Prophetic Perils
End Time Events Revealed

Researched and Written by

Holly Drennan Deyo

Pre-Press and Cover by

Stan Deyo

For Stan: Husband, Best Friend and Partner in Life
Zeh Dodi v'Zeh Rei

Publishers: Deyo Enterprises LLC
Pueblo West, Colorado, The United States of America

Prophetic Perils

End Time Events Revealed

Copyright © Holly Deyo and Stan Deyo 2016

ISBN: 978-0-9852945-6-4

Publishers: Deyo Enterprises LLC
P.O. Box 7711, Pueblo West, Colorado, USA 81007

Web Sites:
http://standeyo.com/
http://daretoprepare.com/
http://standeyo.com/News_Files/Hollys.html

Published Works:
Dare To Prepare (5th Edition)
Prudent Places USA 4th Edition (Book on CD)
Garden Gold: Growing Maximum Veggies With Minimum Effort
The Cosmic Conspiracy – Final Edition 2010
Lectures and Interviews of Stan Deyo Vol. 1: The Garden of Eden and the Solomon Antichrist
The Townsend Brown Legacy (Flash Drive)
The Vindicator Scrolls (Vol. 1)
UFOs Are Here (DVD)
The Gemstone Scrolls (Part 1 of 3)

Email Addresses:
holly@standeyo.com   standeyo@standeyo.com

Table of Contents

Prologue

-- *One* --

Alyssa Riordan hummed her favorite Imagine Dragons tune as she sped along I-25. She visualized lead singer, Dan Reynolds, dancing and pounding that vertical mega-bass drum. He drove his heart into the ground in the final throes of "I Bet My Life". It portrayed everything she thought about her family, the distance, her rebellion, the things they didn't get about her life. As she grew older, Alyssa saw their wisdom, and that distance hurt her soul. She thought of Dan's words to his parents honoring them, *I've told a million lies and now I tell a single truth, there's you in everything I do.* Alyssa winced at Dan's song, an open tribute to his parents. It was a message asking for forgiveness. Alyssa realized it was time to make things right with her mom and dad. Maybe with God, too.

Minutes flew as her little sports car sliced through the miles. Even after 20 years of living in Colorado, gazing at the Rockies never became old. They really were purple in the early hours until the morning sun morphed them dark green.

Ryan would be home in a couple hours and her mind turned to fixing dinner. A picnic on the deck would be just the thing.

It was a perfect Colorado day. The sky was a brilliant blue umbrella and not a chemtrail in sight. Lyssa mulled how wonderful it was to have 75-degree weather in mid-November. Lyssa thought back to her youth when late autumn would have already wrapped its icy fingers around her. She didn't miss Kansas City's long, dreary snow months or its muggy miserable summers.

Lyssa pulled her white Mustang into the driveway and ducked into the garage. Dumping her purse on the kitchen counter, she hauled chicken, salad ingredients and garden corn from the fridge.

Outside, Alyssa deftly lit the grill as she mentally organized her 'to-do' list.

A quiet breeze stirred colorful placemats anchored by blue-rimmed plates. She sighed in contentment thinking life was just about flawless.

Checking her watch, she flipped the chicken breasts to sear the other side. She slid the basting brush over them coated with orange sauce.

Idly she watched Chance and Digger race around the backyard, grateful for the fence. She knew their two cattle dogs would be off visiting neighbors if they weren't corralled. Sniffing the fragrant air, Digger bounded up the steps to see if any tidbits had dropped onto the deck. Wagging a happy tail she looked at Alyssa expectantly.

"Digger I swear, you're led by your nose!" Lyssa chided good-naturedly. "Go play with your brother. Better yet, run off some of these rabbits!" She waved off the Kelpie toward the woodpile.

Digger came by her name righteously. When she and her dog-brother were barely six months, Lyssa caught Digger scratching out her first hole. She and Ryan had laughed seeing dirt fly in all directions. Sensing their amusement, Chance quickly got the message and imitated his sister's busy paws. Lyssa and Ryan gaped in amazement seeing how fast they could tear up the yard. By the time they were three, neither had dared dig another hole after 'excavating' Lyssa's favorite yellow rose bush. The pair rarely saw Alyssa angry, but knew they were in deep trouble when she spotted the wilted plant.

Lyssa turned her attention to the salad tossing it lightly. She contemplated that she and Ryan were genuinely happy – scarily so. What had they done to deserve it? Feeling a little superstitious, she refused to examine it more closely, yet felt thankful.

Alyssa reminisced while the chicken cooked. She and Ryan had met in the oddest way. Lyssa, who worked as a cosmetic consultant for a small downtown boutique, took her lunch hour seriously. It was her time to get away. Everyone wanted to look ten years younger and thought magic could be found in a tube. It was a delicate balance to keep within the bounds of truth and yet sell products and hope.

Often she walked the six blocks to Wagner's Book Nook to thumb through the latest releases. *You can have your e-readers,* she thought vehemently.

Lyssa liked the feel of a book in her hands, bent pages unapologetically she wanted to refer to later and underlined not-to-be forgotten bits of wisdom. Nothing beat a good book while lazing under the warm Colorado sun.

Glancing at her watch, it told her she was going to be uncharacteristically late if she didn't get a move on. Ducking out of Wagner's with her latest purchase, Lyssa started power walking in three-inch heels.

No sooner had she covered 50 yards when her world spun out of control. Book, purse, shoes and dignity flew in every direction. She would have hit the pavement with a mighty thump when a pair of strong arms intervened.

Mortified, she looked into the most intense blue eyes she'd ever seen. Deep sky blue fringed in black lashes. Stammering, Lyssa attempted an explanation, but words eluded her. She was lost those eyes that stared at her with concern.

"Ah-hem, I was…" Lyssa began as she tried to scramble to her feet. Pain shot through her ankle as she disentangled herself from Ryan's arms.

Red oozed up her neck to the roots of her tawny hair. "Gee," Lyssa began again, "I'm not usually this clumsy."

Blue eyes crinkled with mirth. "Sure, whatever." Ryan agreed good-naturedly as he gazed at the pile of delight in front of him.

Alyssa thought she detected the faintest hint of an Irish brogue.

Oh-oh. She warned herself. *Better watch out for this one.*

Quietly, he collected the contents of her purse that lay strewn over the sidewalk.

With a conscious effort, Lyssa attempted to regain her composure tugging down her plum pencil skirt.

"Really, I…" She winced in pain as she realized she wouldn't be wearing those lovely Christian Louboutin's any time soon. No chunky platforms for her, just the exquisite elegance of a designer that knew a woman's heart. The thought of sliding her feet over those signature red leather soles made her smile.

Anxiously she grabbed the battered shoe and her heart sank. She had saved two months to purchase those flamingo pink beauties and her dreams were squashed in a wink. Lyssa examined the skinned and pushed up leather and scolded herself over such extravagance. Worse than the damaged shoe, the heel was hopelessly broken. *I told you so, Lyss,* she scolded herself, *you wasted your money.*

Seeing her discomfiture, Ryan quickly lifted Alyssa to her feet. As she hopped around on one foot, Lyssa bemoaned the loss of the Louboutin.

Grunting, Ryan chastised her. "Be glad it was only a shoe! It could have been your neck. What were you thinking running in those spikes?"

Irritation shot through her veins as Lyssa searched for a zinging retort.

"You don't get it…" She began. Gazing into his dark-fringed eyes, her thoughts drifted, became discombobulated. "I… I have to get back to work." She stammered.

"I don't think you'll get very far in your condition." Ryan predicted. "I'll drive you."

Lyssa was about to protest when arrows of pain stung her ankle. *He's right,* she thought to herself. *I can't very well hobble on one foot and a sore ankle.* Glancing at her watch, her clumsiness had chewed up another ten minutes.

Eyes wide in self-annoyance, Alyssa sighed her gratitude at having at least one decision today taken out of her hands.

"My car's right behind you." He offered.

Gratefully, Lyssa sank into soft pearl leather when she thought, horrified, *I don't even know this guy's name! What am I doing?*

As if reading her mind, her knight in shining armor turned saying. "By the way, I'm Ryan. Ryan Riordan, at your service." He grinned.

Flaming once again, Lyssa smiled her gratitude. "Alyssa." She replied and stuck out her hand.

By car, they arrived at La Boutique sooner than she wished. Lyssa enjoyed their short conversation. Ryan shared he worked at an investment firm just down the street.

Glancing at her watch, Alyssa was relieved to see she had seven minutes to spare. From under thick dark lashes, Alyssa saw her rescuer had square muscular shoulders under his Dolce & Gabbana suit. Its lightweight wool-silk did little to hide his athletic frame.

As though reading her stray thoughts, Ryan offered. "I know it's a bit strange the way we met and maybe too soon, but would you like to have coffee tomorrow?"

Lyssa hesitated for a micro-second. Vivid blue eyes held her gaze. Her heart thrummed an escalating beat and before she could gather common sense, she breathed out a happy, "Yes".

Ryan grinned his pleasure. They agreed to meet at The Bean.

What is going on? This is definitely not me! First, the fall and then falling for a stranger. Well, OK, I'm not falling for him, but I am intrigued. She admitted to herself. *There must be something in the air. It's an off day for sure.* She excused.

Alyssa glanced at her gold and diamond Omega watch. *Three minutes to decide a lifetime. Maybe.* Again, Lyssa was shocked by her thoughts. Cooler and calmer than what she felt, Alyssa wanted to put some distance between her and her unruly feelings.

On the drive back to Burton Stone's offices, Ryan whistled a tuneless song thinking how lovely Alyssa looked sprawled on the sidewalk. Smiling to himself he mused, *this might be my lucky day!*

-- *Two* --

Where was Ryan? Alyssa wondered. He rarely missed dinner at home and was seldom late without phoning. Ryan was always respectful of everyone's time never assuming his was more valuable than someone else's.

Alyssa poked the chicken with metal tongs, testing for doneness. Clear liquid oozed out signaling they'd be ready in another minute. She peeled back a crisp cornhusk and savored the aroma. *They're nearly done, too,* she determined and slipped the husk back into place.

Peach tea on the table, napkins folded, meal ready. All I need is my husband.

An hour later, Ryan still hadn't showed up or called. Instead of being annoyed Alyssa started to worry. By 6 p.m. "Dad" was always home. The soft dark eyes of Digger and Chance looked at her expectantly for answers.

"Guys, I don't know what to tell you. Your dad is really late. You'll just have to wait for your game of laser light."

Tracking the laser's little green dot was the dogs' favorite game. Alyssa marveled how quickly Chance's head pivoted side-to-side when Ryan moved the light in short jerks. Digger knew to let her dog-brother take the lead or else get nipped. This was *his* game, or so he thought. Ryan always shot the light over Chance's back so Digger had a bit of fun, too. Laser chasing left bone chewing in the dirt. Ball retrieval took a backseat too. There was something magical about a dancing green sphere that made their eyes light in anticipation.

As though understanding Alyssa's every word, they curled up close to the picnic table knowing their human dad would settle there first.

By 7:00, Alyssa worried in earnest. Repeatedly she punched in Ryan's cell number and was met with a fast busy signal. Sitting on the deck enjoying the golden-peach sunset, it hadn't occurred to her to turn on the radio. Instead she sat and drank in the early evening quiet in between worrying about Ryan.

The sun had disappeared over an hour ago, abruptly, as it always does in the mountains, and the evening turned distinctly chilly. Alyssa rubbed her arms furiously and she moved the now-cold meal indoors.

Flicking the light switch with one hand, Alyssa remained in darkness.

She glanced over at the stove. It was dark, too. *Great, a power outage,* she muttered, *but that doesn't explain why I can't reach Ryan.*

Alyssa grabbed a flashlight from the kitchen drawer. Instantly the room burst into view while she reached for a perfumed jar candle.

Fumbling for the radio, Alyssa switched it on. Nothing. Thinking she hadn't hit the power button hard enough, she gave it another push. Nothing. *That's odd,* Alyssa thought. *It's plugged in.* Then she remembered. *Lyss, get a grip, no power, girl.* Fleetingly she mused how much she took electricity for granted.

-- *Three* --

Ryan resisted temptation to tap his shoe impatiently as the unexpected brokers' meeting dragged on endlessly. Joshua Baines was giving trainees lessons in cold-calling to snag new clients. "The basic pitch is this: 'I'm going to generate 20% returns a year for you or I'm going to consistently beat the market. Fair enough?' Now before the client has a chance to…"

Ryan's mind drifted to his little family, thinking how he'd rather be there than here, but the boss wanted everyone to rally around the newbies and share how they get it done. Ryan couldn't figure for the life of him why he had to be at the meeting. He was the wildcard – the guy that ran a bit against the crowd. Instead of putting his clients just into stocks to "keep the trades going and the money moving," Ryan offered diversity.

Normally this approach would have guaranteed him being fired at other brokerage houses, but with his strong good looks, extraordinary track record and genuine interest in people, he easily brought in new clients. Ryan made Burton Stone and his clients money. Not only did he have a knack for guiding people to the right stocks, he also put them in cash and precious metals. He stayed away from certificates and urged people to actually take possession of their silver and gold investments.

Ryan glanced at his Rolex and shifted in his chair.

Joshua continued his spiel. "And if he says 'I totally agree with you, but let me talk to my wife, let me do my own homework and I'll think about it,' now is the time to let your closing skills shine. Don't let him slip away. You've got his ear. Keep that hook…"

Suddenly all the lights went out in the conference room.

Joshua stopped short. "What the… Riordan, call maintenance. See what's up. Get some light on in here!" Ryan was already ahead of him.

"Josh, no juice, no phone. They'll get the generators going pretty soon." Thirty minutes later, the ten of them still sat in the dark. To Josh's credit, he held his cool when the rest got antsy. He wanted to finish his presentation, get his new fish swimming in the right direction. "You've got to move money to make money," Joshua always said.

Ryan glanced out of the bronze gold windows and saw nothing, but a sea of darkness. There was not a single light on in the entire DTC complex – Denver Tech Center. Only a few lights flickered at the Hyatt. Ryan wondered idly if the power outage had hit Lone Tree. It was just fifteen minutes to his home there and it didn't look like they were going to get power back on soon.

"Josh, I know you were on a roll, but let's call it a night. We can come in early if you like and pick back up. You need the FlickIt screen and we can't see it sitting here in the dark."

Running his hand through his dark hair, Josh weighed the chances of electricity blazing again. "OK, everybody, we'll have a working lunch tomorrow and finish up." Pushing back their chairs he heard only a few anonymous groans as they gathered up smartphones and messenger bags. "In the morning men, bright and early!"

Randall Maiser, one of the newest to the team asked, "Hey, anybody got a light? Guess we'll be walking down to the parking lot."

"Maiser, you could use a little more walking. It's only ten floors," Luke teased. "Think if you were at the top of the Cash Register, you'd be hiking down fifty." Rand's ears reddened at the implied criticism.

Ryan paused a minute, glad Burton Stone's offices weren't in the Wells Fargo building. He always thought instead of it looking like a cash register the structure resembled a giant mailbox with its oddly curved roof. Ryan knew he should have called Alyssa two hours ago, but didn't figure the meeting would last so long. Ryan tapped the home number before realizing his iPhone wasn't working. *Hmmm, that's weird,* he mused, *its light is on but not calling.*

Ryan climbed into his vintage Porsche and pointed its nose toward I-25. *Even with rush hour done, where's all the cars?* Ryan wondered. *There are always cars.* As he pulled onto the freeway, Ryan slammed on the brakes as he nearly rammed into a Landcruiser. *Geez, that's a bad place to run out of gas. He should have at least pulled off to the side,* Ryan grumbled.

He maneuvered around the 'Cruiser and what his headlights picked up shocked Ryan. Strewn in front of him looked like wreckage after a demolition derby except it seemed endless. Cars had rear-ended each other in a continuous trail of metal and rubber. Those that had managed to avoid the chaos wove carefully around the rest. In the dark people were shouting and honking not yet understanding the magnitude of what lie ahead.

Ryan gave up trying to reach Alyssa and concentrated on driving. What should have taken fifteen minutes to get home ate up an hour. *Boy, Alyssa is going to be steamed. I wonder if they'll have this mess cleaned up by morning.* Ryan mulled.

As Ryan eased the Porsche into the driveway, he saw that the power outage had hit the whole neighborhood. Since the electricity was out, he left his car in the driveway and locked the door. He found Alyssa in the living room reading by candlelight. Instead of anger, concern etched her features. "Ry!" she cried getting up to hug him. "I was so worried. You didn't call." Her voice trailed off as she watched his face.

"Lyss, you wouldn't believe the freeway! I left over an hour ago. It was like playing dodge ball with big hunks of metal. Wrecks all over the place," he explained. "But it was weird, you know. Everything was just so dark. I tried to call you, but nothing. Guess the phone is out too?"

She nodded. "You missed dinner and with the power out, I can't heat it up for you." She mildly chided.

"'S'OK, I'll just have a sandwich."

"Here, take the flashlight," as she passed him the Stanley. She liked this tripod model because its three LEDs could be angled to light a room in all directions.

Sitting at the kitchen bar, Ryan washed down his ham and cheese with a Bud Light. Turning to his wife, Ryan said. "You know, Lyss, there's something strange about this blackout. It's just so, I don't know … all over everything. I didn't see any house anywhere with lights on. It was weird," he repeated.

Alyssa said, "Look Ry, it'll be back on by morning. Finish your sandwich and let's go to bed. Can't do much without electricity."

"Well, I can think of one thing…" Ryan grinned at her with an Irish twinkle in his eye.

-- *Four* --

The next morning, Colorado's brilliant sunshine streamed through the front windows bathing everything in its warmth. Alyssa padded across the tiled kitchen floor expecting to pour a cup of coffee. *Darn! Can't believe I forgot to set the timer.* She noticed the lights were out on the fridge, microwave, ovens, and dishwasher. Even the phone base was dark. Then it all flooded back. The only thing working was the battery-run wall clock.

Ryan appeared in the kitchen doorway. "Lyssa, I need some bottled water. Looks like I'll be taking a PTA bath this morning."

She heard Ryan standing in the shower pouring water from the jug in a quick wash. Idly she wondered how he was going to dry his hair.

Fifteen minutes later Ryan trotted downstairs, smartly dressed in navy Armani. Alyssa noted his still-damp hair and shrugged her shoulders in the direction of the dead appliances.

"Don't worry sweetheart, I'll grab something on the way." Kissing his wife goodbye, Ryan piled into the car and dropped his briefcase into the passenger seat. He nosed the Porsche from Lincoln onto I-25 and to his shock, the sight before him mirrored last night's disaster. However, in broad daylight it took on new dimensions. Cars lay twisted like they were on some nightmarish track. One after another after another. But something didn't look right. Then his brain pinpointed it. There were lots of cars just abandoned that obviously hadn't been hit. They look perfectly fine. *What the heck?* Ryan thought his brow knitting together. It looked like the freeway scene out of Stephen King's *The Stand,* where people just stopped driving because they had died behind the wheel.

He maneuvered the Porsche in and out of free pockets. There wasn't as much traffic as last night, but people milled about moving from one car to another, dazed. Some appeared hurt and where were the ambulances? Seemingly out of nowhere a man dressed in slacks, casual shirt and loafers jumped in front of the Porsche frantically waving his arms. Quickly taking in the scenery, Ryan noticed very few cars were moving. *This is really bizarre!* Ryan thought.

Ryan braked to avoid hitting the guy, slowed and cracked the window. "Do you needs some help?"

"Hey man, can I use your phone? Mine's dead and I've got to call my wife. I've been stuck here all night and something super strange happened. She's going to be worried sick."

Ryan checked his iPhone; no signal. "Sorry friend, can't help you, no bars." The man, Tim Franks, looked surprised. "Really? Nobody's phone is working. It's like we're in the Twilight Zone. Can you at least give me a lift?"

Ryan hesitated knowing he had to get to the office. Ryan quickly assessed the man's neat Chinos, crew neck sweater and Top-Siders. He didn't look dangerous.

"Please…" Tim pleaded. "I'm beat. I have to take a leak and my wife will be frantic. I'm just up the road off Orchard."

Ryan glanced at his watch again, sighed and signaled Tim to get in. *Sheesh, now I am gonna be late. Lyssa always said I couldn't turn anybody down. Guess she's right.*

Tim slid into the soft leather and breathed a sigh of relief. Ryan couldn't help but sniff the air and realized there was no hint of booze or pot. Tim said, "I really appreciate this. It's the darnedest thing ever. I'm driving home and all of a sudden it's like we're all playing bumper cars. People started swerving to avoid getting clobbered, but more cars started slamming into each other. What's really freaky is that a lot of them just flat-out stopped, like mine. No reason. Just stopped."

Ryan sneaked a look at Tim while keeping his eyes on the mess ahead. *This really is just too strange,* giving Tim credit. *He's right. Some of the cars don't look damaged, but were just left there.*

"Here, take a right, here," Tim motioned. "I'm just a few blocks."

As they pulled into the driveway, Tim offered, "Let me give you something for the lift." Reaching for his wallet, he voiced his gratitude. "You really bailed me out."

Ryan waved him off thinking what a story he'd have to share with Alyssa that night. "Hey Tim, hope everything works out."

Tim nodded and gave Ryan a grateful look.

Ten minutes later Ryan pulled into Burton Stone's parking lot only to see that all the newbie brokers had beaten him there. *Hmmm* Ryan mused, *that's good in a way. Hope they keep up this go-get'em attitude.*

As Ryan swung his long legs out of the Porsche, the new fish sidled over. In a micro-second, Ryan assessed something was wrong. If he wasn't mistaken Rand had on the same clothes as yesterday. Bart Biggs looked rumpled, tie loosely knotted, shirt wrinkled. Bart, JJ, Nicholas, Rand, Alex, Adam, Luke, Morgan, heck, they were all here, but it looked like they wore yesterday's clothes. They didn't present the crisp, sharp image Burton Stone demanded.

Ryan gave them a quick disapproving up-and-down glance. Before he could open his moth, Bart jumped in. "Don't say anything. We know we're a mess, but boss, we couldn't help it. None of our cars would start. We stopped to hash over a bit of what Josh, I mean Mr. Baines, said. You drove off and none of our cars would start. I know this sounds crazy…" Bart's voice trailed off. Ryan gave them a skeptical look and then remembered what he'd witnessed on the freeway.

Ryan started to say something, but Bart interrupted. "Wait, you have to hear this. We saw some lights over at the Hyatt so we decided to walk over, get a bite and call home. Their big gennies worked, but just enough to run the bare essentials. No phone service there either. When we got the lay of the land and snagged the last sandwiches, we realized we were going to have to stay here. Everybody else had grabbed the last rooms, so we slept in our cars."

Ryan raised his eyebrows in surprise, but he said nothing. *This is really weird,* he thought for the umpteenth time. *There's just no other word for it.*

"What we don't get Mr. Riordan, is why your car worked and ours didn't."

"I have no idea. She's my lucky girl? An oldie but goodie?" Ryan offered even though it sounded hollow in his own ears. "Have you guys seen Joshua?"

They all shook their heads, no. Ryan turned to retrieve his iPhone. "Mr. Riordan, wait. There's more. Something you need to know."

Hearing the worry in Luke's voice, Ryan stopped mid-step.

"When we were at the Hyatt, we overhead something. I know this is going to sound crazy."

"Go on," Ryan encouraged.

"Well, there's a bunch of old-timers at the Hyatt. They're here for a ham radio convention," Luke continued. "So when the power went out and stayed out, some of them plugged their gear into the generators. They were talking to guys in New York and California and Toronto. Mr. Riordan…" Luke's voice trailed off.

Ryan gave a look that said, *get to the point.*

Luke swallowed hard. "The power outage is all over."

"What, all over Denver?" Ryan queried.

"No, I mean all over the Country."

"Oh, bullsh—"

Luke cut him off. "No, I mean all over America, clear up into Toronto, Winnipeg, Calgary, Vancouver, I mean ALL OVER," his voice rising in obvious distress.

Ryan stared at Luke in disbelief, eyes widening.

"Is there more? Did they say anything else?" Ryan pressed. Silence. "What? Out with it!"

Ryan looked more closely and noticed a number of their eyes were red-rimmed.

Adam took over, Luke too shaken to speak. "They said North Korea sent a sub over and that crazy bastard Kim Jung-un nuked us! He got up to New York's coast and fired a nuke. It went off over South Dakota in something they said was an EMP – an electromagnetic pulse. It took out the electricity here and in Canada."

Ryan sagged back against his Porsche trying to take it all in. "Well, how long is it going to be before it's fixed? Joshua isn't going to be too happy." Ryan looked from JJ to Nick to Adam to Randall. He noticed David's eyes welling and for the first time he spoke up.

"Sir, they aren't." David whispered.

"Aren't what?" Ryan certainly wasn't getting the picture. "Aren't, *what?*" He repeated more forcefully.

David cleared his throat struggling for control. "Power's not coming on any time soon. Maybe a couple of years if we're lucky." David stood straighter and squared his shoulders. "They said, Mr. Riordan, that we might not get electricity back for a couple of years."

Ryan started at him in total disbelief. Looking at their drawn faces he saw they weren't joking.

There has to be a mistake. A couple of years? That can't be what they heard. "I'm going over there myself, see what's what," Ryan announced more casually than he felt.

"I'll come," David volunteered.

"Me too," Morgan piped up. "It's better than hanging out in the parking lot."

All nine of them walked over to the Hyatt. Ryan's stomach growled as he remembered he'd gotten sidetracked from breakfast giving Tim Franks a lift.

"Com'on, guys, breakfast is on me." Ryan offered. Encouraged at the thought of pancakes, eggs and steaming coffee, they picked up the pace, but their anticipation was short-lived. It seemed everybody from the DTC had the same idea in addition to the people that walked from the freeway. There was nothing to eat and no place to sit.

When they found the ham radio guys, they didn't have a lot more to tell. From ham chatter they shared that North Korea had sent up a nuke not far off Long Island and blew it up far overhead. Its pulse knocked out power to most of North America by overloading power lines with electrical charges. Cascading failures took out the big transformers one after another. Chaos and panic were erupting in every large city and the President planned to send out the Army and National Guard. It was going to take them several days to arrive because only part of the military's vehicles and planes were hardened against an EMP. Word was North Korea had bought the missile and nuke from Russia.

In its wake, people rioted and looted. Word traveled fast and frightened folks were clearing grocery stores of food and water. Nobody stopped to pay, just took whatever they could get their hands on. They even dragged out computers, TVs and stacks of jeans and winter coats, baby formula and diapers.

Ryan felt bad for the young men with him. He couldn't even buy them a meal and the news this morning was worse than what they'd shared in the parking lot.

"Com'on, I'll drive you home. There's no point in hanging around here." Ryan offered.

They were relieved, but looked dubiously at his little Porsche.

"OK, so it's going to take a couple of trips. You got some place to go? Pair up by where you live. That should cut down on driving time."

By the time Ryan pulled back into his driveway, his mind reeled by what he'd heard. How was he going to explain this mess, no, this *nightmare* to Alyssa?

-- *Five* --

Chance and Digger were surprised to see their Dad home so early. *Game, Dad?* They wagged their tails expectantly. Hearing Ryan's shoes on the hardwood floor Alyssa bounded out of the kitchen.

"Honey, how come you're home so early?" Alyssa kissed her husband hello.

Ryan gave her a quick hug and set her gently aside. Getting right to the point he said, "Lyss, get your shoes. There's something I need to show you."

Alyssa cocked her blonde head to one side. Sensing his seriousness, she slid into sandals and grabbed her purse. She climbed into the passenger's side of his little black car and strapped in. Ryan slipped it into gear and headed for the freeway.

"Ryan honey, where are we going? You're acting funny." Alyssa asked a bit uneasily.

"I want to show you something, but first we need to get gas." Ryan pulled off University into a deserted Conoco station and it suddenly dawned on him. Confirming his suspicions, a sign hung on the door. "Sorry, No Electricity, No Gas." In a slow circle he wheeled past Lone Tree's golf club. People in signature Polos and golf slacks dotted the course. Ryan puzzled to see golf carts whizzing around the links. *That looks pretty normal.* Ryan chuckled to himself, *guess if the power's out, you might as well play a round.* Down Lincoln Avenue a nearly identical "No Power, No Gas" sign sat in front of Loaf 'N Jug's pumps. Ryan sighed and glanced down at the gauge. He still had a half tank.

A few grocery stores they passed remained open during daylight hours only. All had signs on their doors saying, "Cash Only, Exact Change Appreciated." One store was rationing everything that was shelf stable including batteries, bottled water and Clorox. However, they had slashed prices on meats, milk, eggs and dairy products, and all frozen foods.

Ryan passed Sky Ridge Medical Center on the right, which seemed overly busy. He poked Alyssa to take a look. People filled the parking lot milling about while others sat on the grass waiting to be seen. Lyssa threw Ryan a questioning glance, but he just shrugged his shoulders.

Gazing around, Ryan saw many more stalled vehicles like on the interstate, but they weren't as concentrated in one place or blocking traffic. Saying nothing he realized they were the same cars he'd seen there the day before.

He gave Alyssa a quick reassuring look, but his lips compressed into a grim line. Minutes later he swung onto I-25. Alyssa let out a spontaneous gasp. The freeway looked like the Bronco stadium parking lot at game time – times ten – except there wasn't a football player in sight. Cars and trucks filled the freeway's lanes like a shiny bright metal collage. People roamed about, but others sat on the side of the road obviously injured. Some wore makeshift bandages torn from clothing and tied around bloody heads and limbs. Others walked across lanes of stalled traffic in search of bathrooms, water and breakfast.

Off to their left sat Parkview Meadows. Instead of people loaded down with shopping bags and juggling kids, Colorado's largest shopping mall was dark and quiet. Like the freeway hundreds of cars filled the silent parking lot, waiting for their owners to collect them.

Swinging her eyes back to the freeway, everywhere Alyssa looked she saw mangled cars, doors flung open, some people resting inside, waiting. Dazed people looked around as if searching for answers. Others softly cried, punctuated by occasional screams of pain. Parents grasped children's hands tightly fearful of losing them in the confusion.

Alyssa had heard about Denver's hundred-car pile-ups, but this was way worse. *Where are the ambulances, the tow trucks? Why aren't emergency vehicles on scene and the EMTs?* Alyssa turned her head aside as a woman dressed in linen suddenly bent over and vomited next to her car. Wiping her mouth on her sleeve, she clutched her stomach and seemed disoriented. Alyssa notice a deep gash on her head.

Alyssa said nothing, but cast a worried look at her husband. He squeezed her hand and slowly wove his car in and out of the metal mayhem. Looking down the road Ryan saw a few other vehicles navigating the wreckage when it dawned on him, *all of these cars are older like mine!* Suddenly from seemingly out of nowhere, a disheveled woman ran up and banged on another car's window, wildly waving her arms. She mouthed something and frantically pointed over her shoulder.

Ryan too, wondered where the ambulances were till he took a good look ahead. As far as the eye could see cars, trucks and semis filled the interstate. He hadn't really examined the extent of the freeway's mess because he had been too busy concentrating on what lie in front of him. Off to the right he noticed a distant coal train. There was nothing to stop its chugging down the track to Pueblo. No other train had hit it. Nothing blocked its path. It had just stopped like these thousands of cars and trucks. On the other side of I-25, the RTD, Denver's light rail system looked like a long, silver dead snake. People all up and down the Denver corridor from Lone Tree to Longmont depended on this transportation 24/7. It too, was going nowhere.

"Ryan, look over there," she said, pointing ahead to the right shoulder. "That's a first!"

Ryan's eyes tracked where she indicated and were met by a sea of navy. Weaving in and out of the vehicles they saw what looked like several hundred cops riding bicycles. Obviously their Crown Victorias and Ford Expeditions had gone the same way as the cars on the freeway. Alyssa watched as police methodically stopped at every vehicle checking for injuries and taking reports. Behind them rode a wave of green. Dressed differently than the police it was easier to spot the EMTs and paramedics. Attached to their bikes were bags loaded with bottled water and first aid supplies.

Realization slammed his chest like a physical blow. Besides some people crying and chatting, he noticed just how quiet it was. No radios blared. No planes from Denver International flew overhead. A "V" of Canada geese migrated south, but they were the only things moving in Colorado's blue skies. What the ham operators shared at the Hyatt must be true. Turning to Alyssa, Ryan filled her in on as much detail as he knew. There was no kind way to soften the news, just say it and get it done.

Ryan watched as her face changed from interest to shock to horror. Her pretty features knotted up as she let out a howl of anguish. He pulled the Porsche over and held her as she sobbed out her fears. Gulping back tears, she turned her face upward and whispered, "Ryan, what are we going to do? This can't be real." Tears squeezed from the corners of her eyes.

Holding her tighter Ryan tried to reassure her. "Lyss, we'll get through this like we do everything – together."

"I know Ryan, but this is just so… so, big."

Glancing out the window and taking in the wreckage, the magnitude of events began to take hold. "Oh God, Ryan, it looks like the end of the world!"

"Lyssa, stop! That's just fairytales. Once they get the roads cleared and power back, this will be just like a bad dream."

Keeping his thoughts to himself, Ryan wondered *if cars aren't running, will tow trucks be any better off? Without fuel, they won't be going far for long anyway,* he mused. Then he thought about everything that depended on computers and electricity; banks, utilities, ATMs, food inventories, water purification plants, hospitals, sewage treatment, trash service, Wall Street, credit cards… His mind reeled at the implications.

Ryan didn't want to go there, but his mind tugged back to when his parents dragged him to church. *What was that they'd said? There was a time coming when nobody would be able to buy or sell anything.* Ryan mentally shook his head to clear that possibility, but it stuck like Super Glue. *Is this it? Is this what they talked about?* Involuntarily, his mind turned over one thought. *What if we really are in End Times?*

Chapter 1: Signs, Signs, Everywhere There's Signs

Warning signs are now so apparent even the casually interested person knows something is up. Something is wrong; something isn't normal. They feel it. They sense it. People paying attention see things are really off-kilter. Compared to just two decades ago, life is on a tilt. People in their 50s and older, see it more clearly because they remember when life was less crazy. They expected more, yet were content with less. Life was slower and appreciation greater. For 30-somethings and younger, this current pace and morality is all they've known, so life may not seem strange.

Whether a person is Jewish, Christian, Muslim, Buddhist, New Age, pagan or a non-believer, everyone except the most blind senses something looming. Easy life has switched to one of expectancy. Some wait for the Sword of Damocles to fall. Others expect a slower unraveling that brings great upheaval. Yet others wait for Enlightenment. Some speak of the Great Cleansing. Whatever point of view, nearly everyone senses a coming "adjustment".

"The trigger could be a terrorist attack, a monetary collapse, cataclysmic failure in power generation, or a natural disaster. [They] fear what comes next and have no faith in either their government or human nature.

"'We're not talking about folks walking around wearing tin foil on their heads,' says Virginian prepper Jay Blevins. 'We're not talking about conspiracy theorists. I'm talking about professionals: doctors and lawyers and law enforcement and military. Normal, everyday people. They can't necessarily put their finger on it. But there's something about the uncertainty of our times. They know something isn't quite right.'"[1]

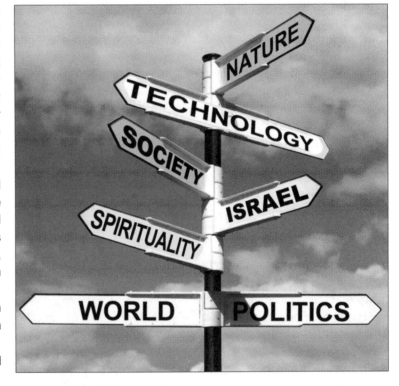

These expected changes can be summed up as End Times events. This doesn't mean the world will no longer exist, nor does it portend man's extinction. It does signal the close of This Age where too much discord, illness, hunger, anxiety, disease and poverty co-exists with great joy, love, appreciation and triumph.

There will be a new beginning – for all – in whatever form it takes, but know that within a very short time, nothing will ever be the same.

So just what are these signs? What should we pay attention to?

These many signposts fall into six main categories: Nature, Society, Spiritual, World Politics, Technology, and Israel. God placed markers for man to see how close he is to End Times and have time to prepare for them, but the sands in the hourglass have nearly run out. After reading this material and seeing the headlines, where we are on the timeline is undeniable. Some of these events could happen at no other place in history. Understanding this is vital because there is no mistaking how close we are. Many of these events have slowly ramped up over decades or years to the point where people might miss the escalation. *Prophetic Perils* shows in words, pictures and specific details exactly how things have "quickened".

When you see all of these signs coming together, overrun each other then know the Grand Finale has arrived. While this is *not* the end of the world, it is the start of the roughest time people ever have experienced. After seven years of hell on earth, collectively called Tribulation, there will be peace, wellness and limitless joy.

These are the major things to watch for:

Nature signs will show weather has turned more violent. Even slumbering volcanoes will awaken and spew, and earthquakes will rattle every part of the planet both more strongly and in unexpected places. Weather-related events people may fob off to global warming, chance or manipulated data, but ask yourself, do things look the same as 20 years ago? Earth changes, in addition to war will fuel famine and disease. Countries that were once food and water stable have sold off important life-sustaining chunks of land. Through our own shortsightedness the odds have multiplied that hunger will spread to places never thought possible. One has only to look at the Dust Bowl Days to see how desperate times can become. No rain, no food. Even the world's richest country can't fix this.

Societal signs include people becoming more materialistic and self-absorbed. Bizarre swaps take place where good things are viewed as evil and vice versa. Societal pressures force people to accept the untenable or be harshly labeled and judged. Morality? Sex was reserved for marriage or at least committed relationships, but hooking up is now a pass-time, something to ward off boredom. Sandwiched between completely selfless acts – sometimes at the cost of their own lives – is an overarching attitude is noninvolvement. Some of the most astonishing behavior is rising to the surface; things we never imagined people doing. Both groups like ISIS and individuals act in the most cold-blooded, shocking manner ever imagined. Personal responsibility? Where has it gone? Instead of self-control, bad behavior is excused away as a "disease" and government is expected to supply everybody's everything. Because of this self-indulgent era and a desire to escape, drug use escalates. This draws gangs, drug cartels and mafias, which bring more violence and disregard for laws.

Spiritual signs include people leaving churches en masse. Part of this stems from people's disillusionment with organized religion, their leaders exhibiting absentee morals and terrible lapses in judgment, and what worshippers see as outdated doctrine. People will increasingly rely on human, rational solutions as prayer and dependence on God take a backseat. They will put their own ingenuity and science before God saying He didn't create the universes. Life is only the product of chance and evolution. When folks abandon faith, something must fill the void. Increasingly it's paganism, cults, witchcraft or a mishmash of religions. People will knock the Bible deeming it an old dusty relic claiming Jesus isn't coming back and that prophecy has already been fulfilled. So don't worry, "fuhgeddaboudit", the worst has already happened. More players will claim to be Jesus Christ. Some will be pretty convincing, but the Bible tells you how to tell the fake from the real. One of the most obvious signs is the growing worldwide persecution of Christians and Jews. Soon a deception will be exposed so diabolical and clever that it fooled most people. It's the wild card as there's much speculation just what that will be. On the plus side in the Last Days, the word of God will have spread everywhere and people will have a greater understanding of prophesy. Secrets will be revealed.

On the **World scene**, countries will become progressively war-driven, involved in even more great conflicts. Nations will realign alliances making for some strange and alarming pairings. Two more large-scale wars will ravage countries before the one "finishing" war – Armageddon. Muslim extremists will push into many countries bringing with them the most horrific aspects of conflict and take those to extremes. "Rules of engagement" are abandoned. They will force millions more from their homes that flood into surrounding nations further fueling world instability. Because of this additional countries will assume a strong war footing acquiring and stockpiling weapons of mass destruction. Many will target Israel. In all this, where is America? That will become all too clear – soon. As peace and economic stability unravel it will be necessary for a global government to take charge. With that will be a single world currency and to stem religious wars, a single united faith.

During these times, **Technology** gives way to greater travel and leaps in communication. Never before have people and machines made such astonishing jumps as in the last 100 years. Buckminster Fuller's research discovered that human knowledge doubled every century till 1900. World War II's end brought it down to every 25 years and today it takes just 13 months. Technical advances are doubling every two years while clinical knowledge doubles every 18 months.[2] According to an IBM paper, the "Internet of things" will lead to knowledge doubling every 12 *hours.*[3] Only when such great advances were made could the Mark of the Beast be implemented. Once in place it will be impossible to hold a job, shop and sell things, pay bills and utilities, receive medical care, take vacations, bank, go to school without this special "permission slip" and it comes at a terrific price. During the 2010 U.S. Census, virtually every house, apartment, mobile home, trailer, cabin and pup tent was pinpointed and mapped with government handheld GPS units. Tracking and NSA's uber data collection center add to government's super snooping into people's lives. It's an unnerving reminder of George Orwell's *1984*, but it's gone far beyond some of his expectations. As much as technology propelled countries to exceptional heights, it's also made them extremely vulnerable with everything riding on the premise that life will continue normally.

Israel is God's master key to End Times. Some signs have been around for quite some time like wars and earthquakes. Societal problems have peppered history since Biblical times, but not to the degree as seen now.

Israel is the *unique clue* because who would think people would come back to their homeland after a 2,600-year absence and become a thriving nation again. That happened on May 14, 1948. Prophecy says that the generation alive when this happened will also be the one that witnesses End Times. As predicted the Jews returned and Jerusalem is re-occupied. Israel is becoming an enormous problem worldwide – as prophesied – and all nations around her are spoiling for war.

No doubt this is a lot to take in, but think about the changes we're seeing. Every box is being ticked off just as prophecy said. Looking at the mountain of evidence is to see we're nearly at the End Times doorstep. It's undeniable. We are poised at the finish line, but there is hope and a solution.

God never releases judgment without ample warning. Sometimes people choose not to see or hear, but the warnings are always there. We are in a season like no other and now is the time to be fully prepared spiritually, mentally and physically. The clock is a minute from midnight. Whether a person welcomes these changes or grabs at the last dirt clod as he tumbles off the cliff, the End of This Age is just a whisper away. Will you be ready?

AUTHOR'S NOTE: Since time began, the world has seen its share of prophets and seers. Some have been uncannily accurate, but only one source is *always* correct. Around 2,000 Biblical prophecies have already come to pass, some written hundreds of years in advance. That's why its predictions are the basis for *Prophetic Perils*. While this book discusses prophecies meant for all countries, it was easiest to acquire specific information on the U.S. because our government and science agencies don't copyright their material. When it was available for other nations, those data were included, too. Regardless, trends are similar around the world, and prophetic signs and their fulfillment have global consequences.

Chapter 2: Earthquakes – The Great Shaking

...And there will be famines, pestilences, and earthquakes in various places. —Matthew 24:7 (NKJV)

There will be great earthquakes, famines and pestilences in various places, and fearful events and great signs from heaven. —Luke 21:11 (NIV)

Earth Changes

This is a topic dear to many peoples' hearts and something frequently watched. It doesn't require fancy instruments to monitor and their impact is felt daily around the world. People track earthquakes and volcanic eruptions and check for coming storms. They report on huge sinkholes appearing under homes and in their yards, and of hearing ominous rumblings within the Earth and above it. Some changes are newer like these weird noises and the increase in gaping holes where land used to be stable while other phenomenon are on a steady grind upward. Often ignored are the less 'exciting' events – those that don't slam us like drought and floods, but often they're more worrisome when their effect kills wide swaths of crops and herds, and then food prices skyrocket in the store.

Another topic of constant discussion, sometimes prompting *heated* debate, is global warming or lack thereof. While the root cause isn't important to this discussion, we do have to deal with the consequences. Weather *is* more extreme. Full stop. In America, the Country is now rarely on the same page for weather. This is also the case in many other nations for those that have a great deal of real estate.

Winter used to be, well, pretty much winter throughout the Country and the same was true of summer. Now when some areas experience bone-cracking cold and feet-deep snow, others have blinding sunshine and shorts-and-sandals weather.

Extremes are the norm. When drought scours the planet, it brings a scorched earth policy instead of bearable dryness. When it rains, it's unrelenting. There is little middle ground.

February 2015, New York City experienced its coldest month in 80 years and snow hit all 50 states the first week of March. Never mind that it was only three weeks from spring. Boston's wretched winter of 2014-15 is now also its snowiest going back to 1872, with 108.6 inches.

While the America's Midwest vacillates between drought and drowning, eastern states frequently receive too much rain. In the west and southwest, it's just the opposite. One could choke on the dust. Some folks ardently argue we're in global warming. Then NOAA, the National Oceanic Atmospheric Administration reported that 2,185 cold records were broken or tied in the last week of February 2015. Contrast that to Summer 2014.

The Japan Meteorological Agency announced that 2014 was *the* hottest year in more than 120 years of recordkeeping – by far.[4]

Andrea Thompson for Climate Central wrote a piece in November, "2014 Set for Record Hot; Record Cold Thing of the Past". Her prediction proved hugely inaccurate. According to NOAA, for 30 days in June 2012, some 3,215 heat records were broken or matched.[5] While places are setting new record high temperatures, extreme cold is also seen. A large swath of America broke all-time record lows in March 2015.[6] Cities in North Dakota to Vermont, from Texas to Florida shivered in bone biting cold and dangerous wind chills. Some cities experienced their coldest temperatures in decades for so late in the season. A "Siberian Express" had trudged down from the North Pole and slapped North America with mind-numbing cold.

On the climate issue, people have a lot of drums to beat and much of it depends on what data they're using. Numbers can lie especially when they're governed by agendas, agencies and money. Even if people could agree on whether Earth is heating or cooling, the cause is another point of disagreement. One thing that is undeniable is its volatility and lack of predictability. It is certainly a sign of the times and events are escalating. Let's examine some specifics.

Earthquakes

Earthquakes are something this author has monitored for over 20 years. In that time we've seen USGS perform some pretty creative accounting when it comes to quake records. It's one thing for a temblor's size to change up or down – and it's usually down – by one magnitude, but not more than that. Whatever agency is closest to the epicenter whether it's EMSC (European-Mediterranean Seismological Centre), Natural Resources Canada, GNS (New Zealand) or Geoscience Australia, they will experience the greatest shaking, and therefore show the highest magnitude. It's also normal for state agencies to record a different magnitude and number of events compared to USGS.

A major adjustment came in 2003 when USGS changed the average number of events for four magnitudes. Above are both sets

Richter	"Old" Annual Average	"New" Annual Average
8.0 – 9.9 Great	2	* 1
7.0 – 7.9 Major	18	** 17
6.0 – 6.9 Strong	120	** 134
5.0 – 5.9 Moderate	800	** 1,319
4.0 - 4.9 Light	6,200	13,000
* Based on observations since 1900. ** Based on observations since 1990.		

expected for each range in any given year. A harder situation to explain is when a large earthquake disappears entirely. It's just weird to have a shaker completely wiped off the map especially when other countries continue to show it.

Despite changing quake counts, temblors generally claim 10,000 lives every year. Exceptions always arise. More than 20,000 people died in the 7.7 jolt that struck Pakistan and India in January 2001. Even worse, over 300,000 people perished in Haiti's devastating 7.0 quake on January 12, 2010. This doesn't count another 8,600 Haitians who died from cholera when their water became contaminated in the aftermath.[7]

FRACK THAT

Scientists share that an increase in smaller quakes is due to fracking in some states. Nearly 450 shakers above mag. 3.0 hit the central and eastern U.S. from 2010-2013. That's over 100 per year compared to just 20 each year from 1970–2000.[8] That dramatic uptick was seen mostly in Colorado, Texas, Arkansas, Oklahoma and Ohio where fracking is prevalent.[9] These quake locations match where companies dispose of wastewater by injecting it into the ground.

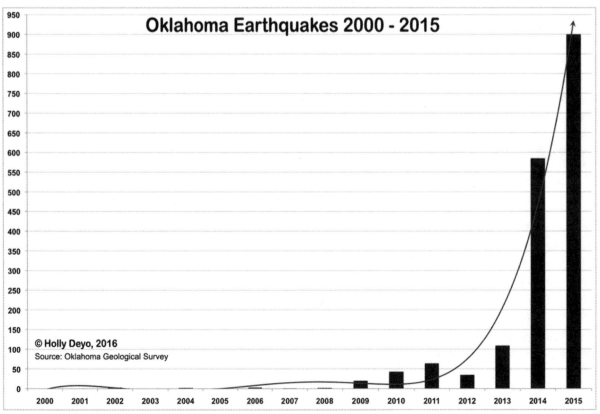

Oklahoma Earthquakes 2000 - 2015
© Holly Deyo, 2016
Source: Oklahoma Geological Survey

In 2014 Oklahoma experienced 585 magnitude 3.0 and higher quakes – more than the last 35 years combined. According to the study, any of these reawakened fault zones, running northeast and northwest, are capable of producing Richter 5 and 6 earthquakes. In 2015, over 900 shakers hit Oklahoma.[10]

In a new study published in *Geophysical Research Letters,* seven geologists found that fracking reawakened formerly snoozing fault lines. Prior to this, Oklahoma's only active fault was Meers. Now there are 12 more.[11] Fault zones, quiet for millennia, prove that even long-dormant ones aren't dead.

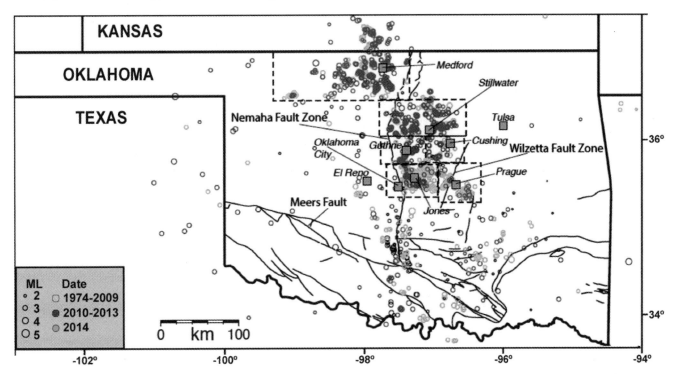

Tulsa petroleum geologist, Bob Jackman, has linked earthquakes to the oil and gas industry for years. Regarding Oklahoma's "unusually aligned faults" Jackson says, "They may trigger an earthquake anyway, but in geological time that may be once every 10,000 years. But here, we are having swarms of them."[12] Residents in the "Sooner State" should prepare for more and larger shakes.

Though scientists are reluctant to say fracking causes shakes stronger than Richter 6, they admit it was responsible for the 5.3 quake near Trinidad, Colorado in 2011 and the 5.6 quake in Prague, Oklahoma that same year. Temblors of this size usually aren't destructive, but the Prague quake knocked bricks from three sides of a home in Sparks, after two earthquakes hit the area in less than a day.

Again, this author isn't debating the root cause of events. Bible prophecy doesn't address this, just that there would be more earthquakes and whatever the source, we must deal with the end result.

DEADLY DUO – DESTRUCTIVE AND DANGEROUS EARTHQUAKES

One point where people disagree without cause is whether or not the number of earthquakes is increasing. They are. There is, without question, a rise in 'dangerous and destructive' temblors since 1950. An undeniable upward trend is shown by this graph. So while USGS hasn't changed their averages for over a dozen years, their own database tells the rising quakes story.

Some scientists try to explain it away due to more monitoring equipment being installed. That might be applicable for *small* magnitude quakes that are harder to detect unless seismometers are close, but that wouldn't be the case for larger events. It especially wouldn't apply by the parameters USGS set up – that dangerous and destructive earthquakes are defined as meeting at least one of the following:

- Causes moderate damage of at least $1 million or more
- Takes 10 or more lives
- Is magnitude 7.5 or higher
- Rates an X or greater on the Modified Mercalli Intensity scale, or
- Generates a tsunami.

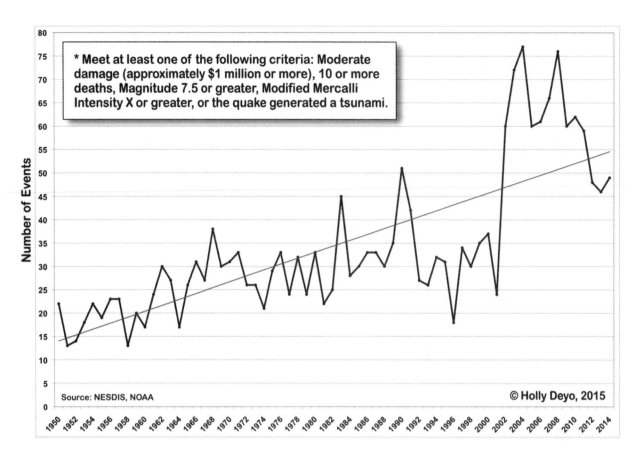

* Meet at least one of the following criteria: Moderate damage (approximately $1 million or more), 10 or more deaths, Magnitude 7.5 or greater, Modified Mercalli Intensity X or greater, or the quake generated a tsunami.

Source: NESDIS, NOAA

© Holly Deyo, 2015

Bigger, Not Better

A third proof comes from a USGS study unveiling there were more big earthquakes – in fact, TWICE as many in the first quarter of 2014 – compared to the same time frame clear back to 1979. Lead author of this study, Tom Parsons, a research geophysicist with USGS in Menlo Park, CA states. "We have recently experienced a period that has had one of the highest rates of great earthquakes ever recorded."[13]

Richter 7.0 Quakes Since 2000

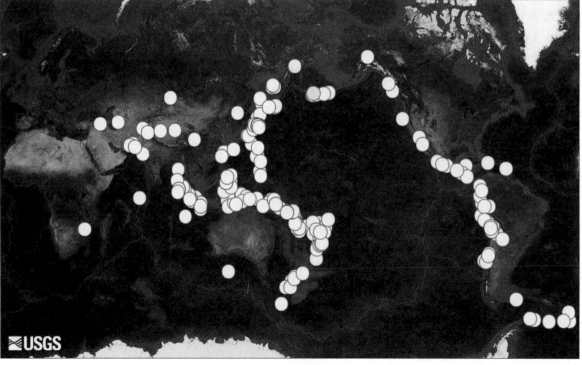

"The average rate of big earthquakes – those larger than magnitude 7 – has been 10 per year since 1979, the study reports. That rate rose to 12.5 per year starting in 1992, and then jumped to 16.7 per year starting in 2010 – a 65 percent increase compared to the rate since 1979. This increase accelerated in the first three months of 2014 to more than double the average since 1979, the researchers report."[14]

What does USGS attribute this to? Random chance.

Examining additional data shows something even more disquieting. According to USGS, "the frequency of earthquakes in the central and eastern U.S. has QUINTUPLED, to an average of 100 a year during the 2011-2013 period, up from only 20 per year during the 30-year period to 2000."[15]

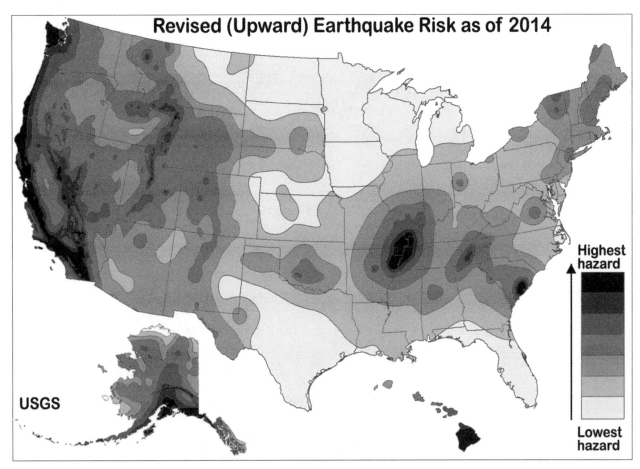

Image: Combining this new quake probability for the New Madrid Seismic Zone and California, and recent understanding that temblors can rupture multiple faults simultaneously, the USGS revised their Earthquake Risk Map in 2014.

"'We know the hazard has increased for small and moderate size earthquakes (in the central and eastern U.S.). We don't know as well how much the hazard has increased for large earthquakes. Our suspicion is it has, but we are working on understanding this,' said William Ellsworth, a scientist with the USGS."[16]

"Insurers are alarmed about higher quake risk. 'I worry that we will wake up one morning and see earthquake damage in our country that is as bad as that [which] has occurred in some developing nations that have experienced large earthquakes,' said Carl Hedde, head of risk accumulation at Munich Re America. 'Beyond building collapse, a large amount of our infrastructure could be immediately damaged. Our roads, bridges and energy transmission systems can be severely impacted.'"[17]

What states are cited as most in danger? Missouri and Illinois are in the Top 10 – the heart of the New Madrid Seismic Zone. According to USGS, earthquakes pose significant risk to 143 million people in 39 states. In 2015 the USGS revised the number of Americans at risk showing FEMA's number of 75 million was way too low. Instead, their data indicate nearly HALF of the population lies in a danger zone. Highest exposure to the strongest shaking is to people living in California followed by Washington, Utah, Tennessee, Oregon, South Carolina, Nevada, Arkansas, Missouri and Illinois. However, these 10 states aren't alone. This is USGS' breakdown of the number of Americans at risk of earthquakes based on 2013 population counts.[18]

State Populations Exposed to Earthquakes

Alabama	2,946,821	Massachusetts	5,713,347	Oregon	3,953,102
Arizona	2,181,934	Mississippi	1,102,354	Pennsylvania	4,149,921
Arkansas	1,918,993	Missouri	3,056,429	Rhode Island	1,010,722
California	38,148,001	Montana	639,536	South Carolina	4,752,617
Colorado	4,441,107	Nebraska	13,568	South Dakota	28,867
Connecticut	3,031,560	Nevada	2,830,256	Tennessee	6,422,565
Delaware	183,092	New Hampshire	1,321,574	Texas	1,173,162
Georgia	4,517,387	New Jersey	7,445,043	Utah	2,884,547
Idaho	1,477,049	New Mexico	1,577,788	Vermont	602,498
Illinois	1,522,342	New York	14,472,574	Virginia	2,316,984
Indiana	1,595,896	North Carolina	2,904,404	Washington	6,927,274
Kentucky	1,527,762	Ohio	367,517	West Virginia	295,602
Maine	1,394,095	Oklahoma	2,019,243	Wyoming	479, 063
Maryland	16,585			TOTAL	~143,000,000

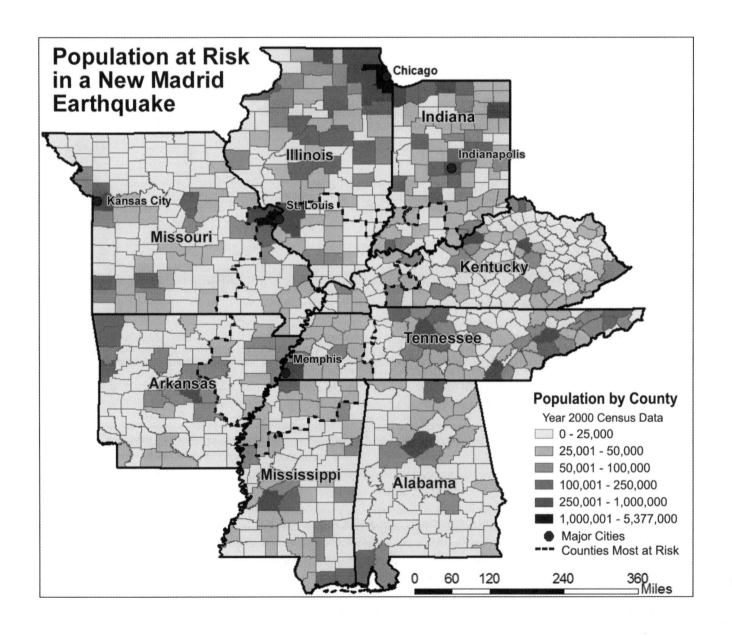

Population at Risk in a New Madrid Earthquake

Chicago · Indiana · Illinois · Indianapolis · Kansas City · St. Louis · Missouri · Kentucky · Tennessee · Memphis · Arkansas · Mississippi · Alabama

Population by County
Year 2000 Census Data
- 0 - 25,000
- 25,001 - 50,000
- 50,001 - 100,000
- 100,001 - 250,000
- 250,001 - 1,000,000
- 1,000,001 - 5,377,000
- ● Major Cities
- - - - Counties Most at Risk

0   60   120   240   360 Miles

FEMA PREPARES

Is a huge New Madrid shake the reason FEMA (Federal Emergency Management Agency) looked for sources where they could buy 144 million MREs in January 2011? (See next page.) They wanted "meals in support of disaster relief efforts based on a catastrophic disaster event within the New Madrid Fault System **for a survivor population** of 7M to be utilized for the sustainment of life during a 10-day period".[19]

A "survivor" population?

FEMA's RFI (Request for Information) was for enough meals to feed 7 million people twice a day for 10 days. (See image next page.)

This ties with the 2009 FEMA-funded study that examines a huge earthquake hitting the New Madrid fault. The following is excerpted from the Executive Summary – emphasis theirs.

"The results indicate that Tennessee, Arkansas, and Missouri are most severely impacted. Illinois and Kentucky are also impacted, though not as severely as the previous three states. Nearly **715,000 buildings are damaged** in the eight – state study region. About **42,000 search and rescue personnel** working in 1,500 teams are required to respond to the earthquakes. Damage to critical infrastructure (essential facilities, transportation and utility lifelines) is substantial in the **140 impacted counties** near the rupture zone, including 3,500 damaged bridges and nearly **425,000 breaks and leaks** to both local and interstate pipelines. Approximately **2.6 million households are without power** after the earthquake. Nearly **86,000 injuries and fatalities** result from damage to infrastructure. Nearly **130 hospitals are damaged** and most are located in the impacted counties near the rupture zone. There is extensive damage and substantial travel delays in both Memphis, Tennessee, and St. Louis, Missouri, thus hampering search and rescue as well as evacuation. Moreover roughly **15 major bridges are unusable**. Three days after the earthquake, **7.2 million people are still displaced** and **2 million people seek temporary shelter**. Direct economic losses for the eight states total **nearly $300 billion**, while indirect losses may be at least twice this amount."[20]

The other states factored into this 153-page study include Indiana, Mississippi and Alabama. One issue examined is what to do with the expected 3,500 that die in the quake plus the others that succumb in the following days if morgues are leveled. Then they looked at how would they secure some 350,000 prisoners.

THE 'BIG ONE'

No one expects scientists to be 'god' or have His knowledge. They are likely to change their published information and opinions as more accurate data becomes available. This is the case for both 'the big one' for California, the Pacific northwest and their earthquake assessment for the entire U.S.

In March 2015, geologists raised the chance of a magnitude 8.0 or greater earthquake hitting California within the next 30 years from 4.7% to 7%. The original time frame was much wider, which looked at a 50-year window at the outside, not 30. When people read 'window' dating, they breathe a sigh of relief thinking that a catastrophic quake won't happen until the furthest out date of 30 years. They automatically block out the word "**within**". The USGS window doesn't "X" off the 29 years up to that point. A nightmarish California mega-quake could happen tomorrow.

Multiple Simultaneous Ruptures

Pivotal to their map revision is the recent discovery that quakes on fault lines aren't necessarily well-behaved staying on the same fracture. Instead, large quakes can rupture simultaneously across multiple faults as far as seven miles apart.[21] One of the authors of this study, Ned Field states, "As we've added more faults, we realized we're not dealing with separate, isolated faults but really an interconnected fault system. The message to the average citizen hasn't changed. You live in earthquake country, and you should live every day like it's the day a Big One could hit."[22] Many faults at risk are in the Los Angeles area, home to some 13 million people, second in size only to New York. Compared to their previous forecast, the likelihood of moderate-sized earthquakes (magnitude 6.5 to 7.5) is lower, but for larger events it's higher.[23]

Four California faults cited by USGS as being particularly "ready" – their word – have enough stored energy to unleash destructive earthquakes right now. These include the Southern San Andreas, the Green Valley, the Hayward–Rodgers Creek and the Calaveras. All of these faults run directly under cities.

Buyers: Login | Register Vendors: Login | Register Accessibility

FEMA

RFI for Pre-Packaged Commercial Meals

Solicitation Number: HSFEHQ-11-R-Meals
Agency: Department of Homeland Security
Office: Federal Emergency Management Agency
Location: Logistics Branch

Notice Details | Packages | Interested Vendors List

Print Link

Complete View

- Original Synopsis
  Sources Sought
  Jan 20, 2011
  11:54 am
- Changed
  Jan 27, 2011
  3:59 pm

Return To Opportunities List

Solicitation Number: HSFEHQ-11-R-Meals

Notice Type: Sources Sought / Cancelled

Synopsis:
Added: Jan 20, 2011 11:54 am

The Federal Emergency Management Agency (FEMA) procures and stores pre-packaged commercial meals to support readiness capability for immediate distribution to disaster survivors routinely. The purpose of this Request for Information is to identify sources of supply for meals in support of disaster relief efforts based on a catastrophic disaster event within the New Madrid Fault System for a survivor population of 7M to be utilized for the sustainment of life during a 10-day period of operations. FEMA is considering the following specifications (14M meals per day):

GENERAL INFORMATION

Notice Type:
Sources Sought / Cancelled

Original Posted Date:
January 20, 2011

Posted Date:
January 27, 2011

Response Date:
Feb 03, 2011 11:59 pm Eastern

Original Response Date:
Feb 03, 2011 11:59 pm Eastern

Archiving Policy:
Automatic, 15 days after response date

Archive Date:
February 18, 2011

Original Set Aside:
N/A

Four California faults cited by USGS as being particularly "ready" – their word – have enough stored energy to unleash destructive earthquakes right now. These include the Southern San Andreas, the Green Valley, the Hayward–Rodgers Creek and the Calaveras. All of these faults run directly under cities.

In March 2015, UC Berkeley scientists discovered that two of California's most dangerous faults, the Hayward and Calaveras, are connected in two areas. One has a lengthy deep connect and the other is a shorter surface bridge. Because of these connections, scientists had to reassess the size of earthquakes that might shake the area. Previously when scientists thought the Hayward and Calaveras faults were separate, they put the quake threat at 6.9 to 7.0. Because of their combined strength, the expected magnitude has now been forecast at 7.3. That's *if* a rupture from Richmond stopped at Gilroy. Lead researcher Estelle Chaussard said, "A rupture from Richmond to Gilroy would produce about a 7.3 magnitude quake, but it would be even greater if the rupture extended south to Hollister, where the Calaveras Fault meets the San Andreas Fault."[24] What a difference 15 miles make.

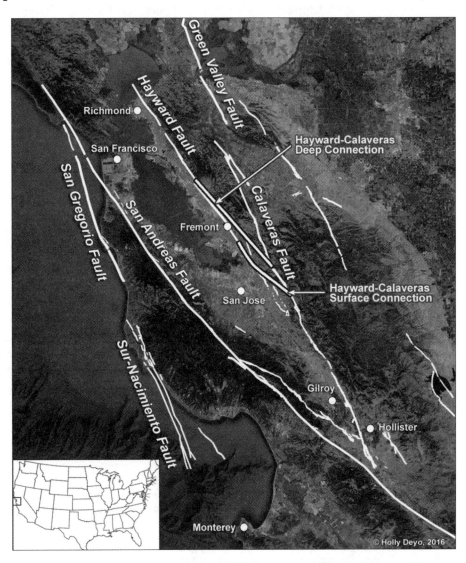

Chaussard and Berkeley colleagues made this new discovery by analyzing 19 years of satellite data and measured how much the south end of the Hayward Fault had moved. They thought it had stopped at Fremont, but it continued further merging with the Calaveras. This means they could rupture together producing a significantly more destructive earthquake than previously thought. But California's "big one" may not be the worst of it.

The Pacific Northwest Time Bomb

The worst natural disaster in America's history is coming say geologists. They are all in agreement. *It is absolutely coming.* This is based on the last 10,000 years' data showing 41 mega-quakes have hit the Pacific Northwest.

All of Canada, America and Mexico sit on the huge North American Plate. To the northwest, just off the coast of Washington, Oregon and California, lies the smaller Juan de Fuca Plate, which is trying to dive under the North American Plate, but it's stuck. When they unlock and snap, it will produce a megathrust earthquake. Within 15 minutes a massive wall of water will travel all the way to Japan and another will slam over the West Coast. Not only will this event unleash a colossal earthquake ripping devastation for some 700 miles, it will generate a 100-foot high tsunami. FEMA official Kenneth Murphy says, "Our operating assumption is that everything west of Interstate 5 will be toast."[25] That's covers up to 100 miles inland.

Seattle, Tacoma, Olympia, Portland, Salem and Eugene – wiped out – affecting about 7 million people. Oregon's Military Department Office of Emergency Management also puts Vancouver, B.C. squarely in the cross hairs and estimates those living in the hazard zone at much higher levels – 15 million.[26] That's many times over what was publicly released in July 2015 and government is notoriously tightlipped downplaying every disaster.

If the quake occurs during summer when tourists and residents line the beaches, the consequences would be catastrophically worse. Ian Madin director of Oregon's Department of Geology and Mineral Industries estimates that 75% of all structures in Oregon aren't designed to withstand a major Cascadia quake. FEMA calculates the temblor and tsunami will destroy about a million buildings, including 3,000 schools plus:

- **Half** of all highway bridges

- **Two-thirds** of all railroads and airports

- **Half** of all police stations

- **Two-thirds** of all hospitals and

- **One-third** of all fire stations.[27]

The fire station issue is a huge concern because one consequence of massive earthquakes is fire due to ruptured gas lines.

In addition to the nearly 13,000 people FEMA estimates will perish, another 27,000 will be injured. FEMA expects they will need to provide shelter for a million displaced people, plus food and water for another 2½ million.

Scientists say this mega-quake *is* coming. There is no doubt. They occur generally every 240 years and this next one is way overdue since the last one struck on January 26, 1700. By drilling into the sea floor they found conclusive evidence that 41 such events have regularly hit America's West Coast over the past 10,000 years. The 1700 mega-quake, which was a full-length rupture of the Cascadia Fault, sent a 600' wall of water all the way to Japan. It's now been over 300 years since the last major event so the next monster temblor could strike at any moment. Of those 41, about half impacted the entire fault line while 22 involved just the southern end with "smaller" temblors ranging from 8.0 – 8.2. Smaller in this sense is definitely a relative term.

Most people aren't aware of the devastation brought about by the 1700 event because American Indians mostly inhabited the area. Because they had no written language, history was kept by oral tradition so it wasn't as readily available to the outside world. The same was true for the First Nations people that lived on Vancouver Island, British Columbia. There "the earthquake shaking collapsed houses of the Cowichan people on Vancouver Island and caused numerous landslides. The shaking was so violent that people could not stand and so prolonged that it made them sick. On the west coast of Vancouver Island, the tsunami completely destroyed the winter village of the Pachena Bay people with no survivors."[28]

Outside of northwestern North America in 1700 people barely knew this country existed. From south-central Alaska to Oregon's Cape Blanco was uncharted until the Spanish and English explored it 70 years later. Yet, when the Juan de Fuca and North America Plates suddenly shifted in 1700, America was on the map. The tsunami that hit Japan flooded their fields and washed away homes. Samurai, merchants, and villagers all recorded the mysterious event, but they saw no storm nor felt an earthquake. So this tsunami became known as an "orphan". Today, with millions of people living in the danger zone combined with the Internet, people would know instantly what happened.

Professor Michio Kaku, physicist and professor at City College of New York agrees with USGS scientists, this mega-quake is coming. Kaku said the severity has not been exaggerated one bit and that it will explode with 30 times the maximum energy of the San Andreas Fault – the one familiar to most people. Hollywood likes to portray "the big one" originating in California and it may well have a big one, but it won't likely be as bad as what hits north on the Cascadia Fault.

AFTERMATH

One of the reasons people will have a difficult time evacuating or relocating after the quake is liquefaction. This makes what used to be solid ground turn into quicksand. Scientists estimate that the expected mega-quake would last a minimum of four minutes followed within 15 minutes by the massive tsunami. Contrast that to the 1989 Loma Prieta 6.9 quake that lasted just 15 seconds. It killed 63 people and caused $6 billion in damages. Japan's government estimates their 2011 9.0-mega-quake and tsunami shook the country for 6 minutes and did about $300 billion in damages.[29]

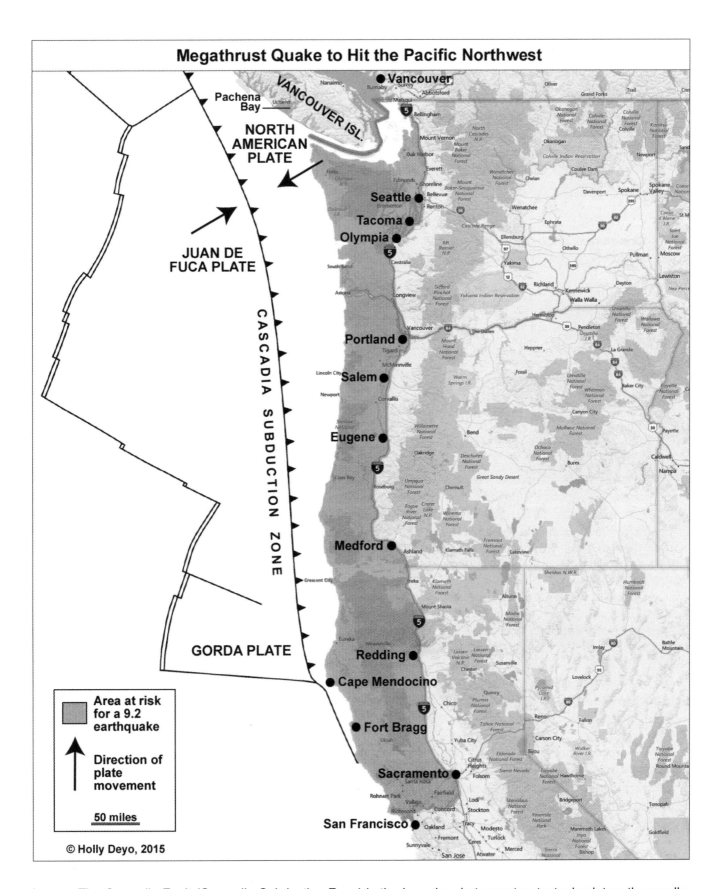

Image: The Cascadia Fault (Cascadia Subduction Zone) is the boundary between two tectonic plates: the smaller offshore Juan de Fuca plate that's sliding northeast under the much larger North American plate, moving southwest. This fault line begins near Cape Mendocino, California, runs along Oregon and Washington, and ends around Vancouver Island, Canada.

Oregon's Seismic Safety Policy Advisory Commission estimates that in the I-5 corridor it will take:

- 1 – 3 months to restore electricity
- 1 – 12 months to restore drinking water and sewer service
- 6 – 12 months to even partially restore major highways, complete restoration – 3 to 5 years with a nationwide effort
- 18 months to restore health-care facilities.

On the coast, those numbers go up. Whoever chooses or has no choice but to stay there will spend:

- 3 – 6 months without electricity
- 1 – 3 years without drinking water and sewage systems
- 3 or more years without hospitals.[30]

Those estimates don't apply to the tsunami-inundation zone, which will remain uninhabitable for years.[31] Ian Madin calculates that the West Coast will permanently drop up to 9 feet and lessening as it goes inland toward Salem.[32]

Kaku said that the 70,000 people at greatest risk – those in the inundation zone – mostly have zero idea that such a danger awaits them; that "it barely rates on their radar screen."[33]

In the mega-quake that hit in 1700, a massive tsunami surged over Japan that originated at the Cascadia Fault. This discovery was made just in the last decade or so. Once physicists were able to connect these two events, they're able to calculate the energy released and the earthquake's magnitude. To show just how mighty a quake of this size is, Kaku shared that a similar sized event with the same fault dynamics created the Himalayan Mountains thrusting up Mt. Everest some 29,000 feet. When Fox News interviewer Shephard Smith asked Michio Kaku since he knows what awaits people on the West Coast if he'd live there, Kaku responded, "I'd have to think twice."[34]

Great Quakes Rising

A fourth piece of evidence comes from a different source: the Geological Society of America. During their annual meeting in Vancouver, British Columbia in October 2014, they shared that the number of 'great' earthquakes nearly TRIPLED over the last decade. Between 2004 and 2014, 18 Richter 8 and larger quakes rattled Earth. That's an increase of 265% when the entire preceding 100 years saw just 71 temblors of this size.[35]

Eric Niiler for *Discovery News* reports, "Many scientists believe we may be entering a time of greater seismic and volcanic activity. Imagine the 1,300-foot glacier acting as a crushing deep-freeze for hot lava coming from the Earth's core. Less ice, more magma."[36] Besides glaciers acting on magma, for earthquakes, the weight of ice depresses the crust where it sits and in essence, keeps it in place. However, when glaciers melt, stresses on earthquake faults can shift leaving them more vulnerable to movement.

Last Thoughts on Increasing Earthquakes

Even if the 'random chance' explanation were true, which is weak in light of all the evidence, much like the global warming debate, we still have to deal with the consequences. Whether or not USGS changes its averages for the annual number of quakes, their own statistics and commentaries show that earthquakes are on the rise for a variety of reasons.

Fracking pumped up quake activity in the U.S. by 400% from 2010 – 2013. A significantly bigger jump showed in 2014 and an even larger increase the next year.

Richter 7 shakers, globally, have taken a dramatic upward turn since 1992, doubling in the first quarter of 2014 compared to 1979.

Richter 8 and larger temblors around the world jumped 265% between 2004 and 2014.

A USGS paper published in 2015 reveals that earthquakes could rupture multiple faults simultaneously making California living a little shakier.

Earthquake risk for the U.S. was determined by USGS scientists to be greater than previously thought, which necessitated their risk map to be redrawn in 2014.

Worst of all, "dangerous and destructive" earthquakes have steadily risen since 1950. We may be in for a bit of a jolt.

Chapter 3: Volcanoes, Earthquakes' Cousins

I will show wonders in the heavens above and signs on the earth below, blood and fire and billows of smoke. The sun will be turned to darkness and the moon to blood before the coming of the great and glorious day of the Lord. —Acts 2:19-20 (NIV)

And I will show wonders in the heavens and in the earth: Blood and fire and pillars of smoke. The sun shall be turned into darkness, and the moon into blood, before the coming of the great and awesome day of the Lord. —Joel 2:30-31 (NKJV)

Volcanoes have played an important part in our lives going back to Biblical times and beyond. They release heat and pressure from the earth's core in addition to producing material used in concrete, roofing and nuclear reactor construction. Volcanoes were instrumental in forming Earth and filled outlying farming areas with mineral-rich soil. The Garden of Eden sits within protective walls of a massive caldera – a huge volcano that fell in on itself. When Adam and Eve were kicked out of paradise, God guarded Eden's pathway with three roiling volcanoes.

However, when volcanoes go on a tear, they can extinguish life in a single blast.

Mount St Helens

Usually volcanoes give notice they're about to erupt, but not always. Sometimes they fool even the experts and deliver an unexpected, terrifying surprise. When Mount St. Helens blew on May 18, 1980, geologists thought an eruption would come 'at some point', but due to their crude monitoring equipment back then, they couldn't pinpoint it. By late April, Helen's bulge grew 5 feet a day. That was extraordinary. Unbelievably, a mere 5.1 temblor pushed her over the edge and she blew out in a rare, phenomenally powerful sideways blast. When geologist David Johnston who was monitoring the volcano 5 miles away saw the quake spike on the seismometer, he hollered excitedly into his radio, "This is it!"[37] Johnston died immediately in that explosion along with 56 others.

Within 15 seconds, the whole north face of the mountain was on the move. ...the north face collapsed, releasing superheated gases and trapped magma in a massive lateral explosion.

The abrupt release of pressure over the magma chamber created a glowing cloud of superheated gas and rock debris blown out of the mountain face moving at nearly supersonic speeds. Everything within eight miles of the blast was wiped out almost instantly. The shockwave rolled over the forest for another 19 miles, leveling century-old trees; all the trunks neatly aligned to the north. Beyond this "tree down zone" the forest remained standing but was seared lifeless. The area devastated by the direct blast force covered an area of nearly 230 square miles. Shortly after the lateral blast, a second, vertical explosion occurred at the summit of the volcano, sending a mushroom cloud of ash and gases more than 12 miles into the air. The cloud of ash darkened the skies, causing street lights to come on as far away as Spokane, Wash., more than 300 miles away. Ash continued to erupt for more than nine hours. Ultimately, an estimated 540 million tons of ash drifted up to 2,200 square miles settling over seven states.

As the north face was blown apart, the heat instantly vaporized glacial ice and snow around the remaining parts of the mountain. By 8:50 a.m., massive mudflows were moving through the river systems to the west and southeast of Mount St. Helens. The hot mud moved in excess of 90 mph, sweeping away everything in its path.[38]

Image: The May 18, 1980 eruption at Mount St. Helens was one of the greatest volcanic explosions ever recorded in North America measured at a VEI 5.[39] The eruption sent an ash plume over 12 miles into the atmosphere. Prevailing winds carried it northeast, where it turned daylight to darkness over 120 miles away. (USGS)

IMPACTS

Ash piled up 10 inches deep as far as 10 miles away and ½ inch deep 300 miles downwind. By day three, the eruptive cloud's murkiness had crossed the entire US. Two weeks later, it had encircled the planet.

The cost was more than just weeks of "bad air" and dead trees. When Mount St. Helens finally quieted six years later, her appearance had been greatly altered. Considered just as beautiful, her size was whittled by over 1,300 feet.

The eruption stole 57 lives. Countless wildlife died. Anything that couldn't "burrow in" to escape the burning explosion was incinerated. Another 7,000 big game animals perished as well. Hatcheries lost 12 million salmon fingerlings. The force of this 24-megaton blast flattened enough trees to build 300,000 two-bedroom homes.

Then came the lahars – those horrific unstoppable mudflows. Their chaos damaged 27 bridges, nearly 200 homes, 650 miles of roads and 16 miles of railroad. Lahar damage was not limited to land. The Cowlitz River was so clogged with slurry, water "flowed" at only 20% of its normal rate. The Columbia River's channel was equally impaired. As the lahar poured in, its depth was reduced from 40 feet to just 14. As a result, 31 ships were stranded in upstream ports. Dredging efforts to make rivers navigable again tallied $215 million."[40]

At the time of the eruption, this author worked at the corporate headquarters of a national building materials center in Kansas City. We purchased a good deal of lumber and dimension wood products from Weyerhaeuser, one of the world's largest producers of softwood lumber.

Weyerhaeuser, who has owned and managed the St. Helens Tree Farm since 1900, was the largest private landowner impacted by the eruption. Nearly 68,000 acres or about 14% of the Tree Farm were devastated besides 26,000 acres of saplings. In addition to trees, Weyerhaeuser lost 650 miles of their own roads and 16 miles of railroad, three logging camps and shops, buildings, equipment and vehicles.

A collective look of disbelief showed on all 121 faces in our Purchasing Department. Most of us had never witnessed such a cataclysmic eruption, certainly nothing this close. The horror people faced "over there" transfixed us and we were privately grateful Kansas City was a good distance from Washington. Meanwhile our corporate officers brainstormed how they would supply lumber to their 120 stores and seven distribution centers. They saw a lot of zeros added to the loss column with supplies of Douglas fir and red cedar greatly impacted. Different priorities.

Weyerhaeuser flew out the VP of Purchasing of our company to see the devastation first hand. What he witnessed via company chopper was beyond staggering. Everything that had thrived and was rich green the day before merged into a field of gray blah. Trees that weren't flattened by the blast were creepy skeletons standing at attention. Some trees and plants were too stubborn to get the message that everything was dead and just waiting to fall over. By June 1987, Weyerhaeuser had completed reforestation of the Tree Farm. In all, over 18 million trees were hand planted, one by one, on over 45,000 acres.

HELENS FUTURE

So is it over, the eruptions? Hardly. In 2004, a swarm of earthquakes culminated in a small eruption on October 1st. The mountain gave one week's notice. Magma began pooling 2½ – 3 miles under the volcano in 2008 and the chamber is slowly refilling.

"It looks like Mt. St. Helens is getting ready to erupt again, and it can happen in the order of years to decades," said USGS seismologist Seth Moran.[41] Since she is the lower 48's most active volcano St Helens bears watching.

So we know something "big" can happen in our lifetime. The next question is when scientists insist a Yellowstone super-eruption isn't likely to occur soon, why are they spending millions of dollars on studies for just such a scenario?

Look how comparatively small Mount St. Helens blast was compared to Yellowstone's mega-eruptions.

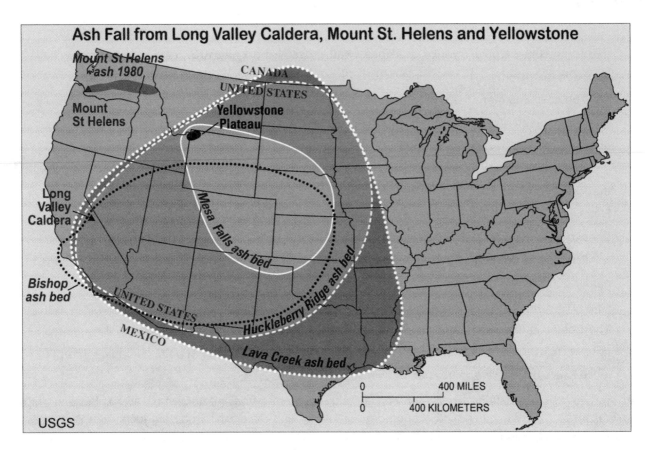

Ash Fall from Long Valley Caldera, Mount St. Helens and Yellowstone

USGS

Supervolcanoes

Scientists estimate there are around 20 supervolcanoes in the world. Some are dormant, some extinct and some simmering. According to two new studies published in the journal *Nature Geoscience*, unlike average volcanoes, supervolcanoes can explode spontaneously and don't need triggers like earthquakes.[42] The European

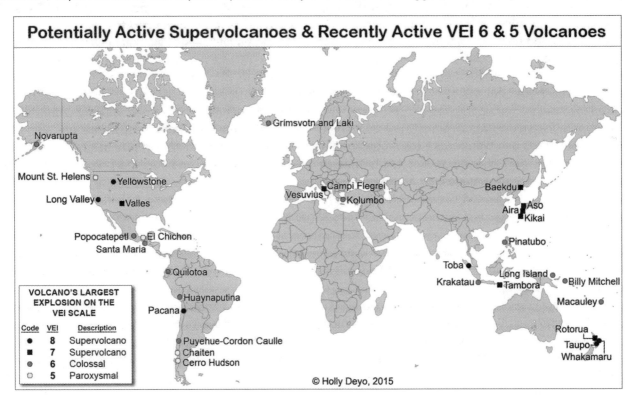

Potentially Active Supervolcanoes & Recently Active VEI 6 & 5 Volcanoes

© Holly Deyo, 2015

Science Foundation says that the rise in volcanic activity on the planet is at a 300-year peak and suggests that a massive eruption could be possible in the not-too-distant future. Their latest report, "Extreme Geo-hazards: Reducing the Disaster Risk and Increasing Resilience," warns global government's have done virtually nothing to prepare.[43]

Scientists overall agree that on the Volcanic Explosivity Index (VEI) – a measurement of volcanoes like Richter is for earthquakes – supervolcanoes must rate a 7 or 8, which describes their eruptions as "colossal". Some VEI 6 volcanoes are also listed – those that have erupted recently, geologically speaking. Smithsonian geologist Ben Andrews states 14 supervolcanoes are still potentially active and include:

VEI	LOCATION	LAST ERUPTION NOTES
8	Yellowstone, NW corner of Wyoming	3 super-eruptions: Huckleberry Ridge 2.1 million years ago; Mesa Falls 1.3 million years ago; Lava Creek eruption 640,000 years ago
8	Long Valley, California	760,000 years ago
8	Pacana Caldera, Chile	Erupted with a VEI-8 explosion 4 million years ago and as recently as, but not with that force, in 2013
8	Lake Toba, North Sumatra, Indonesia	74,000 years ago
8	Whakamaru, North Island, New Zealand	254,000 years ago
8	Lake Taupo, North Island, New Zealand	26,000 years ago, largest known eruption over the past 70,000 years. Erupted in 180. Affected skies over Rome and China.
7	Valles Calderas, New Mexico	1.12 million years ago
7	Campi Flegrei, Naples, Italy	39,280 years ago
7	Mount Tambora, Sumbawa Island, Indonesia	**MOST RECENT SUPERVOLCANO ERUPTION** caused the Year Without a Summer in 1816 in North America and Europe. Crops failed, livestock died in plunging temps, brought worst famine of the 19th. Ejecta shot 28 miles high. The mountain shrunk 4,100 feet when its top blew off. 92,000 people immediately died. Snow fell in England and Canada in June, and frost was present throughout summer. Snow and ash fell into European rivers, causing Typhus outbreaks. Crop losses in Europe also led to starvation. 200,000 people died of Typhus and hunger in 1816.
7	Aira Caldera, Kyosho, Japan	~22,000 years ago with continuing activity
7	Kikai Caldera, Osumai Islands, Japan	6,300 years ago
7	Mount Aso, Island of Kyushu, Japan	4 super eruptions 300,000 to 90,000 years ago
7	Baekdu Mountain, China-N. Korea border	969 AD Limited regional climatic effects.
7	Rotorua Caldera, North Island, NZ	Last major eruption ~240,000 years ago
6	Novarupta	Last major eruption 1912
6	Pinatubo, Luzon, Philippines	Last major eruption 1991
6	Santa Maria, Guatemala	Last major eruption 1902
6	Bardarbunga, Iceland	Last major eruption 1477, last known eruption 1910. August 2014 swarm of 1,600 earthquakes in 48-hours.
6	Billy Mitchell, Bougainville Island, PNG	Last major eruption 1580
6	Laki south of Iceland	1783-1784. Emitted 120 million tons of sulfur dioxide, produced a Volcanic winter in 1783 on the North Hemisphere, crop failures in Europe, may have caused droughts in India. Eruption estimated to have killed over six million people globally, making it the deadliest in historical times.
6	Grímsvotn south of Iceland	1783-1784 Erupted at same time as Laki, but mostly under the glacier. Erupted again in 1998, 2004, 2011. Disrupted air travel in Iceland, Scotland, Norway, Denmark.
6	Long Island, Papua New Guinea	1660
6	Kolumbo, Santorini, Greece	1650

VEI	LOCATION	LAST ERUPTION NOTES
6	Huaynaputina, Peru	1600
6	Macauley Island, Kermadec Islands, NZ	4360 BC
6	Popocatepetl, Mexico	Most active volcano in Mexico with over 15 major eruptions since 1519 and another in 1947. December 2000, tens of thousands of people were evacuated before its largest display in 1,200 years. Other eruptions: 1994, 2005, 2012, 2013, 2014.
6	Puyehue-Cordon Caulle	June 2011 – VEI 5 eruption; at least 4,200 people evacuated. 4.5 million fish and 40-60% of livestock perished (600,000 to 1M sheep and 36,000 goats) from starvation and dehydration when water and forage were covered in ash. Numerous flights disrupted in Paraguay, Uruguay, Chile, Argentina, Brazil closing airports for several days. Widespread flight disruptions in New Zealand, Australia and South Africa.

Yellowstone

In December 2013 scientists revealed that the massive magma pocket under Yellowstone is 2½ times larger than previously thought. Imagine an area of fiery liquid rock 55 miles long by 20 miles on each side and six miles deep. While the chamber continues to fill, right now there is enough material to equal this supervolcano's biggest-ever eruption.[44] It's hard to conceive of something this vast. To put it into perspective, this explosion was 2,000 times the size of the 1980 Mount St. Helens eruption.

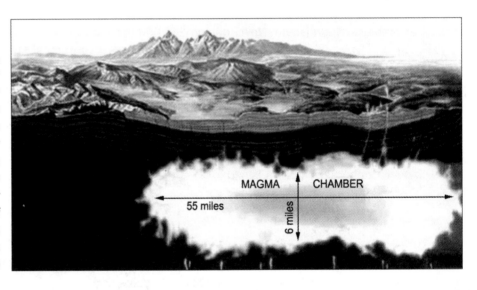

Discoveries didn't end there. In April 2015, seismologists from the University of Utah found a massive reservoir of partly molten rock right under the main chamber. It solved the mystery of why Yellowstone releases more carbon dioxide than could be explained by gases coming from the magma chamber.

The newly discovered reservoir is about 4½ times the size of the main chamber. The amount of magma it contains is simply staggering. Scientists estimate that it's enough to fill the Grand Canyon more than 11 times. If you've never flown over this natural wonder, there is no way to convey just how mammoth it is. Looking from a plane's window, this massive gash in Earth's crust seems to extend endlessly.

Photo: Anasazi Indian granaries were situated high above the Colorado River at Nankoweap Creek. This image is of Marble Canyon on the left bank (South Rim) 500 feet above the Colorado River, looking southwest down the Grand Canyon. (Courtesy Drenaline)

The photo of Marble Canyon shows only the smallest sliver of the Canyon, but illustrates just how dramatic the steep walls are. The Grand Canyon twists and turns for nearly 280 miles and averages about a mile deep. This massive gorge widens to 18 miles across and narrows to only 600 feet in other places. Imagine filling this massive earthen "bowl" 11 times over with magma! That's how much magma and red-hot rock gurgles below Yellowstone.

NEXT SUPER-ERUPTION

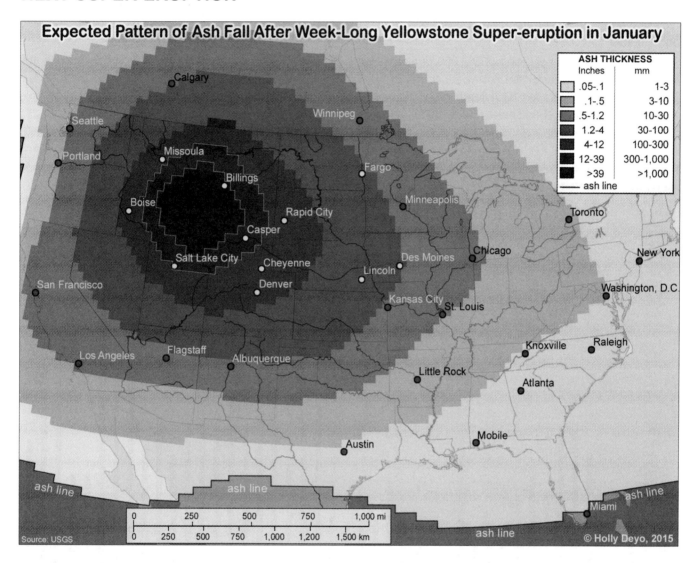

While scientists contend an eruption isn't imminent, they monitor it closely and were compelled to examine a mega-eruption scenario happening at different times of the year covering several timeframes. Because wind blows at various speeds during the year, they made models for January, April, July and October for an eruption lasting three days, a week and a month. None of the outcomes are happy for America – or the rest of the world for that matter. Its ash cloud would encircle Earth many times producing a nuclear winter, blocking out sunlight, fresh air and polluting water. A gagging all-pervasive stench from the dead would be impossible to escape creating monumental misery. People would need LOTS of water filters, breathing masks and stored food just to survive. With good reason, Blackfoot Indians named the Yellowstone area 'the land of evil spirits' and generally shunned it except when collecting obsidian for arrowheads.

YELLOWSTONE SUPERVOLCANO ERUPTIONS WERE EVEN BIGGER

In February 2016, scientists released a disturbing study about Yellowstone's historic explosions. The team discovered that Yellowstone had produced just 12 distinct Yellowstone mega-eruptions, but they were more violent. This coincides with the theory that fewer eruptions generate more violent ones. Lead scientist, Dr. Thomas Knott, of the Leicester University study, "The size and magnitude of this newly defined eruption is as large, if not larger, than better known eruptions at Yellowstone, and it is just the first in an emerging record of newly discovered super-eruptions during a period of intense magmatic activity between 8 and 12 million years ago."[45]

RECENT ACTIVITY

Over three miles of Firehole Lake Drive, between the Old Faithful geyser and Madison Junction, turned into a "soupy mess" and closed the road in July 2014. Park spokesman Dan Hottle described the road melt as "extreme and unusual".[46]

Though Yellowstone gets 1,000-3,000 quakes a year, most are too small to feel. However, a 4.8 quake – the largest in 34 years – struck the northwest corner of the park on March 30, 2014. A flurry of smaller quakes followed. The larger temblor was felt 23 miles away in two small Montana towns, Gardiner and West Yellowstone. People reported feeling the ground shake and items fell off shelves in a local grocery store.[47]

During winter 2014 – 2015, visitors reported that Yellowstone Park's Boiling River was hotter than they'd ever remembered it. On one of the coldest days of winter, the river's temperature climbed to 140 degrees. Normally it hovers around 134. Park scientists admit they have no explanation underscoring that the mechanics of Yellowstone aren't well understand.[48]

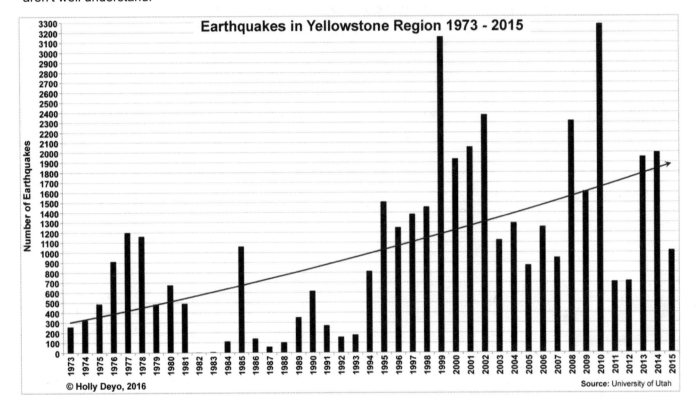

"A report from scientists at the University of Utah shows that the 'supervolcano' underneath Yellowstone has risen at a record rate since mid 2004. The journal *Science* … reported that the caldera floor of the massive volcano has risen 3 inches, per year, for the past three years. This is a rate of growth three times more rapid than ever observed, since records were first kept back in 1923. … According to the US Geological Survey, the rate (of uplift) slowed between 2007 and 2010 to a centimeter (.4 inch) a year or less. However, since the start of the 2004 swelling, ground levels over the volcano have been raised by as much as 10 inches (25 centimeters) in places.

"'It's an extraordinary uplift, because it covers such a large area and the rates are so high,' said the University of Utah's Bob Smith, a long-time expert in Yellowstone's volcanism in an interview with National Geographic.'"[49]

Dan Dzurisin, Yellowstone expert with the USGS Cascades Volcano Observatory in Washington state. "'There has to be magma in the crust, or we wouldn't have all the hydrothermal activity that we have. There is so much heat coming out of Yellowstone right now that if it wasn't being reheated by magma, the whole system would have gone stone cold since the time of the last eruption 70,000 years ago."[50]

The Sun-Moon-Volcano Connection

It's not your imagination. Since 2014 volcanoes have been exploding with greater frequency. Recently they've burped and blown in Iceland, Hawaii, Indonesia, Vanuatu, Ecuador, Chile, Guatemala, Colombia, Mexico, Costa Rica, Japan, Russia, Antarctica, the Philippines and Papua New Guinea. Activity accelerated to the point where scientists are probing the cause and finding interesting patterns.

We all know that the moon affects tides on Earth. Likewise, the Sun and moon both influence our planet's rotation. New research shows that while these changes are extremely small on the surface, their effects on Earth's interior are much greater.

Terra Nova journal published a study in October 2013 outlining an important correlation between major volcanic eruptions and length of a day going back to 1790 AD.[51] They discovered that "relatively large changes in rotation rate were immediately followed by an increase in the number of large volcanic eruptions. And, more than merely being correlated, the authors believe that the rotation changes might actually have triggered these large eruptions."[52]

The massive amount of energy needed to alter the planet's rotation then moves both into the atmosphere and under Earth's surface. This barrage of subterranean energy further stresses volcanoes making it easier for magma to rise to the surface creating more eruptions.

A shortened day is not the only thing scientists found triggering volcanoes and this other factor has even greater impact: melting glaciers.

THE GLACIER FACTOR

Every year Antarctica loses 91.5 billion U.S. tons of ice, which tripled in the last decade.[53]

When the weight of massive glaciers diminishes, there's less force to keep Earth's crust in place so it snaps back from its formerly bent position. For some time now, scientists have gathered information supporting this theory.

Roughly 19,000 years ago, glaciers were at their peak. Between 12,000 and 7,000 years ago, when vast amounts of ice melted "the global level of volcanic activity rose by up to six times. Around the same period the rate of volcanic activity in Iceland soared to at least 30 times today's level."[54] Scientists have found corroborating evidence in Europe, North America and Antarctica.

NASA's lead polar ice researcher, Thomas P. Wagner, stated, "This is really happening. There is nothing to stop it now."[55]

It's common knowledge that volcanic eruptions can alter Earth's climate by throwing up enough ash to block the Sun and drop temperatures. Marion Jegen, a geophysicist at Geomar in Germany, wondered if the reverse were true. Could climate affect volcanic activity?

To test their theory, Jegen and her colleagues looked at core samples drilled in the oceans off South and Central America. The sediment gave a clear view of the last million years of Earth's climate. Periodically, shifts in Earth's orbit, cause rapid warming of the planet, massive glacier melt and then a quick rise in sea levels. Their core samples revealed many layers of volcanic ash after those periods. This was especially apparent around Costa Rica and at other places that saw 5 – 10 times as much volcanic activity when glaciers melted.

The key lay in sea levels rising *rapidly*.

When glaciers melt, it changes the weight distribution on Earth in a double whammy. Pressures on the continents reduce while weight on the ocean's floor crust increase. If this occurs slowly, Earth has time to adjust and there's less impact on volcanism. Jegen's theory panned out. She correlated correctly that the speed of glacier melt determines how intensely volcanic eruptions increase.

So we're in a bit of a paradox. Antarctica loses over 91 billion tons of ice yet numerous scientific articles report that its ice has expanded to record-high levels. How can that be? Maybe the answer once again lies with volcanoes.

Many mountains in Antarctica aren't volcanic, but radar located a number of them deep under the ice and also revealed a layer of ash likely from Mount Waesche's eruption 8,000 years ago. Virtually all are on West Antarctica's side – the portion that's collapsing. In 2013 a newly formed volcano was discovered and it may have already erupted. These subsurface eruptions are likely fueling Antarctica's ice melt. More ice melt = more eruptions.

Last Thoughts on Increasing Volcanic Eruptions

Earth has about 1,500 active volcanoes including 14 supervolcanoes. Eruptions often go hand-in-hand with earthquakes and quake activity is on the rise. So are "significant eruptions" according to NOAA's database. A significant eruption is one that meets at least one of these yardsticks:

- Causes fatalities
- Causes moderate damage of at least $1 million or more
- Has a Volcanic Explosivity Index (VEI) of 6 or higher
- Generates a tsunami, or
- Was associated with a major earthquake.

Mount St. Helens is refueling for another explosion and scientists discovered in 2013 that Yellowstone's magma chamber is 2½ times larger than originally thought. This volcano frequently sees swarms of small earthquakes. However, in September 2013, *three* swarms hit the park simultaneously. Geophysicist Bob Smith stated he'd never witnessed two concurrent quake swarms in 53 years of monitoring seismic activity in and around Yellowstone, let alone three.[56]

In 2014 one of the park's roads melted, a larger-than-usual quake hit and Boiling River's temperature elevated to heights people never before remembered. Its caldera continues to heave and fall like a living breathing giant. Yet scientists assure us this is all perfectly normal.

Based on the previous three mega-eruptions, some people contend Yellowstone is overdue for another such event while others say the three doesn't constitute a trend.

Scientists recently proved that the Sun and moon have an effect on volcanism ramping up on shorter days. Rapidly melting glaciers also increase eruptions by moving weight off continents before Earth has time to absorb the change. This lets Earth's crust "snap" back into place from being bent triggering quakes and eruptions.

Chapter 4: Tornadoes – Nature's Most Violent Storms

Beginning 15 years ago, things started changing with tornadoes. In recent trends, America sees around 1,300 twisters every year[57] though NOAA statistics used to say about 1000[58]occurred. While wild weather isn't producing more of these damaging storms, but they're striking more frequently in clusters or outbreaks. It used to be that 150 days out of the year saw at least one twister. Days with tornadoes have now dropped to 100, but the number of them hitting *on the same day* has more than tripled. More often they're coming in swarms, sometimes by the dozens.

In a U.S. study, scientists looked at six decades of data through 2014 and the change was unmistakable. "On the list of the 10 single days with the most tornadoes since 1954, eight have occurred since 1999, including five since 2011. That year alone had days with 115, 73, 53 and 52 twisters.

"The average number of days annually with at least 20 tornadoes has more than doubled since the 1970s to upwards of five days per year in the past decade."[59] On days that had at least 30 tornadoes, there has been an average of three per year in the past decade, compared to 0.6 days per year in the 1970s. This means preparing for a lot more damage.

This study, published in *Science*, didn't explain the change, but said that more instances of heavy rain are falling all over the world. Couple that with heat and they inferred this could be the cause.

As a kid growing up in Tornado Alley, we lived in a protected vortex. How our family was never in "twister cross hairs" is a mystery. Every family on our street used to watch from our front yards ominous green anvil-shaped clouds traverse the skies. We knew these brought nasty storms, often tornadoes. Yet we all watched. With the escalation of wild weather, we'd have to give this activity a second thought.

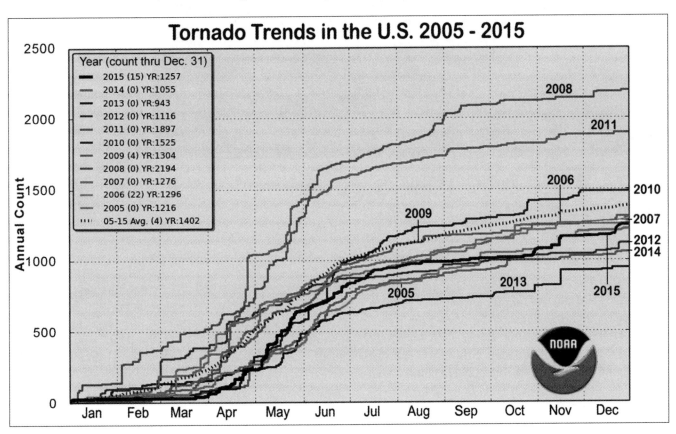

AN INCONVENIENT TWISTER

May 3 and 4, 1999 was a time no Oklahoman will forget. Moore, a suburb of Oklahoma City was slammed with the 5th monster twister in 15 years. The population of 55,000 still couldn't have anticipated what awaited them despite not being strangers to tornadoes. The tornado first touched down at 6:23 p.m. and in less than 21 hours, 76 twisters forged the Oklahoma / Kansas outbreak. At least five were EF4s and EF5s.

Designated as the A9 Bridge Creek tornado, this F5 beast stretched a mile wide and tore up everything in its path. The storm formed about 45 miles southwest of Oklahoma City and rampaged on the ground for four hours angling to the northeast. As skies cleared, residents took in the remains in horror.

Oklahoma officials estimate that nearly 8,100 homes and businesses were damaged or destroyed. Kansas lost over 1,100. Together those two states saw $3 billion in damages.[60] In Mulhall, a town due north of Oklahoma City, more than 75% of it had been destroyed. Even well built homes on the edge of town were nearly flattened. Worst though was the loss of 54 lives. Most of the fatalities occurred in Oklahoma – 45 in all, another four died in Kansas; Texas lost one person and Tennessee another four.

What had been a friendly neighborhood with pristine homes, neatly edged lawns and beautifully tended gardens was now a sea of tan. Homes were flattened or blown off foundations.

Photo: Image of Tornado A9 snapped by general forecaster Erin Maxwell near the Bridge Creek, OK area on May 3, 1999.

Some homes that remained looked from the air like dollhouses with top floors and roofs ripped off. Other streets looked like a precision bomb had detonated in a lumberyard, blowing up houses till they were nothing but sticks of timber. Streets over where houses might be intact, otherwise green lawns were strewn with debris. 2x4's skewered through sides of cars. Trees were debarked and stood naked with not a leaf in sight. The only dots of color in this vast expanse of tan destruction were cars arriving to begin removing mountains of rubble and blue Porta Potties.

RELIVING A NIGHT OF TERROR

Dixie and her husband, Master Sgt. John Szymanski were newlyweds and had just moved into their new home. John had spent the afternoon mowing and planting flowers. That evening the two made dinner and watched the ominous-sounding weather on TV. When the tornado barreled toward their neighborhood, they took refuge in the closet. As the tornado roared closer John wrapped his arms around Dixie as they lay on the floor. John recounted, "And then the house exploded around us, just disintegrated. I was thrown a few feet and just bounced on the ground, and she was gone. I just couldn't hold onto her."

John and Dixie Szymanski

Minutes later, John freed himself and looked around in shock. The neighborhood was gone. "There was nothing left. Must have been 50 houses."

In his anxiety to find Dixie, John didn't realize his left ankle was broken and his right knee was damaged. He found Dixie in the neighbor's yard with the left side of her face smashed. Though the twister had hurled her forcefully to the ground at least Dixie was alive. She and John lost count of the surgeries required to reconstruct her face. Her nose was broken in four places; Dixie's neck was broken along with her left cheek, jaw, skull and the bones around her left eye.

Dixie doesn't remember much as they kept her on morphine. One of the worst procedures involved doctors injecting her eye with a deadening agent so they could sew her eyelids shut. John remembers every horrific detail.

When new storm warnings sound, Dixie and their kids go to bed, but John can't sleep. He stays up, keeps an eye on things so they never go through another such disaster.[61]

Renee Faulkinberry

A decade later, Renee Faulkinberry recalled how she and her 16-year-old daughter huddled in a bedroom closet as the massive twister leveled their home. They felt all of the air being sucked out of their home and then nothing. Faulkinberry could only figure they both blacked out. When they regained consciousness, she frantically called out to her daughter. She was OK.

Renee recounted, "All I could see was blood coming down my arm and down my face. I remember her getting out and me lying there waiting for her to get help. It seemed like forever. I didn't hear anybody, and I kept screaming for help."[62]

Renee remembers far too much. She still sees her psychiatrist and suffers a lot of back pain. Doctors diagnosed her with PTSD – post-traumatic stress disorder and severe depression. She doesn't go outside much anymore. Renee confesses, "I cry a lot and get real scared. Sometimes even on Saturdays, when the siren goes off at 12 noon, it bothers me. A lot." [63]

OUTBREAK!

A single tornado can strike fear and trepidation, but swarms can be terrifying. Unimaginable. April 2011 brought the largest and one of the deadliest outbreaks in history. It lasted 3 days, 7 hours and 18 minutes. During that time, the National Weather Service and other agencies confirmed 355 twisters. This is the most ever for a continuous outbreak. Four were EF5's – the highest rating – meaning winds were clocked at over 200mph.[64]

Photo: Twin tornadoes are spawned from the same super-cell in the Great Plains on September 28, 2010. (NOAA Legacy Photo; OAR/ERL/Wave Propagation Laboratory)

Where these twisters rampaged, people must have thought their world was ending. It is simply impossible to envision 355 tornadoes coming so close together. Alabama and Mississippi were hardest hit; but Arkansas, Georgia, Tennessee and Virginia were also slammed. Every state from Texas to New York was affected. So wide was the destruction, tallies put the cost at $11 billion. Whether it was due to flying debris, the tornadoes themselves, or the softball-sized hail, this outbreak injured over 2000 and took 350 lives – the most since 1936.

"Less than a month later, on May 22, more than 50 tornadoes touched down across an eight-State area, the most powerful of which was a 0.75-mile-wide tornado that cut a 6-mile path through Joplin, MO. The tornado destroyed thousands of homes and caused widespread damage in the city. This historic tornado resulted in 161 fatalities, the most fatalities ever recorded from a single tornado since modern record keeping began in 1950."[65]

Photos Top: Nearly 7,000 homes were leveled by 200mph winds when an EF5 tornado struck Joplin, Missouri the night of May 22, 2011. (Jace Anderson/FEMA). **Bottom**: In an odd quirk of fate, an undamaged teddy bear is stuck on a fence after an EF5 tornado hit El Reno on May 31, 2013. It was the widest tornado in U.S. history at 2.6 miles across and the second EF5 twister to touch down in Oklahoma over a two-week period. (Andrea Booher/FEMA).

O CANADA, YOU NEARLY CLAIMED THE RECORD

July 27, 2015 brought a shock to Canadians on Manitoba's prairies. An exceptionally long-duration twister carved a path of destruction through the province's southwest. Farms near Tilston bore the brunt. Large trees snapped like toothpicks, power poles mysteriously vanished, out buildings and farm crops were flattened, and a semi-trailer flipped on its side. One farmer lost 400 chickens; another lost a sheep. Bridge damage forced closure of Highway 256 west of Melita, from Highway 445 to Highway 345. The accompanying dramatic storm brought flash flooding while eerie lightning lashed the sky and hail pummeled everything below.

Fred Raynor, a farmer near Tilston said, "There were chunks of trees and debris just flying everywhere. Some of it was going clockwise, some of it was going counter-clockwise, all at once. I was sitting on a chair at the (kitchen) table and you could feel the whole house shaking."[66]

Tornado Activity in Canada

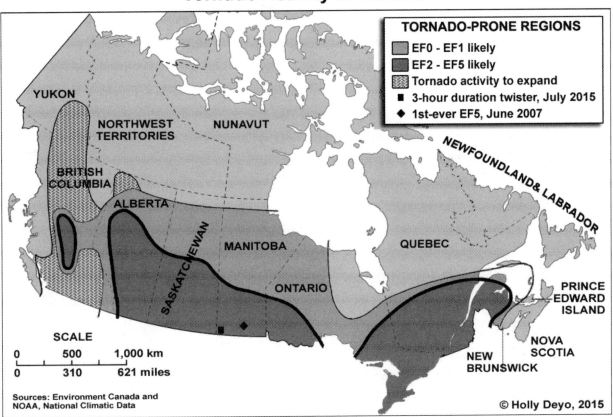

Dakota Radcliffe, 15, and his brother were in their truck trying to get a look at the tornado. However, it caught up with them and forced the boys into a roadside ditch. Dakota recounted, "'we were on the road, we were driving and there was almost no visibility whatsoever. You could feel the truck kind of shaking a bit for a couple miles, and then, all of a sudden at one point, I'd say at least three of the wheels were off the ground while we were still on the highway. We were just praying. It was pretty emotional.'"[67]

Weather experts called Manitoba's "high-end" EF-2 twister "exceptional," "rare," "phenomenal". The amount of energy required to sustain an EF-2 tornado for 3 hours is phenomenal. This monster wedge tornado – meaning it's as wide at the bottom as at the top – had even the most testosterone-driven fleeing to their basements.

Miraculously, during the tornado's nearly 3-hour stay on the ground, left people unscathed. Usually twisters in Canada only touch down for a few minutes. The only other twister that stayed locked to land longer was the Tri-State Tornado in 1925. It's 3½-hour trek through Missouri, Illinois and Indiana killed 695 people.

Environment Canada had issued first tornado warnings shortly after 8 p.m., about a half hour before this beast arrived. People admitted it was really scary because darkness hid its exact location for most of its stay. While still light enough to see, storm chaser and photographer Greg Johnson said at times it put out as many as six finger-like funnels underneath the cloud. "The wind intensity was so strong that there were parts of Highway 256 in the southwest part of the province that literally had the asphalt stripped off the road's surface."

Saskatchewan storm chaser Jenny Andrew saw the tornado in action, but called the hunt off when she arrived in Virden. She noted, "When we left, it was kind of odd because the whole highway was just littered with frogs. There was thousands of them!"[68]

ANOTHER RECORD – CANADA'S FIRST EF-5 TWISTER

On June 22, 2007 Canada was hit with its first-ever EF-5 tornado. EF-5s are so rare they make up less than 1% of all tornadoes. Twisters are nature's most fierce storms and instill fear because even small ones can morph into monsters. Their very unpredictability makes them so unnerving. Long ropy twisters can be just as strong as more awe-inspiring 2½ mile-wide funnels. Until 2007, Canada had been spared the worst nature offers and it's a sure indication that things are ramping up, changing.

Since 1950 only seven EF-5s had struck outside the U.S.: two each in France, Germany, and Italy and one in Russia. Now Canada joins the ranks. This tornado touched down at 6:25 p.m. near Elie, Manitoba, about 25 miles west of Winnipeg and 80 miles north of the U.S. border. The 1,000 foot wide tornado stayed on the ground for about 35 minutes and tracked about 3½ miles before lifting into the air. No fatalities or serious injuries occurred, likely due to many residents being out of town attending a high school graduation. Those at home sheltered in basements or crawled under mattresses.

Photo: Don't be deceived by its seemingly slim presence; it was a brute. F5 tornado as it approached Elie, Manitoba from the southeast on June 22, 2007. (Courtesy storm chaser Justin Hobson)

Winds sandblasted bark from trees and snapped utility poles like tiny twigs. The tornado picked up an entire two-story house and carried it hundreds of feet through the air, where it exploded. Debris covered streets and nearby fields from demolished buildings. Two semi-trailers were shoved off the Trans-Canada Highway and a truck was blown hundreds of feet off the road to the middle of a field twisting it like a pretzel. The funnel destroyed at least 3 homes and left many more damaged as well as vehicles and the town's mill. Like it was "stuck" in one place, the tornado repeatedly slammed the same area of Elie. Simultaneously an EF-3 twister touched down in Oakville, just 10 miles from Elie. That tornado struck rurally destroying several outbuildings and many trees.

'OUT OF SEASON', NOT OUT OF THE ORDINARY

Another change is that tornadoes are striking more often outside the usual season. The term 'season' is misleading, as twisters can occur any day of the year. Historically in America things start to heat up March – April, and kick into highest gear May – June.

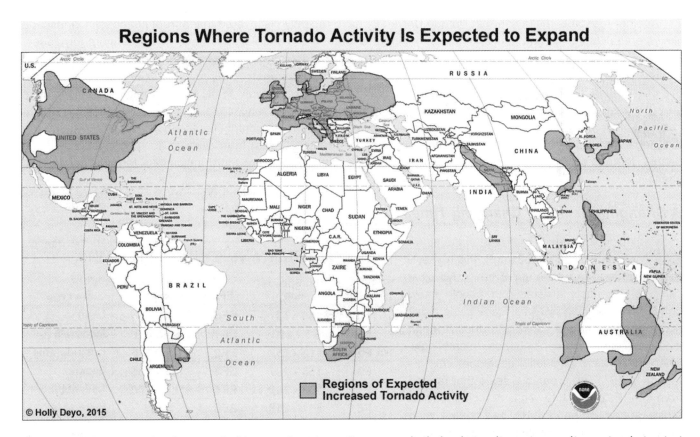

Regions Where Tornado Activity Is Expected to Expand

Regions of Expected Increased Tornado Activity

© Holly Deyo, 2015

"As with the grouping [swarms] of tornanation does, the season's timing is turning extreme: It now tends to start really early or really late. Four of the latest-known 'beginnings' of the season have happened since 1999, and five of the 10 earliest starts have fallen within the same time frame."[69]

In March 2012, more than 80 tornadoes rampaged across America from the Midwest to the Gulf of Mexico in one day. That's more than is typically observed during the entire month. Canada only gets that many in a year. Things are changing. Scientists say that earlier-than-normal tornado outbreaks will become the norm. Tornado season that used to begin in April now starts in February. Atmospheric physicist Anthony Del Genio of the Goddard Institute for Space Studies, part of NASA, stated that thunderstorms will pack a bigger wallop. This is especially true for the central and eastern states.[70] Purdue's atmospheric scientist Robert Trapp and colleagues got a similar result in their 2009 and 2011 studies found that "the number of days when conditions exist to form tornadoes is expected to increase".[71]

A third change is seen in the records for both the most and fewest tornadoes over 12 months. This latest shift came in the last five years, showing that weather is becoming more erratic.

TORNADO ALLEY MORE THAN DOUBLES

A fourth change occurred when the Storm Prediction Center revised their map of 'tornado alley'. It used to encompass the top half of Texas, most of Oklahoma and Nebraska, and the eastern half of South Dakota. The new area also takes in the upper Midwest and Deep South, along with Florida.[72]

Canada ranks #2 in the world with between 80 and 100 tornadoes annually. Meteorologists estimate 80 is at the very low end, that a much higher count is closer to fact. However, "The Great White North" is so vast compared to population density, that twisters may go unreported. To put this in perspective, Canada is just a smidge larger than the U.S., but with 1/10 the people. Tornadoes there most often target the southern two-thirds of Alberta and Saskatchewan, the southern half of Manitoba and Ontario, the southern one-third of Quebec; British Columbia's interior; and most of New Brunswick. Now that may be changing to encompass a greater area of Canada certainly in British Columbia and Alberta.

Not only are existing regions expanding where tornadoes hit in the U.S. and Canada, NOAA's map shows where they expect strike zones to widen around the world. Part of the reason for this is likely due to climate in transition. This may produce more areas where moist hot air collides with cold dry air causing an increase in twisters.

Another reason is researchers at Purdue University have recently discovered that abrupt changes in landscape like where tall buildings and farmlands meet, or where a forest stops and flat land starts generate more tornadoes. This also explains why trailer parks seemed to get smacked more often than averages allowed. Often they are located in open fields just outside city limits making them tornado magnets. Until recently scientists pooh-poohed this observation, but not only do they now admit it, they have an explanation. While this is a relatively new finding, they theorize after studying 62 years of data that radical changes in landscape height may squash or stretch columns of air making them spin faster. They believe this faster spin rate contributes to severe weather forming. As the global population continues to grow and more land is cleared outward from cities to accommodate additional people, tornado target-rich areas will naturally expand as well. These are more indications tornado behavior is changing.[73]

A Changing Scale for Changing Times

Peak Doppler speeds analyzed in the storm were estimated at 281 – 321mph, the highest-ever recorded anywhere on Earth.[74] *No, that can't be,* scientists insisted, but people knew better. Just because NOAA's Fujita scale didn't allow for wind speeds above 318 doesn't mean it couldn't, didn't and can't happen. Interestingly, when Dr. Fujita originally developed his F-ratings in 1971, he created a scale that ranged from F0 – F12, with F12 winds reaching Mach 1 – the speed of sound. He had stated then "tornadoes are not expected to reach F6 wind speeds." Still, Fujita assigned "inconceivable tornado" to describe an F6 event thought it was never used. So it's not that tornadoes that massive couldn't happen, scientists just thought they wouldn't.[75]

OLD FUJITA vs. ENHANCED FUJITA					
FUJITA	Wind Speeds, mph	EF	Wind Speeds, mph	Damage
F0	40 - 72	EF0	65 - 85	Light
F1	73 - 112	EF1	86 - 110	Moderate
F2	113 - 157	EF2	111 - 135	Considerable
F3	158 - 207	EF3	136 - 165	Severe
F4	208 - 260	EF4	166 - 200	Devastating
F5	261 - 318	EF5	>200	Incredible

Further underscoring the possibility of stronger than F5 tornadoes is this caveat from NOAA's Storm Prediction Center. "Even if the winds measured by portable Doppler radar … had been over 318 mph, the [Bridge Creek] tornado still would have been rated "only" F5, since that is the most intense possible damage level. On the Enhanced F-scale, there is no such thing as "EF6" or higher. Damage – no matter how "incredible" the damage or how strong the wind – maxes out at EF-5."[76] In 2007, a reworked Fujita scale went into effect. Scientists wanted to more closely match the EF rating to the damage caused. Since that's their marker, not so much clocking actual wind speed, then it's understandable why they cut off the scale where they did. An EF5's damage is listed as "Total Destruction of Buildings". When that happens there's no place to go. When structures are obliterated, what's left to physically assess? But changing their measuring stick, the real intensity of the storm is hidden.

The Enhanced Fujita Scale now tops out at "greater than 200mph", leaving a lot of leeway for guesswork. One has to wonder how much the controversy over the real wind of Oklahoma's Bridge Creek tornado had to do with scientists changing the scale.

Last Thoughts on Tornadoes

While Stan and I still lived in Australia, we read about the mile-wide twister that hit Moore, Oklahoma. This monster stayed on the ground for an-hour-and-a-half carving ruin along the way. By the end of the day, May 3, 1999, 44 people were dead. We were stunned. Even growing up in tornado alley, we never saw twisters this big.

Sixteen years ago, a mile wide tornado was really impressive, but worse was to come. May 22, 2004 brought an enormous funnel to Hallam, Nebraska. This whirling mass of destruction measured a staggering 2.5 miles wide. Still, on May 31, 2013, the largest tornado ever recorded topped it at 2.6 miles across.

Nate Billings, photographer for *The Oklahoman* said, "I've covered a lot of tornadoes, but this one is, by far, the most destructive. When you're first on the scene, it's hard to tell how big it is but I just kept walking and it just kept getting bigger and bigger and bigger...I've never really seen anything quite like this."[77]

Not only are tornadoes coming 'out of season', they're striking in enormous swarms and taking on monstrous proportions.

Canada experienced a never-before-seen EF-5 tornado and also the world's second longest-on-the-ground event is very telling.

These changes illustrate the trends in more extreme weather that's emerged in recent years. As with other Earth Changes already examined, End Times is more concerned about the events than the cause. The U.S. isn't the only Country to be clobbered with disasters.

Chapter 5: Wildfires

The first [trumpet] sounded, and there came hail and fire, mixed with blood, and they were thrown to the earth; and a third of the earth was burned up, and a third of the trees were burned up, and all the green grass was burned up. —Revelation 8:7 (NASB)

Who could forget this iconic photo? Fire behavior analyst, John McColgan, took this award-winning picture while firefighting in Montana's Bitterroot National Forest. A pair of elk stood in the Bitterroot River finding little relief as a wall of fire descended. In color, this photo is even more stunning. Every tree is backlit with yellow flames contrasting with still-green grass and bushes lining the river. Reflected in the water below, fire turned the river an eerie orange. On August 6, 2000, several fires burned together near Sula, just east of the Idaho border, creating a monster 100,000-acre blaze. From McColgan's vantage point on a bridge over the East Fork of the Bitterroot, he snapped this image. McColgan who had fought fires for 20 years claimed modestly that he just happened to be in the right place at the right time. Animals "know where to go, where their safe zones are. A lot of wildlife did get driven down there to the river. There were some bighorn sheep there. A small deer was standing right underneath me, under the bridge."[78]

Named the Valley Complex Fire, it had swept across more than 300,000 acres by the end of the month. Dry lightning continued to ignite 70-100 new fires a day and almost 90% of the 14,000-acre Sula State Forest burned. It was so badly damaged no one was sure if it could recover. By the end of the month, 30,000 firefighters and support personnel – some from Canada, Australia, and New Zealand – deployed to extinguish the inferno.

Two days after the big burn Gary Frank, hydrologist for the Montana Department of Natural Resources and Conservation, drove his four-wheeler around smoking logs and through piles of ash. Along Lyman Creek he saw a deer's charred corpse and dead trout fingerlings lining the riverbed. In every direction as far as he could see, a blackened wreck was all that remained of the forest. Since the fire, Montana has planted over 1 million Ponderosa pine and Douglas fir seedlings.

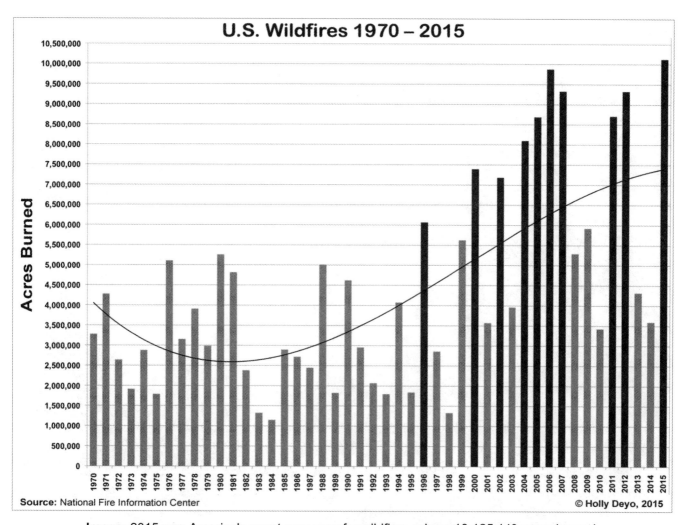

U.S. Wildfires 1970 – 2015

Acres Burned

Source: National Fire Information Center

© Holly Deyo, 2015

Image: 2015 was America's worst-ever year for wildfires, where 10,125,149 acres burned.

While 2000 was really bad for U.S. wildfires, it was by no means the worst. In the last 45 years, the 5 most devastating occurred as of 2006. Since 2000, many western states have experienced the largest wildfires ever in their state's history. All of 2000 saw about the same number of acres scorched as the first 7 months of 2015. Compared to all years from 1960 on (chart below only shows since 1970), 2015 was the worst charring over 10 million acres.

Bigger, Longer, Stronger

Wildfires are increasing in nearly every country around the world. Not only are they getting worse, the time when they generally burn has grown by about ⅓. In the early 1970s wildfire season lasted five months. Now it's seven and a half. The number of large burns – those over 1,000 acres – has jumped too. U.S. Forest Service Chief Tom Tidwell said during a May 2015 congressional hearing, "We are seeing wildfires in the United States grow to sizes that were unimaginable just 20 or 30 years ago."[79]

Several factors are at work. Snow is melting earlier in the U.S. West, which leaves mountainous forests and lower lands less protected. When it rains, it comes in deluges, so instead of the ground absorbing it, water rolls off. However, the moisture is enough to spur undergrowth. Then when drought or prolonged dry periods occur, weeds, grasses and small shrubs die and provide perfect tinder for firestorms.

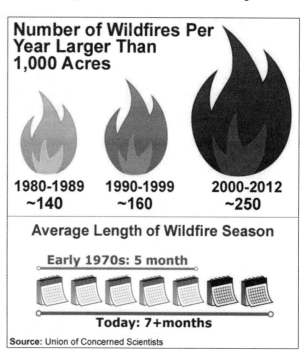

Number of Wildfires Per Year Larger Than 1,000 Acres

| 1980-1989 ~140 | 1990-1999 ~160 | 2000-2012 ~250 |

Average Length of Wildfire Season

Early 1970s: 5 month

Today: 7+months

Source: Union of Concerned Scientists

Especially since the 1980s, temperatures across the U.S. have risen in nearly every region except the southeast. While it's hotter and dryer in the West, it's hotter and wetter in the East.

Scientists predict that wildfires are going to do even more damage expanding in scope and severity. The greatest increases worldwide are expected for parts of western and southern US, southwest Canada, parts of the Mediterranean basin, eastern Siberia, south-central Australia, western South America and much of the arid regions in Asia. Weather extremes again play against humanity and wildlife, and fit right in with End Times prophetic scenarios.

This doesn't mean that wildfires will be the sole reason ⅓ of Earth, trees and grass burn up. They could, however, help set the stage – or finish it. As with a number of End Times prophecies, multiple causes may combine to fulfill a certain event. For example, falling meteors, volcanic eruptions, an EMP cutting off critical coolants for spent nuclear fuel, and/or nuclear weapons could ignite already drought-stricken lands.

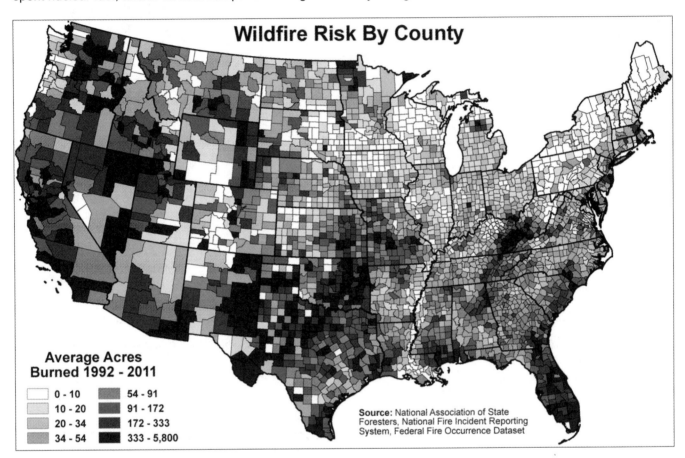

Wildfire Risk By County

Average Acres Burned 1992 - 2011

0 - 10	54 - 91
10 - 20	91 - 172
20 - 34	172 - 333
34 - 54	333 - 5,800

Source: National Association of State Foresters, National Fire Incident Reporting System, Federal Fire Occurrence Dataset

CANADA

On May 8, 2016 the Great White North was in the midst of its worst-ever natural disaster when a massive wildfire engulfed parts of Alberta. Officials declared a local state of emergency on May 1 for the neighborhoods of Prairie Creek and Gregoire, which was soon expanded to cover 10 more localities.

On May 3 the entire town of Fort McMurray – some 88,000 people – was ordered to leave everything behind and evacuate. The next day the fire exploded aided by 45mph winds and within a week over 570,000 acres had burned. Desert-like humidity, unusually high temperatures and vicious winds whipped roaring blazes out of control. The wildfire was unpredictable, completely burning down one street and leaving the next untouched. Fire spread across the province to Canada's oilsands operations knocking out a third of oil production. They lost about one million barrels of oil a day. In the midst of this an outbreak of stomach flu hit some of the evacuation centers.

Fort McMurray resident Shawn Chaulk sat trapped in his car on May 3 with his wife and three children. They, like hundreds of others, were frantically trying to get out of town. He sobbed, "I could see it coming, and I sincerely thought we would all perish in the vehicle. I looked at the sky and it was like Armageddon."[80] People desperate to escape jumped sidewalks with their cars, driving straight down them, even driving on the wrong side of the road.

Chaulk described it as like a scene in a bad movie. Gridlock brought travel to a halt and Chaulk commented that, "If someone had to pee, they literally opened a car door and stood up and peed."[81]

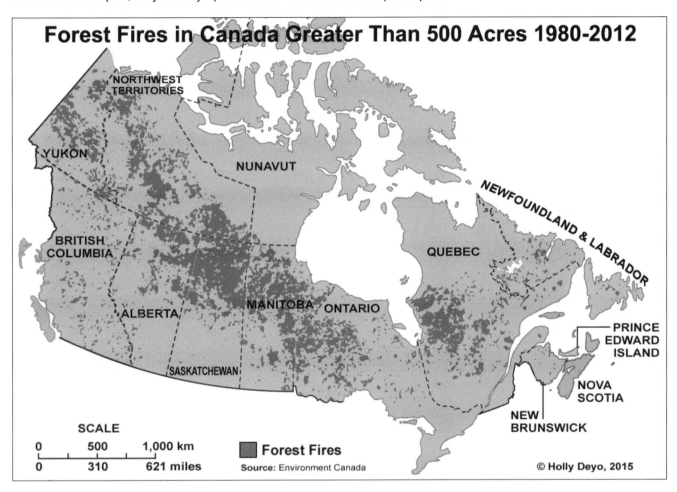

Forest Fires in Canada Greater Than 500 Acres 1980-2012

SCALE
0 — 500 — 1,000 km
0 — 310 — 621 miles

■ Forest Fires

Source: Environment Canada

© Holly Deyo, 2015

By May 10, at least 2,400 homes and structures had burned in Fort McMurray leaving only foundations behind. Whole neighborhoods were obliterated, but the hospital and most schools were intact. On Fort Mac streets, twisted metal is all that remained of most cars. Many evacuees fled 200 miles south to Edmonton seeking safety and shelter. They returned to no gas, undrinkable water and a damaged power grid, but were overjoyed to be reunited with their furry family members. At least two airlines bent the rules and allowed pets to travel inside the cabins.

At the time of this writing, 700 firefighters, 26 helicopters, 13 air tankers and 46 pieces of heavy equipment were still fighting this horrific wildfire.[82]

TERRORIST AGENDA

Ever since 2002, the FBI has been aware that al-Qaeda is calling for lone wolf Western Muslims to start forest fires. The Spring 2012 issue of *Inspire* – the Muslim propaganda magazine – published an article titled "It Is of Your Freedom to Ignite a Firebomb", which gave *very* detailed instructions on how to build an "ember bomb". Pictures, diagrams and explanations showed how to get the most damage, how to set forest remotely and leave no trace for investigators to find. It even discussed "correct wind patterns to set a forest fire in, the right season, the right time of year, the correct temperature – all designed to cause the maximum amount of carnage and death."[83]

The article suggested bombs should be ignited in a U.S. forest and specifically mentioned Montana. The article's author wrote, "In America, there are more houses built in the countryside than in the cities. It is difficult to choose a better place than in the valleys of Montana where the population increases rapidly."

It took more than a year for authorities to release findings on Colorado Springs, CO horrific 2013 event. The Black Forest Fire killed two, destroyed 511 homes, damaged another 28 and racked up over $420 million in insurance costs. To date, uninsured expenses haven't been tallied, but around 80 homes weren't covered. Reluctantly officials admitted it was human caused, but wouldn't go so far as to say arson, let alone terrorists.

At the time then Sheriff Terry Maketa revealed, "One thing that my investigators have given me the authority to state is that they have all but ruled out natural causes as the cause of this fire. I can't really go any further on that, but I can say we are pretty confident it was not, for instance, a lightning strike."[84]

Terrorists' intentions are verified by a treasure trove of materials seized after Navy SEALS killed Osama bin Laden. It gave unprecedented insight into al-Qaida tactics including a detailed campaign for starting fires throughout the American West.

UNDER FUNDED, UNDER APPRECIATED

Besides causing heartache and inconvenience, terrorists' aim in igniting fires is to hurt the economy. In 1995, firefighting made up 13% of the U.S. Forest Service's annual budget. 2015 marked the first time ever that over half of their budget was spent putting out wildfires. That's a 300% jump. This increase deeply cut into the their ability to fund projects that reduce fire threat – the very thing that's shredding their budget. Fire suppression is also chewing into funds that keep forest hiking trails and 15,000 campgrounds pristine. By comparison to other agencies, their budget is small considering it has to cover 193 million acres of national forests, 442 wilderness areas, 20 national grasslands and eight national monuments. It pays for 35,000 scientists, administrators, land managers, seven research units and supports nearly 450,000 jobs.[85] Not only are forests national treasures, they provide much of the oxygen we breathe. According to *Environment Canada,* Canada's national environmental agency, two mature trees can provide all the oxygen needed for a family of four.[86] Throughout the world they supply half of all oxygen created. They're home to 60% of the at-risk species in America and furnish more than 90% of the timber harvested in this country. We lose forests and everybody loses.

The U.S. isn't their only target. They've also set their jihadi eyes on Russia. Rachel Ehrenfeld, terror funding expert at the American Center for Democracy shared that "Russia's security chief, Aleksandr Bortnikov, also has warned, 'Al-Qaida was complicit in recent forest fires in Europe' as part of terrorism's 'strategy of a thousand cuts.'"[87]

Wildfires – A Burning Issue

According to Lloyd's of London 20 countries are most affected by wildfires in terms of economic damage.[88] They arrive at their findings from examining over 100 years of fire disasters from 1900 to 2013. To be counted, at least one of the following criteria has to be met:

- 10 or more people are killed
- 100 people are affected
- A call goes out for international assistance
- Declaration of a state of emergency

Top 20 Countries Most Affected By Wildfire 1900-2013

1. United States	5. Spain	9. Mongolia	13. Israel	17. Argentina
2. Indonesia	6. Australia	10. Italy	14. Malaysia	18. Mexico
3. Canada	7. Greece	11. Chile	15. Yugoslavia	19. Nicaragua
4. Portugal	8. Russia	12. South Africa	16. China	20. Croatia

Source: Lloyd's of London

Lloyd's places the blame on weather extremes, more people on the planet and them moving into less populated areas. The U.S. Forest Service calls this land the Wildland Urban Interface – property that borders or moves into the wilderness. Since 2000 over ⅓ of U.S. housing lies in these fire-prone areas.

Look at these maps and consider over the past 30 to 40 years where those wildfires most often strike. Now factor in that wildfire regions are expanding. It doesn't matter if you're in the camp of global warming and or feel that it's the result of natural heating and cooling cycles. Regardless of the cause, humanity has to deal with it.

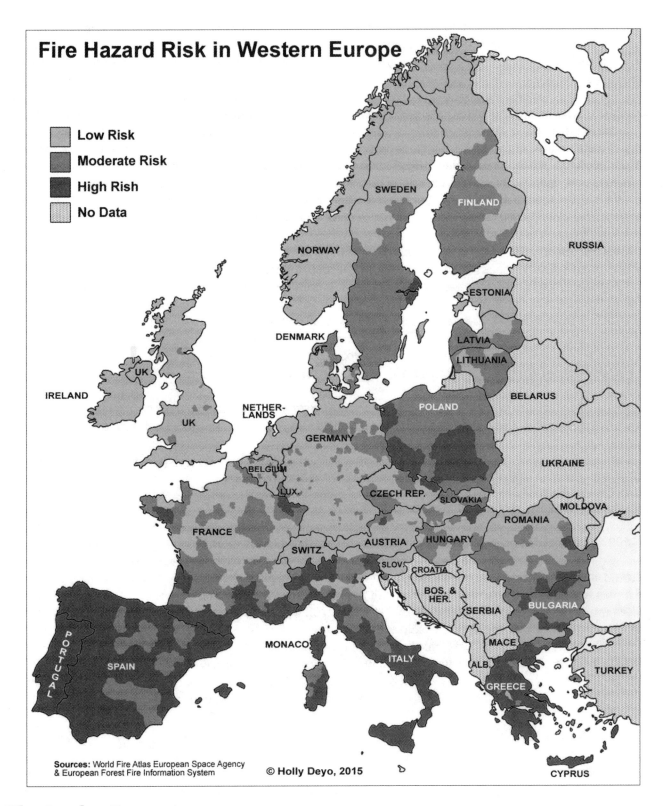

Fire Hazard Risk in Western Europe

Legend:
- Low Risk
- Moderate Risk
- High Rish
- No Data

Sources: World Fire Atlas European Space Agency & European Forest Fire Information System

© Holly Deyo, 2015

The Lucky Country

Due to increasing frequency, size and ferocity, wildfire is now one of the most serious natural disaster threats in southern Australia. They experience more bushfires around the perimeter of the country where the majority of Aussies live because the interior is primarily desert. This map only shows fires since 1997, so it may look like most occur only in the north. New South Wales, Canberra, South Australia and Tasmania have all experienced horrible bushfires in recent years, but Victoria – especially around Melbourne – is the hotbed for wildfire. Four of the five deadliest fires on record in Australia charred Victoria. With drought and heatwaves increasing in intensity and duration, the fire escalation is apparent. Prior to 2000, a wildfire equal to any of the three that occurred in 2003,

2007 and 2009 would have happened only once a generation. Three in rapid-fire succession is something that had never before occurred in living or recorded history.[89]

Exacerbating the problem is the huge number of eucalypt trees that readily explode when exposed to wildfires or intense radiant heat. These living "torches" constitute over 75% of Australia's tree population and grow everywhere except in their too cold alpine area. Gum trees can reach heights of 500 feet and are monumentally flammable. Eucalypts are especially dangerous because they can rocket flames from treetop to treetop. Plus they have a unique ability that shocked even a 20-year veteran firefighter. Matt Dutkiewicz led his team to protect a cottage situated on bare ground – an area ravaged by drought. Matt thought their job would be a piece of cake because it looked like nothing could burn. He was wrong and describes the unbelievable.

"The wind stopped. Then it started pulling in from the valley behind us. The hairs on the back of my neck stood up and I thought, 'There's something not right here.' Then this furnace just hit us. The trees in front of us snapped off and the mirrors of the truck smashed. The flames were 2 meters off the ground to about 8 meters in the air and were weird blues and oranges. It was like the air was on fire.

"A few kilometers away, firefighter Neil Cooper was surrounded by burning vegetation and sought refuge in a bare field locally called the Oval. In theory it would be the safest place to sit out the blaze, but when he got there he saw a 'blanket of flame over the paddock about a meter high, shimmering like oil on water'. It was like nothing he had seen in his 20 years on the job.

"The Canberra firestorm that ravaged Australia's capital in January 2003 surprised everyone. No one expected

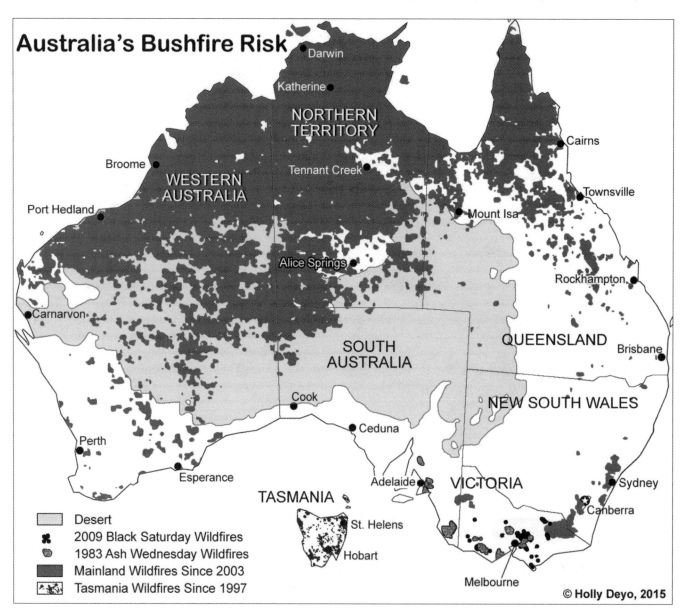

the blaze to reach the city and enter the suburbs with such force, killing four people and destroying almost 500 homes. But for some scientists the biggest mystery of all is what firefighters like Cooper and Dutkiewicz saw. Bare earth shouldn't be able to sustain a fire of such ferocity at ground level, let alone meters up in the air, and flames from burning vegetation should be yellow or orange, not blue. As far as most scientists are concerned, what the firefighters saw was impossible."[90] So eucalyptus trees that cover great swaths of Australia present a huge and growing wildfire threat.

BLACK SATURDAY BUSHFIRES

The most catastrophic wildfire occurred in 2009 when 173 people were killed in a single day making it the world's 8th deadliest wildfire. Lightning, a downed power line and arson combined to char over a million acres and bring unspeakable tragedy.

On February 7, 2009, the worst wildfire "The Lucky Country" ever experienced arrived. It had been blisteringly hot. Melbourne, Victoria recorded its highest ever temperature at 115.5°F with humidity only a dismal 6%. The worst heatwave in Victoria's history struck amid Australia's worst-ever drought – described as 1,000-year event. Two long months of zero moisture and winds whipping over 60mph completed this recipe for disaster. Firefighters came from all over Australia, New Zealand and the United States to extinguish flames that threatened the country's southeastern state. Even so, flames destroyed 2,100 homes, displaced over 7,500 people. Out of those whose lives were taken, 120 died in a single fire in Kinglake alone –halfway between Melbourne and Wandong. The RSPCA, which is similar to the Humane Society, estimates that more than 1 million animals died in the fires including nearly 12,000 head of livestock. Nearly a quarter-million acres of park were damaged. It's estimated that the Black Saturday Bushfires, as they are known, released energy equal to 1,500 Hiroshima atomic bombs.

Pam Ross shares the story of her son, Robert, and his family and how they survived.

Robert lived with his wife, Lee, and their baby son, Riley, near Wandong, about 30 miles north of Melbourne. Rounding out the family was Miffy a Labrador, Jack the Jack Russell, goats Gary and Glitter, two cats named Puddy and Ginger, two horses, two ferrets and fifteen chickens – called 'chooks' Downunder.

"On Black Saturday, things started to look bad so my daughter-in-law Lee left early with the baby and two dogs while my son stayed to try and protect the house and pets. When the wind changed he put all the animals except the horses and chooks in his car. He cut the fences to give the horses their best chance and let the chooks out of their shed. As he was hosing the house he saw the flames coming towards him. He jumped in his car and started to try and out run (sic) the fire. His entry was blocked so had to drive through paddocks smashing through fence after fence. He nearly got bogged in a creek bed but found a way out. He drove blind for about 10 kilometers [6 miles] until he found a road which he followed until he found a dam. He collected all the pets: he put the goats in the dam on their leads and placed the cats and the ferrets in their cages on the edge of the dam half in half out and covered them all with a blanket. Minutes later the fire went right over their heads. After a couple of hours of sitting in the dam and sharing it with about twenty kangaroos, he was found by chance by the CFA [Country Fire Authority]. They took him back to the fire station where he had to stay up all night helping the firemen defend the station. We finally heard from him at 5:30am on Sunday morning.

"Unfortunately they have lost their home and the horses died. They found three chooks still alive and amazingly the chook shed was still standing with five eggs in the nest. Everything else was gone. I can only thank God my son is alive but I grieve the loss of their horses, their home and mostly their dream of living in the country with their beloved pets. They had only been there for four months and were just starting to enjoy their new life."[91]

Officially the Black Saturday Bushfires lasted nearly five weeks from February 7th to March 12th though smaller fires continued for many months after that. In terms of money, conservative estimates put the cost at $4.7 billion in 2015 dollars.

Last Thought on Wildfires

Without question, wildfires are immensely destructive in terms of lives, land, property and businesses. They're increasing around the world in scope and intensity as well as "wildfire season" lengthening. Coupled with weather extremes – prolonged drought, stronger heatwaves, higher wind events – are acts of terrorism whose purpose is to ignite more wildfires. Terrorists have realized at least since 2002 that wildfire is a cheap, effective way to cause heartache and extreme inconvenience while taking billions of dollars out of a country's economy. The only factor people can control is not moving onto land that borders or is a part of wilderness areas where many occur and are more difficult to fight.

In Genesis 9:8-11 God promised never to destroy Earth by water again, but fire is another thing. God used fire on multiple occasions to punish like with Sodom and Gomorrah and also against Egypt and he promises to do so again. Apostle John prophesied in Revelation 17: 1-4, 15-18 that Babylon will be destroyed by fire. 2 Peter 3:7-12 also warns of major destruction by fire.

This natural disaster leaves nearly no country unscathed, but some countries are "touched" more harshly than others and it's only expected to grow.

Chapter 6: Weird Weather Grows Wilder

...On the earth, nations will be in anguish and perplexity at the roaring and tossing of the sea. People will faint from terror, apprehensive of what is coming on the world... —Luke 21:25-26 (NIV)

One sign that's impossible to disguise or dismiss is the global number of weather disasters. NOAA keeps track of U.S. billion-dollar disaster events and maintains detailed accounts dating back to 1980. During those 36 years, America has been hit with 188 such weather catastrophes. Each cost at least a billion, but some were many times this amount. Taken together, they pegged over $1 trillion.

In looking at Billion Dollar Disasters, the greatest number of catastrophes has occurred in the most recent years with one exception: 1998. That year saw *the* worst El Niño ever recorded. Not to blind you with numbers, but out of that $1 trillion, those seven events took 40% of it. So not only are disasters ramping up, they're causing a lot more damage. **NOTE**: NOAA usually releases their yearly disaster data by the first week of April, so the 2015 information is less than a week old. Though NOAA knows these each cost at least a billion, every one of these 10 events may go significantly higher.

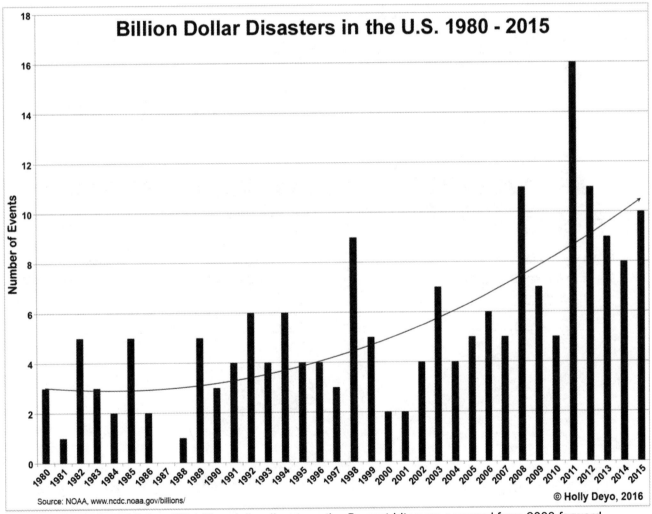

Image: Out of these 188 billion dollar disasters, the 5 worst-hit years occurred from 2008 forward.

The most expensive included:

- Hurricane Katrina August 2005
- Super storm Sandy October 2012

- Hurricane Andrew August 1992
- U.S. Drought/Heatwave Summer 1988
- Midwest Flooding Summer 1993
- Hurricane Ike September 2008
- U.S. Drought/Heatwave 2012

The 2004 – 2005 Hurricane Slam

2004 was a banner year for hurricanes with Charley, Frances, Ivan and Jeanne slamming the Country all within six weeks of each other. People in the southeast and up through the eastern seaboard must have wondered what 'gods' they'd made angry. Frankly, 2004 was just plain ugly, but we hadn't met Katrina yet.

Those storm-weary people had to be relieved when winter 2004 rolled around. Hurricane season was over. At least it was until the next year. 2005 brought, Dennis, Katrina, Rita and Wilma – one every month July through October. To this day, Hurricane Katrina is THE worst weather disaster in U.S. history. Couple this with astonishingly inefficient, ill-prepared FEMA, a horrific catastrophe was made unnecessarily worse.

KATRINA

At least 1,833 people lost their lives and the wicked cruel storm displaced more than 1.5 million people – three times that during the entire Dust Bowl years.

For those without homes or transportation in New Orleans, the Superdome became their residence of last resort for six days. The massive damaged stadium was not equipped to adequately house 40,000 refugees.[92] In the sweltering, sticky heat, the smell became unbearable especially when the toilets failed and people resorted to defecating on the floor.

Of his experience at The Dome, Doug Thornton, regional V.P. of the company that manages the Superdome writes. "We had less than 24 hours to get ready. We never, ever had encountered those conditions before, where you had five to seven days with no running water, no functioning toilets, no way to communicate with the people inside, the heat was oppressive, the conditions there were beyond inhumane and rationing of food, water at the same time, and no way to get out."[93]

Photo: Even at the much cleaner Superdome, it was horribly crowded. (FEMA/Andrea Booher)

60

Photo: New Orleans, LA, September 7, 2005, neighborhoods and highways throughout the area remain flooded as a result of Hurricane Katrina. (Jocelyn Augustino/FEMA)

Dead bodies were left floating in floodwaters and bloating on steaming asphalt. People were too exhausted and occupied with trying to survive to bury the dead.

When conditions in the Superdome became untenable, thousands of people were bussed to the Houston Astrodome.

Well over 2 millions folks were without power for weeks, some for over a month. More than 200,000 homes, mostly in New Orleans and the surrounding area, were completely destroyed. Over 200,000 jobs were lost so even those that had the wherewithal and means to get to work, often found those companies closed.

In the days following we heard reports of rapes, murders and looting. With virtual martial law in place, more than 1,000 firearms were seized in door-to-door searches.[94]

Aftermath

Despite this hellish experience, people survived. Many didn't return to New Orleans after being housed in shelters around the Nation. They adapted. Found work. People shared stories of overwhelming generosity of strangers, of 'getting through", of strength and sadness. A decade later though most have put the experience behind them, scars are forever on their hearts.

This recounting barely scrapes at the volumes of Katrina data and it's just one of 178 catastrophic events to hit America between 1980 and 2014.

A Once-in-a-1000-Year Event

September 2013. Nobody in Colorado had ever witnessed that much rain. 100-year rain or snowfall events are getting quite commonplace. 500-year downpours are more frequent that the half millennia mark dictates. But 1000-year rains? So what is that exactly? It doesn't mean that it will happen once every 1,000 years, but that it has 1/10 of a 1% chance of occurring relative to a specific location. Rare as that is, that's exactly what happened in Colorado. Disaster declarations were signed in 17 counties – one region extends north from Boulder to Glen Haven and the other south from Brighton to Pueblo. The National Weather Service called the event "Biblical," "historic," "unprecedented." Nearly 12½ inches of rain fell over two days breaking their previous record of 5½ inches for an entire month. In a week, at least 21 inches had fallen.

For some states like Louisiana or Mississippi that get 60 inches in a year, 12½ inches wouldn't be that big of a deal, comparatively speaking. That's why the 100-, 500- and 1,000-year events are specific to a certain area.

The historic rains sent 20-foot walls of water slamming down mountainsides, destroying bridges, taking out towns and completely isolating others. In the mountain village of Lyons most trailer parks were obliterated. *Do you need something?* became the town's new greeting. Over the state 20,000 homes were damaged and another 1,600 were demolished.

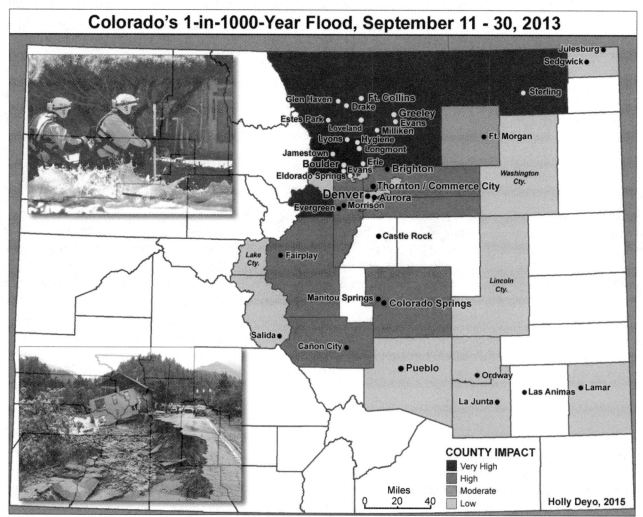

62

At least ten people lost their lives; hundreds more were missing. Officials stated it could take weeks, maybe months, to search through flood-ravaged areas looking for people who died.

Some 1,900 oil and gas wells were shut down so crews could check for damage. Evacuees of Hygiene returned to devastation. Mud blanketed everything even garages and tops of fence posts. St. Vrain Creek, which runs between Longmont and Hygiene left trucks in ditches and carried items two miles downstream.

In Lyons 51 Colorado National Guardsmen, first responders, and civilians had to be rescued when their tactical trucks were swamped. Thirty-six were choppered out by U.S. Army aviators before worsening weather halted the rescue operation. Fifteen others, all first responders and Guardsmen, had to wait out the flood on higher ground. Major roads washed away or were covered by mud and rock slides in mountain towns. The sleepy hamlet of Glen Haven was reduced to rubble while key infrastructure like gas lines and sewers systems were destroyed. Town administrator, Frank Lancaster said hundreds of homes in Estes Park could be unreachable and uninhabitable for up to a year. It would have a devastating effect on this Rocky Mountain tourist town. A full year later 80 properties still didn't have natural gas and scores of others couldn't flush their toilets forcing them to use porta-potties of 5-gallon buckets.

Damage to Colorado's multibillion-dollar agriculture industry was vast. Aerial footage shows huge areas of farmland under water. Row upon row of corn, lettuce, onions and soybeans were submerged up and down the South Platte River. Fields were so soggy it made harvesting produce that had brought in nearly $9 billion the year before, nearly impossible. When veggies could be picked, 500 miles of damaged roads added to the cost of transport and farmers' frustration.

Floods overwhelmed sewage treatment plants. Then Gov. John Hickenlooper estimated that 20 million gallons of raw waste was released and 10 times that much in partly treated effluent. It not only covered farms, but contaminated drinking water and wells throughout eastern Colorado.[95]

Residents like Genevieve Marquez were overwhelmed. "What now? We don't even know where to start. It's not even like a day by day or a month thing. I want to think that far ahead but it's a minute-by-minute thing at this point. And, I guess now it's just help everyone out and try to get our lives back."[96]

Seven 1-in-1,000 Year Rain Events in 7 Years

April showers bring May flowers, but in March 2016, they brought over two feet of rain to northwest Louisiana, Texas and Arkansas. Over 5,000 homes in Louisiana alone were flooded. Roads submerged, sewers backed-up, bridges washed out, cars were abandoned in streams-that-became-rivers. At least five people died. Rivers reached all-time highs and in some instances water reached the height of power lines. Historic flooding closed I-10 at the Texas-Louisiana line for four straight days. One meteorologist called this event a "rain bomb".[97]

News videos showed horses chin deep in water struggling to swim and stay alive. Brenda Maddox who was forced to flee her home of 26 years said, "We'd heard we'd get a lot of rain, but it all came so sudden. We hate to leave, but we thought we'd get out while we can."[98]

Allen DeWeese was living in the Land-o-Pines campground about 75 miles east of Baton Rouge with his 10-year-old son. He joked saying they're now calling it Land-o-Lakes. His trailer was destroyed rendering he and his son homeless. Another couple fearing their mobile home might be looted stayed to the point of desperation and was the last to leave. Floodwaters crept up their front steps while they watched neighbors evacuate. When water was waist-deep on Sam Cassidy and an alligator swam by, he and his wife decided to leave, too.

Making matters worse during the flood, the Sabine River Authority released over 260 billion gallons of water from the Toledo Bend dam. To put this into perspective during this period of release the flow of water was more than twice that of Niagara Falls' average rate. In late April 2016, 105 Texas plaintiffs and 134 from Louisiana sued the Authority alleging in the complaint that they had to know it would damage area homes. The Sabine River Authority contended the reservoir was never built for flood control and felt they had not option except to release the excess. Now it's up to the courts to decide.

It rained. And rained. And rained some more till over 20" fell on South Carolina from Oct. 1 - Oct 5, 2015. One meteorologist estimated the historic deluge dropped 6 *trillion* gallons of water – enough to fill the Rose Bowl stadium to the top more than 65,000 times. Before the wet onslaught, 65% of the state was in drought. Record flooding wiped out infrastructure, contaminated water supplies, inundated thousands of homes and businesses, and cut off entire towns. At least 19 people lost their lives. Eighteen dams were breached or failed entirely as earthen barriers softened. Rising floodwaters closed over 150 bridges and nearly 300 roads including a 75-mile stretch of I-95, the freeway that connects Miami to Washington, D.C. to New York. Boil advisories were issued for the 375,000 people living in Columbia.

When resident Ben Hudson saw water everywhere and neighbors in trouble, he hauled out his 22-foot fishing boat. He knew that while it was ocean-capable, it'd be vulnerable in flood's swift currents and debris. He asked a policeman when were the rescue teams coming and the cop said, *they aren't, they were too overwhelmed.* He told Hudson, "Nobody's coming. There's no one to come. I can't commission you. But if you want to be a hero, this is a good day to start."[99] Hudson and a fellow boater pulled 70 people to safety and found another 30 boaters cruising the waters looking for people to save. Some were on second floors of their homes and some had to climb onto their roofs or into trees, waiting for help to arrive.

The depth and scope of the water was daunting yet Hudson and friends persevered in their rescue efforts. They dodged power lines and every type of debris imaginable. Their boats bumped into floating cars and water-buried bridges. Dams that were supposed to hold back their immense watery burdens were invisible as they too, were under water. Hudson couldn't even see the Lake Katherine dam and he drove right over it.

Environment reporter Sammy Fretwell for *The State* newspaper said, "You've had homes flooded, major intersections flooded out, that people have never seen happen before. You've had standing water in yards, cars underwater – that's been pretty much the legacy of this storm."[100] Insurance companies expect damages to exceed $1 billion. This was the 7th 1-in-1000 year event in 7 years.[101] [102] The March 2016 Louisiana rain-smackdown was #7. The Tennessee flood in May 2010, heavy rain from Hurricane Irene pounding New England and the Mid-Atlantic states in 2011, Colorado flooding in 2013, the Baltimore-Washington D.C deluge in 2014, and massive flooding in Nebraska in May 2015 round out these mind-numbing events. What does this say about what's coming?

Biggest Ever Hurricane

As this is being written, October 23, 2015, the largest-ever Western hemisphere hurricane is hurling its worst at Mexico. Monster 200mph winds propelled category 5 Patricia from Mexico's western side onshore. People had little time to prepare as it morphed from a tropical storm close to shore to a raging Cat 5 'cane in less than 24 hours. Patricia's punishing winds stampeded right through the heart of the county in a narrow cone, which means its forces were highly concentrated. Within hours of Patricia's arrival people had picked grocery stores clean.

"Godzilla" El Niño Forms

The El Niño of 2015-2016 tied the 1997-1998 event as the strongest on record and dubbed Godzilla and Bruce Lee by forecasters. It may even surpass all others, but how strong it becomes won't be known until spring 2016. Since 1950 NOAA's database shows only two comparable in strength to the event now developing. Those occurred in 1982-83 and 1997-98. In those 65 years, 23 El Niños have formed and NOAA ranks them Weak, Moderate, Strong or Very Strong. To rate the strongest, sea surface temperatures have to be 2°C (3.6°F) or more, higher than normal for at least five consecutive overlapping seasons. An upward move of two degrees doesn't sound like much, but think about how vast oceans are. They're always absorbing heat from the Sun and then winter's coldness without much change. In order for oceans to shift this much, they've had to be exposed to massive, continual heating or cooling.

In July 2015, the Climate Prediction Center changed their method for calculating these four categories. In doing this, it put five El Niño events and three La Niñas (the cool phase) into less severe categories by one full rank making everything look closer to normal. This is similar to what USGS did when they changed the average number of earthquakes for four magnitudes in 2003 making everything seem a little "quieter".

Wild Weather Goes Global

Rains are biblical, heatwaves are non-stop, frigid cold is widespread, droughts are crippling, tornadoes strike in savage swarms. Weather has changed radically. Meteorologists said even for a world getting used to wild weather, May 2015 seemed "stuck on strange". Strange included torrential rain in Texas that alternated with driving drought. A heatwave killed at least 2,500 in India. "Apocalyptic" rain flooded Moscow streets while lightning blew up a gas station. Two super typhoons formed in the western Pacific. Four major U.S. tornado outbreaks generated some 460 twister reports. Destructive twisters also hit New Zealand, Mexico, and Germany, which saw two tornado outbreaks. Softball sized hail hammered Colorado. When winter was officially two months past, cold weather in Ukraine killed 37. Record 91° temperatures baked Alaska. Drought began to form in the eastern U.S. states.

Marshall Shepherd, meteorology professor at the University of Georgia noted "when it rains hard, it rains harder than it did 20 to 30 years ago." In these torrential downpours, more rain ends up as runoff rather than recharging dwindling aquifers or nurturing the land. Climate scientist Jennifer Francis at Rutgers University said, "Mother Nature keeps throwing us crazy stuff. It's just been one thing after another."[103]

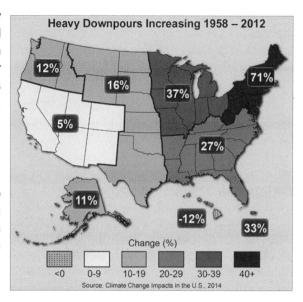

TEXAS, OKLAHOMA, COLORADO

After weeks of heavy rain and flooding, aquifers filled to capacity – and beyond. Colorado, Oklahoma, and Texas each recorded record rain in May 2015. In fact, Oklahoma and Texas had their wettest month of any month – ever – with precipitation totals more than twice the average.

TEXAS

May's torrential downpours caused massive flooding throughout Texas, inundated businesses, invaded homes and streets, knocked out bridges and swept homes off foundations. Over 37 *trillion* gallons of water fell on the Lone Star State in that one month – enough to cover all of Texas in 8 inches of water. Despite repeated warnings to evacuate and not to drive through high water at least 41 people lost their lives in Texas and Oklahoma. More than 10,000 cars were damaged and the next worry was whether people would try to resell them in other states.

Photo: Volunteers help clean up debris from the recent flooding and storms next to Hidden Valley Road in Wimberley, TX. (Courtesy Jocelyn Augustino/FEMA)

Wimberley and Houston were two of the worst hit cities. In Houston alone, 1,400 structures suffered severe damage. When the mighty Blanco River surged into the Ernie Perez's Wimberley home, it blew the door off its frame. Literally. Dirty brown water poured in and swirled his furniture together like a mega Mixmaster. Ernie said, "It turned the living room into a gigantic washing machine" and he knew 911 wasn't going to get to them in time.[104] In the distance Ernie's brother saw firefighters with a rescue boat. He whistled loudly and managed to attract their attention. They were among the lucky ones; others weren't so fortunate and perished. Many homes on Houston's west side filled with three feet of water before it was over.

The Brown family was surprised to hear a knock on their door as water prohibited travel. It was someone whose vehicle got stuck and they desperately needed shelter. Saundra Brown realized with water expected to flood inside their home they'd better form a game plan. "We just told everybody, 'Get on the couches.' Then we put the family on the dining room table. (We moved to) the counters next. And if it was going to rise more, we'd go on the roof."[105]

Oklahoma

While massive, damaging tornadoes are frequent in Oklahoma, few people are insured for devastating floods, let alone know what to do afterwards. Half of the state's counties had flood-damaged homes. Sam Porter, director of Oklahoma Baptist disaster relief said, "In all of my 16 years of disaster relief work, I've never seen such widespread damage. It's a major, major concern. It's truly a big deal in Oklahoma. We've had to take alternative measures we've never done before. Flood recovery is the hardest kind of disaster to clean up. It's heavy, moldy, it's just a mess. You've lost everything, but it's all still there."[106]

Insurance claims in Texas and Oklahoma are expected to top $1 billion.[107]

Colorado

By the 19th, parts of Colorado from one end of the state to the other broke all-time rain records for May. Two months past the official end of spring, the Rockies got another 20 inches of snow and winter storm warnings went into effect. Ten snowplows cleared away 8 inches of hail, which had shut down I-25 in Colorado Springs stranding drivers. Elsewhere golf ball size hail brought highway and street traffic to a standstill and clogged drainage systems across the region. From the South Platte to Poudre to Purgatoire, Colorado rivers bulged and hit flood stage.

With all the rain, came worry for two massive burn scars left by devastating wildfires in 2012 and 2013 – the two worst firestorms in Colorado's history. Flames exploded overnight on June 25, 2012 and mandatory evacuations rocketed from 12,000 to 32,000. The Waldo Canyon Fire ripped through the first and second containment lines and burst into the city of Colorado Springs. Of the nearly 29 square miles scorched, five were charred so severely that plants and roots four inches down were completely gone. There was nothing left to act as anchors. Wildfire experts said it was so barren that the land resembled moonscape. Colorado Springs Fire Chief Rich Brown was short and to the point in an evening news conference that Tuesday, "This is a firestorm of epic proportions,"[108] but worse was to come the very next year.

2013's Black Forest Fire was even more nightmarish burning over 500 homes and killing two people. These two fires combined left massive burn scars visible from space. In floods, instead of just moving water, because there's nothing to hold loose materials, rocks, mud and dead trees can scream downhill creating even greater havoc in its path. So May 2015's flash floods dredged up more anxiety than "just" dealing with too much water.

NASHVILLE

Two to four inches of rain was forecast for Nashville, Tennessee on May 1, 2010. By that afternoon six inches had fallen and it was still pelting down. The city mayor, Karl Dean, was monitoring flash flood reports when a live scene on TV caught his eye. A branch of the Cumberland River was inundating cars and trucks on I-24. Drivers were shocked to see a 40-foot building sail past them in the slow lane.

When the mayor caught sight of the building floating down the freeway he said, "it became very clear to me what an extreme situation we had on our hands."[109]

Rescue teams, fire and police personnel were sent out in boats to answer countless 911 calls. They pulled families off rooftops and employees from flooded warehouses. One rescue involved extracting the driver of an 18-wheeler in water up to his chest. Despite heroic efforts that weekend, 11 people died.

David Edgin, former tugboat captain, had 70 barges and seven boats out on the Cumberland. While the rain continued to hammer down he phoned the U.S. Corp of Engineers for a river-rise forecast. The duty officer reported, "it's blowing up our models. We've never seen anything like this." For safety, the 77 boats were ordered to tie up along the bank and wait the storm out.

Photo: Aerial view over Nashville, Tennessee on May 4, 2010 following severe storms and floods that have damaged or destroyed homes and businesses in April of that year. (David Fine/FEMA)

Rain kept coming. The Cumberland had risen to 35 feet from 15 on Saturday. It was expected to hit 42 and blew by that on Monday finally cresting at 52 – 12 feet above flood stage. Thirteen inches of rain – twice the previous record – had fallen on the city.

Water submerged the world famous Grand Ole Opry. Its manager, Pete Fisher, literally canoed through the entrance and what met his eyes shocked him. Had people been sitting in the front row they would have had seven feet of water overhead. Opry out buildings that housed millions in equipment were similarly flooded. Instruments, electronics, video screens, amps – all under water.

Country Western superstar Brad Paisley who lives in Nashville stated, "I felt powerless in a way I've never felt before with weather. Here in Nashville our weather is manageable, normally. But since that flood, I've never once taken normalcy for granted."[110]

AROUND THE WORLD

Rio

What used to be called 500- or 100-year-events – floods like Nashville experienced – are much more frequent. Three weeks before Nashville's 2010 flood, Rio de Janeiro was slammed by 11 inches of rain in 24 hours. The average for January is less than ½ inch. Between nearly 300 landslides and massive flooding, at least 249 people died.[111] Eight months later Rio was hit by another series of floods and mudslides. Rio received the equivalent of a month's rain in 24 hours. This time over 800 people died[112] and nearly 3,000 people lost their homes. Between the death toll and damages of $13 billion, it was Rio's worst single-day disaster in history.[113]

Photo: Mountainous Teresopolis hardest hit area of Rio by 2011 storms. (Courtesy Vladimir Platonow/ABr[114])

Pakistan

Toward the end of July that same year, record rains in Pakistan caused flooding that affected over 20 million people. In four days, different areas of the country received anywhere from 8½ to 16½ inches of rain. Besides a death toll of nearly 2,000, it's estimated that economic costs hit $43 billion.

Thailand

Thailand was stunned with back-to-back floods in 2010 and 2011. The first was awful, but the 2011 event was beyond dreadful. By late November much of Bangkok was under water and in terms of Thailand as a whole, this event has been described as "the worst flooding yet in terms of the amount of water and people affected".[115] Economically, this was the world's 4th costliest disaster at nearly $46 billion, coming in behind Japan's 2011 earthquake and tsunami, the '95 Kobe quake and 2005's Hurricane Katrina. Nearly 8,000 sq mi of farmland was ruined and hundreds of factories were under water creating a worldwide hard drive shortage. The car and electronics industries were also impacted with damage done to Toyota, Honda, Hitachi, and Canon plants.

Australia

Not be left out, Queensland, Australia experienced a series of devastating floods in December 2010 labeled "unprecedented" and "unpredictable".[116] Thousands of people evacuated, which is why "only" 39 died. Had a similar flood hit the U.S. the death toll might have been much higher. Though Australia occupies about the same real estate as mainland US, they have less than 8% of America's population, so it would be the equivalent of losing 525 Americans. Four days after the initial deluge an area the size of France and Germany was still under water. In addition to the human toll, these floods closed ports and roads, disrupted transportation, and interfered with agriculture and coal industries.

On the other end of the spectrum, drought is also making headlines. Severe drought has hit, Texas, California, Australia, Russia and East Africa. May 2015 brought India's second deadliest heatwave that claimed over 2,500 lives.

Deadly heatwaves struck Europe in 2003, killing over 71,000.[117] [118] Russia lost over 55,000 to this silent killer in 2010 and again in North America and Europe in 2006. At least 225 in the U.S. succumbed to the oppressive heat, as well as over 25,000 cattle and 700,000 fowl in California alone. Canadian provinces closest to the U.S. border were also hit with unrelenting heat. Temperatures in Phoenix pegged 118°F making it the hottest day since 1995 and one of the 11 hottest since 1895.[119] South Dakotans saw a freakish 117°F in Pierre where it's normally 40 degrees cooler.

KILLER HEAT WAVES

May 2015 brought unbearable heat to all of India. Blistering temperatures spiking to 117°F melted roads in New Delhi. Nighttime brought little relief when heat "plummeted" to 100 degrees. Punishing conditions of no air conditioning combined with oppressive humidity made survival for some impossible. Weather Underground's Dr. Jeff Masters wrote, "On May 23 at 14:30, Bhubneshwar [near the northeast coast of India] recorded a temperature of 42.2°C (108°F) with a dew point of 29.3°C (84.7°F), giving an astonishing heat index of 62°C (143.6°F.)"[120] According to Costa Rican weather records researcher Maximiliano Herrera, some stations measured a heat index of up to 65°C (149°F). Experts blame the "heat bomb" on surging hot, dry winds from Pakistan.

Deadly heatwaves struck Europe in 2003, killing over 71,000.[121] [122] Russia lost over 55,000 to this silent killer in 2010 and again in North America and Europe in 2006. At least 225 in the U.S. succumbed to the oppressive heat, as well as over 25,000 cattle and 700,000 fowl in California alone. Canadian provinces closest to the U.S. border were also hit with unrelenting heat. Temperatures in Phoenix pegged 118°F making it the hottest day since 1995 and one of the 11 hottest since 1895.[123] South Dakotans saw a freakish 117°F in Pierre where it's normally 40 degrees cooler.

MAY 2015 "STUCK ON STRANGE"

Extreme weather is becoming the norm. Meteorologists said even for a world getting used to wild weather, May 2015 seemed "stuck on strange". Strange included torrential rain in Texas that alternated with driving drought. A heatwave killed at least 2,500 in India. "Apocalyptic" rainstorms flooded Moscow streets while lightning blew up a gas station. Two top-end typhoons formed in the Northwest Pacific. Four major U.S. tornado outbreaks generated 460 twister reports. Destructive tornadoes also hit New Zealand, Mexico, and Germany, which saw two twister outbreaks. Hail the size of softballs hammered Colorado. After winter was officially two months over, cold weather in Ukraine killed 37. Record 91° temperatures baked *Alaska*. Drought began forming in the U.S. eastern states. Sea ice in the Antarctic grew to the largest expanse ever on record while the Arctic's was the 3rd smallest. Britain shivered in the coolest temps since 1996 while Spain suffered the driest May since 1947.

Marshall Shepherd, meteorology professor at the University of Georgia noted, "When it rains hard, it rains harder than it did 20 to 30 years ago."[124] Climate scientist Jennifer Francis at Rutgers University said, "Mother Nature keeps throwing us crazy stuff. It's just been one thing after another."[125]

Crazy weather didn't stop in May. On the same day massive wildfires charred over 100 sq. miles of Washington, just 200 miles away snow fell in Calgary. While most Canadians soaked up the summer sun on August 22, Albertans were stunned to see the white stuff coating everything. New fires continued to pop up, but the largest – the North Star, which at the time of this writing was just 30% contained, had already burned over 200,000 acres in just three weeks. With still four months to closing out the year, 2015 became Washington's worst-ever year for fires with well over a million acres charred.

GLOBAL CATASTROPHES

Flood, fire, drought, hurricanes, heat and everything in between paint a picture of wild weather gone mad. Since 2010, newscasts have doubled the time spent on weather and natural disaster stories. Since the early 1990s, it's more than quadrupled.[126] A handful of recent headlines tell the story:

- Niagara Falls Has Frozen Over as Extreme Winter Weather Continues Across the East Coast – and It Is Going to Get Even Colder
- Thames Bursts Banks as Cameron Calls UK Floods 'Biblical'
- Britain Grapples Through Worst Torrential Rainfall in 248 Years
- 406 U.S. Record Cold Temperatures in January 2014 – 1073 Snowfall Records
- January 2014 Marks the Coldest Month for the U.S in Over 100 Years, Super Bowl May Be Re-Scheduled
- Nearly 2 Feet of Rain in 24 Hours Hits Florida's Palm Beach County
- The Sea Froze So Fast That It Killed Thousands of Fish Instantly
- 100,000 Bats Fall Dead from the Sky During a Heat Wave in Australia
- Canada Plunges into a Deep Freeze, "Exposed Skin May Freeze in Less Than Five Minutes
- UK Swept By Destructive, '17 Year-High' Tidal Surge
- Turkish Cold Snap Literally Freezes Animals Where They Stand
- Biggest Winter Storm Ever to Wreck Holidays for Millions in UK
- Gale Force Winds Batter Europe, as Thousands in U.K. Face More Flooding
- Typhoon Haiyan: More Cadaver Bags Sent to Philippines as Toll Climbs to 3,633 Dead
- Afghanistan Avalanches: More Than 180 Dead
- Cyclone Marcia: At Least 350 Homes Left Uninhabitable, Says South Australians Told to Leave Homes Due to Catastrophic Bushfire Danger
- North Queensland Hit By Worst Flooding in 30 Years, With More Rain Forecast
- Malawi Floods Leave Grim Legacy of Death, Destruction and Devastation
- Report Warns That Super-storm Sandy Was Not 'The Big One'
- Avalanches Kill Over 200 amid Heavy Snow in Afghanistan
- Bolivia: Thousands Displaced by "Unprecedented" Floods
- After Drought, Rains Plaguing Midwest Farms
- Vanuatu Blames Global Warming as Cyclone Causes Nation's Worst Climate Disaster in Recent Memory
- Study: Climate Change to Trigger Longer, Fiercer 'Mega-droughts'
- California Snowpack Is Alarmingly Low
- New PBS Special 'Extreme Realities' Explores Security Threat from Climate Change
- Photos Document Devastation After Floods Hit Morocco
- Climate Change Is Driving Heat Waves Around the World: Report
- California Heat Wave Drives Power Demand to Highest of the Year
- Nevada Downpour Caused Over $1 Million in Damage
- Record Flood Fills Detroit Freeways
- Big Island of Hawaii Struck by Earthquake as Two Hurricanes Approach
- California Drought Reaches a Terrifying Milestone
- Lake Mead Drops to Lowest Levels Ever as Drought Plagues Southwest
- Report: Coastal Flooding Has Surged Along Eastern Seaboard
- 'Freak' Sandstorm Blankets Iran's Capital, Kills at Least 4
- Weather, Climate-Related Disasters Have Cost the Planet TRILLIONS

Senior scientist, Jay Gulledge, at the Center for Climate and Energy Solutions says, "we know that warming of the Earth's surface is putting more moisture in the atmosphere. We've measured it. The satellites see it. So the chances for extreme weather are going nowhere but up."[127]

Other experts agree that extreme weather is on the rise and likely to escalate, even if they don't agree on the cause. It's unfortunate that the previously used term of "global warming" – implying that it's primarily human caused – has confiscated the more neutral sound of "climate change." It's undeniable that climate *has* changed, but the cause or causes are up for grabs. Regardless, we must deal with the escalating events. That is the point, because even proponents of greenhouse gases say we are too far over the edge to not see their effects.

Dr. Peter Stott, head of climate monitoring at the Met Office Hadley Centre in London says, "Unusual or extreme weather events are of great public concern and interest, yet there are often conflicting messages from scientists about whether such events can be linked to climate change. While it is clear that across the globe there has been an increase in the frequency of extreme heatwaves and of episodes of heavy rainfall, this does not mean that human-induced climate change is to blame for every instance of such damaging weather. However climate change could be changing the odds and it is becoming increasingly clear that it is doing so in such a way as to increase the chances of extremely warm temperatures and reduce the chances of extremely cold temperatures in many places."[128]

Professor Michael Mann, director of the Earth System Science Center at the Penn State Department of Meteorology states, "here in the US, we've seen a doubling in the frequency of record-breaking heat, relative to what we would expect from chance alone. So far this year, we're seeing those records broken at nearly 10 times the rate we would expect without global warming. So there is no question in my mind that the "signal" of climate change has now emerged in our day-to-day weather. We are seeing the loading of the random weather dice toward more "sixes". We are seeing and feeling climate change in the more extreme heat we are witnessing this summer, the outbreak of massive forest fires like the one engulfing Colorado over the past week, and more extreme weather events like the Derecho that knocked out power for millions in the eastern US during a record-breaking heat spell."[129]

Climatologist Michael Oppenheimer of Princeton University, who helped write a recent report on extreme weather stated, "Something has gone wrong. To put it bluntly, we're doing a lousy job keeping up with disasters."[130]

Mega-Disasters Around the World

In 2014, the only continent hit harder with catastrophes than North America was Asia, followed by Europe, then Africa, South America, and finally Australia – Oceania. Australia is usually at the bottom of this list, which is why she's nicknamed The Lucky Country.

Asia accounted for about one-third of all catastrophes, North America roughly 25% and Europe about 20% .The other three are a couple percentage points apart and all are under 10% for their share.

MunichRe is the world's largest reinsurer so tracking natural catastrophes is tops on their 'to do' list. In 2012, they warned other reinsurers that they should consider raising their rates because weather-related disasters have risen so greatly. This warning came on the heels of 2011 when MunichRe was hit with $116 billion in claims. Their study showed the number of weather-related losses in North America *nearly quintupled* in the past 30 years, increased 400% in Asia, 250% in Africa, 200% in Europe and 150% in South America.[131]

Now flash forward to 2014. Even though it was a vicious year for disasters in some parts of the world, North America didn't share in any of the top 5 events. This even takes into account January's bone-crushing Polar Vortex and June's cluster of damaging thunderstorms that nearly wiped Blair, Nebraska off the map.

SAO PAULO MEGA DROUGHT

While many disasters are about what nature does *to* us, southeastern Brazil suffered heavily from something withheld – rain. Sao Paulo is home to some 44 million people and covers more real estate than Britain. Water for their homes and businesses is supplied by a four-lake system collectively called the Cantareira reservoir and the Alto Tiete reservoir network. A top government regulator warned Sao Paulo that if severe rationing weren't implemented they would likely run out of water in 100 days.

As weeks with no rain passed into October, the Cantareira sank to just over 3% capacity and Sao Paulo was on the verge of collapse. This was the worst drought in 80 years. Vicente Andreu, president of Brazil's National Water Agency worried, "If the drought continues, residents will face more dramatic water shortages in the short term. If it doesn't rain, we run the risk that the region will have a collapse like we've never seen before."[132]

This was huge because that one state supplies 40% of the GDP for all Brazil. If Sao Paulo, the country's economic "locomotive" collapsed, the domino effect would have been enormous. Though water was trucked in and rolling power outages were implemented, some businesses were crippled. One meat packing plant permanently shut its doors.

Their rainy season, October – March, came and went with little improvement so Sao Paulo is in the midst of a third consecutive year with soaring temperatures and historically low rainfall. The cost of this drought, just for 2014, hit $5 billion in damages.

YUNNAN PROVINCE, SOUTHWEST CHINA

The afternoon of Aug. 3, 2014, slammed China with a 6.1 earthquake – the strongest to hit the area in 14 years. While not the largest on the Richter scale, the quake and ensuing landslides destroyed more than 12,000 brick homes, damaged 30,000 others, killed 617 people and injured another 2000. Pictures repeatedly showed stunned, vacant faces.

At the onset, people flew from their homes, clutching babies. Repeated aftershocks made them fearful of going back inside for those whose homes were still standing. More than 2,500 troops were dispatched to aid in rescue efforts and when they ran out of stretchers, the injured were carried on doors.

Ma Yaoqi, an 18-year-old resident and volunteer in the quake zone, said that at least half of the buildings had collapsed from the city center of Zhaotong to the worst hit town of Longtou. The rest of the buildings were damaged. Ma said, "I saw dead bodies being wrapped in quilts and carried away. Some were wrapped with small quilts. Those must be kids."[133]

Ma continues. "It's so terrible. The aftermath is much, much worse than what happened after the quake two years ago. I have never felt so strong tremors before. What I can see are all ruins."[134]

Unrelenting rain complicated rescue efforts to bring tents, water, food and other relief supplies to survivors. With roads caved in, much had to be carried in on foot. This disaster's losses, too, ended up around $5 billion.

INDIA AND PAKISTAN FLOODS, SEPT. 2 – 26

The strongest monsoon rains to hit India and Pakistan in more than 50 years devastated the two countries, causing landslides, home collapses, thousands of evacuations, power outages, countless water rescues and unprecedented flooding. Some areas received more than a foot of rain. Pictures of dirty water swirling around peoples' chests told the story. One man waded through chest-deep water in India with his goat slung around his neck. Another image showed four men rescuing two very large hogs from drowning by hoisting them on top of a rickety makeshift bamboo raft. Still other photos showed human chains passing babies down the line in waist-deep water. Temples in India were so engulfed by floodwaters, nothing but statuary on rooftops remained visible.

Six straight days of rain completely inundated more than 980 villages – 450 in India, 530 in Pakistan though a total of 2,600 were affected. Some villages saw water levels over 12 feet high. More than 80,000 people had to flee their homes. In India, over 200,000 people were rescued from raging floodwaters in 2,000+ villages.

During these 3½ weeks of water hell, over 550 people died across the two countries after being swept away by floodwaters, electrocuted from downed power lines, or crushed by landslides and sudden collapse of thousands of homes.

Ghulam Nabi, a resident in Srinagar, India, told the AP, "I'm in my 80s and I've never seen floods like this. If this is how it is in my neighborhood, I cannot imagine the devastation in other areas."[135]

Omar Abdullah, the chief minister of Jammu and Kashmir state in India, tweeted. "This is an unprecedented situation and we are doing the best we can under the circumstances. Please don't panic, we will reach you, I promise."[136] Some were fortunate; for others, rescue didn't come in time.

Losses from the flooding were estimated to be $5.1 billion.

WINTER DAMAGE IN JAPAN

In northern Japan, 18 locations set records for the greatest snow depth on record in the Kanto/Koshin region, which includes Tokyo. So rare is snow in Tokyo the city came to a standstill. About 246,000 homes were without power on the first day. Over 2,100 people were evacuated from their homes over fear they would collapse.

Journalist Minoru Watanabe, who specializes in coverage of disasters and crisis management said, "When 8 cm (3 inches) fell on Tokyo a year ago, the city practically descended into panic. A heavy snowfall would paralyze most of the city's functions and leave the transport network in tatters. The railway switches would fail to function and signal cables snap. The schedules of the subway lines that share their tracks with regular commuter trains would be thrown into disarray. Auto traffic would come to a standstill."[137]

Imagine what 10.6 inches did to Tokyo during the heaviest snowstorm in 45 years.[138] Snow and 53mph wind cancelled 338 flights and caused thousands of car accidents. People there are so ill prepared for this kind of weather that they don't own ski parkas. Women walked around in their kimonos carrying umbrellas.

In Japan's northeastern city of Sendai, the storm dumped nearly 14 inches of the white stuff, making it the heaviest snowfall in 78 years. Fukushima was also blanketed by 17.3 inches. Worst hit was Karuizawa, 93 miles northwest of Tokyo, where the snowfall was just shy of three feet deep.

By the time the record-breaking storm finished it racked up nearly $6 billion in losses. At least 37 people died and another 1,253 were injured.

TROPICAL CYCLONE HUDHUD

Hurricanes aren't new to Asia. They frequently wreck havoc across the region. Hudhud was no different as she slammed into India as a category 4 storm on Oct. 12. The powerful cyclone demolished at least 6,500 homes, killed 124 and affected another half million. While the storm mainly ravaged two states, heavy rain was forecast for six, prompting flooding fears. Hudhud intent on destruction, flattened rice crops, banana and sugarcane plantations, ripped out roads, cut power to millions and forced the evacuation of 500,000.[139] According to the UN, Cyclone Hudhud racked up $ 11 billion worth of losses.[140]

The damage caused by Hudhud not only changed the landscape of port city, Vizag, but it was the first city in India to be directly hit by a cyclone since 1891. Before this, superstorms normally made landfall in the plains and semi-urban areas along the coast. So their targets are shifting to more populated areas.

"Hudhud not only emerged as first high intensity cyclonic storm in 2014 to make landfall at wind speeds of 206 kph [128mph], but also the third highest intensity cyclonic storm out of the 515 cyclonic storms that developed in either the Bay of Bengal or the Arabian Sea since 1891."[141]

As in most crises, potable water was critical. Sai Padma, who lives in an urban neighborhood of Visakhapatnam, stated. "The biggest problem is water. We ran out of our stock of the corporation drinking water yesterday and each 10-litre [2.5 gallon] can of water is being sold at 2,500 rupees [US$40], which is ridiculous. It is appalling that in times of such crises, all some people can think of is making money. The government relief too is nowhere to be seen."[142]

India Aftermath

In reading countless worldwide news article on disasters and their aftermath for three decades, one recurring theme appears: the heart-warming selfless giving of people also suffering juxtaposed to shocking self-centeredness to the point of killing others. So many people around the world knock America, but these two opposite attitudes rule throughout the world, regardless of type of government. Meanwhile in India...

Amid the struggle for survival were allegations that some government officials, who were appointed to distribute milk and water to provide respite to harrowed citizens, were not doing their job properly.

In the midst of this devastation, three important public bodies — GVMC, Vuda and police commissionerate – *are headless*, which is also affecting the relief operations.

I saw a man dumping a sack of water pouches near my house. But before I could lay my hands on them, two men ran out and took the sack away with them. We are dying of thirst as we have no access to drinking water and people (relief workers) do not have the common sense to distribute it properly," an agitated M Ramana said.

Milk vans being sent to distribute free milk to citizens are only giving away a few packets free while rest are being sold in the black market at huge rates," alleged V Mahalakshmi of Peda Waltair.

As the supply of food items in the open market remained scarce, their prices continued with their northward journey, blowing a hole in the pockets of citizens.[143]

This should remind everyone of then FEMA Director Michael Brown during Hurricane Katrina? If it has faded from memory, as a refresher, Michael Brown was more interested in how he'd look in stylish clothes, good on camera than he was about getting aid to millions of suffering people.

Two days after Katrina hit, Marty Bahamonde, one of the only FEMA employees in New Orleans, wrote to Brown that "the situation is past critical" and listed problems including many people near death and food and water running out at the Superdome. Brown's entire response was: "Thanks for the update. Anything specific I need to do or tweak?"[144]

In the midst of the overwhelming destruction caused by the hurricane and enormous problems faced by FEMA, Mr. Brown found time to exchange e-mails about superfluous topics, including "problems finding a dog-sitter," Melancon said. Melancon said that on August 26, just days before Katrina made landfall, Brown e-mailed his press secretary, Sharon Worthy, about his attire, asking: "Tie or not for tonight? Button-down blue shirt?"

A few days later, Worthy advised Brown: "Please roll up the sleeves of your shirt, all shirts. Even the president rolled his sleeves to just below the elbow. In this [crisis] and on TV you just need to look more hard-working."

On August 29, the day of the storm, Brown exchanged e-mails about his attire with Taylor, Melancon said. She told him, "You look fabulous," and Brown replied, "I got it at Nordstroms. ... Are you proud of me?"

An hour later, Brown added: "If you'll look at my lovely FEMA attire, you'll really vomit. I am a fashion god," according to the congressman.[145]

While Brown pondered and emailed these banalities, 1,833 people perished.

Prior to landing work at FEMA, Michael Brown's biggest job was supervising judges at Arabian horse shows.

"People wondered how he got to FEMA as we all did, and certainly what he did with the Arabian Horse Association was nothing [compared to] what he does with FEMA," Arabian Horse Association Regional Director Chuck Mangan.

"Brown was brought into FEMA by his college roommate, Joe Allbaugh, President Bush's first campaign manager and FEMA director. At the time, Brown's only prior experience in emergency services was in a suburb of Oklahoma City in the mid-1970s. He became FEMA director when Allbaugh left in 2003."[146]

People blamed President Bush, but ultimately WE are responsible for our own actions and preparations. So this was on Brown. Not on our superiors though they generally take the hit. Brown let Americans down countrywide in our worst-ever disaster. It is why we advocate NOT depending on government, not on FEMA. Be personally responsible. Always.

Last Thoughts on Disasters

Insurance companies are at the forefront monitoring natural disasters because they don't want to be caught holding the bag for billions of dollars in claims. In the last decade insurance companies, large and small, have axed policies that insure for earthquakes, tornadoes and flooding. FEMA's National Flood Insurance that's always touting, "buy our insurance, get insured!" insures only property at ground level and above, the least vulnerable. Finished basements that are every much a part of peoples' homes and entertainment areas are left without recourse.

Do you see the pattern in these five 2014 disasters? Each account contains words like "rare", "unprecedented", "worst-ever", "strongest", "never seen before", "set records", "record-breaking", "worst in decades".

MunichRe's 2016 chart[147] clearly shows that the number of global catastrophes is growing. No matter the category of Geophysical, Meteorological, Hydrological or Climatological, ALL are ticking up. Quakes and seismic activity are increasing at the smallest rate while severe storms and floods are lifting by huge amounts. Taken together, the trend is unmistakable. Over the last 36 years, disaster intensity, in addition to frequency, is accelerating.

2015 was the worst year for huge disasters since MunichRe has kept figures. Nearly 1,100 natural catastrophes took 23,000 lives – three times higher than the previous year. The upward march is unmistakable. In 1980 and for nearly a decade, big deadly events hovered around 350, give or take. But in 1988, things began to change noticeably and then by 2000, quite sharply. Now in 2015, they've increased 200% without backtracking.

In 2015 the deadliest event by far was the series of earthquakes that struck Nepal and the neighboring India, China and Bangladesh. They claimed 9,000 lives making them among the 15 deadliest earthquakes since 1980.

Heatwaves in May and June caused almost 3,700 deaths in India and Pakistan. Europe too, suffered in hot, dry weather where over 1,200 people died from extreme heat stress. Winter storms hammered the USA, Canada and Europe. Typhoons battered China, Japan and the Philippines and widespread flooding drenched the United Kingdom. Droughts attacked virtually every continent. Without question catastrophic disasters are escalating, leaving no place untouched.

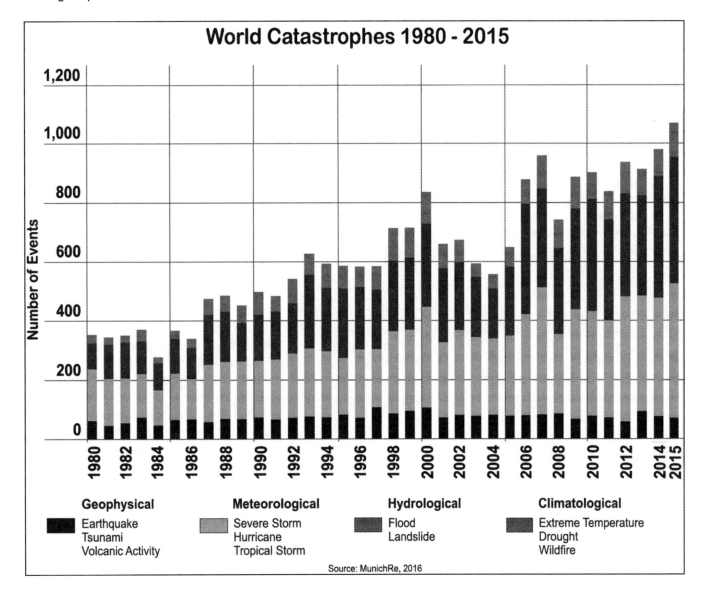

Chapter 7: Signs in the Heavens

There will be signs in sun and moon and stars, and on the earth dismay among nations, in perplexity at the roaring of the sea and the waves, men fainting from fear and the expectation of the things which are coming upon the world; for the powers of the heavens will be shaken. —Luke 21:25-26 (NASB)

I will display wonders in the heavens and on the earth, blood and fire and columns of smoke. The sun will be turned into darkness and the moon into blood before the great and awesome day of the Lord comes. —Joel 2:30-31 (NASB)

The sun will be turned into darkness and the moon into blood, before the great and glorious day of the Lord shall come. —Acts 2:20 (NASB)

And God said, Let there be lights in the expanse of the heavens to separate the day from the night, and let them be signs and tokens [of God's provident care], and [to mark] seasons, days, and years, —Genesis 1:13-15 (AMP)

Mysteries in the Skies

The night's canopy is full of extraordinary beauty and mystery. We depend on the magnificent sky eyes of Hubble, Chandra, Spitzer, Herschel and other space telescopes to bring galaxies and nebulae into our living room. If not for them we would experience their grandeur as mere pinpricks of light, if that. Since the first telescope wasn't invented until the early 17th century, imagine what people missed seeing before then!

However, some objects, some events were simply too huge and too close, relatively speaking, to miss, telescope or not. Four of these are solar and lunar eclipses, blood moons and comets.

Put yourself in their shoes in pre-telescope days. Every night like celestial clockwork, a creamy bright white moon rises and traces a path through the blackened sky. People have tracked the moon to know when to plant crops, designed calendars by its waxing and waning, and planned feasts and festivals around this orb. Every so often, an odd thing happened when it would "disappear" completely. According to NASA, during the 5,000 years between 1999 BC and 3000 AD, some 12,064 lunar eclipses have occurred or will occur, but only 3,479 were total.

Then one night, something really freakish happened and the moon turned an ominous brick red. What could that mean?

Evidently quite a bit during some appearances, especially when they came in tetrads – or four total lunar eclipses in a row. During those same 5,000 years, it will only occur 142 times. Between 1 and 2100 AD, a tetrad has happened just 62 times. That may sound like a lot for such an unusual show.

Here's when this "very unusual event" becomes "rare". During those same 2,100 years, a tetrad occurring on Jewish Feasts – making it a <u>Biblical</u> Tetrad – has happened only seven times. Seven times in 2,100 years... and each time some momentous event took place within a year on either side of those Tetrads.

In the Jewish year of Nisan 5775 (2015), during March-April, the exact same pattern of holidays, Jewish feasts and total solar eclipse was reproduced like was seen in Nisan 3793 (March-April 33 AD), when Jesus was crucified and resurrected.

Biblical Tetrads and Major Events

1. **April 14, 32 – Sept 27, 33. Jesus' Crucifixion.** This first occurrence doesn't qualify as a tetrad since it featured two full blood moons and two half blood moons. It's usually included as it surrounds Christ's crucifixion and resurrection, setting the pace for monumental events surrounding celestial happenings.

2. **April 17, 162 – Sept. 30, 163. Martyrdom, Diaspora and Great Plague.** This tetrad is associated with the Jewish Diaspora, a deadly plague killed off Europeans and the persecution of Christians in the Roman Empire under Marcus Aurelius Antoninus.

3. **April 9, 795 – Sept. 21, 796. Defeat of the Muslim Empire.** During this tetrad millions of Jews and Christians were martyred and the Muslim attempt to conquer the world was thwarted by Charlemagne.

4. **March 30, 842 – Sept. 12, 843. Fall of the Holy Roman Empire.** Muslims rose again this time to defeat the Holy Roman Empire that martyred millions of Jews and Christians.

5. **April 9, 860 – Sept. 22, 861. 2nd Defeat of the Muslim Empire.** During this tetrad, Muslims attempted to conquer the world a second time and were defeated by Europe. In 861 Muhammed al-Mudabbir arrived in Egypt and tripled the tax on Christians and Jews. Because so many couldn't pay, they filled the prisons. Again, millions of Jews and Christians were martyred.

6. **April 2, 1493 – Sept. 15, 1494. Columbus Discovers the New World.** This tetrad was noted for the Spanish Inquisition where the Jews were expelled from Spain. Columbus is credited for discovering America.

7. **April 13, 1949 – Sept. 26, 1950. Nation of Israel Reborn on May 14, 1948.** After being dispersed throughout the world for 2,000 years, the Jewish people reclaimed Israel and declare a nation. One year later, the UN accepted them. Dead Sea Scrolls found.

8. **April 24, 1967 – Oct. 6, 1968. Six Day War June 5–10, 1967.** Jerusalem was restored as the capital of Israel and the Temple Mount was seized by Israel for the first time in 2000 years.

9. **April 15, 2014 – Sept. 28, 2015. Financial markets shaken globally.** Jonathan Cahn wrote the book, *The Mystery of the Shemitah,* tying Biblical tetrads, Shemitahs and major world events together. He says the 2015 Shemitah:

- Wiped out an estimated 16% of the British markets
- Wiped out 18% of the French markets
- Wiped out 25% of the German markets
- Wiped out 4,000 points from the Indian markets
- Wiped out 12,000 points from the Brazilian markets
- Wiped out $2 trillion of the U.S. markets and
- Wiped out a massive $11 trillion from the world's financial realm.[148]

It didn't stop there. Financially 2016 launched *the worst* year since the Great Depression. In the first three weeks the Dow dropped nearly 10%. Fears renewed that Wall Street was entering a downturn dwarfing the one that caused the 2008 recession. January 16th saw the Dow sink 550 points by mid-day. Before closing, the DJIA had recovered 300 points and closed down just 1.56%. In the weeks following, markets jerked up and down like financial rickrack. Leading economists cite the historic drop in oil prices as the leading reason for such volatility. In January crude oil plunged to $26.30 a barrel – the lowest since May 2003 due to a global oil oversupply. Experts argue that it will sink lower. Two other fear factors are the threat of global recession and whether or not big banks will be able to withstand these forces.

During the second week of January, China allowed the biggest fall in the Yuan in five months, which caused stock market trading to be suspended twice. China's currency continued to drop since a 2%-devaluation in August 2015 touched off a global stock market selloff.

In May 2015 the Dow peaked at 18,312.39. Nine months later it'd lost 13%.

Speaking at 2016 World Economic Forum, William White, former chief economist of the Bank of Inter-national Settlements, warned that the global financial system has become dangerously unstable. He said, "The situation is worse than it was in 2007. Our macroeconomic ammunition to fight downturns is essentially all used up. Debts have continued to build up over the last eight years and they have reached such levels in every part of the world that they have become a potent cause for mischief. It will become obvious in the next recession that many of these debts will never be serviced or repaid, and this will be uncomfortable for a lot of people who think they own assets that are worth something. The only question is whether we are able to look reality in the eye and face what is coming in an orderly fashion, or whether it will be disorderly. Things are so bad there is no right answer. If [the Federal Reserve] raise rates it'll be nasty. If they don't raise rates, it just makes matters worse."[149]

In February 2016, CNN Money headlined: "fear has taken over stock markets around the world."[150] Globally stocks officially slipped into a bear market the week of February 8th closing more than 20% below recent highs. Brazil, Canada, China, France, Germany and Japan's market are already in bear status. (Investopedia defines a bear market as a 20% or more downturn in multiple broad market indexes, like the Dow or Standard & Poor's, for at least two months.)[151] The truism used to say that "When America sneezes, the world gets a cold." Financial gurus have added, "As goes China, so goes the world." As of February 13, 2016, the U.S. had avoided bear territory, but with the Dow off 13% from its high and the Nasdaq off 17%, people are strapping in anticipating a wild ride.

While the world spins through 2016, the 2014-2015 Shemitah fallout may not be over.

BIBLICAL TETRADS AND OTHER CELESTIAL EVENTS

The 2014 – 2015 tetrad is like no other as this one also includes a total solar eclipse and a Supermoon. This is when, while in new moon phase, the moon orbits closest to Earth making it look larger. Rabbis teach that blood moons are signs from God indicating judgment on Israel while solar eclipses are signs for judgment on Gentiles. The 2014-2015 Biblical Tetrad is special in yet another way. It's a Shemitah year.

So What's a Shemitah Year?

In the old days as prescribed in Exodus 23:10-11 and Deuteronomy 15:1-11, farmers didn't work their fields every 7th year. No planting or harvesting was done, so farmers and fields alike had time to rest. Whatever crops re-seeded were given freely to anyone. Shemitah, meaning "to release" was also a time when loans to Hebrews were wiped away by creditors. Today, rabbinical measures permit food to be grown, but they are in keeping with various interpretations of how Shemitah should be applied to Israel now. Likewise, rabbinic provisions are in place allowing banks and individual creditors to continue debt collection.

During a Shemitah year, God can raise nations or tear them down. This can affect their economy and wealth, their military and leaders, and the health and wellbeing of the citizens. Is it coincidence that the five greatest economic crashes of the last 40 years – 1973, 1980, 1987, 2001 and 2008 – all occurred in Shemitah years? Or that the Yom Kippur War occurred in the Shemitah year of 1973 and the 9/11 terror attacks coincided with the end of Shemitah in 2001?

Jubilee

If these things weren't enough to pique prophetic interest, factor in that 2015 is also a Jubilee year, which occurs every 50 years. This provided for two consecutive years where people didn't farm, all Israelites who had sold themselves into slavery were set free, and all land that had been sold reverted to its original owners. (See Leviticus 25:8-22) Jubilee hasn't been celebrated in Israel for thousands of years because it involves returning land according to tribal designation. Since it's unclear which tribes today's Jews belong to – most are probably from Judah and Levi – land can't be re-apportioned along tribal lines.

IDENTICAL BIBLICAL TETRADS IN 33 AD AND 2015

Every feast, lunar and solar event lined up identically. On our Gregorian calendar it looks like this:
NOTE: The first Easter or Resurrection Sunday occurred on the Jewish Feast of Firstfruits on Nisan 16, 33 AD

Jewish Calendar 33 A.D. (Nisan 3793) & 2015 (Nisan 5775): Identical Feasts, Holidays, Solar Eclipse & Blood Moon

March

Sun	Mon	Tue	Wed	Thu	Fri	Sat
1	2	3	4	5	6	7
8	9	10	11	12	13	14
15	16	17	18	19	20 First day of Spring Solar Eclipse	21
22	23	24	25	26	27	28
29	30	31				

April

Sun	Mon	Tue	Wed	Thu	Fri	Sat
		1	2	3 ✝ Passover Sacrifice Jesus' crucifixion Good Friday	4 Blood Moon Passover (Pesach) Feast of Unleavened Bread
5 First Fruits Passover (Pesach) Feast of Unleavened Bread – Easter, Resurrection Day	6 Passover (Pesach) Feast of Unleavened Bread	7 Passover (Pesach) Feast of Unleavened Bread	8 Passover (Pesach) Feast of Unleavened Bread	9 Passover (Pesach) Feast of Unleavened Bread	10 Passover (Pesach) Feast of Unleavened Bread	11
12	13	14	15	16	17	18
19	20	21	22	23	24	25
26	27	28	29	30		

© Holly Deyo, 2015

Contrast the positive side of Shemitah and Jubilee with the ominous warnings of a rare Biblical Tetrad and solar eclipse, and it could be a very prophetic time.

After 2015, with or without a Supermoon or solar eclipse, the next Biblical Tetrad won't take place for 568 years.

Jewish Calendar 33 A.D. (Nisan 3793) & 2015 (Nisan 5775): Identical Feasts, Holidays, Solar Eclipse & Blood Moon

September

Sun	Mon	Tue	Wed	Thu	Fri	Sat
		1	2	3	4	5
6	7	8	9	10	11	12
13	14 Rosh Hashana Feast of Trumpets	15	16	17	18	19
20	21	22	23 Yom Kippur Day of Atonement	24	25	26
27	28 Blood Moon Sukkot Feast of Tabernacles	29 Sukkot Feast of Tabernacles	30 Sukkot Feast of Tabernacles			

October

Sun	Mon	Tue	Wed	Thu	Fri	Sat
				1 Sukkot Feast of Tabernacles	2 Sukkot Feast of Tabernacles	3 Sukkot Feast of Tabernacles
4 Sukkot Feast of Tabernacles	5	6	7	8	9	10
11	12	13	14	15	16	17
18	19	20	21	22	23	24
25	26	27	28	29	30	31

© Holly Deyo, 2015

The Star of Bethlehem – 2015

This event is even more remarkable than the very rare Blood Moon Tetrads, but it received a lot less attention.

God issued over 5,000 promises in the Bible and none are so meaningful as those that we can actually see. Every time a rainbow appears Christians remember God's promise that He'd never again destroy the world by water.

The Blood Moon Tetrad was a last *warning*. The second appearance of the Star of Bethlehem is a monumental *promise* of His soon return. It's happened only once since Jesus' birth

over 2000 years ago in summer of 2015. Can it be coincidence that a final warning and a unique promise come within few weeks of each other?

A few nights ago, this author looked out into the pre-dawn sky. It was inky dark in this late October sky. The pending sunrise brought the palest pinks peeking over a slumbering horizon. Everything was dark and peaceful. Quiet. Two vibrant stars burst silently from indigo skies. So astonishingly bright, they blocked out fellow stars with their blinding light. They twinkled between branches of a Honey Locust tree, merging to create a dazzling, mesmerizing superstar.

As exceptional as this it was, it paled compared to when Jupiter and Venus converged three months earlier on June 30. These two planets passed less than ⅓ degree apart making them explode in brilliance.

Scientists try to debunk the importance of the Star of Bethlehem saying it didn't appear over a single night, but over months. This makes the spectacular sight even more inspiring. It was no flash in the pan. These two huge

planets, Jupiter and Venus blended together as one, would have shined as a fierce beacon especially without interference from cities' light pollution. It would have been visible for hundreds of miles – further if the earth weren't curved. They are a message of kindness and love. What else can describe God sending His son to suffer in our place, take on the punishment for believers if not ultimate mercy born out those two gifts?

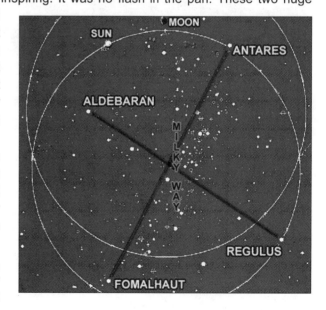

Another important sign is that this conjunction occurs in the constellation of Leo (the Lion), also known as "the Lion of Judah" – another name for Jesus. Not only do Venus and Jupiter appear to be nearly touching, forming the single Star of Bethlehem, the conjunction occurs with Regulus – the "King" star. And Jesus is the King of Kings.

In Leo, the bright star Regulus, one of four "royal stars", sits right below the lion's mane. It, along with the three other royal stars, Aldebaran, Fomalhaut and Antares, form a fixed cross in the heavens.

Few people realize just how amazing God's sky is. Yes, we admire its magnificence especially spectacular viewed away from heavily populated areas. It's even more awe-inspiring when learning that God laid out in 48 constellations the story of Jesus the Redeemer. Most everyone has heard of the 12 zodiac signs, but each constellation has another three small constellations, called side decans, that help flesh out God's revelation in the stars. In yet a third layer, smaller stars flesh out God's message. This is like Biblical skip codes that reveal much prophecy, if done properly using Hebrew.

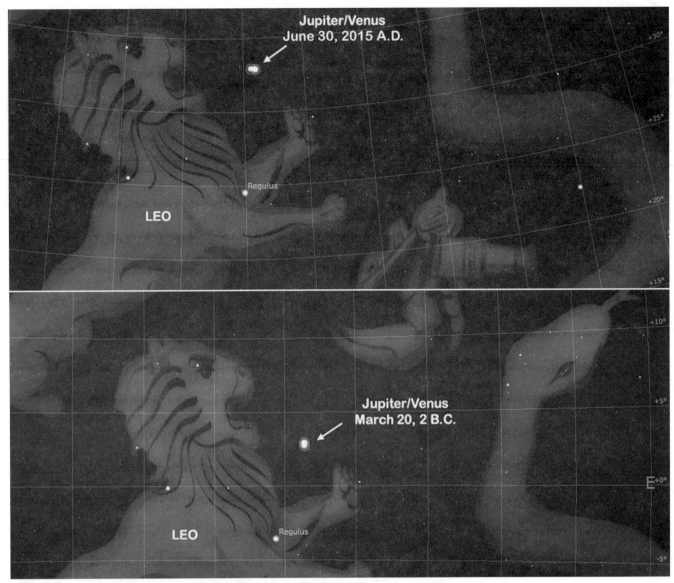

Jupiter/Venus
June 30, 2015 A.D.

LEO

Regulus

Jupiter/Venus
March 20, 2 B.C.

LEO

Regulus

The first 16 constellations, including the 12 smaller ones and the first four major signs, tell the story of his birth and life prophecy. The second four major signs reveal His dealings with His people, the Elect; and the last four tell the story of His coming triumph over Satan. And look what's right next to the Lion of Judah in the sky – the Serpent, juxtaposing ultimate good next to ultimate evil.

THE GOSPEL IN THE STARS

God's astronomy isn't to be confused with astrology as there are important distinguishing differences.

First, God's celestial map doesn't include planets. Astrology does.

Second, astrology has been characterized as "Satan's counterfeit life guide" compared to God's unchanging message presented in the stars, which tells the story of Jesus' birth, crucifixion, resurrection and triumph over Satan.

Third, astronomy is God-centered. Astrology is *self*-centered implying people can get along quite well without the Creator if you just use the tool of astrology.

Fourth, astrology divides the 12 major constellations into neat and tidy segments of 30° each. In God's celestial masterpiece the segments aren't equal. Some constellations "invade" each other's space. This is really how life is – a lot of overlap and connectivity.

Fifth, astrology's zodiac runs counter-clockwise and is presented as seen from above, where Satan arrogantly places himself. God's celestial map is seen as His children would see it from Earth because they are for signs for us, and it "runs" clockwise, the right way, in keeping with the laws of physics.

Sixth, God's astronomical zodiac was created when he made the heavens. Man's astrological zodiac came into being somewhere around 2,000 BC give or take, – some 600 years before Moses penned the Torah, the first five books of the Bible. Three constellations, the Bear, Orion and the Pleiades are mentioned in Job – the oldest book in the Bible, which dates back to 2150 BC While the first organized system of astrology is generally credited to the Babylonians around 1800 BC, "Newer" zodiacs carved in ivory were recently discovered sealed in Croatian caves for over 2,000 years.

Last, according to the *Book of Enoch*, Fallen Angels taught humans astrology and God's good, holy angels taught man astronomy.

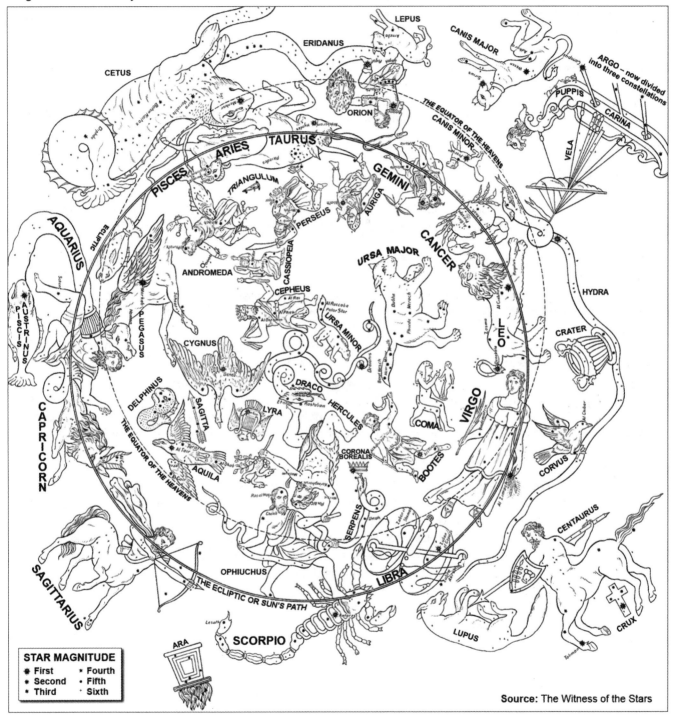

Source: The Witness of the Stars

BOOK OF ENOCH

The *Book of Enoch* (whose validity is sometimes called into question) clearly writes that Fallen Angels, the Watchers, taught mankind astrology, not astronomy.

"And Azazel taught men to make swords, and daggers, and shields, and breastplates. And he showed them the things after these, and the art of making them; bracelets, and ornaments, and the art of making up the eyes, and of beautifying the eyelids, and the most precious stones, and all kinds of colored dyes. And the world was changed. And there was great impiety, and much fornication, and they went astray, and all their ways became corrupt. Amezarak taught all those who cast spells and cut roots, Armaros the release of spells, and Baraqiel astrologers, and Kokabiel portents, and Tamiel taught astrology, and Asradel taught the path of the Moon."[152]

After mankind learned these arts, everything on Earth went sideways. Enoch continues in the next verse. "And at the destruction of men they cried out; and their voices reached Heaven. And then Michael, Gabriel, Suriel and Uriel, looked down from Heaven and saw the mass of blood that was being shed on the earth and all the iniquity that was being done on the earth."

Enoch mentions how Uriel, one of God's good and holy angels gave him information on astronomy. Enoch writes, "And I saw how the stars of Heaven come out, and counted the Gates out of which they come, and wrote down all their outlets, for each one, individually, according to their number. And their names, according to their constellations, their positions, their times, and their months, as the Angel Uriel, who was with me, showed me. And he showed me everything, and wrote it down, and also their names he wrote down for me, and their laws and their functions."[153]

GOD'S MESSAGE

Since the beginning, all 48 constellations have always been represented by the same symbol. Capricorn isn't shown as a goat in one chart and a horse in another. All 48 major and minor constellations form one continuous story when *read in the right order.*

God's celestial map begins at Virgo with Jesus' birth from the Virgin Mary, not at Aries as is done in astrology. Joseph Seiss, American theologian and Lutheran minister, wrote that the interior passages of the Great Pyramid also recount the story of the Redeemer and His People. Keep in mind that this massive stone "science vault" was built at least as early as 2,175 BC. Some date it to 2,560 BC while others put its construction much earlier. Seiss details much in 1882 book, *The Gospel in the Stars,* which you can download for free on the Internet. This stone triumph is also a prophetic calendar for huge events like the destruction of Solomon's Temple in 70 AD, the Exodus of Israel from Egypt in 1446 BC, the start of World War I in 1914 and even the Great Depression in 1929. To decode it, substitute years for inches like in 2 Peter 3:8 when days are substituted for years.

Interestingly the Egyptian zodiac places the Sphinx as a marker between the Woman and the Lion. There is no sphinx or Great Pyramid in constellations so it is a unique designation. The "sphinx", meaning "to bind together closely" in Greek has the head of a woman and the body of a lion, tying together the beginning and the end of this celestial story. In other words it joins together this prophetic story, starting at Virgo and ending at Leo, to read God's eternal message to the world.

God painted it across the skies so everyone could read his message. It's written a universal language that doesn't require translation or bookbinding. It overcomes time, location and possible misunderstandings and is always present for people to read. If you want further information read Rev. Ethelbert William Bullinger's 1893 definitive work, *The Witness of the Stars.* It's free to download on the Internet. The history of Jesus is indisputable for Christians and every other human being. Whether people can read or not, whether they are educated or not, they can look at the stars and see, KNOW, God's unchangeable message.

While the Tetrad is an awesome signal, a warning linked to many events involving Israel and other nations' treatment of her, the reappearance of the Star of Bethlehem, this re-announcement of Jesus' coming, is unique. There is nothing like it. It is a blessing beyond measure of God's mercy, a promise, that He is sending His son – soon.

Chapter 8: Signs in the Sun

"And I will show wonders in the heavens and in the earth: Blood and fire and pillars of smoke. The sun shall be turned into darkness, and the moon into blood, Before the coming of the great and awesome day of the Lord. —Joel 2:30-31 (NKJV)

And there will be signs in the sun, in the moon, and in the stars... —Luke 21:25 (NKJV)

"Immediately after the tribulation of those days the sun will be darkened, and the moon will not give its light; the stars will fall from heaven, and the powers of the heavens will be shaken. —Matthew 24:29 (NKJV)

Most people don't give the Sun a second thought unless it's cloudy and they had planned to work on their tan or too much heat had caused their tomato plants to drop blossoms or roses to shrink. We always think pleasantly of the Sun as that constant fiery disk that keeps us warm and lights our days.

And why wouldn't we? At 4.5 billion years, the Sun's only halfway through its life before running out of fuel. The Sun isn't a stagnant ball of gas. It's gradually, very slowly, getting hotter and brighter.[154] As time passes scientists see more evidence that our star is an evolving body.

People experienced these changes first-hand when sunlight felt like needles piercing their clothes and burned their skin, and caused them to squint more than usual from its blinding rays. Fifteen years ago when we still lived in Australia, the ozone hole was at its largest ever. In Sept. 2000, it stretched over 11.5 million square miles, roughly the size of Africa.[155] While the hole opens up over Antarctica, the absence of its protective shield can be felt all over the globe.

Gardeners report leaves scorched and bleached by harsh rays. On a larger scale, too much UV hurts most grain crops in addition to peas, tomatoes, peppers, cucumbers, cauliflower, beans, squash, broccoli and carrots. People and animals see more skin cancer, cataracts and weakened immune systems. So while we want the Sun to keep steady, it's far from doing so.

The Sun Goes Nuts

In 2003, even those barely interested in the Sun took notice of its wild antics. Our star went nuts and even NASA termed its behavior as "haywire".[156] Even though solar maximum had passed – the supposedly downward, quieter side of its 11-year cycles, the Sun shot off it largest ever X-ray solar flare. To understand just how off the chart exceptional this was, you have to know how solar flares are classed.

It's really simple with flares dumped into four categories, B, C, M, and X. Each of these letter ratings is further divided 1-9. An X has 10 times the strength of an M and 100 times the power of a C. It's like a Richter scale for flares. B's and C's are so run-of-the-mill, no one pays much attention to them. M's start to attract notice as they can cause short radio blackouts at the poles and minor radiation storms that could hurt astronauts and people living on the International Space Station.

X's are literally in a different class and can exceed an X9, but it's rare. It was very impressive when a string of eight X10 and X12 flares pummeled Earth in 1991. That was mighty, but not the best the Sun had to offer. In April 2001, approaching the middle of Solar Cycle 23, the Sun unleashed a CME (coronal mass ejection) on April Fool's Day. Auroras were seen as far south as Mexico and southern Europe. That was nearly unheard of as they mainly display across America's Upper Midwest or across northern Europe.

The very next day the Sun spat off an X20 flare. Fortunately it was aimed away from Earth or the damage could have been disastrous.

Every solar cycle (usually about 11 years) produces flares and sunspots though some are busier than others. On March 10, 1989, the Sun unleashed an X20 flare that targeted Earth. Auroras were seen as far south as Texas and Florida. That was the positive side. It was beautiful. Canada took the brunt and the storm caused a massive power grid failure in Quebec, which lasted 12 hours and March in Canada can be brutal. "In less than 2 minutes, the entire Quebec power grid lost power. During the 12-hour blackout that followed, (6) million people suddenly found themselves in dark office buildings and underground pedestrian tunnels, and in stalled elevators. Most people woke up to cold homes for breakfast. The blackout also closed schools and businesses, kept the Montreal Metro shut during the morning rush hour, and closed Dorval Airport.

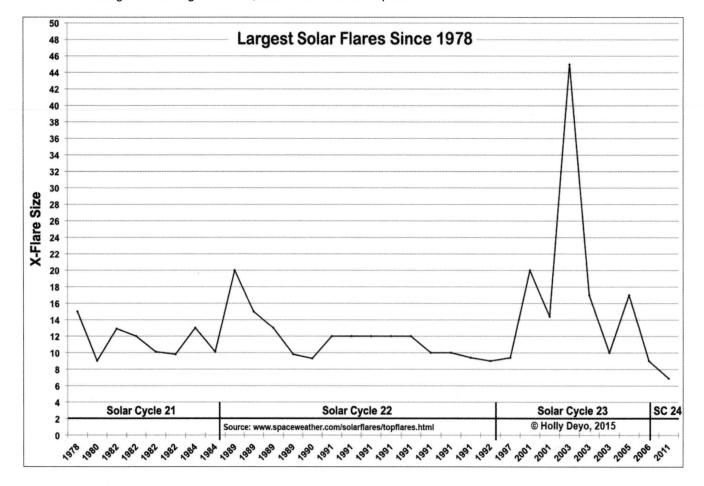

"The Quebec Blackout was by no means a local event. Some of the U.S. electrical utilities had their own cliff-hanger problems to deal with. New York Power lost 150 megawatts the moment the Quebec power grid went down. The New England Power Pool lost 1,410 megawatts at about the same time. Service to 96 electrical utilities in New England was interrupted while other reserves of electrical power were brought online. Luckily, the U.S. had the power to spare at the time…but just barely. Across the United States from coast to coast, over 200 power grid problems erupted within minutes of the start of the March 13 storm. Fortunately none of these caused a blackout."[157]

The Carrington Event

On the morning of September 1, 1859, amateur astronomer Richard Carrington ascended into the private observatory attached to his country estate outside of London. After cranking open the dome's shutter to reveal the clear blue sky, he pointed his brass telescope toward the sun and began to sketch a cluster of enormous dark spots that freckled its surface. Suddenly, Carrington spotted what he described as "two patches of intensely bright and white light" erupting from the sunspots. Five minutes later the fireballs vanished, but within hours their impact would be felt across the globe.

That night, telegraph communications around the world began to fail; there were reports of sparks showering from telegraph machines, shocking operators and setting papers ablaze. All over the planet, colorful auroras illuminated the night-time skies, glowing so brightly that birds began to chirp and laborers started their daily chores, believing the sun had begun rising. Some thought the end of the world was at hand, but Carrington's naked eyes had spotted the true cause for the bizarre happenings: a massive solar flare with the energy of 10 billion atomic bombs. The flare spewed electrified gas and subatomic particles toward Earth, and the resulting geomagnetic storm—dubbed the "Carrington Event"—was the largest on record to have struck the planet."

When telegraphs did come back on line, many were filled with vivid accounts of the celestial light show that had been witnessed the night before. Newspapers from France to Australia featured glowing descriptions of brilliant auroras that had turned night into day. One eyewitness account from a woman on Sullivan's Island in South Carolina ran in the Charleston Mercury: "The eastern sky appeared of a blood red color. It seemed brightest exactly in the east, as though the full moon, or rather the sun, were about to rise. It extended almost to the zenith. The whole island was illuminated. The sea reflected the phenomenon, and no one could look at it without thinking of the passage in the Bible which says, 'the sea was turned to blood.' The shells on the beach, reflecting light, resembled coals of fire."

The sky was so crimson that many who saw it believed that neighboring locales were on fire. Americans in the South were particularly startled by the northern lights, which migrated so close to the equator that they were seen in Cuba and Jamaica. Elsewhere, however, there appeared to be genuine confusion. In Abbeville, South Carolina, masons awoke and began to lay bricks at their job site until they realized the hour and returned to bed. In Bealeton, Virginia, larks were stirred from their sleep at 1 a.m. and began to warble. (Unfortunately for them, a conductor on the Orange & Alexandria Railroad was also awake and shot three of them dead.) In cities across America, people stood in the streets and gazed up at the heavenly pyrotechnics. In Boston, some even caught up on their reading, taking advantage of the celestial fire to peruse the local newspapers.

Ice core samples have determined that the Carrington Event was twice as big as any other solar storm in the last 500 years. What would be the impact of a similar storm today? According to a 2008 report from the National Academy of Sciences, it could cause "extensive social and economic disruptions" due to its impact on power grids, satellite communications and GPS systems. The potential price tag? Between $1 trillion and $2 trillion.[158]

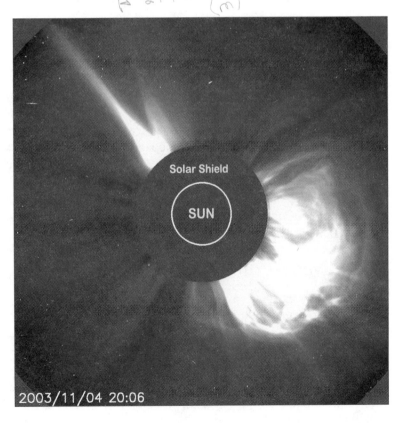

While researchers and writers generally label Carrington as the biggest ever flare, its size has never been pinpointed. Since instruments weren't in place then to give accurate measurements it's hard to get a good accounting. Most scientists don't even hazard a guess.

The Cliver-Svalgaard paper states this event was "exceptionally large", but people want to know just how big and how exceptional. To that end the pair looked at five markers: how severely it disturbed the ionosphere, how fast solar particles traveled to Earth, how strong was the solar wind, how much it interfered with radio communications and how far south auroras reached.

They found that the Carrington flare was a big event, but not the biggest. They discovered that for those five markers it had had close rivals and a few "superiors", but it's the only event in the last ~150 years that's at or near the top for all five. They conclude, "September 1859 was not markedly larger (if it was larger at all) than that of the top tier of subsequent great storms, contrary to the findings of Tsurutani et al. (2003)."[159]

Now why is this important? A century and a half later, the BIGGEST solar event ever shook astronomers' perception of "normal".

The Mother of All Flares

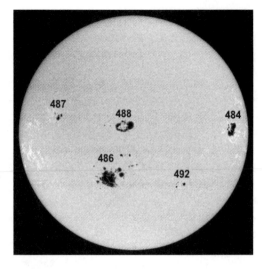

"In November 2003, an 'X' solar flare, the strongest of solar storms, temporarily disabled many satellites, killed one satellite completely and burned out an instrument on a Mars orbiter. The crew of the International Space Station took shelter, reporting elevated radiation readings and 'shooting stars' in their own eyes. In September 2005, a string of 'X' solar flares caused lesser disruptions to major power grids and knocked out the GPS system completely for ten minutes."[160]

For many of us who watch solar activities, it was a time of shock and disbelief seeing something this massive.

El Sol was quiet. The Sun's face had been nearly spotless and Cycle 23's solar maximum had passed two years earlier. Suddenly in late October, three giant sunspots appeared, each one larger than the planet Jupiter. Sunspot 486 was the biggest in 13 years. The Sun was having a really bad face day. Big sunspots usually unleash the largest flares and this was no exception. Over two weeks this triple threat shot off 11 X-class flares, which it took the entire previous year to match.

"Normal" X-flares usually register as an X1 or an X2, but this flare pegged a never-before-seen X28. It took a while for scientists to absorb this rare event. Then it morphed into something freakish. Employing an innovative technique, physicists in New Zealand used the upper atmosphere as a giant X-ray detector. Their findings, published by the *American Geophysical Union* on May 17, 2004, revealed the **true size** of this flare – a colossal, incomprehensible X45! It's unparalleled energy equaled 50 billion atomic bombs. Normally CMEs take two to three days to reach Earth, but this record-breaker shot across the expanse in less than 18 hours.

Researcher Neil Thomson from the University of Otago commented. "'This makes it more than twice as large as any previously recorded flare, and if the accompanying particle and magnetic storm had been aimed at the Earth, the damage to some satellites and electrical networks could have been considerable.' Their calculations show that the flare's x-ray radiation bombarding the atmosphere was equivalent to that of 5,000 Suns, though none of it reached the Earth's surface, the researchers say."[161]

IMPACT!

After the X45 blast, "many satellites in earth orbit began behaving erratically. Airlines redirected polar flights to below the Arctic Circle, resulting in major delays across the US.

"In other parts of the world, the situation wasn't much better. Power grids in Sweden were overloaded resulting in prolonged blackouts. Power consumption at two nuclear stations in New Jersey had to be reduced to prevent similar disruption. In Japan another spacecraft was lost. On the International Space Station astronauts had to take shelter in shielded parts of the station. The effects were felt even farther out in the solar system. The radiation monitors on-board the Mars Odyssey were burnt out, overloaded by the very emission they were build to study. Spectacular auroras were witnessed on Jupiter. The Cassini spacecraft, on its way to Saturn, detected interruptions in radio communications. 6 months later, the CME shockwave was still going, as it brushed past the Voyager 2 spacecraft, then 7 billion miles from Earth."[162]

2012: Near-Catastrophe on Earth

The only thing that saved our bacon on July 23, 2012 was that the CME blast didn't aim at Earth. Had the massive cloud erupted just one week earlier, it was have hit Earth square-on. University of Colorado physicist Daniel Baker warned, "We would still be picking up the pieces" as it was THE most powerful storm in 150 years. Baker continues. "In my view the July 2012 storm was in all respects at least as strong as the 1859 Carrington event. The only difference is, it missed."[163]

Not only was this CME extremely powerful, it exploded off the Sun at rare speed. Normally, CMEs travel about 2,000mph, but this one rocketed away nearly four times that fast. Part of the reason for such extraordinary velocity is that another CME had travelled that same route just four days before. Then BANG! BANG! On July 23, two more CMEs shot off the Sun 10 minutes apart. In essence, the CME that erupted on the 19th ploughed a celestial path, like a bulldozer shoveling a clearing, which made extremely rapid travel possible for the next two. Should that July

2012 CME have had Earth in the cross hairs, you'd be cooking breakfast on a BBQ, not the stove – providing you'd stored enough propane. We missed catastrophe by one week.

WHEN HELL COMES TO EARTH

NASA stated. "Analysts believe that a direct hit … could cause widespread power blackouts, disabling everything that plugs into a wall socket. Most people wouldn't even be able to flush their toilet because urban water supplies largely rely on electric pumps."[164]

Steve Tracton of the *Washington Post's* Capital Weather Gang put it this way. "Electric power grids, communications and navigation systems (including GPS), and satellites (including weather) could be damaged beyond repair for many years. The consequences could be devastating for commerce, transportation, agriculture and food stocks, fuel and water supplies, human health and medical facilities, national security, and daily life in general."[165]

"According to a study by the National Academy of Sciences, the total economic impact could exceed $2 trillion or 20 times greater than the costs of a Hurricane Katrina. Multi-ton transformers damaged by such a storm might take years to repair.[166]

This is a solar EMP – an Electromagnetic Pulse kiss of death. Its effect is similar to a nuclear bomb detonated at high altitude. Today it would cause much more damage than the Carrington Event because people rely on technology for nearly everything. Baker states. "In my view the July 2012 storm was in all respects at least as strong as the 1859 Carrington event. The only difference is, it missed."[167]

"In February 2014, physicist Pete Riley of Predictive Science Inc. published a paper in Space Weather entitled 'On the Probability of Occurrence of Extreme Space Weather Events.' In it, he analyzed records of solar storms going back 50+ years. By extrapolating the frequency of ordinary storms to the extreme, he calculated the odds that a Carrington-class storm would hit Earth in the next ten years.

"The answer: 12%.

"'Initially, I was quite surprised that the odds were so high, but the statistics appear to be correct,' says Riley. 'It is a sobering figure.'"[168]

All of these events show the Sun isn't behaving as it should and possibly setting up for unexpected and unpleasant activities. There's more.

Strange Doings on the Sun

We like the Sun and other major things people count on to be constant. Stable. Reliable. It gives a feeling of control, and we breathe sighs of relief when they act the way they're supposed to. However, the Sun isn't behaving. Something is amiss.

Again, the chart of Solar Cycles 22, 23 and 24, shows where the highest sunspot activity occurred for each of the approximately 11-year cycles. Within a cycle, it's not uncommon for two peaks to occur. The first peak *always* has the largest number of sunspots, which can be followed by a second peak with a lower count. Solar Cycle 24 is the only cycle ever to have more sunspots in its second peak than the first.[169]

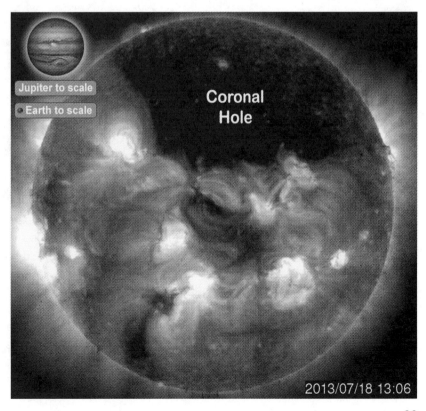

Image: Massive coronal hole on July 18, 2013. (Credit: European Space Agency/SOHO)

A second oddity is 24's extreme weakness. David Hathaway, head of the solar physics at NASA's Marshall Space Flight Center in Huntsville, Alabama states, "'I would say it is the weakest in 200 years.' Scientists say that solar activity is stranger than in a century or more, with the sun producing barely half the number of sunspots as expected and its magnetic poles oddly out of sync."[170] Scientists wonder whether Earth is gearing up for a mini ice age.

In conjunction with this, increased solar activity usually goes hand in hand with more sunspots. The graph for Solar Cycle 24, shows it considerably less busy than in either 22 or 23, yet it shot off a CME that could have altered life as we know for years to come.

A fourth very strange anomaly is how the Sun went through this cycle's magnetic pole reversal – the oddest on record. While scientists stress how weird this was, they say they weren't concerned. During a normal reversal, the magnetic field weakens at both poles to the point of zero and then they re-emerge with the opposite polarity for north and south. They usually do this flip at the same time.

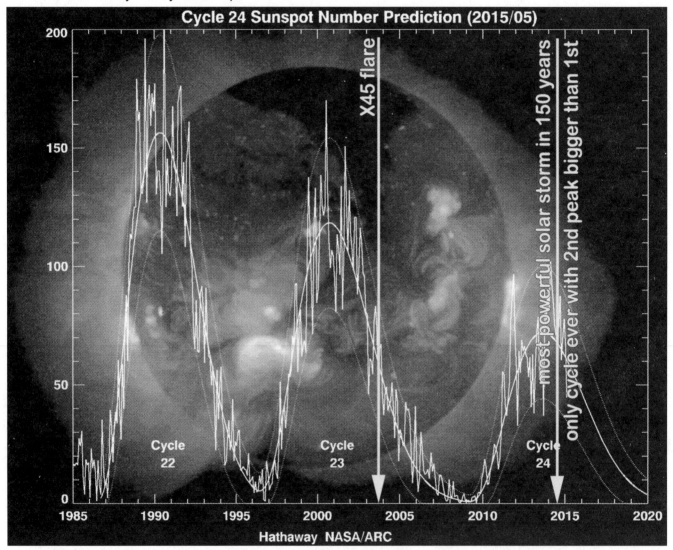

However, in Solar Cycle 24, they reversed about 16 months apart. The North Pole reversed first, so it had the same polarity as the south for a while. Then the South Pole changed and they were once again on track.[171]

A fifth bit of strangeness just has to seen to fully comprehend. It has to do with coronal holes. Coronal "hole" is a bit misleading as there really isn't a hole in the Sun. The dark area contains less solar material and it's cooler than the rest of the Sun. This opening in the magnetic field is where solar winds are most likely to blow out particles three times faster than elsewhere on the Sun.

Skylab first spotted coronal holes in the early 70s and scientists are still learning about them. This much they do know, which pinpoints another oddity in this solar cycle. During solar maximum, the number and size of coronal holes <u>decreases</u> because the magnetic fields on the Sun are about to reverse. Solar Sunspot Cycle 24 produced an unusual double maximum. The first hit at the end of 2012 and the second came in early 2015. Yet this massive hole, formed close to solar maximum and covers about 25% of the Sun's surface that faces Earth. That is massive! Just the visible part is enormous and there's no telling how far it extends on the Sun's back side.

Last Thoughts on Solar Signs

The Sun is evidently changing more than many people thought. Flare instruments were only calibrated to measure up to X17 though two X20s hit in 1989 and 2001. No one thought flares could ever exceed these two monsters or equipment would have been adjusted accordingly. A dozen years ago, the Sun shot off a gargantuan, largest-ever X45 flare that shocked even the most jaded scientists. It occurred when solar activity should have been winding down and was the most potentially lethal flare on record. Its CME had the energy of 50 *billion* atomic bombs and took only one-fourth the time usually required to reach Earth. 2003 saw the fastest, biggest, strongest solar flare ever.

Then in 2014 during one of the Sun's weakest-in-200-years cycles, it shot off the most powerful solar storm in 150 years. In conjunction with low sunspot numbers for Solar Cycle 24, the Sun was still turbulent, when it should have been quieter. Weak Solar Cycle 24 is the only one in history to have twin peaks with the second peak producing more sunspots than the first.

Then 24's magnetic pole swap didn't occur simultaneously as it should have. Instead they reversed in a first-ever event 16 months apart.

Last, El Sol exhibited a monster-size coronal hole close to solar maximum in 2013 when it should have shown much smaller ones. It's unsettling that the Sun is becoming somewhat erratic and unpredictable. One has to wonder what is next on its agenda and if it's gearing up for End Times.

Chapter 9: Signs of Pestilence

...And there will be famines, pestilences, and earthquakes in various places. —Matthew 24:7 (NKJV)

There will be great earthquakes, famines and pestilences in various places, and fearful events and great signs from heaven. —Luke 21:11 (NIV)

Prophecy warns that in End Times pestilence will play a large part and it isn't a matter of events ramping up like for earthquakes, volcanism, chaotic weather and solar activities. Enough diseases are already here to kill every living thing in existence many times over – except maybe cockroaches that have survived for over 300 million years.[172] Several things are a worry: weaponization of bio-toxins and dispersal of same, global proliferation of BSL (**Bio**safety **L**evel) 3 and 4 facilities, the rise of superbugs and, situations where hospitals and pharmaceutical companies are compromised and can no longer provide medicine or treatment.

Bioweapons

March 26, 1975 marked the date when the Biological Weapons Convention (BWC) Treaty went into effect. As of February 2015, 172 countries had signed, but that doesn't mean they've all abided by it and some have yet to ratify it. At least 9, and maybe as many as 17[173] nations are believed to have offensive biological weapons programs. These weapons are still available and some have been used in recent history – *after* the treaty was signed. Granted, individuals and groups, not countries, disbursed them but in order to have vaccines and defense against future bioattacks, storehouses of these bacteria and viruses are kept by many nations. (See section in this chapter on Biosafety Labs.)

Bacteria make ideal candidates because they generally require small amounts to be effective – often only a pound can kill or incapacitate hundreds of thousands of people if released in a metropolitan area. These weapons are invisible, odorless, tasteless, and spread silently. That's part of the terror aspect – that something unseen, undetectable, can cause such mayhem.

Over 1,200 agents could be used to make WMDs – Weapons of Mass Destruction, but relatively few are easy to acquire and weaponize. Top agents, those most desired by those wishing to instill panic and cause harm are in **Category A**. The U.S. health system and government officials give these diseases highest priority. B and C can also be used for bio-terrorism and are far from friendly.

Category A

Highest priority agents pose a risk to national security because they
1. Can be easily disseminated or transmitted person-to-person
2. Cause high mortality with potential for major public health impact including that on health care facilities
3. May cause public panic and social disruption
4. Require special action for public health preparedness

Category B

Second highest priority agents include those that
1. Are moderately easy to disseminate
2. Cause moderate rate of illness and low mortality
3. Require specific enhancement of CDC's diagnostic capacity and enhanced disease surveillance

Category C

Third highest priority agents include emerging pathogens that could be engineered for mass dissemination in the future because of
1. Availability
2. Ease of production and dissemination
3. Potential for high morbidity and mortality rates and major health impact

Potential of Bioterrorism Agents[174]		
Category A	**Category B**	**Category C**
Smallpox	**Bacteria**	Nipah Virus
Anthrax	Q Fever	Hantavirus
Plague	Brucellosis	**Tick Borne Hemorrhagic Fever**
Botulism	Glanders	Far Eastern
Tularemia	Melioidosis	Central European
Viral Hemorrhagic Fevers	Typhus Fever	Kyasanur Forest
Ebola	Psittacosis	Louping III
Marburg	**Viruses**	Powassan
Lassa	Alpha Viruses	Negishi
Argentine	Venezuelan Encephalomyelitis	**Tick Borne Encephalitis Virus**
Machupo	Western Equine Encephalomyelitis	Crimean-Congo
And related viruses	Eastern Equine Encephalomyelitis	Omsk
	Toxins	Kyasanur Forest Disease
	Ricin	Yellow Fever
	Clostridium Perfringens	Multidrug Resistant TB
	Staphylococccus Aureus	
	T2 – Mycotoxins	
	Food or Water Borne Pathogens	
	Salmonella	
	Shigella	
	E. coli	
	Cholera	
	Crypto	
	Typhus Fever	
	Chlamydia	

Lethality

Estimated Casualties in a Biological Attack[175]			
DISEASE	**DOWNWIND IMPACT**	**NUMBER KILLED**	**NUMBER INCAPACITATED**
Rift Valley Fever	.6 miles	400	35,000
Tick Borne Encephalitis	.6 miles	9,500	35,000
Typhus	3 miles	19,500	85,000
Brucellosis	6 miles	500	125,000
Q-Fever	>12½ miles	150	125,000
Tularemia	>12½ miles	30,000	125,000
Anthrax	>12½ miles	95,000	125,000
Based on 110 lbs of an airborne agent dispersed by aircraft 1¼ miles upwind of a 500,000-population center.			

Some biologicals, especially in Categories A and B are extremely deadly. Dr. Stefan Riedel for Baylor University's Medical Center produced an analysis of how many people would perish downwind of this type attack.

ANTHRAX

Anthrax occurs naturally in the ground, is found on every continent and can live for years in the carcasses of dead farm animals or in the soil. While it's not contagious person-to-person, it's a desirable biological weapon because it can be deadly if eaten, inhaled or transmitted by open cuts or insects. All terrorists would need to do is locate a diseased carcass and dry the disease into a powder.

SMALLPOX

Though the World Health Organization declared smallpox eradicated in May 1980, what if it were resurrected? Only two sites – the CDC in Atlanta and the Vector Institute in Koltsovo, Siberia – guard the last known reservoirs of this ultimate killer. A disease earns that title when it's taken an estimated 300 million lives in the 20th century alone, but it wasn't quite done.

On September 11, 1978 Janet Parker, a photographer working at England's University of Birmingham Medical School was the last person to die from smallpox. Professor Henry Bedson who headed the lab believed he was on the verge of a smallpox breakthrough and the World Health Organization agreed and sent him samples of the virus. Because his lab didn't meet safety requirements, and no one would put up the money for improvements WHO's shipments stopped, but the research didn't. Lab people worked on an extremely lethal airborne virus without air locks, without separate showers or changing facilities, and without contamination-prevention clothing. Because Bedson knew his time short, they also handled the virus in the main lab, away from safety cabinets. Though the researchers kept their vaccinations current, Janet hadn't had a shot for 12 years and immunization only lasts three to five.

At first Janet thought she had the sniffles with a headache and some body pain. Doctors thought it was just a drug rash. Then telltale pustules appeared over her entire body and especially on her face. Janet was diagnosed with dreaded smallpox. Since she'd had contact with her parents and close friends, they were quarantined. Hospital workers and the ambulance driver had also been exposed. Altogether 260 people ended up in quarantine.

Prof. Bedson was the first person to die. While his wife was distracted, he went into his garden and slit his throat. Bedson, just 48, left a suicide note in his own handwriting saying, "I am sorry to have misplaced the trust which so many of my friends and colleagues have placed in me and my work and, above all, to have dragged into disrepute my wife and beloved children. I realize that this act is the least sensible thing I have done, but it may in the end allow them to get some peace."[176]

Janet Parker's father died a few days later of a heart attack from the ensuing stress and worry. Janet's mother had contracted it, but was treated and survived. The general consensus is that Janet was inadvertently exposed through the air duct from the lab into her office, which was directly above the lab. She died at 40, one month to the day after feeling "unwell".

"In 1992, Ken Alibek – formerly Colonel Kanatzhan Alibekov – defected from Russia to the US. Alibek served as the first deputy director of Biopreparat, the Soviet Union's biological warfare agency, founded in 1973. After arriving in the US, Alibek began making allegations against his former nation, claiming that the Soviet Union had produced 50 tons of smallpox. Biopreparat, he claimed, had employed a scientific army of 30,000 people who worked on smallpox and other pathogenic weapons, such as Ebola, anthrax and plague."[177] So who knows? Russia is very secretive and they own a lot of real estate – nearly twice that of America.

In 2004, French and Russian scientists found several graves in the Russian republic of Sakha where the corpses were infected with smallpox. British Professor Jonathan Ball writes, "both oil exploration and changes in the climate are capable of releasing not only smallpox, but potentially even viruses we have never seen before."[178]

French and Russian scientists then reanimated a giant 30,000 year-old-virus, Pithovirus, in 2014. A spokeswoman for France's National Centre for Scientific Research said Pithovirus burst back to life when offered the "bait" of living amoeba. She worried, "this study demonstrates that viruses can survive in permafrost – the permanently frozen layer of soil found in the Arctic regions – almost over geological time periods, that is for more than 30,000 years. These findings have important implications in terms of public-health risks related to the exploitation of mining and energy resources in circumpolar regions, which may arise as a result of global warming. The re-emergence of viruses considered eradicated, such as smallpox, whose replication process is similar to Pithovirus, is no longer the domain of science fiction. The probability of this type of scenario needs to be estimated realistically."[179]

So if smallpox makes a comeback, are you safe? Many Boomers were inoculated as kids, but vaccine protection is long gone, lasting about a decade.

RICIN

What's frightening about ricin is it's readily available, easy to produce and extremely lethal. This naturally occurring substance comes from the seeds of castor beans. In pressing, the oil is separated from ricin, which is then disposed. Since castor oil is used worldwide, it's easy to acquire the bean. Ricin, as a poison, can be in the form of powder, mist, pellet, or dissolved in water or weak acid. Whether inhaled, eaten, or injected, it can be lethal in as little as 36 hours.

In a 1978 incident that was nearly James Bond-ish, Bulgarian dissident and author Georgi Markow was assassinated in London while he waited for a bus. Ricin was injected into his thigh with a poisoned dart fired from the tip of an umbrella.[180] Within four days, Markow was dead. An autopsy, conducted with the help of scientists from the UK's germ warfare center at Porton Down, revealed he'd been killed by just 0.2 milligram of ricin. The assassination was detected only because the pellet didn't fully dissolve.

BOTULISM

Botulinum toxin has always been a highly prized bioweapon because of its extreme toxicity – 50 to 100 times stronger orally than sodium cyanide.[181] Even minute amounts can fatally paralyze people if swallowed or breathed. In fact, it's *the* most poisonous substance known. A single gram in crystalline form, dispersed evenly and inhaled, could kill more than 1 million people.[182]

Studies conducted by the U.S. military indicate that Botulinum toxin released through the air from just a single source could incapacitate or kill 10% of the people downwind for ⅓ mile.[183] Releasing it in an enclosed area like a subway, train, concert hall, shopping mall or sports arena would have deadly consequences, especially if multiple disbursements were made simultaneously from different areas.

New Discovery, No Cure

Until recently, *Clostridium botulinum*, the bacterium that causes botulism, had seven strains with their toxins labeled A through G. Scientists discovered an 8th in 2013 – the first in 40 years. They're keeping the particulars very close to the chest because A-G have treatments, IF identified early enough. However, for strain H, there is no antidote and it's feared what would happen if rogue governments or terrorists get their hands on it.[184]

Who's Got It or Had It

Botulinum toxin took center stage when investigators found a vial in Iraq after Saddam Hussein was ousted. Several nations, including the former Soviet Union and Iraq, developed and stockpiled weaponized botulinum toxin despite signing the bioweapons treaty. In 1991, Iraq claimed it had produced more than 5,000 gallons of the toxin – enough to kill everyone on Earth three times over. About 10,000 liters or a little more than half of their stocks were loaded into military weapons.[185] Iran, North Korea and Syria are also known or suspected to have bioweapons programs.[186]

Yet another analyst found this: "No nation publically acknowledges either an offensive biological weapons (BW) program or stockpile. Examination of unclassified sources indicates that several nations are considered, with varying degrees of certainty, to have some BW capability. These are: China, Cuba, Egypt, Iran, Israel, North Korea, Russia, Syria, and Taiwan. Iraq had a biological weapons program prior to the 1991 Persian Gulf War, but ended the program in the 1990s. Libya had in the past been named as a country with a biological weapons program. But after Tripoli announced in 2003 that it would eliminate its WMD programs, no evidence of a biological weapons program was discovered. There is evidence that Al-Qa'ida had a BW program prior to the 2001 U.S.-led invasion of Afghanistan."[187]

When Japan's Aum Shinrikyo cult unleashed an airborne form of this toxin in the early 1990s, all three attacks failed. It's not clear why the attempts fizzled. Possibly they used an ineffective strain or maybe their aerosol equipment didn't work. Afterwards the cult turned to the nerve agent Sarin and met with "better" results.[188]

Food Poisoning

Another ugly scenario involves contaminating food supplies. Botulinum could be sprayed on fruits and vegetables or slipped into any stage of food processing. While this toxin has primarily been seen as poisoning due to poor food canning, its extreme lethality and ease of acquisition will likely make botulinum toxin a prime WMD choice.

BIOLOGICAL WEAPON USE IN RECENT TIMES

In 1991, four people were arrested in Minnesota for planning to kill a U.S. marshal by mixing ricin with DMSO, a commercial solvent, which they planned to coat on the door handles of his vehicle.[189]

"In April 1993 Thomas Lavy, 54, was stopped by Canadian customs officials with four guns, 20,000 rounds of ammunition, $89,000 in cash, a supply of neo-Nazi literature and a plastic bag containing a white powder Lavy identified as ricin. The bag was confiscated and Lavy went home to Arkansas. Months later, Canadian authorities got the powder analyzed and confirmed that it was ricin. According to the FBI, the amount in Lavy's bag could have killed 32,000 people."[190]

In 1994, a Japanese sect of the Aum Shinrikyo cult attempted an aerosolized release of anthrax from the tops of buildings in Tokyo.[191]

In 1995, two members of a Minnesota militia group were convicted of possession of ricin, which they had produced themselves for use in retaliation against local government officials.[192]

In 1996, Ohio man, Larry Wayne Harris, attempted to obtain bubonic plague cultures through the mail.[193] His lawyer claimed Harris was researching material for a book on germ warfare.

In 2001, biologist and perpetrator Bruce E. Ivins mailed anthrax spores to U.S. media and government offices in New York and Washington. Two letters were postmarked September 18, one addressed to Tom Brokaw at NBC-TV and another to the editor of the *New York Post*. Two other letters were stamped October 9 and addressed to Senators Thomas Daschle and Patrick Leahy. After a number of unsuspecting people handled them, 5 people died and another 17 were sickened. Belatedly it was discovered that scores of buildings were contaminated with spores that had leaked from those letters. At least 30,000 people who were deemed at risk required prophylactic antibiotics.[194]

In December 2002, six terror suspects were arrested in Manchester, England when it was discovered that the group, led by a 27-year-old chemist, was using an apartment as a ricin laboratory.[195]

Later, on Jan. 5, 2003, British police raided an apartment near London and foiled Chechen separatists plotting to attack the Russian embassy. The raid netted 22 castor seeds and recipes for making ricin.[196]

On Feb. 3, 2004, three U.S. Senate office buildings were closed after the toxin ricin was found in a White House mailroom that serves Senate Majority Leader Bill Frist's office.[197]

On November 1, 2011, four men were arrested in Georgia for plotting to disperse ricin in Atlanta among other places in the U.S.[198]

Again in 2013, Mississippi man, Paul Kevin Curtis, sent ricin-laced letters to President Obama. It should be noted that it's very deadly because a little amount can be lethal, there's no cure and death can come within 36 to 72 hours.[199]

More Disease Would Just Be Overkill

Many of the possible illnesses are already here and can be divided into three groups: Emerging, Re-Emerging and Deliberately Re-Emerging. In medical terms "emerging" is one that has appeared in a population for the first time or may have existed previously but is rapidly increasing in rate of incidence or geographic range. Normally, "emerging" means that something's new, but in this instance, it can cover several decades.

Re-Emerging diseases are those that have been around for as long as centuries, but have come back in a different form or shown up in another location. Not only do they mutate, but about 75% are "zoonotic" indicating they can jump species like Bird Flu and Lyme Disease.[200] Though there are about 200 such illnesses, the World Health Organization and its partners focus mostly on just a dozen. Fortunately the CDC's scope is broader because diseases from bugs and animals cause three out of five illnesses in humans.[201] These are particularly worrisome because of their ability to survive and morph.

A third category is "Deliberately Re-Emerging", which means they are bio-terror agents that have been intentionally released. These agents can be aerosolized, put in food or water supplies, portable sprayers or any other dispersal methods terrorists or rogue governments dream up. Many of these agents are highly contagious by aerosol, are environmentally stable, can remain infectious for a long time and have no cure. This is a sampling of existing health concerns.

Deadly Emerging and Re-Emerging Diseases

DISEASE	TYPE	TRANSMISSION	EMERGING / RE-EMERGING
AIDS / HIV	Virus	C, O	Emerging
Anthrax	Bacteria	C, B, I	Deliberately Re-Emerging
Antimicrobial resistance	Many	O	Emerging
Bird Flu (H5N1)	Virus	C	Emerging
Botulism	Bacteria	I, B, O	Emerging
Bluetongue	Virus	V	Emerging
Campylobacteriosis	Bacteria	I, C	Emerging
Chagas Disease	Protozoan	V, I, O	Emerging
Chikungunya	Virus	V	Emerging
Cholera	Bacteria	I	Emerging
vCJD Creutzfeldt-jacob Disease	Protein	B, O	Emerging
CRE	Bacteria	C	Emerging
Crypto Cryptosporidiosis	Protozoan	I	Emerging
Dengue	Virus	V	Re-Emerging
Diphtheria	Bacteria	C, B	Re-Emerging
E. Coli	Bacteria	I, C	Emerging
Ebola	Virus	C	Emerging
Enterovirus 71	Virus	C, B	Emerging
Flesh-Eating Disease	Bacteria	C	Emerging
Flu	Virus	C, B, I	Re-Emerging
Hantavirus	Virus	C, B	Emerging
Hendra Virus	Virus	C	Emerging
Hepatitis C	Virus	O	Emerging
Lassa Fever	Virus	C, B, I	Emerging
Legionnaires' Disease	Bacteria	B	Emerging
Leishmaniasis	Protozoan	V	Emerging
Lyme Disease	Bacteria	V	Emerging
Malaria	Protozoan	V	Re-Emerging
Marburg Hemorrhagic Fever	Virus	C	Emerging
Measles	Virus	C, B	Re-Emerging
Monkeypox	Virus	C, B	Re-Emerging
MRSA	Bacteria	C	Emerging
Nipah Virus Encephalitis	Virus	C	Emerging
Onyong-nyong	Virus	V	Re-Emerging
Oropouche	Virus	V	Re-Emerging
"Phantom Menace"	Bacteria	C	Emerging
Plague	Bacteria	V	Re-Emerging
Rift Valley Fever	Virus	V	Re-Emerging
SARS	Virus	B, I	Emerging
Salmonella	Bacteria	I	Emerging
Shlellosis	Bacteria	I, C	Emerging
Sindbis	Virus	V	Re-Emerging
Smallpox	Virus	B, I, C	Re-Emerging
Staph	Bacteria	B	Re-Emerging
Strep	Bacteria	C, B, I	Re-Emerging

Deadly Emerging and Re-Emerging Diseases			
DISEASE	TYPE	TRANSMISSION	EMERGING / RE-EMERGING
TB	Bacteria	B, I	Re-Emerging
Tularemia	Bacteria	V, B, I, C	Re-Emerging
Typhoid	Bacteria	C, I	Re-Emerging
Whitewater Arroyo Virus	Virus	C, B	Emerging
West Nile Virus	Virus	V	Re-Emerging
Whooping Cough	Bacteria	B	Re-Emerging
Yellow Fever	Virus	V	Re-Emerging
Zika	Virus	C, V, O	Emerging
C= contact, B= Breathing, I = Ingestion, V = Vector Borne, O = Other			

Superbugs

At the rate we're over using antibiotics, bioterror agents won't be needed. Because people insist on antibiotics for things they can't cure, like viruses, and doctors cave and prescribe them anyway, it's eating away at their effectiveness. Another factor is giving antibiotics to cattle, chicken, turkeys, etc. to make them grow faster. Theses drugs also leach into rivers, lakes and streams, further lessening their effectiveness. The rise of "superbugs" has become so serious that the CDC ranked the most drug-resistant diseases by how many people they sicken, the

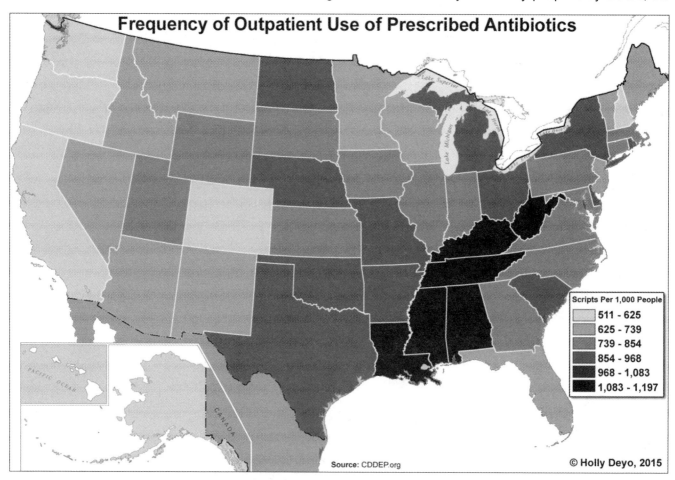

number of folks hospitalized and how many die from them. The threat level for 18 diseases is designated as Urgent, Serious or Concerning. Making matters worse, in addition to antibiotic resistance, some illnesses get the upper hand through spontaneous genetic mutation or by swapping genes with others bugs.

"Antibiotic resistance is a worldwide problem. Many forms of resistance spread with remarkable speed. World health leaders have described antibiotic-resistant microorganisms as 'nightmare bacteria' that 'pose a catastrophic threat' to people in every country in the world."[202] The CDC deems three diseases "Urgent".

URGENT, URGENT

Clostridium Difficile – Causes life-threatening diarrhea. These infections mostly occur in people who have had both recent hospitalization and antibiotics. C. Diff is responsible for killing up to 14,000 people each year and causing a quarter million to be hospitalized. Deaths from C. Diff increased 400% between 2000 and 2007, partly due to the emergence of stronger bacteria.

Drug Resistant Gonorrhea – Gonorrhea is the second most commonly reported notifiable infection in America and is easily transmitted. If it becomes resistant to cephalosporin that would greatly limit treatment options and could cripple efforts to control this STD. Australia, France, Japan, Norway, Sweden and Britain are already reporting cases that don't respond to this drug.[203] In 2011, over 300,000 cases were reported to CDC, but they estimate the true number is over 800,000 that occur annually in America.

CRE (Carbapenem-Resistant Enterobacteriaceae) – These bacteria are related to others commonly found throughout the world that live in the stomach, mucous areas and on some places of the skin. This is true for both humans and animals. What's deadly and different about CRE is that it secretes an enzyme making it immune to nearly all antibiotics. CRE ends up killing half of its victims because there's nothing to treat infections.[204]

America is one the highest users of antibiotics in the developed world. While usage hit its peak in the 1990s, treatment is shifting toward broad-spectrum antibiotics. Within the country, distinct patterns emerge. Antibiotics are most often prescribed in the Southeast and least often in the West. It follows then that antibiotic resistance might be strongest in Louisiana, Mississippi, Alabama, Tennessee, Kentucky and West Virginia.

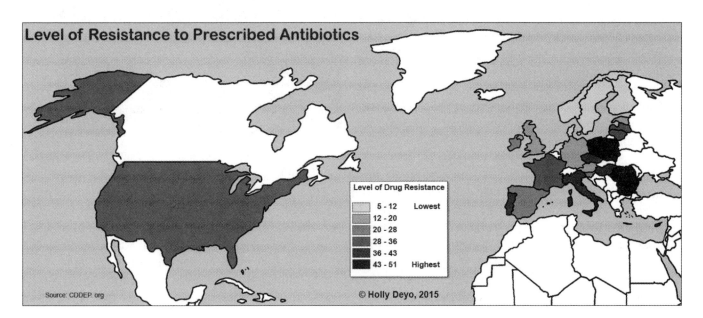

As a whole Europe prescribes antibiotics less frequently than the U.S. and Western Europe's resistance level is on par with America's. Scandinavian nations rank best with Eastern and Southern Europe at the bottom. However, all countries contribute to this disaster-in-the-making where diseases get stronger and the ability to ward them off dwindles. Data was incomplete for Canada, Israel and Turkey so CDDEP didn't include them, nor did they survey Oceana.

Bio-Safety Labs

The potential for accidents at these facilities has moved from science fiction to reality. It's not a stretch to Stephen King's *The Stand* leap into action. The plot is this:

At a government laboratory in rural California, a weaponized version of influenza (called Project Blue) is accidentally released, immediately wiping out everyone on staff except for military policeman

Charles Campion and his family, who flee the base. However, Campion is already infected by the superflu, nicknamed "Captain Trips", and spreads it to the outside world.

Days later, Campion crashes his car at a gas station in East Texas where Stu Redman (Gary Sinise) and some friends have gathered. When they investigate, they find Campion dying of the flu next to his wife and baby daughter, who are already dead. Campion tells Stu with his dying breath that he was followed from the base by a mysterious figure, and says, "You can't outrun the Dark Man".

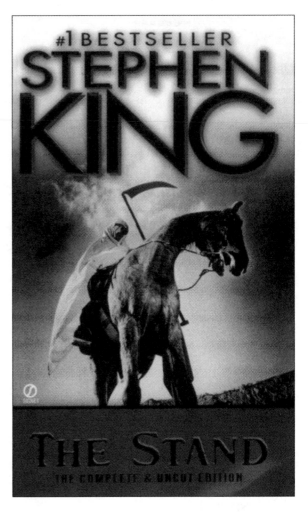

The next day, the U.S. military arrive to quarantine the town. While the other townspeople quickly become ill and die, Stu remains healthy and is confined at a CDC facility in Vermont order to study a possible cure. This proves futile and the superflu rages unchecked, causing civilization to collapse and killing over 99% of the population of the entire world in less than two months.[205]

The plot becomes richly involved taking on the ultimate battle between good and evil, God and Satan. The mini-series evolved from King's original 1978 novel showing what foresight he had when most people didn't know bio-warfare agents even existed. While King says he believes in God, he's a little fuzzy on details especially regarding the afterlife. However, he certainly must have read Revelation or at least be familiar with the Four Horsemen of the Apocalypse. This was one of many book covers for The Stand but probably most accurate.

After the infection runs its course, a small group of immune survivors lies scattered across the country. These include rock star Larry Underwood (Adam Storke), who has just had his big break but is now stranded in New York City; Nick Andros (Rob Lowe) a deaf man in Arkansas; Frannie Goldsmith (Molly Ringwald) a teenager living in Ogunquit, Maine; Lloyd Henreid (Miguel Ferrer) a criminal stuck in a prison cell in Arizona; and "Trashcan Man" (Matt Frewer) a mentally ill scavenger. The survivors soon begin having visions, either from kindly Mother Abagail (Ruby Dee) or from the demonic Randall Flagg (Jamey Sheridan). The two sets of survivors are instructed to either travel to Nebraska to meet Mother Abagail, or to Las Vegas to join Flagg.[206]

HANDLING THE DEADLY

Fifteen BSL-4 labs in the U.S. handle only the most deadly, incurable pathogens like Smallpox, Ebola, Marburg, Lassa, and other hemorrhagic diseases. After 9/11, BSL-3 labs in the U.S. trebled to 1,400. Each state has at least one, some have numerous labs and thousands more exist around the globe.

Level 3s experiment with Bubonic Plague, TB, Brucella, various encephalitis viruses, SARS, Rabies, Rift Valley and others like Anthrax – unless it's weaponized. In that case it's handled in a BSL-4 facility. Even with treatment, these diseases are so deadly that bacteria escaping laboratories could be devastating.

BSL-2s work with agents that pose moderate hazards like Hepatitis A, B, and C; MRSA, Measles and Lyme disease and more. BSL-1 agents don't usually cause disease in healthy people like canine hepatitis and non-infectious bacteria.

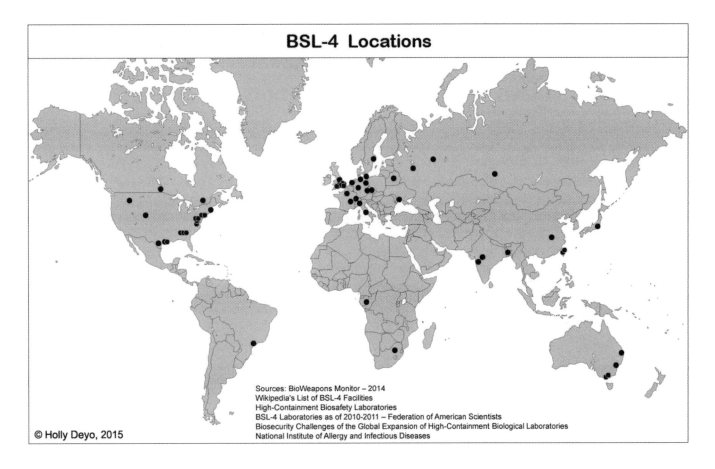

BSL-4 Locations

Sources: BioWeapons Monitor – 2014
Wikipedia's List of BSL-4 Facilities
High-Containment Biosafety Laboratories
BSL-4 Laboratories as of 2010-2011 – Federation of American Scientists
Biosecurity Challenges of the Global Expansion of High-Containment Biological Laboratories
National Institute of Allergy and Infectious Diseases

© Holly Deyo, 2015

Accidents Aren't Waiting to Happen, They Have

One might be tempted to write off *The Stand, Contagion, I Am Legend* or *12 Monkeys* as apocalyptic science fiction. *USA Today's* 2015 investigation reveals a different story. So does *Scientific American*. Between 2006 and 2013, biolabs notified federal regulators of about 1,500 incidents involving "select agent pathogens" – those that affect humans, agriculture or both. In more than 800 cases, workers received medical treatment or evaluation.[207] Some of the accidents and foul ups besides safety violations include:

- Air-purifying respirators failing in H5N1 avian flu experiments
- Missing vials of pathogens
- Cattle infected in vaccine experiments sent to slaughter for human consumption
- Lab mice escaping infected with deadly viruses
- Jabs with infected needles
- Materials stored outside of containment areas
- Wild rats building nests out of research waste
- Spills and other loss of containment
- Holes in biosafety-level-4 (BSL-4) protective suits, and
- Unsafe lab practices

Scientific American corroborates some of the accidents unearthing nearly 400 incidents in the U.S. from 2003 – 2009.[208] It's impossible to obtain a full accounting of accidents and lab-acquired infections because there is no universal, mandatory requirement for reporting.

PUTTING THE "S" IN STUPID

Understandably labs are reluctant to disclose problems because one facility that continually had incidents was supposedly going to be fined $425,000. It would have been the largest fine in the government program's history except it was never levied, just discussed. Among numerous infractions, one the worst at this facility occurred in 2008 when a nearby disease-free herd had one of its cows sickened by brucellosis. The pathogen had escaped the lab.

Brucellosis is highly contagious and causes cattle and other livestock to abort and have stillborns, produce less milk, suffer weight loss, infertility and lameness. Since many other animals on our dining tables can catch Brucellosis – sheep, goats, pigs, deer, bison, elk, moose, and marine mammals – an outbreak could be devastating. Nearly two decades ago Brucellosis cost beef and dairy farmers $30 million a year. Other animals can also be sickened – ones people in Western countries don't normally eat like rats, dogs, horses, water buffalo and camels. So there's a lot of potential for it to spread if it gets loose.

The USDA also cited LSU – Louisiana State University AgCenter – for violating regulations by sending Brucella-infected cattle that had been part of their experimental vaccine program to a slaughterhouse where their meat was sold for human consumption.

Phil Elzer, who at the time ran LSU's Brucella studies, balked at the citation. He said "the practice of sending research cattle to slaughter was declared in the lab's operating procedures that were reviewed and signed off on at each inspection by Federal Select Agent Program regulators." So either the USDA knew of sending infected cattle into the food chain or gave the reports such quick looks they never saw it. Not once. Elzer stated, "To all of a sudden say we were doing it wrong was very surprising."[209]

One has to wonder over how many years, how many times infected meat went onto dinner plates. Louisiana State appealed and the USDA eventually dropped the $425,000 fine.

Brucellosis in Humans

Yes brucellosis can affect humans and in the U.S., there are up to 200 new cases every year. It used to be primarily associated with consuming unpasteurized milk, soft cheese and raw meat from infected cattle, but it can also spread through the air, enter an open wound, by sexual contact and breastfeeding, but **not** by casual contact with a pet.[210] According to the Mayo Clinic symptoms can show up in a few days to a few months. Symptoms are similar to those of the flu – fever, chills, sweats, weakness, fatigue; joint, muscle and back pain, and headaches – so diagnosis can be tricky. Sometimes symptoms disappear for weeks or months and then return. In some people, brucellosis becomes chronic, persisting for years, even after treatment.[211]

Since it's listed as a bio-terror agent, whoever thought intentionally integrating brucellosis-sickened cattle into meat for sale was clever?

CONGRESSIONAL "MUSHROOM" SYNDROME AND BUCK PASSING

Lab regulators at the Federal Select Agent Program refuse interviews despite repeated requests. The program oversees nearly 300 organizations that operate BSL-3 and eight that operate BSL-4 labs. Plus there are hundreds of other facilities not in that program. Who oversees them?

For the most part, labs are self-policing so there's not much incentive to be forthcoming on mishaps and safety failures especially when grants and fines may be at stake. Lab regulators at the Federal Select Agent Program – whose departments often fund the research they oversee, are tight lipped. Info is often only garnered through FOIA requests and even then, highly redacted.

CDC and USDA regulators have cited over 100 labs working with bioterror agents for serious safety and security failures since 2003. Some facilities are repeat offenders:

- 5 labs have had "multiple referrals" for enforcement actions
- 2 labs have been kicked out of the program
- 5 labs were suspended from doing any select agent research
- 33 labs have been put on "performance improvement programs" since 2008 – a voluntary alternative to suspension or other sanctions, for facilities with "repeated failure to correct past observation, biosafety and security concerns"
- 7 more labs just since May 2015 are in performance improvement programs
- Dozens have faced regulatory actions from the USDA and
- 48 investigations resulted in $116,750 in fines.

The CDC won't say who even the worst offenders are. Instead, the CDC and the USDA cites the 2002 bioterrorism law – the Public Health Security and Bioterrorism Preparedness Response Act, (PHSBPRA) – saying it requires keeping this information secret. However, the Federal Select Agent Program – jointly comprised of the

CDC and Animal and Plant Health Inspection Service – says that's wrong, that no law or regulation bars labs from discussing their research or problems they've had. They just aren't supposed to share details of security measures that would give terrorists or any unauthorized person access to pathogens. Somebody is passing the buck all in the name of secrecy.

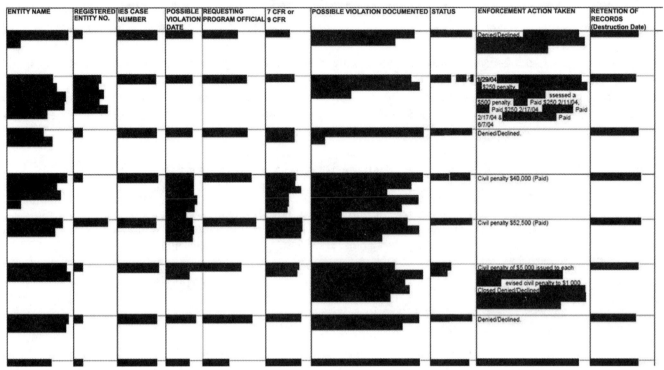

Image: USDA spreadsheet of enforcement actions taken against laboratories that violated regulations for working with deadly pathogens. Notice the last column that reads: RETENTION OF RECORDS (Destruction Date) Evidently Federal Select Agent Program regulators want no trace left behind.

About the only outside oversight encountered is the yearly report Congress requires documenting the number of thefts, losses and releases of these pathogens at labs. However, for nearly 300 labs, Congress gets just three pages of data. Incidents, mistakes and near misses are lumped together by type, no details. Even for really serious screw-ups they provide only vague information. Congress is kept in the dark about what labs put Americans at risk and what they did.

FACILITIES IN OUR MIDST

The government planned well when they built Dugway Proving Ground way out in the Great Salt Lake Desert with mountain ranges on three sides. The massive complex covers nearly 800,000 acres making it larger than Rhode Island. Even set in this remote area didn't prove safe enough. In March 1968, over 6,200 sheep were exposed to the nerve agent VX during open-air tests. The sheep either died outright or were euthanized because they were so severely injured. To this day, the Army admits no culpability, but autopsies proved they had VX in their systems and the military reimbursed farmers for loss of their herds.

Now flash forward 50 years, BSL-4 and BSL-3 labs are sprouting up all over. They are housed in universities and hospitals, on military bases and in stand-alone facilities. In 1990 there were just 12 BSL-4 labs. By 2000 – 17. It jumped wildly in 2010 (spurred by 9/11) to 42 and after 2012 another dozen appeared bumping the total to at least 52. BSL-3 labs, which are nearly as dangerous, number in the thousands and also are located in cities. The more labs, the greater the risk of mistakes, never mind duplicated work that wastes taxpayer dollars.

It's inevitable that in densely populated countries like Taiwan and India, these dangerous labs will be too close to where people live and work. They don't have the luxury of extra real estate compared to the number of residents, but other nations have no excuse.

BSL-4 labs aren't just built in the highly populated U.S. cities of Atlanta, Richmond, VA; Bethesda, MD; San Antonio, but also in Winnipeg, Manitoba; London, Melbourne, Berlin, Prague, Milan, Hamburg, Singapore, Bhopal, Rome, Geneva and others. Europe currently has the largest number of people living in the direct vicinity of BSL-4s. With Asia's newly built facilities and exploding population, they're set to overtake Europe in the next few decades for labs too close to population centers.

Shocker 1: A recent study[212] published in London's BMC Medicine found that because BSL-4 labs are being built in highly populated areas, the risk of an escaped pathogen causing a pandemic is greater than a pandemic that occurs naturally. One scenario is preventable, the other not. The study also found that there is a 500% better chance of containment in rural areas. So why are these labs located in cities where there's lot of people, homes, businesses, restaurants?

Shocker 2: Federal agencies don't know how many or where BSL labs are located. According to the GAO, many fingers play in the BSL lab sandbox. All of the following agencies are involved in various aspects as users, owners, regulators and as funding sources. No wonder they don't know where all the labs are or what they're working with. Jack doesn't talk to Jill and vice versa and there are always turf wars between government agencies. Taxpayer waste, lack of coordination and duplication has to be monumental.

FEDERAL AGENCIES INVOLVED WITH BIOSAFETY LABS

Agency	Has own HCLs	Funds research or building of HCLs	Regulates HCLs with pathogens posing risk to humans	Regulates HCLs with pathogens posing risk to animals & plants	Regulates activities or safety in HCLs	Regulates manufacture of biological products	Researches how to detect or coordinates how to respond to biological attacks	Regulates export of pathogens & equipment for military & civilian use
CDC	X		X					
USDA	X			X				
NIAID	X	X						
NIH					X			
FDA	X					X		
DOC								X
DOD	X	X						
OSHA					X			
DOS	X							X
FBI	X							
DHS	X	X						
DOE	X						X	
DOI	X for Animals							
VA	X for Veterans							
EPA	X						X	
HCL = High Containment Lab								

YIMBY – YES IN MY BACKYARD

As a child through late her late twenties this author grew up in Kansas City, Missouri. Going to the Country Club Plaza for dinner and shopping was always fun. It's home to everything from fine to casual dining and upscale shopping set against a backdrop of Spanish architecture.

Every Thanksgiving night after a day of turkey, family, football and the Macy's Parade, tens of thousands flock to The Plaza for the start of the "Season of Lights". The tradition began over 85 years ago when Charles Pitrat, head of maintenance, hung a strand of 16 colored lights over the door of The Plaza's first building. Now nearly every merchant and restaurateur decorates the historic 15 blocks.

Photo: This fountain is the best known and most-photographed of all of the city's fountains. It's located at the east entrance to the popular Country Club Plaza district. The figures were sculpted by Henri Greber in 1910 and adorned the mansion of Clarence Mackay in Long Island, NY. Over the years the fountain was vandalized and eleven parts were missing. The Nichols family initiated the purchase and installation, funded by the family, the city and private contributions including a collection by school children in the Kansas City area. It was brought to Kansas City in 1951 and refurbished by Herman Frederick Simon and dedicated in 1960. The J. C. Nichols Memorial Fountain has four heroic horsemen, which are said to represent the four rivers of the world: the Mississippi River (the Indian riding the horse and beating off an alligator), the Volga River (with the bear), the Seine and the Rhine.

With fat flakes swirling softly under antique-looking streetlights, people delight in seeing the Country Club Plaza's lights switch on. Then Christmas wasn't controversial. Macy's and nearly every other retailer put on fantastic animated displays and Nativity scenes in their big glass windows. People stroll and carol.

Since so many make this annual pilgrimage they have to park blocks away. Cabs are ready to whisk them to the best viewing vantage point. For a more leisurely ride, horse-drawn carriages clip-clop across Brush Creek Bridge to any destination in the area. Armed with parkas and hot cocoa, people anxiously wait for the 7 p.m. count down when 80 miles of lights transform an already lovely area into one of enchantment. Beside shops and restaurants fully decorated, Kansas City dresses their fountains in jewel tones. Known as the City of Fountains, there is plenty of opportunity in Kansas City. Colored water flows easily from some; others shoot up, spiral and burst into beautiful brilliant droplets. Color shimmers and reflects off Brush Creek that flows some 10½ miles through The Plaza. Everything sparkles like millions of rainbow jewels. To keep decorating tasteful, tower lights are always one color. The Time Tower is always red. Nichols Tower, Zoom Tower, Granfalloon and Ingredient Towers are always green. It's tradition.

It's nice to be able to count on things. But what people didn't count on is having a BSL-3 lab right in their backyard. Literally. Beside shopping and dining, hotels and many apartments are available within walking distance. Just 10 minutes away lurks Midwest Research Institute, now MRIGlobal. Between 2 and 10 minutes from MRIGlobal are several country clubs, a museum, theater, numerous parks, more restaurants and businesses plus multi-million dollar homes in Mission Hills, Kansas, just over State Line.

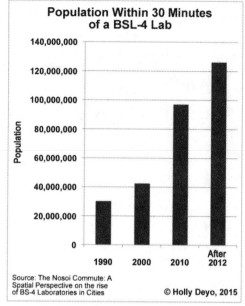

Population Within 30 Minutes of a BSL-4 Lab

Source: The Nosoi Commute: A Spatial Perspective on the rise of BS-4 Laboratories in Cities

© Holly Deyo, 2015

In St. Louis, Doisy Research Center with its BSL-3 lab is just four minutes from many residential subdivisions. Georgia State University's BSL-4 lab is two blocks from the State Capitol. A few more blocks travelled and residential areas are everywhere.

San Antonio's BSL-4 lab is seven minutes from multiple housing divisions.

Boston University's BSL-4 lab is just 11 minutes distant from Back Bay, known for its stately brownstones, Parisian-style boulevards, trendy boutiques, fine dining, and upscale hotels. This BSL-4 is right in the heart of multiple campuses, student housing and residences.

Seattle's BSL-3 lab is in the middle of everything – restaurants, a zoo, shopping, parks, several golf courses and tons of homes.

When Manhattan, Kansas finishes its BSL-4 lab at K-State, it will be two blocks from housing subdivisions.

Homes close to Texas A & M's BSL-3 lab are two minutes to the north and four minutes to the southeast. This facility has experienced multiple power failures and power is central to negative air pressure systems to keep pathogens contained. They work by keeping pressure inside the room less than pressure outside the room, so all air flows in, not out.

In June 2007, lightning hit in and around the CDC's brand new BSL-4 facility bringing down both the main power and backup generators. It showed shortsightedness that the 'gennies' were located off-site and shared with other entities. They were left with batteries only, which were meant to provide limited emergency light in the event of evacuation. As in Texas A & M's power outages, the negative air pressure system was compromised.[213]

The very next year, 2008, the CDC's $214 million facility experienced a repeat of airflow problems. The door to Building 18 housing the germ that causes Q Fever was found sealed with duct tape after a ventilation system malfunction. (Use #1,228 for duct tape?) Nine workers were tested for it, but none were infected. [214]

The list of BSLs too-close-for-comfort goes on and on. What used to be NIMBY – Not In My Back Yard is now YIMBY – Yes, in *My* Back Yard. All it requires is one ambitious terrorist or one careless scientist for a lot of people to have a really bad day.

Careless Practices, Mistakes and Near Misses

May 2015, live anthrax was accidentally sent to 194 laboratories in all states, three territories of Guam, Puerto Rico, and the U.S. Virgin Islands, the District of Columbia plus three labs in Canada. Overseas spores went to Japan, United Kingdom, Australia, Italy, Germany, Norway, Switzerland, and to Osan Air Force Base in South Korea[215] where as many as 22 people were possibly exposed.[216] This is a big jump from the May report that said anthrax had been sent to 18 labs in 9 states. In June the Pentagon corrected itself and added Canada and South Korea. On this latest botch up, Pentagon spokesman, Col. Steve Warren calmed, "There is no known risk to the general public, and there are no suspected or confirmed cases of anthrax infection in potentially exposed lab workers."[217] However, four people in three commercial labs in Delaware, Texas and Wisconsin underwent preventive treatment.

This mistake came on the heels of increased scrutiny for bioterror agents and their oversight around the country. Still, errors are occurring after decades of using poor safety measures. Now Capitol Hill worries that failed lab procedures could extend to other bioterror agents. The Pentagon shut down nine labs until it could be determined that their procedures are safe. Will that be enough?

In June 2014, the CDC inadvertently sent anthrax samples to a low-containment lab and shipped deadly Bird Flu to a USDA (U.S. Department of Agriculture) lab. This followed the discovery of six Smallpox vials in a Food and Drug Administration facility.[218] That same month, 86 CDC employees in Atlanta were exposed to airborne anthrax – the deadliest form.

Remember 2001's bio-terrorism event? Five people died including two postal workers when they processed anthrax-filled letters. Twenty-two people developed infections; 11 became critical.

In December 2014, another screw up at the CDC possibly exposed one or more technicians to Ebola.[219]

Backing up, in 2004, Maryland's Southern Research Institute accidentally sent four teaspoons of anthrax – or about 16 trillion spores – to Children's Hospital Oakland Research Institute in California.[220] According to Medicine.net, inhaling even 10,000-20,000 spores can be lethal.[221] So 16 trillion spores could kill roughly every American twice over – at the low estimation – providing they were in the vicinity of the release.

Experts then recommended that the time for a "live" sample to be declared "dead" should be several days instead of 24 hours. After the CDC's subsequent investigation, they couldn't come up with a good answer of why better safety measures still hadn't been implemented. CDC biosafety officer Dr. Paul Meechan stated, "Why that did not become integrated into the DNA of handling *bacillus anthracis* is a great question. I don't have a good answer."[222]

Reports released in 2008 and 2010 from the Department of Health and Human Services, CDC's parent agency, documented a long list of issues. They concluded that CDC labs even though working with the most lethal agents, didn't always ensure the physical security of the pathogens or restrict access to them, and personnel didn't always receive required training. Some just blew past it ignoring protocols.

In 2012, the Public Health Agency of Canada reviewed one – just one – CDC animal biosafety facility and described their practices as "models", but that doesn't mean to say they all are. Debra Sharpe, who investigated the 2004 incident as director of compliance at Southern Research Institute, questioned the training at the CDC and other U.S. labs. "We spend millions of dollars on these laboratories, but we're not spending the appropriate amount of money on training and safety and implementing management systems. I see a lot of scientists that have come from CDC. Generally, they have poorer practices," [compared with the private sector].[223] More than a decade ago and multiple incidents later, it appears the CDC still hasn't learned valuable lessons.

The UK has a similar track record. From 2010 – 2014, their 600 CL3 labs and nine CL4 labs (same as BSL-3 and BSL-4) reported 116 accidents or near misses. One blunder involved sending live anthrax from a government facility to unsuspecting labs across the UK, exposing other scientists to the disease. Another mishap involved the failure of an air handling system that helped contain foot and mouth disease. Britain's 2007 foot and mouth outbreak was traced to a leak in a containment lab's drainpipes in Pirbright Institute, Surrey. As a result, animals on eight farms were infected and were culled. At least 65% of these accidents were serious enough to warrant investigation.[224]

Last Thoughts on Diseases

Prophecy warns that in End Times pestilence will play a large part in reducing global population by 25%. Enough diseases are already here to kill every living thing in existence many times over. Several factors underscore that disease could easily overrun the world:

1. Weaponization of bio-toxins and dispersal of same – using bioweapons in wartime and by rogue elements has happened for decades. Despite the 1975 BWC treaty in place, a number of countries are thought to still maintain stockpiles.

2. Global proliferation of BSL 3 and 4 facilities. It's surprising that some entity hasn't attempted to penetrate these thousands of facilities around the world. Despite extraordinary security, buildings that house the worst diseases in the world would be very tempting.

3. Rise of superbugs and increasing antibiotic resistance. In addition to many illnesses that can kill the victims that aren't usually fatal, the CDC categorizes at least 18 diseases as Urgent, Serious or Concerning. Not only are they extremely deadly despite intervention, they are now overcoming antibiotics due to mutation and over-prescribing of once-effective antibiotics. Couple these factors with a natural disaster, situations where hospitals and pharmaceutical companies are compromised and can no longer provide medicine or treatment, it clears the path for disease to overtake once healthy communities.

It's well established that in areas where people are packed densely together like in disaster areas, refugee camps and jails, illness thrives. Lack of hygiene, vaccines and education all make disease travel quicker through populations. War and famine – two things prophesied in the scripture at the beginning of this chapter contribute to disease. Couple that with hospitals and morgues probably unavailable in those times, disease could run with little to stop it.

Chapter 10: Famine – It's Coming Again

You will sow much seed in the field but you will harvest little, because locusts will devour it. You will plant vineyards and cultivate them but you will not drink the wine or gather the grapes, because worms will eat them. You will have olive trees throughout your country but you will not use the oil, because the olives will drop off. You will have sons and daughters but you will not keep them, because they will go into captivity. Swarms of locusts will take over all your trees and the crops of your land. —Deuteronomy 28:38-42, 40 (NIV)

The Lord will turn the rain of your country into dust and powder; it will come down from the skies until you are destroyed. —Deuteronomy 28:24 (NIV)

And there will be great earthquakes in various places, and famines and pestilences; and there will be fearful sights and great signs from heaven. —Luke 21:11 (NKJV)

For nation will rise against nation, and kingdom against kingdom, and there will be famines and earthquakes in place after place. —Matthew 24:7 (AMP)

Nation will rise against nation, and kingdom against kingdom. There will be earthquakes in various places, and famines. These are the beginning of birth pains. —Mark 13:8 (NIV)

When He opened the third seal, I heard the third living creature say, "Come and see." So I looked, and behold, a black horse, and he who sat on it had a pair of scales in his hand. And I heard a voice in the midst of the four living creatures saying, "A quart of wheat for a denarius, and three quarts of barley for a denarius; and do not harm the oil and the wine." —Revelation 6:5-8 (NKJV)

Photo: Victor Vasnetsov's 1887 painting, "Four Horsemen of the Apocalypse" clearly depicts events prophesied in Revelation 6:1-8. At the top center is the Lamb of God, the Lion of Judah – Jesus Christ. He opens the first four of seven seals, which summons four beings that ride out on white, red, black, and pale horses symbolizing Conquest, War, Famine, and Death.

A disproportionate amount of time is spent on famine for good reason. No food, no life. Pretty simple. Not everyone suffers around the globe from a single solitary earthquake or hurricane "over there". However, because the world is so globally intertwined and dependent, food availability affects everyone. Countries import and export to each other all over the globe. A few nations are considered self-sufficient like the U.S., Canada, France, Russia, Australia, India, Argentina, Burma and Thailand.

If it got right down to it, America could survive without with delectable kiwis from New Zealand or their lovely Braeburn apples. We could live without limes and other seasonal fruit from Colombia and Mexico or Corona beer. While it's lovely to enjoy nuts from Costa Rica, Brazil, Africa, India and Vietnam, it's not life and death. It might be tougher to lose Brazil's coffee or China's talapia, but this country would still survive.

America's grain production is comparable to Saudi Arabia and oil. They are the big dogs in their respective fields. Those other countries could survive too, quite happily, without importing food, even with a few "holes" in their inventory.

Other nations aren't so fortunate. Over a third of the world imports at least ¼ of their grain. Half of all nations import over 50% of these basics and 13 countries must import all. This traces back to the loss of fertile soil either being contaminated or over-planted or sold off, and rapidly disappearing fresh water.

Unlike other disasters, most don't point to a global event like famine. It IS coming and the groundwork is laid logically, scientifically, irrefutably, and people are partially responsible for this coming catastrophe. God, when He issues judgment, forewarns and stays within the bounds of physics. He doesn't do things via "abracadabra" though He could. There is logic, science, but most often, we small humans haven't stumbled onto the information yet. The 3rd seal is irrevocable. It is coming. Famine *is* coming and the path is indisputable. It is laid with precision to our doorstep and mostly from our own doing.

AND JESUS SAID …

Mankind has been at the mercy of food shortages since he was booted from the Garden of Eden. Famine, primarily the result of natural disaster and war, has snatched tens of millions of lives. Whether fighting countries blocked food transport or obliterated stored grain, blew up irrigation systems or pulled men from tending their crops, war could be counted on to initiate famine. Natural disasters, "acts of God" or however one chooses to label them, take just as many lives. The difference is that one scenario is avoidable; the other isn't. Over the centuries famines have repeatedly carved into the populations of Europe, Russia, Ireland, Iceland, Vietnam, up through the Scandinavian countries, China, the Middle East and even America. These are but a few examples.

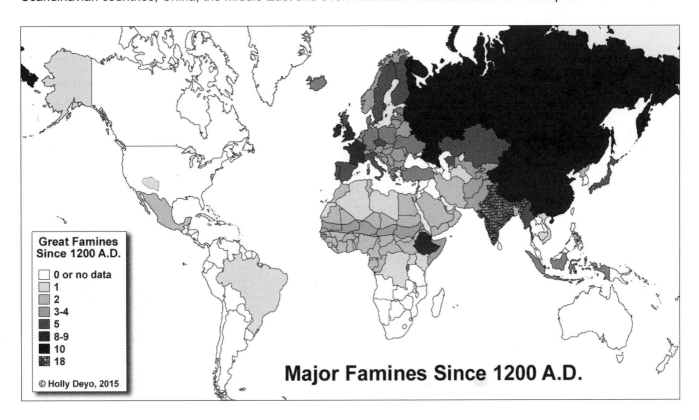

Great Famines Since 1200 A.D.

- 0 or no data
- 1
- 2
- 3-4
- 5
- 8-9
- 10
- 18

© Holly Deyo, 2015

Major Famines Since 1200 A.D.

American Indians

While most famines result from war or natural disaster, a mystery surrounds what exactly happened to the Anasazi. Widespread food shortage is thought to be the prime cause for collapsing the 400-year Puebloan civilization, but there's more. Those that survived migrated some time around 1300 A.D from the Four Corners where Utah, Arizona, New Mexico and Colorado all meet. At least 30,000 people occupied this dramatic 30,000-square-mile landscape of red sandstone canyons, buttes and mesas.

Photo: Cliff Palace in Mesa Verde National Park, Colorado encompassed 225 rooms. It's the largest of about 4,000 preserved cliff dwellings. As large as these cliff homes are, 95% of the Anasazi lived in huge communities on the mesa. To put this in perspective, more people lived in that area of southwest Colorado then than now. (Courtesy Tobi 87)

The Anasazi were exceptional builders. Some structures reached five stories high and boasted 800 rooms. No multi-family dwellings equaled their size in America until the 1870s. One colossal structure in New Mexico's Chaco Canyon required hauling, shaping and placing 30 *million* stones. At least 10 buildings of this size are visible there. 30,000,000 x 10… that's a lot of work. Few trees existed close by and it's estimated they literally dragged 100,000 timbers from 30 miles away for roof beams. Architecture shows their "towns" were carefully planned, constructed and decorated. In Pueblo Bonito, the most widely recognized village in Chaco Canyon, they even remodeled tearing out old walls to build larger structures. Here, in the middle of desert shrubs and low grasses, stood homes for thousands.

They constructed a 500-mile web of roads, each 30 feet wide, radiating from Chaco Canyon. This was really curious since they didn't have the wheel or animals to ride. Whether crossing deserts, high dunes or canyons their roads remained ramrod straight. The Anasazi built a sophisticated astronomical observatory on top of Fajada Butte to track planting seasons and ceremonial times. Evidence of this is seen in spiral petroglyph wall carvings marking sun and moon cycles. Fajada rises 443 feet straight out of the flat canyon floor so for easier access, they constructed a 750-foot ramp.

Life was difficult in the best of times. Then something changed. It got worse – a lot worse. Something awful drove them from their magnificent cities and villages.

Archeologists still can't say conclusively, but they believe tree ring evidence shows a combination of events forced them to leave. In this arid region, cropland below 5,500 feet was too dry and above 7,500 feet it was too cold with a short growing season. Even when good rains came plus having an impressive system of dams and canals with water-diversion gates and water catchment from the canyon rim, they pressed food production to the limit.

Without rain, it was impossible to grow enough corn, squash and beans to support everyone. After a 30-year drought from 1276 to 1299 – one of many extreme dry periods – widespread famine slammed the Ancient Ones. Climate change, violence, war and cannibalism forced them out. Yet more mystery is implied from respected former archeologist Alden Hayes. He writes, "Too much happened too fast to have been a local happening. The jump from one- to five-story buildings, the roads and astronomical observatory, the complex social organization they implied – it's too much to accept without outside influence."[225] What does that mean? Tree rings show that about 1275 an unrelenting drought stuck that became more widespread and protracted than the Anasazi had ever known. It decimated crops, eroded waterways to irrigate fields and lowered the water table. So they abandoned all they had built. Had the Anasazi hung on even a few more years, they would have seen it become very wet. Though rain returned, the Anasazi never did.

Asia

According to John Seach, scientist and founder of *Volcano Live*, Aso in Kyushu, Japan erupted in 1229. One of the most severe effects of a major eruption is "nuclear winter". Million of tons of ash circle the globe blocking the sun, plummeting temperatures on Earth. This kills crops, farm animals – and people. Since Aso is one of world's largest volcanoes it's likely it caused Japan's worst-ever famine.

It wasn't until a couple years ago scientists solved the mystery of what caused another famine in Japan and elsewhere around the world just 30 years later. Another volcano was to blame. This time its eruption was so powerful it kicked off the centuries-long Little Ice Age.

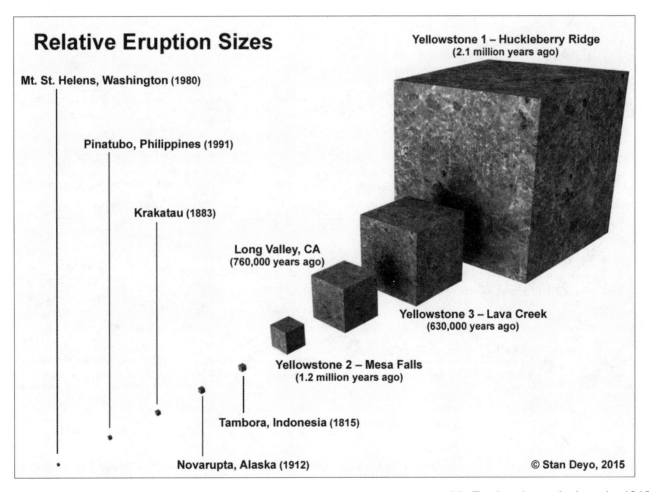

How big was the eruption? This incomprehensible event was on par with Tambora's explosions in 1815. Scientists estimate this blast was 8 times stronger than Krakatoa and it wrecked enough destruction to be called the "Pompeii of the Far East." But what volcano caused it? How could an eruption strong enough to blast ash into the stratosphere be invisible?

Just a few years ago scientists discovered the culprit, the former Samalas volcano, which is now the huge Segara Anak caldera in Lomboc, Indonesia. Like Yellowstone, Samalas belched out so much magma it collapsed in on itself leaving only a caldera and a pile of destruction in its wake. Today, the crater is filled with beautiful turquoise water and from its depths rises the current active cone, Barujari. Small by comparison, sitting inside the caldera, the secret of Samalas was completely disguised. Ancient manuscripts found in a Dutch library cataloged this event as something so horrific it brought "the end to a kingdom". In 2012, scientists from the University of Colorado, Boulder, carbon-dated dead plants and logs from under ice caps on Baffin Island (north of Canada's mainland) and Iceland, as well as sampled ice and sediment cores. Through matching ash deposits, scientists traced the explosion to where Samalas once towered. They found that cold summers and ice grew abruptly between 1275 and 1300 resulting in poor harvests and devastatingly heavy floods. So many people died even in far off London in that "year without a summer", people were shoveled into mass graves. Scientists now point the finger at Samalas as the source of that large-scale famine.

Though China and Russia run neck and neck for repeated food shortages, no country suffered more drought-induced famines up through the 1950s than India. This country is almost entirely dependent on monsoon rains and when they fail, famine follows claiming millions of lives. Southern India is particularly hard hit and often Deccan is mentioned in conjunction with starvation.

Politics also played a role. While Britain still controlled India they seized local farmlands and converted them to foreign-owned plantations. They also restricted internal trade and taxed Indians unmercifully to finance unsuccessful expeditions in Afghanistan. Food prices shot up and few could afford to eat while grains were shipped to Britain. Before India won independence in 1947, the last major famine from 1943 to 1944 killed up to 4 million in Bengal alone on India's eastern side.

Photo: View of Segara Anak Lake from the crater rim – all that's left of Samalas Volcano. In the middle-back of this image rising from the water is the active cone Barujari. (Courtesy Petter Lindgren)

China

Closer to present day, four famines in China – 1810, 1811, 1846, and 1849 – killed at least 45 million. Numerous other famines have subsequently hit China, but of all countries, this one is most secretive regarding internal strife and disasters. However, the 1959-1961 famine caused by Mao Tse-Tung's industrialization drive, the "Great Leap Forward", was too big to hide. In one of the worst food shortages of all times, at least 42 million died.

This monstrous, hellish famine can be squarely laid at their leader's feet. In his book *Mao's Great Famine; The Story of China's Most Devastating Catastrophe*, Frank Dikotter reveals that the People's Republic of China suffered a "staggering degree of violence" surprisingly recorded in Public Security Bureau reports.

The Communist Party viewed farmers as faceless, nameless drones. "For those who committed any acts of disobedience, however minor, punishments were huge. State retribution for tiny thefts such as stealing a potato, even by a child, would include being tied up and thrown into a pond; parents were forced to bury their children alive or were doused in excrement and urine, others were set alight, or had a nose or ear cut off. One record shows how a man was branded with hot metal. People were forced to work naked in the middle of winter; 80 per cent of all the villagers in one region of a quarter of a million Chinese were banned from the official canteen because they were too old or ill to be effective workers, so were deliberately starved to death."[226]

China's eastern province of Anhui recorded 63 instances of cannibalism. "In Damiao commune Chen Zhangying and her husband Zhao Xezhen killed and boiled their 8-year-old son Xiao Qing and ate him. In Wudian commune Wang Lanyong not only picked up dead people to eat, but also sold two jin [2.2 pounds] from their bodies as pork."[227]

Author Yang Jisheng writes in the opening paragraph of his two-volume tome, "I call this book Tombstone. It is a tombstone for my father who died of hunger in 1959, for the 36 million Chinese who also died of hunger, for the system that caused their death, and perhaps for myself for writing this book." Documenting this nightmarish famine a witness told Yang. "I went to one village and saw 100 corpses. Then another village and another 100 corpses. No one paid attention to them. People said that dogs were eating the bodies. Not true, I said. The dogs had long ago been eaten by the people."[228]

On NPR Louisa Lim reported China's famine causing "unbearable hunger making people behave in inhuman ways. Even government records reported cases where people ate human flesh from dead bodies." She quotes from Jisheng's book. "Documents report several thousand cases where people ate other people. Parents ate their own kids. Kids ate their own parents. And we couldn't have imagined there was still grain in the warehouses. At the worst time, the government was still exporting grain."[229]

Europe

Ireland's Potato Famine of 1845-1852 nearly always pops into people's minds. It began quite mysteriously when potato plant leaves suddenly turned black, curled, and then rotted. At the time they didn't know that an airborne fungus had traveled in the holds of ships from North America to England. It was so virulent that a single sick potato plant could infect thousands more in just a few days. In the first year, imported Indian corn and survival of about half of their original potato crop cut down on starvation.

To survive, poor Irish sold off their livestock and whatever else they owned to buy food. Since no potato crop had ever failed for two straight years, they gambled that 1846 would bring brighter days. It didn't. As food supplies dwindled, people subsisted on wild blackberries, root vegetables, old cabbage leaves, seaweed, shellfish, weeds and grass.

Compounding matters, the winter of 1846-47 was hit with the worst storms in living memory as blizzard after blizzard buried homes in snow up to their roofs. Most Irish winters see no snow at all, so people didn't know how to cope with this added disaster. Before "The Great Hunger" was over, it claimed a million lives and another million permanently left Ireland for England, Australia and America.

Because cannibalism is the greatest taboo, reliable records are scarce. In an unpublished 1999 paper, the eminent U.S. historian Perry Curtis observed, "the silences surrounding cannibalism are almost deafening enough to arouse suspicion."

Professor Cormac O'Grada of University College Dublin told a New York conference on world hunger about cannibalism practiced during the Great Potato Famine. O'Grada, a leading expert in this area, said while there were many rumors about it, one documented report involved John Connolly of Connemara on Ireland's West Coast. While being tried for stealing sheep, it came out that his family was in such dire straits Connolly's wife had eaten some of the flesh off the legs and feet of their dead son. When the body was exhumed, nothing but bones remained from where John indicated. His three-month sentence of hard labor was immediately dismissed.[230]

Another instance was printed in the May 23, 1849 edition of *The Times*. In County Mayo, a starving man "extracted the heart and liver...[of] a shipwrecked human body...cast on shore".[231]

Russia

"Cats, dogs, and rats were eaten; the strong overcame the weak, and in the shambles of the public markets human flesh was sold. Multitudes of the dead were found with their mouths stuffed with straw. ...Three Russian famines of comparative recent date were among the most severe in the history of the country. They occurred in 1891, 1906, and 1911. In 1906 the government gave 40 pounds of flour a month to all persons under 18 and over 59 years of age. The suffering was intense and the mortality exceedingly heavy, but the available statistics are not wholly reliable. The famine of 1911 extended over one-third of the empire in Europe. It affected over 30,000,000 people indirectly, while 8,000,000 were reduced to starvation. Weeds, the bark of trees, and bitter bread made from acorns constituted the chief diet for the destitute."[232]

Next to India and China, no country feels famine's thrust more greatly than Russia. Food shortages occur regularly, about every four to five years: 1901, 1906, 1911, 1920, 1921, 1924, 1931, 1936, 1939, 1946, 1948, 1951, 1957, 1963, 1965, 1972, 1975, 1979, 1981, 1984, 1991 and 1995.

During World War I, Russians experienced a violent revolution in 1917 and multiple civil wars. Bolshevik soldiers often forced peasants to sacrifice their food so they just stopped growing crops. If they couldn't eat them, why bother just to feed soldiers. Instead, they ate seeds, which did little to sustain them. By 1921, 5 million Russians had perished.

This wasn't the cruelest. Sometimes government leaders think people are just a nuisance and need to be eradicated.

THE HUNGER

Soviet dictator Josef Stalin would have liked to deport the entire population of Ukraine, but 20 million were too many to move. He found another solution: starvation. Ukrainians call it the Holodomor – the Hunger.

Soviet troops and secret policemen raided Ukraine villages, stole harvests and all food in their homes. "They dropped dead in the streets, lay dying and rotting in their houses, and some women became so desperate for food that they ate their own children. If they managed to fend off starvation, they were deported and shot in the hundreds of thousands.

"So terrible was the famine that Igor Yukhnovsky, director of the Institute of National Memory, the Ukrainian institution researching the Holodomor, believes as many as nine million may have died. For decades the disaster remained a state secret, denied by Stalin and his Soviet government and concealed from the outside world with the help of the 'useful idiots' – as Lenin called Soviet sympathizers in the West."[233]

It wasn't just Ukrainians in the crosshairs. Stalin also wanted to purge the Urals, the Lower Volga and Siberia.

Millions of peasants were deported mainly to Siberia between 1930 and 1931, but 800,000 people rebelled in small uprisings, often murdering local commissars who tried to take their grain. Stalin's response was to send in henchmen shooting farmers by the thousands. The peasants' counter-response was to destroy their crops and slaughter 26 million cattle and 15 million horses to prevent them from falling into the hands of Bolsheviks. War broke out in the north Caucasus, the Volga, southern Russia and central Asia.

More than a million peasants were deported just to Siberia: hundreds of thousands were arrested or shot and Stalin still collected their grains. By December 1931 famine ravaged Ukraine and north Caucasus. "'The peasants ate dogs, horses, rotten potatoes, the bark of trees, anything they could find,' wrote one witness Fedor Bleov.[234]

CONTROL THE FOOD, CONTROL THE PEOPLE

Conditions deteriorated further and cannibalism was rife by 1932. "There are horrific eye-witness accounts of mothers eating their own children. In the Ukrainian city of Poltava, Andriy Melezhyk recalled that neighbors found a pot containing a boiled liver, heart and lungs in the home of one mother who had died. Under a barrel in the cellar they discovered a small hole in which a child's head, feet and hands were buried. It was the remains of the woman's little daughter, Vaska.

"Littering the fields were bodies of starving farmers who'd been combing the potato fields in the hope of finding a fragment of a potato. Some frozen corpses had been lying out there for months."[235]

Why would Stalin have done this?

Besides wanting to rid the country of "useful idiots", historians write that class warfare was designed to "'break the back of the peasantry', a war of the cities against the countryside and… to shatter their independent spirit."[236] Americans, take heed.

There is also another likely reason. Ukraine is Europe's breadbasket – a huge producer and exporter of wheat and corn. Its vast fields of rich dark soil are perfect for growing grains as well as vegetables, sugar beets, sunflower seeds, milk and meat. It could also be an example of the philosophy often attributed to Henry Kissinger: "He who controls the food supply controls the people."

In the face of Russia's frequent food shortages, it would be clever to eventually "annex" the entire country. There is precedence as Mr. Putin invaded and annexed Crimea in 2014. Pro-Russian insurgents also control a strip of land from Novoazovsk to Luhansk in Ukraine's eastern border with Russia.

Africa – Famine Now

In recent times, the largest share of famine deaths have shifted from Asia to Africa. One of the most poignant photos to ever capture the appalling desperation from famine was snapped in 1993 by Kevin Carter entitled "The Vulture and the Child". It shows a tiny naked little girl, maybe 4 years old, with stick thin arms and legs during the Sudan famine. Ribs protrude from her thin brown skin. The child is crawling toward a United Nations food camp a half-mile away, but she can't keep up with the group. She is tired and hungry and lies down in the dirt. In the background not far away a vulture waits for the child to die. This picture first printed in the *New York Times* in March of 1993 shocked the whole world. No one knows what happened to the child, including the photographer. After Carter took the photo, he chased the vulture away and then "sat under a tree, lit a cigarette, talked to God and cried."[237]

Most Recent Deadly African Famines			
Years of Famine	Countries Affected	Cause	Result
2012	Sahel region*	Drought-induced 50% crop failure, insect plague, high food prices, conflict	18,000,000+ faced hunger
2011	Somalia, Djibouti, Ethiopia, Kenya, Uganda	Severe drought, driest conditions in 60 years	260,000 starved – half under age 6; 9.5 million on brink of starvation
2010-2012	Somalia	Drought-induced crop failure; Outside nations waited till conditions hit crisis level to intervene	260,000 starved; 1,000,000+ displaced; 2.7 million needed assistance; 1,000,000+ were refugees in other nations
1998	Sudan	Drought and lack of action; Aid slowed by civil war	70,000+ starved
1991-1992	Somalia	Political unrest, civil war	300,000 starved; 2,000,000+ displaced
1983-1985	Ethiopia	Drought and food gap; Ethiopian government let food aid rot and $$ sent by other countries was used to buy weapons	1,000,000+ starved
1980-1983	Uganda	Drought cut harvest by ⅔	30,000 starved; 250,000 threatened
1972-1973	Ethiopia	Drought-induced crop failure	60,000 starved
1968-1972	Sahel region*	Drought-induced crop failure	1,000,000+ starved
1967-1970	Nigeria	Civil war	1,500,000+ starved
1958	Tigray, Ethiopia	Poverty; Aid sent didn't make it to citizens	100,000 starved
1943-1944	Rwanda & Burundi	Drought-induced crop failure	300,000 starved or displaced
* 1,000 km wide east-west belt spanning Africa from the Atlantic Ocean to the Red Sea			

Journalists at the time were warned never to touch famine victims for fear of disease. He later confided to friends that he wished he had intervened. It preyed on his mind – that and the continued violence he witnessed especially in South Africa. Three months later, and only a week after being bestowed the Pulitzer Prize for this photo, Kevin Carter committed suicide at age 33. A portion of his parting letter read, "the pain of life overrides the joy to the point that joy does not exist … I am haunted by the vivid memories of killings and corpses and anger and pain … of starving or wounded children, of trigger happy madmen…."[238] This story and others just as haunting are repeated around the globe. Stories of famine…

Photo: June 20, 2008 – Fields of corn are decimated and crops are ruined for the year by the flooding waters of the Mississippi River in southern Illinois. (Courtesy Robert Kaufmann/FEMA) In the Great Flood of 1993, at least 15 million acres of farmland were inundated with agricultural losses over $17 billion.

Is Famine Coming to Your Table? The Odds Are Getting Stronger

Would you, could you, ever think that famine might come to America, become a *global* catastrophe? The stage is set and it's further along, more precarious than one might think. Nature plays a huge role in whether or not bellies are full. As weather extremes escalate, famines will plague the globe, increasing in size and scope. Too much rain can submerge fields like what happened in the U.S. Midwest in summers 1993 and 2008. This was just one cornfield out of thousands that excessive rains put under water.

As much as 14" of heavy rain fell across the Midwest during the first two weeks of June 2008, causing the worst floods in 12 years. It broke a dozen tributary river height records and led to widespread flooding. Though a dozen states had most of parts submerged, worst hit was Iowa, where 83 of its 99 counties were declared disaster areas. Iowa's losses alone were in the billions. Levees along Cedar Rapids were built to hold water 22 feet high, well above the estimated 500-year flood level, but water rose 31 feet. Floods affected 36,000 people and put millions of acres of land under water.

In 2008, towns along the Mississippi River from Illinois to Missouri built barriers in an attempt to hold back rising waters. Still 41 levees overtopped and those near Meyer and Gulf Port, Illinois broke on the 18th sending their watery burden into homes and businesses, and over millions of acres of farmland. Though hundreds of people evacuated 24 lost their lives.

IMPACT ON CROPS

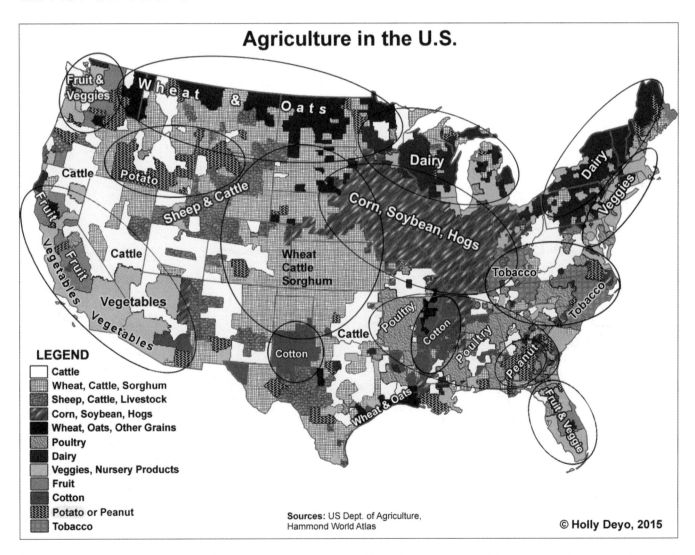

Image: This map indicates the primary growing regions for 19 major U.S. crops. All areas couldn't be marked and still be readable. For example, winter wheat is grown in 42 of the 48 contiguous states. Sugar beets are grown in small portions of 11 states, but other crops took precedence.

America's Corn Belt, which is also home to soybeans, is nearly identical to the 2008 flood area. However the Corn Belt includes Ohio, the top half of Kentucky and the southeast part of North Dakota. These two historic floods covered the vast majority of crop fields. Congress's think tank, the Congressional Research Service, reported that farmers lost 1½ million acres of corn and soybeans.

The American Farm Bureau Federation estimated very early on that crop losses for June 2008 alone would exceed $8 billion. They rightfully expected this figure to rocket because it didn't take into account all the livestock that drowned plus damage to infrastructure, buildings and farm equipment. The final tally came in at nearly double.

This was the *second* 500-year flood in 12 years. An even worse event struck in 1993, causing 48 deaths, economic losses of $34 billion and damages to over 70,000 homes. Roughly 150 major rivers and tributaries had flooded inundating at least 15 million acres of farmland. In 1993, hundreds of levees were breached while in 2008, "only" dozens failed. While they held together better in residential areas, where they broke it flooded crops.

Too much rain fell on America's corn and soybean belt and submerged fields Iowa, Nebraska, Illinois, Indiana, Wisconsin, Ohio, North Dakota, South Dakota, Kansas, Minnesota, Michigan, Kentucky and Missouri. As much as five million acres of crops were thought to be lost entirely inside and outside the Corn Belt.

NOTE: To clear up the misconception about 100-, 500- and 1,000-year floods, it doesn't mean that they occur only every 100, 500 or 1,000 years. Instead, it's a way to measure the odds. A 100-year flood means there is a 1-in-100 or 1% chance of a massive flood event happening. The odds of a 500-year flood means there is a 1-in-500 or .2% chance of it occurring in any given year and for a 1-in-1,000-year event, the odds are just .1%. Theoretically these type floods can occur back-to-back, but it's *highly* unlikely. However, that's nearly what happened. As wild weather escalates, scientists may have to rethink their definitions.

TRANSPORTATION

In 1993, the impact on transportation was mighty. Barge traffic on the Missouri and Mississippi Rivers stopped for nearly two months. Bridges were out or inaccessible on the Mississippi from Davenport, Iowa down to St. Louis, Missouri. On the Missouri, bridges were out from Kansas City to St. Charles, Missouri. Major east-west rail and road transportation was severed, causing major delays and forced rerouting. Numerous interstate highways and

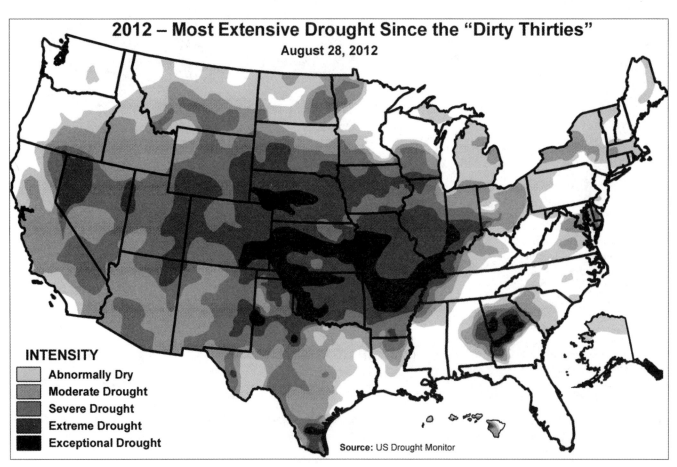

2012 – Most Extensive Drought Since the "Dirty Thirties"
August 28, 2012

INTENSITY
- Abnormally Dry
- Moderate Drought
- Severe Drought
- Extreme Drought
- Exceptional Drought

Source: US Drought Monitor

other roads closed. Ten commercial airports flooded. In 2008 major rail lines in Iowa, Wisconsin, Minnesota, Missouri and Illinois washed out, halting movement completely. Other public infrastructure, such as sewage treatment and water treatment plants, was damaged or destroyed.

The Other End of the Sword

Prolonged drought is more damaging to crops. It's the pit bull of natural disasters when it comes to food. The unbearable drought and ensuing heatwave of 2012 inflicted over $34 billion in damages. The worst US catastrophes since 1980 were Hurricane Katrina and Superstorm Sandy. Those two events didn't impact our food supply, but this massive drought did – in a big way. This is a huge heads-up for those to connect dots to prophetic scripture.

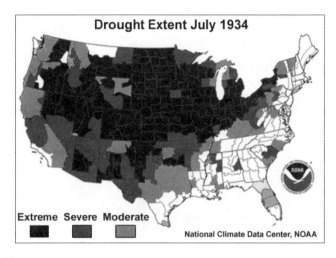

For the entire year of 2012, drought descended on the Nation. What's eerie is that it sat right over the biggest part of our food belt with its fingers stretched out at their worst right at harvest time. This drought was the most extensive ever since the Dust Bowl Days of the 1930s – the Dirty Thirties. Did you ever wonder why it was called that?

The Great Dust Bowl

Where had the precious rain gone? It was like somebody had flipped a switch. In 1931 the rain stopped and black blizzards began. This April 18, 1935 photo shows a typical dust storm – this one rolled over Stratford, Texas just four days after the worst day ever during the Dust Bowl storms – "Black Sunday". It brought a mountain of black dirt that swept across the High Plains and instantly turned a warm, sunny afternoon into the darkest of dark nights. Any unanchored soil turned to dust and blew away in massive clouds and blocked out the Sun. Choking

billows of dirt – named "black blizzards" or "black rollers" – marched cross the Nation reaching New York City and Washington, D.C. Relentless clogging dust prompted the name, the Dirty Thirties. On the Plains, visibility was reduced to three feet or less. Edward Stanley, a Kansas City news editor, coined the term "Dust Bowl" while recounting Robert Geiger's tale of what he experienced in Oklahoma in 1935.

BLACK SUNDAY: APRIL 14, 1935

The Dust Bowl years weren't all dark and dismal. There were days the air actually cleared and people could go outside, plough fields and plant in hopes that rain was around the corner. They went to church, cleaned thick dirt from their homes, picnicked, and appreciated tranquil times instead of the nightmare they often lived.

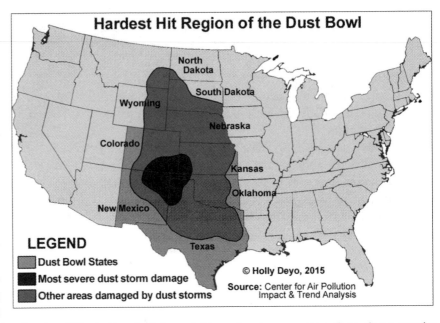

During the afternoon of April 14, under rare blue skies the temperature suddenly plunged and birds chirped fretfully. On the horizon a menacing black cloud fast approached. People on the roads looked for protection in any abandoned building, as it was impossible to navigate the swirling black mass. Those at home and caught outside couldn't even see the doorknobs. "Black Sunday's" punishing cloud came less than three weeks after dust storms wiped out 5 million acres of wheat.

The wall of blowing sand and dust first blasted Oklahoma's eastern panhandle and its northwestern area around 4p.m. It blew south and southeast across the main part of the state that evening, propelled by 40mph winds and plummeting temperatures. Worst hit was the Oklahoma and Texas panhandles, where the massive rolling wall of blowing dust resembled a land-based tsunami. While these "haboobs" are common in Phoenix and the Middle East, this was a strange sight in America's heartland. Winds in the panhandle reached 60mph and the blackness was so complete people couldn't see their outstretched hands.

An Oklahoma woman's letter describes what life was like trying to survive in June 1935. "In the dust-covered desolation of our No Man's Land here, wearing our shade hats, with handkerchiefs tied over our faces and Vaseline in our nostrils, we have been trying to rescue our home from the wind-blown dust which penetrates wherever air can go. It is almost a hopeless task, for there is rarely a day when, at some time the dust clouds do not roll over. 'Visibility' approaches zero and everything is covered again with a silt-like deposit, which may vary in depth from a film to actual ripples on the kitchen floor."[239]

These "dirt walls" were all too common. The weather service reported 14 that first year in 1931 and 38 the next. Any creature living outside risked death. Even with water soaked rags tied around their faces, people spat out dirt clods the size of pencils. A new disease ravaged the Plains: dust pneumonia. Animals died in the fields with two inches of dirt lining their stomachs. How anything survived is a mystery.

This was the decade of the double whammy. The Country was in the midst of the Great Depression when slapped with historic drought. Millions of people were forced out of their homes foreclosed on by banks and headed west looking for work. Two and a half million people comprised America's biggest migration in history. Conditions out West were little better for the struggling masses. They lived in tents erected on wooden platforms and earned

$.75 – $1.25 a day for picking fruit and cotton. Out of that wage, renting a tar paper shack without plumbing, electricity or a floor took 25 cents. Confronted with lack of sanitation and clean water, typhoid, malaria, smallpox and tuberculosis outbreaks were common.

The Dust Bowl was no small thing. It came in waves. In the High Plains it lasted eight excruciating years. At the peak in 1934, 80% of CONUS was in some state of drought.

Was this an isolated event? No, and they're coming more frequently – like quickening heartbeats.

Three More Epic Droughts

The 1950s: Between 1950 and 1956 drought scoured the Great Plains and Southwest. The evil twins of hot temperatures and little rain combined to put 58% of the land in moderate to extreme drought. In some places crops were cut in half. Worst hit Texas experienced a 7-year dry spell worse than the Dust Bowl days. The land baked and cracked and even the hardiest grasses shriveled. Wells dried up, creeks turned to sand, crops withered and cows cried pitifully. Cattlemen couldn't keep their herds alive even with emergency supplies from the federal government. Every person, every animal was desperate for rain. Eighty-year-old rancher Eugene Kelton in west Texas remembered how tough it was. "A cow'd get down and they'd be layin' there bawlin', you know, and those wild hogs be eatin' on 'em. They just started eatin' on her while she's alive. I fell out with hogs right there."[240]

Drought left a nasty imprint and the decade that ended in 1960 saw 100,000 farms and ranches disappear. Afterwards Texas took big steps to ensure drought never again decimated the lands by doubling the number of reservoirs. This worked well until 2005 when a series of droughts again cursed the Lone Star state.

1988-1989: This drought's deadly tentacles stretched across more than a third of the U.S. inflicting nearly $80 billion in damages. Harvests dropped sharply and hurt production of three major grains. Corn fell by a third, soybeans dropped 21% and spring wheat plummeted by <u>half</u>. The next year winter wheat was clobbered. Shocking. Something of this magnitude truly scuttles logic. It shouldn't happen in the world's leading Nation, not in The Land of Plenty. But it did. As fields began to resemble bleached bones, farmers were driven out of business.

The drought brought the worst dirt-blowing events since the Dust Bowl days. In February 1988 South Dakota schools were forced to close. In spring, weather stations set all-time records for lowest rainfalls and the longest time between rains. Summer 1988 saw two record-setting heatwaves like those of 1934 and 1936. NOAA estimates 7,500 people succumbed to heat deaths.[241] During summer 1988, drought led to many wildfires, including catastrophic fires in Yellowstone. Barge traffic, which hauls 45% of all bulk goods like grain, coal and petroleum shipping in the central U.S., halted during June and July. People worked feverishly to dredge the Mississippi to accommodate the 20-foot drop in water, the task wasn't completed before the industry lost a billion dollars.

Though it covered less territory than the Dust Bowl, 1988 ranks as not only the costliest drought in United States history but also the costliest natural disaster second only to Hurricane Katrina. In Canada, drought losses added to another $3.7 billion. The drought drug on and wasn't officially over till 1990.

For farmers it was excruciatingly, but it was overshadowed by many other billion-dollar weather extremes. Nobody really pays attention to drought because it's a "slumber" event. It's not a brain shaking 8.2 earthquake or a volcano eruption. Drought is a slow, more all encompassing, long-range disaster. Because it might not affect people directly until they go to the grocery store and see food prices have jumped 35%, they pretty much put drought on "ignore". It's somebody else's problem.

And Now – The Present:

TEXAS' UNRELENTING DROUGHT

Always in a state of extremes, drought raised its ugly head again in 2005 costing the state over $1.5 billion.[242] Governor Perry declared all 254 counties of Texas disaster areas. By August of the next year, 77% of the hay destined for cattle feed was dead. Crop losses hit a stunning $4.1 billion for the year.[243] If the drought weren't enough to deal with, by the second week of March 2006, wildfires charred about a million acres of the Texas Panhandle, destroyed homes and ranches, and killed 10,000 horses and cattle.

In 2007 weather flipped to the other extreme and Texas was deluged. Victoria, halfway between Houston and Corpus Christi – was drenched with 66 inches of rain.[244] While it helped with the death-dealing dryness, relief was short-lived and dryness was already underway before the year was out. In 2008, Texas was saddled with drought again. It intensified through 2009 dropping the Lone Star state into the worst dry period since 2000.

September 2008 to September 2009 became the driest one-year period *ever* for Texas, costing the state's cattle industry over $1 billion. By August, South Texas had seen less than four inches of rain. Dryland crops - ones that aren't irrigated - were total losses in South and Central Texas, along the Gulf Coast and the Rio Grande Valley. Stocks of goats, sheep, honey and horses were also hit. Climatologists said it was the worst drought in 50 years to hit Texas – that the back of the horrible 2008-2009 drought was finally broken. Except it wasn't. Drought redoubled its angry fist with a vengeance.

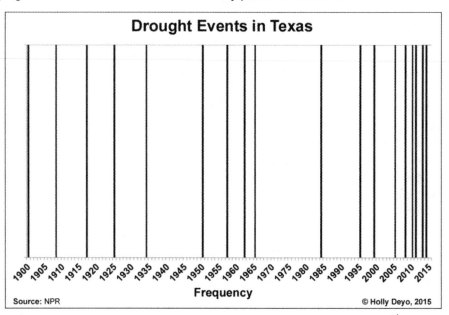

Texas has recently experienced some of the worst drought struggles on record. This has hurt the 2nd largest food-producing state in America and all of the U.S. for that matter. What began in 2008 continued unrelentingly through 2011 when the entire state was gripped in exceptional dryness – the most severe category – on U.S. Drought Monitor maps.

Newspapers showed pictures of exceedingly emaciated cattle and others that simply died of thirst. Cattlemen did their best to get them to market but some didn't make it in time and perished painfully. Other ranchers drove herds north to greener pastures. The *Austin American-Statesman* newspaper printed some of most shocking photos of Texas's dire drought conditions – too graphic to include here. Ranchers weren't being intentionally cruel. Many thought the drought would turn around in the next few months, but it didn't. Photos showed:

- Cows with their ribs and hipbones barely covered by shrunken hides.
- Some stuck in dry-caked former water holes too weak to extricate themselves.
- Farmers making last-ditch efforts bottle feeding full-grown cattle water trying to save their lives.
- Boats stranded on their sides in lake beds that used to contain water.
- Firefighters working in 100°+ weather working to save homes from burning down.
- A farmer kneels in the middle of his 800 acres that should be rich green with cotton. Instead, a few plants fight to stand 8 inches high in tan cracked soil.
- Field upon field of dead corn meets the eye. When corn is even produced, husks are peeled back to reveal few kernels and blackened silks.
- A cow looks for a blade of grass in the bottom of her pond. Instead she's met with 4" of hard cracked mud
- Pastures that should be verdant green are devoid of vegetation.
- Catfish can barely move when their ponds have dwindled to a few inches.
- Millions of dead trees are silhouetted against the morning sky.
- The carcass of a young deer lies on the ground near a dried-up creek likely abandoned by its mother. The fawn's ears, eyes and lips are missing.
- A sign on Pelican Point Resort's boat ramp warning of "No Lifeguard on Duty" and "No Diving" is thousands of feet away from the last remaining speck of water.
- Utility workers repair water main breaks all over Austin where land has sunk and broke the pipes.
- "Pray for Rain" signs tacked to fence posts and barbed wire.
- Emaciated longhorns wait in their pens to be auctioned
- Ranchers gather at a downtown park in Fredericksburg to pray for rain.

MORE IMPACTS

Despite Texas doubling the number of reservoirs after the crippling drought of the 1950s, it wasn't enough to combat the new rounds of extreme dryness.

This author's favorite aunt used to describe blistering miserable days as "hotter than the hinges of hell." Residents of Wichita, Texas, close to the Oklahoma border, must have thought they'd arrived when September 13, 2011 saw the 100th day of 100° weather[245] – and no rain. Some parts got the wet stuff, but not nearly enough.

In January 2010, the *New York Times* reported an end to "the worst drought to strike Texas in the last 50 years," but by May the state climatologist said "areas of Texas [were] facing drought conditions again."[246] The drought that began in the fall of that year resulted in the single driest year in recorded Texas history and hadn't abated by the end of 2014.

In September 2011 wildfires tore across the state. The most devastating fire complex in Bastrop County scorched over 34,000 acres and destroyed more than 1,300 homes. Climatologists said it was the worst drought in 50 years to hit Texas. Farmers and ranchers directly lost nearly $8 billion in crops and livestock in 2011, which is HALF of what Texas contributes to the Nation's food supply every year.[247]

Texas' drought didn't just decimate cattle, hay and pastures. Growers had to abandon the equivalent of 55% planted cotton. Wheat was down 47%. Corn 46%. Grains 50%. Grain sorghum lost a whopping 60%. Losses estimated at nearly $8 billion in 2011 didn't include their all-important contributions of fruits and vegetables, peanuts, horticultural and nursery crops. The 500 million drought-dead trees were valued at $558 for their timber. Those harvested for lumber have trunks 5 inches or larger so this number omitted another $111 million for seedlings and saplings, which are normally more susceptible to severe drought of this magnitude.[248]

One of the more mind-boggling repercussions from the 2011 drought was the staggering loss of trees. The Texas Forest Service estimates that drought wiped out 500 million forest trees and another 5.6 million in urban areas.[249] Imagine looking around your neighborhood, your town, and think how bare it would be without trees. These weren't killed in wildfires or lightning strikes. Drought strangled them.

As drought dragged on into 2013 many smaller ranchers were forced to cull their herds when 40% of the pastureland hit "poor to very poor" conditions. Besides contending with nearly no rain, heat attracted a plague of pests that continued to denude native grazing grasses. Rangelands were in tatters and Mark Svoboda of the National Drought Mitigation Center worried that even when rains returned to normal it would take two to three years for them to get to even 75% of what they should be. In addition to pasture worries, drought took its toll on

newborns. Calves were weighing 100-150 lbs. less than normal and born a month late.

Jay O'Brien owns the oldest privately held ranch covering more than a million acres of the Texas Panhandle. It's been in the family since 1876 and they've endured numerous harsh droughts. Of this one Jay shares their survival strategy.

"Normally we use about half of our country for yearlings and half for cows, and we do that as a safety valve. In 2011, we destocked [sold] all of our yearlings, and so we've spread the cows over the whole ranch. We've been able to maintain our cow herd. Now, if this drought [2013] continues another year, we'll have to sell some cows and we'll just destock in order to maintain the ranch...."[250]

Photo: Over 500 million trees that survived the previous drought succumbed in 2011 like this one in Austin, TX. (Courtesy John S. Quarterman)

At all costs, ranchers want to avoid completely liquidating their 4-legged assets. It's not like when farmers encounter crop-killing drought and can choose to replant or wait for the next growing season. Ranchers still have to provide feed and water no matter what nature throws at them. If they have to sell off an entire herd, with many other owners in the small situation, it forces down the price per head. If they've waited too long, the cattle have likely lost weight further pushing down their value. When it comes time to rebuild their herd, it's usually at a premium. This isn't done overnight as it generally requires at least three years to reestablish a herd. In the meantime, cash is all outgoing while they try to survive. For the consumer, the glut of beef drives down the cost in grocery stores, but prices will boomerang. Within a couple of years prices shoot up. In 2014, prices went up 10% compared to just a year before. In 2011, a pound of hamburger cost Americans $2.95. Four years later, it had doubled. From 2013 to 2014, brisket went up 61%.[251] At this rate, many people won't be able to afford even the most basic cuts of meat.

Texas is one of the most water-conscientious states, considerably better than California, and making it through exceptionally dry times is tops on politicians lists. Of the top three food-producing states – California, Texas and Iowa in that order – the top two are most often hit with killing drought.

Unfortunately the much anticipated rain from the 2015-2016 El Niño was a dud for Southern California. Instead its moisture ended further north from San Francisco to Washington state. As of spring 2016 their hellish drought continues.

CALIFORNIA'S DEADLY DROUGHT

California's extreme drought – the worst in 1,200 years – is well into year four.[252] In 2014, damages had already climbed over $2 billion and eliminated 17,000 jobs. Analysts project 2015's bill to add another $3 billion. This translates to higher costs in grocery stores raising prices for fruits and vegetables from 13% to 34%.[253] Experts report there is no end in sight to the drought either. They estimate that 11 TRILLION gallons of water would be needed to eliminate their extreme dryness.[254]

California's drought got so bad that people began stealing water from canals, fire hydrants, fire trucks, and from each other. One industrious person actually dug under the street and tapped into the water main. Another sneaky individual boosted a tanker while the truck sat idling and made off with 500 gallons. In Oakland, East Bay Municipal Utility District is imposing fines for stealing water from fire hydrants. First time offenders are charged $500 and $1,000 for a second violation. People are desperate for H_2O and none more so than farmers.

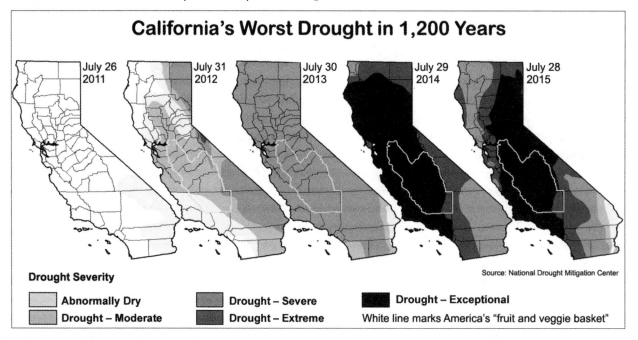

America's Fruit and Veggie Basket

Farmers are facing financial ruin and shoppers are seeing higher prices. More than third of America's vegetables and two-thirds of fruits and nuts are produced in California – over 200 crops. Some are grown nowhere else in the Nation like almonds, artichokes, dates, figs, olives, persimmons, pistachios, pomegranates, prunes, raisins, and walnuts. Only Florida produces more oranges than the Golden State and Texas grows more cotton. To keep animals fed and cereal manufacturers supplied, California produces hay, rice, corn, sugar beets, and wheat in large quantities. California is big into milk, beef cattle, eggs, sheep, turkeys, hogs and horses – the second largest livestock producer right behind Texas.

Of the top five agricultural states, California leads the way in food production followed by Iowa, Texas, Nebraska and Minnesota.[255] In terms of natural disasters, Texas tops all 50 states as hit hardest followed by California. All of these states have dealt with killing drought or waterlogged fields, but the drought gripping The Golden State and The Lone Star is unrelenting. Could this be a cog slipping into place for the prophesied famine?

Here are California's top crops[256] – many of which fill of plates, cover our bodies and fill our homes and businesses with beauty.

Crops and Livestock Where California Leads the Nation[257]				California's Top 20 Commodities[258]
VEGETABLES & MELONS	CA % OF U.S. TOTAL	FRUITS, NUTS & MILK	CA % OF U.S. TOTAL	
Artichokes	**100**	**Almonds**	**100**	Almonds
Asparagus	46	Apples	2	Grapes
Beans	13	Apricots	86	Cattle & Calves
Broccoli	96	Avocados	86	Berries
Cabbage	31	Berries, Blueberries	8	Walnuts
Carrots	83	Berries, Raspberries	56	Lettuce
Cauliflower	89	Berries, Strawberries	91	Hay
Celery	95	Cherries, Sweet	10	Tomatoes
Corn, Sweet	21	**Dates**	**100**	Nursery
Cucumbers	10	**Figs**	**100**	Flowers & Plants
Garlic	**98**	Grapefruit, All	15	Pistachios
Lettuce, Head	72	Grapes, All	88	Broccoli
Lettuce, Leaf	85	**Kiwifruit**	**100**	Rice
Lettuce, Romaine	72	Lemons	91	Oranges
Melons, Cantaloupe	63	Nectarines	94	Cotton
Melons, Honeydew	76	**Olives**	**100**	Carrots
Melons, Watermelon	16	Oranges, All	29	Celery
Mushroom, Agaricus	14	Peaches, Clingstone	73	Peppers
Onions, All	31	Peaches, All	73	Eggs & Chicken
Peppers, Bell	60	Pears, All	24	Other Poultry
Peppers, Chile	69	Pecans	2	
Potatoes, Sweet	18	**Pistachios**	**100**	
Pumpkins	15	**Plums**	**97**	
Rice, Sweet	**99**	**Prunes**	**97**	
Spinach	70	**Pomegranates**	**99**	
Squash	18	Tangerine Family	80	
Tomatoes, Fresh	37	**Walnuts**	**100**	
Tomatoes, Processing	96	Milk & Cream	21	
California is the sole producer (97% or more) of foods in **bold**.				

California is also #1 producer of cut flowers, potted plants, foliage plants, flower bedding plants, and houseplants. Don't start your home veggie gardens from seed? California is also the #1 grower of nursery and vegetable plants.

Taking Its Toll

In both 2014 and 2015, a half million acres of farmland went unplanted, costing the state's agricultural industry $1.5 billion and 17,000 seasonal and part time jobs. Think we can do without California crops? They could always be imported, but at what cost?

Extreme dryness is slowly killing California's agricultural business. Almond, olive and apricot trees are all being demolished at record speed. What once was considered a clever move – to switch to fruit and nut trees that don't have to be replanted every year – like peppers, beans or cauliflower – has now boomeranged. At least with a row crop, the tractor can be parked for the year or the farmer can choose to plant only half of his fields. With orchards, it's a year-round commitment. Fruit and nut trees aren't like tomato or lettuce plants where after a month or two crops are ready for picking. It takes a long time for trees to be mature enough to produce fruit and nuts – sometimes as much as 8 or 10 years depending on variety, its graft stock and a host of other factors.

FISH VS. FARMER

In summer of 2015 those in Tracy's Banta-Carbona Irrigation District, 50 miles due east of San Francisco, were ordered by the state water board to stop pumping river water for crop irrigation. Tracy is located in the heart of America's food basket – at the north end of the San Joaquin Valley – outlined in white in the California drought map. To cut off farmers' water is terribly short sighted. They literally help feed the world.

It all began a decade ago with conservationists wanting to save the smelt – a tiny fish used as bait. Though it's short-lived and rather unremarkable, it was full-throttle to save the smelt. Water was diverted from farmers to support the mighty smelt. A ten-year long battle ensued in court and out. By January 2015, California's notoriously liberal Ninth Circuit Court affirmed that water projects were jeopardizing the delta smelt's existence and that endangered species must be saved "whatever the cost".[259] If Banta-Carbona's irrigation suit is denied in court, they face fines of $22 million *a month* and it could cost farmers another $200 million in the loss of their orchards and vineyards.

WATER WISE-NOTS

Compounding the smelt drama came this once-in-1200-year drought that's strangling crops and farmers' livelihoods. For the first time in the last 40 years, California is trying to get a handle on the water situation. In 2014, legislators asked people to voluntary cut back water usage by 25%. That went completely unheeded. Everyone wanted lush lawns, beautiful landscape and long showers. By 2015, even the most hardheaded Californian realized they were in crisis mode.

California was the only state that didn't regulate groundwater pumping until recently. Though Gov. Brown passed new groundwater controls in 2014, they don't go into effect until 2020, some not for two decades. Senior climatologist Bill Patzert said the Central Valley Aquifer has been there for about 10,000 years. But between uncontrolled pumping and relentless drought not recharging the aquifer, no one can say how much is left or how much longer it will last. Scientists estimate that about 80 million acre-feet have been sucked out since 1962 and one quarter of that just in the last decade.[260]

With new restrictions coming, well diggers are booked as much as two years in advance. They want wells in place before the mighty clamp down takes effect. Central Valley Aquifer wells that used to strike water at 500 feet now have to be drilled to 1,000 feet or more, at a cost of more than $300,000 a well.[261] Despite this unprecedented drought and farmers in dire straits, swimming pool construction could hit the highest level since 2007 with plans for another 13,000 to be built in 2015. Celebrities are apparently tone deaf to the state's demand to cut back. Numerous news outlets report glitterati are totally ignoring the water crisis. However, a few like Jessica Simpson, Cher, Julia Roberts and Jennifer Anniston either have allowed brown patches to creep into their lawns or tore out water-sucking plants and replaced them with watering-saving counterparts. Even notoriously liberal energy conservation activist Barbra Streisand is on the "shame list"[262] – along with quite a few others. The $100 fine for overstepping water usage isn't even enough for the chauffeur's tip.

CALIFORNIA'S SINKING "SHIP"

Alarm bells are clanging. While the Central Valley Aquifer runs about 400 miles under the Sacramento and San Joaquin Valleys, enough water has been extracted to make the entire area sink over a foot and in some parts, nearly 30 feet.[263] This picture of Joseph Poland tells the story of a 29-foot subsidence marked on this telephone pole from 1925 to 1977. Since then drought and groundwater irrigation has deepened the crisis.

Some hotspots are shrinking at incredible rates. The Tulare Basin, which includes Fresno and Bakersfield, sank 13 inches in just 8 months. The Sacramento Valley is sinking ½" every four weeks and the California Aqueduct – a critical network of pipes, canals and tunnels that moves water from the Sierra Nevada Mountains in the north and central part of the state to southern California – has sunk a foot. Most of that occurred in just four months of 2014.[264] Subsidence has cracked irrigation canals, derailed trains, cracked and caused houses to be condemned, disrupted utilities, contaminated ground water and buckled roads. It has already destroyed thousands of public and private groundwater well casings in the San Joaquin Valley.

Photo: Joseph Poland of the U.S. Geological Survey stands next to a utility pole southwest of Mendota in 1977. Poland determined the ground had sunk almost 30 feet between 1925 and 1977. The signs tacked on the pole show where the ground level was at various times during the 52-year period. It gives the location "San Joaquin Valley California BM [bench mark] S661 Subsidence 9M [29½ feet] 1925 – 1977". Since then, the pole has been replaced, and there are no signs now. Scientists believe the ground has sunk another 10 feet since 1977 for a total of nearly 40 feet. (Courtesy US Geological Survey)

More disturbing though, is the subsidence on either side of this aquifer that runs parallel to the San Andreas Fault. (See next map.) Without that water weight to hold the Pacific and North American tectonic plates in place, it could make the state much more vulnerable to earthquakes.

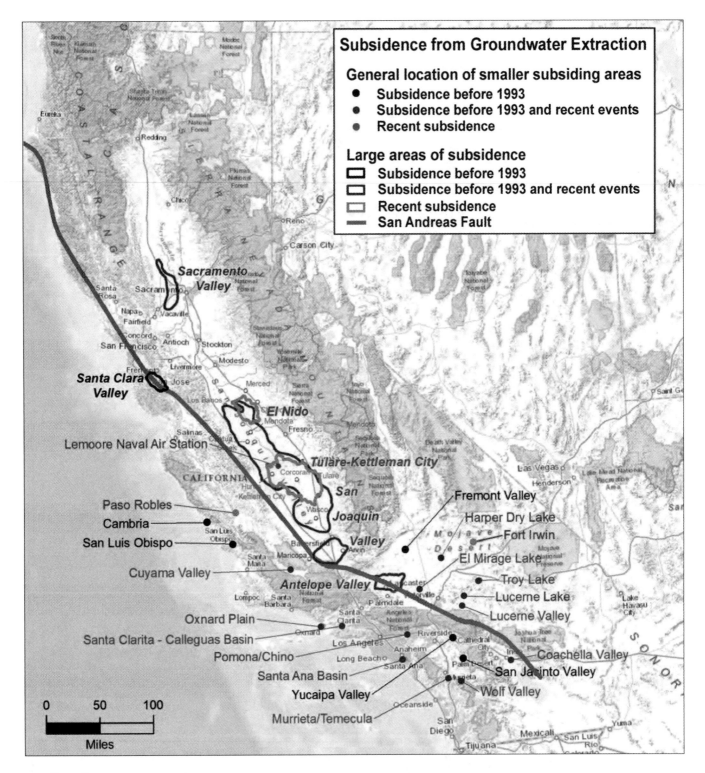

Fukushima Factor

All around Japan their soil, water, plants and animals are contaminated. "A large range of Japanese foodstuffs, including spinach, tea leaves, milk, beef, and freshwater fish up to 200 miles from Fukushima"[265] aren't safe due to high levels of cesium-137. Its half-life is 30 years so it will remain hazardous for decades. Animals higher up the food chain are more highly poisoned since animals accumulate radiation when one animal consumes another. For example, a whale would likely have more amassed radiation than plankton. Hardly anyone talks about strontium-90 that goes into bones. Japanese as well as other Asian people tend to make a lot of fish stews cooking the bones right along with everything else, which add even more radiation.

Nuclear engineer Arnie Gundersen made alarming discoveries when he was in Fukushima for a month in early 2016. He says that one year after the Chernobyl reactor blew up in Ukraine, scientists and engineers knew exactly where its core was. All three cores at Fukushima are "missing". Many experts believe that they burned through the concrete floors of the power plants, broke through containment and are in direct contact with groundwater. In a further comparison to Chernobyl, Gundersen says, "It's absolutely clear that the noble gases like Xenon and Krypton were three times higher [at Fukushima] than Chernobyl. I don't think anybody debates that. The IAEA isn't taking that into account when they look at the exposure to people. To give you an idea of how severe it was, the noble gases over Seattle 400,000 times higher than normal after Fukushima. That's clearly worse than Chernobyl. The one thing that everyone focuses on is cesium and I just got back from a month there and I was chasing cesium all through Fukushima prefecture. There's probably half the cesium that was released form Chernobyl in Fukushima. If you look at it in aggregate, more noble gases, much more liquids [released] and perhaps probably roughly the same amount of cesium, Fukushima was worse than Chernobyl."[266]

Japan's wildlife is suffering terrible repercussions. Gundersen and scientists followed a monkey up into the mountains and picked up its poop and tested it. It measured an astronomical 50,000 becquerels per kilogram. As vegetarians, these monkeys eat everything in the forest so the exposure goes straight into their gut. They're already getting cataracts. A hunter gave Gundersen and his colleagues some wild boar meat, which they tested before thinking to eat it. They found it contained three times the amount of normal background cesium and their studies showed that Japan's forest animals are highly contaminated. Fukushima has also affected vegetables grown in Japan. They found lots of cases of gargantuanism, which is a result of radiation exposure and makes veggies exceptionally large. It shows up in the second-generation vegetables and especially in the third.

Gundersen shared that Tepco, Tokyo Electric Power Company, should do more, but the amount of uninhabitable land is enormous – the size of Vermont. He says Tepco has "no intention of cleaning the whole state. What they've done is they have these bags – 30 million 1-ton bags, 30 million tons of radioactive stuff they've picked up along the sides of the road and directly in the towns' centers and that's it. Once they've cleaned an area they're not going back. But what we've found is that these supposedly clean areas are being re-contaminated. The wind and the rain and the movement of dust everywhere is re-contaminating areas that Tepco claims are clean.

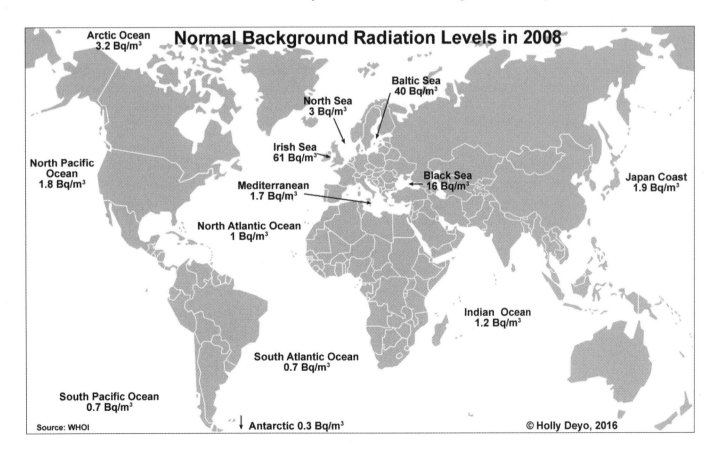

"I was in one spot in a parking lot and there was this black material on the edge of the parking lot so we put our spectro radiation detector down. Ohmygod, it was hotter than a pistol. This is an occupied parking lot with cars and to my right is about 20 of these 1-ton bags in somebody's backyard. Tepco cleaned it up, but didn't move them. And to my left is about 50 of these 1-ton bags in somebody else's yard. The fact is I got more that 100,000 Bq. per kilogram from that black dust in the middle of a town that people are living in.

"The most hideous is on top of Minamisoma town hall. Minamisoma is one of those cities that was evacuated and they've let people back in so there's 60,000 people in this town. We decided to check the sidewalks and they're hotter than a pistol. On the roof of the town hall they had put solar collectors in a year ago and they had completely cleaned the roof and painted the roof and put these beautiful solar collectors in. I noticed this black dust underneath these solar collectors. Oh my god, it's pegging the meter. So what's happening, is how can dust get to the fourth story of a building? It's blowing in the wind. So Tepco doesn't want to acknowledge this airborne dose to children, to adults everything Tepco claimed to have cleaned and I don't think they did a good job – but even assuming they did a good job – everything they claimed to have cleaned is highly radioactive again."[267]

In early 2016, Fukushima power plants were still hemorrhaging. Gundersen said that the Fukushima power plants continue "to bleed into the Pacific every day. But what no one is paying any attention to is that the entire mountain range that runs 100 miles up and down this coast is also contaminated. And as much radiation is pouring out… into the Pacific from the mountain range because it's so contaminated, as from the Fukushima site… In fact, they've got an entire state pouring radiation into the Pacific. So what's in the Pacific? Off of California, they're finding radiation at what I would consider significant levels… In a cubic meter of ocean water they're finding 10 becquerels per cubic meter…and that's going to go on for 300 years. So we have contaminated the biggest source of water on the planet, and there's no way to stop it.

"It used to be that scientists believed dilution is the solution to pollution. But I think we're finding with the biggest body of water on the planet, that you can't dilute this stuff. And we're going to begin to see this bio-accumulation, which is all the fish that are in the ocean are going to uptake the cesium and the strontium and become more and more and more radioactive…"[268]

Fukushima's radioactive ocean water arrived at the U.S. West Coast several years ago. In 2008, cesium-137 background radiation in oceans and seas was sampled around the world by Woods Hole Oceanographic Institution to establish normal levels. Measurements varying from this map indicate something has changed. Woods Hole knew the Irish Sea is elevated due to radioactive releases from England's Sellafield nuclear facility at Seacastle. Levels in the Baltic and Black Seas are higher due to fallout from the 1986 Chernobyl explosion. Japan had some of the best ratings until the Fukushima-Daiichi fiasco. In 2011 waters closest to the Fukushima plant had concentrations of up to 60 *million* becquerels per cubic meter (Bq/m^3) – enough to cause serious reproductive and health problems.[269] **NOTE**: Though Revelation 8:8-10 sounds like it describes a huge meteor crashing down, radiation in water may play a role in how ⅓ of all sea life perish and ⅓ of the world's water is poisoned.

America's Food Basket

It's not just America that depends on homegrown crops. California, Iowa, Illinois, Minnesota, Nebraska and Texas are the top six U.S. food exporters around the world. Out of all the foods shipped from the U.S., six states make up 40%. Rounding out the top ten are Kansas, Indiana, Washington and Ohio. They ship food to 34 different countries from Argentina and Venezuela with the top five being China, Canada, Mexico and Japan. Canada and Mexico used to be the two biggest importers, but from 2008 to 2014 China more than doubled their food purchases from America. This might be one reason China is buying up large portions of America.

Keep in mind the frequent droughts that plague Texas and the unrelenting drought California is suffering, then look again at the map of the epic floods in 1993 and 2008. Every one of the top 10 food-producing states was in the crosshairs of these crop-killing floods except Washington and Ohio. In 2015, Washington, where it normally receives lots of rain, was gripped by drought. This brought the state's most catastrophic ever wildfire season burning over 1 million acres.

The USDA reported in 2015 that California's prolonged drought would have significant impact on fruit, vegetables, beef, nuts, milk and dairy prices.

So when these states have disasters during crop growing time, it doesn't just affect availability and pricing in America, but around the world. All it takes to create food shortages and panic, and in a really bad scenario – famine – is to have disasters affecting several countries at once.

Then there's the stupidity of just-in-time inventory.

Top 30 U.S. Agricultural Destinations

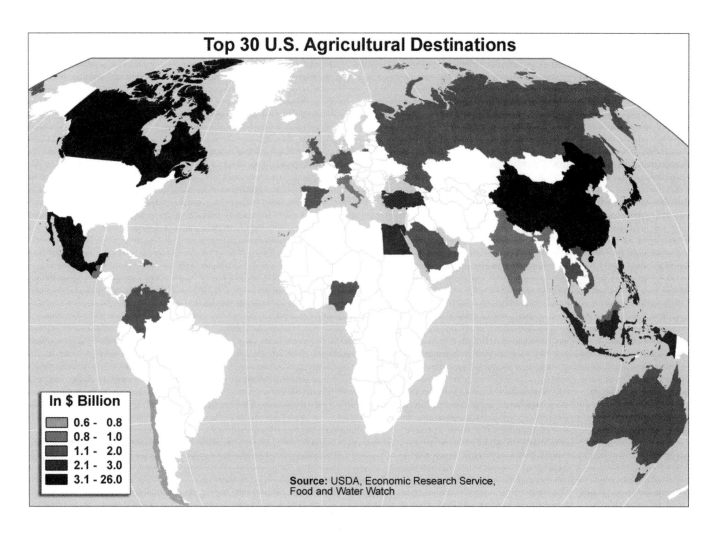

In $ Billion
- 0.6 - 0.8
- 0.8 - 1.0
- 1.1 - 2.0
- 2.1 - 3.0
- 3.1 - 26.0

Source: USDA, Economic Research Service, Food and Water Watch

Food Supplies Severely Impaired: Just-In-Time

In the early 1900s, Americans lived a different lifestyle. More than half of the population lived rurally and produced their food. They had their own water well. They were self-sufficient. By mid-century, only 43% of Americans lived on farms. Today with mechanized farming and years of young people migrating to cities, this number has shrunk to just 1%.

Grocery stores have also changed over the years. In the 1990s fully stocked on-site warehouses vanished and companies switched to just-in-time inventories. Backup stock dropped to a mere 3-day supply. As of 2015, stores have whittled inventory to a shaky 1½-day reserve. Soft drinks, chips, fresh produce and other perishables are brought in daily. Typically little to no back stock exists.

Since 2008 a growing number of people report that when they check grocery store shelves, beyond one or two boxes neatly lining the front edge there is nothing behind them. To the casual eye, shelves look neatly filled, but are barely half to a third stocked.

Replenishing trucks roll to and from stores with the precision of a marching band. What happens when the band stops playing? There is a growing likelihood of an EMP event occurring or a coordinated cyber-attack shutting down GPS and computers logging inventory control. The more frightening event, an ElectroMagnetic Pulse, could effectively kill computer chips in electronics and zap power grids around the world. With "dead" chips, life as we know it stops and would prevent groceries from getting to stores.

Most people don't grow their own food with the exception of little home vegetable gardens. Though over a third of American households have home them, they generally plant only veggies. A few grow fruit, but there's a huge hole in the protein department. Too, folks often don't grow enough for canning to sustain them through winter. Despite an upward trend in home and community food gardening, unless an area has enough rain, plants will die quickly without electricity to get water to gardens from treatment plants.

The other issue paralleling this scenario is food storage. If only freeze-dried or dehydrated foods are kept at home, people will be reduced to eating very crunchy dry chunks. It's better than starving, but not choice. Both of these type foods require an ample and steady supply of potable water for reconstitution. That's why this author recommends in *Dare To Prepare* to keep at least ⅓ of all stored foods in the form of canned goods. They're ready to eat even if heat is unavailable. All that's needed is a can opener.

Who Feeds the World?

It's not just America that depends on this Nation's crops. California, Iowa, Illinois, Minnesota, Nebraska and Texas are the top U.S. food exporters to the world. Six states make up 40% of all food shipped from the U.S. Rounding out the top ten are Kansas, Indiana, Washington and Ohio. When these 10 states have a bad growing season, it doesn't just affect availability and prices in America, but around the world. The U.S. sends food to 34 countries from Argentina to Venezuela with the top four being China, Canada, Mexico and Japan. Canada and Mexico used to be the two biggest importers, but from 2008 to 2014 China more than doubled American food purchases. This is one reason China is buying up large portions of America, Australia and Africa - so they have a guaranteed supply.

Since 2002, the top food exporting countries have remained the same and in this order: United States, Brazil, Netherlands, Germany, France, Canada, China, Spain, Belgium, Argentina, Italy and Australia. The only thing different in 2012 is the *amount* of food that's sent to other countries. It's grown significantly.

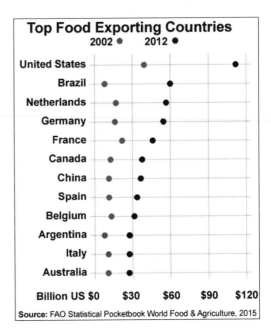

Livestock is the Netherlands' main export. For France, it's wheat, sugar, wine, and beef. Brazil's largest exports are coffee, soybeans, beef, sugar cane, ethanol and frozen chickens. From America foods in highest demand are corn, wheat, soybeans, fruits, nuts, beef and dairy. Canada ships out wheat, canola, cattle and soybeans. Germany's top exports are milk, dairy and cereals. China's main contributions are vegetables, rice, apples, tangerines, oranges and sugarcane. There is a surprising *lack* of export overlap except for beef. So for food supplies, dependency has become a global thing. If one country is unable to export in a given year, it leaves a major hole in world supplies.

RUSSIA

Massive drought hit Russia in 2010 and knocked out 25% of their grain crops. It reminded those alive in the early 60s of the drought that prompted panic slaughtering of livestock.

Extreme weather events – especially drought, which is hardest on crops – are becoming increasingly common in Russia. The 2012 drought confirmed this trend coming right on the heels of the 2010 event. Even after repeated natural disasters, Russia still has only a few crop-saving measures in place. Oxfam, an international organization that analyzes poverty in nations says that in 2012, Russia suffered crop losses in half of its regions with states of emergency declared. They lost 25% of their sugar beet, sunflower,

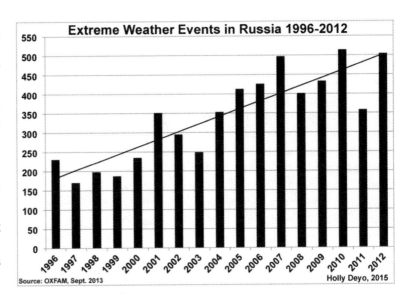

potato and vegetable crops pushing some farmers to the brink of bankruptcy. This is meaningful because small farmers provide well over half of Russia's food. Ranchers with livestock lost even more because the price of grain skyrocketed in 2012-2013. With Russia not being a major exporter and with increasing natural disasters, they will need to import more and more foodstuffs to feed their people.

BRAZIL

As of 2015 Brazil continues to grapple with ongoing drought – the worst in eight decades. Even though Brazil has the largest freshwater reserves in the world, their largest city – Sao Paulo – is running out of water. That's how bad the water shortage is, hurting one of the world's largest agricultural exporter. However, to play in this league, Brazil's farming irrigation accounts for 72% of their water use. This drought is causing massive crop losses in one of the country's agricultural centers.

In 2014 right in the midst of Brazil's worst drought in at least 50 years, it received the equivalent of two months' rain. Nearly 5 inches of rain fell in just a few hours and the hard-packed ground was unable to absorb it. NOAA states that they can expect intense, heavy downpours interspersed by long periods of drought. Not a good forecast for one of the world's food exporters.

U.S. ecologist with Brazil's Amazon Environmental Research Institute, Daniel Nepstad, said the multiple droughts in recent years are worrying. "I think it's reason for some pretty deep concern over the Amazon ecosystem. We're seeing the reliability of the seasons in the Amazon break down."[270]

CANADA

Even though extreme weather put crops under water, effectively drowning them, drought is the biggest crop killer. Extreme events like the 2001 and 2002 droughts and floods of 2010 and 2011 have had a devastating impact on crops with yields cut in half. Drought has primarily hit half of Canada – every province west of Saskatchewan (the middle of their country) and on the other side of the nation, parts of eastern Quebec and covering all of New Brunswick and Nova Scotia.

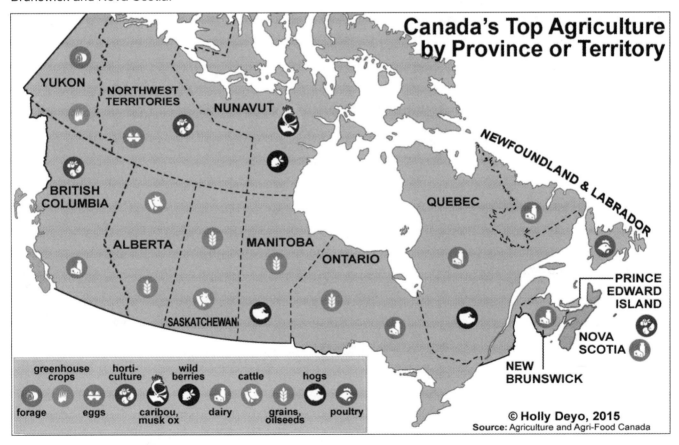

Exceptionally warm summers have also increased livestock deaths from heatwave. This was especially true for poultry, never mind that the 2015 avian flu wave forced the killing of nearly 50 million birds in America.[271] The price of chicken and turkey skyrocketed. Minnesota, the leading turkey producer, has lost nearly 9 million birds. Eggs went through the roof and in some states, egg purchases were rationed. One of America's largest grocery chains, H-E-B, posted signs in their Texas stores warning, "Eggs not for commercial sale. The purchase of eggs is limited to 3 cartons of eggs per customer."[272]

Canada's dry fall of 2013 was followed by the coldest winter in 18 years – the 3rd coldest on record. Harsh conditions in Canada's prairies and northwest Ontario, killed crops and forages, produced underweight cattle and increased livestock's risk of dying. 2014's growing season was tough again for food producers across Canada. They dealt with cool spring temperatures, flooding, drought, hail storms, summer snow and early frost. All of these conditions conspired to reduce crops by up to 30%. Record-cold temperatures also had farmers worrying about grain storage and it prohibited growers from transporting a lot of their grain across country. Droughts reduced milk and dairy production and beef cattle lost considerable weight. As a major exporter, this hurt food availability around the globe.

FRANCE

Since the early 1970s, people working France's farmland diminished by about 60%. This country more than any other in the EU exports more food and is the only European country that's completely self-sufficient. It's a leader in Europe's agricultural exports – chiefly wheat, cereal grains, sugar, wine and beef. However, it needs to import cotton, tobacco, and vegetable oils. No surprise France also grows a lot of fruit – mostly apples, pears, peaches and cherries. France grows crops on over 35% of its land, mostly owned by small farmers. In 2014 hundreds of vineyards and farms suffered "enormous damage" when torrential rains hit the region. Other crops were destroyed when floods overwhelmed greenhouses. They caused millions of dollars of damage in Montpellier alone, a renown grape growing city in southern France. Entire vines were swept away and mud was so deep farmers couldn't get out to assess the damage. Experts see France as "dangerously unprepared for natural disasters.

Here's another rub. Since France has an equal right's inheritance law – meaning you must divide any property equally among all children since there is no such thing as disinheritance. Often if one child wants to sell, it squashes the chance of maintaining the farm if other siblings aren't in a position for buyout. So some of their prime crop-growing lands are now used for businesses other than food production.

GERMANY

For some reason we don't hear much about natural disasters in Germany, but increasingly drought smacks this normally beautifully green country. Since 1951 excessive dryness has become a problem that's reducing grain and cereal crops by as much as 25%. In the European Union, Germany is the third largest producer of agricultural goods right behind France and Italy so when Germany loses, it's a big hit.

THE NETHERLANDS

Situated between Germany and France, it suffers many of the same natural disasters as those two countries. The Netherlands is one of the world's top three leaders in growing vegetables and fruit, supplying 25% of all vegetables exported from Europe. They also produce vast amounts of barley, corn, wheat, sugar beets, and potatoes exporting nearly half of the world's spuds. The Netherlands is also big into pig and dairy farming. Besides dairy cows, they raise beef cattle, chicken, duck, lamb, pork, and turkey. Eggs and beef are the main livestock exports. Add flowers into the mix and The Netherlands pretty much do it all. Timber is their only downfall as they have to import over 90% of all forest products.

According to the UN, the Netherlands is the most vulnerable country in all of Europe to natural disasters – primarily floods and droughts – the fraternal twins of catastrophe. Then there's the issue of sea level rise. The Netherlands has the unfortunate location of sitting below sea level. Their land is very low and very flat with only half of its land sitting three feet above sea level. That's how the country got its name, meaning Lower Countries. On its northwest side, the Netherlands has a number of fingers and islands stretching out into the North Sea. Much of the farmland is reclaimed swamps. While this makes for very rich soil, the swamps can certainly reclaim its land.

CHINA

China ranks first in worldwide farm output consisting mostly of rice, wheat, potatoes, tomato, sorghum, peanuts, tea and spices, millet, barley, cotton, oilseed and soybeans. They also export large quantities of fish and seafood, apples and dairy. Although it has only 8% of Earth's arable land, it produces food for a fifth of the world's people –

the 1.4 billion Chinese. Nine percent used to be the number bandied about for the percentage of their land that could grow crops, but in December 2013 China's Ministry of Land and Resources revealed the results of a 5-year secret study showing farmers had so fouled the farmland 2% – some 8 million acres – is now too polluted to grow food.[273]

Their mass production comes with a heavy price. China has a scandalous reputation for putting poisonous, deadly additives into an array of foodstuffs; incurring repeated salmonella infections, exposing foods to heavy metals and excessive pesticides, misusing veterinary drugs in foods, selling contaminated pork and pet treats, selling fake eggs and marketing fake honey, which tested out to be colored glucose water.[274] One can't forget China's exploding watermelons when farmers "mistakenly" injected them with the growth accelerant forchlorfenuron, Sichuan peppers releasing red dye in water, or cadmium-tainted rice, arsenic-laced soy sauce, chickens injected with barite powder to increase weight, bleach in mushrooms, or the borax detergent put in pork to make it look like beef.[275] They have passed off and sold dead rat as pork and had tens of thousands of lifeless pigs floating down their rivers.[276]

China's Method to Cope With Rising Food Prices – Just Kill 'em

When grain prices rose, small time milk and cattle feed farmers engaged in unethical practices. They began putting additives in milk, including potentially deadly melamine, so it registered a higher amount of protein. Literally hundreds of thousands of children fell ill, five died and 54,000 were hospitalized. This badly damaged China's milk exports and 11 countries banned them entirely. Upon exposure, company executives and officials were arrested and two were executed. Companies went bankrupt.[277] When China was busted on the melamine, they replaced it with something more difficult to detect – hydrolyzed leather protein made from scraps of animal skin.

Just a few months after the milk scandal broke, in October 2008 China was discovered to be adding melamine to eggs. These two terrible deadly disgraces came on the heels of their June 2007 crisis involving adulterated pet food. At least 4,000 dogs and cats died of renal failure and another 17,000 became sick after eating jerky treats from China.[278] The FDA was never able to pinpoint the cause even after running 1,000 tests, but there was no doubt about the country of origin. China.

In 2008 melamine was found in frozen fried chicken China exported to Japan and in powdered eggs shipped to Japan and South Korea. China's baking power exported to Malaysia was also found to contain the deadly chemical.

EXPANSION

In September 2013, Shuanghui International, China's biggest meat products company, purchased Smithfield Foods – a deal valued at $7.1 billion – in an effort to meet their insatiable taste for pork. This is the single largest takeover of an American company by China, which carved out 25% from the U.S. pork industry. Smithfield, whose headquarters is located in Virginia, also owned Armour, Eckrich and Gwaltney. Now China does. The Smithfield acquisition should really bump up China's pig count, as they already owned about 475 million porkers - 60% of the world's supply. Now it's considerably more.

An American woman living in China says that Shuanghui has been "plagued by constant reports here in this country [China] of meat infested with maggots, customers succumbing to food poisoning, and random testing that shows illegal levels of bacteria and illegal additives such as clenbuterol in their meat." Clenbuterol is a banned additive that keeps animals lean and their skin a healthy pink, but is lethal to humans when eaten. After the clenbuterol scandal was exposed, Shuanghui was forced to pull those meat products from store shelves for two years.

The Smithfield takeover "stirred concern among U.S. politicians" – especially Sen. Debbie Stabenow, Democrat from Michigan and chairwoman of the Senate agriculture committee. She worried, "To be sure, the purchase of one American food company does not jeopardize America's food independence. But Smithfield is our largest pork producer – will China or other countries seek to purchase our largest poultry, or dairy, or corn producers next? Is it in America's security interests if in a decade or two our food supply is 30, or 60, or 90 percent foreign owned?" She continued. "…We still do not know if the potential impact on American food security, the transfer of taxpayer funded innovation to a foreign competitor, or China's protectionist trade barriers were considered. It's troubling that taxpayers have received no assurances that these critical issues have been taken into account in transferring control of one of America's largest food producers to a Chinese competitor with a spotty record on food safety."[279]

Between foods standards far below those of the FDA and their extreme lack of hygiene, educated Chinese and those that can afford it shun their restaurants and prefer to cook at home.

Wenonah Hauter, Executive Director of Food & Water Watch, warns, "The recent USDA decision to allow processed chicken imports from China, coupled with news of the Smithfield-Shuanghui merger approval by shareholders and a federal review commission, shows that U.S. regulators are paving the way for meat imported from China – a country with a terrible food safety record.

"Smithfield wants the public to believe this merger is just about exporting pork to China. And the USDA is trying to soothe consumers by promising that imported processed poultry products will be made from U.S.-origin birds. But it is only a matter of time until these initial conditions ease and we are importing meat and poultry from China.

"U.S. consumers should know that the politics of trade are trumping common sense when it comes to our food. Our regulators shouldn't be making it easier for the chicken breasts or pork chops on our plates to be born, raised and slaughtered in China."[280]

Zhang Renwu, a businessman who owns two farms in Utah summed up their intentions quite clearly. "We want to bring American sunshine, land and water back to China."[281]

China's Woeful Water Contaminating Crops?

This same concern for poor food standards has flowed into China's drinking water. China has a huge and growing problem. Water scarcity. And clean water is nearly non-existent.

At first it might seem contradictory that the western side of China is at low risk for water shortage where rainfall isn't plentiful, and most of their 1.4 billion people live on the eastern half where crops are grown and rain is abundant. To put this into perspective, imagine a country roughly the same size as America's 48 states plus Alaska, but with over four times the population and crammed onto the land east of Texas. This heavy concentration of humanity and lack of clean water and food standards have produced toxic mix. Chemical runoff and other pollutants have contaminated 60% of China's aquifers.

Can you imagine any developed country dumping 16,000 dead rotting pigs with internal organs exposed into their drinking water?[282] Hope Lee, market research analyst for Euromonitor International, says you don't dare drink the tap water in China. Not only is their water really filthy before going to treatment plants, it becomes re-contaminated in degraded pipelines on the way to homes.[283] People who expressed fear over food and water contamination and protested these conditions were quickly muzzled. Zhao Lianhai was sentenced to 2½ years in jail for exposing the melamine scandal after his son was made ill from drinking tainted baby milk. He'd set up a website to warn other parents and Lianhai was charged with inciting public disorder.[284] It's like the veil of governmental silence that enveloped Japan after Fukushima's nuclear disaster.

The New York Times writes, "If you think China's air is bad... For visitors, China's water problem becomes apparent upon entering the hotel room. The smell of a polluted river might emanate from the showerhead. Need to quench your thirst? The drip from the tap is rarely potable. Can you trust the bottled water? Many Chinese don't. What about brushing your teeth?

"Measured by the government's own standards, more than half of the country's largest lakes and reservoirs were so contaminated in 2011 that they were unsuitable for human consumption. China's more than 4,700 underground water-quality testing stations show that nearly three-fifths of all water supplies are 'relatively bad' or worse. Roughly half of rural residents lack access to drinking water that meets international standards."[285]

Quality is so bad that those who can afford it buy *foreign* bottled water. Chinese don't even trust their country to uphold decent water standards at their own bottling plants. One of China's biggest water suppliers is Nestle. Nestle predicts China will purchase $16 billion of bottled water by 2017.[286] Where does Nestle get a lot of its water? Straight from Canada, the U.S. Great Lakes and aquifers on California Indian reservations. Wait, isn't California in the midst of an epic drought? Doesn't matter. Nestle sucks 250,000 gallons a day from Lake Michigan[287] 2013 – the last year when reports were available – showed that Nestle tapped into 600 feet of groundwater on the Morongo Reservation, which translates to about 200 million gallons a year.[288]

And Now... Drought

Compounding matters, chronic drought plagues China and 2015 brought the worst one in 60 years. Even before the drought hit aquifers in Inner Mongolia, water levels had dropped over 250 feet. Crops and people suffered. Corn was only half its normal height and lettuce and other vegetable yields shrank. Groundwater levels hit historic lows in northeast and in central China where hundreds of millions of people live. Reservoirs were so dry in agricultural Henan province that Pingdingshan city closed car washes and bathhouses, and people were forced to extract water from puddles.

Over the years farmers and water-hogging industries have sucked dry over half of China's 50,000 significant rivers. Hundreds of cities are now in what the government classifies as "serious scarcity" of water. Not only are coal-fired power plants, steel foundries and other high water-demand industries rapidly depleting aquifers and reservoirs, half a billion Chinese who live in the northeast need water for daily use.

The water situation has become so dire that two Chinese businessmen recently bought two water sources in British Columbia, Canada. Several investors aren't flinching at spending $20 million to buy a Canadian well and set up a bottling plant. Another entrepreneur purchased a well in Chilliwack, B.C. for $17 million. A third man is shipping 200 container loads of B.C. mineral water to China every month. Twelve times a year China sends 1.76 million gallons of water from Canada back home. However, if they follow through on plans to build the "China-Russia-Canada-America" high-speed rail line, some water may ship via train. The line would start in Beijing, cross Siberia, zoom through a tunnel under the Pacific Ocean, cross the Bering Strait and then cut through Alaska and Canada to reach CONUS.

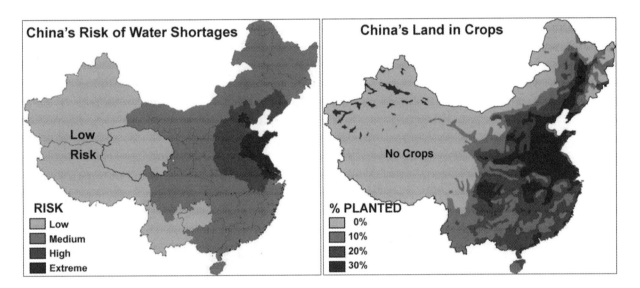

Between droughts, desertification, China's poor hygiene standards, polluted cropland, lack of food and water regulation, and fruits and vegetables grown in a cesspool of liquid infection, what does this say about their food shipped around the world?

WHEN DISASTER STRIKES

All of these giant food supplying countries – America, Brazil, Canada, the Netherlands, Germany, France, Italy, Australia, Argentina and Spain – regularly experience catastrophic natural disasters. What happens when a "prefect storm" arrives and multiple main food-supplying countries are traumatized at once? Foreign owners aren't going to keep crops and livestock in the land where they're grown. They're going to send it home. The foundation is laid for famine and Americans and Australians will be hungry from their own lack of foresight.

Western Food Supplies at Risk – The Rest of the Story

It's one thing to read about drought and heatwaves, floods and challenges of food producers, but their trials usually roll off the average person's back until it affects their wallet. Food prices seem to be on a permanent upward bound escalator. Besides natural disasters hitting farmers and ranchers around the world, something else has crept into our midst – something that has the ability to devastate a nation's food security – foreign ownership.

No nation in their right mind allows foreigners, whether they are corporations or individuals, to purchase large swaths of their food producing land. It is so shortsighted, there are simply no words. Yet this is exactly what the U.S. is allowing – sometimes to the tune of millions of acres per state like in Washington, California, Colorado, Texas, Alabama, Florida and Maine. Arizona, Arkansas, Georgia and Oregon are hot on their tails. In a "food crunch", there is nothing preventing foreign owners from sending fruits, veggies, cattle and other livestock, grains and other produce grown on America soil back to their homeland. This is on top of the massive food exports America sends around the world. The implications are absolutely staggering. Over 26 million acres of prime U.S. agricultural land belong to other countries. If you look at the "Agriculture in the U.S." map shown earlier in this chapter it illustrates what is grown where, you'll see that foreign interests have purchased some of everything including a lot of timber. With the escalation of forest fires, it's an agricultural product as significant as food.

Agricultural land owned by foreign entities has Canada in first place at 28% or 7.2 million acres. The Netherlands owns 19%, Germany – 7%, United Kingdom – 6% and Portugal – 5%. These numbers are as of 2013, when the government issued their last report. Foreign ownership has likely increased in the intervening years as America sells off many of her assets.

FARMLAND – THE HOT COMMODITY

"Farmland has now become the latest scarce 'hot' commodity for all sorts of speculators *who have absolutely no interest in agriculture*," said John Peck, executive director of Wisconsin-based Family Farm Defenders. "No local farmer can compete with $7,000 an acre," he said, citing the going price foreign investors are willing to pay for America's heartland.[289]

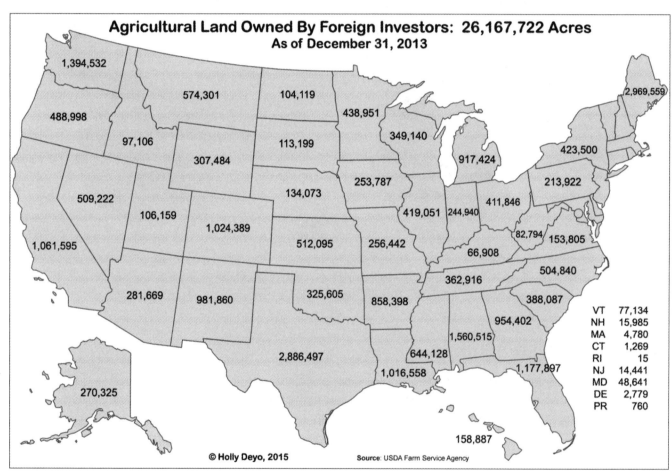

Agricultural Land Owned By Foreign Investors: 26,167,722 Acres
As of December 31, 2013

© Holly Deyo, 2015   Source: USDA Farm Service Agency

When China's Shuanghui International bought America's Smithfield Foods, they really got a deal. Not only did they buy America's largest pork producing company they got 100,000 acres of primo farmland in Missouri, Texas and North Carolina thrown into the deal.

With information just released that China has so polluted some of its precious farmland it can no longer be used, we want those farming practices here? So now they're casting their eyes overseas to America, Chile, Brazil, Russia, Ukraine, Bulgaria and Australia.

The Communist manifesto states that China should be 95% grain self-sufficient, but Mao Tse-tung let his people starve in the 60s rather than import food. Too proud, too stiff-necked. Although the current president Xi Jinping has backed away from grain self-sufficiency quotas, the ideology remains. So they look to usurp other countries' farmland. "The historic notion of food security and self-sufficiency is an incredible source of legitimacy for the Communist Party. This is, after all, a party of peasants that came to power during times of famine," said Jim Harkness, former president of the Minneapolis-based Institute for Agriculture and Trade Policy."[290]

U.S. FARMERS AGING OUT

What's a farmer or rancher to do when he wants to retire and has no one to carry on the family business? This is another aspect of farmers selling out. Fourth-generation Kansas farmer David Taylor, 59, sold his 176-acre soy farm after realizing his children weren't interested. Taylor is just one of many finding himself in this predicament. Nationally the majority of farmers are 55-years-old and fewer young people want to pick up the plowing reins. In just five years from 2007 to 2012, America lost over a staggering 95,000 farms for a variety of reasons.[291] In addition to having no heirs interested in farming, they're tired of battling drought and floods, and getting too little in return for working such grinding hours. If farmers or ranchers are in the big leagues, chances are much better for weathering tough times. But with agricultural land prices soaring and equipment prices through the roof, it's a chance-filled, thankless career. A new harvester can cost up to $500,000. Not many smaller farmers can afford it.

Now factor in genetically altered plants that no longer allow farmers to save seed year to year. These "terminator" seeds have been altered so that plants grown from these seeds don't produce the same wonderful crop that its "parent" did. Farmers are forced to buy more seed every year at an average cost of $300 an acre. This doesn't include watering, fertilizing and pesticides, never mind their time and cost of fuel and the land itself. It's alarming that six companies – Monsanto, Syngenta, DuPont, Bayer, BASF and Dow control 98% of the world's seed sales.[292]

Hybrids are further modified by Monsanto to require specific chemical applications in order to grow. Roundup Ready crops – another Monsanto brainchild – have been bred to accept over-the-top drenchings of this poison. Many now won't grow without it. This author encourages people to have their own little seed banks of non-hybrid, heirloom seeds as written in her book *Garden Gold*. It requires little space in your freezer and assures that you always have the best homegrown veggies possible from now and into the future.

The China Food Takeover in Australia

In Queensland, a Chinese-Japanese consortium bought the 240,000-acre cotton plantation, Cubbie Station, *complete with the largest irrigation system in the Southern Hemisphere*. Water rights alone make this a shocking foreign purchase because Aussies are perpetually in water-crisis mode. Decades ago Australian left-wingers, much like those in America, chose to protect the environment over the welfare of its citizens. Then physicists Dr. Edward Teller and Dr. James Maxfield tried to get the Australian government to capture and make use of water resources. As early as 1968, Teller proposed under Operation Plowshare constructing nuclear craters to hold freshwater. However environmentalists quashed this even when farmers lost harvests and herds in repeated droughts. This is extremely alarming because a country comparable in size to the US 48 states can only grow crops on 6% of the land. Most of the interior is desert.

It doesn't make Americans happy that another country is equally shortsighted, but it underpins the notion that free and blessed countries are selling off to foreigners their most precious possession – self-sustainability.

The largest privately held ranch, S. Kidman & Co., is up for sale. Its 25 million acres cover parts of three states and one territory and is home to 185,000 head of cattle. Asking price is US$234 million for all 10 stations, bull breeding stud farm and feedlot, which will be sold as an "all or nothing" package. Just one of its ranches in South Australia is larger than all of Ireland. Until January October 2016, six to 12 international bidders smacked their lips when Chinese conglomerate Shanghai Pengxin Group edged out other bidders including firms from China and Hong Kong, as well as a Canadian teachers' pension fund. Two Chinese companies, conglomerates Ningbo Xianfeng New Material Company and Rifa Australia, a division of Zhejiang, were on the short list. Canada's Hewitt Cattle Company and London's private equity firm Terra Firma, via Consolidated Pastoral also seriously looked at Kidman. Terra Firma is the outfit that bought the massive cattle interests of James Packer when he unloaded them in 2009 for over US$239 million. These bidders were in addition to unnamed companies in the U.S., Switzerland, South America and Indonesia – all vying for this once-in-a-lifetime property. Just half with their hat in the ring are Australians.

This purchase is on the heels of the Chinese firm, Fucheng, buying another Queensland cattle ranch in September 2015. Their US$20 million outlay bought a 77,000-acre sweet set up in Woodlands in the southern part of the state.

This isn't all.

In July 2015, Chinese ball-bearing billionaire, Xingfa Ma, bought two cattle stations, Wollogorang and Wentworth, in Northern Territory plus 40,000 head of cattle for US$34 million.

In June 2015, Chinese supermarket giant Dashang Group bought Hunter Valley cattle grazing property, Glenrock Station, in Queensland for US$32 million. This got Dashang 76,000 acres of prime cattle breeding land that enjoys regular high rainfall.

In March 2015, Hailiang Group, looking for a shortcut to put Australian beef on Chinese grocery shelves, spent over US$23 million on the Hollymount cattle station in southern Queensland, plus another US$7.2 million for a cattle and crops property nearby. These two land grabs netted China over 125,000 acres.

Historic Tasmanian crop and grazing property, Vaucluse, was recently sold to US food and agriculture conglomerate, Cargill, for over US$14 million.[293] Yes, Americans have jumped into the picture, and so have Middle Easterners, Europeans, Japanese and Koreans though the U.S. is the most food-secure of the lot.

Another foreign mega-deal purchase involved Chinese state-owned, Bright Food, which paid US$400 million for 75% of Australia's Manassen Foods in 2011.

In 2016 one of China's largest beef producers, Chongqing Hondo Agriculture Group, may purchase US$73 million farmland, cattle stations and slaughterhouses.

China's eyeing greedily even more of Australia's agricultural land. Trade agency, Austrade, reported that as many as 300 Chinese companies are currently looking to invest in Australia.[294]

As of 2013, foreigners owned 12.5% of Australia's agricultural land.[295] That's the latest publicly available report and at the rate foreigners are purchasing great chunks of The Lucky Country, that number is likely lagging. Another source says that nearly 125 million acres of Australia's agricultural land has some degree of foreign ownership.[296]

In 2014 attorney Allan Myers sold his Elizabeth Downs cattle operation in Northern Territory to Chinese buyer, Yiang Xiang Assets, for more than US$8.4 million. This brought China over a half million acres, not counting a further purchase of 9,000 head of cattle. The Beef Central website reports this was the first large purchase by China in the Northern Territory and they're already checking out other properties.

Finally alarm bells went off in March 2015 with all of these Chinese buyouts, which resulted in tightened *oversight* of sales. It doesn't prohibit them; it just puts them under scrutiny. The Aussie government cut cumulative foreign land purchases from AU$252 million down to AU$15 million before official clearance is required. This doesn't mean foreign entities can't purchase massive chunks of Australia's food-producing land, they just have to have government OK.[297]

Kevin Van Trump wrote in his daily agricultural newsletter. "It's thought that the line-up of Chinese interests is extensive, with as many as 300 Chinese cattle and cattle-related companies now looking to invest in Australia. From what I understand, they are interested in almost everything and anything dealing with agricultural. According to reports, deals all across the country are getting done much more quickly than anyone could have imagined. Chinese investors are coming in with the 'cash' and making big offers."[298]

Aussie friends, you'd better watch it or you'll be eating rice at every meal and speaking with a funny accent.

Canada, the Right Stuff – With Loopholes

On the surface, the Great White North has the right idea about limiting foreign investment when it comes to their food producing land. Or do they? From British Columbia to Quebec laws vary for how much land foreigners can own. For example, Ontario, Nova Scotia and Prince Edward Island have no restrictions. Alberta allows foreign ownership of up to 20 acres, Saskatchewan: just 10 acres unless it's a partnership with a Canadian, then the number jumps to 320. But then there's a loophole. On Saskatchewan's prairies where foreign ownership used to be fairly controlled, a foreigner can now purchase farmland if he or she is a resident for just six months. They can also get an exemption if they live outside Canada, but *plan* to move there and farm. In Alberta foreigners can lease land for 20 years or acquire an exemption if it will "economically benefit the province". Quebec laws provide for 10 acres of foreign ownership and Manitoba sets the limit at 40. Once again, Canada uses common sense in not giving the farm away – literally.[299]

Canada is seeing what Australia and America have experienced. If primo growing land is available and farmers need to sell, there will always be foreigners willing to step in and do the deed.

Brazil, the Netherlands, France, Spain, Belgium and Italy

Brazil, too, is caught in a bind of needing foreign investment with agriculture to boost their sagging GDP. 2015 saw Latin America's largest economy nosedive in its worst year since 1992. Five years before, it banned selling agricultural land to all foreign interests, but tight times have Brazil relaxing restrictions. This country that was keen on resource nationalism now has to strike a balance between giving up too much to outsiders and finding a path to economic growth.

According to a Food and Agriculture Organization report, Belgium, Germany, France, and the Netherlands have no restrictions on foreigner land ownership. Neither does Italy or Spain except if it's in border areas. It's one thing to happily, voluntarily export food in good times, but quite another for other nations come into a country, buy the land and determine where that food goes. It *will* ship to their homeland, not feed the locals.

So What's Up With the Global Land Grab?

In 2013 the UN released a study showing that world food supplies are being threatened. This threat is mostly a result of drought, underscored by worldwide water wars. While some crops are put under water by massive deluges, the greatest and growing menaces are drought and heatwaves. Their 2007 report was hopeful; the latest is dire. As drought grows, farmers increasingly rely on aquifers for irrigation, but that resource is being sucked dry. Out of the world's 37 largest aquifers, 21 have passed their sustainability tipping point. Two new studies say 13 are in the worst possible shape and are "significantly distressed". Not only are wealthy individuals, corporations and countries buying up farmland around the world for what it can grow, but for what lies underneath. In this era of water wars "blue gold" is a red-hot commodity. Without water, there's no food. No crops. No livestock.

1/3 of World's Largest Aquifers in Serious Trouble

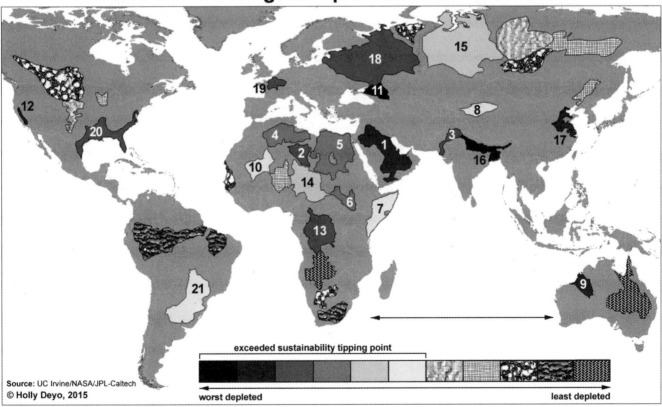

Source: UC Irvine/NASA/JPL-Caltech
© Holly Deyo, 2015

exceeded sustainability tipping point

worst depleted   least depleted

Aquifers supply 35% of all freshwater used by people worldwide. Exceptionally dry times can rocket this figure greatly as it has in California's mega-drought that shot aquifer reliance to 65%. Large basins, which seem like they'd have an endless supply of the wet stuff, rely on snowmelt and rain to recharge. It takes thousands of years to refill them. That's IF they aren't still being sucked dry in the interim.

Over one third are in serious trouble because water is being extracted at a staggering rate. For aquifers to get in this bad of shape they must have a lot of water pulled out while simultaneously not being recharged or refilled.

When those two factors converge, they put groundwater supplies in extreme danger. Eight fall into this worst category and are classified as Overstressed. Not surprisingly most of these are in the Middle East and North Africa. However aquifers in China, Russia, Australia, France, the U.S., South America, Pakistan and India are also in deep trouble.

KEY AQUIFERS IN TROUBLE

The #1 most troubled aquifer in the world, The Arabian, supplies water to some 60 million Saudis. Murzuk-Djado in Africa is #2. In 3rd worst shape is the Indus Basin #3 in India.

Going back to Africa, the next four slots are filled by the Northwestern Sahara Aquifer System (#4), the Nubian #5, the Sudd #6 and Ogaden-Juba #7. The Nubian sits pretty equally over Libya, Egypt, Chad and Sudan – under the vast Sahara Desert. Even though it's large, people are drastically draining the Nubian to grow crops, water livestock and develop projects in Libya and Egypt. Situated in a desert it enjoys very little recharge and what little rain falls, is decreasing. In Egypt alone, water levels have dropped nearly 200 feet.

China lays claim to #9 the most endangered aquifer in the northwest region of Xinjiang, Tarim Basin.

Aquifers numbered #9 – #13 are also seeing massive depletion, but some water does seep back in so they do become somewhat recharged before the "great suck out" begins again. These last five basins are still "Extremely" or "Highly" stressed, depending on how much they refill.

Australia has the most troubled aquifer, Canning Basin #9, situated in the northern part of West Australia. It's been hit by a double whammy of the water-hogging mining industry and a lack of hurricanes that bring drenching rains. When hurricanes do come, only 15% of their rain makes it into the aquifer.[300] This is a huge blow because a vast area from north of Broome down to Port Hedland and 1,000 kilometers inland had been earmarked for agricultural development in the Northern Australia White Paper. However, an international study completed in 2014 concluded that the Canning has the third highest depletion rate in the world.

Slot #10 goes to the Taoudeni-Tanezrouft Basin in Africa's northwest and Russia's North Caucasus Basin in the west captures #11.

California's Central Valley Aquifer System – the area that grows the bulk of America's fruits and vegetables grabs #12.

To put this into perspective, California's Central Valley Aquifer System supplies 20% of the America's groundwater making it the second most pumped aquifer in country after the Ogalallah.[301] As discussed earlier in this chapter the Central Valley Basin is being so sharply depleted with no recharge that the land around it is sinking. It's sinking over the top of the aquifer and next to it. It's also subsiding parallel to the San Andreas Fault as well as right over it. The Central Valley Basin runs half the distance of the San Andreas' 800-mile length, which marks the boundary between the Pacific and North American Plates. This isn't a good scenario with the aquifer's massive weight being removed because it helps keep tectonic plates in place and behaving.

The worst basin, the Congo #13, is in Africa's west central area.

Eight more aquifers are deemed past the tipping point with more water being used than is replenished:

#14 – Lake Chad in Africa

#15 – West Siberian in Russia

#16 – Ganges-Brahmaputra in northeast India. The Ganges-Brahmaputra has more water extracted than any other major aquifer in the world due to high population and irrigation. Its saving grace is lying in a region that gets tons of rain.

#17 – North China situated on the country's east side

#18 – Russia Platform in the country's western-most region

#19 – Paris in northern France

#20 – Atlantic and Gulf Coastal Plains, which covers half of Texas down through its "toe" and down into northeast Mexico. It fully covers the southern states of Louisiana, Mississippi, Florida and South Carolina; plus half of Arkansas, Alabama, Georgia, North Carolina and Virginia.

#21 – Guarani in parts of Brazil, Paraguay, Uruguay and Argentina

NOTE: New Zealand and Alaska don't have any of the world's largest aquifers so weren't included on the map to make it larger.

Over a third of the world's largest aquifers – most of these supply critical moisture for agriculture – are in deep trouble. It's quite simple. No water, no food.

Gimme a Glass of Ethanol

Food riots are rarely stand-alone events and are often the product of escalating prices in other vital areas like fuel, plus political instability and corruption. In the dozen years since 2002, food prices more than doubled with little backtracking. This doesn't take into consideration 2011 when food prices really went off the rails spiking 250%.

Seven countries are home to 65% of the world's hungriest people: India, China, the Democratic Republic of Congo (DRC), Bangladesh, Indonesia, Pakistan, and Ethiopia. Together they make up *half* of the global population.

All of them are in conflict to one degree or another. China, like Russia, is ultra-secretive on national discontent and negative press, and estimated to have over 180,000 protests every year. To keep the Chinese under control, it spends $125 billion annually on an amazing array of "stability maintenance" gear. For an <u>unarmed</u> country of usually very polite, tightly wound people, why are riot gear, bulletproof helmets, armored cars, drones, shields, batons, guns, night-vision goggle, bomb-disposing robots, and the latest high-tech surveillance equipment needed?[302] Maybe they don't want to see what havoc 1.5 billion angry hungry people could produce.

The causes of food riots are multi-faceted and can be traced to:

* Weather disasters and plant diseases
* Low stockpiles
* Dietary improvements demanding better food especially in China and India thereby scooping up formerly readily available surpluses
* A weak and volatile dollar exchange rate
* Export restrictions due to low reserves
* Agricultural land sold off for other uses and
* Biofuel production

Of these food shortage factors, five we can't do anything about; the last two we can. First, major food supplying countries need to stop selling off land to foreigners and losing control over this irreplaceable resource and stop selling prime agricultural land that's flipped for housing or used car lots or another shopping mall.

Second, stop with the biofuels. Out of every 10 ears of corn, four go into gas tanks. Have you tried sucking corn through a gas hose? It doesn't work. Have you enjoyed a glass of ethanol lately? This is beyond shortsighted when hundreds of millions of people are starving. Biofuel can be made from non-edibles like bio-methane from purified biogas or landfill gas or seaweed or algae. The latter would be a good use for those poisonous algal blooms that plague oceans around the world. Why – use – food – for – fuel?

THE TRUTH WILL OUT

Even the UN's notoriously left-wing IPCC, the Intergovernmental Panel on Climate Change, released a report in March 2014 saying very diplomatically that they're not sure biofuels are helping control emissions even to the slightest degree. In fact, they state that biofuel production may actually put more pollution into the air than gas and diesel, not to mention the enormous amount of water needed to produce ethanol. Their statement is softened with politically correct-speak and to reach the true story one must chop through a lot of empty words, but their assessment is clear. The IPCC writes, "Biofuels have direct, fuel-cycle GHG [greenhouse gas] emissions that are typically 30-90% lower than those for gasoline or diesel fuels. However, since for some biofuels indirect emissions – including from land use change – can lead to **greater total emissions than when using petroleum products**, policy support needs to be considered on a case by case basis."[303]

A more straightforward assessment comes from Canada's International Institute for Sustainable Development saying that the climate benefit of replacing petroleum products with biofuels is basically zero. Instead they recommend implementing stricter emission controls on vehicles claiming that would literally be about 100 times more effective.[304] Short, sweet and to the point.

Once people cut through the red tape on the biofuel issue, the intent is clear. It's more about providing *energy* security at the expense of *food* security. If countries can save their petroleum reserves and cut down on those imports, then they can dance a little further from OPEC's scimitar. This thought is underscored by the enormous amount of fracking being done in America when a few years ago that term was barely in anyone's vocabulary. It's all about the gas.

In 2015, 5.25 *billion* bushels of corn went to make 14.5 billion gallons of ethanol. Based on the suggested daily intake of 2,100 calories per person compared to the energy calories in a gallon of gas, those billions of bushels of corn would have fed nearly 600,000,000 people for a year.[305]

In 2000, priorities were different with a food-over-fuel common sense approach. Then just 5% of America's corn went to ethanol and over 90% fed livestock and humans here and around the world. In 2015, the amount of corn given over to ethanol production equaled the amount allocated to feed people and livestock.[306] Corn is in tens of thousands of products from cereals to fillers, as sweeteners in the form of corn syrup in a shocking amount of foods and beverages to even the real food of corn on the cob or corn in a can or frozen.

Much like the coming-of-age TV show One Tree Hill that popularized "hoes over bros", meaning girls put girlfriends before boyfriends, the world needs to re-adopt a "food over fuel" mentality. The idea that ethanol is an environmental-positive approach is a non-starter. Not only is it a push for being beneficial, ethanol may actually put more pollution into the environment than using gas and diesel.

One can only deduce that there is a plan afoot to take food from people, foment discord and political unrest around the world, make more countries food-insecure and starve many millions in the process. On this path, famine is coming.

Food Riots and Other Hungry Behavior

2008 marked the beginning of the Great Recession that still hadn't lifted seven years later. Nearly every food bank and pantry in America was forced to cut back on distributions due to the number of people asking for help. As food prices and food lines increased, availability slumped. People grumbled and bellies rumbled, but no one rioted. 2008 also saw world food prices rocket up 225% in four years.[307] Real turmoil began the year before.

In 2007 through the first half of 2008 food riots broke out in Africa, Egypt, Uzbekistan, Pakistan, Sri Lanka, Bangladesh and Haiti.

Indian farmers committed suicide when crops failed often by swallowing pesticides. In 2007 and 2008, nearly 250,000 took their own lives.[308]

In Africa, 14 of 53 countries saw mass rioting following abrupt spikes in food prices during in those same two years. Riots swept the continent from Egypt and Tunisia in the North, to Burkina Faso, Mauritania, Cameroon and Senegal in the West, and Madagascar, Mozambique and Zimbabwe in the South.

Pasta protests erupted in Italy and tortilla protests blew up in Mexico.

Considering that the average Italian puts away 62 pounds of linguine, fettuccine and spaghetti every year, people balked at the 20% increase while their wages remained flat. In September 2007 protesters called for a countrywide strike against pasta retailers. Central to the problem was the rising cost of wheat worldwide. Since emerging countries demand better diets, which include more meat, the requirement for livestock feed is also rising. Wheat stockpiles are decreasing the world over as grain prices soar. America is the world's largest grain exporter and during the year of the pasta protest, U.S. reserves hit a 33-year low.

In Mexico 75,000 trade unionists, farmers and left-wing party members marched through downtown Mexico City protesting drastic price increases for food staples. Sparking their anger was the cost of their beloved tortillas rising 400%.[309] For Mexico's poor, this is central to their diet and without being able to afford the bare minimum many were at risk of becoming malnourished. Mexico's first response was to clamp down on hoarders.

Food was so tight in Brazil they banned all rice exports and India banned all outgoing rice except for Basmati that commands the highest price.

Likewise China, Indonesia, Vietnam, Madagascar, Cambodia and Egypt imposed strict export bans on rice.

By March 2008 rice prices in Egypt more than doubled in only a few months. Fights in long bread lines left at least six people dead and the government called in the Army to bake bread for the people.

In Burkina Faso, West Africa protestors in the three major cities of Bobo-Dioulasso, Ouhigouya and Banfora attacked government offices, and burned shops, cars and gas stations. On February 21, 100 people were arrested for stoning government officials. Merchants and traders were among those who protested taxes and increasing costs of goods. The government wasn't blind-sided by their actions as an official said violent protests were "expected" due to constantly rising prices for even basic foods, fabric and gasoline.

A week later Cameroon's capital of Yaounde and the major shipping port of Douala were paralyzed after riots erupted in several western towns. Bands of stone-throwing youths barricaded streets with burning tires and wood. Businesses and shops closed as vehicles were smashed and torched. For four days rioters took to the streets while police countered with tear gas dropped from helicopters. Police arrested nearly 1,700[310] hauling them off in trucks and beating some with rifle butts. During the unrest, 24 rioters were shot and killed. The reason? High food and fuel prices in addition to water were becoming "increasingly scarce".[311]

In Yemen, food riots broke out in March 2008 and continued through April. Thousands of armed protesters set up roadblocks and torched police stations. Street protests broke out in Indonesia when the price of food and fuel doubled.

Photo: Shops were looted and goods burned on the streets in Jakarta, Indonesia. Riots were triggered by economic problems including food shortages and mass unemployment.

In Bangladesh 10,000 workers rioted, smashed cars and buses and vandalized factories in anger at food prices doubling in one year. Dozens were injured in the violence.

In Haiti violent food riots hit the country for over a week and caused the deaths of five people. From 2007 to 2008 prices for basic foods including rice, beans, fruit and condensed milk had shot up 50% and fuel costs tripled in just two months. Haitians took to the streets throwing rocks at UN peacekeepers and police protesting the huge rise in the cost of rice, beans, cooking oil and other staples. They blocked national highways and city streets, burned cars and tires, smashed windows and looted. The U.N. fought back with tear gas and rubber bullets. Angry protestors tried to break in the Presidential Palace in Port au Prince and demand that Rene Preval step down. People had been hungry for months and likened their stomach pains to "eating Clorox [bleach]" and were reduced to eating dirt "cookies". Patrick Elie, advisor to president Preval knew how extremely fragile the situation had become. He worried. "I compare this situation to having a bucket full of gasoline and having some people around with a box of matches. As long as the two have a possibility to meet, you're going to have trouble."[312]

LIVING THROUGH A FOOD RIOT

One little boy, who was eight at the time, shared what he saw during the Indonesian food riots. Hindra Martono's parents owned a grocery store, and with food shortages underway, his mom and dad knew they would be targeted. As soon as the banging on their door began, little Hindra, his brother, sister and parents hid in the attic hoping to be spared.

Hindra recalled, "I remember that my brother and sister were also there, frightened. My sister cried so much. They were discussing what if they burned us down along with the house. My mother asked me to pray to God. …Then I remember I saw one of the mob climb up, break our window, and open the door from the inside. The mob flooded in. They took everything. Food, money, electronics, furniture – all of it. Among them, I saw my father's employees, people who were happily playing with me as a kid, carrying our belongings. I do remember that I really hated them at that time. I felt like I was betrayed."[313]

The mob found them in their hiding place and Hindra blocked out how they escaped. Too afraid to go back home, they moved from one relative's house to another. Hindra continued. "When we actually got back, I saw my father's shop and our home in devastating conditions. I can't imagine what my father's feeling was, seeing the shop that he built from scratch for almost 20 years just destroyed like that. …I remember life after that was hard."[314]

Photo: Shelves at a ShopRite in Montgomery, NY are emptied of bottled water on the eve of Hurricane Sandy. This same scene is repeated every time a huge storm is forecast whether it's a blizzard, tornado or hurricane. Within hours stores look like something out of an apocalyptic movie. Shelves are wiped of food, water and other essentials. In their haste people dumped things on the floor that weren't edible.

Last Thoughts on the Coming Famine

Famine isn't new to the world. Repeated, catastrophic food shortages have plagued every continent, killing thousands. In other famines, millions starved. Frequently food shortages are the result of natural disasters including floods and volcanic nuclear winters, insect plagues and fungus infestations, but most often the culprit is unrelenting drought. Other wide-scale famines result from war, political machinations or civil strife and the world today certainly isn't more peaceful.

As countries become more heavily populated, demand on water grows. This is especially punishing for nations prone to drought like North Africa, the Middle East, Mexico, Australia and China. It makes growing crops and raising livestock difficult in the best of times.

Major food exporting countries should expect to get smacked more often by natural disasters as weather becomes even more unpredictable and more extreme. Several of these nations hit at once could have a devastating impact on global food supplies.

One of the worst possible scenarios is an EMP – Electromagnetic Pulse. If it stems from a solar explosion, it could have an even wider impact than an EMP from a nuclear bomb. Well-respected scientists warn that just such a solar eruption will take place. It's a certainty. Most countries' infrastructure, including the U.S., is not protected. We'd get dropped back into the 1800s with few people knowing how to cope, let alone feed themselves. Many nations depend on irrigation for food production and if electricity isn't available, crops would literally die where they stand. There'd be no diesel for harvesters or fuel to transport crops and animals to processing plants, let along get the end products to market.

People thinking they can load up at the local grocery store will have a shock, because everyone who hasn't prepared will be thinking the same thing. Food stores have changed drastically in the last two decades. They used to have huge on-site warehouses with enough stock to keep stores supplied for several months. With the transition to just-in-time inventories, back-up stock is now limited to 1½ days. In a mad scramble for last supplies, food and water will be wiped off shelves within minutes. Then what?

Around the world people flock to stores to purchase food, bottled water and batteries before every forecasted natural disaster. Those are the three biggies. If children are in the family, then formula and diapers disappear too. After 2005's historic Hurricane Katrina, some victims were without electricity for a couple of months, not days. When people realized "juice" wasn't coming back any time soon, generators were grabbed from home improvement centers in record time.

Even those who have prepared, have set food and water aside, they will have only a finite supply, and hungry angry (hangry) people will "storm the Bastille" and take what you have. Even neighbors and friends if they're hungry enough will come banging on your door… or barge through it.

Looting was rampant after Hurricane Katrina and Superstorm Sandy. In New Orleans, besides food, people helped themselves to flat screens, computers, jewelry, designer jeans and sneakers. Sustained emergencies often bring chaos and propel people into actions they wouldn't have considered two decades ago. Everyone thinks he or she would never participate in crime and such uncivilized actions, but history proves different and Hurricane Katrina really opened the floodgates – no pun intended – to bad behavior.

"Around the corner on Canal Street [in New Orleans], the main thoroughfare in the central business district, people sloshed headlong through hip-deep water as looters ripped open the steel gates on the front of several clothing and jewelry stores. One man, who had about 10 pairs of jeans draped over his left arm, was asked if he was salvaging things from his store. 'No,' the man shouted, 'that's *everybody's* store.' Looters filled industrial-sized garbage cans with clothing and jewelry and floated them down the street on bits of plywood and insulation. A man walked down Canal Street with a pallet of food on his head. His wife, who refused to give her name, insisted they weren't stealing from the nearby Winn-Dixie supermarket. 'It's about survival right now,' she said as she held a plastic bag full of purloined items. 'We got to feed our children. I've got eight grandchildren to feed.'"[315]

People justify their actions saying they had family to feed or selfishly, they just don't give a rip and go with "me first, the rest be damned". But what will they do when the stores are emptied? Well-documented histories show cannibalism is a last-resort solution.

Life-sucking, mind-numbing painful hunger brings out the worst in humans. In normal times people would never smack their hungry lips looking at their spouse, their children or a corpse lying by the roadside and think "dinner". Cannibalism goes back way before Biblical days. Hunger drives people to do the unimaginable. World-renown American psychologist Abraham Maslow defined the hierarchy of basic human needs as these seven priorities in this order: air, food, drink, shelter, warmth, sex, sleep.

If you can't breathe, everything else is moot. Assuming you have oxygen, the strongest driving force is food. Clawing hunger inspires people to do the forbidden as the Old Testament shows. Nothing has changed.

Deuteronomy 28:53-57 reveals a very dire, disgusting warning about famine,

"Then you will eat the offspring of your own body [to avoid starvation], the flesh of your sons and daughters whom the Lord your God has given you, during the siege and the misery by which your enemy will oppress you. The man who is most refined and well-bred among you will be cruel and hostile toward his brother and toward the wife he cherishes and toward the rest of his children who remain, so that he will not give even one of them any of

the flesh of his children which he will eat, because he has nothing else left, during the siege and the misery by which your enemy will oppress you in all your cities. The most refined and well-bred woman among you, who would not venture to set the sole of her foot on the ground because she is so delicate and pampered, will be cruel and hostile toward the husband she cherishes and toward her son and daughter, and toward her afterbirth that comes from between her legs and toward the children whom she bears; for she will eat them secretly for lack of anything else, during the siege and the misery by which your enemy will oppress you in your cities." —Amplified Bible

Further underscoring coming famines beyond the impact of weather disasters, war and associated problems; major food growing countries are selling off their fresh water and prized agricultural land to foreigners. Smaller farmers are being pushed off their land, which is then bought by corporations. More frequently it's sold to countries strapped for food and water, and when the crunch hits, they'll send their crops and livestock home, not sell it to the hungry citizens they bought it from.

Increasingly farmers and ranchers have no one to hand over their backbreaking, grueling family business. Kids want to move to the city, do something else, "get out of this boring, small town". Canada is seeing the same thing. Often they must sell farmland that's been in the family for generations. In just five years from 2007 to 2012, America lost over 95,000 farms. This precious fertile land is then transformed into housing developments, industry or another shopping mall.

Unscrupulous conglomerates have bought up and patented 98% of all self-replicating, heirloom seeds that farmers depended on year to year for their next crops. This forces them to buy what was once an unending gift from God besides spraying on poisonous chemicals to even make them grow.

The pieces are in place and paint an ugly picture. Famine is ripe and ready to strike. All it needs is the right and terrifying trigger.

Chapter 11: Signs in Society

Increase in Fake Messiahs

For many will come in My name, saying, 'I am the Christ,' and will deceive many. —Matthew 24:5 and Mark 13:6 (NKJV)

And He [Jesus] said: "Take heed that you not be deceived. For many will come in My name, saying, 'I am He,' and, 'The time has drawn near.' Therefore do not go after them. —Luke 21:8 (NKJV)

For false christs and false prophets will rise and show signs and wonders to deceive, if possible, even the elect [God's chosen]. —Mark 13:22 (NKJV)

Multiple verses warn about people claiming to be Christ in End Times. It's that important and God doesn't want people taken in. Though all three of the world's major religions have messianic claimants those pertaining to Judaism and Islam can be ruled out since the New Testament would only be addressing Christianity. We can also rule out those who have already died unless they're going to reincarnate.

People with messianic delusions have dotted the planet since the 1700s, which saw a small handful. Nine were born in the 1800s. Nearly 30 throughout the world were born during the 1900s, which is probably the best century for a meaningful false christ to appear. Someone born in the 21st century would be too young as time is just too short waiting for them to grow up.

If people looked into the backgrounds of some of the possible "candidates", they would toss their claim on the rubbish heap in a fat hurry. Jesus was flawless, perfect though human. These guys are far from it.

- Australian-born Alan John Miller seemed a little "off" so his mother tried to have him committed. Before Miller realized he was Jesus in 2007, Miller was a property developer and IT specialist, married with two children. He was a senior member of Jehovah's Witness but booted out when he dumped his wife for Karen. His current girlfriend, Mary Suzanne Luck, Miller named Mary Magdalene, though she wasn't his first MM designee. [316]
- Miami-based Jose Luis de Jesus Miranda who has 666 tattooed on his arm,[317] simultaneously claimed to be both Jesus and the Antichrist. Jesus Miranda "claims he is greater than Jesus Christ and that his teachings supersede those of Christ" …and "since He is Christ, worship of Jesus Christ is invalid. His followers are now also receiving 666 tattoos to declare their allegiance to him."[318]
- The U.S., Britain and Venezuela all booted 68-year-old Brazilian-born Inri Cristo out of their countries.[319] Inri has mostly female adherents (and no, he is *not* good looking), all dressed in pale blue belted gowns. One might be tempted to chuckle if this weren't so sad. One poor dear, Abevere, who was 88 in 2016, has been trotting around with this "messiah" for 34 years.
- Russia's Sergey Anatolyevitch Torop a.k.a. Vissarion was a former traffic cop before being fired in 1990.[320] The "Christ of Siberia" has about 5,000 followers. Dressed in thick white furry parkas with nothing but frost-reddened cheeks, eyes and mouths visible, they nearly blend in with their wintry surroundings. It's blisteringly cold in those remote Siberian woods. You've got to give his followers an "A" for true grit kneeling in front of him in the snow with the wind howling. When Vissarion isn't preaching on Skype, or playing with his seven kids while luxuriating in his Western style lavish home (his followers live in wooden huts in relative poverty), he's jetting off to hobnob with spiritual friends in India. The Russian government worries about the growing spiritual vacuum in their country. They estimate about that 4,000 religious movements and cults – involving up to 800,000 people are filling the void.[321]
- Convicted child predator Wayne Bent, a.k.a. Michael Travesser was serving 10 years in a New Mexico prison till illness intervened.[322] Travesser had a "bent" for lying in bed with naked underage girls. Bent claimed they were just "spiritual exercises". A judge ruled in January 2016 that Bent, now 74, should be released from jail after being diagnosed with skin cancer.[323] (Wonder if any followers commented that the real Jesus would be above such human afflictions?)
- Two other candidates popped up in South Africa: Moses Hlongwane[324] and Phetole Selepe,[325] equally disqualified.

- Then there's the hatchet-carrying California homeless man named Jett Simmons McBride who claims to be Jesus.[326]
- Not even Benjamin Creme's Maitreya qualifies though 93-year-old Creme claims his guy "is the same as the Christ, the Imam Mahdi, Krishna and the Messiah."[327] You have to give Creme an "A" for persistence since he's been pushing his candidate via radio appearances, books and Share International since 1982. Boy, is he going to have a surprise pretty soon!

Here is the only scripture needed to know these people are fakes. Jesus' coming will be a BIG EVENT. Everyone will know, not just a few anointed people stuck in the boondocks. Matthew 24:23-27 Jesus warns us there will be imposters and His return will be unmistakable. He says, *Then if anyone says to you, 'Look, here is the Christ,' or 'There He is,' do not believe it. For false christs and false prophets will arise and show great signs and wonders to deceive, if possible, even the elect. Listen, I have told you beforehand. "So, if they say to you, 'Look, He is in the desert,' do not go there; or, 'Look, He is in the private chambers,' do not believe it. For as the lightning comes from the east and flashes to the west, so will be the coming of the Son of Man."*

Growing Bad Behavior

People will be lovers of themselves, lovers of money, boastful, proud, abusive, disobedient to their parents, ungrateful, unholy, without love, unforgiving, slanderous, without self-control, brutal, not lovers of the good, treacherous, rash, conceited, lovers of pleasure rather than lovers of God —2 Timothy 3:2-4 (NIV)

Another sign of the End Times is society's self-absorption, preoccupation with (over)-indulgence, indifference to brutality and treachery, and distancing one's self from the truth.

- Korean Air's 2015 ad campaign sums it up nicely with their slogan "it's all about you."

- Jamaica's adults-only Hedonism resorts host nudist and swingers conventions and known for drug use. One friend, Kathy, who traveled there with her husband in the mid-80s and not knowing what to expect, came back somewhat shocked saying, "Everything you could ever want, anything you can think of, is there for the asking." Travel brochures didn't exactly spell this out and it was pre-Internet days for most folks so they had no way of knowing. One 2010 Hedonism guest talked about oral sex in hot tubs and orgies held behind closed doors.[328] Since this was 25 years later maybe they weren't so "hedonistic" when Kathy and Steven vacationed there.

- *Thank you* is said too little and *What's in it for me?* spoken too often.

- Lies roll off tongues like mercury – slippery and toxic. During this 2016 election year, never have campaign speeches been riddled with so many "factually-lacking statements". Finger pointing has replaced gesturing and lies have replaced substance.

- Today every kid participating in a contest or race, deserving or not, gets a trophy or ribbon conveying the concept that "everyone is a winner". It used to be there were winners and losers. If you didn't come in first that time, it was incentive to try harder or study more for the next time. Somebody always comes in first and the rest fall somewhere afterwards. Now everyone is the proverbial chief and no one is a brave. Said another way, everyone is a general and soldiers are MIA – missing in action. There has to be a boss. This might be insight why when a parent tells a child to clean his room he informs them "later" or "when I get ready." Or, when a parent a grounds a teen, they're apt to be met with a *"F*** you!"* and slam out of the house. Had Boomers talked like that to our parents, we'd still be bouncing off the walls. While this author's parents never hit or spanked, behavior like this would have bent that needle. It simply wasn't considered let alone tolerated.

- Schools have changed – a lot. There were always kids that got in trouble, ones that flunked out and those that arrived and left stoned. Back then the principal still administered swats to younger kids. It came as a shock to see 19 states in the U.S. still allow it. Swats didn't happen to students often, but being sent to The

Office never meant a "get out of class free card". By the look of things, lack of disciple isn't helping. Now students bring knives and guns to class, mouth off to teachers and show up *if* they feel like it. No wonder teachers are quitting the educational system. They spend as much time filling out paperwork as teaching. Often they are glorified baby-sitters or stand-in parents. With two parents working, sometimes they have zero idea what's happening at school until there's a real problem. Everybody is busy and trying to survive, overworked and often taken for granted.

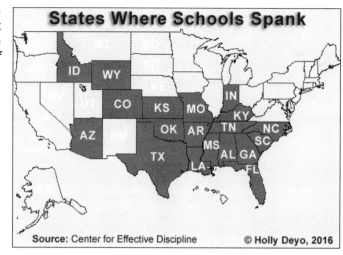

Source: Center for Effective Discipline   © Holly Deyo, 2016

- "Generation Me" is the name Jean Twenge, professor of psychology at San Diego State University, gave to the current generation of young people. She maintains that the values of many born now are much more narcissistic than Baby Boomers.[329]

- Greed was iconized by fictional character Gordon Gekko in the 1987 film *Wall Street* when he proclaimed, "Greed, for lack of a better word, is good." Real life stockbroker Bernie Madoff catapulted this concept to new heights when he defrauded tens of billions from investors.[330]

- Language is now littered with "selfie," "mini me" and "me time." Selfies gave rise to "photobombing" where folks, sometimes strangers, unexpectedly insert themselves into other people's pictures.

- Social media has also played a role giving everyone an "eternal spotlight". Instead of 15 minutes of fame, this kind can last forever. Once something goes viral on the Internet, it's extremely hard to remove all traces. Even when people have "scrubbed" their websites or pulled photos off social media, some sites keep them anyway, sometimes hidden, sometimes not, or delay a month removing material from servers.

- Social media's lure has encouraged people, celebrities and unknowns unlike, to put up nearly naked photos of them. Some users share information they later regret or reveal more than they intended just to keep their name relevant. People tweet that they're going to a sold out concert or "next big thing" restaurant that Friday night only to come home and find they've been burglarized. It's lifted bragging to an art form and gives the illusion that people actually care what someone had for breakfast. If photos are lurid, you can be sure millions of people will download them and pass them around.

- Taken to the extreme, a Florida man was found guilty in 2015 of his wife's murder after he uploaded pictures of his wife's bloody, bullet-riddled body on Facebook. He then posted "Im (sic) going to prison or death sentence for killing my wife love you guys miss you guys takecare (sic) Facebook people you will see me in the news."[331]

- Sexting seems to have a life of its own. These digital "breadcrumbs" hang around with the strength of steel. How often has a teenage girl sent nudies to her boyfriend, only to have them texted to their circles of friends and beyond?

- A notch higher, there's revenge porn. At the time, it might seem an intimate thing to do – take sexy photos or videos of the two of you together. Alone. Then someone cheats, the other person is hurt and uploads those formerly private pics to embarrass that former boyfriend or girlfriend. Sometimes the victim isn't even aware of the invasion until someone alerts them. Nonconsensual pornography has become so commonplace that at least 26 states have revenge porn laws.

- If you're tired of your partner and don't have the moral courage to tell that person face-to-face, people are delivering the bad news via text. SlyDial lets a person leave a "personal" message, but bypasses ringing and goes straight to voicemail.

- The Breakup Shop, an online breakup service, will end their customers' relationship in a variety of ways depending on how much you want to spend. They offer a simple text or email for $10 to something more elaborate besides the "you're now single" message plus cookies, wineglasses and a movie.

- It had to come – websites that promote marital cheating. One of the first was Ashley Madison launched in 2001. As of July 2015 it boasted over 37 million users. Then there's Meet2Cheat, Vaulty Stocks, Call and Text Eraser (CATE), which uses the slogans, "Save your marriage – everyone deserves privacy" and "Love is blind, we keep it that way." Heated Affairs' slogan is "No one has to know" plus they offer married hook-up advice. Married Secrets, Gleeden and Lonely Housewives are just a drop in the marital cheating bucket, plus there's a multitude of other sites with names so raw they can't be published.

These activities have resulted in many ruined marriages. A survey commissioned by the law firm Slater and Gordon, found that postings on Facebook, Skype, Snapchat, Instagram, Twitter, What'sApp and other social media were cited in 1 out of 7 divorces. FacebookCheating.com puts that number at 1 in 5. Nearly 20% of people say they have daily fights because of these Internet sites.[332]

Australian singer-songwriter superstar Tina Arena addressed her concerns about the selfie culture. "It's so narcissistic. It's highly perturbing. It's hugely detrimental long-term. People are unbelievably obsessed with the superficial and don't understand what goes on internally. There's an enormous loss of empathy, which is really scary. As soon as the human being loses his or her empathy there's nothing left. There's a lot of apathy, but no empathy. There's a culture of being famous for the sake of it on reality TV and they've done the same thing in music… We have crossed the line where we're desensitized, we don't give a sh*t anymore."[333]

Increased Violence and Lawlessness

Because lawlessness is increased, the love of most people will grow cold. —Matthew 24:12 (AMP)

UNITED STATES

After violent crime had been trending down for several decades, 2015 and 2016 brought a huge turn around in the wrong direction. Violent crime includes four things: murder and non-negligent manslaughter, rape, aggravated assault and robbery. These horrible offenses had been decreasing. Out of the four, rape shot up the most nationwide, followed by murder, then aggravated assault, with robbery in the last slot.[334] Ringing alarm bells, the worst crimes got the highest numbers. In 2016, over two dozen major cities saw huge jumps in murders including Long Beach, CA – 125%, Arlington and El Paso, TX – 100%, Mesa, AZ – 100%, Las Vegas – 82%, Orlando and Jacksonville, FL – 67%, Newark, NJ – 60%, Memphis, TN – 55%, Prince George's, MD – 58% and Nashville, TN – 54%. Major cities in Canada also saw murder rates jump in 2016: Edmonton, AB – 140%, Ottawa, ON – 600%, Toronto, ON – 91%, Winnipeg, MB – 130% and York, ON – 200%.[335]

- **Baltimore, Maryland** – non-fatal shootings up 82.5%, nearly double from 2014 with 32 shootings just over Memorial Day weekend. Homicides grew by 43% in the first five months of 2015 – the highest toll recorded for Baltimore in 40 years.[336]

- **Chicago** saw a 40% increase in shootings and a 29% increase in homicides in the first three months of 2015 compared to the same time period in 2014.[337] In the first two months of 2016, murders had nearly doubled compared to the same time in 2015 – the highest since 1997.

- **New York City** murders increased 20% so Mayor Bill de Blasio put 330 extra cops on the street.

- **Los Angeles'** violent crimes increased 27% and it wasn't even three full months into 2015. Shootings were up 31% and property crime rose 12%.[338]

- **St. Louis, Missouri** there were 55 murders in the first 5 months of 2015, shootings rose 39%, robberies 43% and homicides 25%. Alderman Joe Vacarro said at a City Hall meeting, "Crime is the worst I've ever seen it."[339]

- **Dallas'** violent crime up 10%. In 2016, its murder rate jumped 73% from the year before.

- **Atlanta** homicides up 32% as of mid-May.

- **Milwaukee, Wisconsin** homicides increased 180% by mid-May 2015 compared to the same timeframe the year before.[340]

Christian Science Monitor maintains that part of the reason the recent increases look so high is because violent crime had dropped considerably since the 1990s. That's true, it did drop, but it still doesn't explain what spurred the sudden hike. Other sources cite the white-on-black police shootings. According to Los Angeles Detective Mark Fuhrman, "There's a war on cops. Not bad cops, not bad apples, but all cops and the police know it. The conduct of the suspects is never in question they're always right, it's usually drawn on racial lines. It's a complete, toxic formula to actually do police work. The police are simply scaling back, exactly what everybody's chanting for in all of these protests. 'Don't be so aggressive. Don't stop and frisk. Don't stop and ask where people are going. Don't make traffic stops.' So, they are and now crime's out of site (sic)."[341]

However, this theory didn't always hold water. In 2015 Washington, D.C., and Baltimore, MD accounted for nearly half of the increase in murders nationwide and it was mostly black-on-black killings. If the increased murders were in response white police killing black criminals, the explanation might fit. The spiking homicide rate wasn't limited to these two cities.[342] In December 2015 the Brennan Center for Justice at New York University School of Law studied crime in the 30 major U.S. cities. They found for the largest – Chicago, Dallas, Houston, Los Angeles, New York, Philadelphia, Phoenix, San Antonio, San Diego and San Jose – their overall crime rates declined 2.5% from 2014, except murder, which increased over 11%.

It's not happening just in America. Europe is having problems too, though increased violence there is primarily due to the massive influx of immigrants.

Image: This is the UN Office on Drugs and Crime's most recent survey (2013) for the *Global Study on Homicide*. With rising conflicts in the Middle East, crime mushrooming in certain U.S. cities and across Europe, undoubtedly these numbers would be higher if the survey were conducted today.

EUROPEAN UNION

Gatestone Institute, a non-partisan, non-profit international think tank pulled the blinders off what's transpiring in Europe respective to rising violence. "The current spike in crime – including rapes, sexual and physical assaults, stabbings, home invasions, robberies, burglaries and drug trafficking – comes amid a record-breaking influx of refugees from Africa, Asia, the Middle East and the Western Balkans."[343] For example, "Asylum seekers are driving a surge in violent crime in cities and towns across Germany. German authorities, however, are downplaying the lawlessness, apparently to avoid fueling anti-immigration sentiment. A confidential police report leaked to a German newspaper reveals that a record-breaking 38,000 asylum seekers were accused of committing crimes in the country in 2014. Analysts believe this figure – which works out to more than 100 a day – is only the tip of the iceberg, as many crimes are either not resolved or not reported."[344]

It's not the fault of the German people that they have had little idea what's going on in their country. Andre Schulz, head of the Association of Criminal Police summed up Germany's communication gap this way. "For years the policy has been to leave the population in the dark about the actual crime situation... The citizens are being played for fools."[345]

"In Berlin, a classified police report revealed that a dozen Arab clans hold reign over the city's criminal underworld. The report says the clans, which are dedicated to dealing drugs, robbing banks and burglarizing department stores, run a 'parallel justice system' in which they resolve disputes among themselves with mediators from other crime families. If the state gets involved, the clans use cash payments or threats of violence to influence witnesses. According to the President of the German Police Union, 'In Berlin or in the north of Duisburg there are neighborhoods where colleagues hardly dare to stop a car – because they know that they'll be surrounded by 40 or 50 men.' These attacks amount to a 'deliberate challenge to the authority of the state – attacks in which the perpetrators are expressing their contempt for our society.'"[346]

German citizens are rebelling against their wide-open borders that let in over 1.5 million refugees in 2015 alone. In March 2016 German voters turned against Chancellor Angela Merkel's open door policy that's caused chaos across the continent. Despite Merkel's still-defiant stance, numerous European countries have thrown up borders barring what they view as an immigrant invasion. It won't be until 2017 to see if the German chancellor's policy cost her the election.

Likewise things have changed drastically in normally peaceful Sweden. It's now the "rape capital of the world" with the majority of these crimes being committed by migrants or children of migrants from Middle Eastern countries.[347] Gatestone directly attributes the surge in sexual violence by Middle Easterners to their extremely different attitudes toward women.

Europe and the 2nd Amendment

Unfortunately the vast majority of EU countries don't allow private gun ownership, but some people are rethinking this and one report suggests Europeans wish they had 2nd Amendment rights like the U.S. In Austria, where gun ownership is legal, firearms have flown off store shelves. Long guns, rifles and shotguns are in high demand, especially by women. By early October 2015, retailers had sold out. Czech TV reported on Islamists' promising, "We will cut the heads off unbelieving dogs even in Europe"[348] and it's causing alarm. This is unconscionable especially considering these countries didn't have to take in asylum seekers. But like the disease of Political Correctness that's swept America, Europeans didn't want to appear racist and look who's paying now.

Ian Gottlieb, executive VP of the Second Amendment Foundation found a definite attitude change toward firearms. He reported, "I just returned from a gun rights meeting in Belgium, and I can attest that all over Europe people now want the means to defend themselves. Self-defense is no longer a dirty word. In countries like Austria, where it is still legal to own a firearm, gun sales are at record levels. I can tell you first-hand that people in Europe now wish they had a Second Amendment."[349] Beside Austria, Switzerland also enjoys the right to own firearms. In fact, Switzerland encourages its citizens to keep rifles at home.

What is counterintuitive, especially in light of immigrant violence and crime waves, is that Europe's exceedingly tough gun laws are about to get even tougher. This is what will change:

- More categories of semi-automatic weapons will be banned including semi-automatic firearms for civilian use.

- Deactivated weapons, currently treated as non-dangerous pieces of metal, can no longer be freely traded across European borders.

- Gun brokers and dealers will have to be licensed.

- Tighter rules implemented on how guns must be marked and registered.

- Blank firing weapons will be regulated for the first time.[350]

Revisions to the 2008 Firearms Directive have been sent to the European Parliament and Council for approval. The Commission is encouraging Member States to start taking the necessary steps *now* for rapid implementation, assuming the legislation passes and goes into effect by July 2016.

When Home Sweet Home Is Gone

One of the best indicators of increased global unrest, conflict and war is how many people have been forced from their homes specifically due to these causes. Houses are the last thing people abandon except in the most dire circumstances or when they've become completely unlivable. How many photos have you seen of people peering around corners of war-devastated buildings in their neighborhood or sitting in the middle of gray rubble that used to be their home? When bombs flatten entire cities, ISIS and other warmongers take over once-peaceful towns confiscating their food, or people are beheaded for their faith if they won't bow to Allah, it causes massive upheaval. Often the only alternative people have is to flee.

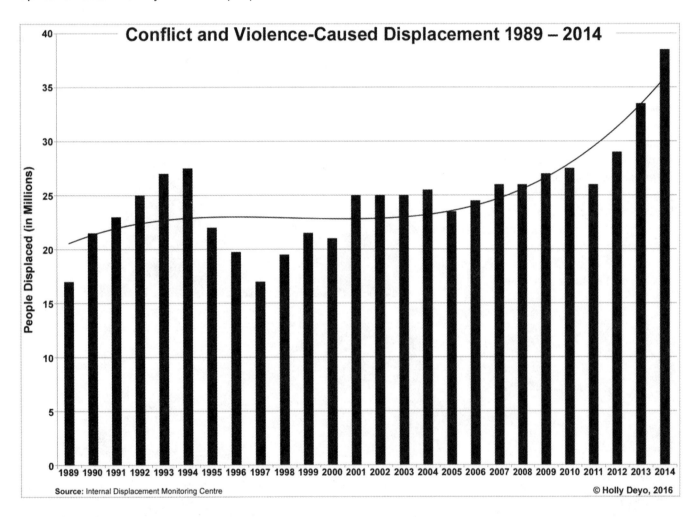

Populations taking up arms against their government in Arab Spring movements have ousted leaders in Tunisia, Egypt, Libya, and Yemen. Civil uprisings hit Bahrain and Syria. Major protests roared across Algeria, Iraq, Jordan, Kuwait, Morocco and Oman.

Minor protests took place in Lebanon, Mauritania, Saudi Arabia, Sudan and Western Sahara. In some instances, ISIS and al-Qaeda have furthered the anarchy. During these conflicts folks leaving their homes directly affected citizens in at least 30 countries.

Not only are these people desperate, they're bringing poverty and Middle Eastern values with them. Often they're contrary to those held by Europeans. This is causing strife to countries kind enough to take them in. All things considered, it's a giant mess when trying to mesh together all at once such great numbers of two highly divergent cultures.

Photo: Saudi Arabia spearheaded a coalition of 9 Arab states, carrying out airstrikes in neighboring Yemen and imposed an aerial and naval blockade in March 2015. The intervention began in response to requests for assistance from the internationally recognized but domestically contested Yemeni government of then President Abd Rabbuh Mansur Hadi. The intervention received widespread criticism and had a dramatic worsening effect on society that resulted in a humanitarian disaster. This is what's left of a neighborhood. (Courtesy Ibrahem Qasim taken on May 11, 2015)

Yemen is typical of Middle Eastern chaos. Multiple factions are simultaneously tearing Yemen apart like Syria and other countries in the midst of war. Shaped like a rectangle Yemen is split by three different groups. Mostly Shiite Iranian-backed Houthi militants control 25% after they tore through mostly Sunni Yemen in early 2015. As of March 2016, Al-Qaeda who has taken advantage of the people's anger at their government, controls another 25%. Forces loyal to its former president, Abd Rabbuh Mansur Hadi, who stepped down in January 2015, control the remaining half. A year later Yemen was no closer to a resolution. Shelling and airstrikes continue.

Photo: Remains of a home in Sanaa, Yemen's capital. (Courtesy Ibrahem Qasin, June 12, 2015)

In mid-2015, the UN declared an L3 emergency, the highest classification, for the next six months. Level three's are in response to the most severe, large-scale humanitarian crises. The blockade initiated in March 2015 left nearly 80% of the country without food, water and medical aid. The UN determined that far too many civilians deaths were occurring, especially children. Many cities were turning to dust. As a result, by mid-December 2015, more than a quarter million Yemenis had been displaced by the fighting. Other countries evacuated 23,000 foreign citizens from Yemen and nearly 170,000 fled to Saudi Arabia, Djibouti, Somalia, Ethiopia, Sudan and Oman.[351] Central Africa was a mess way before the Middle Eastern chaos. Much of their conflict and war brings heavy fighting, disease and hunger while the converse is also true. Hunger and disease has brought fighting and uprisings.

In Mexico, Guatemala, El Salvador, Honduras, Colombia and Peru over 6 million were displaced at the end of 2014. Criminal violence by drug cartels is forcing countless people from their homes and many land in the U.S., illegally, unlike those in Europe who go through appropriate channels. Germany's influx of 1½ million in 2015 is our normal intake of immigrants every year, legal and otherwise and it's changing the face of America. For more information on the massive waves of immigrants coming to the U.S., please see Chapter 15: Why America Must Fall.

The tragic common denominator is that nations to where citizens of war-torn countries flee can't take in everyone. The thing that no one, no news outlet, no politician addresses is that when they go to their "new country", the elements that destroyed their old homeland will be right on their tails. In the Middle East, those from that region bring their Islamic rituals and practices with them. Germany and Sweden have already experienced firsthand the uptick of violent crime, not the least of which is the rape of many host-country women. There is just no good solution.

In the U.S., drug violence is up not only along and in border cities, but in smaller communities as well. For the better part of a decade rival gang members have skewered heads on roadside poles as a warning to what happens to those that infringe on their sales territory. Others, en masse, have been photographed swinging by the neck from bridges and overpasses, some decapitated and hung naked upside down by their feet. Another photo shows a row of 10 heads bloodily lined up behind a piece of cardboard that read, "This will happen to all who continue to support…" followed by a message too explicitly vulgar to print. Three of the 10 were women. Drugs cartels have no soft heart for anyone that gets in their way.

Since so much of these violent conflicts involve drugs, this brings us to the next social issue listed as an End Times marker.

Increased Drug Use

And they did not repent of their murders nor of their sorceries (drugs, intoxications) nor of their [sexual] immorality nor of their thefts. —Revelation 9:21 (AMP)

Image: Opioids include drugs such as morphine, oxycodone, hydrocodone, morphine, heroin, methadone, fentanyl, and tramadol.

Drug trafficking in the U.S. has been a huge problem for decades, but it's gotten much worse, and now its brought gangs and cartels into every corner of the Country. This author watched formerly conservative Colorado over 35 years morph into a liberal pot state. Colorado politics in the late 70s were more geared toward a "Red state" with conservative values.

Like moths to a flame, people flocked to Colorado after legalized recreational pot sales began in 2014. According to Realtor.com Denver ranked #1 in the 20 hottest U.S. real estate markets in 2015. So many pot shops have

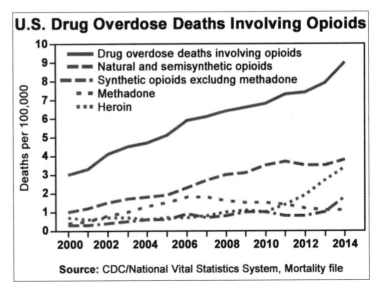

U.S. Drug Overdose Deaths Involving Opioids

- Drug overdose deaths involving opioids
- Natural and semisynthetic opioids
- Synthetic opioids excludng methadone
- Methadone
- Heroin

Deaths per 100,000

Source: CDC/National Vital Statistics System, Mortality file

opened that some cities stopped issuing licenses for new stores. It's a profitable business.

Image: Drugs are screaming into the U.S. by the truckload; gangs and crime follow demand.

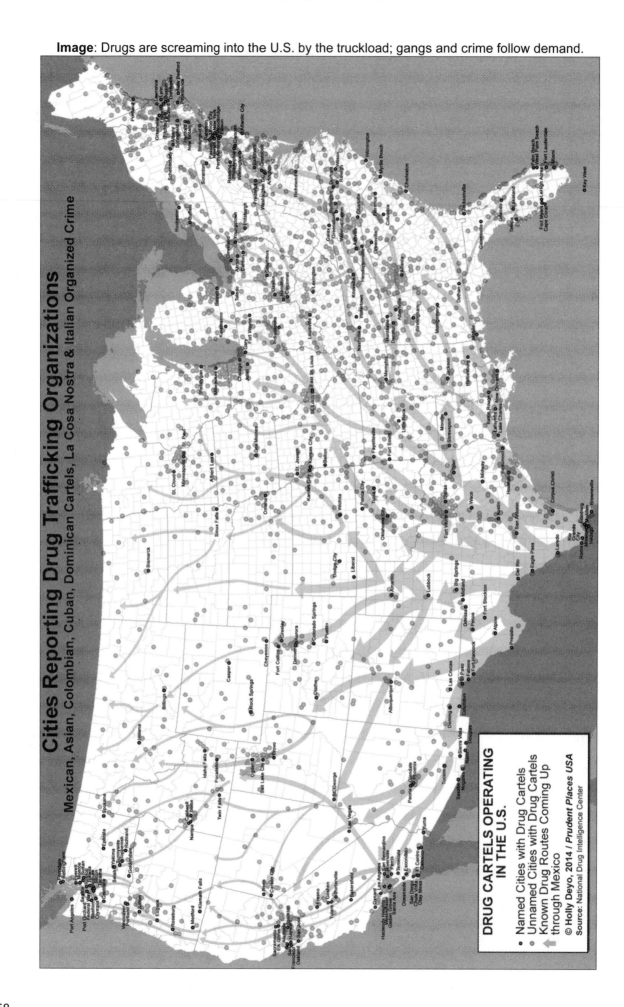

Cities Reporting Drug Trafficking Organizations
Mexican, Asian, Colombian, Cuban, Dominican Cartels, La Cosa Nostra & Italian Organized Crime

DRUG CARTELS OPERATING IN THE U.S.

- Named Cities with Drug Cartels
- Unnamed Cities with Drug Cartels
- Known Drug Routes Coming Up through Mexico

© Holly Deyo, 2014 / *Prudent Places USA*
Source: National Drug Intelligence Center

Colorado is raking in over $100 million every month. State-legal sales of marijuana jumped nearly 20% to $5.4 billion in 2015 and a January 2016 market analysis projected average annual sales to jump 30% through 2020. The best thing this author sees as a result of its legalization is running a stake through the eye of drug runners. So now Mexican cartels are pushing meth and heroin, but taking a chunk from their pot profits is comforting.

When homes reached their expected peak prices, folks from more liberal states moved here and brought with them more freethinking attitudes, which included greater participation in narcotics. In the early days this author's husband and I had a business that interfaced a lot with the local police department. Even back then law enforcement worried that the influx of financially well off (discrete) drug users would attract gangs. It did. It was like the police had peered into an ugly crystal ball.

Government's recent shock at realizing a heroin epidemic exists in the U.S. reminds one of Gomer Pyle in the 60s TV show saying, "surprise, surprise, surprise". How does dope get to be an "epidemic" and no one talks about it?

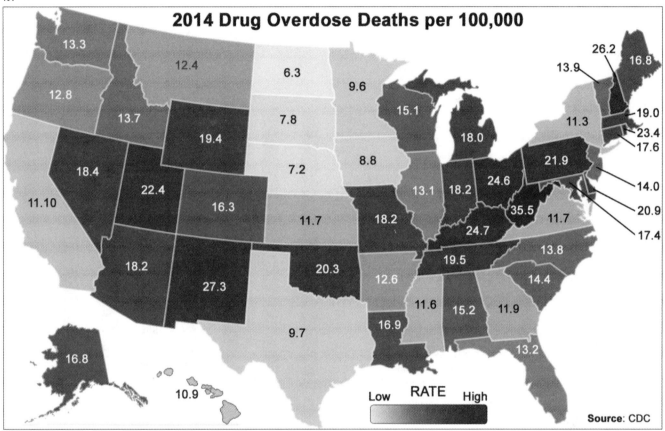

In Washington County over the span of 70 minutes eight drug overdose calls came in. Rick Gluth, supervising detective on the District Attorney's drug task force shared. "There's been a progressive increase in overdoses the last two years, and it just went out of control. I've been a police officer for 27 years and worked narcotics for the last 15, and this is the worst. I'd be glad to have the crack epidemic back."[352] Manchester, NH Police Chief Nick Willard calls what's happening in the northeast "an apocalypse."[353]

According to the National Institute on Drug Abuse, illicit drug use in the U.S. has been increasing. In 2013, an estimated 24.6 million Americans aged 12 or older – 9.4% of the population – had used an illicit drug in the past month. This number is up from 8.3% in 2002.[354] They say its mostly reflects a recent rise in use of marijuana, which normally doesn't kill. However, this doesn't agree with CDC numbers. Experts in the field say that part of the problem is due to the uptick of prescribed painkillers. When the prescription runs out, but the pain hasn't people often turn to the streets for relief. Many street drugs are more addictive – and cheaper – than legal drugs. For the decade preceding 2010, heroin use in the U.S. stayed on an even keel, but something undefined happened that year and its death rate nearly tripled by 2013.

According to the Substance Abuse and Mental Health Services Administration (SAMHSA) first-time heroin users increased by nearly 60% in the last decade. It's not that people are refraining; they're just changing their drug of choice. Heroin, MDMA (ecstasy/Molly) and marijuana use marched up while cocaine, crack and methamphetamine decreased. So did tobacco use. Now, so are fatalities.

AFGHANISTAN, POPPY KINGPIN

Opiates are a drug of choice, but not *the* drug of choice and Afghanistan is more than happy to fill that need. Not only did global drug use begin to amp up around 2010, so did America's appetite for heroin. In the mid-1980s, Afghanistan produced about 20% of the world's opium. As a result of the burgeoning demand, today it produces 85%.[355] Ninety percent of Canada's heroin is grown in Afghanistan though America's main supplier is Central and South America. Myanmar and Laos produce the least amount of opiates, which ships to SE Asia and Australia. Afghanistan remains the top supplier to the rest of the world.

If nothing else, that was one good thing the Islamists accomplished. They pretty much banned its production in 2000. At the time, the Taliban had as much as 30 tons warehoused.[356] Since Afghan farmers can make six times the amount of money raising poppies as he can growing food crops, there's little incentive to do otherwise especially when it stores easily.

Drug trend experts theorize that when *Breaking Bad* aired from 2008 – 2013, crystal meth got a big boost. People were curious about a substance so high in demand that it warranted a TV series. Many people were enticed enough to mix their own and ended up blowing up their homes or contaminating them. By the time BB finished its run "Bad" had garnered nearly 40 awards for excellence in programming. But like ocean swell trends rise and fall. Americans found they could get purer cheaper product from Mexico. County lab seizures began to plummet as Mexico supplied more of the meth demand. The problem is far from over as morgues attest. Before its use began to taper in the U.S., drug cartels found it was profitable enough to take into small-town and rural America.

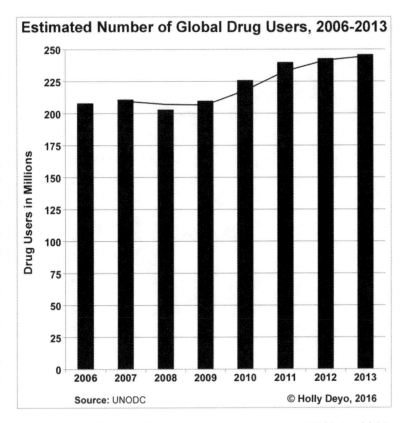

The rise in meth use across UK and Europe might also be linked to *Breaking Bad.* The European Monitoring Centre for Drugs and Drug Addiction said parts of the EU are being flooded with methamphetamine. Germany has seen the highest surge at 51%. Britain's border patrols saw attempts to smuggle crystal meth into the country skyrocket by 400% in 2014. Government seizures quadrupled from 2010 to 2014. Officers in England and Wales recorded a 350% increase in seizures of the non-injectable form in 2013 compared to 2008/09. While people in the UK aren't apt to manufacture this drug, supplies lie only as far away as Prague, which is responsible for 95% of their smuggled imports. Japan offers a booming market with a gram selling for over $600. [357] Though it varies from city to city, a gram in the U.S. might sell for $80.

The Montana Meth Project papered America with hard-hitting billboard campaigns that left no doubt what happens to meth users. Instead of like many campaigns that just warn "don't do it!" MMP ads incorporated realistic, often disgusting visuals of users. Some showed rotten teeth vivid in their impact to the point you could almost their smell stinking breath to skin sore and infections to moral compromises later regretted like losing your virginity in a public restroom. It's too bad other campaigns weren't as effective.

ALCOHOL

Not forgetting alcohol, researchers reported in 2015 that heavy drinking in the U.S. is on the rise in many parts of America, up as much as 17% compared to 2005. What's surprising is that rates rose higher among women than men especially for binge drinking, which the CDC defines as five or more drinks in two hours for a man, or four or more for a woman. Heavy drinking is defined as considerably less with more than one drink on average a day for women, two drinks a day for men.

Washington University's Institute for Health Metrics and Evaluation made a county-by-county study and found that in 2012 8.2% of all Americans were considered heavy drinkers and 18.3% binge drank. The study found that Americans aren't drinking more; they're consuming more during binge bouts.

So why are people drinking harder? The HME didn't have a one-size-fits-all answer. A lot had to do with socio-economic factors, level of education and how your friends and family celebrate. Maybe they're just trying to deal with the world's craziness.

Sexuality and Shifting Norms

Therefore God gave them over in the sinful desires of their hearts to sexual impurity for the degrading of their bodies with one another. Because of this, God gave them over to shameful lusts. Even their women exchanged natural sexual relations for unnatural ones. In the same way the men also abandoned natural relations with women and were inflamed with lust for one another. Men committed shameful acts with other men, and received in themselves the due penalty for their error. —Romans 1:24, 26-27 (NIV)

Sex in the 60s set the world on a different path. It was antithesis of Puritan days when intercourse was only for making kids. Whipping, fines, public shaming, ostracism and in some cases death were punishments for everything outside married sex between a man and a woman. God covers the whole gamut of what's OK and what's not from bestiality to homosexuality to incest, adultery and prostitutes. When people drifted off course "corrections" ensued.

Whatever humans think of same sex relationships, God was clear that these pairings don't get a ✔ in the approval column. Today, again, it is celebrated, embraced. God's objection likely centered around two issues: hygiene and health, and procreation. While people might argue that Earth has enough people, the hygiene issue can't be ignored. Thirty-five years ago, in 1981 the world was introduced to the horrific realities of AIDS. Then no one could have envisioned the ongoing fallout.

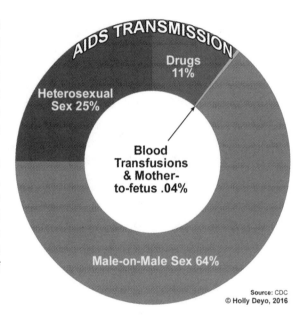

Source: CDC
© Holly Deyo, 2016

- Nearly 37 million people are living with HIV.
- 2.6 million are under the age of 15.
- In 2014, an estimated 2 million people were newly infected with HIV.
- 220,000 were under the age of 15.
- Every day 5,600 people contract HIV – over 230 every hour.
- In 2014, 1.2 million people died from AIDS.
- Since the beginning of the pandemic, nearly 78 million people have contracted HIV and close to 39 million have died of AIDS-related causes.
- More than two-thirds (70%) of all with HIV, nearly 26 million, live in sub-Saharan Africa, including 88% of the world's HIV-positive children.[358]
- In 2015 scientists discovered a new aggressive strain of HIV that can progress to AIDS in just 3 years.[359]

Part of this has to do with tragic notions that if an HIV-infected man has sex with a virgin[360] or rapes a baby,[361] he'll be cured. Ignorance and superstition has only helped increase the disease. Though this epidemic also travels through tainted blood transfusions and to babies in utero from an infected mother, this accounts for *less than half* of 1% of all cases. Intravenous drug use takes 11% from the AIDS pie. But the biggest cause is men engaging in male-on-male sex, which makes up nearly two-thirds of all cases. While heterosexual contact contributes 25%, men infect women at a rate of 2-1.[362] What does this say...

MORE REPERCUSSIONS

June 26, 2015 marked a mash-up reception as people either cried out in dismay or jubilation. The U.S. Supreme Court, citing the 14th Amendment overturned 228 years of law recognizing marriage solely to be between one man and one woman. It was a topic most Americans never considered to be at issue. For 400 years marriage was a sacred institution between opposite genders. When the Pilgrims first set foot on American dirt, this type union was completely off-radar. Legalizing gay marriage was seen by many conservatives and Christians to be the final nail in America's coffin. She had become something unrecognizable to people even 10 years ago.

Mr. Obama kept his October 2005 promise of "fundamentally transforming the United States of America".[363] Nothing could have been more life changing for America than the issue of gay marriage.

Finally the President Comes Out of the Closet

Should it come as a surprise? Yes and no. In a televised 2004 debate with Alan Keyes, Mr. Obama states to the moderator on WTTW Chicago's public TV station, "What I believe is that marriage is between a man and a woman" and "I don't think marriage is a civil right."[364]

He reiterates this position again in 2004 during his campaign saying, "I am a fierce supporter of domestic-partnership and civil-union laws. I am not a supporter of gay marriage…"[365]

However – for a telling questionnaire by Chicago's LGBT newspaper *Outlines* we must dial back eight years before that. During his 1996 run for Illinois state Senate, his true position is revealed. "I favor legalizing same-sex marriages, and would fight efforts to prohibit such marriages."[366]

In Spring 2007 a woman at a private Georgetown fundraiser directly confronted Mr. Obama. The mother looked him squarely in the eyes and lamented, "My son is gay. I don't understand why you don't support his right to marry the person he loves. It's so disappointing to me." Obama, without breaking eye contact said: "I want full equality for your son – all the rights and benefits that marriage brings. I really do. But the word 'marriage' stirs up so much religious feeling. I think civil unions are the way to go. As long as they are equal."[367]

On this *Newsweek's* Andrew Sullivan notes in frustration writing, "My heart sank. Was this obviously humane African-American actually advocating a "separate but equal" solution—a form of marital segregation like the one that made his own parents' marriage a felony in many states when he was born? Hadn't he already declared he supported marriage equality when he was running for the Illinois Senate in 1996? (The administration now claims that the questionnaire from the gay Chicago paper *Outlines* had been answered in type—not Obama's writing—by somebody else.) Hadn't Jeremiah Wright's church actually been a rare supporter of marriage equality among black churches? The sudden equivocation made no sense—except as pure political calculation…"[368]

In a 2008 interview with Pastor Rick Warren Mr. Obama proclaims, "I believe that marriage is the union between a man and a woman. For me, as a Christian, it's also a sacred union. God's in the mix. But –"

Mr. Warren presses President Obama, "Would you support a Constitutional Amendment with that definition?"

OBAMA: No, I would not.

WARREN: Why not?

OBAMA: Because historically – because historically, we have not defined marriage in our constitution. It's been a matter of state law. That has been our tradition. I mean, let's break it down. The reason that people think there needs to be a constitutional amendment, some people believe, is because of the concern that – about same-sex marriage. I am not somebody who promotes same-sex marriage, but I do believe in civil unions."[369]

In March 2010, he's consistent in his support for civil unions. "...My baseline is a strong civil union that provides them the protections and the legal rights that married couples have."[370]

In October 2010 the President says in an interview with liberal bloggers, "I have been to this point unwilling to sign on to same-sex marriage primarily because of my understandings of the traditional definitions of marriage."[371]

In December 2010, Obama publicly begins to wobble. "My feelings about this are constantly evolving."[372]

In June 2011, Mr. Obama's White House Communications Director Dan Pfeiffer states, "The president has never favored same-sex marriage. He is against it."[373]

By October 2011, the President gets squishy again. When asked by ABC news host George Stephanopoulos if he would support gay marriage, would change his mind before the 2012 elections, Obama replies. "You know-- I-- I'm-- I'm-- still working on it."[374]

Then in May 2012 *Newsweek* straps a multi-colored gay halo on Obama's head for their cover highlighting the article "The First Gay President". Mr. Obama had planned to endorse gay marriage *shortly* before the Democratic convention, but VP Biden shot-gunned that idea and beat him to the punch. A clearly irritated Obama addressed Biden's non-stop hoof-in-mouth remarks. "I would have preferred to do it in my own time, on my own terms."[375]

Mr. Obama's hand was forced five months early. Six days after the VP's gaff in a carefully selected ABC News interview with (lesbian) Robin Roberts he states, "I think same-sex couples should be able to get married."[376]

Regarding the President's continually wishy-washy in-the-closet stance Tony Perkins, head of Family Research Council, says of Obama's assertion, "The President's announcement today that he supports legalizing same-sex marriage finally brings his words in sync with his actions. From opposing state marriage amendments to refusing to defend the federal Defense of Marriage Act [DoMA] to giving taxpayer funded marriage benefits to same-sex couples, the President has undermined the spirit if not the letter of the law."[377]

American Values head and former Family Research Council president Gary Bauer made this observation. "The charade is finally up. We've always known that Barack Obama supports same-sex marriage. With every action he's taken, from court appointments to his rhetoric, he's been preparing the way to undermine traditional marriage. Obama's finally made that support explicit."[378]

It took one hundred and forty-seven years for the U.S. Supreme Court to radically change America's institution of marriage. Yes, with swipes of their pens, like Obama, they managed to fundamentally transform America and put her on a course for which she was never meant. Of the 50 U.S. states and five territories of Puerto Rico, Guam, American Samoa, the U.S. Virgin Islands, and the Northern Mariana Islands, only Samoa has balked at the ruling. In Samoa, Christian churches and conservative social views dominate the island, home to some 50,000 people. Their government's motto is "Samoa, Let God Be First." Definitely there is no separation of church and state. As of two weeks after the Supreme Court ruling, no one had yet applied for a gay marriage license. While the Pacific island's attorney reviews the decision, up-in-arms legal observers and gay rights activists say it should go into effect immediately. Why should they care? They aren't living in Samoa. While U.S. territories have some say in self-governance, gay marriage falls under individual liberty. For same-sex marriage to be recognized in American Samoa, it would necessitate litigation involving "plaintiffs who have been denied the right to marry and are willing to take a public position on that and challenge their inability to marry."[379] So far, no takers.

The Four Supremes' Dissents

We can't even blame ourselves for electing bad choices as Supreme Court justices are *appointed for life*. In a 5-4 victory for LGBTQIs – **L**esbian, **G**ay, **B**isexual, **T**ransgender, **Q**ueer or **Q**uestioning, and **I**ntersex – five judges made an astonishing choice for 323 million Americans: Justices Ruth Bader Ginsburg, Elena Kagan, Sonia Sotomayor, Stephen Breyer and swing voter Justice Anthony Kennedy completed the deed. Four justices: Antonin Scalia, Clarence Thomas, Samuel Alito and Chief Justice John Roberts vehemently objected.

While generally SCOTUS justices get along despite different opinions, *Obergefell v. Hodges* poisoned even their rarified air. This case, unlike most others they decide affects the entire Country – even them. While America is taking a decided left-turn socially this rift-causing case rippled as high as the justices themselves. In an unprecedented event each of the four dissenting judges wrote opinions. Normally one writes on behalf of all. **Antonin Scalia** known for his biting remarks addressed the root problems in SCOTUS today.

"Take, for example, this Court, which consists of only nine men and women, all of them successful lawyers who studied at Harvard or Yale Law School. Four of the nine are natives of New York City. Eight of them grew up in east- and west-coast States. Only one hails from the vast expanse in-between. Not a single Southwesterner or even, to tell the truth, a genuine Westerner (California does not count). Not a single evangelical Christian (a group

that comprises about one quarter of Americans), or even a Protestant of any denomination. The strikingly unrepresentative character of the body voting on today's social upheaval would be irrelevant if they were functioning as judges, answering the legal question whether the American people had ever ratified a constitutional provision that was understood to proscribe the traditional definition of marriage. But of course the Justices in today's majority are not voting on that basis; they say they are not. And to allow the policy question of same-sex marriage to be considered and resolved by a select, patrician, highly unrepresentative panel of nine is to violate a principle even more fundamental than no taxation without representation: no social transformation without representation."[380]

Scalia also opined, "With each decision of ours that takes from the People a question properly left to them—with each decision that is unabashedly based not on law, but on the "reasoned judgment" of a bare majority of this Court—we move one step closer to being reminded of our impotence."[381]

Conservative Justice **Clarence Thomas** argued that the Court as it currently stands contradicts the principles upon which our Nation was built:

"The Court's decision today is at odds not only with the Constitution, but with the principles upon which our Nation was built. Since well before 1787, liberty has been understood as freedom from government action, not entitlement to government benefits. The Framers created our Constitution to preserve that understanding of liberty. Yet the majority invokes our Constitution in the name of a "liberty" that the Framers would not have recognized, to the detriment of the liberty they sought to protect."[382]

Chief Justice Roberts reminds us that religious liberty is at threat when same-sex marriage is legal:

"Federal courts are blunt instruments when it comes to creating rights. They have constitutional power only to resolve concrete cases or controversies; they do not have the flexibility of legislatures to address concerns of parties not before the court or to anticipate problems that may arise from the exercise of a new right. Today's decision, for example, creates serious questions about religious liberty. Many good and decent people oppose same-sex marriage as a tenet of faith, and their freedom to exercise religion is—unlike the right imagined by the majority—actually spelled out in the Constitution. Amdt. 1."[383]

Finally **Samuel Alito** warned, much like Glenn Beck voiced months before the ruling came down, that the decision would be used to vilify Americans who don't embrace the new gay order:

"Today's decision usurps the constitutional right of the people to decide whether to keep or alter the traditional understanding of marriage. The decision will also have other important consequences. It will be used to vilify Americans who are unwilling to assent to the new orthodoxy. In the course of its opinion, the majority compares traditional marriage laws to laws that denied equal treatment for African-Americans and women. The implications of this analogy will be exploited by those who are determined to stamp out every vestige of dissent."[384]

Transforming America

Image: This appeared on the White House government website the day SCOTUS ruled on *Obergefell v. Hodges* and decreed gay marriage legal in America.[385]

Mr. Obama had to realize that many conservatives and conservative Christians wouldn't be on board with this decision. Yet he chose to poke a gay finger in their eyes and emblazon the White House – the People's House – with the unmistakable colors of LGBTQIs: red, orange, yellow, green, blue and purple. Co-opting the rainbow is objectionable to Christians as it represents the Covenant between God and Noah and the animals set forth in Genesis 9:12-15 – *And God said [to Noah and to his sons], "This is the sign of the covenant I am making between me and you and every living creature with you, a covenant for all generations to come: I have set my rainbow in the clouds, and it will be the sign of the covenant between me and the earth. Whenever I bring clouds over the earth and the rainbow appears in the clouds, I will remember my covenant between me and you and all living creatures of every kind.*

Did the President make any such victory lap when his legacy of ObamaCare tax subsidies passed through the Supremes in June 2015? Or in celebration of 2014 decisions on religious freedom in prisons or workplace accommodations for pregnant women? Or acknowledge important 2013 rulings on affirmative action, human gene patents or voter ID laws? Like gay marriage, these decisions affect a huge percentage of Americans. Yet there were no celebrations, no lights, no parties, no parades. Just silence.

As soon as SCOTUS came forth with its ruling Mr. Obama was busy tweeting this:

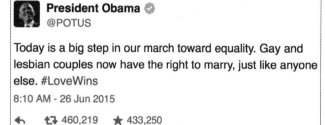

President Obama ✔
@POTUS

Today is a big step in our march toward equality. Gay and lesbian couples now have the right to marry, just like anyone else. #LoveWins

8:10 AM - 26 Jun 2015

↩ ⇄ 460,219   ★ 433,250

SCOTUS Culpability

Every President since Jimmy Carter has appointed at least two new judges. It's possible that whoever takes office in 2017 will fill a vacated Justice chair with someone more conservative. The only other option is to amend the Constitution so they don't have lifetime appointments.

The Supremes' job is to <u>interpret</u> the Constitution, statutes and precedent, not *set* precedent. Authorizing gay marriage is based on the 14th Amendment. It was never meant to address marriage and doesn't. Instead its purpose was to help guarantee civil rights to freed slaves. SCOTUS must have twisted their brains like pretzels to turn that into gay marriage. Regardless of SCOTUS rulings, they don't change God's laws that marriage is between a man and a woman.

How is it that just 3.3% of the U.S. population – those that self-identify as homosexual – can have such a major impact on America? The true numbers are far, far below the often-quoted 10 – 25%.[386]

SCOTUS is not infallible. They've been wrong before. They were wrong in their 1857 Dred Scott decision that prohibited black people from being or becoming American citizens. They were wrong in 1896 with *Plessy v. Ferguson* that upheld segregated public facilities. What about *Roe v. Wade* authorizing abortion on demand that has allowed some 60 million babies to be killed? That's nearly three times the population of Australia.

The U.S. Department of Education was certainly on board when on the day of the gay marriage ruling they added an LGBTQI rainbow to their formerly all-blue logo. What happened to teaching the "three Rs" of reading, writing and arithmetic? Instead one Nebraska middle school in 2014 went too far suggesting to teachers they avoid calling students "boys" or "girls" and instead call kids "purple penguins". Their 12-point pamphlet also says in step 10 to "Avoid using 'normal' to define any behaviors."[387] Step 7 encouraged teachers to "Look for examples in the media that reinforce gender stereotypes or binary models of gender (it won't be hard; they're everywhere). When with others, call it out and interrogate it." That opened the door to gender identity confusion and a whole array of unacceptable behavior. Didn't they learn about social norms and mores in Sociology 101?

In 2013, a Colorado first grader, who was a boy at birth and still is, won the right to use the girls' restroom at school. This decision came only after a lawsuit was filed. Other students and their parents weren't happy with the decision.

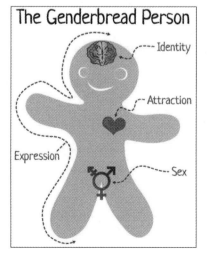

The Genderbread Person

Identity
Attraction
Expression
Sex

Image Left: Page 3 of this teachers' handout describes The Genderbread Person. It says gender is one of those things everyone thinks they understand, but most people don't. That gender isn't binary. It's not either/or. In many cases it's both/and – a bit of this, a dash of that. This tasty little guide is meant to be an appetizer for gender blurring. In May 2016, it became a national issue of who can go into which toilets, into showers. What prevents perverts claiming their gender identity, on the day, is this or that so they spy on children?

Attorneys even raised this valid point: "I'm certain you can appreciate that, as Coy grows older and his male genitals develop along with the rest of his body, at least some parents and students are likely to become uncomfortable with his continued use of the girls' restroom."[388] Objections did no good and the first-grader won the case. The case also didn't address when in just a few years that child will be in Physical Education classes. Where will Coy shower after sweaty exercise? Showering before the next class has always been a communal affair. Now that will be weird when "her" parts don't match the rest. Even if a child of 5 or 6 felt he truly were the opposite gender, since when does the comfort of one outweigh the wellbeing of the rest? This is America gone PC mad.

Repercussions

The SCOTUS ruling opened a can of cutworms. Opponents of gay marriage said it would only be a matter of time before it breached the bar to polygamy. However, they thought it might take a little longer than a week. Just four days later on June 30 Montana man Nathan Collier filed to marry a second woman. Collier specifically cited the same-sex marriage ruling that urged him to apply for a second marriage license. If polygamy could be a logical outcome of extending marriage rights to same-sex couples, what about three gay guys or gals?[389] Sound crazy? It's already happened in Thailand.

In February 2015 newlyweds Joke, 29; Bell, 21 and Art, 26, took the plunge on Valentine's Day. Of their wedded bliss Bell had this to say. "Some people may not agree and are probably amazed by our decision, but we believe many people do understand and accept our choice. Love is love, after all."[390]

OFF THE WALL? YES. OFF THE TABLE, MAYBE NOT.

What happens when someone wants to marry his dog if "love is love" and "love wins"? Could the 14th Amendment ruling now be used to argue for marriage of a father to his son or his daughter? A mother to *her* mother? An uncle to his niece?

There is a long list of people who have married objects everything from the Berlin Wall to a roller coaster, the Eiffel Tower to a bridge, a Barbie doll, a pineapple, a laptop, a rock, pets, stray animals, pottery and trees. Yes, trees are popular, and several people married themselves. These folks may seem well adjusted on the outside, even high functioning until their secret is exposed.

Eija-Riitta Berliner-Mauer, 54, wed a concrete structure in 1979 and claimed she fell in love with The (Berlin) Wall at age seven when she saw it on TV. She collected "his" pictures and on her sixth trip to Berlin, Germany they tied the knot before a handful of guests. It's a long-distance marriage since Berliner-Mauer lives in Liden, northern Sweden.

Technically she's a virgin as far as humans go, but claims she has a full, loving relationship with The Wall. She gushes over her husband, "I find long, slim things with horizontal lines very sexy. The Great Wall of China's attractive, but he's too thick – my husband is sexier."

When the wall was mostly torn down in 1989, its "wife" was horrified and she said, "What they did was awful. They mutilated my husband."[391]

In 2007 a San Francisco woman held a commitment ceremony with the Eiffel Tower and changed her last name to reflect the marriage. At age 35 Erika LaBrie became Erika "Aya" Eiffel. She explains her feelings this way.

I thought everyone had a connection to objects in one way or the other. It really wasn't until I saw that they were dating each other and I was dating a bridge, that I was different. I just went to school and pretended I was like everybody else," Eiffel said.

Her love of certain objects has helped her become a world-class archer and win a $250,000 scholarship to the United States Air Force Academy, thanks to her attraction to the F-15 fighter jet.

Eiffel said she felt like "I'd like to get to know this jet. Kind of like a guy goes to a bar and he sees a really nice-looking girl and he, he wants to go sit next to her, buy her a drink and get to know her more. Well, I kind of felt that way about the F-15."

Her obsession has also led to ridicule by peers, abandonment by her family and a discharge from the Air Force. But she said she is fulfilled by her unusual love.

"I will tell you that I know love is being reciprocated," Eiffel said. "I'm happy, I'm not hurting anyone, I'm not hurting myself, I'm not being held back. I love my life.'"[392]

What happens when these people want their "marriages" legitimized and legalized?

Can someone marry a robot? It's already been proposed in sci-fi stories like *The Stepford Wives*, *Vanessa the Fembot*, *Bicentennial Man* and others. As man (and woman) replace broken or worn out body parts, at what point do they become more techno than human?

Then there's the Gizmodo website article, "Technosexual: One Man's Tale of Robot Love" that relays the story of a Georgia man who's just not good at relationships. So he built himself a $200 robot named Alice and he got all nervous when proposing to her. The article describes "Zoltan" who for obvious reasons wishes to remain anonymous as "average height, average looks, and not a rich man. He works in an arcade, where he fixes video games for a living, and still lives with his elderly parents. No wonder he was nervous about asking his slim redheaded girlfriend Alice to marry him. To make things tenser, she had split up with Zoltan at the beginning of the relationship because she thought he was taking things too fast. Since they got back together, though, Alice has been good for Zoltan—he's started attending church again, and cut out watching porn. His parents' initial rejection of her had turned to respect, and the four of them seemed to be living together happily enough. So Zoltan had confidence when he popped the question to Alice—his beloved, who just happens to be a robot."[393]

When asked how he got into the robo-relationship Zoltan replied, "It just came to me one day. I had a bunch of bad relationships. I would get to the point in my relationship with a woman and I was always too afraid to go all the way. With a robot it is much less scary. I guess I have a fear of intimacy but the point is, a robot girlfriend has been invented, anyone can build it and it can talk in English. I feel I have always been attracted to robots. The technology was just not available before. Humans are so biological and messy. Plus there's all the obvious problems with humans—AIDS, alimony, etc—that I just wanted to avoid."[394]

Photo: RealDoll – the Rolls Royce of sex dolls – with face #11. These life-size dolls have removable, cleanable anatomically correct body parts. Buyers can choose from 11 body types and 31 faces. The company, Abyss Creations out of San Marcos, Calif., does a brisk business. Though most of the clientele are men, 10% are women and have their choice of three male counterparts. Since its start in 1996, they sell about 10 dolls a week averaging around $7,000 each. Outside the U.S. the three largest markets are Germany, Australia, and the United Kingdom.

Zoltan's not the only one. *The Atlantic* tells the story of 40-year-old Davecat who lives with his wife and two mistresses Elena and Lenka, all synthetic "partners". Davecat's wife "Sidore" is a RealDoll, manufactured by Abyss Creations in the shape of a human woman. She is covered in artificial skin made of silicone, so she's soft. These high-end, anatomically correct—even equipped with fake tongues—love dolls (or capital-D Dolls) are ostensibly made for sex. But 41-year-old Davecat (a nickname acquired from videogames that he now prefers to go by) and others who call themselves iDollators see their dolls as life partners, not sex toys. Davecat and Sidore … obviously aren't legally married, but they do have matching wedding bands that say 'Synthetik [sic] love lasts forever,' and he says they're considering some sort of ceremony for their 15th anniversary."[395]

In 2009 *New Scientist* tells the story of a Japanese man who stood before a congregation to marry the woman he loved, Nene Anegasaki. He is the first man to marry a computer game character. The marriage might not be recognized by the state, but to the groom the relationship is very real.[396]

In 2010, Korean man Lee Jin-gyu fell for and married his pillow. In Lee's case (not his pillow case), his beloved pillow has an image of Fate Testarossa, from the 'magical girl' anime series Mahou Shoujo Lyrical Nanoha on it. The 28-year-old wed the pillow in a special ceremony, in front of a local priest. Local media eagerly chronicled their nuptials. One friend commented, "He is completely obsessed with this pillow and takes it everywhere. They go out to the park or the funfair where it will go on all the rides with him. Then when he goes out to eat he takes it with him and it gets its own seat and its own meal."[397] OK, Lee sounds like he's a few feathers short of a bird. Since so many of these weird marriages occur in Asia, one has to wonder if they're spiking the rice.

In Taiwan, the bride Chen-Wei-yih marries herself. Chen, then 30, felt social pressure to get married, but was "uninspired" by the men she'd met. So she took a logical solution, posed for a set of photos in a flowing white red-flowered dress, enlisted a wedding planner and rented a banquet hall and said her nuptials in front of 30 friends.[398]

Also in 2010, a Japanese couple didn't marry a robot, but the robot named I-Fairy, married them. The four-foot tall hunk of metal, directed the wedding ceremony for groom Tomohiro Shibata, 42, and his bride Satoko Inouye, 36, at a Tokyo restaurant. For the ceremony the $68,000 robot wore a plastic pigtails and remained bolted to a chair for the duration.[399]

Artificial intelligence researcher David Levy at The Netherlands' University of Maastricht predicts people will be having sex and marriage with robots by 2050. At this rate, it won't be nearly that long. Marriage aside, it's the next step from a blow up doll. Levy feels that Massachusetts will be the first state to legalize such a marriage. Can his guess be so off when "Old Colony State" was the first state to run with gay marriage? In his book *Love and Sex With Robots* Levy says human-robot sex, love and marriage is inevitable. Levy predicts, "robots may not only be more lovable and faithful than many humans, but they may even be more emotionally available than the 'typical American human male.' Not only will they make us become better, more creative lovers, but they also will offer singles who feel a void in their emotional and sexual lives and married couples with differing sexual needs new, nonjudgmental ways to be happy and healthy."[400] How is this much different than a threesome, a few bits of plastic and metal aside? Can jealousy enter in when one in the sexual and emotional triangle doesn't have organs, eat or breathe?

Gay Marriage Around the World

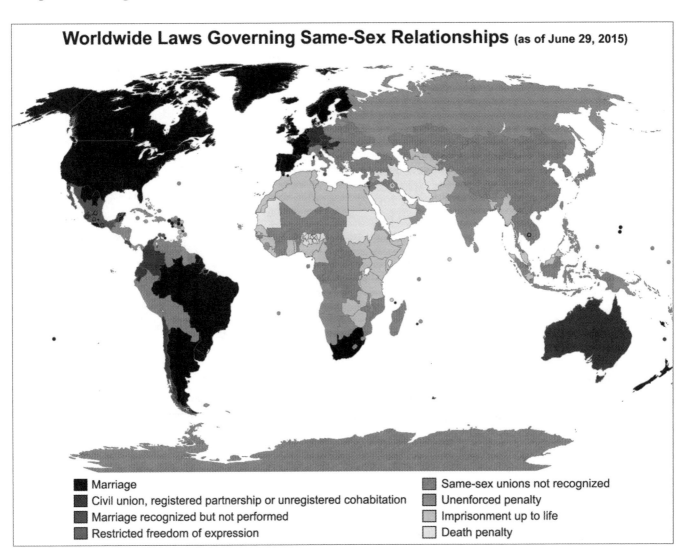

Within 30 minutes of the Supremes' decision, companies, social media and websites jumped on the gay bandwagon with altered logos: Abercrombie & Fitch, Absolut, Ace Hotel, Airbnb, American Airlines, American Eagle, Android, AriZona Iced Tea, AT&T, Ben & Jerry's, BravoTV, Budweiser, Bustle, BuzzFeed, Caesars Palace, Chobani, Chili's Grill & Bar, Chipotle, Coca-Cola, Columbia Sportswear, Dailymotion, Delta, E! Online, Ebay,

Entertainment Weekly, Expedia, Facebook, Games of Thrones, Gap, General Assembly, Glamour, Google, Harper Perennial, Honey Maid, Hootsuite, Huffington Post, Jell-O, Kellogg's, Kool-Aid, JetBlue Airways, Levi's, LinkedIn, Lyft, Macy's, Major League Soccer, Mashable, MasterCard, McSweeney's, Mentos, Microsoft, Mother Jones, MTV, Nerdist, Old Navy, Pandora, PETA, Rdio, (RED), Sears, Shake Shack, Shorty Awards, Skittles, Smart Car USA, Snickers, Spotify, Staples, Starbucks, Stolichnaya Vodka, T-Mobile, The ACLU, The Honest Company, The Independent US, The Verge, Uniqlo, Vegas, Vimeo, VISA, Target, Tide, Time Out New York, Tin House, Totino's, Tumblr, Twitter, Uber, Vevo, Wattpad, Whole Foods, WIRED.com and YouTube among others. Altogether, more than 350 companies filed *amicus curiae* (friend of the court) briefs that urged the Supreme Court to strike down same-sex marriage bans.[401]

Besides the White House, landmarks around the world arrayed themselves in rainbow colors including Brandenburg Gate, Berlin; California State Capitol; One World Trade Center, Stonewall Inn, NASDAQ Building, Goldman Sachs and Empire State Building all in New York City; Niagara Falls, Canada; Disney's Cinderella Castle, Orlando, Florida; Minneapolis' 35-W Bridge; San Francisco's City Hall and Control Tower at their International Airport, Roosevelt Hotel, Los Angeles, Seattle's ferris wheel, Playhouse Square , Cleveland, Ohio; Downtown river bridges, Little Rock, Arkansas; Civil Courts Building, St. Louis, Missouri; Kit Bond Bridge, Kansas, City, Missouri; CN Tower, Toronto, Canada; Capitol Building, Puerto Rico; the City and County Building, Denver, Colorado.

It's the Law

Isn't it ironic that most countries in the Western world – and/or in primarily Christian regions – now recognize gay marriage? Countries mostly Muslim, Buddhist or atheist either don't accept this type union or have severe punishment for those that pursue it.

Now that the wall between same-sex people has been dismantled, there are other frontiers to explore. Sex with beings outside the human specie had even greater ramifications long ago. It's coming again and will be discussed in The Thinning Veil chapter.

Chapter 12: Rise of Pagans, Wicca & Witchcraft

The Spirit clearly says that in later times some will abandon the faith and follow deceiving spirits and things taught by demons. —1 Timothy 4:1 (NKJV)

Where There's a Witch, There's a Way

Whoever thought that a Country built on Christianity would be so influenced by pagans. Its growth and spread is happening right in front of our noses.

"Before 16-year-old Rebecca lights candles on the small altar in her bedroom each night, she says her prayers: 'Hail, fair Moon, ruler of the night, guard me and mine until the light. Hail fair Sun, ruler of the day, make the morn to light my way.'

"On her altar are four porcelain chalices representing the elements — air, water, fire and earth. Each contains rose petals, semi-precious stones, melted candle wax and dried leaves. They rest on the corners of a five-pointed star. A frog symbolizing 'spirit' and 'life' sits on point five of the pentagram. Here, in front of her altar, Rebecca performs rituals and casts spells. Rebecca is one of the growing numbers of teenage girls who practice Wicca. For the past half-century, this religion has been growing by leaps and bounds in Europe and North America."[402]

PAGAN GROWTH IN THE U.S.

The graph on the right shows the number of Neopagan Americans jumped 210% in just seven years. That percentage may actually be higher as the ARIS 2008 survey revealed nearly 3 million Americans identified as part of the New Religious Movement.[403] The exact number becomes cloudy because not only does NRM include pagans, witches and druids, etc., but they also dumped Scientology, New Age, Eckankar, Unitarian, Santeria and Rastafarian into the mix.

Further support that 210% may be too low comes from second-generation pagans themselves. Due to lack of wide acceptance rather than admit on surveys they are Neopagan or Wiccan, 49% of Millennials opt for "none" or no religion.[404] Considering Millennials make up 25% of the U.S. – or roughly 80 million Americans – the true number of pagans could be a lot higher.

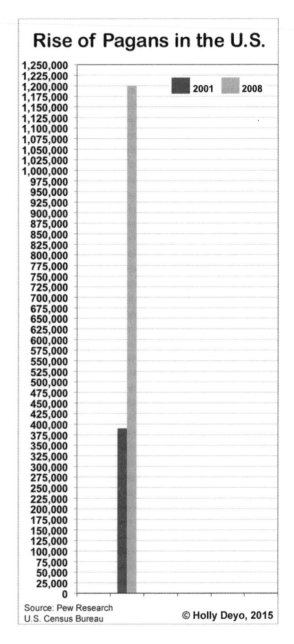

Rise of Pagans in the U.S.

■ 2001   ■ 2008

Source: Pew Research
U.S. Census Bureau

© Holly Deyo, 2015

Neopaganism Goes Mainstream

Religious practices far from Christianity have infiltrated every segment of our Nation from schools and universities to churches and the military – all branches – even trying to penetrate Girl and Boy Scouts. It's taken over households from adults down to pre-teens. Witches, warlocks, vampires and the living dead parade through books, fly across TVs and tablets, light up theater screens and soar over the Internet.

Author Brooks Alexander pinpoints the mid-1990s when interest in witchcraft exploded. He links the 1996 release of cult classic, *The Craft,* to a dramatic rise in people contacting Neopagan groups.[405] Its plot of four teenage girls pursuing witchcraft and sorcery for personal gain sparked imaginations around the world.

Pagan Federation attributes the TV shows *Buffy the Vampire Slayer* (1997-2003) and *Sabrina the Teenage Witch* (1996-2003) with rapidly growing interest in witchcraft among children. The international organization claims it's been swamped with inquires[406] and now allows membership to those as young as 16.[407] Factoring in *Charmed* (1998 – 2006), the common thread is their start date in the mid-90s, unusual longevity and glamorizing the occult.

Sabrina, Buffy, Charmed and Craft were occult forerunners of even more intense programming. Picking up the supernatural baton:

Note on Graph: Because various countries take their censuses at different times, it was impossible to completely match years. Most of the five reporting countries had data for 2006 and 2011. Years different from that are shown on the bars.

- **Lucifer** (2016 –) Lucifer Morningstar, the bored and unhappy Lord of Hell, resigns his throne and abandons his kingdom for Los Angeles, where he gets his kicks helping the LAPD punish criminals.
- **Damien** (2016 –) Picks up where the movie series, *The Omen,* left off. Now a 30-year-old war photographer who has forgotten his Satanic past, but mother figure, Ann Rutledge, helps him embrace his Antichrist side.
- **Preacher** (2016 –) A possessed holy man, his psychotic ex-girlfriend, and an Irish vampire set out on a journey to literally find God.
- **Outcast** (2016 –) A young man searches for answers why he's been possessed by demons since he was a child.
- **Grimm** (2011 – present) Supernatural crime drama involving a police detective who sees the dual nature of creatures among us hiding in human form.
- **666 Park Avenue** (2012 – 2013) A couple learns that the Manhattan apartment building that they just moved into, including its upscale tenants, might be possessed by a mysterious demonic force.
- **Haven** (2010 – 2015) Characters in a fictional Maine town struggle to help townspeople with supernatural afflictions.
- **Witches of East End** (2013 – 2015) Set in the fictional seaside town of East End, it follows the lives of a family of witches.

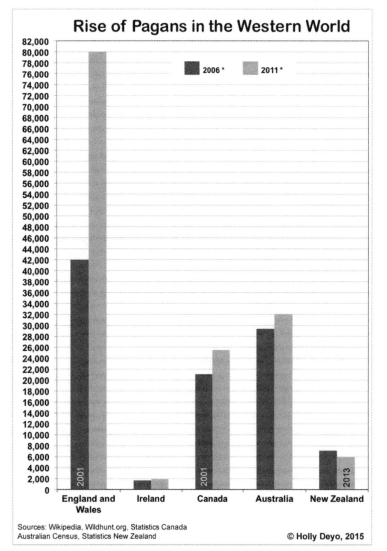

Rise of Pagans in the Western World

Sources: Wikipedia, Wildhunt.org, Statistics Canada
Australian Census, Statistics New Zealand

© Holly Deyo, 2015

- **Angel From Hell** (2016 – 2016) An angel named Amy, acts as a guardian for Allison, forms an unlikely friendship. Cancelled after 5 episodes.
- **The Originals** (2013 – present) Many years ago, an original family of vampires lived in New Orleans. However, their happy lives changed and it's up to them to take back what they built.
- **The Vampire Diaries** (2009 – present) Teenage girl is torn between two vampire brothers.
- **Teen Wolf** (2011 – present) Awkward teen is attacked by a werewolf and inherits the curse as well as the enemies that come with it.
- **Supernatural** (2005 – present) Two brothers follow their father's footsteps as "hunters" fighting evil supernatural beings including monsters, demons, and gods that roam the earth.
- **Once Upon a Time** (2011 – present) Residents of small-town Storybrooke, Maine are characters from various fairy tales transported to the "real world" town and robbed of their real memories by a powerful curse.
- **The Haunting Hour** (2010 – 2014) R.L. Stine leads young viewers on a creepy tour of tales featuring life-sized dolls, werewolves and carnival clowns that are stalking children.

- **The Secret Circle** (2011 – 2012) 16-year-old girl moves to Chance Harbor, Washington to live with her grandmother after her mother mysteriously dies and discovers she's a witch along with 5 other teens.
- **Angel** (1999 – 2004) Vampire Angel, cursed with a soul, moves to Los Angeles and aids people with supernatural-related problems while questing for his own redemption.
- **Being Human**, UK series (2008 – 2013) A werewolf, a vampire, and a ghost try to live together and get along.
- **Being Human**, North American series (2011 – 2014) Three 20-somethings share a house and try to live a normal life despite being a ghost, a werewolf, and a vampire.
- **Hex** (2004 – 2005) Shy college girl discovers she possesses dangerous powers, and is being drawn into a world far beyond her control.
- **The Walking Dead** (2010 – present) Sheriff's Deputy leads group of survivors in a world overrun by zombies.
- **American Horror Story** (2011 – present) Anthology series that centers on different characters and locations, including a haunted house, an insane asylum, a witch coven, a freak show and a hotel.
- **Lost Girl** (2012 – 2015) Charismatic woman learns she is a succubus, a supernatural being who feeds off the sexual energy of humans.

EARLY EXPOSURE

Kids are embracing Neo-paganism through many venues on the Internet, books, movies, games and TV. While dabbling in the dark has always had its appeal, nothing sparked interest like JK Rowling's Harry Potter series. Christian writer Hillary White observes, "Sorcery and witchcraft have become the hottest themes in youth culture and education for the first time in modern Western civilization."[408]

Those who think books like the Harry Potter series are harmless and exert no influence, think again.

Steve Wohlberg, bestselling author of *Exposing Harry Potter and Witchcraft: The Menace Beneath the Magic* has read all the Potter books. While not on a mission to bash witches, he is concerned about the "Potter effect" on teens. JK Rowling's books were no passing craze. Her series of seven, which have been translated into 77 languages, took the author from flat broke to billionaire selling over 400 million copies. The last book sold 11 million units in the first 24 hours.[409] With Pottermania spread to movies, DVDs and music, video games, clothes, shoes and jewelry, home décor, Potter-themed candy, cookies and gum products, and a theme park in Orlando, Fla., the brand's worth is an estimated $15 billion.[410]

Wohlberg states, "There's plenty of real occultism embedded in Rowling's fantasy works and in spite of naïve popular opinion, Pottermania is aiding Wicca's growth." He warns that "when Wiccans summon 'nature spirits' in their rituals, they are entering dangerous territory. 'Occultism has a dark side practitioners can easily become trapped like a fly in a spider web.'"[411]

When the *San Francisco Chronicle* polled kids about Rowling's 4th book *Harry Potter and the Goblet of Fire*" kids responded overwhelmingly positively. Ten-year-old Gioia Bishop of Napa, California writes. "I was eager to get to Hogwarts first because I like what they learned there and I want to be a witch."[412]

Wohlberg cites several examples bearing out his concern. "During one radio interview (live from Seattle, KGNW, WA) with me as the guest a caller named Melissa phoned the show and told host Thor Tolo and me that her 14-year-old daughter read the first Harry Potter book and then promptly went back to the bookstore to purchase books about Wicca.

"A friend of mine has a daughter who works at a Barnes & Nobel bookstore in Nashville, TN. She said that many young people purchase both Harry Potter and Wicca books together.

"Another teenage friend told me that she met a Wiccan in an Internet chat room who confessed that it was Harry Potter that first created his interest in spells and magic.

"The founder of a large Internet witchcraft school has publicly stated in a press release that Harry Potter teaches Wiccan philosophy and is aiding the Wiccan cause – big time."[413]

TWILIGHT TIME

Not to be overlooked, the hugely successful *Twilight* series has to be included. Author Stephenie Meyer tells the story in four books of Bella Swan, a teenage girl who falls in love with a 104-year-old vampire, Edward Cullen. Later the story line turns into a love triangle with werewolf, Jacob Black. The series was penned in rapid succession from 2005 through 2008 and the idea for *Twilight* came to her in a dream. By November 2011, they had sold over

120 million copies worldwide with translations into 39 different languages. Between the books that were turned into movies, the *Twilight* franchise garnered $5.7 billion.[414] After snagging the #1 position on several bestsellers lists including *the New York Times* Best Seller List for Children's Chapter Books, *Twilight* was trumpeted as the "spiritual successor" to Harry Potter.[415] In 2010 Meyer released *The Host,* where parasitic aliens called "Souls" take over human bodies. Meyer plans to turn this book into a trilogy.

HEARD IT ON THE STREET

Even *Sesame Street* with viewers as young as three introduced a vampire character in 1972 and Count von Count still lives today. He's dressed in typically black vamp attire, has orchid colored skin and the expected pointy fangs. The Count lives in a cobweb infested castle with many bat "children" and a cat named Fatatita.

The program burst into living rooms in 1969 with high ratings and positive reviews, which has only gained momentum. In 2001 it snagged over 120 million viewers and by the show's 40th anniversary, was broadcast in more than 140 countries. That same year *Sesame Street* was the 15th-highest rated children's TV show in America. By 1996, 95% of all American kids had watched the show by the time they were three.[416]

In the early 1970s, the Count laughed maniacally accompanied by thunder and lightning. He used hypnotic powers to stun people by simply waving his hands. This was discontinued a few years later over concern that it would frighten children. The Count became friendlier, they removed his hypnotic powers, and he interacted more with show characters. His laugh changed from maniacal to a victorious, stereotypical Dracula guffaw. So there was a concerted effort to make vampires kid friendly.

Something Wiccan This Way Comes

It's amazing how many Neopagan sites on the Internet are geared specifically to teenagers. Some introduce them to covens, others to spells, some to the finer details of sexuality, and still others for the basics of deities, how-to's, festivals, familiars and a whole range of topics. If they don't find what they need, there's always The Witches' Voice (WitchVox).

This website lists just shy of 3,000 covens and meet-up groups in the U.S., Canada, the U.K. and Australia. Contacts are further broken down by state or province and by age group of those at the helm whether they are high priests and priestesses or elders. To make it easy for newcomers to find the best fit, they can select covens for families or adults only, college age or teens. A special arm of the site is dedicated to teen witches and their essays. The phenomenally popular website lists over 8,000 links and by mid-2015, enjoyed over a half billion hits since launching in February 1997.

The Witches' Voice is in good company as it's estimated there are over 9,000 pagan sites on the web.[417]

Scouting Our Scouts

Some time back, Wiccans thought to snake their tentacles in Scouting, a youth group begun in 1907 and respected the world over. Nearly every kid this author knew started as a Cub or Brownie. We rose up through the ranks of participation learning self-sufficiency, outdoor and survival skills, human decency, community service and giving to others. We kept to the Law of the Girl Scouts' Promise "On my honor, I will try: To serve God and my country, To help people at all times, And to live by the Girl Scout Law", which is "I will do my best to be honest and fair, friendly and helpful, considerate and caring, courageous and strong, and responsible for what I say and do, and to respect myself and others, respect authority, use resources wisely, make the world a better place, and be a sister to every Girl Scout."

Boy Scouts were similarly bound by their Promise of "On my honor, I will do my best to do my duty to God and my country and to obey the Scout Law; To help other people at all times; To keep myself physically strong, mentally awake and morally straight," with the oath of "Duty to God and country, Duty to other people, and Duty to self" – in that order.

We all strived to live by that code of conduct. We learned a lot and some of it was pretty tough, but it built backbone and character. Everyone worked for badges. They required time, skill, personal investment and sweat. This author still has her green sash full of brightly colored merit badges. Scouting is ever evolving and some of their new badges are directed toward Dentistry, Outdoor Adventure, Cinematography, Archery, Ultimate Recreation Challenge, Nuclear Science and Railroading.

Never, not once did we worry witches would infiltrate the ranks. It was simply not on the radar. Today it's another paradigm. Today witches want their place on Scout sashes, which makes one do a head-twist like to Linda Blair in *The Exorcist*.

THE COVENANT OF THE GODDESS

This group of over 100 covens and single Wiccan practitioners is one of the oldest and largest of its kind. They were instrumental in getting the Department of Veterans Affairs to approve pentacles for military headstones. CoG tried for recognition within the Scouts' religious emblem program that studies other belief systems. Though these religious programs are created, administered and awarded by outside groups, each program must be recognized by the Boy Scouts. As of 2007, the BSA recognizes 35 different denominations including Catholic, Jewish, LDS, Buddhist, Lutheran and Protestant.

CoG calls for children as young as 8 to be exposed to Wicca. Their programs are "Over the Moon" for ages 8–11, "Hart and Crescent" for ages 12–18, and the Distinguished Youth Service Award for adults working with youth. The Boy Scouts of America have refused to recognize the Goddess' programs and its members can't officially wear the emblems on their uniforms. In order for the CoG to be chartered, at least 25 Boy Scout troops would have to be on board. Thus far, no takers.

Pagans and Witches Infiltrate the Military

So who goes there? Atreiyuh Cammen was 14 in 2006 when he became a witch. He is now a witch in the U.S. military. Back in the day, as a kid, he'd read fantasy books, but it was the Harry Potter series that "fueled his interest in the Wiccan faith".[418] Cammen isn't the only one. He said that 'hundreds of military trainees chose to study witchcraft at the base and its coven. One such trainee is 19-year-old Jesse McCrady also a witch who attends services on Texas' Lackland Air Force base. McCrady from North Texas claims he's been "in the craft" since age 10.

At Lackland, Tony Gatlin is the coven's high priest and his wife, the high priestess. He's the grandson of a Southern Baptist preacher who became dissatisfied with his church and converted to Wicca over 14 years ago.[419] Gatlin explains, "The Christian faith may have prayer. The Catholics may pray the Rosary. We have things we call spells...".[420]

Gatlin says, "I knew I had a spiritual side that needed to be nurtured. Just by chance, I met a witch, and it was transformational for me from then on.[421] Gatlin shared that he had spent 25 years active duty in the military and then at the Pentagon during Sept. 11. Now his mission is to guide other interested trainees at Lackland into witchcraft. Their services are the largest in the world with 400 in attendance.[422]

The American Religious Identification Survey 2008 estimated there were 1,200,000 Pagans and Wiccans in America. In 2007, the Pentagon counted over 1,500 Wiccans in the Air Force and 350 in the Marines. Though the Navy and Army are much larger branches, no one keeps tabs on pagan membership.

"Members of Circle Sanctuary – a Wiccan church based in Wisconsin that serves Pagans globally – puts the current estimates of military Pagans around 10,000, but even that number is a guess. Retired U.S. Army Major Michelle Boshears – herself a Green Craft Wiccan – says those numbers reflect only active duty military who claim Paganism as their religion on official forms. When Boshears served 15 years ago (in 2012), the only option for Pagans was to mark "No Preference" or "Other." For that reason, she estimates that the numbers of Pagans in uniform could be closer to 20,000."[423]

ACCOMMODATION, THE FIRST STEP OF ACCEPTANCE

The US Army's 2001 chaplain's handbook dedicates six pages to Wicca describing their practices, festivals, beliefs and organizational structure. Following a lawsuit in 2007, the military approved a pentagram (the Pagan five-pointed star) to be carved on military headstones in Arlington National Cemetery and other burial sites around the country.[424] To meet the growing number of military practicing various forms of paganism, every branch of U.S. armed forces now allows this form of worship.

Practitioners of paganism can encompass a wide variety of traditions including Druidism, Heathens, Witches, Neo-Paganism, Norse, Earth Religion, Old Religion, Jainism, Eclectic Paganism, Shamanism and Wiccan that worship polytheistic, nature and animistic "gods". The different practices under the umbrella of paganism don't worship the Christian God or Jesus, but often include Mother Earth and elementals. Generally pagans are pantheists, polytheists or duotheists.

Hanna Rosin for the *Washington Post* wrote in 1999, "to date, no other group as off-beat as the wiccans has asked for approval. But the Army's Handbook for Chaplains lists a few of the myriad possibilities open to soldiers: Church of Satan, Black Judaism, Scientology, Temple of Set – all candidates for potential approval, considered case by case."[425]

Photo: Notice the pentagram overlaid by the American Eagle on this military patch.

Nearly 40 bases across America and overseas, including on ships and in war zones have U.S. military-recognized places of worship. Covenant of the Goddess with at least 100,000 member covens and Circle Sanctuaries are open to Wiccans, Druids, Pagans and many other alternatives.

Republican Georgia Congressman Bob Barr, tried to stem the growth of pagan gatherings on military bases, but this movement died a quiet death in June 1999. It was hard to fight the 1986 Federal Court of Appeals decision – Dettmer v. Landon – that ruled Wicca a religion. However, opposition remained. In 2006 U.S. Army Chaplain Captain Don Larsen was dismissed from his post in Iraq after changing his religious affiliation from Pentecostal Christianity to Wicca. He'd had also applied to become the first Wiccan military chaplain.

Ft. Hood, in Austin, Texas allowed the first pagan worship area to be built on base in 1997. It's the longest running such site comprised of 100 active duty soldiers, dependents, and military retirees.[426]

Photo: Cadet Chapel Falcon Circle is dedicated May 6, 2011. (Courtesy Mike Kaplan)

By 1999, "every full moon, a few dozen off-duty soldiers have gathered at an open campsite at Fort Hood, America's largest military post. By day, they are privates and sergeants in the U.S. Army, training for deployment to Korea, Bosnia, Kosovo. But at these lunar assemblies they trade in their Army fatigues for hooded robes, chant to the lead of their chosen high priestess and dance around a fire well into the night. They are America's first official Army witches, with all that double duty implies: buzz cuts and pentagram rings, moon tattoos under uniforms. One typical dog tag reads: NAME: Philip Campanaro. UNIT: USAG III Corps. RELIGIOUS PREFERENCE: Wicca."[427]

For pagans at the Air Force Academy in Colorado Springs, Colorado, Falcon Circle (see photo prwevious page) was dedicated in May 2011. The inner circle sits like a mini Stonehenge surrounding a propane-lit stone fire pit. This sits atop 1,225 sq. feet of flagstone enclosed by a massive ring of boulders, dug from the Rockies. The Academy spent $80,000 to erect this outdoor worship circle, including more than $26,000 for erosion control. This necessary expense insured against a repeat incident of boulders crashing from their 7,200-foot perch into the Visitor's Center. Compared to the magnificent Christian chapel $80K is a pittance, but opponents argue that it was a lot of money to accommodate just three pagans out of 4,300 cadets. The majority at USAFA comprise over 98% Christian. [428]

Next to the U.S., England and Wales combined has the highest number of Neo-Pagan believers. Ministry of Defence figures show 770 members in the Navy, Army and Royal Air Force. While it's unknown if they have official on-base worship sites, just as for any religion, servicemen and women of these alternative faiths can request time off to celebrate festivals. Their commanding officers are encouraged to make every effort to accommodate them.[429]

Last Thoughts on the Rise of Pagans

While the occult has existed for ages, the last 20 years saw mighty gains for mainstream acceptance. In a decade the number of pagan practitioners doubled in England and Wales. However in just seven years, new adherents in America shot up nearly 150% and that may be a low figure.

Many churches treated lightly the witchcraft so clearly promoted in the Harry Potter series and they didn't even bother addressing the Twilight saga.

Wicca is frequently in music, especially Heavy Metal, compared to Stevie Nicks' rare-for-then song "Rhiannon". Nicks penned this haunting tune in 1974 about an old Welsh witch. It's a far cry from heavy metal, black metal and death metal bands with Satanic names and album topics too disgusting to acknowledge.

Neopaganism depicted in TV, movies, books and games is now mainstream reaching out to children as young as three. While some is full of gore, grim and the gruesome, other depictions make it kid-friendly, fun, enticing to teens. Children as young as 10 are already practicing witches.

A plethora of websites makes occult information easily available to impressionable minds. While some Neopagan sites have age restrictions, how would they know how old someone is? Witches' Voice is a one-stop shop for people looking to find their "right fit" coven or meet-up group with nearly 3,000 listings and over 8,000 links. This is just one of an estimated 9,000 plus pagan sites.

For anyone not on-line and wants books and paraphernalia virtually every bookstore has a dedicated occult-magick-pagan-witches-Satan-etc. section. Plugging in "occult books" on Barnes & Noble's website brings up nearly 43,000 results. Amazon returns over 80,000 hits plus all the "extras" an aspiring witch might want.

Halloween sales are booming and second only to Christmas. In 2014, Americans spent $7.4 billion[430] on everything Spooksville. By comparison, Canada put the U.S. to shame shelling out over $1 billion[431]. Considering Canada's population is about 1/10 that of the U.S., that's a phenomenal amount.

Since the 1986 Federal Court ruling that Wicca is a recognized religion, it cleared the path for inclusion in the military. Now some 40 U.S. bases have places for pagan worship complete with officiating high priests and priestesses and veterans are allowed to have pentagrams on their headstones. Military "dog tags" can read Wicca, Druid, Pagan or whatever designation is desired.

Like other takeovers, it begins with small things. Gradual change is effective change and it perfectly encapsulates what's happening in America and the other Western Nations. *WE ARE THERE.*

Chapter 13: Christian Persecution

"If the world hates you, you know that it hated Me before it hated you. If you were of the world, the world would love its own. Yet because you are not of the world, but I chose you out of the world, therefore the world hates you. Remember the word that I said to you, ... If they persecuted Me, they will also persecute you. ... But all these things they will do to you for My name's sake, because they do not know Him who sent Me." —John 15:18-21 (NKJV)

Then you will be handed over to be persecuted and put to death, and you will be hated by all nations because of me. At that time many will turn away from the faith and will betray and hate each other —Matthew 24:9-10 (NIV)

"These things I have spoken to you, that you should not be made to stumble. They will put you out of the synagogues; yes, the time is coming that whoever kills you will think that he offers God service. And these things they will do to you because they have not known the Father nor Me. But these things I have told you, that when the time comes, you may remember that I told you of them. ... —John 16:1-4 (NKJV)

And I saw thrones on which were seated those who had been given authority to judge. And I saw the souls of those who had been beheaded because of their testimony about Jesus and because of the word of God. ... —Revelation 20:4 (NIV)

Though this is an End Time sign, Christian persecution has existed since the time of Jesus. It's unrelenting and occurs the world over. However, with the Internet's worldwide reach recruiting people to come against Christianity is easier than ever and we are more aware of the atrocities ramping up.

In recent months, stories of Christian persecution have seemed more like pages ripped from the Book of Exodus than modern-day news reports. Author David Curry penned:

A Christian couple beaten to death and then burned in a kiln...more than 200 schoolgirls kidnapped in Nigeria … a mother forced to give birth in chains in Sudan … the mass exodus of families forced from their homes in Syria and Iraq, driven out by the brutality of ISIS … The violence and cruelty seem to know no bounds.

These don't even take into account the untold stories of persecution happening in closed countries like North Korea. Kenneth Bae's capture, imprisonment and then fortunate release only highlights the instability of the country and suppression of religion there. There is no question that millions of Christians around the world live in constant danger simply because of their choice of religion.

I urge you to not forget about those living without the rights you enjoy. Do not forget about those who fear for their lives simply because they own and read a Bible. Do not forget about those who have watched their children die simply because of their faith. Remember and pray for them.

The rise of Islamist extremism and the ongoing suppression of faith by communist regimes continue to drive persecution of Christians and other religious groups. For far too long, much of the free world has done little to oppose the persecution of Christians. It is time for those of us who are living with the blessing of freedom of religion to advocate for those who are not.[432]

Justin D. Long's research concludes this is the Age of Martyrs. "During this century, we have documented cases in excess of 26 million martyrs. From AD 33 to 1900, we have documented 14 million martyrs."[433] More Christians have died for their faith in this current century than all other centuries of church history combined.

OpenDoorsUSA.org states that each month 322 Christians are killed for their faith, 214 churches and Christian properties are destroyed and, 722 acts of violence are committed against Christians. This includes beatings, physical torture, confinement, isolation, rape, severe punishment, imprisonment, slavery, discrimination in education and employment, forced marriage and even death.

This map pinpoints the top 50 countries where Christian persecution occurs. According to Pew Research Center, over 75% of the world's population lives in areas with severe religious restrictions and many are Christians. The U.S. Department of State says that Christians in over 60 countries face persecution from their governments or surrounding neighbors simply because of their belief in Jesus Christ.

2015 WORLD WATCH LIST

PERSECUTION LEVEL														
EXTREME	4	Syria	11	Maldives	18	Qatar	25	Myanmar	32	Comoros	39	Oman	46	Azerbaijan
SEVERE	5	Afghanistan	12	Saudi Arabia	19	Kenya	26	Palestinian Terr.	33	Tanzania	40	Mali	47	Indonesia
MODERATE	6	Sudan	13	Libya	20	Turkmenistan	27	Brunei	34	Algeria	41	Turkey	48	Mauritania
SPARSE	7	Iran	14	Yemen	21	India	28	Laos	35	Colombia	42	Kazakhstan	49	United Arab Emirates
1 North Korea	8	Pakistan	15	Uzbekistan	22	Ethiopia	29	China	36	Tunisia	43	Bangladesh	50	Kuwait
2 Somalia	9	Eritrea	16	Vietnam	23	Egypt	30	Jordan	37	Malaysia	44	Sri Lanka		
3 Iraq	10	Nigeria	17	Cen. African Rep.	24	Djibouti	31	Bhutan	38	Mexico	45	Tajikistan		

WorldWatchList
OpenDoorsUSA.org

Over 125,000 Christians were kidnapped in 2014 alone. These people were dissident Sunnis, Kurds, Armenians, Chaldeans and Yazidis.

Many Christians in China are forced to worship quietly in 'home' churches only. All are scrutinized. Human rights group, China Aid, reveals "brutal religious oppression" is "sweeping Communist China" and that persecution jumped 300% from 2013 to 2014.

Dan Weber, president of the Association of Mature American Citizens stated, "Although the Chinese persecutors might be described as tame compared to the atrocities of the jihadists or so-called 'holy warriors' in Arabia and Africa, the China Aid report suggests that Christians have become a target of choice on a global scale."[434]

Christian persecution isn't just occurring "over there". The planks of persecution are being laid in America.

Hostility to Christianity in America

It started in just the tiniest measures. Most people thought these were just one off things. Somebody had a bad day and wanted to pick a fight. Lash out. First one atheist complained that they were "offended" seeing a cross at a war memorial. Then someone sued to have the Ten Commandments removed from on top of Florida's Dixie County Courthouse. Another person challenged that a similar monument be removed from the rotunda of the Alabama Judicial Building. Then another suit was filed over a Ten Commandments monument resting on the lawn of Oklahoma's Haskell County Courthouse. In October 2014, a man was held for allegedly urinating on and crashing into the Oklahoma State Capitol monument.[435] This photo is what he left...

Stores came on board with a cold shoulder toward Christianity. The American Family Association compiled a list of companies that support Christmas or not. AFA grouped them by those who were "For Christmas", "Marginal", or "Against Christmas". Banana Republic, Barnes & Noble, Family Dollar, Foot Locker, Gap Stores, L.L. Bean, Office Depot, Old Navy, Radio Shack, Staples, and Victoria's Secret among others were cited as hostile to Christmas.[436]

"Happy Holidays" replaced "Merry Christmas" on lips of store clerks. Christmas trees are now all inclusive Holiday trees. After backlash from the public, retailers re-examined whether it was clever to eradicate Christ and Christmas.

In 2008, Tonia Thomas stated she was terminated from Counts-Oakes Resorts Properties Inc. for refusing to say "Happy Holidays". The company fired back she was "a disgruntled employee" in what NBC called "a one-sided version of what happened". While Andy Phillips, the company's president assures, "We are a Christian company and we celebrate Christmas", labor attorney G. Thomas Harper advises employees to just ignore the season.[437]

In June 2011, NBC cut 'one nation under God' from the Pledge of Allegiance during the US Open golf tourney. NBC was forced to address this issue on air after receiving a barrage of irate Tweets. During NBC's weak apology, sports host Dan Hicks still couldn't say the omitted words and referred to them as "a portion of the Pledge of Allegiance".

"We began our coverage of this final round just about three hours ago and when we did it was our intent to begin the coverage of this U.S. Open Championship with a feature that captured the patriotism of our national championship being held in our nation's capital for the third time. Regrettably, a portion of the Pledge of Allegiance that was in that feature was edited out. It was not done to upset anyone and we'd like to apologize to those of you who were offended by it."[438] This wasn't the last time NBC cut the phrase. "Under God" was conspicuously absent in 2015 during their commercial for TV spy thriller "Allegiance".[439]

In 2011, James Hudspeth petitioned the White House to remove "under God" from the U.S. Pledge of Allegiance. After four years, he had only gathered 20,000 signatures out of more than 320 million Americans.[440]

In November 2013, President Obama omitted 'under God' when he read the Gettysburg Address.[441]

Public bans are put on Nativity displays where before they were commonplace. Removal of a Ten Commandments plaque that had hung in a courtroom for decades is demanded. We're seeing Christian suppression in schools where Christmas carols are no longer allowed.

Then a real shocker – the Pentagon who is the hub of military action – where there are "no atheists in foxholes" released a statement in May 2013 confirming that soldiers could be prosecuted for promoting their faith: "Religious proselytization is not permitted within the Department of Defense…Court martials and non-judicial punishments are decided on a case-by-case basis…"[442]

TODAY'S LESSON: NO TEN COMMANDMENTS

A single atheist brought uproar to a small Oklahoma town: Muldrow, population 3,400. Gage Pulliam, a chubby cheeked bespectacled junior at Muldrow High, sent a photo of one of the school's religious plaques to Freedom From Religion Foundation (FFRF). The national non-profit organization fired off a letter to the school's superintendent asking that the plaques be removed and intimated a lawsuit would be forthcoming if they didn't comply. Their letter brought intense backlash from the townspeople.

At a school board meeting county residents arrived with Bibles in hand and Christian sayings on their cars and clothes. Teachers, students, parents, state lawmakers and church leaders all came supporting the Ten Commandment plaques. Hundreds of people signed a petition in support and a local church gave out free Ten Commandments t-shirts. Despite massive backing to keep them, down came the plaques.

"'I moved here in 2001 from Texas. The first thing I saw when I went to a parent-teacher conference was the Ten Commandments,' Rob McGee told the *Sequoyah County Times*. 'Then I noticed the lack of school violence, lower number of teen pregnancies. It was a pleasant surprise.'

"'Now it's almost like a fear is gripping this small community because God is being removed and when God is removed something else will take its place. It's like the last vestige of protection is being removed from our schools, our students and the teachers. If most of the people of Muldrow want to continue to have the Ten Commandments posted, then what right does some outsider have to come in and tell us we can't post them?'"[443]

Church officials and politicians alike addressed what they called a "war on Christianity". Pastor John Moore of the Muldrow First Baptist Church stated. "It's Christianity under attack within our own country. The irony can't be missed by anyone who's lived in this country or grown up in this country… it's promised in Scripture."[444]

Other schools and government buildings have met with similar action. In Kentucky, the ACLU sued three counties: Harlan, McCreary and Pulaski. Harlan County complied and removed the offending plaques, but the other two counties fought, lost and racked up $450,000 in legal fees.[445]

In 2012, the FFRF set their sights on Pennsylvanian schools in New Kensington and Connellsville for displaying Ten Commandments demanding they be removed.[446]

And the same happened in Marion, Ohio[447] and Narrows, Virginia.[448]

In 2013, Tennessean schools bent over backwards to accommodate non-Christians. Springfield High in Robertson County not only took down the Ten Commandments, they replaced it with five of the Pillars of Islam.[449]

Next the FFRF initiated actions against the Ten Commandments display in a Newland, North Carolina Town Hall.[450]

Here is a rich irony. This atheist group, the FFRF based in Madison, Wisconsin, operates out of a former church rectory.[451]

In 2012, the ACLU filed a lawsuit on behalf of two wiccans against the city of Bloomfield, NM regarding a Ten Commandments display on city hall property. The six-foot-tall, 3,000-pound monument was placed there in July 2011 and officially dedicated by former city councilmember Kevin Mauzy. With regard to the lawsuit, Mayor Scott Eckstein expressed surprise. He stated. "I am surprised (by the decision) and had never really considered the judge ruling against it because it's a historical document, just like the Declaration of Independence and the Bill of Rights. The intent from the beginning was that the lawn was going to be used for historical purposes, and that's what the council voted on."[452]

In October 2014 29-year-old Michael Tate Reed Jr. was arrested by the Secret Service after destroying a six-foot monument of the 10 Commandments. He committed this act the morning after he'd stormed into the Oklahoma City Federal Building and threatened to kill President Obama and spit on his picture. Reed drove over the granite monument with his truck, knocking it off its base and smashing it into five pieces. He completed the vandalism by urinating on it. Reed was admitted the next day to a mental health facility and formal charges were never filed.

The controversy didn't end there. Though privately funded by the family of Republican Rep. Mike Ritze, it sat on public land and was center stage of an ACLU lawsuit. After Reed's actions, the Satanic Temple released this statement. "The Satanic Temple was appalled to learn of the act of destructive vandalism laid upon the 10 Commandments monument in Oklahoma today. As many are aware, we are seeking to have a Satanic monument erected alongside the 10 Commandments – and *only* alongside the 10 Commandments. We do not want our monument to stand alone. If our monument stands at the state Capitol, we want it to compliment and contrast the 10 Commandments, with both standing unmolested as a testament to American religious freedom and tolerance."[453]

In June 2015, Oklahoma's Supreme Court ordered the monument's removal in a 7-2 decision. Using a heavy-duty crane and cutting tools workmen completed the task under the cloak of darkness to dodge protesters. Oklahoma Highway Patrol troopers provided security during its relocation to outside the Oklahoma Council of Public Affairs Office. Now locked in place with epoxy and rebar, the removal cost as estimated $5000.[454]

Full Scale Battle Against Christians

In March 2015, Rev. Franklin Graham gave an ominous warning to Christians living in America. He cautioned on how religious freedoms are being eroded stateside while believers are simultaneously being persecuted throughout the world.

Rev. Graham advised during a recent appearance on the Christian-based 700 Club. "We're going to see persecution, I believe, in this country, because our president is very sympathetic to Islam and the reason I say that … is because his father was a Muslim, gave him a Muslim name, Barack Hussein Obama. His mother married another Muslim man, they moved to Indonesia, he went to Indonesian schools. So, growing up his frame of reference and his influence as a young man was Islam. It wasn't Christianity, [it was] Islam."[455]

America's Judeo-Christian Roots

America was built on Judeo-Christian principles, not Islam, as President Obama has repeatedly tried to instill. He cited that Thomas Jefferson owned a Quran. Yes, he did. Jefferson had an inquisitive mind for history, religion and litigation. If anything, Jefferson was trying to understand the minds of Islamic Barbary Coast pirates and how to deal with them.

Photo: Reverends Franklin Graham and Bill Graham in Cleveland Stadium, in Cleveland Ohio, in June 1994. (Courtesy Paul M. Walsh)

Between 1530 and 1780 roughly 1.5 million Europeans and Americans were enslaved in Islamic North Africa.[456] "Islam, and what its Barbary followers justified doing in the name of their prophet and their god, disturbed Jefferson quite deeply. America had a tradition of religious tolerance, in fact Jefferson himself had co-authored the Virginia Statute for Religious Freedom, but fundamentalist Islam was like no other religion the world had ever seen. A religion based upon supremacism whose holy book not only condoned but mandated violence against unbelievers was unacceptable to him."[457]

Obama's attempt at linking Islam to America's roots dates back to his Senatorial days. He stated on June 28, 2006 to a liberal Christian group, "Whatever we once were, we are no longer a Christian nation – at least, not just. We are also a Jewish nation, a Muslim nation, a Buddhist nation, and a Hindu nation, and a nation of nonbelievers."[458]

On April 6, 2009, he said in a joint presser with then President Gul of Turkey, "Although as I mentioned, we have a very large Christian population, we do not consider ourselves a Christian nation or a Jewish nation or a Muslim nation; we consider ourselves a nation of citizens who are bound by ideals and a set of values. I think Turkey was – modern Turkey was founded with a similar set of principles...."[459]

Au contraire Mr. President. Most Americans *do* consider the U.S. a Christian nation while modern Turkey, founded in 1923, has a nearly 98% Muslim population.

He tries again in February 2015. "Here in America, Islam has been woven into the fabric of our country since its founding."[460]

"That does not mean that there were no Muslims in America at the founding – many African slaves were originally Muslim, and were forcibly converted from that faith. But to say that Islam as a religion has been 'woven into the fabric of our country since our founding' is simply false. The first wave of Muslim immigrants [which amounted to only 'several thousand'] to the United States did not begin until well after the Civil War. The first mosque in the United States was not built until 1915, by most reports."[461]

So Islam had zero impact on America's Founding Fathers.

On this issue, son of world-renowned evangelist Billy Graham, Franklin commented further.

"'I agree with diversity but what's happening with this country is all these religions are getting front row and Christians are being pushed – and we're the majority – are being pushed back to the back of the room,' said Rev. Graham in an interview with WNCN News about his recent call for Duke University to end its policy on having a Muslim Call to Prayer at the campus's Christian chapel.

"'This country was built on Christian principles, it was men and women who believed in God and believed in His Son Jesus Christ who built this country," said Rev. Graham. ... It wasn't built by Islam, and it wasn't built by any other group. It was those who supported and believed in the Lord Jesus Christ."[462]

9/11 Terrorism Leaves Indelible Marks

Beyond the immediate tragedy of 9/11, the attacks left permanent scars. First and foremost is the loss of 2,977 victims and the sorrow of their family and friends. And those who suffer survivor guilt...

Health issues of first responders linger to this day. More than a thousand people who lived or worked near ground zero, including first responders, have been diagnosed with cancer related to the attacks.[463] Over 18,000 people suffered from illnesses linked to dust from the exploding World Trade Center.[464]

Countless thousands suffered PTSD – especially children who saw images on TV played in an endless loop.[465]

The economy was also hurt. In one week following, the Dow Jones fell 1369.7 points (14.3%), its largest one-week drop in history and US stocks lost $1.2 trillion in value.[466]

Manhattan alone lost an estimated 100,000 jobs. 18,000 businesses were destroyed, disrupted or forced to relocate.[467]

For the first time ever air travel across the US and Canada was almost completely suspended for three days, which affected events with closures, postponements, cancellations and evacuations. Other countries imposed similar restrictions.[468] The airline industry lost about $100 billion annually in the years after the attacks before rebounding.[469]

Insurance companies were hit with an estimated $40 billion bill[470] and the cost to rebuild the World Trade Center into the new National September 11 Memorial and Museum took another $700 million.[471]

Photo: Out of the debris from 6 World Trade Center remained an untouched 20-foot cross – plus several others found in the wreckage – that had been a part of the building's steel beam fabrication. Atheists sued in 2014 to have it removed from its permanent location in front of the 9/11 Museum. Judges stuck down the suit noting that the cross became a "symbol of hope and healing for all persons" after the tragedy. It would have been cruel irony to the Muslim extremists that perpetrated these unthinkable acts, had they not committed suicide, to see several Christian crosses emerge. (Courtesy U.S. Customs and Border Protection)

LONGER TERM IMPACTS

Onerous legislation passed into law, most importantly 2001's PATRIOT Act and 2012's National Defense Authorization Act, and furthered governmental invasion of privacy.

It impacted all future air travel with long lines, full body scans and TSA feel-ups and pat-downs. Restrictions were levied on what and what size products could be taken on board. Every day things like manicure scissors, gel shoe inserts and cigarette lighters were eyed as potential weapons.

One of the worst impacts was being thrust into Middle East wars that now span nearly 15 years. Those too, brought consequences with thousands of service people killed, many suicided, tens of thousands wounded.

In an effort to hunt al-Qaeda, many, many – *too many* – innocent civilians lost their lives overseas in drone attacks and imprecise targeting. Experts estimate the cost of Afghanistan and Iraq wars will peg a staggering $4 - $6 trillion,[472] not the paltry $50 billion Donald Rumsfeld put forth before going in.

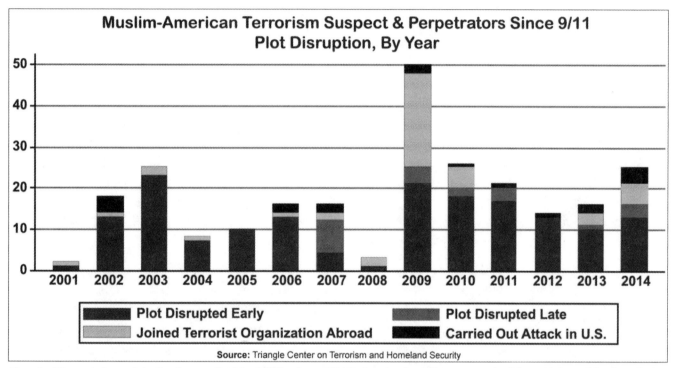

Source: Triangle Center on Terrorism and Homeland Security

Graph: Though terrorist attacks peaked in 2009, since 2012, they're trending up again. Threats from Muslim clerics to hang their flag over the White House and kill President Obama have done nothing to soften feelings toward them. Nearly 150 Muslim-Americans have plotted acts of terrorism in the U.S. since 9/11.[473] This is something the government prefers to keep under wraps.

Then there's the issue that 9/11 perpetrators probably didn't consider – increased negative feelings toward Muslims, not just in America, but around the globe. If they wanted any understanding, *any* sympathy, they missed the mark. In the 9/11 aftermath, tensions rose between the two faiths and even people who weren't Muslim, but may have looked like it, took unfair hits, physically and verbally. Bullets smashed windows at a mosque in Irving, Texas. "A Muslim student at Harvard was harassed by four men who tried to take off her hijab while reportedly saying, 'What are you doing here? Go home to your own country.' And Balbir Singh Sodhi, a turbaned Sikh man mistaken for a Muslim, was shot and killed at a gas station in Mesa, Ariz."[474]

While negative opinion toward Islam grows, overt animosity directed at Muslims faded rather quickly after 2002, considering… However, those horrific 9/11 attacks left a permanent bad taste in the mouths of most Americans. Couple that with the 2013 Boston Marathon bombings, which killed 5 people and wounded 264 others – carried out by Muslim radicals Dzhokhar and Tamerlan Tsarnaev – and even more attacks, it reignited distrust of peaceful Muslims. Factor in countless beheadings splashed across news headlines in horrific detail, stabbings, fighting and wars brought by Muslim groups, what was just a "bad taste" has morphed into a genuine bad opinion of Islam by the majority of Americans.

That animosity toward Islam grows is documented through polls conducted by CBS News, Gallup and *Huffington Post*. According to a 2006 CBS survey, the number of Americans who view Islam negatively rose from

33% in 2002 to 45% in 2006.[475] Gallup's January 2010 poll showed it shot up to 53%.[476] By 2015, the number inched even higher to 55%.[477] With reason. More attacks.

Distrust of Muslims grew further when text in the Quran was spotlighted saying it's OK to lie to "infidels" and to kill those that are their enemy – the "People of the Book" (Christians and Jews). This was particularly significant as liberal leaning publications and mainstream media tend to shy away from anything that puts Islam in a poor light.

Photos: Images of Boston Marathon bombing, courtesy Dave Bowman (top) Aaron Tang (bottom).

On the lack of public outrage over these terrorist acts, Reverend Franklin Graham had this to say. "First of all, you don't have condemnation outside of this country. You'll have clerics in this country who'll condemn these acts. But these acts of terrorism are not condemned by the mullahs in Saudi Arabia or in Egypt, or Iraq or Syria. The reason is, is because the Quran teaches this and so, if they condemned it, they would be condemning the Quran, and they're not going to condemn the Quran. So, the teaching of the Quran permits slavery, it permits the killing of Jews, permits the killing of Christians, and it's a very, very dangerous world in which we live and we need to be aware of the truth."[478] Americans aren't the only people Muslim radicals target. More attacks from them are occurring the world over.

Terrorist Attacks in Canada

February 2015 – The RCMP (Royal Canadian Mounted Police) arrest Ottawa man Awso Peshdary who they say has been financing others' travel to Syria to join ISIS. Peshdary is detained by authorities in 2010, but not arrested – during what is then Canada's most extensive anti-terrorism investigation, Project Samossa. He posts on his Facebook page (since removed) an image of an assault rifle laid across a map of Canada and America. Another caption says not to think of those "killed in the cause of Allah" as dead. He wrote beside a Facebook post about a child who had frozen to death in Syria. "WAKE UP Muslims," "And what is the matter with you that you fight not in the cause of Allah and for the oppressed young men, women and children."[479]

Fall 2014 – Jahanzeb Malik, 33, from Pakistan who has lived in Toronto for a decade is the target of a 6-month surveillance. Malik brags about taking "weapons, combat and landmine training" in Libya. He even is alleged to want to bring the undercover officer in on a scheme "to blow up the U.S. consulate and other buildings in the financial district in Toronto." Canada is in the process of trying to deport Malik.[480]

October 2014 – On the morning of October 22, Michael Zehaf-Bibeau, a 32-year-old Muslim drug addict shoots and kills Cpl. Nathan Cirillo while the 24 year old stands guard at the War Memorial in Ottawa, Ontario. ISIS claims to be the inspiration in this attack as well as similar ones on Australia and the U.S. The November 21, 2014 edition their propaganda magazine *Dabiq,* says, "The significance of these attacks and others is enormous and cannot be underestimated. By calling on Muslims around the world to rise up in arms, the sheikh launched attacks in Canada, America and Australia … without nothing more than words and a shared belief in the act of worship that is jihad."[481]

October 2014 – Martin "Ahmad" Couture-Rouleau, a recent Muslim convert, runs down two Canadian Armed Forces members in the 2014 Saint-Jean-sur-Richelieu ramming attack. Warrant officer Patrice Vincent dies of his injuries. Couture-Rouleau is eventually gunned down and killed. *The Toronto Sun* reports that Couture-Rouleau calls 911 during the chase and tells the operator – after hitting the soldiers with his car – he carried out these acts in the name of Allah. ISIS takes credit saying they inspired the attacks and were "the direct result" of its call for violence in countries that had joined the international military campaign against the terrorist group.[482]

July 2013 – Canada Day participants at the British Columbia Provincial Legislature Buildings are targets of an alleged plot by Surrey residents John Stewart Nuttall, 38, and Amanda Korody, 29, to plant pressure-cooker bombs as inspired by al-Qaida. Investigation by RCMP and CSIS prevent implementation of the plot. Former friend, Ashley Volpatti said she met Nuttall and Korody at a corner store, and described the former street kids as "really, really nice people" who were attending a local mosque. Then she noticed a change in their attitude. "In one conversation, Nuttall became quite angry, saying his brother had served with the Canadian military, but that he believed Canadian soldiers shouldn't be over 'on Muslim soil.'"[483]

April 2013 – Chiheb Esseghaier and Raed Jaser of Montreal and Toronto, respectively, are charged as part of an alleged Al Qaeda plot to derail a New York to Toronto train on the Canadian side of the border. According to an undercover FBI agent, Esseghaier pondered getting the Yellowstone volcano to erupt. The agent testified in a Toronto court that the PhD student believed an eruption would cause a national disaster for his "worst enemies". Reconsidering, he thinks that that would be too difficult so he shifts back to disrupting the passenger train and planned to cut out 15 or 20 feet of track.[484]

February 2013 – The head of CSIS, the Canadian Security Intelligence Service, Richard Fadden tells Parliament that the threat posed by al-Qaeda is changing and becoming harder for authorities to track. He states. "Al-Qaeda in the [Afghanistan/Pakistan] area was the directing brain that caused 9/11. It has been much weakened. But on the other hand, all of their affiliates…they are much, much more operational than they used to be. They are beginning to communicate between themselves far more than they used to. And in every single case, there are

Canadians who have joined them. CSIS is currently aware of dozens of Canadians – many in their early 20s – who have travelled or attempted to travel overseas to engage in terrorism-related activities in recent years," he tells the Senate committee on National Security and Defense in Ottawa.[485]

August 2010 – Police arrest three men in an alleged plot to commit acts of terror on Canadian soil. Misbahuddin Ahmed, 26, of Ottawa is convicted of two terrorism-related offences in July 2014. Hiva Mohammad Alizadeh, 30, pleads guilty in September to possessing explosives with intent to do harm and is sentenced to 24 years in prison. In May 2012 new charges are levied against Ahmed and Alizadeh. The third man arrested in 2010, Khurram Syed Sher, 30, was initially acquitted now faces charges of conspiring to facilitate terrorism.[486]

March 2009 – Software engineer Momin Khawaja, 30, the first person charged under Canada's Anti-Terrorism Act, is convicted for his role in a plot to plant fertilizer bombs in the United Kingdom. In December 2010 he is given a life sentence. Khawaja denies the charges and appeals to Canada's Supreme Court along with two men who are fighting extradition to the U.S. Pratheepan Nadarajah and Suresh Sriskandarajah are both accused of terrorist activities in the States: U.S. prosecutors say that Nadarajah attempted to purchase US$1 million worth of missiles and AK-47s for the Tamil Tigers – a guerrilla organization in northern and eastern Sri Lanka. U.S. prosecutors allege that Suresh Sriskandarajah, a.k.a. "Waterloo Suresh," helped launder money for the Tamil Tigers and conspired to procure equipment for them.[487]

June 2006 – In this Ontario plot, Canadian counter-terrorism forces arrest 18 al-Qaeda inspired terrorists (dubbed the "Toronto 18" – 14 adults and four youths – one age 15). They are accused of planning to detonate truck bombs in downtown Toronto including at the Toronto Stock Exchange, to open fire in a crowded area, and to storm the Canadian Broadcasting Center, the Canadian Parliament building, the Canadian Security Intelligence Service (CSIS) headquarters, and the parliamentary Peace Tower, to take hostages and to behead the Prime Minister and other leaders.[488]

Eleven are ultimately convicted of terrorist offences. In January 2010, co-leader Zakaria Amara, 24, of Mississauga, Ont., was sentenced to life in prison. Ringleader, Fahim Ahmad, 25, is sentenced to 16 years in prison after pleading guilty to importing firearms, participating in a terrorist group and instructing others to carry out activities for that group. Shareef Abdelhaleem, 34, convicted of participating in a bomb plot, is sentenced to life in prison with no chance of parole for 10 years. Fellow suspect Saad Gaya, 22, from Oakville, Ont., is sentenced to 12 years. Bomb plotter, Saad Khalid, 23, pleads guilty and is sentenced to 14 years.[489] Ali Mohamed Dirie, 26, a Canadian born in Somalia is sentenced to seven years. On tape, he calls white people the "number 1 filthiest people on the face of the planet. They don't have Islam. They're the most filthiest people. In Islam there is no racism, we only hate kufar (non-Muslims)." In September 2013, Dirie is reportedly killed fighting with rebels in Syrian after entering that country using someone else's passport.[490] Five others are charged and sentenced. Seven others have charges stayed or dropped.

Terrorist Attacks in Australia

April 2015 – British police say a 14-year-old boy from northern England is arrested on April 2 in connection with an alleged plot to target an Anzac Day, marking the date of the first Gallipoli landings in 1915, where large numbers of Australian and New Zealand troops fought and died. The same alleged plot saw five teenagers, all aged between 18 and 19, arrested in Melbourne on April 18, including Sevdet Ramadan Besim, 18, who was charged with conspiring to commit a terrorist act. Besim drafted on his mobile phone why he intended to carry out the terror attack, and instructed his family on how he wanted his grave set and what they could do with his car and possessions. He and co-accused Harun Causevic planned to run down a police officer with a car, behead that officer with a knife and seize the officer's gun and embark on a shooting rampage.[491] [492]

February 2015 – Police arrest and charge Omar Al-Kutobi, 24, and Mohammad Kiad, 25, with planning to carry out an imminent attack on February 10, 2015, saying they seized a hunting knife, an IS flag and a video describing an attack. A neighbor, Roberto Macatangay said, "I'm scared that I'm living with these people. They seemed to be really nice. They were sarcastic people but I didn't mind that. We used to joke about religion, about Mohammad and Jesus Christ."[493]

December 2014 – Australian gunman Man Haron Monis, a self-styled cleric originally from Iran, takes 17 people hostage in a cafe in the center of Sydney. Monis and two hostages are killed after a 16-hour siege. In 2001, using the name Ayatollah Manteghi Boroujerdi, he claims in an interview with ABC Radio National's The Religion Report that he had been involved with the Iranian ministry of intelligence and security, and that his criticism of the regime and secret information he possessed resulted in his persecution as well as the detention of his wife and children. He claimed that his family's detention was a result of views the Iranian government believed to be "dangerously liberal". Monis migrates to Australia as a refugee in 1996 seeking political asylum. In 2003, Monis marries a woman who was a client of his black magic business.[494]

September 2014 – 18-year-old Numan Haider is shot dead after he stabs two counter-terrorism officers in Endeavour Hills, a suburb of Melbourne, Victoria. Haider was one of 40 to 50 people who had had his passport cancelled due to concerns he would travel abroad to join ISIS. He is reportedly seen with an ISIS flag. In the police station's parking lot, Haider produces a knife, slashes one officer across the arm, turns on the second officer and stabs him in the face and chest. When the second officer collapses, Haider climbs on top of him and repeatedly stabs him.[495][496]

September 2014 – Police thwart a plot by supporters of Islamic State to carry out beheadings in Australia. They detain 15 people and raid more than a dozen properties across Sydney. The raids involve 800 federal and state police officers – the largest participation in the country's history. Attorney General George Brandis confirms that an Afghani who had spent time in Australia and now works with ISIS in the Middle East, ordered the Australian beheadings and to videotape the killings. Mohammad Ali Baryalei, believed to be Australia's most senior member of Islamic State, is named as a co-conspirator, along with an unnamed Australian. Additional raids are conducted in the eastern cities of Brisbane and Logan, Queensland. In the prior week, Australian police arrest two men in Brisbane for allegedly preparing to fight in Syria, recruiting jihadists and raising money for the al-Qaida offshoot group, Jabhat al-Nusra, also known as the Nusra Front. The government believes about 100 Australians are actively supporting extremist groups within the country, recruiting, grooming suicide bombers and providing funds and equipment.[497]

December 2011 – Justice Betty King sentences three men, Saney Aweys, 28; Nayev El Sayed, 27, and Libyan Wissam Fattal, 35, to 18 years in prison with minimum terms of 13½ years. She states they were all "unrepentant radical Muslims and would remain a threat to the public while they held extremist views". Judge King continues. "The fact that Australia welcomed all of you, and nurtured you and your families, is something that should cause you all to hang your heads in shame that this was the way you planned to show your thanks for that support. Your views about Australia and Australians, and your attitude towards the country's armed forces, its civilians, and its government, were clear. Your plans were evil. All of you believe in the principle of martyrdom. All of you believe it is your obligation to oppose and deal with those you describe as infidels. It is an unfortunate but widely known fact that some Muslims hold extremist views of not only their religion, but of their obligation under their religion to martyrdom, (and) have engaged in worldwide terrorism." El Sayed shouts, "God is with us" at the end of the sentencing.[498]

August 2006 – Joseph T. Thomas (a.k.a. "Jihad Jack") is the first person to be convicted under the Australian Anti-Terrorism Act 2005 for receiving funds from Al-Qaeda. It was later overturned on appeal. The milkman turned Islamic convert travelled to Afghanistan in 2001 to train with the Taliban and returned in 2003.[499]

July 2004 – November 2005 "The Sydney Five" – Khaled Cheikho, Moustafa Cheikho, Mohamed Ali Elomar, Abdul Rakib Hasan and Mohammed Omar Jamal – part of a 9-man Victoria-based cell are found guilty of conspiring to commit acts of terrorism. They order or buy hundreds of liters of chemicals, which could be used to make explosives. They also buy firearms and thousands of rounds of ammunitions from gun shops in western Sydney. At least one Sydney member was close to Abdul Nacer Benbrika, a Melbourne extremist since jailed over a plot to blow up targets including the Melbourne Cricket Ground. Four of the 9 – Mirsad Mulahalilovic, Khaled Sharrouf, Mazen Touma and Omar Baladjam admitted terrorism offences and were jailed for 23 to 28 years.[500]

October 2003 – French Islamist al-Qaeda recruit Mohammed Abderrahman a.k.a. "Willie Brigitte, lived with Faheem Lodhi while in Australia in 2003. Just 10 days after arriving, Brigitte marries Melanie Brown, a recent convert to Islam and former Aussie Army signaler. Brown wasn't aware that she was Brigitte's third wife. He is arrested in Sydney by Australian immigration officials six weeks after the marriage and deported to France. Upon arrival he's immediately arrested. Brigitte allegedly was preparing attacks on Sydney's Lucas Heights nuclear reactor and Pine Gap, the U.S. base in Australia's Northern Territory.[501] December 2006, it's reported that the basis for French terrorism-related charges against him is an allegation that he aided the murderers of Ahmad Shah Masood by supplying them with fake identity documents.[502] In 2007, France sentenced Brigitte to nine years in jail for planning the terror attacks on Australia.

October 2003 – Pakistani born Australian architect, Faheem Khalid Lodhi, a.k.a. Abu Hamzu, is accused of plotting to bomb the national electricity grid or Sydney defense sites in addition to the Victoria Barracks, HMAS Penguin naval base and the Holsworthy Barracks. Lodhi is convicted by the New South Wales Supreme Court in June 2006 on these terrorism-related offences: 1) preparing for terrorist attacks by seeking information for constructing bombs, 2) seeking information and collecting maps of Sydney's electricity grid and possessing 38 aerial photos of military installations, 3) possessing terrorist manuals detailing how to manufacture poisons, detonators, explosives and incendiary devices. Lodhi is sentenced to 20 years in prison.[503]

Obama's "Secret" Muslim Meeting

Further tilting America away from Christianity is the growing Muslin influence on U.S. foreign policy. Though Muslims were invited to the White House after 9/11 under the Bush administration, participants said the February 2015 meeting was the first time a president has held a round-table with Muslim-American leaders. Rev. Graham feels that Mr. Obama's courtship of Muslims will lead to further persecution of Christians in America.

For two days in February 2015, the White House stonewalled refusing two news agencies the names of 14 American Muslim leaders President Obama met with to "discuss a range of domestic and foreign policy issues."[504] One tweet reveals a little more. Hoda Elshishtaw's Twitter account reads, **"At White House meeting @HodaHawa discussed increasing American Muslim participation in government:** http://bit.ly/1vuIVBu via @mpac_national".[505]

On the MPAC-linked page Elshishtawy writes, "I personally handed the President a list of highly qualified American Muslim professionals to consider for appointed positions within the Administration. These individuals come from a variety of industries including STEM, national security, foreign policy and education. These Americans are building bridges between our nation and Muslim communities worldwide and are eager to serve our country at the highest levels possible."[506]

US-Islamic World
@usislam

At White House meeting @HodaHawa discussed increasing American Muslim participation in government: bit.ly/1vuIVBu via @mpac_national

↩ ⇄ 4 ★ 2 ...

Her recommendations are in addition to Muslims already in key positions advising Mr. Obama:

Arif Alikhan, Assistant Secretary for Policy Development for the U.S. Department of Homeland Security (DHS)

Mohammed Elibiary, Homeland Security Adviser. Elibiary appeared at a conference honoring Ayatollah Khomeini and made attacks on prosecution of terrorist fundraisers, actively promoted jihadist ideology godfather Sayyid Qutb, and threatened a *Dallas Morning News* journalist who repeatedly exposed his extremist views.[507]

Rashad Hussain, Special Envoy to the Organization of the Islamic Conference (OIC) and Special Envoy for Strategic Counterterrorism Communications. In his role as OIC Envoy, he advised the Administration on policy issues related to the Muslims.

Salam al-Marayati, Obama Adviser, founder Muslim Public Affairs Council and its current executive director; and a Muslim leader who said that Israel should have been added to the "suspect list" for the Sept. 11, 2001, terrorist attacks.

Imam Mohamed Magid, Obama's Sharia Czar and President of the Islamic Society of North America (ISNA). *Time Magazine* profiled him and the *Huffington Post* dubbed him "America's Imam". *PJ Media* writes, "his ubiquitous presence across the Obama administration undoubtedly makes him the most influential and sought after Muslim authority in the country."[508]

Eboo Patel, Advisory Council on Faith-Based Neighborhood Partnerships and Obama's faith advisor.

ROUND TABLE ATTENDEES

Those who attended President Obama's hushed up round-table included these Muslim luminaries:

Farhana Khera, executive director of Muslim Advocates spearheaded the effort to get Muslim leaders to the White House

Imam Magid, representative of the Adams Center, a large mosque in Sterling, Virginia and former president of the Islamic Society of North America (ISNA) and adviser to the White House National Security Council

Bilqis Abdul-Qaadir, woman who played college basketball at Indiana State while covered head to toe except for her hands – currently graduate assistant with Indiana State's Women's Basketball team

Arshia Wajid, founder of American Muslim Health Professionals

Dean Obeidallah, comedian and left-wing pundit

Kameelah Mu'Min Rashad, founder of Muslim Wellness Foundation and Muslim chaplain at the University of Pennsylvania, in Philadelphia

Diego Arancibia, board member and associate director of the Ta'leef Collective, converted to Islam from Christianity in 1998.

Farhan Latif, chief operating officer at the Institute for Social Policy and Understanding (ISPU), a think tank in Dearborn founded and led by Muslim Americans

Dr. Sherman Jackson, a.k.a. Abdul Hakim Jackson serves as the King Faisal Chair of Islamic Thought at the University of Southern California. One lecture Dr. Jackson gave has been described as a "call to battle" between Muslims and the West. In 2009 and 2012 he was named among the 500 most influential Muslims in the world by the Royal Islamic Strategic Studies Center in Amman, Jordan, and the Prince Alwaleed Bin Talal Center for Muslim-Christian Understanding.

Azhar Azeed, president of the Islamic Society of North America (ISNA). He is also the founder and the past President of Islamic Association of Carrollton, Texas one of the large mosques in the suburbs of Dallas.

Rahat Hussain, president and Legislative Policy Director for Shiite advocacy group Universal Muslim Association of America (UMAA)

Hoda Elshishtawy Hawa, national policy adviser of the Muslim Public Affairs Council (MPAC), founded by members of the Egyptian Muslim Brotherhood

Maya Berry, executive director of the Arab American Institute

Haroon Mokhtarzada, co-founder and former VP of Innovation for Webs, a do-it-yourself website building product. Webs was acquired by Vistaprint in 2011 where he is VP of Digital Products.

AFTER THE ROUND TABLE

Farhana Khera asked Obama "to use his bully pulpit" to speak out against "anti-Muslim hate and bigotry." (According to the latest FBI statistics, Muslims are victims of only 13.7% of religiously motivated hate crimes while American Jews experience almost five times that amount.)[509] She also asked Obama to nominate a Muslim American as a federal judge, saying there hasn't been a federal judge in the U.S. who is Muslim.

This misstep would be another foot in the door for Sharia law – something that would directly conflict with the U.S. Constitution.

At the conclusion of the hour-long round-table, Muslim-American leaders said they were told they shouldn't talk afterward to the news media about what Obama said during the discussion. Some listened, some didn't. Doesn't this raise concern?

With Islam America's fastest growing religion[510] – and the world's[511] – is it any wonder we're seeing a shrinkage in Christianity? People are converting from Christianity to Islam and according to San Diego's KPBS, the group seeing the greatest "domestic conversion" is California Latinos.[512] That partnered with America and many other Nation's adopting a more secular view, Christianity is experiencing a step-away. The subtle pressure to do just that is seen in these many examples.

May 2015 – 16-year-old Christian girl attending Florida's Polk State College is given four "zeroes" on an assignment when she refuses to concede that Christianity is false.[513]

May 2015 – Feds will now regulate Christmas decorations, including "stars, wreathes, candles without shades, light sculptures, blow-molded (plastic) figures, and animated figures."[514]

February 2015 – A Florida student is reprimanded for saying "God bless America" at the conclusion of morning announcements. Reportedly, two atheist students complained about the off-the-cuff declaration to the American Humanist Association, who sent a letter to the school through their Appignani Humanist Legal Center.[515]

January 2015 – The EEOC determines a New Jersey school district violated law when it fires a teacher who hands a Bible to a student. The Equal Employment Opportunity Commission admitted that religion and retaliation played a factor in Walt Tutka's termination.[516]

December 2014 – A group of out-of-state atheists tries to keep an east Alabama town from celebrating the birth of Christ in their Christmas parade. Earlier that year, they threatened Piedmont with a lawsuit if the high school football team didn't stop praying before its games.[517]

December 2014, 2013, 2012, 2011, 2010, 2009 – The annual White House Christmas cards focus on Bo, the First Dog, instead of traditional faith, family, freedom or Christmas. 2010 was the exception with just a generic picture of the White House in snow. In 2009, White House Christmas tree ornaments featured figures of Chinese dictator Mao Tse-Tung, drag queen Hedda Lettuce and Obama's face crudely pasted onto Mt. Rushmore. To put your likeness alongside presidential greatness of (left to right) George Washington, Thomas Jefferson, Theodore Roosevelt, and Abraham Lincoln requires a very high opinion of oneself. Most Americans would be too humbled to even have that comparison made, let alone publicly displayed for millions of people that tour the White House, especially at Christmas.[518 519 520 521 522 523]

November 2014 – A Maryland school district scrubs Christmas, Easter – all Christian and Jewish holidays – from the school calendar so to not offend Muslims.[524]

October 2014 – Houston issues subpoenas demanding a group of pastors turn over sermons dealing with homosexuality, gender identity or Annise Parker, the city's first openly lesbian mayor.[525]

October 2014 – Students at a Long Island, New York high school are – for a second year – denied the right to form a Christian club. The first attempt occurred the preceding December. Law can't prohibit Christian clubs as an extracurricular activity.[526]

October 2014 – Though fine with staging productions about rape and incest, a North Carolina college orders a student to "dumb down" his faith-based magic show. Fellow drama club students at Cape Fear Community College loved the idea and unanimously approved the project, but the school's drama club adviser overruled the students.[527]

September 2014 – California charter school removes all books from its library either written by a Christian author or with a Christian message. Despite a "long-established Supreme Court precedent that strongly disapproves of school libraries removing books based on opposition to their content or message", the school superintendent ignored their cease-and-desist letter.[528]

September 2014 – Football players at Arkansas State University are ordered to either remove a Christian cross decal from their helmets or modify it. The athletics director Terry Mohajir said he wanted to fight the decision because the decal honored former player Markel Owens and equipment manager Barry Weyer, who both passed away that year.[529]

July 2014 – California school orders 18-year-old student not to mention God in his graduation speech. School officials reject three versions of Brooks Hamby's salutatorian (scholastically second best in the class) address. One administrator went so far as to redact every religious reference with a black marker like it was a top-secret government document.[530]

June 2014 – 18-year-old Connecticut high school finds all websites associated with Jesus, Republicans and the NRA blocked. When Andrew Lampart's law class was instructed to prepare for a debate on gun control, all websites on this topic were mysteriously unavailable through the school's Internet service. Pro-gun control sites were not. The Connecticut Republican Party website – blocked. The Connecticut Democratic Party website – not blocked. National Right to Life – blocked. Planned Parenthood – not blocked. Connecticut Family, a pro-traditional marriage group – blocked. LGBT Nation – not blocked.[531]

April 2014 – West Virginia wrestling team told to remove their 10-year motto emblazoned across the back of team shirts. "I can do all things through Him that strengthens me" must go.[532]

April 2014 – Family sues a New Jersey school district and its superintendent to remove the phrase "under God" from the Pledge of Allegiance that students recite. The suit claims a daily affirmation of God reinforces a prejudice against atheists and Humanists. It further claims that studies show atheists are the most disliked and distrusted minority group in the country, ranking below recent (illegal) immigrants, Muslims and gays.[533]

March 2014 – Orlando, Florida teacher tells 5-year-old girl to quit praying before eating lunch.[534]

December 2013 – When boys and girls returned from Thanksgiving break, they discovered that their teachers' Christmas cards had been removed – under orders from the Georgia school's administration. For as long as anyone could remember, teachers at Brooklet Elementary School have posted Christmas cards in the hallways outside their classrooms until now.[535]

June 2013 – The Department of Justice, under President Obama, defunds Louisiana Young Marines chapter because their oath mentions God and also a youth program because it permits voluntary student-led prayer.[536]

February 2013 – Obama Administration legislation for the Affordable Care Act forces religiously affiliated organizations and companies to provide birth control and abortion-inducing drugs despite faith-based objections.[537] In June 2014, the Supreme Court ruled for an exemption in favor of Hobby Lobby.[538]

January 2013 – Pastor Louie Giglio is pressured to remove himself from praying at the inauguration after it's discovered he once preached a sermon supporting the Biblical definition of marriage.[539]

February 2012 – The Obama administration forgives student loans in exchange for public service if that public service is not related to religion.[540]

December 2011 – Hillary Rodham Clinton, while Secretary of State under Obama, vilifies other countries' religious beliefs in deference to LGBTQI – **L**esbian, **G**ay, **B**isexual, Transgender, **Q**ueer or **Q**uestioning, and Intersex – rights.[541]

November 2011 – Obama administration objects to including President Franklin Roosevelt's famous D-Day prayer on the WWII Memorial in Washington D.C. that "gave solace, comfort and strength to our Nation and our brave warriors as we fought against tyranny and oppression".[542]

November 2011 – Although Thanksgiving is a holiday traditionally steeped in giving thanks and praise to God and recognized as such by previous presidents, Obama omits God from his Thanksgiving speech.[543]

Photo: The Mojave Cross has been at the center of a Christian vs. secular battle for decades.

August 2011 – The Obama administration releases its new health care rules that disregard "freedom of conscience" protection for medical workers regarding abortion and contraception.[544]

June 2010 – Federal judge Barbara Crabb rules National Day of Prayer unconstitutional saying it calls for religious action.[545] Federal Appeals court overturns Crabb's ruling.[546]

April 2011 – In landmark legislation Obama presses for passage of EDNA (S.815, H.R.1397) forcing religious organizations to hire people that oppose their moral codes and faith standards. It passes the Senate in November 2013 and goes before the House in 2015.[547]

February 2011 – Although President Obama has no trouble quickly filling Cabinet and czar positions, it takes him over 2 years to appoint a religious freedom ambassador and it is only done after he succumbs to public and Congressional pressure.[548]

January 2011 – After a federal law is passed to transfer a WWI Memorial in the Mojave Desert to private ownership, the U. S. Supreme Court rules that the cross can continue to stand, but the Obama administration refuses to allow the land to be transferred as required by law.[549] Stretching out a decades-long battle the Supreme Court refuses to hear the case saying it must first go through the 9th U.S. Circuit Court of Appeals.

Military Christians in the Cross Hairs

Jacqueline Klimas writes. "Soon there may only be atheists in the foxholes" and she may be right.[550] Every month the clamps tighten on Christian soldiers and chaplains. What use to be viewed as normal activity in military ministry is being systematically squashed.

Military chaplains are forbidden to pray for soldiers? That just doesn't seem possible, yet chaplains are under considerable scrutiny.

In 1999 and 2000 the Navy faced lawsuits from 50 chaplains stating the Navy discriminates against evangelical and Pentecostal clerics. Rev. Billy Baugham is executive director of the Greenville, S.C.-based International Conference of Evangelical Chaplain Endorsers. He oversees 350 chaplains concerned about the military's new religious guidelines. The Air Force Academy in Colorado Springs, Colorado requires "a brief, non-sectarian prayer" during military ceremonies "to add a heightened sense of seriousness or solemnity, not to advance specific religious beliefs." Baugham asks, "'So, to what deity do you address your prayer to? No one knows. And who gets to write the prayers? Once the government becomes the approving authority, the poor chaplain is forced to be an agent of the state.'" Rev. Baugham said he "just got a call from an Army chaplain in Iraq who says he'd be hammered if he used Jesus' name. Chaplains are scared to death."[551]

In 2005, Navy Lt. Gordon Klingenschmitt became the center of this fight when he was censored for praying in the name of Jesus. Seventy-three members of Congress went to bat for him in an open letter to President Bush. They wrote that 80% of U.S. troops are Christian and that censorship of chaplains' prayers disenfranchises "hundreds of thousands of Christian soldiers in the military who look to their chaplains for comfort, inspiration and support."[552] Klingenschmitt shared that during his training at the Navy Chaplains School in Newport, R.I., "they have clipboards and evaluators who evaluate your prayers, and they praise you if you pray just to God. But if you pray in Jesus' name, they counsel you."[553]

While the military has made tremendous inroads to include Pagan, Wiccans, and even Satanists, the clamps are tightening on Christians.

MIKEY WEINSTEIN AND MRFF

In April 2013, Mikey Weinstein, lawyer and founder/president of the Military Religious Freedom Foundation, called the practice of Christians in the service sharing their faith "spiritual rape." When Weinstein tried to push the Pentagon to vigorously enforce an existing policy against proselytizing, they issued this statement:

"Religious proselytization is not permitted within the Department of Defense. Court-martials and non-judicial punishments are decided on a case-by-case basis."[554]

Following that statement backlash erupted and the Pentagon was forced to back pedal. Their new pronouncement read, "Service members can share their faith (evangelize), but must not force unwanted, intrusive attempts to convert others of any faith or no faith to one's beliefs (proselytization)."[555]

Retired U.S. Army Lt. Gen. Jerry Boykin, now executive vice president of the Family Research Council agrees there should be no coercion, but felt the Pentagon's words left too much grey area. Boykin said the "concern over an erosion on religious freedom in the military is legitimate because 'open hostility' against Christians is well documented and getting worse in the Armed Forces. Boykin claimed 'the (Obama) administration would be very happy if the vestiges of Christianity' were removed from the military."[556]

In another incident, a chaplain at Alaska's Joint Base Elmendorf-Richardson was ordered to remove a religious column he had written titled, "No Atheists in Foxholes: Chaplains Gave All in World War II," because it supposedly offended atheists on the base. Within five hours of the request, Lt. Col. Kenneth Reyes' column was removed.

The Military Religious Freedom Foundation accused Reyes of going on an "anti-secular diatribe" and publicly denigrating "those without religion", but Reyes hadn't attacked or insulted non-believers in the essay. Blake Page on behalf of MRFF wrote to Col. Duffy. "In the civilian world, such anti-secular diatribe is protected free speech. Beyond his most obvious failure in upholding regulations through redundant use of the bigoted, religious supremacist phrase, 'no atheists in foxholes,' he defiles the dignity of service members by telling them that regardless of their personally held philosophical beliefs they must have faith."[557]

Page went on to accuse Reyes of "faith based hate" and urged that he be punished. Ron Crews, executive director of Chaplain Alliance for Religious Liberty said. "Chaplains have religious liberty as well to speak to issues. Mr. Weinstein appears to want to silence any speech of faith in the military. It is a sad day for the Air Force and for our country when officers obey every command from Weinstein to silence even chaplains from talking about their faith."[558]

MILITARY POLITICAL CORRECTNESS RUNS AMUCK

In June 2013 the Air Force, along with the Pentagon, required Ron Dicianni's painting to be removed from the Mountain Home Air Force Base's dining hall where it had hung for many years. "Blessed Are the Peacemakers" referenced one of the eight blessings in the book of Matthew. "Peacemakers" is part of a collection of five paintings to honor the heroes who responded to the 9-11 terrorist attacks.

In Dicianni's words: 'It depicts a policeman in the foreground with a "ghosted" figure of a medieval knight behind him, as a symbol of the proverbial, "White Knight" that defends the innocent and comes to the rescue of the oppressed, and is a deterrent to all who mean harm to the helpless. I was spurred on to do the paintings of these brave people because my own son was a firefighter during that September attack. He asked me to do something visually for those brave men and women, thus the "Hero Series" was born. I am still trying to piece together the reasons that the print of Blessed Are The Peacemakers was found to be so offensive. Was it the policeman? Was it the 'White Knight'? Was it the reference to Jesus' words, "Blessed are the peacemakers…"?

"If it was the policeman, then I am mystified why anyone would be offended by those we call to protect us in an emergency. If it was the 'White Knight' I wonder what about that symbolism is offensive, since most would want their daughters to be rescued by a 'White Knight', wouldn't they? If it is the title from Matthew 5 then it clearly points to a hatred and despise of Christ and the Bible, which our nation was founded on. I am unable to perceive how such a positive message could be so offensive to a few that would seek to remove it."[559]

Photo: DiCianni's beautiful inspirational work of art, "Blessed Are the Peacemakers" to honor heroes of Sept. 11, 2001, is painted in ruby red, warm gold, soft white and rich blue.

DiCianni concluded stating. "We want to be clear that here at Tapestry Productions, we have the utmost respect for the men and women of this great Country who wear the uniform of our Armed Forces and who have sacrificed so much to defend America. I am certain that religious censorship does not reflect their values nor does it reflect the beliefs upon which this Nation was founded. However, given the events of the last few months, it appears that the Pentagon, under the leadership of Defense Secretary Hagel, has undertaken a censorship campaign to rid the military of any vestige of Christianity."[560]

Christianity Continually Stripped from Armed Services

Armed forces face unbelievable challenges and lethal encounters that defy even the best authors to accurately convey. They are separated from friends and family, often shipped out of their town – out of their Country for the first time. Everything is strange, foreign. The language is different. The smells are different. Due to severe budget cuts, soldiers are sometimes thrust into war without adequate personal protection,[561] not enough bullets and sub-adequate vehicle armor. They have been forced to harden their Humvees with "plywood, sandbags, and armor salvaged from old Iraqi tanks".[562] Vehicle protection hadn't improved three years after *60 Minutes* exposed this insanity.[563] So soldiers are much more at risk for IEDs – Improvised Explosive Devices that line every roadway. *Is anyone listening?* Troops must wonder.

Meals are often less-than-tasty MREs – Meals Ready to Eat. Soldiers serve in debilitating heat that the enemy is used to – in full uniform, not the floaty garb that Middle Easterners wear. They miss home, holidays, anniversaries and frequently the birth of their first child. Troops are no longer availed of "normal life", of the mundane that comprises most lives of people back home. Language is strange and customs stranger. Sometimes unseen forces of chemical and biological weapons attack our soldiers. No wonder they suffer from PTSD.

The edict mandated from Obama to cut both funding and forces, expects American forces to perform better, longer and more often with less. It will be cut to the smallest since World War II. Big cuts to President Obama's 2016 Pentagon budget that once would have been unthinkable were openly discussed in early May 2015 on Capitol Hill.[564] Obama's new military budget will shrink by more than $75 *billion* and deeper cuts are expected if sequestration returns in fiscal year 2016.[565] Old soldiers, retired and discharged, not members of the National Guard or Reserve, were *involuntarily* recalled to active duty.[566] That's how deep the cuts run. Where can they further cut an already bleeding armed forces? Additionally young soldiers are called to make multiple tours of duty without any time to recover.

"The cycles of combat have been so long and so frequent that nearly 13,000 soldiers now have spent three to four cumulative years at war in Iraq or Afghanistan, according to Army records. About 500 GIs have spent more than four years in combat, the Army says.

'Undoubtedly this is unprecedented,' says Stephen Maxner, a military historian and director of the Vietnam Center and Archive in Lubbock, Texas."[567]

No wonder soldiers suffer from PSTD. Literally every day soldiers face life-threatening scenarios. Their stress is undeniable and cumulative.[568] Is it any wonder that military suicide rates are excruciatingly high? Losing soldiers to suicide at a rate of 1 every 18 hours is a national disgrace.[569] They need help.

Sometimes the only solace, the only comfort they have is from chaplains, a belief in God, soldiers reading their Bibles and being able to discuss their fears and tightly held Christian beliefs openly. Yet the military requires them to keep a lid on it.

Christian persecution within the military is so onerous that former Arkansas Gov. Mike Huckabee told young Americans to wait until President Barack Obama is out of office to enlist because his administration has "an open hostility toward the Christian faith." Huckabee continued: "Why would they want to be in a military that would be openly hostile and not just simply bring some scorn to their faith, but would punish them for it?"[570]

These are a few examples of how Christianity is being systematically purged from the military – those that should be in the forefront of knees on the ground asking for God's protection – not shunning him.

June 2014 – U.S. Navy orders Bibles to be removed from base hotels and lodges.[571]

March 2014 – Maxell Air Force Base suddenly bans Gideons from handing out Bibles to willing recruits, a practice that has taken place for years.[572]

March 2014 – "Ask an Atheist Day" is promoted by the Air Force Academy one week after a cadet is forced to take down a Bible verse from his dorm room white board.[573]

February 2014 – Lance Corporal Monifa Sterling is court martialed after not following orders to take down a Bible verse from her work station which read: 'No weapons formed against me shall prosper.' Sterling is busted down from lance corporal to private and given a dishonorable discharge.[574]

December 2013 – Guantanamo Bay Naval Base orders two nativity scenes be removed from the dining hall and confined to the base chapel's courtyard. This happens after complaints from 18 on a base with a population of nearly 6,000.[575]

October 2013 – Soldiers in a counter-intelligence briefing at Fort Hood – site of mass murder by a radicalized Muslim soldier Nidal Hasan – are told that evangelical Christians are a threat to America and that for a soldier to donate to such a group "was punishable under military regulations".[576]

October 2013 – Fifty Catholic priests hired to serve as military chaplains are prohibited from performing Mass services at base chapels during partial government financial shutdown. When offered to perform Mass free of charge, they are denied permission and threatened with termination.[577]

October 2013 – The Air Force Academy, in response to a complaint from Mikey Weinstein's Military Religious Freedom Foundation, makes "so help me God" optional in cadet honor oath.[578]

August 2013 – A Department of Defense training manual teaches soldiers that people who talk about "individual liberties, states' rights, and how to make the world a better place" are "potential extremists." It also lists supporters of former presidential candidates Ron Paul, Chuck Baldwin, and Bob Barr as potential "militia" influenced terrorists".[579]

August 2013 – A Senior Master Sergeant is relieved of duty for refusing his lesbian commander's order to say he supports gay marriage and being punished for his traditional Christian beliefs.[580]

August 2013 – The military provides taxpayer-funded extended leave of up to 10 days in order to enter a same-sex marriage. These special bonuses aren't granted to heterosexual couples.[581]

August 2013 – The Air Force, while cracking down on Christianity, invites drag queens to perform at a base, which one airman deems "totally inappropriate and offensive. "We can't even have Bibles on our desks".[582]

July 2013 – When an Air Force sergeant with 27 years' service sends a complaint to the chaplain at West Point about a same-sex marriage ceremony performed in their chapel, he receives a letter of reprimand. It tells him to get in line with military policy or get out. They tear up his new 6-year reenlistment contract and replace it with 1-year agreement and warn "be prepared to retire at the end of this year."[583]

June 2013 – The Obama Administration "strongly objects" to a proposed amendment to the National Defense Authorization Act that would protect the religious rights of soldiers – including evangelical Christian service members who are facing growing hostility towards their religion.[584]

June 2013 – The Pentagon orders removal of an Air Force video honoring first sergeants because it mentions the word "God", which some fear would insult atheists or Muslims. The video is a twist on the famous "So God Made a Farmer" commentary written and narrated by the late radio broadcaster Paul Harvey, which is later used as the basis of a commercial for the Super Bowl.[585]

June 2013 – An unidentified Army master sergeant is investigated, reprimanded, threatened with judicial action, given a bad efficiency report and told he is "no longer a team player and not performing up to standards" because he served Chick-fil-A sandwiches at a party. Chick-fil-A had been boycotted by gays because they supported the Defense of Marriage Act as does the master sergeant.[586]

May 2013 – Air Force officer, Lt. Col. Laurel Tingley, is required to remove a personal Bible from his desk because it "may" appear he is condoning a particular religion. Rep. Louie Gohmert (R-TX) takes issue with the demand and tells Fox News. "If that is the standard, then Christianity will be over because there will always be somebody who is uncomfortable no matter what someone's belief is when it comes to Judeo-Christian beliefs. It appears it is getting more and more difficult to be a Christian and serve in the military."[587]

April 2013 – Soldiers in the U.S. military are told in a training briefing that evangelical Christians are the No. 1 extremist threat to America – ahead of the Muslim Brotherhood, KKK, Nation of Islam, al-Qaida, Hamas and others.[588]

April 2013 – Military Religious Freedom Foundation's President Mikey Weinstein and others meet privately with Pentagon officials to enforce a regulation prohibiting proselytizing. The MRFF pushes for those caught to be court-martialed. Weinstein says U.S. troops who do are guilty of sedition and treason and should be punished – by the hundreds if necessary – to stave off what he calls a "tidal wave of fundamentalists" and compares Christian evangelism to rape.[589]

January 2013 – President Obama voices his opposition to and calls it "ill-advised" a provision in the 2013 National Defense Authorization Act that allows military chaplains to opt-out of performing gay marriages.[590]

June 2012 – Bowing to a complaint from the MRFF, the Pentagon withdraws consent for publisher LifeWay Christian Resources to use official military emblems on Bibles. Covers were designed for one of the four service branches. Includes patriotic essays, transcribed prayers from past and present American military, battle-themed hymns, the Armed Forces Code of Conduct, and the Pledge of Allegiance. Ironically, these Bibles no longer sold on base have imprinted on the back, "The book that defines true liberty and freedom for all time".[591]

February 2012 – Due to pressure from the anti-Christian groups VoteVets.org and Military Religious Freedom Foundation, three-star Army general and war hero, Lt. Gen. William G. Boykin, is forced to withdraw from speaking at West Point.[592]

February 2012 – The U.S. Air Force provokes outrage by removing a Latin reference to God on its Rapid Capabilities Office patch after complaints from a military atheist group.[593]

February 2012 – The Army orders Catholic chaplains not to read a letter to parishioners that their archbishop asks them to read. The letter calls on Catholics to resist the Obama Administration policy that would force institutions affiliated with religious groups to provide coverage for birth control, sterilization and agents that induce abortions.[594]

November 2011 – The Air Force Academy withdraws support for Operation Christmas Child, a program that sends toys and toiletries in shoeboxes to needy kids around the world.[595]

September 2011 – Air Force Chief of Staff prohibits commanders from notifying airmen of programs and services available to them and leaves this solely in the hands of chaplains.[596]

September 2011 – The Navy issues guidelines for Walter Reed Medical Center stipulating, "No religious items (i.e. Bibles, reading materials and/or artifacts) are to be given away or used during a visit."[597] Under heavy pressure from Congress and religious leaders, the Navy rescinds this policy three months later.[598]

August 2011 – After 20 years, the Air Force stops teaching the "Just War theory" class to officers at Vandenberg AFB. The course, taught by chaplains, used Scripture from both the Old and New Testaments to show missile launch officers that it can be moral to go to war.[599]

June 2011 – Department of Veterans Affairs censors prayer by banning the words "God" and "Jesus" during funeral services at Houston National Cemetery. Volunteer service group, the National Memorial Ladies, are told they must stop telling families "God bless you" at funerals and remove the words "God bless" from condolence cards.[600]

January 2010 – The U.S. Army directs troops to scratch off with a Dremel-type tool and then cover in black paint a Bible inscription etched into their gun sights. Defense contractor Trijicon said after 30 years of doing so, they will no longer stamp scripture into the weapons' serial numbers.[601]

THE BOTTOM LINE

Gen. Jerry Boykin summed it up best, that it is "discrimination against Christians" and that the "climate of intimidation within the Air Force has worsened to such an extend that even chaplains now fear carrying out the most basic duties of their job. In this case, a chaplain has been censored for expressing his beliefs about the role of faith in the lives of service members. There has to be a recognition that this is discrimination against Christians. Chaplains are placed there for a purpose. Why do we have chaplains if they aren't allowed to fulfill that purpose? When anti-Christian activists like Mikey Weinstein are dictating the rules for what chaplains are allowed to do, then why we must ask the question why we have chaplains?"[602]

Turning Up the Heat

As with any revolution, it begins with planting a tiny seed. Like gas price signs at filling stations advertising $2.49/gallon. That's normal. Then OPEC gets a burr under its saddle or somebody blows up Middle East oil wells and prices skyrocket over night in retribution to $3.35/gallon. Diesel shoots up 20¢ more. In the ensuing weeks, gas edges up another 10¢, 20¢, 50¢. After enough public outrage and people greatly decrease driving, OPEC gets a big heart and reduces prices by 50¢ compared to 14 days ago. You're thankful to pay even 25¢ below the high. Prices sit there for a while. We get used to the new high and then the "edge up" starts all over again. That's how it is with animosity toward Christians. Little bit by little bit.

Politicians shrink from saying radical Muslims are responsible for most attacks on Christians. Instead it's labeled "workplace violence". It's called anything but what it is. Politicians don't want to "offend"... And so it grows when people don't speak up.

Addressing a group of Muslims in California Omar Ahmad, Founder of the Council on American-Islamic Relations (CAIR) proclaims. "Islam isn't in America to be equal to any other faith, but to become dominant. The Koran, the Muslim book of scripture, should be the highest authority in America, and Islam the only accepted religion on Earth."[603] A friend of Daniel Pipes, Rev. Austin Miles of Oakley, California, knew of his interest in CAIR. Miles sent Pipes the newspaper clipping in 2001 from the *San Ramon Valley Herald*. CAIR trying to do damage control released a presser saying Ahmed's statement was "false and pure fabrication" on the reporter's part. But nothing ever came of it. Reportedly they never even contacted the *Valley Herald.* Combine that with Quran's instruction that at least six different types of lying are sanctioned between its covers (discussed later in this chapter) it should be a cautionary tale. It's yet another axe chipping at the tree of Christianity.

In 2012, Liberty Institute and the Family Research Council, two organizations committed to protecting and advancing religious liberty rights in the U.S. released a joint project *The Survey of Religious Hostility in America*. It chronicled more than 600 incidents,[604] most occurring over the last decade. In 2013 they published *Undeniable: The Survey of Hostility to Religion in America*, which tracked 1,200 cases, nearly doubling the number in the previous year. In 2014, their catalog showed a 133% increase of Christian attacks since their first publication. These cases resulted in litigation, but left a multitude of others on the table.

Christian Girls, Women Kidnapped, Raped, Beaten to Convert to Islam

This is a repellent topic by anyone's standards. The UN published a report in January 2016 that shows ISIS is currently holding about 3,500 sex slaves, most women and children from the Yezidi community, but a number are also from other ethnic and religious minority communities. Non-Muslim women who refuse the Islamic "rite of rape" are murdered.[605]

Martyrs Beheaded Throughout History

This form of capital punishment dates back to earliest times in the 3rd century, which included 38 Catholic saints. In Biblical times John the Baptist lost his head for criticizing then ruler Herod Antipater for divorcing his first wife.

Most people remember the Biblical story of David and Goliath. It relays the tale of normal sized David killing the giant, Goliath. By all odds the fight shouldn't have gone in his favor, but it did. It is recorded as this:

"The account of the battle between David and Goliath is told in 1 Samuel, chapter 17. Saul and the Israelites are facing the Philistines near the Valley of Elah. Twice a day for 40 days, Goliath, the champion of the Philistines, comes out between the lines and challenges the Israelites to send out a champion of their own to decide the outcome in single combat, but Saul and all the Israelites are afraid. David, bringing food for his elder brothers, hears that Saul has promised to reward any man who defeats Goliath, and accepts the challenge. Saul reluctantly agrees and offers his armor, which David declines, taking only his sling and 5 stones from a brook.

"David and Goliath confront each other, Goliath with his armor and shield, David with his staff and sling. "The Philistine cursed David by his gods." but David replies: "This day Jehovah (Jesus) will deliver you into my hand, and I will strike you down; and I will give the dead bodies of the host of the Philistines this day to the birds of the air and to the wild beasts of the earth; that all the earth may know that there is a God in Israel, and that all this assembly may know that God saves not with sword and spear; for the battle is God's, and he will give you into our hand."

"David hurls a stone from his sling with all his might and hits Goliath in the center of his forehead, Goliath falls on his face to the ground, and David cuts off his head."[606]

Centuries later in 1076 Britain – beheadings were conducted because it was cheap, and swords and axes were readily available.

However, nearly 400 years later, just 93 decapitations were performed at London's famous 'Towers'.

BEHEADINGS ABANDONED

Britain outlawed beheadings altogether by 1747 and France by 1792. It took Scandinavian countries until the early 1900s to abandon them. However, Europe has completely turned away from capital punishment.

By 1903, beheading was universally banned throughout Europe and Asia with one exception.

NAZI GERMANY

Friedrich Lorenz, born in what is today's Hildesheim district of Lower Saxony to postman Klein Freden in 1897. The family moved to Hildesheim in 1902. Here Lorenz made first contact with the Catholic Church, the Missionary Oblates of Mary Immaculate. He attended St. Karl Oblate boarding school in Limburg in the Netherlands from 1911 to 1916. Though he joined the Novitiate of the Oblates at Maria Engelport Monastery, one month later they had to release him for military duty. In WWI, he fought as a NCO (non-commissioned officer) on the Western Front and was awarded the Iron Cross, second class, for bravery.

After the war, he re-joined the monastery and took eternal vows in July 1923. A year later, he was ordained as a priest by the Bishop of Fulda, Joseph Damian Schmitt. Lorenz was assigned his first posting to the People's Mission and was later transferred to Schwerin, Germany.

On September 1, 1939, Lorenz was recalled to the military as a chaplain when WWII loomed. Once again, he received the Iron Cross for bravery.

In 1940, Lorenz returned to Schwerin and participated with the "Wednesday Circle", a discussion group for men from the Stettin pastoral area.

On February 4, 1943, Gestapo stormed the Wednesday Circle. Forty people were arrested, including Lorenz. The Reichskriegsgericht in Torgau sentenced him to death on July 28, 1944 for "listening to enemy broadcasts", "undermining the fighting forces", and "helping the enemy". Lorenz was beheaded on November 13, 1944 in Halle, Germany.[607]

Friedrich Lorenz was just one of approximately 16,500 men, women and one 17-year-old boy, Helmuth Hubener, that fell under the guillotine's blade. This practice ended in 1945 with the fall of Nazi Germany.[608]

CURRENT ACCOUNTS

While still allowed by law in Yemen and Iran, though none have been conducted there, Saudi Arabia is the only country to still perform beheadings. From 2007 through 2013, they held at least 643 such executions and they were done humanely. However, in 2015, Saudi Arabia carried out 158 beheadings – the highest number in two decades. This death sentence is reserved for serious crimes of rape, murder, apostasy, sorcery, armed robbery, drug trafficking and repeated drug use. Before 2004, beheadings were nearly non-existent. This is yet another sign of the times.

BEHEADINGS WITH "HUMANITY"

This might seem like a strange concept, but properly done with one blow from a sharp instrument, beheading can be swift and nearly painless compared to other methods like crucifixion or being burned at the stake or botched lethal injection.

If a chopping block or guillotine isn't used, the person to be executed kneels blindfolded and hands are cuffed or tied behind their back. Being blindfolded prevents the victim from flinching and the executioner missing his target. A sharp instrument is then poked into the middle of his or her back. This immediately causes the person to arch the neck backwards, making a clean strike much easier.

Before carrying out the penalty, those to be executed are given tranquilizers and taken by police van to a public area after noon prayers. After a blindfold is in place, they are led to the middle of a 4 by 4 foot plastic sheet spread out on the ground.

Dressed in either their own clothes or in a white robe, but barefoot, their hands and feet are shackled. While kneeling and facing Mecca, an Interior Minister reads the victim's name and crime(s) to those that have gathered.

A policeman hands the executioner a traditional 43 – 47 inch-long Arab scimitar. He takes a few practice swings. The prisoner is then jabbed in the back causing him to raise his head. Usually the deed is completed with one swing sending the head flying some two to three feet away. With a gloved hand the attending doctor stems the spurting blood and sews the head back on. The body is then wrapped in the plastic sheet and carried off by ambulance to be buried in an unmarked grave for prisoners.[609]

So while beheadings *were* a thing of the past for some 100 years, events are reversing. Now there is a resurgence. In the numbers following this author does not include unrelated accounts like beheadings from great white shark attacks or ones due to car accidents or botched hangings.

Now take a look at what's happening around us.

Modern Day Beheadings

Islamic extremists are bringing their gruesome executions back in ways heretofore unthinkable. Instead of beheading as an expedient, near-painless death, they are dragging it out to excruciating torment.

1999

Australians aren't as filtered as Americans on vital news. They show their citizens what's really going on in the world. Circa 1999, nightly news aired a load of Indonesian Christians in the back of a pick-up. The shocking thing is that these people had all been macheteed and landed in the back of the truck, literally in pieces. Legs, arms, torsos and heads were all jumbled up, atop each other. Tossed together like a human salad. There was no respect for life, certainly none for Christians. As has been maintained by this author, when firearms are removed, thieves, murderers and terrorists will resort to knives, poisons, bioweapons, broken glass, baseball bats, 2x4s – whatever is at their disposal.

2002

DANNY PEARL

The first modern-day beheading that garnered worldwide attention began with American journalist, Daniel Pearl. Pearl was an American with Israeli citizenship – the perfect combination as Muslim extremists view Jews as "apes and dogs" (Quran Surahs 2:65, 5:60, and 7:166). 'People of the Book', which includes Christians, are also fair game, despite living a Godly, charitable life. If a person isn't Muslim, they are considered infidels and targets for murder, sanctioned by the Quran, (Surah 2:191-193)

From the Daniel Pearl Foundation they share:

"Danny was born on October 10, 1963, in Princeton, New Jersey, and grew up in Los Angeles, where he displayed an insatiable curiosity for music, academics and sports.

"Music turned out to be an essential form of expression for Danny and led him to become a fixture in several bands throughout the world, where he improvised on the electric violin, fiddle, or mandolin. Today, friends and colleagues still recall how quickly he would pick up an instrument when he sensed an occasion, such as writing a song for a pregnant friend past her due date, or the Christmas night when he entertained downhearted co-workers at his office.

"Danny exuded compassion and joy wherever he went. As his best friend said, "Danny was the only one who didn't know he was charismatic." He endeared himself to others with an easy humor and appreciation for the absurd, always keeping an open mind to other perspectives, cultures, and backgrounds. He was humble, generous and loved life and people. World leaders and peasants, Rabbis and Mullahs, all considered him a friend.

"A gifted writer from a very young age, Danny's aptitude for journalism became apparent as a student at Stanford University where he co-founded the student newspaper *Stanford Commentary*.

"In October of 2000, they moved to Bombay, where Danny became the South Asia Bureau Chief for the Wall Street Journal.

"It was from Bombay that Danny covered the "war on terrorism," occasionally venturing into Pakistan. He was retracing the steps of "shoe bomber" Richard Reid and hoped to meet with Sheik Gilani, a spiritual leader, when he was abducted in Karachi on January 23, 2002. For weeks, millions around the world — from heads of state, to religious leaders and ordinary people — rallied for Danny's release. In Danny, the terrorists believed they abducted a media figure, an American, and a Jew. But they had much more — a true citizen of the world and an embodiment of civilized values, whose death, like his life, would inspire millions of people in the cause of decency and cultural understanding. Several weeks elapsed without word of his fate; his murder was confirmed on February 21, 2002. Four of the kidnappers were convicted on July 15, 2002, including mastermind Omar Saeed Sheik, although others believed to be involved are still at large.

"Two days before his abduction, Danny learned that his wife Mariane was expecting a baby boy; he chose the name Adam for their son. In May, just three months after his murder, Mariane Pearl gave birth to Adam.

Danny's death in 2002 began a dangerous resurgence of beheadings, ones designed to inflict maximum pain and terror.[610]

Two years later, a rash of beheadings commenced.

2004

KODA SHOSEI

Japanese citizen, Koda Shosei, 24, was kidnapped while touring Iraq. Shosei was warned not to go, but he wanted to see conditions in Iraq for himself. He and his family were members of the United Church of Christ and Koda's arm bore a Christian cross tattoo. Somewhere between October 20 and 29, 2004, **Abu Musab al-Zarqawi**'s group abducted Koda. His captors threatened Koda's life if Japan didn't withdraw its forces from Iraq within 48 hours. Japan refused to negotiate with terrorists and the payment was his head, his body wrapped in an American flag. Koda was the first Japanese person beheaded in Iraq and ironically his last name, Shoesei, means 'proof of life'.

June 22, 2004 brought the decapitation of South Korean interpreter and Christian missionary, Kim Sun-il. Kim arrived in Iraq on June 15, 2003, and worked for Gana General Trading Company, a South Korean company contracted to the U.S. military. Kim was abducted in Fallujah not quite a year later at the end of May by the Islamist group Jama'at al-Tawhid wal-Jihad ("Oneness of God and Jihad").

KIM SUN-IL

While held hostage, the Islamic group tried to force S. Korea to cancel plans of sending 3,000 additional troops to Iraq. They also demanded that the 660 military medics and engineers already there be withdrawn. S Korea refused to yield. Like with the decapitation victims, Kim was dressed in an orange jumpsuit and blindfolded. On June 22, like Nick Berg, five men assault Kim with a knife and his head is sawed off. Kim was just 33.

During the video airing of this decapitation, the terrorists read a statement. "To the South Korean citizens: We warned you. This is the result of your own doings. Enough lies, or cheatings. Your soldiers here are not for the sake for the Iraqis, but they are here for the cursed America."[611]

Revealed by the Pentagon, in another heartless act, Kim's body had been booby-trapped with explosives.

EUGENE ARMSTRONG, JACK HENSLEY, KENNETH JOHN BIGLEY

British civil engineer Kenneth John Bigley was kidnapped in the al-Mansour district of Baghdad on September 16, along with Americans Jack Hensley and Eugene Armstrong. The three men worked for a Kuwaiti company, Gulf Supplies and Commercial Services, on reconstruction projects in Iraq. The men knew their home was being watched and realized they were in grave danger when their Iraqi house guard quit due to threats by militias for protecting U.S. and British workers. Regardless, Bigley and the two Americans continued to live in the house.

On September 18, the Islamic extremist group, led by Jordanian Abu Musab al-Zarqawi, posted a video of the three men kneeling in front of a Tawhid and Jihad banner. The kidnappers said they would kill the men within 48 hours if their demands for the release of Iraqi women prisoners held by coalition forces weren't met.

The British denied they had Iraqi women prisoners, but they did have two scientists: British-educated Dr. Rihab Taha and US-educated Dr. Huda Salih Mahdi Ammash. Taha, dubbed Dr. Germ, was cited by the U.S. Joint Chiefs of Staff and the U.S. Defense Intelligence Agency as one of the world's most dangerous women. Ammash nicknamed by Western press as Mrs. Anthrax and Chemical Sally was number 53 on the Pentagon's list of the 55 most wanted. Both of these women were highly involved in Saddam Hussein's bio-weapons program.

Ammash, who obtained her Ph.D from the University of Missouri, 'built' Saddam's chemical program with Taha at the helm. The deadline arrived and these dangerous scientists were not released. Armstrong was first to decapitated on September 20. Abu Musab al-Zarqawi personally beheaded Armstrong. Hensley was similarly murdered 24 hours later by a group of men from Tawhid and Jihad.

For some reason Bigley's execution didn't take place till some two weeks later on October 7. Despite the attempted intervention by the Muslim Council of Britain and the indirect intervention of the British government, plus video pleading from Bigley himself to then Prime Minister Tony Blair, all went unheeded. All were subsequently decapitated.

PAUL MARSHALL JOHNSON, JR.

At the time of his kidnapping, Johnson, a native of New Jersey, lived in Saudi Arabia. Trained as a helicopter engineer he worked for Lockheed Martin on upgrading Saudi AH-64A Apache attack helicopters. This was during a time when Saudi Arabia experienced surging violence against foreigners. The week preceding, four people had been shot: BBC journalists Frank Gardner and Simon Cumbers, and two Americans in Riyadh. Johnson was stopped and abducted at a fake checkpoint by a group of Muslim extremists called Al-Qaeda in the Arabian Peninsula.

A video filmed by this group, showed a blindfolded Johnson being held hostage in exchange for al-Qaeda prisoners held in Saudi jails. Their demands were not fulfilled and Johnson was decapitated somewhere around June 18, just six days after his capture. Five weeks later Johnson's severed head was found in a refrigerator by Saudi security official.

NICHOLAS EVAN BERG

American freelance radio-tower repairman, Nick Berg, 26, travelled to Iraq in December 2003 for work and to visit family, an Iraqi man married to Nick's late aunt. On February 1 he returned home to Philadelphia and six weeks later, travelled back to Iraq only to find the promised work no longer existed.

The last Nick's family heard from him was on April 9, 2004 and he never returned to his hotel. Since he and his family remained in close contact by phone and email, they knew something was terribly wrong. Berg had been abducted and somewhere in the interim – beheaded. He was found by a U.S. military patrol, dumped on an overpass, wearing the traditional orange jumpsuit signifying a captive of extremists with his severed head sitting on top of his body.

On May 2004, jihadist group Muntada al-Ansar posted a 5-minute video with the opening title of "Abu Musab al-Zarqawi Slaughters an American". In it Nick identifies himself, his family and where he lived just outside Philadelphia, PA.

In the video Berg is surrounded by 5 men wearing ski masks and shemaghs – the traditional Muslim scarf headdress. They then converge on Berg. While two of them hold Nick down a third saws off his head with a knife. This execution was meant to be excruciating. As this barbaric act is committed, Berg screams and his captors shout *Allahu Akbar"* – God is greatest. The severed head is held up to the camera and then set on Nick's body.

Following this, in 2005 three Christian girls were beheaded in Indonesia. They were so young, just 14 and 15. Now flash forward to 2013. Beheadings are ramping up to the days of old.

2013

LEE RIGBY

On May 2013, British Army soldier, Lee Rigby of the Royal Regiment of Fusiliers, was run down with a car and then nearly beheaded with knives and a cleaver. Rigby was off duty and walking along Wellington Street when he was attacked and killed by Michael Adebolajo, 28, and Michael Adebowal, 22. Both are British of Nigerian descent, raised as Christians, and then converted to Islam. The pair chose Rigby simply because he was the first soldier to appear on the South London street where they laid in wait on May 22.

When questioned about the murder Adebolajo stated, "This is how we kill our animals in Islam. He may be my enemy but he is a man...so I struck at the neck and attempted to remove his head."

"During the first interview he ranted for 40 minutes, often wagging a finger in the air, about British troops 'committing mass murder' in Muslim lands. He said there was a 'war between Muslims and the British people' and he was a 'soldier of Allah'. Rigby was a drummer, not a fighter.

"When asked about the soldier's killing, he said: 'He was struck on the neck with a sharp implement and it was sawn until his head, you know, became almost unattached.'

When finally subdued and apprehended, Adebolajo was covered in Rigby's blood with the knife and cleaver still clutched in red hands. On December 19, 2013, both of the attackers were found guilty of Rigby's murder and sentenced to life imprisonment.

Friends described Rigby as witty and extremely popular, well liked and respected among the Second Fusiliers. Just 25, Rigby leaves behind his 2-year-old son and wife of 5 years.[612]

HANNY TAWADROS AND AMGAD KONDS

In February 2013, 29-year-old Muslim, Yusuf Ibrahim, beheaded two Coptic Christians in New Jersey, 25-year-old Hanny Tawadros and 27-year-old Amgad Konds. This clearly brought the horror of Islamic beheadings to America. Pamela Geller who blogs at *Atlas Shrugged* said the act "appears to have been a ritual killing, religious in nature," though no motive was given by police. Ibrahim was taken into custody after their severed hands and heads were found in a shallow grave, buried separately from the bodies. The suspect drove one of the victim's white Mercedes to Philadelphia and tried to set it on fire. Police tracked and arrested at him at his Bayonne, New Jersey apartment. Ibrahim was indicted on two counts each of murder, felony murder, kidnapping, robbery and desecrating human remains and mutilation of the bodies. He faces up to two life sentences on the murder charges and is being held on a $3.3 million, cash-only bail.[613]

JAMES FOLEY, STEVEN SOTLOFF, DAVID HAINES, ALAN HENNING, PETER KASSIG

In rapid succession during 2014, ISIS beheaded American journalists **James Foley**, Steven Sotloff and British aid workers, David Haines and Alan Henning and Peter Kassig. Foley began his career as a teacher before switching to journalism. In 2009, he worked for USAID-funded development projects in Baghdad. He organized conferences and training seminars designed to rebuild Iraq's civil service. The next year he left Iraq and applied to become an embedded freelance journalist. He was assigned to U.S. troops in Iraq and joined *Stars and Stripes* as a reporter in Afghanistan. In 2011, Foley travelled to Libya to cover the uprising against Muammar Gaddafi, embedding himself with rebel fighters. This is where everything went south.

In 2011, he and two other reporters, American Clare Morgana Gillis and Spanish photographer Manu Brabo were detained in Brega, Libya, by Gaddafi's forces. In the ensuing encounter, another journalist, Anton Hammerl was killed and the three of them were beaten. After being jailed 44 days, Foley was released and he returned home to Milwaukee. Foley should have taken a lesson, but instead, travelled back to Libya in short order.

Foley was captured again November 22, 2012. Negotiations through August 19, 2014 failed and ISIS beheaded him.

Jihadi John

It was released on February 26, 2015, that the perpetrator, known as "Jihadi John" is actually Mohammed Emwazi. Emwazi was so nicknamed by hostages after John Lennon of The Beatles referring to their British accents. Other members of this ISIS terror cell were dubbed George, Paul and Ringo. While dapper in public life, during beheadings, Emwazi always wore head-to-toe black with only his eyes and the bridge of his nose visible.

This 26-year-old Kuwaiti-born British man grew up in West London in a well-to-do family. He graduated from the Westminster University with a degree in computer programming. Desiring to get out of England, he tried ardently to get to Somalia, but was detained at the Amsterdam airport. Emwazi returned to Britain and in a bit of irony, complained bitterly that he had been "very unfairly treated". It is hard to reconcile a man described as polite, intelligent, having a penchant for wearing stylish clothes and planning his wedding to this picture of unfathomable savagery.

"Jihadi John" notoriously beheaded James Foley, Steven Sotloff, David Haines, Alan Henning, Peter Kassig, and Japanese Haruna Yukawa and Kenji Goto Jogo. He then led the group of 21 Egyptian Christians to their slaughter on the beach in Syria.

After this savagery, ISIS reveals they are holding another American journalist, **Steven Sotloff**. They promise he will be killed if Obama doesn't halt air strikes against ISIS. Obama refuses and they released a video showing the beheading of Sotloff on September 2, 2014.

Peter Haines, father of two, resided in Sisak, Croatia prior to his capture. He had been an aircraft engineer in the Royal Air Force before shifting to humanitarian aid in 1999. There his job was to help victims of conflict in former Yugoslavia, Africa and the Middle East. In 2012, he was an unarmed security worker for a civilian peacekeeping group in South Sudan.

In March 2013, Haines' luck ran out. An armed gang kidnapped him while working in a camp for displaced Syrian people. He was abducted, along with Italian aid worker, Federico Motka, but the translator and driver were left alone. The translator relayed that the two had been taken after their tires had been shot out while traveling on a country road.

Much like with Foley and Sotloff, a rescue attempt was made, but failed.

ISIS released a video on September 13, 2014, which followed the same format as for Foley and Sotloff. It shows Haines delivering a prepared speech and then his executioner makes a statement. He puts a knife to Haines' throat and makes sawing motion as the video fades out. In the last frames, his captor holds the orange jumpsuit of the fourth captive, Alan Henning, and threatens England's Prime Minister. "If you, Cameron, insist on fighting the Islamic State then you, like your master Obama, will have the blood of your people on your hands."

Alan Henning was captured in December 2013 during the ISIS occupation of the Syrian city, Al-Dana. Like Haines, he was in-country to provide humanitarian relief. Though Henning had been warned not to cross into Syria, he said he wanted to make sure supplies were being delivered into the right hands. He was simply an ambulance driver for Rochdale Aid 4 Syria, which raised aid money for those caught in warzones.

Henning was a kind man. You can see the softness in his nice brown eyes. To ISIS, it doesn't matter. Life doesn't matter.

David Cameron said Britain would do all it could "to hunt down these murderers and bring them to justice", but either they didn't or their mission failed. This father of two, 47, in the dreaded orange jumpsuit, was beheaded. The act was verified on October 3, 2014 when the video was released. In it showed a clip of the next man to suffer at the hands of Muslim extremists – **Peter Kassig**.

Peter, like Haines and Henning, was a humanitarian aid worker. After graduation in 2006 from North Central High School in Indianapolis, he became a U.S. Army Ranger, with an army special operations unit, serving from June 2006 to September 2007. After a medical discharge, Kassig majored in political science.

Following this, Kassig worked in Syria and Lebanon as a humanitarian. He helped Syrian refugees via Special Emergency Response and Assistance (SERA), a non-governmental organization he founded in the Fall of 2012. It gave refugees medical assistance, supplies, clothing, and food. As a trained medical assistant Kassig also provided trauma care to Syrians.

ISIS took Kassig hostage on October 1, 2013 while delivering food and medical supplies to refugees in Deir Ezzour, eastern Syria. Though he had converted from Christianity to Islam before his capture, it didn't matter to ISIS as Kassig was beheaded on November 16, 2014.

PALMIRA SILVA

Palmira Silva was beheaded in broad daylight in a suburban north London backyard. The 25-year-old Muslim perpetrator, Nicholas Salvadore had beheaded a cat and was covered in blood. He was in the process of sodomizing a dog, when the 82-year-old grandmother tried to intervene. The suspect then turned his machete on Silva, stabbed her repeatedly. As he severed her head, the suspect was heard yelling, *"Allahu Akbar! Allahu Akbar!!"*

Two other would-be victims were more fortunate after the assailant tried to attack them. The suspect was finally tasered and brought down after more than 20 police showed up on the scene.

The widowed cafe owner still went to the family business every day, loved gardening and described by one neighbor as "such a sweet lady".

"One neighbor told of her narrow escape. Freda Odame, 30, a catering worker, said she heard a commotion and pulled back her curtains to see a man in his mid-20s with a knife.

"Someone was shouting and the door was banging. I could hear the screaming but I could not hear what he was saying," she said. "I could see that he had a big curved knife, about the size of an arm's length and he was crouching as if frantically searching for something. He had a crazed look in his eyes so I closed my curtains because I was scared."[614]

WOMEN DECAPITATED IN LONDON

Alarmingly, the story of Palmira Silva isn't an isolated instance. She was the third woman to be beheaded in London in 2014. On June 3rd, Tahira Ahmed, a 38-year-old mother-of-two was decapitated at her home in West London. She had been stabbed, both of her arms broken and then decapitated following an intense argument. Tahira's family described her as "the kindest, most patient and gentle individual, who lived for her children and family, and had devoted her life to the welfare of her children and their best possible upbringing. A barbaric man, with out-dated and backward ideals cut her life was cut short in the most brutal manner. He caused untold pain, which will forever haunt Tahira's family and friends."[615] Naveed Ahmed has been jailed for life, a minimum of 22 years, for her murder.

In April, 60-year-old Judith Nibbs was beheaded in Shoreditch, an inner city district in London's historic East End. Her 67-year-old estranged husband was found at the scene. Police didn't look for anyone else. The day after Judith died, her daughter who is severely disabled tweeted the single word: 'Mum?'

In June 2013, Aras Hussain, 21, decapitated his girlfriend Reema Ramzan, who was just 18.

The year before, in October 2012, Catherine Gowing, 39, was decapitated and raped by serial rapist Clive Sharp, 47.

In March of the same year Elizabeth Coriat, 76, was decapitated by her son Daniel Coriat, 43.

Earlier that same month, Tony McCluskie, 36, decapitated his sister, Gemma McCluskie, 29.[616]

2015

MOAZ AL-KASSASBEH

Just before his jet crashed, Jordanian pilot Moaz al-Kassasbeh ejected. Though it's not certain what caused the jet's malfunction, al-Kassasbeh purportedly told *Dabiq* his craft had been hit by a heat-seeking missile. Since *Dabiq* is an ISIS-run propaganda publication, the truth of this statement is in question.

NOTE: Not only is *Dabiq* an ISIS magazine, it is the name of the town in Muslim eschatology of the site where the final battle occurs between Muslims and Christians and where the Land of Islam was created. The battle is seen as ushering in the End of Times.

Lt. Kassasbeh had been on a mission to destroy anti-aircraft batteries over Raqqa in northeastern Syria. Upon hearing of his son's capture, Moaz's father prayed that "Allah will plant mercy in their hearts and they will release him." This did not happen.

On Feb. 3, 2015, ISIS posted a video of Moaz dressed in an orange jumpsuit housed in a cage on the scorching desert sands. He is doused with fuel and white phosphorus, a substance used to burn metal. Moaz is set on fire and struggles terribly as the blaze consumes him. He finally gives up in a corner of the cage.

As follow-up, in case one tiny cell of 27-year-old first-lieutenant Moaz al-Kassasbeh remained, a front end loader dumps concrete on his incinerated body – just to make sure his life was truly extinguished – and for effect.[617]

21 COPTIC CHRISTIANS SLAUGHTERED

In February 2015, 21 Christians were beheaded for being Christians and over 100 Jewish graves were vandalized in France. These Christians did nothing offensive and were kidnapped in two attacks in December 2014 and January 2015 from the coastal town of Sirte, eastern Libya. On Feb 12, these 21 men, Coptic *Christians* recognized by Egypt as such, but not by Pres. Obama, were marched down the Libyan beach to their death. They were clothed in traditional orange jumpsuits and made to kneel at the water's edge. The men were then beheaded, in turn, with their lifeforce literally turning the ocean red.

The Obama administration refused to link these executions to Islam and used adjectives of "cowardly," "wanton" and "unconstrained by faith, sect, or ethnicity," but determinedly avoided mentioning these men were all Christians. Instead they were referred to as "people of the region".[618]

At the National Prayer Breakfast on this issue President Obama said. "We see ISIL, a brutal, vicious death cult that, in the name of religion, carries out unspeakable acts of barbarism – terrorizing religious minorities like the Yezidis, subjecting women to rape as a weapon of war, and claiming the mantle of religious authority for such actions. And lest we get on our high horse and think this is unique to some other place, remember that during the Crusades and the Inquisition, people committed terrible deeds in the name of Christ."[619]

News agencies skewered him for those remarks. Fox News reporter Ed Henry asked White House Press Secretary Josh Earnest. "You talked about the murder of 21 citizens. I'm just curious, why didn't you mention it was 21 Christians killed by Muslims? Is that relevant?"[620]

Earnest responded – finally. "'It sure is, because the ISIL extremists that carried out this attack indicated that the reason they were killing them is not just because they were Egyptian but because they were Christian.' ...Obama likened the crimes of the Islamic State to those committed hundreds of years ago by Christians during the Inquisition and the Crusades.' The White House continued to backtrack on their original statement, now recognizing that the murder was rooted in the victims' Christian faith."[621]

President Obama's comparison of radical Muslims' acts of horror to the Inquisition and the Crusades infuriated Christians around the world and they received much backlash from secular communities as well.

Catholic League President Bill Donohue called the comments, "'insulting' and 'pernicious' in a statement, and said Obama was trying to 'deflect guilt from Muslim madmen.'"[622]

Radio talk show host Rush Limbaugh said he "insulted the whole gamut of Christians."[623]

Former GOP governor of Virginia, Jim Gilmore, called the comments "the most offensive I've ever heard a president make in my lifetime" and that they go 'further to the point that Mr. Obama does not believe in America or the values we all share.'"[624]

Republican governor of Louisiana, Bobby Jindal, referred to the remarks as a "history lesson" that ignores "the issue right in front of his nose." Continuing, "we will be happy to keep an eye out for runaway Christians, but it would be nice if he would face the reality of the situation today. The Medieval Christian threat is under control, Mr. President. Please deal with the Radical Islamic threat today."[625]

Former Pennsylvania Senator Rick Santorum said. "Today's remarks by the President were inappropriate and his choice of venue was insulting to every person of faith at a time when Christians are being crucified, beheaded, and persecuted across the Middle East. While Christians of today are taught to live their lives as the reflection of Christ's love, the radicals of ISIS use their holy texts as a rationale for violence. To insinuate modern Christians – the same Christian faith that led the abolitionist movement, the Civil Rights Movement, and global charitable efforts fighting disease and poverty – cannot stand up against the scourge we see in the Middle East is wrong."[626]

Well-known Christian evangelist Franklin Graham best summed up Mr. Obama's remarks on Facebook. "Mr. President – Many people in history have used the name of Jesus Christ to accomplish evil things for their own desires. But Jesus taught peace, love and forgiveness. He came to give His life for the sins of mankind, not to take life. Mohammad on the contrary was a warrior and killed many innocent people. True followers of Christ emulate Christ—true followers of Mohammed emulate Mohammed."[627]

"Last week, Pope Francis prayed for God to welcome the 21 Coptic Christians as martyrs since they had their 'throats slit for the sole reason of being Christians.'"[628]

ISLAMIC STATE ABDUCTS ABOUT 350 CHRISTIANS, MURDERS 15

In the pre-dawn hours of February 15, 2015, at least 90 people are abducted from Assyrian Christian villages in northeastern Syria. The Syrian Kurdish militia, with help of U.S.-led air strikes and the Iraqi Peshmerga, shelled the nearby border, which is held by the Islamic State. This area is important to ISIS because it borders territory currently controlled by their group in Iraq. Instead of fighting fairly, ISIS chooses to kidnap these Christians, including women, children and the elderly, living in rural villages.

Another 3,000 manage to flee the attack and find refuge in Hassakeh and Qamishli. Frantic relatives have a difficult time getting information as landlines are cut and cell phones are made inactive. In the next few days, ISIS continues to seize Assyrian villages. According to Osama Edward, founder of the Assyrian Human Rights Network, the Islamic fanatics captures even more hostages over three days swelling the number to about 350.[629]

In February 2014, one woman is beheaded, two men are shot and it's unknown how the other 12 are killed.

Sharlet and Romel David, in Modesto, California, told KCRA TV that 12 of their family members are believed to be among those kidnapped by IS and they fear for their safety.

"'We pray, we pray all the time,' said Romel. 'What we've heard is it was like a sea of black uniforms marching through all the villages, burning down the churches, desecrating the crosses and wreaking havoc.'"[630]

On the heels of the Assyrian village raids, a 5-minute video shows ISIS thugs in an Iraqi museum smashing with sledgehammers ancient artifacts – some dating back over 2,000 years. This is likely to be the first of many such actions since this region is home to nearly 1,800 of Iraq's 12,000 registered archaeological sites. Demolition of these treasures comes as IS continues to target shrines, as they 'cleanse' what they believe is heresy. Ironically, the on-going destruction includes Muslim holy sites. If IS truly believed these artifacts were heretical and were keeping true to their faith, they wouldn't be selling them on the black market to finance their campaign.[631]

Then May 2015 brought horrifying news.

ISLAMIC STATE KILLS 800, BURIES SOME ALIVE

In summer 2014, Islamic State militants attacked Yazidis in villages of northern Iraq. After seizing Sinjar they executed at least 500 of these Christians and buried some of them alive including women and children. During the offensive they took another 300 women for slaves and about 40,000 people were kidnapped at gunpoint. The captured Yazidis, who are viewed by Muslims as "devil worshipers" were told to convert to Islam or face death.

In March 2015, the UN published a horrifying report describing killings, torture, rape and sexual slavery of Yazidis by Islamic State, as well as the use of child soldiers. Investigators reported that the Jihadis separated out Yazidi men and boys over the age of 14 to be executed. The younger boys were forced to become child soldiers while women and girls were carried off as 'spoils of war'.

"In a telephone interview, Iraq's human rights minister Mohammed Shia al-Sudani said, "Some of the victims, including women and children were buried alive in scattered mass graves in and around Sinjar."[632]

"Legislator Mahma Khalil said he spoke to four different people with knowledge of what happened inside the camp. 'The militants want to spread horror among them to force them to convert to Islam or to do something else'."[633]

About 50,000 Yazidis – half of them children – fled to the mountains outside Sinjar and are now at risk of starvation.

In early May 2015, Islamic State rounded up over 300 prisoners near Mosul in Iraq and shot them.

ISLAMIC STATE EXECUTES DOZENS OF ETHIOPIAN CHRISTIANS IN LIBYA

In April 2015, ISIS delivers more carnage as they orchestrated and filmed executions of 30 men. They were ordered to pay a tax or preferably deny their Christian faith. They did neither. In a highly produced 39-minute video, prisoners were divided into two groups and led off. Those in orange jumpsuits were beheaded on a Mediterranean Sea beach with a long knife. The remainder dressed in black were led into the desert and shot in the back of the head.

The video's narrator says in Arabic, "All praise be to Allah, the Lord and cherisher of the world and may peace and blessings be upon the Prophet Mohammed. To the nation of the cross, we are back again on the sands, where the companions of the Prophet, peace be upon him, have stepped on before, telling you: Muslim blood that was shed under the hands of your religion is not cheap. In fact, their blood is the purest blood because there is a nation behind them (which) inherits revenge. And we swear to Allah: the one who disgraced you by our hands, you will not have safety, even in your dreams, until you embrace Islam."[634] "We owe nothing except the edge of the sword."[635]

MUSLIM MIGRANTS THROW CHRISTIANS OVERBOARD – LITERALLY

In yet another gruesome set of murders, 15 Muslim migrants in a fracas with Christians dumped them overboard as they set a course for Italy. The rubber dinghy with 105 passengers on board set off from Africa. During the course of the trip, a fight broke out when victims "professed the Christian faith while the aggressors were Muslim".[636] The Muslims threw 12 Christians overboard letting them drown. The death toll would have been higher except survivors formed human chains.

Mission of Islamic State

ISIS (Islamic State of Iraq and Syria) or ISIL (Islamic State of Iraq and the Levant) or IS (Islamic State), SIC (State of the Islamic Caliphate) or Da'ish (a name widely used by Arabs, but disdained by the group) or The State, al-Dawla, for short, the name they prefer, whichever term used, they are the group responsible for increasingly horrific acts. These people's complete lack of regard and reverence for life is indoctrinating kids to their life of terrorism and torture as young as five. "Author and former radical Islamist Maajid Nawaz told Fox & Friends Monday [Feb. 2, 2015] 'Islamic State from the beginning has been saying that they're planning not just to build a state but a new generation of jihadists who have been raised on their diet of blood and violence.' "[637]

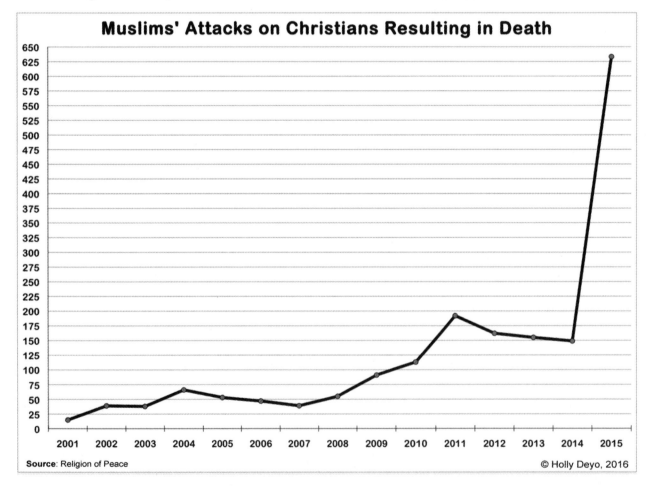

Muslims' Attacks on Christians Resulting in Death

Source: Religion of Peace

© Holly Deyo, 2016

ISIS' clearly stated objective is to target Christians. "When the Islamic State began enslaving people, even some of its supporters balked. Nonetheless, the caliphate has continued to embrace slavery and crucifixion without apology. 'We will conquer your Rome, break your crosses, and enslave your women,' Adnani, the spokesman, promised in one of his periodic valentines to the West."

"The Quran contains at least 109 verses that call Muslims to war with nonbelievers for the sake of Islamic rule. Some are quite graphic, with commands to chop off heads and fingers and kill infidels wherever they may be hiding. Muslims who do not join the fight are called 'hypocrites' and warned that Allah will send them to Hell if they do not join the slaughter." – "I will cast terror into the hearts of those who disbelieve. Therefore strike off their heads and strike off every fingertip of them". (Quran 8:12) No reasonable person would interpret this to mean a spiritual struggle."[638]

As of March 2015, ISIS now had a presence and military allies in Algeria, Libya, Lebanon, Syria, Iran, Afghanistan, Pakistan, Egypt, Indonesia, Gaza, Philippines and Jordan, with plans to establish its own caliphate.

Alarmingly, in March 2015, the world's worst terrorist organization, pledged allegiance to IS – Islamic State. While IS is terrible, the Nigerian terror group Boko Haram, killed 17,000 men, women and children in 2014 – the deadliest year since 2007. This doesn't include combatant deaths, meaning that the combined number could be as high as 47,000 people.[639] That these two groups have unified, should send a trickle of worry up the spine.

Terrorism Spreading

On September 21, 2013, Islamist al-Shabaab militants brought mayhem and death to an upscale shopping center in Nairobi, Kenya. For 80 hours, attackers continued their slaughter killing at least 63 and injuring over 175. It took just four people to manage this chaos before being fatally shot.

Their plan worked so well that on February 21, 2015, the same al-Qaeda linked terror group, al-Shabaab, called for attacks on Western malls. Specifically named were the Mall of America in Minnesota, the West Edmonton Mall in Alberta, Canada, and London's Oxford Street. Like Nairobi's Westgate Mall, these possible targets feature fine dining and exclusive shopping. West Edmonton is the largest mall in North America and the Mall of America attract the most visitors of any shopping area in the world – at least 40 million every year. Similarly, Oxford Street is the busiest shopping street in all of Europe.

These three malls are very desirable targets for such misguided people. Past and current activities guarantee acts by 'lone wolves', if nothing grander.

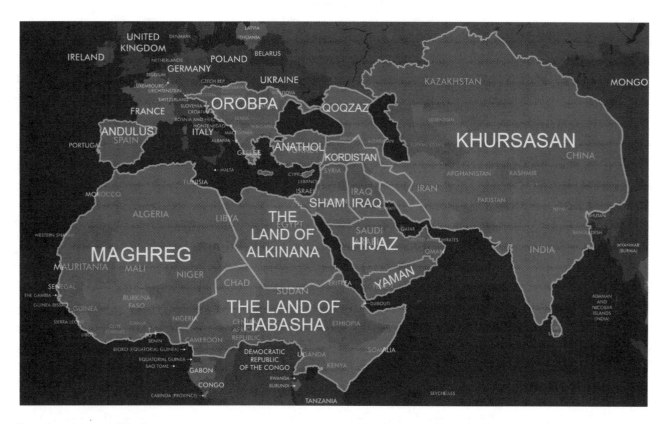

The New Caliphate

Islamic State made it clear they plan to establish a caliphate stretching from Spain to China, including Greece, Romania, Austria and Bulgaria. Kurdistan, Iraq, Syria and Lebanon are to be the pillars. They made this chilling announcement July 2014 and plan for global domination within five years. Considering the size and scope, this is an ambitious endeavor. The goal is to remove secular governments and replace them with a pan-Islamic caliphate. Maybe with the help of Fethullah Gulen.

Fethullah Gulen's Wish for a New Caliphate

Imam Fethullah Gulen spearheads and funds his endeavors through an amassed fortune that's valued close to $50 billion.[640] Born in Erzurum, Turkey, Gulen secured a green card in 2001 pleading health issues and moved to a sprawling 28-acre property in the Poconos of Saylorsburg, PA. From there he leads the Gulen Movement – a transnational religious and social operation that spans 160 countries. Under its wing are some 2,000 educational institutions – charter schools, university departments, language centers and religious courses.[641] The movement also has a bank, media companies, hospitals, an insurance company and a university.[642] That is a *very* far-reaching arm with influence in diverse realms.

Muslim Equivalent of Scientology

Millions of Muslims worldwide idolize Gulen; view him as their guru. While there is little doubt the Movement's schools are above average scholastically with a waiting list of two for every student, they also pack a healthy punch of indoctrination. Students are educated throughout the world in so-called "houses of light," a combination student residence and Koran school. They are strictly controlled within "cemaats", Turkish for religious communities. TV, music and books are closely monitored. Anything that goes against Gulen's teachings is prohibited in some houses of light. Often students are housed free of charge, but in return they are expected to devote their lives to "hizmet" – service to Islam.

In his book *Fasildan Fasila*, translated as *From Time to Time*, Gulen writes "a pupil must be 'on the go day and night' and cannot be seen sleeping. [Sleep deprivation is a well-established indoctrination technique.] 'If possible, he sleeps three hours a day, has two hours for other needs, and must devote the rest entirely to hizmet. In essence, he has no personal life, except in a few specific situations.'

"Residents of the houses of light are also expected to proselytize, and Gulen even offers advice in his writings on how to go about it. The students should befriend infidels, even if it means having to hide their true motives. 'With the patience of a spider, we lay our web to wait for people to get caught in the web.'"[643]

The Gulen Movement has two sides – one that faces the world and another that hides from it. Members are encouraged, but not required to marry within the Movement. Rich businessmen donate millions to Gulen projects, and civil servants and skilled manual workers also contribute. "Fethullahics" donate an average of 10% of their income to the community and some give up to 70%.

Some who broke with the group liken it to Scientology. They describe Fethullah Gulen as "an ideologue who tolerates no dissent, and who is only interested in power and influence, not understanding and tolerance. They say that he dreams of a new age in which Islam will dominate the West."[644] Those courageous enough to speak out only do so anonymously as the Imam's retribution is fierce. Their peers, business partners and the religious community ostracize critics and those who break with the Movement. In short everyone and everything they've known for years shun them. Renegades who dare speak against Gulen fear for their jobs, family and health.

GULEN EXPOSED

Though presenting a seemingly innocuous outreach, Imam Fethullah Gulen's true intentions were revealed. Gulen "studied at a mosque in Erzurum, a city in eastern Turkey, together with Cemaleddin Kaplan, who later moved to Germany where he was known as the 'Caliph of Cologne' because of his radical preaching. At the same time, Gulen encountered the teachings of Said Nursi, a Kurdish Sufi preacher, and joined his community.

"In one of his sermons, he called upon his students to establish a new Muslim age advising supporters to undermine the Turkish state and act conspiratorially until the time was ripe to assume power."[645]

His 1999 Turkish sermon provides valuable insights into his tactics. "You must move in the arteries of the system without anyone noticing your existence until you reach all the power centers ... until the conditions are ripe, they [the followers] must continue like this. If they do something prematurely, the world will crush our heads, and Muslims will suffer everywhere, like in the tragedies in Algeria, like in 1982 [in] Syria ... like in the yearly disasters and tragedies in Egypt. The time is not yet right. You must wait for the time when you are complete and conditions are ripe, until we can shoulder the entire world and carry it ... You must wait until such time as you have gotten all the state power, until you have brought to your side all the power of the constitutional institutions in Turkey ... Until that time, any step taken would be too early – like breaking an egg without waiting the full forty days for it to hatch. It would be like killing the chick inside. The work to be done is [in] confronting the world. Now, I have expressed my feelings and thoughts to you all – in confidence ... trusting your loyalty and secrecy. I know that when you leave here – [just] as you discard your empty juice boxes, you must discard the thoughts and the feelings that I expressed here."[646]

Gulen pleads that his words were taken out of context, but how can one mangle/misinterpret an entire lengthy paragraph? So does Gulen have America's best interests at heart while living in our Country, let alone the world's? Instead, it reinforces evidence that this Imam has a vicious, sneaky hand-in-a-velvet-glove take-over plan.

GULEN, TURKEY, SAUDI ARABIA AND THE U.S.

Today while Turkey's government has moved away from the West, particularly the U.S. and Israel, Gulen has been busy infiltrating many aspects of America. His massive network tentacles into U.S. politics via huge political donations, aggressive lobbying and free trips to Turkey for Congress and staff. Gulen has inserted many of his five million followers into major U.S. engineering firms, NASA, the White House, universities and Hollywood. Through State Department contacts, he acquires H1-B visas to staff his schools with Turkish followers. The primary requirement for an H1-B is employment, which the Gulen Movement readily supplies. Hand in glove.

The Saudis, with whom America is much aligned, are motivated by resurgence of the Sunni Caliphate. They have played a significant role in Turkey's rise in the Muslim world. It appears America is blind to these activities especially since Turkey is pursuing a more radical version of Islam much like the Saudi Wahhabi extremists. Further though Saudi Arabia still denies involvement in the attacks on 9/11, 15 of the 19 aircraft hijackers were Saudi citizens.

While still mayor, Recep Tayyip Erdogan now Turkey's President, was thrown in jail for 10 months by "provoking enmity and hatred" at a 1997 rally with these words: "The mosques are our barracks, the domes are our helmets, the minarets are our bayonets, and the faithful are our soldiers."[647] His imprisonment woke up Muslims to being more patient, stealthier in their goals, tying to what Gulen advised in his 1999 Turkish sermon.

Erdogan was also quoted saying. "Democracy is like a streetcar. You ride it until you arrive at your destination, and then you step off. We believe that democracy can never be the objective; it's only a tool."[648] It seems a well-defined case of both Turkey and Saudi Arabia massaging America's back while simultaneously plunging in a stiletto.

Islam and Christianity – Religions of Obvious Difference

Westerners will never completely wrap their minds around a religion that so readily embraces death, much more than it loves the gift of life. Another major difference is the ethics of lying – something clearly condoned in Islam. In Christianity, #9 of the Ten Commandments is unambiguous about not lying. Islam has no such compunctions and permits at least six different types of lies.

1. *Taqiyya*: deceit for the purpose of spreading Islam. "*Taqiyya* is inspired by the example and sayings of the Prophet Mohammed praised in the Hadiths (the sayings of the Prophet) as 'the greatest deceiver', and praised in the Koran. Muslims have used *taqiyya* defined as 'precautionary dissimulation,' 'religiously-sanctioned deception,' 'lying' or 'deception' and 'keeping one's convictions secret' and 'holy deception'."[649]

Taqiyya: Their doctrine that permits deceit in order to spread islam

Instances in the Quran are pointedly shown by Muhammad's own actions.

Though not called *Taqiyya* by name, Muhammad clearly deceived when he signed a 10-year treaty with the Meccans that allowed him access to their city while he secretly prepared its takeover. The unsuspecting residents were easy conquered when Muhammad broke the treaty two years later and people in the city who trusted him were executed.

Another example is when Muhammad tricked his enemies into letting down their guard by pretending to seek peace. This happened to Ka'b bin al-Ashraf and a Jewish leader in Medina and again later with Usayr ibn Zarim. At the time, Usayr ibn Zarim was attempting to gather armed forces against the Muslims from among a tribe allied with the Quraish – a group on whom Muhammad had already declared war. Muhammad's messengers went to ibn Zarim and persuaded him to meet with the prophet of Islam in Medina to discuss peace. As soon as they were vulnerable, the Muslims massacred ibn Zarim and his 30 companions (Ibn Ishaq 981).

Muslims had such a bad reputation for lying and killing former nonbelievers even after they accepted Islam, they still didn't feel safe. Such was the case of Jadhima. When Muslim "missionaries" approached their tribe, one of the members insisted that they would be murdered despite converting to Islam to avoid execution. However, the others believed they could trust the Muslim leader's promise of safety if they didn't resist. After convincing the skeptic to lay down his arms, the unarmed tribesmen were quickly tied up and beheaded. (Ibn Ishaq 834 & 837).[650]

2. **Kitman**: deceit by omission – telling someone a partial truth or a gross distortion of it.[651] The most common example is when a Muslim says that jihad really refers to 'an internal, spiritual struggle', he is not telling the whole truth. The Quran uses jihad and its derivatives 59 times. Of those, only 16 could be considered 'internal' with no object or person as the target of the struggle based on the context of the surah.[652]

Another common form of *kitman* is to quote only the few peaceful passages from the Quran, knowing full well that that passage was later replaced by a more militant, contradictory verse.[653]

3. **Tawriya**: deceit by ambiguity – a doctrine that allows lying in virtually all circumstances – including to fellow Muslims and by swearing to Allah – provided the liar is creative enough to articulate his deceit in a way that is true to him.[654]

4. **Taysir**: deceit through facilitation, not having to observe all the tenets of Sharia. For instance, Muslims traveling during the month of Ramadan or engaged in jihad don't need to observe the required fast.[655]

5. **Darura**: deceit through necessity allowing to engage in something *Haram* or forbidden. *Darura* says that if you are forced to do something un-Islamic, you will not be called to account for your actions in this world or in the hereafter.[656]

6. **Muruna**: temporary suspension of Sharia in order that Muslim immigrants appear moderate. Few Westerners know that the Sunni Muslim Brotherhood revived the doctrine of *muruna*, which literally means "stealth" or "flexibility." It is far worse than *taqiyya*, since it sanctions all prohibitions that block Muslim interests, even blasphemous ones. It allows Muslims to sow division and confusion in the Western world and was designed to catapult and advance Sharia by using Western means.[657] *Muruna* allows Muslims to break their own codes to avoid detection like shave off their beards, wear western clothing, or even drink alcohol to blend in. "Nothing is more valuable these days to the Islamists than a blue-eyed Caucasian Muslim willing to engage in terrorism. Another common way of using *muruna* is for a Muslim to marry a non-Muslim or to behave like a non-Muslim so their true agenda will not be suspected."[658]

One other type of *muruna* allows what amounts to legalized prostitution. "A Sunni Muslim male may enter into a contract with a woman … for sexual gratification without the financial obligation necessary to maintain a wife. As a consequence, the sin of adultery never takes place because the sex contract is an official marriage license."[659]

HOW THIS DIFFERS FROM CHRISTIANITY

Christians are governed by "your word is your bond", not telling falsehoods. Matthew 5:37 says "Let your Yes be simply Yes, and your No be simply No; anything more than that comes from the evil one." Scripture doesn't condone recruiting, conducting business or doing God's work by deceit and lies. That is Islam's plan of action. It should be a *big* heads up about Islam.

Last Thoughts on Christian Persecution

While beheadings were considered humane, by the late 1700s, only two countries practiced this method of execution: Germany and Saudi Arabia. Beheading ended across the Reich when Nazi Germany fell in 1945. Throughout the world only Saudi Arabia still decapitates criminals, but humanely. Effectively, beheading became extinct some 70 years ago.

Until now. It's seeing a resurrection mainly employed against Christians and Jews and used as a bargaining chip by Muslim extremists. Since 2001, Muslim fanatics have murdered well over 1,200 people by their brutal method of sawing off heads.

As prophesied in Revelation 20:4, the world will see martyrs that give their heads, their lives, for Christ Jesus. 2002 marked the beginning of this resurgence with Danny Pearl.

Chapter 14: Apostasy – Defection from Christianity

For the time will come when people will not put up with sound doctrine. Instead, to suit their own desires, they will gather around them a great number of teachers to say what their itching ears want to hear. —2 Timothy 4:3-4 (NIV)

But relative to the coming of our Lord Jesus Christ (the Messiah) and our gathering together to [meet] Him, ... Let no one deceive or beguile you in any way, for that day will not come except the apostasy comes first [unless the predicted great falling away of those who have professed to be Christians has come], and the man of lawlessness (sin) is revealed, who is the son of doom (of perdition) —2 Thessalonians 2:1,3 (AMP)

Faith Shrinkage

Americans' faith in God is measurably declining and those who don't identify with any religion are also growing rapidly. According to the Pew Research Center, adults 18 and older who describe themselves as Christian dropped by nearly 8% in just seven years, from 78.4% in 2007 to 70.6% in 2014.[660] In just two years post-Christians jumped from 36% in 2013 to 44% in 2015.[661]

By 2015 nearly 23% of Americans are religiously unaffiliated – the "nones" – up from 16% in 2007.[662] They are at the highest level in Pew's history. Lack of religious affiliation doesn't automatically mean they're atheists. In 2007, just 5% felt "There

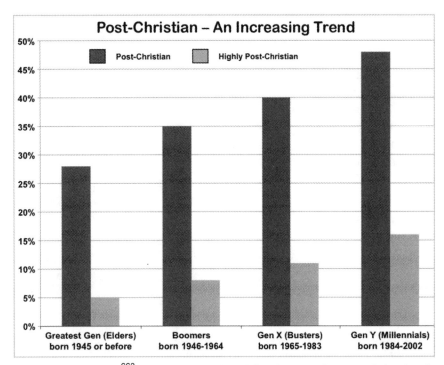

is no God," but that number nearly doubled in 2015 to 9%.[663] Christians in the U.S. who say they are "absolutely certain" God exists dropped sharply in 2015 to 63% from 71% in 2007.[664]

Barna, a market research firm specializing in studying religious beliefs, outlined 15 variables that define Post-Christian. They must meet 9 or more of these factors and Highly Post-Christians have 12 or more characteristics:

1. Don't believe in God
2. Identify as atheist or agnostic
3. Disagree that faith is important in their lives
4. Haven't prayed to God in the last year
5. Have never made a commitment to Jesus
6. Disagree the Bible is accurate
7. Haven't donated money to a church (in the last year)
8. Haven't attended a Christian church (in the last year)
9. Believe Jesus committed sins
10. Don't feel a responsibility to "share their faith"
11. Haven't read the Bible (in the last week)
12. Haven't volunteered at church (in the last week)
13. Haven't attended Sunday school (in the last week)
14. Haven't attended religious small group (in the last week)
15. Don't participate in a house church (in the last year)

In 1972 those who claimed "no religion" were a scant 5%.[665] Twenty years later, it had crept up to 8%. Then it shot up and shows no sign of stopping. The number of Americans backing away from Christianity since 1970 is striking.

From 2007 to 2014, unaffiliated American adults increased to nearly 7%.[666] This includes over 13 million atheists and agnostics, as well as nearly 33 million who say they have no particular religious affiliation.

Of the unaffiliated:

- 88% aren't "looking for a religion"
- 30% had a religious or mystical experience
- 30% believe in spiritual energy in physical things like mountains, trees and crystals
- 28% believe yoga is a spiritual practice
- 25% believe in astrology and reincarnation
- 58% say they feel a deep connection with nature and Mother Earth
- 31% have been in touch with someone who is dead
- 15% have consulted a psychic or fortuneteller
- 19% have seen or been in the presence of a ghost
- 12% describe their religion as atheist, 17% agnostic, and 71% "nothing in particular"

Only a little over half of Americans see religion as very important any more, but both groups – those who are religious and the "nones" – see religion is losing its influence. It's not just the U.S. backing away from religion and Christianity in particular. Other Western countries are expected to see the same.

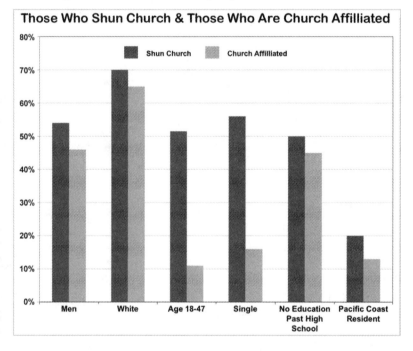

Those Who Shun Church & Those Who Are Church Affilliated

Why People Don't Go to Church

Part of the backing away from churches has to do with people's disillusionment. Many pastors aren't meeting the needs of congregants and instead, are taking advantage of them. Some people see churches as outdated and somewhat irrelevant. Other words used to describe church are boring, exclusive, homophobic, hypocritical and judgmental.

Folks who are done being played by politicians, scammers and religious leaders are consequently opting out of everything. Sex scandals in the U.S., England, Africa, India and Asia played their part in turning people from organized religion.

Churches that focus too much on money and power put people off. Pastors who preach "prosperity gospel" and build themselves mega-mansions with air-conditioned doghouses, hit up congregations for luxury private jets and over-the-top perks further degrade trust.

Then there's the Vatican's vast wealth in artwork, jewels, gold and treasures, and big investments in banking, insurance, chemicals, steel, construction and real estate. People see their tithes and donations going to enrich clergy and houses of God in extreme luxury instead of spreading the Gospel and helping the poor. No wonder Christians are disillusioned, but this is a tiny bit of the pull-away pie.

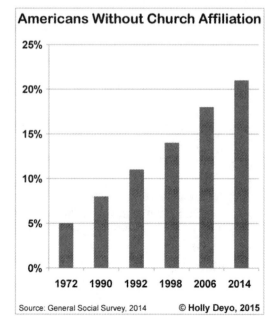

Americans Without Church Affiliation

Source: General Social Survey, 2014   © Holly Deyo, 2015

Countries That Will No Longer Have a Christian Majority in 2050

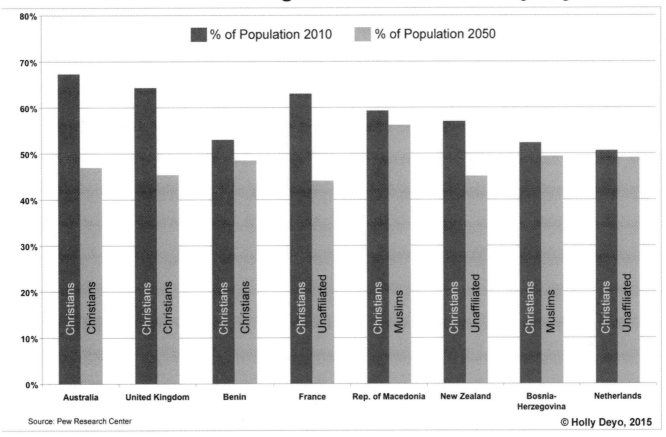

■ % of Population 2010   ■ % of Population 2050

Source: Pew Research Center

© Holly Deyo, 2015

Let's start with the Vatican. Cardinal George Pell, secretary for the Vatican's economy, wrote recently in the *Catholic Herald:*

> Apart from the pension fund, which needs to be strengthened for the demands on it in 15 or 20 years, the Holy See is paying its way, while possessing substantial assets and investments.

> In fact, we have discovered that the situation is much healthier than it seemed, because some hundreds of millions of euros were tucked away in particular sectional accounts and did not appear on the balance sheet.

> So exactly how much is the Vatican worth? It's hard to say. The Catholic Church has a history of opacity about its finances, something Pell says is slowly changing.

> And much of its assets are near impossible to value because they will never be sold off, such as its gold-laden palatial church property and priceless works of art by the likes of Michelangelo and Raphael.

> It also owns a global network of churches and religious buildings, many of which contain precious historical treasures, serving the world's 1.2 billion Catholics.

> What we do know is that Vatican Bank, officially titled the Institute for the Works of Religion, manages €5.9bn ($9.8bn, £6.5bn) of assets on behalf of its 17,400 customers. And it manages €700m of equity which it owns. Another tidbit to emerge is that it keeps gold reserves worth over $20m with the US Federal Reserve.

> The bank has been caught up in a number of scandals, including the funding of priests caught up in sex abuse allegations and of money laundering for the Mafia and former Nazis.[667]

> According to best guesses of bankers, Vatican wealth is between $10 and $15 billion.[668]

Disenchantment With Religion

As a strong sign of End Times, nothing says it more clearly, or shows it more sharply than a global defection from religion and God. Various factors have shaken and stirred disbelief from Communism to humanism to intellectualism to disillusionment to perceived irrelevancy, to breakdown of the family and to a certain extent loosening moral codes and wavering moral compasses. The following four maps show the decline in religion, in belief in God over 150 years.

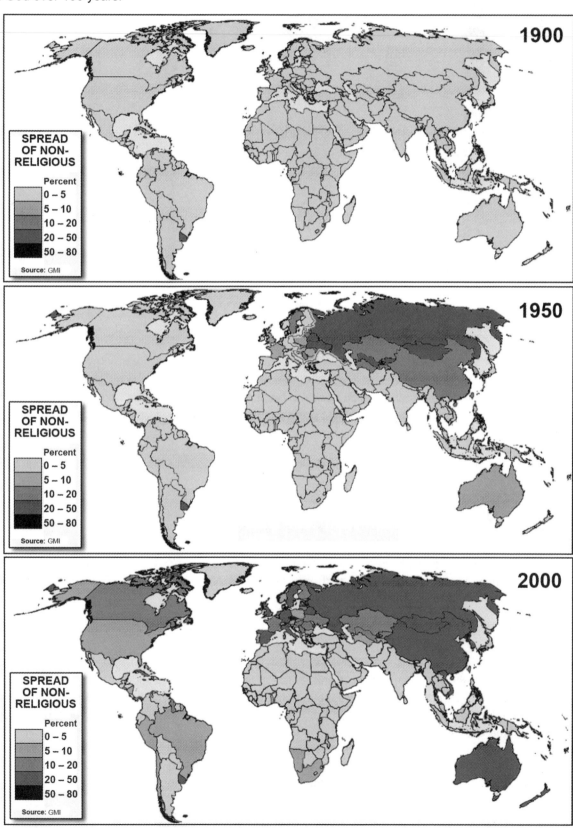

Other reasons given were boring sermons, church members were rude or unfriendly, lack of family involvement, lack of familiarity of the Bible, indifference, have better things to do, it's their only day to sleep, have to work, pressure to become a member, seen as always asking for money and lack of social acceptance like interracial marriages or homosexuality. More often bumper stickers read "Good Without God." Some people say they are sick of the hypocrisy.

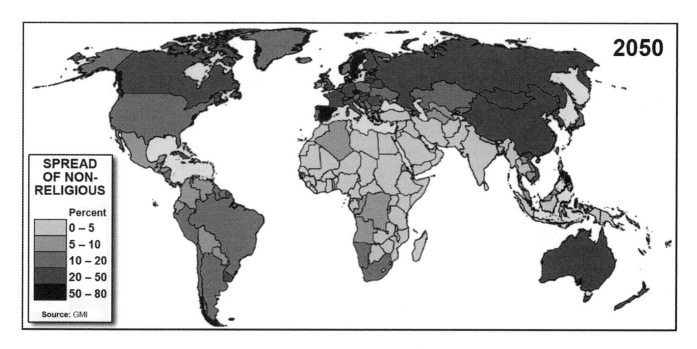

On Catholics, Protestants and Evangelical Christians...

This is not to denigrate Catholics or Protestants or Evangelicals. It IS to point out that in this End of Days there is error on all sides. The devil is at work and he is busy, as he's only got a flyspeck of time left.

It is to encourage every single person to read scripture, to receive its truth, to not be taken in by cults, to not be swayed by slick words. Rely on Christ's words alone. If you feel a twinge in your spirit that something's not right, it's probably not. Churches these days are tainted and often well, a mess. It's best to read scripture, talk with other like-minded Christians. Go back to the days of Jesus when churches met in private homes and there was no such thing as a preacher, no collection plates. Everyone taught everyone to his degree of discernment. As scripture says, let no man call another "teacher". Matthew 23:8-12.

Scandalous Scandals

Though other scandals erupted in years past, they really ramped up in 2006. The following isn't an all-inclusive list as it would require a ream of paper, but it's some of the banner-making bad examples.

Who could forget, Jimmy Swaggart's tearful confession on nationwide TV *"I have sinned against you, my Lord"*. While he wept, tears dotting his glasses and one couldn't help but feel a little bit of the "carny" atmosphere, so much so that one would find it hard to believe his confession was not a little to theatrical. Swaggart's downfall began when he attacked fellow televangelists Marvin Gorman and Jim Bakker. He exposed Gorman's affair with one of his congregants, who in turn, was more than happy to descend on Bakker.

Swaggart's transgressions multiplied when he railed against social ills, promiscuity, homosexuality and pornography but forgot to check his own backyard. The fiery Louisiana preacher was defrocked in 1988 by the national Assemblies of God presbytery. Three years later he was implicated in another prostitute sex scandal. This time, instead of pleading for forgiveness, he told those at Family Worship Center, "The Lord told me it's flat none of your business."[669] Swaggart returned to the airwaves in 2010 on SonLife Broadcasting Network at age 75.

Some preachers have even done jail time for their crimes, but it hasn't lessened the taste of rot in congregants' mouths. It doesn't end with the Vatican. A lot of clergy have recently been caught in embezzlement and sex scandals.

Give Me the High Life

Church members discovered over $66,000 disappeared during Pastor John Albert Jackson Sr.'s 19-year-stint at Goodwill Baptist Church in North Carolina. He and his 38-year-old son were charged on three counts of embezzlement and three counts of malfeasance. Jackson Sr. was sentenced to nine months in the North Carolina Department of Corrections.[670] [671]

Texas pastor Russell Thomas Jr., deposited more than $284,000 in a secret bank account over the span of two years. In March 2014, he was indicted on theft charges.[672]

Georgia pastor Ephren Taylor II masterminded what officials dubbed the "Christian Ponzi Scheme" where he scammed $16 million from churchgoers. Taylor visited numerous churches in America on his "Building Wealth Tour" falsely promising that 20% of the profits would go to charity. It didn't, and the scheme collapsed in 2010. In 2015, the judge sentenced him to 19 years and seven months in the Federal pen plus restitution of $15,590,752.81.[673]

Illinois televangelist Howard Richmond convinced 24 big time investors to part with enough money to finance plans for a megachurch and promised big returns. One guy even forked over a million bucks. Richmond sold his scheme by showing investors fake documents alleging his church had millions in assets. Instead of putting investors' dollars toward the ministry he spent it on a BMW, luxury hotels, a trip to Hawaii, clothes and jewelry. December 2013, he was sentenced to 12 years' jail time.[674]

Quentin L. Respress pleaded guilty November 2013 to one count of theft and one count of forgery in a plea agreement. While pastor of Ohio's Macedonia Baptist Church, he stole over $54,000 from the congregation. Edna Payne told Respress, "You robbed us blind. You have demonstrated uncontrollable greed." Respress was ordered to repay the amount stolen and is on 5 years probation. Violation of probation results in an automatic two-year jail sentence.[675]

Texas Baptist minister Charles Gilford and his wife, Adriane Gilford "misappropriated" $430,000 from churchgoers and gambled it away in Louisiana casinos. The duo were indicted in June 2012 and charged with aggregate theft and "misapplication of fiduciary property." Two years prior, Adriane was arrested on felony charges for writing bad checks.[676] Charles was sentenced to 5 years in prison and his wife got two.

Joe Seephis Hardie, former pastor of New Mt. Zion Missionary Baptist Church, was found guilty of scheme to defraud, grand theft of over $100,000, money laundering of more than $20,000, and two counts of money laundering over $300. The State Attorney's Office determined he took money from the church for personal use throughout 2007 and 2008 as well as some months in 2009. The sentence includes 90 days in jail, 90 days in a jail weekend work release program, two years of house arrest followed by 18 years of probation and repaying the debt at a rate of $500/month.[677]

Chicago South Side Methodist minister, Bernard Johnson, was sentenced in 2014 to 15 years in prison and restitution of $10,000. His crime? He scammed congregants out of $50,000 in 2008 and 2010, and spent it on dining, travel, clothing and entertainment. He was previously convicted in 2009 for stealing over $43,000 from an Alabama school.[678]

Bruce Anthony Stark, now former pastor of a Lakeport, California church stole over $100,000. Stark, between 2002 and 2007, treated Hilltop Apostolic Church as his personal ATM. In February 2014, he was sentenced to three years in jail. Deputy District Attorney Sharon Lerman-Hubert said. "It's hard to imagine a more egregious crime, stealing from one's own church."[679]

Stealing Trust

Gilbert Deya, while in Kenya, was accused of child trafficking and capitalizing on Mary's immaculate conception, stating that he had the power to give barren female followers "miracle babies." Accusations were made that Deya stole five infants between ages 22 months and 4½ years. The pastor as of 2014 was still hiding out in England.[680]

Another religious leader, Tony Alamo, 79, was sentenced in 2009 to 175 years jail time on 10 counts of sexual immorality with underage girls ages 12 to 14. When his home was raided in Arkansas, six young girls were seized and it was suspected he'd forced them into child porn. Among other charges were child abuse, tax evasion and threatening to kidnap a federal judge.[681] After evading arrest for years, Alamo served four years in prison during the 1990s for not paying $10 million in federal taxes. Seven women who were allegedly sexually abused by Alamo were awarded $525 million in February 2014.[682]

In June 2013 Geronimo "Pastor G" Aguilar who founded Richmond Outreach Center (ROC) was forced to resign, along with three other pastors, after an explosive sex scandal was revealed. Pastor Aguilar was awarded $115,000 in salary and housing in his severance package despite adultery and disgrace.[683] All the resignations stemmed from Pastor G's extradition to Texas in late May to face seven felony charges.

A criminal past isn't the only source of Aguilar's troubles. Several women have come out of the woodwork claiming to have had sex with the pastor. Amber Baker started attending the ROC when she was five. Baker claims that when Pastor Aguilar's wife was out of town, he took her, two other young women and her 16-year-old sister to a timeshare.

"'He brought us alcohol, we got drunk and the rest is history. I had just turned 18. We had sex. It was wrong. Just because it is not illegal doesn't mean it is not wrong and he was my pastor. I moved to Richmond to serve God.' She claims Pastor G also had sex with other members of her family. 'My mother, my aunt and myself have all been involved with him sexually.'"[684]

In June 2105, Aguilar was convicted on all seven counts of the indictment. Two counts of aggravated sexual assault of a child that carry a maximum sentence of life in prison. Three counts of sexual assault of a child under 17. Two molested sisters were just 11 and 13 and the elder said she had been raped. Last, two counts of indecency with a child, each second-degree felonies that carry maximum sentences of 20 years.[685] Aguilar was sentenced to 40 years in prison and the counts will be served concurrently.[686] Aguilar must serve 20 years in a Texas before he's eligible for parole.

Bigger Isn't Better?

All of these examples of immorality took place in mega-churches. One has to wonder if building a congregation from something small into an enormous entity isn't too much of an ego stroke. Did they get confused on just who was to be worshipped? In the beginning "church" was held in homes with small numbers of people. Often no single person was an all-the-time leader. People took turns presenting the lesson for that week. The alternative was to decide on a passage to read and think about for the next Sunday and then everyone gave input and shared insight. Home churches eliminated the need for "passing the plate," which automatically removed the possibility of embezzlement. It also removed focusing on raising funds to erect buildings and Christians got back to basics. With everyone taking a turn at leading the fellowship, no one got a "God complex" or thought seducing or having affairs with church members was clever. Sometimes bigger isn't better.

Sex and Servants of God

Sexual immorality in the Catholic Church continues to make headlines. With unaccustomed speed, the Vatican expelled New Jersey man, Michael Fugee, from the priesthood in 2014 after defying a lifetime ban on ministry to children. Charges stem back to 2001 when he admitted to police he had fondled a teenage boy's genitals. After becoming sexually aroused he realized it was a "violation". However, Fugee's suspect behavior goes back to 1994.[687]

St. Louis priest, William F. Vatterott was sentenced to three years in federal prison on a child pornography charge in April 2013. The boy's mother read a statement in court alleging Vatterott's actions that went beyond child porn. The archdiocese said Vatterott had been on administrative leave from St. Cecilia since June 2011, due to "allegations involving inappropriate electronic communications received by a minor and an incident of underage drinking."[688] The priest apologized for his behavior and blamed his actions on alcoholism.

All of these things are enough to put anyone off, but then there are the never-ending accounts of priests' pedophilia, homosexuality and rape. Instead of the Catholic Church dealing with this immense shame straight on, they've ignored it, swept it under the carpet, denied these burgeoning accusations and shunted off offending priests to new parishes. Now they're messing with new victims. Pope Francis revealed in July 2015 that 1 in 50 priests is a pedophile and a "leprosy" that's infecting the Catholic Church.[689]

Cases originate all over the Americas and have spread across the pond to Ireland, Britain, Belgium, France, Germany, Poland, New Zealand and Australia. "From 2001 to 2010 the Holy See, the central governing body of the Catholic Church, 'considered sex abuse allegations concerning about 3,000 priests dating back up to 50 years', according to the Vatican's Promoter of Justice. … In Ireland, a report was made which covered six decades (from the 1950s) and noted 'endemic' sexual abuse in Catholic boys' institutions, with church leaders aware of what was going on and government inspectors failing to 'stop beatings, rapes and humiliation.' The commission's report on church abuse ran to five volumes. Police in the Irish Republic are examining if criminal charges can be brought over a damning report on child sex abuse at Catholic institutions."[690] The true number of rapes and underage sex will never be known as the Vatican relegated many cases be dealt with locally, if at all.

PAT MCEWAN

Pat McEwan from Scotland, now 62 and a recovering alcoholic, described his rape when he was just 8-years-old and fell prey to a *ring* pedophile of priests. His main abuser, his parish priest, encouraged Pat to visit him, appeared to slip into a trance. Pat shook him. 'I've just been talking to Jesus and he says would you like to go to heaven?' said the priest. Then he asked, 'Do you love your mummy?' Yes Father. 'Do you love your daddy?' Yes Father. 'Do you love me? Because this is our little secret and you mustn't tell your mummy or daddy or you will go to the burny fire.'

Pat continued. "I ran home shaking like a dog. I had wee short trousers on and the shite was running down my leg. My mum and my auntie had to wipe me down."

This was the 1950s and the priest arranged for Pat's devout mother to visit Carfin Grotto, leaving the boy with a priest friend of his. Pat watched through the window while his mother disappeared into the grotto. "As soon as she did, the priest turned to him. 'I want you to do for me what you have done for your parish priest,' he said. Then he raped him. Afterwards, he tried to quieten the child's tears before his mother returned. 'God doesn't like boys who cry. Be a soldier of Christ.'

ANN MATTHEWS

The abuse isn't relegated to boys. Sometimes priests look to the opposite sex. Like Pat, Ann Matthews also lived in Bishop Devine's diocese. During the 80s, her priest regularly abused her from age 11 to 17. Ann never told her parents, as he was a regular guest in their home – saying prayers. Unbelievably, when visiting Ann's dying grandma, he tried to have sex with her on the sofa. These experiences left Ann broken. She suffers from eating and sleep disorders, anxiety, depression, can't hold a job and is often suicidal. Of her life, she summaries, "Sometimes, it feels like I died a long time ago, that there's this body that walks around the earth and doesn't know it should lie down."[691]

CARDINAL KEITH O'BRIEN

Britain's most senior Roman Catholic cleric, Cardinal Keith O'Brien, acknowledged in March 2013 that he was guilty of sexual misconduct, a week after he announced his resignation. This followed formal complaints from three current and one former priest accusing him of inappropriate sexual contact dating back at least to 1980. O'Brien, 74, was the highest-ranking person in the Church's recent history to confess to such actions. O'Brien's generalized apology was especially shocking as he widely condemned homosexuality as immoral and a "grotesque subversion,"[692] but had privately been making advances to his own priests for years.

One of four unnamed priests, after submitting his complaint, said the church had targeted him, not the offending Cardinal. They were warned not to make their complaints public because *they* would cause "immense further damage to the church".[693] The priest stated the church failed to act quickly and appropriately, and expressed fears the matter would be swept under the carpet. "It tends to cover up and protect the system at all costs. The church is beautiful, but it has a dark side and that has to do with accountability."[694]

SHRINK LINKS SEXUAL ABUSE AND CELIBACY

Richard Sipe, an American psychotherapist and ex-priest who has spent many years researching celibacy and abuse stated. "The clerical power structure not only protects clergy who are sexually active but sets them up to live double lives. Corruption comes from the top down. Superiors, rectors and bishops do have sexually active lives and protect each other – a kind of holy blackmail."[695] … Sipe continued citing studies that suggest that 70% of priests are psychosexually immature and that 6% of them will have sex with minors. Sipe has linked abuse and celibacy. He published a study in 1990 showing that at any time 50% of priest had been sexually active in the past three years. Those same figures hold true in Spain, Holland, Switzerland and South Africa except in Australia where abuse by Catholic priest is six times higher than other churches combined.

DAVID AND PETER

David corroborates this from his own experiences in Australia and New Zealand. When he was just 14, he rebuffed sexual advances of a 65-year-old Jesuit in New Zealand. He later joined the priesthood and was approached sexually in a Cistercian order and in a seminary. In Australia, he met with the same thing. This time it was a senior priest in a priory. Pressed to keep quiet, David left the priesthood.

He met a man, "Peter" with whom he had an affair and who had also left the seminary in Rome. They traveled to Peter's old haunts including a convent he frequented for weekly confession. Peter revealed that his confession was always heard *last*, after the nuns left, by a priest who later became a bishop and operated at the highest levels of the Vatican. David shared about Peter's experiences, "At the top of the convent there was a comfortable room set aside for confession. But what started as confession turned into a weekly lover's tryst. Peter, who was somewhat bitter about having quit Rome, was eager during that holiday to tell me the exact nature of their lovemaking. It involved anal intercourse."[696]

WHEN DOES IT STOP?

Charisma Magazine reports, "Of course, everyone is unfortunately familiar with the Catholic pedophilia scandals that the Church is still trying to wade through even as new scandals arise."[697] And arise they have.

In September 2015, every Catholic was over the moon about Pope Francis coming to America. He travelled through 15 countries, spent six days in America before meeting with sexual abuse survivors. Francis was met with chants of "Ho, ho, hey, hey, welcome to the U.S.A." and "We love Francis, yes we do. We love Francis, how about you?"[698]

He was met with much adoration before getting down to some of the ugly business – meeting sexual abuse survivors he called "true heralds of mercy." For them Francis humbled himself saying, "God weeps for the sexual abuse of children. I am overwhelmed by the shame that people who were in charge of caring for those young ones raped them and caused them great damages. Humbly, we owe each of them our gratitude for their value as they have had to suffer terrible abuse."[699] In 2015 the Pope had to accept resignations of three American bishops while a Pennsylvania priest was found guilty in September this same year of sexually abusing three boys at a Honduran orphanage.

The numbers continue to climb in this ultimate abuse of trust, but as of September 2015, these are the shocking numbers:

- 3,400 sexual abuse cases referred to the Vatican 2004 – 2014
- 2,572 priests sentenced to a lifetime of penance
- 848 more defrocked over the last decade
- Pope Benedict XVI defrocked 384 priests in 2 years
- The majority of priests' victims were male
- 64% of all abuse allegations against a priest were made only by males
- 85% of the accusers were 8 to 10-years-old
- $150,747,387 – the amount spent between July 2013 and June 2014 on costs "related to child protection efforts and to allegations of clergy sexual abuse of minors"[700]

Abuse of Nuns By Priests

Most people are familiar with Catholic clergy's too-frequent ventures into pedophilia and homosexuality, but lesser known are the many rapes of nuns committed by their very own priests. Sister Marie McDonald, mother superior of the Missionaries of Our Lady of Africa first chronicled these horrendous abuses in a November 1998 paper entitled "The Problem of the Sexual Abuse of African Religious in Africa and Rome". Her paper was presented to a Catholic group – the Council of 16 – that meets three times each year with delegates from three entities:

1. The Union of Superiors General – an association of men's religious communities based in Rome
2. The International Union of Superiors General, a similar group for women, and
3. The Congregation for Institutes of Consecrated Life and Societies of Apostolic Life, the Vatican office that oversees religious life.

In September 2000, sister Esther Fangman, a psychology counselor and president of the Federation of St. Scholastica in Alabama, brought this problem to the attention of 250 Benedictine abbots in Rome. This Federation is made up of 20 monasteries, 18 in the U.S. and two in Mexico. As a result, a considerable geographic area was covered with this exposé.

On Feb. 18, 1995, physician Sr. Maura O'Donohue briefed Vatican prefect Cardinal Eduardo Martínez and members of his staff on the widespread abuse.

So the rapes were well documented within the Vatican and it was at crisis level particularly in Africa where AIDS was prevalent. Previously, priests used the services of prostitutes, but fearing they might get infected, looked elsewhere.

Abstinence and nuns are usually synonymous, and with the rise of AIDS in the 70s African priests realized their female counterparts would be clever sex partners, willing or not. Sex in Africa is extremely common, even among priests. Sister McDonald documents this extensively stating that discussing sex and AIDS is taboo. However, *having* sex is not. It occurs often and under a variety of conditions including premarital, recreational, obligatory, rape, sex as a "gift", sugar-daddy sex, extramarital and second family sex, and multiple partners.[701] It's quite acceptable even for African Catholic priests and as one explained, many consider their vow of celibacy to mean they won't marry, but intercourse is a given and sometimes, so are the resulting children.

With this much sexual activity and ignorance, AIDS exploded and so did the abuse of nuns.

There and in other undeveloped countries, women are still largely behind in gender equality and just accept what men demand of them. Most accosted nuns were unwilling and had had years of submissiveness drilled into them. Some nuns acquiesced because who, in a healthy life, doesn't desire physical intimacy. Other nuns who took their vows seriously and clearly guarded their 'women parts', didn't count on being targeted by priests.

O'Donohue wrote, "'a superior of a community of sisters in one country was approached by priests requesting that sisters would be made available to them for sexual favors. When the superior refused, the priests explained that they would otherwise be obliged to go to the village to find women, and might thus get AIDS.' O'Donohue continued that at first she reacted with "'shock and disbelief' at the 'magnitude' of the problem she was encountering through her contacts with 'a great number of sisters during the course of my visits' in a number of countries."[702]

When nuns were raped and became pregnant, some aborted. Others produced 'miracle babies' as they claimed ignorance of how it happened. Some that had received zero sex education believed the myth that you couldn't become pregnant while menstruating or during a full moon or right after giving birth or some other wives' tales. Other nuns literally lost their minds at their predicament and some died in childbirth.

Especially in educationally under developed countries like Africa, priests calculated that a woman who previously hadn't had sex – or at least none in years – would be clean – free of AIDS. Hence nuns became prized tools for their sexual gratification.

These rapes didn't start nor end there. O'Donohue's paper lists 23 countries where nun abuse was reported: Botswana, Burundi, Brazil, Colombia, Ghana, India, Ireland, Italy, Kenya, Lesotho, Malawi, Nigeria, Papua New Guinea, Philippines, South Africa, Sierra Leone, Tanzania, Tonga, Uganda, United States, Zambia, Zaire, Zimbabwe.[703]

Megachurches – Mega Scandals

In 2007 Sen. Charles Grassley launched financial investigations into six of the country's largest churches. His complaints covered the pastors' "extravagant lifestyles and questions about whether the churches' tax-exempt status is being abused. That includes the personal use of Rolls Royce cars (and Bentleys), private jets and multimillion-dollar homes. Grassley is also looking into exorbitant salaries, so called 'love offerings' or cash payments to ministers; a justification for layovers in Hawaii and the Fiji Islands; and in one case, the purchase of a $23,000 commode with a marble top."[704] Two televangelists in Missouri and one in Irving, Texas told Grassley they have since made changes in how they govern their ministries or set compensation. Four in Newark, Texas; College Park, Georgia; Tampa, Florida and Lithonia, Georgia refused to cooperate in supplying information.[705]

In the end, "Grassley staffers determined that they did not have 'time or resources' to issue subpoenas to the four ministries that did not completely respond to their inquiries. They instead issued reports based on public records, third parties and insiders. Among their findings:

"Insiders [at the] … Fort Worth, Texas [megachurch] said they were intimidated from speaking with committee staff, with one former employee saying they were told 'God will blight our finances' if they talked.

"[The] Georgia pastor['s] ministry was called the 'least cooperative' with staffers unable to determine the names of board members.

"The majority of questions asked by Grassley staffers of [the] megachurch in Lithonia, Ga., remained unanswered, including the amount of [the pastor's] salary.

"Several former staffers at [the] megachurch in Tampa, Fla., wanted to speak with staffers but 'were afraid of being sued by the church,' and at least one was reminded by a church lawyer of a previously signed confidentiality agreement."[706]

JACK A.

2013 saw a Hammond, Indiana megachurch pastor, Jack A., step down after admitting to a long-term affair. In March, he was sentenced to 12 years in prison on charges stemming from a sexual relationship he had with a 16-year-old member he was counseling. Jack, then a married man with two children, tried to blame the victim. "The girl wrote in her victim impact statement, 'I was raised by my parents and teachers to trust and obey my pastor. He was a celebrity to me, a father figure and a man of God. As my pastor, I sought guidance and counseling from [Jack] when I was in need of help. [Jack] violated my trust. But when it was being violated, I didn't even know it because he made me believe what we were doing was OK and right in the eyes of God. When I asked him if it was wrong, he told me no and that I was his precious gift from God. I felt so special when he texted me from the holy altar during his sermons.'"[707]

FLORIDA

Jack's debacle followed three separate Orlando megachurch leader scandals.[708] One involved the younger brother of a well-known Dallas evangelist, who was publicly re-ordained in August 2011, just 8 months after stepping down. The cause was a 4-year long affair while married. Six other bishops were also re-ordained in that same ceremony. Among those was the senior pastor of Healing Place Church in Baton Rouge, LA who had resigned in July 2012. After initially citing health issues, it was later revealed the real cause was an affair.

Then a 36-year-old megachurch founder fatally shot himself in December 2013, a year after stepping down as lead pastor from Summit Church. He'd been in an affair with the church secretary and filed for divorce after 14 years of marriage. His wife countered with charges of drug, alcohol and domestic abuse.[709]

The third involved the former lead pastor of Discovery Church who resigned in May 2013 after admitting to an affair. Though he was not reinstated, it's doubly tragic because Discovery was recognized as "one of the 10 healthiest churches in America". [The pastor] was noted in the book *America's Most Influential Churches* as "one of the top 20 Christian leaders in the US to watch."[710] Of these moral failures, the senior pastor of Orlando's First Presbyterian Church summed it best. "I have an overwhelming feeling of sadness. It's sad for that church, sad for [him] and his family, and sad for what it means to the larger Christian church. It harms the view people have of Christians and Christian leaders."[711]

GEORGIA

Former senior pastor of megachurch New Birth Missionary Baptist Church was accused of having sex with young boys and photos were leaked. Five young men, teenagers at the time of the alleged abuse, filed lawsuits accusing him of coercing them into sexual acts during overnight trips and lavishing them with gifts. The suits were settled out of court in 2011. He was later embroiled in other "offensive dramas, real estate lawsuits and financial scandals."712

BISHOP TERRY

Charismatic Bishop Terry, 52, in Arlington, Texas was found guilty in 2006 of drugging and sexually assaulting three women, two of them members in his congregation. Terry and his wife appeared to have it all with their sprawling mansion, luxury cars and successful megachurch. But drug addiction and domestic violence ripped their marriage in two. His wife confessed in an interview. "There were times when he would actually hold me captive in the bathroom for hours and hours belittling me, stripping me of my value, blaming me for no reason at all."[713] He'd brought the three women to a Euless apartment, drugged them with GHB – the date rape drug – and then sexually assaulted. Despite earlier rumors he'd been sleeping with other church members, [she] stood by her husband. With the rape charges, their marriage unraveled.[714] In 2006 he was sentenced to 15 years in prison and fined $30,000.[715]

FORT LAUDERDALE

The megachurch pastor abruptly resigned on April 3, 2014 from Calvary Chapel in Fort Lauderdale. It was a shock to the congregation as he had led this church for 30 years. Its 20,000-strong membership mushroomed under his teachings with satellite locations in Boynton Beach, Boca Raton, West Boca, Plantation, Hollywood, and the Keys. It's not clear what led to the resignation, but the pastor admitted to multiple counts of adultery and a penchant for porn. While not present for the reading of his resignation letter, he admitted to "moral failing".[716] During affairs pastors probably don't consider how their exposed assignations and failings might affect congregants. Marie Harris wrote on Facebook, "My heart is breaking for my Church, my Pastor and his family." Also on Facebook, church member Anne Marie Giri wrote, "everyone was visibly upset."[717]

Back Story

At 21, this pastor, Bob, got a job at Capitol Records in Detroit, and he says "I was living the life of sex, drugs, and rock n roll, literally..." Years later, he began to abuse drugs and alcohol, and after multiple traffic tickets, some of which included driving under the influence he lost his driver's license. With his music industry career ruined he moved to Las Vegas and got a job in property management, but his talent in entertainment lead to him becoming an entertainment director of a casino in Las Vegas.

"Up until 1984 he continued to live his life of sex and drugs, but then on the day after Christmas his life changed. Bob's brother, Jim, who had recently married and 'got' religion, gave him a place to stay after he came to Jim's house from a party at the casino filled with alcohol and cocaine. Jim let Bob stay in his living room and he gave him a pillow, blanket, and a Bible. Bob threw the Bible back at Jim and said 'Jim will you shut up with your Jesus stuff.'

"So with the Bible still on the floor, Jim and his wife went to bed, but Bob says he couldn't sleep because the Bible was 'calling out to him'. Bob picked that Bible up opened it to the Gospel of John and began reading, and he says that when he got to 3:16 he began to weep uncontrollably. Jim and his wife came from around the corner and Jim said to Bob 'God just woke me up and told me I'm supposed to pray for you.' After that day at his brother's home he says he hasn't been the same since.

"In the following days Bob quit his job at the casino and began to serve as an associate pastor at Calvary Chapel Las Vegas. In 1985, [he] and his wife, moved to South Florida and began Calvary Chapel Fort Lauderdale."[718]

JOSHUA AND C.J.

In 2014, two megachurch pastors, Joshua and C.J., left the leadership council of The Gospel Coalition, after overseeing a trial involving child abuse at Covenant Life Church in Gaithersburg, Md. Questions arose after the May 2014 trial of what they knew about the abuse and why they did nothing to prevent it. In 2015 C.J. released a statement saying Covenant Life leaders said they didn't know about the abuse until "many years later."

The case involved a 56-year-old (convicted May 15, 2014) of sexually abusing at least four underage boys in the 1980s when he was a youth leader at Covenant Life. Jeremy, who he victimized around 50 times during church-related sleepovers testified at the trial and is now hailed a hero. His abuser currently serves a 40-year sentence.[719] C.J.'s brother-in-law initially counseled him to keep quiet to police about the abuse since it was years after the sexual exploitation took place. The brother-in-law stepped down from his role at Covenant Life in March 2014. C.J., who had founded Covenant Life in 1977, handed the reins over to Joshua in 2004 and led Sovereign Grace Church of Louisville, Ky. Joshua remained at Covenant Life Church until January 2015. In October 2012, the same month that a lawsuit was filed, C.J. stepped down from Sovereign Grace Ministries to focus on pastoral ministry. Two subsequent civil suits were dismissed.

DAVID AND SON

David, 78, founded Yoido Full Gospel Church, an Assemblies of God-affiliated denomination in 1973. This Seoul, South Korean church is officially the world's largest with more than 1 million members. Though it seats 26,000 people in the main building, overflow visitors can watch on television screens in nearby buildings. Seven services are given every Sunday, which are translated into 16 languages.

February 2014 David, its head pastor, was sentenced to three years in prison for embezzling $12 million in church funds. Long time friend and fellow pastor Bob of Evangel World Prayer Center, in Louisville, Kentucky set the record straight. David chose not to accuse his son in court, but he was at the root of the crime. His son was indicted on the same charges and immediately taken into custody after being sentenced to three years in prison.

Twelve years ago David's son devised a stock purchase plan to acquire shares at triple the price. The scheme ended in financial losses of over $12 million and his father was on the hook because he signed the papers authorizing the action. David testified that since he trusted his son and the church elders, he hadn't read the papers and just put his name on the signature line. The judge considered David's lifelong commitment to the Yoido Church. David hadn't received even a dime from the stock scheme, had raised and personally given to the church over $170 million, lived modestly in a 1,000 sq ft apartment and didn't even own a car. Charges against David resulted in probation while his son went straight to prison.[720] [721]

HIS OWN CHURCH WANTED HIM GONE

August 2014 brought a bizarre departure from sex scandals. Pastor Mark found his own parishioners picketing his megachurch urging him to repent of his sins. He came under fire the year before for multiple scandals. Some involved him posting "vulgar and misogynistic comments on the church's online forum fourteen years ago under the pseudonym William Wallace II".[722] Among other allegations critics cited plagiarism, misusing church funds to bolster book sales and silencing anyone that questioned him. "His Mars Hill Church (including its 15 franchised satellite locations) attracts nearly 15,000 weekly. [His] podcast has 250,000 regular listeners worldwide, and his 2012 book, *Real Marriage,* topped a *New York Times* best-seller list. This questionable allocation of church money is indicative of a wider problem that rankles those in [his] growing flock of critics: the lack of transparency around Driscoll and church funds."[723] Amidst the controversy, congregants began leaving his Mars Hill Church in droves. Twenty-one pastors and elders at Mars Hill brought un-refuted charges of bullying and intimidation against him. Finally in October 14, 2014 the pastor stepped down.[724]

JIM AND TAMMY FAYE BAKKER

Besides Jimmy Swaggart when one thinks of church scandal, Jim Bakker jumps to mind. While Swaggart's troubles were primarily confined to his own moral demons, Bakker's dramas encompassed a much larger scope. He teamed up with two prosperity gospel pastors and created the "Praise the Lord" (PTL) show for their joint network Trinity Broadcasting.

In 1978, the Bakkers opened Heritage USA in Fort Mill, South Carolina. Then it was the third most successful theme park in America, employing 2,500 and attracting 6 million visitors by 1986. Contributions requested from viewers were estimated to exceed $1 million a week to finance the theme park and PTL. During Heritage's heyday, the *Charlotte Observer* launched an investigation and their world began to unravel. It led to criminal charges leveled at Bakker and his subsequent incarceration.

The Bakkers embraced the prosperity gospel lifestyle like penguins to snow. Frances FitzGerald in an April 1987 *New Yorker* article wrote, "They epitomized the excesses of the 1980s; the greed, the love of glitz, and the shamelessness; which in their case was so pure as to almost amount to a kind of innocence." Detractors had their own interpretation for PTL: Pass the Loot, Preachers Taking Loot, Providing Tammy with Lipstick, or Perverts for the Licentiousness.[725]

The Bakkers greatly oversold 4-day vacations to the theme park's hotel at least $1000 a pop, which brought in $68 –165 million, or more, depending on which source is checked. Some contributors gave $7000 so the amount truly gleaned isn't known. "With accommodations for just 25,000 vacationers, Bakker oversold an additional 43,000 memberships, diverting $3.7 million to his own personal use. … When Bakker's former personal assistant David Taggart, himself previously convicted of fraud, took the stand, he cataloged Bakker's lavish lifestyle: condominiums, houses, mink coats, diamonds, two Rolls Royces, and a Mercedes, all paid for out of donations."[726] Nothing epitomized their excesses quite like the $4,500 air-conditioned doghouse Tammy Faye had custom built.

Things came to a head in 1989 when a jury found him guilty on 24 counts involving mail fraud, wire fraud and conspiracy. He was sentenced to 45 years in prison and ordered to pay $500,000 in fines. The scandals, jail time and his dalliance with his secretary, Jessica Hahn, took their toll and Tammy Faye divorced him in 1992. In an appeals decision, the court wiped clean the fine and reduced his sentence to eight years of which he served fewer than five. Bakker eventually remarried, as did Tammy Faye. In his 1996 book, *I Was Wrong,* Bakker renounced prosperity gospel and currently has another ministry headquartered in Branson, Missouri.[727]

TED

In 2006, an evangelical pastor Ted admitted to engaging in an inappropriate relationship with a 20-year-old male volunteer. Like Swaggert, his transgressions wouldn't have been half so egregious if he hadn't condemned them from the pulpit. The pastor arrived in Colorado Springs, Colorado in 1984 after he received a vision of God about forming a church there. It began in the basement of their home with just 22 people. Eventually it grew into megachurch New Life Church with more than 14,000 congregants. His became a household name. He counseled foreign dignitaries and was invited to the White House on several occasions during Bush 2's administration. Eventually he was elected president of the National Association of Evangelicals.[728]

The pastor then 52, said the incident was "an indicator of the compulsive behavior" that ruled him at the time. However, he said he has been undergoing therapy during the two years since and "working it out."

In November 2006 the disgraced pastor stepped down from the pulpit of the megachurch he founded. He admitted to Oprah Winfrey in an interview what he described as a "dark and repulsive" secret part of his life. "It was the first time that dark area of my life I'd worked so hard to fight against was coming to the surface. And to say it, and to talk about it, was so shameful and shocking. Even to me."[729]

After the scandal and a generous severance package in hand, he and his wife moved to Arizona where he sold insurance. Part of the agreement with New Life was that he left the area, but that stipulation expired in 2008 and they moved back to Colorado Springs. In 2010, the pastor started a new church in Colorado Springs home, St. James, which marked the beginning of a remarkable comeback.

Fatal Blows?

Conservative author and talk show host Glenn Beck is known for making seemingly unbelievable predictions that eventually come to pass. In May 2015 he made two more such pronouncements. This time he predicted people would leave churches in droves if the Supreme Court legalized gay marriage, which it did on June 26 in a 5-4 decision, regardless of what individual states voted.

First, if pastors still choose to preach against homosexuality, churches will lose tax exempt status. They will be forced to cave on this issue or close.

Pressure will then be exerted on congregants. Initially one might think it'd be just the opposite – steadfast believers would rally, stand and fight, claiming 1st Amendment rights. *Something.* Instead Beck paints a different scenario, one that has Christians buckling and fleeing to save their hide.

He predicts, "The stigma of going to church will be too much and Americans would not want to risk losing their jobs, livelihoods, or reputations. Persecution is coming. If this goes through, persecution is coming. I mean *serious* persecution. Mark my words. Fifty percent," Beck reiterated. "Within five years, 50 percent of the people you sit next to in church will not be there … because they'll say: 'I can't do that. I will lose my job. People are picketing at my house. I just can't do that.'"[730]

Could this be another spear thrust into the heart of Christianity?

Communism Infiltrates Christian Churches

Every Christian has heard of the coming "Great Apostasy" and wondered whatever could cause this. It was always this big mystery – one of those burning questions we hope to notch off as answered before we die. The answer lies in the 1800s, back to the middle of the 19th century when most church denominations had only one branch. Then, there was a sense of unity. The Civil War did more than split our Nation; it separated denominations on social issues. Once divided, churches weakened against an invading enemy.

Ten years before the turn of the century, Marxist "social gospel" was introduced to major American seminaries and schools of divinity. Theologians returning from studies in Europe and Germany planted these seeds. They espoused the very poison that changed Europe's spiritual and moral fiber.

Walter Ranschenbusch graduated from the prestigious Rochester Theological Seminary in 1885 thoroughly indoctrinated with "Iluminism" that substitutes faith in God with faith in man. Seven years later, Ranschenbusch, Leighton Williams and a group of like-minded individuals organized "The Brotherhood of the Kingdom" to promote their radical beliefs of Fabian Socialism, which embraces evolutionary socialism rather than revolution. "Walter Ranschenbusch declared: "If ever Socialism is to succeed, it cannot succeed in an irreligious country. It must start in the churches."[731]

And so it did.

Another Marxist, Reverend F.D. Huntington in New York, occupied himself establishing America's branch of the Christian Socialist Movement – the religious arm of the Fabian Socialist Society. By 1900 the Marxist plan to infiltrate American churches was fully on track.

In February 1900, 25 leading churchmen met to establish the National Federation of Churches, most of which were ardent Fabians. One of Ranschenbusch's English protégés was Communist Harry F. Ward. In the 1953 hearings of the House Committee of Un-American Activities, Manning Johnson testified "Dr. Harry F. Ward, for many years, has been the chief architect for Communist envision and subversion in the religious field.... He was a member of the Communist Party while I was a member... I would say that he is the *Red Dean of the Communist Party* in the religious field."[732]

One year later, the National Federation of Churches met in Philadelphia, which eventually gave birth to a much larger Communist organization and changed America's history. In 1902, they met in Chicago with numerous prominent NFC clergy actively involved.

Next came the Committee on Correspondence comprised of radical ministers or laymen. They toured America's seminaries infusing them with their propaganda. Deliberations in New York on November 15, 1905 influenced thousands of religious thereafter and it was then that the Federal Council of Churches, now the National Council of Churches, was formally proposed.

By 1907 the groundwork had been laid and Dr. Rauschenbusch returned to England fully committed to Fabian thinking to subvert America's churches.

At the end of 1908, Rauschenbusch and Harry Ward set up a 9-day conference in Philadelphia that officially formed the Federal Council of Churches of Christ in America (FCC) with 29 representatives of Protestant and Eastern Orthodox denominations. They chose the same constitution by Socialists at the 1905 Inter-Church Conference on Federation and adopted Ward's "The Social Creed of the Churches". The latter had been submitted to and approved by Nikolai Lenin, founder of the Bolsheviks, leader of the Russian Revolution and first head of the USSR. By 1914 the FCC had become one of the major propagandists for Marxist America.

On February 10th of that year, conspirators met in the home of millionaire Andrew Carnegie and designed plans for "the Church Peace Union", which was connected to the FCC. By the early 1920s, the Communist Party had a good foothold to infiltrate American churches led by Harry F. Ward, Jerome Davis, William B. Spofford, and Albert Rhys Williams. In testimony, former top Communist Benjamin Gitlow told the House Committee on Un-American Activities: "This group wielded tremendous influence in the religious field and did Trojan Horse work in advancing the Communist conspiracy in religion. The number of clergymen who followed the Communist Party line grew by leaps and bounds."[733]

Dr. Ward travelled to Moscow in 1924 and 1929 to plan with Stalin how to use American churches in furthering the goals of the International Communist Conspiracy. In '25, Ward travelled to China where he lectured throughout their clergy. At the Communist International meeting it was agreed that "the missions and church institutions in China could be used... to cover up Communist espionage activities... "That was also the case in this country, where the Federal Council already had a budget of $350,000 and an office in Washington from which it promoted Communist interests.[734]

By 1935, Communists had fully infiltrated America's churches. The FCC revealed their cooperation to push the Communist line issuing a report that ultimately called for:

- A world government of delegated powers
- Complete abandonment of U.S. isolationism
- Strong immediate limitations on national sovereignty
- International control of all armies and navies
- A universal system of money
- Worldwide freedom of immigration
- Progressive elimination of all tariff and quota restrictions on world trade and
- A "democratically controlled" international bank

They've obviously obtained the majority of their goals.

In 1945, the Federal Council of Churches was one of only 42 NGOs – non-governmental organizations – invited to send delegates to the international conference in San Francisco. This was significant because the FCC called for the founding of the United Nations,[735] presided over by Communist agent Alger Hiss.

After a beating from Conservatives in the 40s, the FCC took on four important agencies: the Church World Service, the Interseminary Committee, the Protestant Film Commission, and the Protestant Radio Commission. It was on November 29, 1950 the name formally changed to National Council of the Churches of Christ in the U.S.A., but they maintained their old Marxist leaders.

"In the formal constitution of the National Council of Churches in Cleveland, one representative from each of the participating denominations signed the official book ('Dies Committee on Un-American Activities') which became the Document of Record. Eleven of these 29 signers of the official book have public records of affiliation with pro-Communist enterprises.... There were 358 clergymen who were voting delegates to the constituting convention.... Of these clergymen, 123 (or 34%) have had affiliations with Communist projects and enterprises. That represents a high degree of Communist penetration. The overlap between the old Council and the new was almost complete....

"The Communist Party, U.S.A., has instructed many of its members to join churches and church groups, to take control whenever possible, and to influence the thoughts and actions of as many church-goers as they can.... The party tries to get leading churchmen to support Communist policies disguised as welfare work for minorities. Earl Browder, former head of the American Communist party, once admitted: 'By going among the religious masses, we are for the first time able to bring our anti-religious ideas to them.'"[736]

Last Thoughts on Apostasy

Today Christian ministers, pastors and priests are in a bind. Without changing to more liberal attitudes, people increasingly view the church as out-dated. But by moving the lines of what's acceptable like "there are many ways to Heaven", putting practicing gay preachers in the pulpit and, and performing same-sex marriages, the church's formerly firm stance on Biblical teachings has weakened. Black and white have blurred to dingy grey.

Many in ministry have lost sight of salvation. They look to fill pews rather than churchgoers' hearts with God. As society shifts and accepts the formerly unacceptable, people don't want to be seen as judgmental and are further pushed by political correctness. Congregants now hear more of "let the good times roll" rather than it's time for self-examination. One regular member of Joel Osteen's Texas megachurch said he likes to attend there because he always came away feeling good. He felt criticized at work all week and didn't need it on Sunday too.

Ministers who preach prosperity gospel have their eye ever on the collection plate and less on the word of God.

There is nothing wrong with being wealthy, but scripture reminds us that it's harder for those Christians to remain on-track. Matthew 19:24 says that "it's easier for a camel to go through the eye of a needle than for someone who's rich to enter the kingdom of God." When life gets too easy, people don't rely on God.

Besides giving weakened messages and falling victim to moral failures, some preachers surprise in ways one wouldn't imagine.

While this author still lived in Perth, Australia, we were invited to a cocktail party. It was a wide, interesting mix of the intellectually stimulating, those with considerable means and members of clergy. During conversation with an Episcopal priest, he said he couldn't remember if something were one of the Ten Commandments or not. A look of incredulity flashed across my face followed by crazy blinking at his obvious ignorance. This was in 1997 and hopefully since then, he's brushed up on the Bible.

Another example came in 1996, shortly after my mother passed away. Years before while living in the Midwest, she'd been hugely active in her church. She'd lived in the same house with my dad since 1959. When he passed, we moved her to Colorado. She had nice neighbors and as always, got along stupendously with everyone. When most people have a spouse, party invitations for singles can be scarce so it's harder to

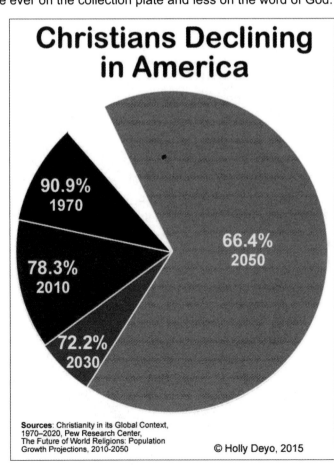

Christians Declining in America

90.9%
1970

78.3%
2010

72.2%
2030

66.4%
2050

Sources: Christianity in its Global Context,
1970–2020, Pew Research Center,
The Future of World Religions: Population
Growth Projections, 2010-2050   © Holly Deyo, 2015

integrate. Mom lived in her Colorado home for four years before she was taken from her family and friends. In lieu of flowers, we asked that donations be made to our church. When they were handed over, the minister shocked us by demanding, *"is that all there is?"* It's little signs like these that reveal spiritual shortcomings.

Some clergy's messages lack power for lasting impressions, but part of the problem lies with churchgoers when apathy takes over. After the terrorists' attacks of Sept. 11, 2001, people were desperate to go to church. Shock and disbelief drove folks out of bed Sunday mornings. Pews, hearts and collection plates filled and attendance rose by 20%. As survivor Priscilla Warner observed, "Sept. 11 brought God out of the closet."[737] Within weeks, the horror wore off and attendance returned to pre-attack levels. Even after Hurricane Katrina, Superstorm Sandy, the Boston Marathon bombing, Virginia Tech and Columbine killings, the 2008 economic crash and ensuing recession, nothing drives Americans permanently into church pews.

Besides churches changing, broad stroke, to suit the times, moral failings of church leaders have done much to damage people's faith. Some say that preachers, pastors and priests are "only human". That's true, but they are also in charge of setting examples of good character and leadership. They have a higher moral bar to meet simply by the position they hold. Taken together, all these things have lessened churches' impact and members are drifting away.

Without a steady compass people change course, fall away. It will take some major event, something so horrific and frightening to make enough people say, no God could ever let this happen. While we've witnessed a "little apostasy", over the past several decades, the Great Apostasy will dwarf these events and leave Christians at great spiritual risk.

Chapter 15: Why America Must Fall

The United States is notable in End Time scriptures due to her obvious absence.

In order for a number of End Times prophecies to complete America must be taken out of the picture. One theory why America is not in scripture during the End of Days is that it's been reduced to a state of insignificance or near destruction. So many things could bring this once great Country to its knees. This could either be done physically, meaning that America is catastrophically attacked from within, or more likely, from an outside force, or she crumbles financially under the weight of crushing, crippling debt – or both.

Image: Flying the American flag upside down is an SOS signal. Section 8a of the United States Flag Code states, "The flag should never be displayed with the union down, except as a signal of dire distress in instances of extreme danger to life or property."

While she is still the world's leading super power, chinks in her strength began appearing in 1980.

Chink 1: Crippling Debt

It's hard to remember when financial pundits didn't speak about the U.S. national debt in terms of the "T" word. It took 200 years to hit the first trillion of debt and just six years under President Ronald Reagan for it to double. Much as many look back fondly at this optimistic, can-do, feel-good President, under his command the national debt soared 184%. America was truly launched on financial skids through deficit spending. President Reagan's contribution to the national debt was just the opening volley. Today, 35 years since the beginning of the "Reagan Revolution," when the Nation politically realigned to more conservative values, the U.S. national debt has rocketed by over 1750%!

George H.W. Bush followed suit mushrooming the debt 55% in just four years. By the end of his presidency in 1993, the national debt had doubled again to $4 trillion.

America elected Bill Clinton in 1993. Probably the most ridiculous statement ever voiced by a U.S. President other than "I did not have sexual relations with that woman [White House intern], Miss Lewinsky," and denied urging her to lie about an affair[738] – also uttered by Mr. Clinton – was his 1996 State of the Union declaration that "the era of big government is over."[739]

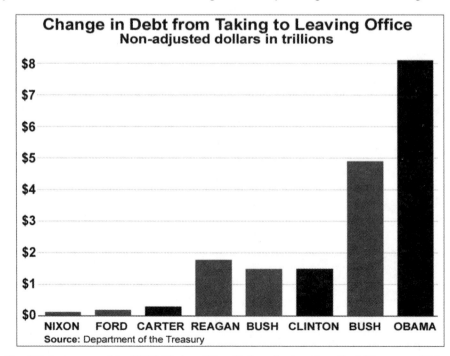

Change in Debt from Taking to Leaving Office
Non-adjusted dollars in trillions

Bars (left to right): NIXON, FORD, CARTER, REAGAN, BUSH, CLINTON, BUSH, OBAMA
Source: Department of the Treasury

He promised pre-election to overhaul the Federal government so that it "serves better and costs less".[740] He was a master at promising much and delivering deceptively little, which may be why he earned the name "Slick Willie". Or, it may be because he survived impeachment on perjury and obstruction of justice charges. **NOTE**: For clarification, Mr. Clinton was impeached for *lying to Congress* when questioned about Monica Lewinsky, not for the affair itself. This widely publicized misconception was even published in Australian papers that his presidency was in jeopardy for having an affair. Both charges, the perjuries and obstruction of justice, were related to events stemming from sexual misconduct, not the acts themselves. Or maybe the Slick Willie moniker stuck because President Clinton survived 10 scandals in his first year alone: Gennifer Flowers affair, "I didn't inhale", Rose Law firm, draft dodging; don't ask, don't tell, Travelgate, Vice Foster suicide, Whitewater, healthcare and Troopergate. Clinton was so skillful dodging an assortment of scandals that he dubbed himself "the comeback kid."[741] Regardless of how he managed to stay in office Mr. Clinton was slapped with a $250,000 fine and disbarred for five years. Between 1993 and 2001, Mr. Clinton increased the national debt $1.5 trillion.

Not only did these presidents massively grow government, they set the stage for shocking jumps in the national debt.

Four weeks after taking office in January 2001, George W. Bush delivered another unfulfilled promise on the Nation's finances: "Many of you have talked about the need to pay down our national debt. I listened, and I agree. We owe it to our children and grandchildren to act now, and I hope you will join me to pay down $2 trillion in debt during the next 10 years. At the end of those 10 years, we will have paid down all the debt that is available to retire. That is more debt, repaid more quickly than has ever been repaid by any nation at any time in history."[742]

By the end of his first term, the national debt had climbed to $7.6 trillion. 2006 added another trillion. The last day September 2008, the total national debt pushed through the $10 trillion invisible Maginot Line in the worst financial crisis since the Great Depression. By the end 2009, the national debt leapfrogged to $12.3 trillion. Mr. Bush's two terms in office had tacked on nearly $5 trillion.

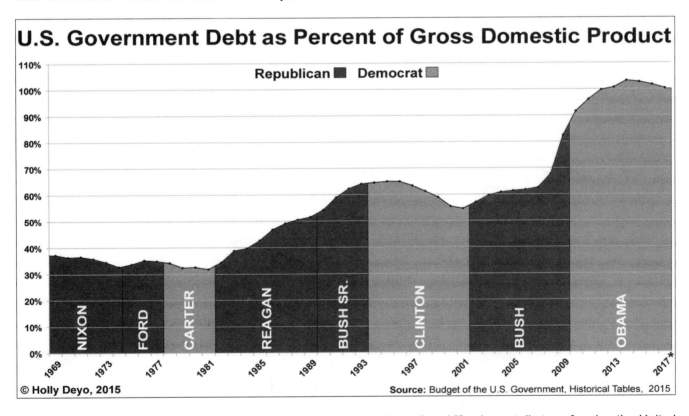

In 2009, Barack Hussein Obama's promises of "hope and change" and "fundamentally transforming the United States of America" couldn't have proved truer.[743] As they say, be careful what you wish for. His presidency would be more accurately described as "shock and horror". All that "free" ObamaCare and free Obama phones, to proposed free community college, more sick leave, faster Internet and second-earner tax credits come at a price. In this election year, Presidential candidates and admitted socialist Bernie Sanders and Hillary Clinton, proposed free college tuition for all. A conservative estimate put the yearly Federal bill for this at $47 billion and the states left with a $23 billion tab.[744] The math simply doesn't work. It's fiscal suicide.

We have a lot of "takers," not all, but way too many. Much of this is the fault of government who act as enablers encouraging people to rely on entitlements and reward generational welfare recipients. These are people who are physically and mentally capable of working, but choose not to because it's all they've ever known.

President Obama reduced the definition of full time work in America down to 30 hours a week from the standard 40. During the Great Recession Mr. Obama refilled the work place with minimum-to-low-end paying jobs instead of the former higher paying work. During his presidency, the U.S. government morphed into a gigantic income-redistribution machine. Americans for Tax Reform said in an April 14, 2015 press release that President Obama had proposed 442 tax hikes[745] since taking office. Brace for more and not just from the current administration. People are objecting so strenuously to onerous taxation that nearly 14,000 Americans have renounced citizenship since 2010.[746]

As of this day, March 6, 2016, the national debt stands at $19.1 trillion. By the time Mr. Obama leaves office, it's estimated he will have brought the debt to a staggering $20 trillion, nearly doubling it. It's one thing to double it when it stands at $1 trillion, and quite another to jump it to $20.

SOCIAL SECURITY ON LIFE SUPPORT

Another huge reason entitlements are in trouble is the way social security is run. Economics expert Dr. Allen W. Smith explains what happened to social security. It was a looting of the people's, not government's, retirement piggy bank. Smith is no lightweight. He's authored numerous books on the subject and retired as Professor of Economics at Eastern Illinois University after teaching econ for 30 years. His book, *Understanding Economics,* published by Random House, was used in over 600 schools in 48 states.

In a huge over simplification here, Smith details in "Ronald Reagan and the Great Social Security Heist" why this fund is now broke. In 1982, President Ronald Reagan warned that social security was in deep trouble. To fix the problem, Federal Reserve Chairman Alan Greenspan, Mr. Reagan and his advisors designed the Social Security Amendments of 1983. This tax hike, which generated $2.7 trillion in surplus revenue, was earmarked and to be set aside to cover its increasing costs. Smith writes, "This surplus revenue was supposed to be saved and invested in marketable U.S. Treasury bonds that would be held in the trust fund until the baby boomers began to retire in about 2010. But not one dime of that money went to Social Security."[747] Instead it funded wars, tax cuts for the wealthy and other government programs. Smith maintains that SS was not close to bankruptcy in the early 80s, but promoting this concept was a way to generate cash. The $2.7 trillion was never repaid and in 2010, social security began permanently running in the red. In 2010 alone, the government borrowed $49 billion to pay these benefits and its spurting red ink ever since.

David C. John, senior research fellow at the Heritage Foundation, paints a grim picture of social security's future. In less than a decade from the first year social security ran in the red, that deficit amount will double. By 2025, less than a decade from now, government will have to borrow about $220 billion to cover payouts. Then in another seven years, in 2032, social security will owe recipients about $350 billion.[748] Where will they find the $$?

SIMPLY UNSUSTAINABLE

Notice that Social Security and Health issues account for the biggest slices of the pie. Fifty cents of every dollar goes to these bloated entitlements. Keep in mind that in 2015, the Feds spent $1.4 trillion more than in 2015.

Prior to June 1933, government spending was kept in line because every dollar was tied to an actual piece of gold. With the Great Depression fresh in their minds and possible bank failures looming, people began to hoard gold. This wasn't helping an already shaky economy.

According to Keynesian theory, one way to fight off an economic downturn is to inflate the money supply. Increasing the amount of gold held by the Federal Reserve grew its ability to inflate the money supply. In 1933 President Roosevelt denied creditors the right to demand payment in gold, imposed a seven day bank holiday to halt the month long bank runs, and forbade them to pay out gold or export it. In April Roosevelt ordered all gold coins, bullion and gold certificates in denominations greater than $100 to be turned in for other money. People received $20.67 per ounce of gold. In 1934, government raised the price of gold to $35 per ounce, increasing the Federal Reserve's balance sheets by 69%. In 1971 President Nixon proclaimed that the U.S. would no longer convert dollars to gold at the official exchange rate. This completed abandoning the gold standard, which Britain had dropped in 1931. Now the U.S. dollar isn't tied to anything but a printing press.

Image: The first number right after the category is the amount of the 2015 budget allocated to this expense. The second number is how much these areas have increased in 2015 compared to 2005. All went up except Education. These amounts have all been normalized to 2015 dollars. *Income Security* includes federal employee retirement and disability, unemployment compensation, food and housing assistance, veterans' benefits, and other federal income security programs. *National Defense* includes overseas contingency operations.

The U.S. has so over-extended itself that it must borrow money to pay bills despite taking in a stunning $3.3 *trillion* in 2015. The Federal government has been consistently going in the hole since 1960 minus four years in the Clinton administration. Since the mid-70s the U.S. generated truly staggering deficits – the difference between what government takes in and what it spends. From 2008 to 2009, the deficit jumped over 200%! In the

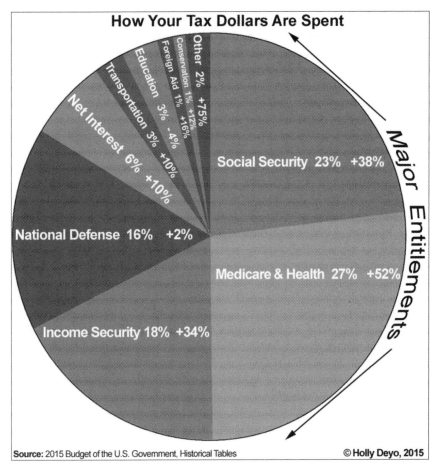

How Your Tax Dollars Are Spent

Major Entitlements

Other 2% +75%
Conservation 1% +12%
Foreign Aid 1% +16%
Education 3% - 4%
Transportation 3% +10%
Net Interest 6% +10%
Social Security 23% +38%
National Defense 16% +2%
Medicare & Health 27% +52%
Income Security 18% +34%

Source: 2015 Budget of the U.S. Government, Historical Tables   © Holly Deyo, 2015

decade from 2005 to 2015, the deficit leaped from $318,346,000,000 to $563,564,000,000 despite the Feds having an extra $1.2 trillion to spend! This is a "kind" comparison because in the four years of 2009-2012, the Obama administration racked up over $5 trillion in deficit spending. If any business ran accounting like this, it would be *out* of business! Bankrupt.

In case your brain goes numb trying to visualize what a trillion dollars is, this comparison puts it into perspective. How tall is a trillion dollars in $1000 bills?

Stacked on top of each other $1000 bills equal:

- $1 million = 4 inches high
- $1 billion = 364 feet high
- $1 trillion = 63 miles high

Said another way, how long ago is a trillion seconds? Counting backwards:

- 1 million seconds = 12 days ago
- 1 billion seconds = 31 years ago
- 1 trillion seconds = 30,000 BC

In case you don't have one of these "Hamiltons" in your hip pocket, this is what they looked like with Founding Father Alexander Hamilton on the front. They're pretty scarce considering the $1000 bill was discontinued in 1969 and there are only a little over 165,000 still in existence.

The country is hemorrhaging money and the government keeps raising the debt ceiling. So who owns all this debt?

We weren't always in this mess. Between 1901 and 1916, the budget was very close to balancing every year.

World War I brought large deficits that totaled $23 billion for 1917–1919. Throughout the 1920s, the budget was in surplus. However, the Great Depression and World War II resulted in unrelenting, unprecedented deficits. By 1946 Federal debt, held by the public, had mushroomed to $242 billion.

This is even more eye popping considering until the start of the Civil War, the U.S. relied solely on customs duties to finance the government. In the 19th century, selling public land supplemented the customs duties. By the 1860s they piled on excise taxes, followed by estate and gift taxes. It wasn't until 1913, Americans were hit with income taxes and by 1930 it made up 60% of government revenue. You know the rest of the story.

WHO OWES WHOM? AND WHO OWNS WHOM?

By 2019, the U.S. Debt Clock projects that we'll have a national debt of over $20 trillion. Since it predicts tax revenue to grow by 111% that means we'll all be paying more income tax. Despite this, the Federal government is expected to rack up about a $370 billion deficit with spending up 157%. Every single year they spend more than they collect. This is unsustainable and either the economy will implode or our creditors will come knocking. When the U.S. government fails, it's going to take a lot of economies along with it.

About that debt... As of November 9, 2015, it stood at $18.6 trillion. About 75% is held by the public, which includes debt purchased by pension funds, foreign governments, foreign investors, American investors and Federal Reserve Banks. This is often in the form of Treasury Bills. The other 25% is held by government agencies. It's like robbing Peter to pay Paul. One of the biggest loaners was the Social Security fund, but with more Baby Boomers retiring and sluggish economic growth its viability is rapidly coming to a close. Then where does government go for a piggy bank?

As of August 2015, foreign countries owned $6 trillion of U.S. debt. Not surprisingly China and Japan are the biggest stakeholders with about $1.2 each trillion. After that comes a group of banks in the Caribbean, then a group of oil exporters from South America, the Middle East, North Africa and Indonesia. The remaining top 10 are rounded out by Brazil, the UK, Switzerland, Ireland, Hong Kong and Luxembourg. Even Russia, Mexico and Kazakhstan get in on the action. Kazakhstan? Really?

GOVERNMENT WASTE

This could be a whole book in itself. Take the Post Office for example. For the decade ending in 2014, the U.S. Post Office lost over $47 billion and $26 billion of it accumulated between 2012 and 2014. It's wallowing in a tsunami of red ink and could be more efficiently run by the public sector. It can't keep its head above water despite being given $18 billion in subsidies every year. Salaries and benefits for its 617,000 employees tap this agency for $1.8 billion every two weeks.[749] That's the equivalent of earning $36.45/hour. Who wouldn't want that? An annual salary and perks of $76,000 is well above the national average of $56,000.[750]

Drowning in Bureaucracy

Apparently it takes 645 agencies to run America. When questioned by business expert Stuart Varney, Presidential hopeful Dr. Ben Carson commented on burgeoning government. "We have 645 government agencies and sub agencies. Each of which has a budget. In many cases a very substantial budget. I personally believe that you can cut three or four percent of fat out of each one of those budgets. Anybody who tells me you can't, like Nancy Pelosi... What a bunch of crap."[751] But it goes beyond this. Too many agencies overlap each other.

In 2013, the GAO – Government Accountability Office – reported there are 198 areas where the executive branch agencies or Congress can reduce, eliminate, or better manage fragmentation, overlap, or duplication to save money.[752] For example, 10 agencies help minorities with AIDS.[753] Autism research is handled by over 11 different agencies.[754] Eight different Defense of Department agencies are looking for prisoners of war and those missing in action.[755] Schriever Air Force Base in Colorado Springs has eight different satellite control centers to control 10 satellite programs.[756]

Another huge area the GAO identified is the overlapping of disability and unemployment benefits. Their report shows that 117,000 people got duplicated benefit payments from the disability insurance and unemployment insurance programs in one year, costing taxpayers $850 million. As legislation currently stands, it doesn't preclude receiving overlapping benefits.[757]

Though this is the 4th year the GAO has generated these reports and Mr. Obama asked Congress to fast-track these budget repairs and government reorganization, it's either partly done or not done at all. House Oversight Chairman Darrell Issa said, "One of the most troubling things in GAO's report is the number of agencies that have no idea just how much taxpayer money they are spending on their programs."[758]

I See Dead People

In 2015, the U.S. government was still trying unsuccessfully to halt benefit payments to the deceased by introducing the Stopping Improper Payments to Deceased People Act, S 1073 bill. This would hopefully help stem the nearly $125 billion – an uptick of $19 billion more in 2013 – outlay to the deceased. It would require agencies to use more accurate and complete lists of deceased individuals to confirm payment eligibility. Not only is Social Securities Master Death Files not kept current by their sources, other agencies that dispense the benefits don't have access to the SSA's complete files.[759] Estimates say only 35 people worldwide are 112-years-old, yet the Social Security's Master Death Files showed about 6.5 million people on their books.[760]

Pentagon – A Black Hole on Unaccountability

Likewise, the Pentagon is plagued with problems that end up costing taxpayers *trillions*. They say the payroll system for America's 2.1 million active-duty and Reserve soldiers, sailors, airmen and Marines is nearly impossible to update. Other problems include clerical errors, vanished documents and old, incompatible computer systems. A Reuters investigation found that errors in the military are widespread. A law in place since 1996 requires all federal agencies to undergo annual audits. All have complied – all except the Pentagon, which lets billions swirl down a dark, murky hole. To rectify this problem, in 1997 the DoD test ran Defense Integrated Military Human Resources System, or DIMHRS, software they hoped would make it easier for solders' information to be updated. The Pentagon told Congress it would cost $577 million – cheap considering it would eliminate 88 pay and personnel systems. The phase-in began in 2004. After more than a decade of development and over $1 billion of taxpayer money, DIMHRS was declared unusable.[761]

Photo: Aerial shot of the Pentagon, headquarters of the U.S. Department of Defense, snapped in January 2008. (Courtesy David B. Gleason)

When submitting monthly financials to the Treasury, the Navy's Defense Finance and Accounting Service (DFAS) often used "plugs" – fake numbers to make their totals match the Treasury's. Why plugs? Because of "the Pentagon's chronic failure to keep track of its money – how much it has, how much it pays out and how much is wasted or stolen."[762] Plug usage is rampant as DFAS not only used it for Army, Navy, Air Force and other defense agencies' accounting, but it's common practice throughout services at the operational level to compensate for lost or missing information.

It wasn't just the billions in screwed up service pay that inflicted hardship on soldiers and sunk morale. This was only a fraction of the money problems. From 2003 to 2011, the Army lost track of nearly $6 billion in supplies. Reuters found that "the Pentagon is largely incapable of keeping track of its vast stores of weapons, ammunition and other supplies; thus it continues to spend money on new supplies it doesn't need and on storing others long out of date. It has amassed a backlog of more than half a trillion dollars in unaudited contracts with outside vendors; how much of that money paid for actual goods and services delivered isn't known. And it repeatedly falls prey to fraud and theft that can go undiscovered for years, often eventually detected by external law enforcement agencies."[763]

Too Much Stuff

Navy Vice Admiral Mark Harnitchek, director of the Defense Logistics Agency admitted, "We have about $14 billion of inventory for lots of reasons, and probably half of that is excess to what we need."[764] That's probably why the military left behind $1 billion worth of Humvees in Iran that ISIS later commandeered. Those 2,300 vehicles were what ISIS got in Mosul alone. But that doesn't stop the Pentagon from buying more stuff. Sept. 30, 2012, the DLA and military services had $733 million worth of excess supplies and equipment stacked warehouse shelves. That figure was up 21% from $609 million a year earlier.

In another movement of Pentagon brilliance, the Army committed to train Iraqi soldiers in an effort to turn them into a viable unit. Some 3,000 U.S. soldiers stationed in Iraq were assigned to the training. Congress financed this by hiding $1.2 billion into an omnibus bill. This is in addition to the $25 billion spent on the same training from 2003 to 2011. So how'd the 2015 effort work out? The 30,000-strong Iraqi army fled like scaled cats when faced with 1,000 ISIS fighters. Shortly after came an encore performance that sent 10,000 Iraqis running when confronted by just 400 Islamic State fighters.[765] Apparent you can't buy courage and determination, but the Pentagon can waste more $$.

One of the more notable examples of Pentagon waste occurred after all this equipment fell to ISIS. To counteract this unhappy turn of events, the U.S. military sent into Iraq 175 M1A1 Abrams main battle tanks, 55,000 rounds of main tank-gun ammunition, $600 million in howitzers and trucks, $700 million worth of Hellfire missiles and 2,000 AT-4 rockets. The purpose? To destroy the American armor ISIS had acquired. Imagine the irony of American weapons used to destroy American weapons.

Secretary of Defense under President George W. Bush, Donald Rumsfeld told the Pentagon. "Our financial systems are decades old. According to some estimates, we cannot track $2.3 *trillion* in transactions." The importance of the issue, he said was not "about business practices, nor is the goal to improve figures on the bottom line. It's really about the security of the United States of America. And let there be no mistake, it is a matter of life and death."[766] The next day was 9/11 so the Pentagon's compliance transgressions slunk into the background for another decade.

Since the Pentagon has thumbed its nose at the required audits since 1996, they still haven't accounted for $8.5 trillion forked over to them by Congress, courtesy of the taxpayer. How can the Pentagon continually get away without submitting to audits? Their accounting is so screwed up they plead to Congress for extensions that are granted and the missing audits aren't revisited. This happens year after year without oversight or enforcement. Can you imagine if IRS gave you the ugly notice of a forthcoming audit and you say you can't find a bunch of receipts so just go away, that they'd be OK with that? No, IRS would throw you in jail and hound you till you died. Shudder to think what they'd do if it came to light you'd used a lot of bogus numbers in tax returns.

In a decade the Pentagon wasted billions to modernize is accounting systems, but these programs have either failed or not lived up to expectations. Nine projects are underway to find a workable solution. The programs were pitched at a cost of $7.2 billion to develop and implement, but as of 2013 they had already chewed up more than double dollars. Several won't even be completed until 2017, so it's anyone's guess how much beyond that $15 billion will be required.[767] In the meantime, the Pentagon continues to use plugs, lose vast sums of money and never held accountable.

Oink Oink – Government Waste From the Pig Book

Now for a little pork barrel "fun". **C**itizens **A**gainst **G**overnment **W**aste, CAGW, a nonpartisan, nonprofit organization began chronicling government fraud, abuse and mismanagement in 1991. In 2002 they launched

Piglet Books that expose these activities at a state level. For similar transgressions on a national level, check their *Congressional Pig Books* and online database of pork. CAGW documents that out of each tax dollar, 31¢ pays interest on debt, 23¢ pays for services to Americans and 46¢ is wasted. In their publication *Prime Cuts*, they lay out a 5-year road map to save taxpayers $2.6 trillion. In October 2015, Congress was finally shamed into killing Alaska's infamous "bridge to nowhere." This $400 million project slipped into a transportation bill became the symbol of Washington pork. It proposed to link Alaska's far southwest city of Ketchikan to its airport. In light of abysmal post-recession economic growth they thought it was too extravagant, too expensive. It was.

Since 2010 former Republican Senator Dr. Tom Coburn (2005-2015) published *Wastebook,* an annual tally of

government's most absurdly wasteful spending. He opens his 2014 book with a scathing assessment of Congress and the woeful state of government saying "leadership in our nation's capital is ever more distant, disconnected, and absent."

Sen. Coburn revealed that, "Congress actually forced federal agencies to waste billions of dollars for purely parochial, political purposes. Mississippi lawmakers, for example, attached a rider to a larger bill requiring NASA to build a $350 million launch pad tower, which was moth balled as soon as it was completed because the rockets it was designed to test were scrapped years ago. Likewise, when USDA attempted to close an unneeded sheep research station in Idaho costing nearly $2 million every year to operate, politicians in the region stepped in to keep it open. Washington politicians are more focused on their own political futures than the future of our country. And with no one watching over the vast bureaucracy, the problem again isn't just what Washington isn't doing, but what it is doing."[768]

As a result of a 2006 law co-sponsored by Dr. Coburn, the "Federal Funding Accountability and Transparency Act", a.k.a. "Google Your Government Act" citizens could track their tax dollars through the website www.usaspending.gov. At least they could until Dr. Coburn left office. Adam Andrzejewski then picked up the charge and founded American Transparency (www.openthebooks.com) and named Coburn honorary chairman. The goal of American Transparency is to put every dime of government spending—on all levels—online, in real time.

Because Dr. Coburn believed in term limits, he chose not to run in 2016. As a result, Americans lost valuable insight via this fiscal conservative and whistleblower. With his departure, the public lost a strong voice exposing government's unrestrained, outrageous spending.

In 2010 Congress banned earmarks, yet with Dr. Coburn's final edition of *Wastebook 2014*, it's clear wild spending is still rampant. The following are just a few examples of government waste. Some are so egregious it's enough to make your eyes bleed.

- $465 million for continued development of an obsolete fighter engine
- $15 million gift for Ireland
- $4.2 million for local weapons of mass destruction support team
- $3.8 million to save part of a baseball stadium from demolition... for the memories
- $1.9 million for water taxi service at Pleasure Beach, CT
- $951,500 for "green" street lights in Detroit
- $500,000 to maintain a WW1 statue... in France!
- $200,000 for a tattoo removal program in California
- $615,000 to help the University of California-Santa Cruz digitize its Grateful Dead memorabilia
- $1.5 million on a video game that teaches parents how to feed their kids vegetables
- $371,026 study to see if moms love dogs as much as their kids
- $202,000 for National Science Foundation study on why Wikipedia is sexist
- $387,000 on Swedish massages for rascally rabbits
- Pentagon to Spend $1 Billion to Destroy $16 Billion in Unneeded Ammunition
- $856,000 to test mountain lions skills on a treadmill
- $171,000 on study of gambling habits monkeys

- $307,524 on synchronized swimming for sea monkeys
- $50,000 USDA grant to process, package, and market "Poop Paks," plant fertilizer made from Alpaca manure
- $697,177 for a "painfully long, awkward" global warming musical, *The Great Immensity*
- $930 million on unnecessary printing costs
- $175 million on an unused monkey house (and other structures)
- $112 million on fraudulent tax reimbursements to prisoners
- $47.6 million for a streetcar system that runs the same rout as the subway system below it
- $15.68 million for an unprofitable shooting range
- $18.5 million for bus service for federal government employees. Many shuttles run empty rather than pick up workers from neighboring agencies, creating redundant routes.
- $2.9 million on a study of World of Warcraft and other computer games
- $2.5 million for a U.S. Census critically derided 30-second commercial that appeared during the Super Bowl
- $2 million for a study about posting pictures online
- $1.5 million for a laundry-folding robot
- $1 million for a study about baby names
- $150,000 to build "critter crossings" in Vermont
- $997,766 to enhance zoos in Arkansas, Illinois, Louisiana, Wisconsin, and Florida with poetry
- $124.3 million to "flush" security clearance investigations "like a dead goldfish"
- $331,000 study of spouses stabbing voodoo dolls when "hangry" (anger when hungry)
- $146 million for sports stadium subsidies
- $10,000 to watch grass grow in Florida
- $117,521 to chronicle Vermont's 1970s hippie movement
- $41,000 to boost morale at Penn State following former football coach Jerry Sandusky's conviction of sexually abusing ten boys
- $90 million to promote U.S. culture around the world including a nose flutist, or more accurately, a "snoutist"
- $1 billion to destroy $16 viable military-grade surplus ammunition
- $392,000 NASA study to see how humans will react to meeting space aliens
- $16 million to build road through Fresno, CA "ghost mall" to scare up business
- $1.25 million for a Grammy Museum in Cleveland, MS
- $202,291 FEMA rebuilds golf course instead of helping flood victims in Texas
- $1.4 million in guarantees to give Disney Polynesian Resort a makeover
- $15,000 to NASA to hunt for lost tomb of Genghis Khan
- $15 million to transform abandoned Pennsylvania mall into East Coast Hollywood
- $35 million on unused Department of Homeland Security (DHS) vehicles
- $80 million to the Department of Defense to build a real-life "Iron Man" suit
- $95,000 for Drug Enforcement Administration (DEA) museum
- $7.6 million for unused Virgin Island ferries
- $5 million airport tree-trimming project morphs into 27-hole golf course renovation in Iowa
- $1.2+ million for an airport to nowhere in New York
- $30,000 for a NASA study to predict the collapse of civilization
- $1.97 million to create a new communication network for fossil enthusiasts and professionals
- $180,000 for two dozen teachers to travel to Germany for lessons in Bach and Baroque dancing
- $160,000 that was supposed to go to reduce road crashes used to restore non-working lighthouses
- $200,000 Gateway to the Blues" museum funded over deteriorating bridges
- $533,376 for study explaining the science of meditation
- $5 million for students at the University of Tennessee to dress up as fruits and vegetables to promote healthy eating
- $2 million for USDA contest to build wooden skyscraper
- $34 million on project to convince Afghans to grow soybeans they won't eat
- $965,000 for an unused, unneeded ice house in Louisiana
- $3 billion in food stamps traded for cash and drugs
- $9 million, DOD pays 16 times the going price for helicopter parts
- $468 million, fleet of 20 refurbished Italian planes intended to be backbone of Afghanistan's Air Force scrapped due to a barrage of problems, recouped only $32,000

- $1 million toward the Eisenhower Memorial, burning through cash paid commissions to Frank Gehry's architecture firm at $16.4 million, not counting an additional $13.3 million "to the multiple parties responsible for managing the design process and providing administrative support." The question on everyone's mind uttered by Justin Shubow, president of the National Civic Art Society is, "Everyone wants to know, where is the money going?"[769]
- $500,000 for butterfly farm in Oklahoma
- $4.2 billion on bogus tax returns
- $1,523,133 to study who attends science festivals
- $544,338 spent by the Dept. of Justice to buy premium LinkedIn account to promote jobs during the hiring freeze (and yes, Obama replaced formerly high-paying with minimum wage jobs. No wonder people are lobbying for $15/hr. to flip burgers.)
- $682,570 to study shrimp on a treadmill

These are only a few ridiculous expenditures cataloged by CAGW and Senator Coburn. To get the full scope, please read their annual publications and check out the American Transparency website. This author is positive that nearly anyone, any American could run the government budget more efficiently, cut waste and streamline agencies where this Country actually operated in the black instead of an unending avalanche of red ink. Literally hundreds of billions, no *trillions*, could have been saved in lieu of these silly projects. Like ObamaCare, had these excess expenditures been refunded to us, the taxpayer, every American would own their home outright and be debt free. The flunkies elected to serve in the White House and suck from the pork barrel's teat would actually have to find work that is productive.

Instead, a bloated government, no oversight and a bought Congress put us on a downward spiral of extreme and crushing debt. Who in government, any more, is out there working, being a voice the people instead of lining their own pockets and focusing on their own reelection? It's likely only new senators and Congressional representatives that haven't yet been enticed, paid for and indoctrinated.

OBAMACARE WITHOUT CONSENT

This logo is laughable to all Americans. The "Patient Protection and Affordable Care Act", a.k.a. ObamaCare was passed without people knowing what was in it and shoved down our throats. There was no such thing as "choice." The most shocking in-your-face statement on ObamaCare was uttered in March 2010 by then Speaker of the House, Nancy Pelosi, "We have to pass the bill so that you can find out what is in it..."[770] Never before had America operated like this. Congress, for the most part, passed this 2,700-page behemoth without even thumbing

through it, let alone having read it. That was the opening volley. In three years, ObamaCare added over 20,000 pages of regulations making a print out 7'3" high. Those figures were from 2013. There's no telling how much more it has mushroomed in the years following.

Photo: ObamaCare bill and regulations stacked 7'3" high, courtesy of Senator Mitch McConnell's (R-KY) Twitter account, which he described as a #RedTapeTower. He wrote. "Just take a look at this giant stack: one day's worth of ObamaCare regulations. 828 pages in one day. Overall, there are nearly 20,000 pages – with many, many more to come. This is the owner's manual for the health care law that's supposed to make things better. Are you kidding? This law is a disaster waiting to happen. ObamaCare is just too expensive, and it's not working the way Washington Democrats promised. That's why ObamaCare needs to be repealed. And that's why I will continue to push for its repeal."[771]

The Obama administration refused to disclose healthcare hikes for 2015 until after the November election. Regarding this secrecy Tim Phillips, president of free-market Americans for Prosperity stated, "This is more than just a glitch. The administration's decision to withhold the costs of this law until after Election Day is just more proof that ObamaCare is a bad deal for

Americans."[772] With this election in the rear view mirror, it's reported that ObamaCare premiums will soar another 20.3% on average instead of the 7.5% claimed by federal officials. Obama's administration only calculated cost raises for the Silver program ignoring data for the Bronze, Gold and Platinum plans.[773] That put a whole other shine on it.

So how cost-effective and money savings was the promised ObamaCare? Zip. Zero. Nada. Just the reverse and Americans were sold another pile of lies. Comparing premiums in 2013 before its implementation to those afterwards in 2014, some premiums rose an eye-popping 78%.[774] Not only were many Americans staggered from sticker shock, at least 6.3 million people lost their coverage under newly imposed ObamaCare. It underscored the lie of his now infamous promise of "If you like your health care plan, you can keep it". His statement earned Politifact's 2013 "Lie of the Year", which is still being broken with the potential to be worse than before.[775] Why people are so angry can be summed up quite easily. ObamaCare plans cost more and cover less. He had promised middle incomes families their taxes wouldn't go up "one single dime" from his healthcare plan. Yet, 21 associated taxes will extract $1 trillion over a decade.[776]

Not to beat a dead horse, but the government's website for Obama's health care has cost taxpayers $2.1 BILLION so far. How inadequate, how ignorant do you have to be to squander this amount of money, never mind that for the first year after its rollout, it was an unusable fiasco? Truly, most people can self-teach html coding and put together a comprehensive website for hundreds of millions less. It was truly astonishing. No words. It reveals the ongoing inadequacies and dead brain people in government and those they choose to hire.

Last and certainly not the least of it, President Obama's healthcare system that was supposed to save so much money is projected to add $6.2 trillion to the national deficit.[777] Following are additional lies, er, uh, "factual failings" stated by Mr. Obama on his healthcare legacy. Mr. Obama's Affordable Care Act has been anything but. For example, the President promised one thing and delivered another.

No wonder during his last year in office, he cast about for another legacy.

The Truth About ObamaCare

PROMISED	DELIVERED
Obama: "If you like your health care plan, you'll be able to keep your health care plan, period."[778]	At least 6.3 million Americans lost their coverage due to ObamaCare.[779]
Obama: "If you like your doctor, you will be able to keep your doctor."[780]	Many Americans couldn't keep their current doctor without paying extra.[781] [782]
Obama: "In an Obama administration, we'll lower premiums by up to $2,500 for a typical family per year."[783]	Premiums for people purchasing coverage in the individual market have significantly increased in a majority of states –many by over 100%.[784]
Obama: "For the 85% and 90% of Americans who already have health insurance, this thing's already happened. And their only impact is that their insurance is stronger, better and more secure than it was before. Full stop. That's it. They don't have to worry about anything else."[785]	ObamaCare mandates DO increase the cost of coverage. Federal regulations written in 2010 assumed "that the increases in insurance benefits will be directly passed on to the consumer in the form of higher premiums. These assumptions bias the estimates of premium changes upward."[786] [787]
Obama: "Under my plan, no family making less than $250,000 a year will see any form of tax increase."[788]	ObamaCare contains 21 separate tax hikes, fees, and penalties, many of which heavily impact the middle class. Altogether, they will amass over $1 trillion in new revenue over a 10-year period. Among the taxes that will hit the middle class are the individual mandate tax, the medical device tax, and new penalties and limits on health savings accounts and flexible spending accounts.[789]
Obama: "I will not sign a plan that adds one dime to our deficits – either now or in the future."[790]	ObamaCare's new spending is unsustainable. It was passed into law relying on a wide variety of unrealistic budget projections. A report released February 26, 2013 by the Government Accountability Office shows it will add at least $6.2 *trillion* to the national deficit.[791]
Obama: "Whatever ideas exist in terms of bending the cost curve and starting to reduce	A report from Richard S. Foster, the chief actuary for the Centers for Medicare and Medicaid Services (CMS) – a nonpolitical civil

The Truth About ObamaCare	
PROMISED	**DELIVERED**
costs for families, businesses, and government, those elements are in this bill."[792]	service employee – estimates the total national health expenditures will increase by $234 billion between 2010 and 2019.[793]
Obama: "I will protect Medicare."[794]	ObamaCare cut Medicare spending making unprecedented and unrealistic payment reductions to Medicare providers and Medicare Advantage plans to finance new spending in the law. The cuts amount to $716 billion from 2013 to 2022, which will significantly impact seniors' ability to access care.[795]
Obama: "I will sign a universal health care bill into law by the end of my first term as president that will cover every American."[796]	The nonpartisan Congressional Budget Office and Joint Committee on Taxation project there will still be 31 million uninsured adults in America by 2025, demonstrating that this law would create universal coverage was incorrect.[797]
Obama: "So this law means more choice, more competition, lower costs for millions of Americans."[798]	In most states, the number of insurers competing in the state's exchange is less than the number of carriers that previously sold individual market policies. At the local level, for 27% of the nation's counties, exchange enrollees will have a choice of plans from only two insurers. In 6% of counties, consumers will have no choice with only one carrier offering coverage in the exchange.[799]

EXTREME NERVE

The U.S. Treasury is kind enough to allow us to help pay down debt they incurred, which is now *our* debt and about $160,000 per taxpayer. This is after rampaging through our wallets via burdensome taxes. If you feel so inclined you can "gift" the Fed in any amount by credit or debit card, PayPal, checking account, or savings account. They want to make it easy for you. That's really rich. Amazingly they managed to collect about $4 million in 2015 from hardworking taxpayers. That's a .000021% drop in an ocean of $19 trillion red ink. Yes, they need some more taxpayer money to waste.

Chink 2: Runaway Illegal Immigration

There is plenty of blame in both political parties. Republicans want to please big donors who press for cheap labor and Democrats want guaranteed voters. Both are rolling out the welcome mat much to the detriment of America.

AMNESTIES BY ADMINISTRATION		
PRESIDENT	**YEAR**	**HOW MANY GIVEN A FREE PASS**
Ronald Reagan	1986	Blanket amnesty for 2.7 million, supposedly a one time only deal event
George H.W. Bush	1989	Amnesty for 1.5 million family members
Bill Clinton	1994	Rolling amnesty for 578,000
Bill Clinton	1997	Extension of the rolling amnesty created in 1994
Bill Clinton	1997	Amnesty for close to 1 million from Central America
Bill Clinton	1998	Amnesty for 125,000 from Haiti
Bill Clinton	2000	Amnesty for 400,000 who claim they should have been amnestied in 1986
Bill Clinton	2000	Amnesty for an estimated 900,000
Barack Obama *	2015	Amnesty for an estimated 5 million

*NOTE: Congress passed all of these amnesties except Mr. Obama's, which was accomplished through Executive Action on November 20, 2014. E.A.s are not a formal executive order, but it was a simple implementation of a series of DHS memos usually employed when it involves something controversial.

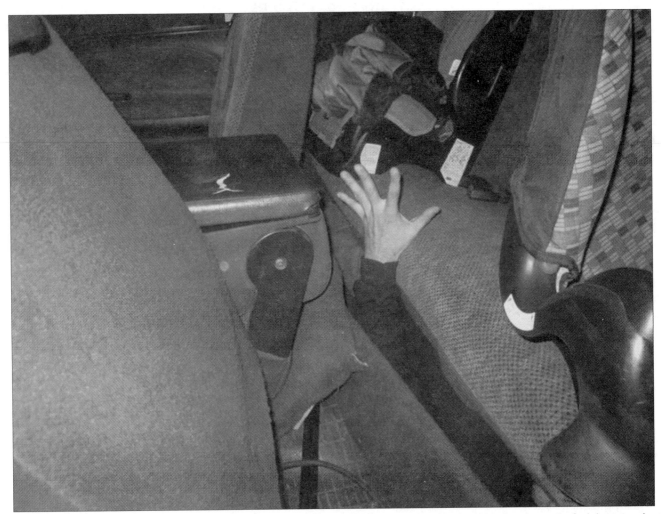

Photo: U.S. Customs and Border Protection officers find a hidden man wedged under back seat of pickup truck at Otay Mesa Border checkpoint. (Courtesy U.S. Customs and Border Protection)

In May 2015, Border Patrol agents saw a spike in the number of people hiding in vehicles trying to sneak through highway checkpoints. Yesenia Lopez, a U.S. Border Patrol agent in the El Paso area said, "It [is] something that we see that's very dangerous."[800] People are hiding in trunks and braver ones are crammed under seats and behind fake dashboards or stashed like animals into 18-wheelers. Some die in the process though coyotes still collect their fees.

Why wouldn't undocumented migrants want to come to the U.S. with all of the benefits offered them? Some freebies are obtained just by being an illegal immigrant, others by using forged documents. Benefits they can receive include Social Security, Medicare, driver's licenses in some states, free education K-12, in-state college tuition, grants, professional accreditations, loans, WIC (federal food assistance for **W**omen, **I**nfants and **C**hildren), disability, public housing, food stamps, unemployment benefits, and tax credits from state and federal agencies. Through President Obama's amnesty program Illegal immigrants who are given work permits and Social Security Numbers could get up to $9,182 – in cash benefits from the federal government – every year.

PINGING A FALSE NARRATIVE

Repeatedly Mr. Obama defended the mighty influx illegal immigrants saying they help the economy by bringing jobs. That is just not so. The educated and skilled are staying in Mexico and those needing a handout look north to America.

The New York Times carried an enlightening piece in 2013 about the rise of Mexico's new middle class.[801] It tells the story of Ivan Zamora, then 23, who graduated from a brand new university in Guanajuato, which is about dead center in Mexico. Zamora says that a decade ago he might have already left for the United States, but that opportunities are opening in his country so he wants to stay.

After graduation Zamora took an internship at one of the many multinational companies close to the university campus and was soon hired by Volkswagen. With the nice salary he's earning, Zamora is helping his sister pursue her dream of studying marine biology.

Another man, Mauricio Martinez, 29, works as an engineer in Guanajuato at the Italian tiremaker *Pirelli*. He makes good money and his job afforded him credit so his wife could start her own gourmet salad shop business. Both drive to work (yes, that *is* a luxury in Mexico), just purchased a 3-bedroom townhouse in a brand new development, enjoy their tiny yard and a new flat screen TV.

The key is education. While businesses are booming and moving to Mexico, the article reveals that the country is encountering problems finding people educated enough to work these careers. So while the intelligent and educated are staying put, making a decent life, the others look to America.

The low end of the educational scale paves the wave for a life of crime, black market businesses and excruciating poverty.

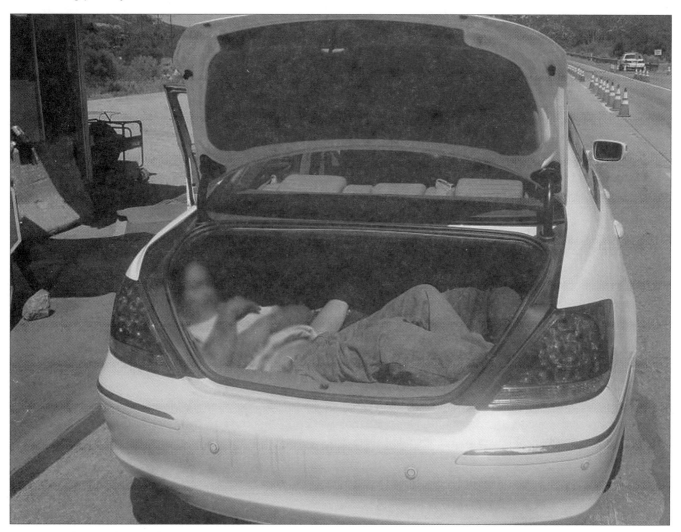

Photo: On April 13, 2014, U.S. Border Patrol agents arrest a 41-year-old man for human smuggling at the I-8 San Diego Sector checkpoint. Agents discovered two men locked in the trunk of a 2005 Acura RL sedan and sweating profusely. This is but one of hundreds of thousands of coyote efforts to bring across illegals and terrorists into America. (Courtesy U.S. Customs and Border Protection)

DOING WHAT'S NECESSARY TO SURVIVE

This author has visited Mexico many times. It is a lovely exquisite country with blindingly beautiful white beaches and clear turquoise water. The people were always friendly, welcoming. My husband and I on one visit in the 1990s ventured off into the "real" Mexico. We drove up and down crazily winding roads with no signs warning of impending danger. They were obviously needed as crashed cars were left to rust and disintegrate in ditches.

People were too poor to haul them off, let alone have them repaired. Where cars "died" there they stayed. We drove into the desert on what could barely be described as a wide path, let alone a road, no grass in sight, no homes. Just endless crummy land and cactus.

We came upon a lovely couple. She was a large squat woman, grey hair pinned in a bun, wearing a faded, formerly bright dress to cover her girth. Her husband was equally short, maybe about 5'4", shirt hanging outside faded trousers and skinny as a pole. Pablo was grizzled and darkened by long years working in the unrelenting sun. They welcomed us by using hand signs and with a smattering of Spanglish, we managed to communicate just fine.

What rocked us both was their home. They were so poor that they couldn't complete the building. Instead, three sides of a cinder block structure stood about six feet high, waiting for a roof and a front-facing wall. For all intents, they were still out in the elements and Rosa extended her hand in a near-toothless smile. Welcoming us to their folding chairs – a source of pride to offer seating.

Eva

The Washington Post tells the story of Eva Ortiz[802] who lives about 4½ hours southeast of Guanajuato in Chalco. She was orphaned as an infant, a maid at 10, raped at 14 and a mother at 15. Ortiz never saw the inside of a classroom. Not once. She began selling bootleg VHS tapes of Disney cartoons for a buck each.

Over the years both drug cartels and the Mexican federal police paid her visits. Since cartels control the majority of the black market DVD business they weren't happy about her enterprise. Three armed thugs broke into her house and held her daughter at gunpoint until Eva withdrew her life savings from the bank. She had counted on that money to take her and her family to a safer neighborhood.

Three times in 2012, the Federales raided her business and made off with thousands of dollars worth of her merchandise. Despite those setbacks and zero education, Ortiz was eventually able to afford a 3-year-old Chevy SUV and a cement-block home for her and her four daughters.

DOING THE WORK AMERICANS WON'T? NOT SO.

The millions of Mexicans that come here illegally aren't bringing jobs or skills nor are they coming here to do the work that Americans won't. They just do it for cheaper dollars or off-book.

According to Bureau of Labor Statistics,[803] Americans fill 66% – 78% of all unskilled positions in food prep and serving; cleaning and maintenance; construction, and assembly line jobs. Illegal immigrant workers fill the rest. Additionally, the non-partisan, non-profit Center for Immigration Studies finds that since President Obama took office, 67% of employment "growth" went to immigrants both legal and illegal, not to Americans.[804] That translates to jobs with lower pay, part time hours and no benefits.

Bottom line, the U.S. has an illegal immigration problem that draws the poorest, the uneducated, drug cartels, the desperate and coyotes (human smugglers). It's not attracting the best of the best and when that doesn't happen, an entire nation can be dragged down to the lowest common denominator.

AMERICA 1892: GIVE ME YOUR HUDDLED MASSES, NOT THE DISEASED, THE CRAZY, THE LAWBREAKERS

Lobbyists and groups promoting illegal and legal immigration often quote Emma Lazarus' 1883 poem *The New Colossus,*

> Give me your tired, your poor,
> Your huddled masses yearning to breathe free,
> The wretched refuse of your teeming shore.
> Send these, the homeless, tempest-tossed, to me:
> I lift my lamp beside the golden door.

The verse said nothing about welcoming the diseased, the lazy, the crazy and the felon. This was the era when America needed warm and able bodies. Can you imagine America with just 6% of the population it has today? The Country wanted people that were *willing to assimilate,* become Americans yet share the best their culture, skills and talent had to offer. Now those that come often wish not to assimilate and want their culture to replace ours. Instead of melding in, little oases of subcultures remain mostly isolated, choosing not to learn English, which further isolates them. When 350 languages are spoken within a nation, it fractures a country, not unifies it.

In a May 2015 video filmmaker Ami Horowitz went to a Somali neighborhood in Minneapolis, Minnesota and asked Muslims about Sharia law and life in America. When asked if they preferred to live under American law or Sharia law, their answer wasn't surprising. All anted Sharia, even the women. "Sharia law," said one man in sunglasses. Another man holding coffee seconded the sentiment: "I'm a Muslim, I prefer Sharia law." Another added: "Sharia law, yes." A fourth said, "Sharia, of course if you're Muslim, yeah." They all said it was OK to kill anyone who insulted the prophet Muhammad that it was easy to be Muslim in America, but all would rather live in a Muslim country. "I want to live in a Muslim country with my people." One man went so far as to say, "I'm not Americanized. I just speak fluent. I'm articulate, you know what I mean? As far as my culture, my preferences and everything, it's still Somali."[805]

People that came through Ellis Island in 1892 searching for The Promised Land had to be declared mentally and physically fit. Immigrants often stood for hours in the elements waiting to be processed. After registering, doctors scanned each immigrant briefly in what was termed "six-second physicals". Every person was assessed. An "H" marked on their clothing indicated a possible heart condition while "LCD" meant Loathsome Contagious Disease, an "X" indicated mental problems, an "L" for lameness and so on. Unless they had someone already in America willing to pay for their treatment – and this didn't mean the taxpayer – they were turned away, which applied to only 2%.[806] Back then there were immigration *standards*. Now we let in every Tom, Dick and Harry, legal and illegal, and this Country now has a resurging problem with formerly eradicated diseases like TB, Dengue Fever, Swine Flu[807] and Chicken Pox[808].

For whatever reason, officials are "dramatically" downplaying the issue. Dr. Elizabeth Lee Vliet, experienced physician and nationally recognized speaker said, "Many people are trying to diminish the seriousness of this. They say, 'We have these diseases in the U.S.' Well yes, we do, but they've been well controlled, we have good hygiene, and most of our parents keep children home when they're sick."[809]

"So far a slew of sicknesses have been brought into the U.S. by the recent tidal wave of illegal immigrants. [In] an outbreak of scabies in one housing facility for unaccompanied border minors – the infestation was contracted by numerous Border Patrol agents. Other additional illnesses have also been noted. We are starting to see chicken pox, MRSA staph infections, we are starting to see different viruses," said Rio Grande Valley Border Patrol agent Chris Cabrera.[810]

"Once the flu bug, TB, or any infectious disease is released – once they are brought across the border–they're just going to keep infecting more people. One person can infect a thousand people, and then that thousand can infect thousands more. There is an exponential increase. It's a very real risk," Vliet warned. "It could get out of hand very quickly; but since these are common disease that people have heard of, the risk isn't necessarily taken seriously."

The doctor concluded, "First and foremost we need to enforce immigration laws. The migrants should be quarantined until we can determine what they have. This is a national security risk, it is a public health risk, and it is going to overwhelm the healthcare system for U.S. citizens."[811]

Worse, illegals that consider themselves "entitled" to America's aid, suck dry the Country's annual entitlement budget to the tune of HALF of the annual financial plan. In 2015 shockingly HALF of the nearly $4 **trillion** budget went to "entitlements".

Immigration Services collected manifests from incoming ships, which contained passenger names as well as answers to important questions. An inspector asked each passenger about potential destinations and job prospects. Freeloaders weren't appreciated. If they failed the medical or immigration inspection, they were placed in detention until a hearing was scheduled in front of the Board of Special Inquiry, made up of inspectors. Only about 10% of immigrants underwent hearings about their health, economic conditions and beliefs. Even then exclusion was often reversed if someone posted bond or an aid society took responsibility for that immigrant. Though only about 2% of immigrants were deported on medical or economic grounds, at least the Country had a handle and procedure for those who wanted to come here. When they passed these light tests and inspections, immigrants had to pay 50¢ or less than $17 in today's money. This contributed to funding the Office of Immigration for other immigrants seeking a new life.

In the 1600s, there was no political or business agenda for admitting immigrants. They sought a better economic life, not looking for a handout, wanting religious freedom – not freedom *from* religion many now advocate. Democrats weren't looking for guaranteed voters pumping the liberal agenda and Republicans weren't ignoring borders in favor of cheap labor. Immigrants had to come to America, legally, not sneaking through the borders.

Photo: Deyo House in New Paltz, New York. The story of Christian Deyo's journey from Europe to the rugged frontier of the New World has always given Mary Etta Schneider a sense of pride and a belief that anything is possible. Like other Deyo descendants, Schneider refers to him as grandpere (grandfather), and like those who know American history, he is an elder statesman of New Paltz. Deyo was one of 12 Huguenots who met with the Esopus Indians in 1677 and bought 40,000 acres stretching from the Shawangunk Mountains to the Hudson River. In exchange, the Esopus tribe was given farming tools, clothing, blankets, wine, horses, tobacco and gunpowder. Both the settlers and the Esopus signed the land deed. A fair deal. The hearty band of French Protestants (and Belgian Walloons) set sail for the New World to escape religious persecution. To this day, their settlement on the east bank of the Wallkill River remains intact and open as Historic Huguenot Street to visitors from all over the world. Schneider said: "When you think of these tiny ships they came on into the wilderness, it is striking. My mom, Marian Deyo, instilled in me early on that anything is possible, especially when I think of what my ancestors did to get here, so it has helped to form a big part of who I am."[812]

NOTE: This author's family immigrated in 1685 and her husband's ancestors arrived in 1654 from Ireland, France and Germany. America was *very* primitive in those days. It's hard to imagine land not covered in houses and concrete, with trees filling half the country, and wild grasses and buffalo herds populating the rest. Those ancestors like many other stalwarts paved the way for other Americans. They must have been awestruck when traveling west by covered wagon and first laying eyes on the Rocky Mountains. Who knew what lie on the other side? Did it fall off into the ocean? No roads or tunnels existed to make travel easier. How their rickety wagons ever made it over the rocks, ravines and high altitudes remain a mystery and a testament to their drive and fortitude.

Her husband's family, Deyo, has the oldest home still standing on the oldest street in America in New Paltz, New York. Stan's father's side of the family, Solomon Lefevre Deyo, was the chief engineer of the Interboro Rapid Transit Subway System. Lines 1, 2, 3, 4, 6 and 9 still exist today as part of New York City's mass transit. The author's family was primarily writers, doctors, merchants, teachers and law enforcement. They all came here with hopes, dreams and goals, and hard-work ethics.

Can this be said of all illegals now breaking through our borders and expecting retribution for America supposedly "stealing" Mexico? Correction of misconception: The United States purchased the Spanish Possessions in 1848 for $15 million. That was the equivalent of three quarters of a billion dollars today. Not stole, *bought*. Then population was about 20 million not 320 million. Real estate was cheap and land could be homesteaded for free. Water was clean, gold and silver was theirs for the taking if you worked hard and sacrificed nearly everything.

Now we have a lot of takers, not all, but way too many. Much of this is the fault of government who act as enablers encouraging people to rely on entitlements and rewarding generational welfare recipients. In the 1600s, there was no political or business agenda for admitting immigrants. They sought a better life economically, but didn't look for a handout, wanting religious freedom – not freedom *from* religion many now advocate. Democrats weren't looking for guaranteed voters pumping the liberal agenda and Republicans weren't ignoring borders in favor of cheap labor. Immigrants had to come to America, legally, not sneaking through the borders.

Border Patrol Hog-Tied While DHS Lies

U.S. Border Patrol estimates that 3 out of every 4 illegal aliens that cross the border evade apprehension.[813] Agent Chris Cabrera, VP of the National Border Patrol Council Local 3307, a union for border agents testified before the Senate Homeland Security and Government Affairs Committee in March 2015. He said, "Ask any line Agent in the field and he or she will tell you that at best we apprehend 35-40% of the illegal immigrants attempting to cross. This number is even lower for drug smugglers who are much more adept at eluding capture." He also stated that agents who report groups of more than 20 illegals are punished. Cabrera said agents who report these groups get paybacks and are removed from the field and assigned processing jobs or reassigned to sectors where fewer illegal immigrants come across.

Cabrera stated, "I want to address whether or not the border is secure. If you ask this question of the Department of Homeland Security (DHS) or senior management at Customs and Border Protection (CBP), they will tell you the border is secure." [During a Senate hearing on immigration reform, then Homeland Security Secretary Janet Napolitano insisted that U.S. borders have 'never been stronger.'][814] Cabrera continued, "They may even point to statistics and metrics showing that the Border Patrol is 75 percent effective in apprehending illegal immigrants and drug smugglers. However, I want to be crystal clear – *the border is **not** secure*. How can this enormous gap exist between what the DHS tells you here in Washington and what our Agents know to be the truth in the field? Frankly, it is how you manipulate the statistics."[815]

The goal of tamping down the impact and number of illegals pushing through our borders is underscored by the near absence of their photos on the Border Patrol's Flicker and CBP sites. They have hundreds of images posted focusing on drug seizures, memorials to fallen agents, participation in 5K runs, police week valor ceremonies, Asian American heritage month, seizures of counterfeit $100 bills, game jerseys, golf equipment and guitars; seizures of hazardous toy dolls, candlelight vigils, honor guard competition, signing ceremonies of trade agreements with Kenya and Uruguay, agriculture inspection, their Tethered Aerostat Radar System and electronic devices, Super Bowl security, and a helicopter retirement ceremony.

Only 8 photos were posted having anything to do with illegal immigrants. Only photos of a *secure* border fence were seen. None showing where fences were either non-existent, of using barely there barbed wired or fences completely broken down. No pictures were available of the thousands of illegals marching through the deserts. They exist. Lots of them. For years mainstream news outlets have published these photos illustrating their articles. Websites like Secure Border Intel, Desert Invasion, Desert Invasion-U.S., American Patrol, Americans for Legal Immigration PAC and IllegalAliens.US have no trouble photo-documenting illegals streaming across the southern border.

Instead the U.S. Border Patrol, likely under the direction of Homeland Security, concentrates on photos of ceremonies and drug interdiction. Based on the literal tons of dope smuggled into America every year, interception is laughable. This is not to disparage hardworking Border Patrol agents, but to shine a light on Homeland Security's false narrative.

VULNERABLE

In 2010, Border Patrol Agent Jesus Mesa was surrounded and pummeled by four rock throwers who were illegally trying to cross the border through an opening in the fence. Some of the rocks, as shown on Breitbart's news site,[816] were seven inches long. This is a far cry from the false narrative that it's "kids throwing pebbles". These attacks most often come in remote areas where a lone agent may be 1½-hours away from backup. Compounding matters, due to remote locations their radios don't work because the necessary infrastructure is missing.

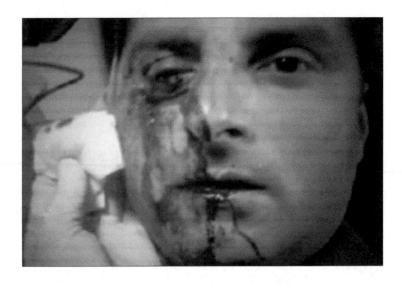

Photo: Border Patrol Agent Jesus Mesa after would-be borders jumpers pound him with rocks.

Agent Brian Terry

For years mountaintop spotters on the U.S. side have given America's Border Patrol headaches. Though agents know these criminals are present, their hands are tied by rules of engagement, which dictate they must use non-lethal *bean bags* first for defense. In March 2014, Border Patrol Chief Michael Fisher issued a directive instructing his agents to retreat when illegals threw rocks and other objects at them, and to avoid blocking drug smugglers' vehicles by stepping away.[817] This was a big heads up to an agenda.

Such one-sided means of defense got Border Patrol agent Brian Terry killed in December 2010 proving that bean bags don't work against AK47s. Under a 4-year gag order, what really happened that day wasn't made public until February 2014. Terry's team was on a hill above a ravine when a ground sensor went off alerting them to approaching smugglers. As instructed they yelled "Police" in Spanish and the smugglers turned and fired.

"Fellow agent Gabriel Fragoza testified in court. 'I saw some members of the group point their weapons at us. Agent Castano and I deployed less lethal bean bag rounds as the individuals began to shoot at us. I saw muzzle flashes coming from the individuals, then heard Agent Terry say *"I'm hit! I'm hit! I can't feel my legs."*

"Agent William Castano gave a similar account, saying, 'I heard shooting which was coming from the wash. I heard Agent Terry say, *"I'm hit."* I went to Agent Terry to administer first aid. At this time, he said, *"I can't feel my legs. I'm paralyzed."* Agent Terry soon lost consciousness and died at the scene.'"[818]

Chopper Downed

In June 2015, a U.S. Border patrol helicopter operating in U.S. airspace was fired on five times by someone or multiple people on the Mexican side of the border. The area patrolled, near the Rio Grande in Laredo, Texas, is notorious for drug smuggling and illegal immigrant crossings. Of the five rounds fired, the chopper took two and was forced to make an emergency landing in Texas. As of this writing, searches continue on both sides of the border for the perpetrators.[819]

HOMELAND SECURITY WORKING *AGAINST* BORDER PATROL

In January 2015, news reporting agency, Breitbart obtained leaked internal training documents from a U.S. Customs and Border Protection (CBP) agent. It revealed CBP agents are receiving guidelines instructing them that the vast majority of illegal immigrants coming to and those already in America are off limits to federal agents. They are basically immune to detention and deportation. Every agent now has to sign a paper acknowledging he has received this training. Don't detain anyone unless they are a direct threat.

Homeland Security Secretary Jeh Johnson sent out a memo indicating agents should only arrest someone *they directly see* cross the border, if they are wanted by the police or are convicted felons, have an extensive or violent criminal history, or pose a national security or public safety threat. To detain the majority coming through requires specific approval from leadership.

> The source clarified this and said, "Nothing says don't arrest, but it clearly says don't waste your time because the alien will not be put into detention, sent back or deported. There is literally no reason to arrest an illegal alien because they are specifically telling Border Patrol there will be no consequence for the illegal alien. It is a waste of time and resources to arrest someone who is off limits for detainment or deportation and the documents make that fact clear. Border Patrol agents are now being trained to be social workers, not law enforcement."

This is not how it was before. Border Patrol used to arrest, process, and turn the illegal alien over to Immigration and Customs Enforcement (ICE) and the courts. Under this new program, the majority of illegal aliens will be released directly from the Border Patrol with no appointments or expectation that they ever have to show up for a hearing.

Before these changes, all illegal aliens arrested by Border Patrol were required to enter the deportation system where they would be scheduled for a deportation hearing at a future date. Under this new system, the illegal aliens are not even required to show up for a hearing ever. Not only are we releasing these people with no hearings scheduled, no notice to appear, but the DHS [Department of Homeland Security] is forcing Border Patrol to prepare the initial paperwork for the illegal aliens' work permits." The source added, "Americans really need to think about the terrorism-related implications of this. Illegal aliens who are suspected of having terrorism ties, but not convicted, could be permitted to stay in the country.[820]

Image: While the Obama administration continues to insist that our borders are more secure than ever and that they are deporting more illegals than ever. On December 22, 2015, Homeland Security put out a false press release saying, "The number of convicted criminals removed from the interior continued to increase…"[821]

One way government has "massaged" the figures to make the number of deported illegal aliens look falsely better is by what they now count as a deportation or removal. Immigration and Customs Enforcement (ICE) used to include only those that were actually IN the U.S. and then deported. Now ICE counts those even turned away at the border as deportations. This makes

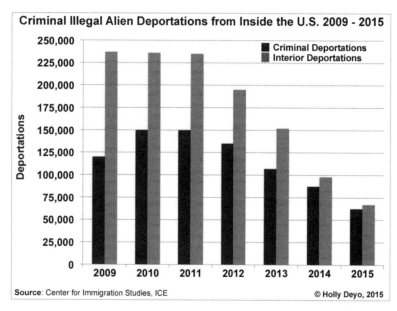

deportation numbers look erroneously high compared to previous administrations. In the same Senate hearing described in the next paragraph, Senator Jeff Sessions explained the "apples and oranges" discrepancy. "What did happen is that ICE, when their numbers began to plummet, started counting border removals as part of their removals [deportations]. It was a misrepresentation – and deliberate – to hide the weakness that was occurring."822 It was also revealed in this hearing that ICE estimates about 2 million illegal alien criminals are now living in the U.S. Their crimes aren't for traffic tickets or failing to appear before a deportation. They are serious criminal offenses including rape, murder, attempted murder, child abuse, drug trafficking and aggravated assault.

In testimony before a December 2015 Senate Judiciary Committee Jessica Vaughan, Director of Policy Studies for the Center for Immigration Studies gave this statement: "These abysmal deportation numbers are the result of deliberate policy choices made by President Obama to dismantle immigration enforcement, all the while telling Congress and the public that he was accomplishing "record" deportations. This willful neglect has imposed enormous costs on American communities. In addition to the distorted labor markets and higher tax bills for social welfare benefits that result from uncontrolled illegal immigration, the Obama administration's anti-enforcement policies represent a threat to public safety from criminal aliens that ICE officers are told to release instead of detain and remove. The administration's mandate that ICE focus only on the 'worst of the worst' convicted criminal aliens means that too many of 'the worst' deportable criminal aliens are still at large in our communities. We are likely to see a further drop in deportations in the coming year, following the implementation of the administration's Priority Enforcement Program. Known as PEP, this program further limits ICE officers, requiring them to ignore prior deportees and other deportable aliens who were formerly priorities, and explicitly allows state and local governments to obstruct enforcement with sanctuary policies."823

No wonder the Border Patrol is disheartened. They are, in essence, being sent on a fool's mission. Three decades ago, in a business where this author worked, a Vietnam vet came in frequently. Since there were stretches of down time, he'd sit and chat. As time progressed, we became friends and he shared things that he saw and experienced in Nam.

Mike gave some pretty astounding accounts during those conversations. Some were about times they made arduous trips up hills or through jungles and when in position, with "Charlie" in sight, were given "stand down" orders. Don't engage. Don't shoot. This happened repeatedly, not once or twice. Mike shared that one of his biggest emotions after the war was anger. A while into his tour of duty, he realized there were other agendas at play besides winning. Mike came home, spit on for doing a job he didn't want to do, in a place he didn't want to be – and gave his right leg in the process. It was at that point this author realized things aren't always what they seem, nor were governments. So like Vietnam, this nonsense of free passes for illegal aliens through the border has a purpose and not one with a good ending.

NOW LET'S DEFUND THEM

It was bad enough when President Obama implemented his catch and release policy, but now he wants to cut border protection funding. Department of Homeland Security will propose to Congress to cut $110 million from Immigration and Custom Enforcement's budget and give it to other agencies that have nothing to do with protecting our borders. DHS' reasoning runs something like this according to an ICE insider. 'Well, ICE, you're not using all of your budget, and, it's coming from bed and deportation money, because you can't arrest people and you can't detain people. So it doesn't makes sense that you're not using your budget, so we are going to take it away from you and give it to other divisions of homeland security.'"[824]

One source on Capitol Hill stated, "ICE has been getting decimated. All the money goes to border patrol because they can't deport people, while ICE – who actually are in charge of deportations – are handcuffed, silenced and stifled. This is how we get flooded with illegal immigrants: catch-and-release."[825]

Hand-in-hand with catch-and release is the policy of don't catch them in the first place. Less than 1% of more than 480,000 immigrants who overstayed their visas were deported in 2015. Ever since 2009 there's been a steady decline in the deportations of overstays. At most, Immigration deported only 2.6% in any year as of 2009, so in round numbers, America "inherited" another 3.3 million Mexicans in seven years. This only applies to people who came on visas for work or pleasure or through the Visa Waiver Program. It does not include other visa categories, like Mexican nationals who use Border Crossing Cards[826] so this 3.3 million figure is likely even higher. Add this to the border jumpers and the numbers skyrocket.

THE SAGA OF COMPEAN AND RAMOS

Before Brian Terry came Compean and Ramos. In February 2005 the two are on routine patrol in Fabens, Texas, a suburb of El Paso along the Tex-Mex border. Jose Compean notices a border breach and radios it in. They give chase and the border breaker, Osvaldo Aldrete-Davila, abandons his van and heads for Mexico on foot some 120 yards away. Other border patrol agents are now on scene and join the pursuit. The illegal immigrant confronts Compean on the other side of a drainage ditch on his way back to Mexico. Compean tries to arrest him, they get into a scuffle and shots are fired. No one is hit.

Meanwhile Ramos climbs down the ditch to help Compean when he hears shots. He sees Compean on the ground while the drug smuggler is running away and thinks Aldrete-Davila has a gun because he sees something "shiny" in his hand, but can't be sure. Ramos, to defend Compean fires off a round, which gives Aldrete-Davila a non-fatal buttock wound. Aldrete-Davila appears to be fine because he's still running and escapes across the Mexican border. On the Mexican side, people are waiting to pick him up. As Ramos and Compean walk back, they see that inside the van is about 750 pounds of marijuana – a million dollars worth. The mistake? They don't orally report the shooting because they think no one was hurt, and supervisors and seven other agents are on the scene – plenty of witnesses. The supervisors are required to file a written report. They don't.

The Back Story

Homeland Security gets involved and opens an investigation. Enter now Arizona Border Patrol agent Rene Sanchez. Drug smuggler Aldrete-Davila grew up with Rene Sanchez in Mexico and now lives in Wilcox, Arizona. They are good friends. Rene Sanchez was best friends with Aldrete-Davila's brother growing up. He even accompanied Aldrete-Davila's sister on her 15th birthday.

In a DHS memo, Christopher Sanchez outlines how the investigation into Ramos and Compean began. On March 10, 2005, Christopher Sanchez receives a phone call from Border Patrol agent Rene Sanchez, who tells him about Aldrete-Davila's encounter with Ramos and Compean.

According to the document, Rene Sanchez writes that Osvaldo Aldrete-Davila's mother, Marcadia Aldrete-Davila, contacted his (Sanchez's) mother-in-law, Gregoria Toquinto, and tells her about the Border Patrol agent shooting Aldrete-Davila. Toquinto tells her son-in-law, Rene Sanchez, about it and he talks to Osvaldo on the phone in Mexico. One has to wonder how and why a U.S. Border Patrol agent and his family are so buddy-buddy with a long-time drug smuggler and his family.

DHS sends investigator Christopher Sanchez to Fabens, Texas and eventually into Mexico to find Aldrete-Davila. Christopher Sanchez offers Aldrete-Davila immunity, free border crossing cards and free healthcare to come back to the U.S. and testify against Ramos and Compean.

Now the Lies Begin

At this point Ramos and Compean are arrested, charged with shooting Aldrete-Davila and then trying to cover up the incident. The other agents on the scene at the time change their story – radically so upon also being given a type of immunity – and are encouraged to tell the "real" story. They testify that Aldrete-Davila had no gun.

The reporter who broke this story nationally, Sara Carter, goes down to Mexico to interview Aldrete-Davila's family. They confess he's run drugs since age 14 – for more than a decade – is never seen without a gun and would never have crossed into the U.S. carrying a dope load worth a million dollars without one. The mother offers that Aldrete-Davila is a middleman in the drug smuggling ring associated with the Juarez Cartel then led by Vicente Carrillo Fuentes.

Four months before the trial, Aldrete-Davila sneaks another truckload of drugs across the border. The government goes before the judge and asks that all of that evidence be sealed so the jury would never hear it. Long time investigator into the Ramos-Compean case, Tara Setmayer obtains a copy of the DEA report. It verifies that Aldrete-Davila was identified as having dropped off 800 pounds of drugs at a Texas stash house in October 2005, but is never arrested.

During the trial Aldrete-Davila is painted as an innocent just running drugs the one time to get money for his poor sick mother. She must have been really "sick" because pharmaceuticals in Mexico are dirt cheap and an 800-pound truckload of pot would buy a lot of "medicine".

At trial, Ignacio Ramos and Jose Compean are found guilty in March 2006 and receive 11- and 12-year prison sentences, respectively that they begin serving on January 17, 2007. Ramos and Compean are thrown into solitary confinement and both are shocked at being treated so harshly. Ramos is a skilled, dedicated officer capturing nearly 100 drug smugglers and seizing countless thousands of pounds of narcotics. He's also nominated Border Patrol Agent of the Year in March 2005, but that goes out the window with Aldrete-Davila. None of Ramos' good work history is admissible in court.

Congress Wakes Up

In September 2006 members of Congress begin to investigate and ask Homeland Security for a briefing to find out what's really going on. Homeland Security officials tell the Congressional investigating team that: 1) Ramos and Compean confessed; 2) they knew Aldrete-Davila was unarmed; and 3) they said they wanted to shoot some Mexicans that day.

Really? Why would they shoot people also of Hispanic decent?

Those three allegations rub Congress raw. They ask for proof and none is ever provided. Four and a half months later, the official investigative report used to prosecute Ramos and Compean is still not finished, let alone released. It takes members of Congress complaining and going public about the debacle for DHS to turn over the report. When they finally do, it's classified. Under great pressure, DHS finally releases a redacted version, but none of what they alleged is in report.

In a biting letter, Congressman Dana Rohrabacher (R-CA) blasted President George W. Bush and his administration for treating terrorists better than they treat the two convicted Border Patrol agents, Ignacio Ramos and Jose Compean.

Rep. Rohrabacher called on the Bush administration to conduct a thorough review of the harsh treatment the two decorated border agents are receiving while in solitary confinement. The popular conservative wrote to President Bush that for 10 months Ramos and Compean have been in conditions more severe than experienced by alleged terrorists held by the US at the Naval Base in Guantanamo Bay, Cuba.

Rohrabacher told the news media in a statement that he has written a letter to Manhattan federal trial judge Michael Mukasey, Bush's nominee to replace Alberto Gonzales as US Attorney General, demanding that upon confirmation Mukasey conduct an unbiased review of the agents' prosecution. "Given the close personal relationship between the prosecuting US Attorney Johnny Sutton, former Attorney General Alberto Gonzales and President Bush, past requests for inquiries into prosecutorial misconduct in this case have been ignored," Rohrabacher claimed in his statement. "Conflicting statements made by Mr. Sutton [Aldrete-Davila's attorney] during Senate testimony in July and to the press have yet to be clarified," Rohrabacher continued, "and newly obtained information regarding the treatment of the officers in solitary confinement for the last 10 months reveals conditions that are harsh and unnecessarily punitive in nature."[827]

"In response to the public outrage, the U.S. Senate and the House of Representatives have held several hearings on the prosecution and more than 100 Members of Congress have called on President Bush to pardon or commute the sentences of Agents Ramos and Compean. But the White House continues to remain silent on the issue after promising nearly a year ago to look into the matter."[828] In December 2007 a 3-judge panel, in the Fifth Circuit Court of Appeals heard arguments by Ramos and Compean's attorneys. Judge E. Grady Jolly blasts, "It does seem to me like the government overreacted here. There were plenty of statutes you could have charged."[829]

Just Deserts

In 2007 the 753-pound load of smuggled drugs came back to bite Osvaldo Aldrete-Davila. A federal grand jury indicted him on October 17th for intent to distribute a controlled substance, conspiracy to import a controlled substance, and conspiracy to possess a controlled substance with intent to distribute. The indictment was sealed until November 15, 2007 the date DEA agents arrested Aldrete-Davila at the border. Osvaldo Aldrete-Davila was convicted of drug smuggling in August 2008 and sentenced to 9½ years in jail.

On January 19, 2009 during his final full day in office, President Bush, commuted the sentences of both Ramos and Compean, ending their prison term on March 20, 2009. They were released on February 17, 2009 and spent the last month in home confinement. When U.S. courts side with criminals over law abiding, citizen-protecting Americans, there is something severely out of kilter.

Plot Thickens

Everyone wondered what took Mr. Bush so long to commute the sentences. Despite repeated requests, appeals were ignored. Maybe something else was afoot.

Rep. Ted Poe, R-Texas, called for a congressional investigation into alleged prosecutorial misconduct by Aldrete-Davila's attorney Johnny Sutton. Poe also called for an investigation into the alleged push by the Mexican government demanding Ramos and Compean's prosecution. That Mexico was truly interfering looked more and more likely. As soon their sentences were changed, Mexico put up a big stink. On this Rep. Poe comments.

"As soon as President Bush commuted Ramos and Compean's sentences, the Mexican government registered a large protest. In their protest, the Mexican government admitted their involvement in the case without specifying what their involvement was. So I think the first order of business is for the U.S. Congress to investigate what role the Mexican government had in demanding the Bush administration prosecute this case. Mexico should not be meddling into U.S. criminal cases."[830]

Obama's Catch and Release Policy

In 2012, Mr. Obama proposed in a secret draft document that low-priority illegal immigrants be released. It was intended to lighten the detention load and release into the public those who sneaked into America, but had no criminal record. The policy was detailed in an internal memo obtained by House Judiciary Committee Chairman Lamar Smith. The memo allowed ICE to use their discretion on whether or not to prosecute. This document also pointedly warned to make no public mention of it so it wouldn't be subjected to FOIA requests. The memo admits that the policy was drafted to appease immigration rights groups.

Chris Cabrera, local Border Patrol council president, said "there are no consequences for people coming over illegally and the hundreds of thousands of dollars spent trying to divert illegal immigration are pointless without enforcement. 'What they are doing is like a backdoor amnesty or an amnesty through policy. They can't get everybody in the right way so they are just going to release everybody on their own recognizance pending a court date that hasn't been set, knowing that over 85 percent of the people don't show up for the court date.'"[831]

George McCubbin III, president of the National Border Patrol Council, the union that represents agents and their support personnel, warned that his policy would send the wrong message and that it was tacit permission to fiddle immigration statistics. Because of the great latitude, numbers could be bent so they didn't show too many prosecutions or deportations. McCubbin said he wished his agents had been consulted. He fumed, "It's frickin' unbelievable. They should be talking to the rank and file, the folks that should be doing the job."[832]

Photo: U.S. Customs and Border Protection provide assistance to unaccompanied alien children after they have crossed the south Texas border into America on June 29, 2014. (Courtesy Barry Bahler)

Like many slippery slopes, this one slid downhill on greased rails. Of this policy Smith said, "Rather than allow Border Patrol agents to do their job, the Obama administration instead would like them to roll out the welcome mat for illegal immigrants. This 'catch and release' policy undermines border security, our immigration system, and CBP's mission."[833]

Now flash forward just 1½-years. As of April 2014, Homeland Security released nearly 166,000 *convicted criminal* illegal aliens. Their crimes? Not jaywalking or running red lights, but rape, murder, aggravated assault and kidnapping.[834]

Besides the nearly 166,000 criminals that were supposed to be deported, over 700,000 other illegals were ordered to leave. In total, of the 872,900 illegal immigrants that were free to roam the country, none self-deported as ordered by the courts, according to *Judicial Watch*.[835]

Later in 2014, Federal officers released another 30,000 criminal illegal immigrants. Though the new ICE Director, Sarah Saldana says she's "determined to continue to take every possible measure to ensure the public's safety and the removal of dangerous criminals", it's little comfort after the criminal horses are out the barn door. ICE claims it doesn't have the promised prosecutorial discretion and when felon illegals are refused re-entry by their own countries they have to be released after a period of time.[836]

In March 2016, ICE revealed that 124 illegal immigrant criminals released from jail by the Obama administration since 2010 have been subsequently charged with 135 murders. Besides the murders, these aliens had 464 criminal convictions prior to being released by ICE, "ranging from drug crimes to DUI and other driving offenses to larceny and theft."[837] Jessica Vaughan, Director of Policy Studies for the Center for Immigration Studies, said that 75% were released on court orders or because their countries wouldn't take them back.

At no time was the horrible impact of harboring criminal illegal aliens felt more acutely than on July 2, 2015.

"Sanctuary City" Debacle

When it comes to illegal immigration America is a house divided. Decades prior to 2014, Federal law was in place that clearly stated undocumented immigrants were to be apprehended and deported – not released into the populace on the *hope* they'd show up for their hearing. Others requesting asylum were to be detained and processed. Determining what to do with 30 million illegals is a political football both parties kick all over the field. (Yes, that number has jumped mightily from the old figure of 11-12 million according the Border agents[838] and Mexico's former ambassador.[839]) No one wants to touch it – and don't. In some areas a functioning, challenging border fence exists between the U.S. and Canada and the U.S. and Mexico. In other sections a "fence" consists of broken barbed wire, if that. There is no consistency.

As of 2014 President Obama began openly disregarding Federal law on apprehension and detention of illegal immigrants and went further by doing amnesty end-arounds on Congress. Even further, Mr. Obama released tens of thousands of convicted felon illegals and repeat offenders back among Americans.

Complicating matters and frustrating Border Patrol Agents is the proliferation of "sanctuary cities". These grew out of the 1980s "Sanctuary Movement" – a group of 150 churches and synagogues dedicated to protecting Salvadorans and Guatemalans fleeing civil wars. Nearly 1 million refugees crossed the U.S. southern border, seeking asylum. Due to laws then, many were detained and sent home or their hearing took too long to be heard. Thousands of others made their way to major cities including Washington, DC; Los Angeles, San Francisco, Boston, New York and Chicago and simply blended into the masses.

Early on Rev. John Fife of Southside Presbyterian Church in Tucson announced that his church would openly defy Immigration and become a "sanctuary" for Central Americans. Once Congress passed legislation allowing Temporary Protected Status for people needing a temporary safe haven and the Immigration and Nationality Act, sanctuaries were no longer needed for Central Americans.

Since the 80s, the concept has morphed into something entirely different from protecting asylum seekers to outward defiance of Federal law designed to protect national security to one that harbors convicted felons. The movement has spread from individual churches and synagogues to entire states and a few cities in Canada. Now "sanctuary jurisdictions" provide safe harbor for illegal aliens who are convicted felons, among others, choosing to ignore detainers. These are notifications from Immigrations and Customs Enforcement (ICE) to local law enforcement that they will apprehend a jailed illegal immigrant usually within two to five days. These undocumented immigrants have obviously some criminal act or they wouldn't be in jail in the first place. Not only do sanctuary cities refuse to hold them for ICE, some jurisdictions like Santa Fe, New Mexico have an unspoken "don't ask, don't tell" policy and won't notify ICE of an illegal immigrant's presence or arrest, let alone hold them. Before 2014 was even finished, state and local law "enforcement" officials ignored and declined to honor 10,182 detainers.[840]

If a Lie Is Repeated Often Enough, It's Still a Lie

Now step back a moment to consider the probability that there are **three times** the number of illegal immigrants in the U.S. than what is regularly and consistently touted by mainstream news outlets and the Government. (Hat tip to 10 times *New York Times* bestselling author Ann Coulter for shining a light on this massive discrepancy.)

Coulter unearthed two very significant studies that dispute the count of illegal immigrants. That number of 11 million has stalled since 2005. People on top of this issue no doubt have viewed dozens of videos and hundreds of photographs documenting steady streams stampeding through the U.S. "borders". "Border" is truly a euphemism these days. These two studies, conducted before Mr. Obama came into office, underscores that an open border policy is condoned by both parties and stemmed by neither. Ditto for the president of Mexico.

In 2006, global investment bank and brokerage firm, Bear Stearns, conducted their own study about the real number of illegal immigrants in America. They had no dog in this race except how to best financially advise clients since unchecked immigration greatly impacts many segments of the economy. Bear Stearns shared unbiased findings because if their research is wrong, then clients lose money. *Lots* of $$. For this reason, their conclusion bears extra attention that the true number of illegals even in 2005 was closer to 20 million and has only mushroomed since. Their figure is based on these factors among others:

1. Money sent back to Mexico tracked by World Bank
2. The booming number of housing permits in gateway communities
3. The upsurge in school enrollment and
4. The sheer numbers crossing the border.

From these, Bear Stearns concluded six important points:

1. The number of illegal immigrants in America may be as high as 20 million people [in 2005], more than double the official 9 million people estimated by the Census Bureau.
2. The total number of legalized immigrants entering the U.S. since 1990 has averaged 962,000 per year. Several credible studies indicate that the number of *illegal entries has recently crept up to 3 million per year*, triple the authorized figure.
3. Undocumented immigrants are gaining a larger share of the job market, and hold approximately 12 to 15 million jobs in the U.S. (8% of the employed [in 2005]).
4. Four to six million jobs have shifted to the underground market, as small businesses take advantage of the vulnerability of illegal residents.
5. In addition to circumventing the Immigration Reform and Control Act of 1986, many employers of illegal workers have taken to using unrecorded revenue receipts. Employer enforcement has succumbed to political pressure.
6. Cell phones, Internet and low-cost travel have allowed immigrants easier illegal access to the U.S. and increased their ability to find employment and circumvent immigration laws.[841]

Of equal importance is a groundbreaking 2006 report conducted by Donald Barlett and James Steele for *Time* magazine. This investigative duo has earned over 50 national awards for their excellence in journalism including two Pulitzers. (Move over Woodward and Bernstein a la Watergate.) Barlett and Steele broke with mainstream news parroting the party line and confronted the overwhelming issue of illegal immigrants. They found that the number of illegals streaming into America in 2006 was at least 3 million. 3.1 million if one is picky. Just from "October [2005] through Aug. 25, [2006] it [the Border Patrol] apprehended nearly 1.1 million illegals in all its operations around the U.S. But for every person it picks up, at least three make it into the country safely."[842]

Take the more realistic number of 20 million illegal aliens in the U.S. in 2005 and add 3 million more arriving yearly, the Census Bureau's fake number of 9 million may be light by as many as 30 million. That aside, if not even one single person had sneaked through the border in 10 years the Census Bureau's stale number is about 11 million short of reality. Considering the huge numbers piling through the borders day and night, there is no way the figure proffered by the U.S. Census Bureau hasn't budged in over 10 years. It's one giant falsehood. Government doesn't want to reveal the true number especially in view of tough employment and the billions it costs taxpayers to keep them here.

Another gem highlighted is that undocumented workers are taking jobs that Americans won't do **not** because of the *type of work*, but due to low pay. When companies continually hire people under the table, which lets them dodge paying taxes and the company avoid paying FICA and healthcare plus vacation and other benefits, it perpetuates companies paying low wages. It's America's answer to cheap Asian and Latin American workers, but it's bred a much deeper problem – the alluring welfare state.

On the other end of the scale, some people are demanding $15/hr. for flipping burgers. That is simply beyond ridiculous! That may take about two brain cells. These folks have lost all perspective. Flipping burgers isn't intended to warrant a living wage. When a person is in high school or university, they expect to work these entry-level, part-time jobs and be glad to have work! After completing five years of university, this author started at the bottom rung, expected to "pay dues", but prove yourself through time, effort, diligence and hard work. Salary began at a fraction of what these burger-flippers demand. We have totally gone socialist upside-down if a persons thinks a salary is *owed*, not earned. And for a little more "lost" perspective…

Illegals Demand a Say!

Everybody has a "thing" that really gets up his or her nose. That's a British phrase from many years living in Australia. "Up your nose" is something that really irks – *a lot*. Illegals do mine, as do they to *hundreds of millions* of other taxpayers. This simple news story tweaked many noses and pointed out more stupidity of Political Correctness: ***Oregon Driver Cards: Immigrants Sue to Reverse Measure 88 Defeat***. Really? Since when do non-Americans get to **demand** rights in our Country? In short, a group of illegal immigrants in normally (very liberal Oregon) sued the state for rights to obtain driver's licenses. Voters in 2014 resoundingly slapped down that ballot measure by ⅔. Thirty-five of Oregon's 36 counties voted "no". They broke our laws by stampeding the borders and then think they can demand rights that give them better jobs here? Is this crazy or what?!? It gets worse.

In November 2015, an immigrants-rights group came up with their own "Bill or Rights". These are their demands:

1. People aren't allowed to say "Illegal" or "Alien" and change it to "Undocumented American" and acknowledge they are already here.
2. Affirmation they are to be treated with dignity and respect.
3. Guaranteed pathway to citizenship.
4. U.S. birth certificates for anchor-baby children.
5. No deportation or incarceration without charges, hearings or representation.
6. Public education, in-state tuition (they already get free K-12 education and when applying to college no birth certificate is require. With a high school diploma it would be assumed they live in that state so in-state tuition shouldn't be an issue.)
7. Guaranteed wage equality (There is no such thing even for Americans, ask many women.)
8. Medical care (They already get this because when they need a doctor even for a cold, they go to emergency rooms. Whether they are able to pay or not they are treated.)
9. No deportation after reporting crimes.
10. Guaranteed rights same as American citizens.[843]

To even contemplate such multi-faceted demands from people that shouldn't even be here in the first place, borders insanity.

Somewhere, *somewhere* along the line America has to understand that runaway immigration is going to be our undoing. We will no longer have a country.

Shoe on Other Foot

Most countries have exceedingly strict criteria for non-citizens entering their nation. Mexico is unapologetically restrictive about letting in foreigners, yet calls repeatedly for open borders into America. Mexico will boot a person without second thoughts if outsiders don't improve the country's 'economic or national interests' or are 'not found to be physically or mentally healthy'." Illegal entry into Mexico is punishable by two years jail time. A second offense gets 10 years. Applicants must pass a barrage of exams including produce a birth certificate, provide a bank statement proving economic independence, pass a test, and prove they can provide their own health care. There are no sanctuary cities in Mexico nor do they tolerate the concept of police ignoring detainers. By national mandate all law enforcement officials must comply with immigration laws. Mexico can and does involve the military in immigration enforcement ops and citizens can arrest illegals and turn them in to authorities.[844]

Felon Illegals Killing Americans

KATE STEINLE

July 2, 2015 brought squarely into focus why the Dept. of Homeland Security's catch-and-release policy, the release of convicted felons into the populace and sanctuary cities, states and municipalities is not only unlawful, but also dangerous. That was the day five times deported and seven times convicted felon Francisco Lopez-Sanchez fatally shot Kate Steinle. While walking with her dad and a friend on Pier 14 in San Francisco 32-year-old Kate's life ended. Mr. Lopez-Sanchez – a.k.a. Jose Inez Garcia Zarate and several other names – claimed he found the weapon wrapped in a T-shirt under a pier bench. Allegedly when he picked it up, it fired – three times.[845]

After serving time in a Texas federal prison, Lopez-Sanchez was sent to California to face felony marijuana charges. Since San Francisco doesn't comply with Immigration detainers, when the charges were dismissed, Mr. Lopez-Sanchez was released from custody on April 15, 2015. Two and a half months later Kate Steinle was dead. Sanchez admitted he chose to live in San Francisco specifically because it's a sanctuary city.

Described by her dad, Jim, as "strong-willed and beautiful," Kate fought hard to live. While lying on the ground, she pleaded, "Dad, help me, help me."[846] Her mother, Liz, said that though she fought for her life Kate's heart had stopped twice and then was restarted in the ambulance. She died two hours later at San Francisco General Hospital.

MARILYN PHARIS

Later that same month, an illegal alien from Mexico murdered another California woman. While Marilyn Pharis, 64, slept in her bed, 29-year-old Victor Aureliano Martinez Ramirez, broke into her home, brutally beat her with a hammer and raped her. She died 8 days later. *The Santa Maria Times* reported that Ramirez was charged with "attempted murder, first-degree burglary with person present, assault with intent to commit rape, sexual penetration by foreign object and resisting a peace officer."[847] After the violent assault Ramirez fled the scene and Marilyn called for help. A police dog tracked Ramirez to another home he had broken into and was hiding.

Ramirez was on probation for committing battery against another woman in May of 2014, while in possession of methamphetamine. He was charged twice in 2015 for violating probation, once for possessing a concealed knife and the other for drugs.[848] Immigration officials said they had asked police authorities to notify them before Martinez was released in 2014 from the Santa Barbara County Jail, but they didn't. Though Santa Barbara is not listed as a Sanctuary City, their actions suggest they should be.

A week later, police charged a second man, 20-year-old Jose Villagomez, with Marilyn's rape and attempted murder. It wasn't stated, Villagomez or Ramirez, who raped her first. Villagomez had been arrested on July 28 on unrelated charges and a week later, when police discovered his participation, those crimes were added to his charges. While Villagomez lived in Santa Maria, it's unclear if he too, were in the U.S. illegally.

Dangerous Sanctuary Cities

If laws were enforced against Sanctuary Cities and other such illegal immigrant protecting jurisdictions, Kate Steinle and Marilyn Pharis might still be alive. However, that boat may have already tipped too far into the drink. At some point during 2014 the number of Hispanics in California now outnumber Caucasians. Ditto for New Mexico. Since California's overwhelmingly liberal population supports President Obama's amnesty, it's doubtful things will change.

In late July 2015, the House passed a bill by 241-179 to withhold some federal law enforcement grants to sanctuary cities. Another bill called "Kate's Law" – Establishing Mandatory Minimums for Illegal Reentry Act of 2015 – was presented to the Senate. It would penalize sanctuaries and impose a 5-year mandatory jail sentence for illegal immigrants who re-enter the United States after being convicted of an aggravated felony or have three strikes for trying to enter the country illegally. Mr. Obama has already threatened to veto it and instead called on Congress "to legalize illegal immigrants as the way to solve the problem of criminals who shouldn't be on the streets."[849] As of May 2016, "Kate's Law" still hadn't passed.

Cosponsor of Kate's Law Sen. Ted Cruz (R-Texas) stated, "What happened to this young woman on a pier in San Francisco is heartbreaking. And the heartbreak is even more tragic given the circumstances. Clearly, our laws are not adequately deterring those who have already been deported from illegally reentering the country. And as we have seen in this case, and sadly, in too many others – the consequences of failing to keep these aliens from returning are dangerous and can be deadly.

Cruz continued: "Too many Americans have been victimized by illegal aliens who had previously been deported. We must send the message that defiance of our laws will no longer be tolerated. Of course, stiff penalties alone will not suffice. Congress must also discourage cities from harboring illegal aliens, and it must hold this Administration accountable for its failure – if not its outright refusal – to enforce federal immigration laws and ensure the safety and security of the American people."[850]

Image: Roughly 340 cities, counties and a few states are considered "sanctuary jurisdictions". For a larger version of this map and its key for specific locations, see Appendix 1. The concept of sanctuary cities has also spread to Canada. In 2013, Toronto, Ontario became Canada's first sanctuary city and Hamilton claimed that status the following year. British Columbia is also attempted to become a sanctuary city, but so far has lacked coordination of police and emergency departments, access to food banks, public transportation and other services to qualify.

Cruz further stated, "I authored and filed legislation for Kate's Law, and just last week tried to get the Senate to pass it. But the leader [John Boehner] of our own party blocked it. The problem is that most of our party [Republican] don't want to enforce immigration laws."[851]

Sanctuary jurisdictions were furious Federal funding might be cut if they continued to defy Federal law. When has state law ever superseded Federal? Exactly never, except in the case of sanctuary cities. Federal law can't apply to one section of the country and not to all or chaos follows. In October 2015, Kate's Law was struck down by a single person, Democrat Harry Reid,[852] contrary to the wishes of the majority of Americans.[853] In one stroke, Reid simultaneously put all 322 million Americans at risk and shoved all immigrants that want to come here legally at the back of the line.

The Juicy Plum to Mexico's North

In a country of 125 million people 45% live in poverty and another 35% are at risk of crossing that line.[854] Less than 2% of the population is extremely wealthy. Most are at the other end of the stick though the middle class is growing. Not surprising, the greater number of poor live in Mexico's southern and central states. The best off are closest to the U.S.

Those that excel financially do so mainly through crime. At the 2011 Occupy movement in Mexico, though poorly attended, one man's placard read, "THE STATE CAN ONLY SUSTAIN ITSELF THROUGH CRIME." Mexico simply can't support their largely uneducated masses and it has greater person density on less real estate. It would be like cramming 40% of all Americans onto ¼ of our land.

Multinational companies are investing there, job opportunities are opening, but the pay is a fraction of that in America for the same work. A factory worker might make $3.65/hr. While wage inflation in China makes Mexico more attractive to global manufacturers, they don't have the education to perform. With only 36% of Mexicans having earned the equivalent of a high school diploma, crime is the fast earning track. Combine that with the huge drug cartel problem and a barely there corrupt justice system, and it all conspires to keep Mexicans down and out. And out appears to be the U.S.

258

This many people can't expect to live at a decent level, so they look to America and it behooves their government to shove them north. Americans pay the price.

Image: Despite America's faltering economy, things look better in los Estados Unidos (the United States).

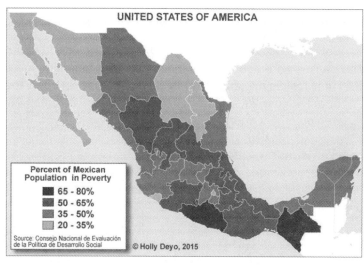

Mexico Facilitating Illegals Into America

Once the Obama Administration promised amnesty or a "path to citizenship", wave upon wave of immigrants flooded the borders and continues to this day. In 2014, a steady stream of migrant kids sneaking across the border turned into a flood that overwhelmed Border Patrol agents. By June 2014, the U.S. expected over 90,000 – maybe more – unaccompanied migrant kids would flood across America's southern border by year's end. While most still came from Mexico, many arrived from El Salvador, Guatemala and Honduras.

With Border Patrol agents given quiet orders by DHS to let all non-dangerous illegals through, they were reduced to caregivers. Union president Brandon Judd said in an interview. "…We can't do our jobs. Forty percent of our agents have been pulled from the field to babysit, clean cells, change diapers. We're actually making burritos. That's not our job. Our job is to protect the border."[855]

With such tight restrictions put on U.S. Border Patrol agents, under-staffed police forces and a porous-to-nearly non-existent border fence, high numbers of illegal immigrants and terrorists slipping through should shock no one.

An elite, widely respected law-enforcement friendly agency released corroborating information about America's lack of spine on immigration. The El Paso Intelligence Center (EPIC) July 7, 2014 intel report concludes. "In late May, the U.S. Border Patrol interviewed unaccompanied children (UAC) and migrant families apprehended in the Rio Grande Valley. Of the 230 total migrants interviewed, 219 cited the primary reason for migrating to the United States was the perception of U.S. immigration laws granting free passes or *permisos* to UAC and adult female OTMs traveling with minors. Migrants indicated that knowledge of *permisos* was widespread across Central America due to word of mouth, local, and international media messaging – prompting many to depart for the United States within 30 days of becoming aware of these perceived benefits, according to the same reporting."[856]

The Mexican government was defensive when caught printing and handing out a 32-page comic book style pamphlet, *Guia Del Migrante Mexicano (Guide for the Mexican Migrant),* that gives pointers on navigating deserts and swimming rivers safely as well as what to pack, how to deal with Border Patrol agents and tips on how to hide once in the U.S.

Why would they do this and more importantly, why is the American government obviously turning a blind eye and what are the implications?

It's not just floods of immigrants looking for a better life that stream through the border. It's the prime entry point due to such easy access.

OTMS – OTHER THAN MEXICANS

Between October 2003 and August 2004 nearly 50,000 non-Mexican illegal immigrants, OTMs – **O**ther **T**han **M**exicans – were apprehended. Due to limited detention facilities, they were released free to roam throughout the U.S. until their immigration hearing. Most never show up for it and blend into the background.

In an August 2004 letter to President Bush, Solomon Ortiz, then Congressman for Corpus Christi in Texas: "Law enforcement agencies across the south-west border are alarmed that the US is releasing thousands of OTMs [Other than Mexicans]. Those released include individuals from nations the US defines as state sponsors of potential terrorism, or from those nations that have produced large numbers of al-Qaeda militants."[857]

Based on those numbers and the fact that the U.S. hasn't improved border security would suggest nearly 300,000 OTMs were caught and released into the population. The number that has sneaked in from those countries and *not* caught would be simply staggering. How many of them are potential terrorists? Mr. Ortiz said similar incidents are "happening all over the place. It's very, very scary".[858] According to Judicial Watch, U.S. Border Patrol estimates three out of every four illegal aliens who cross the border evade apprehension.[859]

In July 2004 border agents from Arizona and Texas anonymously report recent encounters with dozens of Arab men.

In June that same year one Arizona newspaper reported 77 males "of Middle Eastern descent" were caught in two separate incidents trekking through the Chiricahua Mountains. One field agent observed, "These guys didn't speak Spanish and they were speaking to each other in Arabic. It's ridiculous that we don't take this more seriously. We're told not to say a thing to the media. If you want to enter the US illegally, the way to do it is to get to Mexico first."[860]

The possibility of a southern border loophole aiding the terrorist scenario wasn't recognized until 2003. Steve McCraw, assistant director of the FBI's Office of Intelligence, testified before Congress. "The ability of foreign nationals to use [the hearings procedure] to create a well-documented but fictitious identity in the United States, provides an opportunity for terrorists to move freely within the US without triggering name-based watch lists. It also enables them to board planes without revealing their true identity".[861]

OTM Apprehensions

Source: U.S. Customs and Border Protection © Holly Deyo, 2015

While still director of the FBI, Robert Mueller and other U.S. officials also raised serious concerns over OTMs crossing the southwest border at "alarming rates". "Mueller testified before the House Appropriations Committee in March 2005 'there are individuals from countries with known Al Qaeda connections who are changing their Islamic surnames to Hispanic-sounding names and obtaining false Hispanic identities, learning to speak Spanish and pretending to be Hispanic.'"[862]

GOVERNMENT SLIGHT OF HAND

Don't be fooled thinking government is all over this, that it looks like they're apprehending more OTMs. Four things to consider:

1) Their numbers don't emphasize the increase of ALL illegal immigrants flooding through our borders. So while apprehensions have increased so have the number of border crossers.

2) More importantly, while the U.S. was such a desirable place to come two decades ago, when the economy was booming, Border Patrol's statistic gathering wasn't exemplary. Assessing how many illegals have really streamed through is anyone's guess.

3) Since most Americans take a dim view of extremist Muslims, it looks better to Americans to hear reports of more are being apprehended whether it's fact or not. (See McCubbin's comments on fiddling immigration statistics under *Obama's Catch and Release Policy*.)

4) From the earliest Bush administration years this author had interest in the number of illegal aliens flooding into America. Then one could check the Border Patrol site and get the numbers of Mexicans and OTMs – *by country* – who were coming through and caught. In the last decade this information was hidden from the public and now they are all lumped together under OTMs without country designation. The information is available, but only obtainable through a FOIA – Freedom of Information Act. The majority now pounding our borders *is* from terrorist sponsored countries, not Mexico.

Photo: Chiricahua Mountains in southeastern Arizona where 77 Middle Eastern men were caught sneaking into the U.S. (Courtesy Karen Fasimpaur)

In 2010 the Department of Homeland Security had in custody thousands of detainees from Afghanistan, Egypt, Iraq, Iran, Pakistan, Saudi Arabia and Yemen. U.S. Border Patrol statistics indicate that there were 108,025 OTMs detained in 2006, compared to 165,178 in 2005 and 75,389 in 2004.[863] Now look at the escalation after 2011.

In a July 2012 hearing before the full U.S. House of Representatives Committee on Homeland Security, DHS Secretary Janet Napolitano confirms that terrorists have crossed the Southwest border intending to harm Americans.[864]

In May 2013 Mike Vickers who owns a 1,000-acre Texas ranch finds an Urdu-to-English dictionary along his fence. Vickers' property runs along Highway 281, close to the Falfurrias Border Patrol station. The station, about 70 miles north of the Rio Grande, is the first highway checkpoint for vehicles coming from Mexico in an area known for heavy illegal alien and drug traffic. "Local ranchers have to contend with torn-up fences, broken water lines, contaminated wells and robbery on a daily basis from illegal immigrants tramping through their land. One Texas

Border Patrol agent said there is "no doubt" that among the hordes of Central Americans are also crossers from Pakistan and Afghanistan, raising significant national security concerns."[865] While there was no one in the area at the time, the dictionary appeared to have been there from several days to weeks due to weather exposure damage.

In June 2014, six Middle Easterners are picked up in Laredo, Texas, "right along [the area] with the ranchers in Texas finding prayer rugs in their ranches."[866]

September 2014, Sheriff Gary Painter of Midland County, Texas received intel of growing threats from ISIS and was warned to be on the look out for them trying to cross the border. "We have found Muslim clothing. They have found Koran books that are laying on the side of the trail. So we know that there are Muslims that have come across and are being smuggled into the United States." It's easy to pick up on Painter's frustration as he vents to Fox News host Elisabeth Hasselbeck. "The border is wide open. ... There's always a way to get across. ... If they show their ugly head in our area, we'll send them to hell. I would like for 'em [U.S. military] to hit 'em so hard and so often that every time they hear a propeller on a plane or a jet aircraft engine that they urinate down both legs. When you do that, then you've accomplished a lot."[867]

Early in October 2014 over a period of 36 hours, four ISIS terrorists are apprehended in McAllen and Pharr, Texas.[868]

October 7, 2014, California Congressman Duncan Hunter, a former Marine Corp Major and member of the House Armed Services Committee reveals on Fox News that "at least 10" Islamic State fighters have been caught trying to cross the U.S.-Mexico border into Texas. He said that Border Patrol agents had nabbed them, but "you know there's going to be dozens more that did not get caught by the Border Patrol. If you really want to protect Americans from ISIS, you secure the southern border. It's that simple. ISIS doesn't have a navy, they don't have an air force, they don't have nuclear weapons. The only way that ISIS is going to harm Americans is by coming in through the southern border – which they already have." The three-term congressmen continued: "They aren't flying B-1 bombers, bombing American cities, but they are going to be bombing American cities coming across from Mexico."[869]

It's likely most of these incidences aren't reported by mainstream news, or when they are, it's done quickly and quietly. Ed Turzanski, former U.S. intelligence officer and professor of political science and government at La Salle University sheds light on this. He warned that government agencies wouldn't admit discovering prayer rugs, etc. to the press. Turzanski said officials in President Obama's administration forbid the Border Patrol from speaking about anything that "goes against the administration's border security narrative."[870]

Tom Fitton, president of Judicial Watch President warned. "When you have an administration that pushes illegal alien amnesty, permits illegal alien sanctuary policies, and attacks states like Arizona for seeking to enforce the rule of law, it sends a signal to our enemies to cross the border illegally and to do their worst. The Obama administration continues to allow our borders to spiral out of control. These numbers are simply astonishing. Our country cannot secure our borders soon enough!"[871]

Not Isolated Instances

With Mr. Obama's open door policy, more and more people come through unchecked. It's more a case of who's *not* coming through. Border Patrol regularly apprehends SIAs (**S**pecial **I**nterest **A**liens) from 35 "special interest countries" – many that specialize in and support terrorism: Afghanistan, Algeria, Bahrain, Bangladesh, Djibouti, Egypt, Eritrea, Indonesia, Iran, Iraq, Jordan, Kazakhstan, Kuwait, Lebanon, Libya, Malaysia, Mauritania, Morocco, North Korea, Oman, Pakistan, Philippines, Qatar, Saudi Arabia, Somalia, Sudan, Syria, Tajikistan, Thailand, Tunisia, Turkey, Turkmenistan, United Arab Emirates, Uzbekistan, Yemen, Territories of Gaza and West Bank. The U.S. intelligence community designates these nations as countries that could export terrorists to America. Especially leaving the southern border wide open for terrorists, places targets all U.S. citizens.

In August 2007 former Director of National Intelligence Mike McConnell states that not only do terrorists use the Southwest border to enter America but that they will continue to do so as long as it's available.[872] "'The Afghanis and Iraqis,' one official explained, paid the Mexicans $20,000 or 'the equivalent in weapons' for their help in getting into the U.S., and "shaved their beards so as not to appear to be Middle Easterners.'"[873]

Chink 3: Enemies Among Us

In February 2001 Mahmoud Kourani (the brother of Hezbollah's security chief in southern Lebanon) comes across the border from Tijuana into California in the trunk of a car, after bribing a Mexican embassy official in Beirut with $3000 to get a visa. In 2005, he is sentenced to 4½ years in prison after admitting that he helped raise money for Hezbollah while living in Dearborn, Michigan.[874]

In December 2002, Salim Boughader is arrested for smuggling 200 Lebanese, including Hezbollah operatives, across the border from Tijuana into California. Boughader had previously worked for Hezbollah's Al-Manar TV satellite network.[875]

In June of 2004, U.S. Border Patrol agents detain 53 Arabic-speaking males in Arizona near the Mexican border, part of a larger contingent of approximately 100 illegal aliens in the Chiricacha Mountain foothills. A second incident on June 21 in which 24 Arabic-speaking males were seized after a chase of a larger group of border-crossers, most of whom are still at large. The June 21 incident occurred in the area of Pierce and Sunsites approximately 25 miles northeast of Tombstone and not far from the Chiricacha foothills.[876]

In July 2004, 25 Chechans suspected of having links to Islamist terrorists reportedly cross illegally from Mexico. They enter into a mountainous part of Arizona that's difficult for U.S. Border Patrol agents to monitor.[877]

Also in July 2004, a woman named Farida Goolam Mohamed Ahmed is arrested at a Texas airport boarding a flight to New York after she either walks or swims across the Mexican border into Texas. According to *The Washington Post*, she is connected to a Pakistani terrorist group and believed to be ferrying instructions to U.S.-based Al Qaeda operatives.[878]

In December 2004, a Bangladeshi Muslim named Fakhrul Islam is arrested crossing the Texas border from Mexico. With him are members of the Mara Salvatruchas gang (MS-13), which has ties to Al-Qaeda.[879]

In January 2005, two Hamas operatives, Mahmoud Khalil and Ziad Saleh, are arrested as part of a criminal enterprise in Los Angeles. Both enter the U.S. after paying a smuggler $10,000 each to take them across the border.[880]

In November 2005, captured Al Qaeda Egyptian Jihadist Sharif al-Masri tells US interrogators that al-Qaeda is looking to exploit America's porous southern border to smuggle in radiological material from Mexico.[881]

In November 2005 an Iraqi national and al-Qaeda member on the FBI's terrorist list is apprehended by Mexican authorities and handed over to the Texas Hudspeth County sheriff.[882]

In 2006, U.S. immigration authorities discover items along the banks of the Rio Grande River that suggest ties to terrorist organizations. Backing them up, Sheriff Sigifredo Gonzalez of Zapata County, Texas, reports they frequently find currency and clothing along the river.[883] That same year, the Border Patrol in Jim Hogg County, Texas finds a jacket with patches from countries where al-Qaeda is known to operate. One patch is an Arabic military badge depicting an airplane flying over a building and heading towards a tower. The other is an image of a lion's head with wings and a parachute emanating from the animal. The bottom of one patch reads, "martyr," "way to eternal life" or "way to immortality."[884]

In May 2007, after more than a year of being surveilled by the FBI, six foreign-born Muslim men are arrested and charged with plotting an attack on Fort Dix Army Base in New Jersey. They are planning on killing as many soldiers as possible in an armed assault with high-powered weapons, according to the FBI.[885]

Also in May 2007, the FBI issues an advisory about a plan by 60 jihadists in league with Mexican drug lords to cross the border via underground tunnels and attack the intelligence-training center at Fort Huachuca, Arizona, 20 miles from the Mexican border. The advisory warns that, "The Afghanis and Iraqis shaved their beards so as not to appear to be Middle Easterners". They paid Mexican drug lords "$20,000 'or the equivalent in weapons' for the cartel's assistance in smuggling them and their weapons through tunnels along the border into the U.S. The weapons would be sent through tunnels that supposedly ended in Arizona and New Mexico, but the Islamist terrorists would be smuggled through Laredo, Texas, and join the weapons later."[886]

In March 2009 Michael Braun, former Drug Enforcement Administration chief of operations, is quoted as saying, "Hezbollah relies on the same criminal weapons smugglers, document traffickers and transportation experts as the drug cartels. ... They work together; they rely on the same shadow facilitators. One way or another, they are all connected. They'll leverage those relationships to their benefit, to smuggle contraband and humans into the U.S.; in fact, they already are."[887]

In 2009, Muslim cleric and professor Abdullah Al-Nafisi explains in a sermon from his mosque, "Four pounds of anthrax – in a suitcase this big [his hands are about one foot apart] – carried by a fighter through tunnels from Mexico into the US, are guaranteed to kill 330,000 Americans within a single hour, if it is properly spread in population centers there. [Al-Nafisi chuckles.] What a horrifying idea. [He raises his hands in mock fright.] 9/11 will be small change in comparison."[888] (His audience laughs.)

Photo: This tunnel, which zigzags the length of nearly six football fields, links warehouses in Tijuana and San Diego's Otay Mesa industrial area. Authorities seized 8½ tons of marijuana and 327 pounds of cocaine in connection with the tunnel's discovery. The DEA says a tunnel like this, equipped with power, vents and rail system takes hundreds of thousands of man-hours and millions of dollars to complete. Between 1990 and 2012 over 150 secret tunnels have been located. Not just for narcotics, illegal aliens use them to gain entry into America. (Courtesy U.S. Customs and Border Protection)

In 2009, nearly 300 violent Somalis go missing in America. ICE agent Thomas Eyre, reveals the following in a sworn affidavit. Anthony Joseph Tracy, a.k.a. Yusuf Tracy a.k.a. Yusuf Noor, 35, converts to Islam while in prison in the 1990s. In April 2009 Tracy travels to Kenya and helps 272 Somalis obtain visas. In Somalia he makes contact with Harakat al-Shabaab Mujahideen a.k.a. al-Shabaab, the violent, brutal Somali arm of al-Qaeda responsible for worldwide suicide bombings. Tracy's business, Noor Services Ltd., obtains fake documents to acquire visas for these Somalis to go to Cuba. From Kenya they travel to Dubai to Moscow to Cuba, then onto South America, then Mexico and up through the U.S. Southern border. Upon arrival in Mexico, Tracy then advises them how to smuggle themselves into America. Once in America, they vanish. Assistant U.S. Attorney Jeanine Linehan tells U.S. District Judge Leonie Brinkema at a 2010 hearing. "We believe all the individuals are present in the United States. But by the virtue of [Tracy's] successful smuggling scheme, we are having difficulty finding them."[889]

NOTE: Since the early 1990s, the U.S. State Department's refugee-resettlement program has placed more than 100,000 Somalis into U.S cities and towns – nearly all of them Muslims selected by the UN's refugee agency. Minnesota is the destination of choice, with secondary hotspots in Maine, Ohio, Texas and Georgia. More than 800 new refugees from Somalia arrive in the United States every month, according to Refugee Resettlement Watch. The constant influx has earned parts of Minneapolis the nickname "Little Mogadishu".[890] See the full list of Somali Cities of Refuge in Appendix 2.

In February 2010 three men; Khaled Safadi, 56, and 43-year-old Emilio Gonzalez, both of Miami; and 46-year-old Ulises Talavera-Campos, a citizen of Paraguay are charged with financing Hezbollah.[891]

In March 2010, Ahmed Muhammad Dhakane is charged with operating a large-scale alien-smuggling ring out of Brazil responsible for smuggling several hundred Somalis and other East Africans into the U.S. The indictment alleges that those Dhakane's organization sneaked in included people associated with al-Itihaad al-Islamiya (AIAI), a militant group linked to al Qaeda.[892] "Dhakane smuggled in people he knew were violent jihadists 'with the full knowledge that if the decision was made by the [terrorist group], for which he was associated with in the past, to commit terrorist acts in the United States, these jihadists would commit violent acts in and against the United States'."[893]

In April 2010, Jamal Yousef is apprehended in New York City. During interrogation, he admits to stealing weapons from Iraq for Hezbollah. "Yousef alone knew of a Hezbollah stockpile in Mexico that included 100 M-16 assault rifles, 100 AR-15 rifles, 2500 hand grenades, C4 explosives and anti-tank weapons."[894] In July 2010 Mexican authorities announced that they had broken up a Hezbollah network operating in Tijuana, right on America's doorstep.

Also in July 2010, a car bomb explodes near the U.S. border in Ciudad Juarez killing four – two federal agents, one municipal police officer and an emergency medical technician, and wounded 9 other people. Juarez officials said that bomb made with 20 pounds of explosives, possibly C-4, was detonated from a remote location by cell phone. Local experts state the Juarez and Sinaloa drug cartels apparently have adopted terrorists' tactics.[895] [896] [897]

In August 2010 the Southern District Court of New York hands down an indictment showing a connection between Hezbollah and the drug cartels that violently plague the U.S.-Mexico border. Well-known international arms dealer and Mexican national, Jameel Nasr, tries to orchestrate an arms-for-drugs deal. Cocaine from FARC – the Revolutionary Armed Forces of Colombia, which works with Mexican drug cartels to take cocaine into America – is to be traded for thousands of weapons housed by a Hezbollah operative in Mexico.[898]

On January 25, 2011 a U.S. Border Patrol agent from the Casa Grande substation made a disturbing discovery. His normal route includes the eastern border of the Tohono O'odham Nation Reservation as well as the Eloy and Phoenix metro areas. While patrolling the well-worn route for smuggling illegal immigrants and drugs – Terrorist Alley – a.k.a. Cocaine Alley (see map on next page), he finds a copy of *In Memory of Our Martyrs*. This book published in Iran contains short biographies of Islamic suicide bombers and other Islamic militants who died carrying out attacks.

U.S. Customs and Border Protection documents reveals, "The book also includes [final] letters from suicide attackers to their families, as well as some of their last wills and testaments. Each biographical page contains "the terrorist's name, date of death, and how they died."[899] The book cover features a yellow sun and below it are three scarlet blood-dripping bullet holes. Nice.

In May 2011, Iranian-American car seller Manssor Arbabsiar who lives in Corpus Christi, Texas, offers a man that he believes is a member of the Mexican cartel Los Zetas US$1.5 million to murder the Saudi ambassador to the U.S. The plan calls for a bomb to be detonated at a Washington restaurant while Adel al-Jubeir dines.[900]

In September 2012 three members of Hezbollah – including a US citizen named Rafic Mohammad Labboun Allaboun – are arrested in Merida, Mexico and turned over the US authorities. Allaboun is carrying a fake passport identifying him as a citizen of Belize at the time of arrest. Once a prominent Muslim leader in Northern California, Labboun spends over two years in prison for credit card fraud. Authorities suspect that the $100,000 in credit card fraud is linked to Hezbollah's money laundering.[901]

In October 2012 a report shows "hundreds of thousands of Middle Easterners living in Mexico, and a small percentage of them may be radicals using routes established by drug networks to sneak into the U.S. The ties linking Mexico to Islamic terrorism were underscored earlier this year [2012] when an alleged Iranian operative plotted to assassinate a Saudi diplomat in Washington using a hired gun on loan from a Mexican drug cartel. Rep. Sue Myrick (R-N.C.) says mounting evidence of a Hezbollah presence in Mexico is being ignored by the Department of Homeland Security."[902]

In December 2013, newly radicalized Terry Lee Loewen, 58 is arrested in an FBI sting at a Wichita, Kansas airport. Friends and family are stunned as Loewen is seen as a laid-back, warm-hearted avionics technician. Since he is late coming to violent jihad Loewen feels he must make up for lost time by causing "maximum carnage + death." With easy access to the tarmac at Wichita's Mid-Continent Airport, Loewen's plan is to detonate a truck bomb situated between two terminals "to cause the most damage".[903]

In June 2014, Michael Wolf, 24, is arrested on the jetway at Houston's Bush Intercontinental Airport as he prepares to leave the country and join with ISIS in Syria to engage in jihad. To avoid detection, he plans to fly to Canada, then Iceland and on to Denmark where he would eventually make his way to Turkey. Wolf is sentenced in June 2015 to seven years in prison followed by five years of supervised release.[904]

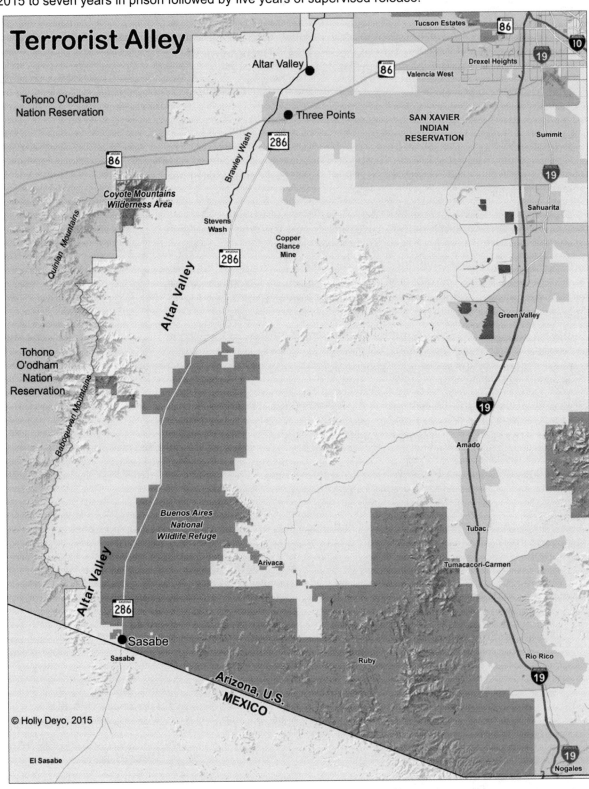

In January 2015, 20-year-old Christopher Lee Cornell, a.k.a. Raheel Mahrus Ubaydah tells an FBI informant they should "wage jihad," and shows his plans for bombing the Capitol and shooting people. Cornell is arrested after purchasing two semi-automatic rifles and about 600 rounds of ammo. Either Cornell's father is in denial or unaware of his son's violent plans saying that Christopher "was a 'momma's boy who never left the house.' He said his son endured frequent incidents of abuse as a practicing Muslim. 'Everything you're hearing in the media right now, they've already painted him as some kind of terrorist,' John Cornell told the newspaper. ... 'They've painted him as some kind of jihadist. ... (Christopher) is one of the most peace-loving people I know.'" Peace-loving Cornell planned to detonate pipe bombs at and near the Capitol and then shoot and kill employees and officials, all of which Cornell had saved money to fund the attack.[905]

In February 2015, a 31-year-old Shiite Muslim Ahmed Adnan Taha, Al Khafaji is apprehended sneaking across the Mexican border into Pharr, Texas. The Border Patrol express concern that the Iraqi is sent by Russia, largely due to the man's history as a military trainer and his skill in speaking several languages, including Russian, and having lived in Crimea. A Ukrainian paid $4,000 for him to get to the U.S., however, the Iraqi refuses to identify the Ukrainian to U.S. authorities.[906]

Also in February 2015, Abdirahman Sheik Mohamud, 23, of Columbus, Ohio is accused of traveling to Syria for terrorist training, then returning to the U.S. with the intention of killing police or soldiers. His training includes firing weapons, breaking into houses, explosives, and hand-to-hand combat. According to court papers, when he returns to America, he has two objectives: to "commit an act of terrorism" and target "armed forces, police officers, or any uniformed individuals" and "go to a military base in Texas and kill three or four Americans execution style."[907]

In February 2015 Abdurasul Hasanovich Juraboev, 24, Akhror Saidakhmetov, 19, and Abror Habibov, 30, are taken into custody for allegedly plotting to join ISIS and help that terror group in America, if they can't travel overseas. Juraboev and Habibov are both Brooklyn residents and citizens of Uzbekistan, while Saidakhmetov, also living in Brooklyn is Kazakhstani. In August 2014 Juraboev posts on an Uzbeki-speaking website that promotes ISIS' ideology, saying he'll kill President Obama if ordered to do so by ISIS. He writes, "I am in USA now … But is it possible to commit ourselves as dedicated martyrs anyway while here? What I'm saying is, to shoot Obama and then get shot ourselves, will it do? That will strike fear in the hearts of infidels." If convicted, each defendant faces a maximum sentence of 15 years in prison.[908]

In April 2015 John T. Booker Jr., 20, is arrested outside Fort Riley military base as he allegedly tries to connect wires to what he believes is a 1000-pound bomb inside a van. His plan is to blow up the device in the name of ISIS and to "kill as many soldiers as possible". Booker is charged with attempting to use a weapon of mass destruction, attempting to damage property by means of an explosive and of attempting to provide material support to ISIS. The FBI is tipped off after Booker tries to join the Army and posts on Facebook he is ready to wage a holy war. "Getting ready to be killed in jihad is a HUGE adrenaline rush!! I am so nervous. NOT because I'm scared to die but I am eager to meet my lord."[909] He faces life in prison.

In April 2015 an Army National Guard soldier and his cousin are arrested after allegedly plotting to fight for ISIS in the Middle East and in America. Guard Specialist Hasan Edmonds, 22, is arrested at a Chicago airport trying to board a plane bound for Egypt while Jonas Edmonds, 29, is arrested at his Aurora, Illinois home. The two men planned to rack up a body count of 120 using AK47s and grenades. Hasan Edmonds had plans to fight for ISIS overseas and Jonas Edmonds would attack a U.S. military installation in northern Illinois.[910]

In April 2015, a 30-year-old Philadelphia mother is charged with planning to go overseas to join ISIS and martyr herself. Known as YoungLioness on Twitter, she posts "If we truly knew the realities ... we all would be rushing to join our brothers in the front lines pray ALLAH accept us as shuhada [martyrs]." After applying for a passport and purchasing her ticket to Turkey in March, she tells a friend that she will deactivate her Twitter account "till I (sic) leave for sham [greater Syria] ... don't want to draw attention of the kuffar [non-believers]." Despite having two children and other family Thomas allegedly tells an ISIS fighter of her desire to die a martyr, "That would be amazing... A girl can only wish."[911]

Also in April 2015, Noelle Velentzas, 28, and Asia Siddiqui, 31, are accused of plotting to plant bombs in America. Allegedly Siddiqui is in possession of multiple propane tanks and instructions for how to turn those tanks into explosive devices. Siddiqui repeatedly contacts members of al-Qaida overseas to offer her support as well as offering it to Mohammed Mohamud, the man arrested in November 2010 after trying to blow up a Christmas-tree lighting ceremony in Portland, Oregon. Velentzas idolizes Osama bin Laden and praises the 9/11 attacks. Velentzas is "obsessed" with pressure cookers and wants to make explosive devices using the cookware to kill multiple people at once.

They also discuss using burner phones, and how to make homemade grenades and pipe bombs. Velentzas is quoted in the complaint saying, "If we get arrested, the police will point their guns at us from the back and maybe from the front. If we can get even one of their weapons, we can shoot them. They will probably kill us but we will be martyrs automatically and receive Allah's blessing." The complaint further paints a picture of a disturbing trend in homegrown violent extremism – and one that increasingly involves women.[912]

In May 2015 a second man, Alexander E. Blair, 28, tied to the April Fort Riley bomb plot is charged with conspiracy. Blair allegedly not only knew about Booker's bomb plans and fails to report it, but also supplies him with money for a storage unit where Booker could store components for the bomb.[913]

In June, the FBI arrest 19-year-old Justin Nojan Sullivan of Morganton, North Carolina as his parents express their shock. He plots attacks on the U.S. homeland hoping to kill 1,000 Americans and send a video of his exploits to ISIS. He considers using biological weapons, bullets coated in cyanide and "set off a gas bomb to finish off the rest." He also mulls over using a car bomb and "a U-Haul packed with bombs." Rich and Eleanor Sullivan alert the FBI two months prior to his arrest when he begins destroying Buddhas and other religious items. Following this, the FBI assigns an undercover agent to communicate with Sullivan and the teen asks him for a silencer. He also asks the agent to kill his parents and said he'd provide their location and money. Sullivan describes himself as a Muslim convert and one engaged in Jihad. He brags, "I'll be doing shootings of my own before then … I'm excited."[914]

"Lone Wolves" Turn Pack Animals

On June 13, 2015 the FBI's Joint Terrorism Task Force arrest college student Munther Omar Saleh, 20, in New York City and charge him with providing material support to the Islamic State. Another conspirator, unnamed, is also taken into custody. In interviews Saleh admits that his group (other members' arrests listed below) plans to bomb New York landmarks, take a vehicle and run down police officers, and then use their weapons to attack others – all on behalf of ISIS. Saleh comes to the attention of law enforcement when he begins posting radical statements on social media. In March he is discovered examining for two consecutive days the George Washington Bridge, which runs between New York and New Jersey.

Saleh denies researching anti-surveillance techniques and how to elude law enforcement, training techniques, and what equipment could be used to carry out violent attacks and bombings. Searches for this information are found on his computer. Also on his computer are downloads of instructions for building pressure-cooker bombs, the possibility of using Crock-Pots, beads, propane, vacuum cleaners, lamps and watches; and information on weapons including knives, axes, and firearms, plus how to disguise equipment and electronics. Saleh's computer history also reveals searches for disguises including beards and wigs. He is spotted the month before his arrest walking into a spy store in Queens that sells microphone detectors and hidden cameras.[915] During this time Saleh is enrolled in a college electrical engineering course that would teach him skills useful for building a bomb.

Saleh's actions reveal how quickly Muslims can become radicalized. Just 12 months prior to planning terror attacks, he is obsessed with video games, most important to him is Pokemon. Saleh spends his time talking online about it and Pokemon TV shows, posts Pokemon commentaries on YouTube and other social media sites for at least six years. Abruptly his videos change from adoring Pokemon to promoting al-Nusra Front, al-Qaeda's Syrian arm and publicly criticizing al-Qaeda for being "too moderate".[916]

On June 15, co-conspirator 21-year-old Fareed Mumuni is taken into custody, but not before Mumuni tries to stab the arresting FBI agent. They arrive at his Staten Island home shortly after 6:30 a.m., issue a search warrant and order him to remain seated on the sofa. Instead Mumuni lunges at an agent with a large kitchen knife and tries repeatedly to plunge it into his chest. None of the stabbings penetrate as the agent is wearing body armor. Again friends and neighbors are shocked by Mumuni's arrest. Neighbor Don Dwonkowski is in denial saying, "I just don't believe it's true. He's a beautiful person; he was a really, really respectful neighbor; helped me all the time; always available. His demeanor – never; I don't believe it, I just don't believe it."[917]

Long time family friend Sherrell Jordan, however, is not taken in and realizes something is terribly wrong. "I noticed some changes in his appearance. About a year ago, he was very friendly and outgoing, but the last six months, he changed his appearance, grew a beard, shaved his head and his demeanor was totally different now, more dogmatic."[918] Mumuni is charged with attempted murder, plotting a bombing and plotting an ISIS attack in America. If convicted, Mumuni faces a maximum sentence of 20 years in prison.

Another member of this terror group is Samuel Rahamin Topaz, 21, of Fort Lee, New Jersey. Rahamin is arrested on June 16 and charged with conspiracy to provide material support to the Islamic State. Electronic communications recovered from Topaz's phone corroborate plans to travel overseas to join ISIS. Friends are shocked by Topaz's actions. His mother is Christian and his father is Jewish. In high school he is recognized for his acting abilities and beautiful singing voice. He is a member of a community theater group that another member describes as "family". He also plays football and runs track. Topaz is accepted into Boston's prestigious Berklee College of Music. He is a recent convert to Islam and posts on Facebook that he is "the angel of carnage" with selfies showing him in jihadist-style scarves.[919] Topaz is held without bail and faces a maximum of 15 years in prison and a fine of $250,000.[920]

On June 28 another New Jersey man 23-year-old Alaa Saadeh is arrested for conspiring to provide personnel and services to ISIS terrorists. According to the court document, his "violent agenda" calls for mass killings and beheadings. Saadeh's unnamed radicalized brother is also arrested after traveling to his native Jordan with plans to join ISIS forces. All in this group plan terror attacks should they be prevented from traveling to Jordan. The complaint reveals Saadeh's motivations, that he "felt that something crazy was going to happen ever since he was a child and now everything crazy is happening," and "there is more to life than continuing with school."[921] If convicted, Saadeh faces a maximum of 20 years in prison as well as a fine of $250,000 for each count.[922]

Technology Aiding Terrorists

By the end of June 2015 America's homeland was the target of 71 *publicly known* Islamist terrorist plots or attacks since 9/11 according to the Heritage Foundation. The first half of 2015 saw the most intense time of terrorist plotting since the Twin Towers attacks. Law enforcement and intel agencies batted a thousand in 2015, but it only takes a single miss for people to have a really unhappy day.

Terrorists are getting cleverer, learning how to improve their skill sets, switching up plans to cause the most carnage and fear. They make the best use of social media to recruit and radicalize others and to share last minute details of plans nearly in motion. They use the Internet to learn how to make explosives, buy components and weapons, and inspire jihadi "virgins" with on-line videos and venomous rants. To thwart planned actions coming to attention of authorities, they hide their IP addresses, use publicly available email encryption software and delve into the "deep web" where really lowlifes go for anonymous contact and purchases.

Since the Deep Web isn't accessible using normal search engines of Yahoo, Google or Bing, most people don't even know it exists or how to access it though experts estimate that it's probably 400 to 500 times the size of what most people use every day – the Surface Web. For the first time in September 2014, the number of active websites hit 1 billion[923] so the Deep Web is unbelievably massive.

Specialized software can peel away layers of the Surface Web revealing the Undernet – the Deep Web. This software maintains the privacy of both the source and the people who access it. It's home to marketplaces for controlled substances, armories selling all kinds of weapons, political dissidents, hardcore child porn, money laundering, credit card fraud, identity theft and any other slimy venture people can conjure. Once terrorists begin to use the Deep Web in earnest, it will be much more difficult, if not nearly impossible for intel agencies to intercept plans before they're carried out.

Terrorists – The Enemy Within

The blind and too-tolerant U.S. government allows Islamic terrorist training camps to proliferate and thrive in America. It's a shocking thought, but happening nonetheless. Due to our laws and free speech, one can't be accused until a law actually is broken or someone is hurt or dies. That is part of this Country's fabric and for the most part, it works.

"A 2007 FBI record states that members of the group [Muslims of America] have been involved in at least 10 murders, one disappearance, three firebombings, one attempted firebombing, two explosive bombings and one attempted bombing.

"'The documented propensity for violence by this organization supports the belief the leadership of the MOA extols membership to pursue a policy of jihad or holy war against individuals or groups it considers enemies of Islam, which includes the U.S. Government,' the document states. 'Members of the MOA are encouraged to travel to Pakistan to receive religious and military/terrorist training from Sheikh Gilani.'

"The document also says Muslims of America is now 'an autonomous organization which possesses an infrastructure capable of planning and mounting terrorist campaigns overseas and within the U.S.'"[924]

A 2006 DOJ – Department of Justice – report states Jamaat ul-Fuqra 'has ... more than 3,000 members spread across the United States, all in support of one goal: the purification of Islam through violence.'" In 2005, the Department of Homeland Security predicted the group would continue to carry out attacks in the U.S. Muslim leaders urge, "act like you are his friend. Then kill him," says Gilani (Muslims of the Americas leader, Sheikh Mubarak Gilani) in the recruitment video, explaining how to handle American "infidels.'"[925]

Additional reports state 2002's Beltway Snipers, John Allen Muhammad and Lee Boyd Malvo, and failed shoe bomber, Richard Reid, all trained at these camps.

Are Terrorists Living Next to You?

This is not paranoia. On February 25, 2015 FBI Director James Comey revealed that there are now ISIS recruits in all 50 states. This doesn't mean necessarily one; it could be hundreds. Alaska was the last state to fall victim. Then in October of that same year Comey delivered a stunning statement that 900 investigations were underway against ISIS operatives, recruits and those ISIS has inspired. Comey had testified to Congress, "When the final counting is done, 2014 will have been the most lethal year for global terrorism in the 45 years such data has been compiled. ISIL in particular is putting out a siren song with their slick propaganda through social media."[926] Comey was right. In 2014 terrorists murdered nearly 33,000 in almost 13,500 attacks around the world. That's up from just over 18,000 deaths in nearly 10,000 attacks in 2013. ISIS and Boko Haram were the two groups primarily responsible for nearly doubling the murders and tripling the kidnappings.[927]

This is Islamic State's carrion (not clarion) cry, their recruiting pitch. "Troubled soul, come to the caliphate, you will live a life of glory, these are the apocalyptic end times, you will find a life of meaning here, fighting for our so-called caliphate. And if you can't come, kill somebody where you are."[928]

In May 2015, Director Comey revealed that Islamic State's influence is growing in America. He stated there are "hundreds, maybe thousands" of people across the country who are receiving recruitment overtures or directives to attack the U.S. They're making brilliant use of social media to spread their poison and hatred sending messages to "disturbed people" via smartphone that could be pushed to launch assaults on U.S. targets. Comey said, "It's like the devil sitting on their shoulders, saying *'kill, kill, kill.'"[929]* Comey continued his warnings saying that fewer Americans are traveling to fight with ISIS overseas yet the number of recruits is rising. That leads to the uneasy conclusion that these dangerous individuals loyal to the Islamic State and its vicious lethal ideology are plotting more violent acts on American soil.

CREEPING SHARIA

With some states attempting to allow Islamic law to supersede state law, there is certainly a whiff of creeping Sharia. Others reading the Islamic fortune cookies have already taken necessary preventative steps. Alabama, Arizona, Kansas, Louisiana, North Carolina, Oklahoma, South Dakota and Tennessee have put Sharia law – Islamic law – off-limits. Other states considering similar bans include Arkansas, Florida, Indiana, Iowa, Kentucky, Mississippi, South Carolina, Texas, Virginia, Washington, West Virginia and Wyoming.[930]

Apparently Texas wasn't 100% sure about a ban and opened the barn door. As of 2015, Irving, Texas – a town situated halfway between Dallas and Ft. Worth – is the first site where an Islamic tribunal in America operates. Texas? Who'd a thought... Texas. Dr. Taher El-Badawi, one of its four judges is quick to reassure, "Sharia, it is exactly Islamic law, it is from God, it is from Allah. It's full of mercy. I know you have a lot of bad experience and a lot of bad examples around us, I agree with you. But not just in Islam, it is everywhere."[931]

In 2015, Hamtramck, Michigan became the first Muslim-majority U.S. city in 2013, mostly immigrating from Yemen and Bangladesh. Then in 2015 Hamtramck made history again by electing the nation's first majority Muslim council. Following the election results, Ibrahim Algahim, a member of the Yemeni community was caught on cell phone video saying, "Today we show the Polish and everybody else that we are united."[932]

Understandably residents were not happy with his divisive comment. Cathie Lisinki-Gordon, a former councilmember, expressed surprise at Algahim's supremacist language. "I'm shocked that he said that. I'm a very good friend of his. I cannot believe that he would ever profile any select group. Especially when his community has felt ostracized and profiled for many years."[933]

Today Hamtramck's population of 22,000 is 40% immigrant with 26 languages spoken. Many people aren't bothering to learn English, so how do kids learn in school? Even the different Muslim groups don't mix much due to language barriers. For more than a century and even as recently as 1970, Hamtramck was a 90% Polish, Catholic town. Today, it's only 11% Catholic. Six mosques dominate the town – the most per capita anywhere in America.

When residents wanted to build a Catholic church on the main drag back then, they were denied. Mosque leaders bought one of the city's largest commercial buildings in the heart of the business district. Now the town's 7th and largest mosque, Al-Islah Mosque, a.k.a. the Al-Islah Islamic Center, will be right on the main thoroughfare at 11301-11303 Joseph Campau. Business owners within 500 feet of the mosques can't obtain a liquor license. The 20,000 sq ft building will hold up to 2,000 worshippers when renovations are completed. The building will be unmistakable topped with the traditional onion-shaped dome and minarets.[934]

Right across the street at 2733 Caniff was another mosque too small to accommodate the estimated 25,000 Muslims in and around the area of Hamtramck. Since 2004, five times a day, loud speakers blast down the streets calls to prayer and longtime residents are struggling to adjust. That's the year residents realized their town had changed irrevocably. Resident and shop owner Karen Majewski whose family emigrated from Poland in the early 20th century voices concerns similar to other residents. "There's definitely a strong feeling that Muslims are the other," she said. "It's about culture, what kind of place Hamtramck will become. There's definitely a fear, and to some degree, I share it."[935]

Dr. Frank Gaffney, president of the Center for Security Policy, has a different take. He worries, "If a woman for example wants her divorce to be recognized in the Islamic community, then she must get it through the Sharia process." Despite Dr. El-Badawi's mild manner Gaffney argues that allowing any Sharia here will undermine U.S. laws and protections for Muslims, especially women and children. He points out what's already happened in Europe.

"In places like Britain we've seen a separate court system take effect. You now have something like 87 different Sharia courts recognized by the British government that operate kind of in parallel with the courts of the English common law. In our country we've both seen this kind of effort made, mostly through arbitration councils to this point, now this tribunal, but also an effort made to penetrate our actual own American court system and this is very troubling."[936]

This is how Islamic law infiltrates non-Muslim countries. Quietly, unobtrusively. It is like bindweed. First small pink and white flowers appear. It looks pretty, petals nod in the summer breeze. Then a short time passes. It's climbed on, intertwined and choked everything in its path with roots some 20 feet deep so it's nearly impossible to eradicate. Creeping Sharia.

CREEPING SHARIAH, NOW AT A TROT

Though people are waking up to the conflict between Sharia law and the American justice system, some cities are trying different avenues and succeeding. In 2013, Dearborn, Michigan voted 4-3 becoming the first US city to officially implement all aspects of Sharia Law. This accommodates their nearly 100,000-strong Muslim population.[937]

A 2015 documentary revealed that some American Muslims champion the thought of Sharia law in the U.S. Filmmaker Ami Horowitz who travels throughout the world, noted that what stood out most to him in European countries was the lack of Muslim integration into countries where they chose to move. Instead of adapting to their new home and its culture, they want to bring in and implement Sharia. During Horowitz's interview with men-on-the-street in Minneapolis, Minnesota a number of them voiced it should be against the law to insult the prophet Mohammed thereby obliterating the First Amendment.[938]

In this same interview, Fox News host Sean Hannity questioned the director of *Jihad Watch,* Robert Spencer, whether or not new immigrants in America must assimilate, must agree with American law, American values and the Constitution. Spencer responds, "Absolutely Sean. This used to be taken for granted among immigrants. ... Now it's a very different case. There have been four separate and independent studies in mosques in the United States conducted since 1998 and they all came to the identical result that 80%, *80%* Sean, of mosques in the U.S. teach the superiority of Sharia over Constitutional law and the necessity ultimately to replace one with the other. ... They are all based on studies of what is actually taught in these mosques and they show that this is a major problem."[939]

Their intent is unmistakable. Underscoring these studies are signs carried in various protests Muslims reading:

• Shariah Will Dominate the World
• Islam Will Dominate the World – Freedom Can Go to Hell

- Shariah the Solution for the East and West
- Muslim Rise Up! Establish the Shariah
- Man Made Law to Hell – Our Way (Shariah) or the High Way" (sic)
- Shariah the Future for UK
- Democracy Is Falling Shariah Is Returning
- Shariah the Only Solution
- Shari'ah for Britain
- Need for Allah's Law, Not Man Made Law
- Islam is the Answer Democracy is Cancer
- No Democracy We Want Just Islam (sign carried in Dearborn, Michigan)
- Islam is Superior and Nothing Will Supercede It
- Shari'ah the Only Option
- Islam Is the Perfect System for all Mankind
- Shariah for France
- Islam the Solution for France
- Ban Democracy Implement Islam
- Shariah 4 France
- Shariah for the Netherlands
- Muslims Will Destroy the Crusade & Implement Islam!
- The Veil: Liberation from Man Made Law

December 15, 2011 Nancy Qualls-Shehata writes on the Muslimah on Progress blog: "Once again Islam is in the news as a major kerfluffle (sic) is underway due to Lowe's decision to pull advertising from the TLC reality show "All-American Muslim". Islamophobes opine about creeping sharia law, while Muslims try to reassure them that, no, we don't want sharia, we are perfectly content with American law and we are fully integrated in society. Well, time for me to confess. For religious Muslims, that's a load of horse hockey. We want sharia law. We want Islamic law to be the law of the land, the law of the planet, the law of the universe. May as well just put it out there. It's the truth, and no amount of pandering to non-Muslims will change that fact."[940]

In 2010 New Jersey judge Joseph Charles ruled in favor a Muslim man who admitted to repeatedly forcing his wife to have intercourse and she had sought a restraining order. Because under Islam there is no such thing as rape, even in U.S. courts, the wife had no standing. The wife, a Moroccan woman who had recently immigrated to the U.S. at the time of the attacks alleged:

"Defendant forced plaintiff to have sex with him while she cried. Plaintiff testified that defendant always told her 'this is according to our religion. You are my wife, I c[an] do anything to you. The woman, she should submit and do anything I ask her to do.'"[941] An appellate court overturned the decision – *this* time.

Cully Stimson, domestic violence prosecutor and expert in criminal and military law assessed the New Jersey case. "This is not the last we will hear of such attempts, however, as Sharia-loving extremists are determined to establish an Islamic Caliphate around the world, especially in America. As Andy McCarthy has written, 'Our enemies are those who want Sharia to supplant American law and Western culture.' We cannot allow that to happen."[942] But it is.

Take for example under Sharia law, collecting or paying interest is prohibited. In order to increase housing, Seattle's mayor, Ed Murray, is looking for how he can introduce Sharia law that foregoes interest. While on the surface it looks attractive to most people not having to pay loan interest, but it's how banks make money so they actually have funds to lend. How is that fair that Muslims get interest-free loans and the rest don't? In order to accommodate them either non-Muslim borrowers will do so at a higher interest rate or the fees for credit cards, checking, ATM access and overdraft protection will rise – or all of the above.

Implementing laws specifically labeled Sharia is a dangerous precedent. Shariah Finance Watch writes, "Islamists are attempting to impose Shariah Compliant Finance (SCF) on Western institutions to use our own financial strengths against us. The most serious problem with SCF is that it legitimates and institutionalizes Shariah law… a theo-political, legal doctrine violently opposed to Western values."[943]

For a decade Sharia has slowly oozed into America. Besides interest-free loans, the Muslim financial concept of *sukuk* is taking root around the world. Sukuks are Sharia-compliant bonds, tied to a physical asset. Investors are rewarded with a share of the asset's profit in lieu of interest. Goldman Sachs, CitiBank, GE Capital and HSBC are among western financial corporations that have introduced sukuk in recent years. As of 2014 four non-Muslim countries have tapped into the sukuk market. First, the UK, then Hong Kong, then South Africa and Luxembourg followed suit.[944]

"In 2008, Rep. Frank Wolf, R-Va., and then-Rep. Sue Myrick, R-N.C., sent AIG then-Chairman Edward Liddy a letter condemning the company's move to offer Sharia-compliant insurance programs: 'You may defend your decision to offer Sharia products and will probably state that they have no real ties to Sharia law, and therefore pose no threat. You are wrong. Like Britain, the way to America's legal code is through its wallet, and if Sharia law gains a strong footing in the United States, it will be through Sharia finance and Sharia products.'"[945]

Some non-Muslim countries already have Islamic family law courts available for their minority Muslim population: Eritrea, Ethiopia, Ghana, India, Israel, Kenya, Tanzania, Singapore, Sri Lanka, Thailand, Uganda, and the United Kingdom.[946]

So You Think Sharia Is Good? Think Again

According to Kamal Saleem, former Muslim radical who grew up in Lebanon, states it is stealthy and quite dangerous, especially for non-Muslims to be under its rule, as Westerners don't think this way. Most Americans see it as the little yellow ducky drifting on the pond, but don't look deeper and see its feet paddling furiously beneath the water. To see Sharia implement completely would tie the brains and hearts of most Americans and citizen of other non-Muslim countries into knots.

Saleem at one time, had been involved with the PLO and the Muslim Brotherhood, learned about jihad by age 7. After participating in considerable Middle East conflict, he was sent to America to infiltrate our society. He worked with the Muslim Brotherhood here, before becoming Christian, so he shares a unique, insider's perspective. Saleem states that Sharia's main principle is to subjugate nations to Islamic laws even indirectly and that there are 3 levels for advancing it:

- When Muslims comprise 1% or less of a nation's population, they keep Sharia hidden and are peaceful. Then practice Islam within a small sphere of family and friends.
- When Muslims comprise 2% or less of a nation's population, they infiltrate the jail system, poor neighborhoods, universities, government and lobby for Sharia Law.
- When Muslims become a large part of a nation's population, they apply pressure by intimidation on a society.[947]

The U.S. is already well into Stage 2 and France has hit #3.

In 2004 Italian journalist, author and political interviewer, Oriana Fallaci observed, "Europe becomes more and more a province of Islam, a colony of Islam. And Italy is an outpost of that province, a stronghold of that colony...In each of our cities lies a second city: a Muslim city, a city run by the Quran. A stage in the Islamic expansionism."[948]

In 2012, CBN News' Erick Stakelbeck interviewed political activist Anjem Choudary, "the face of radical Islam" in Great Britain. He's known for holding frequent rallies calling for Sharia law to be imposed on the UK. Stakelbeck located Choudary in London and asked, "So you believe America, Great Britain, all of Europe, will be Islamic states living under Sharia?"

Choudary replies, "I am convinced. I am 100 percent certain that the Sharia will be implemented in America and in Britain one day. The question is, 'when?' and how it will come to fruition." Unapologetic about its implementation he continues. "If people are afraid of having their hands cut, don't steal. If you don't want to be stoned to death, don't commit adultery. It seems to me that people want all of the vices and they want to get away with it as well. But it doesn't work like that. The seeds for the call for Sharia in America have been there for many decades. We have the Sharia4America project, where we present what we consider to be an alternative to democracy and freedom and the kind of life that people lead in America."[949]

On establishing Sharia law in non-Muslims countries through jihad Anjem Choudary replied, "If we have enough authority and we have enough power, then we are obliged as Muslims to take the authority away from those who have it and implement Sharia. Now I hope that can come in a very peaceful way. I hope we can do that in a way where there is no bloodshed,"[950] but gives no guarantees of peace.

Chicago-based political group Hizb Ut-Tahrir America also pushes the pro-Sharia message in America. Its website states it's "a political party whose ideology is Islam, so politics is its work and Islam is its ideology. It works within the Ummah [community] and together with her, so that she adopts Islam as her cause and is led to restore the Khilafah [Caliphate] and the ruling by what Allah (swt) revealed. ['Swt' is an acronym added after 'Allah' that roughly translates to 'The most glorified, the most high' – a way to honor Allah when mentioning His name.] Hizb ut-Tahrir is a political group and not a priestly one. Nor is it an academic, educational or a charity group. The Islamic thought is the soul of its body, its core and the secret of its life."[951]

The group Sharia4 has also spawned other similar branches: Sharia4UK, Sharia4America, Sharia4Holland, Sharia4Italy and Sharia4Belgium.

Photo: Sign snapped by David Shankbone at a 2010 rally protesting the planned construction of a massive 13-story Islamic community center and mosque near Ground Zero. Hundreds attended and this was just one in a sea of protest signs.

Others read, *"Land of the free. Stop Sharia before it stops you,"* referring to Islamic law. Another sign said, *"No mosque here. Preserve the dignity of our loved ones killed on 9/11."* And, *"Building a mosque at Ground Zero is like building a memorial to Hitler at Auschwitz."* Some saw the proposed Muslim complex as particularly insensitive when nearly 3,000 people died at the hand of Muslims on September 11, 2001.

Sharif El-Gamal, developer behind the "Ground Zero mosque", managed to infuriate area residents a second time. El-Gamal had allegedly "'knowingly' used the ground-floor retail space at 69 Leonard St. for illegal 'religious gatherings' and 'loud parties,' and even stuffed 'religious classes' for children into a basement that didn't have proper fire exits, prompting the FDNY to issue violations", landlord GG1 LLC charges.[952] The noise was so irksome it forced the abrupt lease termination of another resident, who paid nearly $8,000 a month to live there. As of August 2014, El-Gamal, had plans to build a 39-story condo tower and a downsized mosque.

Stoned – Muslim Style

More abhorrent than imagined, stoning – also called lapidation – is still practiced or authorized by Muslim law. In Iran, Mauritania, Nigeria (in 12 northern states), Pakistan, Qatar, Saudi Arabia, Somalia, Sudan, the United Arab Emirates, and Yemen, stoning is a legal punishment. Of these countries, only in Iran, Pakistan and Somalia have stonings actually occurred. In Pakistan all instances have occurred outside the legal system. While stoning isn't condoned in Afghanistan, Iraq, and Mali as national legislation, non-state participants carry out lapidation executions. In Aceh, Indonesia and Malaysia, the practice is sanctioned regionally, but banned nationally.[953]

Stoning is most often used as punishment for sexual relationships outside marriage or for homosexual encounters whether the people are married or not. Women are most often the recipients, especially in cases of rape. Frequently they are charged with having an "illicit affair" rather than seen as victims of forced sex. Because proving adultery is very difficult unless someone is caught outright or a baby results, Article 105 of the Islamic Penal Code allows a judge to use discretion – meaning he can act on his own 'knowledge' or 'gut feeling' instead of the evidence presented.[954]

Before lapidation is carried out, both accused men and women are wrapped in white cotton shrouds secured in three places with rope: around the neck, the torso and knees. Vertical pits are dug just shoulder-wide. Women are stood on their feet and buried to breast height. Men undergo the same treatment, but are buried only to their waists. Iran's Penal Code even specifies the size rocks to be used ensuring a slow and painful death usually lasting about 20 minutes. "The stones used should not be large enough to kill the person by one or two strikes; nor should they be so small that they could not be defined as stones (pebbles)." If a victim is somehow able to escape, which is unlikely while buried and trussed, he or she may go free, but it's virtually impossible for women with ¾ of their bodies held in place with dirt.[955]

CASES

While getting specifics on Middle East stonings can be difficult because of the often-rural locations where they're carried out, cases are surfacing. Recent cases. This author won't belabor the point because lapidation is a vile, unforgivable method of execution. However, people need to know what Sharia Law sanctions and practices. Here are eight cases.

Kurdistan Aziz

On May 17 2008, Kurdistan Aziz, 16, was stoned to death in Sulaymaniya, a modern city of 1.5 million in northeast Iraq. Her crime? Kurdistan followed her heart and eloped with a man her family didn't approve. Since she was well aware of the potential consequences for her actions, Kurdistan had gone to both the police and the Kurdish Democratic Party (KDP) for help. They palmed off her to the corrupt Department of Domestic Violence. Instead of protecting her, they handed her back to the family, after receiving a bribe from Kurdistan's father. Her relatives, who considered Kudistan's actions to have brought shame upon them, stoned her to death on Hawre Mountain.

Before she was murdered, a local women's organization had alerted the authorities in the Sulaymaniya Governate, which was controlled by the Patriotic Union of Kurdistan (PUK). They refused to intervene in, what they called, a 'tribal issue'. Instead of helping, the PUK put the onus on the women's organization to provide a photograph of Kurdistan, risking their own safety. Kurdistan was stoned to death as the result of a corrupt system and her family's so-called "honor".[956]

Du'a Khalil Aswad

On April 7, 2007, a beautiful 17-year-old woman with long auburn hair was murdered in Urgu, a district in Afghanistan's northeastern Badakhshan province. Her crime? She'd fallen in love with the wrong person. Du'a Khalil Aswad was Yezidi and her unnamed boyfriend, Sunni. Both groups fiercely hate each other, so Du'a and her boyfriend would meet secretly and planned their escape to Ba'ashiqah (Bashiqa), near Mosul, some 2,500 miles away. Her family notified the police of her disappearance and the couple was located a few days later. Du'a was arrested and thrown in jail. The tribal leader, believed to be her uncle, assured police that Du'a wouldn't be punished. He lied.

Once home she was brought outside in a headlock to face hundreds of men – no women. An enormous crowd surrounded Du'a jockeying for the best position to watch as nine men attacked her. Du'a was stripped naked from the waist down and viciously beaten.

The *UK Daily Mail* details the profoundly disturbing murder. "One man kicks her hard between the legs as she screams in agony. Du'a tries to lift herself up, but someone hurls a concrete block into her face. Another man stamps on her face. Someone kicks her in the stomach. Police officers stand idly by, some of them apparently enjoying the spectacle as much as anyone else."[957]

After 30 minutes of this savagery, Du'a succumbs in a bloody heap. Her family's "honor" is restored. According to the tribal leader, her family didn't want her stoned, but this brutalization and humiliation was better? Iraqi police arrested two men, but they were later released without being charged. Six others fled town, two of which were reportedly her uncles and another her brother, who appeared in the videos several spectators "thoughtfully" recorded on cell phones.

Du'a was laid to rest in an unmarked grave, but her slumber was short-lived. Kurdish authorities had her dug up and examined to see if she were still a virgin. She was. Du'a had been murdered for a "crime" she hadn't committed. And what happened to her young man? The last report said he was in hiding for a while, but no charges were brought against him.[958]

Amina

In April 2005, 29-year-old woman Amina was stoned to death for committing adultery in Urgu, a district in Afghanistan's northeastern Badakhshan province. The accused man was lashed approximately 80 times and then freed. Local courts are presided over by armed groups and hand down death sentences on very little evidence. The central judicial system has been unable to stop these local courts from making such decisions.[959]

Arifa Bibi

In July 2013, an illegal tribal court, Panchayat, ordered a young Pakistani mother of two stoned to death by her relatives. Her crime? Arifa Bibi was caught using a mobile phone. According to news media her uncle, cousins and other relatives threw stones and bricks until Arifa died. That alone was unusual as bricks aren't on the approved Islamic "weapons list" for stonings. Arifa was buried in a desert far from her village. No family, not even her children attended, as they weren't allowed to participate in the funeral.[960] [961]

Faddah Ahmad

In July 2014, Syria carried out two back-to-back stonings, both on adultery charges. A preacher read the verdict and then a truck dumped stones by Bajaa Garden in the city of Raqqa. Jihadi fighters then brought in Faddah Ahmad, clad tip to toe in black, and stood her in the prescribed hole. When residents gathered, Islamic State fighters ordered them to commence stoning. When none stepped forward, Islamic State jihadis carried out the sentence.

Shamseh Abdullah

The day before 26-year-old Shamseh Abdullah met the same fate. Shamseh lived nearby in Tabqa and residents there were prodded to stone her. In the end only Islamic State members participated pelting her with rocks. What was tragically ridiculous awful about Shamseh's "crime" is that she was a widow and her new husband was shocked to discover the previously married woman was not a virgin. Activist Hadi Salameh said the woman's family didn't even know what her new husband had done until it was too late. The UK-based Syrian Observatory for Human Rights verified these murders despite news being slow to surface. Witnesses, minus a few human rights activists, remain silent on these atrocities due to threats of "death by sword" from Islamic State.[962] [963]

Farzana Parveen

On May 27, 2014, her family in Lahore, Pakistan stoned 25-year-old Farzana Parveen to death. Lahore is no backwater town or tribal village, but is the capital of Punjab Province, the second largest metro area in the country. The stoning didn't take place under the cloak of night, but in the bright afternoon sunshine right outside a high court. Farzana was waiting to testify that she hadn't been kidnapped, but married Mohammad Iqbal of her own free will.

Farzana's crime? She married the man she loved, but had wed him without the family's permission. Iqbal and the Parveens had been neighbors and it had been agreed in 2013 that the two would wed. The arrangement was sealed when Iqbal gave Farzana's father 80,000 rupees (about $800) and gold jewelry. Then in December of that year Farzana's mother died and her father and brother changed their minds about her marrying Iqbal. Regardless the two married January 7, 2014, which enraged her family since they had decided for her to marry the cousin. Her father demanded another $1000, but Iqbal couldn't pay it because he was a poor farmer. That's when the family filed charges that she had been abducted.

About 20 people who had been hiding among the cars, began attacking Farzana and Mohammad with sticks and bricks as they waited for court to open. Among the attackers were her father, two brothers and former fiancé – her cousin. One family member made a rough cloth noose around her neck while her brothers smashed bricks into her skull. Mohammad survived the brutal attacks; Farzana did not. She had been three months pregnant at the time of her murder.

Aisha Ibrahim Duhulow

In October 2008, a 13-year-old Somali girl, Aisha Ibrahim Duhulow, was buried up to her neck and stoned by over 50 men. Eyewitnesses reported it was carried out at a football stadium in Kismayo in front of 1,000 people. Her father told Amnesty International she had been raped by three men. When she tried to report the rape to the al-Shabaab militia in control of the city, Aisha was accused of adultery.

After the crowd had gathered for the stoning, the Islamic administration in Kismayo brought her out. Aisha begged for her life saying, *'Don't kill me, don't kill me,'* but it fell on deaf ears. Though cameras were banned, reporters and radio journalists were allowed to watch. Normally conviction a girl of 13 for adultery would be illegal under Islamic law, but there was confusion as to her real age some saying she was 23. Her father and aunt confirmed Aisha really was just a 13-year-old child. Though she begged for mercy, Aisha was executed. Spectators who crowded in to watch said it was "awful". What did they expect with such barbaric punishment? A witness who wished to remain anonymous observed, "People were saying this was not good for Sharia law, this was not good for human rights, this was not good for anything."[964] Yet no one did anything to stop it. During this horrible tragedy, this monumental stuff-up and miscarriage of justice, a boy was shot in the confusion.

So this is part of Sharia Law, Islamic Law. Pakistani law allows murderers to nominate someone to do the killing, then forgive him.[965] Sharia permits stoning and more importantly, it's engrained in Islamic culture. It's central to their all-pervasive concept of honor and shame. It ranks above everything.

According to Human Rights Commission of Pakistan, 869 women were victims of honor killings in 2013 and over 800 others committed suicide.[966] The Aurat Foundation puts the number of Pakistani honor killings at 1,000, but says it's likely much higher since their numbers are gathered from newspaper reports.[967] Their suspicion that the number is much higher ties closer to the UN's estimates of over 5,000 honor killings every year.[968] A fourth publication, *The Middle East Quarterly,* says that the 5,000 figure "might be reasonable for Pakistan alone, but worldwide the numbers are much greater" – maybe as much as fourfold.[969]

Honor Killings in the Western World

While this phenomenon is usually associated with Muslim nations, increasingly it's popping up in Western courtrooms. Honor violence in America and other western countries is concentrated among their more recent immigrants – primarily Muslims. Honor killings are mainly Muslim-on-Muslim crimes whether worldwide or in the West. Phyllis Chesler, Professor Emerita Richmond College of the City University of New York is an expert on honor killings. Her study shows that worldwide 91% of the people who commit these murders are Muslims and the remaining 9% are Sikhs and Hindus. In North America 84% are Muslims. Muslims comprise an even larger majority in Europe – 96% and in Islamic countries, no surprise, they make up 100%.

Chesler cites a common problem why these crimes are proliferating – tolerance, anti-racism and political correctness. There's another, more insidious reason. Willful blindness. "Most honor killings are not classified as such, are rarely prosecuted, or when prosecuted in the Muslim world, result in relatively light sentences. When an honor killing occurs in the West, many people, including the police, still shy away from calling it an honor killing. In the West, both Islamist and feminist groups, including domestic violence activists, continue to insist that honor killings are a form of Western-style domestic violence…. They are not."[970]

Detective Chris Boughey of the Violent Crimes Unit in the Peoria, Arizona Police Department and lead investigator in the Noor Almaleki honor killing observes. "The prevalence of honor violence and honor killings in the US will only increase, unless we act now. We have a duty to protect these young women and to be a voice for them. Most importantly, it is the right thing to do."[971]

Palestina Isa

One of the earliest honor killings involved 16-year-old Palestina Isa who was murdered by her father Palestinian, Zein and Brazilian mother, Maria. Living in St. Louis, Missouri her parents became increasingly angry over Tina's adoption of Western culture. She liked American pop music, dated a non-Muslim black man and had taken a part-time job without her parents' consent. Tina played high school soccer, tennis, made the cheerleading squad and was an honor student. Tina was known as a free spirit, not in a sexual way, but fun-loving, which often got her in trouble at home. Instead of agreeing to be married off and live in her father's minuscule native West Bank village of Beiteen, Tina wanted to use her mind, go to St. Louis University, study aeronautical engineering and become a pilot.

For two years before Tina's death, FBI agents strongly suspected Zein Isa was a member of the Abu Nidal Organization, a recognized terrorist group. Prior to Zein murdering his daughter, the FBI discovered his group planned to bomb the Israeli Embassy in Washington, D.C. Because of this vital intel, the FBI had bugged Isa's apartment and consequently, Tina's every excruciating scream and cry for help was recorded.

On the night of Tina's murder, Nov. 6, 1989, her parents confront her about her job at Wendy's fast food restaurant. "Where were you, bitch?" Her mother accuses. This was her first day as a counter girl. It should have been a happy time with her promotion. Instead Zein hisses that she is a she-devil and further accuses Tina about her boyfriend Clifford Walker. Zein shouted. "He wants to sleep with you in bed. Don't you feel any shame? Don't you have a conscience? It's fornication!"[972] The conversation escalated and her dad blindsided her with threats:

"Here, listen, my dear daughter, do you know that this is the last day. Tonight, you're going to die?"

In shock Tina asks: "Huh?"

Zein repeats: "Do you know that you are going to die tonight?"

Maria asks about things in her school bag when it dawns on Tina that her parents are deadly serious and she begins to shriek.

"Keep still, Tina!" Zein orders.

She begs her mother for help. Maria is unmoved.

Tina screams again, and her mother asks: "Are you going to listen? *Are you going to listen?"*

Screaming louder, Tina gasps: "Yes! Yes! Yes, I am!" Coughing can be heard and she pleads, *"No. Please!"*

The mother barks, "Shut up!"

Tina continues to cry, her words indecipherable. Zeins stab her repeatedly in the breast.

"Die! Die quickly! Die quickly!" the father ordered.

The girl moans, seems to quiet, then screams one last time.

"Quiet, little one! Die my daughter, die!"[973]

Zein had stabbed his daughter six times before she succumbed.

Bob Craddick, assistant prosecutor for seven years said about the 7-minute tape, "It's worse than any movie, any film, anything I thought that I would ever hear in my life."[974]

Tina's parents were arrested, convicted of first-degree murder and sentenced to death by lethal injection. They showed no remorse. Maria's shocking response to Judge Charles Shaw said it all. "My daughter was very disrespectful and very rebellious. We should not have to pay with our lives for something she did."[975]

Sandeela Kanwal

In 2009 a dad murdered his 25-year-old daughter. Around 1 a.m. police received several 911 calls from a home in Jonesboro, Georgia, suburb of Atlanta. The first was from a man who says, "My daughter's dead." Fifty-five minutes later a call comes in from Gina Rashid, Sandeela's stepmother. "I hear a lot of hollering and screaming and I just woke up and I asked my family what's going on. They're from Pakistan. They're not speaking any English to me. They're not telling me nothing. Sandeela's dead. *Sandeela's dead."*[976]

When police arrive, they found 57-year-old pizza shop owner, Chaudry Rashid, sitting cross-legged on his driveway, smoking a cigarette. Inside, Sandeela, still dressed in her Wal-Mart uniform, was sprawled on her bedroom flood. Her dad admitted to the murder saying his daughter wasn't being true to her religion and wanted out of her marriage to a Pakistani man.

In 2002, Sandeela had agreed to an arranged marriage with her cousin, the son of the uncle who had raised her in Pakistan, so he could legally move to the U.S. He finally arrived in 2008 and immediately moved to Chicago leaving Sandeela behind. Since she had fulfilled her purpose to get this man into America and he was nowhere around, Sandeela wanted out. In her father's mind, murdering her was a God-given right – an honor killing because Sandeela had brought shame on the family.

Chaudry Rashid strangled Sandeela with a bungee cord – the burned remains found in the garage. In a conversation with his family Rashid admitted: "I put the rope around her neck and squeezed her. She disgraced our family."[977]

Sgt. Stefan Schindler, a 13-year veteran of the Clayton County Police Department commented, "I've never encountered anything like this. This was the first time."[978]

Rashid's lawyer, Alan Begner said, "For me, and my upbringing, nothing in your life prepares you for that." Rashid was jailed without bail and charged with murder and other felonies, and sentenced to life in prison. Begner worried self-servingly, "Here in Georgia, this is going to make me sound like a backwoods cracker, but we don't have many Muslims. Not too much diversity down here, at least that I'm aware of."[979]

Begner didn't know how to deal with an honor killing and went into political correctness mode. He hoped the state wouldn't make her murder about Islam or ethnicity saying her death could have happened in any culture, with any family.

No it couldn't.

Amina and Sarah Said

New Year's Day 2008 the double murder of beautiful Sarah and Amina Said, 17 and 18-years-olds, caught the Nation's, no, the *world's*, attention. Their honor killings had been chillingly predicted by Amina, the elder sister.

Their bodies were found in the back of a taxicab left in an Irving, Texas hotel parking lot. Irving, Texas ring a bell? It's the location of the first-ever Islamic-Sharia tribunal in America as of 2015.

Sarah was more athletic. Amina did well enough in school to earn a scholarship and loved anything pink. Yaser, their father, obsessed with his video camera, filmed the girls' every move. When that wasn't enough, he put a bug in Amina's car. Sarah and Amina were forbidden to have boyfriends so they dated in secret. In 2007 Yaser found out that they had Hispanic boyfriends and was furious. Both had proposed and the girls had accepted. It had been Yaser's plan to marry the girls off to Muslim men in Egypt.

Patricia, Yaser's wife, met the Egyptian-born Said brothers: Mohsen, Yousri, Yassein and Yaser where they worked at a neighborhood convenience store, a Circle K. They were here on student visas. Yaser boasted of owning valuable real estate in Egypt, promised Patricia a good life where she wouldn't have to work. Within two weeks they were married. Patricia Owen was just 15 and quite poor when she wed 29-year-old Yaser in 1987. At the wedding one of Yaser's brothers asked Patricia's aunt, Gail Gartrell, to marry him. A shocked Gail asked, "Are you crazy?" They hadn't even dated. Gail said she thought the brothers were attempting "access into the Country by just latching on any American citizen". Patricia admitted right after their wedding, they filled out his papers for his green card.

A year after her first child, Islam, was born Yaser began to regularly beat his Baptist wife, Patricia, known to her family as Tissie. The following two years produced Amina and then Sarah. By the time Tissie was 18, she had three children with Yasir and little education. Years passed; the beatings continued at the slightest provocation. Frightened for the safety of she and her daughters, Tissie phoned her sister, Connie Maggio at work, crying, saying she had to leave Yaser. He had threatened to kill the girls. She phoned Connie again on Christmas Day 2007 saying she had left. Tissie, Amina and Sarah had piled into the car and drove to pick up the girls' boyfriends. They arrived in Oklahoma

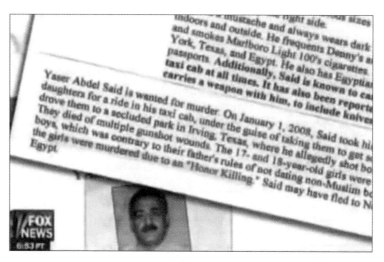

where they boys had jobs waiting. Tissie's brother-in-law called and begged her to phone Yaser; he was worried. Yaser pleaded with her to come home, to not uproot the girls from school; all was forgiven. Everything was OK. So Tissie and the girls drove back to Texas, but everything was far from OK. Yaser lied.[980]

Tissie and Sarah returned home first. Amina stayed with her boyfriend two more days. When she returned New Year's Day 2008, Yaser was waiting. He kissed Amina and Tissie said that for the first in their 20-year marriage she saw a tear form in Yaser 's eye. Amina said, "Mom I'm hungry."

Tissie offered to make her something, but Yaser insisted he wanted to take the girls out for a quick bite – alone. Instead of taking the girls for dinner, he drove 14 miles to Las Colinas, pulled out a gun and began firing.

Somehow Sarah managed to call for help. 911 call recorded her last frantic words: "Help, help! My dad shot me, my sister, help, and now I'm dying, I'm dying! … Oh my God! Not again, *not again…* Stop it, *Stop, Stop it,* Stop…"[981] Then silence…

Yaser shot them 11 times in the back of his cab parked at the Omni Mandalay Hotel.

After the police notified Tissie of her daughters' murders she called Yaser's brother and asked where he was. Moshen said he didn't know, but that Yaser "didn't want to raise whores as daughters."

After Yaser Said shot his daughters, he fled Irving and remains at large. The FBI has offered up to $100,000 for information leading to his arrest and he's on the top ten FBI wanted list. Even after family members said Amina's and Sarah's deaths were honor killings, Irving policeman, Dave Tull, was filmed by Fox News saying they didn't know the motive. Political correctness strikes again, but it wasn't just local cops afraid to call a spade a spade. The FBI, 10 months after the girls' murders, issued a wanted poster for Yaser Said. Originally it contained the phrase "the girls were murdered due to an 'Honor Killing'". Just days later the FBI scrubbed that text. According to Steve Pomerantz who served with the FBI for 27 years and became Chief of Counter-Terrorism, said the Agency is sensitive to criticism and needs the cooperation of the Muslim community so they bowed to their wishes so not to "offend".

Terrorist Training Camps in America

The next map shows locations of terrorist training camps and Islamic 'villages', the primary areas where they live and train with small arms and in military tactics. That is not to say they can't and won't multiply and/or move. Some of these camps have been in operation for nearly 30 years. Although the FBI is aware of at least 22 of these Muslim of America (MOA) enclaves associated with Jamaat ul-Fuqra, reports state there are as many as 35, mostly located in rural areas ranging in size from 30 to 300 acres.[982]

States in gray indicate areas of Muslims of the Americas (MOAs) and/or Jamaat ul-Fuqra activity including murder and attempted murder, fire attacks and bombings, schemes to get money through fraud, and other criminal activity.

MOA Islamic 'villages' ignore their real names and prefer to retag them like Islamberg, Mahmoudberg and Ahmadabad West.

LOCATIONS AND THEIR ISLAMIC NAME (WHERE AVAILABLE)[983] [984] [985]

- Anchorage, AK
- Marion, AL
- Badger, CA *(Baladulla)* [compound abandoned]
- Oak Hills, CA
- Buena Vista, CO [raided and shut down in 1992]
- Commerce, GA (Madinah Village)
- Jesup, GA
- Macon / Odum, GA *(Aliville)*
- Springfield, MA
- Hyattsville, MD
- Coldwater, MI
- Deposit, NY *(Mariaville)*
- Hancock, NY – national headquarters *(Islamberg)*
- Talihina, OK
- Philadelphia, PA
- York, SC (Holy Islamville)
- Dover, TN (Islamville)
- Houston, TX [outreach center]
- Sweeny, TX (Mahmoudberg)
- Fairfax, VA
- Red House, VA (Ahmadabad West)
- Meherrin, VA
- Onalaska, WA
- Bethany, WV
- Barry's Bay, Ontario; Canada (Hasanville)

NOTE: Islamic designations are in italics:

Since these camps belong to al-Fuqra / Muslims of the Americas the logical question is why are they allowed to exist in America especially when they've said they wish to "purify through violence"? The U.S. State Department, Counterterrorism, outlines three qualifications for an organization to be put on the official terrorist list:[986]

1) It must be a foreign organization.

2) The organization must engage in terrorist activity or have the capability and intent to engage in terrorist activity. (Kidnapping, assassination, hijacking; using nuclear, biological, or chemical agents, using firearms or other dangerous devices etc. It also includes planning or executing a terrorist activity, soliciting others to do so, providing material support to them, soliciting funds, or recruitment.[987]

3) The organization's terrorist activity must threaten the security of U.S. nationals or U.S. national security. Fuqra members in America have been convicted of crimes, including murder and fraud.[988]

In *Patterns of Global Terrorism 1999,* the U.S. State Department listed Jamaat al-Fuqra on their "Designated Foreign Terrorist Organizations".[989] Then poof. The next year, just months before 9/11, al-Fuqra disappears off their radar, never to return even though the State Department's terrorism report has this to say about them:

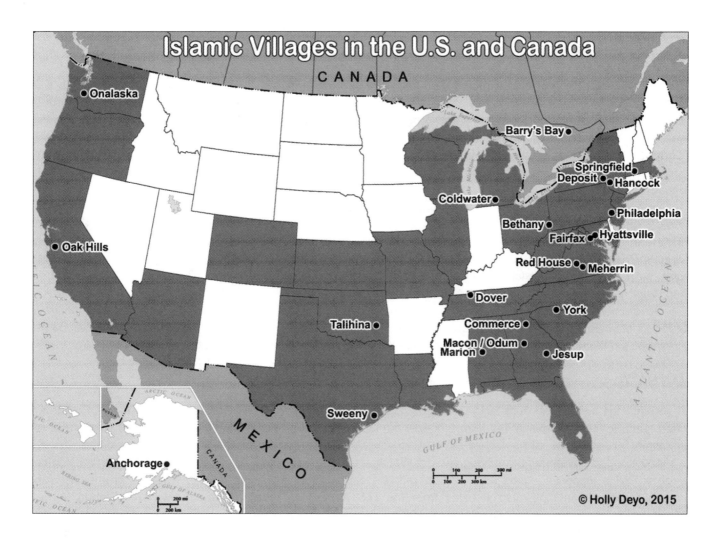

Islamic Villages in the U.S. and Canada

© Holly Deyo, 2015

Jamaat ul-Fuqra Description

Islamic sect that seeks to purify Islam through violence. Led by Pakistani cleric Shaykh Mubarik Ali Gilani, who established the organization in the early 1980s. Gilani now resides in Pakistan, but most cells are located in North America and the Caribbean. Members have purchased isolated rural compounds in North America to live communally, practice their faith, and insulate themselves from Western culture.

Activities

Fuqra members have attacked a variety of targets that they view as enemies of Islam, including Muslims they regard as heretics and Hindus. Attacks during the 1980s included assassinations and firebombings across the United States. Fuqra members in the United States have been convicted of crimes, including murder and fraud."[990]

This is even more curious since the Clarion Project downloaded documents from the FBI that "clearly identify MOA [Muslims of the Americas] as a terrorist organization".[991]

In 2005, the *New York Times* reported on an internal Homeland Security document that "assesses terrorist organizations, their anticipated targets and preferred weapons". It concluded that Jamaat al-Fuqra is a "threat to the United States" and specifically pinpoints them as a possible sponsor of terrorism "linked to Muslims of America; Jamaat al Tabligh, an Islamic missionary organization that has a presence in the United States; and the American Dar Al Islam Movement."[992]

Terrorists In Our Backyard

For over a decade border patrol agents have "found copies of the Koran, ... prayer rugs, ... [and] a lot of stuff written in Arabic, so it's not just people from Mexico coming across that border,"[993] explains former House Representative Tom Tancredo. This is in addition to the staggering tonnage of trash illegal immigrants leave in their wake from Tijuana to Texas. Every year Arizona alone has to deal with 2,000 tons of immigrant refuse[994] including dirty diapers, plastic bottles, backpacks, human waste, toilet paper, clothes, blankets, food containers and even abandoned vehicles.

In 2005, the U.S. projected a record 4,000 immigrants from so-called "high risk" countries in the Middle East and Asia would be arrested trying to enter America illegally, but stated they knew far more would get through undetected. It's not just personal items and drugs they're bringing. That same year, Mexico seized high-powered weapons and rocket launchers in Tijuana. Janice Kephart, former counsel to the 9/11 Commission stated, "Terrorists will use any means to get here. They are using alien smugglers and document forgers to help move people through Iran and Pakistan and it would only make common sense they would use it again to get in the United States."[995]

Nothing seems to stop them and they're flooding across the border where it's least expected – right under the nose of the military, even during target practice. The Barry Goldwater Range northwest of Tucson where Air Force pilots are trained in A-10s, F-16s and F-35s. Illegal immigrants are streaming through by the thousands. Range Director Chas Buchannan said, "It's very hard to control access to a million acres, it's not all fenced in as you might think, we're not staffed to watch every inch of the land to see who is out there. We don't want to see them there, we don't want to see them get hurt, because of the business we're doing."[996] Yet still they come.

Government knows they're coming, has known for over a decade they're already here. Lone wolf, individual terrorists act independently, often without the "go button" pressed by ISIS, al-Qaeda, or whoever. That means any event can set them into motion. Anywhere they are they can create mayhem and death.

ISIS Closes In

Rumblings surfaced in April 2015 that ISIS was close, just over the Texas border from El Paso.[997] People are often numb to these warnings, but then it happened, just a little thing, not like 9/11 but they broke through for the first time.

According to government watchdog Judicial Watch sources – a Mexican Army field grade officer and a Mexican Federal Police Inspector – said ISIS was operating a camp just a few miles from El Paso. More precisely, the camp's location was pinpointed 8 miles from the U.S. border in "Anapra" situated west of Ciudad Juarez, Chihuahua. The same sources revealed a second camp in Puerto Palomas, Chihuahua just 5 minutes from Columbus, New Mexico. The two ISIS camps are less than 75 miles apart via New Mexico State Highway 9, making movement between the two quite easy. Taking the southern route on Mexico's Federal Highway 2 the distance between Anapra and Palomas is less than 100 miles, safe from the U.S. Border Patrol. One camp is equipped with numerous nearby natural water supplies. Sierra de Cristo Rey and Sierra de Juarez forests border the other settlement. Both sites have valuable assets for "camping" terrorists. Positioned in the suburb of Anapra, it would be simple to get "lost" in its population of 3 million and blend into this binational region. Would-be terrorists from the Middle East prefer to come across the U.S.-Mexico border because they know they're easily mistaken for Hispanics, which is why many of them learn Spanish before making the trip.

While performing joint ops during the week of April 6, 2015, U.S. law enforcement and the Mexican Army found documents in Arabic and Urdu, as well as a paper showing the layout of Fort Bliss. ISIS could have downloaded a reasonably detailed public domain map from Wikipedia. This sprawling military installation, which borders Biggs Army Airfield, houses the U.S. Army's 1st Armored Division. It's also home to the 32nd Army Air & Missile Defense Command, the 11th Air Defense Artillery Brigade, the 1st Armored Division Artillery Brigade, the 402nd Field Artillery Brigade and headquarters for a federal tactical operational intelligence center as well as the Department of Defense's counterpart. It looks small on this tiny map, but Bliss covers about 1,700 square miles – bigger than the state of Rhode Island and is the Army's second-largest installation. Breaking into Bliss and doing damage would be a terrorists' coup. In addition to finding a dropped "blueprint" of Fort Bliss, they recovered Muslim prayer rugs.

Those same sources said the "coyotes" that smuggle illegal immigrants and work for the Juarez Cartel, guide ISIS terrorists through the desert between Santa Teresa and Sunland Park, New Mexico. They're also running ISIS the 5 miles between Acala and Fort Hancock, Texas, about 50 miles southeast of El Paso. ISIS prefers to cross in these areas because local police forces are thin and large-scale drug rings have already proved they can travel there unchecked.

Mexican intel sources reveal that ISIS plans to use the airport and rail lines around Santa Teresa, NM. ISIS situates "spotters" in the East Potrillo Mountains armed with binoculars, guns and cell phones to facilitate their movements. Spotters are easily seen and estimates put their numbers into the hundreds. Low-level cartel employees plus people who owe them favors act as spotters and have been seen 75 miles into the U.S. in New Mexico's Sonoran Desert[998] and twice that distance clear to Phoenix, AZ.

ISIS is reportedly performing recon excursions of regional universities, White Sands Missile Range, government facilities in Alamogordo, NM; Ft. Bliss in Texas, and the electrical power facilities near Anapra and Chaparral, NM, which is 30 miles north of El Paso.[999]

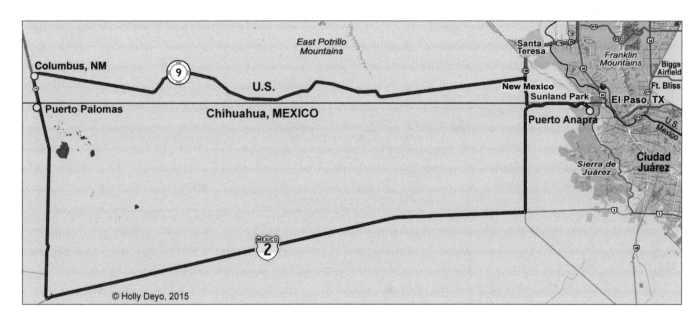

© Holly Deyo, 2015

ISIS' First Attack on American Soil

ISIS may have accomplished their first attack on U.S. soil. May 3, 2015, Garland, Texas. A WCCO investigation found that a Minneapolis man wanted for terrorism encouraged one of the shooters. Twitter accounts showed 25-year-old Minnesotan, Mujahid Miski, a.k.a. Muhammed Abdullahi Hassan, had communicated online about the Texas event before it happened. Hassan left Minneapolis in 2008 to join al-Shabaab in Somalia and was indicted in 2009 on terror charges. During 2015 under the Twitter name of "The Minnesotan3", he urged ISIS supporters in the U.S. and abroad to kill Jews and behead former Homeland Security adviser Fran Townsend.[1000] According to the jihadist monitoring service SITE Intel Group ISIS read a statement on their Al Bayan radio station said that "two soldiers of the caliphate" carried out the Texas attack.[1001]

Roommates Elton Simpson, 30, and Nadir Hamid Soofi, 34, attempted mass slaughter by opening fire outside the Curtis Caldwell Center. Though warned against raising the ire of Muslims, event planner Pamela Geller insisted, "They're just cartoons. We're holding this exhibit and cartoon contest to show how insane the world has become – with people in the free world tiptoeing in terror around supremacist thugs who actually commit murder over cartoons. If we can't stand up for the freedom of speech, we will lose it – and with it, free society."[1002] Despite the Islamic terrorist attack on the French magazine *Charlie Hebdo* in January 2015, Geller plowed onward. The contest featured images drawn of Islam's prophet Mohammed in both historical and contemporary settings with the winner being awarded $10,000. Muslims view any depiction of their "prophet" as sacrilege.

Simpson and Soofi stormed the event in body armor and AK47 assault rifles hoping to inflict major damage. About 40 Garland officers including SWAT and bomb squads, FBI, ATF and Garland ISD security officers protected the attendees inside. Just prior to the shootings, the FBI had warned Garland police, but the bulletin's vagueness didn't give any specifics.

When the terrorist duo began firing semi-automatic assault rifles, a Garland traffic cop shot both attackers with his police Glock. Members of the SWAT team finished them, but not before they shot a security guard in the ankle. It's strongly suspected rather than being directly

> **Shariah is Light** @atawaakul · 3h
> The bro with me and myself have given bay'ah to Amirul Mu'mineen. May Allah accept us as mujahideen.
> Make dua
>
> #texasattack
> ↩ ♺ 37 ★ 24 •••

affiliated with ISIS, they were lone wolf followers and planned the attack themselves. At least one of the gunmen was an ISIS sympathizer, of Pakistani descent. Just before the attack, Simpson posted one last tweet on Twitter referencing his soon attack in Garland: #texasattack: "May Allah accept us as mujahideen [jihadis]."

The pledged allegiance to "Amirul Mu'mineen" – meaning "the leader of the faithful," which analysts feel likely refers to ISIS leader Abu Bakr al-Baghdadi.[1003] [1004]

Among those who retweeted this last post prior to the attack was Junaid Hussain (@_AbuHu55ain), a young computer expert and influential recruiter from Birmingham, England. He moved to Syria in 2013, joined Islamic State and became one of their premier hackers, able to break through bank security systems. He tweeted two telling messages: one a dire warning and the other linking Simpson and Soofi to the Garland, Texas shootout. "QaribanQariba" means "soon, soon", which seems to indicate al-Britani knew about the attacks in advance.

> **AbuHussainAlBritani** @_AbuHu55ain 7h
> Allahu Akbar!!!!! 2 of our brothers just opened fire at the Prophet Muhammad (s.a.w) art exhibition in texas! #TexasAttack
> ↩ ♻ 10 ★ 8 •••

> **AbuHussainAlBritani** @_AbuHu55ain 4h
> The knives have been sharpened, soon we will come to your street with death and slaughter! #QaribanQariba
> ↩ ♻ 15 ★ 8 •••

Shortly after the shootings al-Britani fires off another tweet beginning with "Allahu Akbar" meaning "God is the greatest" or "God is great" followed by a sentence that needs no translation except for "s.a.w." which translates as "Peace Be Upon Him." It's common for Muslims to write "s.a.w." or the acronym "PBUH" after using Mohammed's name.

ISIS claimed responsibility and warned of more attacks to come. "We tell America that what is coming will be even bigger and more bitter, and that you will see the soldiers of the Islamic State do terrible things."[1005] While the White House acknowledges that this was an act of terrorism, they say it's too early to link it to ISIS.

JUNE 2, 2015

Usaamah Rahim, 26, is fatally shot after waving a menacing military knife at police officers in Boston. He originally plotted to behead Pamela Geller just a short trip away in New York for violating Sharia blasphemy laws by organizing the "draw Muhammad" contest the month before. Just hours prior to the confrontation with Boston police, Rahim phones a relative, David Wright, a.k.a. Dawud Sharif Abdul-Khaliq and Dawud Sharif Wright, 24, to notify him of a change in plans. Instead of beheading Geller, Rahim is heard on a recorded conversation saying, "Yeah I'm going to be on vacation right here in Massachusetts. ... I'm just going to go, ah, go after them, those boys in blue, Cause, ah, it's the easiest target and, ah, the most common is the easiest for me."[1006] Rahim also addressed changing his plans to behead Ms. Geller saying, "I can't wait that long."[1007] The FBI said that "going on vacation" was code for going on a mission of violent jihad.

Wright reportedly advised Rahim to destroy his smartphone, wipe his laptop computer and prepare his will. The FBI charged Wright with obstructing a federal investigation by destroying electronic evidence on Rahim's smartphone. When taken into custody it required two sets of handcuffs to restrain him.

It is believed Rahim had been radicalized online by ISIS and had bought three fighting knives and a sharpener on or before May 26 from Amazon.com. In an earlier conversation, Rahim and Wright were heard talking about "thinking with your head on your chest," referencing ISIS videos showing severed heads on the chests of victims they had beheaded. About those weapons Rahim said, "I just got myself a nice little tool. You know it's good for carving wood and like, you know, carving sculptures... and you know..."[1008]

American Cities in ISIS Crosshairs

These actions were just a warm up. March 2015, ISIS released a list of U.S. cities they plan to attack. That's one commonality among Muslim terrorists regardless if it's al-Qaeda, Boko Haram, Islamic State, Muslim Brotherhood or their zillion other branches, they aren't given to idle threats. Whether Islamic State contacts lone wolf Islamic sympathizers or new converts in America or ISIS agents already here or their overseas operatives come over to do the deeds is unknown. In the 18 months ending November 2015 at least 66 men and women had been charged with plotting ISIS-related terror attacks on American soil. By that same date, the FBI had nearly 1,000 active ISIS probes underway in all 50 states.[1009] (See next map.)

With attacks ramping up in America, Europe and Australia, not to mention horrific, ongoing events in the Middle East, people don't feel safe and are arming themselves.

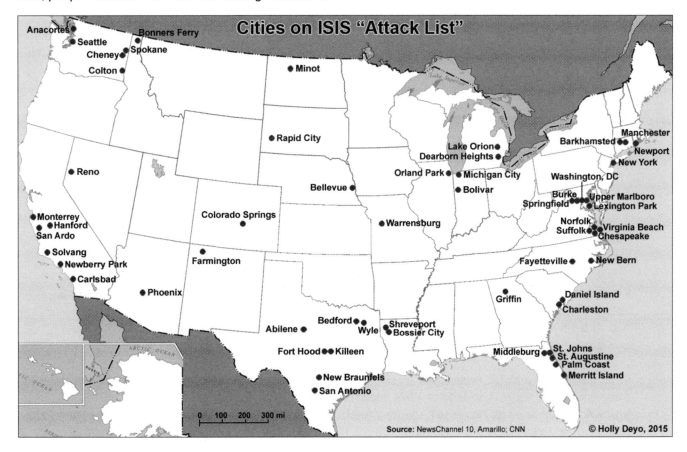

Cities on ISIS "Attack List"

Source: NewsChannel 10, Amarillo; CNN   © Holly Deyo, 2015

ISIS and Weapons of Mass Destruction

In July 2014, ISIS seized enough radioactive material for a large dirty bomb. Jihadis grabbed 88 pounds of uranium compounds from a Mosul University science lab[1010] and radioactive material from government facilities.[1011] While a dirty bomb doesn't have the killing power of a nuke, it has the ability to inspire fear – something ISIS strives for seen by them hitting non-military, soft targets. Former IAEA weapons inspector David Albright said, "Any uranium in the hands of a terrorist group is concerning, since it shows interest in nuclear material and their interest is unlikely to be for peaceful purposes."[1012]

While officials downplayed the threat, Russian Foreign Ministry spokesman Alexander Lukashevich stated. "The sheer fact that the terrorists ... show unmistakable interest in nuclear and chemical materials is, of course, very alarming."[1013]

It's not just nuclear material that was stolen, but also biological and chemical stockpiles. ISIS' threat is considered so severe that Australia Group, a 40-nation bloc dedicated to ending chemical weapons held a session on this issue in Perth in June 2015.

ISIS using WMDs is beyond the hypothetical. They already attacked Iraqi soldiers with roadside bombs filled with chlorine gas in Tikrit. This was verified in film footage showing orange smoke coming from the bombs. Unconfirmed are reports that gases were also used during the siege of Kobani, Syria. Previously it was thought by experts that ISIS' desire for chemical weapons was aspirational, but Julie Bishop, Australia's Foreign Minister said, "The use of chlorine by Da'esh [Isis], and its recruitment of highly trained professionals, including from the West, have revealed far more serious efforts in chemical weapons development." Bishop further stated that ISIS is now undertaking "serious efforts" to develop their chemical weapons arsenal.[1014] This was further underscored in July 2014 when Iraqi U.N. Ambassador Mohammed Ali Alhakim revealed to U.N. Secretary General Ban Ki-Moon that ISIS had stolen more than 2,000 sarin-filled rockets in Mosul in addition to the uranium.[1015]

Though it takes skill to weaponize a dirty bomb, experts feel that it is entirely likely that somewhere in their massive terrorist group, someone has the necessary knowledge. An easier way for ISIS to attain their goal would be to pay Pakistan for a nuclear weapon. They have literally billions at their disposal after taking cash from banks in Middle East cities they'd plundered. Also in their arsenal are tanks, rocket launchers, missile systems, and anti-aircraft systems. Next step on their shopping list? Aircraft.

In the May 2015 edition of their propaganda and recruitment magazine *Dabiq,* they laid out the exact scenario that the FBI warned about back in May 2007. British journalist John Cantlie held hostage by ISIS for two years writes in *Dabiq.*

> What's happening now is a pooling of skills and experience that poses the greatest danger the West has seen in modern times. When you have that amount of battle-hardened mujahidin [one who engages in jihad] all cooperating and exchanging information for the first time under one flag, the potential for operations on a previously unseen level rises exponentially.

> Let me throw a hypothetical operation onto the table. The Islamic State has billions of dollars in the bank, so they call on their wilayah [authority and governance] in Pakistan to purchase a nuclear device through weapons dealers with links to corrupt officials in the region. The weapon is then transported overland until it makes it to Libya, where the mujahidin move it south to Nigeria. Drug shipments from Columbia bound for Europe pass through West Africa, so moving other types of contraband from East to West is just as possible. The nuke and accompanying mujahidin arrive on the shorelines of South America and are transported through the porous borders of Central America before arriving in Mexico and up to the border with the United States. From there it's just a quick hop through a smuggling tunnel and hey presto, they're mingling with another 12 million "illegal" aliens in America with a nuclear bomb in the trunk of their car.

> …And if not a nuke, what about a few thousand tons of ammonium nitrate explosive? That's easy enough to make. The Islamic State make no secret of the fact they have every intention of attacking America on its home soil and they're not going to mince about with two mujahidin taking down a dozen casualties if it originates from the Caliphate. They'll be looking to do something big, something that would make any past operation look like a squirrel shoot, and the more groups that pledge allegiance the more possible it becomes to pull off something truly epic.

> …Perhaps once there was a chance that an attack inside the West or on Western borders by the Islamic State could be averted through negotiations, but no longer. As the territory of the Islamic State crosses from one border to another like a wildfire that is burning out of control, it'll be only a matter of time before the Islamic State reaches the Western world.[1016]

"JV" ISLAMIC STATE GETS TOUCHDOWN WHILE TEAM OBAMA FUMBLES

ISIS has grown larger and more deadly vicious much quicker that experts predicted. Certainly more so that Mr. Obama thought possible. It emerged in February 2016 during Director of National Intelligence James Clapper's testimony that Islamic State has not only used chemical weapons, but has made them.[1017] On July 6, 2015, Mr. Obama stated in a press conference, "Ideologies are not defeated with guns, they are defeated by better ideas and more attractive and more compelling vision."[1018] President Obama still hasn't grasped the seriousness of the threat. They don't want "better ideas." They want a Muslim world. Their philosophy is simple: convert or die. Mr. Obama's lack of understanding was underscored when in January 2014 he referred to Islamic State as the "JV" team compared to Osama bin Laden or when he declared during the 2012 election campaign that al-Qaeda had been "decimated".[1019]

One of the most stunning examples was when Obama called the slaughter of at least 130 people and injuring another 368 in Paris a "setback". Obama's remarks were made to defend his current strategy to defeat ISIS. "There will be an intensification of the strategy that we've put forward. But the strategy that we are putting forward is the strategy that ultimately is going to work. It will take time."[1020] He continued to insist that the U.S. has not "underestimated" the ISIS threat.

This November 13, 2015 attack followed two weeks after a Russian plane was bombed over Egypt. Islamic State claimed responsibility killing all 224 aboard. Does this look like winning?

WHEN "LEGACY" TURNS LETHAL

During half of Mr. Obama's presidency he cast about for a legacy rather than steer America's ship. We ended up with ObamaCare that the majority of Americans detest and an Iran-favored nuclear pact that puts the world in glowing cross hairs. A third leg he's still trying to ram through is global warming. He revisited periodically his early Presidential campaign pledge to close Guantanamo Bay. However, Obama wants to bring detainees to the U.S. and imprison them here. This alternative brought warnings from terrorism experts warning that these actions would encourage jihadis to come to the towns where they are held, take residents captive and unleash violence on the communities until their "heroes" were released. Once on U.S. soil they would be entitled to all the rights Americans enjoy under our legal system.

Pete Hegseth, correspondent for Fox News and former military guard at Guantanamo Bay in 2004-05, shares how "bad" inmates have it. Most prisoners in America would give their left arm for such amenities. The reality is so different compared to what the Obama Administration put out in an effort to close it down. The 2002 bare-bones facility with concertina wire was replaced early on by a top-of-the-line hi-tech facility. Here's what detained jihadis enjoy:

- The exact same healthcare as for U.S. troops
- A 20,000-book library, including their religious books
- Thousands of movies and video games
- Wireless TV sets to watch 300 satellite channels
- Clean clothes and fresh bed linen
- All their religious items and even their beds are marked as to which way Mecca lies

One of the 1,200 guards currently assigned to Gitmo said, "We treat them with dignity and respect. Even when they don't deserve it. Even when they're throwing feces, or urine, or spitting on guards, or scratching guards."[1021]

NOTE: No civilized person would dream of touching bodily eliminations, but in the Middle East some do. It's one reason why Arab men wear gowns or wide pants so they can pull out a loose pant leg and urinate in public – I saw it in Cairo firsthand – while having a pleasant conversation. No need to stop talking and find a toilet. Urine just runs down street gutters. It's also why many of their poor wipe their backsides after defecating with the left hand and eat with the right hand.

Gitmo guards have endured more than 300 assaults. Nearly 700 detainees have been released since 2002 and 30% have returned to terrorism. Just 90 detainees remain as of March 2016.

A fifth legacy Mr. Obama's trying his best to shuck off is his failure to end the "Bush wars" and reverse counterterrorism policies of his predecessor. Three legacies Americans are already paying for – literally. Iran has yet to set off a nuke, but you can bet their scientists have been given the directive to build, *build, build* and Gimto's fate is still up in the air.

It's clear that Mr. Obama operated under a deadly delusional fiction that he understood how to deal with terrorists. It's likely his policies will be viewed as ones that actually mushroomed terrorism and did nothing to halt threats from Islamic State.

A mere 9 hours before the unspeakable slaughter of 130 in Paris, Obama confidently told ABC's George Stephanopoulos that ISIS had been "contained."[1022] In prior years, Mr. Obama falsely described al-Qaeda as "decimated" and "on the run".[1023] He ruled out that al-Qaeda had a direct role in the 2012 Benghazi terrorist attacks. He still claimed that al-Qaeda was on the "road to defeat".[1024] One would think that when he realized toe jam left a bad taste in the mouth, he'd have pulled his foot out. Instead, at least 32 times after Benghazi, Mr. Obama touted al-Qaeda's demise.

To keep Mr. Obama's narrative false narrative alive, more than 50 intelligence analysts claimed their information was "cooked". These agents are paid to give honest assessments on the ISIS war, but what happens when their reports were "inappropriately altered" by senior officials? Two senior analysts at the U.S. military's Central Command signed a written complaint in July 2015 and sent it to the Defense Department inspector general exposing this debacle. Some analyses were briefed to Mr. Obama and portrayed terror groups as weaker than what their intel showed. CENTCOM higher-ups allegedly changed these reports to keep them in line with the Obama administration's public line that the U.S. is winning the battle against ISIS and other terror groups. The complaint said that either key elements were removed or that reports deemed too negative were sent back for a re-write. Because of the hostile work atmosphere, other analysts self-censored, putting a rosy hue on an ugly picture.[1025]

ISLAMIC BONNIE AND CLYDE + HATE

The Christmas party for 75-80 people should have been fun, a happy time of socializing at the Inland Regional Center in San Bernardino, CA. Lighted Christmas trees were everywhere and decorated tables reflected the conference room's holiday cheer.

U.S.-born Syed Rizwan Farook, 28, of Pakistani descent and his Pakistani wife, Tashfeen Malik, 29, changed all that in less than a minute.

In the worst case of Islamic terrorism in America since 9/11, these Muslim jihadis shot dead 14 co-workers and injured another 21.

NOTE: This statement doesn't take into account Muslim Army major Nidal Malik Hasan who shot and killed 13 and injured another 32 at Fort Hood in November 2009. Six years later, Mr. Obama still refused to acknowledge the obvious. Instead he labeled this atrocity "workplace violence" even though Hasan shouted "Allahu Akbar" as his itchy finger repeatedly pulled the trigger.

Though the Farook-Malik murders took place a little over two weeks following the ISIS massacre in France, these killers had plans in place long before. Police found in their townhouse: 2,000 9mm rounds; 2,500 .223 rounds, several hundred .22 rifle rounds, 19 pipe bombs, hundreds of IED tools, material and components for more bombs, and bombs attached to kids' remote controlled cars. They were armed with two AK-47s and two semi-auto handguns. Their SUV housed another 1,400 assault rifle rounds and 200 handgun rounds.

The Farooks had tried to wipe away all traces of their digital footprint. Days before they destroyed their hard drives, removed the computers' motherboards, broke their cell phones and booby-trapped their home.

In the weeks before neighbors noticed a lot of people coming and going from their rented Redlands, CA home along with numerous boxes delivered by UPS within "a short amount of time". Yet no one stepped forward fearing they would be labeled Islmaphobes, racist, or profilers.

Two weeks before the killing spree, Farook had clashed with a Jewish man over Farook's "religion of peace". Nicholas Thalasinos was one of his 14 victims. It's no coincidence these Muslim extremists chose a Christmas party to execute mayhem.

Like so many instances of Islamic terrorism, no one really noticed anything amiss. Not even his mother, Rafia, or so she said. This is doubtful as their garage was described as a "bomb-making factory" and she lived with them. She's also an active member of Islamic Circle of North America (ICNA), a Muslim organization that promotes establishing a caliphate and tied to the radical Pakistani political group, Jamaat-e-Islami.[1026]

Co-workers remarked that Farook was a devout Muslim, but didn't talk about his religion. Former colleague Griselda Reisinger, "He never struck me as a fanatic, he never struck me as suspicious."[1027] This seems to be a common thread and unfortunately, it will cause people to raise eyebrows at innocent Muslims wondering if he or she has secretly radicalized. Farook was described as a good neighbor, a nice guy. He and his wife, initially here on a K-1 fiancée visa, had a 6-month-old little girl. People noticed this jihadi had grown out his beard and the day of the massacre a co-worker had teased him about it before he stormed out of the party.

Farook traveled to Mecca in 2013 for Muslims' once-in-a-lifetime-required Hajj pilgrimage. He returned to Saudi Arabia in July 2014 to pick up Malik and bring her to America. In July 2015, she was granted a permanent residency green card after passing *five different agencies'* background checks including FBI and Homeland Security as well as an interview at the U.S. embassy in Pakistan. Nothing came up when she was fingerprinted and checked against two databases nor anything click when her name and photo was matched against a terror watch list.[1028] It's astonishing and alarming the Feds completely failed to pick her up as a deadly threat.

NOTE: If this is government's idea of good vetting, what does this say about the thousands of Syrian refugees that Mr. Obama wants to bring here predicated on the identical vetting process? Oddly, Farook's back-to-back Mecca trips didn't sound alarm bells at federal agencies because he was gone less than a month each time.

People said Farook had been a constant presence at the Dar-al-Uloom al-Islamiyah of America mosque for two years and had recently memorized the Quran. That's considered quite a feat for anyone. He and Malik had met online in 2013 and married in Mecca by the Muslims' sacred black stone. Before their child was born, his co-workers they callously slaughtered on December 2, 2015 had thrown them a baby shower.

The morning of the party, they left their infant daughter with his mother, who lived with them, saying they had a doctor's appointment. How people can bring about such unspeakable carnage while "living the American dream" and raising a new daughter is a true brain twist. Farook reportedly liked his job as a restaurant health inspector, enjoyed working on old cars and was studying for his Master's degree. Later that day, he returned to the party, with wife in tow, both wearing black military tactical attire and masks to deliver death and heartache.

Few knew what Tashfeen Malik looked like as she kept her face veiled with a *niqab*. The only close up photo of Syed Farook is from his driver's license. It showed a man with dead eyes. For a while authorities wondered who radicalized who, but now based on how far back their individual activities extended, they each did their own thing world's apart and joined together for a match made in Hades.

These two didn't act entirely alone. Long-time friend, Mexican-American U.S born, Enrique Marquez and recent convert to Islam, acquired the AK-47s for them. He also bought the smokeless powder for the pipe bombs. Marquez and Farook had been busy discussing radical Islam since 2007, but it would be four years before they actively tried to implement mayhem. In 2011-'12, they had planned to kill students at Riverside Community College where both men had previously attended. This was before radical Malik was on the scene. Their attack called for throwing pipe bombs from the second floor into the crowded cafeteria and library below. They had already calculated exactly where to launch the bombs for maximum carnage. Another plan involved throwing pipe bombs onto the 91 Freeway from overhead during rush hour. It has a long stretch without exits so the cars would all jam up allowing Farook to mow down drivers. Marquez's priority was to shoot police, then first responders.[1029] They abandoned these plans when the Feds made terrorist arrests close by.

Image: 14 months of ISIS-related interdictions

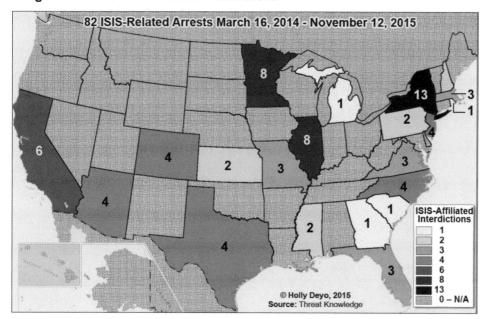

Marquez, 24, and Farook were also related by marriage. He wed Russian émigré, Mariya Chernykh on November 29, 2014. Three years earlier her sister Tatiana married Syed's brother Faheel. In return for his part in the marriage scam Chernykh paid him $200/month, which is supported by bank records. Further silencing any doubt about a fake marriage was Marquez's own words. He told investigators that his wife lived in Ontario, CA with her boyfriend Oscar Romero (while married to Marquez) and that Romero was the father of her daughter. When questioned about Chernykh, Romero said she had already moved on and didn't know her whereabouts.[1030] Not only is she here through immigration fraud, she and her anchor baby are likely enjoying welfare – unless she's found another willing pawn.

Farook and Malik got justice before they could carry out other plans. With in four minutes of them firing 75 rounds into co-workers, police arrived, but the two had already fled the scene. Twenty-three police fired off 380 rounds during a car chase. Malik, in the back of the SUV shot 76 rifle rounds. Somewhere in the melee, both Muslim nuts died. As for Marquez, he's quivering in his jihadi boots. The day after the massacre, he phoned 911 saying, "The f****** a****** used my gun in the shooting. They can trace all the guns back to me."[1031] On December 17, 2015 Marquez was charged with conspiring to provide material support to terrorism, making a false statement in connection with acquiring firearms, and immigration fraud. He's also accused of entering a fake marriage and plotting attacks. If convicted, which looks like a sure thing, he faces a lot of years in prison.

On the day of the San Bernardino massacre, Malik posted on Facebook her "pledge of allegiance to ISIS" swearing loyalty to Muslim fanatic Abu Bakr al-Bagdadi.[1032] Authorities initially believed there could be a "deeper terror matrix" behind the shootings because the Feds revealed Farook had been in contact with both the al-Qaeda-affiliated al-Nusra Front in Syria and the radical al-Shabab group in Somalia.[1033] At the time of this writing the FBI and Homeland Security were investigating alleged communications between Farook and known terrorist recruiter Muhammed Abdullahi Hassan. Hassan who used to live in Minnesota and relocated to Somalia, masterminded the failed 2015 attack in Garland, Texas.

Five days after the San Bernardino murders, Mr. Obama was still trying to decide whether it was terrorism or workplace violence. In a rare address from the Oval Office, the president refused to call them "radical Islamic terrorists", and instead referred to them as "thugs and killers" that were part of a "cult of death".[1034] On the third day the FBI openly acknowledged it was terrorism. Funny, no one else had this problem. How many dots does Obama need?

WHY GO ABROAD, KILL HERE

Shortly before the San Bernardino murders, Threat Knowledge released a terrorism report with these key points:[1035]

- 82 ISIS-affiliated individuals in the U.S. were intercepted by law enforcement March 2014 to November 2015.
- Over 250 Americans have joined or attempted to join ISIS in Syria and Iraq.
- The FBI currently has nearly 1,000 ongoing ISIS probes in the U.S.
- ISIS is recruiting within the U.S. at about 3 times the rate of al-Qaeda.
- Ali Shukri Amin, a 17-year-old Islamic State supporter from Manassas, Virginia, recently sentenced to 11 years in prison for conspiring to provide support to ISIS, had nearly 4,000 Twitter followers, under the alias, 'Amreeki Witness.'
- Ahmad Musa Jibril, an Arab-American Islamist preacher living in Dearborn, Michigan, had 38,000 Twitter followers before his site went silent. A report by the International Centre for the Study of Radicalisation (ICSR) found that 60% of surveyed foreign fighters in Iraq and Syria followed Jibril on Twitter.
- These numbers show ISIS has a significant support base in the U.S., including both those who have already traveled to Iraq and Syria to fight as jihadis, as well as terror suspects who have been intercepted while attempting to travel there, provide support to ISIS in other tangible ways, or attempt attacks.
- Nearly ⅓ of the domestic ISIS cases in the past 18 months involved people who planned to carry out attacks against Americans on U.S. soil. In other words, ⅓ of those intercepted thought the best way to serve Islamic State and its Caliph, Abu Bakr al Baghdadi, is to wage jihad in America.
- The number of followers of ISIS propagandists Ali Shukri Amin and Ahmad Musa Jibril, shows that domestic support for ISIS may reach well into the thousands. With Syrian refugees starting to arrive in the U.S., these numbers may increase.

WELL-FUNDED, WELL ARMED

As of February 2015 the CIA put their loyal fighters at over 31,000, but others estimate their numbers at 200,000. This compares to just 1,000 in 2004 when it began as al-Qaeda.[1036] By June 2015, ISIS controls more than half of Syria, parts of Iraq, has made inroads in Libya and is linked with cells in the Sinai Peninsula, but much more worrisome is its cancerous spread to Southeast Asia.

$1 billion in Humvees the U.S. left behind aided ISIS' brutal stomp through the Middle East. When Islamic State overran Mosul June 2014, they captured 2,300 of those armored vehicles in that city alone plus a lot of weapons.[1037] In addition to Humvees, ISIS secured at least 40 M1A1 main battle tanks, 74,000 machine guns, small arms and ammo, and 52 M198 howitzers.[1038]

Meanwhile Congress mulls sending to Iraq another $13 billion worth of 175 Abrams tanks and tens of thousands of rounds of 120mm ammo, 1,000 Humvees, 700 commercial utility cargo vehicles, machine guns, grenade launchers, long-range radio systems and other gear, fearing that too may fall into the hands of ISIS.[1039] Combine all that equipment and ISIS' bulging bank accounts, with military training and strong motivation, they have morphed from wannabes to a serious international threat.

Islamic State is a well-funded, disciplined, brutal force with one goal in mind. Initially ISIS relied on wealthy donors to fund the terror group. Now firmly established and self-sustaining, it's estimated they earn about $3 million a day. Besides controlling over 60% of the oil fields in Syria and Iraq, they rake in heaps through opium and heroin harvests, kidnapping, taxing the people whose cities they've overrun, human trafficking, selling priceless artifacts on the black market and looting financial institutions.[1040] Earning $110 billion a year, no wonder they've been dubbed the "world's richest terror army."

THE REFUGEE DEBATE

One of the bombers who perpetrated attacks on Paris in November 2015 had a Syrian refugee passport. This isn't the first "refugee" who was actually a terrorist that sneaked into position through kindnesses of the hosting country. Six Bosnian immigrants, three from Missouri, two Illinois and one from New York, were charged in

February 2015 with sending money and military equipment to terrorist groups in Syria including ISIS and the Al-Nusra Front arm of al-Qaeda. Of the six, three became naturalized citizens and three have refugee or legal resident status. Of the 2,184 Syrian refugees the U.S. has taken in, only 2.4% are Christian while 96% are Muslim. Every month the U.S. takes in over 800 Somalis, which is a full Islamic nation. See the complete list of Somali Cities of Refuge in Appendix 2.

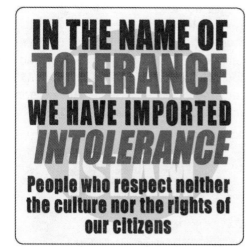

Every year, the U.S. takes in nearly 140,000 refugees often with low-to-no skills. These aren't the million or so legal immigrants this Country admits yearly. Assimilation and self-sufficiency are no longer goals in the government's refugee program. They have access to welfare on the same basis as a U.S. citizen making this program a global magnet. All 15 federal programs bloat the cost of taking in refugees to at least $10-20 billion a year. Unreported are "loans" made to refugees for their transportation to America. Some 47% is never repaid running up a tab of a half billion dollars, not counting the interest that's written off.

Other sets of fingers in the refugee pie are the nine VOLAGs – Voluntary Agencies. Their umbrella name alone is laughable because they get big $$ for every refugee they import. They earn at least a billion every year for resettlement, which is over and above what the refugees receive – $20 billion a year in welfare. These nine agencies have another 350 subcontractors working in 180 cities[1041]:

- US Conference of Catholic Bishops (USCCB)
- Lutheran Immigrant Aid Society (LIRS)
- International Rescue Committee (IRC)
- World Relief Corporation
- Immigrant and Refugee Services of America (IRSA)
- Hebrew Immigrant Aid Society (HIAS)
- Church World Service (CWS)
- Domestic and Foreign Missionary Service of the Episcopal Church of the USA
- Ethiopian Community Development Center (ECDC)

Another little known fact is the Obama administration has put a priority on LGBTQI – **L**esbian, **G**ay, **B**isexual, **T**ransgender, **Q**ueer or **Q**uestioning, and **I**ntersex – asylum and refugee seekers. At the 2012 conference of refugee contractors one contractor demanded that Medicaid pay for sex change operations for refugees.

Arab immigrants in the Muslim enclave of Dearborn, Michigan are also wary of Syrian refugees. This town's population of 98,000 is half Arab, Muslims that are generally Shiite, sworn enemies of ISIS who are Sunni Muslims. Hicham Dawil, of Arab descent, immigrated to Dearborn 30 years ago had this to say about bringing in more Syrians right now. "We don't need no more troubles, you know? I feel bad for the people. On the other hand, look what's happening in France. This is crazy, you know. It's just evil."[1042]

Importing Terrorists

One of the strongest arguments against taking in more of Syria's displaced persons is concern over importing terrorists. In November 2015, Senator Jeff Sessions (R-AL) shared a list of 12 vetted refugees admitted from January to August of 2015 who quickly joined jihad plots to attack America. While Obama proposes to admit over 10,000 new Syrian migrants, his track record underscores flaws in the vetting system. One has only to look at Tashfeen Malik, the female half of the duo that slaughtered 14 in San Bernardino Dec. 2015. She went through the same vetting process Syrians will undergo. Top U.S. security officials say they can't be vetted because it's impossible to know what they were doing before applying for refugee status. FBI Director James Comey agrees. In an October 2015 congressional hearing he testified, "If we don't know much about somebody, there won't be anything in our data. I can't sit here and offer anybody an absolute assurance that there's no risk associated with this."[1043]

Investigative reporter Aaron Diamant dug through a decade worth of immigration data from 2003 to 2013. He found that federal authorities deported 1,033 refugees. In that group, 713 refugees got kicked out of the U.S. for committing aggravated felonies, including dozens of assaults, sex crimes, drug crimes and homicides.[1044]

It's not just adults. Think about Chechen brothers, Tamerlan and Dzhokhar Tsarnaev, who carried out the Boston Marathon bombing. They killed three and injured over 250. One Capitol Hill aid said, "This list – which only covers 2015 and not the many jihadis from prior years – illustrates just how incapable our government is of vetting refugees or predicting post-entry radicalization. Yet the president wants a completely blank-check [in the appropriations bill] to fund not only all of these existing refugee programs from across the globe, but to add a permanent Syrian resettlement program to it – funded directly out of Americans' paychecks and retirement accounts."[1045]

Photo: Close-up view of the Za'atri camp in Jordan for over 600,000 Syrian refugees as seen on July 18, 2013, from a helicopter carrying U.S. Secretary of State John Kerry and Jordanian Foreign Minister Nasser Judeh. (Courtesy U.S. Department of State)

Passport and Visa Snafus

It gets worse. Since 2001, the U.S. revoked over 122,000 visas – 9,500 because they were deemed terrorist threats.[1046] The U.S. allows in people from 38 countries without visas. All a terrorist would have to do is travel to one of those countries first before entering the U.S. and voilà, he's home free.

Some terrorism experts say Americans should be very worried about taking more refugees. Marc Thiessen, American Enterprise Institute fellow and former senior policy adviser to the Senate Foreign Relations Committee chairman stated, "There are serious security concerns. The vast majority of Syrian refugees are legitimate victims of terror and persecution, but it only takes a handful of ISIS infiltrators hiding among them to bring the carnage we saw in Paris to our streets. Moreover, polls show that while the vast majority of refugees oppose ISIS, about 13% support the terror network. We need to help these people, but admitting them into the U.S. is not the best way to do it."[1047]

DHS' utter ineptitude was showcased during a House Oversight Committee hearing on December 17, 2015. Chairman Jason Chaffetz grilled the State Dept. and Homeland Security for not looking at social media posted by people coming into the U.S. Partway through the 4½-hour proceeding in well-deserved irritation and complete disbelief Chaffetz said to Michele Bond, assistant secretary for the Bureau of Consular Affairs, *"You don't have a clue do you?"* She just sat there quietly, face twitching in her discomfort. You could see she wished a sinkhole would open and swallow her. The following is a snippet of the very telling and alarming hearing showing DHS is about 10 years behind in protecting Americans.

Jason Chaffetz, Chairman of the House Oversight Committee opens: The immigration screening process is a critical element in protecting the American people. You got to lock down that border, you got to get rid of the people who are here committing crimes for goodness sake. They're here illegally committing crimes and you all release them back out in the public. Some 60 plus thousand times you did that. These are the criminal element. Don't tell me about the nice, you know, lady who is just trying to help her family. These are people committing crimes, get caught, they get convicted, they are in your hands, and then Homeland Security says 'go back out in the community'.

Mark Meadows (R-NC) to **Alan Bersin**, Asst. Secy. of International Affairs & Chief Diplomatic Officer at DHS: What is the number of that internal document you've seen?

Bersin: Well, I'm uh, uh, it's, it's less than uh, than uh…

Meadows: What's the number? Now you've got a two-inch binder there. It has all kinds of research. It's our pictures, our bios, so you've done good research so you knew I was going to ask this question I assume.

Chaffetz: Of the revoked visas, do you give those to the Dept. of Homeland Security?

Michele Thoren Bond, Asst. Secy. for the Bureau of Consular Affairs: Exactly. We revoke the visa and the information is … (she looks blank and slightly shakes her head)

Chaffetz: So Homeland Security, how many of the revoked visas are still in the United States of America?

Bersin: Mr. Chairman, uh, I don't have that uh, that uh, number.

Chaffetz: You don't have a clue do you?

Anne Richard, Asst. Secy. for the Bureau of Population, Refugees, and Migration: I think we have a very, very strong robust vetting process.

Mick Mulvaney (R-SC): Mr. Rodriguez (director of U.S. Citizenship and Immigration Services), Mr. Bersin just said this is an evolving threat and they're changing the way they do business. Have you changed the way you've vetted in the last 6 months? Aren't we going to learn something about the visa fiancée process and apply it to the refugee process? Are you going to look at social media?

Richard: That I have to differ [sic, should be *defer*] to Leon Rodriguez on.

Chaffetz to Bond: She couldn't even tell me if they were coming in by sea, by land or by air. She thinks most people are coming in by air and *she's* in charge of screening! You can see why **we're scared to death** that this administration, the Department of Homeland Security, the State Department is *not* protecting the American people.[1048]

The week before, DHS was on the hot seat again looking incredibly inept. Homeland Security official Kelli Burriesci was unable to answer even basic questions on visa waivers and terrorism. Rep. Jim Jordan (R-OH) summed up her testimony like this: "Ms. Burriesci, I've asked you the number of Americans who've traveled to Syria, you don't know. The number of Americans who may have traveled and returned, you don't know. The number of Syrian refugees who've entered the country in the last year, you don't know. The number of visa waiver program overstays, you don't know. The number of visa waiver overstays who may have been to Syria before they came here, you don't know. And the number of American citizens on the no-fly list and you don't know. And yet you are the Deputy Assistant Secretary for Screening Coordination, Office of Policy, Department of Homeland Security in front of the oversight committee and you can't give us one single number to some, I think, pretty basic questions?"[1049] Burriesci must have prayed for a sinkhole too.

Fake Passports

Now cobble together Homeland Security's lethargy, bloat, ignorance and incompetence with Islamic State's new ability to create high-quality fake Syrian passports, people have a right to be very wary of the refugee program. This allows terrorists to travel to the U.S., Europe as well as many other countries. "It's very scary," Northeastern University professor Max Abrahms said of reports indicating the barbaric jihadists are creating their own falsified Syrian passports as a means of spreading its fighters around the world.

"'There's a real sense that our porous borders are posing a very real terrorist threat to the United States. At least two of the perpetrators of the Paris attacks got into the country through Greece using fake identification – and of course you have Tashfeen Malik in San Bernardino, who got into the country by misrepresenting herself on her fiancée visa."[1050] Is it too much to expect that Homeland Security's over 240,000 employees could do a better job at keep us safe?

Syrians' Long Trek

By the end of 2015 the U.N. estimates that number of Syrian refugees could hit 4.27 million. This tragic situation has seen tens of thousands stream across the land into Jordan and Lebanon with nothing but what they can carry. Often that is a child. Without question this is the worst humanitarian disaster of our time. Nearly 2 million have sought asylum in Turkey and another million in Lebanon. Over 600,000 fled to Jordan while more than 150,000 poured into Egypt and North Africa.

One has to wonder what's up with the six richest Gulf States taking in no Syrians. Bahrain, Kuwait, Oman, Qatar, Saudi Arabia, and the United Arab Emirates (UAE) have amassed vast wealth through oil, speak Arabic and have historic ties to Syria, yet have taken in zero. These are Muslim nations. It should be a natural fit. So the Syrians are forced to leave.

From Syria, Turkey is a straight hike north and tiny Lebanon is due west. Those thinking to find sanctuary stampede across their borders. This is the short story.

Some board dangerous inflatable boats with twice the human cargo they're rated for. They resemble upright human sardines, probably praying the entire time for calm seas. Many trek through Turkey on foot and then boat through the Aegean Sea hoping their feet will land in Greece. Some drown like Aylan Kurdi whose small body washed up on Turkey's shore while boating to Greece. His story is one of over 3,500 who died in the Mediterranean in 2015.

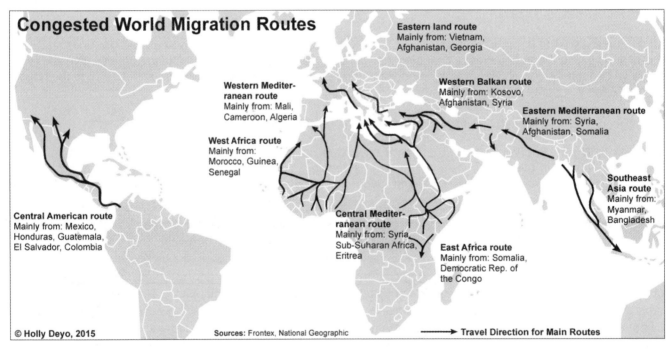

It's not just Syrians. Civil war and those looking for jobs and better lives are leaving Afghanistan, Kosovo, Iraq, Albania, Pakistan, Serbia and Ukraine. The top half of Africa has also migrated to Europe as far north as Sweden and east into Moscow looking for that better life.

From North Africa, it's a short boat trip across the Sea into Spain or Italy. Once in Europe they journey northwest or northeast into the promised lands of Germany, Sweden, Italy, France, Hungary, the UK, Austria, Switzerland, and even Scandinavia.

The refugee situation has gotten so severe countries in the EU have taken measures to stem the hoards. Some countries are up to their eyeteeth with immigrants and accept no more. There is no way to communicate just how enormous these flowing masses of humanity have become. From overhead, swarms of moving colored dots contrast brightly to the tan fields they plow through. Every one is a person. Every life matters. Down steep hillsides, marching along railroad tracks, through ravines and gullies they come. Through highly vegetated areas and deserty places they come. Everywhere trash and refuse reveal the path of their travels. On boats, trains, dinghies and by foot they come. Women wearing hijabs and men praying Muslim style, minus their rugs, when their feet touch land again. It is an unarmed invasion.

Hungary built a 13-foot high fence along its border with Serbia. Macedonia, now the new hub of thousands to reach the EU, is arresting them if they don't leave the country within three days. Determined migrants jumped razor wire to cross into Macedonia near the southern city of Gevgelija. In August 2015 after several attempts, thousands broke through the cordon of special police forces at the border between Greece and Macedonia. Riots broke out in Macedonia that required police to use batons, tear gas and stun guns to force back some 3,000 looking for a new life. Afterwards migrants blocked the rail link between the two countries in protest after police closed the border near the Greek village of Idomeni.

Germany's police are demanding re-introduction of passport controls across Europe.

Bulgaria built a 5-foot thick razor wire fence along its border with Turkey.

Without regard for law or borders, what Europe is experiencing America has many more, with up to 30 million illegal immigrants, according to Mexico's former ambassador, Arturo Sarukhan,[1051] who have pushed into our Country.

It's not just displaced people from Afghanistan and Syria. According to the U.N., 2014 saw the highest-ever level of refugees. Some 59.5 million people left their homes – 8.3 million more people than the year before.[1052]

AMERICA – THE MODERN TOWER OF BABEL

During the week of November 16, 2015, the Syrian crisis debate heated up. It started as a murmur among a handful of U.S. governors that turned into a roar. Within two weeks, 31 governors opposed dropping Syrian refugees into their states.[1053] This was met by a promised veto by President Obama. Those 31 governors say their first obligation is to protect citizens in their state. The bill aimed at improving screening for Syrian refugees including FBI background checks and sign-offs by top officials before bringing more into the Country.

House Homeland Security Committee Chairman Michael McCaul, R-Texas, said in a statement, "America has a proud tradition of welcoming refugees into our country, and we lead the world in humanitarian assistance. However, we also must put proper measures in place to ensure our country's safety."[1054]

Setting security issues aside, Mr. Obama countered, "Slamming the door in the face of refugees would betray our deepest values. That's not who we are. And it's not what we're going to do."[1055]

Rep. Richard Hudson, (R-NC) also endorsed the House bill and governors' concern saying, "America is a compassionate nation. No country on Earth does more or spends more to care for our fellow man. But being compassionate doesn't mean we have to have reckless policies that put American lives at risk."[1056] And he's right. We have taken in millions, still do, but our own people are suffering. Since when is it right to take in countless others at the expense of U.S. citizens. That is Mr. Obama's protocol. Those who grasp the seriousness of the global situation see America first or we can't help the other millions in need. It's like the prophecy of when Babylon is taken out and the world grieves, not because we are gone, but because they have no one to buy their wares.

Since the 1965 Immigration Reform Act, we've imported over 100 million people to America jumping from 194 million then to 300 million in 2006. That's about ⅓ of entire our Country to which we welcomed with open arms. No other country on this planet has been so giving. But now we're suffering. Greatly. Now we're at 322 million people. To put this into perspective Australia with roughly the same real estate as CONUS only has 23 million people. That's just 7% of people in the U.S.

Canada, compared to the U.S., even when including Alaska and Hawaii is still over 200,000 sq. miles larger, but has only 36 million. Why must the U.S. take on more immigrants at the expense of our own people? No country does that. No one.

Rooting Out the Problem

Since 1970 women of 1st world nations – Canada, Europe, Australia and the U.S. – only had two children or less on average. Birth rates equaled the sustainability of available resources like clean air and water, forests, personal finances, crop-growing land and so on.

Third world countries haven't practiced birth control for the last 50 years and now their countries can't provide for their burgeoning masses. They will *add 1 billion every 12 years* to the world's population. For the most part, they are uneducated and contribute nothing. Hard facts, but they are the facts.

Our four countries, or group of countries in the case of Europe, can't take in all of the applying immigrants and illegal immigrants, or our own nations will be destroyed by the financial and resource burden. Then we, these four entities, can help no one. It is the true parable of the Titanic in today's perspective. These four counties, collectively the Titanic, are unable to save everyone. Their lifeboats can only hold so many yet thousands jump overboard and cling to the lifeboats. Under this added weight the boats sink and **all** perish. This is a mathematical fact of Exponential Growth.

On the present course provided by the Immigration Reform Act, America is poised to add another 138 million in the next 35 years not taking into account the unending flow of illegal immigrants. This is unequivocally undeniably irrefutably unsustainable. California adds 1,654 people every single day in both legal and illegal immigrants, which account for 98% of that state's growth. The world adds another 10,000 babies every hour.[1057] Already America takes in over 1 million immigrants and refugees every single year. No other country on Earth does this and so why are we asked to take on even more? It's insanity.

Illegal aliens have more rights than Americans. They have rights to jobs, Section 8 housing, free breakfasts and lunches for their children, free medical for their babies, and are paid under the table at a lower wage and usually pay no taxes. No wonder they're happy with all of these benefits, which are further enticements for more to come here illegally.

Americans – the Growing Poor

This helped throw 10 million Americans out of work while 46 million Americans subsist on food stamps. As of February 2015, more than 30 million American workers can't get jobs or are underemployed according to Gallup. This is far worse than the unemployment number Obama's administration puts out of 5.6%. Government puts a rosy face on unemployment three ways:

1. If a person is so hopelessly out of work they've stopped looking over the past four weeks, the Department of Labor doesn't count them as unemployed.

2. If a person is an out-of-work engineer or teacher yet perform a minimum of 1 hour of work in a week and paid at least $20 even for mowing a lawn or digging a ditch, that person isn't officially counted as unemployed.

3. If a person has a chemistry or math degree and working only 10 hours part time because it's all they can find and is severely underemployed, they aren't counted.

Gallup calls government's unemployment numbers The Big Lie.[1058] Despite what media reports, Americans aren't feeling any rosy outlook.

Piling On

Instead of illegal immigrant wages being circulated into the U.S. economy, they're sending $50 billion every year, called remittances, back to their home countries according to the Bureau of Economic Analysis. However, estimates from the World Bank report that the figure is significantly higher, closer to $100 billion a year.[1059] The double whammy comes when U.S. taxpayers are forced to pick up the $113 billion-a-year tab for the care and feeding of illegal immigrants.[1060] Not only is America being bled to death, illegals are taking poverty level work and undercutting the American worker so they can't get jobs. Regular taxpayers' income goes to pay for all their freebies and their welfare payments.

Stanford professor Dr. Otis Graham wrote in his book *Unguarded Gates: A History of America's Immigration Crisis.* "Most western elites continue urging the wealthy west **not** to 'stem the migrant tide' but to absorb our global brothers and sisters until the horrid ordeal has been endured and shared by all, ten billion humans packed onto an ecologically devastated planet. In this vision of human solidarity, immigration will have equally overpopulated and culturally altered every society. One result may well be the end of mass migration to the United States, because in that crowded place it will be risky to drink the water. Or perhaps it will be the *former* United States, its power for global mischief fragmented into successor regions in a post-nationalist, post-American future. ...Mass migration seems in these times to meet with the approval of American and European elites, but it tends to have disruptive political effects among ordinary citizens in receiving societies. ...**Many have wondered how long the United**

States, the nation receiving more immigrants than all of Europe together, [emphasis mine] can avoid this pattern of populist churning and new leaders and parties combining mass migration backlash with other complaints against ossified and unresponsive governments."[1061]

According to the U.N. 2014 saw highest-ever levels of people forcibly displaced. Some 59.5 million people left their homes – 8.3 million more people than the year before. They are all looking for someplace to go. It is the unarmed invasion.[1062]

The U.S. takes in 100,000 legal immigrants *every 30 days* and has done so for decades, enough to fill the Rose Bowl once every month – in addition to all the illegal immigrants. This author thinks we've done our part and then some. The great bulk of undocumented immigrants are going on welfare. Between this and the increased terrorist threat of admitting primarily Muslims without papers into this country, especially when ISIS and al-Qaeda both have the U.S. in the crosshairs, it is foolish, no *suicidal*, to open our door even farther.

As of the Census Bureau's November 2015 release at least 350 languages are spoken in American homes.[1063] We have become the modern day Tower of Babel.

That is one of the problems encountered when people don't want to assimilate into their "adopted" country and everything has to be written and taught in several languages. Go into any home improvement center, any grocery store, signs are often written in both English and Spanish. As a result of school classes being required to teach in both languages, education has been effectively been cut in half with the same information given twice.

The EU is now encountering this language barrier, along with the financial burden and where to house and process them in trying to deal with this giant influx. It's likely the vast majority of these refugees only want a better life, but it would be so easy for terrorists just to slip into the marching crowds. Without papers, it's hard to prove who they really are. Then again, with the vast amount of funds at ISIS' hands, getting forged documents would be as easier than igniting a backpack bomb.

Image: *Tower of Babel* painted by Pieter Brugel circa 1563, hangs in the Museum Boijmans Van Beuningen, Rotterdam.

Roosevelt had something to say about the massive immigrant problem. Clear back in 1915 he saw the future. "The one absolutely certain way of bringing this nation to ruin, of preventing all possibility of its continuing to be a nation at all, would be to permit it to become a tangle of squabbling nationalities… each preserving its separate nationality."[1064]

Quoting world-renowned immigration expert Frosty Wooldridge, "Any culture that will not defend itself against displacement through mass immigration faces extinction. That includes both time-tested and successful cultures. Embracing diversity is cultural suicide. America's multicultural path guarantees its destruction via cultural clashes and conflict such as Islam, Mexican and African cultures that diametrically oppose American culture. The more diverse a country, the more destructive and broken-down its future. The more people, the more it destroys its quality of life and standard of living. The more it adds immigrants, the more destruction to its environment. The more it imports refugees, the faster America, Canada, Europe and Australia lose their own ability to function. Exponential growth of any civilization cannot be sustained. It leads to ultimate collapse. You are seeing it in Africa, India and China today. You will see it in Europe, Canada, Australia and America in the coming years, IF Western countries don't stop all forms of immigration."[1065]

THAT ELEPHANT IN THE ROOM

What is the common denominator? Except for the Serbs and Ukrainians, refugees are mostly Muslims migrating to non-Muslim countries. It doesn't help engender welcoming feelings when Muslims display such disrespect to refugee-hosting countries. During a November 17, 2015 soccer match between Greece and Turkey a moment of silence was held for the 129 victims killed in the Parris attacks. Instead of honoring this small token of respect, Turkish fans booed the silent tribute and then roared "Allahu Akbar".

Yes, America is a nation of immigrants. We have always welcomed them, but to assimilate, not fragment the Country. That aside, we are at that tipping point where we can't even provide jobs for many of our own taxpaying citizens. Infrastructure is falling apart. The National Grid needs to be hardened against an EMP attack that would only cost about 2 billion. In comparison to what it costs to take on more immigrants, it's that proverbial drop in the bucket. Yet we still bring in more at the urging of big business, the President, both political parties and blind humanitarians who have zero insight. It's time now to put a *pause,* and only a pause, on immigration before runaway numbers put a stake in America's heart and the other three 1st world nations. This is Chink #2. Runaway Immigration will take America down.

HELP FROM HOME

Until March 2015, ISIS was a barbaric threat "over there". ISIS self-proclaimed U.S. "brothers" and others from Western countries generally traveled overseas to join the fight. Now they are camped just south of the U.S. border and are increasingly focused on waging jihad in America.

Fordham Law School's Center on National Security June 2015 study discovered some alarming shifts. "Beginning in late March 2015, there has been a substantial increase in cases involving individuals accused of plotting attacks in the United States in the name of ISIS. Out of the 59 individuals, 17 are domestic plotters, 15 of whom were identified or indicted since late March 2015."[1066] The George Washington University Program on Extremism goes further calling ISIS-related mobilization in the U.S. "unprecedented".

Thwarted plots and attacks on U.S. soil are ramping up. In the first seven months of 2015, the Justice Department brought 48 cases compared to 14 in the preceding 10 months. Karen Greenberg, director of the Center said these perpetrators couldn't be profiled due to ethnic diversity saying they are African, African American, Caucasian, Central Asian, Eastern European, and South Asian. Few are of Arab descent.

(Author's Note: If one looks at accompanying photos to the reports, the vast majority of these individuals are black whether they are African or African American.)

Fordham's and George Washington University studies have profiled them to this extent and found:

- 80% are U.S. citizens.
- Average age is 26.
- 86% are men.
- 40% converted to Islam.

- Only 8 had a previous felony conviction.
- 51% of those charged with ISIS-related activities had attempted to travel abroad or had successfully made the trip.
- 250 Americans traveled or attempted to travel to Syria and Iraq to join ISIS as of Fall 2015.
- 300 American and/or U.S.-based ISIS sympathizers were found active on social media, spreading propaganda, and interacting with like-minded individuals.
- Over 50% are from 4 states: Minnesota, North Carolina, New York and Illinois.[1067] [1068]

Photo: 2012 protest against the film Innocence of Muslims held at the Pitt Street Mall in Sydney, New South Wales, Australia. During the event 19 protesters and six police were injured. (Courtesy Jamie Kennedy)

In the aftermath of the 2015 Paris attacks and attacks in Mali, Obama urges to bring in yet more refugees. A day or so after the Paris attacks the 6th Syrian with a fake passport was captured in Honduras on their way to America. FBI Director James Comey admits it's "impossible" to vet every Syrian refugee.[1069] All it takes is one death-driven nutcase to cause a nightmare, inflict death and shut down our fragile economy.

Chink 4: The Fragile, Vulnerable Electric Grid

Two things besides a cyberattack on the power grid could make Western nations have a really bad day – for several years. It could also affect less developed countries that then would no longer receive shipments of food and medical supplies, and products that can't manufacture, build or grow themselves. It would crush global trade and efforts to give aid to countries overseas. Just because an EMP – electromagnetic pulse – fried electronics and electrical grids doesn't mean other disasters stop. Such a life-altering event would hinder rescue efforts especially ones that require connecting overseas. There would be no traveling to affected countries to help in disasters like the 2004 tsunami that pummeled Indonesia, or Haiti's 2010 earthquake that left a quarter million dead or the 7.6 earthquake that struck Pakistan in 2005 – the same year that also brought devastating Hurricane Katrina. No rescue teams from Australia, Japan, America, Britain, Singapore and Taiwan could fly to New Zealand like when Christchurch was reduced to seismic rubble in 2011. Of equal immediate need there would be no working bulldozers to bury the dead and move debris. No ships could sail aid to Japan in the next Fukushima or Australians and Americans lending hot shots to fight wildfires in each other's country. Canada and the U.S. often send firefighters when flames engulf the other's forests, but how would they fight fires without water transported?

This could be the scenario when a huge solar flare, whose CME (**C**oronal **M**ass **Ej**ection) points at Earth and delivers devastating consequences. By luck of the draw or grace of God, violent X-class flares – the worst – have usually either pointed away or a bit off dead center of Earth. For the most part, we've escaped what could be the worst day our planet has ever known. But not always. There is precedence and scientists have issued new dire warnings.

In December 2015 scientists spotted a huge superflare on a star alarmingly like our own. This prompted

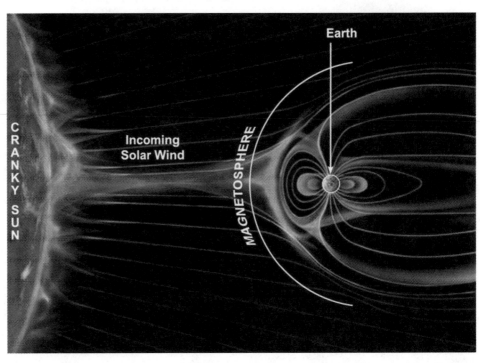

the strongest warning ever that our Sun could unleash just such a flare – one large enough to destroy much of our infrastructure. Energy from that superflare equaled the power of a billion one-megaton nuclear bombs – a thousand times more powerful than any ever recorded. Should such an event erupt from the Sun and point toward Earth, life would radically change within hours.[1070]

BACKGROUNDER

Every day an invisible shield, the magnetosphere, which extends thousands of miles into space, protects Earth from deadly solar rays. Radiation ramps up when the Sun goes through one of its temper tantrums and hurls off flares and CMEs. They can rocket toward Earth as "jet propelled" solar wind instead of its quieter, steadier behavior. It's the magnetosphere's job to deflect most of it, but this protection isn't absolute, especially when bombarded by a hammering CME.

Then it depresses under the onslaught and the overloaded magnetosphere acts like a sieve. In the best case, this brings spectacular sky displays, the Aurora Borealis that dances colorfully across northern regions and less frequently in southern zones. Geomagnetic storms often interrupt radio broadcasts with fading reception or crackly noises, but these are passing events. In the worst case, high voltages can build and travel across long transmission and pipelines that act like conductors. When long power lines are too overloaded, transformers can overheat and their copper insulation melts. Because of the deep interconnectivity of the grid involving with multiple power lines and higher demand for electricity, when one transformer fails, others follow. This can result in catastrophic power failures that knock out power to entire to regions like what Quebec and the U.S. northeast experienced in 1989. This higher demand for power has really become concerning as the electricity used to run air conditioners now is greater than the juice to run all appliances in the 1950s.

Normally CMEs impact countries located in high-to-mid latitudes, but scientists recently made an unnerving discovery about New Zealand's 2001 power outage. On November 6, SOHO (the Solar and Heliospheric Observatory satellite) recorded usually dense solar wind. It zipped toward Earth traveling over 620,000 miles a second. Within 30 minutes, power grid alarms tripped in the middle of New Zealand's South Island. A transformer failed catastrophically. Prior to this New Zealand was considered too far south for CME worries. Now they know differently. The 5-week long power outage brought Auckland to its knees.

Part of the problem is that some countries like the UK and the U.S. haven't invested enough in maintaining critical infrastructure. However, Canada and Finland have installed relays that protect transformers. Despite a 1998 warning, New Zealand didn't make changes. That year four main cables failed that delivered power to the CBD –

the Central Business District. Power was out for 10 weeks in more than two miles of Auckland's economic heart. What previously been considered "unthinkable" by Mercury Energy and politicians became their reality.

Money once again is at the heart of the problem as Dr. Thomas Zurbuchen points out in his 2012 paper. "When interviewed, technology leaders of one U.S. power company as well as government agencies that deal with multiple power companies revealed the pressures on technologists not to include any mechanisms that might hurt the reliability of the power grid. Relays that are supposed to protect the transformers can register false warnings that shut off power when there is no actual danger to the system. Such unwarranted shutoffs are, of course, costly to the power companies and to the U.S. economy. This makes power companies extra sensitive to introducing any technologies, such as new GIC [Geomagnetically Induced Currents] transformer protector relays, that might exacerbate such problems."[1071] So we live with the problem and hold our collective breath, but we may not have long to wait.

OVER-BURDENED AND OLDER THAN DIRT

Another factor weighing heavily on the grid is the crushing demand for electricity. America's power grid built 50 to 60 years ago has outlived its life expectancy by at least a decade. One of these days someone or something is going to administer last rites and we won't even know it until the grid's funeral is underway. Its 2.7 million miles of distribution lines of which more than 450,000 miles transmit high-voltage[1072] and over 2,100 extra-high voltage transformers plus the 6,000 power plants get no time off. 24 hours a day, 7 days a week, 365 days a year they churn out the magic that keeps life moving. The grid was never designed to deliver this much energy yet the demand gets larger every year. In the U.S. electricity usage has grown 1300% from 1940 to 2001.

The biggest juice hog and greatest strain on the grid is air conditioners. Not only can more people afford them, with increased use of computers, large screen TVs and more gadgets and appliances, more heat is added to every home. Who doesn't want to be cool and comfortable? To put this demand into perspective, America's current electricity use just to fuel air conditioning is about the same as the entire energy consumption in the 1950s.[1073] Now add in electric cars. Between 2010 and 2015 the U.S. had sold about 400,000. Charging every car is the equivalent of adding three houses to the grid and EVs sold today can draw 2-5 times more power than those from just a couple of years ago.[1074] One can almost hear it groaning in protest as its fragile bones wear out, yet it's asked to give more and more.

THE CARRINGTON EVENT

Earth was hit by a horrific solar storm in 1859 known as the Carrington Event, named after British astronomer Richard Carrington, who spotted the megaflare. Because this was a little over two decades before electricity came into use, life went on reasonably well. There was no Internet, no ATMs, no gasoline stations, no online banking or automated inventory control. No cell phones, planes or automobiles. No TV, no electrical appliances or video games. No online health records or Facebook or grocery stores with hundreds of the same thing lining shelves. Though trains then ran on coal/steam, today their switching systems are mechanized. However, it did manage to screw up their one bit of worldwide modernity – telegraph systems. Telegraph wires throughout Canada and the U.S. shorted out causing widespread fires. Vivid auroras were visible as far south as Cuba and Hawaii.

1989 DOUBLE WHAMMY

The Sun had been cranky during Solar Cycle 22 and it was about to take it out on Earth. On March 6, 1989 the Sun belched out a large and violent X15 flare. Then on the 10th, another major flare erupted – an X8 – and this was aimed right at the Blue Marble. A CME 36 times the size of Earth ripped form the Sun's surface and hurtled toward Earth at a million miles an hour. Two days later the gas cloud crashed into Earth's protective magnetosphere sending spectacular auroras as far south as Florida, Cuba, and even Honduras. Reddish glows could be seen from most places around the world and those who'd never witnessed the "Northern Lights" thought someone had set off a nuke.

In space some satellites malfunctioned and tumbled out of control for several hours. Back then there were far fewer in orbit and life didn't depend on them to the extent it does today. On Earth, electric currents, those GICs, traveled through the ground. Surges hit power grids all over North America and northern Europe destroying a transformer at a New Jersey nuclear power plant. At 2:45 a.m., on March 13, Canada took it on the chin when Hydro-Quebec's grid crashed knocking out power to 6 million. During the 36-hour blackout[1075] people found themselves stranded in dark offices and in stalled elevators. They awoke to cold showers and cold breakfasts. Schools and businesses remained closed since the Montreal Metro couldn't operate during rush hour.

When Quebec's grid went down both New York Power and New England Power Pool lost many megawatts of power. In New England service to 96 electrical utilities was interrupted. From coast to U.S. coast, over 200 power grid problems erupted. Fortunately none of these caused a blackout. Then just 5 months later on August 16 a massive X20 flare erupted. Its solar storm affected microchips and halted Toronto's stock market trades. More recently the Sun shot off what scientists guesstimate was an X45 flare in November 2003. (See chapter on Signs in the Sun) If that had hit Earth head on, life would have changed radically.

NEAR MISS: SOLAR SUPERSTORM OF 2012

In 2014, scientist Daniel Baker of the University of Colorado and NASA colleagues published a paper on just how perilously close Earth came to disaster in July 2012. He said, "I have come away from our recent studies more convinced than ever that Earth and its inhabitants were incredibly fortunate that the 2012 eruption happened when it did. If the eruption had occurred only one week earlier, Earth would have been in the line of fire. In my view the July 2012 storm was in all respects at least as strong as the 1859 Carrington event. The only difference is, it missed."[1076]

PROGNOSIS GRIM

An analysis of the 1921 storm, which was 10 times more powerful than the 1989 event, estimated that if it occurred today, would leave 130 million people without power. "A severe storm… has the potential for long-duration catastrophic impacts to the power grid. Potable water distribution would be affected within several hours, perishable foods and medications lost in about 12-24 hours; and immediate or eventual loss of heating/air conditioning, sewage disposal, phone service, transportation, fuel resupply"[1077] and nearly every other aspect of daily life would be negatively impacted. Total recovery from a larger storm like the Carrington event, could take 4 to 10 years.

John Kappenman from Metatech Corporation presented his analysis of electrical power systems and came to equally dismal conclusions. "Historically large storms have a potential to cause power grid blackout and transformer damage of unprecedented proportions, long-term blackouts, and lengthy restoration times, and chronic shortages for multiple years are possible. Kappenman summed it up as, 'an event that could incapacitate the network for a long time could be one of the largest natural disasters that we could face.'"[1078]

In February 2014, physicist Pete Riley of Predictive Science Inc. published a paper in *Space Weather* entitled "On the Probability of Occurrence of Extreme Space Weather Events." He analyzed records of solar storms going back more than 50 years. By extrapolating the frequency of ordinary solar storms to the extreme, he calculated the odds of a Carrington-type event hitting Earth in a decade. He determined the likelihood is 12% or about 1 in 8.

Riley's findings shocked him. "Initially, I was quite surprised that the odds were so high, but the statistics appear to be correct. It is a sobering figure." He continued. "If that CME had hit Earth, the resulting geomagnetic storm would have [been] comparable to the Carrington Event and twice as bad as the March 1989 Quebec blackout."[1079]

Daniel Baker warns, "We need to be prepared."[1080] America isn't.

That Other Grim Scenario

A nuclear weapon detonated in or above Earth's atmosphere can create an electromagnetic pulse (EMP), a high-density electrical field. It acts like a stroke of lightning but it's stronger, faster, briefer. Its pulse can seriously damage electronic devices whether connected to power sources and antennas or not. This includes communication systems, computers, electrical appliances, automobile and aircraft ignition systems and their computer-driven modules, plus the all-important electrical grid. Damage can range from a minor interruption to burning out components by overloading them with current to the point where they either blow out or are fried from the inside. Most electronic equipment within 1,000 miles of a high-altitude nuclear detonation (HEMP) could be affected.

Although an EMP isn't likely to hurt people, it could damage pacemakers or other implanted electronic devices. Battery powered radios with short antennas usually survive.

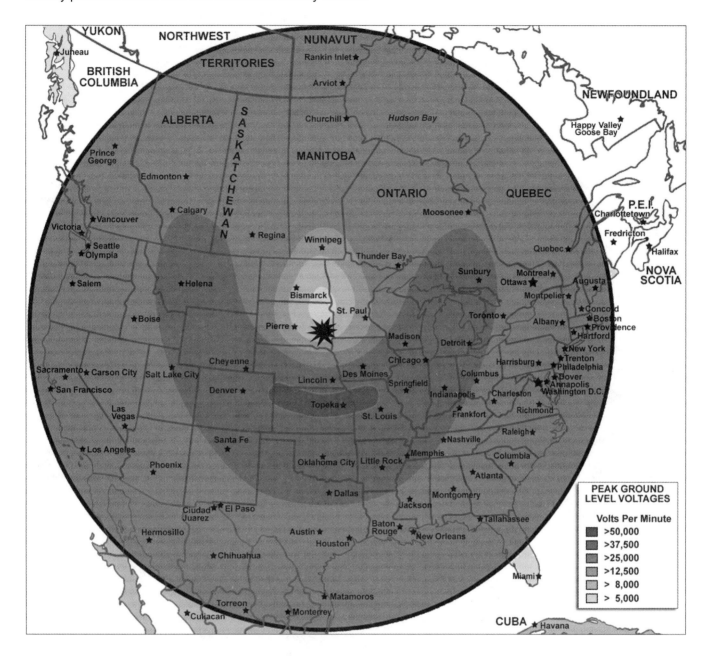

Image: Because of the Earth's curvature and its magnetic field tilts downward at high latitudes, the harsher blast areas form a "U". Maximum EMP occurs south of the explosion.[1081] For example, in the image above, even though the point of detonation was roughly over Huron, SD, the worst hit area would be around Topeka, KS and fanning out from there. This depiction assumes a weapon of more than 1 Megaton exploded about 300 miles overhead with a reach of about 3,000 miles. If that bomb were exploded 120 miles overhead, coverage would about 2,000 miles. The last scenario of an airburst 30 miles overhead would cover about 960 miles or about ⅓ of America. Any of these scenarios would make a grim outcome.

9 OUT OF 10 COULD DIE

A 500-kiloton atomic bomb like those first developed in 1953 and exploded 300 miles above the center of America could so damage electric and electronic infrastructure that it would instantly destroy the nation's economy. Equally devastating would be the psychological effects. Even a 100-kiloton bomb, detonated at the right altitude in the right location, could collapse the electrical grid. Though nukes have advanced far beyond this in size, all nuclear powers – Russia, China, the UK, France, the U.S., Israel, India, Pakistan, Iran and even unstable North Korea either already have these weapons or are capable of building or buying them. Iran, who is hell-bent on stepping up Armageddon to usher in their messiah, the Mahdi, is one of the four likeliest countries to set off an EMP in addition to Russia, China and unstable North Korea. All it would take is a nuke launched off America's coast and the deed would be done. China and Russia have both sneaked within 12 miles of U.S. coasts, entering U.S. territorial waters.

Should such an event happen today, either by a weapon or an enormous solar storm, we wouldn't get blasted to the Stone Age, but would likely spend years like the Pioneers of the early 1800s. How would people survive? Many can't even cook without a TV dinner and microwave. Frank Gaffney, president of the Center for Security Policy, expressed a very dim view of surviving an EMP. "Within a year of that attack, nine out of 10 Americans would be dead, because we can't support a population of the present size in urban centers and the like without electricity. And that is exactly what I believe the Iranians are working towards."[1082]

Photo: Tsar Bomba, a.k.a. Big Ivan, is the largest nuclear weapon ever tested. Russia detonated the 57-megaton behemoth on October 30, 1961 over Mityushikha Bay in the Barents Sea. The ground below was completely leveled like a skating rink for 35 miles.

Windows in homes shattered some 800 miles away in Finland and Norway. Nikita Khrushchev's "baby" was 1,350 to 1,570 times the combined power of the bombs dropped on Nagasaki and Hiroshima. Its energy was 10 times the entire firepower of WWII and a quarter of the force of Krakatoa's 1883 eruption. Khrushchev wanted to teach America a lesson of fear and intimidation in hopes to quash the spread of capitalism and built this beast four times larger than anything the U.S. possessed.

Though dumped from a specially modified plane from 2½ miles overhead, its fireball reached nearly as high and the subsequent mushroom cloud traveled 40 miles upward. Big Ivan was originally intended to be twice as large, but since immediate fallout would have reached Soviet land and meant suicide for the plane's crew, they scaled back the test.

This didn't stop the Russians from building a second Tsar Bomba with a yield of 100 megatons. A bomb doesn't need to be even a fraction of this size to create a very damaging EMP.

THE WEAKEST LINK

Such an attack would literally cost trillions in damaged transformer failures. Unlike other countries, America's electrical grid is so interdependent that when one section goes down, the rest can follow.

America's grids are becoming more vulnerable to disruption because of this interconnectivity, but it provides cheaper power by shunting it through high voltage power lines to whichever utility is in need. This power sharing has inadvertently escalated the risks.

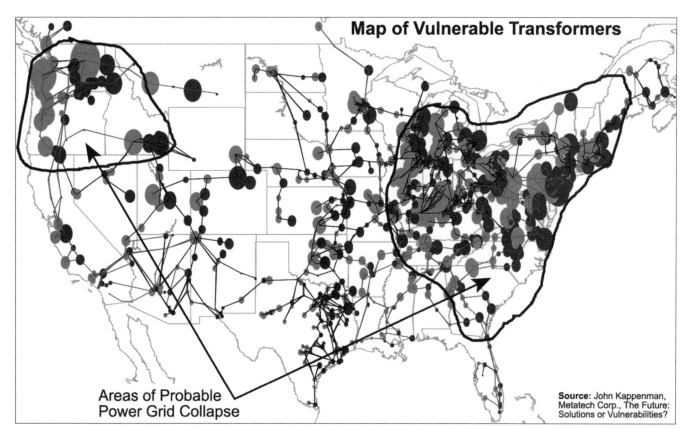

Map of Vulnerable Transformers

Areas of Probable
Power Grid Collapse

Source: John Kappenman, Metatech Corp., The Future: Solutions or Vulnerabilities?

Image: John Kappenman's map showing a geomagnetic disturbance at latitude 50°N, which would run close to the Canadian cities of Kamloops, BC; Calgary, AB; Regina, SK; Winnipeg, MB; Kenora, ON and Port-Cartier-Ouest, According to a National Academy of Sciences workshop and report, more than 300 Extra High Voltage (EHV) transformers in America are at risk of permanent damage and would need to be replaced[1083] when the next geomagnetic superstorm like those in 1921 or 1859 occurs. As a result, Metatech's scientists and engineers expect the areas circled on the next map – the Pacific Northwest and most everything east of Missouri down to Florida – to collapse.

Image: This drawing is a bit deceiving because large power transformers cover a huge footprint.

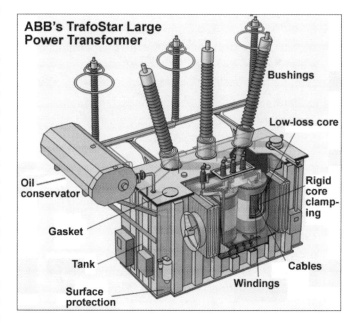

ABB's TrafoStar Large Power Transformer

Bushings

Low-loss core

Oil conservator

Rigid core clamping

Gasket

Tank

Cables

Windings

Surface protection

Recently manufacturers of EHV transformers were backlogged by nearly three years. Three plants in America are capable of manufacturing transformers up to 500kV and only one in Memphis, TN is set up to manufacture a 765kV unit. These two sizes make up the largest group of At-Risk transformers in the U.S. Between Canada and Mexico, four plants can produce transformers up to 500Kv and another one in Quebec can build them as large as 800Kv. Out of these nine facilities five lie within the areas expected to collapse. What good can they do if electricity is caput? You have to have electricity for manufacturing so this is truly a giant catch-22 fiasco.

Then they would need to be transported to the U.S. Some weighing over 820,000 pounds require specially built freight cars called Schnabels and only 30 exist in America plus few others worldwide.

Because transformers are so expensive, upwards of $8 million apiece, few replacements are on hand. They have to be specially ordered and custom-built. To replace even one of America's 2,100 large transformers can take up to 24 months if produced outside the U.S. Inside might take just 16 months. According to the Dept. of Energy's

2014 report that lead-time could extend to **5 years** if the manufacturer has trouble obtaining bushings and other raw materials like copper and special electrical steel.[1084]

Some are so massive – the size of a new single family home measuring 45 feet high and covering some 2,200 sq. feet – that transportation is another hurdle.

Image: Attacks on the U.S. energy grid and critical manufacturing make up 60% of all cyberattacks. Critical Manufacturing includes iron, steel and aluminum production; manufacturing of engines, turbines, electrical and power transmission equipment; and transportation covers all aspects of vehicles, planes, aerospace and their parts as well as all things railroad. In other words all the manufacturing industries essential to many other critical infrastructure sectors.

To further brighten the day, large transformers are exceedingly vulnerable to hack and physical attacks. One manufacturer stated, if someone were to intentionally try ... it is a surprisingly simple task and there are a large number of ways to conceivably damage a transformer beyond repair."[1085] This doesn't take into account the over 200,000 miles of high-voltage lines.

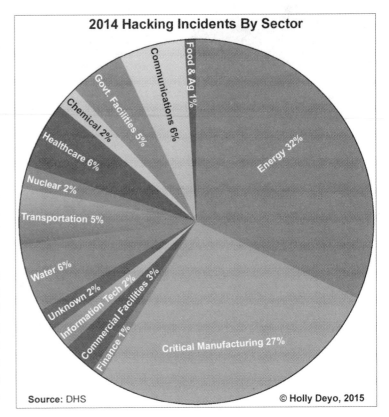

2014 Hacking Incidents By Sector

Food & Ag 1%
Communications 6%
Govt. Facilities 5%
Chemical 2%
Healthcare 6%
Nuclear 2%
Transportation 5%
Water 6%
Unknown 2%
Information Tech 2%
Commercial Facilities 3%
Finance 1%
Energy 32%
Critical Manufacturing 27%

Source: DHS   © Holly Deyo, 2015

HACK ATTACKS

According to Rep. Randy Weber, (R-TX) in his testimony to the House Subcommittee on Research and Technology on how to protect the grid from cyberattacks, he stated that every four days, part of the nation's power grid is struck by a cyber or physical attack.[1086] Global transformer manufacturer ABB echoed his statement.[1087] Between 2011 and 2014 electric utilities reported to the Dept. of Energy 362 physical and cyber attacks. In 300 "significant" attacks, the suspects were never identified.

When these mega-structures are so vital to every day life, it's astonishing they're so poorly protected. Most are enclosed by only chain link fencing and are easily identified by their size and appearance.

In 2013 attackers severely damaged the Metcalf, California substation. First they cut six underground fiber optic lines and then fired over 100 rounds of ammo at the transformers. Due to the extent of damage, police felt more than one gunman participated, but they were never caught. They didn't manage to knock out power, but their destructive actions cost Pacific Gas & Electric over $15 million. More importantly it brought power station vulnerabilities to national attention.

Other recent attacks include – and these are just four out of hundreds:

- **2011**: An intruder accessed a critical hydroelectric converter station in Vermont by smashing a lock on the door.
- **2013**: A gunman fired multiple shots at a gas turbine power plant along the Missouri-Kansas border.
- **2013**: Four bullets were fired from a highway and hit a power substation outside Colorado Springs.
- **2013**: Security officers at Florida's Jacksonville Electric Authority noticed a man climbing a fence surrounding St. Johns River Power Park, which generates energy for 250,000 households. Though he was later seen trying to break into a second facility, he fled and was never caught.[1088]

If one substation is hit, it can cause a power outage for a day or so, or several weeks and is "relatively" easy to fix. However if multiple stations are clobbered simultaneously, that's a different ballgame. It could leave millions in the dark for months – maybe longer with cascading failures.

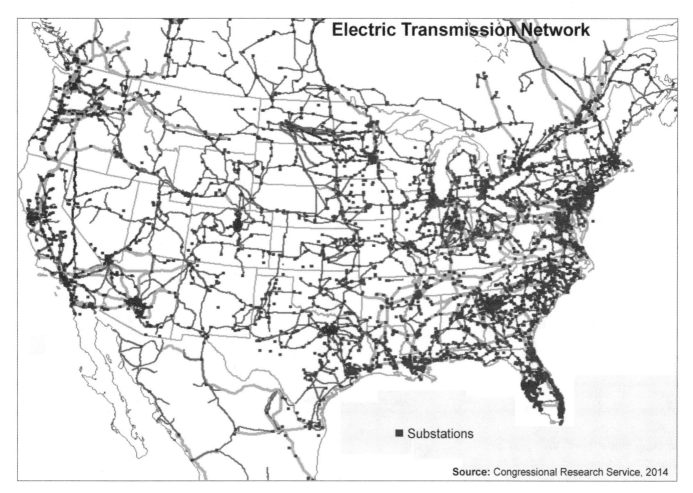

Image: As seen from this image, the U.S. power grid extends into Canada and Mexico.

While no cyberattack has successfully brought long-term power outages, attempts are ratcheting up. Department of Homeland Security received 151 incident reports in 2013 alone – up from 111 in 2012 and 31 in 2011.[1089] Now attacks have really blown up. Think about that statement – *no long-term power outages…* It certainly implies that short-term outages *have* succeeded.

It only takes one victorious try to make millions suffer greatly. As the grid is increasingly meshed with the Internet, ultimately becoming a full Smart Grid, hackers affiliated with rogue nations and terrorist groups are working tirelessly to bring a nationwide crisis. Besides crashing systems outright, hackers are planting malware in the industrial control systems of critical infrastructure. The most recent malicious software – *BlackEnergy* (and its variants), *Havex* and *Sandworm* – were found in these systems. Unfortunately Smart technology provides even more access points because it's heavily tied to the Internet, making a teetering and fragile power grid more vulnerable.

Rep. Suzanne Bonamici (D-OR) shared that, "In just one month, the PJM interconnection – which coordinates electricity transactions in 13 states and in D.C. – experienced 4,090 documented cyber attempts to attack their system. That's more than five and a half attacks on their electrical power system per hour."[1090] This number is vastly different from what Homeland Security divulged. Keep in mind that PJM [the regional transmission organization for the RFC region] is only one of the 8 interconnections besides being one of the smaller sectors. If one were to extrapolate from this, true the number of hack attempts could 10 times higher. "Brent Stacey, an associate lab director at the Idaho National Laboratory, told lawmakers there has been a '32% increase in the number of attacks on the energy sector' and it continues to increase."[1091] Lawmakers were shocked at this and you'd think they'd be whipped into action. Didn't happen.

It may be that the RFC is targeted more often since Washington, D.C. is in this grouping. Then there's always lack of government transparency despite what Presidents promise. Bennet Gaines, senior vice president at First Energy Service Company confirms this saying, "In some cases there's a three-to-six-month lag" before the government shares any details on cyberattacks.[1092]

PEARL HARBOR 2.0

In October 2012 then Defense Secretary Leon Panetta warned that America is facing the possibility of a "cyber-Pearl Harbor" and is increasingly vulnerable to foreign hackers who could dismantle the nation's power grid, transportation system, financial networks and government. He continued. "An aggressor nation or extremist group could use these kinds of cyber tools to gain control of critical switches. They could derail passenger trains, or even more dangerous, derail passenger trains loaded with lethal chemicals. They could contaminate the water supply in major cities, or shut down the power grid across large parts of the country." He concluded by saying the most destructive scenarios involve "cyber-actors launching several attacks on our critical infrastructure at one time, in combination with a physical attack."[1093] Taking over vehicles, planes and trains is becoming more of a reality.

As early as 2012 Charlie Miller, security engineer at Twitter, and Chris Valasek, director of security intelligence at the Seattle consultancy IOActive, found alarming flaws in later model cars. With just a laptop connected to its diagnostics port they were able to continuously blast its horn, drain its battery, change the speedometer and gas gauges at will, abruptly tighten seat belts, accelerate or brake at will, turn headlights on and off, and disable or jerk the steering wheel.

For years hackers have warned that passenger jets are vulnerable to cyberattacks. For obvious reasons, airlines and airplane manufacturers have downplayed the warnings, but now too much proof exists for the public not to worry. You now have to ask yourself *how lucky do you feel boarding a plane?* As with newer cars, recently designed aircraft like Boeing's 787 Dreamliner and long-haul Airbus models A350 and A380 are vulnerable. Chris Roberts, IT expert and founder of security company One World Labs, claimed that he successfully hacked into their onboard entertainment systems 15-20 times between 2011 and 2014. He did this by hooking his laptop up to the Seat Electronic Box (SEB), which is usually located under each passenger seat and using Ethernet. He accessed the SEB just by "wiggling and squeezing" its cover.

Roberts also claimed that in 2005 or 2006 he hacked the International Space Station and changed its temperature. Roberts and his team also toyed with taking Mars' Curiosity Rover "for a spin", but eventually ditched the plan. Roberts said, "We got yelled at by NASA. If they're going to leave open sh*t that's not encrypted, that's their own damn silly fault. ... The closest we've done is figure out exactly how they're [NASA and the Rover] communicating, how they're controlling it, and we might have one or two of the passwords for some of the software that we know are still in default mode. But the problem is actually getting into it without breaking more laws than we're used to breaking. No, I think NASA would probably really get pissed at me for that one."[1094]

Why did Roberts do it? He was given an $80,000 grant by the Pentagon to find vulnerabilities. Later an FBI agent told him that accessing airplane networks without authorization is a violation of federal statute. Roberts has never been charged with a crime so maybe the agent's comment was meant to dissuade others from trying.

Regional Entities
Florida Reliability Coordinating Council (FRCC)
Midwest Reliability Organization (MRO)
Northeast Power Coordinating Council (NPCC)
ReliabilityFirst Corporation (RFC)
SERC Reliability Corporation (SERC)
Southwest Power Pool, RE (SPP)
Texas Reliability Entity (TRE)
Western Electricity Coordinating Council (WECC)

Electric Grid Sectors

Not affiliated

Source: NERC

Dr. Anuja Sonalker, lead scientist and program manager at non-profit Battelle warns, "I think they [Black Hat hackers] have the pieces. If you follow the last several years, they've demonstrated successful hacks into cars, health-care devices, pacemakers, TVs, everything. So the pieces are there, and the Internet of things is not going away. It's here."[1095] The point remains that successfully penetrating transportation control systems are the prelude to hacking not just America's electric grid, but to take out power to all western nations.

China, Russia and other countries have already penetrated the U.S electric grid. They could launch a war without firing a single bullet. At the time they didn't damage the infrastructure, just mapped the systems, but intelligence agencies discovered malware they left behind. Presumably if relations really sour or we go to war with them, the destructive software would be activated. Likely North Korea and Iran also have these hacking capabilities if they haven't already used them. As early as 2008 a cyberattack took out power equipment in multiple regions outside the U.S. Extortion demands followed the blackout.[1096]

James Clapper, director of national intelligence said, "Unknown Russian actors successfully compromised the product supply chains of at least three [industrial control system] vendors so that customers downloaded malicious software designed to facilitate exploitation directly from the vendors' websites along with legitimate software updates…"[1097] Six years later Clapper revealed this despite utility executives trying to downplay the problem, saying hacking is getting worse. "Cyber threats to U.S. national and economic security are increasing in frequency, scale, sophistication and severity of impact."[1098]

In October 2014 the *Washington Free Beacon* reported that Russian hackers had penetrated critical water and energy systems. Malicious software *BlackEnergy* and a variant were discovered implanted in numerous control systems, which gave the hacker remote access. *BlackEnergy* has been around since at least 2007 and sold through the cyber underground and pushed primarily by the Russian gang, Quedagh. It's unknown how many individuals or nation states have it and *BlackEnergy* was likely used to attack Ukraine.

Red Dragon hackers have also intruded into sensitive U.S. infrastructure. In May 2013 *International Business Times* reported that China had breached the U.S. Army Corps of Engineers dams database. This site contains information and data on the vulnerabilities of thousands of dams. Not only could access put America's water supplies at risk, it could jeopardize the power grid. Further, if any of the over 8,100 dams failed, the database includes estimates of how many would perish.[1099]

It's not just China. In 2013 Iranian hackers also penetrated the control system of a small dam 20 miles from New York City. However, this information wasn't released until more than two years after the incident and it's still classified. It's like when Earth has a near miss with an asteroid, NASA says *oops, that was close* the day after it happens. Officials feel this "probing" intrusion was just a practice run.

While our infrastructure is becoming increasingly integrated, these systems are shockingly unprotected. This puts prime targets of the power grid, factories, pipelines, bridges and dams at huge risk. In a conventional war, a country usually knows its enemy. In the case of cyberattacks signals can bounce all over the globe making the point of origin nearly impossible to pinpoint. How can you fight an invisible opponent? The only way is to have all infrastructure hardened in the first place, which we don't. Security experts say operators don't even think about security and therefore have done little.

ISIS, too, has already tried to hack America's grid, but government officials refuse to say when or where their attempts were made. Just that they had failed. John Riggi, section chief in the FBI's cyber division expressed concern over ISIS. "Strong intent. Thankfully, low capability. But the concern is that they'll buy that capability."[1100]

Utah's critical infrastructure protection coordinator, Mark Lemery downplayed ISIS' attempts. "They'd love to do damage, but they just don't have the capability. Terrorists have not gotten to the point where they're causing physical damage."[1101] It's comments like these that are the real worry. They give a false sense of security and then Congress falls back, does nothing – again. If money is all that's holding ISIS back, then our hair should be on fire. With ISIS raking in $3 million a *day*, money is literally no problem.

Energy company execs claim that since the U.S. grid is a patchwork the likelihood of it being taken down is extremely low. These unnamed people in CNN's article say, "it would take a large, expensive team of highly technical spies to understand the layout of computers and machines at an energy company. Then it takes stellar hackers to sneak in. And even if they do manage to flip a switch – which companies maintain has never happened here in the United States – the attack might only take out electricity fed to a tiny portion of land, maybe a section of a city. An entirely different type of attack would be needed to carry that over to the next power plant."[1102] Really? If $$ and know how is all that's holding them back, we should be very concerned. ISIS has plenty of cash and that can buy the other. Maybe the reason ISIS hasn't hit the grid yet is that they've been otherwise occupied. They've been busy blowing up people and chopping off heads. When they put their mind to it, *really* make it a priority; it's only a matter of time.

Admiral Michael Rogers, who also serves the dual role as head of U.S. Cyber Command said there are "already groups within the U.S. cyber architecture who seek to cause major damage to corporate and other critical sectors of the American economy." He said that these people, cyber hit men for hire and nation-states all have the U.S. in their crosshairs and that "it is only a matter of the when, not the if, that we are going to see something traumatic."[1103] The year before outgoing Homeland Security Secretary Janet Napolitano left a warning for her successor: "A massive and 'serious' cyber attack on the U.S. homeland is coming, and a natural disaster - the likes of which the nation has never seen – is also likely on its way."[1104]

EXECUTIVE ORDERS AND WILLFUL BLINDNESS

In August 2012 a group of Republicans, led by Senator John McCain (AZ), killed a cybersecurity bill that had been a national security priority saying it would be too burdensome for corporations. However, Mr. Obama signed on February 12, 2013 Executive Order 13636, "Improving Critical Infrastructure Cybersecurity" and PPD-21, which looks at the cascading consequences of infrastructure failures.

He followed this on February 13, 2015 with Executive Order 13691 – "Promoting Private Sector Cybersecurity Information Sharing". This EO urges companies to share cybersecurity-threat information with one another and the federal government – something many companies are reluctant to do.

On its heels came Memorandum signed February 25, 2015 "Establishment of the Cyber Threat Intelligence Integration Center". Its mission is to connect intel from government agencies when a crisis occurs.

Then on April 1, 2015, Mr. Obama issued his third cybersecurity EO 13694 "Blocking the Property of Certain Persons Engaging in Significant Malicious Cyber-Enabled Activities," which allows the government to impose penalties on foreign individuals or entities that engage in hacking the U.S.

All the EOs in the world will do little if strong measures aren't implemented to harden all areas of our infrastructure. Action talks and nonsense walks.

Ted Koppel legendary broadcaster and host of ABC's Nightline shared a grim picture of America's cybersecurity. He said that the one agency that should be most prepared – Dept. of Homeland Security – isn't. Koppel said, "I've talked to every former Secretary of Homeland Security, and they all acknowledge there is no plan." Mr. Obama's current Secretary, Jeh Johnson responded to Koppel's prodding queries about America's disaster plans with an alarming comment. "He [Johnson] just sort of pointed up at a shelf filled with white binders and he said, 'Look, I'm sure there's something up there somewhere.'"[1105] Levelheaded Koppel realized there wasn't much he could do to fix the cybersecurity mess and government's lack of action so he bought at least six months of water and freeze-dried food for he and his family including the seven grandkids.

So just how bad is it? We'll never have a true understanding of the hacking extent until the lights go out.

THAT RADIOACTIVE DINOSAUR IN THE ROOM

Think Fukushima multiplied by 100. This is nearly too ugly to contemplate, but it's a real and deadly scenario if some entity takes out the grid – and they want to. In a do or die scenario, people will either walk or peddle to the nearest water source to quench their thirst. Water weighs eight pounds per gallon. The average person can bike maybe two-to-four gallons from a nearby water source to home with a jerry-rigged carrying set-up. This water weighs 16 to 32 pounds. How much can be transported greatly depends on the terrain between home and destination, that person's physical fitness, climate (if a person is biking over icy winter roads) and physical impediments like police roadblocks or destroyed bridges and roads, or traveling over uneven, rocky fields. To "quench" a nuclear plant's water needs would be virtually impossible without electricity since their storage pools are typically 40 feet deep by 40 or more feet wide and long. That means about a half million gallons to fill them.

In an EMP event or a pervasive grid hack, without power water can't be transported to cool the rods. In simplest terms, they then overheat and spew radiation into the air, which is then carried around the world on air currents. After a 9.0 earthquake and tsunami slammed northern Honshu, Japan in March 2011, three reactors exploded and went into nuclear meltdown. Four years later radioactive readings in some U.S. states are still off the charts. Look at all the dead wildlife especially off the U.S. and Canadian west coast clear up to Alaska from Japan's Fukushima. It is truly tragic especially for all the Japanese who've been continually lied to about the health dangers right under their noses.

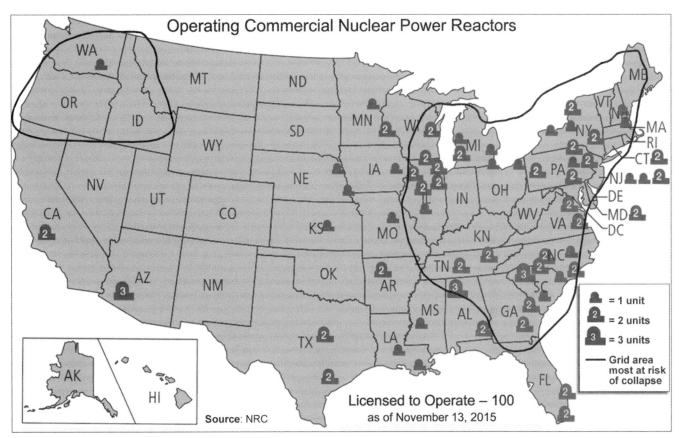

Operating Commercial Nuclear Power Reactors

= 1 unit
= 2 units
= 3 units
— Grid area most at risk of collapse

Licensed to Operate – 100
as of November 13, 2015

Source: NRC

Image: Map of 100 operational nuclear power plants as of the end of 2015. More than 75% lie within the two most fragile areas of the grid as per John Kappenman's and Metatech's assessment of vulnerable transformers. As of September 2015, applications for 19 new power plants had been submitted to the NRC. Ten of these also lie in the vulnerable regions. Prevailing wind blows west to east to where the highest concentrations of people live in the least grid-secure area. In a nuclear emergency, there would no place to evacuate tens of millions.

Image: Yucca Mountain test tunnel in Nevada built by the DOE to determine if the location was suitable as a deep geological nuclear waste repository. (Courtesy Department of Energy.)

As of November 2015 the U.S. had 100 operational nuclear plants. Seventy-two of these, plus another planned 10 lay within the two areas of likely grid collapse. Ten others in these same-circled areas are undergoing decommissioning and about that same number are already mothballed, plus six more sites are independent spent fuel storage installations. Whether nuclear plants are online or decommissioned, *all* store spent nuclear fuel (SNF) onsite. There's simply no place else to put it. There was a "best place" out in the deserts of Nevada called Yucca Mountain, until Mr. Obama killed that project in 2011 without public knowledge or input. There sailed another $15 billion[1106] out the window. Yucca Mountain was a viable scenario because radioactive waste was to be isolated by 1,000 feet of dry rock overhead yet 1,000 feet above the water table.

No place is perfect, but Yucca Mountain is certainly safer than having highly radioactive material scattered at 145 sites around the country. More importantly many of these locations have or are running out of room for the 85,000 tons, yes *tons*, of nuke waste. Every year America churns out about 2,600 tons of hot spent fuel with no place for it to go. With this deadly material a thousand feet underground, it's a lot smarter than trying to safeguard 145 sites.

That same year, 2011, that Mr. Obama killed the national repository several entities – South Carolina, Washington state, the National Association of Regulatory Utility Commissioners and Nye County, Nevada – filed a joint suit requiring the NRC to restart licensing proceedings. They were court-ordered to comply in November 2013. After the licensing requirements were met in 2015, Yucca hit another snag or two. The Dept. of Energy isn't the sole owner of the land that the repository is on and Nevada refuses to give the necessary water rights. So

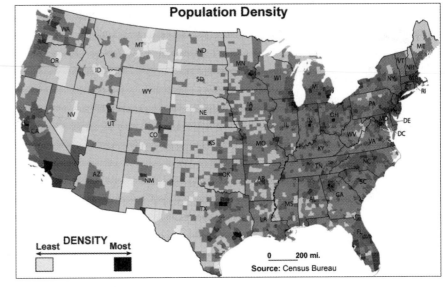

while Yucca Mountain was given the go ahead through the courts, the project has been defunded.

JUST FIX IT!

On June 18, 2013, Rep. Trent Franks introduced HR 2417 – the Secure High-voltage Infrastructure for Electricity from Lethal Damage Act. Commonly known as the Shield Act, in the three days following its introduction it went to three different committees: Energy and Commerce, House Budget and the Subcommittee on Energy and Power. And there it sits. It requires any "owner, user or operator of the domestic bulk-power system to implement measures to protect the system against specified vulnerabilities."

Astronomer Donald Goldsmith estimates "grid down" would cost up to $2 trillion[1107] in economic damages yet to harden it would only require about $2 billion.[1108] This is less than 2% of what America sends on illegal aliens <u>every year</u>. Why government hasn't followed through is a mystery to many. This is not only a real threat, but one that could end America's life as we know it. Remember Revelation 18:9-11: *And the kings and political leaders of the earth, who committed immorality and lived luxuriously with her, will weep and beat their chests [in mourning] over her when they see the smoke of her burning, standing a long way off, in fear of her torment, saying, 'Woe, woe, the great city, the strong city, Babylon! In a single hour your judgment has come.' "And merchants of the earth will weep and grieve over her, because no one buys their cargo (goods, merchandise) anymore."*

Chink 5: The Fundamental Transformation of America

There's more to consider if people aren't yet convinced America is in grave trouble. Mr. Obama promised in 2008 to "fundamentally transform" America and he at least kept his word on this. The voting block that endorsed Obama thought he meant, idealistically, an end to racism was within grasp. Instead, this divide became a gaping growing festering boil. Likely only those on the radical left realized what he really meant. From apologizing for American exceptionalism to embarking on an "apology" tour to kissing up to enemies and alienating allies, Americans began an 8-year trip on Obama's train of change.

Following is a partial list of Obama's legacy and fundamental transformations:

- Failed and shortsighted foreign policy
- Less secure America with sagging national security
- Increased racial divide to a gaping chasm
- Decimated the U.S. military to lowest numbers since WWI
- Fomented open hostility toward Israel – the only U.S. ally in the Middle East

- Redistributed wealth from middle class to rich and poor
- Nearly doubled food stamp use to 47 million in a decade and more than doubled its cost from $29 billion to $64 billion *a year*
- Brought about the lowest labor participation rate in 37 years
- Shoved through high-impact legislation without Congress knowing what it contained, e.g., ObamaCare
- Cut the standard 40-hour work week down to 29
- Awarded unprecedented entitlements at taxpayers' expense
- Racked up even more scandals than the Billary Clintons
- Actively supported gay marriage and gender redefinition
- Single-handedly brought the highest deficit – more than the combined Presidents through the Nixon administration
- Increased federal spending by 20% and national debt by 66%
- Caused highest-ever utility bills with onerous environmental regulations through its wars on coal, carbon, and on "ponds and ditches"
- Involved military in another Iraq war after pledging to withdraw our troops
- Continually tried to refocus Nation's attention on global warming rather than on terrorism and the economy
- Promoted an anti-Christian agenda and rhetoric
- Implemented dangerous "catch and release" immigration policy and released tens of thousands of illegal immigrant felons into the populace
- Unprecedented crackdown against whistleblowers

To be fair, where in all of the above, minus the Executive Order-driven changes, was Congress? Americans weren't pleased with the changes and expressed their ire at the ballot box. Since Obama took office Democrats lost over 1,000 seats: 14 Senate seats, 69 House seats, 12 governorships and 910 state legislature seats. In November 2015, non-partisan pollster Gallup found that just 11% of Americans approved of the Congress. This was bested only in Fall 2013 when four polling groups including Gallup, CBS and Fox News each showed Congress had a 9% approval rate.

The downward trend is unmistakable. In 2001, this legislative body according to Gallup enjoyed its highest approval rating of 84 since 1993. It remained steady in the 45s and 50s till March 2003. Then the love affair ended and their numbers declined consistently into the teens during the Obama years.[1109] The curious thing is that despite Americans' obvious disgust with elected representatives, few seem willing to make permanent changes. Is it a case of the enemy you know is better than the one you don't? Or is it indicative of #8.5 on the Life Cycle of a Country?

The Supremes

One of the more profound, enduring changes is that in the Supreme Court. It has morphed from a body that *interprets* law to one that's making it. The fact that something as momentous, so nation changing as gay marriage – was decided not by vote, but by nine people – is astonishing. The balance of power and law hangs on just a few. Presidents come and go and onerous legislation can be overturned, but The Supremes' decisions have the staying power of Super Glue.

Death of Antonin Scalia, Death of Conservatism?

On Valentine's Day Eve 2016 Judge Scalia passed away in Texas. But was it murder? Owner of Cibolo Creek Ranch John Poindexter tried to awaken Scalia about 8:30 that morning. The judge's door was locked and he didn't answer. Three hours later after returning from an outing, Poindexter and one of the judge's friends opened his door. Scalia's body was cold. Poindexter shared, "We discovered the judge in bed, a pillow over his head. His bedclothes were unwrinkled. He was lying very restfully. It looked like he had not quite awakened from a nap."[1110] Who goes to sleep with a pillow over their face? On the other hand, why would a murderer leave evidence in place?

In yet a third walk-back or "clarification" describing how the judge was found Poindexter said the "pillow was over his head," [1111] against the headboard. With all of the different stories, we will never know the truth.

Even stranger, Presidio County Judge Cinderela Guevara pronounced that he'd died of natural causes after first saying it was a heart attack. This statement was made without seeing the body or an autopsy being performed, which is permitted under Texas law.[1112] One of his nine kids was supposed to have accompanied the judge to Cibolo Creek Ranch, but at the last minute couldn't make it. Maybe if he'd been able to go, the judge wouldn't be dead. This isn't judgment, but if foul play were afoot, maybe his son being there would have thwarted opportunity since the judge had declined security detail.

Sotomayor Breyer Alito Kagan

Thomas Scalia Roberts Kennedy Ginsburg

Photo: Generally speaking these judges are liberal: Ruth Bader Ginsburg, Sonia Sotomayor, Stephen G. Breyer and Elena Kagan. On the other end of the spectrum are Clarence Thomas, Antonin Scalia, Chief Justice John G. Roberts, and Justice Samuel A. Alito, Jr. Anthony M. Kennedy is often viewed as the swing vote. This assessment means something, but not a lot as consistently conservative Chief Justice John G. Roberts unexpectedly changed in the last hours to vote for ObamaCare. His was the vote that catapulted ObamaCare into law.

With the premiere conservative SCOTUS voice gone, the scale has tipped dangerously in favor of liberal-leaning America. The Supremes were due to rule on numerous vital cases in 2016 on immigration, religious freedom, ObamaCare, affirmative action, voting rights and maybe most importantly, limiting Presidential powers – something Mr. Obama has frequently over-stepped. Regarding the latter Judge Scalia and Mr. Obama were complete opposites. Mr. Obama continually "reinterpreted" the Constitution to further his goals. Mr. Scalia was a textualist meaning he interpreted written law, in this case the Constitution, without going beyond the intent of the legislators who wrote it. Without textualism, Scalia said it opened the door to abandoning the liberties that America's Founding Fathers considered essential.

Judge Scalia's death will further divide this Nation because at no time in history has America been on such divergent paths. The schism between conservative and progressive, black and white, poor and rich has never been more apparent. The last two Supreme Court judges appointed were Sonia Sotomayor and Elena Kagan. Both are liberal-leaning judges who filled similar seats. For years on key issues, the court has broken 5-4 in favor of liberalism, which has dragged Conservatives on a hellish ride. In his last few months as President, Mr. Obama will certainly try to appoint a liberal judge, which would tip the scales further in that direction by 6-3.

When the Founder Father's framed the Constitution setting SCOTUS judges for life, people only lived to be about 50. After sufficient learning and training, then working as lawyers and judges in lower courts, this left maybe 10 years on the Supreme Court. In 2016, Kennedy had served 28 years at nearly 80 and Ginsburg had served over 22 years and at nearly 83. Ginsburg is liberal and Kennedy is seen as a "flipper" though generally considered conservative. Their passing or stepping down may or may not change the balance, but Scalia's replacement may fundamentally transform America, as Mr. Obama stated he wanted to do. Since some of his "legacy" is going down in flames, this may be a way to leave an unwanted thumbprint for 30 or 40 years.

Either way another divide was set in motion February 13, 2016 – to find a judge that at least 60 out of 100 Senators can agree on. Sixty votes may be a high bar for Obama, whose liberal party holds 46 Senate seats including two independents. Anyway it comes down there will be a long-term price to pay following a bloodbath over the vacated SCOTUS seat.

No Longer the Home of the Free

September 11, 2001 paved the way for onerous legislation including that year's PATRIOT Act and 2012's National Defense Authorization Act, which furthered government's invasion of privacy. While the NSA has monitored Americans' communications for years without their knowledge, after 9/11 the U.S. mushroomed into a surveillance state. Utah is home to a behemoth NSA facility that admits it "touches" 29 petabytes, or 29 million gigabytes, of data every day.[1113]

The state of America's eroding freedom was underscored in a joint 2015 study from the Cato Institute, Fraser Institute and the Swiss Liberales Institut. The authors of The Human Freedom Index, Ian Vasquez and Tanja Porcnik, looked at 76 indicators to determine just how free people are to enjoy liberties such as freedom of speech and religion. They also looked at size of government, restrictive laws, property rights, freedom of movement, women's freedoms, crime and violence, economic freedom, legal discrimination against homosexual relationships and regulation of credit, labor and business. (This study was released after the Supreme Court's June 2015 ruling in favor of gay marriage.)

From 2008 to 2012 – the most recent year for which there was enough data – the U.S. dropped from 17th to 20th out of 152 countries. Canada, the U.K., Germany, Sweden, Ireland, Scandinavia, Australia and New Zealand all ranked higher. Even Hong Kong and Chile rated better. Not surprisingly, Iran ranked dead last. Generally speaking countries in Africa and the Middle East didn't fare well.[1114]

Vasquez and Porcnik explained the poor rating saying that since 2000, the U.S. has declined in economic freedom. Other major factors contributing to the low rating were government's use of eminent domain to take private property and growing invasion of privacy from the war on drugs and war on terror.

THE PATRIOT ACT

The Uniting and Strengthening America by Providing Appropriate Tools Required to Intercept and Obstruct Terrorism Act of 2001, otherwise known as the (USA) PATRIOT Act, was signed into law just 45 days after 9/11. Department of Justice explains the bill's intent as equipping "federal law enforcement and intelligence officials with the tools they need to mount an effective, coordinated campaign against our nation's terrorist enemies. The Act revised counterproductive legal restraints that impaired law enforcement's ability to gather, analyze, and share critical terrorism-related intelligence information. The Act also updated decades-old federal laws to account for the technological breakthroughs seen in recent years... the Act enhanced America's criminal laws against terrorism, in some cases increasing the penalties for planning and participating in terrorist attacks and aiding terrorists. The Act also clarified that existing laws against terrorism apply to the new types of attacks planned by al Qaeda and other international terrorist organizations."[1115]

But does it go too far? Here are the main objections:

1. The Patriot Act allows for "sneak and peek" granting search of a person's property without warrant or notification bypassing the 4th Amendment.

2. It allows agencies to share any and all evidence or information with each other (illegal immigrants strongly object to this since if they were picked up for criminal activity, they could be reported to Immigration and Customs.)

3. It cleared the way for data mining – the mass collection of information about American citizens whether they are targets of criminal investigations or not.

4. It allows "roving wiretaps" so government agencies can legally tap every single form of communication that a person of interest uses, not just a single phone.

5. Most shocking, it permits indefinite detention of immigrants and other non-citizens. There is no requirement that those who are detained indefinitely be removable because they are terrorists.

The speed with which both parties overwhelmingly passed this law is reminiscent of the firearms removal in Australia.

Australia Disarmed

During the terrible Port Arthur Massacre in Tasmania, Martin Bryant shot dead 35 people and wounded another 23. Just six months later, September 30, 1996, Australia disarmed the entire country. Haste and fear voted through this onerous law and now leaves its citizens much more vulnerable. At the time of disarmament, this author and her husband lived in Perth. Stan and I looked at each other in horror realizing that Australians, while having the best of intentions thinking no guns equaled no crime, rushed to pass it. No so. We both keep in touch with friends in that country and the consensus about this legislation is one of regret. People even turned in collector's pieces, held in families for generations that can never be replaced.

Catherine Rushforth and Jenny Mouzo wrote one of the most naive statements ever printed in their 2003 report, *Trends and Issues in Crime and Criminal Justice No. 269: Firearm Related Deaths in Australia, 1991–2001.* It stated that since the 1996 buyback, gun related crime had significantly decreased in Australia. What they didn't address is that criminals simply use other weapons. Knives, broken bottles, dirty needles, nail guns, farm tools like axes, adzes, and the like all suffice nicely. Additionally, suicides and crime were already in a downward trend in Australia before the disarmament, so the Rushforth-Mouzo report doubly gives a wrong picture.

Under tightly controlled circumstances Australians can still have firearms *if* a person owns a farm property and requires a weapon to put down injured animals, etc. or, *if* a person belongs to a gun club. They must have proof of membership and regularly attend. Personal protection as a reason on the application doesn't qualify. Gun owners must have passed background checks, plus re-apply and re-qualify for their license every one to five years depending on the permit.

"Regret" over the general loss of firearm ownership is seen in their statistics. By 2010, the number of privately held firearms was back to the level of 1996. "While Australia's population grew by 19% between 1997 and 2010, the total number of guns soared by 45%. If gun control advocates are correct, gun crimes or suicides should have plunged in 1997 but gradually increased after that."[1116]

So did America, too, act in haste?

NATIONAL DEFENSE AUTHORIZATION ACT

On the surface the NDAA looks to tighten the screws against possible further terrorism. However, the bill has two highly objectionable sections that infringe on Constitutionally granted freedoms:

It allows the U.S. government to put investigations and interrogations of domestic terror into the hands of the military.

It allows the indefinite detention of anyone, including American citizens, as long as the government calls them terrorists bypassing the 6th Amendment.

The vagueness of this bill gives government a *lot* of leeway. While NSA had monitored citizens' communications unbeknownst to them for years, after 9/11, America mushroomed into a surveillance state. Now Utah houses a behemoth NSA facility that performs massive, invasive surveillance of Americans daily.

SHRINKING MILITARY – JUST KEEP YOUR MOUTH SHUT

President Obama reshaped the U.S. military and not for the better. In addition to Christianity being constantly road-blocked when not completely eradicated – a foundation of this Nation and American armed forces, the military was simultaneously neutered at the top. Purging seasoned Generals down through Majors primes the Country for trouble when a less experienced command is at the helm. In 2009, the Obama administration ordered massive reductions, resulting in many officers who were near retirement to be involuntarily separated without retirement or medical benefits. The majority of involuntary top brass separations occurred between 2011 and 2013 for 20 Commanding Generals and Admirals and another 79 Naval Officers. 2012 terminations added 157 Majors.

At least four generals were willing to speak out. Retired Army Major General Paul Vallely stated. "The White House protects their own. That's why they stalled on the investigation into Fast and Furious, Benghazi and ObamaCare. He's intentionally weakening and gutting our military, Pentagon and reducing us as a superpower, and anyone in the ranks who disagrees or speaks out is being purged."[1117] Retired Army Major General Patrick Brady said, "There is no doubt he (Obama) is intent on emasculating the military and will fire anyone who disagrees with him." Retired Army Lt. General William G. "Jerry" Boykin shared, "Over the past three years, it is unprecedented for the number of four-star generals to be relieved of duty, and not necessarily relieved for cause."[1118] Retired Navy Captain Joseph John added, "I believe there are more than 137 [this number has been updated, see above] officers who have been forced out or given bad evaluation reports so they will never make Flag (officer), because of their failure to comply to certain views."[1119]

A Pentagon official who asked to remain anonymous said even "young officers, down through the ranks have been told not to talk about Obama or the politics of the White House. They are purging everyone and if you want to keep your job – just keep your mouth shut."[1120] Mr. Obama must have been unfamiliar with Cicero's admonishment: "Do not hold the delusion that your advancement will be accomplished by crushing others."

THE SHAME OF IGNORING OUR VETERANS

To care for him who shall have borne the battle and for his window, and his orphan. —Abraham Lincoln, Department of Veterans Affairs motto. Guess that got lost in the files... That will make sense in the next page or two.

One of the most shameful actions in recent years involves our Veterans – those people who fought and died for this Country, and others, so they and we could live free. Since the Gulf Wars began, treatment of our service people has slid into a state of disgrace. In 2014 the Veterans Administration scandal blew up. Outrage grew daily as more details emerged. Dozens and maybe hundreds of veterans died from neglect and unbelievably long wait times. Former Senator Tom Coburn reported that more than 1,000 may have died waiting.[1121] Literally thousands of medical test orders were purged *en masse* to eliminate backlogs. "That means the patients did not receive the tests or treatment that had been ordered, but rather the orders for the follow-up procedures were simply deleted from the agency's records."[1122]

Image: Bundled claim folders at risk of fire and water damage, inadvertent loss and misplacement. However the filing fiasco didn't end here and this wasn't the worst of it. At the same office, in as much as the camera lens could capture of the 6th floor, at least 60 file cabinets lined just one isle. More could be seen in the background, but were too small to count. Judging from the depth of the shot, there were many more such set ups out of frame.

Avik Roy catalogued in *Forbes* some of the atrocities that emerged over a couple of weeks.[1123]

- Administrators at the Phoenix VA kept a secret, separate waiting list for treating veterans, to cover up they weren't meeting the VA's 2-week timeliness targets
- VA employees in Fort Collins, Colorado cooked the books to hide long wait times
- A scheduling clerk alleged that at VA hospitals in Austin and San Antonio, workers were "verbally directed by lead clerks, supervisors, and during training" to list official wait times "as close to zero days as possible"
- CBS found an email at the Cheyenne, Wyoming VA with instructions on "gaming the system" in order to keep "the front office [from getting] very upset"
- The Durham, North Carolina VA put two employees on administrative leave due to "inappropriate scheduling practices"
- The chief of psychiatry at the St. Louis VA alleged he was demoted and harassed for trying to increase the number of mental-health patients treated by the department and
- A Chicago VA social worker alleged employee bonuses were tied to manipulating wait time data.

Image: Tops of file cabinets were also completely covered by another 15-18 inches of folders. There was so much weight in this room, floor supports had given away and had begun to slope. (Courtesy Assistant Inspector General for Audits and Evaluations)

Over a year later, the Veterans Affairs' Office of Inspector General reported that one of the troubled regional offices had sent unopened claims from veterans directly to the shredder.[1124] Many politicians suggested after the scandal broke that the VA would be better served by the private sector. A hand-over would be a stab to Obama, in essence admitting that private health insurance is better than ObamaCare. Frankly any time the government gets involved, goals get swaddled in red tape and costs escalate. VA hospitals are heavily unionized, which creates unnecessary expenses and inefficiencies. One examiner noted that the current system is unlikely to change, even at our vets' expense, because too many non-vets benefit. Sen. Coburn continued about the VA budget: " From unwarranted and excessive bonuses for staff (in 2013, when much of the federal government was furloughing employees as a result of sequestration-imposed budget cuts, the VHA paid $27.3 million in bonuses) to construction projects way over budget to unnecessary duplicative programs and paperwork, the VA should better focus on its resources towards services for veterans."[1125] If there is any question the VA needs a major overhaul, check the filing system at the region office in Winston-Salem, North Carolina. (Courtesy Asst. Inspector General for Audits, Evaluations)

Image: In yet another photo – too good to leave out – cabinets were so close together files at the back couldn't be accessed since the drawers couldn't be pulled out all the way. To get folders at the back, drawers had to be unpacked first. And what are all those stains on the floor? The reports found, "We estimated that approximately 37,000 claims folders were stored on top of file cabinets. We also observed files stored on the floor and stacked, as space permitted, in boxes along walls. The photos provide illustrations of the excessive and unsafe file storage at this VARO [North Carolina VA Regional Office]."[1126] Hopefully the other 117 regional offices and facilities aren't in this bad shape. If any clerk, anywhere in America kept their workplace filing system like this, they'd hear someone in a Donald Trump voice shout, *"You're fired!"* (Courtesy Asst. Inspector General for Audits, Evaluations)

PUTTING NON-AMERICANS BEFORE AMERICANS

Every month the U.S. takes in over 800 Somalis and nearly 140,000 refugees annually. This doesn't include the million or so legal immigrants America admits year after year plus the thousands of illegal immigrants who sneak across the border. It's *inconceivable* that the U.S. opens wide her doors to millions of foreigners when nearly 600,000 Americans are homeless. In 2014 about 25% were children under 18 and 50,000 are veterans. How does this happen in the world's superpower?

Some of their stories shed light on this and how they fight to survive.

Maria and Sherice

Open-heart surgery, diabetes and arthritis kept Sherice Bennett from working. Without employment she couldn't afford her medicine and ended up homeless. Sherice waited over two years for an opportunity to convince a judge that she qualifies for federal disability benefits. Maria Ruiz, 62, is bipolar and has been in and out of psychiatric wards. At the time of this writing she hadn't been able to purchase her meds for four months. Maria is one of a dozen Florida residents with disabilities who've filed suit in federal court alleging they have endured unreasonably long wait times, most over two years, to go before a Social Security judge. Miami has *the* longest wait time in the country, averaging 22 months, according to the federal agency's own website. Others have literally died waiting.[1127]

Both of these women live in Miami, the city with the longest wait time in the Country for getting heard in appeals court. According to their own website, 22 months is average before a case comes before a Social Security judge. This is placing people in disastrous, uncontrollable, sometimes life threatening situations.

Angelica Gonzalez

Angelica left home at age 11. All she wanted was a safe place where she could go back to school. Abandoned by her mentally ill mother, she raised herself on the streets of Phoenix, never attended school, and narrowly avoided the gangs and crime that seemed to be everywhere. Gonzalez said, "I just knew if I stayed there, something really bad was going to happen. You never knew when your luck would finally run out."[1128] Years passed. Life went up and then down by the time she turned 26. Angelica married and gave birth to two daughters.

Image: Causes based on a survey of 34,397 homeless people

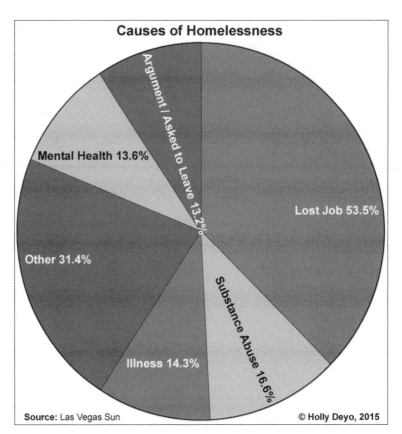

She put herself through college and ended up divorced. Her ex-husband rarely sent child support, but what little she received pushed her over the qualifying limit for subsidy. Child care of $800 a month gobbled up more than half of her paycheck. She had to scale back to unreliable, unlicensed childcare for her girls, one and seven. Between the cost of childcare, her failed marriage, health problems and rising rent, Angelica and her girls ended up homeless.

Rebecca

"Two things happened when I turned 12. My father who used to beat the hell out of us left home and the other thing that happened is I started using drugs... One of my friends said 'Here try this it will make you feel better', and it did. When I turned 13, my Mum found a new partner who lived at home with us. He raped me regularly and abused my younger sisters as well. I was only 13. He also used to beat Mum up and it was hell on earth. For about a year I suffered through it but when I was fourteen I couldn't take it anymore, so I said to Mum 'You have to get rid of this guy, either he goes or I go.' Mum chose him and I landed on the streets.

"Initially I stayed with friends, and then slept with guys from the neighborhood to keep a roof over my head. Eventually I had to leave the suburbs for the city streets. Sleeping in abandoned houses and buildings, I lived on the streets with other young people who were like me. The cuts all up my arm are from slashing up. I slash myself to turn emotional pain into controllable physical pain. It's not usually to kill myself, just to help cope with the pain of the past. The last time I tried to kill myself I only had a syringe to slash up with so I was hacking at myself trying to get myself bleeding properly. Then I sniffed paint until I blacked out. I wanted to bleed to death but it didn't work because someone found me lying in the alley and called an ambulance. You just give up, that's it, it's the end. As soon as you get to that stage where you don't care if you live or die you end up so upset, so depressed, so hurt with everything that you just cant handle even the day in front of you."[1129]

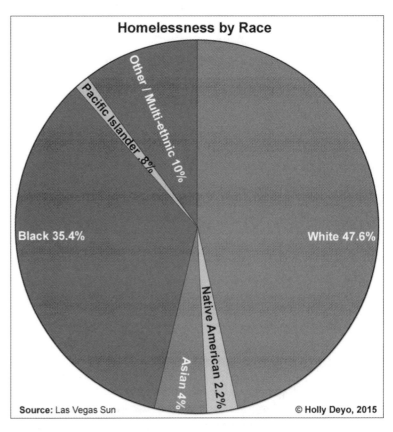

Willie Woods

Willie grew up in Washington, DC just seven blocks from the White House. He said he "grew up too fast", didn't finish high school and wanted to be free of his parents' authority. After a stint in reform school, Woods at 16 decided not to go back home and became homeless. The streets taught him all about drug and alcohol abuse. After three homeless years, his mother helped him enlist in the U.S. Marine Corps. After a few terrific years in the USMC, Woods admitted without elaboration he'd "screwed up" and was dishonorably discharged. Now into his second period of homelessness, Woods suffered from undiagnosed clinical depression. His second round of homelessness lasted 12 years after leaving the Marines. Woods acknowledged, "I was a nasty looking drug addict. I didn't beg. I stole and I conned people out of their money. Conning people was the way I survived." Eventually, Woods earned his GED through a shelter program and married a preacher. Today, at age 54, he attends the University of the District of Columbia. Woods is one of the success stories.[1130]

Herold Noel

When "Iraqi Freedom" began, Private First Class Herold Noel was a soldier in the U.S. Army's 3rd Infantry Division, pounding a path into Baghdad. He recalled, "I fought for this country. I shed blood for this country. I watched friends die." Once home, Herold was diagnosed with PTSD. Unemployed, married with three kids, he couldn't get a job. Like many others Noel came home a hero, but wound up homeless. He lived out of his Jeep after most of his clothes and all of his military medals were stolen at a homeless shelter. Peter Dougherty of the Department of Veterans Affairs said, "The physical war is over. The mental war has just begun."[1131] It was understandable why Dougherty described Noel "a solder at rock bottom". He had applied for housing only to be met with chaos. "I put applications in. I did all that. They lost my application three f^&@# times!" When a city housing agency gave him the runaround yet again, Herold's anger rose. "What are you telling me man? I have three kids out there man! I fought for my country man. My country shouldn't be doing this to me." Herold was one of the lucky ones. Someone heard his story and anonymously paid his rent for a year. While this formerly homeless vet is off the streets – for now – dozens more will take his place.

Photo: Unidentified homeless man living on the streets of New York City. (Courtesy Daivd Shankbone, August 2008)

Soldiers Need "Stand Down"

In 1988 soldier-turned-psychologist, Jon Nachison started "Stand Down" – a military term for when a solider can put down his weapon and stop fighting. Stand Down, now nationwide, is a combo health clinic, jobs fair, and sobriety meeting. Nearly a thousand military vets assembled all night for entrance into San Diego's 3-day camp. It was a time to reclaim dignity, have a hot meal, a warm shower, find clean clothes and a bit of hope. In 2010 veterans returning from Iraq and Afghanistan came home to a deep recession and found themselves homeless.

That year, about 9,000 former military lived on the streets. In 2015, it's 5½ times that many. Nachison said, "This group is becoming homeless quicker than the Vietnam veteran. Vietnam vets came back, it took about eight to ten years before we started really seeing them on the street homeless. This group is coming back and within a year they're ending up on the street. And my best hunch is that for many of them it's these redeployments again and again." Redeployment up to five times – six tours of duty – means layers and layers of traumatization.[1132] Different now among the population of homeless veterans are growing numbers of women who find themselves in these circumstances. Since women now make up 14% of U.S. armed forces, their numbers will grow.

Marguerite Somers

Marguerite was one of the 947 at that Stand Down-San Diego. She, like many vets male and female, had a difficult time transitioning from military life to civilian. Shortly after discharging from the Navy she got divorced and began drinking heavily and using meth. After three months of these personal battles Somers has a clearer perspective, wants help for her addictions. "I lost my son a year ago because of my abuse issues. I owned a home. I lost that. I lost my family's support. I lost my job. Wound up with a bunch of legal issues. You know, I was facing prison time. Just nothing good came out of it."[1133] For Marguerite, it was her lucky day. She was one of 68 selected for rehab. Stand Down only has so much money to stretch and they look for the most motivated to put through the program.

Chris

Chris, now in his early 60s, shares his story of intermittent homelessness. His struggle began 30 years ago when he was honorably discharged from the Army. Chris was diagnosed with PTSD and couldn't hold a job. Drug abuse and alcohol became his method of coping. He shared what led to his post-traumatic distress illness. Chris vividly remembers sitting in a tank, in freezing temperatures, waiting for orders. It was claustrophobic sitting in the tank with engines running. Black smoke filled the air making it difficult to breathe and nearly impossible to see. Dread was his constant companion "not knowing what was going to happen, just waiting, and just feeling helpless too often." For his service Chris was awarded the National Defense Service Medal, which he lost while on the streets. About his time on the streets Chris shared, "It's wretched. You disconnect from everything. All ya think about is, ya know, where you're gonna get your next meal. Your next change of clothes, how you're gonna get clean, where you're gonna sleep. Ya gotta stay busy because if ya don't you go crazy."[1134]

Stephanie

Stephanie, 60, lost her husband two years ago and then had a good jewelry business. She was able to get her blind spouse into hospice when he became terminally ill. The financial burden became too great and two months later, Stephanie lost her home. With her husband's failing health she became stressed, lost her jewelry business and says she now lives on God's good grace. She took a bus to Las Vegas to find a way out of her mess. She spent the first two nights at a mission and mice got into her one bag. A woman suggested she go to a shelter, but Stephanie had heard it had bedbugs. Instead she chose to sleep outside the Joan of Arc church on her tablecloth saying she felt safe there. Stephanie had received 30 awards and won two championships for her jewelry, but was barred from selling at her Vegas location because it was competition for someone selling from a kiosk. She laments, "For a city that takes in the kind of money this city does, I'm appalled by the conditions. Americans are such a blessed people, and they're usually very generous, but what I've seen here is the opposite. The dirty looks I get from some of the ladies who pass by. One of them told me to sell my body. These people don't understand – it can happen to any one of us."[1135]

BOTTOM LINE

Through 2012, some 2.6 million soldiers have served in Iraq and Afghanistan in Operations Iraqi Freedom, Enduring Freedom and New Dawn. The VA estimates that 11-20% of soldiers serving in these three ops suffer from PTSD. Every day 22 veterans take their life.

This chronic homelessness and preferring to bring in even more immigrants to taking care of our citizens is madness, priorities screwed, a national shame. Much as some say we can do both, a decades-long track record says otherwise. The homeless don't need criticism and judgment. They need to be cleaned up and lifted up with a leg up. Judging by the tens of billions spent on entitlements for legal immigrants, illegal immigrants and refugees, you'd think our government could find in the bloated budget enough money for our own people first. Jesus said, *"The poor will always be with you..."* —Matthew 26:11, Mark 14:7, Deuteronomy 15:11, John 12:8, but that doesn't mean look the other way because the problem seems too big, too overwhelming.

Green Lady Down

A Nation on this trajectory cannot sustain itself. America's government as envisioned and set up by our Founding Fathers was formed to be a unifying force, under the control and watchful eye of The People with checks and balances in place. Government worked *for* the People. Not the other way around. This concept was the core of the 2nd Amendment to keep government in check by force if necessary. This is now the principal reason government periodically tries to implement guns bans, limit ammo purchases and allow only certain firearms. We see where that got Australia in 1997 and now they regret all that nonsense.

In present day America, it's gone topsy-turvy. They rule. We pay. A Nation on this trajectory cannot sustain itself. We are on the road to this:

THE LIFE OF A COUNTRY

Scottish history professor Alexander Tyler at the University of Edinburgh is often credited with summing up the life cycle of a country. He observed, "A democracy is always temporary in nature; it simply cannot exist as a permanent form of government. A democracy will continue to exist up until the time that voters discover that they can vote themselves generous gifts from the public treasury. From that moment on, the majority always votes for the candidates who promise the most benefits from the public treasury, with the result that every democracy will finally collapse due to loose fiscal policy, which is always followed by a dictatorship.

"The average age of the worlds greatest civilizations from the beginning of history, has been about 200 years. During those 200 years, these nations always progressed through the following sequence:

1. From Bondage to spiritual faith
2. From Spiritual faith to great courage
3. From Courage to liberty
4. From Liberty to abundance
5. From Abundance to selfishness
6. From Selfishness to complacency
7. From Complacency to apathy
8. From Apathy to dependence
9. From Dependence back into bondage"[1136]

We are at 8.5.

Americans Arming Up

Americans didn't feel safe after the San Bernardino massacres despite presidential reassurances. That slaughter reawakened fears that had receded after 9/11 and the Boston bombings. It didn't help that the President appeared to be living on a different planet – or golf course – when he said the U.S. is safe from an ISIS attack. He tried to reassure saying, "[ISIS] is not going to pose an existential threat to us."[1137] What is meant by an "existential threat" is one that won't wipe out a country, its government or its people. In that sense, Obama is likely right, but a whole lot of misery can be delivered before a nation is completely exterminated. Bet he counted on people not knowing what "existential threat" meant or them looking it up. There's a whole lot of distance between being safe and annihilation.

The President made this remark less than three weeks after Islamic State killed 130 people in Paris, and **the day** after the San Bernardino, Calif. massacre. Hearing the Commander-in-Chief brush aside the reality of terrorism made people feel less safe, more fearful. Americans felt like no one was at the helm and that the one currently occupying that position was inept and hugely out of touch. As a result, Mr. Obama's plan backfired and people chose to further arm themselves.

FIREARMS AND THE SECOND AMENDMENT

During the first seven years of Mr. Obama's presidency, Americans bought nearly 130 million firearms. In 2015 alone the National Instant Background Check System processed over 23 million applications – an all-time high – over two million more than any previous year. This spike followed record-breaking sales for each month of May, June, July, August, September, October, November, and December 2015. If that weren't telling enough about sales, another record was smashed when two million more applications were submitted just in the first *quarter* of 2016 compared to the first three months of 2015.[1138]

Photo: A group of women line up to try different firearms, from handguns to flintlock rifles on March 10, 2012. (Courtesy Wendy Dial, Florida Wildlife & Conservation, //creativecommons.org/licenses/by-nd/2.0/)

Why the uptick? Mr. Obama repeatedly tried to greatly restrict ammo and gun ownership if not implement total disarmament all while various government agencies bought guns and ammo into the billions. Without shame, after a mass shooting occurred, he took that opportunity to politicize his agenda even before victims were buried. Alan Gottlieb of the Second Amendment Foundation explains. "A day has not gone by without a major media assault on gun rights or an Obama administration call for new additional restrictions on gun ownership. Americans have voted with their dollars and bought record levels of guns and ammunition."[1139] Also fresh in everyone's mind were the recent terrorist attacks in Paris and San Bernardino, California and the pervasive feeling that government can't and aren't keeping people safe.

THE NUMBERS TALK

FBI statistics support this. Gun sales always escalate around Christmas where either someone asked for a firearm or loved ones wanted to give the gift of safety, sport shooting or hunting.

After 9/11, firearms sales spiked 16% in October 2001 – the highest month that year except for December. Even with the idea of terrorism on U.S. soil sinking in, the rise in gun sales wasn't huge. However, three other interesting spikes showed up. Two directly corresponded with Mr. Obama's election and re-election. The other came when Mr. Obama returned from another vacation and announced in January 2016 that he was "all fired up" to get moving on gun control. He made a big announcement on his latest Executive Order saying he planned to really tighten applications. That Obama addressed his desire to circumvent Congress yet again with an E.O. was surprising because they are usually implemented by a quiet stroke of the pen. House Leader Paul Ryan called this end-around a "subversion of Congress".[1140]

(NOTE: This chart shows the number of backgrounds checks performed by the FBI, not actual sales. Though it's not an exact 1-to-1 ratio of checks to sales, it's the only way to monitor purchases. Numbers could deviate if someone wanted to purchase a firearm and was turned down, or bought more than one weapon during a single sale.) Even though many Americans *were* enchanted with Barack Obama enough to put him in office, others saw what would take place with his promise to "fundamentally transform America".

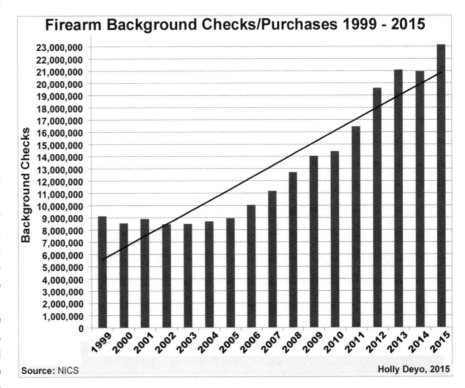

They knew firearms would be targeted. Immediately following his first election firearms sales jumped steadily higher for the next five months. A significantly higher spike took place surrounding the five months after his re-election in 2012. Gun sales for the first time ever hit over 2 million *each month* for November and December 2012 and continued through January, February and March 2013. Then December 2015, when the President promised further gun control, purchases hit the stratosphere of 3,314,594.

MORE GUNS, LESS CRIME

While about three times as many men as women own firearms, more ladies are taking responsibility for their own safety. Florida resident and single mother of two, Michele Powell typifies women's views. "It [see Sheriff Ivey's comments below] made it [purchasing a handgun] feel like a smart move. It made it feel like a proactive move, rather than an aggressive move. It's not coming from aggression at all. It's coming from a personal desire to protect my family. I'd rather have the ability to do something, if faced with that horrible situation, than to simply duck."[1141]

It's estimated firearm ownership in 2015 is somewhere between 310 and 357 million.[1142] Even though about 1% break or are destroyed every year, the number of firearms owned adds up.

Despite liberal media trying to spin it otherwise, homicides rate **dropped 49%** over the past two decades while firearm ownership soared.[1143] A 2012 Congressional study found the plunge in gun-related murders even more impressive – a 51.5% decline while gun ownership doubled.[1144]

Pew Research points out an obvious disconnect – that perception is just the opposite. Americans believe gun deaths and homicides are increasing.[1145] Much of this misunderstanding had to do with Mr. Obama and other gun control advocates beating that thin, tired drum – loudly and liberal new media following his lead. In fact, gun violence is declining everywhere **except** in gun-free zones.[1146]

John Lott, president of the Crime Prevention Research Center and author of *More Guns, Less Crime* had this to say. "Since at least 1950, all but two public mass shootings in America have taken place where general citizens are banned from carrying guns. In Europe, there have been no exceptions. Every mass public shooting – and there have been plenty of mass shootings in Europe – has occurred in a gun-free zone. In addition, they have had three of the six worst K-12 school shootings, and Europe experienced by far the worst mass public shooting perpetrated by a single individual (Norway in 2011, which from the shooting alone left 67 people dead and 110 wounded). Mass killers have even explicitly talked about their desire to attack gun-free zones. The Charleston, S.C., church shooting in June was instead almost a college shooting. But that killer changed his plans after realizing that the College of Charleston had armed guards."[1147]

People primarily "arm up" for three reasons. They don't trust government to tell them the truth, they don't feel safe and they feel that eventually those that want to repeal the 2nd Amendment will gain the upper hand. Alan Gottlieb, the head of the Second Amendment Foundation observed, "Barrack Obama and Hillary Clinton are the best gun salespeople on the planet. The more they scream for new gun control laws the more guns walk off the shelves at gun stores."[1148]

SHERIFFS, YOUR NEXT BEST DEFENSE

Since at least 2013, a coalition of hundreds of U.S. sheriffs vowing to defend 2nd Amendment rights has gotten larger and more vocal. After the December 2, 2015 San Bernardino massacre, people realized more than ever that their lives and that of their families had become a personal matter. While police chiefs are mostly anti-firearm because anti-gun mayors appoint them, sheriffs elected by the people they serve, hold a much different view. Next to the ordinary citizen, they are the last line of defense between the public and criminals. This is typical of their gun rights' advocacy.

Milwaukee County Sheriff David A. Clarke, has repeatedly articulated the importance of law-abiding citizens to defend themselves against violent criminals and the right to bear arms. Clarke said, "We, in law enforcement, have an obligation to be on the side of crime victims. Not on the side of the criminal element. Gun control has nothing to do with the crime and violence that these chiefs see in their cities on a daily basis and they know it. But many of them, especially in your large urban centers, are under the thumb of anti-gun, soft on crime, mayors. And they have to sing from the same sheet of music that their mayors are singing from.

"But the crime and violence we see in our cities and counties is not the result of a lack of background checks, and these chiefs know that. The research and data are there. Criminals don't care about laws in general and they don't care about gun laws or gun restrictions. They will find a way to get around those. And that's why I ultimately say that the chiefs' push for more gun control has nothing to do with reducing violence. Rather, it has to do with gun confiscation."[1149]

Clarke continued saying personal safety is no longer a spectator sport and he urged people to arm themselves. "I need you [the public] in the game. With officers laid off and furloughed, simply calling 911 and waiting is no longer your best option. You can beg for mercy from a violent criminal, hide under the bed, or you can fight back. ... Consider taking a certified safety course in handling a firearm so you can defend yourself until we get there."[1150]

In a "what's good for the goose" challenge, Clark told Fox News Sean Hannity, "I am done asking people in my community to outsource their personal safety to the government. But here's my challenge to the president of the United States [Mr. Obama], you think this is so easy. Forego your Secret Service protection, for you, for the first lady, and your children, and see what it is like to have to [de]fend yourself. And then we'll sit down and have a conversation so you know what we here at ground level have to deal with on a daily base in terms of self-defense."[1151]

Arizona Sheriff Paul Babeu told his residents, "We want a citizen to add to the equation. Be armed to protect yourself, protect your family until we can get there. A lot of people, I go and talk to a lot of citizens in my county and throughout the state, and they're concerned about additional threats in the community. We are STRONG defenders of our 2nd Amendment rights. We call for Arizona licensed concealed carry permit holders to step up and defend themselves, their families, and others, when faced with an armed attacker prior to law enforcement arrival."[1152]

Paul J. Van Blarcum, Sheriff of Ulster County, NY, rallied residents on Facebook to be the county's front lines against terrorism. "In light of recent events that have occurred in the United States and around the world, I want to encourage citizens of Ulster County who are licensed to carry a firearm to PLEASE DO SO. I urge you to responsibly take advantage of your legal right to carry a firearm. To ensure the safety of yourself and others, make sure you are comfortable and proficient with your weapon, and knowledgeable of the laws in New York State with regards to carrying a weapon and when it is legal to use it."[1153]

Florida's Brevard County Sheriff Wayne Ivey echoed Blarcum's statement, "Let there be no mistake … The only thing that stops a bad guy with a gun is a good guy with a gun. If you're a person who is legally licensed to carry a firearm, now is the time more than ever to realize that you, and you alone, may very well be the first line of defense for you and your family."[1154]

A fourth sheriff, Michael A. Helmig from Boone County, Kentucky, reiterated that armed citizens have a responsibility to protect others. "I have reminded my current and retired deputy sheriffs of their responsibility to carry their firearms while off-duty. I would also like to remind the people who have applied, been trained, and issued a license to carry a Concealed Deadly Weapon (CCDW) that they also have a responsibility to carry their firearm, which they are proficient with, for the safety of themselves and others. Each of us, as proud Kentuckians, has a great responsibility to uphold the values of the United States Constitution and protect this great nation from acts of foreign or domestic terrorism. United We Stand, Divided We Fall."[1155]

Stephens County, OK sheriff Wayne McKinney wrote on Facebook that the San Bernardino slaughter proves America is under attack, and that armed citizens must be the first line of defense. "As your sheriff, I encourage all who are LEGALLY ELIGIBLE and TRAINED to carry concealed weapons to do so. I do not want any of us to be helpless victims if we should fall under attack. We may never be able to stop someone from attempting to carry out a violent attack, but we, as armed citizens, can mitigate the damage."[1156]

To help citizens willing to protect Americans, three Missouri county sheriffs in Laclede, St. Clair and Vernon lowered the cost of concealed-carry permits from $100 to $65. Laclede County Sheriff Wayne Merritt stated, "The government has already said they can't keep track of all these home-grown terrorists, so we can't be everywhere at the same time, so people have to be able to defend themselves."[1157]

Chink 6: National Division

A Nation divided cannot stand. That famous phrase, "United we stand, divided we fall" was first penned in John Dickinson's 1768 *Liberty Song*:

"Then join hand in hand brave Americans all,
By uniting we stand, by dividing we fall;
In so righteous a cause let us hope to succeed,
For heaven approves of each generous deed.

One could almost believe Dickinson had a premonition of what was to come. His slogan permeated history. During the Civil War, it was the rallying cry for the Union. In the early 20th century, unions glommed onto it. During WWII it wasn't just the adage of American patriotism, but became the motto of the Allied Forces, which The

Netherlands' Queen Wilhelmina stated in her 1942 address to Congress. Most recently, after 9/11, it became the unifying cry for a Nation wounded. No finer visual of this unity was portrayed in the raising of the Flag by three firefighters at Ground Zero. It was so reminiscent of the iconic photo of the American flag planted at Iwo Jima.

HOPI INDIANS

Stan Deyo said, "When Holly and I were guests of the Hopi Indians at the Shungopavi Tribe, Second Mesa, [village in Arizona] their prophecy keepers told us that America would have a multi-faceted, multi-sided civil war very shortly. Black against white, Puerto Rican against black, Mexican against white whatever; Muslims against Christians, Jews; extreme right, extreme left; poor-rich; all these kinds of different directions will tear America apart once the economy starts to fail and America will eventually be invaded."[1158] This echoes what so many Christian prophets have been shown and the stage is set.

2015: THE YEAR EVERYONE WAS OFFENDED BY EVERYTHING

Never has this author seen such a time with more national angst and ire. Everyone is offended about something. In fact, 2015 was named *The Year Everyone Was Offended By Absolutely Everything.* Being offended became the recreational activity of choice. Sharing opinions and free speech increasingly came under fire. Whatever happened to manning up – oops, you can't say that either now – having a thick skin and getting on with life. That year in excruciating repetition, people were perpetually offended. If they didn't walk the line of censoring everything that rolled off pen and tongue, they were accused of racism, even when the term didn't apply.

A few examples include:

- In 2015 transgenders were offended Caitlyn Jenner, formerly Olympic gold medalist Bruce Jenner, wasn't praised enough for his-now-her transformation.

- That same year transgenders were offended Caitlyn remained politically conservative.

- Gays were offended by Kentucky clerk, Kim Davis, who didn't want her name on gay marriages licenses.

- Muslims were outraged that Ahmed Mohamed a.k.a., Clock Boy, was pulled out of school after building a clock that looked *exactly* like a bomb, which he then brought to school. Could the school be blamed for mistaking it when the clock was placed in a suitcase instead of regular clock housing? Clock Boy's parents were so offended, Ahmed, mom and dad moved to Qatar and demanded $15 million in damages and apologies.

- Muslims were offended that people drew likenesses of their prophet Muhammad.

- Illegal aliens were offended because Donald Trump said some sneaking across the border were criminals, murderers, drug dealers, and rapists. Reread Homeland Security's own statistics to see how tens of thousands of these felons were released into the public.

- "Illegal aliens" were offended at this description and now want to be called "undocumented Americans". (Hint, they're aren't citizens.)

- "Illegal aliens" were offended at being called "illegal" and championed for *all* country borders to be demolished. (Why wouldn't they be living in a 3rd world country and wanting to partake of countless freebies that all employed Americans pay for? The EU removed country borders and now they are overrun with asylum seekers and refugees. Some countries are slowly and surely losing their own laws and cultural identity like France overrun with Muslims who have created their own no-go zones barring even law enforcement. Out of generosity of heart, they have now unwittingly let in 5th columnists. Marseilles is nearly 40% Muslim now and ranked as Europe's most dangerous city.[1159] A decade ago France had 750 no-zones, taken over by Muslims where the country's law enforcement is even afraid to enter. How many of these no-go zones exist now with the continued influx and whose fault is that?)

- Parents were offended when errors on their kid's homework and tests were corrected in red.

- Parents were offended when their kids flunked and demanded they be passed onto the next grade, even when they couldn't read, just so the children wouldn't have hurt feelings or diminished self-respect.

- People were offended by the Confederate flag and demanded its removal. Some discussing this issue voiced the opinion that if the Confederate flag offended and had to be removed, why isn't the multi-colored gay pride flag banned?

- Lawmakers are being deluged with requests to "cleanse" history, erase cultural heritage by removing statues, renaming parks, schools and streets named after Confederate leaders. Much as this was an abhorrent time in America, one can't erase slavery by rewriting history. As Ben Jones, former Georgia Congressman wrote in a *USA Today* op-ed, America is under siege in a "feeding frenzy of cultural cleansing". He continued: "To those 70 million of us whose ancestors fought for the South, it is a symbol of family members who fought for what they thought was right in their time, and whose valor became legendary in military history. This is not nostalgia. It is our legacy. The current attacks on that legacy, 150 years after the event, are to us an insult that mends no fences nor builds any bridges."[1160]

- Specific examples include:

- Tennessee lawmakers demanded a bust of Nathan Bedford Forrest be removed from the statehouse

- Washington D.C. likewise discussed removing eight Confederate-related statues from the Capitol, including one of Jefferson Davis, former president of the Confederacy

- After months of public shouting matches and sharply penned op-eds, the New Orleans City Council voted to remove four Confederate statues from around the city

- Baltimore lawmakers want to rename Robert E. Lee Park

- Dallas lawmakers are considering demands to rename Stonewall Jackson Elementary School and remove Confederate statues from public property

- St. Louis lawmakers are debating over the future of a Confederate statue in a city park

- Commissioners in Hillsborough, North Carolina are debating whether to remove the words "Confederate Memorial" from a Confederate memorial

- The Memphis City Council voted in 2013 to rename three parks – Confederate Park, Jefferson Davis Park and Nathan Bedford Forrest Park

- In a case of P.C. gone overboard, Warner Bros. announced it halted production of toys and replicas of the Dukes of Hazzard sports car known as the General Lee. Seen from overhead, the Confederate flag covered the roof of "good ol' boys" Bo and Luke's '69 Dodge Charger. Back then, most boys – and some girls – clamored for this orange muscle car.

- In a further act of political correctness gone awry, TV Land yanked reruns of the iconic 1980s *Dukes of Hazzard* program. The Confederate flag controversy blew up after Dylann Roof gunned down nine people in a Charleston, South Carolina church. It wasn't the flag that prompted the murders, but hatred within Roof.
  NOTE: While no one wanted to see war among fellow Americans and remember how it ripped families apart, it is a facet of America's history. To remove these legacies is to dishonor the 620,000 men – roughly 2% of the population – who lost their lives in the Civil War. Today, if a similar heartbreaking war occurred, it would mean nearly 10 million Americans would be sacrificed.

- People were offended by Christmas trees, Jesus and Merry Christmas.

- Afrikan Black Coalition called for black people to revolt and overthrow the Constitution, citing the need to "stop white people" in the "white supremacist world" of America.

- College campuses were often at the center of the too politically correct movement.

- Protesters at Amherst College want school president to denounce actions of students who displayed "All Lives Matter" and "Free Speech" posters. They demanded she warn the student body that future "racially insensitive" speeches would incur disciplinary actions.

- University of California students removed offensive American flag from 'inclusive' space.

- Cornell to students and staff: Mistletoe doesn't create an inclusive environment

- University of Tennessee – Knoxville replaced "Secret Santa" with "secret gift exchange"

- Ohio State urged students and staff to avoid red and green colors in favor of an "inclusive holiday spirit"

- University of Minnesota student government was so afraid of offending Muslims, it opted not to hold a moment of silence for the 9/11 victims

- Ole Miss student said a Christmas event was 'too Christian'

The 1st Amendment that guarantees free speech came under more attacks in 2015, often by universities formerly noted for their open-mindedness, of voicing opinions and engaging in intellectual exchange. However, political correctness has gotten so ridiculous throughout the country Alabama National Guard Infantry Officer and second-year law student, Jordan Thompson wrote on Facebook:

> "I'm offended that everyone is offended by something. I'm offended that because I'm a white male, people automatically classify me as privileged, regardless of knowing where I've come from or what I've been through. I'm offended that our First Amendment has turned into freedom of speech [just as long as it doesn't hurt anyone's feelings]. I'm offended that people assume I'm racist because I believe in economic development by way of Capitalism and a free-market economy.

> I'm offended that people who are too afraid to ask for food stamps, disability, or unemployment (because they don't want a handout) are probably the ones who could use it most, yet the majority of recipients who do in fact receive handouts abuse their "privilege" and continue to make frivolous purchases.

> I'm offended that people care more about taking down an outdated Confederate flag but don't get riled up when their American flag is being burned in the street. I'm offended that fast food workers get paid more than my soldiers yet still expect to get paid more than nurses.

> I'm offended by people who claim how offended they are, while they do nothing but gripe about it on their phones or laptops, when they could be writing or calling their respective representatives to

actually get something accomplished. I'm offended by the lack of initiative, hard work, and tenacity in this country. I'm offended by complainers who pity themselves and just want to take as much as they can. ...I just pray that we can one day change our country for the better. And hope that our offenses can turn into progress."[1161]

Universities added more "offensive" words to the politically incorrect list like:

- Lame, Thug, Trash and Third World
- "African American" replaced "black" even when that person was neither African or American
- "Person of size" replaced "fat"
- "Differently abled" instead of "handicapped"
- "Caucasian" had to go away to be replaced by the more acceptable "European-American individuals"
- "Elderly" was replaced by "people of an advanced age"
- "Healthy" no longer OK, replaced by "non-disabled individual"
- "Homosexual" out; LGBTQIPO – in, which stands for Lesbian, Gay, Bisexual, Trans, Questioning, Intersex, Pansexual or Omnisexual
- "Boyfriend"/"girlfriend" with the more inclusive "partner" or "significant other"
- "Crazy" replaced by "mental illness"
- "Ghetto" replaced by "economically disadvantaged area"
- "Founding Fathers" considered too sexist. New term: "The Founders"

In 2015, the Dept. of Justice added "felon" and "convict" to the list of no-no's in favor of "person who committed a crime" and "individual who was incarcerated."[1162] According to the University of Wisconsin – Milwaukee, the phrase "politically correct" is now politically correct.

RACE

Black on White

The Knockout Game, which is mostly a black-on-white assault crime, didn't come into media focus till around 2012. It involves someone picking a random target and then trying to punch the victim unconscious with a single blow. This practice of sucker-punching is also called "One-Hitter Quitter," "Pick 'Em Out and Knock 'Em Out," "Catch and Wreck," "Point-em-out, Knock-em-out," "Knockout King," and "Polar Bear Hunting – a pointed reference to white victims.

Some people actually died in these rituals. Others were left with internal bleeding, bruised brains, severe whiplash, broken eye sockets and worse. Age, gender, pregnant or disabled doesn't matter. All are fair game. One of the game players said, "We used to walk to where a lot of people be at and hit 'em. If one of the homeboys didn't knock him out, then the other would come. Whoever knock him out would be king."[1163]

The wave began in the East and swept across the U.S. to California before media quit tippy-toeing around the obvious black-white component. Not only had America become nauseatingly politically correct, but we now had a black President. Glaringly liberally-biased news outlets happily ignored this inconvenient activity until it reached San Diego. This senseless crime has also shown up in Canada, England and Australia.

According to the US Department of Justice, blacks accounted for 52.5% of homicide offenders from 1980 to 2008, with whites 45.3% and "Other" 2.2%, keeping in mind there are 5 times as many whites in the U.S. as blacks. The offender rate for blacks was almost 8 times higher than whites, and the victim rate six times higher. Most homicides were intraracial with 84% of white victims killed by whites, and 93% of black victims killed by blacks.[1164] [1165]

In a broader look, during 2012-2013, blacks committed an average of 560,600 violent crimes (excluding homicide) against whites, whereas whites committed 99,403 such crimes against blacks. This means blacks were the offenders in 85% of violent crimes involving both ethnic groups. This number is consistent with reports from 2008, the last year DOJ released similar statistics.[1166]

White on Black – Trayvon Martin

In summer 2013, racial tensions accelerated with the shooting of Trayvon Martin, a black 17-year-old, killed by neighborhood watch coordinator George Zimmerman, 32. Born in Virginia, Zimmerman is of Peruvian and German descent. Martin had been temporarily staying in a gated community where the shooting took place. No one, absolutely no one in that upscale community wore hoodies. Zimmerman's testimony was that he had been watching a "suspicious" man who jumped him in the rain. Zimmerman told investigators Martin had threatened him putting his hand over his nose and mouth to the point where he couldn't breathe saying, "You're going to die tonight," while repeatedly slamming his head into the pavement.[1167]

Zimmerman was treated for head injuries and a broken nose, which corroborated his story. After being questioned for five hours, he was released. Six weeks after the shooting, amid widespread, intense media coverage, Zimmerman was charged with murder. It was the first time a President of the United States had ever intervened in a crime. Mr. Obama was to do so in subsequent cases further creating the appearance of racial favoritism. Sixteen months after the shooting, Zimmerman was acquitted of second-degree murder and manslaughter when both a grand jury and a Department of Justice investigation called it justified.

What shocked the Nation as much as anything was President Obama coming out while tensions were at their highest saying, "If I had a son, he'd look like Trayvon."[1168] Clearly at that point Mr. Obama chose racial lines rather than be the unifying force he promised in 2008.

Dylann Roof

Thousands of hate crimes occur every year in the U.S., but rarely do they scale the heights of the June 2015 massacre in a South Carolina church. In a shooting that shocked the Country, 21-year-old white supremacist Dylann Roof shot nine people including the pastor attending a Bible study. Before gunning them down, he reportedly told the victims, "I have to do it. You're raping our women and taking over the country. You have to go."[1169] Authorities found his manifesto where Roof claimed to have developed his views after the 2012 shooting of Trayvon Martin and ongoing "black-on-white crime". His website LastRhodesian.com, since removed, also contained racist rants about Jews, Hispanics, East Asians and patriotism. Roof is currently in jail, charged with nine counts of murder and three of attempted murder. His trial is slated to start on July 11, 2016. **NOTE**: Ironically, it was the Trayvon Martin-George Zimmerman shooting that motivated both Roof and the Black Lives Matter movement.

Black Lives Matter

This led to the growth of a divisive movement, Black Lives Matter and others, which have further polarized America along racial lines. Without question some of the high profile cases of white police officers shooting black suspects have been horrible, but mainstream media failing to correct misconceptions and falsehoods, exacerbated the problem.

It started with a hashtag. People thought it would fade with time like the Occupy Wall Street Movement. Instead it blazed and mushroomed. Today it's still rising and polarizing. Its origin can be traced back to Opal Tometi who was unhappy with George Zimmerman's acquittal. Tometi says, "We created #BlackLivesMatter. We created a platform. We used our social media presence online in order to forward a conversation about what is taking place in black communities... This was actually a racial justice project for black people."[1170] That division was fomented, promulgated, fanned and exacerbated until it became a cauldron of anger and hatred.

On New Year's Day 2016, a group of 50 activists from Black Lives Matter Chicago, the Black Youth Project and Assata's Daughters harassed patrons at Dove's Luncheonette, Kanela Breakfast Club and at least three other eateries in Chicago. Members participated in a back and forth chant while patrons ate breakfast. BLM had hoped this would garner sympathy from the general public. The protesters marched down Damen and Milwaukee Avenues in Wicker Park for two hours, chanting "I believe that we will win" and "F*&k police" and "We Ready, We Coming!"[1171]

It's unclear how their stated purpose (written under a raised fist on the BLM website) fits into disrupting diners: "Black Lives Matter affirms the lives of Black queer and trans folks, disabled folks, Black-undocumented folks, folks with records, women and all Black lives along the gender spectrum. It centers those that have been marginalized within Black liberation movements. It is a tactic to (re)build the Black liberation movement." It also states that 2.8 million blacks are incarcerated, 500,000 blacks are in the U.S. illegally and that "Black queer and trans folks bear a unique burden from a hetero-patriarchal society that disposes of us like garbage and simultaneously fetishizes us and profits off of us."[1172] **NOTE**: In the 70s Wicker Park was mostly Hispanic. By the late 80s, it had become one of the most racially and economically integrated neighborhoods in Chicago. In the 90s, a transformation emerged changing the community into a place for white-collar working-class residents and artists. Today residents are mostly white-collar, college educated young professionals.[1173]

Continued Media Bias – Michael Brown

Take for instance the 2014 case in Ferguson, Missouri where white police officer, Darren Wilson, shot an unarmed black man, Michael Brown. This man media persists in calling a "boy" was 18 and legally an adult, 6-foot-3, and weighed nearly 300 pounds.[1174] Testimony from credible witnesses said Brown charged Wilson while Wilson was in his squad car and "fought for his gun." One bullet was found lodged in the car door and Brown had a graze wound on his right thumb and gunshot residue indicating a gun had been fired at close range. Blood spatter direction supported the officer's account that Brown continued to charge.

Some blacks took this opportunity to spread the falsehood that Michael Brown had his hands up, which gave birth to the mantra "Hands Up, Don't Shoot".

Brown's accomplice in the store robbery, Michael Johnson, is credited with starting this wrong-based slogan.[1175] Nevertheless it caught fire and mainstream news did nothing to correct this view. The premise of Brown's surrender was obviously not true and Wilson wasn't indicted. However, due to public outrage and death threats, Wilson had to quit his job and move away.

Image: Looted and burned-out QuikTrip gas station and "Quick Stop" in Ferguson, Missouri taken on August 15, 2015. (Courtesy Loaves of Bread)

Following the shooting, protests and riots came in three waves. The first lasted over two weeks. At least 12 businesses that had nothing to do with the incident were looted and burned out. Police cars and others vehicles were set ablaze. Activists took to streets across the country organizing dozens of protests in several states. One woman Shannon White, 20, said, "I feel people have every right to get violent. It's a form of retaliation. People are tired of being treated this way by the system."[1176] What made no sense was the lashing out and stealing from shopkeepers that kept their small community alive. Many of the victims were black too, yet paid the price.

Symptomatic of the problem was a South Carolina police officer shooting a black man in the back. Caught on tape Michael Slager, 33, said he feared for his life after he and Walter Scott, 50, scuffled. Scott had taken Slager's stun gun and then while running away, Slager pumped 8 bullets in Scott's back. Caught on tape, Slager was clearly guilty of killing him. Slager was charged with murder, held without bail and no trial date has been set as of December 2015.

FUEL FROM THE ORIGINAL FIRE

O.J. Simpson

Racism jumped in just four years rocketing past the days of fury over the O.J. Simpson verdict and the Rodney King case four years later.

As recap, black former pro football star and actor O.J. Simpson was put on trial for murdering his stunningly beautiful German ex-wife Nicole Brown Simpson and friend, Ronald Goldman. During their 7-year marriage Simpson pleaded no contest to spousal abuse. Her undated letter to O.J. accused him of verbal abuse, wife beating and infidelity.[1177] Two years after the divorce, Nicole and Goldman were found dead *outside* her home. She had been stabbed multiple times in the head and neck with her head nearly severed. Goldman's jugular had also been sliced, multiple stabs appeared on the head and then the fatal knife wounds plunged into the heart and lung. These were deemed acts of extreme personal rage.

Friends said the Simpsons had tried to reconcile, but those attempts ended several weeks before Nicole and Goldman's murders. Forensics found Goldman likely interrupted Nicole's murder when he had stopped by to return her mother's glasses lost outside the restaurant where he worked as a waiter.

Simpson's black lawyer, Johnnie L Cochran, came up with a spectacular defense of, "You must acquit, if it doesn't fit." Cochran continually invoked this phrase to persuade the jury that Simpson couldn't have murdered

Nicole and Ronald. The jury must have been brain dead. Simpson was found not guilty in an extremely controversial criminal trial.

Three years later, in 1997 Simpson was found liable for Nicole and Ronald's deaths in a civil suit brought by their families. He was ordered to pay more than $33 million for their wrongful deaths. Simpson is currently serving a prison sentence in Nevada for kidnapping, robbery, burglary, assault with a deadly weapon and other charges for trying to obtain memorabilia he claims belonged to him.

In a bout of total narcissism, Simpson wrote a book about his wife's murder entitled *IF I Did It*. No one doubted he did. Subsequently, the Goldman family purchased those book rights.

Who, in their arrogance, would write such an in-your-face book basically confessing to such heinous crimes? Who would do that unless seeking a shocking amount of attention to the point of self-incrimination? Simpson was a football hero. He was pretty. He had a "name". People worshipped O.J. and he was the representative star of Hertz Renta-a-Car commercials, able to leap racial barriers in a single bound. Now Simpson is where he belongs, in jail and unworshipped.

Rodney King

Taxi cab driver Rodney King became nationally known after being beaten by Los Angeles police officers. Unknown to the cops George Holliday video recorded the entire scene. Prior to the beating, King and a couple of friends had been drinking and watching basketball at a friend's house. King, who is black, admitted trying to outrun police at dangerously high speeds at times over 115mph. A DUI charge would violate his parole for a prior robbery conviction. King also had other convictions for assault, battery and robbery. Once the high-speed chase was over, four white police officers delivered 56 baton swings and kicks to the mostly prone King. The officers who claimed they acted in self-defense were tried before a jury of nine whites, one biracial, one Asian and one Latino in a white middle-class suburb of Los Angeles. On April 29, 1992, all four men, Sgt. Stacey C. Koon, 41; Officers Laurence Powell, 29; Theodore Briseno, 39; and Timothy Wind, 31, were acquitted.[1178]

The verdict shocked the Nation and touched off an angry firestorm. Rioters burned nearly 3,800 buildings destroying some 1,100, smashed storefronts and looted stores racking up over a billion in property damage. Innocent passing motorists were considered fair game and beaten in predominantly black downtown L.A. During six days of rioting immediately following the verdict, 55 people were killed and over 2,000 were injured. Civil unrest got so out of control Mayor Tom Bradley declared a state of emergency and Gov. Pete Wilson called in 4,000 members of the National Guard. In the ensuing weeks, over 11,000 people were arrested.

Aftermath

Three years after the Rodney King riots and right after the O.J. Simpson trial, racial tensions shot up. According to a CNN/Kaiser Family Foundation poll, 41% of Americans saw race as a "big problem" in 1995. In 2011 in the midst of the love-fest with Mr. Obama who promised to be the Great Unifier, just 28% viewed race as a major social issue. But when Obama morphed into the Great Divider and reality set in, 49% of Americans viewed race as a "big problem".[1179] *The Washington Examiner* reported evidence continues to mount that by the time he leaves office in 2017, his legacy will be the one of the most-ever polarizing presidents. In his last year at the helm, instead of softening he's "doubling down on programs and policies that are certain to divide the country even further."[1180] This isn't solely the observation of the *Examiner*. Notoriously liberal *Boston Globe* wrote, "Obama insisted that [partisanship and rancor] would change when he was president. The toxic style of politics wasn't inescapable. Give me the highest office in the land, he assured a rapturous crowd in Ohio two days before the 2008 election, and 'we can end it once and for all.' Millions of voters believed him. They took to heart his vow to transfigure American public life. They looked forward to the uplifting leadership he promised. What they got instead was the most polarizing and divisive presidency in modern times."[1181]

LET THE NUMBERS SPEAK

While racial issues take center stage again, often citing interactions between white police and black people, a few numbers put some of this into perspective.

According to the U.S. Justice Department, despite making up just 13% of the population blacks commit 52% of homicides while whites were responsible for 45%.[1182] According to 2013 FBI data, black criminals committed 38%

of murders, compared to 31% for whites, though there are over five times more white people in America.[1183] By 2014, the percentages were more evenly divided by actual incidents with black criminals at 47.2% and white criminals at 48%.[1184] Keep in mind the ratio of more than 5 white persons for every black.[1185] Said another way, based on the number of whites to blacks, this means blacks accounted for a 560% increase in 2014's homicides.

Between 2011 and 2013, 38.5% of those arrested for murder, manslaughter, rape, robbery and aggravated assault were black. Considering black males aged 15-34 only make up about 3% of the population, but are responsible for the vast majority of these crimes, the number becomes very sobering.[1186]

Though outnumbered by whites 5-to1, blacks commit 8 times more crimes against whites than the reverse, according to FBI statistics from 2007. A black male is 40 times as likely to assault a white person as the reverse.[1187] Data also show that interracial rape is almost exclusively black on white, not white on black.[1188] **NOTE**: For at least six consecutive years, the FBI broke out, albeit somewhat obscurely, rape and sexual assault statistics for three groups: White on Black, Black on White and Black on Black. Out of the nearly 300,000 reported rapes, 52% were committed Black on Black; 48% were Black on White and White on Black was 0. Strangely, the year that Mr. Obama took office in 2009 these statistics were omitted from FBI reports much like the OTMs (**O**ther **T**han **M**exicans) are lumped together for the last decade without country designation.

REVERSE DISCRIMINATION OF AFFIRMATIVE ACTION

This policy initiated by President John F. Kennedy in the early 60s, ideally implemented would have leveled the employment playing field for women and minorities. Businesses incorporated on nearly every piece of literature the phrase "Company 'X' is an Equal Opportunity Employer". It was a small hedge against charges of discrimination.

For years people complained rightfully that white men were often paid more than counterparts doing the same job. In practice this policy produced racial and gender quotas both in college admissions and the workplace. For example, to reach a diversity that reflected the population it served, police departments were required to turn away more qualified, more skilled applicants in order to comply with this policy. Instead of assuring employment *equality*, it led to reverse discrimination.

Reverse discrimination also became apparent at universities. In 2009, Princeton sociologist Thomas Espenshade and researcher Alexandria Walton Radford published their findings on college admissions discrimination. To enter a top private university they found Asians needed nearly perfect SAT scores of 1550 (out of 1600); whites were admitted scoring 1410, and blacks sailed through on a score of 1100.[1189] Maybe for unskilled labor this is acceptable, but especially for work that requires skill and training, who wants "second tier"? Said another way, if you're undergoing a heart transplant do you want someone tinkering with your parts that isn't the most qualified? In firefighting, often they are required to physically carry people overcome by smoke. Is it wise to ask a 140-pound female to hoist 200 pounds of dead weight? Your life may depend on it.

In 2010, the Justice Department forced the Dayton, Ohio police department to lower its test standards score of 72 to 58 so more minorities could pass. The same thing happened at a fire company in New York.[1190] For the first time in history, the New York Fire Department let a woman into "the house" that failed her running test six times. Wendy Tapia, 34, was sworn in after her first failure blaming a foot injury, failed five more attempts and finally resigned in November 2013. One FDNY member said, "She'll graduate, no question. The department doesn't want another black eye."[1191] He referred to a $98 million federal lawsuit that alleged discrimination against minority applicants.

As of 2015 Colorado Springs police officers will no longer have to take physical fitness tests. In November that year 12 women over age 40 filed a civil suit claiming physical fitness tests were discriminatory. They had to pass two running tests, do 52 push-ups in 2 minutes and 45 sit-ups in 2 minutes. That shouldn't be too tough on someone in decent physical shape. If they can't pass even the basic tests, how are they going to apprehend the bad guys? Colorado Springs residents were in an uproar over the court's decision, which will be appealed in 2016. Resident Mary Jo Piccin worried, "I think it's a mistake. I think the police need to be able to chase down them criminals." And that gets harder for those in blue honoring Homer Simpson's mantra: donut donut donut.[1192]

In 2008 Abigail Fisher filed suit against the University of Texas when she was admittedly rejected under "holistic review," which takes a person's race into account. Fisher graduated with a 3.59 GPA, earned 1180 on her SAT, did volunteer work and played the cello. Still she was denied acceptance because she was white. Her suit claimed that UT accepted nonwhite students with lower grades and fewer extracurricular activities. Yet even the Fifth Circuit Court of Appeals upheld the university's affirmative action policy. Subsequently Fisher graduated from Louisiana State University in 2012 and works as a business analyst in Austin, but felt she might have snagged a better job graduating from UT. The U.S. Supreme Court heard her case in December 2015, but no decision is expected any time soon.

Harvard came under attack in 2015 for allegedly limiting its number of Asian students. The case argues that Asian Americans are held to higher scholastic standards than other ethnic groups, but are disproportionately denied admission. Their case studies uphold the finding of Espenshade-Radford. One Asian denied entrance to Harvard ranked first out of 460 in his graduating class and scored 100% on his ACT college-admissions exam. If the suit is successful it could end a 40-year Supreme Court decision that favored blacks and Hispanics.

REPARATIONS CONTROVERSY

"Forty acres of land and a mule" – a staple of black history and the name of Spike Lee's film company. What most people haven't heard is that black leaders, not General Sherman, really generated the idea.[1193] Toward the end of the Civil War, Union General William Tecumseh Sherman promised slaves this is what they'd receive, which President Andrew Johnson later withdrew. This promise was out of line since Sherman was just a general, not President. Then Sherman's Field Order No. 15 applied only to the South, redistributing about 400,000 acres. According to Order No. 15 it involved, "The islands from Charleston, south, the abandoned rice fields along the rivers for thirty miles back from the sea, and the country bordering the St. Johns river, Florida." [1194] More importantly, two sections of this Order specified they would be governed entirely by blacks and no whites could reside there. If this isn't segregation, what is?

To straighten out a bit of history, there was never a mule promised by Sherman. He just prescribed the land. The mules came later. (See William T. Sherman's Special Field Order #5.[1195])

Since blacks today represent 42.5 million of Americans, extrapolated reparations would require 1,700,800,000 acres of land, which is more than half of the U.S. Researcher Thomas Craemer of the University of Connecticut, estimated that reparations would cost between $6 and $14 trillion. That's about three quarters of the national debt. Craemer based his calculations on guessing hours slaves worked from when the country was officially established in 1776 to 1865, when slavery was abolished. He multiplied the time worked by average wages and added compounding interest of 3%, which more than compensates for inflation.[1196]

To say the least, reparations are completely unrealistic and the majority of Americans aren't in favor of them. (Could that have anything to do with whites outnumbering blacks by more than 5-to-1?) Slavery ended 150 years ago. Every American today, plus their parents and grandparents, weren't even around then. The majority of our ancestors back to the 1600s weren't even a part of this horrible black blot on American history. Why should they and we be held liable?

Craemer said he "felt good" because his country, Germany, paid $89 billion as of 2012 to Jewish victims of Nazism. This was compensation for slave labor during the Holocaust, lost livelihoods, billions in stolen irreplaceable art and priceless jewelry – and the outright slaughter of 6 million people. The utter irony is that Hitler likely had Jewish and black roots.[1197]

These two issues, the Holocaust and slavery, are hardly comparable, and not one penny can make up for a life taken in either country. Hitler ordered 6 million Jews exterminated – either shot or buried alive when not gassed naked, shivering and starved. He was motivated by extreme hatred; American South slavery by greed and ignorance. While many blacks under slavery endured the nearly unendurable, many lived decent lives, taken out of African poverty that exists today. Some were treated as family members, but other "owners" viewed them as little better than animals, not even permitting them to marry, hence "jumping the broom" was born. As if this is any different or makes slavery in the least excusable, Hitler's Holocaust encompassed at least 6 million and America's slavery involved about 3.9 million.[1198]

NOTE: Mounting evidence shows that Hitler and his wife, Eva Braun, escaped to Argentina and he didn't die until 1962. No one actually saw Hitler commit suicide and the two bodies were never positively ID'ed. A 2010 book,[1199] among others, showed Hitler escaped from Berlin to Denmark, back to Travenmunde, Germany; then to Reus, Spain; then the Canary Islands and ultimately to Mar Del Plata, Argentina in the province of Rio Negro. He reportedly lived outside Bariloche in the spectacular setting of the Andes Mountains until the age of 73. (Some people picture him in a different setting surrounded by red-hot flames and lots of screaming.)

Regardless, the reparations debate pretty much falls on deaf ears. Healing needs to move past this completely impractical "solution". On the other hand, pundits say that without it, America will never heal and this division will continue to fester.

GROWING ECONOMIC DISPARITY

Nothing quite shines a light on national division than the disappearing middle class. It's the primary engine that drives small business, creating 65% of all jobs.[1200] Its shrinkage means fewer decent employment opportunities and a whole lot of mediocrity in the job market. According to the *Wall Street Journal* the U.S hit its highest-ever cumulative wealth in 2013.[1201] Credit Suisse ranks America's wealth per person at a staggering $352,996 for every adult. The U.S. has by far the greatest number of people in the top 1% global wealth group and accounts for 46% of the world's millionaires[1202] but this doesn't translate to the average, middle class American. Instead most wealth is concentrated at the top of the food chain.

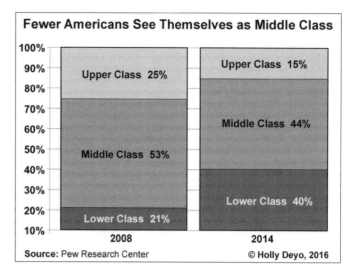

The middle 60% of Americans used to earn over half of the Country's income as far back as 1967. By 1988 it dropped below 50% for the first time and it's now dwindled to 45.8% in 2013. Contributing to this downward trend is the declining manufacturing sector with automation, centralization and outsourcing taking bigger bites.

Between 2000 and 2010, the U.S. lost 5.7 million manufacturing jobs.[1203] Of the 20 job fields the Census Bureau sees as declining from 2014 to 2024, 11 are in manufacturing. Of 15 fastest growing occupations nine are in the healthcare industry. (Does that mean more people are expected to become sick or not as many are choosing these careers?)

What Is Middle Class?

"Middle class" is often defined by economists as Americans making within 50% of the median income. For 2014, this meant a range from $26,828 to $80,485. However, it greatly depends on location. If a person lives in New York or San Jose, California or the Silicon Valley an average home might cost $1 or $2 million and be quite modest. Likewise, salaries there are proportionally higher, but so is the cost of living. Regardless, *in just seven years,* Americans experienced a huge shift in personal wealth. The top financial tier shrunk 40%; the middle class shrunk by 17%, and those in the poorest category nearly doubled.

When the Great Recession of 2008 hit, nearly 8.7 million jobs were lost – many forever.[1204] The jobs that replaced them were lower paying, part-time and without the former benefits. Full-time work, which has always consisted of a 40-hour week, was knocked back to 30 after the implementation of ObamaCare. No other country in the developed world – not Australia, Belgium, Brazil, Chile, Denmark, France, Germany, Iceland, India, Israel, Italy, Netherlands, Poland, Russia, Sweden, Taiwan or the United Kingdom – have so few hours required to constitute a full work week, except Canada. Some countries' work standards are a lot higher. India requires 60 hours and Taiwan over 72 to constitute a complete workweek. Only

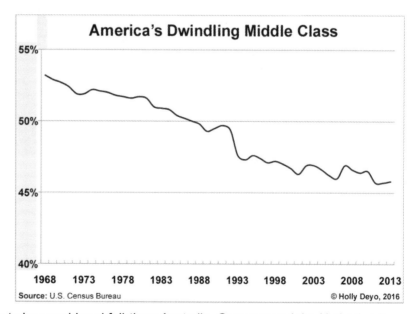

three come close with a minimum of 36 hours to be considered full-time: Australia, Germany and the Netherlands.

ObamaCare forced companies to provide healthcare for more employees. In the double whammy of a dead economy and government-required healthcare, businesses were forced to do more with a lot less. So they went with less. To survive they stopped hiring and replaced full-time employees with part-timers. ObamaCare was supposed to help people, but it hurt the job market and their chances of finding work because businesses couldn't afford the staggering cost of healthcare.

The Obama administration liked to say all those lost jobs were recovered, but with what? The sad fact is the higher-paying jobs in construction, manufacturing and banking were replaced with low-paying positions at restaurants, hotels and temp agencies. Many people were forced to work two jobs to pay the bills.

Meanwhile, the U.S. continues to import foreigners and keep borders porous so illegals can be hired for cheap dollars. Immigrants legal and otherwise are a short-term boost to the economy. They need housing, transportation, medical care, food and social services, which keeps money moving. However, the long-term effect is economically negative while further diluting the Nation's culture.

Another Slap – H-1B Visas

Kept quiet is the practice of universities and industry executives importing foreign professionals instead of hiring Americans. They're bringing in a workforce of at least 100,000 over and above the annual cap of 85,000 new H-1B visas. 2014 was just as bad with over 160,000[1205] brought in on H-1Bs blowing by the cap. Less than 17% qualified as "high-tech" computer experts further inflaming the outsourcing controversy. Under the table, they've hired 21,754 professors, lecturers and instructors; 20,566 doctors, clinicians and therapists; 25,175 researchers, post-docs and biologists; and 30,000 assorted financial planners, P.R. experts, writers, editors, sports coaches, designers, accountants, economists, statisticians, lawyers, architects and computer experts.[1206] One exception to the highly educated is if a person qualifies as a fashion model.[1207] Universities have zero legal obligations to recruit Americans for these jobs. Instead these guest workers are being hired at lower wages than what it would cost to employ Americans with the same skills. Once here, H-1Bs allow the guest workers to move to different companies.

If they don't want to head back home after their 6-year stint is up, during this period they can apply for a "green card" giving them permanent residency. Spouses and kids are also allowed to come on H-4 visas where they can attend our schools, but not work. (How many employers would think to ask, *are you here on an H-4 visa?*)

Another facet to this controversy is that American professionals displaced by foreign nationals are forced into lower paying careers. This hidden enclave of two million foreign white-collar guest workers has now replaced America's professionals. All these factors combine to drive down white-collar wages.

Last Thoughts

America must be taken down before the hammer can smash Israel. The U.S. is the only entity standing between it and annihilation. Too many countries hate us for what we have and what we stand for in addition to an abrasive, hegemonic foreign policy. Israel is poised for that promised smackdown when all nations come against her and there will be no country to intervene.

Chapter 16: Visions of America's Destruction

"And I will send fire on Magog [Russia] and on those who live in security in the coastlands. Then they shall know that I am the Lord." —Ezekiel 39:6 (NKJV)

NOTE: In other Biblical translations, "coastlands" is substituted for "isles". Both of these descriptions could describe the United States because over half of the population lives along the oceans and before 9/11, America thought it imperious to attack being an "island", surrounded and protected by distance and water.

GEORGE WASHINGTON

This vision occurred circa 1777 and told to a reporter named Wesley Bradshaw by an officer, Anthony Sherman, serving under General Washington at Valley Forge. It showed three great trials that would greatly challenge the Union: the Revolutionary War, the Civil War, and the greatest war, which was to be fought on U.S. soil. Many believe it takes place close to End Times and Jesus' return. Washington used to go into a thicket often to pray in private so it shouldn't be surprising that an angel appeared to him. This particular afternoon while working on a dispatch he looked up to see a very beautiful female. He'd given orders not to be disturbed and when she intruded he asked her four times what she wanted, but received no answer. When she broke the silence it was to say "Son of the Republic, look and learn," while pointing east. Washington saw a heavy white vapor in the distance rising fold upon fold, which gradually dissipated. All the countries of the world – Europe, Asia, Africa and America were spread out in one vast plain. The Atlantic Ocean roiled between Europe and America, as did the Pacific between Asia and America.

The figure repeated her instruction to Washington to "look and learn." There floated a dark, shadowy being, like an angel, between Europe and America. He sprinkled some ocean water on America with his right hand, while his left did the same on Europe. A cloud raised from these countries, joined mid-ocean, eventually enveloping America. Flashes of lightning shot from it Washington heard groans and cries of the American people.

The angel sprinkled water like before and another cloud formed. When it fell back into the ocean, the female figure again commanded Washington to "look and learn". This new scene revealed America's growth with villages, towns and cities springing up from the Atlantic to the Pacific.

The mysterious female said "Son of the Republic, the end of the century cometh, look and learn." He again saw the dark angel look south toward Africa and an ill-omened specter approached America. It glided over every town and city and people turned on each other in battle. Then a bright angel appeared and on its forehead was a crown of light with the word "Union" inscribed on it. He carried the American flag, which he put between the divided Nation and instructed, "Remember ye are brethren." The inhabitants immediately stopped fighting, became friends again, united around the flag.

Image: U.S. flag in 1777

The next vision after hearing the now-familiar instruction, "Son of the Republic, look and learn" revealed the dark, shadowy angel placing a trumpet to his mouth. He gave it three distinct blasts and again sprinkled ocean water on Europe, Asia and Africa. A terrible scene unfolded with thick black clouds over each country that then joined together as one. Throughout the cloud shone a dark red light and Washington saw hordes of armed men march by land and sail by sea to America. That ominous cloud enveloped America and the cities and towns he saw spring up were devastated and burned by that massive army.

Through the sounds of war Washington heard the female's voice order, "Son of the Republic, look and learn". When she finished, the shadowy angel blew his trumpet again, this time in a single, loud, fearful blast. Instantly a light as bright as a thousand suns broke into fragments the dark cloud that enveloped America. Simultaneously the angel wearing the "Union" crown with America's flag in one hand and a sword in the other came down from the heavens attended by legions of white spirits. They immediately joined the people of America who Washington felt were about to be overcome. They were immediately encouraged, closed their broken ranks to fight on.

In the midst of conflict the beautiful female angel said "Son of the Republic, look and learn." When she finished the dark angel again sprinkled ocean water on America. Immediately the dark cloud rolled back taking the armies with it and leaving the inhabitants victorious.

Once again he saw America rebuild her cities and towns while the bright angel with the crown cried out, "While the stars remain, and the heavens send down dew upon the earth, so long shall the Union last." Taking the crown from his head with the word "Union" emblazoned on it he placed it on the Standard while the people knelt and said "Amen."

The scene faded and Washington saw nothing except the rising, curling vapor he first witnessed. This too disappeared and he was left to gaze at the beautiful female angel who said, "Son of the Republic, what you have seen is thus interpreted: Three great perils will come upon the Republic. The most fearful is the third, but in this greatest conflict the whole world united shall not prevail against her. Let every child of the Republic learn to live for his God, his land and the Union." With those words the angel vanished and Washington felt he'd been shown America's birth, progress and destiny.[1208]

DAVID WILKERSON

David Wilkerson wrote *Set the Trumpet to Thy Mouth* in 1985. He was one the first to I.D. America as modern Babylon of End Times prophecy. He wrote, "I believe modern Babylon is present-day America, including its corrupt society and its whorish church system. No other nation on earth fits the description in Revelation 18 but America, the world's biggest fornicator with the merchants of all nations." If you want a really exceptional book on this topic, there is no finer work than Rick Coombes, *America, The Babylon*. It's an exhaustive, convincing study. Like many others who study prophecy, this author used to think many years ago that modern Babylon would be the same as the first in what's now Iraq. However, some of the identifying factors didn't fit for modern physical Babylon to be in the Middle East like exporting its culture abroad, land of immigrants, highest living standard, people sensual and materialist, center of merchandising and marketing, respected and envied, yet **hated** by the whole world. Then there's that pesky detail of a city in New York actually named Babylon. A lot of other identifying features are outlined primarily in Revelation, Jeremiah and Isaiah. Doubt crept in that it could be Iraq. It certainly isn't a land of immigrants. Nor is it rich with 25% of Iraqis living below the poverty line. It has one main export – oil. That's it, so Iraq's not a hub of trade. While it's bursting with cultural heritage, Iraq doesn't export it. Then one telling clue hit right between the eyes. At the time, this author was researching and writing *Prudent Places USA* – a map-driven book on all aspects of America. The original of the following river map was 2x3 feet, letting the viewer see in detail just how covered the U.S. is with water. In color it's astonishing with rivers of blue throbbing throughout. Every bit of gray you see here is a river or stream. (Image next page.) Her 3.5 million miles of rivers could encircle the globe 140 times with water to spare. That, together with all the other indicators changed my mind. America is modern Babylon.

Wilkerson lists these warning events:

"Before the great holocaust there will be smaller holocausts – the oil fields of the Middle East will be ablaze, and the smoke will rise night and day as a warning of the greater holocaust yet to come. There will be bombs falling on oil fields, on shipping docks and storage thanks. There will be panic among all oil producers, and shippers, and upon all nations dependent on that oil.

"Soon, very soon, an economic nightmare will explode into reality. What frightful news it will be! *[O Babylon] you who live by many waters, rich in treasures, your end has come, and the line measuring your life is cut.* — Jeremiah 51:13 (AMP). America is about to face a time of mass hysteria, as banks close and financial institutions crumble and our economy spins totally out of control. Gold and silver will also lose their value. *They will throw their silver into the streets, And their gold will be like refuse; Their silver and their gold will not be able to deliver them In the day of the wrath of the LORD; They will not satisfy their souls, Nor fill their stomachs, Because it became their stumbling block of iniquity.* —Ezekiel 7:19 (NKJV). Government can't stop the coming chaos. Ezekiel warned, *the king will mourn, the prince will be clothed with horror, and the hands of the people of the land will tremble. According to their conduct I will deal with them, and by their judgments I will judge them. And they will know that I am the Lord.* —Ezekiel 7:27 (NKJV). These prophecies once again reveal God's judgmental decrees to wicked nations.

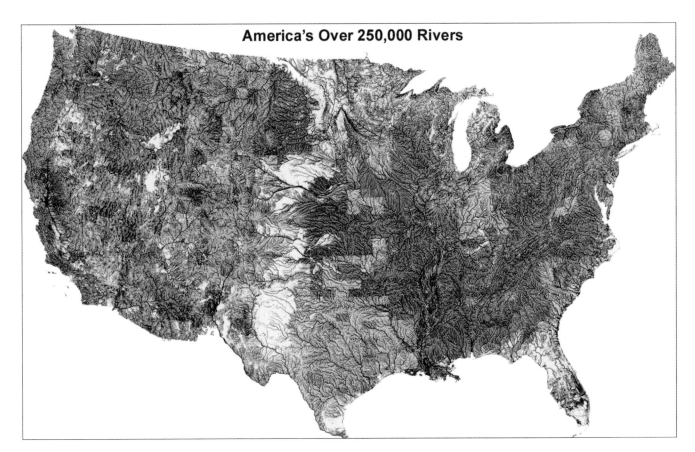

America's Over 250,000 Rivers

"Scoff if you choose, but the underlying fears about a collapse will soon become a tragic reality. Numerous cracks will appear in our fragile prosperity, and soon even the most pessimistic will know in their hearts that a total collapse is certain. Senators and congressmen will sit in stunned silence as they realize no one can stop the tailspin into chaos. Business, political and economic leaders will be terrorized by its suddenness and its far-reaching effect. *Son of man, if a country sins against Me by committing unfaithfulness, and I stretch out My hand against it, destroy its supply of bread, send famine against it and cut off from it both man and beast.* —Ezekiel 14:13 (NASB). The great holocaust follows an economic collapse in America. The enemy will make its move when we are weak and helpless."

On September 7, 1997 Wilkerson wrote, "'I have had a recurring vision of a thousand fires burning at one time in New York City. I am convinced race riots will soon explode. New York is a powder keg. Federal and state, now listen to what he predicted in '92, welfare cutbacks will be the spark that ignites the fuse. There will be 100,000 angry men on the streets in a rage because they have been cut off from government benefits.'"[1209]

In March 2009 Wilkerson expanded on his visions saying "about a thousand fires [are] coming to New York City. It will engulf the whole megaplex, including areas of New Jersey and Connecticut. Major cities all across America will experience riots and blazing fires-such as we saw in Watts, Los Angeles, years ago. There will be riots and fires in cities worldwide. There will be looting-including Times Square, New York City." He said that in major cities, grocery stores would be emptied in an hour at the sign of an impending disaster as in small towns and rural areas. Though he wasn't selling anything he advised if you are able to do so to "lay in store a thirty-day supply of non-perishable food, toiletries and other essentials".[1210] After the economic collapse when America is on her back, Russia will invade.

PERRY STONE

In Stone's May 2008 vision he stood by an unnamed river and could see for 180 degrees. He counted at least five major U.S. cities where rioting and fighting were taking place. This was happening inside sections of the poorer areas among ethnic groups. They were literally burning these cities down. Tangentially, Stone says, "...there's been other people confirm it, California, parts of New York – they got a governor in New Jersey that finally put his foot down and got that mess straightened out there, but there are five major cities right now that are on the verge of complete bankruptcy. If they start cutting money out of the unions, which is the police force, and they've already done it in some places, and if there is any kind of a cutback in benefits that goes to some of the people in some of these areas, I promise you, you will see fighting and burning of cities In the United States like we've never seen it before."[1211]

NOTE: This vision occurred in 2008 and an Internet search[1212] turned up more than five cities and municipalities close to bankruptcy. Some of these cities have already filed; some are teetering. Let the author emphasize Perry Stone cited **no specific city**. These cities may or may not be ones he saw, plus with our precarious economy, others locations could find themselves in trouble.

Filed for Bankruptcy Protection

- Vallejo, California – 2008
- Stockton, California – 2012
- Mammoth Lakes, California – 2012
- San Bernardino, California – 2012
- Harrisburg, Pennsylvania – 2011
- Central Falls, Rhode Island – 2011
- Boise County, Idaho – 2011
- Detroit – 2013
- Jefferson County, Alabama – 2011Prichard, Alabama – 2009
- Washington Park, Illinois – 2009
- Gould, Arkansas – 2008

Facing Bankruptcy

- Scranton, Pennsylvania Bell, California
- San Diego, California
- Hamtramck, Michigan
- Jefferson County, Alabama
- Central Falls, Rhode Island
- Gary, Indiana
- Flint, Michigan

Additional Cities Possibly in Financial Trouble

- Los Angeles, San Diego, San Jose and San Francisco, California
- Baltimore, Maryland
- Washington, DC.
- Honolulu, Hawaii
- Chicago, Illinois
- Cincinnati, Ohio
- Camden, New Jersey

WILLIAM BRANHAM

American Christian minister Branham who passed away in 1965 was generally acknowledged as initiating the healing revival after World War II. American historian, David Edwin Harrell Jr. described him as: "an unlikely leader… his preaching was halting and simple. But William Branham became a prophet to a generation. A small, meek, middle-aged man with piercing eyes, he held audiences spellbound with tales of constant communication with God and angels. Night after night, before thousands of awed believers he discerned the diseases of the sick and pronounced them healed."[1213]

Branham experienced a series of seven prophetic visions in 1933. Visions six and seven both pertained to the U.S. with the final one showing America's complete destruction. The progression is important giving a timeline and also validation. So far the first five have come to pass and in some cases, warning was given decades in advance. In visions six and seven a woman rises to great power in America, which could either be a literal woman or symbolic. In the final part, he saw a massive explosion that turned America into ashes from coast to coast. This was symbolic as no single nuclear weapon has that much power. Branham couldn't fathom what this meant because it wasn't till little later that year on September 12, 1933, Hungarian-American physicist and inventor Leo Szilard conceived the idea of nuclear chain reaction.

Vision One: He saw in a vision that the dictator of Italy, Benito Mussolini, would invade Ethiopia and according to the voice speaking to him, Ethiopia "would fall at his (Mussolini's) steps". However, the voice continued and prophesied a dreadful end of the dictator. He would have a horrible death and his own people would literally spit on him. **NOTE**: This came to pass two years after his vision when Italy invaded Ethiopia on October 3, 1935.

Vision Two: The next vision indicated America would be drawn into a world war against Germany, which would be headed up by Austrian Adolph Hitler. The voice predicted that this terrible war would overthrow Hitler and he would come to a mysterious "end". In this vision he was shown the Siegfried Line where many Americans would die, but Hitler would be defeated. **NOTE**: It wasn't until the early 1960s that German films surfaced, which forced the American government to admit what really happened. Hitler had escaped. This vision predicted WWII, which began on September 1, 1939 and ended September 2, 1945.

Vision Three: The third part of the vision showed three 'ism's' in the world: Fascism, Nazism, Communism. The first two would come to nothing, but Communism would flourish. The voice specifically warned to keep eyes on Russia, not the Soviet Union, concerning future involvements. Fascism and Nazism would end up in Communism. **NOTE**: Though there are still remnants of Fascism and Nazism, neither have the force of earlier years. However, Communism never disappeared. Its doctrine promised eventual world takeover and even though it appeared to wane, it would again surge. Communism is still the law of the land in China, Cuba, Laos, North Korea and Vietnam.

Vision Four: Predicted tremendous technological advances right after the war. In his vision an egg-shaped car with a plastic bubble roof symbolized this going down beautiful highways by remote control. The car had no steering wheel and the passengers were playing a game like checkers. **NOTE**: The first truly self-sufficient cars appeared in the 1980s though not on the road. It wasn't until 2013 four U.S. states and the UK even permitted testing these vehicles on public roads. In May 2014, Google presented a new concept for their driverless car that had neither a steering wheel nor pedals.[1214] In 2015, a few Google self-driving cars appeared on the roads, but probably wouldn't be available to the public till 2017-2020.

Image: Google self-driving car motors past a double-deck commuter bus at Google's headquarters in Mountain View, CA on October 21, 2015. (Courtesy Michael Francis Shick) It's egg-shaped just like Branham's vision showed.

Vision Five: The fifth scene addressed the fast moral decay of women. The woman in the vision began to wear revealing clothes, bobbed her hair and donned men's attire. Finally it showed her all but naked covering herself with a tiny apron about the size and shape of a fig leaf. With her womanhood so little valued, terrible moral decay would envelop the earth and with it, perversion as described in the Bible.

NOTE: Bobbed hairstyles first appeared in the 20s, but for the most part still dressed conservatively. Then "swimsuits" consisted of knee-high socks, bloomers to the knees and a short-sleeve top up to the neck. Occasionally "skimpier" versions chucked the socks. By the 50s, swimwear was still modest by today's standards consisting mostly of 1-piece suits, strapped or strapless tops. French fashion designer Jacques Heim first introduced the bikini in 1946, but it didn't catch on worldwide till two decades later. And you pretty much know the rest of the story today with bare-there swimsuits and nude beaches. It's interesting that Branham specifically mentioned a woman covering herself with something about the size and shape of a fig leaf. In 2003 radical PETA – **P**eople for the **E**thical **T**reatment of **A**nimals – launched the *Turn Over a New Leaf – Try Vegetarian* campaign. It featured actress Pamela Anderson in a string bikini with a rhinestone-encrusted lettuce leaf for the bottom and two leaves for the top.[1215] The pantsuit was introduced in the 1920s, "when a small number of women adopted a *masculine style,* including pantsuits, hats, and even canes and monocles."[1216] In the 60s this author attended a Southern Baptist Church with her friend across the street on Wednesday and Sunday nights and her parent's church Sunday mornings. The Baptist pastor's daughters were never allowed to wear pants except with a dress over the top. It wasn't until 1993 that women were allowed to wear pants of any kind on the U.S. Senate floor. Now they are a staple in every female's wardrobe.

Vision Six: Then a beautiful woman arose in the U.S., clothed in splendor, and given great power. She was lovely, but with a hardness difficult to describe. She was also cruel, wicked and cunning. Her authority dominated the land and she had complete power over the people. The vision indicated that either this woman would be a literal person or represented an organization, which is scripturally characterized as female. Though the voice in the vision didn't reveal who she was, Branham felt in his heart she represented the rising Roman Catholic Church, which he noted in parenthesis at the end of this vision he'd written out.

Vision Seven: The voice bade him look once more. He saw a great explosion tear the entire land and left America a smoldering, chaotic ruin. As far as the eye could see there was nothing but craters, smoking piles of debris and no humanity in sight. With that, the vision faded away.[1217]

DUMITRU DUDUMAN

Romanian pastor Dumitru Duduman is known for smuggling 300,000 Bibles into the Soviet Union. In August 1980 he was arrested for these activities by the Romanian Secret Police, tortured and interrogated for five months. He was beaten almost daily and repeatedly shocked in an electric chair. Unable to break Duduman, authorities gave him three choices; a mental hospital, prison or expulsion to the U.S. He, his wife and daughter moved to America with few possessions, broke, no place to live, and not knowing the language. One night in despair while walking around outside he cried out. "God! Why did you punish me? Why did you bring me into this country? I can't understand anybody. If I try to ask anybody anything, all I hear is, 'I don't know.'"

A familiar angel's voice, one he'd heard many times while in prison, came to him in a bright light. He urged Dumitru to have patience, "to get on something" that he didn't know what it was. Duduman did as instructed, was fully awake and being awake, says what he was shown wasn't in a vision. The angel showed him all of California and said, "This is Sodom and Gomorrah! All of this, in one day it will burn! Its sin has reached the Holy One." Then he took Dumitru to Las Vegas. "This is Sodom and Gomorrah. In one day it will burn." Then, he took Dumitru to New York State and then Florida naming each state saying, "This is Sodom and Gomorrah! In one day it will burn."

The reason for the coming destruction was simple. He said, "I want to save the church, but the churches have forsaken me. The people praise themselves. The honor that the people are supposed to give Jesus Christ, they take upon themselves. In the churches there are divorces. There is adultery in the churches. There are homosexuals in the churches. There is abortion in the churches and all other sins that are possible. Because of all the sin, I have left some of the churches. You must yell in a loud voice that they must put an end to their sinning. They must turn toward the Lord. The Lord never gets tired of forgiving. They must draw close to the Lord, and live a clean life. If they have sinned until now, they must put an end to it, and start a new life as the Bible tells them to live."

The angel encouraged Dumitru because he was poor and no one knew him. The angel said, "Don't worry yourself. I will go before you. I will do a lot of healing in the American churches and I will open the doors for you. But do not say anything else besides what I tell you. This country will burn!"

Duduman asked how America would burn and the angel answered, "The Russian spies have discovered where the nuclear warehouses are in America.

NOTE: In a video[1218] of Dumitru, his grandson Michael Boldea, who is his interpreter, translates the phrase "nuclear warehouses" as "nuclear plants". This puts a whole different meaning on what areas would be bombed. The U.S. has 9 main nuclear arsenal sites, which are different from the locations of 100 nuclear power plants.

When the Americans will think that there is peace and safety – from the middle of the country, some of the people will start fighting against the government. The government will be busy with internal problems. A revolution will be started by the Communists. Then from the ocean, Russia, Cuba, Nicaragua, Central America, Mexico..." (and two other countries he couldn't remember) will defeat America. "...They will bomb the nuclear warehouses. When they explode, America will burn!"

Dumitru shared that the angel explains "Mystery Babylon". He said, "Tell them because all the nations of the world immigrated into America and America accepted them. America accepted Buddha, the devil church, the sodomite church, the Mormon Church and all kinds of wickedness. America was a Christian nation. Instead of stopping them, they went after their gods. Because of this, He named them "the Mystery Babylon." [1219]

NOTE: In that same video Dumitru refuses to share this information if it weren't in the Bible. The angel asks him if he's read Jeremiah 51. He says that describes America (new Babylon) not the Babylon of old, while Revelation 18 refers to the old one in Iraq.

It's really sad that some Christians have turned their backs – and worse – on their Jewish brother and sisters. Scripture is super clear how much God loves them. In the very first book of the Bible He said, *And I will bless them that bless you [Israel], and curse him that curses you...* —Genesis 12:3 That's how precious they are, not to mention it was the tribe of Judah into which Jesus was born. The Israelites **are** His chosen people. This plays an important part in the rest of Dumitru's prophecy.

The angel continued, "I have blessed this country because of the Jewish people who are in this country. I have seven million Jews in this country, but they do not want to recognize the Lord. They didn't want to thank God for the blessing they received in this country. Israel doesn't want to recognize Jesus Christ. They put their faith in the Jewish people in America. But, when America burns, the Lord will raise China, Japan, and other nations to go against the Russians. They will beat the Russians and push them all the way to the gates of Paris. Over there they will make a treaty, and appoint the Russians as their leaders. They will then unite against Israel. When Israel realizes she does not have the strength of America behind her, she will be frightened. That's when she will turn to the Messiah for deliverance."

Dumitru had one last question for the angel. "How will I know that this is for real, that it will really happen?" The angel replied, "As a sign that I have spoken to you, tomorrow before you wake, I will send someone to bring you a bed, and at noon I will send you a car and a bucket of honey. After which I will send someone to pay your rent." True to his word, the next day someone brought a bed. At noon a car arrived with the bucket of honey and his rent was paid, as God had promised him. [1220]

In a 1996 vision Dumitru was shown the presidents of Russia and China, who was described as short and chubby, and two other presidents from countries he didn't understand, but thought they were from Russian-controlled countries. The Russian said to the Chinese, "I will give you the land with all the people, but you must free Taiwan of the Americans. Do not fear; we will attack them from behind."

The voice of the man showing Dumitru what was to happen to America instructed, "Watch where the Russians penetrate America." Then I saw these words written: *Alaska, Minnesota, Florida.* "When America goes to war with China, the Russians will strike without warning." Russia wants America out of the picture so they can do as they please with Europe.

All four presidents shook hands, hugged and signed a contract plotting America's destruction. Each already had a pre-planned point of attack though none were named other than the three. One of them said, "We're sure that Korea and Cuba will be on our side, too. Without a doubt, together, we can destroy America."

The angel warned Duduman that these presidents will act as America's friends all the while plotting her demise.

One point of hope is the man showing Dumitru America's fate said that while God would allow the Country's destruction, help was coming. The man said. "God, however, still has people that worship Him with a clean heart as they do His work. He has prepared a heavenly army to save these people." Dumitru saw a great army that was well armed and dressed in white. The man said, "This army will go to battle to save My chosen ones. Then, the difference between the Godly and the ungodly will be evident." [1221]

HENRY GRUVER

Gruver, an American evangelist and prayer walker, turned 73 in 2016.

The Prince Charles Vision – 2nd Vision, 1985 or '86

Henry's detailed second vision shows both America and England targeted by chemical weapons and a huge invading army. He was visited by an angel who instructed Henry to take his family in their van to a pull off on Highway 26 on Mt. Hood. He was to drive to Government Camp, Oregon staying on Highway 26 miles and drive exactly five miles to this pull off on the right.

After finding the pull off, they walked down a switchback trail into a canyon. Once at a clearing they were met by an English butler, dressed in a tuxedo with a white towel or napkin over his left arm. He greeted them as though they were expected and instructed them to follow. Before reaching the designated place Henry looked down from a ledge he saw five rows of chairs set up, 12 seats in each row in front of a stage or platform. By the chairs, he saw a senator he felt he knew and a 4-star general who he didn't recognize. When Henry and his family reached the duo, the butler introduced them and the general responded, "Yes, you are the one, and

the family, which we've been hearing about." [In other videos, Gruver says it's the general he knows, but not the senator.] The senator also greeted Henry, asked how he was and he thought *I guess I do know him.*

After chatting a bit, the butler announced, "You need to be seated; all of the guests have arrived and it is time to begin." Looking around Henry saw all the seats had filled. He didn't recognize anyone, nor could he remember them afterwards, just the senator and general. They sat with the senator on Henry's right and the general to his right. While still standing the general said something to the butler who pulled out a walkie-talkie, spoke into it and then he moved back to the clearing. Then they heard a tandem-rotor helicopter approach from behind and saw it carried a portable construction office on wheels painted in "United Nations blue", which was very gently set down. The cable releases and the chopper flies off.

The butler walked over to the office, unlatched the door and to Henry's astonishment out walked Great Britain's Prince Charles. While the butler stood at full attention Charles emerged wearing desert-tan shorts, a short sleeve shirt and brown safari hat, wide-brimmed like British soldiers wore in Africa or the Middle East. Charles' face was red and puffy, and his eyes were red like he'd been crying and Henry wondered why he was so distressed.

As Charles approached, everyone rose. He looked at Henry, came towards him saying, "You are the family I have heard about. Thank you for coming; you are here today by my request. I have a message for you. Please be seated."

He then spoke a little with the general who nodded. Charles walked back to the microphone and said, "Thank you all for coming today. I have a message for you; please take heed. I must inform you your nation is at war, and that you have a battle to fight; but the saddest thing is, is that you must fight it without God."

The general behind him took exception to this statement, got up in Charles' face and said sarcastically, "We know we are at war. We know we have a battle to fight; but we did not know *God* had anything to do with it!" Prince Charles reacted by pointing his right finger between the general's eyes and responded with clipped authority, "And sir, *that* is your mistake!" As the argument progressed, the audience listened attentively.

Suddenly in Henry's peripheral vision to the left he saw an enormous, house-sized frog. **NOTE**: In scripture, frogs normally symbolize judgment. See Exodus 8:2 and Psalm 105:30.

The motion that had caught Henry's attention was the frog getting ready to fill its air sac. Utter terror filled him and he wanted to shout, *"Let's get out of here! If that thing opens its mouth, one lap of the tongue and my family will be gone!"* He refrained because he didn't want to interrupt Charles and the general. He looked back and forth between the frog, the general and the people. All were oblivious. Henry looked back to the

frog and saw its head tilt backwards preparing to croak. He saw its air sac fill and turn yellowish. He leaned toward his family and said, *"If that frog opens its mouth and croaks, we're all dead!"* Still no one paid attention to the frog. Right then the frog opened its mouth. Instead of a croaking sound white smoke billowed out enveloping Charles and the general. It was just about to hit Henry's wife when the scene changed.

Henry was immediately swept up into the heavens looking down on Earth. A huge square appeared much like Trafalgar Square in London. In Henry's vision its famous four colossal lions, fountains and statue of Lord Nelson were absent. It was empty but surrounded by lots of buildings housing government offices, commerce, churches, libraries and museums. He thought of Trafalgar Square because it was a representation of the British Empire in its glory encompassing everything to run an empire.

People started running of out of these buildings into the open square wearing the clothes and uniforms of their occupation. He saw a nurse with her nurse's hat on and a doctor with a stethoscope around his neck. A welder wore his leather apron and goggle type hat and a military man dressed in uniform. Whatever this event is caught them and they ran out, fully aware. They ran into the middle of the square and pointed up into the sky on Henry's left where the frog was. They laughed mockingly and jeered, "You can't hurt us. We're not afraid of you. You don't have any power any more!"

Then Henry's eye caught sight of the army stretching clear into the heavens to the height from where he watched. The massive army, which numbered into the hundreds of thousands was armed and stood at attention. As Henry watched the troops, he noticed to his immediate left and at his same level, the army's commanding general. He was an impressive sight in a full-dress military uniform adorned with gold braid and many decorations on his chest.

Hearing the mockery, Henry thought, *No! No! Don't say that!* The same terror swept over him as when he saw the frog. The general became furious at their laughing and jeering. As he clenched his fist, his face turned red. Rage was obvious as his neck muscles bulged and his body shook. Raising his arm, he barked out orders. "Present arms! Aim! Fire!" This massive army of footmen had jumped down to the level of the people in The Square. They were in full chemical warfare gear.

Henry said he didn't learn what they were wearing until a man came back from maneuvers in Afghanistan. Upon hearing the description, he said, "Henry, you have perfectly described the Russian chemical warfare uniform. He said, "I didn't even know they had that kind of uniform till I went over there myself and saw it. We didn't even have pictures to training for these because this is the latest of gear they have. Your description of their chests looking like a ribbed locust in the desert, that's what they looked like. Their faces kinda look like a horse, in a way, and they have big googly eyes. He explained to me that the googly eyes are like goggles of their head covering. Their snoot that looks like a horse has a pre-filtration system, a breathing apparatus that goes back down into the ribbed-looking chest that has multiple filtration systems. That is the most advanced chemical weapons gear you can get on the face of the earth. We didn't have anything to match it. They fired chemicals across and some of my men got into those chemicals and their chemical warfare gear began to melt right off them. I don't know what kind of material they had, but we'd better find out. From that time on, I was scared to death over there. One blast of this vapor could wipe out my whole platoon."

As they fired the first on these people in The Square, Henry said he believed that he witnessed something he believes we're being prepared for today. **It totally caught these people by surprise.** They sincerely with their whole heart did not believe that that massive military had any power and they did not believe that they would fire on them. They were caught by total surprise and total panic. They were totally surprised even though they knew the army existed. [Sound familiar?][1222]

In another recounting of this vision, Henry also described the general as looking like Alexander Lebed, a Russian general with bushy eyebrows and black hair who commanded during the Afghan war. He held in his right hand an enormous rectangular weapon full of cylindrical holes. Once again he commanded, "Fire!" Something akin to lightning shot from the holes and across the heavens.

Henry's attention drew back to The Square. He heard gunfire roaring and thunder coming from the light beams that shot through the heavens. People ran back and forth in The Square, screaming. Henry thought it odd that even though he could hear bullets thudding into their bodies and see their clothes pierced, no one fell. The surrounding buildings, vehicles and every tangible thing around The Square disappeared or turned to dust and fell to the ground. With that, the vision finished. **NOTE**: Lebed died in Siberia, 2002, at the age of 52 in a mysterious helicopter crash. Supposedly the chopper went down with its 20 passengers and crew when it became entangled in power lines.[1223] General Lebed is recognized for revealing the existence of suitcase nukes developed by the KGB (now the FSB). Lebed told Congress in 1997 that after the Soviet Union dissolved, they were unable to account for

48 of the 132 devices and they carried 1 kiloton of explosives, the equivalent of 1000 tons of TNT.[1224] Soon after Russia viewed Lebed as a political liability. Maybe they "took care of" that liability with the chopper crash. General Vladimir Dvorkin, too, confirmed the existence of suitcase nukes in 1999 on a PBS special[1225] as well as by former Russian military intelligence officer Stanislav Lunev in 1998.[1226] It's rumored that those portable nukes were sneaked into the U.S. years ago and secondarily, that Muslim extremists may have acquired some on the black market. Regardless, any such device built in the early 90s would have a dead battery by now. Supposing they could be refurbished, people would have to understand how to bypass safeguards and anti-tampering devices. According to the Federation of American Scientists, a 1-kiloton blast set off from a low-flying airplane would level most of the buildings in a crowded city spreading lethal radiation in a half-mile radius. Detonated in Lower Manhattan, causalities could reach 200,000.[1227]

Henry Gruver – Russian Invasion of America

He shares: I went up the Eagle Tower and later I only learned it as Eagle Tower. When I got to the top of it, it had 8 kinds of knobby-looking things aiming in 8 different directions, north, south, east, west and in between. I kind of looked at them and they were in these notches where you could fire arrows out from and I was standing there looking out over the island of Anglesey.

All of a sudden, in this vision I was shot up into the heavens and looking down on Earth like you would look at a satellite picture. You see that every time you see the weather. It looked so much similar and I had supernatural vision. I looked down and I saw a massive military movement coming out of the Icelandic waters above Iceland. I couldn't believe my eyes in what I saw. I saw this massive military movement coming out of the here [pointing on a map]. It came in between the United States and Europe. It was marine and air as you can see the airplanes.

This was my first confirmation in the sense from General Walker. General Walker has given me many confirmations. This was my first picture of an assault taking place. It also shows the movement coming out of Europe to take these countries. NATO command center is right in here [pointing on a map]. You're looking at some very serious fronts that Russia has been building. This massive military movement down between the United States and Europe troubled me as I'm watching it so then I looked off across at the United States because I wondered if they were doing that [large movement] across the Atlantic what are they doing on the United States. That's too big to be just a maneuver.

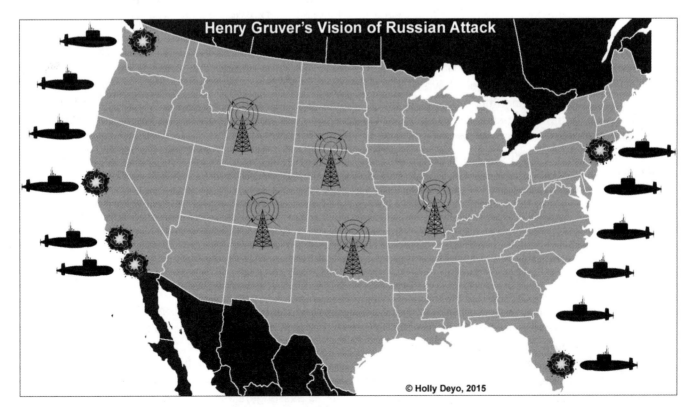

Henry Gruver's Vision of Russian Attack

© Holly Deyo, 2015

I looked down and as I looked at the United States I first saw the Atlantic seaboard, the eastern seaboard and I saw these submarines that looked like they were parked right along our beaches all along the East Coast.

What I mean by "all along the beaches" is the sand. If you fly and look down in the ocean, at the clear water in the ocean, you will see the point where the beaches begin and the white sands begin to turn darker. You can see the edge of the beach so to speak – the sand where it's washed back into the sea. They were parked with their hulls right at that point where the sand was beginning to discolor and the floor of the ocean was coming through.

I couldn't believe my eyes. They were all along there. So I looked because at the time we lived in Portland, Oregon so I looked off across toward Portland, Oregon. I saw the submarines along the Pacific Coast. I looked all the way down to San Diego and they were all along our coasts. As I was looking down toward San Diego, all of a sudden I saw motion all across the United States. These radio towers, it was like they were coming out of the ground and going up into the air and they were dotting their lines out like they were broadcasting. I was made to know that they were sounding the alarm. But as they were beginning to sound the alarm, all of a sudden the broadcasting signals went out and sprinkled to the ground like dust. I was made totally aware in the vision that their warning was not getting through.

I shouted in the Heavens and I said, " Oh no! Lord, the warning isn't getting through. They won't even know what hit 'em!" As I said that, all of a sudden the first missile fired out of a submarine. It went up and hit right over New York City. I watched that city literally disintegrate into the atmosphere as that massive explosion took place. I mean it was gone, folks. There'll be nothing left of that city. Then all of a sudden I looked down along the coast and I would say about where Miami, Florida would be… I told them this down there [Florida] last night and they weren't too happy to hear that. And Miami disappears…

Then all of a sudden because I was seeing this here, I looked away then so I don't know if there were more explosions that took place between those two along the coastal area. I didn't see it. My concern was over toward Oregon again because my family was in Portland at that time. As I was looking over toward Portland I saw another explosion. It looked like it was in the area of Seattle, Bellevue. That area went up just like New York and Miami. Then all of a sudden I looked down and here's another one was going off. It looked like the San Francisco area. Then down just to about Los Angeles and then San Diego. I saw those six nuclear-looking explosions and I tell you, they literally devastated everything. Whatever was in their path, it went into the Heavens. In the Russian invasion vision, I saw that massive military… I saw them hitting on the Nation, I saw them hitting the coasts and pounding them.

Then all of a sudden I was down on the Eagle Tower looking down at the village – automatic because that was the position I was looking from the Heavens. I watched the village, the cars were going normal speed, people were walking, talking normal. I thought, and I don't know how long I stood there and watched thinking, well, are the alarms going to go off at any minute? If this is happening in the United States, they've got to know it, got to sound the alarms if there's that kind of military going down across the Atlantic, there's got to be some kind of alarms set off. No alarm went off.

So I began to settle in on the understanding and I uttered these words. "Oh God, if this has not happened, then what will be the sign of it happening and of its time?" Those were my words standing there. As I spoke these words, words were spoken very clearly back to me.

"December 14th, 1986 when Russia opens her gates and lets the masses go, the free world will occupy themselves with transporting, housing, and caring for the masses. We'll begin to let our weapons down crying 'peace and safety'. And that's when it will happen."[1228]

Astoria, Washington Vision

In Henry's February 1980 "night vision", he was called to a ship at the port of Astoria, Washington where the Columbia River flows into the Pacific Ocean. In this vision I was standing on the bridge. That's where the wheel is where they steer it with a captain I believe was from the Philippines, Captain Estacion, of the *Atlantic Pioneer*. I was standing on the bridge and we were talking. All of sudden I glanced out over the inlet to the Columbia River and I saw all of these ships coming in loaded with troops. I was watching the troops ships go right around the ship we were on as though they didn't even see it. They didn't fire one shot at the men on the decks. The crew was down there walking around. They didn't fire any shots and I thought, "This is interesting," watching this phenomena when all of a sudden I began to see them coming up to the docks and where there were no ladders, they threw these hook ladders up and troops began climbing up onto the ports and anybody they saw, they shot them. We're watching this and all of a sudden the captain says, "Your Nation is under siege." I said, "Yes it is, but look this. This is different."

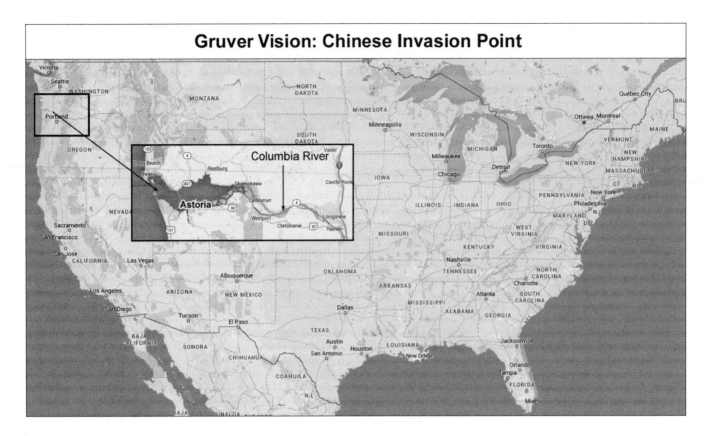

Gruver Vision: Chinese Invasion Point

About that time we were looking over the bow of the ship and out from under the docks came these WWII vintage planes. American planes with the star on them and the American flag. I believe that's very significant in today's world. You will be able to understand a little more regarding while it would be WWII-type planes. I don't understand the coming out from under the docks, but I believe God was showing me many things in this vision. They were going up into the air and firing on the motherships that all of these troop carriers were coming out of.

I saw of couple of them hit and go down. I watched this war literally take place. I hear the screams of the people of the city of Astoria as these troops are running through the streets and ousting people from their houses and just shooting them. I don't see anybody, any military coming to return fire. It's as though we have no defense. I'm looking at these troops I realize these are Chinese. What are they doing here? That was the end of the vision when I realized they were Chinese.[1229]

A. A. ALLEN

In 1954 Pentecostal Evangelical and faith healer witnessed Russia destroy America. He saw Russians invade the U.S. and launch a nerve gas attack across major portions of America's heartland. Then Russia attacked America on both coasts with nukes.

Allen's vision began from the perspective of standing on top of the Empire State Building, looking at the Statue of Liberty – the gateway to the world. The Lord spread out a huge animated map. He heard a voice he knew instinctively that it came from the Lord saying, *For the eyes of the Lord run to and fro throughout the whole earth, to show Himself strong on behalf of those whose heart is loyal to Him. In this you have done foolishly; therefore from now on you shall have wars.* —2 Chronicles 16:9 (NKJV)

He looked through one of the telescopes on Liberty and saw much farther than he should have been able to. Instead of seeing Liberty in the Jersey Bay, he saw her situated much further south in the Gulf of Mexico. He could see the U.S. like it had been compressed through the eye of the scope: Seattle and Portland far to the Northwest. Down the West Coast lay San Francisco and Los Angeles. New Orleans was closer, at the center of the Gulf Coast area. To the West were the great towering ranges of the Rocky Mountains and the Continental Divide. A giant hand reached out, probably like that in Stephen King's *The Stand*. It reached toward Liberty and her torch was ripped away, replaced by a cup. From that cup came a brilliantly shining sword, a sharp, glistening, dangerous sword that seemed to threaten the world. He heard that great voice again, this time saying, "Thus saith the Lord of hosts, Drink ye and be drunken, spew and fall, and rise no more, because of the sword which I will send."

350

The mighty hand forced Liberty to drink every drop from the cup and Allen knew it was punishment. He said, "I knew that the sword merely typified war, death, and destruction, which is no doubt on the way. Then as one drunken on too much wine, I saw the Statue of Liberty become unsteady on her feet and begin to stagger, and to lose her balance. I saw her splashing in the Gulf, trying to regain her balance. I saw her stagger again and again, and fall to her knees. As I saw her desperate attempts to regain her balance, and rise to her feet again, my heart was moved as never before with compassion for her struggles. But as she staggered there in the Gulf, once again I heard these words, 'Ye shall drink and be drunken, and spew, and fall, and rise no more because of the sword that I shall send among you.'"

Allen's horrible vision didn't end there. As he watched a huge black cloud arose and took the shape of an enormous skull. The dark figure was complete down to its waist finishing with two black arms and hands. Its eerie blackness was broken only by unholy white eye sockets and a mouth hole. The figure bent at the waist toward, skirting Canada and stretched one hand toward the East and one toward the West, one toward New York and one toward Seattle. That horrible black cloud had one interest – to destroy multitudes.

The skeleton, with its arms around America began to blow white vapor toward New York City until it covered all of the eastern part of the U.S. Then it turned its attention west and blew that same vapor from its nose and mouth covering the entire West Coast and Los Angeles. The skeleton blew out a third vapor aimed at America's mid-section enveloping St. Louis, Kansas City and New Orleans. Liberty reeled and staggered as the vapors engulfed her. Allen could see she was in great pain, in mortal agony as he described it. She gave one final cough, and made a last desperate effort to rise from her knees, and then fell face forward into the Gulf waters.

The nightmare vision didn't end there. Millions of people fell screaming and moaning in the streets and on the sidewalks. They coughed as though their lungs were on fire. Above the agony he heard these words: *A noise will come to the ends of the earth, for the Lord has a controversy with the nations. He will plead His case with all flesh. He will give those who are wicked to the sword, says the Lord. Thus says the Lord of hosts: "Behold, disaster shall go forth from nation to nation, and a great whirlwind shall be raised up from the farthest parts of the earth. And at that day the slain of the Lord shall be from one end of the earth even to the other end of the earth. They shall not be lamented, or gathered, or buried; they shall become refuse on the ground.* —Jeremiah 25:31-33 (NKJV)

Suddenly from the Atlantic and Pacific, and the Gulf, rocket-like objects came up out of the water and shot high into the air. Each headed in a different direction, but all targeted the U.S. What appeared to Allen were interceptors, but they weren't able to take out the ocean rockets. The rockets exploded simultaneously producing massive fireballs, which he likened to an H-bomb he'd seen detonate in the South Pacific. Then it was over.[1230]

NOTE: Boris Yeltsin signed the international Chemical Weapons Convention agreement in January 1993, even though it didn't go into effect until December 1997. Much doubt exists that Russia abided by it. The London *Sunday Times* reported in 1994 that Russia had developed a new "superplague powder" so lethal that 440 pounds sprayed from an airplane or dispersed in air burst bombs could kill 500,000 people. At the time of the article the West had no antidote.[1231] Of all the countries in the world, only four haven't signed the CC agreement as of the close of 2015: Egypt, South Sudan, North Korea and Israel. Though Syria signed, nearly 60 attacks have been launched against their people using chlorine, mustard, Sarin and BZ.[1232] Likely accessing the Syrian army stockpile – said to be one of the world's largest – Islamic State and the Syrian government have been confirmed to use these in the civil war. Though reports say these chemical attacks continued at least through August 2015, between March and August 2013 nearly 1,500 Syrians had been gassed, including over 400 children. It's not known what the real number of nerve gas deaths is at present. Rafael Foley, part of Organization for the Prohibition of Chemical Weapons said that "The sad reality is that chemical weapons use is becoming routine in the Syrian civil war."[1233] Alarmingly diplomatic sources said it's possible that Islamic State had gained the ability to make it.

Chapter 17: One World Government, One World Economy and One World Religion

Then I stood on the sand of the sea. And I saw a beast rising up out of the sea, having seven heads and ten horns, and on his horns ten crowns, and on his heads a blasphemous name. Now the beast which I saw was like a leopard, his feet were like the feet of a bear, and his mouth like the mouth of a lion. The dragon gave him his power, his throne, and great authority. And I saw one of his heads as if it had been mortally wounded, and his deadly wound was healed. And all the world marveled and followed the beast. So they worshiped the dragon who gave authority to the beast; and they worshiped the beast, saying, "Who is like the beast? Who is able to make war with him?"

And he was given a mouth speaking great things and blasphemies, and he was given authority to continue for forty-two months. Then he opened his mouth in blasphemy against God, to blaspheme His name, His tabernacle, and those who dwell in heaven. It was granted to him to make war with the saints and to overcome them. And authority was given him over every tribe, tongue, and nation. All who dwell on the earth will worship him, whose names have not been written in the Book of Life of the Lamb slain from the foundation of the world.

If anyone has an ear, let him hear. He who leads into captivity shall go into captivity; he who kills with the sword must be killed with the sword. Here is the patience and the faith of the saints.

Then I saw another beast coming up out of the earth, and he had two horns like a lamb and spoke like a dragon. And he exercises all the authority of the first beast in his presence, and causes the earth and those who dwell in it to worship the first beast, whose deadly wound was healed. He performs great signs, so that he even makes fire come down from heaven on the earth in the sight of men. And he deceives those who dwell on the earth by those signs which he was granted to do in the sight of the beast, telling those who dwell on the earth to make an image to the beast who was wounded by the sword and lived. He was granted power to give breath to the image of the beast, that the image of the beast should both speak and cause as many as would not worship the image of the beast to be killed. He causes all, both small and great, rich and poor, free and slave, to receive a mark on their right hand or on their foreheads, and that no one may buy or sell except one who has the mark or the name of the beast, or the number of his name.

Here is wisdom. Let him who has understanding calculate the number of the beast, for it is the number of a man: His number is 666. —Revelation 13:1-18 (NKJV)

"Thus the angel said, 'The fourth beast shall be a fourth kingdom on earth, which will be different from all other kingdoms and will devour the whole earth and tread it down, and crush it. As for the ten horns, out of this kingdom ten kings will arise; and another will arise after them, and he will be different from the former ones, and he will subdue three kings. He will speak words against the Most High [God] and wear down the saints of the Most High, and he will intend to change the times and the law; and they will be given into his hand for a time, [two] times, and half a time [three and one-half years]. —Daniel 7:23-25 (AMP)

A Different World Coming

The Bible doesn't use the phrases "one-world government" or "one-world currency", but provides plenty of evidence to accurately draw these conclusions. It warns that both of these things will come to pass under the Antichrist. By combining Daniel's vision with John's from Revelation, it's clear that a one world government will be implemented by the Antichrist, the most powerful "horn" or king who will defeat the nine other rulers.

It's hard to imagine that every other country – especially those enjoying first-world status – would willingly place itself under a single person's control. Maybe a global catastrophe takes place so monumental that people beg for relief in any form and from any source. Regardless the Antichrist will either crush these nine other regions or reduce leaders to mere figureheads. Enter global government. He commands them under an iron rule including all commerce, which is how

the idea of a one-world currency emerges. By controlling all commerce, "the mark" is instituted that allows people to work, buy food, clothing, pay their bills, utilities and mortgages – literally everything. Maybe it will begin under the auspices of the UN. Maybe not.

World Notables Promoting the New World Order

Bill Gates, founder of Microsoft and one the world's richest men, says that both the UN and NATO have failed miserably. Gates told the *Huffington Post* in January 2015 that the world "badly needed" **global government**. *"Take the UN, it has been created especially for the security in the world. We are ready for war, because we have taken every precaution. We have NATO, we have divisions, jeeps, trained people. But what is with epidemics? How many doctors do we have as much planes, tents, what scientists? If there were such a thing as **a world government**, we would be better prepared."*[1234]

Gates isn't the only one touting the New World Order. While George Herbert Walker Bush is considered the "father" of the New World Order, its formulation began decades before and its push hasn't stopped. World leaders and members of the elite all stump for the same transition.

George H.W. Bush, 41st President of the U.S, January 29, 1991: *"We are Americans, part of something larger than ourselves. … What is at stake is more than one small country; it is a big idea: **a new world order**, where diverse nations are drawn together in common cause to achieve the universal aspirations of mankind – peace and security, freedom, and the rule of law. Such is a world worthy of our struggle and worthy of our children's future…. The world can, therefore, seize this opportunity to fulfill the long-held promise of **a new world order**."*[1235]

George H.W. Bush, January 16, 1991: *"If we do not follow the dictates of our inner moral compass and stand up for human life, then his lawlessness will threaten the peace and democracy of the emerging **new world order** we now see, this long dreamed-of vision we've all worked toward for so long."*[1236]

George H.W. Bush, March 6, 1991: *"Now, we can see a new world coming into view. A world in which there is the very real prospect of **a new world order**. In the words of Winston Churchill, **a world order** in which 'the principles of justice and fair play protect the weak against the strong. …' A world where the United Nations, freed from cold war stalemate, is poised to fulfill the historic vision of its founders. A world in which freedom and respect for human rights find a home among all nations. The Gulf War put this new world to its first test. And my fellow Americans, we passed that test. … Even **the new world order** cannot guarantee an era of perpetual peace. But enduring peace must be our mission. Our success in the Gulf will shape not only **the new world order** we seek but our mission here at home."*[1237]

George H.W. Bush, September 11, 1990: *"A new partnership of nations has begun. ... Out of these troubled times, our fifth objective – **a new world order** – can emerge: a new era – freer from the threat of terror, stronger in the pursuit of justice, and more secure in the quest for peace. ... Today that new world is struggling to be born, a world quite different from the one we've known. A world where the rule of law supplants the rule of the jungle. A world in which nations recognize the shared responsibility for freedom and justice. Once again, Americans have stepped forward to share a tearful goodbye with their families before leaving for a strange and distant shore. At this very moment, they serve together with Arabs, Europeans, Asians, and Africans in defense of principle and the dream of a **new world order**.*"[1238]

Jimmy Carter, 39th President of the United States, July 29, 1977: *"This Voyager spacecraft was constructed by the United States of America. We are a community of 240 million human beings among the more than 4 billion who inhabit the planet Earth. We human beings are still divided into nation states, but these states are rapidly becoming **a single global civilization**.*"[1239]

Barack Hussein Obama, 44th President of the U.S. July 22, 2014: *"Part of peoples' concern is just the sense that around the world the old order isn't holding and we're not quite yet to where we need to be in terms of **a new order** that's based on a different set of principles...*"[1240]

Barack Hussein Obama, April 5, 2009: *"All nations must come together to build a stronger **global regime**.*"[1241]

Joe Biden, VP under Barack Obama, April 5, 2013: *"The affirmative task we have now is to actually create **a new world order**, because the global order is changing again, and the institutions of the world worked so well in the post-World War II era for decades, they need to be strengthened, and some need to be changed.*"[1242]

Joe Biden, May 29, 2014: *"I believe we, and mainly you [Air Force Academy Cadets], have an incredible opportunity to lead in shaping **a new world order** for the twenty-first century in a way consistent with American interests and common interests. ... There was an overwhelming desire of our grandparents and my parent's generation to bring home every single one of the 12 million forces stationed in Europe and Asia. They knew they had to lay a foundation for **a new world order**, an order that brought the longest period of sustained and peace in Europe and Asia.*"[1243]

Joe Biden, August 24, 2008: *"Collective security today must encompass not only the security of nations, but also mankind's security in a global environment that has proven vulnerable to debilitating changes wrought by man's own endeavors. Thus, in setting an American agenda for **a new world order**, we must begin with a profound alteration in traditional thought.*"[1244]

Joe Biden, "How I Learned to Love the **New World Order**", article penned by Biden published in the *Wall Street Journal*, April 23, 1992.   Then he was Chairman of the Senate Foreign Relations European Affairs Committee.[1245]

Strobe Talbott, Deputy Secretary of State under President Bill Clinton, July 20, 1992: *"In the next century, nations as we know it will be obsolete; all states will recognize **a single, global authority**. National sovereignty wasn't such a great idea after all.*"[1246]

Al Gore, former Vice President under Bill Clinton and global warming activist, July 3, 2009: *"It is the awareness itself that will drive the change. And one of the ways it will drive the change is through **global governance** and global agreements.*"[1247]

Richard Nixon, 37th President of the U.S., 1967: *"The developing coherence of Asian regional thinking is reflected in a disposition to consider problems and loyalties in regional terms, and to evolve regional approaches to development needs and to the evolution of **a new world order**.*"[1248]

Richard Nixon, 1972: *"It is not our common beliefs that have brought us together here, but our common interest and our common hopes; the interest that each of us has to maintain our interdependence and the security of our people, and the hope that each of us has to build **a new world order**.*"[1249]

Walter Cronkite, legendary CBS news anchor, October 19, 1999: *"It seems to many of us that if we are to avoid the eventual catastrophic world conflict we must strengthen the United Nations as a first step toward **a world government** patterned after our own government with a legislature, executive and judiciary, and police to enforce its international laws and keep the peace. To do that, of course, we Americans will have to yield up some of our sovereignty. That would be a bitter pill. It would take a lot of courage, a lot of faith in **the new order**.*"[1250]

Gordon Brown, Prime Minister of the United Kingdom, October 22, 2011: *"I do not envisage **a new world** founded on the narrow and conventional idea of isolated states pursuing their own selfish interests. Instead, I see a* *world that harnesses for the common good the growing interdependence of nations, cultures, and peoples that makes a **true global society**."[1251]*

Gordon Brown, February 22, 2009: *"We need a global New Deal – **a grand bargain between the countries and continents of this world** – so that the world economy can not only recover but... so the banking system can be based on... best principles."[1252]*

Mahmoud Ahmadinejad, former president of Iran, July 1, 2010: *"Iran and Syria have a joint mission to create **a new world order** on the basis of justice, humanity and belief in God."[1253]*

Henry Kissinger, former National Security Adviser and Secretary of State under Presidents Nixon and Ford, on implementing the New World Order, August 29, 2014: *"The contemporary quest for **world order** will require a coherent strategy to establish a concept of order within the various regions and to relate these regional orders to one another. These goals are not necessarily self-reconciling... **A world order** of states affirming individual dignity and participatory governance, and cooperating internationally in accordance with agreed-upon rules, can be our hope and should be our inspiration. But progress toward it will need to be sustained through a series of intermediary stages. "My country's history, Mr. President, tells us that it is possible to fashion unity while cherishing diversity, that common action is possible despite the variety of races, interests, and beliefs we see here in this chamber. Progress and peace and justice are attainable. So we say to all peoples and governments: Let us fashion together **a new world order.**"[1254]*

Henry Kissinger, November 1, 2014: *"Kissinger describes four models of 'world order' extant: Europe's Westphalian model of nation-states with equal status; the U.S. model; China's notion of itself as a great regional power; and an Islamic system of believers and infidels. These parallel universes can find common ground only if a **'globalistic second culture and concept of order'** is created. The United States cannot lead, but is an indispensable agent for peace and diplomacy."[1255]*

Henry Kissinger, January 6, 2009: *"The president-elect [Obama] is coming into office at a moment when there is upheaval in many parts of the world simultaneously. You have India, Pakistan; you have the jihadist movement. So he can't really say there is one problem, that it's the most important one. But he can give new impetus to American foreign policy partly because the reception of him is so extraordinary around the world. His task will be to develop an overall strategy for America in this period when, really, **a new world order** can be created. It's a great opportunity, it isn't just a crisis."[1256]*

Henry Kissinger, January 12, 2009: *Kissinger warned that "the alternative to **a new international order** is chaos" in a New York Times piece opined about Obama becoming a key player. "The extraordinary impact of the president-elect on the imagination of humanity is an important element in shaping **a new world order**. ... The role of China in a new world order is equally crucial."[1257]*

David Rockefeller, Chair and CEO of Chase Manhattan, member of the Council on Foreign Relations, Bilderberg Group and Trilateral Commission, 2003: *"We have before us the opportunity to forge for ourselves and for future generations **a new world order**, a world where the rule of law, not the rule of the jungle, governs the conduct of nations. When we are successful, and we will be, we have a real chance at this **new world order**, an order in which a credible United Nations can use its peacekeeping role to fulfill the promise and vision of the U.N.'s founders."[1258]*

Larry P. McDonald, former Rep. (D-GA): *"The drive of the Rockefellers and their allies is to create a **one-world government** combining supercapitalism and Communism under the same tent, all under their control. Do I mean a conspiracy? Yes, I do. I am convinced there is such a plot, international in scope, generations old in planning, incredibly evil in intent."[1259]*

Vladimir Putin, president of Russia: While Mr. Putin is more low-key in his comments his goal is obvious. He is achieving this much like Zbigniew Brzezinski observed in 1995 – slowly and regionally at first, then incorporating more areas. Alex Newman summarized, *"A crucial component of the **globalist new world order** is the eventual creation of truly global monetary and financial governance. On both fronts, Putin has helped lead the charge. In 2009, the Kremlin even published a statement outlining its priorities ahead of the G20 summit, demanding the creation of a "supranational reserve currency to be issued by international institutions as part of a reform of the global financial system." The IMF, the Kremlin statement said, should consider using its proto-global currency known as 'Special Drawing Rights,' or SDRs, as a 'super-reserve currency accepted by the whole of the international community.' The basket of national currencies undergirding the SDR would be expanded, too. The same year, Putin protege Dmitry Medvedev, then serving as Russia's 'president,' pulled what he called a '**united***

future world currency' coin out of his pocket at a G8 summit. The coin featured the words 'unity in diversity.' Then, he explained to the audience that it 'means they're getting ready.'"[1260]

Mikhail Gorbachev, former president of the Soviet Union, October 19, 2011: *"We saw deterioration where there should have been positive movement toward **a new world order**."* —Addressing students at Lafayette College in Easton, PA, in a message entitled "Perspectives on Global Change."[1261]

Zbigniew Brzezinski, National Security Adviser to President Jimmy Carter, September 29, 1995: *"We do not have **a new world order**, we cannot leap into **world government** in one quick step."*[1262]

Jacques Chirac, former president of France, November 20, 2000: *"For the first time, humanity is instituting a genuine instrument of **global governance**. ... By acting together, by building this unprecedented instrument, the first component of an authentic **global governance**, we are working for dialogue and peace."*[1263]

Richard A. Falk, American professor emeritus of international law at Princeton University: *"The existing order is breaking down at a rapid rate and the main uncertainty is whether mankind can exert a positive role in shaping a **new world order**... We believe **a new order** will be born no later than early in the next century."*[1264]

Richard A. Falk, *"My overriding concern is to foster an abolitionist movement against war and aggression as social institutions, which implies the gradual construction of **a new world order** that assures basic human needs of all people, that safeguards the environment, that protects the fundamental human rights of all individuals and groups without encroaching upon the precarious resources of cultural diversity, and that works toward the non-violent resolution of intersocietal conflicts."*[1265]

George McGovern, U.S. Senator and Democratic Party presidential nominee in 1972 stated February 14, 1991: *"I would support a presidential candidate who pledged to take the following steps... At the end of the war in the Persian Gulf, press for a comprehensive Middle East settlement and for a **new world order** based not upon a Pax Americana, but on peace through law with a stronger U.N. and World Court."*[1266]

Robert Muller, former Assistant Secretary General of U.N. from Belgium: *"We must move as quickly as possible to a **one-world government, one-world religion, under a one-world leader.**"*[1267]

Robert Muller, written about him, November 21, 2008: *"Mr. Muller is very likely a very decent person, however, he is one of several who have pushed the **one world government** and **one world religion** agenda for many years and it is always a liberal humanist anti-theist agenda – oh yes, religion will be there but only a state-approved one. For such people, it is very simple: they reason that if you can get rid of religious differences there will be world peace."*[1268]

Pope John Paul II, January 1, 2004: *"More than ever, we need **a new international order** that draws on the experience and results achieved in these years by the United Nations. [It] would be able to provide solutions to the problems of today... based on the dignity of human beings, an integrated development of society, solidarity between rich and poor nations, and on the sharing of resources and the extraordinary results of scientific and technological progress."*[1269]

Pope Benedict XVI, November 10, 2010: *"...the pope sent words of encouragement to the leaders of the world's 20 advanced and emerging market nations who will get together in Seoul on Thursday and Friday to work out **a global financial roadmap**."* Pope Benedict XVI calls on G-20 nations to serve common global interests, November 10, 2010. —Letter to South Korean president Lee Myung-bak released by the Catholic Bishops' Conference of Korea[1270]

Pope Benedict XVI: *"One of his most senior advisers, cardinal Renato Martino, said: 'The encyclical is not asking for a super- or world government.' But it comes very close to doing so. It proposes a **'true world political authority'** that 'would need to be universally recognized and to be vested with the effective power to ensure security for all, regard for justice and respect for rights.' It would be asked to **'manage the global economy**; to revive economies hit by the crisis [and] to avoid any deterioration of the present crisis.'"*[1271]

Pope Benedict XVI: *"In the face of the unrelenting growth of global interdependence there is a strongly felt need even in the midst of a global recession... of **a true world political authority**. Furthermore, such an authority would need to be universally recognized and to be vested with the effective power to ensure security for all."*[1272]

Jorge Mario Bergoglio, now Pope Francis was introduced by *Time* as the new World Pope in their March 13, 2013 issue.[1273]

Pope Francis: During his visit to Ecuador on July 8, 2015, the pope gave an impassioned plea for *"**a new economic and ecological world order** where the goods of the Earth are shared by everyone."*[1274]

Pope Francis: Then in Bolivia the next day, he repeated his call for a **new economic order** and criticized Capitalism.[1275] Bolivia's Marxist leader, Evo Morales, presented the pope with a gift – a carved wooden hammer-and-sickle cross with the figure of a crucified Christ on it.

Pope Francis: While he didn't utter the words "a new world order" in this instance, he said something very telling on February 18, 2016. "A person who thinks only about building walls, wherever they may be, and not building bridges, is not Christian."[1276] The Pope's remarks were in response to Presidential candidate Donald Trump's promise, that if elected, he would build the desperately needed border wall between the U.S. and Mexico. Trump responded, "For a religious leader to question a person's faith is disgraceful. If and when the Vatican is attacked by ISIS, which, as everyone knows, is ISIS' ultimate trophy, I can promise you that the pope would have only wished and prayed that Donald Trump would have been President."[1277] Trump also commented that for someone who didn't think the border wall should be built that the pope has a mighty big wall around the Vatican. Maybe he hasn't heard the old proverb, "Good fences make good neighbors."

Image: Screen snap of the nearly 2-mile, 40-foot high wall surrounding Vatican City. One Catholic who visited the sovereign state described it as a "literal fortress."[1278]

According to *New York Times* quoting Gerard Mannion, professor of Catholic Studies at Georgetown University, "There are, to be sure, formidable walls in Vatican City, and much of the site, including the gardens and the modest guesthouse that is home to Francis, is set behind them. ... Some of the walls in Vatican City were built in the ninth century by Pope Leo IV in an attempt to protect it from attacks by pirates and other marauders, historians said. But other stretches of wall were built during the 15th and 16th centuries less as a defensive measure and more as 'a political and cultural statement' about the cultural and political power of the pope."[1279] How is this any different than America wishing to protect herself?

To further drive the point home, the pope gave a mass the day before just across the border from El Paso, Texas in Juarez – a huge point of entry for illegal aliens. The mass was for all the migrants who died while trying to enter America illegally. Within his speech was a tacit criticism for not opening wide our borders.

In order for the New World Order to be implemented, America must be taken out. This can be done bit by bit or with a huge hammer coming down like an EMP, a dollar collapse or civil war. The slower process would be to remove America from Super Power status by throwing open our borders to every immigrant that wants entry. When this happens it overburdens our schools, hospitals, entitlements, muddies our culture and takes jobs that Americans need. This is in progress as you read this.

In February 2016, Mr. Obama gave the "stand down" order to Border Patrol agents. This new federal directive forces agents to release most illegal immigrants they arrest and bans ordering them to return for deportation hearings.

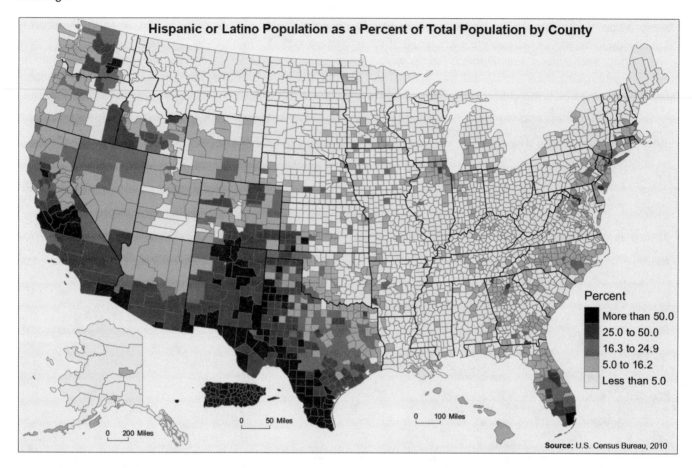

Image: This map, produced by the U.S. Census Bureau, uses data from the 2010 census. Between then and 2016, Mr. Obama has backed sanctuary cities, refused to enforce immigration laws already on the books and worst of all, threw open the doors to illegal immigrants in February 2016. Six years after these data were compiled many of the counties would likely have their percentages shoved higher in light of the President's immigration policies. Not only is the word out in other countries that no illegal immigration laws are enforced now, but would-be illegals worry that when a new President is elected, their opportunities to sneak across the border will diminish.

It's no coincidence that states bordering Mexico have the highest percentage of Hispanics and Latinos and with that, we are well on the way to becoming Mexamerica – just what the New World Order prescribed.

Brandon Judd, president of the National Border Patrol Council, testified before the House Subcommittee on Immigration and Border Security February 2nd. "Immigration laws today appear to be mere suggestions, there are little-to-no consequences for breaking the laws and that fact is well known in other countries."[1280]

Arizona and Texas have 11 border posts though three aren't even operational. Inspector General officials for Homeland Security visited seven in 2015. They questioned 14 employees working in the Tucson Sector. Ten admitted the manual gate was "repeatedly left open." Time and time again they asked that broken security cameras be fixed. The first request came in January 2013. Nothing was done. The second request was made in August 2014. That request too, was ignored because somebody had marked the work order "closed". The problem still wasn't fixed in April 2015 when the inspectors arrived. So it seems there is a concerted effort to make illegals' attempts to "c'mon over" much easier.

NO PURGE FOR THE SURGE

Illegal immigrants know their time may be short depending on who is elected next as President. Several candidates have promised to secure the border, build that fence. How many times have Americans heard that before? Because the next President *might* do something, another surge of illegals began in earnest in 2015. In just the two months of November and December there was a 173% increase in detentions compared to the same time in 2014.

A repeat of this was seen after Obama renewed diplomatic relations with Cuba. The last three months of 2015 saw a dramatic surge in Cubans coming here illegally, too. By year's end 2015 showed an 84% increase over the year before. This doesn't include the more than 20,000 Cubans admitted legally every year or those that overstay tourist visas. "Many have cited a bleak Cuban economy and said they feared the U.S. would soon revoke their special status, which generally allows them to stay, *with benefits,* once they arrive in the U.S."[1281]

So many are coming through the border from Central American countries the government has plans to open five new shelters in Colorado, Florida and New Mexico. This is in addition to the one opened outside Dallas in December 2015. The site in Lakewood, Colorado was scrapped in February 2016 because just that one facility would have cost between $28 and $37 million.[1282]

When Gil Kerlikowske, commissioner of U.S. Customs and Border Protection, admits that illegal aliens sneaking through our borders may be "the new normal", this has to be by design. Bob Goodlatte (R-VA), "The word is, come on ahead and the border is open, the Obama administration is going to take good care of you."[1283]

Carl Gallups, author and pastor of Hickory Hammock Baptist Church had this to say about the pope's comments. "Why is the pope so concerned about America's borders, immigration laws and citizenship requirements when it is a known fact that the Vatican has one of the highest border walls, some of the world's strictest immigration laws and some of the most stringent citizenship requirements? I say the pope has no business in America's business – especially the business of border security and homeland defense. When America can tell the pope how to manage the borders of the Vatican, I would consider listening to his opinions about our laws."[1284] Gallups also cited scripture for the biblical mandate of national defense: "What about Israel's walls? What about Nehemiah's walls – and defending them with deadly weapons against the terrorists of his day?"[1285]

To Kill a Country

Global elites began actively infecting schools and universities with their anti-democracy rhetoric after Communism moved into churches in 1935. If God had remained at the center of the Country He blessed beyond description, their plan could never have succeeded.

Schools now offer "education lite" and practice Common Core that teaches students to pass tests, but not to think. Kids receive only *half* the taught material Baby Boomers did because the same lessons must be repeated in both English and Spanish.

Drugs are ever more present with recreational marijuana legal in Alaska, Colorado, Oregon and Washington, plus another 19 states are ready to board the pot train. Medical marijuana is legal in nearly half of the U.S.[1286] and the majority of Americans support it. Heroin is now epidemic in the U.S. because it's so much cheaper than prescribed painkillers.

Last, Americans have witnessed the grandest transfer of wealth in history from their wallets to big business, big pharma and big banks. Quantitative Easing 1, 2 and 3 did nothing to stimulate the economy. Instead of the money filtering throughout the Country, banks and transnational businesses kept it. American college teacher Paul Buchheit notes stunning details about this unfathomable wealth transfer:

- Since 2008's Great Recession, America's richest 1% gained $2.3 trillion to $5.7 trillion *every year.*[1287]
- Almost none of the 1 percent's wealth led to innovation or jobs.[1288]
- 10% of the world's combined wealth was taken by the global 1% in the past three years.[1289]
- In just three years, the world's top 1% grew their wealth from $100 trillion to $127 trillion.[1290]

So why are these comments focused on America? She's the leader in world democracy. Americans are independent, demand Constitutionally granted rights, are armed and feel very squeezed by their government. America is the last bastion between freedom and government strangulation. But she's in trouble. The Nation is broke with over one-third of the Country permanently out of work. In people's angst over whatever, many have turned to drugs even for a few hours escape. Our kids' and grandkids' education is on the skids. In tests that gauged 15-year-olds' skills in math and science, out of 76 countries, the U.S. ranked a woeful 28.[1291] It's no shocker Asian countries topped the list, but Canada, Australia, the UK, New Zealand and even the Czech Republic scored better. So did France, Estonia and Poland. At other end of the scale Qatar was nearly in the gutter. In short, we're being dumbed down and drugged out while the UN and Global Elites steal our Country and our wealth.

Agenda 2030, the Uglier Version of Agenda 21

America usually comes to the world's aid first when catastrophes strike. With the U.S. out of the way, too broke, corralled by global treaties or spread too thinly in world conflicts, other countries could fall or be forced to dance to the foul tune of Agenda 2030. Controlling America is a necessary requirement to implement One World Government. Part of that control is to remove America's firearms.

The UN and Global Elites – "gold-collar workers" – rule the world by tugging on the reins harnessed to every nation right down to individual bank accounts. They moved at a trot with Baby Boomers. Now they're at full gallop with dirt clods flying. Agenda 21 (indicating agenda for the 21st century) started with a world convention in Rio de Janeiro in 1992 where 179 nations signed off on the plan.

Then Earth Summit Secretary-General Maurice Strong opened the summit with this statement. "Current lifestyles and consumption patterns of the affluent middle class – involving high meat intake, the use of fossil fuels,

electrical appliances, home and work-place air-conditioning and suburban housing – are not sustainable."[1292] Environmental activist and attorney Daniel Sitarz spelled it out even more clearly. "Agenda 21 proposes an array of actions which are intended to be implemented by every person on Earth. Effective execution of Agenda 21 will require a profound reorientation of all human society unlike anything the world has ever experienced – *a major shift in the priorities of both governments and individuals and an unprecedented redeployment of human and financial resources.*"[1293]

Right on the summit's heels, in June 1993, President Clinton signed Executive Order 12852, which established the President's Council for Sustainable Development.

If you thought Agenda 21 was bad, you're going to hate Agenda 2030.

Agenda 21's goal when it was first introduced in 1992 primarily focused on the environment. Looking through the 351-page document, the word "sustainable" was a common thread. Implemented, we're seeing it through Federal land grabs, designated UN Biospheres and MAB Programs, and mounting onerous EPA regulations. The first sentence of its preamble set the theme for Agenda 2030:

"Humanity stands at a defining moment in history. We are confronted with a perpetuation of disparities between and within nations, a worsening of poverty, hunger, ill health and illiteracy, and the continuing deterioration of the ecosystems on which we depend for our wellbeing. However, integration of environment and development concerns and greater attention to them will lead to the fulfillment of basic needs, improved living standards for all, better protected and managed ecosystems and a safer, more prosperous future. No nation can achieve this on its own; but together we can – in a **global partnership** for **sustainable development.**"[1294]

Image: The MaB (Man and the Biosphere Program) acronym overlays a blue, green, white and red rainbow topped with an Egyptian ankh. The rainbow's four colors represent blue for water, green for forests and grassland, white for snow-covered mountains and red for deserts and dry lands. Beginning in 1970 the UN designated 651 such sites in 120 countries. Western nation locations make up nearly half of all Biosphere Reserves. Within these 311 sites are: Australia – 14, Canada – 16, Ireland – 2, UK – 5 and US – 47. The next highest contender is Russia with 41.

MaB is another UN program focusing on climate change, geared to put the environment before humanity. Legitimate concerns arise about how biosphere reserves operate regarding national sovereignty, the status of private property within these reserves, the amount of control the UN has over land management in biosphere reserves, and the effect BRs might have on the economy of neighboring communities. Interestingly, in the 34-country governing body, the UK is the only western nation included.

For the right of getting screwed, U.S. taxpayers "contributed" $3 billion to the UN in 2015 – more than 185 other countries combined.[1295] Every member nation (there are 193) pays a set percentage of whatever is the UN's budget for any given year. Most countries pay less than 1%. Top paying nations include:

> U.S. – 22% (plus 25% of the peacekeeping budget)
> Japan – 10.83%
> Germany – 7.14%
> France – 5.59%
> Britain – 5.18%
> China (with the second largest economy) – just 5.15%

Those last four permanent members, combined, still pay less than the U.S. at $2.5 billion. Second tier payers include:

> Italy – 4.45%
> Canada – 2.98%
> Spain – 2.97%
> Brazil – 2.93%
> Russia – 2.44%
> Australia – 2.07%[1296]

Something is *really* wrong here considering 56 countries of the Organization of Islamic Cooperation (OIC) – which include 10 of the world's 20 top oil-producing nations – will contribute *together,* not each, just $360 million.[1297]

NOTES ON THE UN: John D. Rockefeller donated the 18 acres where the UN buildings sit. If they had to purchase that land, adjusting for inflation today, it would exceed $107 million and that's not factoring in location, location, location. It's a fantastic property overlooking the East River, just a mile and a half from Central Park. In New York City, 18 acres would be priceless. On top of that donation and the nasty "contribution" America forks over to them every year, the U.S. loaned them $65 million interest-free to build it.[1298] In 2006 the Federal Reserve Bank of New York put a price tag of $2,100 a *square foot* on NYC's undeveloped property. In today's dollars that'd be a cool $1.6 billion, give or take.[1299] While the UN buildings sit on prime U.S. land, those 18 acres were deeded over in a treaty that gives them complete sovereignty. In exchange for the U.S. providing them local police, fire protection and other services, the UN agrees to acknowledge *most* local, state, and federal laws.[1300] How much is "most"? And because they agree to *acknowledge* our laws doesn't mean they respect or obey them. With all of these concessions, one has to wonder why we wanted the UN here so desperately.

THE AGENDA

In the UN's document "Transforming Our World: The 2030 Agenda for Sustainable Development," it sets out 17 Goals and 169 Targets to change the world. At first sniff, it smells pretty rosy. Who wouldn't want the world to be cleaner (that means you China) and every person have plenty of potable water and nutritious food and live in dignity. The equality-for-all dream. Yes, a dream. Since mankind populated Earth, it has never existed and never will, not until Jesus returns and sets the planet on the right course. Earth isn't Utopia; we're still stomping around in reality.

This isn't an endorsement to do nothing, but there's a whole lot of space between where the world is now and what the UN wants to achieve in its collective hallucination. Most of these "goals" involve more wealth redistribution, greater government control, relinquishing personal freedoms, giving away cultural and national identity, tearing down national borders and making the world a metaphoric "race of tan" a la New Ager T. Lobsang Rampa in his book, *Twilight*.

A lot of these unobtainable ambitions hinge on the Global Warming/Climate Change issue. Globalists unrelentingly hammer this lynchpin because it's a way to achieve global control and knock America down 42 pegs. The overall plan is to cram the most people onto the smallest amount of *designated* space, generally forsake owning automobiles and bike or hike to work, the grocery store, entertainment and hospitals. The sick and dying would take mass transit if still breathing and didn't have the decency to self-terminate. Yes, more countries are endorsing this.

It's hard to imagine what the UN attendees are breathing to think these goals and targets are remotely possible. That doesn't mean they won't try.

Goal 1. End poverty in all its forms everywhere

Goal 2. End hunger, achieve food security and improved nutrition and promote sustainable agriculture

Goal 3. Ensure healthy lives and promote well-being for all at all ages

Goal 4. Ensure inclusive and equitable quality education and promote lifelong learning opportunities for all

Goal 5. Achieve gender equality and empower all women and girls

Goal 6. Ensure availability and sustainable management of water and sanitation for all

Goal 7. Ensure access to affordable, reliable, sustainable and modern energy for all

Goal 8. Promote sustained, inclusive and sustainable economic growth, full and productive employment and decent work for all

Goal 9. Build resilient infrastructure, promote inclusive and sustainable industrialization and foster innovation

Goal 10. Reduce inequality within and among countries

Goal 11. Make cities and human settlements inclusive, safe, resilient and sustainable

Goal 12. Ensure sustainable consumption and production patterns

Goal 13. Take urgent action to combat climate change and its impacts, and acknowledge that the UN is the primary forum for negotiating global response

Goal 14. Conserve and sustainably use the oceans, seas and marine resources for sustainable development

Goal 15. Protect, restore and promote sustainable use of terrestrial ecosystems, sustainably manage forests, combat desertification, and halt and reverse land degradation and halt biodiversity loss

Goal 16. Promote peaceful and inclusive societies for sustainable development, provide access to justice for all and build effective, accountable and inclusive institutions at all levels

Goal 17. Strengthen the means of implementation and revitalize the global partnership for sustainable development[1301]

In fact, the plans are well underway. Put into a search engine your "town, state" along with "sustainable city" or contact your Board of County Commissioners. Don't be surprised if there's not already an entire website dedicated to it. Besides "sustainable development", when you see or hear phrases like these, know it's all about Agenda 2030:

- Affordable Housing
- Asset Mapping
- Biodiversity
- Bioregional
- Buffer Zones
- Cap and Trade
- Carbon Footprint
- Climate Change
- Common Good
- Community Engagement
- Community Visioning
- Compact City
- Complete Streets
- Comprehensive Land Use Plan
- Comprehensive Planning/Re-Zoning
- Conservation Easement
- Consumption Based Impact
- Cooperativeness
- Downsizing
- Eco-footprint
- Eco-village
- Ecocity
- Equity and Local Economy

- Livable Communities
- Local and Sustainable Food
- Mixed-Use Development
- Multi-family Buildings
- New Urbanism
- Non-Compete
- Non-Elected Boards
- One Planet Living
- Open Space
- Preservation Development
- Priority Development Areas
- Public-Private Partnerships
- Quality of Life
- Redevelopment Commissions
- Reduced Tenant Footprint
- Regional Visioning Projects
- Regionalism
- Resilient Cities
- Rewilding
- Sensitive Lands
- Small Footprint
- Smart Streets
- Smart Cities

- Endangered Species
- Environmental Impact
- Environmental Justice
- Green Code=House Modified
- Green/Alternative Projects
- Greenbelts
- Greener Developments
- Green Marketing
- Greenways
- Green Transport
- Growth Management
- Habitat
- Inclusive
- Integrated Design
- Smart Growth
- Stack and Pack Housing
- Sustainable Communities Initiative
- Sustainable Communities Strategies
- Sustainable Lifestyles
- Sustainable Development
- Sustainable Transport
- Sustainable Water
- Urban Growth Boundary
- Urban Intensification
- Walkable Cities
- Walkable Communities
- Wetlands
- Wildlands Project

Why so many names? J. Gary Lawrence, advisor to President Clinton's Council on Sustainable Development explained the subterfuge. "Participating in a UN advocated planning process would very likely bring out many of the conspiracy-fixated groups and individuals in our society... This segment of our society who fear 'one-world government' and a UN invasion of the United States through which our individual freedom would be stripped away would actively work to defeat any elected official who joined 'the conspiracy' by undertaking LA21 [Local Agenda 21]. So we call our process something else, such as comprehensive planning, growth management or smart growth."[1302]

EARTH FIRST

Think back how many nature and conservation shows have aired on TV in the last two decades. While captivating they are meant to soften viewers to the Earth First movement and now the plans are full throttle. Before 2015, previous attempts to pass climate change initiatives failed, but when Mr. Obama enacted a new string of EPA regulations, it paved the way.

Participating countries agreed it needed a $30 billion "push" to get the United Nations Paris Agreement launched. From 2010 to 2016, Mr. Obama had given over $2.5 billion to the initiative.[1303] Regardless of a global climate agreement, Mr. Obama "pushed" a lot on America. He cost taxpayers at least $10.5 billion investing in failed green energy companies.[1304]

On the global agreement because the President knew its costly and unrealistic goals would be met with rock-hard opposition, he performed another end-around Congress. Since the Senate must ratify foreign treaties Obama bypassed that legislative body. To this end Secretary of State John Kerry and other diplomats were charged with making sure it didn't qualify as a treaty.[1305] Outraged Senator Roy Blunt wrote "Just as we witnessed throughout recent negotiations with Iran and during the previous climate agreement with China, President Obama and his administration act as if Congress has no role in these discussions. That's just flat-out wrong."[1306]

Under Obama the EPA – Environmental Protection Agency – went completely out of control. In 2014 Mr. Obama's "war on coal" took center stage when the EPA tried to implement their Mercury and Air Toxics Standards (MATS) policy. It would have amounted to shutting down 300 coal-fired plants across America, closing coal mines and chopping over 125,000 jobs. The GAO, Government Accounting Office, calculated the EPA would be cutting off enough generated power to run 26 million homes. The issue landed in the Supreme Court and something very interesting, something unique took place in February 2016.

In a shocking first the Supreme Court (SCOTUS) granted a Stay of Request from 29 states and coal power plants after what they claim was "an unprecedented power grab" by the EPA. Here's what traditionally takes place.

After the EPA announces a new regulation, they take effect at the end of 30 days. If the rule is challenged it still stays in effect during ensuing litigation. The challengers took it to court and they ruled the new regs would stay in place. The challengers then took it to the Supreme Court, which did something it has never done in history. They told the lower court that it must prevent the EPA from enforcing its own new rules while they were being challenged. This happened because the last time the court overturned an EPA case, it cost the suing entities $10 billion to comply in the interim. Rather than make the power plants waste billions for a rule that will probably be thrown out anyway, the Supremes decided to bar enforcement of the regs during litigation. The bottom line is that the Supreme Court believes the EPA has gone way beyond what Congress intended to keep air clean at the expense of coal plants having to shut down. Judge Andrew Napolitano opined that since the EPA has been slapped down twice now on this issue by the Supremes, this part of Obama's "legacy" is doomed to failure.[1307]

Also in 2014, the EPA attempted "the greatest water grab that we have seen by the federal government in the United States," according to Rep. Scott Tipton.[1308] Instead of just controlling large bodies of water, they want to expand the rule to include streams, riverbanks, wetlands and floodplains. Cattle rancher Jack Field from Washington state said, "It sounds to me once that drop falls out of the sky it's under the EPA's jurisdiction."[1309] Tom Woods, a custom-home business owner worried this would mean costly delays while the EPA decided if a road ditch is considered part of the United States' water.

In 2015 the EPA initiated an unprecedented power grab implementing a rarely used section of the Clean Air Act called the Clean Power Plan. It requires every state to regulate how much power it produces, transmits and consumes. While in theory participation is somewhat voluntary, "strong encouragement" is offered including the threat of halting a significant portion of a state's ability to generate power. In practice, consumers could experience rolling brownouts or blackouts, which are one reason Smart Meters have been installed on nearly every home.

Of the Global Climate Change accord, legal or not, Mr. Kerry remarked, "The world has come together around an agreement that will empower us to chart a new path for our planet."[1310] This cemented another cog in the wheel of Agenda 2030. Still this wasn't enough. Lou Leonard, vice president for climate change policy with the conservation group World Wildlife Fund said, "In fact the U.S. must do more than just deliver on this pledge – the 28 percent domestic target can and must be a floor, not a ceiling."[1311]

Tiny Footprints

In lockstep is a program called Tiny House Nation. 2016 marked its third successful season. "There's a trend in the U.S. housing market, albeit a very small one. Drawn to the prospect of financial freedom, a simpler lifestyle, and **limiting one's environmental footprint**, more buyers are opting to downsize – in some cases, to spaces no larger than 300 square feet – and this series celebrates the "tiny house" movement."[1312] With some homes as small as 100 sq ft this movement has spread around the world to Canada, England, Australia, Japan, Spain, Germany, Scotland and Russia. In August 2015, Tiny House Jamboree held an event in Colorado Springs, Colorado expecting about 10,000 attendees. Twenty-eight houselets were on display, none larger than 200 sq ft That's the size of a single car garage. It's hard to imagine their shock when 40,000 people showed up.[1313]

Image: This 128 sq ft houselet in Portland, Oregon belongs to Tammy Strobel and her husband Logan Smith. To bathe, a video tour showed they had to move the composting toilet out of a cubicle since it doubled as a shower. It sits on wheels and cost $33,000 to build. They moved into it October 2011 and four years later decided it was time to find a more realistic home. After deciding to keep it as a vacation place, they moved into a "spacious" 480 sq ft apartment. (Courtesy Tammy Strobel, creativecommons.org/licenses/by/2.0/).

The UN has done a great job of covertly planting the tiny house seed. It's become a big deal. However, once reality sets in the romance wears off when needing to store clothes for changing seasons, cooking meals on miniscule countertops, doing laundry and literally running into other family members. There is no such thing as privacy. Needless to say, these houselets wouldn't fare well in Tornado Alley.

ECO-VILLAGES

Bioregional is one "green building" pioneer active in England, France, Luxembourg, Canada, the U.S., Australia, Tanzania and South Africa. Their one-planet living motto is "A vision of a world in which people enjoy happy, healthy lives within their fair share of the earth's resources, leaving space for wildlife and wilderness."[1314] This is where Agenda 2030 proponents preferred you lived.

One thing that has always baffled is the utter impracticality of these housing concepts. Taking a bus would be nearly a requirement in bad weather. The average person still has only two hands and often one is occupied with a briefcase, a purse or both. Without a car it would necessitate going to the grocery store every day. Qué pena! (What a pain!) Heaven forbid trying to plan for a party. For that matter there's no room for extra bodies. BedZED apartments are only 540 to 904 sq ft.

Photo: Beddington Zero Energy Development (BedZED) is one of the first large-scale environmentally friendly housing developments to be built. Located in Hackbridge, London it was designed to produce zero carbon emissions, protect the environment and promote a "sustainable" lifestyle. Its 100 homes and 15,120 sq ft of workspace were completed in 2002. Cars are discouraged so only 100 parking spaces were provided, however, no vehicles are pictured in this photograph so there's no indication where they are allowed and where would guests park? These projects instead encourage using public transportation, biking and walking.

While BedZED won several awards in the sustainable living category, the project encountered numerous problems. The biomass wood chip boiler had both technical and reliability problems so a gas boiler is now used. No explanation was offered, but for some reason, the local authorities didn't allow the wood chip boiler to run at night. The initial investment of purchasing the boiler is the disadvantage most often cited. Also in the heating arena, BedZED's passive solar aspect wasn't sufficient.

Their expensive 'Living Machine' water recycler failed to clean the water and despite their target of a "1 planet" footprint, it still used 1.7. A "planet" is the length of time it takes Earth to replenish resources and absorb waste a person makes. For example, if a person's footprint were 2 planets it would take Earth two years to regenerate what was used. It's no surprise that BedZED started in England as they are leading the pack with Agenda 2030 compliance. In fact, the U.S. arm of Agenda 2030 is modeling much of its activities after the EU. As innovative as BedZED looks, it is this author's idea of hell on earth. There's no place for a veggie garden, no place for kids or dogs to run and play unless that one thinks that minuscule swatch of grass is adequate. Additionally too many studies prove that people packed tightly together leads to aggression. Likely you wouldn't want to spend too much time outside in that "yard". Since recycling was a major consideration for BedZED the land on which this eco-village sits was used for many years as a dumping ground for sewage sludge from the nearby plant.[1315] Don't kids eat dirt?

SUSTAINABLE CITIES

This concept has caught on like wildfire since it first ignited in 1990 with ICLEI – International Council for Local Environmental Initiatives. At the UN's inaugural conference, The World Congress of **Local Governments** for a **Sustainable Future**, in New York more than 200 local governments from 43 countries attended. In 2003, ICLEI officially changed its name to ICLEI-Local Governments for Sustainability. Two decades later, ICLEI had over 9,000 cities mapped that were actively participating.

Then in 2012, they removed the map from their site so this image is from web archives. Larger maps are available in Appendix 3 for Australia, Canada, European Union, Italy, New Zealand, the UK, and the U.S. with separate maps for Alaska and Hawaii. Maybe this is because some communities woke up and realized the insidious nature of this UN agenda program.

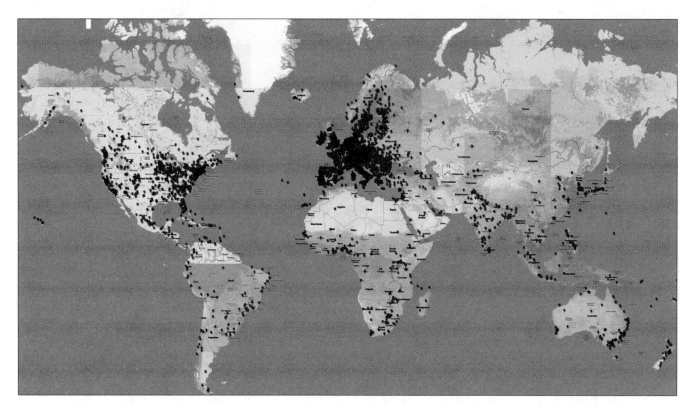

By region, it's easy to see that Europe dominated in 2012 with 6,348 cities, North America – 1,594, Asia – 396, Oceania – 284, Africa – 209 and South America – 176. Now four years later, that number has changed. Some communities when they understood the UN's insidious plan have dropped out and others have joined. On the current ICLEI site, they list countries and cities participating, but for the U.S. they no longer show specific cities. Instead a "member" total is given for each state. Not surprisingly California is the frontrunner with New York next in line followed by Florida, Washington and Massachusetts.

SIGNS YOUR COMMUNITY DRANK THE KOOL-AID

Two requirements for an ICLEI sustainable city membership are a commitment to climate protection and an annual fee of up to $9,500 based on population or a city's operating budget. And for what? For council members to admit a town was blind enough to sign onto this global program? If a city wanted to implement these measures they could do so without paying heavy fees every year. Most people residing in these towns would likely want the money put to better use. Interestingly each community defines what its participation will look like so they can do as little or as much as they want as long as they pay up.

Let's take a look at Pueblo, CO, which is the nearest city to where this author and family live in an unincorporated area of Pueblo County. Their website states its initiative: "The city sees "sustainability" in the broadest sense possible, from solar panels and recycling, to **smart land use** and storm water policies. We also see general trail, sidewalk, and urban design improvements to walkability and bikeability as paths to general health and a more sustainable city."[1316]

One of the first indicators a city has joined is the emergence of bike lanes. All it requires is some road paint and a few bike signs to tack up. For example, in the older area of the city of Pueblo, Colorado, smaller homes were built close together compared to typical residences today. Cars are forced to park on the street. This left two lanes for vehicular traffic. However, in 2014 the city's Planning and Development Dept. turned the right lane into a bike lane and buffer zone. Now traffic frequently backs up. Drivers already frustrated with the speed limit at a 30mph crawl sometimes drive in the bike lane to pass slower cars. At least when there were two lanes, traffic flowed better. This was exceptionally shortsighted because this road leads from the hospital. And yes, a $95 ticket is issued if a person violates the bike lane even if no one is using it.

In another piece of brilliance in the same area of the city when they didn't have enough space to donate an existing lane to bicyclists, bikers are now allowed to drive in the car lane. What made no sense was turning over vehicle lanes to bikes especially when getting to the hospital might be a matter of life and death.

It's not like this state is hurting for bike and hike trails. Due to its exceptional weather and year-round outdoor activities, Colorado literally had hundreds and hundreds of bike lane miles before ICLEI was even an agenda. This includes at least 45 miles of trails through the 10,000 acres surrounding Lake Pueblo.

It's not just Colorado. Map My Run (dot) com gives a plotted course for cities in every state plus Australia, Canada, France, Germany, Ireland, Italy, Japan, Netherlands, New Zealand, Singapore, South Africa, Spain, and the UK. This site lets visitors plug in a city and how long a trail is desired. Its searchable database allows for customization for bikes, hikes, runs and walks and supplies a smartphone app.

MEGA-REGIONS

In tandem with being squeezed onto even smaller pieces of land, Agenda 2030 wants to "rewild" greater portions of countries. Rewilding can't begin until people are properly corralled.

While Agenda 2030 can't require nations to relocate its residents, countries can "encourage" its citizens to move to more populated areas. America 2050 examined regions of high population density based on the U.S. Census Bureau and melded it with economic data. They looked at the more than 3,000 counties for four things:

- Population change from 1970 to 2006
- Employment change from 1970 to 2006
- Wage change from 1970 to 2006 and
- Average wages in 2006.

This gave them a picture of where's hot and where's not for population centers. From the data, 11 mega-regions emerged where 75% of people lived in 2006. Their end game was to figure out "a national growth strategy" that covered "economic development, landscape conservation, smart growth and urban revitalization."[1317] (Notice the last three are Agenda 2030 catch phrases.) All of these mega-regions are the fastest growing areas in America except the Great Lakes and Gulf Coast.

INCENTIVES TO HERD THE MASSES

These 11 areas will be first to get the best infrastructure and the most federal dollars. Taking a page from Agenda 2030, America 2050 lists five major challenges: global competitiveness, infrastructure, fairness and opportunity, climate change and energy, and rapid population growth. Central to their plan is a high-speed rail system for each mega-region, but what does this require for people to take advantage of it? People concentrated in specific areas. A high-speed rail system won't be available to the 16% of America that live in the 75% of the Country outside mega-regions. They call these areas "white spaces". Government could in effect force people into cities by:

- Implementing more toll roads
- Increasing fees on existing toll roads
- Raising gasoline taxes
- Choosing not to give federal funds to fix roads
- Withholding environmental approval for big projects based on carbon footprint. This could mean large delays and challenges for say roads out into the suburbs. So if you wanted traffic congestion fixed or a new Interstate connect to speed the commute, the 'burbs won't get it
- Imposing taxes that charge drivers by the mile could further penalize people living in less populated areas.

Oregon launched its pay-by-the-mile program in 2015 and according to Mileage-Based User Fee Alliance, 25 states are in various stages of following. This plan is already in force in Germany, Austria, Switzerland, the Czech Republic and New Zealand.[1318] These plans all redistribute wealth on a massive scale from the suburbs to the cities.

Like the eco-villages that started in England, America 2050 was inspired by the European Union in their study.

SQUEEZE PLAY IN PRACTICE

Where this author and family lives in Pueblo West, an unincorporated area of Pueblo County, CO (not to be confused with Pueblo City 12 miles to the east), we've seen it firsthand. Pueblo would like nothing better than to annex our community and it's been a simmering boil for the 15 years we've lived here. Our community has roughly 33,000 people spread over 70 sq mi. Pueblo the city has 108,000 people crammed into 45 sq mi. Their population density runs 2,265 per sq mi compared to ours at 471. We moved here for good reasons – elbow room and clean air, reasonably priced land for a small orchard and gardens, a place for our Kelpie cattle dogs to run, no city sales tax and to enjoy space between neighbors, nice as they are. Additionally there's a 360-acre "wilderness" area literally across the street where folks like to hike.

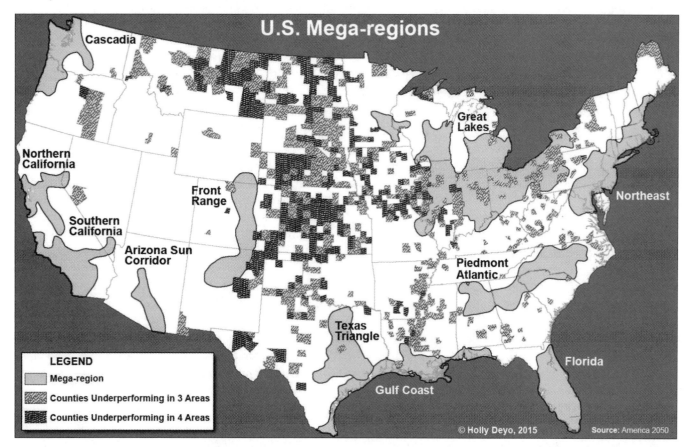

The animus from Pueblo to Pueblo West was really strange. As newcomers we didn't understand it, but witnessed it firsthand. Right after 9/11, Pueblo held a public meeting addressing terrorism. I approached the then County Commissioner and gave her a copy of my book, *Dare To Prepare*. She was really pleased, said she wanted to talk more about preparedness. Then she asked where we lived and I responded, Pueblo West. Immediately an iron curtain descended. She turned on her heel and said she had to go.

We were stunned at the quick cold shoulder. We had no idea about the ongoing desire of Pueblo to annex Pueblo West. They want our tax dollars. Until the last few years when Pueblo West got a Safeway, Walmart, Walgreens, etc. and its own hospital arm of Parkview Medical Center, we still had to shop in Pueblo or preferably, trot 45 minutes north to Colorado Springs. This was way before ICLEI hit Pueblo, but Pueblo covets our space, our land, our clean air and most importantly, our tax dollars.

Living with elbow-room doesn't mesh with Agenda 21 or 2030. Suburbanites and rural dwellers will be penalized. Dr. Stanley Kurtz, Harvard anthropologist and author of *Spreading the Wealth: How Obama Is Robbing the Suburbs to Pay for the Cities* said it's an effort to "Manhattanize America".[1319] In 2013, in tandem with Mr. Obama's "Argonne speech", the Dept. of Energy released a series of reports called "Transportation Energy Futures". Its strategy aims at reducing America's greenhouse gas emissions up to 80% by around 2050.

Kurtz writes, "Arguably the most controversial of those reports covers the 'effects of the built environment on transportation.'" To put it plainly, the 'built environment' report lays out strategies the federal government can use to force development away from suburbs and into cities, supposedly for the sake of reducing carbon dioxide emissions given off by all those suburban commuters. The Obama administration wants to force so-called smart growth policies on the country: get out of your car, stay out of the suburbs, move into small, tightly-packed urban apartment complexes, and walk or take public transportation instead of driving."[1320]

Transportation Energy Futures sets out Mr. Obama's strategies quite clearly in this 5-point Federal plan:

- **Technical and planning assistance** – distribute information to local communities up through federal agencies on how to implement "walkable neighborhoods"
- **Marketing and outreach** – "persuasion" campaigns aimed at the general public

- **Funding** – money disbursed *only* if in agreement with smart growth
- **Tax policy** – which would influence land development
- **Regulations** – applied at all levels from local communities up through federal agencies that would withhold transportation funding if land use aimed at smart growth isn't at the forefront[1321]

So this would be yet another incentive for Pueblo to incorporate Pueblo West. If Pueblo County is viewed as being unable to control populated areas within its border it could greatly impact whether or not the county received Federal funds for various projects – primarily roads and other infrastructure.

EXECUTIVE ORDER 13575 – LOCKSTEP WITH UN AGENDAS

In June 9, 2011, President Obama addressed "white spaces" signing Executive Order 13575 establishing the White House Rural Council (WHRC). Following the drumbeat of Agenda 21 and 2030, it aims is to exert broad municipal powers over nearly every aspect of life for the 16% that live rurally. There's already been a huge shift in people moving to cities. According to America 2050 25% of Americans lived rurally or in the 'burbs in 2006. The Census Bureau showed that number had shrunk to 19.3% in 2010 and[1322] Mr. Obama cited the number as 16%. He could be wrong since he said America has 57 states.[1323] Regardless, the number of people living in white spaces is diminishing.

Section 1 gives the Rural Council's game away. *"Sixteen percent of the American population lives in rural counties. Strong, sustainable rural communities are essential to winning the future and ensuring American competitiveness in the years ahead. These communities supply our food, fiber, and energy, safeguard our natural resources, and are essential in the development of science and innovation. Though rural communities face numerous challenges, they also present enormous economic potential. The Federal Government has an important role to play in order to expand access to the capital necessary for economic growth, promote innovation, improve access to health care and education, and expand outdoor recreational activities on public lands."*[1324]

Section 4b gives an uncomfortable preview of how the WHRC will insinuate its tentacles. It plans to *"coordinate and increase the effectiveness of Federal engagement with rural stakeholders, including agricultural organizations, small businesses, education and training institutions, health-care providers, telecommunications services providers, research and land grant institutions, law enforcement, State, local, and tribal governments, and nongovernmental organizations regarding the needs of rural America."*[1325]

On the surface it may sound great, but Mr. Obama stating the Feds have "an important role" and will team up with big corporations to involve themselves with rural America should raise concern. Most rural economies don't want the Federal government to come in and take over. Austrian-British economist and philosopher F.A. Hayek warned. "Economic control is not merely control of a sector of human life which can be separated from the rest; it is the control of the means for all our ends. And whoever has sole control of the means must also determine which ends are to be served, which values are to be rated higher and which lower, in short, what men should believe and strive for."[1326]

The EO states it wants greater control over food, fiber and energy – necessities of life – in these rural areas. To do this the White House called on Tom Vilsack, the current Secretary of Agriculture to chair this Council plus the heads of 25 other top government agencies:

Agriculture *

Commerce *

Council of Economic Advisers

Council on Environmental Quality

Defense *

Domestic Policy Council

Education *

Energy *

Environmental Protection Agency *

Federal Communications Commission

Health and Human Services *

Homeland Security *

Housing and Urban Development *

Interior *

Justice *

Labor *

National Economic Council

Office of Cabinet Affairs (liaison between White House and Cabinet)

Office of Management and Budget

Office of National Drug Control Policy

Office of Public Engagement & Intergovernmental Affairs (spinmeisters from White House to public)

Office of Science and Technology Policy

Small Business Administration

Transportation *

Treasury *

Veterans Affairs *

NOTES: Bold type indicates they are Cabinet members or enjoy Cabinet rank. An asterisk shows they are the 15 largest Federal Agencies. Italics indicate other Agencies that enjoy "closest-advisor" status.[1327]

That's a shocking amount of "government participation". In addition to these 26 people, the Ag Secretary can add more personnel at his or her discretion from "other executive branch departments, agencies, and offices". What some of these agencies have to do with rural America is a mystery, but it's obvious government wants to exert even more control over every aspect and it's leaving nothing to chance or any possible loopholes unzipped.

Since one of the biggest goals is to herd people onto smaller and smaller pieces of land, now would be a good time to purchase acreages in rural areas. People who have stood their ground and refused to be put off their land are winning – unless the government uses eminent domain. However, if you live in a big city in a large apartment, expect your quarters to be squeezed till you can't breathe. You are already in the grips of Agenda 2030. While there's no way to stop Agenda 2030 projects at the Federal level, locally there is a better chance. Local Agenda 2030 endeavors are different from private conservation groups, which are fine and valuable. But make no mistake; a local Agenda 2030 entity has a different goal from private conservation groups.

REWILDING

We all love animals and nature. Who hasn't stopped to watch a herd of deer grazing or sighed in awe over majestic mountain peaks or paused to observe a colorful butterfly. Nature plays an important part in most peoples' lives or they wouldn't have put Central Park in the heart of Manhattan nor would it attract 40 million visitors every year. Nature plays a vital role, both short- and long-term in our mental and physical health. It doesn't and shouldn't come before humans, but this doesn't mean giving a license to abuse God's creation.

Genesis 1:26-28 – at the very start of the Bible because it's that important – clearly puts humans above nature. *And God said, Let us make man in our image, after our likeness: and let them have dominion over the fish of the sea, and over the birds of the heavens, and over the cattle, and over all the earth, and over every creeping thing that creepeth upon the earth. And God created man in his own image, in the image of God created he him; male and female created he them. And God blessed them: and God said unto them, Be fruitful, and multiply, and replenish the earth, and subdue it; and have dominion over the fish of the sea, and over the birds of the heavens, and over every living thing that moveth upon the earth.* Clearly some people have a different agenda.

"Rewilding" was coined by environmental activist Dave Foreman and developed in the mid-90s by conservation biologist Michael Soule. Since then, it has broadened in definition to cover two aspects: mass restoration of ecosystems starting with large carnivores at the top of the food chain working down to the smallest creature and second, to rewild places where humans live.

Dave Foreman, co-founder of the Earth First! Movement and president of the Rewilding Institute stated. "We must make this place an insecure and inhospitable place for Capitalists and their projects – we must reclaim the roads and plowed lands, halt dam construction, tear down existing dams, free shackled rivers and return to wilderness millions of tens of millions of acres of presently settled land."[1328] In another flamboyant comment he stated, "My three main goals would be to reduce human population to about 100 million worldwide, destroy the industrial infrastructure and see wilderness, with it's full complement of species, returning throughout the world."[1329] However, this author's personal favorite Foremanism is "Phasing out the human race will solve every problem on earth, social and environmental."[1330] What he seems to miss is that without humanity, Foreman wouldn't be around to enjoy nature either.

Because Agenda 21 evokes such negative feelings, "rewilding" morphed into "wildlife corridors" and renamed as such by the Western Governors' Association in February 2007. Like "sustainable cities" the same phrase can wear various disguises. Some more innocuous phrases for rewilding include: Wilderness Conservation, Ecological Integrity, Native Species Diversity, Big Wilderness-Area Complex, Landscape-Level Ecological Restoration, Biodiversity, Continental Wildways, Wildland Project and Wildlife Movement.

WILDLANDS NETWORK THEN AND NOW

Before returning large portions of Earth back to nature, people have to move onto smaller and smaller pieces on land. You've likely seen Dr. Michael Coffman's largely red and yellow map of America simulating what UN MaB (Man and Biosphere) Core Reserves, Corridors and Buffer Zones might look like. He paints a maze of unrealistic segments designated for people and animals. It is nature friendly, human hostile. This map, though a model, was not an exaggeration of the fate that could befall Americans if the UN gets their way.

Dr. Coffman, president of Environmental Perspectives, Inc. taught forest ecology for many years at Michigan Technological University – a leading forestry school. He's a respected scientist, ecologist and friend of the environment. He uses common sense and is a stalwart advocate of the UN butting out of our business. He puts people first.

ANATOMY OF A BIOSPHERE RESERVE

© Holly Deyo, 2016

His map showed how up to 50% of America might have been in UN wilderness reserves and buffer zones if the Senate had ratified the 1992 Biodiversity Treaty, more correctly called the Convention on Biological Diversity (CBD). The U.S. hasn't signed the other two biodiversity treaties either: the 2000 Cartagena Protocol on Biosafety and 2010's Nagoya Protocol on Access and Benefit-sharing. While America signed the CBD in June 1993 as of March 2016, it's not been ratified. Coffman's map was instrumental in halting the U.S from taking a very dangerous step. This is what happened.

The Sneaky Treaty

The CBD's concepts were first introduced in 1981 by the International Union for the Conservation of Nature. Before being presented at the 1992 Earth Summit in Rio its core principles appeared in numerous UN documents and was incorporated into other agendas. This allowed the American Sheep Industry Association (ASI) to examine its core content in advance.

In 1991, the Sheep Association in conjunction with Colorado's Keystone Center conducted a joint study. Not liking what they saw the ASI adopted official policy contrary to it. At the 1992 Summit, President Bush refused to sign after seeing what was in it. His victory was short-lived.

Pres. Clinton signed it on June 4, 1993 with an army of environmental groups backing him. The State Department in November requested that the Senate put ratification on "fast-track" to avoid public discussion and it was Senator George Mitchell's job to get this done. Every senator except five piled onboard as did VP Al Gore who was busy building his Task Force to implement it. The Senate Foreign Relations Committee held hearings on the Treaty in April 1994, at which time ratification was recommended and voted on favorably 16-3 two months later.

On July 5, in what would be a monumental uphill battle, Tom McDonnell, Director of Natural Resources at ASI and Henry Lamb from the Environmental Conservation Organization joined forces to defeat it. Lamb drafted a letter to be signed by all organizations involved in property rights and natural resources. They immediately faxed it to 75 like-minded groups with the request that they refax it to other similar groups. The Alliance for America, an association dedicated to property rights, faxed it to an additional 4,400. The opposition was officially off and running.

Then on July 14 the Foreign Relations Committee released a report raising questions that hadn't been addressed in their committee hearings. This gave the anti-Treaty side a two-week delay to investigate further.

On July 28, 1994 the ASI unveiled their 100-page bombshell study. It revealed the "smoking gun" – the existence of a draft of the *Global Biodiversity Assessment (GBA),* required by the Treaty, which identified the "Wildlands Project" as a primary mechanism for Treaty implementation. In an August 1 teleconference, McDonnell reviewed with staff of the Republican Policy Committee and the Foreign Relations committee ASI's analysis.

On August 3, Senator Mitchell announced that the Treaty vote would take place on August 8. Throughout the night of August 3, a fax written by Coffman went out to 4,400 organizations and individuals asking them to oppose the Treaty. On August 4 fifty Senate staffers and reps from the American Farm Bureau and the National Cattlemen's Association met for an in-depth presentation on the ASI's treaty analysis. All day long, messages urging Senators to kill the Treaty lit Senate fax machines and switchboards. On August 5, Senator Dole issued a letter to George Mitchell, signed by 35 Republican Senators saying they wouldn't ratify the Treaty until questions raised by the Minority Report had been fully answered. So the vote scheduled for later that day was cancelled.

Then Congress recessed August 26 – September 12. When it reconvened the Environmental Conservation Organization mailed letters to 1,050 Mayors, urging them to oppose the Treaty. On September 19 every Senator received that letter co-signed by 293 organizations. Once again, Senate switchboards and fax machines lit up.

On September 30, 1994, the day of the vote, Senator Kay Bailey Hutchison (R-TX) struck the fatal blow. Armed with 6-foot posters of Dr. Coffman's damning red and yellow map and excerpts from the treaty, the rest of the Senate understood clearly what was afoot. In the 103rd Congress Senators Burns, Craig, Helms, Nickles and Wallop also spoke against the GBA and the treaty was withdrawn.

It's likely bogged for the time being in the sludgy progress known as government waiting for a GBA-friendly Senate. Regardless of ratification, government is shuffling billions toward implementation.

In addition to government, organizations have pushed ahead with rewilding.

Besides Earth First! another group that has sniffed a little too much ozone is the Wildlands Network. It was originally founded and named by Dr. Michael Soule in 1991 as the Wildlands Project. It boasts an impressive group of science advisors that echo Dave Foreman's mantra of Earth First! When Agenda 21 and the Biodiversity Treaty met the Wildlands Network (then still Project) it was a threesome made in rewilding heaven. This is not unlike the UN's Biosphere Reserve concept of where people and animals exist in their own zones with a buffer between the two, but more human-restrictive.

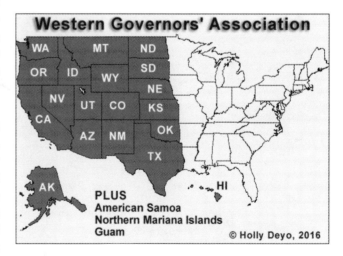

The Wildlands Network's aims is to return huge chunks of North America back to wolves, cougars, lynx, wolverines, grizzly and black bears, jaguars and other large animals. Since they require enormous tracts of land to survive and thrive, this necessitates cramming people into smaller areas of the cities to create buffer zones between human places and animals spaces. This would greatly impede people's ability to camp, hike and bike in parks and wildness areas for fear of coming in contact with any of the above. So that end, theses activist would implement the three "C"s: Cores, Corridors and Carnivores and guess what gets top priority. It's not humans.

THE GOVERNORS

At that 2007 Western Governors' meeting they unanimously approved a policy resolution, "Protecting Wildlife Migration Corridors and Crucial Wildlife Habitat in the West" and published their findings in the comprehensive study, *WGA Wildlife Corridors Initiative Report.*[1331] They aren't looking to "take over" human areas, but to protect existing wildlife habitats, help animals thrive and repopulate. With forest fires and changing weather animals are having a hard enough time surviving. In 2008, the most recent number, showed vehicles hit large animals over a million times every year. That's a 50% jump up from the previous 15 years, so that figure is likely significantly higher now.[1332] This is vastly different than rewilding projects.

REWILDING AROUND THE WORLD

North America

The Wildland Network premise is to connect existing protected areas with new healthy habitats – on a massive scale. Their vision involved four exceptionally large wildlife corridors from Canada, down through America, Mexico and Central America, and ending at South America. Their plans call for taking half of Mexico, half of Central America and large swaths of the U.S. and Canada. Of course they want the best these places have to offer – according to their website "our national parks, scenic rivers, majestic mountains, crystal clear lakes, continental trails, and vibrant grasslands and forests."[1333]

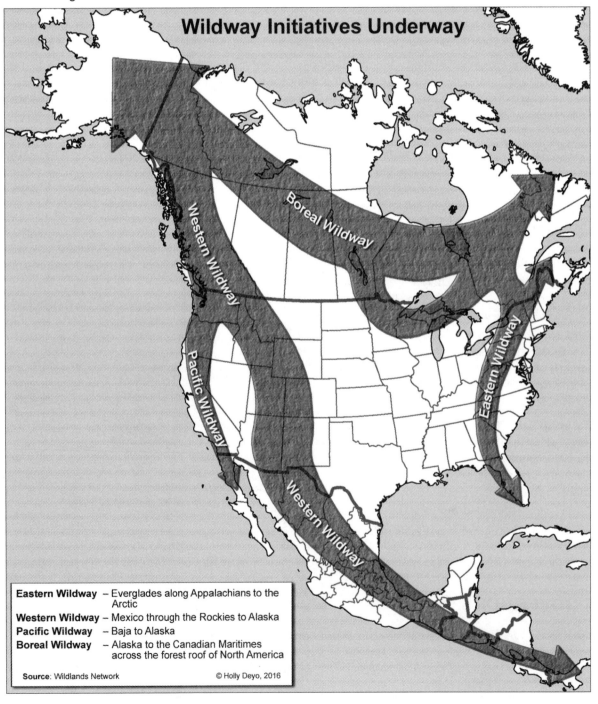

Wildway Initiatives Underway

Eastern Wildway – Everglades along Appalachians to the Arctic

Western Wildway – Mexico through the Rockies to Alaska

Pacific Wildway – Baja to Alaska

Boreal Wildway – Alaska to the Canadian Maritimes across the forest roof of North America

Source: Wildlands Network   © Holly Deyo, 2016

The big "gum up" for the Eastern Wildway is that a lot of the areas they want to incorporate are close to the large cities of Montreal, Québec City, New York, Boston, Philadelphia, Washington, DC and Atlanta. They are in a dilemma since Wildland Project founders envisioned this: "It is estimated that large carnivores and ungulates require reserves on the scale of 2.5 to 25 million acres.... For a minimum viable population of 1000 [large mammals], the figures would be 242 million acres for grizzly bears, 200 million acres for wolverines, and 100 million acres for wolves. Core reserves should be managed as roadless areas (wilderness). All roads should be permanently closed."[1334] So doesn't it make sense that the Global Biodiversity Assessment Treaty, the UN, Agendas 21 and 2030 under the guise of smart cities and these environmental extremists, want to cram us onto smaller and smaller tracts of land?

The Western Wildway is the largest initiative covering some 5,000 miles. It is a massive undertaking to convert this much land into an international coalition. Literally hundreds of organizations are on board to make this happen including some well known actors like the Sierra Club, the Rewilding Institute, The Wilderness Society, Western Wildlife Conservancy, Biodiversity Conservation Alliance, Canadian Parks and Wilderness Society, the Wildlife Conservation Society Canada and many more.

Their network includes partners from four arenas: conservation, foundation, artist and zoological. Within and outside these groups they have onboard government agencies, community coalitions, the Dept. of Transportation and highway authorities, zoos, aquariums, private landowners, foundations and individual supporters. It's a formidable group, but most people in North America still believe humans trump the rest.

The Netherlands

The Dutch government began one of the first initiatives in the 1980s. Oostvaardersplassen is a 22-sq mi nature reserve that's home to both birds and large animals. Because willow trees started sprouting in the marshy parts, they brought in herds of deer, ponies and cattle. Since Oostvaardersplassen sits below sea level, the dyke surrounding it keeps out natural predators. That forces rangers shoot 30-60% of the animals to keep the numbers down. Sadly others die of starvation because the reserve is too small and flat to offer shelter. Doesn't exactly sound like a natural scenario.

Europe

Europe has much larger goals than just these eight areas. Their plan is to transform 2.5 million acres by 2020: "We believe that all kinds of landscapes, from city centres to wilderness areas, can and need to be rewilded. Not all of them becoming pure wilderness of course, but all habitats can become quite a bit wilder. Including all areas under different levels of legal protection. If the level of "wildness" could be measured on a scale from 0 to 10, where zero is a city centre and 10 a remote wilderness, we would like to see all of Europe move up a notch or two or three along that scale."[1335]

At the May 2009 "Conference on Wilderness and Large Natural Habitat Areas" in Prague they asked for nominations. Over 30 were submitted to what is now known as Rewilding Europe. Eight areas are already underway with two more earmarked. More than 25 organizations have partnered with Rewilding Europe including national, nature and archaeological parks, UNESCO Biosphere Reserves, universities, foundations, local communities, and NGOs.

Western Iberia – Located in Spain close to the border of Portugal, over 500,000 acres have already been set aside for conservation. In this unique reserve, over 2,000 outdoor rock carvings dating back 22,000 years ago mostly show animals that populated this region back then including aurochs, wild horse, red deer, ibex and fish. Because of poor land management and over hunting the area was pretty much without animals. Horses, cattle, deer and ibex have been reintroduced.

Danube Delta – Europe's largest wetland covers 1.5 million acres. It's home to all kinds of waterbirds including pelicans, herons, storks, cormorants and terns; and has the largest number of fish species in all Europe.

Southern Carpathians – located in Romania this area is already surrounded by over 2.5 million acres of protected land. In its rolling, forested hills many species of animals roam including wolves, Eurasian lynx, brown bear, wild cat, deer, wild boar, chamois and bison.

Velebit – located in Croatia this area is also a Man and Biosphere Reserve and is on a tentative list to be declared a World Heritage site. It has dramatic scenery with old-growth forests and deep canyons, and home to Balkan chamois, red deer, brown bear, wolf and lynx. Wild horses are already in place, and soon possibly again also ibex.

Central Apennines – located in central Italy and covers more than 2.5 million acres in beech wood forests, open hillsides and alpine grasslands. It's home to deer, wild boar, brown bears, horses, cattle and wolves. Chamois, vulture and eagles also thrive here.

Rhodope Mountains – this 500,000-acre reserve situated in Bulgaria is home to 4,329 animals including brown bears, wolves, jackals; 278 bird species and 2,000 different plants

Image: Rewilding Europe has chosen these 8 areas to focus on first. Others sites will follow.

Eastern Carpathians – located in the triangle where Poland, Slovakia and Ukraine meet is one of the few places in Europe with nearly all of its original native wildlife

Oder Delta – spans over 600,000 acres Germany and Poland of which more than 170,000 are the open waters of a lagoon. It's an important stopping area to more than a quarter of a million migrating bird species and permanent home for otters, beaver, salmon, sea trout and many other species. Dry land is home to wolves, bison and elk.

Rewilding England

In England their projects include reclaiming the **Wandle River**, which flows for nearly 9 miles through south London. It's described as an "urban sewer" having been a dumping ground for bleach and dyes from the 90 mills along its length.

Next on their list is the 3,500 acres of **Knepp Castle** in West Sussex. It's now home to cattle, ponies, pigs, deer, purple emperor butterflies and a variety of birds.

On the northwestern edge of the Lake District National Park in Cumbria lies the remote **Ennerdale Valley**, which covers 10,626 acres. Previously too many sheep had eaten native grasses to the bone. In the last decade all boundary fences have been removed and the land has been turned over to beneficial cattle grazing.

The UN must be very happy because it's estimated that by 2020 80% of all Europeans will live in cities and towns. This makes rewilding fairly easy. By mid-2012 the EU had designated 26,406 conservation sites covering a total of 18% of the land or nearly 200 million acres. Six countries have set aside more than a quarter of their land for conservation: Bulgaria (34%), Greece (27%), Cyprus (28%), Slovakia (30%), Slovenia (36%), and Spain (27%).[1336]

Wales

Wales has one project underway and its sizeable compared to the country. **Cambrian Wildwood** covers some 7,500 acres. Their goal is to reintroduce pine martens, red squirrels, wild boar and beaver.

Scotland

Community of Arran Seabed Trust (COAST) is working for the protection and restoration of the marine environment around Arran and the Clyde.

Creag Meagaidh National Nature Reserve covers nearly 9,900 acres in the south of the Monadhliath north of Loch Laggan in Scotland. Large-scale sheep farming and high deer numbers had devastated Creag Meagaidh to the point where trees weren't growing there. It's taken 30 years, but trees are now regenerating.

Glenlude is the focus for regenerating this former 368-acre sheep farm and conifer plantation. Besides reforesting the area, they're reintroducing deer, pine martens, foxes, mountain hares, red squirrels, water voles, buzzards, hen harriers, barn owls, and red and black grouse in addition to a wide range of invertebrates & amphibians.

The John Muir Trust, the same group that owns Glenlude, bought 3,000 acres of land on the remote Knoydart peninsula 30 years ago, named **Li and Coire Dhorrcail**. It too, had suffered deforestation, large-scale sheep farming and heavy grazing by deer. In 1987, the land was bare for the most part, grazed to the bone first by sheep and then by high populations of deer. Since going to the Trust volunteers have hand-plants thousands of Scots pine, birch, juniper, hazel, rowan, ash and oak that are now above head-height.

The Trees for Life organization have planted over 1 million trees since in an effort to restore the **Caledonian Forest** that used to cover much of Scotland. Once again deer had overgrazed down to the ground. The charity plans to bring in red squirrels, capercaillie (a member of the grouse family), beaver, wild boar, lynx and wolves back to their native habitats. It has already established an experimental population of wild boar in an enclosure.

Carrifran Wildwood's is the brainchild of a group of local friends with a vision for restoring its 1,606 acres. The Borders Forest Trust bought the nearly 1,600 acres of Corehead and the adjacent 4,448 acres Talla and Gameshope estates. Their aim is to restore this to a wild and largely wooded land of 6,000 years ago. In the first decade they planted over half a million trees in the lower valley plus thousands of shrubs and trees in the high hanging valleys. Carrifran Wildwood's is different because volunteers are maintaining the fences to keep out sheep and goats and have killed a significant amount of roe deer. This project is more about the trees and shrubs and less so about the animals except woodland birds.

Glenfeshie is one of the most dramatic examples of rewilding in the UK. A few years ago, it was a forest of deer at the expense of the forest. This resulted in 42,000 acres of a dying Caledonian pine forest. Trees couldn't replenish because deer ate every tree seedling trying to grow here. In fact, it was here that Edwin Landseer painted his famous 'The Monarch of the Glen' oil painting in 1851. In 2004, the then Deer Commission for Scotland undertook action deer culling and the baby trees are thriving.

Abernethy is a 30,000-acre nature reserve in the Cairngorms National Park. Like most of Scotland's native woods, Abernethy suffered deforestation over the centuries with sheep and deer munching new tree growth. The Royal Society for the Protection of Birds (RSPB) has a 200-year vision to revitalize the Abernathy plantation back to the old Caledonian Forest. Another 8,648 acres at Abernethy could support some tree cover. The goal is to expand the forests plus encourage areas of mire, grassland, rock, scree (small stones that cover a mountain slope), and bog woodland. The plan is to achieve this without fencing, so deer numbers need to be maintained at a level the land can sustain. Besides the pines birch, aspen, alder and willow trees have all but disappeared from the edge of the existing forest. It's hoped that in time Abernethy will reconnect with Glenfeshie.

Last is **Mar Lodge**. It's a 72,500-acre estate also in Cairngorms National Park. Despite the pine forest suffering Mar Lodge is home to golden eagles, capercaillie, dotterel (a small bird in the plover family), snow bunting, pine martens and many others. After thinning the deer herds, nearly 500 acres of pines and broadleaf trees have regenerated. The goal is to reconnect Mar Lodge with the forests in Abernethy and Glenfeshie.

Australia

Their rewilding program primarily consists of reintroducing Tiger and Easer Quolls, plus the Tasmanian Devil back to mainland Australia. All are marsupials. Australia enjoys an incredible amount of biodiversity, but over the last two centuries the Lucky Country has lost 10% of its native mammals species – the highest rate anywhere in the world. To help remedy these alarming losses, experts are considering reintroducing native dingoes. Dingo numbers have dwindled due to hunting and trapping, but mostly the fault lies with the Dingo Barrier Fence (DBF). This record-breaking long fence runs for about 3,480 miles on the eastern side of Australia and another 727 miles on the west where it's called the State Barrier Fence of Western Australia.

Western Australia's government has plans to add another 304 miles, which would create a largely continuous barrier through five bioregions from north of Geraldton to Cape Arid. The DBF was originally built in the late 1800s and stretched from eastern Queensland all the way to the South Australian coastline. These fences were erected to protect

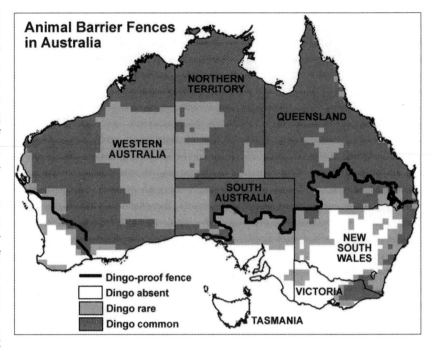

crops from rabbits, then later modified livestock from dingoes. Because nature wasn't allowed to take its course smaller predators like feral cats and red foxes have invaded. Besides stopping dingoes in W.A. they're also stopping the emus and kangaroos, but failed to stop feral rabbits from invading farms. Unfortunately a large number of emus are dying after becoming entangled in the fence. One unforeseen repercussion from the emus perishing is the impact and plant life. They travel long distances and "deposit" up to 200 plant species along the way.

New Zealand

Indisputably New Zealand is one of the most beautiful countries in the southern hemisphere, but it's had trouble with its animals. The only native mammal is a bat and animals never took hold till NZ became colonized. However both large islands that make up this country were rich in bird life with at least 115 species found nowhere else.

When the Maori arrived, they brought rats, dogs, cats, weasels, ferrets and pigs. Between humans hunting and invasive mammals eating them, the islands lost over 40% of their bird species. Instead of "fixing" either North or South Island, conservationists chose one of NZ's small islands, Rotorua, just 82 acres.

Rotorua Island, due east of Auckland, has an interesting history. It used to be a treatment center for men with alcohol and drug issues. The facility closed in 2005, but since the island needed to be self-sufficient, the island was cleared of forests and native vegetation to make way for the facility and crops. After its closure, rats overran the island so in addition to exterminating them, before they could bring in any animals, 400,000 native plants were planted. Even the birds had abandoned Rotorua so the conservationists literally started from the ground up.

In May of 2014 conservationists released 40 North Island saddleback and 40 whitehead birds. Then in October they brought over the first kiwi chicks. In February the first reptiles arrived: 50 moko skinks (a rare lizard) and the first takahe, one of the country's most imperiled birds with only about 300 in existence. Head ecologist Jo Ritchie pointed out one very enviable aspect for this project. "The work on Rotoroa has taken one fourth of the time it would normally take to do such a project … there is no bureaucracy – ideas are formulated, issues are raised – solutions found and decisions made quickly to get work done."[1337] Wouldn't it be a pleasant change if all governments worked this way.

SUMMARY

In all these examples except for North America, there is a common thread. Have you seen it? All of the European projects and in Australia and New Zealand, they want to restore the land and animals without putting people into small boxes. Granted, there are two important differences. For the most part, many of these areas were already uninhabited and second, Europeans generally live in much smaller homes and apartments, spaced closely together. But The Wildlands Network basically wants a world without people or as few as possible. It's the UN Agendas 21 and 2030 without the UN.

One World Religion

Bible students and even those in the secular world know this is a huge sign of End Times. Its possibility became really visible in 2001. Polish artist, Piotr Mlodozeniec, designed the original COEXIST graphic for an exhibit in Jerusalem's Museum on the Seam. Piotr's artwork featured three religions: Islam, Judaism and Christianity with prominent letters representing each. "C" for the Muslim crescent, "X" for the Jewish Star of David, and "T" for the Christian cross. In between were "oe" and "is" – to complete the **COEXIST** message. Since its inception, people have modified it to one of its current incarnations.

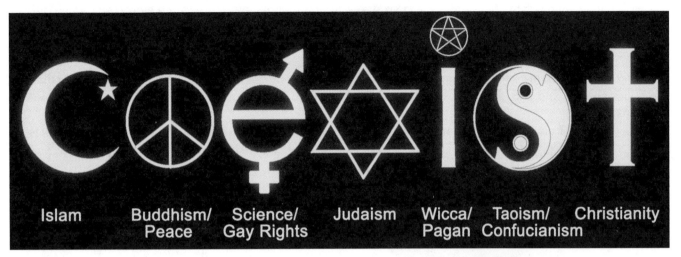

| Islam | Buddhism/ Peace | Science/ Gay Rights | Judaism | Wicca/ Pagan | Taoism/ Confucianism | Christianity |

Coexist has turned up on t-shirts, patches, mugs, bumper stickers, key chains, jewelry, in wall art and comics, and yes, even tattoos. Push back against this concept is seen in this bumper sticker. Two follow-up sentiments on t-shirts and bumper stickers address the impossibility of coexistence. The first asks, *"How can you coexist with people who want to kill you?"* One thing about bumper stickers, they're an interesting barometer of public opinion, right or wrong.

The second says, *"We must learn to coexist, but let's not pretend that they don't contradict."* This is never more evident than in these core differences. Muslims don't believe:

1) In the Trinity
2) That Jesus died on the cross then resurrected, which is essential to Christians
3) Jesus is Divine, but views Him as a mere prophet on par with Mohammad
4) In Original Sin
5) Muslims view Christianity as a religion created by Paul and the Romans in 325 AD, not followers of Christ
6) Muslims place high value on death (Surah 9:38). Christians treasure life as a gift from God.

While some people advocate that Islam isn't a religion of peace, those that haven't gone to the extreme are peace loving and just want to live their lives. Many critics of Christianity also point out its past violence during the Crusades. They ended in 1291. Right now it's Islam taking center stage for violence and cruelty the world over.

Rasmussen's January 2015 poll reflected American's opinions about Islam, which are likely held by other countries as well:

- 52% believe Islam as practiced today encourages violence more than most other religions.
- 64% think there is a global conflict today between Western civilization and Islam.
- 75% agree that Islamic religious leaders need to do more to emphasize the peace in their faith.
- 86% said radical Islamic terrorism is a threat to the U.S.[1338]

Surveys conducted since 2012 found these views have changed very little.

JEWS AS PIGS AND APES?

How can anyone want to be "brothers and sisters" with those who think Hebrews are simian and swine and lop off Christian's heads?

There is much debate whether or not the Quran actually calls Jewish people pigs and apes, but when Muslim clerics do so in sermons, it further embeds the anti-Semitic notion. On January 30, 2015 one such clerk said the following: "Many Muslims are being harmed these days by a group whose hearts were sealed by Allah. 'He made of them [Jews] apes and pigs and slaves of deities' (Quran, 5:60). They are harming the livelihood of the believers [Muslims]."[1339]

Kids do learn from their parents, each other and their religious leaders. On September 12, 2014 a Palestinian youth recited this poem on official PA TV, demonizing Jews as apes and pigs:

"You have been condemned to humiliation and hardship
O Sons of Zion, O most evil among creations
O barbaric apes, O wretched pigs..."[1340]

In December 2015, South Florida Muslim leader Sofian Zakkout called Jews the "grandsons of monkeys and pigs," while commemorating the 28th anniversary of Hamas. Zakkout is well known and respected among Muslims in the Sunshine State. He is Director of the American Muslim Association of North America (AMANA) with ties to two dozen area mosques. So his message against Jews has a long arm. Zakkout has also been exposed for his two-faced behavior. When he wants to be perceived as a man of peace, he speaks and writes in English. When he's on a rant, cursing Jews or calling for violence, he uses Arabic.

This violence showed up again in February 2014. Over a graphic of two dead Hamas founders, Zakkout wrote in Arabic, "It is an obligation to kill those who left our religion. It is an obligation to kill those who fight our religion and to intimidate our enemies and the enemies of the religion. Everything is from the Quran, not from me." He signed it "Sofian."[1341]

Five months later in July, Zakkout organized a pro-Hamas rally outside the Israeli Consulate in Miami. Rally goers kept shouting, "We are Hamas!" Afterward Zakkout posted in Arabic on Facebook above photos from the event: "Thank God, every day we conquer the American Jews like our conquests over the Jews of Israel!" He signed it "Br. Sofian Zakkout."[1342]

In October 2014, Imam Mohammed al-Khaled Samha from a Danish mosque blasted his audience with another anti-Semitic rant. "How can we – or any free Muslim with faith in his heart – accept the division of Palestine between [the Palestinians] and a gang of Jews, the offspring of apes and pigs... Palestine has been and will remain the land of Islam. It is the land of the great battle, in which the Muslims will fight the Jews, and the trees and the stones will say: 'Oh Muslim, oh servant of Allah! There is a Jew behind me. Come and kill him.'"[1343]

This wasn't the first time Samha spewed his garbage. In 2005 after a magazine published a picture of their prophet Mohammad, which isn't allowed, Samha traveled to the Middle East, incited hatred and riots that killed hundreds.

These are but a few out of hundreds of examples that show deep-seated loathing.

JEWISH-MUSLIM ANIMOSITY

This wound goes back to Biblical times over 4,000 years ago to the story of Abraham, his wife Sarah, and her maidservant, Hagar. The short version is that Sarah desperately wanted a child, but she had become old and barren. She prayed for a child and God told her to be patient. As she grew older she thought God had forgotten His promise and took matters into her own hands. To say the least, it was a terrible, *terrible,* fateful decision with present-day repercussions.

Sarah asked her husband to make Hagar pregnant. Hagar, though a servant, began to get attitude once with child, which made Sarah very irritated with her. When she complained to Abraham, he said, *Look, she's your servant, do what you want.* So Sarah was harsh to her (no specifics given) and Hagar ran off into the wilderness. While there an angel appeared to Hagar, prophesying that her son Ishmael would "live in hostility toward all his brothers" (Genesis 16:12 AMP) and told her to go back home.

The Amplified Bible says, *"He (Ishmael) will be a wild donkey of a man; His hand will be against every man [continually fighting] and every man's hand against him; and he will dwell in defiance of all his brothers."* The American Standard Version is even stronger calling Ishmael "a wild ass". At the time of Ishmael's birth, Abraham was 86.

The story continued in Genesis 17. God came to Abraham when he was 99, some 13 years after Ishmael was born. The Lord told him He's going to bless Sarah with a son. Abraham's face must have been priceless as he fell on the ground laughing, and said to himself, *What? Sarah's 90, have a child?*

Now flash forward to Genesis 21. Sarah was 91 when she gave birth to Isaac. After he was weaned, which is assumed to be around two though the Bible isn't specific, this made Ishmael about 16. When Sarah saw Ishmael mocking Isaac Sarah demanded Abraham kick them both out. Abraham understandably distressed at his older son's departure received the promise from God in Genesis 21:12-13 that great nations would come from both of Ishmael and Isaac. From those nations came Judaism from Isaac's line and Islam from Ishmael's. It must have raised Muslims' ire when God pronounced in Genesis 22:2 that Isaac was Abraham's only son.

The obvious conclusion is if Abraham and Sarah had trusted God, believed God when He promised they would have a son, Sarah would never have encouraged Abraham to bed Hagar and Islam would never exist.

MODERN TIMES

Now this festering boil centers on the tug of war over Jerusalem. In Genesis 12:7, 13:14-15, 15:18-21 and 17:8 God promised the land of Canaan (Israel) to Abraham and his descendants – the Hebrews – forever. In the Jewish Diaspora when the Assyrians conquered them and later Nebuchadnezzar deported them, the Jews were literally scattered all over the world. Arabs then took over that land known as Palestine. After 2,545 years[1344] enough Hebrews had returned to Israel and it was officially declared a Jewish nation on May 14, 1948. Understandably Arabs were angry over this and being mostly Muslim didn't recognize God's promise documented in the Bible. Additionally, even though born of a servant, Muslims thought first-born Ishmael should have top consideration.

Jerusalem is *the* most sacred city to Jews and Christians, and third most to Muslims after Mecca and Medina. In the vicinity of King Solomon's temple and later King Herod's built on top of it, stands the Al-Aqsa Mosque and a little way away the Dome of the Rock and Dome of the Chain. It's also the site where the third and final Jewish temple will be built. How this will be accomplished is a puzzle when Muslims occupy this land. Varying theories exist of where exactly Solomon and Herod's temples were built. Scholarly examination, which is much too complex to dig into here locate them in different places, but all within the Temple Mount. It's thought that underneath the Al-Aqsa Mosque or a few yards to the north lies the buried Ark of the Covenant. Located by ground penetrating radar, before the area was sealed off, a 20-ton rock was found blocking off a large tunnel. It's there the Holy of Holies may rest, but we may never know as that real estate is in the hands of Muslims.

In 1990, the Jerusalem Islamic Waqf (an Islamic trust) acquired a permit to use the area that used to be Solomon's stables on the pretext of having an alternate place of worship for occasionally rainy days during Ramadan. Construction under the former stables finally started in 1996. In reality this gave Muslims a stronger claim over the Temple Mount as they intend the El-Marwani Mosque to house 10,000. More importantly this mosque, the largest in Israel, prevents Jews from using the area as a place of prayer.

2014 - 2015

On October 8, 2014, when the Temple Mount opened to non-Muslim visitors, clashes erupted almost immediately between masked Palestinians and police officers. Palestinian rioters threw rocks, pieces of metal, large cinder blocks and Molotov cocktails and sprayed flammable materials at the cops. Non-Muslim visitors are only allowed to come in through the Mugrabi entrance. In pre-planned treachery, the Palestinians had placed large objects blocking police access to the area. Then they poured flammable liquid on objects inside that they later tried to set on fire with Molotov cocktails.

Police chased rioters into the Al-Aqsa Mosque who then barricaded the doors with large marble slabs, furniture and wood posts. From inside they pummeled police with bricks, rocks and fireworks, and sprayed them with an unidentified flammable substance that made it hard for them to breathe. The ensuing chaos and fire inside the mosque caused extensive, permanent damage. Three officers were injured from the rocks and fireworks; five Palestinians were arrested and dozens were hurt.

A week and a half later, Palestinian Authority President Mahmoud Abbas gave a speech in which he stated, "We have to prevent the settlers from entering the Temple Mount by any means. It is our mosque and they have no right to enter and desecrate it".[1345] That was really rich since it was Palestinians that planned and carried out the attacks and caused the damage.

Two weeks later on the 30th, prominent rabbi Yehuda Glick, who had worked feverishly to restore Jewish rights to visit the Temple Mount, was nearly assassinated. He was just leaving a conference where he spoke about the Jewish presence on the Temple Mount when someone drove by on a motorcycle and shot him. Glick often prayed and performed Jewish rituals at the Temple Mount, which is strictly forbidden by Israeli police. Understandably this infuriated Muslims who reacted angrily to his presence. Police tracked down the shooter to arrest him, but previously convicted Palestinian terrorist Moataz Hejazi was fatally shot in crossfire. Released in 2012, Hejazi had spent the previous 11½ years in prison for serial arson, some at Jerusalem schools. In prison he razored two wardens in the face in 2001, which earned him time in solitary confinement. Two years later he wounded another warden in the face and in a third incident, poured boiling water over another prisoner.[1346]

November saw repeated episodes of Palestinians flinging rocks, Molotov cocktails, cinder blocks and other assorted items at Israeli security forces. Video footage shown to over 60 foreign Ambassadors and Diplomats stationed in Israel clearly documented Palestinians committing the damage done to the Al-Aqsa Mosque.

Then in early 2015, Palestinian women began to "protect" the Mosque from Jews. One woman stated, "Everybody must protect Al-Aqsa so the Jews don't take it. They have their eyes on it."[1347] The dean of Islamic studies at Al-Quds University, Mustafa Abu Sway, stated that "there is no similar situation" in Islamic history where women had taken such an active role in guarding a holy site. Muslim women hurled anti-Semitic slurs and chased Jewish people, which led to some of them being banned from the Temple Mount. Other Palestinian women shouted, "The army of Muhammad is coming!"[1348] Since November 2015, many more clashes involving Palestinians and Israeli security forces have taken place. They mostly involved the former throwing Molotov cocktails and large rocks at the latter.

To further erase Jewish connections to holy sites, in October 2015 six Arab states – Algeria, Egypt, Kuwait, Morocco, Tunisia and the UAE on behalf if Palestinians convinced the UN to list the Cave of the Patriarchs in Hebron and Rachel's Tomb in Bethlehem as Muslim sites. The U.S., UK, Germany, Netherlands, Czech Republic and Estonia voted against the resolution. Regardless, the approved resolution passed despite these sites' significance in Jewish history and tradition. The Arabs also tried to get the Western Wall designated as an extension of and part of the Al-Aqsa Mosque. A firestorm of international protest volleyed at UNESCO's Director-General shut down the attempt.

And so it goes. Endless rounds of violence between Jews and Muslim. But it's not just Muslims at fault. Christians and Jews must share the blame as well.

TOP REASONS CHRISTIANS ARE HATED

That Christians would be hated should be no surprise. Jesus prophesied it in John 15: 18-19: "If the world hates you, keep in mind that it hated me first. If you belonged to the world, it would love you as its own. As it is, you do not belong to the world, but I have chosen you out of the world. That is why the world hates you." That was a preview. Christians have brought most of the animosity on themselves. We can come across as:

- Harsh
- Self-Righteous
- Unforgiving
- Intolerant
- Inflexible

Then there's always the regretful, shameful history of violence:

- The Crusades
- The Inquisition

- Witch hunts
- Support of slavery
- The Holocaust
- Catholic sexual abuse

Yes, there is plenty for Christians to answer for.

TOP REASONS JEWS ARE HATED

Like Biblical prophesy of hatred toward Christians, Zechariah 12:2-3 predicted it for Jews: *"Behold, I am going to make Jerusalem a cup that causes reeling to all the peoples around; and when the siege is against Jerusalem, it will also be against Judah. It will come about in that day that I will make Jerusalem a heavy stone for all the peoples; all who lift it will be severely injured. And all the nations of the earth will be gathered against it."*

God warned in Deuteronomy 28:65 that they would be persecuted the world over. *"And among those nations you shall find no rest, and there shall be no resting place for the sole of your foot; but there the Lord will give you a trembling heart, failing of eyes, and despair of soul."* More specifically they are despised, rightly or wrongly for these reasons among others:

- They are God's "Chosen" (Deuteronomy 14:2)
- Through them God gave the world His Word
- Through them God provided the world's Savior
- Perception they have taken over business, banking and cinema resulting in …
- Disproportionate success
- Zionist movement that re-established the Jewish homeland resulting in …
- Conflict between Jews and Palestinians
- Garnering "blind" support of U.S. and disproportionate amount of financial aid from America
- Jealousy over maintained national identity and culture
- Blamed for death of Jesus

Among the three major world religions there is much rancor and there's little doubt it's growing like a cancer.

THE BIG "3" AT A GLANCE

Here is a summary of the major distinctions between Christianity, Judaism and Islam. Some differences are bridgeable; others aren't.

Comparisons Between Christianity, Islam and Judaism			
Topic	**Christianity**	**Islam**	**Judaism**
Nature of God	One God, who exists in three distinct persons (The Trinity): Father, Son and Holy Spirit (Matthew 28:19).	One God, *Allah*, who is not a trinity (Quran 112:1).	One God in English is 'Yahweh' or 'Jehovah' (Deuteronomy 6:4).
On Their Faith	One true religion.	One true religion.	Teaches Judaism is the way for Jews, not the way for everyone.[1349]
Jesus Christ	The second person of the Trinity and born of the Virgin Mary. "...true God from true God" (Nicene Creed)	A prophet, sent by Allah and born of the Virgin Mary, but not divine (Quran 5:17).	An ordinary Jew, not the Messiah, nor a divine person.
Jesus' Mission	To reconcile Man to God, through His death as a sacrifice for the sins of all mankind.	To proclaim the *Injil*, or gospel. This gospel has been corrupted over time by human additions and alterations.	Since Judaism rejects the idea of Jesus as Messiah, His mission is of no relevance.

Comparisons Between Christianity, Islam and Judaism

Topic	Christianity	Islam	Judaism
Jesus' Death	"...For our sake he was cruci-fied...he suffered death and was buried. On the third day he rose again...he ascended into heaven..." (Nicene Creed)	Jesus was not crucified (Quran 4:157), but was raised to Heaven by Allah (Quran 4:158).	Jesus was crucified for His claim to be divine.
Holy Spirit	The third person of the Trinity, truly divine: "...with the Father and the Son He is worshipped and glorified." (Nicene Creed)	Identical to Angel Gabriel, who appeared to the Prophet Mohammed giving him the Quranic text.	Not a distinct person, but a divine power, which for example, was given to the Prophets.
Sin	We inherit a sinful nature through our common ancestor Adam, who rebelled against God. Jesus Christ atoned for our sins through His death on the Cross (Romans 5:12-17).	There is no concept of origi-nal sin, nor vicarious atone-ment. All Humans are born sinless, but human weak-ness leads to sin.	Rejects the doctrine of original sin. Atonement for sins is made through seeking forgiveness from God in prayer and repent-ance especially on *Yom Kippur*, the day of atonement.
Salvation	By grace through faith in Jesus Christ (Ephesians 2:8-9).	Achieved through good works, thus personal right-eousness must outweigh personal sin (Quran 23:101-103).	Through good works, prayer and the grace of God. There is no parallel to the Christian view of substitutionary atonement.
Hell	A place of everlasting punish-ment for the unrighteous (Matthew 25:46). There is no crossover between Heaven and Hell.	Jahannam – a place of tor-ment and fire (Quran 25:65, 104:6-7). Its seven levels depend on degree of of-fense.	Concept of Gehinnom or Ge-henna – those who die in sin may suffer temporary punish-ment, but certain sins merit eter-nal punishment.
Lying	Strictly forbidden in the Ten Commandments (Exodus 20:16).	6 different types of lying are sanctioned.	"Thou shall not bear false wit-ness" (Exodus 20:16).
Jihad	No concept.	Generally misinterpreted as "holy war", it means "strug-gle." However, some Mus-lims take this to the extreme and carry out violent murders and beheadings. Allowed by Surah 9:38-39 and Vol. 1, Book 2, #35 * and in Vol. 9, Book 93, #555 ** of the Had-ith. [1350]	No concept.
Death for Converting to a Different Faith	No.	Yes.	No, but may be ostracized.

* The Prophet said, "The person who participates in (Holy battles) in Allah's cause and nothing compels him to do so except belief in Allah and His Apostles, will be recompensed by Allah either with a reward, or booty (if he survives) or will be admitted to Paradise (if he is killed in the battle as a martyr). Had I not found it difficult for my followers, then I would not remain behind any sariya going for Jihad and I would have loved to be martyred in Allah's cause and then made alive, and then martyred and then made alive, and then again martyred in His cause," (Volume 1, Book 2, No 35, Narrated Abu Huraira).

** "Allah's Apostle said, "Allah guarantees (the person who carries out Jihad in His Cause and nothing compelled him to go out but Jihad in His Cause and the belief in His Word) that He will either admit him into Paradise (Martyrdom) or return him with reward or booty he has earned to his residence from where he went out," (Volume 9, Book 93, No. 555: Narrated Abu Huraira).

When people fight, slaughter and create havoc, it's impossible for governments to maintain control. Islamic State doesn't look like it's going away any time soon and may be gathering momentum and recruits. It's the single largest source of religious world conflict. Christians aren't blowing themselves up and taking groups of innocent people with them. Jews aren't entering restaurants, theaters, businesses, schools and shopping malls with AK47s mowing down entire roomfuls of adults and children. Hindus aren't wielding machetes and dismembering humans and throwing body parts in the back of pickups. And Buddhists aren't filming themselves sawing off Christians' heads and posting their atrocities online in gruesome detail. Yet radical Muslims cast aside life and take as many as they can with them to become martyrs and get those 72 virgins. Martyred women get nothing.

The promise of the 72 virginal prizes isn't even in the Quran, but mentioned in a Hadith, which is a collection of Islamic tradition. In the collection compiled by Imam Abu Isa Muhammad at-Tirmidhi, Hadith 2687 says, "The Prophet Muhammad was heard saying: 'The smallest reward for the people of paradise is an abode where there are 80,000 servants and 72 wives, over which stands a dome decorated with pearls, aquamarine, and ruby, as wide as the distance from Al-Jabiyyah [a Damascus suburb] to Sana'a [Yemen]'."[1351]

So if this promise is relegated to "tradition" instead of written in their holy book, maybe it's more rumor or maybe they end up with 72 Hagatha the Horribles instead of exceptionally lovely houris – voluptuously beautiful maidens.

LAYING THE GROUNDWORK FOR A ONE WORLD RELIGION

This violence in world religions is regrettable especially among Jews, Christians and Muslims since Judaism is the parent of the other two, arguably founded about 1714 BC. Judaism began when God made the Covenant with Abraham promising Israel their lands forever. (Genesis 12:7-8)

Christianity and Judaism are the two most closely linked. They share the Old Testament in common and throughout the Christian Bible, Jewish and Christian histories are intertwined. Most scholars agree that Jewish authors, with the possible exception of Luke, even wrote the New Testament, which follows the framework of Judaism. Nowhere in the Bible is the prophet Mohammed, Allah, Muslims or Islam because it didn't form till about 580 years after Christianity.

Unless something monumental, something of unimaginable command takes control worldwide, there can be no reconciliation after hundreds of years of death and hate. With anger growing globally toward radical Muslims

who tarnish peaceful practitioners, the rise of anti-Semitism and Christian persecution, it's nearly impossible to see a unifying resolution. Yet the foundations are being laid right before our eyes for the False Prophet's one world religion (Revelation 13:11-18) that will support the Antichrist's one world government (Revelation 13:1-10).

Chrislam

This author first heard about Chrislam in January 2006 through a *Christian Science Monitor* article entitled, "New Religion in Africa: Islam and Christianity Blended – and Growing". This group began as "Chris-lam-herb" mixing Christianity, Islam and medicine before morphing into Chrislam. Though gaining a recognizable foothold today it's not new. Two branches began decades ago: *Ifeoluwa* founded by Tela Tella in the 70s and 80s and *Oke-Tude* started by Samson Saka in 1999. People of faith point out that the world's two largest religions have irreconcilable differences of insurmountable chasms, but followers of Chrislam urge unity.

Since these two movements originated in Nigeria, most of the western world had never heard of it till recently, but it's now spread to America. In 2011 churches from Alaska to Wyoming agreed to hold a Chrislam service. Participants covered a wide segment of denominations including Catholic, Methodist, Church of Christ, United Church of Christ, Episcopal, Unitarian, Presbyterian, Baha'i, Ecumenical and various independent congregations.

In 2014, Berlin began construction on The House of One where Muslims, Jews and Christians will worship together. Their vision: "Berlin is soon to become home to something truly unique. Jews, Christians, and Muslims are planning to build a house of worship here – one that brings a synagogue, a church, and a mosque together under one roof. One communal room in the center of the building will link the three sections. This will serve as a meeting place, where worshippers and members of the public can come together and learn more about the religions and each other."[1352] As of January 2016 construction isn't complete and they are actively seeking donations.

"UNITED" RELIGIOUS ORGANIZATIONS

The United Religions Initiative (URI) interfaith network was the brainchild of retired Episcopal bishop William Swing, but it wasn't established till seven years later in June 2000. Its vision sounded all warm and fuzzy "to engage in community action such as conflict resolution and reconciliation, **environmental sustainability**, education, women's and youth programs, and advocacy for human rights." Notice the specific reference to "environmental sustainability" – that popular phrase of Agendas 21 and 2030,[1353] which should be no surprise since it was a model to the UN. As of January 2016, 94 countries had signed on. The size of their network had increased six-fold in a decade and they're growing at a rate of 23% per year.[1354]

Source: United Religions Initiative

Every little square represents one of their 763 Interfaith Cooperation Circles for Christians, Buddhists, Muslims, Hindus, Indigenous Africans and Native Americans. To form a Circle, groups of at least seven people from at least three different religions independently must organize, self-govern and self-fund. Even though the Circles are stand-alone entities, like for membership to ICLEI's sustainable cities, URI still wants Circles to pay into Headquarters or give a "gift" or a service. Their site says, "CCs [Cooperation Circles] have the responsibility to develop financial and other resources to help meet their needs and help meet the needs of other parts of the URI. In order to help support the worldwide URI community, CCs are asked to make a financial gift or contribution of service. Discuss what kind of financial gift or contribution of service your CC would like to offer."[1355]

Its Preamble says, "We believe that our religious, spiritual lives, rather than dividing us, guide us to build community and respect for one another. Therefore, as interdependent people rooted in our traditions, we now unite for the benefit of our Earth community. ...We unite to heal and protect the Earth."[1356] The Purpose echoes the same sentiment. "The purpose of the United Religions Initiative is to promote enduring, daily interfaith cooperation, to end religiously motivated violence and to create cultures of peace, justice and healing for the Earth and all living beings."[1357]

Their Charter wants "to create cultures of peace, justice and healing for the Earth and all living beings," and to "act from **sound ecological practices to protect and preserve the Earth** for both present and future generations." Notice again the emphasis to the environment.[1358] What has this to do with religion and God ... unless you've made the environment and Earth your religion?

COMMON POISONOUS SEEDS

The world has moved on from the original Coexist bumper sticker that acknowledged just the three world major religions of Christianity, Judaism and Islam to embracing everything from obscure sects to gays to peace and science, to pagans and atheists and every religion in between. This trek down the road to universalism – that One World Religion – is unmistakable. Christianity says there is one road to salvation, not through enlightenment of psilocybin mushrooms, acid (LSD) or scopolamine that makes you regurgitate a lot before you "get there".

New Agers and Ecumenicalists say the road to God is something else, something all encompassing. It's so easy to get off onto that path. Be enticed and seduced especially in light of political correctness that says we must accept everything in the name of tolerance. Jesus was quite specific in John 14:6. "I am the way, the truth, and the life. No one comes to the Father except through me." But this is the road that the New World Order would have us take and it's popping up everywhere. Other organizations like the World Religions Conference, Shared Faith, European Interreligious Forum for Religious Freedom (EIFRF), Parliament of the World's Religions, World Council of Churches and Interfaith Summit Conference also promote this same objective.

Universalism and the Deception of Inclusiveness

The Spirit and Truth Sanctuary, founded in 2012 by Pastors DE and Brandi Paulk is one of a growing trend toward ecumenism. If that surname sounds familiar that's because DE's family was embroiled in decades of scandals. One involved a Sarah-Abraham-Hagar scenario among others.[1359] Coming out of a Charismatic church Pastor Paulk embraces Universalism, the belief that all people will be saved regardless of what they've done or believed. Behind the pulpit is a beautiful stained glass window blazing with symbols of many faiths surrounding a dove. Over their clerical robes they wear stoles stamped or embroidered with the same symbols as their logo:

The Trendiest, Friendliest, Most Radically Inclusive Worship Experience in Atlanta

Paulk even penned a book, *The Holy Bible of Inclusion*. Numerous publications are devoted to the subject like:

- Bishop Carlton Pearson's The Gospel of Inclusion: Reaching Beyond Religious Fundamentalism to the True Love of God and Self
- Richard Scott Thornton's Inclusive Christianity: A Progressive Look at Faith
- Rev. Dr. Mark D. Roberts Christian Inclusiveness, Witness Lee's The All-Inclusiveness and Unlimitedness of Christ
- Steven Greenebaum's The Interfaith Alternative: Embracing Spiritual Diversity
- Reverend Stephanie Rutt's Getting to the Heart of Interfaith: The Interfaith Worship Manual
- Ted Brownstein's The Interfaith Prayer Book

- Dr. Eboo Patel's Interfaith Leadership: A Primer
- Matthew Fox's One River, Many Wells

In one of the most bizarre and dangerous statements ever uttered by a pastor, this has to be in the top 10. Every pastor, minister and priest this author has heard preach, at the end of sermons issues an altar call or a call to decision where people that want the gift of salvation must make a purposeful conscious choice to tell God what you've done wrong (list your sins), promise to not do them anymore, ask forgiveness, ask the Lord into your life and accept the gift of salvation. It's not something left all loosey-goosey. Just because Jesus offers salvation as a gift doesn't mean you automatically get it and don't have to actively accept it. On this Pastor Paulk has something else to say.

"Whether or not we must 'choose' of our own free will to be saved or not has become a huge subject of controversy of late among Christians. Those who argue that we must use our free will to make a decision would say that each of us is saved by our own faith in Jesus and the work He did on the cross.

"Ephesians 4:8-10, however, says this: For by grace you have been saved through faith, and that not of yourselves; it is the gift of God, not of works, lest anyone should boast. For we are His workmanship, created in Christ Jesus for good works, which God prepared beforehand that we should walk in them.

"So, if Jesus is the 'author and finisher' of our faith, and if Paul tells us in Ephesians that we are 'saved' through faith that is 'not of ourselves' but rather is the gift of God, then is it really our faith (our decision) that saves us? Or does our faith in the finished work of Jesus merely connect us to what He has already completed? In other words, do we have faith in Jesus, or do we have faith in faith?"[1360] This tunnels into the absurd.

WHAT MUST I DO TO BE SAVED?

Both Jesus and the aspostles (guided by the Holy Spirit) taught that to be saved, one must:

Hear	Romans 10:13-17 John 6:45 Revelation 1:3
Believe	John 2:30-31 Hebrews 11:6 Acts 16:31
Repent	Luke 13:3-5 Acts 2:38 Acts 17:30-31
Confess	Matthew 10:32-33 Romans 10:9-10
Be Baptized	Mark 16:15-16 1 Peter 3:21 Acts 2:38 Acts 22:16
Live Godly	Titus 2:11-14 Romans 12:1-2 2 Peter 1:5-11

POPES

However, the big guns came out with popes promoting ecumenism and unification because they reach billions more than Pastor Paulk.

In 2014 former president Shimon Peres held talks with Pope Francis. In a shocking statement, Peres said, "Now, given the fact that the United Nations has had its day, what is needed is an Organization of United Religions, a U.N. of religions."[1361]

This was an overt entreaty to promote a One World Religion. Nothing hidden, he just put it out there. Peres called it the "United Religions." This concept used to be anathema to most Christians, but over the years and with the formation of numerous groups aimed at this objective, its grating on ears is beginning to dull.

In 2000 then Cardinal Ratzinger who became Pope Benedict XVI in 2005, said non-Catholic churches are "gravely deficient," that they were "not churches in the proper sense."[1362] In the 16-page document entitled, *Dominus Iesus: On the Unicity and Salvific Universality of Jesus Christ and the Church*, he went on to say Orthodox churches suffer a "wound" because they don't accept the authority of the pope and that wound is "still more profound" in Protestant denominations. Ratzinger continued. "Despite the fact that this teaching has created no little distress ... it is nevertheless difficult to see how the title of 'Church' could possibly be attributed to them."[1363] He topped off his commentary saying that other churches aren't real churches nor are their priests real priests because they can't trace their origins back to Peter and the apostles. Not surprisingly, that went down with Protestants like swallowing razor blades.

Why all the nasties? The Catholic Church is still chapped over the Orthodox Schism that began in 1054 followed by the Protestant Reformation starting 1517. This was never more obvious than when Benedict wrote in *Dominus Iesus*, "The lack of unity among Christians is certainly a wound for the [Catholic] church in that it hinders the complete fulfillment of her universality in history."[1364] Your prophetic hairs should be standing at attention. Popes are determined to bring the "gravely deficient" Protestant daughters back into the fold – to have them move back home and submit.

Photo: Vatican viewed from the Tiber River on September 2, 2007

Isaiah 47:1, God identifies a "daughter of Babylon," which is different from old Babylon in Iraq – a daughter that comes out of that system and exists in End Times. In Biblical prophecy, when it references a woman or daughter, it means a church. This connection is made when scripture talks about God's Church indicating the woman or bride (the body of believers) who will marry Jesus Christ. (See Ephesians 5 and Revelation 19:7). But Isaiah 47 refers to a great *false* church. There can be no mistake that Mystery Babylon indicates the Catholic Church as Revelation 17 lays out its description. Today Mystery Babylon of the End Times has grown so large, its reach extends worldwide as indicated in Revelation 17:15. Globally Catholics number more than 1.2 billion from many countries who speak many different languages. Now it strives for even greater control and power wanting to bring back into the fold all Orthodox and Protestants.

John Paul II, in his 1995 encyclical, "Ut Unum Sint" ("To Be One"), said the objective of ecumenism was to unite other churches under the "Magisterium of the church" – Roman Catholic Church authority. The document states: "To believe in Christ means to desire unity; to desire unity means to desire the [Catholic] Church."[1365]

Regarding what looked like concessions, including accepting of some "Christian communities" as "churches," a November 27, 2003 Global News Wire article observed, "These concessions represent neither a shift nor a softening of the dogmatic positions long held by the Roman church. Rather, the dogma remains deeply entrenched and the concessions are merely a part of the strategy or means by which 'other Christians' will be led to accept and unite under Catholic dogma."[1366]

Argentina's Pope Francis broadens the quest of ecumenism by cozying up to Islam. In an historic first he "opened the door to Muslim prayers and Quran readings at the Vatican last year [2014]. Palestinian President Mahmoud Abbas and Israeli President Shimon Peres joined the pontiff in the Vatican gardens for a prayer meeting."[1367]

During his South America tour Francis called for "a new economic and ecological world order where "the goods of the Earth are shared by everyone, not just exploited by the rich."[1368]

What can't be achieved in denigration and overtures to bring other churches under the Catholic wing is coupled with global warming shaming and calls for a New World Order.

Pope Francis climbed on the global warming bandwagon when he addressed the UN and Congress in September 2015 – one of the rallying points of unification around the world. Pope Francis refers to it as climate as "a common good."[1369]

Global warming, promoted globally by the UN, is a common theme central to wealth redistribution, the New World Order and ecumenism leading to a One World Religion. Even a decade ago, who would have thought these things could be tied to global warming?

Image: Video screen snap of Pope Francis unifying religions in 2016. Clockwise left-bottom is Christianity, Buddhism, Islam and Judaism.[1370]

TREADING ON DANGEROUS TERRITORY

Church leaders, especially Catholic and Protestant leaders are paving the way to the One World Religion with misplaced tolerance. We're seeing it in government and in the economy and in faith. In 1989 Archbishop of the Anglican Church, Robert Runcie, called for all Christians to accept the Pope as "a common leader presiding in love" during his first official visit to the Vatican during an evening prayer. Runcie continued. "For the universal church, I renew the plea. Could not all Christians come to reconsider the kind of primacy the bishop of Rome (pope) exercised within the early church, a 'presiding in love' for the sake of the unity of the churches in the diversity of their mission?"[1371]

Chapter 18: Israel, God's Prophetic Time Clock

Psalms 83, Ezekiel 38 and 39

The one thing that sets Biblical prophecy apart from all others is that it's always correct, no exceptions. Out of approximately 2,500 prophecies about 2,000 have been fulfilled to the letter. Dr. Hugh Ross calculated the odds of this accuracy is less than one in 10^{2000} – that's 10 with 2,000 zeros after it.[1372] Many for Israel already have a ✓next to them like enemies would move into the land of Israel, their temple would be destroyed, they would be scattered throughout the world, they would return to their land and its desert would bloom. Some of the most significant prophecies will be fulfilled during or close to Tribulation:

- Israel will undergo unprecedented trouble (Jeremiah 30:7, Daniel 12:1)
- Arab nations will attack Israel and try to annihilate her. (Psalm 83)
- Israel will defeat them. (Zechariah 12:6)
- Israel will then live in security and prosper with greatly expanded borders. (Ezekiel 38:11)
- A Russian-led coalition of Muslim nations will invade Israel in the Gog-Magog War. (Ezekiel 38:1-17)
- God will destroy the Gog-Magog attackers supernaturally. (Ezekiel 38:18-23, Ezekiel 39:1-8)
- The Antichrist will guarantee Israel's security and enable the Jews to rebuild their Temple. (Daniel 9:27)
- 3½ years into the guarantee, the Antichrist will enter the new Temple in Jerusalem and declare he is God in what's known as the Abomination of Desolation. (Daniel 9:27, Matthew 24:15-18, 2 Thessalonians 2:3-4)
- The Jews will reject the Antichrist and in retaliation he'll try to annihilate them, killing two-thirds. (Revelation 12:13-17, Zechariah 13:8-9).
- At the end of the 7 years, when the Jews are nearly destroyed, they will recognize Yeshua (Jewish word for Jesus) as the Messiah. (Zechariah 12:10, Romans 9:27-28, Romans 11:25-27)
- Jesus returns and brings all believing Jews to Israel. (Deuteronomy 30:1-9)
- Israel will be established as the world's leading nation. (Isaiah 2:1-4, Micah 4:1-7)

What's is in store for God's prophetic clock? It will be mighty, overall mighty terrible, but ultimately mighty miraculous.

Small But Mighty

Imagine a country no bigger than New Jersey surrounded by enemies. At its narrowest, Israel is less than 10 miles across, which makes it even more vulnerable. To say the land stretches some 290 miles north to south is deceptive because the southern half comes to a sharp "V", which is filled with desert. So half of its 8½ million people live along the shoreline and in urban areas.

Jesus lived and ministered mostly around Galilee, Jerusalem and Judea. But he also walked east of the Jordan River, which dumps into the Dead Sea, into Perea and Decapolis in Jordan and Syria, and up to Sidon, which was about 20 miles north of Tyre in Lebanon.

Because the country is so small they would have encountered mountains, plains, rich agricultural land and desert just minutes apart. Several mountain ranges run the length of the country so He and the apostles likely traveled closer to the seas and through valleys. Even so, on foot it would have taken quite awhile to make the rounds.

I Will Bless Those Who Bless You...

After being scattered throughout the world for over 2,500 years, it truly was a miracle that Jews retained their culture, traditions and language, let alone returned to re-establish their Nation. In this effort, the U.S. played a key role and its favorable treatment of Israel ensured America's blessings. God is very clear about Israel. In Genesis 12:3 He said, *I will bless those who bless you, And I will curse him who curses you.* Bill Koenig in his 2008 book *Eye to Eye - Facing the Consequences of Dividing Israel,* chronicles major disasters occurring within 24 hours of Presidents Bush, Clinton and Bush II who applied pressure on Israel to trade her land for promises of "peace and security" or made major public statements calling for a Palestinian state. The correlation is undeniable.

Twelve U.S. Presidents, soon to be 13, have taken office since Israel became a nation again. Beginning with Harry S. Truman, regardless of party affiliation, they were generally very supportive of Israel or at least did them no harm until Gerald Ford entered the picture. Worse than Ford was Jimmy Carter with his barely concealed racism.

Surprisingly one of the greatest advocates for Israel was Lyndon Johnson. His grandfather, who was a fundamentalist Christian, along with other members of the Johnson family, believed the Hebrews would return to Palestine one day. He told Lyndon, "Take care of the Jews, God's Chosen People. Consider them your friends and help them any way you can."[1373] By the time Jimmy Carter finished his term, his anti-Israel policies leapt off news pages including his own book *Palestine: Peace Not Apartheid.* In fact, history shows the peanut farmer was *the* most anti-Israel President only trumped by Barack Obama.

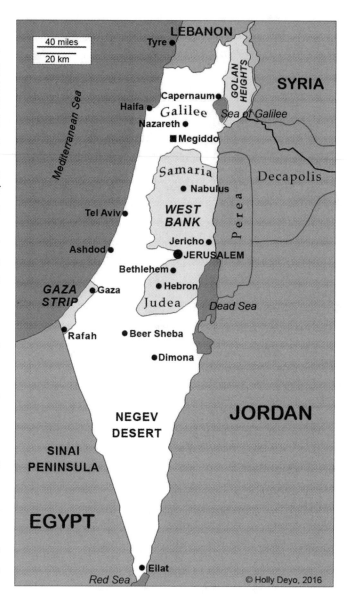

© Holly Deyo, 2016

Presidents' Treatment of Israel			
President	**Friend**	**Foe**	**Comment**
Truman 1945 – 1953	X		Condemned Hitler as "mad" and called those that carried out the atrocities – the "systematic slaughter" of Hebrews – "Nazi beasts".[1374] Brought 80,000 Jewish refugees into the U.S,[1375] instituted an arms embargo in hopes of bringing Middle East peace.
Eisenhower 1953 – 1961	X	X	Publicly supported Israel, but quietly applied great pressure for Israel to withdraw from the Sinai Peninsula after the Suez War ended in 1956.[1376] Continued Truman's arms embargo.
Kennedy 1961 – 1963	X		Strongly supported Israel and lifted Truman's arms embargo. Extended first informal security guarantees in 1962. In 1963, authorized sale of advanced U.S. weaponry, including surface-to-air Hawk missiles,[1377] but opposed Israel developing nukes. His brother, Bobby, was also a strong supporter of Israel. During his 1968 Presidential campaign, he declared he would maintain "clear and compelling support for Israel."[1378]
Johnson	X		Became Israel's chief diplomatic ally and primary arms supplier especially during the

Presidents' Treatment of Israel			
President	**Friend**	**Foe**	**Comment**
1963 – 1969			1967 Six Day War. Rescued hundreds of Jews during the Holocaust – actions that could have thrown him out of Congress and into jail.[1379] Closely supervised crafting of 1967 UN Resolution 242 guaranteeing Israel's "secure and recognized boundaries."
Nixon 1969 – 1974	X		During a surprise invasion of Israel in the 1973 Yom Kippur War, Nixon responded immediately with overwhelming aid to counter the offensive,[1380] despite knowing it would alienate the Arab World and greatly irritate the Soviet Union. Even today, Nixon is greatly admired by the Israelis and viewed "as the man who saved Israel."[1381]
Ford 1974 – 1977		X	Took a hard line against Israel demanding they withdraw from the Sinai. Sent such a threatening letter to PM Yitzhak Rabin that 76 Senators demanded Ford "make it clear the U.S., acting in its own national interests, stands firm with Israel."[1382]
Carter 1977 – 1981	X	X	Brokered deal between Israel and Egypt, which provided for complete withdrawal of Israel from the Sinai Peninsula.[1383] After leaving office, his personal writings revealed him to be a rabid anti-Semite. He also called for international recognition of Hamas when war broke out between them and Israelis in 2014.[1384] Demanded the UN investigate Israel for war crimes.[1385] Complained there was "too many Jews" on the government's Holocaust Memorial Council.[1386] Penned the highly controversial anti-Semitic book, *Palestine: Peace Not Apartheid*. Viewed as so anti-Israel and pro-Hamas that both PM Benjamin Netanyahu and President Reuven Rivlin declined Carter's request to meet when he visited Israel in 2015.[1387] **NOTE**: The *only* reason Carter gets any positive marks is that the peace he brokered for the Middle East allowed Israel 40 years of breathing room to prosper and build their military and technology.
Reagan 1981 – 1989	X	X	Publicly supported Israel, but had numerous harsh confrontations with them.[1388] Reagan worked to free Soviet Jews and approved the CIA rescuing 500 Ethiopian Jews in 1985. He helped to reform Israel's economy. In 1985, following a severe economic crisis, which sent Israel's inflation rates as high as 445%, the U.S. approved a $1.5 billion emergency assistance package. Reagan helped formulate Israel's successful economic stabilization plan and began sending them $3 billion every year in foreign aid.[1389]
George H. W. Bush 1989 – 1993		X	His anti-Semitic Secretary of State, James Baker, demanded Israel negotiate with a Palestinian delegation from East Jerusalem and the West Bank, and publicly supported Palestinian "right of return," which would have ended the Jewish state.[1390] In 1991 Bush stated East Jerusalem was "occupied territory," though Israel had officially annexed it in 1980.[1391]
Clinton 1983 – 2001	X		Strong friend of Jewish people and Israel. Clinton had 5 Jews in his Cabinet, appointed 2 Jews to the Supreme Court, and had many others in key positions.[1392] Despite giving substantial financial aid he favored land-for-peace.[1393]
George W. Bush 2001 – 2009		X	Claimed to be Israel's friend, but was the first President to call for a Palestinian state.[1394]
Obama 2009 – 2017		X	Most anti-Israel President in history. Repeatedly called Israel's settlements "illegitimate" and treated Netanyahu with disdain during White House visits. Gives famous June 2009 apology speech in Egypt to the Muslim nations of the Middle East.[1395] In July 2009, Obama announced that it was time for "daylight" between the United States and Israel.[1396] In May 2011 Obama demanded on national TV that Israel return to 1967 borders. That same month Obama became first President to officially call for a two-state solution for the Israel-Palestinian conflict.[1397] On November 3, 2011, in what Obama thought was a private conversation with French President Nicolas Sarkozy, their open mics transmitted their true feelings. Sarkozy to Obama: "I cannot stand him [Netanyahu]. He is a liar." Obama replied:

Presidents' Treatment of Israel

President	Friend	Foe	Comment
			"You're fed up with him, but I have to deal with him every day!"[1398] In a 2012 September speech to the UN Obama said, "The future must not belong to those who slander the prophet of Islam." (Message aimed at Israel)[1399] In August 2014, in the midst of an Israeli war with Hamas, Obama withholds weapons shipments to Israel.[1400] Over the years, the Obama Administration made *many* leaks to the press about Israel.[1401] In January 2015, Obama issued a directive that goods from the West Bank must be labeled as such, which amounts to a boycott.[1402] In March 2015, Obama declassified document revealing Israel's "highly covert" nuclear program.[1403] In July 2015, Obama pushed through the UN the infamous nuclear deal with Iran that threatens Israel's survival.[1404]

President names in bold indicate they were with the Democrat Party.

Consequences of Trying to Divide Israel

In Zechariah 2:1-8, God says that Israel is the "apple of His eye" and anyone that who messes with her, "plunders" her or tries to divide her will see disastrous consequences. Several Presidents tried, as did Israel's 5th Prime Minister Yitzhak Rabin. It's no coincidence that Rabin was assassinated on November 4, 1995. This happened right at the end of a rally, which supported the Oslo Accords and his killer didn't support a divided Israel.[1405] Was this an example of God delivering a mighty swat?

Presidential Actions Against Israel and Their Consequences

Date	Action	Date	Consequence
October 18, 1991	The U.S. announced the Madrid Conference with Arabs, the U.S., Israel, the USSR and Palestinians, which paved the way for more talks. Bush said, "Territorial compromise is essential for peace."[1406]	October 1-31, 1991	**Oakland (California) Firestorm** burned over 3,000 homes, did nearly $6 billion in damages and killed 25.[1407]
February 18-25, 1993	George H. W. Bush's Secretary of State Warren Christopher traveled to Israel and 7 Arab countries to restart the peace process.[1408]	February 26, 1993	**World Trade Center Bombing** – terrorist attack killed 6 and injured over a thousand.[1409]
September 13, 1993	The Oslo Peace Accords – the Land for Peace accord – Palestinians would recognize Israel and Israeli forces would withdraw from parts of the Gaza Strip and West Bank, giving Palestine the right to self-govern in those areas.[1410]	September 1, – November 30, 1993	**California Wildfires**: Dry weather, high winds and wildfires in Southern California killed 4 and racked up $2.3 billion in damages.[1411]
January 16, 1994	Clinton and Syrian President Hafez al-Assad made statements supporting Oslo Accord as first step to peace, which involved Israel giving up the Golan Heights.	January 17, 1994	**Northridge Earthquake** killed at least 60 and injured more than 9,000. The 6.7-quake caused widespread damage in the San Fernando Valley. It was the most devastating temblor to hit Calif. since the 1906 San Francisco event and the costliest in U.S. history at $72 billion.
September 28, 1998	Clinton, Netanyahu and Arafat met at the White House where Arafat called for a Palestinian state by 1999.[1412]	September 28, 1998	**Hurricane Georges** That same day, Cat 2 Georges ploughed through the Gulf Coast and dumped up to 30 inches

Presidential Actions Against Israel and Their Consequences

Date	Action	Date	Consequence
			of rain in 2 days. It was the costliest 'cane since Andrew, causing $9.6 billion of damage and killed over 600.[1413]
October 15, 1998	Secretary of State Madeleine Albright finishes agreement, which requires Israel to surrender 13% of the West Bank. President Bill Clinton meets with Yasser Arafat and Netanyahu at the White House to finalize another Israel land-for- peace" deal.[1414]	October 16 – 24, 1998	**Texas Flooding** Torrential rains of up to 25 inches in 5 days and thunderstorms cause flooding across much of southeast Texas. Storms left 31 dead and caused over $1.4 billion in damages.[1415]
May 3, 1999	Arafat had been scheduled to declare Palestinian state with Jerusalem as its capital.[1416] Declaration postponed.	May 3-6, 1999	**Oklahoma and Kansas Tornadoes** Devastating F4-F5 twisters rip through Oklahoma and Kansas, killing 55 and causing $3 billion in damages.
June 8, 2001	George W. Bush sent Secretary Tenet to Jerusalem with a proposal to exchange land for a "Roadmap to Peace."	June 5-17, 2001	**Tropical Storm Allison** dumped up to 40 inches of rain in Texas and Louisiana, causing severe flooding especially in the Houston area. The storm left 43 dead and caused $11.7 billion in damages.[1417]
September 10, 2001	Pres. Bush, his Secretary of State Colin Powell, U.S. Ambassador to Israel Daniel Kurtzer and the Saudis had been working on the most comprehensive two-state plan for Israel and Palestine, which was mostly completed on Sept. 10.[1418]	September 11, 2001	**Terrorist Attacks in New York City and the Pentagon plus one intended for the White House**, but it crashed in Pennsylvania due to brave efforts of the passengers. Nineteen Islamic terrorists from Saudi Arabia killed nearly 3,000 including 343 firefighters and paramedics, 23 NYC police and 37 Port Authority officers.
August 15 – 22, 2005	Settlers in Gaza and Northern Samaria given eviction notices. U.S. Secretary Condoleezza Rice tells Israel evacuation "cannot be Gaza only." Israeli PM Ariel Sharon authorizes mandatory evac of residents refusing to leave Gaza. 9,000+ Israeli soldiers evacuate 25 communities. Many were forcibly removed, and then 3,000+ homes were bulldozed. President Bush states to Congress, "We'll continue working for the day when the map of the Middle East shows two democratic states, Israel and Palestine living side by side in Peace and security."[1419] He later states, "My vision, my hope, is that one day we'll see two states, two democratic states, living side by side in peace."[1420]	August 25 – 31, 2005	**Hurricane Katrina**, the most deadly hurricane and costliest natural disaster to strike the U.S. It caused over $156 billion in damages and left 1,833 dead, destroyed 225,000 homes and displaced over a million. Striking hardest in New Orleans, over a decade later some areas were still uninhabitable.[1421]
Summer 2008	Presidential candidate, Sen. Barack Obama gives support in a meeting with Palestinian Authority Chairman and Fatah leader Mahmoud Abbas for a new Arab sate within Israeli borders.[1422]	January 1 – December 31, 2008	**U.S. Drought and Heatwave** caused nearly $8 billion in agricultural losses. By the end of August about 19% of CONUS was in moderate to extreme drought.[1423]
May 14, 2015	President Obama said a two-state solution for Israel and Palestinians was "absolutely vital" for Middle East peace.	May 5 – 10, 2015 May 21 – 26,	**Southern Plains Tornado** outbreak across 7 states. Some 122 tornadoes took 4 lives and caused at least $1 billion in damages.

Presidential Actions Against Israel and Their Consequences				
Date	Action	Date	Consequence	
		2015	**Texas and Oklahoma Flooding and Severe Weather** killed at least 31 and created at least $1 billion in losses. Between 350 and 400 homes disappeared in Texas and over a thousand more were damaged.[1424]	
November 5, 2015	Obama administration officially abandons two-state agenda.[1425]			
NOTE: All damages listed under Consequences are in 2016 dollars.				

Rise of anti-Semitism

The trend today, even among Christians, is to denigrate Jewish people. It's gone beyond sly comments in private conversations. Defacing property, heckling and other verbal abuse along with spray painted racial slurs on property, arson, swastikas painted on synagogues and schools, mezuzahs vandalized, harassment, discrimination, physical violence and even murder. This author's husband stopped guesting on one prominent talk show due to the host's repeated anti-Jewish rants. Her behavior wasn't only shocking, but extremely disappointing especially since she proclaimed her Christianity. We thought such sickening behavior would never be revisited after the Holocaust. However it's another prophesied event in End Times – the ugly rise again of anti-Semitism. According to the prophet Jeremiah, God said, *"I will make them [Jews] hated by all the kingdoms of the earth. People will curse them…"* — Jeremiah 29:18 (NCV). And they do.

Part of anti-Semitism's resurgence stems from ongoing conflicts with Palestinians. Some has to do with people buying into a spurious document, *The Protocols of the Elders of Zion*. Its intent was supposedly to paint Jewish people as the creators of the Illuminati. Portions of the Protocols were "borrowed" from Maurice Joly's 1864 fictional work *Dialogue in Hell,* a thinly veiled attack on the political ambitions of Napoleon. Joly, in turn "borrowed" themes from Eugene Sue's 1856 novel *Les Mysteres Du Peuple*.

Professor Norman Cohn documented in his book *Warrant for Genocide,* the world-control myth was lifted from a 19th century French political satire, which put forth the plotters weren't even Jewish.[1426]

Researcher and editor Ken Adachi wrote this about the Protocol's history: "In 1884, the daughter of a Russian general living in Paris, Mademoiselle Justine Glinka, paid Joseph Schoerst (alias Shapiro), a member of the Jewish Mizraim Masonic Lodge, the sum of 2,500 francs [~$250 then and ~$8,500 in 2016] for a 'document [which] contained extraordinary dictated writings from assorted speeches which would later be included in the final compilation of the Protocols of Zion.'

"…The ideas and beliefs expressed in these protocols are so hideous and repugnant to the sensibilities of any normal person of good will, that the English translator, Victor E. Marsden, could only work on translating Nilus' 1905 Russian version of the Protocols (at the British Museum) for one hour per day due to his revulsion with the concepts being promoted."[1427]

AROUND THE WORLD IN "HATEY" DAYS

Since 2009 hate crimes against Jews noticeably ratcheted up. Attacks on Jews raged globally across Europe, Canada, America and Australia. 2014 was the worst year in a decade. In Europe, France saw the most instances of Jewish people targeted, followed by Britain and Germany. Though France's population is only 1% Jewish, they suffer 50% of all racist attacks.[1428] Experts say this new trend in anti-Semitism can be traced directly to the influx of Muslims in these countries[1429] and especially in cities with large Muslim populations.[1430]

Pew Research put France's Muslim population in 2010 at 7.5% – nearly 5 million – with some areas like Paris at 15% and Marseilles at 40%. Recent estimates show the UK had about 5% Muslims with Belgium, Germany and the Netherlands each at 6%.[1431] From 1990 to 2010, Muslim numbers have increased 300% to 44 million across Europe, which brings serious concerns about integration.[1432]

United Kingdom

In 2014 anti-Semitic hate crimes in the UK more than doubled in just one year.[1433] Then in the first six months of 2015, the number shot up 38% compared to the same time frame in 2014.

Anti-Semitism is fueling migration back to Israel and to the U.S. From 2013 to summer of 2015, well over 14,000 French Jews left for Israel. Honey Gould, a Jewish mother of two in the UK said she, her husband and kids were moving to Arizona. "I know there are plenty of people who simply want to live a peaceful coexistence," she said, "but there is so much anti-Semitism in Britain, and it's coming from all sides. Our local Jewish schools look like prison camps. They're surrounded by wire fences. There are guards on patrol, some with dogs. On Saturdays, you see police walking the street with members of the CST [Community Security Trust]. I don't want to sit at home panicking when my husband goes to the synagogue. I just want to live in peace."[1434]

U.S.

European Jews choosing America as home seemed natural. The U.S., as a rule, has been Israel's most ardent friend, until Jew-hating President Carter, the lesser-so Bushes and then the worst of the worst Pres. Obama. Rabbi Joseph Potasnik, executive VP for the New York Board of Rabbis said, "Unfortunately anti-Semitism has become fashionable again. It's not a big deal to hate the Jews. The first group that gets attacked is the Jews."[1435] "Fashionable" and anti-Semitism should be mutually exclusive.

Ugly behavior toward Jews hit over a hundred U.S. college campuses in 2015. Not surprising in the 28 states where it occurred, it often happened where the number of mosques is greatest: California, New York, Florida, Illinois, New Jersey and Massachusetts.[1436] [1437] It's gotten so bad that Tammi Rossman-Benjamin of the University of California – Santa Cruz co-founded the AMCHA (Hebrew for "Your People") Initiative. This is an online database for reporting anti-Semitic incidents that take place on American college campuses. The following is an example of what's on the database.

One female student athlete at Delaware Valley College tweeted out in December 2013, "Can I kill all the [expletive deleted] Jews in Lakewood *pleeeasse?!?!!*"[1438] It took 15 months for this ugly post to be brought to the attention of school administrators. The irony is that a rabbi, Joseph Krauskopf, founded this Pennsylvania college in 1896.

In February 2015, a Boise, Idaho a woman attacked her Jewish neighbor, Annette Guidry, kicked her in the stomach and groin, dragged her by the hair, and stood on her neck until she said she believed in Jesus. Two days later she cut up this woman's mail and scratched "death" on her mailbox. Marguerite Haragan was charged with two felony counts of malicious harassment and faces up to five years in jail.

Swastikas were spray painted on 30 homes in Madison, Wisconsin. Jim Stein, an 18-year resident of the city's west side woke Valentine's Day 2015 to see "F**k Jews" spray-painted on a garage door across the street. Garage doors, driveways and vehicles were targeted with anti-Semitic slogans, obscene drawings, derogatory remarks about women and drawings of Confederate flags with "KKK" next to them.[1439]

In January 2015, pro-Palestinian activists stormed a New York City Council meeting that was discussing commemorating the 70th anniversary of Auschwitz's liberation. Protesters in the Council chamber's balcony unfurled a Palestinian flag and began yelling "Palestinian lives matter" and "Don't support genocide." Several dozen disrupters had to be forcibly removed. Afterwards Councilman David Greenfield accused them of anti-Semitism in an impassioned speech. "What you saw here today was naked, blind anti-Semitism. That's what you saw, and that's what you watched, and that's what you witnessed – people who were upset for one reason. Do you want to know why they're upset, do you want to know why they're angry, do you want to know why they unfurled that flag today? Because Hitler did not finish the job. He only wiped out *half* of my family."[1440]

In California, swastikas were spray painted onto the wall and doorstep of the Jewish Alpha Epsilon Pi fraternity at UC Davis.[1441]

These examples all happened during the first six weeks of 2015. The year before a gang carrying Palestinian flags attacked a Jewish couple on New York's Upper East Side.

Also in 2014 Frazier Glenn Cross who had a long history of spewing anti-Semitism rhetoric shot to death a boy and his grandpa outside a Jewish community center in Overland Park, Kansas. He then turned his gun on a woman at a nearby Jewish assisted living facility. When arrested, he was heard shouting "Heil Hitler" from the back of the police car.

Much as Muslims like to say they are the biggest targets of hate crimes, the FBI reports that at least 6 out of 10 attacks are directed at Jews. They also admitted that number might be higher since their data only comes from voluntary reports.[1442]

Canada

Canada is seeing the same thing. Hate crimes on university campuses and on the streets jumped 28% in 2014, making it their "worst year" too, for anti-Semitism.[1443] Though Canadians are more apt to call it anti-Zionism, it still refers to the same activities. Blame for Israeli government policy on Palestinians is now directed at the Jewish people as a whole.

In Quebec's Val-Morin municipality more than a dozen Hasidic homes were vandalized, and one was completely destroyed by arson.

In Penticton, BC, a mattress was set on fire with the words 'burnt Jew' written across the top.

In Montreal two Muslims, Omar Bulphred and Azim Ibragimov were responsible for multiple attacks against the city's Jewish community. This included firebombing the Snowdon community center plus setting fire to the Skver-Toldos Orthodox Jewish Boys School in Outremont.

Also in Montreal, multiple cars were spray painted with swastikas. Still in Montreal, a man slapped a Hasidic woman sitting on a park bench as he rode by on his bicycle.

In Calgary multiple Jews were attacked and injured by Palestinians. In July 2014 a pro-Palestinian demonstration just outside Calgary's City Hall quickly became an anti-Israel/anti-Jewish hate rally. People chanted, "Kill the Jews" and "Hitler was right". Some Jewish people were beaten.

In Toronto two weeks earlier the same thing happened. Even though the violent crowd was taped beating Jews only one man was arrested. One Jewish man severely beaten was shown bleeding and being led away by paramedics.

Also in Toronto in August 2014, security video caught a man walking his mixed poodle up to Beth Joseph Lubavitch Synagogue and smearing dog feces on the door.

"According to the Toronto Police Service annual Hate Crime Report, in 2014 Toronto's Jewish community was the single most victimized group. In nearly one in every three reported hate crime incidents in Toronto, Jews were the victims, with similar results seen in other Canadian cities."[1444]

Australia

Aussies were surprised and dismayed seeing anti-Semitism grow in the Lucky Country even though it's not to the degree sweeping Europe. According to the 2014 annual Report on Anti-Semitic Incidents, hate crimes against Jews in Australia jumped 35% compared to the year before. One of the most disturbing finds is that physical attacks tripled. The Executive Council of Australian Jewry's report showed slightly different numbers, but the bottom line was the same – physical attacks against Jews rose 200% compared to the previous year, threatening emails were up 180% and property damage rose 66%.[1445]

In March 2015, Australia got a nasty taste. While retired British colonel Richard Kemp lectured at Sydney University on military tactics, at least a dozen students burst through the doors disrupting his talk. They proceeded to intimidate the attendees, which included elderly people, got right in the faces, and positioned themselves between Kemp and the audience. They fought with other students and bullied the largely Jewish audience. Over megaphones the disrupting group shouted, "Richard Kemp, you can't hide, you support genocide."[1446] Demonstrators stood on chairs, pushed students and shouted at those who objected to their behavior.

Even more over the top was Associate Professor Jake Lynch and another senior lecturer, which both led and encouraged the protesters. Lynch was seen standing on his chair, waving money at Jewish people implying "greedy Jew" and yelling in the faces of students. Lynch, Director of the Center for Peace and Conflict Studies, is under investigation by the University. The demonstration continued for about 20 minutes when campus security forcibly hauled them off.

In August 2014 a gang of eight drunken teens, aged 15-17, boarded a Sydney school bus transporting Jewish kids, aged 5-12. They threatened to slit the children's throats and yelled, "Must kill the Jews" and "Heil

Hitler." Though no one was hurt, the kids were traumatized, as were the parents. Eventually five teens were arrested, but later released into their parents' custody. No charges were pressed.

Numerous people felt this incident was a decided turning point because Aussies see things have changed in their country. Isabelle Stanton who emigrated from Belgium in 2007 and whose daughter was on that bus said, "I am shocked, I am more than shocked, I am disgusted, I am horrified, I am flabbergasted. I can't say Australia is as bad [as Europe], and we haven't reached that level of hatred for the Jews, but there is this feeling that we have to be vigilant, and that we have to be discreet in our way of being Jewish here and I don't like it."[1447]

In October 2015 a 22-year-old Jewish man visiting Melbourne was injured when an attacker punched him in the neck and called him a "f***ing Jew."[1448] The offender was drunk and verbally abusive before he became physical. Coincidentally another Jew driving by interceded, otherwise the victim's injuries could have been worse.

In Melbourne July 2014, a man was attacked for wearing a shirt with the IDF logo and Hebrew writing. While walking home at night, two Arabic-speaking Muslim men attacked 28-year-old Zachary Gomo. He said, "I noticed them when it was too late. They jumped on me, started punching, screaming 'kalb Yehud!' (Jewish dog), 'Allahu akbar' (God is great) and something about Gaza in Arabic."[1449]

Anti-Semitism spread across the country from Melbourne to Perth, which is about like going from Charleston, SC to Los Angeles. In August 2014, Avraham Shalom Halberstam and his assistant from Jerusalem landed in Perth – the next stop on a lecture tour. When their ride arrived to take them to their destination six teens banged on the car surrounding and spitting on it. The driver Danny Mayer said, "They were telling us to 'F*** off', that we were killers and they wanted to 'fix us up'. They literally wanted us to come out and fight with them. It's very frightening. Obviously something you don't expect in a suburban shopping center to be accosted and treated this way."[1450]

Danny, a modern Orthodox Jew admitted, "I'm a bit shaken from [Monday]. I'm the one who pretty much rescued the rebbe. They were surrounding him, so I raced over to get him into the car and they surrounded the car screaming, 'You are killing babies in Gaza.' I've been in Israel for seven years and it wasn't too far from being in an Arab village and trapped in a car. We absolutely felt threatened."[1451]

"The incident comes less than two weeks after the walls of Perth's only Jewish school were painted with graffiti that read 'Zionist scum.' It also comes in the wake of police confirming that a Perth-based Islamic preacher who described Jews as 'filthy rapists' won't be prosecuted under the state's race-hate laws."[1452]

Prof. Mark Baker, director of the Jewish center at Melbourne's Monash University said, "There has been a seismic shift. It's as though the images that we once viewed on television have popped out of the computer screen and landed in our bedrooms. People feel as though they are living inside the experience of ISIS beheadings, anti-Israel demonstrations and the Gaza Israel war. Everyone is talking about this incessantly, fearing that the world is no longer recognizable, and living in fear of an impending catastrophe. The community is in a tailspin and looking for answers."[1453]

New Zealand

New Zealand's Jewish community has lived there since before the country was settled, is considered well integrated and the people are valued for their contributions. Jewish people came to Kiwiland before New Zealand became a British colony in 1840 and helped establish trade with Australia and Britain. Even as remote as this beautiful country is, it's not been spared the ugliness of anti-Semitism. Headstones in Wellington's historic cemetery were desecrated with swastikas and the number "88", a code of neo-Nazis, meaning "Heil Hitler". (Since "H" is the 8th letter in the alphabet they use "88" for "Heil Hitler".) More than 20 graves – all over 130 years old – were spray painted with ugly sentiments including "f*** Israel" and "don't f*** with us" scrawled on them. What saddened Kiwis most, besides the obvious hate, is that some of these were graves belonging to New Zealand's Jewish founders.[1454] In 2015 more headstones were defaced, this time in Dunedin, which is on the South Island. Two were hit with so much force they broke in half.

A man about 20 slapped a four-year-old little boy hard on top of his head. At the time he was walking home from his preschool with his mom, his brother and a friend. Both boys wore yarmulkes – Jewish skullcaps – when the man reportedly of "Middle-Eastern appearance" approached and hit him. The attacker then jumped into a car with four other men, laughing and sped off. This incident left both the little boy and his mother traumatized. In October 2014, men riding in a car yelled a curse at a little Jewish boy walking in Remuera, a suburb of Auckland. The next month in another Auckland suburb, Mt. Eden, an adult man attacked a small child wearing a yarmulke. Who takes out their hate and racism on children?

Stephen Goodman, president of the New Zealand Jewish Council, shared that "young Middle Eastern-looking men had yelled in Arabic at a young Jewish girl in the train station, while men in a car yelled, 'F****n' Jews' at a young boy walking in Remuera.[1455]

Even the Prime Minister, John Key, a non-practicing Jew who openly acknowledges his ancestry, had his 2014 campaign election poster defaced. On a billboard was scrawled the words "Lying Jew c****ucker". Key's image was painted over with a black hat and traditional ultra-Orthodox sidelocks. Key is blond with very short hair. His own mother narrowly escaped the Holocaust. Key said, "I just find it disappointing for the Jewish community. I have a Jewish past, which is extremely well known. My mother was Jewish, and some of my mother's family went to the concentration camps. But for the Jewish community in New Zealand, they are hard-working, decent people and they don't deserve to be brought into some sort of personal campaign that's directed at me."[1456] During that same election, Steve Gibson, Key's opponent posted a message on Facebook so vile only the last half can be printed here. "...nasty little creep with a nasty evil and vindictive sneer." The post was later deleted. Gibson's Labor Party – the political equivalent of Democrats in America – censured him for his actions. For the record, Key won handily in 2014 and is currently serving a third term. Gibson quit the Labor Party after being threatened with expulsion.

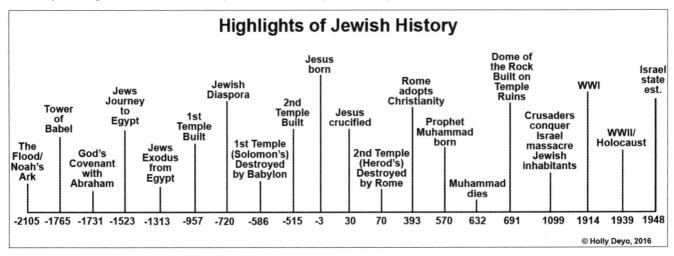

Israel's Rocky History

"Israel is the very embodiment of Jewish continuity: It is the only nation on earth that inhabits the same land, bears the same name, speaks the same language, and worships the same God that it did 3,000 years ago. You dig the soil and you find pottery from Davidic times, coins from Bar Kokhba [rebellion of Jews against the Roman Empire circa 132–136 BC], and 2,000-year-old scrolls written in a script remarkably like the one that today advertises ice cream at the corner candy store."[1457]—Dr. Charles Krauthammer, American Pulitzer Prize-winning syndicated columnist, author, political commentator, and physician

One can't ever accuse the Hebrews of having it easy. They've been displaced, conquered, persecuted, exiled, reviled, slaughtered, blamed for killing Jesus and for spreading the Black Plague. While life has often been difficult in the extreme, it's caused them to be very practical, pragmatic people and exude "Israeli passion", to treasure every day and embrace each to its fullest. There is a price for being the "apple of God's eye". In *Fiddler on the Roof,* Tevye who's a Jewish peasant in pre-revolutionary Russia lamented to God. "I know, I know. We are Your chosen people. But, once in a while, can't You choose someone else?"[1458] He had a point and their lot is about to get radically more difficult.

After all this you'd think their numbers would be decimated especially since Hitler wiped out 40% of their people. Today, seven decades later, about 15 million Jews survive. Israel and America are home to most with about 8.5 million in Israel and 5 million in America. Another million reside in the European Union. After that France and Canada share about 800,000 with handfuls scattered around the world. It's hard to get an exact count with more moving back to Israel. For such a remarkable history and such extreme hardships, it's amazing that that many survived. It has taken all these years for the Jewish people to equal their numbers right before the Holocaust.

Today, surrounded by enemy nations, Jews experience frequent bombings in public places. They never know when Hamas will let more rockets fly like they did in 2014. During those 50 days Hamas and their allies fired off 4,500 rockets at Israeli soldiers. Some 875 were duds or misfires and fell inside Gaza on their own people, but the Jews were blamed for those deaths.

Hamas said they started with 10,000 rockets and had 3,000 left, so maybe they shot off more than the "official" number.[1459] Iran has often promised to "erase Israel" in one way or another since 2000.[1460] Ironically in 2005 then Iranian president Mahmoud Ahmadinejad promised to do just that, when he, like Hitler, was shown to have Jewish roots.[1461] Where they differ is that Hitler also had African ancestry.[1462] This map shows the current degree of global anti-Semitism.

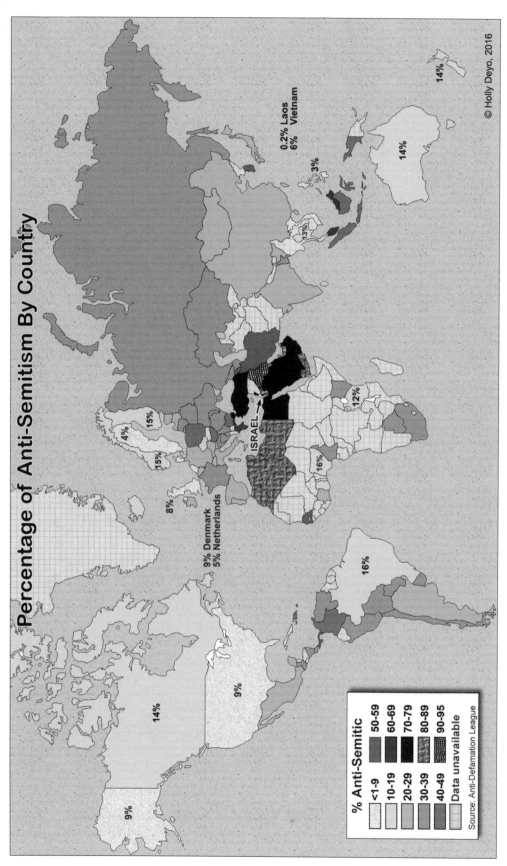

Percentage of Anti-Semitism By Country

© Holly Deyo, 2016

% Anti-Semitic	
	<1-9
50-59	10-19
60-69	20-29
70-79	30-39
80-89	40-49
90-95	Data unavailable

Source: Anti-Defamation League

Prophecy and Israel Fulfilled

- Miraculously the Jews people returned to their homeland and Israel was re-established as a nation in May 1948 as promised in Isaiah 11:11-12.

- As of June 7, 1967 they once again occupy Jerusalem – prophesied in Zechariah 8:4-8.

- Their language was resurrected during the 19th and 20th centuries as set out in Zephaniah 3:9.

- Ezekiel 36:34-35 predicted how Israel's land would be like the Garden of Eden. This began in the 20th century and continues today.

- The Sanhedrin Council would be re-established. This is less straightforward and has much to do with the building of the 3rd Temple. This body, which is like a combination Supreme Court and Congress, met for the first time on October 13, 2004.[1463] The original Sanhedrin consisted of 71 rabbis with Moses at the helm. The 2004 meeting in Tiberias is significant since it's the place where the Council last gathered in 425 AD and now meets in Jerusalem every month. Mainstream press largely ignored this event, probably because they didn't understand its significance.

- In June 2005 the Sanhedrin called for detailed architectural plans to rebuild the new Jewish Temple,[1464] which will be covered in the next section.

- All nations around the world are coming against Israel as prophesied in Zechariah 12:2-3. God warns, "I am going to make Jerusalem a cup of reeling before all the surrounding nations. And when there is a siege against Judah, it is also against Jerusalem. And it will be on that day that I will set Jerusalem as a weighty stone to all the peoples. All who carry it will surely gash themselves, and all the nations of the land will be gathered against it."

- **NOTE**: One has only to look at the preceding map to see this is well underway especially by nations physically closest to Israel. You can't get much more hate in a country than 92% of Iraqis, 81% of Jordanians, 75% of Egyptians, 71% of Turks, 74% of Saudis, 78% of Lebanese, 93% of Palestinians and 56% of Iranians. That's only a partial list. In the months and years to come, in whatever time is left before the Great Middle East War and the Gog-Magog War, the number of people will grow in countries that already hate Israel. Add to them nations that are currently friendly to Israel like America, Canada, the UK, Australia, New Zealand, Sweden, Denmark, Norway, Finland and some Asian nations. They too, will harden their hearts.

Like many other prophecies God doesn't flip a switch and *presto* it's done. Most are a process to completion.

Prophecy and Israel to Be Fulfilled

That brings us to prophecies that will be fulfilled before the great battle of Armageddon. Those occurring then won't be discussed here as most people will have either died, are considered lost souls in God's eyes or have been raptured.

RED HEIFER

Before the Temple can be rebuilt, a perfect red heifer must be born. This is no small feat to qualify as "the one". She must be completely red with not even two hairs of a different color, have no physical injuries or defects, have never been used for work, her owner must never have profited from the heifer and she must be a virgin. To produce this special animal ranchers are mating Red Angus, Shetlands and others with a red bull. They've gotten close, but aren't quite there yet.

Israelis have looked for the special heifer since at least 1997, maybe even 1987 when the Temple Institute was formed. However, when a prospective heifer has been offered the cow was rejected for one reason or another. Ranchers in Oklahoma and Texas have also tried to birth the perfect animal, but have only produced males. As of

2015 a rancher in the Negev Desert began implanting frozen Red Angus embryos in Israeli domestic cattle, which will introduce Red Angus to Israel. A number of red males have been born, but so far no females. They are getting close and she is the prerequisite for building the Temple.

Photo: This heifer is one produced by an Oklahoma rancher for Israel, but she didn't qualify. Behind her is a traditional Black Angus.

Israel's Coming Third Temple

For as long as this author can remember, there's always been talk about Israel building its third and final temple. While waiting to acquire the necessary land, Jewish craftsmen are wasting no time. They've been busy making some of the most important pieces to be used in the temple. Each of their 70+ sacred vessels and vestments is beautifully made, highly polished, intricately decorated and fashioned according to exact Biblical requirements. Every piece is a work of art made from pure gold, silver or copper as prescribed in Exodus 31:3-5. The 200-pound Menorah alone is covered with 95 pounds of gold with a price tag of $2 million.[1465] The high priest's robes of azure weaves, gold thread and a breastplate with 12 precious stones, took 11 years to research and $150,000 to complete.[1466]

Nine craftsmen and artisans didn't need to wait for the temple to be built to make these ready. The Temple Institute already has them on display. Judging from their intricacy and perfection, it's no surprise they were 25 years in the making. These are some of the Temple Mount's highlights.

On the east side is the **Golden Gate**, now blocked, is a holy site in both Judaism and Christianity. It's the entrance through which Jesus came on Palm Sunday. For Jews, it's the entrance through which the Messiah will come. It is also the doorway through which the Shekhinah, the Divine Presence of God, appeared. Its blockage fulfilled Ezekiel 44:1-3: *Then He brought me [Ezekiel] back to the outer gate of the sanctuary, which faces toward the east, but it was shut. And the Lord said to me, "This gate shall be shut; it shall not be opened, and no man shall enter by it, because the Lord God of Israel has entered by it; therefore it shall be shut. As for the prince [the Messiah], because he is the prince, he may sit in it to eat bread before the Lord; he shall enter by way of the vestibule of the gateway, and go out the same way.* In order to prevent the Messiah's entrance Ottoman Turk Sultan Suleiman the Magnificent walled it off in 1541. The Ottomans also plunked a cemetery in front of it hoping to further discourage the Messiah's entry.

Photo: Golden Gate built through the old city wall of Jerusalem as seen on Mary 22, 2009. (Courtesy of geologist Mark A. Wilson) Built from Jerusalem Stone the rocks are a warm, rich rosy-golden color. In the forefront and behind the trees is the cemetery that the Ottoman Turks built in hopes to bar the Messiah. In Islamic tradition the gate is also where some of the events of Judgment Day will occur.

NOTE: What's interesting is that this prophecy was written nearly 2,000 before its fulfillment. It's not something monumental like predicting the Hebrews would come back to their land, intact, over 2,600 years later.

Or, that the prophet Isaiah predicted a conqueror named Cyrus would destroy seemingly impregnable Babylon and subdue Egypt along with most of the rest of the known world. Isaiah made this prophecy 150 years before Cyrus was born and 180 years before he destroyed Babylon (Isaiah 44:28; 45:1,13).

Or, in approximately 700 BC, the prophet Micah named the small village of Bethlehem as the birthplace of Israel's Messiah (Micah 5:2). This prophecy fulfilled in the birth of Christ is one of the most widely known and celebrated facts in history.

Prophecy, seemingly not a big deal, about a gate getting blocked off, but predicted 2,000 years in advance is precisely why it *is* a big deal. Little details, even small prophecies that appear insignificant, further solidify for even the ardent skeptic, that predictions through God's Biblical prophets always, *always* come true.

Dome of the Rock is the Muslim shrine to commemorate the prophet Muhammad's ascension into heaven accompanied by the angel Gabriel. It was built in late 600 AD on top of the site of the Second Temple, restored by King Herod and then destroyed by the Roman siege of Jerusalem in 70 AD.

Continuing around the Temple Mount, **Solomon's Stables** are under the southeastern courtyard. It's thought that the Crusaders, not Solomon, used this area as stables. The stables were recently converted to the El-Marwani Mosque, which can hold 10,000 worshippers.

Temple Mount / Noble Sanctuary

Golden Gate (blocked)

North Gardens

Dome of Suleiman Pasha

Dome of the Rock

Dome of the Chain

East Gardens

Solomon's Stables

Single Gate (blocked)

Triple Gate (blocked)

Dome of Solomon

Dome of the Ascension

Dome of Tablets

Al-Nahawiyya Dome

Dome of Joseph

Ruined Towers

Double Gate (blocked)

Archeological Excavations

Muslim Quarter

Gate of the Chain (Muslim entrance)

Bab al-Silsila Minaret

Dome of Moses

Wilson's Arch

Western Wall

Mughrabi Gate (non-Muslim entrance)

Likely location of Ark of the Covenant

Islamic Museum

al-Aqsa Mosque

White Tower

Dome of Yusuf Agha

Women's Mosque

Jewish Quarter

N   E   S   W

Ruined Towers are the city walls that were destroyed in a 1033 earthquake. A new tower was built to protect the Double Gate entrance. After the city fell to the Crusaders, the Knights Templar expanded the tower and converted it into a massive defensible structure, blocking the Double Gate.

Just inside the massive wall at the Ruined Towers is **Al-Aqsa Mosque**, meaning "the farthest mosque," also known as Bayt al-Muqaddas. Thought to have been originally constructed in 705 AD it sits on top of King Herod's temple extension. Somewhere in this area is the likely location of the Ark of the Covenant. The Knights Templar headquartered in a wing of the royal palace in the captured Al-Aqsa. Much of the mosque, as it stands, dates to its rebuilding after the earthquake.

Immediately west of it is **Dome of Yusuf Agha**. It's thought to be built by Saladin, the first sultan of Egypt and Syria in the late 1100s after his armies recaptured Palestine from the Crusaders, who had conquered it 88 years earlier.

On the west side is the **Islamic Museum**, established by the Supreme Muslim Council in 1923. It's housed in a wing added by the Knights Templar during their short stay on the Temple Mount in the early 1100s.

Next is the **Mughrabi Gate** built in the early 1200s and named after residents from a nearby neighborhood who had come to Jerusalem from Morocco during the days of Saladin. The gate is accessed by a covered wooden bridge and is the only entrance to the Al-Aqsa Mosque for non-Muslims.

Close by is the **Western Wall.** The exposed portion is situated closest to the holiest center of previous temples. People, especially Jews in Israel and around the world, come here to pray. Like many places of antiquity the Wall is a building marvel. Altogether it stretches 105 feet high; 43 feet are underground. Most of the boulders were likely dug either at Zedekiah's Cave, the largest quarry in Jerusalem, or about 2½ miles northwest of the Old City at Ramat Shlomo. Each stone weighs between 2 and 8 tons, some even more. One boulder in Wilson's Arch, which lies perpendicular to the Western Wall, weighs about 570 tons. How they moved this is as much a mystery as the stones in the Great Pyramid at Giza.

Just beyond the **Dome of Moses** is the **Bab al-Silsila Minaret**, which was built in 1329 and further north is the **Gate of the Chain** through which Muslims enter.

For the new temple, the Temple Mount Faithful have already cut the cornerstones from 6-ton stones using diamonds. They've been consecrated with water from the Biblical pool of Siloam and are waiting to be used. Since the Levite priests have already been specially trained, all they need is the Temple itself. However, the Al-Aqsa Mosque is in the vicinity of where the temple must be built and Muslims would never permit it being built as long as they control the Temple Mount.

Ray Gano writes about building the new Temple. He said that a meeting held in November 1990 with religious and political leaders, scientists and archaeologists, they determined it would take 1-2 years. This is just for the temple itself, not its ornamental work. An altar would be raised somewhere west of the temple construction site and once priests resume daily sacrifices, temple construction would begin.[1467]

To that end, the Temple Institute released in January 2011 a three-dimensional model of the future Third Holy Temple. While Jews say they have to wait to build it after the Dome of the Rock and mosques are cleared, they are constructing its stone altar off-site. The Institute says that as soon as it can be moved to its proper location on the Mount, offerings can begin before the building of the Temple itself.

Black Gold

Ezekiel 36:8-11 prophesied that Israel would become very wealthy. In December 2010 Noble Energy discovered Leviathan. Not the mythical creature lurking underwater, but a massive natural gas field offshore in the Mediterranean. Seismic tests estimate this deep-water "gold mine" might contain 16 trillion cubic feet. The second stage of exploration drilled down nearly 24,000 feet, which revealed another natural gas reserve and maybe 6.6 billion barrels of oil.[1468] Until August 2015 Leviathan was the largest natural gas field found until discovery of the Zohr in Egyptian waters. It surpasses Leviathan by roughly 14 trillion cubic feet, doubling Egypt's reserves, but there's plenty for both countries with heaps left over.

Bonanza #2! Oil companies in Israel hit the jackpot in October 2015. To borrow a line from the Beverly Hillbillies' theme song – with a twist, *"And up through the ground came a bubblin' crude. Oil that is, black gold, Texas tea. Well the first thing you know ol' Israel's a billionaire…"*

While it didn't exactly bubble up, they drilled to black gold. Even today (March 2016) with crude around $40/barrel it's enough to keep them fat and happy with sufficient oil to supply their needs for decades – IF there were that much time left. This will make Israel an energy player, an exporter for the first time in history.

Energy independence will free them from having to purchase 75% of their oil from the Kurds. When Israel jumps into the picture, it will please the Iraqis because they weren't happy when the Kurds began selling their oil. The loss of Israel will cut into Kurdish revenues. Israel's bounty may further anger the Kurds by cutting their sales to Italy, France, Spain, Netherlands, Croatia and Egypt. However, Egypt may no longer need it with the Zohr find.

While Israel has maybe 60-some oil fields, those would be amateur hour compared to this new Genie Energy discovery. On the first map of Israel in this chapter, Genie's bonanza would be about just under the GH of the Golan Heights.

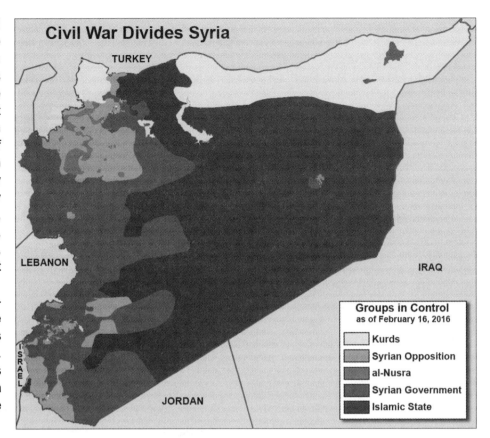

Civil War Divides Syria

Groups in Control
as of February 16, 2016

- Kurds
- Syrian Opposition
- al-Nusra
- Syrian Government
- Islamic State

TROUBLE HEAD

Fly #1: There is more than one fly in the proverbial oil ointment. The first "fly" is Genie Energy, an American company and its subsidiary, Afek Oil & Gas that dug the exploratory wells. Besides Genie's CEO, Howard Jonas, major shareholders include media magnate Rupert Murdoch, British investment banker Lord Jacob Rothschild; former Vice President Dick Cheney, American hedge fund manager Michael Steinhardt, former CIA director James Woolsey, former head of the US Treasury Larry Summers, and an ex-ambassador to the UN and energy secretary Bill Richardson – all 1%ers – the Who's Who of the world's richest. You have to wonder how much of the revenue and oil would actually go to Israel.

Fly #2: Though Israel has occupied the Golan Heights since 1967 and then annexed it in December 1981 this real estate originally belonged to Syria. Syria is in chaos with civil war and their oil supplies are dwindling. This country has become a train wreck. It devolved from peaceful protests in 2011 to civil wars between Assad's persecuted Alawite sect, aligned with Shiite fighters from Iran and Hezbollah in Lebanon, against Sunni rebel groups. The chaos has facilitated ISIS taking over part of the Middle East. Syria's wars have killed 250,000 and displaced half of the population. Syria is in shreds with five entities tugging for control including the Syrian government, the Kurds, Islamic State, al-Nusra Front and the Syrian opposition. Their country looks like a war zone because it is, with entire cities flattened. Syria has morphed into a proxy war with Russia and Iran pitted against the U.S. and her allies. When, IF, the country settles down, they may come for the Golan. With nothing to lose they'll need BIG revenue to rebuild.

Fly #3: It may be that Israel's newfound black-gold wealth is a main reason "all the countries in the world" come against it. It was always a puzzle what could be at the center of Zechariah 12:3.

In September 2014, the U.S. and UK leveled sanctions on Russia for its actions against Ukraine. Those hurt, but not nearly as bad as the great downturn in gas prices. Oil had accounted for over half of Russia's federal budget. Russia was the world's largest producer of crude, the third-largest producer in 2014 of petroleum (after Saudi Arabia and the U.S.) and second-largest producer in 2013 of natural gas.[1469] It's estimated that for every dollar drop in oil prices, Russia losses US$2 billion in revenue. This may be a strong reason why Russia has been so driven to lay claim to gas, oil and mineral rights in the Arctic.

The vast majority of Russian crude exports, over 70%, went to European countries, particularly Germany, Netherlands, Belarus and Poland. When Israel's oil comes online, flooding the market with more black gold, this may further cut Russia's revenues.

Despite president Vladimir Putin's personal wealth estimated at $40 billion[1470] to $200 billion,[1471] the country is in rough financial shape. In 2015, food prices rose by a third, car sales were down 40%, people stopped buying homes and many are cold inside. Valery Fedorov, director general of Vciom, a Russian public opinion research center worried. "People are more alarmed and more tense, because now we are speaking not only about their well-being, but their lives in general."[1472]

Much like what America's government does – distract-deflect-deny – experts say that Russia is trying to take people's minds from domestic economic woes. To this end they're airing on state-run TV the possibility of a global war.

Bill Browder from Hermitage Capital Management observed, "The crisis is suddenly filtering into people's daily lives. 55pc [55%] of consumer goods in Russia are imported and these are doubling in price. People are buying anything they can that keeps its value. ...It's going to be worse than the default crisis in 1998. This time you have a situation where the West is against them. Russian companies are shut out of the global capital markets. The country can't turn to the IMF because Washington will block it. There is no lender of last resort."[1473] To help Russia's economy, sanctions need to turn around soon, which they could if Russia butted out of Ukraine. However, it's unlikely gas prices will skyrocket and the world will have one angry Russian bear on its hands.

Who else would be hurt by Israel's mammoth oil supplies? OPEC for one. Formed in September 1960 the oil consortium now has 14 members: Algeria, Angola, Ecuador, Gabon, Indonesia, Iran, Iraq, Kuwait, Libya, Nigeria, Qatar, Saudi Arabia, United Arab Emirates and Venezuela. Most of the countries derive over 75% of their revenues from oil. It's hard to think of Saudi Arabia in a cash bind, when so many of their princes have solid gold "thises and thats". They've become so strapped that the Saudi deputy crown prince considered selling part of Saudi Aramco – the kingdom's crown jewel. Still, Saudi Arabia keeps pumping out large oil supplies, which, while it protects their market share, puts pressure on neighboring rivals and forces prices to stay extremely low. It really is a catch-22.

However, they're far from broke. When King Salman arrived in Washington in September 2015 for a meeting with President Obama, his entourage took over the 222-room Four Seasons Hotel. Eyewitnesses reported crates of gilded furniture and accessories being wheeled into the hotel to make the multi-billionaire feel at home. One Four Seasons regular said, "'everything is gold. Gold mirrors, gold end tables, gold lamps, even gold hat racks.' Red carpets have been laid down in hallways and even in the parking garage, so the king and his family never have to touch asphalt when departing their custom Mercedes caravan."[1474]

Venezuela, an original OPEC member, is in tough shape. Experts say it's going through the worst economic crisis in its history. Between 2014 and 2016, their economy was expected to shrink 16.5%. Add to that inflation soaring above 1000% and they're in deep weeds.

Nigeria, another OPEC member, is in serious trouble since oil is its biggest income generator. Nigeria has to import a great percentage of its food, so without oil revenue, the country is in a double bind.

In February 2016 OPEC members agreed to freeze oil production at the January level in order to stem the cash hemorrhage. "Morgan Stanley analysts say that oil 'in the $20s' is possible if China devalues its currency further, and Standard Chartered Bank predicts that prices could hit just $10 a barrel."[1475] In 2014, oil was at $115/barrel and has been as low as $20 a barrel so it's easy to see why big oil producing countries are gnashing their teeth.

Brazil's economy is also shrinking while unemployment is rising. Then they were further whammied by China's currency devaluation. Brazil even had to sell off some of their prime agricultural land. In 2014 their stock market was down 22% from the previous year and sank another 2% in 2015. Brazil in 2014, produced just shy of 3 billion barrels of oil, so while other countries were harder hit, it was another wound. Brazil's largest trading partner was China. They went from buying US$2 billion in 2000 to $83 billion in 2013. Now that China's economy is flailing, they've drastically cut back on imports. This too has smacked Brazil.

THE COMING FURY AGAINST ISRAEL

Now with Israel drilling some of the largest reserves, this will not only further hurt Saudi Arabia's economy, but also Russia's as Israel looks to supply the European Union, the Palestinians, Turkey, Egypt and maybe Greece. These are all non-OPEC countries, but rest assured OPEC won't be pleased that Israel has come into great wealth that could impact their own. It may also hurt to varying degrees every other gas and oil supplier on the map. So oil could very well be the spark that brings all nations against it. While this is a likely component of End Times prophecies why countries come against Israel, it's probably not the whole story.

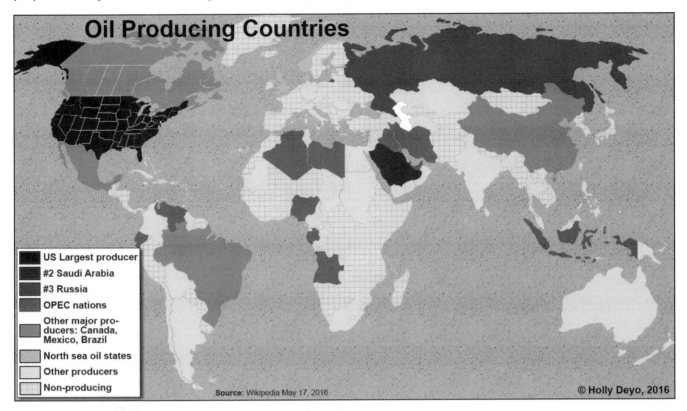

Anti-Semitism never seems to die. With countries like Iran wanting to "wipe Israel off the map" and Hitler having tried to exterminate them plus the well-documented resurgence of Jewish race-hate, that too, could be another cause. Another leg may be the never-ending animus of Muslims towards Jews and Christians, the tug o' war over Jerusalem and the Temple Mount. Israel's immediate neighbors will come against her in the Great Middle East War, followed by the Gog-Magog War – WWIII. Oil and wealth envy could be the igniter for global hatred-turned-war. And what if Israel gives rise to the Antichrist as some eschatological scholars suggest citing John 5:43? They say he will be a Jew from the tribe of Dan. Still others point to a Muslim or the pope. Scripture never explained why Israel draws the world's wrath, just that it does. The reasons put forth may be a part of it or one or more may be all of it.

End Times Prophecy for Israel and the World

God warned in Ezekiel 38 and 39 that Russia and Iran, along with a coalition of Muslim allies including Turkey, Libya, Sudan and Ethiopia would invade Israel. It reveals this war will take place after Israel has re-gathered as a nation, which officially occurred on May 14, 1948.

U.S. RECOGNIZES JEWISH STATE

"WASHINGTON, Saturday, May 16, 1948. —Ten minutes after the termination of the British Mandate on Friday, the White House released a formal statement by President Truman that the U.S. Government intended to recognize the Provisional Jewish Government as the *de facto* authority representing the Jewish State.

"The U.S. is also considering lifting the arms embargo but it is not known whether to Palestine only or the entire Middle East, and the establishment of diplomatic relations with the Jewish Provisional Government.

"The White House press secretary, Mr. Charles Ross, told correspondents today that the reaction so far to the recognition had been overwhelmingly favourable. He said this step had been discussed with Mr. Marshall and Mr. Lovett before action was taken, and it had their complete support.

"Mr. Ross said that the president had decided several days to grant American recognition to the new Jewish State, but due to personnel regulations he could not announce his policy until a formal letter arrived. "We were able to move very quickly when the messenger brought the letter," he said, "because the President had already determined the course of action to be taken."

In End Times prophecies, the United States isn't mentioned because she ceases to exist as a world power or is removed altogether. This is further reinforced in that Israel will face the invading hoards alone. If America were still viable, she surely would have come to help her only Middle East ally, unless the U.S. has also joined the global band of hate.

Image: It's hard to read so the article announcing the U.S. recognizing Israel as a State is typed on the preceding page. There is another image of this paper, which allowed the rest of the last paragraph to be viewed, but the quality is so poor, it's nearly unreadable.

MEGIDDO

The Jezreel Valley as it was called in the Old Testament and Esdraelon Plain in the NT, spreads out in a massive triangle to the north, east and south of Tel (meaning "mound" or "hill") Megiddo. On the next map, the teardrop is where the inhabited Megiddo Kibbutz sits. This is different than Tel Megiddo, which is slightly higher than the kibbutz and is the lookout for protecting the valley below. Tel Megiddo is situated on an irregular triangle of land immediately northwest of the teardrop, ½ mile from the kibbutz. Today Megiddo covers 15 acres and rises 200 feet[1476] from the valley floor. It gave great views for many miles in all directions – an important advantage in battle.

Israel is located at the juncture of three continents: Africa, Asia and Europe. Whoever controlled Megiddo, controlled a narrow strategic "international highway" to the Mediterranean. This roadway linked major trades routes and empires from Egypt to what's now Iraq.

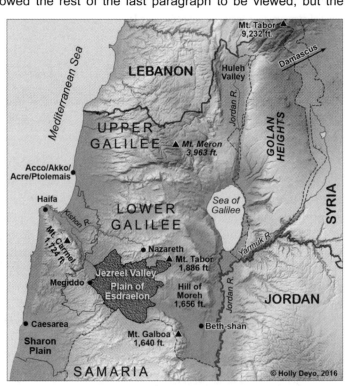

Photo: The Plain of Jezreel or Plain of Esdraelon is Israel's breadbasket. It stretches across northern Israel, from the northwestern base of Mount Carmel to the Jordan Valley covering a little over 95 sq miles. (Background image courtesy DigitalGlobe © 2016)

The plain is so large and unobstructed that when Napoleon Bonaparte first saw it he remarked, "All the armies of the world could maneuver their forces on this vast plain…There is no place in the whole world more suited for war that this…[It is] the most natural battle-ground of the whole earth." With that he routed the much larger Turkish army in 1799.

More battles have been fought on this plain than anywhere else in the world. Assyrians, Canaanites, Egyptians, Greeks, Israelites, Persians, Philistines and Romans have all entered into armed conflicts here. Though Megiddo has been abandoned since 586 BC, a crucial battle took place here. In 1918 British Field Marshal Edmund Allenby led British, Indian, Australian and New Zealand troops against the Ottoman Turks and gained control of the Holy Land. In this Battle of Megiddo, it took Allenby from September 19th to the 25th, 1918 to complete the Allied offensive.

Photo: Aerial view on April 15, 2011 of Tel Megiddo, northern Israel.

PHOTO: This image is an enlargement of the ruins on Tel Megiddo. At its height Megiddo was a wealthy sophisticated city. Its multi-chambered gate and water system are two indicators of the city's superiority. One sign of its wealth was a treasure trove of nearly 400 carved ivory artifacts, ornaments, women's cosmetic tools, combs and game pieces. These were discovered in one room of a Canaanite palace when the royal residence was destroyed in 12th century BC. One box measuring roughly 3" x 5.25" x 4.75" was carved from a single piece of ivory. On the outside were intricately carved lions and sphinxes. Gold artifacts were also found, but it seems the material of choice was ivory.

Megiddo was the crown jewel of all cities in Canaan and Israel. It became an Israelite city sometime between the 10th and 9th centuries and served as the administrative center for the fertile plain below and to the north. In the following pages, this author will spend a bit of time showing how these people lived on Tel Megiddo because this area has never stopped being important. It is without a doubt the most contested piece of dirt in the world. Very soon the ground below and north of it will be the site of yet another epic battle. Megiddo is *the* perfect place for this final human battle.

DO "TEL"

In ancient times, civilizations built right on top of previous ones that had either been conquered or had burned down. This is particularly evident on Tel Megiddo. Since 1925 archeologists have unearthed 26 different layers of civilizations spanning 35 centuries. People chose this site time and again since earliest times because of its strategic location.

Tel Megiddo inhabitants had built a remarkable survival city. Though the best view of its remaining wall is from the north, the Tel was entirely enclosed. Access gates were three-deep in Solomonic style. If one gate were breached, intruders had two more to penetrate. In the southwest corner, the city had a marvelous water system.

A constantly running stream fed all their water needs though today the level fluctuates with the water table. An ingenious shaft/tunnel duo was constructed during King Ahab's reign c. 874 – 853 BC. Despite earning the reputation as *the* most evil king of Israel with four entire chapters in 1Kings devoted to his horrible actions, he was respected as a great builder. He also married the infamous Jezebel known for her immense cruelty, sex intrigues, prostitution and murder.

SIDE NOTE ON AHAB AND JEZEBEL: Ahab married pagan princess Jezebel from Phoenicia, what's now Lebanon, and they were a bad duo. As queen of Israel she forbade worshipping God and tried to convert all of

Israel to Baalism, honoring the god of rain. This involved the detestable practices of homosexual prostitution and burning children alive during bi-sexual orgies.[1477] In keeping with her upbringing Jezebel had two heathen sanctuaries built – one in Samaria and the other on Megiddo. Between the two, they were home to 850 pagan priests. She tried to drive out God's prophets and became the first female persecutor.

After imposing terrible cruelties on the people, they turned on the priests and slaughtered all 850. As just one example of Jezebel's horrid nature, Ahab fancied a vineyard next to them at Megiddo. When he offered to buy it, the owner Naboth, declined because it'd been in the family for generations. Ahab took to his bed in a monumental pout and went on a hunger strike. Jezebel said *get up, be happy, I'll take care of it*. She arranged for Naboth's arrest on trumped up charges of blasphemy. After she paid witnesses to lie in court, he was found guilty and stoned to death. This enabled Ahab to acquire the coveted vineyard.

Photo: This is one altar found on Megiddo used during the time of Jezebel and Ahab. This one was probably meant for incense or grain burning, as it was too small for animal sacrifice. However it's 2¼ ft. x 3 ft. size might have worked for sacrificing babies. Blood of living sacrifices was then smeared on the four horns (corners) to consecrate it.

Later Ahab died in battle in 874 BC at Ramoth-Gilead, about 10 miles from present-day Daraa, Syria. At the end of His patience with Ahab's family, God commanded Jehu, the 10th king of Israel, to wipe them out. Though Ahab was already dead, there was still Jezebel and her three adult kids. So in 843 BC Jehu rode out to Megiddo and saw Jezebel standing in her tower. A couple of eunuch servants stood by her and Jehu ordered them to toss her out the window. They did, and horses stomped out what life remained after her fall. Jehu then dined inside her palace and before she could be buried, feral dogs ate Jezebel – everything except her head, hands and feet. 2Kings 9:37 commented on her demise that there would be no place for her to be buried and that her carcass would be dog feces in the field.

Whatever bad Ahab did as king, he was an innovative builder. Megiddo workers carried out his clever idea for their water system 150 years before King Hezekiah dug his water tunnel in Jerusalem. Access to water on Tel Megiddo was designed so that inhabitants never had to leave their walled hill. This was especially vital when under siege. Workers dug a 6-foot wide vertical shaft 200 feet down to a horizontal tunnel that ran 400 feet to the spring. This took them just outside city walls as the spring is in a cave. When construction was finished, the outside entrance to the spring was sealed with a massive stone wall and covered with dirt and rocks so enemies never knew it was there.

The finished tunnel was nothing short of a great engineering achievement. Considering their water system was constructed without modern equipment nearly 3,000 years ago, the mind boggles. Archeologists believe the ramrod straight tunnel was chiseled by teams of workers starting at each end and meeting in the middle. That would be quite a feat without seismic imaging or ground penetrating radar. People could then get water simply by lowering buckets into the shaft and hauling it up.

Photo: The round altar in the middle of this picture is on the north side of Tel Megiddo marked on the layout "Bronze Age temples and sacrificial altar." Built with fieldstones, it measures 28 feet in diameter and stands 5 feet high with a staircase ascending from the east. Large quantities of animal bones and pottery shards were found between the altar and the excavated walls. It ceased to be used before 1900 BC. In the lower right is the corner of one of three rectangular temples. Where the palm trees stand is the dirt level today, which is about 20 feet higher than the altar. (Courtesy Hanay, Wikipedia Commons)

Another interesting feature was their grain silo located in the center of the Tel. From the angle of the layout photo, it's impossible to appreciate just how huge their grain bin was. Twenty-three foot high walls were built by stacking similar-sized rocks one on top the other. Across its 36-foot diameter were two staircases opposite each other. The stairs looked really narrow – maybe only a foot wide and without a railing. They likely had designated one specifically for each direction since there was literally no room for two people to pass each other. Two staircases circumvented the confusion. William Holladay, noted lexicon editor, calculated that a silo that size could hold 588 cubic yards of grain – enough to feed 350 horses for up to 150 days. A dome likely covered it to protect the seeds from insects and rain.

Some argue whether the two areas marked "stables" were actually that or storerooms, marketplaces or barracks. Right now it looks more weighted toward stables. To back this up, between 1927 and 1934 excavators unearthed both sets of stables, one grouping in the north and other on the south side. Stables were about 70 feet long and 36 feet wide, housing 30 horses each. The buildings themselves were divided into three sections with two long stone aisles next to a main corridor that was paved with lime. A series of stone pillars separated the main corridor from outside aisles. Bolstering the argument for the stables theory were mangers situated between the pillars, which held food and water for the animals. Holes were bored into the pillars so horses could be tied up. The courtyard in front of the south stables was likely an exercise area for the animals. Still you have to wonder why they built stables so close to their water source. With 12 stables in the north group and 4 by the palace, Tel Megiddo could house 480 horses, chariots and charioteers. These structures used to be referred to as Solomon's stables. Now they're now attributed to either King Omri or King Ahab.

The Coming Last Battle – and Two Just Around the Corner

Christians, Jews, Muslims and the secular world all know the concept of Armageddon. Since 1997 people have co-opted the last half of the word and hooked it onto epic events.

- **Snowmageddon** – a vicious storm that dumped nearly 40 inches of the white stuff in 2010 on the north Atlantic states. It also became the name of a 2011 movie.
- **Carmageddon** – first used for a video game in 1997. In 2011 it referred to monster traffic jams in Los Angeles following the closure of I-405.
- **Pharmadeddon** – when medicine and the pharmaceuticals industry do more harm than good. David Healy used as his book title in a searing indictment of big pharma. Generically it's used to describe how America got hooked on prescribed painkillers.
- **Obamageddon** – In 2013 Wayne Allyn Root used it in his book title exposing how Barack Obama was killing capitalism via crushing deficits, too many entitlements and massive tax hikes. Generically it's used to describe America's decline during Obama's administration.

Armageddon. The word evolved from the Hebrew "*har* Meghiddo" in Revelation 16:16 meaning, "mount of Megiddo" though it's really just a hill, a *har*. The King James Version translates it as "Armageddon". *And they (demons) gathered the kings and armies of the world together at the place, which in Hebrew is called Har-Magedon* (Armageddon). During the seven soul shaking, crisis years described in Revelation 6-18, 20 judgments slam Earth culminating in Armageddon. Most people still on the planet at the beginning of the seven years, those that weren't supernaturally removed by God, die in these horrific events. Those are the lucky ones. Revelation 9:6 says that people will try to commit suicide, but can't. Of those that survive, the majority of the remaining defiant ones still give God the middle finger, much to His great sadness. He gives this final "great shaking" in hopes of them acknowledging He *is* God. He doesn't want them to forfeit their lives, but it's their choice.

Because this event is so far down the road in the End Times, it's not a sign, but a termination of man's evil and defiance. However, there is another grand war, WWIII, that will have survivors and it's nearly on our doorstep. This is the Gog-Magog War. But first comes the Great Middle East War.

PLAYERS IN WORLD WAR III

God warned in Ezekiel 38 and 39 that Russia and Iran would invade Israel, along with a coalition of Muslim allies including Turkey, Libya, Sudan and Ethiopia. Other players might be Algeria and Tunisia plus some or all of "The Stans": Kazakhstan, Tajikistan, Uzbekistan, Kyrgyzstan, Turkmenistan and Afghanistan. The common thread is that all are Muslim countries with the exception of Russia.

MISSING FROM ACTION? NOT SO FAST: THE GREAT MIDDLE EAST WAR

Isn't it odd countries closest to Israel and that hate her most – Syria, Egypt, Saudi Arabia, Jordan, and Lebanon – don't join the conflict? The reason is simple. They've already been wiped out. Psalm 83:1-8 tells of another coalition of Muslim nations that invade Israel before the massive Russian-led incursion. They're described as "all those [nations] around them [Israelites] who despise them." (Ezekiel 38:26)

Without question Israel has no friends in the Middle East. The least anti-Semitic country close by is Russia, which will lead the invasion of Israel in the Gog-Magog War. As the saying goes, *with friends like these, who needs enemies?* Imagine being surrounded by countries where 8 or 9 people out of every 10 hate your guts. When people understand just how tiny Israel is – about the size of New Jersey – and what she's up against, no wonder God will intervene supernaturally to save His people.

This Great Middle East War takes place after enough Jews have gone back to Israel and the country is reestablished as a nation. That officially occurred on May 14, 1948. In End Time prophecies, the United States isn't mentioned because she ceases to exist as a world power. This is further reinforced because Israel faces the invading hoards alone. If America were still viable, she would have come to help her only Middle East ally. How her super power status is extinguished likely comes in two volleys. The first results from overwhelming debt. When money is substituted for God, He, in divine justice, could use it as a destroyer. Following is likely a nuclear attack as described in many dreams in the chapter about prophetic visions of America's destruction. With America out of the way these countries have a clear path to invade Israel.

Image: Israel is a near-flyspeck compared to all countries that come against it. It will truly be a David and Goliath event. Without God's supernatural intervention, the invasion would squash Israel in a nanosecond. While these are the likely players, the boundaries have changed since Biblical times. Put may also include Algeria and Tunisia. Besides Meshech, Tubal, Gomer, Beth-to-garmah in Turkey, Azerbaijan and Armenia may participate as part of the Muslim consortium. Magog and the Muslim contingency may incorporate The Stans: Kazakhstan, Kyrgyzstan, Uzbekistan, Turkmenistan, Tajikistan and Afghanistan.

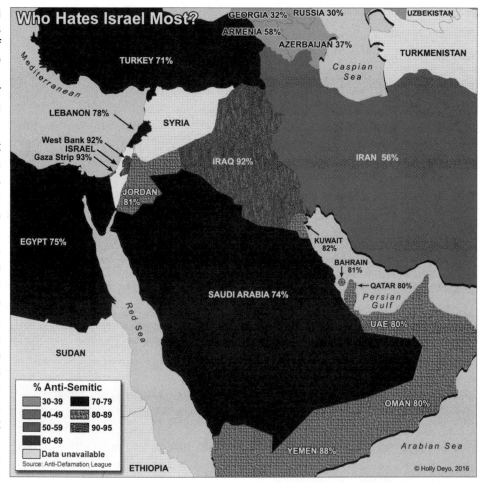

Arabs in southern Israel, Palestinian refugees and Hamas in the Gaza Strip accompany this group of five nations that strike Israel. Their goal is to stop Israel from being a nation (Psalm 83:4). In short, Muslims hate Israel because:

- She threatens their belief in the Koran and their religion – one that post-dates Judaism by nearly 2,000 years.
- Muslims believe that the Jews lost their right to the land because of their disobedience.
- Whatever land Muslims occupied at one time, the Koran teaches that they have a right to take back.
- Islam teaches Muslims to kill Jews and Christians because they are infidels.

Image: This regional map and the global map earlier in this chapter show the degree of anti-Semitism based on the Anti-Defamation League's data. No information is available for Syria because the country is in such upheaval.

The attack in the Great Middle East War will be like a flash-bang grenade that starts quickly and ends faster, with the Muslim armies killed by the IDF – Israeli Defense Force. Verses 13 and 14 say Israel's military will come against the invading Arabs like a whirlwind and sweep them away like chaff or tumbleweeds, and then consume them like fire burning a forest. The purpose (verses 16-18) is to show Arab Muslims that the God of Israel is the one true God. All of this is accomplished in a single night (Isaiah 17:14).

Some have confused the Psalm 83 War and the Gog-Magog war as the same event. They are distinctly two different conflicts with different players and different outcomes.

416

TWO IMMINENT WARS	
The Great Middle East War Players **Psalm 83** (verses 1-8)	**Gog-Magog War, WWIII Players** **Ezekiel 38 & 39**
Tents of Edom (decedents of Esau) = Palestinian refugees & southern Jordanians **Ishmaelites** = Saudi Arabians **Moab** = Palestinians refugees & central Jordanians **Hagrites** = Egyptians **Gebal** = Hezbollah & northern Lebanese **Ammon** = Palestinian refugees & northern Jordanians **Philista** = Palestinian refugees & Hamas in the Gaza Strip **Inhabitants of Tyre** = Hezbollah & southern Lebanese **Assyria** = Syrians & northern Iraqis **Children of Lot (Moab and Ammon)** = Jordanians **Amalek** = Arabs of the Sinai Peninsula including Bahrain, UAE, Oman, Yemen, Kuwait, Qatar	**Magog, Rosh** = Russia & former Soviet republics **Persia** = Iran **Cush** = Sudan & Ethiopia **Put** = Libya, Algeria & Tunisa **Gomer, Meshech, Beth-togarmah & Tubal** = Turkey plus possibly Germany & Austria, Armenia, and the Turkish-speaking people of Asia Minor & Central Asia
Led By: Arab confederacy	**Led By:** Russia and Iran
Arab's Purpose: End Israel as a nation **God's Purpose:** Punish Israel because she has forgotten God	**Purpose:** Russia is forced by God to invade Israel possibly in retaliation for attack(s) on its allies

Here is another big clue why the Psalm 83 nations will be taken out. Ezekiel 28:24 says *"And there will no longer be a briar or a painful thorn to prick the house of Israel from all those around them who treated them with contempt; then they will know [with clarity] that I am the Lord GOD."*

Image: Isaiah 17:1 predicts Damascus will become a "ruinous heap". (Background image courtesy Bernard Gagnon)

DAMASCUS DEMISE

One of the most notable outcomes from the Psalm 83 War is the total destruction of Damascus. The Syrian capital is the oldest continually inhabited city in the world. For it to be completely destroyed will be an unmistakable event. Isaiah 17:1 says it will cease being a city and become a ruinous heap. This can only mean a nuclear attack. Today's nukes are so much larger than Fat Man and Little Boy dropped on Hiroshima and Nagasaki. Since they were detonated overhead, fallout was considerably less than in a ground burst, so the cities are still inhabited. Since Damascus is relatively small, about 40 sq. miles, one large or several small nukes detonated in a ground strike could leave it leveled and unlivable.

THE SAMSON OPTION AND SYRIA'S BIO-CHEMICAL THREAT

Israel has maintained the Samson Option defense policy as a last resort if she is ever overrun by enemies or is about to be defeated. While never openly admitting to having a nuclear arsenal, Israel is thought to have around 80. Israel's nukes aren't part of their normal war weaponry, but a strategy used only when pushed to the brink. Nuclear security experts Hans Kristensen and Robert Norris theorize theirs are high-yield bombs, something large enough to get the job done. The 2014 study concludes Israel has:

- 80 nuclear warheads to be delivered by 24 mobile Jericho missiles
- 2 nuclear-capable fighter squadrons capable of carrying 20 bombs each, and
- A small inventory of nuclear-capable submarine-based cruise missiles[1478]

Syria's Chemical Weapons

Further supporting Israel using nukes on Damascus, keeping in mind they are "weapons of last resort," Isaiah 17:4-6 says that Israel's north and central regions incur serious damage and casualties. Since Syria has used chemical on its own people dozens of times, Syria may hurl these agents against Israel's military to incapacitate them. Syria is believed to have one of the world's largest stockpiles of chemical weapons and threatened in 2013 it would use them in the event of foreign intervention. So far seven facilities in Syria have been identified. Sites in Al-Safir, Latakia where Russia has an eavesdropping post, Al-Salamiyah and Homs produce theses agents. Al-Furqlus, Al-Dumayr, Masyaf and Baniyas are storage locations, and research is conducted in Damascus.[1479] [1480]

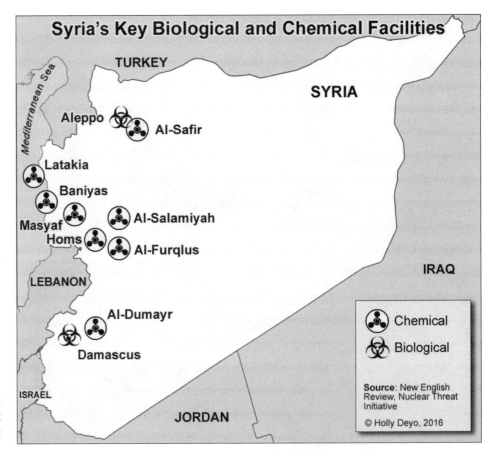

Syria's Bioweapons

Officially Syria doesn't have biological weapons, but according to NATO Consultant Dr. Jill Dekker, they've worked on developing quite an array including aflatoxin, anthrax, botulism, camelpox, cholera, plague, ricin, smallpox and tularemia. Russia has helped them install anthrax in missile warheads, fitted to Scuds and standard artillery shells.

Dekker states that while the U.S. downplays Syria's bioweapons capability, their program is sophisticated and advanced. They have mastered both making them more virulent and being able to spread them through the air.

Some agents were acquired during natural outbreaks. Others were obtained from Russia, North Korea, Iran and Iraq.[1481] Syria has disguised these programs. They're hidden in chemical and defense labs, and in veterinary vaccine research facilities in Damascus and Aleppo. Syria sees nothing morally wrong in using bio-warfare and considers them part of their normal weapons program. This could be the impetus for Israel nuking Damascus. Notice how all nine facilities are on Syria's western border, so close to Israel.

MIDDLE EAST WAR "PRACTICE?"

For almost a month, beginning Valentine's Day 2016, Muslim nations participated in the largest-ever military exercise for the area. "North Thunder" maneuvers held on the Arabian Peninsula included 150,000 soldiers, 2,540 warplanes, 20,000 tanks and 460 helicopters. Many of the participants – Bahrain, Chad, Comoros, Djibouti, Egypt, Jordan, Kuwait, Malaysia, Maldives, Mauritania, Mauritius, Morocco, Oman, Pakistan, Qatar, Saudi Arabia, Senegal, Sudan, the UAE and Tunis will be Psalm 83 players. Officially North Thunder's purpose was "to send a message to the world that Saudi Arabia will not be a passive observer to the massacres of civilians and mayhem in Syria and Iran's ambitions in the region."[1482] Political analyst Hamdan Al-Shehri said the aim was to unify Arab and Islamic countries.

They may invade Syria to stop the massacres because the rest of the world, in their opinion, hasn't stepped up. Their other stated purpose is to curtail Iran's increasing muscle flexing. According to Ali Reza Zakani, a member of Iranian parliament, four Arab capitals of Damascus, Baghdad, Beirut and Sanaa are under Iran's control and have joined the Islamic Iranian revolution.[1483] All of these countries either border Israel or are very near it except for Yemen. It's ironic that Iran who is the least anti-Semitic country of the bunch has indicated on numerous occasions that it wants to eliminate Israel from the planet. However, Syria, Iran, Lebanon and Yemen are near the top on the Israel hate-gauge.

ISRAEL'S SECURITY

As a result of their defeat in the Great Middle East War, Israel greatly expands her territory back to Biblical times encompassing Lebanon and Jordan, and parts of Syria, the Egyptian peninsula and the northern part of Saudi Arabia.

How far south it goes into Saudi Arabia is up for discussion. It's not set out in Genesis. These countries come against Israel and in their defeat, Israel regains her rightful land as outlined in Genesis 15:18 and Deuteronomy 11:24.

These verses detail the parameters of the Abrahamic Covenant that guarantees Israel's land ownership for always. The Nile River and the Mediterranean Sea border Israel's west side and the Euphrates River on the east. Plus she has a mighty army to protect her. Israel's border expansion puts

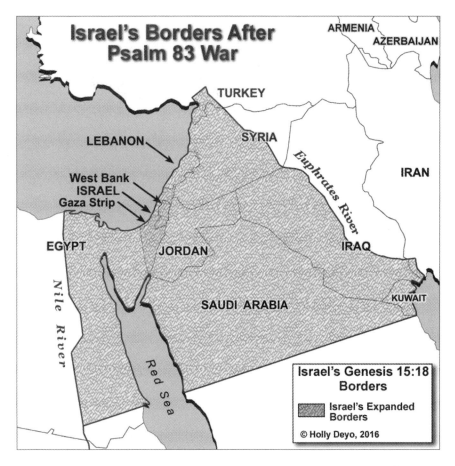

distance between she and her enemies, and the country now lives in relative peace, though not for long. This is why Israel is confidently living in "unwalled cities".

The Psalm 83 countries should never have pressed Israel, never invaded her, never have targeted her riches of the Dead Sea and oil fields as they get their backsides handed to them. This clearly separates the Great Middle East War and the Gog-Magog War, and explains why these countries are noticeably absent from WWIII, the Gog-Magog War.

Why Is Israel Invaded in the Gog-Magog War?

Two secular reasons stand out above all else:

1) Jews have always been envied and hated for reasons already covered. Anti-Semitism is reaching new heights. Instead of one person, Hitler, wanting their deaths, numerous countries will unite in bloodlust.
2) Newfound mega-oilfields will give "God's country" profound riches. It will make nations' greed fester to the point where they will kill for Israel's vast wealth. This is clearly described in Ezekiel 38:11-12.

Those work on a secular level, but the premier reason God permits Israel to be attacked is their attitude toward Him. God says in Ezekiel 39:7 that He will no longer allow Israel to profane His name. He warns this war – WWIII – *is coming*. Israel will be taught a lesson at the hands of Russia and Iran and the other invaders. However in Ezekiel 39:18 and through the rest the chapter, reveals the punishment coming to the attackers is worse than any Stephen King horror story.

RUSSIA FORCED INTO WAR

Just when things look like they are all over for Israel, God doesn't give the foreign armies a spanking; He annihilates them. In "blazing rage", God sends an earthquake to Israel so enormous that everything breathing – people and animals alike are terrified. The temblor is so strong it flattens mountains and causes massive landslides. The invading armies will turn against one another and slaughter each other in confusion and panic. A pandemic follows undoubtedly from the decaying bodies and lack of hygiene.

God isn't done yet. He calls in all the birds of prey and wild animals to feast on the dead till they're full. Even with help of the animals, it takes Israel seven months to bury the bodies. The burial site (Ezekiel 39:14-16) is a place east of the Dead Sea, about 15

miles into what used to be Jordan, but is once again, part of Israel. This is the Valley of Hamon Gog (the multitudes of Gog) and the city at the site of what's now Dibon (Dhiban) will be renamed Hamonah (hoard). It will take seven *years* for Israel to burn all of the weapons left in the aftermath.

There is good reason to believe nuclear weapons will be used in this war too. Ezekiel 39:14-16 says after the war is over and the dead are buried, search parties will go out and look for any unburied bones. Instead of performing the disposal task, they are only to flag any remaining bones and others specifically assigned to burial will perform that task. This suggests contamination likely from radioactivity.

SO WHAT'S THE POINT?

The answer is two-part. Israel is invaded as punishment for "profaning God's Name. The decimation of Russia and many Muslim nations will show Israel and every other country that God *is* Lord. Muslims around the world will be shocked seeing God crush Middle East Muslims in defense of Israel. They will witness Biblical prophecies being fulfilled and not those in the Koran. It will make many Muslims choose to follow the God of Israel.

Ezekiel 36:18-21 explains why God has been so angry for over 2,700 years with the Jews. After being expelled from their land in 720 BC, they violated sacred things and disrespected God. Many have ignored God's laws altogether. Other Jews have become atheists or very secular at the least and are indifferent to God. God has a very definite opinion of indifference to Him saying it's the worst position to take. *So then, because you are lukewarm, and neither cold nor hot, I will vomit you out of My mouth.* (Revelation 3:16 NKJV)

One example of this disrespect was the behavior of Ashkenazi Jews in Portugal and Spain through the Middle Ages. During *vegio,* the customary celebration on the eve of a child's circumcision, these observances deteriorated into full-fledged parties. People got drunk and indulged in "irreverent behavior" that attracted both Jews and Gentiles to the festivities.[1484] The Covenant of Circumcision (Abrahamic Covenant) was a solemn event. Laid out in Genesis 12-17, it was God's promise to Abraham that He would make him the father of many nations giving him many children. It also promised "the whole land of Canaan" from Egypt to the Euphrates to his descendants forever. But it was more than that. Circumcision was also a permanent reminder for Israel to stop being stiff-necked (Deuteronomy 10:16 and Leviticus 26:40-42) and to obey God's laws (Romans 2:25). So it wasn't something to be taken lightly yet they took these occasions to party hearty.

Other Jews are observant without considering why they're performing certain rituals. Jewish authors Dennis Prager and Joseph Telushkin brought to light a real head-scratcher. "According to Judaism, one can be a good Jew while doubting God's existence, so long as one acts in accordance with Jewish law. But the converse does not hold true, for a Jew who believes in God but acts contrary to Jewish law cannot be considered a good Jew."[1485]

More recently Jews got mixed up in cults and religions they shouldn't have. In the 1960s, some in the U.S. became involved in polytheism like the cult of Asherah that was practiced in Solomon's Temple. Others participated in witchcraft like Jewitchery. Jews at the Kohenet Institute run one of the most recent forms of neopaganism. The Kohenet Institute trains Jewish priestesses to act as rabbis and their adherents pray to Anat, Asherah, Lilith and other deities.[1486]

Dominos Lining Up for Gog-Magog War

The chess pieces are lining up for Russia to begin the Gog-Magog War. In Ezekiel 38:4 God foretold nearly 2,600 years ago that Russia would be forced to invade Israel having 'hooks put in its jaws'. This may be driven by defense pacts and economic agreements Russia has with Syria, Iran, and other Islamic nations. Damascus getting nuked in the Great Middle East War could be the trigger or an Israeli pre-emptive strike on Iran's nuclear facilities. Even though Russia would be reluctant to do so, it has a number of incentives to nurture its relationship with Syria even if it means being pulled into war. Senator Sam Brownback said, "For years Russia and Syria have had what Russian President Putin recently termed a 'special relationship.'"[1487]

It's evident by these nine points that Russia and Syria enjoy a mutually beneficial relationship that won't easily be dislodged.

1. On October 8, 1980, Syria and the Soviet Union signed a Treaty of Friendship and Cooperation. The two countries have a long-standing relationship dating back to 1944. (Russia and China signed a similar Friendship Treaty in 2001.)
2. Russia wants to keep its naval installation at Syria's Tartus port since it's their only access to the Mediterranean and Russia desires to strengthen its naval presence there.
3. Cash poor Russia, due to the plunge in oil revenues, wants to maintain its energy contracts with Syria.
4. Syria backs Russia because Moscow blocks the UN Security Council from passing anything that might hurt Bashar al-Assad's regime.
5. Russia is Syria's largest arms supplier (as well as Iran's), sales in the billions.
6. Russia wants to maintain its largest eavesdropping post outside Russia in Latakia, northwestern Syria. This is just an hour up the coast from Russia's naval base.
7. In 2013, Syria and Russia signed an agreement for joint oil exploration off the Mediterranean coast.
8. On August 26, 2015, the Kremlin made an open-ended time commitment to its military deployment in Syria, which Mr. Putin began withdrawing seven months later.
9. In 2016, Russia agreed to cancel nearly three-quarters of Syria's $13.4 billion debt.

RUSSIA REGAINS ITS MOJO

While Mr. Obama sat back preferring a minor role in the Middle East and elsewhere in the world, Vladimir Putin made great inroads. Russia is once again positioning itself to move into Super Power status.

Putin's forged new relationships with once-distant countries. He's built up his military to be an astounding force as well as supplying arms to many surrounding countries. Russia, the second largest arms exporter, has poured tons of heavy weapons into Armenia to the tune of US $200 million.[1488] This relatively small country is armed with a virtual cannon pointed at critical U.S. allies of Azerbaijan and Georgia.

In February 2016, Russia announced closer military cooperation with Iran in Syria. Russian Defense Minister Sergei Shoigu said recently while visiting Moscow, "We are seriously with the Syrian government and nation and we have had decisive cooperation with Russia, which has resulted in a change of power balance and creation of a new situation for Syria."[1489]

Photo: President Bashar al-Assad of Syria and President Vladimir Putin of Russia met in Moscow in October 2015 to discuss military operations in Syria. (Courtesy Press Service of the President of Russia)

TURNING TURKEY

In 2001, Turkey still saw itself aligned with the U.S., Western Europe and Israel. It's always been the counted-on bridge between Muslim and Christian countries. Shortly after PM Recep Tayyip Erdogan took the reins in 2003, staunchly secular Turkey began steadily to shift away from the West. Erdogan kept his strict Muslim beliefs veiled for a while, but slowly morphed into an openly pro-Muslim giant. Turkey now has cultivated close ties, financial and ideological, with Iran, Syria, Sudan and the Gulf countries, as well as with Hamas and Russia. In short, "Trade with the country's [Turkey] eight nearest neighbors – including Syria, Iran and Iraq – nearly doubled between 2005 and 2008, from $7.3 billion to $14.3 billion."[1490]

This started in 2003, when Saudi Arabia and oil-rich Persian Gulf countries pumped nearly $4 billion cash into the coffers of Erdogan's party, the AKP. By 2006 Turkish economists estimated that "gift" was undervalued even at $12 billion. Then in 2015 Saudi Arabia announced it would invest another $613 billion in Turkey by 2020.[1491] Though Turkey is a NATO member, it now has zero love for the West. It ranks #2 right behind Egypt and Jordan for hating America and Americans, followed by Russia, the Palestinian territories and Lebanon. Turkey, unlike other countries, doesn't distinguish between Americans and U.S. government policies.[1492]

SAUDI ARABIA – FRENEMIES

Saudi Arabia, who the U.S. publicly considers a strong ally, is a thinly veiled enemy. According to Oscar Wilde, "True friends stab you in the front." So what does that make Saudi Arabia? In 1973 the Saudis and their oil-producing friends imposed an embargo against America for supporting Israel in the war with Egypt and Syria. It resulted in quadrupling the price of oil. This author remembers *very* long gas lines at service stations that stretched for several blocks. If you were short on fuel, you prayed you wouldn't run out before your turn at the pump.[1493] President Nixon asked gas stations to not sell fuel on Saturday nights or on Sundays, and 90% complied. Some stations had no fuel at all.

Over the years, America's "best friend" repeatedly inflicted gas price pain. In 2008 when oil was over $127 a barrel, President Bush asked the Saudis to produce more oil and bring down the cost. For the second time that year, they refused.

In 2001, Crown Prince Abdullah, a backer of the Palestinian intifada, didn't think America was doing enough to rein in Israel's actions in the Palestinian territories. When newly elected President Bush invited him to visit the White House in May 2001, Abdullah declined with an arrogant response, "A time comes when peoples and nations part. We are at a crossroads. It is time for the United States and Saudi Arabia to look at their separate interests. Those governments that don't feel the pulse of their people and respond to it will suffer the fate of the Shah of Iran."[1494] (Due to his friendly relations with the U.S. and Israel, Mohammad Reza Shah Pahlavi a.k.a. The Shaw lost support of Muslim clerics. That and charges of corruption plus his push toward modernization alienated him from both Iran's clergy and the working class. After 38 years as monarch, The Shaw was forced to flee Iran and died in exile in Egypt.)

There's little doubt the Saudis were behind the September 11, 2001 attacks on the World Trade Center and Pentagon. Afterwards, Saudi Arabia issued a statement calling it "regrettable and inhuman" and two months later, the Bush administration still publicly praised Saudi support for the war on terrorism. At this point it hadn't come to light that 15 of the 19 terrorists were Saudi nationals. They repeatedly stalled when the U.S. wanted to examine the hijackers' background files and interview their families. Zero cooperation.

Now the shoe is on the other foot. Saudi Arabia has multiple challenges on its solid gold plate. Why America maintains the charade of friendship is mystifying. Unless, it has everything to do with money and the old adage: the enemy of my enemy is my friend.

In July 2014 former U.S. Ambassador to Saudi Arabia James Smith described their challenges as "a maelstrom." He listed several major issues:

- Pressures created by Islamic State attacks
- King Abdullah's death
- Collapse of the Saudi-backed transitional government in neighboring Yemen
- Plummeting oil prices
- Russian military intervention in Syria
- Fallout from the July 2015 nuclear deal with Iran, which led to removing sanctions on their chief rival[1495]

The U.S and Saudi Arabia have close defense and security ties, 9/11 aside, as well as mutual financial interests. In just five years from October 2010 through November 2015, the U.S. was poised to ink over $111 billion in defense sales to the Saudis.[1496] That's a big incentive to stay buddies. On the other side, Saudi Arabia has been America's biggest oil supplier right after Canada.[1497] The Saudis are probably praying the price of oil begins to rise again. All things considered, the two nations maintain a shaky relationship… for now.

IRAN – THE 2-FACED WILD CARD

Contrary to U.S. law and other civilized nations that assume someone is innocent till proven guilty, let's start with the premise that Iran is not our friend. It hasn't been for many years and they've been greatly helped by Mr. Obama. Iran has a long history of out-maneuvering the U.S.

Take for instance the January 2016 prisoner exchange. Four Americans detained in Iran got to come home: a *Washington Post* reporter, a Christian pastor, a former Marine and one other man. In return, Iran got **seven** people released that had been accused or convicted of violating U.S. sanctions. Additionally, the U.S. dropped Interpol's arrest warrants on 14 Iranian fugitives it sought.

Then there's Robert Levinson. He disappeared in Iran in March 2007 while working an off-book operation for the CIA. American officials are unsure if the former FBI agent is even still alive. If so, he'd be the longest-held hostage in American history. In late 2010, Bob's family received "irrefutable proof" of life, but press couldn't share what that was due to safety concerns for Mr. Levinson. Then in January 2013, his family released photos to the media that had been taken nearly two years earlier. It showed Bob had lost considerable weight, had long gray hair, and wore an orange jumpsuit holding a sign that read, "Help Me". Nearly a decade later, Bob would be 67. This becomes increasingly unlikely since he had high blood pressure and was diabetic. The Iranians have always denied knowing his location, but if Mr. Obama had made Levinson's release a priority and IF Iran were remotely interested, they could find him.

Now we come to the *coup de grace* of stupid deals – Obama's 2015 Iran nuke agreement, officially the Joint Comprehensive Plan of Action (JCPOA). Even the *Washington Post* called it "the worst agreement in U.S. diplomatic history."[1498] Since beginning his second term, Mr. Obama had cast about looking to establish his legacy, something he can be proud of. One thing he longed to hook his name to was brokering peace in the Middle East. In 2015, with time running out, he sent Secretary of State, John Kerry, to bring Iran to heel, except it went sideways. Kerry came back with a deal all right, but the U.S. got screwed. Again. So did the rest of the world. Within a few days of the agreement, Iran held a "Death to America" rally. It's not just America that will suffer. At least, the dumb deal doesn't rest solely with the U.S. as the U.K., Russia, China, France, Germany and the EU all agreed to the July 2015 Iran deal.

For nuke signers getting to tout *"there is an agreement!"* this is how it shakes out.

Pros for Iran

- Got $150 billion unfrozen assets. Once restored, they can't be taken back. Most of the money held in escrow accounts in China, India, Japan, S. Korea and Turkey was restored as of January 16, 2016.[1499]
- Sanctions relief not tied to compliance.
- Iran gets to determine what sites are verified for compliance and what scientists can be interviewed.
- Inspectors must give Iran 24 days' notice before gaining access, allowing Iran to hide banned activities.
- No condition in the agreement prohibits Iran from continuing to export terrorism.
- Iran will further destabilize the Middle East. Though it's widely recognized that Israel has about 80 nukes to be used as last line of defense only, other Middle East nations curbed their pursuit of these weapons if Iran didn't acquire them. Now Saudi Arabia and other Middle East countries are pursuing nukes to protect themselves from Iranian interference.
- Israel's tenuous safety just got torpedoed.
- Deal does nothing to stop Iran's development of ballistic missiles, which combined with nuclear weapons, would threaten every country around the world.
- Iran doesn't have to come clean on past nuclear activity, which leaves inspectors little ability to verify prohibited advances.
- Deal lifts sanctions on two Iranian atomic scientists who worked on Iran's illegal nuke program and on a nuke proliferator who previously helped smuggle nuclear components.
- Iran is allowed to conduct advanced research and development that paves the way for modern centrifuges. They will be able to enrich huge amounts of uranium that shortens their "ready" time for a bomb.
- Deal lifts UN ban on Iran for conventional weapons in 5 years and 8 years for ballistic missile technology.[1500]

Pros for the Rest of the World

- Obama's "legacy". What form the fallout takes has yet to be determined.

All things considered the Iran nuclear deal is a joke. Mr. Obama pushed hard for the UN to vote on this deal by-passing U.S. elected representatives. Several 2016 Presidential candidates promised to rip up the deal should they be elected. Likewise, Iran takes the agreement with a grain of salt evidenced by them threatening to walk away after performing a fourth banned missile test on March 8, 2016. One of those two missiles had this phrase emblazoned on its side, *"Israel should be wiped off the Earth"* written in Hebrew. They wanted to make sure Israelis could read it.[1501] Iran only agreed to the deal to get back their billions and have sanctions removed. Once they had their $150B in hand, it didn't matter if the some nations imposed sanctions again. Iran's got money in the bank and Russia in their corner as both a business partner and military supplier. Watch for Iran's "muscles" to flex further.

ISRAEL

It's widely recognized that Israel has about 80 nukes for defense purposes only. Thirty-six years of sanctions never deterred Iran from their nuclear ambitions. Now with those restraints removed, Iran's plans for an atomic arsenal will soar. Israel has more reasons than ever to be concerned. Though ranked #1 for militarization in the Middle East, Israel is so small and surrounded by enemies she will be the little mouse that roared. Malcolm Gladwell, author of *David and Goliath: Underdogs, Misfits, and the Art of Battling Giants* wrote this about intimidating adversaries: "What the Israelites saw, from high on the ridge, was an intimidating giant. In reality, the very thing that gave the giant his size was also the source of his greatest weakness. There is an important lesson in that for battles with all kinds of giants. The powerful and the strong are not always what they seem."[1502] This is especially true when God is on your side and Jews are His chosen people.

While once they count on America to defend them unfailingly, the Obama Administration has hung them out to dry. Repeatedly. On the Iran nuclear deal, Israel's Prime Minister Benjamin Netanyahu summarized: "In an ideal situation, you wouldn't have countries seeking to annihilate the state of Israel and openly saying that. ... So I think the real problem in the Middle East is not the democracy of Israel that has shown restraint and responsibility, but it's countries like Iran that pursue nuclear weapons with the explicit goal first of annihilating us, but also ultimately of conquering the Middle East and threatening you."[1503]

In September 2012, Mr. Netanyahu who knew what Iran was up to pled his case for the umpteenth time. Netanyahu has continuously clashed with President Obama over the urgency of military action against Iran. It fell on deaf ears. To make the situation abundantly clear Israel's PM held up a poster drawing of a bomb with a fuse. Netanyahu literally drew a red line just below a label reading "final stage" to a bomb where Iran was 90% along to having enough weapons-grade material. Mr. Netanyahu said Iran would be on the brink of developing a nuclear weapon in less than a year.

Screen Snap: Holding up a simplified drawing of a bomb with a lit fuse, Netanyahu drew a red line just below the label reading "final stage" to a bomb, in which Iran was 90% of the way to having sufficient weapons-grade material.

Instead of Netanyahu's requests resulting in even more sanctions levied on Iran, less than three years later, they were completely removed. That was in 2012. Four years later it's a worry how much closer is Iran to that red line. Israel has never ruled out a pre-emptive strike on Iran's nuclear plants. According to Iran Watch, Iran's stockpile in November 2015 of low-enriched uranium was sufficient, after further enrichment, to fuel approximately seven nuclear warheads.[1504]

After Iran's March 2016 illegal missile tests, Islamic Revolutionary Guard Corps Brig. Gen. Amir Ali Hajizadeh threatened. "Iran has built missiles that can hit targets at 2,000 km. They are designed to hit Israel at such a distance. Israel has been surrounded by Islamic countries and its life is short."[1505] No wonder Israel is very concerned. Israel's Sword of Damocles is swinging ever closer.

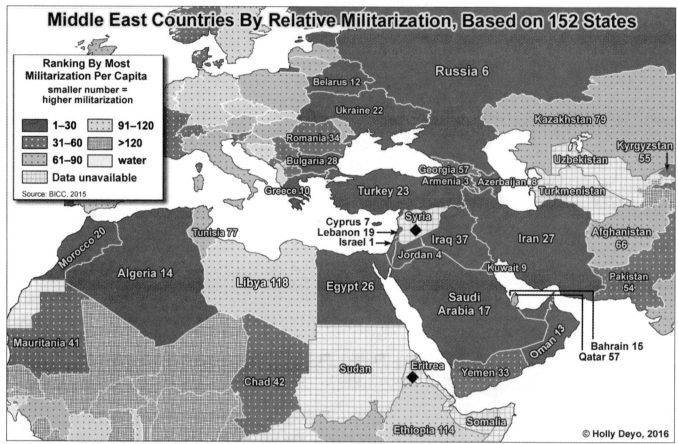

Image: The Bonn International Center for Conversion (BINN) based in Germany performs annual assessments of the degree of militarization around the globe for 152 countries. Their Global Militarization Index (GMI) shows the relative weight and importance of the military compared to its society as a whole. Rank is based on military spending compared to the GDP, number of personnel compared to the whole population and the number of heavy weapons systems compared to the population.

MILITARY MOVERS AND SHAKERS

Other Middle East nations like Saudi Arabia said they would curb their pursuit of these weapons if Iran didn't acquire them. Now in addition to Israel and Iran, the nuclear race is on with United Arab Emirates whose first reactor will be completed in 2017, Egypt, Turkey, Jordan and Saudi Arabia – Iran's archrival.[1506]

In February 2016 a top Israeli government minister warned that several Gulf Arab states in the Middle East are trying to acquire nuclear missiles. Though defense minister Moshe Ya'alon didn't reveal the states, two are thought to be Saudi Arabia and the United Arab Emirates.[1507]

The Middle East continues to lead the world in militarized nations. From 2009 to 2015, 13 Middle East countries rose markedly in boosting their military and war toys. Egypt and Kuwait dropped two places, but they are so high up on the list of 152, a slight change doesn't mean much. For two countries, Syria and Eritrea noted by a diamond, no current numbers were available, but the Bonn International Center for Conversion (BICC) believes Eritrea, which came in at #1 in 2009, is still "very highly" militarized. They made the same assessment for Syria, which was #2 then, but it's so torn by civil war, information isn't available.

Iraq which didn't even make the list in 2009, jumped in at #37 in 2015.

Little Qatar will probably see a bump next year as it announced in 2014 that it was making a $24 billion investment in modern weapons systems. In fact Qatar and its regional neighbors spent nearly $100 billion on arms purchases that year. Their shopping spree covered tanks as well as helicopters, warships, missiles and artillery.[1508]

Russia, which will lead the Gog-Magog War, moved from #13 in 2009 to #7.

Though Iran in 2015 came in at #27, they just got a huge cash infusion in January 2016 courtesy of the nuclear deal just outlined. Two weeks after the sanctions were lifted, Iran hit the shopping trail spending about $18 billion in Europe. They bought 118 planes from Airbus worth $27 billion total. They also inked deals in shipping, health, agriculture and water provisions. Then onto Russia, where they bought hardware.

President Obama and John Kerry *assured* U.S. senators that Iran would use the billions to benefit the Iranian people, but they're immediately beefing their military. Russia and Iran signed deals in January 2016 to manufacture helicopters and planes. Plus Russia is already delivering to Iran powerful Almaz-Antey S-300 air and missile defense systems. One senior U.S. Marine Corps aviator said it's a deadly threat to everything except the most advanced stealth fighters and bombers. "A complete game changer for all fourth-gen aircraft [like the F-15, F-16 and F/A-18]. That thing is a beast and you don't want to get near it."[1509]

With low crude prices and major sanctions imposed, Iran hadn't been able to modernize its dilapidated military. Russian presidential aide Vladimir Kozhin revealed, "When all restrictions and all sanctions are lifted [which they now are], I think we will have a rather serious development in the sphere of military-technical cooperation, it partially now embraces items not covered by sanctions, and we hope for very large projects in the future. The interest of the Iranian side is huge. They really need serious upgrade of their entire armed forces. Taking into account that it is a large country with large armed forces, of course, the talk will be about very large contracts, worth billions." [1510]

Photo: 9A83ME launcher from the S-300VM Almaz-Antey anti-ballistic missile system. According to Wikipedia it will knock out short- and medium-range ballistic missiles, aeroballistic and cruise missiles, fixed-wing aircraft, as well as loitering ECM platforms and precision-guided munitions. (Courtesy Vitaly V. Kuzmin) This beast is one of Iran's new Russian-made toys valued at $175 million. Since 2015/16 Russia is offering both the S300PMU and S300V/VM to Iran.[1511]

Since Western hardware will likely be unavailable to Iran, they are truly cementing their relationship with Russia. Furthering the Middle East's nightmare is Iran's purchase of Russian-made Sukhoi Su-30 Flanker fighters. These would greatly enhance Iran's air power. The shopping list also includes: T90 tanks and relevant air defense systems, Sukhoi Su-30 multipurpose jets, MI-17 and MI-8 helicopters, Yak-130 advanced jet trainer and light attack aircraft; Bastion mobile coastal defense missile systems equipped with Yakhont anti-ship missiles, coastal missile defense systems, and maritime technology of diesel-powered and electrical submarines.[1512] Money and common ideology make strong partners.

It's significant that of all countries that will be players in the Great Middle East War and the Gog-Magog War, 21 are in the top 25% of militarized countries worldwide.

Chapter 19: The Thinning Veil

The coming of the [Antichrist, the lawless] one is through the activity of Satan, [attended] with great power [all kinds of counterfeit miracles] and [deceptive] signs and false wonders [all of them lies], and by unlimited seduction to evil and with all the deception of wickedness for those who are perishing, because they did not welcome the love of the truth [of the gospel] so as to be saved [they were spiritually blind, and rejected the truth that would have saved them]. Because of this God will send upon them a misleading influence, [an activity of error and deception] so they will believe the lie —2 Thessalonians 2:9-11 (AMP)

Then the king [the Antichrist] will do exactly as he pleases; he will exalt himself and magnify himself above every god and will speak astounding and disgusting things against the God of gods and he will prosper until the indignation is finished, for that which is determined [by God] will be done. He will have no regard for the gods of his fathers or for the desire of women, nor will he have regard for any other god, for he shall magnify himself above them all. Instead, he will honor a god of fortresses, a god whom his fathers did not know; he will honor him with gold and silver, with precious stones and with expensive things. He will act against the strongest fortresses with the help of a foreign god; he will give great honor to those who acknowledge him and he will cause them to rule over the many, and will parcel out land for a price. —Daniel 11:36-39 (AMP)

Jesus answered, "Be careful that no one misleads you [deceiving you and leading you into error]. For many will come in My name [misusing it, and appropriating the strength of the name which belongs to Me], saying, 'I am the Christ (the Messiah, the Anointed),' and they will mislead many. ... For false Christs and false prophets will appear and they will provide great signs and wonders, so as to deceive, if possible, even the elect [God's chosen ones] —Matthew 24:4-5, 11 (AMP)

The Corruption of Mankind

Now it happened, when men began to multiply on the face of the land, and daughters were born to them, that the sons of God [fallen angels, see Job 1:6] saw that the daughters of men were beautiful and desirable; and they took wives for themselves, whomever they chose and desired. Then the Lord said, "My Spirit shall not strive and remain with man forever, because he is indeed flesh [sinful, corrupt – given over to sensual appetites]; nevertheless his days shall yet be a hundred and twenty years." There were Nephilim (men of stature, notorious men) on the earth in those days – and also afterward – when the sons of God lived with the daughters of men, and they gave birth to their children. These were the mighty men who were of old, men of renown (great reputation, fame).

The Lord saw that the wickedness (depravity) of man was great on the earth, and that every imagination or intent of the thoughts of his heart were only evil continually. The Lord regretted that He had made mankind on the earth, and He was [deeply] grieved in His heart. So the Lord said, "I will destroy (annihilate) mankind whom I have created from the surface of the earth – not only man, but the animals and the crawling things and the birds of the air – because it [deeply] grieves Me [to see mankind's sin] and I regret that I have made them." But Noah found favor and grace in the eyes of the Lord.

The [population of the] earth was corrupt [absolutely depraved—spiritually and morally putrid] in God's sight, and the land was filled with violence [desecration, infringement, outrage, assault, and lust for power]. God looked on the earth and saw how debased and degenerate it was, for all humanity had corrupted their way on the earth and lost their true direction. —Genesis 6:1-8, 11-12 (AMP)

As you saw iron mixed with ceramic clay, they will mingle with the seed of men; but they will not adhere to one another, just as iron does not mix with clay. —Daniel 2:43 (NKJV)

God said to Noah, "I intend to make an end of all that lives, for through men the land is filled with violence; and behold, I am about to destroy them together with the land. Make yourself an ark... —Genesis 6:13-14 (AMP)

Signs of Christ's Return

For the coming of the Son of Man (the Messiah) will be just like the days of Noah. For as in those days before the flood they were eating and drinking, marrying and giving in marriage, until the [very] day when Noah entered the ark, and they did not know or understand until the flood came and swept them all away; so will the coming of the Son of Man be [unexpected judgment]. —Matthew 24:37-39 (AMP)

Spiritism Forbidden

"When you enter the land which the Lord your God is giving you, you shall not learn to imitate the detestable (repulsive) practices of those nations. There shall not be found among you anyone who makes his son or daughter pass through the fire [as a sacrifice], one who uses divination and fortune-telling, one who practices witchcraft, or one who interprets omens, or a sorcerer, or one who casts a charm or spell, or a medium, or a spiritist, or a necromancer [who seeks the dead]. For everyone who does these things is utterly repulsive to the Lord... —Deuteronomy 18:9-14 (AMP)

The Battle Against Evil

For our fight is not against flesh and blood, but against principalities, against powers, against the rulers of the darkness of this world, and against spiritual forces of evil in the heavenly places. —Ephesians 6:12 (MEV)

Therefore rejoice, O heavens, and you who dwell in them! Woe to the inhabitants of the earth and the sea! For the devil has come down to you, having great wrath, because he knows that he has a short time." —Revelation 12:12 (NKJV)

Prediction of Apostasy

But the [Holy] Spirit explicitly and unmistakably declares that in later times some will turn away from the faith, paying attention instead to deceitful and seductive spirits and doctrines of demons, [misled] by the hypocrisy of liars whose consciences are seared as with a branding iron [leaving them incapable of ethical functioning], who forbid marriage and advocate abstaining from [certain kinds of] foods which God has created to be gratefully shared by those who believe and have [a clear] knowledge of the truth. —1 Timothy 4:1-5 (AMP)

Hell Exists

As soon as Moses finished speaking all these words, the ground under them split open; and the earth opened its mouth and swallowed them and their households, and all the men who supported Korah [led revolt against God's divinely appointed leaders], with all their possessions. So they and all that belonged to them went down alive to Sheol; and the earth closed over them... —Numbers 16:29-33 (AMP)

Demons in Hell

For if God spared not angels when they sinned, but cast them down to hell, and committed them to [pits of darkness, to be reserved unto judgment; and spared not the ancient world, but preserved Noah with seven others, —2 Peter 2:4-5 (ASV)

Demons to Be Released

And he opened the bottomless pit, and smoke arose out of the pit like the smoke of a great furnace. So the sun and the air were darkened because of the smoke of the pit. Then out of the smoke locusts came upon the earth. And to them was given power, as the scorpions of the earth have power. They were commanded not to harm the grass of the earth, or any green thing, or any tree, but only those men who do not have the seal of God on their foreheads. —Revelation 9:2-5 (NKJV)

What the "H" Was That!

People are freaking from what they see and dream. They witness things they don't want to see, dream nightmares that are all too real. We know something is different; something is invading our peace, something uninvited. Where people used to be able to shut things out, "bar the door, Katie," make that go away, "it", something is breaking through normalcy.

Aliens and UFOs, angels fallen and otherwise, cattle mutilations, crop circles, demons, ghosts, old hags, orbs, poltergeists, portals and shadow people – the veil is thinning between the paranormal and what we call Real Life. Let this author state from the get-go she's had zero encounters with any of the aforementioned, but have heard numerous interviews and read considerably on the topics.

Prior to 1980, some events in the paranormal category didn't exist. Others were rare, but unquestionably something is trashing the barrier between the seen and the unseen. Scientists and theologians theorize that the unseen world is right next to us. A parallel universe would explain how angels are always hovering close by, sometimes interceding on our behalf. They are that invisible hand who magically jerks a car back onto the road or that mysterious person who appeared to someone lost in the wilderness and guided them back to the hiking trail, then vanished in a microsecond. Countless stories of angel assistance have been recorded – so much so that numerous books detail their lifesaving, comforting presence.

Bold and Beautiful

For Boomers, crop circles, cattle mutilations and shadow people didn't exist when we were kids. While some of the paranormal are intriguing, even beautiful, like angels and crop formations, the majority add an element of fear and loathing.

Photo: This crop circle was made in Switzerland in July 2007. Those little specks are people, which give an idea of this circle's size.

The first crop circles discovered in the 1970s were fairly simple. Initially designs were modest and hoaxers like Doug Bower and David Chorley, who confessed to making at least 250, muddied the field, so to speak. Then formations became so complex incorporating mathematical equations and scientific aspects that investigators concluded human hands couldn't have created them. Designs grew to be over 400 feet across and incorporated more than 2,000 individual shapes so intricately arranged they were invisible to the casual observer.

Circles and formations usually appear overnight often in farmer's fields taking advantage of their uniform crop height. There's no evidence of equipment used to flatten plants. Grain stalks are evenly bent over, not broken. No footprints or tire marks mar the surrounding field.

By 2000, formations exploded around the world particularly in the UK, Russia, Japan, the U.S., Canada, South America and Australia. By 2011, over 10,000 patterns around the world had been documented.

Colin Andrews, who has researched crop circles since 1983, believes 80% are man-made. That leaves 20% made by some *thing*, something else.

The Creepy and Frightening

On the other end of the "beautiful" spectrum are repulsive, terrifying encounters. It wasn't until 2001 that this author fist heard of shadow people. A caller to Art Bell on the program he started, *Coast To Coast AM* now hosted by George Noory, first introduced this paranormal oddity. Since then countless people have experienced these things. They appear featureless and black and don't engage humans. Usually they move silently across the floor without attempting to engage whoever is in the room. Then in 2016 one of these creatures became openly evil, threatening. That was a new wrinkle. It was as though these 'things' have gained new powers. On a few occasions people have reported shadow animals.

The Old Hag or Night Hag Syndrome

When tired and longing for your pillow, the last thing you want is a visit from the Night Hag. Though encounters have been documented for hundreds of years around the world, they are becoming more prevalent, more malevolent. Here are a few.

One woman described it like this: "It happened for the first time when I was 14. I couldn't move, didn't understand what it was. My most prominent time having to experience sleep paralysis was last year while lying in bed. I fell asleep pretty quick, but then woken up with the pressure of a hand on my right shoulder. When I could turn around, I saw the old hag! She had long, craggy gray hair, pale greenish face, long nose, and – creepiest of all – her eyes were all black. She smiled at me... then took off. That's when I snapped out of the paralysis."[1513]

Photo: *The Nightmare,* painted by Henry Fuseli in 1781 is considered one of the classic depictions of the Night Hag where its victims experience sleep paralysis.

Scientists attribute these unsettling experiences to Sleep Paralysis. However, that doesn't account for some people reporting accompanying strange smells, the sound of approaching footsteps, apparitions of weird shadows or glowing eyes, or the oppressive weight on their chest, making it difficult, if not impossible, to breathe.

Another person shared their story:

"I am 42 and first had a nightmare about a terrifying witch at the age of 16. She kneels on my chest and stares into my face, slowly getting nearer and nearer. I am completely terrified. She wears a black cloak and hood. Her face is like a witch and evil generates from her, surrounds me from her. Other times, I can be lying on my stomach and she will creep her hand up the back of my head, down my face, and hook her fingers under my top teeth and pull my head back. Other times, she will bite, sit on the bed, knock the door, call my name, and generally scare the crap out of me."[1514]

Mat shared: "I have had various experiences of sleep paralysis. I've seen my bed covers pushed down onto my face, unable to move or shout. A female voice has hissed in my ear, bringing feelings of terror. Once I saw the old woman looking at me through my bed covers. She was gray and had an (sic) menacing grin. I started hitting the covers where this misty gray face was staring from. My wife woke up at this point and screamed, saying she saw the woman's face, too. I think there's more to it than just the scientific explanation. I think it's part physical and part supernatural. I think our brains pick up a more expansive signal when we are between sleep and an awake state."[1515]

And yet another:

"I was watching TV around 1 a.m. at my grandma's house. My granddad was in his room asleep across from the room that my grandma and I were in. She was asleep as well. I heard a grunting noise, like someone was trying to yell for help, but was being choked. I also heard an old woman and a man laughing. I was afraid and awoke my grandmother. We ran to my granddad's room. He was trying to wiggle himself free - and some old woman was sitting on him, holding him down. A bald man was sitting in his chair looking at us and laughing. We could slightly see through both of them, and we knew they weren't human, but evil spirits.

We struggling with trying to free granddad, and the ghost thought it was so funny that we couldn't touch her; our hands and arms went right through her to his body. The bald man stood up tall over us. He was angry that we tried to wake granddad. I turned on the room's light, and the spirits rose up and disappeared."[1516]

Shadow People – Hat Man

This author first became familiar with the concept in 2001 so they are a more recent phenomenon. Shadow People and "Hat Man" entities are different from ghosts, which have been reported for millennia. Ghosts usually either appear like real people or pets of either gender with definable facial features and fully attired in clothing appropriate to the time in which they lived. Some ghosts have been described as white misty beings or recognized as deceased family members who try to communicate with humans.

Most people describe Shadow People as black human-shaped silhouettes though more recently a few shadow animals have been seen. Usually Shadow People are just masses with no discernable facial features. Seen in a person's peripheral vision they move across a room slowly at first like being on a flat escalator, then rapidly jump to another part of a witness' surroundings. They are usually accompanied by a feeling of dread.

Once these things sense detection they'd disintegrate or move between walls, which suggests interdimensional travel.

That was then. Now they have "matured" in their human interactions and appearance. More often people are seeing them straight on for longer periods of time and some witnesses report Shadow People with red glowing eyes. Their actions were described as more benign where they were skulking around the periphery. Once they began to engage people using eye contact, they became distinctly malevolent and often violent.

In eastern Canada, an 8-year-old child woke up around 3 a.m. "Mary", felt compelled to look at her bedroom door and to her horror saw the shadow of a person in a top hat. In the dim hallway light she saw he held a knife menacingly at face height. Mary thought he wanted to kill her and in the only defense she knew, dove under the covers. That was the first and last time she saw Hat Man.

Sandra, who was 15 at the time, had her first experience in 2005. It was a typical hot, sticky summer Missouri night. She was listening to music while reading and trying too cool off. Inexplicably Sandra became cold all over and filled with fear. When she took off her headphones, Sandra nearly passed out from freight. Right in front of her was an entity about five feet tall with blood red eyes. She only saw it momentarily before it ran through the wall toward the outside of the house. Not realizing at first it wasn't human she expected to hear a thud as her room was on the second floor of the house.

Sandra was about to drift off to sleep at 2 a.m. when it happened again. This time seven entities appeared on the ceiling digging their claws and toes into the drywall to hang on. Paralyzed with fear, but able to breathe, she saw they all had glowing red eyes. They hung there for a while watching her, assessing. Then she blinked and they disappeared. The next morning Sandra expected to see claw marks, but there weren't any, nor on any of their subsequent visits.

A husband shares his dual experience with his wife:

"In December, 2007, my wife and I were sleeping in bed when I knew or felt my wife was being attacked. I woke to find a Shadow Person on top of her, choking her! I jumped out of bed and shared several French profanities with it. As I moved toward it to confront it, it moved away into the wall. I turned to see my wife still choking and woke her. She stated that she dreamed that she was being choked by a person on top of her.

Normally, you would dismiss it, but how do two people have simultaneous experiences? She would later have a similar experience in the Army where her roommate woke to see a person choking her!"[1517]

These things have attacked Christians and non-Christians alike. Some people reported that when they called on the Name of Jesus these entities disappear.

Cattle Mutilations

The *Denver Post* wrote about the strange death of Snippy, a 3-year-old Appaloosa. Her real name was Lady, but reporters nicknamed her Snippy because at the time of her death, Lady was thoroughly cut up. This was a first for the quiet little town of Hooper, 20 miles north of Alamosa. Lady belonged to Nellie Lewis and she kept her beloved horse on Harry King's ranch, which belonged to her brother. Nellie would ride Lady whenever she made the short trip from Alamosa. One night, Lady missed her drink from the water trough and then again the next morning. What Harry found when he looked for her that morning shocked and sickened him.

Lady had died on the night of September 7, 1967 with all flesh removed from her neck up. The laser-sharp bloodless border appeared cauterized. Her bones were bleached white like they'd been in the sun for months. Odd thing was, there was no blood anywhere. A neighbor who had seen Lady shortly after her strange skinning shared this: "From the neck up that horse was peeled. It was just pure white bones. The horse had only been dead for a night but it looked like it had been dead for months. Nellie was there with us and she found a piece of metal next to the horse. It was covered in horse hair. When she picked it up it burned her hand and she screamed and dropped it. Her hand was badly burned. I was there. I saw it."[1518] Lady's spinal cord was missing along with her heart, abdominal organs and brain.

U.S. Forest Service and Ranger, Duane Martin, was sent to investigate. He happened to have a Geiger counter with him and Nellie Lewis' boots tested radioactive. Martin found "a considerable increase in radioactivity"[1519] as far away as two city blocks from Lady's body, but readings directly over the horse were negative. For two years after her death, no grass grew where she was found.

Berle, Nellie's husband, said that circles were pressed into the ground close to Lady's body. They were two inches in diameter and four inches deep and were part of larger circles that were about three feet around. Over a half-mile area, 15 of these circles were burned into the ground. Berle said that they "looked like they'd been made by exhaust pipes."[1520] Yet, no footprints appeared anywhere around Lady's body.

Photo: Twenty minutes straight north from Alamosa up Colorado Highway 17 is the tiny town of Hooper, population 101. Both are situated in the San Luis Valley, sparsely populated and unencumbered by light pollution. For decades this area has been the Nation's UFO hotspot, some sightings dating back to the 1600s. It was this and a failed cattle ranch that prompted Judy Messoline to build the UFO Watchtower in 2000. People from around the world come to view the sky phenomena. Messoline said, "During the day, we see silver balls and saucer-shaped objects. We've also had reports of people driving down the country roads out here who've seen saucers flying right next to them."[1521]

On the same day that the article, "Dead Horse Riddle Sparks UFO Buffs," was published in the *Pueblo Chieftain*, came an account by Superior Court Judge Charles E. Bennett of Denver. Bennett and his wife, Dorothy Jean, and his mother had witnessed three reddish-orange rings in the Denver sky. They maintained a triangular formation, moved at a high speed and made a humming sound.[1522] This ignited the cattle mutilation-UFO connection.

CATTLE MUTILATIONS EXPLODE

Kansas farmers first reported 40 bizarre and sad incidents in Fall 1973. By September 1974, the cattle phenomena had spread to Nebraska with at least 50 cases. In Fall 1974, they began to taper off in Nebraska and moved into South Dakota and Minnesota. Mid-December 1974 a cow was found mutilated near Kimball, Minnesota. At the same time, a number of UFOs had been sighted in the state.

From 1974 – 1976 over 1,500 cattle in 22 states had been killed in the same manner.[1523] By 1999 that number had jumped to over 22,000[1524] and found in every state except Maine, Hawaii and Alaska. At least six Canadian provinces were similarly struck: Alberta, British Columbia, Manitoba, New Brunswick, Quebec and Saskatchewan.[1525]

Local sheriffs and state bureaus of investigation were baffled. In those and subsequent occurrences the ear, eyeball, jaw flesh, tongue, lips, tail, udder, genitals and/or rectum were removed. Another common feature is that there were no tracks surrounding the animal. One cow was even discovered in a large mud hole, but still there were no footprints. Even in snow, there are no tracks apart from the victimized animal. Often they are drained of blood through precise, smoothly cut holes and there is no blood, not a drop, on the ground. It's as though they were scooped up from overhead, surgically excised, drained of blood, and then dropped back on the ground. Some reports read that all four of the animal's legs were fractured, consistent with being dropped.

Also in Colorado, in San Luis about an hour south of Hooper, Manuel Sanchez found his 4th mysteriously slaughtered calf in a month. That was in 2009. Then two more appeared by 2011. In Manuel's 50+ years of raising cattle, he has no explanation for the missing eyes and ears or the tongues and genitals excised by fine cuts. The 72-year-old had always lived among the piñon-patched pastures where his father and grandfather cattle ranched. They were used to having mountain lions and coyotes kill cattle, elk and deer, but the remains of the mutilated cows showed it couldn't be predators. Nor would it be rustlers leaving the choice meat behind. Sanchez explained. "A lion will drag its kill. Coyotes rip and tear flesh. These were perfect cuts – like with a laser or like a scalpel. And what would take the waste – all the guts – and leave the nice, tender meat? No tracks. No blood. No nothing. I got nothing to go by. They don't leave no trace."[1526] Every other rancher reporting similar cattle deaths described them the same way.

1999 ELK ABDUCTION

On February 25, 1999 near Mt. St. Helens in the Cascade Mountains of Washington state multiple witnesses saw something unnerving, something inexplicable. These weren't people out to stir sensationalism or indulging in hallucinogenics. Instead they were 14 U.S. Forest Service workers who saw something shocking. This is what they shared.

A few minutes before noon forest workers had just broken for lunch and were heading for the crew vehicle. "Francisco" and "Augustine" were nearly at the turnout some 1900 ft. in elevation. "Manuel" and two others were walking up the slope from an old access road and were about 300 feet further down. The remaining 11 were scattered between the two groups on the hill's north side.

Francisco stopped to rest and watched 14 head of elk that had been hanging out all morning on the slope to their northeast. That's when Francisco spotted a strange object moving in the northeast. The UFO skimmed the clear-cut terrain at brush-top level while hugging the contour of the hill, heading toward the animals. The object's initial location was about 800 yards distant and 200 ft. below Francisco.

It moved silently with a slight, but a noticeable wobble. They realized it wasn't a paraglider as they'd first thought. The craft appeared to be about 5 to 6 feet wide and 7 to 8 feet long, dull-red color on the right half and bright white like enamel paint on the right. The rest of the disc was gray. Francisco, Augustine and Manuel were able to calculate the craft's size comparing it to the elk and it made one full revolution every 2–2½ seconds.

They watched the craft move toward the all-female herd, which remained calm until it was very close. Alarmed, they bolted and ran up the slope to their east. For some reason, one adult separated herself from the rest and trotted north. The disc quickly positioned itself directly above the lone elk and lifted her off the ground. The strange part was, no visible means were used to hoist the animal. She ascended like she was on a Star Trek tractor beam. At this point the 500-pound elk quit struggling and appeared unconscious. Her head was plastered right to the bottom of the craft with her body "standing" stiffly beneath. The kidnapped elk moved like the disc did as though she were welded to it.

Once the craft moved over the edge of the forest, continuing north, it ascended at a 45° angle until clouds obscured it. All this took place during a three to five minute span. Afterwards the rest of the herd remained closely huddled together, closer than before the extraction. The unnerved workers admitted they did too.

Since then the mutilations have gone global to Central and South America, Australia and Europe including the UK. Though 90% involve cattle, this phenomenon includes sheep, horses, goats, pigs, rabbits, cats, dogs, deer, elk[1527] and yes, in rare instances, humans. Government has tried fob off these happenings saying they're due to predators or blowflies, but it doesn't wash, particularly with long-time ranchers. Other popular explanations include:

- Satanic cults and ritual sacrifices
- Sex deviants
- Intelligence agencies secretly testing for nuclear or chemical weapon contamination
- Testing for BSE – Mad Cow Disease
- Extraterrestrial experiments

The truth could be all, some or none of these explanations. Fifty years after the fist mutilation with no concrete answer, we may never know what's behind these bizarre happenings.

Takeaways

The common theme is that these animals are dead, bloodless with soft tissue missing. No tracks appear around the deceased. Domestic animals are visibly agitated, fearful and avoid getting too close to the dead animals. Scavenging coyotes and wolves keep their distance for days without touching the carcasses. High levels of radiation have been detected near the mutilated. UFO sightings were reported around the time when animals were mutilated, but not always. Maybe they were missed or maybe they were absent.

UFOs, Aliens and the Nephilim

We are not alone in the universe. Most Americans, Brits and Germans believe aliens exist and more people are coming to that conclusion. September 2015's poll shows that over half of those surveyed accept that intelligent extraterrestrial life is a reality. The poll, conducted by the market-research group YouGov, found that 56% of Germans, 54% of Americans and 52% of Britons believe in the existence of ETs and EBEs – extraterrestrial biological entities. A distinction has to be made because EBEs imply something living and some extraterrestrials are thought to be robots. Those who hold this belief greatly outnumber those who don't and those who are undecided are the fewest.[1528] National Geographic's 2012 poll found that 77% of Americans think aliens have visited Earth.[1529] About 79% judge the U.S. government is hiding information about UFOs and 55% believe real-life Men in Black agents threaten into silence people who've had UFO encounters.[1530]

BELIEVERS BY THE NUMBERS

If the concept of aliens or extraterrestrials (ETs) seems far-fetched, very notable and respected people accept they are real and here. Some have had personal sightings and/or abductions whose numbers are growing every year. Others feel their presence is logical based on the amount of planets that have all the requirements for life.

In 2013 scientists found a dozen new potentially habitable exoplanets. Less than two years later they discovered another eight, including two that are the most Earth-like yet. As of 2014 astronomers had confirmed the existence of over 1,700 exoplanets.

The Milk Way alone may contain 60 billion such planets that orbit red dwarf stars.[1531] NASA scientists used to think there should be one Earth-size sphere in the life-supporting zone of each red dwarf. Now researchers have doubled that estimate after factoring in how cloud cover could help those planets support life. Clouds play an important part because they both cool and warm planets, and absorb radiation. Other researchers put that number at 100 million.[1532] Either way, 60 billion or 100

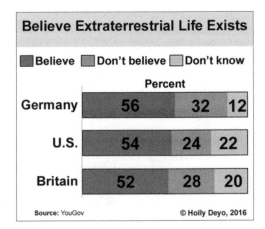

Believe Extraterrestrial Life Exists

■ Believe ■ Don't believe ☐ Don't know

Percent

Germany	56	32	12
U.S.	54	24	22
Britain	52	28	20

Source: YouGov   © Holly Deyo, 2016

million, by the numbers of alone, the chance for intelligent life is strong and everyone is looking for signs of life. Even the Pope is skywatching, but for what... admittedly, in part, for extra-terrestrials.

Image: Artist's rendition of sunset seen through the tenuous atmosphere of a hypothetical moon. As the suns dip below the horizon, the gas giant comes into view. The moon's landscape remains illuminated by sunlight reflected off the planet. (Courtesy NASA/JPL-Caltech)

POPE SCOPES THE SKIES

In 1993, the Vatican erected a 6-foot telescope on Arizona's Mt. Graham. The Tucson was chosen for its lack of light pollution and its clear dark nights. While VATT (Vatican Advanced Technology Telescope) takes pictures, a next door monumentally huge scope, oddly enough named Lucifer, watches for UFOs and aliens.

Lucifer is one of the world's most advanced telescopes using twin 28-foot mirrors. Either of its mirrors would make it the second-largest optical telescope in continental North America. Lucifer is a collaborative effort among Germany, the U.S. and Italy's astronomical communities.

Photo: This (VATT) is the original "Pope Scope", owned by the Vatican / Catholic Church. It's situated on Mt. Graham in southeast Arizona and operated by the Vatican Observatory, one of the oldest astronomical research institutions in the world, partnered with the University of Arizona. First starlight streamed through the telescope in 1993. Ironically this "eye in the sky" sits right next to another scope on Mt. Graham, christened Lucifer – **L**arge **B**inocular Telescope Near-infrared **U**tility with **C**amera and **I**ntegral **F**ield Unit for **E**xtragalactic **R**esearch.

Besides VATT in Tucson, the Vatican has an ambitious astronomy program in Castel Gandolfo, 15 miles southeast of Rome. An Argentinean Jesuit named Father Jose Gabriel Funes who's also scouting for ETs runs it. Funes maintains there's no conflict between believing there is intelligent alien life and the teachings of the Catholic Church.

Pope Francis agreed with this statement when he said in 2014 he would baptize aliens if they came to the Vatican. One of former Pope Benedict XVI's astronomers said, "Any entity – no matter how many tentacles it has – has a soul."[1533] And some are definitely lost.

Funes said in 2008, "Just as there is a multiplicity of creatures on Earth, there can be other beings, even intelligent, created by God. This is not in contrast with our faith because we can't put limits on God's creative freedom. To say it as St. Francis [of Assisi], if we consider some earthly creatures as 'brother' and 'sister,' why couldn't we also talk of an 'extraterrestrial brother'?"[1534] Not everyone shares that viewpoint.

UFO WITNESSES

Some of the most famous sightings include the 1945 and '47 UFO crashes in Socorro and Roswell, New Mexico, the 1942 UFO battle over Los Angeles, a UFO that flew for six hours over the White House in 1952, the 1980 UFO landing in England's Rendlesham Forest and the 1997 Phoenix Lights. This craft covered the span of several blocks and was witnessed by thousands flying over Arizona and Nevada. For 106 minutes on March 13, people were stunned. Among those who saw the UFO was Fife Symington, Arizona's governor at the time.

The field of extraterrestrials believers is becoming exceptionally wide and credible. Hundreds of scientists, military personnel, government and people working in intelligence agencies have witnessed them as documented by Dr. Steven Greer. Here are a few notables with recognizable names.

Professor Stephen Hawking, revered physicist and cosmologist who maintains that humans should be taking steps to avoid them rather than seek them out.

Lord Rees, Britain's royal astronomer said in 2010 he believed aliens could well exist and warned that they might prove to be beyond human understanding.

Lachezar Filipov, deputy director of the Space Research Institute of the Bulgarian Academy of Sciences. He and his colleagues claimed in 2009 they were already in contact with extraterrestrial life and that "Aliens are currently all around us, and are watching us all the time."[1535]

Edgar Mitchell, former NASA astronaut in the 1971 Apollo 14 moon mission. Mitchell stated in 2009 that alien life exists, but that the US government is covering up the evidence.

Jimmy Carter, U.S. President 1976-1980. He said: "I don't laugh at people any more when they say they've seen UFOs. I've seen one myself."[1536]

July 29, 1977 on the occasion of NASA launching Voyager 1 and Voyager 2, they put a gold-plated copper record aboard containing a message meant for extraterrestrials. "We cast this message into the cosmos… This is a present from a small distant world, a token of our sounds, our science, our images, our music, our thoughts, and our feelings. We are attempting to survive our time so we may live into yours. We hope someday, having solved the problems we face, to join a community of galactic civilizations."[1537]

General Douglas MacArthur, Korean and WWII soldier. He said in 1955 "the next war will be an interplanetary war. The nations of the earth must someday make a common front against attack by people from other planets."[1538]

Monsignor Corrado Balducci, Vatican theologian, said: "Extraterrestrial contact is a real phenomenon. The Vatican is receiving much information about extraterrestrials and their contacts with humans from its embassies in various countries, such as Mexico, Chile and Venezuela."[1539]

Air Chief Marshal Lord Dowding, WWII RAF Fighter commander during the Battle of Britain. "I am convinced that these objects [UFOs] do exist and that they are not manufactured by any nations on earth."[1540]

Ronald Reagan, U.S. President 1980-1988. Upon seeing a UFO himself he said, "I looked out the window and saw this white light. It was zigzagging around. I went up to the pilot and said, 'Have you ever seen anything like that?' He was shocked and he said, 'Nope.' And I said to him: 'Let's follow it!' We followed it for several minutes. It was a bright white light. We followed it to Bakersfield, and all of a sudden to our utter amazement it went straight up into the heavens. When I got off the plane I told Nancy all about it."[1541]

During the September 1985 Peace Conference in Geneva Reagan asked Soviet rival Mikhail Gorbachev for help fighting an alien invasion from extra terrestrial life. Reagan repeated his concerns and warning when he spoke to a group of Maryland high school students upon returning to the US. Afterwards his advisers removed any mention of aliens from his speeches. President Reagan's "casual references to invasions from outer space made [Colin] Powell [Reagan's National Security Advisor] uneasy. He worried that people might think Reagan was really concerned about interplanetary invasions if he kept raising the issue. When the subject came up, Powell would roll his eyes and say to his staff, 'Here come the little green men again.'"[1542]

In Dr. David Clarke's book, *How UFOs Conquered the World,* writes, "Ronald Reagan was a born-again Christian and saw no contradiction between his faith and a belief in aliens."[1543]

Mikhail Gorbachev, USSR's last head of state warned, "The phenomenon of UFOs does exist, and it must be treated seriously."[1544]

Nick Pope, who worked from 1985 to 2006 in the British Government's Ministry of Defense department said, "I suspect there are thousands and millions of civilizations out there. We all hope it's just going to be ET-style fluffy aliens as opposed to a terrifying alien invasion."[1545]

Paul Hellyer, member of Canadian Parliament from 1949 to 1974 and Defense Minister from 1963 to 1967 publicly stated: "UFOs, are as real as the airplanes that fly over your head."[1546]

Dr. Herman Oberth, German rocket engineer taken by the US after WWII said, "It is my thesis that flying saucers are real and that they are spaceships from another solar system. There is no doubt in my mind that these objects are interplanetary craft of some sort. I and my colleagues are confident that they do not originate in our solar system."[1547]

Richard Nixon U.S. President 1969-1974 said in a press conference, "I'm not at liberty to discuss the government's knowledge of extraterrestrial UFO's at this time. I am still personally being briefed on the subject."[1548]

Jackie Gleason, former comedian, actor, and musician, and close friend of Nixon was reportedly taken to Homestead Air Force Base in Florida where Nixon showed him bodies of ETs. His former wife, Beverly McKittrick, said Jackie described the aliens as small beings that are "only about two feet tall with bald heads and disproportionately large ears."[1549]

Dr. J Allen Hynek, former director the U.S. Air Force's of Project Blue Book. "When the long-awaited solution to the UFO problem comes, I believe that it will prove to be not merely the next small step in the march of science, but a mighty and totally unexpected quantum leap... we had a job to do, whether right or wrong, to keep the public from getting excited."[1550]

Gordon Cooper, former NASA astronaut in the 1960s for the Mercury-Atlas 9 and Gemini 5 missions, wrote a letter to the UN in 1978 asking them to set up a research program to study UFOs. Cooper had spotted saucers in 1951 while flying an F-86 over Germany.

In 1957, Cooper was in charge of several advanced projects, including the installation of a precision landing system. While at Edwards Air Force Base in California, Cooper said, "I had a camera crew filming the installation when they spotted a saucer. They filmed it as it flew overhead, then hovered, extended three legs as landing gear, and slowly came down to land on a dry lake bed! These guys were all pro cameramen, so the picture quality was very good. The camera crew managed to get within 20 or 30 yards of it, filming all the time. It was a classic saucer, shiny silver and smooth, about 30 feet across. It was pretty clear it was an alien craft. As they approached closer it took off."[1551]

Lord Hugh Caswall Tremenheere Dowding, Air Chief Marshal in the Battle of Britain said, "I am convinced that these objects [UFOs] do exist and that they are not manufactured by any nations on earth."[1552]

J Edgar Hoover established the FBI and worked under six Presidents. In 1942 when flying saucers flew over Los Angeles, they were fired at, according to reports. In a statement to the press Hoover said, "We must insist upon full access to disks recovered. For instance, in the LA case the Army grabbed it and would not let us have it for cursory examination."[1553]

Walter Cronkite, American broadcast journalist and anchorman for CBS Evening News for 19 years, and respected "voice of the truth for America." In the 1950s, Cronkite was invited to a Pacific island with other reporters to observe an Air Force display of their new missile. As it was about to launch, a 50-60 foot disc-shaped UFO hovered in the sky. It was dull gray and had no visible means of propulsion. As Air Force guards ran toward the UFO with their dogs, the disc hovered about 30 feet off the ground. It suddenly sent out a blue beam of light, which simultaneously struck the missile, a guard and a dog. The missile froze in mid-air about 70 feet from the launcher. The guard froze in mid-step and a dog froze in mid-air as he jumped at the disc. This all happened within five minutes or less. Thirty minutes later, Cronkite and other reporters were warned by an Air Force Colonel not to report the incident.[1554]

Robert James Lee "Bob" Hawke, Sr., Australian Prime Minister 1983-1991 said. "I believe that the most important thing that will happen in the new millennium... will be the proof of extraterrestrial intelligence. While this will have many aspects of profound significance, nothing is more important in my estimation than the hope that this event will serve to bind together the peoples of planet earth and serve to emphasize the total futility of human conflict between groups and nations."[1555]

Dr. Walther Riedel, research director and chief designer at Germany's rocket center in Peenemunde, Usedom. Though Riedel had never seen a saucer, for several years he kept records of UFO sightings all over the world. He told *LIFE* magazine in April 7, 1952: "I am completely convinced that they have an out-of-world basis."[1556]

THE DISCLOSURE PROJECT

In 1996 retired physician and founder of the Disclosure Project, Steven Greer, and his staff interviewed over 400 government, military, and intelligence community witnesses about UFOs and extraterrestrials. Interviews covered their firsthand experiences with UFOs, ETs, ET technology and related cover-ups. In 1997, Greer and several other members of the Center for the Study of Extraterrestrial Intelligence (CSETI) made a presentation to Congress. The Disclosure Project's goal was to get amnesty for government whistle-blowers who violated their security oaths by sharing insider knowledge about UFOs. That meeting didn't progress far. Congress remained tone deaf and did nothing.

Then in May 9, 2001, over 20 military, intelligence, government, corporate and scientific witnesses came forward at the National Press Club in Washington DC to present basically the same evidence. This presentation didn't make much of a dent either. Maybe the Disclosure Project feels it's making progress, possibly in the sense of increased public awareness. However, in the arena of the U.S. government discussing this topic, except in the most dismissive terms, nothing has changed.

On *Jeff Rense*, former Canadian MoD Paul Hellyer commented, "The secrecy involved in all matters pertaining to the Roswell incident was unparalleled. The classification was, from the outset, above top secret, so the vast majority of U.S. officials and politicians, let alone a mere allied minister of defense, were never in-the-loop."

Government officials steadfastly ignore urgings for disclosure and open dialogue about UFOs and extraterrestrials. Their reasons are many:

1. **War weary.** After WWII they felt the public would be too traumatized to come against another "foe" so soon and one much greater, more powerful than what they just encountered.
2. **Technology**. Reversed engineered alien technology and that gained by trade with them (more about this in a bit), would effectively kill the oil industry worldwide. There would be no need for the petrochemical industry, which would destabilize countries globally as well as end major revenue streams for elites. Retooling and reinventing a world economy based primarily on oil would be nearly cost-prohibitive.
3. **Loss of control.** It would end inequality, hunger and poverty among nations, which would quash control by the New World Order. ET advanced technology in free energy would eliminate these "puppet strings".
4. **Lies damned lies.** After seven decades of government cover-ups and denials, it would be extremely difficult and embarrassing to admit their endless deceit and fabrications. People would lose what faith they have left in governing bodies.
5. **Panic.** Public would freak over creatures much more powerful and intelligent than humans especially when their "experiments" and possible intentions were revealed.
6. **Religious fallout.** People's faiths and belief systems might be shaken.
7. **Impotency.** Government is powerless to stop ET intrusion and abductions.
8. **Money.** Significant numbers of secret government operations would be exposed, which would partly explain where countless trillions have disappeared.
9. **Reprisals and threats of death.** Several Presidents have promised to pull the facade away on the ET/UFO arena, but once in office, only silence ensues, even when pressed.
10. **Ignorance**. Those in the Shadow Government see Presidents as short-term "leaders" lasting at most eight years so there's no reason to bring them into the loop.

11. **Economy.** People fearing the worst might pull investments from the stock market and other institutions, further destabilizing a fragile global economy.

WEAPONS IN SPACE

Part of Dr. Greer's stated agenda is to get governments to not weaponize space, but he's a little late for that. Without most people noticing, the U.S., China and Russia have been deploying new and more sophisticated weaponry into "the final frontier."

In September 2005 Canada's Paul Hellyer made a startling speech at the University of Toronto capturing the attention of mainstream media. "The United States military are preparing weapons which could be used against the aliens, and they could get us into an intergalactic war without us ever having any warning. The Bush administration has finally agreed to let the military build a forward base on the moon, which will put them in a better position to keep track of the goings and comings of the visitors from space, and to shoot at them, if they so decide."[1557] Hellyer further stated "he believes the U.S. has developed new forms of energy at secret 'black operation' units using alien technology and that a 'shadow government' is behind this activity."[1558]

Missiles may not sound very sexy used as weapons against ETs, but according to Colonel Philip J. Corso (Ret.) the first shootdown of an alien craft took place in 1974 over Ramstein Air Force Base in Germany.[1559]

Nuclear Time Bombs

Needless to say, a space war could have very detrimental effects on the nearly 1,400 satellites orbiting earth. At least 34 military sats have plutonium onboard.[1560] According to Australian physician, author and anti-nuclear advocate, Dr. Helen Caldicott, "one of the most deadly [radioactive isotopes] is plutonium, name after Pluto, god of the Underworld. One-millionth of a gram, if you inhale it, will give you cancer. Hypothetically, one pound of evenly distributed plutonium [dust] will give everyone on earth cancer."[1561]

It's a much bigger problem than most people imagine. Case in point:

The Soviet Kosmos 954 satellite was powered by a nuclear reactor with 110 pounds of Uranium-235. It was supposed to be a Soviet eye in the sky for a long time but by December 1977, just four months after its September 18th launch, NORAD detected that it was moving erratically. Its orbit changed going up 50 miles. Due to its fairly high angle, in principle, it posed a threat to almost all of the world's major population centers.[1562]

Down it came breaking into hundreds of pieces spewing radiation everywhere. Most of the Uranium-235 survived reentry, contaminating a 370-mile long area between Great Slave Lake in Alberta, up through Saskatchewan continuing northeast to Baker Lake in the Northwest Territories.

Between January and April 1978, a team of Canadians and Americans swept 48,000 sq. miles looking for debris. They found a dozen large pieces emitting 1.1 sieverts per hour. One fragment released 500 roentgens per hour (equal to 5 sieverts), "which is sufficient to kill a person remaining in contact with the piece for a few hours."[1563] It's usually lethal for humans within five hours.

Canada billed Russia $6 million for the cleanup, but only paid half, which in 2016 dollars is $12 million received. Despite the massive efforts, less than 1% was recovered and properly disposed of. Today, there are still thousands of lost pieces of radioactive, contaminated satellite, waiting to be found by some unlucky individuals.

Crowded Space

In 2011, the National Research Council warned NASA that the amount of space debris had reached a "tipping point." Their report found there is so much "currently in orbit to continually collide and create even more debris, raising the risk of spacecraft failures…" and that "collisions with debris have disabled and even destroyed satellites in the past" including "a recent near-miss of the International Space Station." [1564] So we don't need a war in space.

The U.S. and China have already used anti-satellite (ASAT) devices. In 2007 China shot down its own FY-1C weather satellite. Not only did it demonstrate that it could be done, but the blast sent debris hurtling at nearly 16,000mph along the path of other orbiting spacecraft. The missile's impact produced the largest-ever debris-creating event in history, which could have easily damaged other satellites. No wonder countries freaked with China's space mess and their government had serious egg on its face. Factoring in the plutonium, the rocketing debris could have spelled disaster if it'd hit any of plutonium-carrying satellites. This was the first time a satellite had been shot down since the Reagan administration blasted an orbiting solar observatory in 1985. China has repeated the exercise several times since in 2010, 2013 and 2014 using CSS-X-11 ballistic missiles. This time though they called them "missile defense" tests using hit-to-kill technology.

As of 2016, of the nearly 1,400 satellites, over 40% belong to the U.S. Not only do they continuously snap micro-detailed photographs of earth, they transmit critical data on GPS, surveys, scientific research, weather, and environmental monitoring like oil spills and the extent of forest fires. They send television and communication signals, enable superior military surveillance, perform inspections, and instant credit card authorizations. Other satellites were launched to check on failed equipment. One of their lesser-known tasks is waiting for commands to disable or destroy satellites belonging to potential enemies. While an EMP could toss us back to the 17th century, loss of satellites would send us back to the Industrial Age.

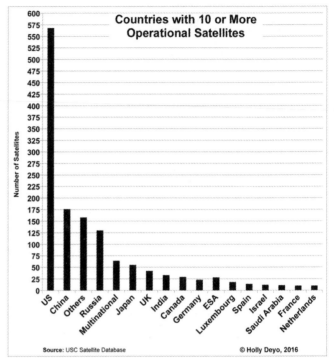

THE *REAL* STAR WARS

Before the Strategic Defense Initiative (SDI), a.k.a. Star Wars, no defense against an alien threat existed. Star Wars' real purpose was to shoot down extraterrestrials, not incoming Soviet warheads though that's how it was packaged to the public. To be sure Star Wars enabled the U.S. to knock down enemy satellites, kill electronic guidance systems of incoming enemy warheads and disable enemy spacecraft, but it had another, unstated, secret benefit. It could take down alien craft. With the policy of Mutually Assured Destruction (MAD) in place, neither the U.S. nor the Soviets would fire missiles at each other. Publicly, SDI was protection from war with the Soviets, which if that were the case, it would give the U.S. a tremendous leg up and inflame Soviet ire. However, Mikhail Gorbachev was secretly relieved to see this technology become reality because President Reagan guaranteed that America would throw this protective shield around the Soviet Union, too.

Other defense technologies exist besides missiles. Publicly, directed-energy weapons utilizing lasers, high-powered microwaves, and particle beams are still in development, but have been in operation since the late 1970s. That fits leaked information regarding the 35-50 year gap between when technology is released to the public and how much earlier it was developed. If only these were enough because as our technology progressed so did that of off-worlders. The threat hasn't lessened and they are still coming here. They are still experimenting on God's children like we are guinea pigs. They are still taking people against their will and doing unspeakable things to them – things that terrorize and inflict enormous physical pain. For this to happen in such great numbers there had to be government knowledge of aliens' presence and what they're doing. Government's response, as a whole, is denial to try and keep a lid on it, but some have hinted strongly at an agenda or come forward. In order to keep their invading forces secret, a pact formed between aliens, who are the Fallen and Government. I know this sounds crazy, but it's fact, and President Reagan tried to warn the public, saying it without saying it, letting us know what was happening.

President Ronald Reagan on the Alien Threat

Referring to a 5-hour private conversation with Gorbachev Mr. Reagan revealed so much more than what most Americans realized. In 1985 Mr. Reagan stated, "I couldn't help but say to [Mr. Gorbachev] just think how easy his task and mine might be in these meetings that we held if suddenly there was a threat to this world from another planet."[1565]

Even more important is the very publicly stated, recorded speech of President Reagan to the UN on September 21, 1987: "Perhaps we need some outside universal threat. I occasionally think how quickly our differences worldwide would vanish if we were facing an alien threat from outside this world." Then his next line revealed something crucial. "And yet I ask, is not an alien force already among us?"[1566]

He made nearly identical remarks in a speech at Fallston High School in Fallston, Maryland on December 4, 1985, "I couldn't help but at one point in our discussions, privately, with General Secretary Gorbachev when you stop to think that we're all God's children wherever we may live in the world, I couldn't help but say to him, just think how easy his task and mine might be in these meetings that we held if suddenly there was a threat to this world from some other species from another planet outside in the universe, we'd forget all those little local differences we had between our countries and we'd find out once and for all, that really are all human beings here on this earth together. Well, I don't suppose we can wait for an alien race to come down and threaten us...[1567]

He also repeated these same thoughts on other occasions. The fictional President Thomas Whitmore in the 1996 movie *Independence Day* stated it a little more eloquently when he addressed the U.S. fighter pilots.

"Good morning. Good morning. In less than an hour, aircraft from here will join others from around the world, and you will be launching the largest aerial battle in the history of mankind. Mankind... that word should have new meaning for all of us today. We can't be consumed by our petty differences any more. We will be united in our common interest.

"Perhaps it's fate that today is the 4th of July, and you will once again be fighting for our freedom. Not from tyranny, oppression, or persecution, but from annihilation. We're fighting for our right to live, to exist – and should we win the day, the 4th of July will no longer be known as an American holiday, but as the day when the world declared in one voice, [voice soaring, emphatic] 'We will not go quietly into the night! We will not vanish without a fight! We're going to live on, we're going to survive.' Today we celebrate our Independence Day!"

If only that were reality.

FROM THERE TO HERE AND BACK

While some scientists say that extraterrestrials and UFOs "contradict virtually all of the basic laws of physics, chemistry and biology on which modern science depends"[1568] let's assume they are unfamiliar with the physics fields that explore parallel universes, wormholes and folding space and time. These concepts are much too involved to delve into here, but the short version is that they explain craft rapidly covering vast amounts of space in a very short time. If this topic interests you, a good starting place is the lectures and books of Michio Kaku, professor of Theoretical Physics at the City College of New York. You can also hear numerous interviews on YouTube. Kaku has a gift for making some of the more complex scientific concepts readily understandable to the novice.

Riding Gravity Waves

In February 2016, scientists finally proved what Einstein theorized a hundred years ago. It was the last piece of his Theory of Relativity to be confirmed.

Under his theory, space and time are interwoven into "spacetime" – the 4th dimension. Einstein predicted that mass warps space-time through by gravity. Imagine space-time as a trampoline, and mass as a big ball sitting on it (next image left). Objects on the trampoline's surface will "fall" towards the center – representing gravity. When objects with mass speed up, like when two black holes spiral toward each other, they send waves along the curved space-time around them at the speed of light, like ripples on a pond (next image right).

Science Magazine explains the discovery best. "Long ago, deep in space, two massive black holes – the ultrastrong gravitational fields left behind by gigantic stars that collapsed to infinitesimal points – slowly drew together. The stellar ghosts spiraled ever closer, until, about 1.3 billion years ago, they whirled about each other at half the speed of light and finally merged. The collision sent a shudder through the universe: ripples in the fabric of space and time called gravitational waves."[1569] Scientists say it was the most powerful explosion ever, minus the Big Bang. It released 50 times more energy than that of all the stars in the observable universe. So while humans are still plodding along, this goes a long way proving time travel – something that aliens are likely using.

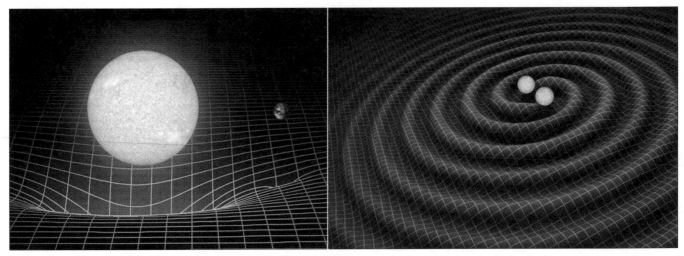

Images: Two illustrations of how gravitational waves behave. **Left:** Artist's impression of gravitational waves generated by binary neutron stars. (Courtesy T. Pyle / Caltech / MIT / LIGO Lab) **Right:** Artist's impression of gravitational waves generated by binary neutron stars. (Courtesy R. Hurt / Caltech-JPL)

Wormholes

Another way to travel is by using wormholes, something else Einstein predicted, which are basically "shortcuts" or "bridges" through space. Scientists say wormholes could either be straight as the illustration shows or winding as in the movie Contact. Either way they agree that these cosmic tunnels would likely be unstable, which is one of their arguments against them being viable. However, in 2015 Spanish physicists created a wormhole in their lab.

Jordi Prat-Camps, doctoral candidate in physics at Spain's Autonomous University of Barcelona said, "This device can transmit the magnetic field from one point in space to another point, through a path that is magnetically invisible. From a magnetic point of view, this device acts like a wormhole, as if the magnetic field was transferred through an extra special dimension."[1570] With wormhole discoveries this far advanced by humans, they are probably a done deal by aliens, Satan's demonic entities. More likely they are right here beside us, just a dimension away. All they need is a gate.

Image: This image shows how "folding" time and space theoretically works, connected by a wormhole. In simplest terms a tunnel connects Point A and Point B, greatly cutting the distance between the two. Albert Einstein and Nathan Rosen first proposed this theory in 1935 earning wormholes a fancier name of Einstein-Rosen Bridges.

Parallel Dimensions

But why go all through this drama when just stepping "next door" into a parallel dimension is possible? This is something physicist Michio Kaku and other renowned scientists acknowledge and have discussed at length saying there's reason to believe parallel dimensions are more than products of sci-fi writers' imaginations. Despite centuries of sky observation, only 4% of the universe is known because the rest is made up of dark matter and dark energy, which leaves a lot of unchartered territory. One man may have made a vital new discovery.

Caltech cosmologist Ranga-Ram Chary thinks he's found proof of a parallel universe. In his 2015 study published in *Astrophysical Journal,* Chary described evidence of cosmic bruising where one universe bumps against another.

Chary mapped a cosmic anomaly using data from the European Space Agency's (ESA) space telescope Planck. He then compared his map with the entire night sky. It showed what looked like a blob made of bright light that was a different color from what it should have been.

Part of CERN's (European Organization for Nuclear Research) job has been to probe the origins and structure of the universe. Scientists hope their Large Hadron Collider will give proof of parallel dimensions.

Photo: Ranga-Ram Chary, a cosmologist from Caltech, has discovered scientific evidence that could prove the existence of multiple and parallel universes. He found an anomaly in the cosmic microwave background that points to the possibility of pocket universes having been created with the expansion of the main universe itself. (Courtesy Lauro Roger McAllister, https://creativecommons.org/licenses/by/2.0/)

When CERN makes its colossal collisions, scientists track the resulting billions of particles at four laboratories around the globe. They're monitoring the particles to see when and how they come together and what shapes they take. Scientists say this could give clear signs of other dimensions beyond the basics of length, breadth, depth and time. They think parallel universes could be hidden within these dimensions. French particle physicist at the European Organization for Nuclear Research (CERN) Aurelien Barrau stated, "The idea of multiple universes is more than a fantastic invention – it appears naturally within several scientific theories, and deserves to be taken seriously."[1571]

Parallel dimensions seem to make the most sense as far as travel and movement between the heavenly, the demonic and earthly realms. It supports people's accounts of entities magically appearing and disappearing and seeming to walk through walls, etc.

"Folding" the universe and using wormholes also could explain why craft are visible one minute and seconds later appear clear across the sky. Logic dictates that travel at those apparent velocities just isn't possible – at lease not in the public arena.

While for the most part earth scientists are relatively still in pre-school regarding parallel universes, advanced travel and the like, Fallen Angel technology has aliens at comparative doctorate levels and beyond. What seems magic to humans is normal to them.

GATING AND PORTALS

The concept of a device that creates wormholes was popularized by the wildly successful 1994-2009 Stargate franchise. Many science fiction technologies that aired 30 and 40 years ago, in the theoretical realm only are now in use or nearly there. Think *Star Trek, Stargate, 2001 A Space Odyessy, Star Wars, Babylon 5, Blade Runner* and *Terminator*. Here are few examples of technologies that 50 years ago might have seemed impossible: Purdue's cloaking device, transparent armor, tractor beams, hyposprays, phasers, universal translators, replicators (3D printers), tricorders, Visor – **V**isual **I**nstrument and **S**ensory **O**rgan **R**eplacement, computerized virtual assistant, flying cars, holograms, brain activated body limbs, voice command recognition, genetic profiling, holodecks (virtual reality) and tablets.

More people accept jumpgates as likely and less like science fiction. In theory stargates allow jumpers to visit planets without craft or any other technology. They make traveling to intra- and even intergalactic distances nearly instantaneous. Some folks believe these gates exist naturally around the world independent of man's creation.

Scriptures talk about gates – heavenly gates.

Photo: Stargate recreation at Japan Expo July 4, 2009 (Courtesy Jamiecat)

And they said, Go to, let us build us a city and a tower, whose top may reach unto heaven; and let us make us a name, lest we be scattered abroad upon the face of the whole earth. And the Lord came down to see the city and the tower, which the children of men builded. And the Lord said, Behold, the people is one, and they have all one language; and this they begin to do: and now nothing will be restrained from them, which they have imagined to do. Go to, let us go down, and there confound their language, that they may not understand one another's speech. So the Lord scattered them abroad from thence upon the face of all the earth: and they left off to build the city. Therefore is the name of it called Babel*; because the Lord did there confound the language of all the earth: and from thence did the Lord scatter them abroad upon the face of all the earth. —Genesis 11:3-9 (KJV)

* NOTE: In Hebrew, Babel has special significance. "Bab" = gate and "el" = God. Quite literally Babel meant "Gate of God".

Then Jacob awoke from his sleep and said, "Surely the Lord is in this place, and I did not know it." And he was afraid and said, "How awesome is this place! This is none other than the house of God, and this is the gate of heaven!" —Genesis 28:16-17 (NKJV)

Lift up your heads, O you gates! And be lifted up, you everlasting doors! And the King of glory shall come in. —Psalm 24:7 (NKJV)

Blessed is the man who listens to me, watching daily at my gates, waiting at the posts of my doors. —Proverbs 8:34 (NKJV)

After these things I looked, and behold, a door standing open in heaven. And the first voice which I heard was like a trumpet speaking with me, saying, "Come up here, and I will show you things which must take place after this." Immediately I was in the Spirit; and behold, a throne set in heaven, and One sat on the throne. —Revelation 4:1-2 (NKJV)

Then He [Jesus] said to him [Nathanael], "I assure you and most solemnly say to you, you will see heaven opened and the angels of God ascending and descending on the Son of Man [the bridge between heaven and earth]." —John 1:51 (AMP)

A half dozen scriptures talk about portals and gates to heaven, but eight times as many discuss those leading to hell or hell itself. This is a sharp warning about how close is the demonic element. The Veil, that thin divider between evil and earth has been eroding over the millennia and parts are nearly transparent. It explains why so many, many people are seeing, sensing, feeling, experiencing demonic attacks and visitations.

UFO SIGHTINGS ARE INCREASING

Best estimates say 80% of UFO sightings can be explained as hoaxes, natural phenomena or human technology mistaken for UFOs. That leaves another 20%, literally numbering in the thousands that are likely of extraterrestrial origin. Some people believe inhabitants of those off-world craft are our space brothers, here to help, protect earth and "save" us. Others have had horrific, unspeakable experiences taking places repeatedly, over decades. More about this in bit. As testament to just how close the veil is to being ripped apart, check the huge uptick in sightings. Couple this with new demonic entities appearing on the scene as well as so many people having dreaded encounters, the veil is coming down. Literally, all hell is breaking loose.

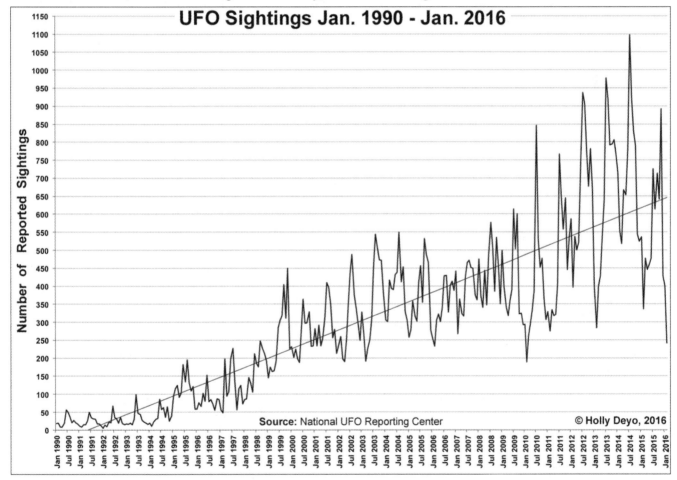

So says Peter Davenport, director of the National UFO Reporting Center (UFORC) since 1994. He is so low-key and unpretentious you'd never know he'd earned an M.S. degree in the Genetics and Biochemistry of Fish from the College of Fisheries, as well as an M.B.A. in Finance and International Business from the Graduate School of Business. His bio says he's worked as a college instructor, commercial fisherman, Russian translator in the Soviet Union, fisheries observer aboard Soviet fishing vessels, flight instructor and businessman. Davenport also founded and was president of a Seattle-based biotechnology company, BioSyn, which currently employs over 300 scientists and technicians. He regularly reports on the most current UFO sightings on talk radio programs including *Coast To Coast AM* and *Jeff Rense*.

MORE SIGHTINGS IN THE UNITED KINGDOM

Increased UFO sightings in the UK are similar to the trend in the U.S. In June 2013 their National Archives released 4,300 pages of UFO-related documents, drawings, letters, photos and parliamentary questions covering the final two years of the Ministry of Defense's UFO Desk. These files were the 10th and final collection released. Between 2000 and 2007, the UK received about 100-200 sightings reports per year. Then in 2008, the number doubled and then tripled in 2009. Since the UFO Desk offices closed, it's anyone's guess how large the number of sightings is now. Minister of Defense offices explained that it was this deluge of UFO reports that strained their resources. As a result, in November 2009, the MoD pulled the plug on Britain's "X-Files".

THE ALIEN COVER-UP

For anyone that has had a passing interest in extraterrestrials and UFOs, they surely would have come across the name of Colonel Philip J. Corso (Ret.). He, along with Bill Burns, authored *The Day After Roswell.* Corso was a member of President Eisenhower's National Security Council and former head of the Foreign Technology Desk at the U.S. Army's Research & Development department. He served 21 years in the Army and fought in both WWII and the Korean War earning numerous awards including the Bronze Star and Legion of Merit. It is what he participated in – guarding alien artifacts brought back from the July 5, 1947 crash in Roswell, NM that gained him the most notoriety. Rather than recount these famous crashes, let's go from there and consider what they're after and what they want.

THEY AREN'T OUR SPACE "BROTHERS"

Whether or not people believe contacting them is a good idea is another matter. Physicist Stephen Hawking believes that intelligent life on other planets likely exists, but that if aliens had visited Earth it would have been a "much more unpleasant" experience[1572] and that humans would be better off avoiding contact. In a Discovery Channel documentary Hawking stated. "If aliens visit us, the outcome would be much as when Columbus landed in America, which didn't turn out well for the Native Americans."[1573] Hawking warns, "We only have to look at ourselves to see how intelligent life might develop into something we wouldn't want to meet."[1574] If aliens were to land today, the majority say the would react much like Hawking, echoing his concerns: 22% would try to befriend them, 15% would run away, 13% would lock their doors, and 2% would try to inflict bodily harm.[1575]

Often it's people who consider themselves New Agers that believe extraterrestrials are here to help. Typical was Sheldan Nidle's Ground Crew's, now the Planetary Activation Organization (PAO), August 1997 plea, "An Urgent Message to Humanity." Here are some highlights.

> The planet is about to enter into a complete state of emergency. When Earth's birthing process fully begins, you will need to be in a safe place. The Galactic Federation, which is sent to us by God, is fully prepared to move you to either a "holographic environment" or to a temporary residence aboard one of their star ships.

> Due to the global magnitude of the Earth changes, many of you may have to be evacuated by space ships. There are currently millions of these ships waiting around the planet to take people from various parts of the Earth to live temporarily in holograms on large mother ships. These ships are presently cloaked, but will become visible at the appropriate time. You will live in these holograms on the mother ships until the Earth's holographic environments are complete.

> Our friends from other planets have highly advanced scientific and technical capabilities by which they can create holograms (energy fields of light) that will exactly replicate your present home. The sun, moon and weather patterns will appear the same as you have known them and you will have housing, food, clothing and all you need to survive.

> There will be no homelessness and no poverty. You will not have to go to work, pay bills or taxes, do housework, grow, cook or buy food. Replicators, like in the TV series "Star Trek", will provide your food and clothing. Everything you need in order to live will be provided for you until you are returned to Mother Earth.

After your Ascension, you will be in full consciousness. You will be able to create the way you look, manifest perfect health, create your own dwelling. You will be able to live for hundreds or thousands of years. … You will have to choose whether or not you want to participate in this evacuation… There is life on other planets. We have benevolent space brothers and sisters who love us and care deeply about us. They will be here to help us through this tumultuous time on our planet.[1576]

According to Wikipedia, " Nidle is known for his prediction that the world would end on December 17, 1996. Nidle, then residing in Walnut Creek, California, predicted that it would happen with the arrival of 16 million spaceships and a host of angels from the 'photon belt'. When this did not occur, Nidle claimed the angels had transferred humanity into a holographic projection in order to give it a second chance. Following his prediction's failure, Nidle removed all reference to it from his website. Nidle was 'awarded' a Pigasus award, an award designed to expose psychic frauds, for his failed prediction."[1577]

Granted Nidle sounds ridiculous, but some people actually believe this. PAO has members in Great Britain, Europe, Central and South America, the U.S. Australia, New Zealand, Canada and Mexico. The site neglected to say how many of these folks have been in contact with beings from the over 200,000 member star nations including "our galactic neighbors" the Andromedans, Arcturians, Bellatricians, Centaurians, Mintakans, Tau Cetians, Pegasians, Fomalhautans and Procyonans.

One common thread on websites and in books that promote aliens-are-our-space-brothers like the PAO, is that Buddha and Jesus Christ are both "very high Ascended Masters of Light." This author doesn't know if this is a promotion for Buddha, but it's certain a demotion for the Son of God.

Little evidence exists of alien friendly activities except in those "memories" purposely planted into abductees' minds. False memories make them believe encounters with them are pleasant and that they have our best interests at heart when quite the opposite is the truth.

THE PLAYERS

The term Watchers is used to indicate "good" aliens in the sense of beings who try to help humans without interfering in their free will, as well as referring to fallen angels. The *Books of Enoch* shed light on both and their activities. The first *Book of Enoch* details the angels' fall from favor, the Watchers who went bad. The second book covers the Watchers who are in the 5th heaven where the fall took place and it lists the leaders of the 200 fallen ones. The last book talks about the unfallen Watchers or good angels.

Watchers were originally sent to Earth to look after humans. However, they took a left turn, gave people forbidden knowledge and mated with human women. Fallen angels were reportedly attracted to women's long hair, which gave rise to the Catholic and Islamic custom of covering their tresses. Their union produced the race of giants and some say, also the gods of mythology. The Fallen Ones thrust forbidden knowledge on mankind, which was supposed to be given to humans gradually. It wasn't that God didn't want people to "know", but he wanted them to mature and learn how to responsibly use the knowledge. This new information included things like weaponry, cosmetics, mining, metallurgy, jewelry making, medicine and healing, reading and writing, the use mirrors and sorcery.

Offspring of Fallen Angels, the Nephilim, managed to thoroughly sexually corrupt humans with orgies, homosexuality, cruelty, violence and promiscuity along with introducing disgusting dining habits that included cannibalism. Nothing good came of matings between celestial beings and humans so God put an end to them with the Great Flood.

The first time Fallen Ones came to earth their intent was to corrupt the human race. Now their agenda is something much worse.

THE THREAT

Dr. David Jacobs published *The Threat: Revealing the Secret Alien Agenda* in 1998. It couldn't have landed on bookshelves much before this author devoured it. Somebody somewhere had to have the answers of why maybe as many as a million human beings have been abducted – something that continues to this very day. Jacobs came to his conclusions reluctantly with about as much enthusiasm as someone wanting to be burned alive. He had a reputation to maintain, but moreover, he hated his findings.

Jacobs earned his Ph.D. from the University of Wisconsin – Madison in 1973, in the field of intellectual history and is a respected faculty member at Temple University's History Department. He's lectured widely, been interviewed endlessly, and participated in numerous television and radio shows discussing alien abductions. Over the course of his 50+ year Ufology career, Dr. Jacobs has conducted over 1,150 hypnotic regressions with abductees. One has to appreciate his precarious position balancing his professorship, which is normally in the realm of stodgy folks, and going out there on that alien limb. Because he enjoys such impeccable credentials, I couldn't wait to see what he knew.

After finishing *The Threat* about 20 years ago, it felt unsatisfying, disturbing, lacking answers, but hinted around the edges about some ill-defined horror. After that he published *UFOs and Abductions: Challenging the Borders of Knowledge* in 2000. For someone eagerly waiting answers Dr. Jacobs was painfully slow between books.

During the course of his UFO career, he taught a course for over 25 years on "UFOs in American Society" at Temple U. As with most professors and those that use hypnotherapy, he is meticulous and methodical, careful to not lead his subjects down any particular path. During these sessions with abductees, Question A led to Question B, Question B led to Question C and so on. If something were unclear Jacobs would backtrack probing for

specific answers, calling for detailed explanations. If someone were fabricating under such scrutiny, it would surely come to light. Jacobs knows hypnosis can lead to faulty memories, but he also realizes it's an invaluable tool in uncovering the truth and helping people deal with what's happening to them. Even if a few folks could be deemed to express faulty memories, over the years, Dr. Jacobs uncovered disturbingly similar details and experiences from the victims.

Photo: Some folks believe this petroglyph depicts ancient astronauts. It's scratched into the surface of red rocks at Capitol Reef National Park, Utah and may date back as early as 1,275 AD. More than 20,000 such images have been found in neighboring New Mexico's West Mesa.

When

Photo: This geoglyph, named The Astronaut, is one of Nazca's most controversial images, as it fits nothing natives could have referenced back then. Measuring 105 feet in length, it has an unusually round head, like someone in a helmet, in addition to wearing boots while pointing skyward. (Courtesy Diego Delso, Wikimedia Commons, License CC-BY-SA 4.0)

Some researchers believe extraterrestrials began visiting Earth many millennia ago based on cave paintings, folklore, myth, petroglyphs, and art, but the breeding program is a much newer development.

Other artwork dating much earlier simply defies explanation. One of the best cases for ancient travel and flight is the Nazca Lines that stretch for 50 miles between Nazca and Palpa in Peru. Hundreds of individual geoglyphs from the complex to the simple cover the plains. Peruvian archaeologist Toribio Mejia Xesspe first studied these stylized hummingbirds, spiders, monkeys, fish, sharks, orcas, dogs, birds and lizards in 1926. Scholars believe they were created as early as 500 BC and we're no closer to understanding their purpose.

According to *National Geographic,* the Nazca complex contains over 800 straight lines, 300 geometric figures and 70 animal and plant designs. Due to their immense size, at least one measuring 935 feet –

that's over three football fields – they would be nearly impossible to create without an overhead perspective, let alone be appreciated. From ground level, they just look like a bunch of light-colored lines stretching off into the distance.

All of the geoglyphs were made by removing the land's reddish pebbles down to a depth of 4 to 12 inches, leaving whitish/grayish ground beneath. The lines remain mostly intact since this isolated area is so arid, nearly windless and stays a fairly constant 75°F.

Photo: The Condor, which is 440 feet from beak to tail, is less than half the size of the largest geoglyphs at Nazca. Since it has askew wings, mismatched feet and other asymmetrical features it likely wasn't produced by laying out grids. (Courtesy Diego Delso, Wikimedia Commons, License CC-BY-SA 4.0)

Though Dr. Jacobs believes extraterrestrials have been coming to earth for hundreds of years, his research indicates abductions didn't begin till the late 19th century, at the earliest, or we'd all be victims by now. Other investigators estimate it's only been going on for about a hundred years. In theory, Jacobs points out if the abduction phenomenon started in America with one million people, it would require about seven generations for everyone to be taken. One point of agreement is that abductions are intergenerational, meaning that if you were abducted, it's likely that one or both of your parents and grandparents were taken, back for generations, as will be your children, their children and their grandchildren. Fellow ufologist, Budd Hopkins, artist and writer first discovered this in 1981. Abductions normally begin in infancy and continue through old age.

Exact numbers are unclear just how many people have been taken. About 2% of people have abduction-like experiences, but that doesn't guarantee they were taken. These frightening extractions are a worldwide phenomena and Dr. Jacobs guesses the percentages of abductees may be fairly similar throughout various countries.

Research shows anyone is fair game regardless of gender, race and sexual orientation. For some reason a disproportionate number of Native Americans, Irish and Celtic are taken.

How

People are taken through walls, windows, and ceilings, often while in bed next to their blissfully sleeping spouse. Abductees commonly report being chased on the road by a UFO when their cars' electrical systems mysteriously malfunction. As their cars glide to a halt, they are overcome first by curiosity and then fear, especially those who remember what's been done to them during other abductions. Those whose memories have broken through describe being lifted into a craft and then either returned to their home or car with several hours or several days missing. Fight as they will, people are taken against their will, usually without other people observing it. Sometimes though, there are witnesses when alien have made errors. Folks have reported seeing very bright lights and think their neighbor's house is on fire. One big question is *how is it that the government isn't aware of what's happening?* The truth is, some do.

Backgrounder – Stan's Story

In 1971, this author's husband was recruited by Dr. James R. Maxfield to go to Australia and work on anti-gravity. This is the same Maxfield that was good friends with Dr. Edward Teller, father of the hydrogen bomb. Their relationship was a natural fit as Maxfield, along with brother, Jack, owned the Maxfield Radiological Clinic in Dallas. Somehow Maxfield knew Stan was working on anti-gravity and advanced propulsion in his home office, which was odd because he never discussed it with anyone. A go-between, Ted Iwanski, who worked in the same Dallas business with Stan, repeatedly, pressed Stan to meet with Dr. Maxfield without explaining why. Eventually, to get rid of him, Stan agreed and was met by a tall garrulous man dressed in cowboy boots and a green lab coat, sucking on a cigar. He sported a crew cut and was an imposing, impressive big man.

Photo: Stan Deyo on our hobby farm northwest of Melbourne, Australia, summer 1999.

In Maxfield's office was a photo of him and Dr. Teller drinking champagne as their submarine traveled under, yes *under,* the edge of the South Pole. Maxfield proceeded to tell him about other research projects conducted under the watchful eye of Edward Teller. It was a lot to process. Maxfield urged Stan to consider his offer to get out of the IT field and focus his talents on advanced propulsion. He revealed they had sponsored other young bright minds to go "Downunder" and work on anti-gravity, to please consider it. In fact Maxfield said, over 50 anti-gravity research projects had been underway since 1948. That was 45 years ago. Now it's a done deal.

In the end, Stan moved to Melbourne. Once there he was introduced to Sir John Williams and some other "cotton tops" as Australians call them. These were men with a few years under their belts and tons of cash at their disposal. They were Australia's elite and the behind-the-scenes controllers. When invited to lunch at the private and very prestigious Melbourne Club with Sir John and Sir Henry Somerset, Stan was more than a little impressed. However, during the meal, at one point the conversation turned somber between Sir John and Sir Henry.

Sir John pointed his hand in the air off to his right and said, "Henry, we're losing control... They're moving in." A nod from Sir Henry was followed by an obvious pause in the conversation.

Puzzled by the vague reference, Stan sought clarification with a simple question, "By 'they' did you mean the European Economic Community?"

The two 'cotton tops' looked at him with blank expressions and then answered, "No" to Stan's inappropriate question. Sir John then asked Sir Henry in his aristocratic voice if he were going fishing on his property on the weekend. It was obvious to Stan that he was supposed to have been briefed on the 'they' issue, but it hadn't happened. The rest of conversation was held over fine port and cigars in the 'gentlemen's lounge' adjoining the restaurant.

Cutting to the chase, Stan later discovered that there was a covert, joint program between aliens and the military financed by a multi-national industrial complex. For how long it had been underway, Stan didn't know. He did find out that the agreement had been made in exchange for technology way beyond what humans presently had for allowing ETs to abduct people. Heaven alone knew then for what purpose. Now it is chillingly clear. Evidently this agreement worked OK – for a while – and then went sideways when extraterrestrials gained control.

Forty-five years later, it's terrifying to understand how much further along is the alien agenda. That will become clear shortly.

This author realizes how perfectly ridiculous this sounds even to her own ears, but my husband lived it and I've heard the story told dozens of times with no variation. It fits what others have shared since first hearing this 20 years ago. So what *is* the alien agenda?

What Are They Doing?

- Using our resources.
- Controlling, torturing and experimenting.
- Sexual harvesting.
- Creating hybrids.
- Walking among us.

That's the CliffsNotes version though there are considerable sub-texts.

Resources is pretty self-explanatory, but without a definitive answer. One possibility put forth by Zecharia Sitchin and others is that ETs are using our minerals, mining them. For a couple of decades people all over the world have reported hearing strange hums, drilling noises and feeling odd widespread vibrations underfoot. Most people have attributed those phenomena to the world's wealthy constructing underground cities for when the SHTF – "**S**tuff" **H**its **T**he **F**an – or else they put it in the "I don't know, it's just weird" bucket. In this scenario the elites don't plan to be topside when the rest of the world deals with the ensuing chaos from an economic collapse or a major natural or technological disaster. However, if back before the Great Flood, Fallen Angels taught humans metallurgy, surely in the intervening years, they'd have figured out how to make their own rare minerals.

Other abductees say extraterrestrials need our water. From information gleaned by those taken and returned, aliens view Earth as unique in the universe for its vast water supplies and abundant biodiversity, not to mention humans. It's not that they are concerned for man's welfare when we engage in war or have monumental screw-ups like Fukushima and continually ruin the environment.

ETs are worried about mankind for *their* sake, not ours. They are concerned we're going to render this planet uninhabitable, which is why they implant horror-visions in abductees' minds of natural disasters and dying species. They want us to care for Earth, but not for the reasons one might imagine.

It's on record that ETs shut down nuclear missiles both in the U.S. and UK. Captain Robert Salas witnessed such an event on March 16, 1967 at Malmstrom Air Force Base in Montana. He was on duty at the time and said, "The missiles shut down – 10 Minuteman missiles. And the same thing happened at another site a week later. There's a strong interest in our missiles by these objects, wherever they come from. I personally think they're not from planet Earth."[1578] Colonel Charles Halt witnessed the same thing in December 1980 at the former military base RAF Bentwaters, England. Halt was Deputy Base Commander at the time when three patrolmen investigated strange lights in the nearby forest. They reported approaching a triangular craft, "approximately three meters on a side, dark metallic in appearance with strange markings. They were observing it for a period of time, and then it very quickly and silently vanished at high speed."[1579] Two nights later it was back. "Halt found indentations in the ground, broken branches, and low-level background radiation. He and his team also witnessed various lights moving silently in the sky, one of which was 'shedding something like molten metal.' Another shined a beam of light down towards them."[1580]

Former Captain Bruce Fenstermacher was a Minuteman III launch officer in 1976 stationed at Warren AFB near Cheyenne, Wyoming. He heard a call over the radio about a 60-foot UFO shaped like a "fat cigar" hovering above a launch site. He said, "As a serviceman who followed orders for 20 years, I have reservations about mentioning this incident. One of my concerns was that you all think I'm a kook. And I'm old enough now that I don't care anymore."[1581]

Declassified KGB documents revealed similar incidents happened at Soviet sites and also in Ukraine in 1982. A disc-shaped UFO hovered above the base when launch countdowns were activated for 15 seconds. These nuclear missile shutdowns didn't begin happening until 1948 or they may have intervened at Hiroshima and Nagasaki.

For six decades reports have existed of UFOs hovering over nuclear plants. They've been spotted "harvesting" fuel in the U.S., Mexico, Brazil, Japan, Israel, France, Belgium and in other countries. Dr. Donald A. Johnson, psychologist and owner of Sun River Research, an employee and managerial assessment company has had a long-term interest in the UFO phenomenon. Johnson also maintains a database of over 150,000 UFO reports for the J. Allen Hynek Center for UFO Studies. He summarizes:

- For populations of 50,000-101,000, UFO *sightings* are about 37 per 100,000 people in counties with nuclear facilities – 2.6 times higher than in counties without them.
- For *close encounters*, the rate is about 2.6 per 100,000 in counties with nuke plants compared to 1.8 in non-nuke counties.
- 92 nuclear site counties are considered UFO "hotspots" with 4 or more UFO close encounters, while only 70 of non-nuclear counties are viewed as UFO hotspots.[1582]

So it appears there is a connection with needing nuclear energy.

Control, torture and experimentation. One excruciating and terrifying aspect of alien encounters is their complete and total disregard for human discomfort. Often during abductions victims are made to strip naked and lie on a table while being subjected to the most horrendous physical, mental and psychological intrusions imaginable. Long needles have been inserted into sinus cavities, up the nose, through the navel, ear and eye, and into sexual organs. People have been poked, prodded and examined in every part of their bodies like scientists examining a new species. They've taken samples of saliva; eye, brain and spinal fluids, as well as urine, stool, hair and nails. Sometimes they remove tissue scrapings from subject's ears, eyes, nose, calves, thighs and hips. This is all done without anesthesia, just through the staring of their big bug eyes, exerting a type of mind control. Victims can still see, feel and think; they just can't move or escape.

Direct eye contact is used to scan abductees' recent memories, control bodily functions, erase memories and implant new ones, create emotions and insert post-hypnotic suggestions. That's one thing extraterrestrials make sure to do – is either wipe their memory of being taken or implant a visual that is unrelated.

Image: Typical Gray, generally considered just a robot grunt in the alien hierarchy.

During "procedures" victim's terrified and pain-filled screams are ignored as though aliens are deaf or just don't care. Abductees are later returned home or to their vehicles that magically work again. Sometimes people are dropped off at the wrong location and left wondering how they heck they got there. Other returnees are stymied why their clothing is turned inside out or a shoe is missing. Depending on what's been done to them, they may still be in pain with inexplicable bruises on their skin or discover strange cuts or scoop marks in their flesh.

Dr. Roger Leir noted Ventura, California podiatrist had always believed UFOs existed, but he seriously doubted that abductions were real. Instead he chalked them up to flights of fancy and set out to prove it when everything changed in 1995. Leir had heard of a woman complaining that she'd had an implant so he offered to remove it free of charge. Before his passing in 2014, Leir performed a dozen of these surgeries, some filmed, each time finding a small object. About 75% are small metal pieces shaped like thin rods or a "T". The other 25% resemble non-metallic BBs. Both are covered in dense shiny membranes. Often implants have been attached to nerves so that moving them even under anesthesia is exceptionally painful. Most people, once these things are located, want them removed at all costs. Others choose to leave them in place like Whitley Strieber, author and talk show host, who has one behind his right ear. What the purpose is, no one is sure, perhaps it's a monitoring device. It's probably not a tracker because ETs have no difficulty locating victims time and again because whether or not an abductee has an implant, repeated endless abductions occur.

Sexual harvesting is one of extraterrestrials' grimmer activities. This is their means to create hybrid "babies". For decades women shared bizarre stories of being told by their gynecologist that they were pregnant, often when they knew they shouldn't be. Joy ensued only to be replaced by shock, disappointment and disbelief when the baby disappeared. These weren't false pregnancies. Women displayed all the normal physical signs of expecting, but around 9-11 weeks, suddenly there was no fetus. People would have thought they were losing their minds except for doctors' tests showing there indeed was a baby. But where'd the baby go? What happened?

Once the embryo is taken, it usually goes into a tube of fluid until it's viable, like being born from a giant test tube or incubatorium. Abductees report seeing row upon row of the alien incubators. This could, in part, explain the countless cattle carcasses mysteriously drained of all fluids. They may be used to create quantities of amniotic fluid in which alien-human embryos grow.

Women under hypnosis appeared somewhat more forthcoming about horrendous "exams" performed aboard alien craft. Usually they were checked for viable eggs by means of a tube inserted through her navel. Once confirmed eggs were extracted for purposes no one understood then. Impregnated women were extremely traumatized after these mortifying ordeals. Men had similar procedures performed to extract sperm, which was done either through mechanical means, sexual interaction, or powerful thought projections from aliens in attendance. Though these procedures are out of their control, both men and women experience a sense of shame.

> The aforementioned is a huge clue these creatures, these evil beings are not our friends. They are not our "space brothers". They do not have our best interests at heart. They are not benevolent. The evidence becomes more compelling as you will see and after digesting it, there can be no doubt, *none*, a demonic force is at work. This time, they mean to finish the job.

Creating hybrids. This is every bit as repugnant as it sounds. Once they combine egg and sperm, along with alien DNA, the embryo is inserted into the womb during another abduction. Evidence indicates that human eggs were needed in the earlier stages, but not now with the last stage hybrids, the hubrids.

Dr. David Jacobs, through all of the abductee hypnosis sessions, interviews and decades of study, reveals that the hybridization process has five levels. As each generation is brought forward they look less freakishly skinny, with the over-sized heads and large almond-shaped eyes, pointed chins and tuffs of thin wispy hair. They started out as very alien-looking humanoids and have now progressed to nearly perfect humans. Except they aren't, human that is.

Each stage of hybrid performs specific duties. The genetically closer they are to hubrids, the greater their independence and the more responsibilities they undertake. Early and middle stage hybrids care for hybrid babies and toddlers, perform procedures on humans and escort them to where they need to be on alien craft. Earliest stage hybrids have the added task of cleaning up abductees' vomit and urine. This should underscore the amount of fear experienced by those taken.

Late stage hybrids also perform procedures on people and spend considerable time on earth, but don't live here. They can easily pass as human except for telltale too-large irises and are often devoid of pubic and body hair. However, head hair looks perfectly natural. They are also capable of having sexual relations with abductees and inflicting cruelty – something their earlier-stage predecessors couldn't do. They bring abductees aboard UFOs and develop relationships with them. One of their more important duties is to make sure abductees comply with the program, maintain secrecy about The Change and enforce the rules. They help hubrids integrate and get their life organized on Earth like acquiring housing.

The last stage, fully passing-as-human hubrids, live on Earth and blend in seamlessly. Whereas Grays never speak aloud, only telepathetically, hubrids can do either. They appear fully human, living independently or in groups of two or three while still maintaining contact with their UFOs. Hubrids have one distinct ability that separate them from humanity. They can override human actions and thoughts, often with humans unaware of their input, controlling everything from fear to sexual arousal to crowd restraint.

Walking among us. This is the really creepy part. It boggles the mind thinking that maybe a co-worker, neighbor or store clerk might be one of *them*. Though some people maintain aliens already occupy high places in public office, this is doubtful as it's Jacobs' understanding, and others, that hubrids – those nearly perfectly-passing as human – still have trouble with concepts like countries, things that denote individualism. They're kind of like Communists. What's yours is mine. Hubrids still have trouble grasping the concept of morality and ethics. For example forcing their will on humans is a natural way of dealing with us. In their society there are no consequences for immorality as it's an alien concept – no pun intended. For example, hubrids think nothing of using a memory screen on clerks to block out that it had just stolen clothing from a store.

Another thing hubrids lack is empathy. They can fake it, but it's not a part of their make-up. In social settings and in human relationships, on a scale of 1 to 10 with 1 being the least capable, they are somewhere around a 7 as far as fitting in goes. People in government must be well versed in politics, history, diplomacy, and how the world ticks. Hybrids are able to hold jobs and chit chat at a cocktail party, but they're by no means skilled enough to hold public office where every syllable is scrutinized. That isn't to say those in office haven't been abducted or are alien-sympathizers.

Why?

While they can and do mate with human women, desiring us and not their own kind, (sound familiar?) the hubrids' main goal isn't to corrupt the genetic line, as did Fallen Angels before The Flood though that's a bonus. It's far worse than that. They want to *replace* us. That is not an End Game of "space brother" beings that have our interests at heart. Abductees share that a remnant of humanity will be kept for breeding purposes. IF things go really wrong on Earth (they must not have read the Book of Revelation), aliens will have to do some serious repopulating. For that humans will be needed. Other than this people may be kept around to do grunt work. This amounts to human enslavement. Beyond these two possibilities, we are expendable once Earth's inhabitants are mostly hubrids and their agenda is complete. They look down on humans as inferior but necessary to their plans.

Abductees' participation in the alien-agenda is accomplished, in part, through their long-time association with hybrids and hubrids. Some abductees suffer something akin to Stockholm syndrome and brainwashing techniques, and others are just straight-out threatened into compliance.

While onboard craft most abductees are taught over numerous sessions to perform the same mind scanning, telepathic skills that ETs possess. In their early training, touching a human's head or staring into their eyes was necessary to make them feel, see, believe or do something. The more developed their skills become they can perform these tasks at a distance, which is a frightening thought.

Abductees have another purpose, besides being sperm and egg donors and bonding/teaching their alien offspring, which is to help hubrids and hybrids that are already on Earth. Hubrids and hybrids will require human assistance in the coming takeover, especially in the area of crowd control. Though abductees work with hubrids, sometimes willingly, most often not, many feel they are betraying humanity especially in light of the coming takeover.

One big "flaw" humans have that makes it necessary for alien factions to remove us for the most part is Free Will. It was a gift from God and it made His creations unique. Because of that uniqueness and our ingrained sense of independence, alien control over humans is vital.

It has to be exceedingly frustrating and irritating to aliens, IF they had emotions, and incomprehensible to them that we are so "messy". We are often ruled by our emotions and not often by Vulcan-like dispassionate logic. Alien hierarchy is rigid, orderly, structured. It is goal and task-oriented. Fun isn't in their vocabulary. They wouldn't have a clue what to do with "free time" if such a thing existed in their world.

Isn't it curious just as aliens see our desire to be self-determining and independent as a flaw, governments have an issue with it, too, and clamp down to maintain order? Nearly every bit of human life is now tagged, bagged and recorded. It *is* all about control and it certainly wouldn't do for the public to get wind of what's happening. Talk about mass panic. People might shoot anybody and everybody that exhibits perceived differences fearing they are hubrids or hybrids.

You would think with hubrids "befriending" abductees, inasmuch as they are capable, that sharing information would be a two-way street. It's not the case. Hubrids are to be permitted to answer little. Relationships, even ones spanning decades, are mostly one-sided. Hubrids do most of the questioning in an effort to gather information on integrating. When questions go in the opposition direction, hubrids either clam up and say they aren't allowed to discuss it or are frustratingly evasive.

Regardless they are here, likely in the tens of millions by now. It's not understood what ratio of hubrids, hybrids and abductees to real humans must be achieved to completely achieve takeover, but it can't be far off.

Think about the warning in Matthew 24, *"Many false prophets will appear and mislead many. So when you see the abomination of desolation (Satan) [the appalling sacrilege that astonishes and makes desolate], spoken of by the prophet Daniel, standing in the Holy Place (let the reader understand), then let those who are in Judea flee to the mountains [for refuge]. Whoever is on the housetop must not go down to get the things that are in his house [because there will not be enough time]. Whoever is in the field must not turn back to get his coat. Pray that your flight [from persecution and suffering] will not be in winter, or on a Sabbath [when Jewish laws prohibit travel].* **For at that time there will be a great tribulation (pressure, distress, oppression), such as has not occurred since the beginning of the world until now, nor ever will [again]. And if those days [of tribulation] had not been cut short, no human life would be saved; but for the sake of the elect (God's chosen ones) those days will be shortened.** *Listen carefully, I have told you in advance."* —Matthew 24:11, 15-18, 20-22, 25 (AMP)

The critical message here is that a deception is coming so clever, so subtle, so secret that people aren't going to have much of a chance. It will be *fait accompli* before people realize what's happened. By then it will be too late. Most churches aren't preaching this message. New Agers have swallowed the alien pill thinking they're going to be saved by their space brothers, taken to a safe place and they're following the false drumbeat of Ascended Masters. This author's heart breaks for them as many are the kindest, most loving and selfless people on the planet, but they've lost the plot. They've been taken in.

There *is* a change coming, but it's not of the 1938 "War of the Worlds" obvious invasion. In Tom Cruise's 2005 movie version, though aliens were huge and menacing compared to people, humanity had a chance of winning. What's happening now and has been taking place over millennia is not an open militaristic invasion, but it's an invasion, a takeover nonetheless – one much more ominous in its subtlety. In the "War of the Worlds" it was easy to see who the enemy was. Most people in this real event will be blindsided because they literally can't see the enemy coming because it's already here.

Jude 6 tells that Fallen Angels are already chained and will stay that way until Judgment Day. However, that's only that first 200 that produced the Nephilim. Hebrews 12:22 indicates God has "an innumerable company" of angels. While two-third stayed loyal to God, the remaining third rebelled. Back then there was no concept like million or billion so it's impossible to wrap an exact number around just how large an innumerable company means. Suffice it to say, it's a lot more than 200. Satan knows this is his last shot to claim the prize he feels he deserves, so he's reserved his worst angels and the most for the task at hand. That's why God assures that if He didn't cut these days short, no one would survive.

The obvious question is, *Is there hope? An answer? Is there help for humanity?* Of course! God never leaves His kids without direction, but these times are going to be like nothing ever experienced. We have no point of reference so it will be vital, imperative, to depend on God.

Chapter 20: Message of Hope and Beyond

CliffsNotes

Earth changes in every arena have ramped up. Oklahoma is bouncing around like a ping pong ball. The Sooner State used to get about 20 shakes a year up until 2000. 2015 alone saw over 900. California and the Pacific Northwest are both long overdue for major earthquakes. FEMA has laid in 144 million MREs for the New Madrid region. Big temblors around the world – those larger than magnitude 7 – numbered 10 per year since 1979. In 1992 it rose to 12.5 a year, then in 2010 it jumped to 16.7, which is 67% more compared to 1979-1991. Then in first quarter of 2014, when this study was released, major quakes had more than doubled the average since 1979.

Twenty active and potentially active supervolcanoes occupy every continent except Africa and Antarctica, and Africa sits extremely close to three. Like horseshoes and hand grenades, closeness counts with volcanoes. Every year or two scientists discover something unsettling about Yellowstone, that its magma pools are deeper and wider or that past mega-eruptions were bigger and more intense than previously thought. Earthquakes around this supervolcano have been increasing in number since 1973. NOAA's data verifies that eruptions worldwide have increased significantly since 1855.

Tornadoes are becoming more violent, striking places that never used to see them and more often, they are occurring year-round. Australia, major parts of Western Europe, most of the U.S., half of Canada and bits of South America and Asia are all on target for greater twister activity. In America tornadoes have taken on mammoth proportions, some 2½ miles wide. They're arriving in "families", staying on the ground way too long and frequently maxing out the Fujita Scale.

Wildfires, too, have gotten hotter, harsher and char more land, homes and forests than ever before. Calm wasn't helped when terrorists promised to ignite America's western forests. 2015 went down in record books as the worst-ever fire season burning over 10 million acres in the U.S. alone. This wasn't a one-off event. In the last 45 years, the five most devastating years for U.S. wildfires occurred in the last decade. Just seven years ago, Australia experienced its worst bushfire in the country's history. It's not even summer and Canada is engulfed in one of, if not the worst wildfire in its history. Time will tell since as of May 5, 2016 the fire is still raging. It's already destroyed over 1,600 homes and buildings, and drove out nearly the entire population of 88,000 people in Fort McMurray.[1583] Globally wildfires are increasing in scope and intensity as well as "wildfire season" is lengthening.

Looking at catastrophic disasters in the U.S. the number of billion dollar weather events has definitely increased since NOAA starting collecting data in 1980. The five worst have occurred since 2007. People used to be shocked at 100-year rainfall events, but those are becoming quite common. 500-year downpours are more frequent than the half millennia mark dictates. But 1000-year rains? They were practically unheard of yet **seven** occurred between 2010 and 2016.

Other countries like Australia, Pakistan, Europe, Thailand, India and Brazil are getting similarly hammered. Meteorologists said even for a world getting used to wild weather, May 2015 seemed "stuck on strange". Since 2010, newscasts have doubled the time spent on weather and natural disasters and it's quadrupled since the 1990s. MunichRe's latest study showed the number of weather-related losses in North America has *nearly quintupled* in the past 30 years. Other countries are experiencing the same thing: Asia's weather disasters up 400%, Africa up 250%, Europe up 200% and South America up 150%. The upward march is unmistakable. In 1980 and for nearly a decade, big deadly events hovered around 350, give or take. In 1988, things changed noticeably and then by 2000, quite sharply. By 2015, they had increased 200% without backtracking.

Looking up, signs in the skies are evident. Two really rare events took place in 2014 and 2015. First, the Biblical Tetrads of four blood moons appeared within a year and a half of each other. Only a handful of Biblical Tetrads have occurred since 2,000 BC and the next one won't come for nearly 600 years. Then in June 2015, the unique alignment that comprised the Star of Bethlehem reappeared for the first time since Jesus' birth and blazed in the morning sky for nearly two months.

Also in the heavenly realm of prophecy is the Sun. Though it's been a bit quiet in the present year for solar flares, the Sun's exhibited some very unusual traits. In 2013, 2015 and 2016 it displayed some of the largest-ever coronal holes. They look like yawning black caverns, but they're really large regions that are cooler than the surrounding areas. Then in 2014 during one of its weakest cycles in two centuries, it belched out the most powerful solar storm in 150 years. The last Solar Cycle, #23, was absolutely bizarre when the Sun threw off the largest-ever solar flare – an unbelievable X45. In 2003, scientists were at a loss to explain our star's behavior and said it had gone "haywire".

With Earth changes and war come the deadly twins of famine and disease. Prophecy said there would be an increase in both. Humans are partly to blame for the rise in disease in the overuse and misuse of prescribed antibiotics. It's led to Superbugs – diseases that have extreme resistance to standard treatment. Some are now incurable. As strains mutate, doctors are further stymied how to treat infections. Another facet is the continued risk of biowarfare agents. Laboratories don't have enough security and some facilities that contain the deadliest strains are in highly populated residential areas. While many governments have signed treaties banning these agents, they reason quietly behind closed doors that in order for them to protect us against other countries or rogue agents using them, they must be *and are* stockpiled. In 2015 Syria and ISIS both deployed them against civilians and militaries.

Crops around the world have been impacted by bad weather from drought to floods to hail, to freezes and extreme heat. Famine is nothing new and with 7½ billion individuals on the planet, people especially in underdeveloped countries clamor for food and decent water. Then there's China that's buying up huge tracts of land in other countries to feed their 1½ billion people. Primarily they have their sights set on Australia's land, but with China's deplorable track record for contaminating water resources, no amount of $$ is worth the trade. China's farming practices have polluted 60% of their own aquifers. Then there was the whole 16,000-rotting-pig debacle. Chinese farmers dumped those swine carcasses in rivers – where they get their drinking water. So even *if* it were possible sometime in the future to buy back that land, it would probably be unusable.

The issue of countries selling off prime agricultural land has to be one of the dumbest ideas to hit the planet. More real estate isn't magically going to materialize and when that huge resource goes, there's no getting it back. As of December 2013, the U.S. had sold off over 26 *million* acres of prime agricultural land. Today, it's probably a lot more. Every year, like clockwork the USDA published reports detailing foreign ownership of our precious food-producing land. For an entire decade they did this, every year. Then in 2013, it stopped. For six months this author phoned and wrote asking when a new report was coming. The release date has changed three times getting later and later. The last promised date was spring 2016. It's spring. No report. Beside agricultural land in the U.S. and Australia, Canada is selling off vast water supplies – mostly to, you guessed it, China. After 2008's deep recession even more of America disappeared into foreign hands. From bridges to freeways, from banks and shopping malls to her largest meat company to iconic landmarks like the Chrysler Building, NYC's Plaza Hotel and the John Hancock Life building – gone. Even some water resources are foreign owned. Budweiser, French's Mustard, Gerber, Ben & Jerrys and Purina may have been started by Americans, but are no longer owned by them. Frigidaire and Firestone are gone, too. All of this foreign ownership doesn't bode well for the coming economic collapse. When countries forfeit their food and water supplies, it shows extreme shortsightedness. We can do without a hotel or mall, but food and water resources are another matter.

Australia is in a similar fix with the S. Kidman cattle ranch up for sale. It's literally the world's largest property covering some 25 million acres. That's bigger than all of Ireland by over four million acres and China is top bidder. Likewise China is buying huge swaths of Africa. When food gets very scarce like it did during the Dust Bowl Days, people will wish they'd hung onto their land. Not that you're going to eat metal, but China is also snatching up Australia's gold mines.

Hand-in-hand with food is vital water. Fully ⅓ of the world's aquifers are in trouble. Not a single continent has been spared. With increasing heatwaves and droughts, these precious water reservoirs are being dangerously depleted. Now factor in Fukushima. It's still belching vast amounts of radiation into the ocean and water currents swirl its poison around the globe. Fish and wildlife are ingesting huge amounts of radiation and what do people eat? Fish and wildlife.

Nuclear engineer Arnie Gunderson returned in April 2016 from an extensive survey of Japan's radiation problem. Water is still being contaminated at an alarming rate and they're dumping it into the ocean. There is no place to put it Gunderson shared. "Well, they pumped – they needed to empty tanks on site because the tanks had concentrations of liquid that were 500 times what was permissible. But the stuff they needed to put in them was much more radioactive than that. So the 11,000 tons that they pumped overboard today was to clear tanks so that more radioactive liquid could come behind it. The leak that they just fixed, though, for the last couple of weeks has been leaking something on the order of 7 tons a day – not of the 500-times concentration, but of the much more concentrated radioactivity into the ocean. So there's a lot of radiation in the ocean."[1584]

When the reactors melted and spewed their radiation into the highlands, it's now flowing down from mountain streams. The Japanese government has no intention, due to astronomical costs, of cleaning up their country except minimally – certainly not to the degree where millions of cancers won't surface in the coming years. Japanese fishermen are selling their catches to unsuspecting nations. Plus Gunderson shared that while the U.S. is still importing Japan's fish and seafood, inspectors aren't looking too closely at country of origin. Maybe one of these days we'll all glow in the dark. Out of America's currently operational 100 nuclear power plants 23 are Boiling Water Reactors just like the Fukushima Daiichi plant, many built over or too close to earthquake fault lines.

Before the One World Government can be put into action and before Israel can be successfully attacked, the U.S. has to be taken out of the picture. As strong as she appears on the surface, if you remove the facade and see what's propping her up, you'd be astonished. She is burdened with crippling debt, while government spending is at an all-time high. Too many agencies overlap wasting other millions. Government still funds impossibly pointless projects, which are chronicled yearly in *Congressional Pig Books*. Jobs are sent overseas while America's middle class is asked to fork over more of their paychecks to fund their waste and spending.

The U.S. is being weighted down by runaway illegal immigration that costs taxpayers $113 *billion* a year. That makes the eyes bleed. The numbers are absolutely staggering and with the present administration's open-door, catch-and-release policy, it's only getting worse. Every system is bogged down with people that jump to the front of the line pushing ahead of those that want to come here legally. Hospitals, schools, social services and every entitlement imaginable we give to border jumpers, which is unfair to other would-be immigrants.

Along with illegals undoubtedly are terrorists walking right over the border. Undeniable evidence of their intentions is left strewn along the 2,000-mile open border in addition to tons of their trash. Muslim extremists have set up entire enclaves in various U.S. cities with at least 22 terrorist training camps in place. This is just stupid on a stick. Many of these camps are al-Fuqra Muslims that for some reason have not yet been declared a terrorist organization. Many of their Imams spout anti-American, anti-Christian rhetoric and have proven ties to terrorist groups, yet are allowed to stay here. They laugh at our blind trust, us thinking they will behave like rational people when even moderate Muslims know they won't and don't want them around.

Never before has the U.S. been so divided, not even during the Civil War. We just haven't picked up the guns yet. Then there was one issue dividing the Nation. Today there are many and anger is roiling.

One of the most dangerous chinks in America is the fragile electric grid. It's vulnerable to hacking and EMPs from both the Sun and nuclear attack. While other problems are sinking America at a slower place the power grid going down would be blindingly quick. Almost nothing would work because nearly everything from food and water, to banking, gasoline, utilities, sewage treatment plants, and even city water purification is computer-controlled and electricity dependent. No computers and life as we know it stops.

In the last decade, the world witnessed many nations form new alliances for geo-political and financial reasons. Iran repeatedly states it will wipe Israel off the map. Then there's the Korean father and son nut-jobs, Kim Jong-il and Kim Jong-un who continually threaten to nuke America. Kim senior passed in 2011, but his even crazier son is head of state. Both Iran and North Korea have made great inroads into buying or building nuclear-capable missiles carrying deadly payloads. North Korea is certainly making progress in the scenario set forth in Ryan and Alyssa's story as Korea successfully launched a ballistic missile from a submarine on April 23, 2016.[1585] A sub-based attack on the U.S. was "seen" by Henry Gruver in 1985 though it was Russia perpetrating the assault. Russia has turned from the West and firmly gotten into bed with Syria and other Middle East nations and the European Union. If England chooses to leave the European Union, what effect will that have on the stability of Europe and prophecy? This is a unique event, a clue.

A vital, unique clue that has happened at no other time in history is Israel reestablishing as a nation after Jews were flung across the world for 2,600 years. This officially occurred on May 14, 1948. The date is paramount because prophecy says that the generation alive when this happened will also be the one that witnesses End Times. Also prophesied was Israel recapturing Jerusalem, which they did in 1967. Isaiah 41:18-21 predicted that this last generation would see Israel bloom again. While the Arabs occupied this land, it was a lifeless desert.

Middle East countries held their largest-ever war exercises in spring of 2016. The size of armies in the Middle East – even minute Bahrain's – is staggering. They are preparing for something and that first "something" on their list is Israel. The next major Middle East war will involve Israel's closest neighbors trying to annihilate her. This will be a relatively short war preceding the dreaded Gog-Magog War. It will be a time of unprecedented ugliness.

In hopes of thwarting these events no less than 25 presidents, world leaders and heads of state, popes, dignitaries and business magnates have all spoken openly about the need for a New World Order. For nearly five decades they've planted these seeds and are now clearly pushing this agenda. To meet the goal, America has to be fundamentally transformed, which Mr. Obama promised to do in 2008. The changes that took place during his eight years in office are staggering. Disarming the American public will be a must because no matter how many military personnel are enlisted to carry out their plans and enact martial law, it will be no match for 323 million *really* angry armed Americans.

To make it easier for this New World Government to control people, they are being coerced and enticed to live on smaller and smaller pieces of land, preferably in Eco-villages and other "sustainable" communities. To keep this massive agenda from gaining to much attention, they go under at least 75 different names. Nature and Mother Earth take precedence over humanity.

For about a month now one of these organizations, Vital Ground, which is dedicated to carving out land for grizzly bears, has been heavily advertising on Colorado radio stations. Colorado has no grizzlies nor is there plans to import them. This Montana-based group wants to "enhance and conserve nearly 600,000 acres of crucial wildlife habitat in Montana, Idaho, Wyoming, Alaska, and British Columbia"[1586] for the bear population. This group, which was founded in 1990, wants people to donate – in addition to money – land easements that go into a trust or better yet, give them your land if you live in one of the aforementioned states or provinces. Vital Ground goes hand-in-glove with a zillion other like-minded groups.

The UN is making a global attempt to gather more cities into this ICLEI – International Council for Local Environmental Initiatives – movement. It's a clever plan. Who doesn't love and enjoy nature? Make people give up their land for animals and plants and put them in cramped living quarters. It's a win-win scenario to aid the One World Government. We are already being conditioned through a bad economy to rent or build small homes, live in highly communalized complexes like BedZED and the growing tiny house movement.

The takeover will likely begin with an economic collapse and in order to maintain control, the One World Government will slip into place. Whether the U.S., the European Union or China teeters first, financial institutions will be in a world of hurt as other nations fall like dominos. To keep things calmer, a One World Religion will be instituted. With so much religious unrest in the world, mostly stemming from Muslim extremists and escalating hatred of Christians and Jews – also prophesied – a single religion where people can all worship side-by-side will seem like the perfect solution. It just won't be Jesus who is worshipped.

This may be less difficult than one might think as people are becoming more disillusioned with institutionalized churches. Over the course of 60 years more people have turned from Christianity to embrace paganism, witchcraft – or nothing also prophesied in End Times.

Conflict will be riotous and with the world in chaos people will demand someone do something, *please do something!* That's his cue. At some point in this scenario, the Antichrist will step onto the scene, allowing Israel's temple to be built and bringing a short-lived peace to the world. The Antichrist will look like a "savior" amidst the upheaval. Further controls will be needed and the One World Economy will come to the forefront, along with the Mark of the Beast. It will be impossible to hold a job, shop and sell things, pay bills and utilities, receive medical care, take vacations, bank, go to school without permission.

During the 2010 U.S. Census, virtually every house, apartment and mobile home was pinpointed and mapped with government GPS. Even if you own everything outright, most county governments don't let homeowners pay property taxes in advance. That gives people one-year leeway at the outside. In short, if something requires an exchange of money, it will be off-limits without the Antichrist's literal stamp of approval on people's heads or hands. There's just one catch. In order to receive this mark, every person will have to worship the Antichrist. There is no going back once people make this huge error in judgment. It is a forever deal and one that signs their death warrant.

Then there was the Great Deception that was conceived millennia ago and failed nearly 4,500 years past, which brought more fallen angels to try again. Their plot is grander, cleverer and yet subtler with much more at stake. Their plan, this time, isn't to corrupt the human genetic line, but to *replace* it. In these latter years people are seeing the veil break down between this world and the invisible dimension that's right next to us. Crop circles, cattle mutilations, shadow people and old hags only hint at what exists there. It's also one place where extraterrestrials exist. Numerous highly placed, well-known people from around the world have hinted, some not too discretely, about the alien factor and their presence. Government, wishing to keep a lid on this, has uniformly reacted with derision whenever whistleblowers balked and talked. However, with abductions and genetic experiments numbering in the millions, a truth explosion is coming. People are divided whether these beings bring enlightenment or horror, but their true nature is seen in their actions of physical and mental torture of humans without empathy or conscience as told by countless abductees. These creatures are not our "space brothers" here to help, but fallen angels and their helpers. Their goals will be fully revealed soon in the ultimate battle between good and evil, and it's nearly upon us.

End Times Rescue

Many Christians are so pleased, so happy, feel so *blessed* to be alive in this time. See prophecy come to fruition. This author is not one of them. It's going to be horrific, hard beyond words, which doesn't begin to describe it. What's coming is so far past Earth-speak, because we've never seen it, never had to face such a challenge, nor has any human being since time began. These Christians may be focused on seeing an end to chaos as The Divine reclaims Earth. But, there is great distance between this promised Utopia and what's about to take place. Tribulation will be really, *really* ugly punctuated by moments of victory and joy. It's something many Christians have not truly visualized let alone internalized. People will have to make extremely difficult choices. Those who don't see the truth during Tribulation will try to persuade loved ones to take the Antichrist's deal, accept the Mark of the Beast to survive. However, there is a catch. People will be required to bow down and worship the Antichrist, which assures that person won't see saved loved ones again.

This time of judgment lasts seven years and those still alive during this time will witness more sadness and terrifying things than are imaginable. It will make the worst horror film look like a happy trot around a park. Luke 21:26 warns that during Tribulation men's hearts will just quit because they are so frightened.

When these terrible times are done, Isaiah 25:8 promises that God will "swallow up death forever and ... wipe away tears from all faces." If you've lost family and friends in End Times or any time before, you will be given supernatural understanding to see the big picture. God will remove the memory of what you've gone through.

There is a way out. God gave His kids an escape plan. Pray daily. Pray for forgiveness. Pray for grace and insight.

Dear God,

I admit I am a sinner and ask your forgiveness. I believe that Jesus Christ died in my place paying the penalty for my sins. I am willing right now to turn from my sin and accept Jesus Christ as my personal Savior and Lord. I commit myself to You and ask You to send the Holy spirit into my life, to fill me and take control, and to help me become the kind of person You want me to be. Thank you Father for loving me. In Jesus' Name. Amen (Romans 10:9)

Pray that you are found worthy to be spared participating in what's coming. Luke 21:36 says, *Watch therefore, and pray always that you may be counted worthy to escape all these things that will come to pass, and to stand before the Son of Man.* For those of us who believe in the Rapture that means we look forward to the Blessed Hope promised in Titus 2:13 and keep in our hearts the message of 1 Thessalonians 4:17 (AMP): *Then we who are alive and remain [on the earth] will simultaneously be caught up (raptured) together with them [the resurrected ones] in the clouds to meet the Lord in the air, and so we will always be with the Lord!* In the meantime and until that time, 1 Thessalonians 5:11 reminds us to encourage and comfort one another.

Tips and Thoughts on Preparing

I know these times sound beyond grim and scary, they are, and so very close. People ask if End Times are set in stone. The short answer is yes. This doesn't mean our lives are predestined. We have free will. Every day we make decisions and choices: what clothes to wear, who to vote for, on what to spend money, career path, whether to drink and drive, who to marry, and where to live. However, God has set the big things as immutable events. It's how we react to them that count. Those are our choices. He has set out in scripture what's going to happen and with Him batting 100% in prophecy, that's a record hard to ignore.

With that in mind, there are practical, physical measures to take, things to do and ways to prepare. This includes storing food and water, and having methods to purify it if it's unavailable by normal means, as in turning on the faucet.

Think of physically preparing in this order: water, food, heating and light/alternative power, medical supplies, fuel, and then everything else. This is just a suggested order. Water is paramount. People can live only three days without water, but survive three weeks without food. However, if a person is severely diabetic, insulin may take precedence.

People are of varying minds just how long should be the minimum time frame for storing food, water and other supplies. Unfortunately this author doesn't have a magic answer, but will offer some things for you to consider. Then you can prepare for what's right for you and your family and as money and urgency dictate.

If you believe an economic meltdown or collapse is imminent, hopefully you've already finished. Self-sufficiency or being close to it doesn't happen overnight. It takes time and $$. When Stan and I lived in Australia, it required two full years of doing nothing except getting our 10-acre farmlet to where we could close gates for a year and not need anything. Today, we are in totally different circumstances living back in the U.S. in the county. Our town is somewhere between suburbia and rural, and unincorporated into any city. We don't enjoy the nearly off-grid setting we did 15 years ago, so we make do and become as prepared as possible. There is such a thing as being too remote. For example if a household member becomes incapacitated or ill and there are no neighbors, it could be unnecessarily challenging, if not impossible, to do everything yourself.

Living in a big city is probably the worst-case scenario. Large numbers of people concentrated together tend to breed violence when it's hot. Factor in fear, extended hunger, thirst, panic, grief and confusion when everything they've counted on for life to run smoothly is gone. Imagine cities without functioning sewers, trash collection and normal utilities. People living in hi-rises would have to walk up and down many stairs just to take pets outside. Imagine that many people in close quarters without necessities of life and FEMA unable to provide it. Cities baking in the summer swelter without air conditioning would be awful especially with trash and waste piling up in the streets, not to mention the smell of decomposing bodies. In an EMP scenario clearing all those stalled vehicles would be nearly impossible. People in apartments usually have less space for storable food so living in crowded cities definitely presents extra challenges.

If you live close to nuclear reactors and can't relocate, do all the preps outlined in my book, **Dare To Prepare.** As with a nuclear attack, these aren't death sentences. They *are* survivable, but you need to know in advance what measures to take, assess wind direction and walk perpendicularly to wherever the anvil-shaped cloud is heading. There's obviously more to do, and much of the information is very encouraging, but that discussion is too long for here as several chapters in "Dare" are dedicated to it.

If protein food sources like chickens, beef, wild game and birds, fish, etc. become contaminated, you want "clean" food already in place. Radiation accumulates in organs and bones so avoid having to eat such foods at all costs because it's not excreted like fiber. You don't want to be in a Fukushima-type situation where few alternatives exist except to eat radioactive poison.

FOOD STORAGE

Most freeze-dried food produced today lasts upwards of 25 years so you can't go wrong purchasing it. Length of shelf life depends a lot on where and at what temperature it's kept. The lower the temperature the longer its shelf life. Rule of thumb: for every 10 degrees lower in the food storage room, it doubles viability. For example, food held at a <u>constant</u> 70 degrees F. would last about 10 years. Compare the same things stored at 90 degrees they might only be good for 2½ years. It doesn't mean you can't eat them then, but they won't have the same nutritional value or texture and maybe they'll taste a little funny. Of the six enemies of food – temperature, time, pests, oxygen, humidity and light – heat is hardest on it. Keeping your food supplies at optimal temperature should be a priority, which means not putting them in a hot garage, shed or attic.

For quantities needed, some people have tucked away as much as a decade's worth and that is likely overkill. On the flip side of the coin, extra food can be bartered for things you overlooked, didn't think would be needed, circumstances changed, or there weren't enough funds at the time or given to placate those who would take what you have.

It's smart to have about ⅓ of your stored foods in canned goods. All you need for a meal is a can opener. Freeze-dried meats and veggies, etc., have to be reconstituted, which requires water and heat. Freeze dried fruits at least require water. Even dehydrated soups, pancakes, powders, breads, casseroles, milk and beverages, etc. must have water and many need to be cooked or baked. Even though canned goods don't have a 25-year shelf life, it's a lot longer than you'd think and they are listed in *Dare To Prepare.*

Don't forget your pets. They need food and water too. Most 4-leggeds are considered family members and it's our responsibility to provide for them as well. Especially in times of great upheaval and turmoil, they are great stress relievers and companions. So if you want them around, plan for their needs including any medications. Most pet food has a shelf life of about 18 months. Freeze-dried pet food is available, but it's pretty pricy.

OTHER CONSIDERATIONS

Vitamins are a good investment because stress depletes them more rapidly and it will be vital to stay as healthy as possible.

Speaking of stress, this is no time for cigarette smokers to go cold turkey. Think of all the folks dependent on tobacco, booze or a cornucopia of drugs paired with sudden unavailability. Millions of people will undergo withdrawals simultaneously. A hospice worker shared that druggies are dumpster diving and scouring landfills looking for thrown away prescriptions and these are still relatively normal times. Especially in cities, expect to see a rise in home, pharmacy and hospital break-ins as people frantically search for a way to silence their demons.

With that and other likely scenarios in mind, Stan and I have always recommended having firearms. That is a personal choice, of course, but End Times aren't likely to bring out the best in people. If nothing else, they are a good deterrent to intruders and can be used to hunt.

Replenish and update medical supplies and first aid kits. There is a long list of shelf lives for both prescribed and over-the-counter drugs and medications in *Dare To Prepare* available nowhere else. They vary by product, but are viable a lot longer than the labels say when stored properly. Instead of buying readymade first aid kits, assemble one yourself because supplies in a kit, especially purchased online, can conceal expirations dates. Plus you might be buying a bunch of stuff you don't need or bandages in the wrong sizes.

Cash on hand is a must. As a reminder in the story of Ryan and Alyssa, without electricity, cash is paramount. If possible, purchase some small denomination silver and gold coins. Precious metals are a recognizable form of money the world over. James 5:3 warns that eventually it will become useless, but it has a place when credit cards can't be used and paper money is worthless. Additionally if you want to pay for something valued at $50, it's easier to carry three one-ounce silver coins than a #10 can of diced chicken. These are examples only to illustrate the point since today, mid-April 2016, a one-ounce silver dollar is worth $16.25, which will likely go up when the economic axe falls, and the chicken was priced at $53.

There are many more physical preps you can do to ease the burden of End Times or for any disaster scenario. They are spelled out in great detail in *Dare To Prepare* and are easy to understand. Besides individuals, preparedness groups, businesses and churches, "Dare" is used by police departments, universities, anti-terrorist training units as well as paramilitary units, and sells literally the world over. "Dare" enjoys a 5-star rating on Amazon with countless shining reviews. They are a humbling validation of its practical usefulness and why it's widely recognized as the preparedness "bible".

In addition to "Dare", we have an entire website with free preparedness information at *http://standeyo.com*. There is also a free food planner on my prep site: *http://DareToPrepare.com* as well as in the book.

Being physically prepared is part of the battle. Spiritual attacks will be hard enough but they'll be easier to withstand and you can think more clearly and function better on a full stomach and without overwhelming thirst. It's a lot to consider especially if you haven't done any prep stuff yet. Think baby steps and small bites, but in hurry-up mode. For us, it's second nature as I've done it all my life and Stan's now 20 years into it. Living 24 years in the Midwest, lessons came year round in the form of blizzards, tornadoes, floods, ice storms and power outages. Buy a little extra every time you go to the grocery store. Put in a small garden using non-hybrid seeds. For people in mobile homes and apartments, practice container gardening. There are always answers; some just are just a little tougher to find than others.

More importantly, stay close to our Creator. Be attuned to deception. Pray daily and appreciate all the gifts you've been given. Trust and know that something a lot better is close at hand, but first we have to get through these coming these Prophetic Perils.

Appendix 1 – Sanctuary Jurisdictions

How to Read the Key for Sanctuary Jurisdictions:

Sanctuary Cities used to be just that – cities. Now many counties have taken on this status it applies to all cities within that county. Sanctuary Counties are listed by state in **bold type**. On the map, they are marked by a white numbered dot. Numbering starts over for each state.

Sanctuary Cities are listed by state followed by what county they're in. On the map, they are designated with a black numbered dot. When a city has been specifically identified as a Sanctuary City that lies in a Sanctuary County – it's followed by the phrase *Sanctuary city additionally named in this county.*

When a Sanctuary City is listed, but its county isn't, it's noted with the phrase *Sanctuary city specifically named in XXXX County.*

When Sanctuary Cities and/or sanctuary suburbs are very close together, they are designated with only one numbered dot to prevent the map from becoming unreadable. For example, in #13 in California represents **Los Angeles County**, but it also includes 17 cities and suburbs specifically named for that immediate area.

Eleven states have designated themselves as Sanctuary Jurisdictions: California, Colorado, Connecticut, Maine, New Mexico, North Dakota, Oregon, Rhode Island, Texas, Utah and Vermont as well as the District of Columbia. Sanctuary States and Washington, D.C. are in **bold type**.

One exception is in Colorado where all county jails are sanctuary jurisdictions.

CAVEAT

As more unfavorable light is shined on problems in Sanctuary Jurisdictions, they may choose to stop ignoring detainers from ICE and thumbing their noses at federal law. Most jurisdictions don't have a formal policy in place and have instituted "don't ask, don't tell". Other locations are quite open about it. On November 10, 2009 Pennsylvania mayor Michael Nutter signed Executive Order No. 8-09 "Policy Concerning Access of Immigrants to City Services"[1587] that prohibits police from inquiring about a person's immigration status or disclosing that "confidential information" except in a very few specific instances.

Some states, too, aren't concerned about breaking federal law. In 2011, Utah passed HB116 that provides for a guest worker program and a migrant worker partnership with Mexico. By law, illegal immigrants aren't to be knowingly employed by U.S. businesses. Period. Though HB116 went into effect in mid-2013 Democrat Rep. Brian King from Salt Lake complained, "It (sic) unconstitutional. Clearly we shouldn't be wasting our time with it. We shouldn't be wasting our money with it."[1588]

Many of sanctuary jurisdictions without formal written policy have bowed to pressure from illegal immigration support groups like La Raza (The Race), League of United Latin American Citizens, and Mexican American Legal Defense & Education Fund, and turn a blind eye. When unwanted attention comes to these sanctuary cities they can claim they have no such legislation in place, but their lack of compliance with ICE detainers, hiring illegals and fostering protection for undocumented immigrants reveal the truth.

SANCTUARY CITIES, COUNTIES & STATES

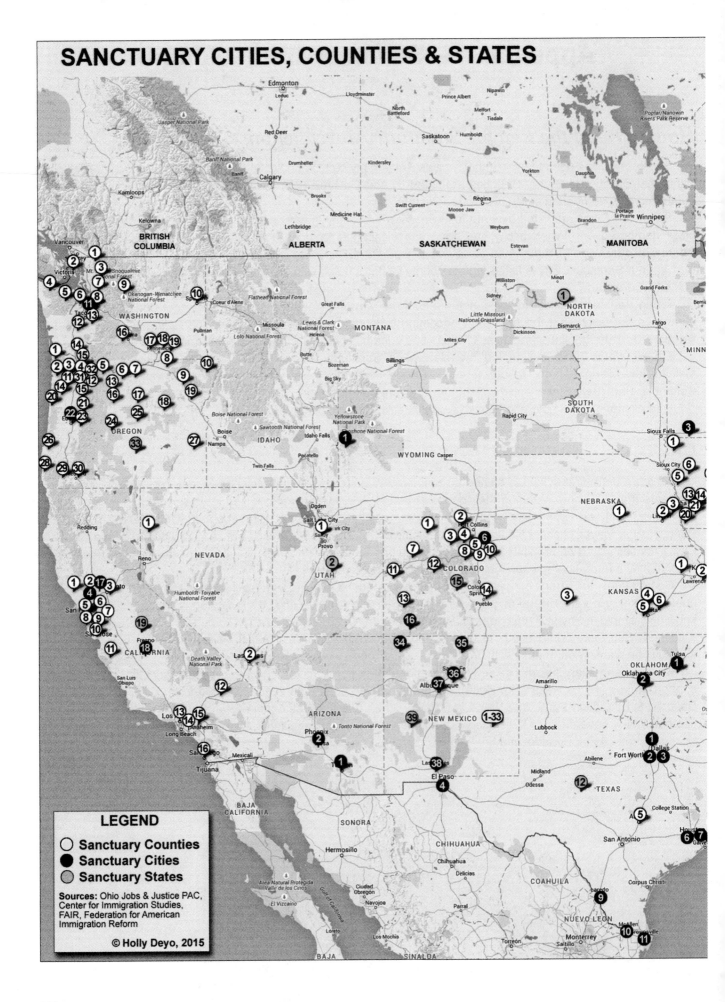

LEGEND

○ **Sanctuary Counties**
● **Sanctuary Cities**
◐ **Sanctuary States**

Sources: Ohio Jobs & Justice PAC,
Center for Immigration Studies,
FAIR, Federation for American
Immigration Reform

© Holly Deyo, 2015

SANCTUARY CITIES, COUNTIES & STATES

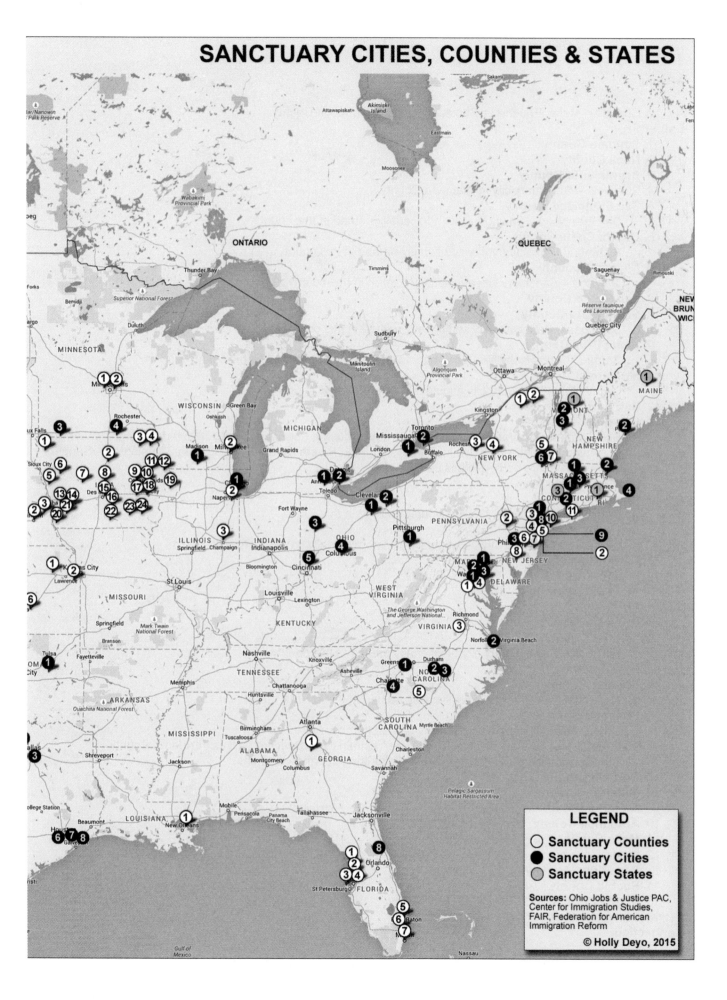

LEGEND

○ Sanctuary Counties
● Sanctuary Cities
● Sanctuary States

Sources: Ohio Jobs & Justice PAC, Center for Immigration Studies, FAIR, Federation for American Immigration Reform

© Holly Deyo, 2015

The Key

Arizona
1. Tucson
2. Chandler, Mesa, Phoenix – Sanctuary cities in Maricopa County

California
1. **Sonoma County**
2. **Napa County**
3. **Sacramento County**
4. Berkeley – Sanctuary city in Alameda County
5. **San Francisco County**
   San Francisco – Sanctuary city additionally named in this county
6. **Contra Costa County**
   Richmond – Sanctuary city additionally named in this county
7. **Alameda County**
   Oakland – Sanctuary city additionally named in this county
8. **San Mateo County**
9. **Santa Clara County**
   San Jose – Sanctuary city additionally named in this county
10. **Santa Cruz County**
    Santa Cruz, Watsonville – Sanctuary cities additionally named in this county
11. **Monterey County**
    Greenfield – Sanctuary city additionally named in this county
12. **San Bernardino County**
13. **Los Angeles County**
    Bell Gardens, Commerce, Cypress, Downey, Industry, Lakewood, Long Beach, Los Angeles, Lynwood, Maywood, Montebello, Norwalk, Paramount, Pico Rivera, South Gate, Vernon, Wilmington – Sanctuary cities additionally named in this county
14. **Orange County**
15. **Riverside County**
    Coachella – Sanctuary city additionally named in this county
16. **San Diego County**
    San Diego, National City – Sanctuary cities additionally named in this county
17. Davis – Sanctuary city in Yolo County
18. Fresno – Sanctuary city in Fresno County
19. **State of California**

Colorado
1. **Routt County**
2. **Larimer County**
   Fort Collins – Sanctuary city additionally named in this county
3. **Grand County**
4. **Boulder County**
   Lafayette – Sanctuary city additionally named in this county
5. **Denver County**
   Denver – Sanctuary city additionally named in this county
6. Commerce City, Federal Heights, Thornton, Westminster – Sanctuary cities in Adams County; Aurora (Sanctuary city that lies in both Adams & Arapahoe counties)
7. **Garfield County**
8. **Jefferson County**
9. **All Colorado County Jails**
10. **Arapahoe County**
11. **Mesa County**
12. **Pitkin County**
13. **San Miguel County**
14. **Pueblo County**
15. **State of Colorado**
16. Durango – Sanctuary city in La Plata County

Connecticut
1. Hartford
2. New Haven

        3. **State of Connecticut**
District of Columbia
Florida
        1. **Hernando County**
        2. **Pasco County**
        3. **Pinellas County**
        4. **Hillsborough County**
        5. **Palm Beach County**
                Jupiter, Lake Worth – Sanctuary cities additionally named in this county
        6. **Broward County**
        7. **Miami-Dade County**
                Miami – Sanctuary city additionally named in this county
        8. De Leon Springs, Deltona – Sanctuary cities in Volusia County
Georgia
        1. **Clayton County**
Illinois
        1. Chicago, Cicero, Evanston – Sanctuary cities in Cook County
        2. **Cook County**
        3. **Champaign County**
Iowa
        1. **Sioux County**
        2. **Franklin County**
        3. **Winneshiek County**
        4. **Allamakee County**
        5. **Monona County**
        6. **Ida County**
        7. **Greene County**
        8. **Story County**
        9. **Benton County**
        10. **Linn County**
        11. **Delaware County**
        12. **Dubuque County**
        13. **Pottawattamie County**
        14. **Cass County**
        15. **Polk County**
        16. **Marion County**
        17. **Iowa County**
        18. **Johnson County**
        19. **Clinton County**
        20. **Fremont County**
        21. **Montgomery County**
        22. **Marion County**
        23. **Wapello County**
        24. **Jefferson County**
Kansas
        1. **Shawnee County**
        2. **Johnson County**
        3. **Finney County**
        4. **Harvey County**
        5. **Sedgwick County**
        6. **Butler County**
Louisiana
        1. **New Orleans**
        2. **Lafayette Parrish**
Massachusetts
        1. Amherst, Northampton – Sanctuary cities in Volusia County
        2. Boston, Chelsea – Sanctuary cities in Suffolk County; Cambridge, Somerville – Sanctuary cities in Middlesex County
        3. Springfield – Sanctuary city in Hampden County
        4. Orleans – Sanctuary city in Barnstable County

Maine

    1. State of Maine

    2. Portland – Sanctuary city in Cumberland County

Maryland

    1. Baltimore – Sanctuary city in Baltimore County

    2. Montgomery County

        Gaithersburg, Takoma Park – Sanctuary cities additionally named in this county

    3. Mt. Rainier – Sanctuary city in Prince George's County

Michigan

    1. Ann Arbor – Sanctuary city in Washtenaw County

    2. Detroit – Sanctuary city in Wayne County

Minnesota

    1. Hennepin County

        Minneapolis – Sanctuary city additionally named in this county

    2. Ramsey County

        St. Paul – Sanctuary city additionally named in this county

    3. Austin – Sanctuary city in Mower County

    4. Worthington – Sanctuary city in Nobles County

Nebraska

    1. Hall County

    2. Lancaster County

    3. Sarpy County

    4. Douglas County

Nevada

    1. Washoe County

    2. Clark County

New Jersey

    1. Fort Lee – Sanctuary city in Bergen County

    2. Newark – Sanctuary city in Essex County

    3. Jersey City, North Bergen, Union City, West New York – Sanctuary cities in Hudson County

    4. Union County

    5. Middlesex County

    6. Hightstown, Trenton – Sanctuary cities in Mercer County

    7. Ocean County

    8. Camden – Sanctuary city in Camden County

New Mexico

    1. – 33. **All Counties** including: Bernalillo, Catron, Chaves, Cibola, Colfax, Curry, De Baca, Dona Ana, Eddy, Grant, Guadalupe, Harding, Hidalgo, Lea, Lincoln, Los Alamos, Luna, McKinley, Mora, Otero, Quay, Rio Arriba, Roosevelt, San Juan, San Miguel, Sandoval, Santa Fe

    34. Aztec – Sanctuary city in San Juan County

    35. Taos – Sanctuary city in Taos County

    36. Santa Fe – Sanctuary city in Santa Fe County

    37. Albuquerque – Sanctuary city in Bernalillo County

    38. San Miguel – Sanctuary city in San Miguel County

    39. State of New Mexico

New York

    1. St. Lawrence County

    2. Franklin County

    3. Wayne County

    4. Onondaga County

    5. Saratoga County

    6. Albany – Sanctuary city in Albany County

    7. Rensselaer County

    8. Spring Valley Village – Sanctuary city in Rockland County

    9. New York City

    10. Nassau County

        Uniondale, Westbury – Sanctuary cities additionally named in this county

    11. Suffolk County

        Bay Shore, Brentwood, Central Islip, Farmingville, Riverhead, Shirley/Mastic – Sanctuary cities additionally named in this county

North Carolina
1. Winston-Salem – Sanctuary city in Forsyth County
2. Carrboro, Chapel Hill, Durham – Sanctuary cities in Orange County
3. Raleigh – Sanctuary city in Wake County
4. Charlotte – Sanctuary city in Mecklenburg County
5. **Chatham County**

North Dakota
1. **State of North Dakota**

Ohio
1. Lorain, Oberlin – Sanctuary cities in Lorain County
2. Painesville – Sanctuary city in Lake County
3. Lima – Sanctuary city in Allen County
4. Columbus – Sanctuary city in Franklin County
5. Dayton – Sanctuary city in Montgomery County

Oklahoma
1. Tulsa – Sanctuary city in Tulsa County
2. Oklahoma City – Sanctuary city in Oklahoma County

Oregon
1. **Clatsop County**
2. **Tillamook County**
3. **Washington County**
   Gaston – Sanctuary city additionally named in this county
4. **Multnomah County**
   Portland – Sanctuary city additionally named in this county
5. **Hood River County**
6. **Sherman County**
7. **Gilliam County**
8. **Umatilla County**
9. **Union County**
10. **Wallowa County**
11. **Yamhill County**
12. **Clackamas County**
13. **Wasco County**
14. **Polk County**
15. **Marion County**
16. **Jefferson County**
17. **Wheeler County**
18. **Grant County**
19. **Baker County**
20. **Lincoln County**
21. **Linn County**
22. **Springfield**
23. **Lane County**
24. **Deschutes County**
25. **Crook County**
26. **Coos County**
27. **Malheur County**
28. **Curry County**
29. **Josephine County**
30. **Jackson County**
    Ashland – Sanctuary city additionally named in this county
31. **Marion County**
32. **Multnomah County**
33. **State of Oregon**

Pennsylvania
1. Pittsburgh
2. **Lehigh County**
3. Philadelphia

Rhode Island
1. **State of Rhode Island**

Texas
1. Denton – Sanctuary city in Denton County
2. Ft. Worth – Sanctuary city in Tarrant County
3. Dallas – Sanctuary city in Dallas County
4. El Paso – Sanctuary city in El Paso County
5. **Travis County**
    Austin – Sanctuary city additionally named in this county
6. Houston, Katy – Sanctuary cities in Harris County
7. Baytown, Channelview – Sanctuary cities in Harris County
8. Port Arthur – Sanctuary city in Jefferson County
9. El Cenizo, Laredo – Sanctuary cities in Webb County
10. McAllen – Sanctuary city in Hidalgo County
11. Brownsville – Sanctuary city in Cameron County
12. **State of Texas**

Utah
1. **Salt Lake City**
2. **State of Utah**

Virginia
1. **Fairfax County**
    Alexandria – Independent Sanctuary city additionally named (closest to Fairfax County)
2. Virginia Beach
3. **Chesterfield County**

Vermont
1. **State of Vermont**
2. Burlington – Sanctuary city in Chittenden County
3. Middlebury – Sanctuary city in Addison County

Washington
1. **Whatcom County**
2. **San Juan County**
3. **Skagit County**
4. **Clallam County**
5. **Jefferson County**
6. **Kitsap County**
7. **Snohomish County**
8. **King County**
    Seattle – Sanctuary city additionally named in this county
9. **Chelan County**
10. **Spokane County**
11. Kent – Sanctuary city in King County
12. **Thurston County**
13. **Pierce County**
14. **Cowlitz County**
15. **Clark County**
16. **Yakima County**
17. **Benton County**
18. **Franklin County**
19. **Walla Walla County**

Wisconsin
1. Madison
2. **Milwaukee County**
    Milwaukee – Sanctuary city additionally named in this county

Wyoming
1. Jackson Hole – Sanctuary city in Teton County

CANADA

Ontario
1. Hamilton – (as of February 2014)
2. Toronto – (as of February 2013)

Appendix 2 – Somali Cities of Refuge

Somali Cities of Refuge			
Alabama	**Idaho**	**Minnesota**	**Pennsylvania**
Mobile	Boise	St. Cloud	Harrisburg
Alaska	Twin Falls	**Mississippi**	Lancaster
Anchorage	**Illinois**	Biloxi	Philadelphia
Arizona	Aurora	**Missouri**	Pittsburgh
Glendale	Chicago	Columbia	Roslyn
Phoenix	Moline	Kansas City	Scranton
Tucson	Rockford	Saint Louis	**Puerto Rico**
Arkansas	Wheaton	Jackson	San Juan
Springdale	**Indiana**	**Nebraska**	**Rhode Island**
California	Fort Wayne	Lincoln	Providence
Anaheim	Gary	Omaha	**South Carolina**
Fullerton	Indianapolis	Durham	Columbia
Garden Grove	South Bend	Greensboro	**South Dakota**
Glendale	**Iowa**	**North Carolina**	Huron
Los Angeles	Cedar Rapids	High Point	Sioux Falls
Los Gatos	Des Moines	New Bern	**Tennessee**
Modesto	**Kansas**	Raleigh	Chattanooga
Oakland	Kansas City	Wilmington	Knoxville
Sacramento	Wichita	**New Hampshire**	Memphis
San Bernardino	**Kentucky**	Concord	Nashville
San Diego	Bowling Green	Manchester	**Texas**
San Francisco	Lexington	**New Jersey**	Abilene
San Jose	Louisville	**Nevada**	Amarillo
Santa Rosa	Owensboro	Las Vegas	Austin
Turlock	**Louisiana**	Camden	Corpus Christi
Walnut Creek	Alexandria	East Orange	Dallas
Colorado	Baton Rouge	Elizabeth	El Paso
Colorado Springs	Lafayette	**New Mexico**	Fort Worth
Denver	Metairie	Albuquerque	Houston
Greeley	**Maryland**	**New York**	San Antonio
Connecticut	Baltimore	Albany	**Utah**
Bridgeport	Glen Burnie	Amityville	Salt Lake City
Hartford	Rockville	Binghamton	**Vermont**
New Haven	Silver Spring	Brooklyn	Colchester
Delaware	**Massachusetts**	Buffalo	**Virginia**
Wilmington	Boston	New York	Arlington
District of Columbia	Framingham	Rochester	Charlottesville
Washington DC	Jamaica Plain	Syracuse	Falls Church
Florida	Lowell	Utica	Fredericksburg
Clearwater	South Boston	**North Carolina**	Harrisonburg
Delray Beach	Springfield	Charlotte	Newport News
Doral	Waltham	**North Dakota**	Richmond
Jacksonville	West Springfield	Bismarck	Roanoke
Miami	Worcester	Fargo	**Washington**
Miami Springs	**Michigan**	Grand Forks	Kent
Naples	Ann Arbor	**Ohio**	Richland
North Port	Battle Creek	Akron	Seattle
Orlando	Clinton Township	Cincinnati	Spokane

Somali Cities of Refuge

Palm Springs	Dearborn	Cleveland	Tacoma
Pensacola	Grand Rapids	Columbus	Vancouver
Plantation	Lansing	Dayton	Green Bay
Riviera Beach	Troy	Toledo	Madison
Tallahassee	*Maine*	*Oklahoma*	Milwaukee
Tampa	Portland	Oklahoma City	Oshkosh
Georgia	*Minnesota*	Tulsa	Sheboygan
Atlanta	Minneapolis	Portland	Charleston
Savannah	Richfield	*Pennsylvania*	*Wyoming*
Stone Mountain	Rochester	Allentown	Casper
Hawaii	Saint Paul	Erie	
Honolulu			

Appendix 3 – ICLEI Cities Around the World

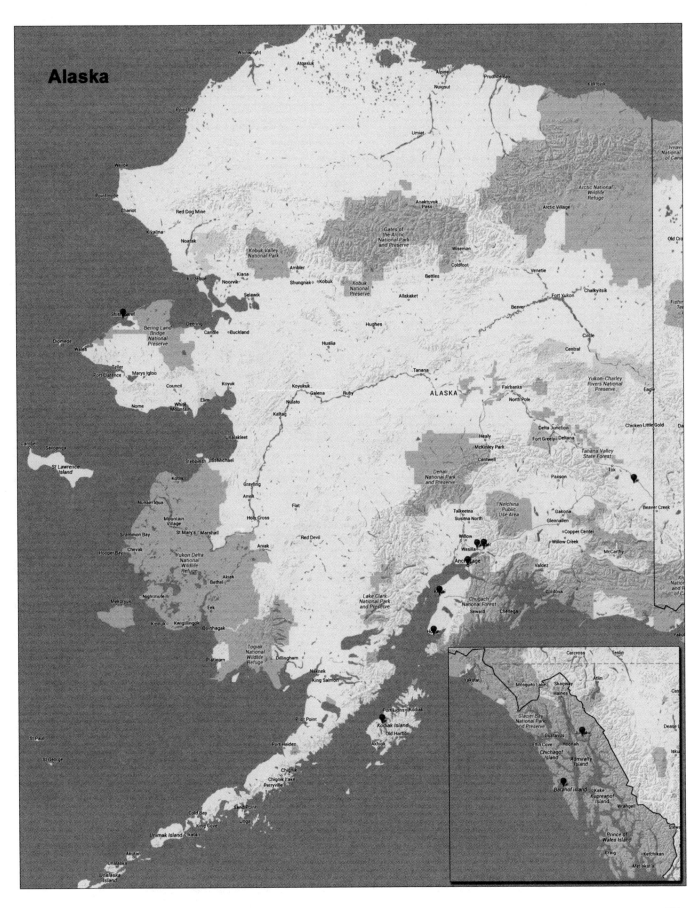

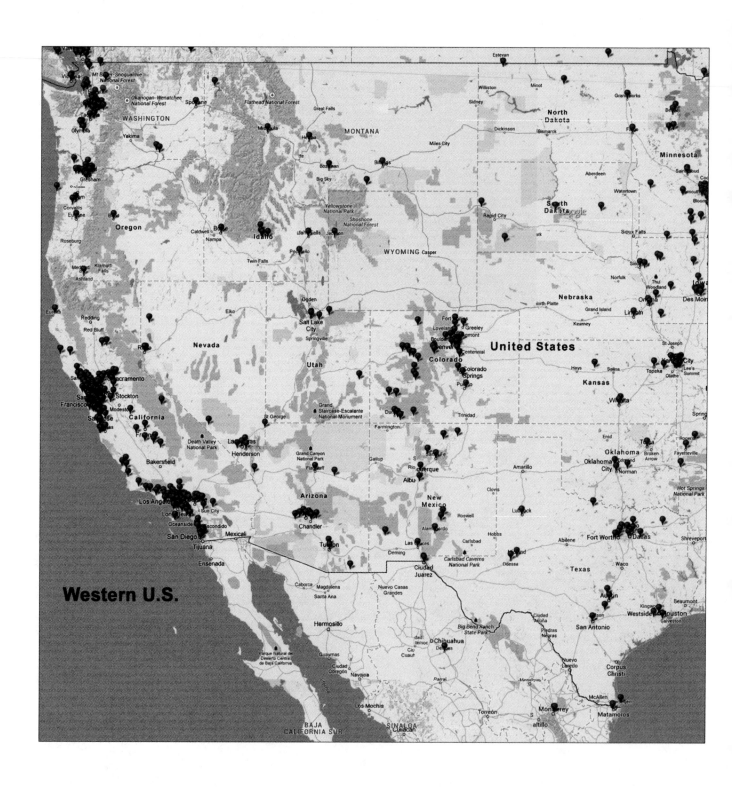

Western U.S.

476

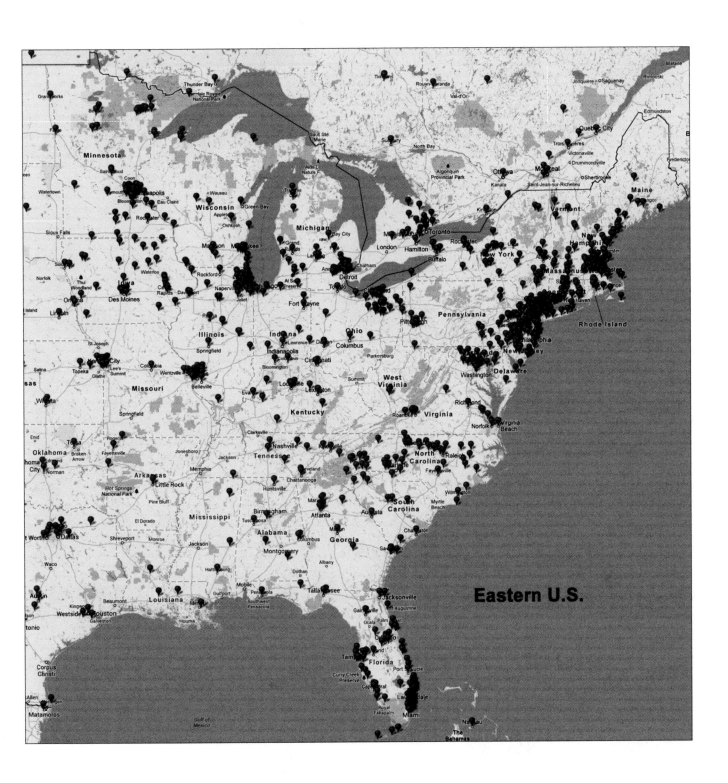

Eastern U.S.

477

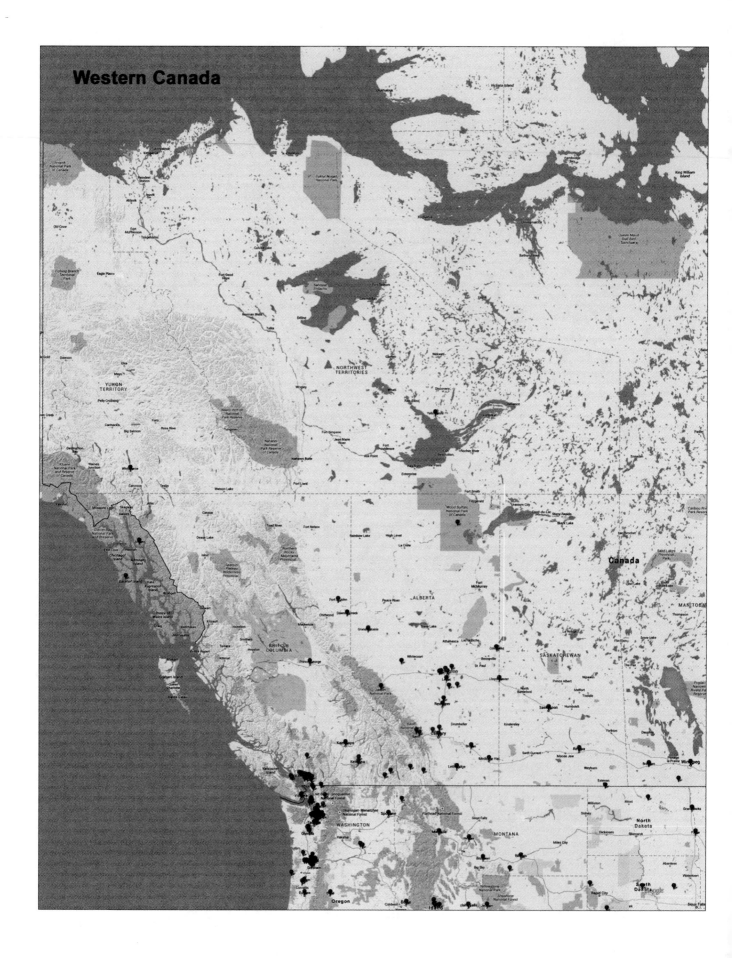

Western Canada

478

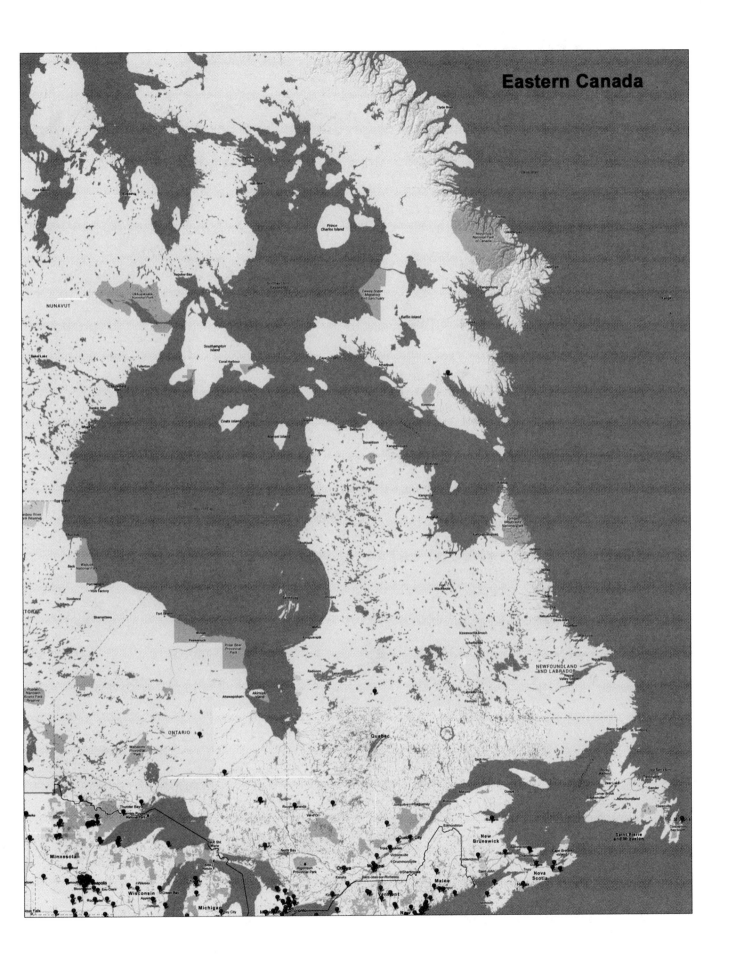

Eastern Canada

479

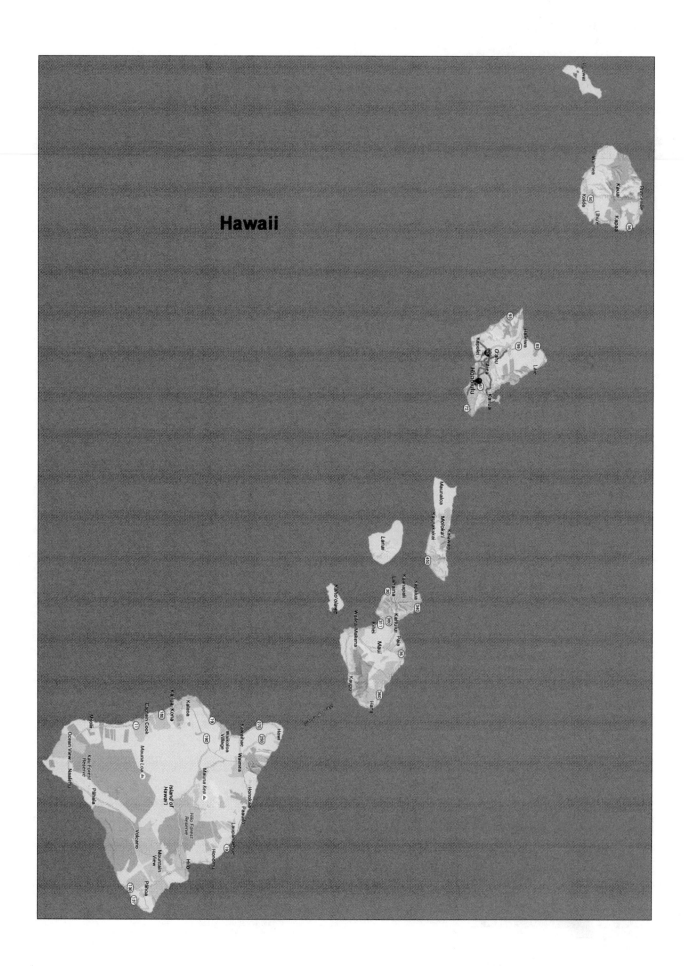

Hawaii

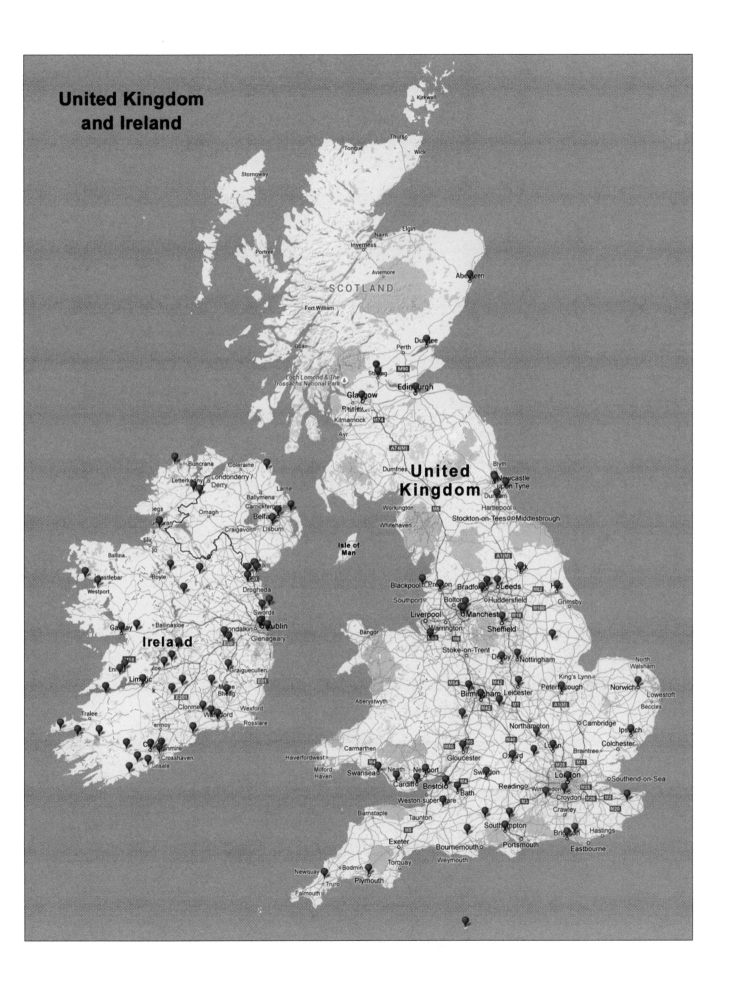

United Kingdom
and Ireland

United Kingdom

Ireland

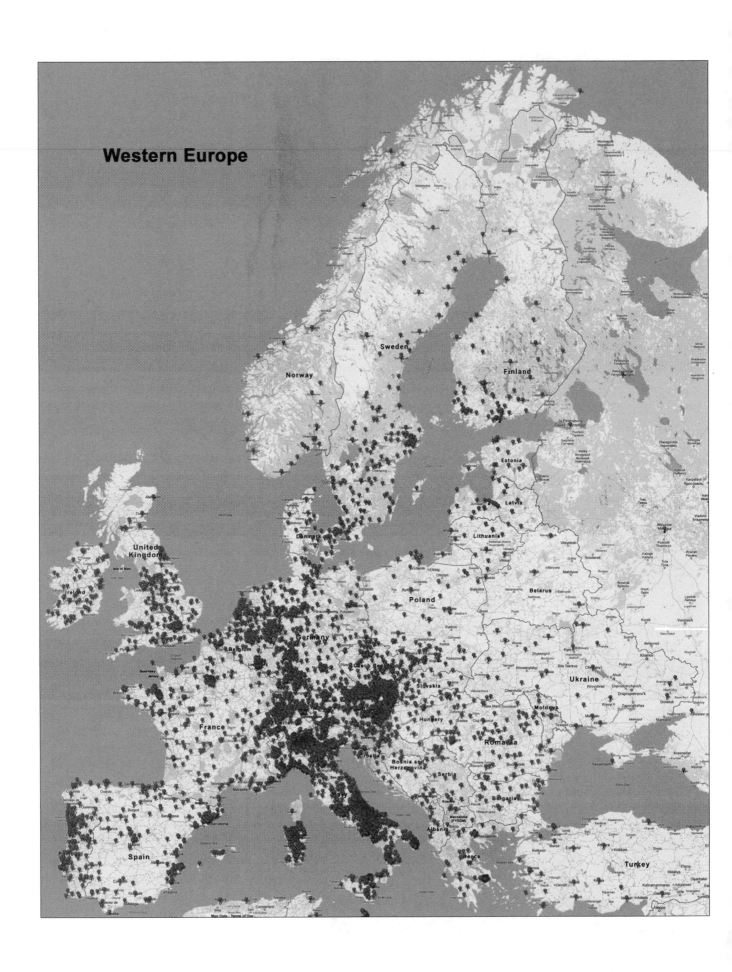

Western Europe

Australia

483

New Zealand

ENDNOTES

[1] Waghorn, Dominic, "Increasing Number of Families Prepping for Catastrophe," *Sky News,* December 23, 2014, http://news.sky.com/story/1395842/us-families-prepare-for-modern-day-apocalypse

[2] Egelhoff, Tom, "How Fast Is Knowledge Doubling?" August 21, 2014, KMMS AM 1450, Bozeman, Montana, http://kmmsam.com/how-fast-is-knowledge-doubling/

[3] "The Toxic Terabyte," IBM, July 2006, http://www-935.ibm.com/services/no/cio/leverage/levinfo_wp_gts_thetoxic.pdf

[4] Romm, Joe, "2014 Was the Hottest Year on Record Globally By Far," January 2015, http://thinkprogress.org/climate/2015/01/05/3607735/2014-hottest-year-by-far/

[5] Thompson, Andrea, "2014 Set for Record Hot; Record Cold Thing of the Past" Climate Central, November 20, 2014, http://www.climatecentral.org/news/2014-set-for-record-hot-record-cold-thing-of-the-past-18360

[6] Dolce, Chris, "Record-Breaking Cold: All-Time March Record Lows Set," *The Weather Channel,* March 7, 2015, http://www.weather.com/storms/winter/news/record-cold-early-march

[7] Haiti Earthquake Fast Facts, CNN, January 6, 2015, http://www.cnn.com/2013/12/12/world/haiti-earthquake-fast-facts/

[8] Ellsworth, W; Robertson, J. & Hook, C., "Man-Made Earthquakes Update," USGS, January 17, 2014, http://www.usgs.gov/blogs/features/usgs_top_story/man-made-earthquakes/

[9] "Induced Earthquakes," USGS, January 1, 2015, http://earthquake.usgs.gov/research/induced/

[10] Strassman, Mark, "What Is Causing Oklahoma's Record Earthquakes?" *CBS News,* January 4, 2016, http://www.cbsnews.com/news/is-fracking-causing-oklahomas-earthquakes/

[11] *Ibid.*

[12] Wade, Jarrel, "New Study Explains Surge of Oklahoma Earthquakes, Predicts Major Ones," *Tulsa World,* March 17, 2015, http://www.tulsaworld.com/newshomepage1/new-study-addresses-surge-of-oklahoma-earthquakes-predicts-major-ones/article_1f76113c-233c-5cb3-b298-da1347ee9a18.html

[13] Oskin, Becky, "Big Earthquakes Double in 2014, But Scientists Say They're Not Linked," *Live Science,* July 1, 2014, http://www.livescience.com/46576-more-earthquakes-still-random-process.html

[14] *Ibid.*

[15] Millman, Gregory J, "Earthquake Risk Rising in Central U.S., Where Many People Are Unprepared," *Wall Street Journal*, July 18, 2014, http://blogs.wsj.com/riskandcompliance/2014/07/18/earthquake-risk-rising-in-central-u-s-with-many-unprepared/

[16] *Ibid.*

[17] *Ibid.*

[18] Jaiswal, K. & Robertson, J., "Nearly Half of Americans Exposed to Potentially Damaging Earthquakes," USGS, August 10, 2015, http://www.usgs.gov/blogs/features/usgs_top_story/nearly-half-of-americans-exposed-to-potentially-damaging-earthquakes/

[19] RFI (Request for Information) for Pre-Packaged Commercial Meals, Solicitation Number: HSFEHQ-11-R-Meals, Agency: Department of Homeland Security, January 20, 2011, https://www.fbo.gov/index?s=opportunity&mode=form&id=40c5ec4c02287bcf1b3a974770d871a1&tab=core&tabmode=list&=

[20] Elnashai, A. S., Jefferson, T., Fiedrich, F., Cleveland, J. L., & Gress, Timothy, "Impact of New Madrid Seismic Zone Earthquakes on the Central USA," Executive Summary, October 2009, https://www.ideals.illinois.edu/bitstream/handle/2142/14810/ImpactofNewMadridSeismicZoneEarthquakeso%20theCentral%20USAVol1.pdf, p. vi,

[21] Xia, Rosanna, "Risk of 8.0 Earthquake in California Rises, USGS Says," *Los Angeles Times,* March 10, 2015, http://touch.latimes.com/#section/-1/article/p2p-83023244/

[22] *Ibid.*

[23] "UCERF3: A New Earthquake Forecast for California's Complex Fault System," USGS Fact Sheet 2015–3009, March 2015, http://pubs.usgs.gov/fs/2015/3009/pdf/fs2015-3009.pdf

[24] Sanders, Robert, "Calaveras-Hayward Fault Link Means Potentially Larger Quakes," *Berkeley News,* April 2, 2015, http://news.berkeley.edu/2015/04/02/calaveras-hayward-fault-link-means-potentially-larger-quakes/

[25] Schultz, Kathryn, "The Really Big One," *The New Yorker,* July 20, 2015, http://www.newyorker.com/magazine/2015/07/20/the-really-big-one

[26] "The Impacts of the Cascadia Subduction Zone Earthquake on Oregon," Oregon Military Department, Office of Emergency Management, 2014, http://www.oregon.gov/OMD/OEM/docs/earth_tsunami/2014%20Impacts%20on%20Oregon.pdf, p. 11

[27] Schultz, Kathryn, "The Really Big One," *The New Yorker,* July 20, 2015, http://www.newyorker.com/magazine/2015/07/20/the-really-big-one

[28] "The M9 Cascadia Megathrust Earthquake of January 26, 1700," Natural Resources Canada, http://www.earthquakescanada.nrcan.gc.ca/histor/15-19th-eme/1700/1700-eng.php

[29] Oskin, Becky, "Japan Earthquake & Tsunami of 2011: Facts and Information," *Live Science,* May 7, 2015, http://www.livescience.com/39110-japan-2011-earthquake-tsunami-facts.html

[30] "The Impacts of the Cascadia Subduction Zone Earthquake on Oregon," Oregon Military Department, Office of Emergency Management, 2014, http://www.oregon.gov/OMD/OEM/docs/earth_tsunami/2014%20Impacts%20on%20Oregon.pdf, p. 11

[31] Schultz, Kathryn, "The Really Big One," *The New Yorker,* July 20, 2015, http://www.newyorker.com/magazine/2015/07/20/the-really-big-one

[32] Madin, Ian, "Cascadia Subduction Earthquake Hazard in Curry County," Oregon Department of Geology and Mineral Industries, April 21, 2014, http://www.co.curry.or.us/Portals/0/Documents/BOC/Full%20Packet.pdf

[33] Smith, Shepard, "Report: Mega-quake Could Kill 13,000 in Pacific Northwest, Video," *Fox News,* July 15, 2015, http://video.foxnews.com/v/4356513070001/report-mega-quake-could-kill-13000-in-pacific-northwest/

[34] *Ibid.*

[35] Carroll, Linda, "Worldwide Surge in 'Great' Earthquakes Seen in Past 10 Years," October 25, 2014, *NBC News,* http://www.nbcnews.com/science/science-news/worldwide-surge-great-earthquakes-seen-past-10-years-n233661

[36] Niiler, Eric, "Quake vs. Volcano: Which One's Worse?" *Discovery News,* August 26, 2014, http://news.discovery.com/earth/earthquakes-vs-volcanoes-which-is-more-powerful-140826.htm

[37] Bagley, Mary, "Mount St. Helens Eruption: Facts & Information," *Live Science,* February 28, 2013, http://www.livescience.com/27553-mount-st-helens-eruption.html

[38] *Ibid.*

[39] "Comparisons With Other Eruptions," USGS, June 26, 1997, http://pubs.usgs.gov/gip/msh/comparisons.html

[40] Deyo, Holly. Prudent Places USA. Pueblo West: Deyo Enterprises, 2014

[41] Paulu, Tom, "Mt. St Helens: Is It Ready to Erupt Again?" *Christian Science Monitor,* September 29, 2014, http://www.csmonitor.com/Environment/Latest-News-Wires/2014/0929/Mt.-St-Helens-Is-it-ready-to-erupt-again

[42] "Supervolcanoes Erupt Without External Triggers," *Nature World News,* January 6, 2014, http://www.natureworldnews.com/articles/5534/20140106/supervolcanoes-erupt-without-external-triggers.htm

[43] Austin, Jon, "Yellowstone About to Blow? Scientists Warning Over Super-Volcano That Could Kill Millions," *UK Express,* January 7, 2016, http://www.express.co.uk/news/science/632054/Yellowstone-about-to-blow-1-in-10-chance-super-volcano-will-kill-millions

[44] "Yellowstone Magma Much Bigger Than Thought, Study Says," *Fox News,* December 17, 2013, http://www.foxnews.com/science/2013/12/17/yellowstone-magma-much-bigger-than-thought-study-says/

[45] Beck, Christina, "Massive Supervolcano Eruptions Once Rocked Yellowstone," *Christian Science Monitor,* March 26, 2016, http://www.csmonitor.com/Science/2016/0326/Yellowstone-supervolcano-eruptions-were-even-bigger-than-we-thought

[46] Srikrishnan, Maya, "Yellowstone National Park Road Melts into 'Soupy Mess'," *Los Angeles Times,* July 11, 2014, http://www.latimes.com/nation/nationnow/la-na-nn-yellowstone-melted-road-20140711-story.html

[47] Zuckerman, Laura, "Yellowstone National Park Rattled By Largest Earthquake in 34 Years," *Reuters,* March 30, 2014, http://www.reuters.com/article/2014/03/31/us-usa-earthquake-yellowstone-idUSBREA2U01920140331

[48] Kearney, Liz, "Yellowstone Park's Boiling River Running Warmer, at Nearly 140 Degrees," *The Missoulian,* March 1, 2015, http://missoulian.com/news/state-and-regional/yellowstone-park-s-boiling-river-running-warmer-at-nearly-degrees/article_4d238eb8-411c-5281-a9e6-c26702f494df.html

[49] "The Yellowstone Supervolcano: New Finding - 'Potential to Erupt With 2,000 Times the Force of Mount St. Helens'," *The Daily Galaxy,* December 21, 2013, http://www.dailygalaxy.com/my_weblog/2013/12/the-yellowstone-supervolcano-2-12-times-larger-than-earlier-estimates-potential-to-erupt-2000-times-.html

[50] *Ibid.*

[51] Palladino, D. M. & Sottili, G., "Earth's Spin and Volcanic Eruptions: Evidence for Mutual Cause-And-Effect Interactions?" *Terra Nova,* October 17, 2013, http://onlinelibrary.wiley.com/doi/10.1111/ter.12073/abstract

[52] Wylie, Robin, "Science Explains Why Volcanoes Are Erupting All Over the Place Right Now," *The Washington Post,* September 29, 2014, http://www.washingtonpost.com/posteverything/wp/2014/09/29/science-explains-why-volcanoes-are-erupting-all-over-the-place-right-now/

[53] "West Antarctic Melt Rate Has Tripled: UC Irvine-NASA," *UCI News,* December 2, 2014, http://news.uci.edu/press-releases/west-antarctic-melt-rate-has-tripled-uc-irvine-nasa/

[54] Wylie, Robin, "Science Explains Why Volcanoes Are Erupting All Over the Place Right Now," *The Washington Post,* September 29, 2014, http://www.washingtonpost.com/posteverything/wp/2014/09/29/science-explains-why-volcanoes-are-erupting-all-over-the-place-right-now/

[55] Gillis, J., & Chang, K., "Scientists Warn of Rising Oceans From Polar Melt," *The New York Times,* May 12, 2014, http://www.nytimes.com/2014/05/13/science/earth/collapse-of-parts-of-west-antarctica-ice-sheet-has-begun-scientists-say.html

[56] Koshmrl, Mike, "Triple Swarm of Earthquakes Shakes Yellowstone," *KOMO News,* September 22, 2013, http://www.komonews.com/news/national/Swarm-of-earthquakes-shakes-Yellowstone-224773612.html

[57] "10 Facts You Want to Know about Tornadoes," May 24, 2011, *AccuWeather,* http://www.accuweather.com/en/weather-news/10-facts-you-want-to-know-abou/50076

[58] "U.S. Tornado Climatology," NOAA, Accessed July 31, 2015, http://www.ncdc.noaa.gov/climate-information/extreme-events/us-tornado-climatology

[59] Dunham, William, "Severe Weather Alert: U.S. Study Finds Tornadoes Coming in Swarms," *Reuters,* October 16, 2014, http://www.reuters.com/article/2014/10/16/us-science-tornadoes-idUSKCN0I52EQ20141016

[60] "Frequently Asked Questions About the May 3, 1999 Bridge Creek/OKC Area Tornado," National Weather Service, Accessed August 3, 2015, http://www.srh.noaa.gov/oun/?n=events-19990503-may3faqs

[61] Raymond, Ken, "Survivor Remembers: 'I Just Kept Screaming for Help'," *The Oklahoman,* May 1, 2009, http://newsok.com/survivor-remembers-i-just-kept-screaming-for-help/article/3365878/

[62] *Ibid.*

[63] *Ibid.*

[64] "April 25–28, 2011 Tornado Outbreak," Wikipedia, https://en.wikipedia.org/wiki/April_25-28,_2011_tornado_outbreak

[65] "Spring 2011 Tornadoes: April 25-28 and May 22," FEMA, May 2012, http://www.fema.gov/media-library-data/20130726-1827-25045-2783/tornado_mat_frontmatter_508.pdf, p. i

[66] Pursaga, Joyanne, "Tornado Touches Down in Southwestern Manitoba," *Winnipeg Sun,* July 28, 2015, http://www.winnipegsun.com/2015/07/28/tornado-touches-down-in-southwestern-manitoba

[67] Geary, Aidan, "'It Was Just Mother Nature Showing Us She's the Boss'," *Winnipeg Free Press,* July 29, 2015, http://www.winnipegfreepress.com/local/Tornadoes-leave-little-damage-in-fierce-path-through-Manitoba-318824411.html

[68] Markewich, Courtney, "Path of Damage Left By Tornado in southwest Manitoba," News Talk 650 CKOM, Saskatoon, Saskatchewan; July 28, 2015, http://ckom.com/story/photos-path-damage-left-tornado-southwest-manitoba/571183

[69] Metcalfe, John, "Tornado Swarms Are Now Upon Us," *City Lab,* October 16, 2014, http://www.citylab.com/weather/2014/10/tornado-swarms-are-now-upon-us/381527/

[70] Begley, Sharon, "Scientists See Rise in Tornado-Creating Conditions," *Reuters,* March 5, 2012, http://www.reuters.com/article/2012/03/05/us-usa-weather-storms-research-idUSTRE8241W620120305

[71] *Ibid.*

[72] Rice, Doyle, "'Tornado Alley' Grows Wider, Report Says," *USA Today,* April 10, 2012, http://usatoday30.usatoday.com/weather/storms/tornadoes/story/2012-04-09/tornado-alley/54157872/1

[73] Heineman, Karin, "Landscape Changes Could Spawn Tornadoes," *Inside Science,* August 14, 2014, http://www.insidescience.org/content/landscape-changes-could-spawn-tornadoes/1896

[74] "The List of the Strongest Tornadoes Ever Recorded: Part III," *Extreme Planet,* October 3, 2012, http://extremeplanet.me/2012/10/03/the-indefinitive-list-of-the-strongest-tornadoes-ever-recorded-part-iii/

[75] "Climate-Watch," NOAA, May 1999, Accessed February 5, 2015, https://www.ncdc.noaa.gov/oa/climate/extremes/1999/may/extremes0599.html

[76] Edwards, Roger, "The Online Tornado FAQ," NOAA, Storm Prediction Center, Accessed August 3, 2015, http://www.spc.noaa.gov/faq/tornado/

[77] "Deadly Second Act: 1999 Moore, Okla. Tornado vs. 2013's Devastating Storm," *CBS News, May 21, 2013,* http://www.cbsnews.com/news/deadly-second-act-1999-moore-okla-tornado-vs-2013s-devastating-storm/

[78] Nix, Steve, "Most Famous Wildfire Photograph Ever Taken!" About Forestry, http://forestry.about.com/od/fireinforests/a/Most-Famous-Wildfire-Photograph-Ever-Taken.htm

[79] Worland, Justin, "This Graphic Shows How 'Unimaginable' Wildfires Are on the Rise," *Time,* August 29, 2015, http://time.com/4005231/wildfires-graph/

[80] Klinkenberg, Marty, "'It Was Like Armageddon': Fort McMurray Residents Share Their Stories," *The Globe and Mail,* May 6, 2016, http://www.theglobeandmail.com/news/alberta/it-was-like-armageddon-fort-mcmurray-residents-share-their-stories/article29932472/

[81] *Ibid.*

[82] "Alberta Premier Says It'S Important for Oilsands to Restart, Trudeau Set to Visit Fort McMurray," *The Star,* May 10, 2016, https://www.thestar.com/news/canada/2016/05/10/fort-mcmurray-residents-to-wait-2-weeks-for-plan-to-return.html

[83] Thomas, George, "Al Qaeda Magazine Encourages Forest Fire Attacks," *CBN News,* May 5, 2012, http://www.cbn.com/cbnnews/world/2012/May/Magazine-Gives-Step-By-Step-Guide-to-Terrorism/

[84] "Are Terrorists Setting U.S. Wildfires," *Global Geopolitics,* September 12, 2013, https://glblgeopolitics.wordpress.com/2013/09/12/are-terrorists-setting-u-s-wildfires/

[85] "Fiscal Year 2016 Budget Overview," USDA Forest Service, February 2015, http://www.fs.fed.us/sites/default/files/media/2015/07/fy2016-budget-overview-update.pdf, pp. 2, 19

[86] Helmenstine, Anne Marie, " How Much Oxygen Does One Tree Produce," About Education, April 20, 2016, http://chemistry.about.com/od/environmentalchemistry/f/oxygen-produced-by-trees.htm

[87] Kovacs, Joe, "Are Terrorists Setting U.S. Wildfires," *WND,* September 11, 2013, http://www.wnd.com/2013/09/are-terrorists-setting-u-s-wildfires/

[88] "Wildfire: A Burning Issue for Insurers?" Lloyd's of London," September 2013, https://www.lloyds.com/~/media/lloyds/reports/emerging%20risk%20reports/wildfire%20final.pdf, p. 18

[89] "Preliminary Report: Impact of the 2009 Victorian Bushfires on Nature and Wildlife," The Wilderness Society, July 31, 2015, https://www.wilderness.org.au/articles/preliminary-report-impact-2009-victorian-bushfires-nature-and-wildlife

[90] Williams, Caroline, "Ignition Impossible: When Wildfires Set the Air Alight," *New Scientist,* August 7, 2007, http://www.sciencearchive.org.au/nova/newscientist/103ns_003.htm, p. 38

[91] Ross, Pam, "A Story of Survival – Victorian Bushfires," The Lost Dogs Home, http://dogshome.com/story-survival-victorian-bushfires/

[92] Duncan, Jeff, "Shelter From the Storm: Doug Thornton Reflects on the Superdome in Katrina," *The Times-Picayune,* January 29, 2013, http://www.nola.com/superbowl/index.ssf/2013/01/superdome_series_catching_up_w_2.html

[93] *Ibid.*

[94] Flaherty, Clay, "New Orleans Mayor Declared Martial Law During Katrina Aftermath," Jurist, August 31, 2011, http://jurist.org/thisday/2011/08/new-orleans-mayor-declared-martial-law-during-katrina-aftermath.php

[95] "Economic Impacts of Colorado Flooding: Identifying the Dimensions and Estimating the Impacts of Reduced Tourism in Estes Park," Colorado State University, October 2, 2013, http://outreach.colostate.edu/rei/rei-docs/Economic%20issues%20of%20flood%20recovery%20Final.pdf

[96] "Death Toll in Colorado Flooding Rises to 8 as Rescue Crews Scour Rubble in Search for Missing," *Fox News,* September 16, 2013, http://www.foxnews.com/weather/2013/09/16/colorado-braces-for-more-heavy-rain-deadly-floods/

[97] "Rain Bomb' Explodes Over Louisiana and Arkansas," MSN video of March 15, 2016, http://www.msn.com/en-us/video/tunedin/rain-bomb-explodes-over-louisiana-and-arkansas/vp-BBquNsJ

[98] "Louisiana Reels From Days of Pounding Rain," *Fox News,* March 11, 2016, http://www.foxnews.com/us/2016/03/11/louisiana-braces-for-even-more-rain-after-record-floods.html

[99] Wilkinson, Jeff, "Flood of 2015: Citizen Rescuers Step Up When 'There's No One to Come'," *Myrtle Beach Online,* October 18, 2015, http://www.myrtlebeachonline.com/news/state/article39664677.html

[100] *Ibid.*

[101] Rice, Doyle, "S.C. Flood Is 6th 1,000-year Rain Since 2010," *USA Today,* October 6, 2015, http://www.usatoday.com/story/weather/2015/10/05/south-carolina-flooding-climate-change/73385778/

[102] Freedman, Andrew, "Flooding Continues in Louisiana in Wake of 1,000-year Rains," *Mashable,* March 15, 2016, http://mashable.com/2016/03/15/nasa-visualization-louisiana-flooding/

[103] Borenstein, Seth, "'Stew' of Factors Cook Up Extreme Weather Around World This Month", *The Denver Post,* May 30, 2015, http://www.denverpost.com/weathernews/ci_28216999/stew-factors-cook-up-extreme-weather-around-world

[104] Knight, Nerissa and CNN Wire, " Death Toll Rises in Texas Amid Severe Flooding; More Rain Forecast," KTLA-TV, Los Angeles, May 28, 2015, http://ktla.com/2015/05/28/death-toll-rises-in-texas-as-forecasters-predict-more-rain-amid-severe-flooding

[105] *Ibid.*

[106] Sherman, Bill, "Baptist Disaster Relief Chief Has Never Seen Such Widespread Damage," *Tulsa World,* May 30, 2015, http://www.tulsaworld.com/homepagelatest/baptist-disaster-relief-chief-has-never-seen-such-widespread-damage/article_a0719189-b0ed-5006-9e42-caf8f1630f9d.html

[107] "Claims Expected to Exceed $1 Billion in Recent Texas, Oklahoma Floods," *Insurance Financial Advisor,* June 8, 2015, http://ifawebnews.com/2015/06/08/claims-expected-to-exceed-1-billion-in-recent-texas-oklahoma-floods/

[108] Holden, Will C., "Waldo Canyon Fire Rips Through Colorado Springs City Limits," *Fox 31,* Denver, June 27, 2012, http://kdvr.com/2012/06/27/waldo-canyon-fire-rips-through-colorado-springs-city-limits/

[109] Miller, Peter, "Extreme Weather," *National Geographic,* September 2012, http://ngm.nationalgeographic.com/2012/09/extreme-weather/miller-text

[110] *Ibid.*

[111] "April 2010 Rio de Janeiro Floods and Mudslides," Wikipedia, Accessed March 15, 2015, http://en.wikipedia.org/wiki/April_2010_Rio_de_Janeiro_floods_and_mudslides

[112] "Death Toll from Flooding in Brazil Surpasses 800," *CNN,* January 24, 2011, http://www.cnn.com/2011/WORLD/americas/01/24/brazil.flooding/

[113] Romm, Joe, "Masters on Brazilian Floods: Brazil's Deadliest Natural Disaster in History," *Climate Progress,* January 16, 2011, http://thinkprogress.org/climate/2011/01/16/207348/brazilian-floods-brazil-deadliest-natural-disaster-in-history/

[114] "April 2011 Rio de Janeiro Floods and Mudslides," Wikipedia, Accessed March 15, 2015, http://en.wikipedia.org/wiki/January_2011_Rio_de_Janeiro_floods_and_mudslides

[115] "2011 Thailand Floods," Wikipedia, Accessed March 15, 2015, http://en.wikipedia.org/wiki/2011_Thailand_floods

[116] "Queensland Floods Unprecedented," *Australian Geographic*, January 11, 2011, http://www.australiangeographic.com.au/news/2011/01/queensland-floods-unprecedented

[117] Hickman, Leo, "Is It Now Possible to Blame Extreme Weather on Global Warming," *The Guardian*, July 3, 2012, http://www.theguardian.com/environment/blog/2012/jul/03/weather-extreme-blame-global-warming

[118] Masters, Jeff, "India's 2nd Deadliest Heat Wave in History Ends as the Monsoon Arrives," *Weather Underground,* June 8, 2015, http://www.wunderground.com/blog/JeffMasters/comment.html?entrynum=3011

[119] "2006 North American Heat Wave," Wikipedia, Accessed March 30, 2015, http://en.wikipedia.org/wiki/2006_North_American_heat_wave

[120] Masters, Jeff, "India's 2nd Deadliest Heat Wave in History Ends as the Monsoon Arrives," *Weather Underground,* June 8, 2015, http://www.wunderground.com/blog/JeffMasters/comment.html?entrynum=3011

[121] Hickman, Leo, "Is It Now Possible to Blame Extreme Weather on Global Warming," *The Guardian*, July 3, 2012, http://www.theguardian.com/environment/blog/2012/jul/03/weather-extreme-blame-global-warming

[122] Masters, Jeff, "India's 2nd Deadliest Heat Wave in History Ends as the Monsoon Arrives," *Weather Underground,* June 8, 2015, http://www.wunderground.com/blog/JeffMasters/comment.html?entrynum=3011

[123] "2006 North American Heat Wave," Wikipedia, Accessed March 30, 2015, http://en.wikipedia.org/wiki/2006_North_American_heat_wave

[124] Borenstein, Seth, "'Stew' of Factors Cook Up Extreme Weather Around World This Month", *The Denver Post,* May 30, 2015, http://www.denverpost.com/weathernews/ci_28216999/stew-factors-cook-up-extreme-weather-around-world

[125] *Ibid.*

[126] "Weather Porn? Network Newscasts Spending More Time on Dramatic Weather," *AP,* December 12, 2014, http://www.foxnews.com/entertainment/2014/12/12/weather-porn-network-newscasts-spending-more-time-on-dramatic-weather/

[127] "Extreme Weather," *National Geographic,* September 2012, http://ngm.nationalgeographic.com/2012/09/extreme-weather/miller-text

[128] Hickman, Leo, "Is It Now Possible to Blame Extreme Weather on Global Warming," *The Guardian*, July 3, 2012, http://www.theguardian.com/environment/blog/2012/jul/03/weather-extreme-blame-global-warming

[129] *Ibid.*

[130] "Extreme Weather," *National Geographic,* September 2012, http://ngm.nationalgeographic.com/2012/09/extreme-weather/miller-text

[131] Mortimer, Sarah, "Reinsurers Should Price in Rise in Natural Disasters - Munich Re," *Reuters,* October 17, 2012, http://www.reuters.com/article/2012/10/17/reinsurance-climate-idUSL5E8LHMK120121017

[132] Baida, Vanessa, "Water Crisis Seen Worsening as Sao Paulo Nears 'Collapse'," *Bloomberg,* October 21, 2014, http://www.bloomberg.com/news/articles/2014-10-21/sao-paulo-warned-to-brace-for-more-dramatic-water-shortages

[133] "Death Toll in Chinese Earthquake Nears 400 as Premier Issues Edict," *AP,* August 4, 2014, http://www.cbc.ca/news/world/death-toll-in-chinese-earthquake-nears-400-as-premier-issues-edict-1.2726849

[134] Chappell, Bill, "'It's So Terrible': Quake Reportedly Kills Hundreds in Southwest China," *NPR,* August 3, 2014, http://www.npr.org/blogs/thetwo-way/2014/08/03/337541731/its-so-terrible-quake-reportedly-kills-at-least-150-in-southwest-china

[135] Zerkel, Eric, "India, Pakistan Flooding Update: Nearly 1,000 Villages Completely Flooded as the Death Toll Climbs," *The Weather Channel,* September 8, 2014, http://www.weather.com/news/news/india-pakistan-flooding-update-20140908

[136] *Ibid.*

[137] "Tokyo Can't Handle Heavy Snowfall," *Japan Today,* January 13, 2014, http://www.japantoday.com/category/kuchikomi/view/tokyo-cant-handle-heavy-snowfall

[138] "'Worst in Decades': 11 Dead, 1,200 Injured in Japan Snowstorm," *RT,* February 9, 2014, http://rt.com/news/japan-worst-snowstorm-decades-260/

[139] "Cyclone Hudhud: 500,000 Evacuated as Storm Bears Down on India's East Coast," *ABC News,* October 12, 2014, http://www.abc.net.au/news/2014-10-11/thousands-evacuated-as-cyclone-hudhub-bears-down-on-india/5807178

[140] "Cyclone Hudhud Caused $ 11 Billion Worth of Losses: UN," *The Economic Times,* February 26, 2015, http://articles.economictimes.indiatimes.com/2015-02-26/news/59541541_1_natural-disasters-asia-pacific-region-cyclone-hudhud

[141] Rao, V. Kamalakara, "Vizag First Indian City Directly Hit By Cyclone Hudhud," *Times of India,* October 18, 2014, http://timesofindia.indiatimes.com/city/visakhapatnam/Vizag-first-Indian-city-directly-hit-by-Cyclone-Hudhud/articleshow/44864271.cms

[142] Rao, V Kamalakara & Manish, "Cyclone Hudhud: on Day 3, Vizag Sees No End to Woes," *Times of India,* October 15, 2014, http://timesofindia.indiatimes.com/india/Cyclone-Hudhud-On-Day-3-Vizag-sees-no-end-to-woes/articleshow/44818530.cms

[143] *Ibid.*

[144] "'Can I Quit Now?' FEMA Chief Wrote as Katrina Raged," *CNN,* November 4, 2005, http://www.cnn.com/2005/US/11/03/brown.fema.emails/

[145] *Ibid.*

[146] Myers, Lisa & the NBC Investigative Unit, "Critics Question FEMA Director's Qualifications," *NBC News,* September 13, 2005, http://www.nbcnews.com/id/9325977/ns/nbc_nightly_news_with_brian_williams-nbc_news_investigates/t/critics-question-fema-directors-qualifications/

[147] "Natural Catastrophes 2014 Analyses, Assessments, Positions," MunichRe, 2016 Issue, http://www.munichre.com/site/touch-publications/get/documents_E1273659874/mr/assetpool.shared/Documents/5_Touch/_Publications/302-08875_en.pdf, p. 56

[148] Cahn, Jonathan, "Shemitah Impact? See Evidence For Yourself," *WND,* January 20, 2016, http://www.wnd.com/2016/01/the-sword-of-the-shemitah-and-how-it-just-changed-your-world/

[149] Evans-Pritchard, Ambrose, "World Faces Wave of Epic Debt Defaults, Fears Central Bank Veteran," *UK Telegraph,* January 19, 2016, http://www.telegraph.co.uk/finance/financetopics/davos/12108569/World-faces-wave-of-epic-debt-defaults-fears-central-bank-veteran.html

[150] "Fear Has Taken Over Stock Markets Around the world," *CNN Money,* February 12, 2016, http://money.cnn.com/2016/02/12/investing/bear-market-global-stocks/

[151] "Bear Market," Investopedia, Accessed April 2, 2015, http://www.investopedia.com/terms/b/bearmarket.asp

[152] *Book of Enoch,* Section 8.1-8.3, http://www.ccel.org/c/charles/otpseudepig/enoch/ENOCH_1.HTM

[153] *Book of Enoch,* Section 33.3-33.4, http://www.ccel.org/c/charles/otpseudepig/enoch/ENOCH_1.HTM

[154] Kollipara, Puneet, "Earth Won't Die as Soon as Thought," *American Association for the Advancement of Science,* January 22, 2014, http://news.sciencemag.org/climate/2014/01/earth-wont-die-soon-thought

[155] Dearden, Lizzie, "Hole in Ozone Layer Above Antarctica Reaches Size of North America," *UK Independent,* November 1, 2014, http://www.independent.co.uk/news/science/hole-in-ozone-layer-above-antarctica-reaches-size-of-north-america-9833341.html

[156] "The Sun Goes Haywire," *Science-at-NASA,* November 12, 2003, http://science.nasa.gov/science-news/science-at-nasa/2003/12nov_haywire/

[157] Odenwald, Sten, "The Day the Sun Brought Darkness," NASA, March 13, 2009, http://www.nasa.gov/topics/earth/features/sun_darkness.html

[158] Klein, Christopher, "A Perfect Solar Superstorm: The 1859 Carrington Event," *History,* March 14, 2012, http://www.history.com/news/a-perfect-solar-superstorm-the-1859-carrington-event

[159] Cliver, E. W. & Svalgaard, L., "The 1859 Solar–Terrestrial Disturbance and the Current Limits of Extreme Space Weather Activity," Solar-Terrestrial Environment Laboratory, October 8, 2004, http://www.leif.org/research/1859%20Storm%20-%20Extreme%20Space%20Weather.pdf

[160] "If the Massive Solar Flare of 1859 (the "Carrington Flare") Happened Today," HubPages, October 25, 2014, http://greekgeek.hubpages.com/hub/massive-solar-flare-1859

[161] "Biggest Ever Solar Flare Was Even Bigger Than Thought," *American Geophysical Union,* March 15, 2004, http://www.spaceref.com/news/viewpr.html?pid=13844

[162] Young, C. Alex, "X17 Solar Flare and Solar Storm of October 28, 2003," *The Sun Today,* http://www.thesuntoday.org/historical-sun/x17-solar-flare-and-solar-storm-of-october-28-2003/

[163] Samenow, Jason, "How a Solar Storm Two Years Ago Nearly Caused a Catastrophe on Earth," *The Washington Post,* July 23, 2014, http://www.washingtonpost.com/blogs/capital-weather-gang/wp/2014/07/23/how-a-solar-storm-nearly-destroyed-life-as-we-know-it-two-years-ago/

[164] *Ibid.*

[165] Tracton, Steve, "Do Solar Storms Threaten Life as We Know It," *The Washington Post,* April 6, 2009, http://voices.washingtonpost.com/capitalweathergang/2009/04/do_solar_storms_threaten_civil.html

[166] Samenow, Jason, "How a Solar Storm Two Years Ago Nearly Caused a Catastrophe on Earth," *The Washington Post,* July 23, 2014, http://www.washingtonpost.com/blogs/capital-weather-gang/wp/2014/07/23/how-a-solar-storm-nearly-destroyed-life-as-we-know-it-two-years-ago/

[167] *Ibid.*

[168] Phillips, Tony, "Near Miss: The Solar Superstorm of July 2012," *NASA Science News,* July 23, 2014, http://science.nasa.gov/science-news/science-at-nasa/2014/23jul_superstorm/

[169] Hathaway, David H., "Solar Cycle Prediction," NASA, January 14, 2015, http://solarscience.msfc.nasa.gov/predict.shtml

[170] Hotz, Robert Lee, "Strange Doings on the Sun," *The Wall Street Journal,* Nov. 10, 2013, http://www.wsj.com/articles/SB10001424052702304672404579183940409194498

[171] Sun, X., Hoeksema, J. T., Yang, L. & Zhao, J., "On Polar Magnetic Field Reversal and Surface Flux Transport During Solar Cycle 24," October 31, 2014, Cornell University Library, http://arxiv.org/abs/1410.8867

[172] "German Cockroaches," Penn State College of Agricultural Sciences, March 2002 Revised January 2013, http://ento.psu.edu/extension/factsheets/german-cockroaches

[173] Pezim, Michael E., "Anthrax as a Biological Weapon," MediResource, June 7, 2008, http://chealth.canoe.ca/channel_section_details.asp?text_id=1484&channel_id=1020

[174] "Overview of Potential Agents of Biological Terrorism, Table 1: Potential Agents of Bioterrorism," Southern Illinois University School of Medicine, December 15, 2014, http://www.siumed.edu/medicine/id/bioterrorism.htm

[175] Riedel, Stefan, "Biological Warfare and Bioterrorism: A Historical Review," Baylor University Medical Center, October 2004, http://www.ncbi.nlm.nih.gov/pmc/articles/PMC1200679/pdf/bumc0017-0400.pdf

[176] "Media 'Harried' Suicide Professor," *The Glasgow Herald,* September 9, 1978, https://news.google.com/newspapers?nid=2507&dat=19780909&id=PwI-AAAAIBAJ&sjid=cUkMAAAAIBAJ&pg=5226,1912288&hl=en

[177] Nuwer, Rachel, "Smallpox: Last Refuge of an Ultimate Killer," *BBC,* January 31, 2014, http://www.bbc.com/future/story/20140130-last-refuge-of-an-ultimate-killer

[178] Ball, Jonathan, "The Chilling Implications of an Ancient Virus Dug Up in Siberia: Diseases from the Past Could Once Again Ravage Humanity," *UK Daily Mail,* March 12, 2014, http://www.dailymail.co.uk/sciencetech/article-2579732/The-chilling-implications-ancient-virus-dug-Siberia-Diseases-past-ravage-humanity.html

[179] Connor, Steve, "Scientists Revive Giant 30,000-Year-Old Virus From Siberian Permafrost – and Say It Could Signal Return of Smallpox in Modern Times," *The UK Independent,* March 4, 2014, http://www.independent.co.uk/news/science/scientists-revive-giant-30000yearold-virus-from-siberian-permafrost--and-say-it-could-signal-return-of-smallpox-in-modern-times-9168442.html

[180] "A Primer of Biological Weapons" October 5, 2001, *NBC News,* http://abcnews.go.com/Health/story?id=117205&page=1&singlePage=true

[181] Hanson, Doug, "Botulinum Toxin: A Bioterrorism Weapon," *EMS World,* April 1, 2004, http://www.emsworld.com/article/10324792/botulinum-toxin-a-bioterrorism-weapon

[182] Arnon, S. & Schechter, R., "Botulinum Toxin as a Biological Weapon," American Medical Association, 2001, http://www.bt.cdc.gov/agent/botulism/botulismconsensus.pdf

[183] Hanson, Doug, "Botulinum Toxin: A Bioterrorism Weapon," *EMS World,* April 1, 2004, http://www.emsworld.com/article/10324792/botulinum-toxin-a-bioterrorism-weapon

[184] Branswell, Helen, "Researchers keep Mum on Botulism Discovery," *Scientific American,* October 22, 2013, http://www.scientificamerican.com/article/researchers-keep-mum-on-botulism-discovery/

[185] Croddy, E. A., Wirtz, J. & Larsen, J. Weapons of Mass Destruction: An Encyclopedia of Worldwide Policy. Santa Barbara: ABC-CLIO, Inc., 2005, p. 72

[186] Branswell, Helen, "Researchers Keep Mum on Botulism Discovery," Scientific American, October 22, 2013, http://www.scientificamerican.com/article/researchers-keep-mum-on-botulism-discovery/

[187] Kerr, Paul K., "CRS Report for Congress: Nuclear, Biological, and Chemical Weapons and Missiles: Status and Trends," February 20, 2008, http://usiraq.procon.org/sourcefiles/CRS_2-20-08.pdf, pp. 13-14

[188] Hanson, Doug, "Botulinum Toxin: A Bioterrorism Weapon," EMS World, April 1, 2004, http://www.emsworld.com/article/10324792/botulinum-toxin-a-bioterrorism-weapon

[189] Borowski, Susan, "From Beans to Weapon: The Discovery of Ricin," American Association for the Advancement of Science, July 11, 2012, http://membercentral.aaas.org/blogs/scientia/beans-weapon-discovery-and-development-ricin

[190] "A Shadow Over the Olympics," Newsweek, May 5, 1996, http://www.newsweek.com/shadow-over-olympics-178358

[191] Hooker, Edmond, "Biological Warfare," December 30, 2014, http://www.emedicinehealth.com/biological_warfare/page3_em.htm

[192] "A Shadow Over the Olympics," Newsweek, May 5, 1996, http://www.newsweek.com/shadow-over-olympics-178358

[193] Vick, Karl, "Plea Bargain Rejected in Bubonic Plague Case," The Washington Post, April 3, 1996, https://www.washingtonpost.com/archive/politics/1996/04/03/plea-bargain-rejected-in-bubonic-plague-case/e5c9150c-1b68-467e-a57c-db88c0e8d0e4/, p. A8

[194] Cole, Leonard A., "Bioterrorism: Still a Threat to the United States," Combating Terrorism Center, January 18, 2012, https://www.ctc.usma.edu/posts/bioterrorism-still-a-threat-to-the-united-states

[195] Warrick, Joby, "FBI Investigation of 2001 Anthrax Attacks Concluded; U.S. Releases Details," The Washington Post, February 20, 2010, http://www.washingtonpost.com/wp-dyn/content/article/2010/02/19/AR2010021902369.html

[196] Ibid.

[197] Hooker, Edmond, "Biological Warfare," December 30, 2014, http://www.emedicinehealth.com/biological_warfare/page3_em.htm

[198] Warrick, Joby, "FBI Investigation of 2001 Anthrax Attacks Concluded; U.S. Releases Details," The Washington Post, February 20, 2010, http://www.washingtonpost.com/wp-dyn/content/article/2010/02/19/AR2010021902369.html

[199] Pearce, Matt, "Mississippi Taekwondo Teacher Charged With a Ricin Plot - Again," Los Angeles Times, November 21, 2013, http://articles.latimes.com/2013/nov/21/nation/la-na-nn-mississippi-ricin-20131121

[200] "Infectious Diseases Still Major Public Health Threat, Fauci Says," Science Daily, March 29, 2005, http://www.sciencedaily.com/releases/2005/03/050325150035.htm

[201] "CDC and Zoonotic Disease," CDC, January 22, 2015, http://www.cdc.gov/24-7/cdcfastfacts/zoonotic.html

[202] "Antibiotic Resistance Threats in the United States, 2013," CDC, http://www.cdc.gov/drugresistance/threat-report-2013/pdf/ar-threats-2013-508.pdf

[203] "WHO: Sexually-transmitted Superbug Could Be Major Crisis," CNN, June 6, 2012, http://thechart.blogs.cnn.com/2012/06/06/who-sexually-transmitted-superbug-could-be-major-crisis/

[204] "Antibiotic Resistance Threats in the United States, 2013," CDC, http://www.cdc.gov/drugresistance/threat-report-2013/pdf/ar-threats-2013-508.pdf

[205] "The Stand Miniseries," Wikipedia, Accessed May 12, 2015, http://en.wikipedia.org/wiki/The_Stand_(miniseries)

[206] "The Stand," IMDB, http://www.imdb.com/title/tt0108941/synopsis

[207] Young, A. & Penzenstadler, N., "Inside America's Secretive Biolabs," USA Today, May 28, 2015, http://www.usatoday.com/story/news/2015/05/28/biolabs-pathogens-location-incidents/26587505/

[208] Harmon, Katherine, "Nearly 400 Accidents with Dangerous Pathogens and Biotoxins Reported in U.S. Labs over 7 Years," Scientific American, October 3, 2011, http://blogs.scientificamerican.com/observations/2011/10/03/nearly-400-accidents-with-dangerous-pathogens-and-bio-toxins-reported-in-u-s-labs-over-seven-years/

[209] Young, A. & Penzenstadler, N., "Inside America's Secretive Biolabs," USA Today, May 28, 2015, http://www.usatoday.com/story/news/2015/05/28/biolabs-pathogens-location-incidents/26587505/

[210] "What Is Brucellosis," Healthline, July 25, 2012, http://www.healthline.com/health/brucellosis

[211] "Brucellosis Diseases and Conditions," Mayo Clinic, January 2, 2014, http://www.mayoclinic.org/diseases-conditions/brucellosis/basics/symptoms/con-20028263

[212] Merler S., Ajelli M., Fumanelli L., & Vespignani A., "Containing the Accidental Laboratory Escape of Potential Pandemic Influenza Viruses," BMC Medicine, November 28, 2013, http://www.biomedcentral.com/content/pdf/1741-7015-11-252.pdf, p. 9

[213] "Testimony Before the Subcommittee on Oversight and Investigations, Committee on Energy and Commerce, House of Representatives, Statement of Keith Rhodes, Chief Technologist," GAO Report GAO-08-108T, October 4, 2007, http://www.gao.gov/new.items/d08108t.pdf

[214] Young, Alison, "Airflow Problems Plague CDC Bioterror Lab," USA Today, June 12, 2012, http://usatoday30.usatoday.com/news/nation/story/2012-06-13/cdc-bioterror-lab/55557704/1?AID=10709313

[215] Stone, Judy, "Pentagon Now Admits It Shipped Live Anthrax to All States, Nine Countries," Forbes, September 3, 2015, http://www.forbes.com/sites/judystone/2015/09/03/pentagon-now-admits-it-shipped-live-anthrax-to-all-states-nine-countries/

[216] "CDC Investigating Error That Caused Live Anthrax Shipments," Boston Herald, May 28, 2015, http://www.bostonherald.com/news_opinion/national/2015/05/cdc_investigating_error_that_caused_live_anthrax_shipments

[217] "Pentagon: Military Mistakenly Shipped Live Anthrax Samples," *Boston Herald,* May 27, 2015, http://www.bostonherald.com/news_opinion/national/2015/05/pentagon_military_mistakenly_shipped_live_anthrax_samples

[218] Roos, Robert, "More Voices Call for Action on Lab Biosafety," *CIDRAP News,* July 31, 2014, http://www.cidrap.umn.edu/news-perspective/2014/07/more-voices-call-action-lab-biosafety

[219] Aegerter, G. & Fox, M., "CDC Reports Possible Ebola Exposure at Containment Lab," *NBC News,* December 24, 2014, http://www.nbcnews.com/storyline/ebola-virus-outbreak/cdc-reports-possible-ebola-exposure-containment-lab-n274561

[220] "Updated Anthrax Guidelines", Accessed April 29, 2016, http://www.cleaningpro.com/ANTHRAX.cfm

[221] "Anthrax, Then and Now", April 10, 2007, http://www.medicinenet.com/script/main/art.asp?articlekey=18812&pf=2

[222] "Anthrax Scare: CDC Lab Didn't Heed Its Own Lessons," *NBC News,* June 29 2014, http://www.nbcnews.com/health/health-news/anthrax-scare-cdc-lab-didnt-heed-its-own-lessons-n143736

[223] *Ibid.*

[224] Sample, Ian, "Revealed: 100 Safety Breaches at UK Labs Handling Potentially Deadly Diseases," *The UK Guardian,* December 14, 2014, http://www.theguardian.com/science/2014/dec/04/-sp-100-safety-breaches-uk-labs-potentially-deadly-diseases

[225] Canby, Thomas Y., "The Anasazi - Riddles in the Ruins," 1982, Norwell Public Schools, http://www.norwellschools.org/cms/lib02/MA01001453/Centricity/Domain/192/The%20Anasazi.pdf

[226] Akbar, Arifa, "Mao's Great Leap Forward 'Killed 45 Million in Four Years'," *The UK Independent,* September 17, 2010, http://www.independent.co.uk/arts-entertainment/books/news/maos-great-leap-forward-killed-45-million-in-four-years-2081630.html

[227] Becker, Jasper, Hungry Ghosts: Mao's Secret Famine. New York: Holt Paperbacks, 1998, pp. 137-138

[228] Applebaum, Anne, "When China Starved," *The Washington Post,* August 12, 2008, http://www.washingtonpost.com/wp-dyn/content/article/2008/08/11/AR2008081102015.html

[229] Lim, Louisa, "A Grim Chronicle of China's Great Famine," *NPR,* November 10, 2012, http://www.npr.org/2012/11/10/164732497/a-grim-chronicle-of-chinas-great-famine

[230] O'Grada, Cormac, "Carleton & Others on Famine's Darkest Secret," August 2012, Presentation at the Carleton Summer School, Clogher, County Tyrone, Ireland, http://www.williamcarletonsociety.org/pdfsanddocs/talkssourefiles/Carleton_Famine.docx

[231] 'Dowd, Niall, "Cannibalism Was Likely Practiced in Irish Famine Says Leading Expert," *Irish Central,* May 15, 2012, http://www.irishcentral.com/news/cannibalism-was-likely-practiced-in-irish-famine-says-leading-expert-151504185-237447661.html

[232] Graves, Ralph, "Fearful Famines of the Past," *National Geographic*, July 1917, p. 89

[233] Montefiore, Simon Sebag, "Holocaust By Hunger: The Truth Behind Stalin's Great Famine," *UK Daily Mail,* July 25, 2008, http://www.dailymail.co.uk/news/article-1038774/Holocaust-hunger-The-truth-Stalins-Great-Famine.html

[234] Montefiore, Simon Sebag, *Stalin: The Court of the Red Tsar,* Weidenfeld and Nicolson, 2003, p. 82

[235] Montefiore, Simon Sebag, "Holocaust By Hunger: The Truth Behind Stalin's Great Famine," *UK Daily Mail,* July 25, 2008, http://www.dailymail.co.uk/news/article-1038774/Holocaust-hunger-The-truth-Stalins-Great-Famine.html

[236] *Ibid.*

[237] "Photograph Analysis of Iconic "Vulture Stalking a Child," February 22, 2012, The Animal Rescue Blog, https://theanimalrescueblog.wordpress.com/2012/02/22/photograph-analysis/

[238] *Ibid.*

[239] "Surviving the Dust Bowl," *PBS,* November 15, 2009, http://www.pbs.org/wgbh/americanexperience/features/general-article/dustbowl-drought/

[240] Burnett, John, "How One Drought Changed Texas Agriculture Forever," *NPR,* July 7, 2012, http://www.npr.org/2012/07/07/155995881/how-one-drought-changed-texas-agriculture-forever

[241] Unger, David J., "'Billion-dollar Weather': The 10 Most Expensive US Natural Disasters," *Christian Science Monitor,* June 27, 2013, http://www.csmonitor.com/Environment/2013/0627/Billion-dollar-weather-The-10-most-expensive-US-natural-disasters/Drought-and-heat-wave-1988-78.8-billion

[242] "Drought 2005," NOAA, August 3, 2009, http://www.srh.noaa.gov/shv/?n=drought_2005

[243] McRoberts, B. & Nielsen-Gammon, J., "An Assessment of the Meteorological Severity of the 2008-09 Texas Drought Through July 2009," Texas A&M University, August 12, 2009, http://climatexas.tamu.edu/files/osc_pubs/august_2009_drought.pdf, p. 4

[244] *Ibid.*, p. 2

[245] "Wichita Falls Makes Texas History with 100th Triple-Digit Day," *Inside Climate News,* http://insideclimatenews.org/content/wichita-falls-makes-texas-history-100th-triple-digit-day

[246] "Everything You Need to Know About the Texas Drought," *State Impact/NPR,* https://stateimpact.npr.org/texas/tag/drought/

[247] Anderson, D., Welch, J.M. & Robinson, J., "Agricultural Impacts of Texas's Driest Year on Record," *Choices,* 3rd Quarter, 2012, http://www.choicesmagazine.org/choices-magazine/theme-articles/what-happens-when-the-well-goes-dry-and-other-agricultural-disasters/agricultural-impacts-of-texass-driest-year-on-record

[248] *Ibid.*

[249] Henry, Terrence, "The Drought Killed Texas Trees, But Not How You Might Think," *State Impact/NPR,* July 23, 2012, https://stateimpact.npr.org/texas/2012/07/23/the-drought-killed-texas-trees-but-not-how-you-might-think

[250] Morgan, Tyne, "Texas Drought Takes Toll on Cattle - and Ranchers," AgWeb, June 7, 2013, http://www.agweb.com/article/texas_drought_takes_toll_on_cattle_and_ranchers/

[251] Vaughn, Daniel, "The End of Cheap Beef," *Texas Monthly,* January 6, 2015, http://www.tmbbq.com/the-end-of-cheap-beef/

[252] "California Drought Is the Most Severe in at Least 1,200 Years," *ZME Science,* December 5, 2014, http://www.zmescience.com/ecology/environmental-issues/california-drought-tree-ring-05122014/

[253] Morath, Eric, "Attention Shoppers: Fruit and Vegetable Prices Are Rising," *Wall Street Journal*, April 15, 2014, http://blogs.wsj.com/economics/2014/04/15/attention-shoppers-fruit-and-vegetable-prices-rising/

[254] Koba, Mark, "The Consequence of California's Severe Drought: Higher Wine Prices," *Fortune,* February 3, 2015, http://fortune.com/2015/02/03/the-consequence-of-californias-severe-drought-higher-wine-prices/

[255] "Farm Income and Wealth Statistics," USDA Economic Research Service, 2014, http://www.ers.usda.gov/faqs.aspx

[256] "California Agricultural Statistics 2013 Crop Year," USDA, April 2015, http://www.nass.usda.gov/ca

[257] "California Drought: Farm and Food Impacts," USDA, July 23, 2015, http://www.ers.usda.gov/topics/in-the-news/california-drought-farm-and-food-impacts/california-drought-crop-sectors.aspx

[258] "California Agricultural Statistics 2013 Crop Year," USDA, April 2015, http://www.nass.usda.gov/Statistics_by_State/California/Publications/California_Ag_Statistics/Reports/2013cas-all.pdf

[259] Smith, Scott, "California Farmers Told to Stop Irrigating Seek Court Order," *Yahoo News,* June 18, 2015, http://news.yahoo.com/california-farmers-told-stop-irrigating-seek-court-order-014947919.html

[260] Boxall, Bettina, "Overpumping of Central Valley Groundwater Creating a Crisis, Experts Say," *Los Angeles Times,* March 18, 2015, http://www.latimes.com/local/california/la-me-groundwater-20150318-story.html

[261] Dimick, Dennis, "If You Think the Water Crisis Can't Get Worse, Wait Until the Aquifers Are Drained," *National Geographic,* August 21, 2014, http://news.nationalgeographic.com/news/2014/08/140819-groundwater-california-drought-aquifers-hidden-crisis/

[262] Collman, Ashley, "The Grass IS Greener in Hollywood: Aerial Photos Expose How Stars Like Kim K, J.Lo and Streisand Are Wasting Water to Keep Their Gardens Lush Despite State's Worst Drought in History," *The Daily Mail,* May 10, 2015, http://www.dailymail.co.uk/news/article-3075906/What-drought-Aerial-photos-expose-Kim-Kardashian-Jennifer-Lopez-Barbra-Streisand-greedy-celebrities-wasting-water-lush-lawns-green-midst-California-s-worst-drought-history.html

[263] Borchers, J.W. & Carpenter, M., "Land Subsidence from Groundwater Use in California," Luhdorff & Scalmanini Consulting Engineers, April 2014, http://www.waterplan.water.ca.gov/docs/cwpu2013/Final/vol4/groundwater/13Land_Subsidence_Groundwater_Use.pdf

[264] Farr, T. G., Jones, C. & Liu, Z., "NASA: California Drought Causing Valley Land to Sink," NASA/JPL, August 19, 2015, http://www.jpl.nasa.gov/news/news.php?feature=4693

[265] Starr, Steven, "Costs and Consequences of the Fukushima Daiichi Disaster," Physicians for Social Responsibility, http://www.psr.org/environment-and-health/environmental-health-policy-institute/responses/costs-and-consequences-of-fukushima.html

[266] Gundersen, Arnie, "On the Road Again...Japan Speaking Tour Series No. 1," Fairwinds, February 12, 2016, http://www.fairewinds.org/podcast//on-the-road-againjapan-speaking-tour-series-no-1

[267] "Fukushima and Nuclear Issues," Arnie Gundersen interviewed by Linda Moulton Howe on *Coast To Coast AM,* March 31, 2016, http://www.coasttocoastam.com/show/2016/03/31

[268] Gundersen, Arnie, "On the Road Again...Japan Speaking Tour Series No. 1," Fairwinds, February 12, 2016, http://www.fairewinds.org/podcast//on-the-road-againjapan-speaking-tour-series-no-1

[269] Pacchioli, David, "Radioisotopes in the Ocean," WHOI, May 1, 2013, http://www.whoi.edu/oceanus/feature/radioisotopes-in-the-ocean

[270] Valentine, Katie, "In the Midst of Its Worst Drought In 50 Years, Brazil Hit By Deadly Flooding," *Think Progress,* December 11, 2013, http://thinkprogress.org/climate/2013/12/11/3047731/brazil-flooding-drought/

[271] Entis, Laura, "Will the Worst Bird Flu Outbreak in US History Finally Make Us Reconsider Factory Farming Chicken," *UK Guardian,* July 14, 2015, http://www.theguardian.com/vital-signs/2015/jul/14/bird-flu-devastation-highlights-unsustainability-of-commercial-chicken-farming

[272] Ferdman, Roberto A., "Egg Rationing in America Has Officially Begun," *The Washington Post,* June 5, 2015, http://www.washingtonpost.com/news/wonkblog/wp/2015/06/05/the-largest-grocer-in-the-texas-is-now-rationing-eggs/

[273] Demick, Barbara, "China Looks Abroad for Greener Pastures," *Los Angeles Times,* March 20, 2014, http://www.latimes.com/world/asia/la-fg-china-foreign-farmland-20140329-story.html

[274] Boehler, Patrick, "China's Next Food Scandal: Honey Laundering," *South China Morning Post,* June 19, 2013, http://www.scmp.com/news/china/article/1264335/chinas-next-food-scandal-honey-laundering

[275] Watts, Jonathan, "Exploding Watermelons Put Spotlight on Chinese Farming Practices," *UK Guardian,* May 17, 2011, http://www.theguardian.com/world/2011/may/17/exploding-watermelons-chinese-farming, 2011

[276] Davison, Nicola, "Rivers of Blood: The Dead Pigs Rotting in China's Water Supply," *UK Guardian,* March 29, 2013, http://www.theguardian.com/world/2013/mar/29/dead-pigs-china-water-supply

[277] "China Milk Scandal: Families of Sick Children Fight to Find Out True Scale of the Problem," *UK Telegraph,* December 3, 2008, http://www.telegraph.co.uk/news/worldnews/asia/china/3545733/China-milk-scandal-Families-of-sick-children-fight-to-find-out-true-scale-of-the-problem.html

[278] Hauter, Wenonah, "A Decade of Dangerous Food Imports from China," *Food & Water Watch,* June 10, 2011, http://www.foodandwaterwatch.org/blogs/a-decade-of-dangerous-food-imports-from-china/

[279] Palmer, Doug, "U.S. Approves Purchase of Smithfield," *Politico,* September 6, 2013, http://www.politico.com/story/2013/09/us-china-smithfield-096399

[280] Rakestraw, Darcey, "Outsourcing Our Meat to China," *Food & Water Watch,* September 24, 2013, http://www.foodandwaterwatch.org/pressreleases/outsourcing-our-meat-to-china/

[281] Demick, Barbara, "China Looks Abroad for Greener Pastures," *Los Angeles Times,* March 20, 2014, http://www.latimes.com/world/asia/la-fg-china-foreign-farmland-20140329-story.html

[282] "Chinese River Choked With Pig Carcasses," *CBS News,* March 11, 2013, http://www.cbsnews.com/news/chinese-river-choked-with-pig-carcasses/

[283] Doherty, Dermot, "China's Unsafe Water Is Nestle's Opportunity," *Bloomberg,* January 24, 2013, http://www.bloomberg.com/bw/articles/2013-01-24/chinas-unsafe-water-is-nestl-s-opportunity

[284] "Chinese Tainted Baby Milk Activist Won't Appeal Against Sentence," *UK Guardian,* November 22, 2010, http://www.theguardian.com/world/2010/nov/22/chinese-babymilk-activist-drops-appeal

[285] Ma, D. & Adams, W., "If You Think China's Air Is Bad..." *New York Times*, November 7, 2013, http://www.nytimes.com/2013/11/08/opinion/if-you-think-chinas-air-is-bad.html

[286] Doherty, Dermot, "China's Unsafe Water Is Nestle's Opportunity," *Bloomberg,* January 24, 2013, http://www.bloomberg.com/bw/articles/2013-01-24/chinas-unsafe-water-is-nestl-s-opportunity

[287] "Where Do They Get Bottled Water," Street Directory, 2007, http://www.streetdirectory.com/food_editorials/beverages/beverages/where_do_they_get_bottled_water.html

[288] Brodwin, Erin, "People Are Furious That Nestle Is Still Bottling and Selling California's Water in the Middle of the Drought," *Business Insider,* April 10, 2015, http://www.businessinsider.com/nestle-is-bottling-water-from-california-2015-4

[289] Holt, Steve, "Here's Why Foreign Investors Are Trying to Buy American Farmland," *Yahoo News,* February 12, 2014, http://news.yahoo.com/39-why-foreign-investors-trying-buy-american-farmland-214444600.html

[290] Demick, Barbara, "China Looks Abroad for Greener Pastures, *Los Angeles Times,* March 29, 2014, http://www.latimes.com/world/asia/la-fg-china-foreign-farmland-20140329-story.html

[291] "Change in Number of Farms: 2007 to 2012," USDA, National Agricultural Statistics Service, 12-M002, http://www.agcensus.usda.gov/Publications/2012/Online_Resources/Ag_Atlas_Maps/Farms/Number/12-M002-RGBDot2-largetext.pdf

[292] Deyo, Holly, <u>Garden Gold</u>, Pueblo West: Deyo Enterprises, 2012, p. 126

[293] "Rural Property Set for Strong Spring Sales," Real Estate Conversation, September 25, 2015, http://www.therealestateconversation.com.au/2015/09/25/rural-property-set-strong-spring-sales/1443148135

[294] "Foreign Investors on Hunt for Aussie Farms," *Sunday Night Channel 7,* July 5, 2015, https://au.news.yahoo.com/sunday-night/a/28634435/foreign-investors-on-hunt-for-aussie-farms/

[295] Robertson, Joshua, "Beef, Big Bucks and Buy-Ups: Are Chinese Investors Changing the Face of Australia," *UK Guardian,* August 6, 2015, http://www.theguardian.com/australia-news/2015/aug/06/beef-big-bucks-and-buy-ups-are-chinese-investors-changing-the-face-of-australia

[296] "Foreign Investors on Hunt for Aussie Farms, July 5, 2015, *Sunday Night Channel 7, Yahoo News,* https://au.news.yahoo.com/sunday-night/a/28634435/foreign-investors-on-hunt-for-aussie-farms/

[297] Verdin, Mike, "China Makes Another Cattle Ranch Purchase in Australia," *Agrimoney,* September 15, 2015, http://www.agrimoney.com/news/china-makes-another-cattle-ranch-purchase-in-australia--8773.html

[298] Van Trump, Kevin, "China Buying a Large Number of Australian Cattle Farms," *The Van Trump Report,* May 20, 2015, http://vantrumpreport.com/china-buying-a-large-number-of-australian-cattle-farms

[299] Winters, Julia, "Restrictions on Foreign Ownership of Agricultural Land in Canada," Gowling WLG, March 1, 2014, https://gowlingwlg.com/en/canada/insights-resources/restrictions-on-foreign-ownership-of-agricultural-land-in-canada

[300] "Our North, Our Future: White Paper on Developing Northern Australia," Australian Government, June 2015, http://apo.org.au/files/Resource/northern_australia_white_paper.pdf, p. 40

[301] "California's Central Valley," USGS, Accessed July 27, 2015, http://ca.water.usgs.gov/projects/central-valley/about-central-valley.html

[302] "China Spends $125 Billion Per Year on Riot Gear and 'Stability Maintenance'," *Business Insider,* May 19, 2015, http://www.businessinsider.com/china-now-spends-125-billion-per-year-on-riot-gear-and-stability-maintenance-2013-5

[303] Sims R., Schaeffer, R., Creutzig, F., Cruz-Nunez, X., D'Agosto, M., Dimitriu, D., & Fulton, L. ..., "Climate Change 2014: Mitigation of Climate Change," Intergovernmental Panel on Climate Change, http://www.ipcc.ch/report/ar5/wg3/, p. 616

[304] "Biofuels – At What Cost? A Review of Costs and Benefits of EU Biofuel Policies," International Institute for Sustainable Development, April 2013, http://www.iisd.org/gsi/sites/default/files/biofuels_subsidies_eu_review.pdf, p. 85

[305] Albino, D.K., Bertrand, K.Z. & Bar-Yam, Y, "Food for Fuel: The Price of Ethanol," New England Complex Systems Institute, October 4, 2012, http://necsi.edu/research/social/foodprices/foodforfuel/, p. 2

[306] Wisner, Robert, "Ethanol Usage Projections & Corn Balance Sheet," Iowa State University, October 13, 2015, https://www.extension.iastate.edu/agdm/crops/outlook/cornbalancesheet.pdf

[307] Berazneva, J. & Lee, D.R., "Explaining the African Food Riots of 2007-2008: An Empirical Analysis," Cornell University, March 2011, http://www.csae.ox.ac.uk/conferences/2011-edia/papers/711-berazneva.pdf

[308] "Farmer Suicides in India," National Crime Records Bureau, 2011, http://ncrb.nic.in/CD-ADSI2011/suicides-11.pdf

[309] "Mexicans Stage Tortilla Protest," *BBC,* February 1, 2007, http://news.bbc.co.uk/2/hi/6319093.stm

[310] Forbinake, Nkendem, "Cameroon: Over 1600 Arrests So Far," *All Africa,* March 7, 2008, http://allafrica.com/stories/200803070387.html

[311] "Anti-government Rioting Spreads in Cameroon," *New York Times,* February 27, 2008, http://www.nytimes.com/2008/02/27/world/africa/27iht-27cameroon.10504780.html

[312] Ryan, Orla, "Food Riots Grip Haiti," *The UK Guardian,* April 9, 2008, http://www.theguardian.com/world/2008/apr/09/11

[313] Mafrtono, Hindra, "What Was It Like to Be a Victim of the May 1998 Riots in Indonesia," *Slate,* February 4, 2014, http://www.slate.com/blogs/quora/2014/02/04/what_was_it_like_to_be_a_victim_of_the_may_1998_riots_in_indonesia.html

[314] *Ibid.*

[315] "Looters Take Advantage of New Orleans Mess," August 30, 2005, *NBC News,* http://www.nbcnews.com/id/9131493/ns/us_news-katrina_the_long_road_back/t/looters-take-advantage-new-orleans-mess/

[316] Miller, Alan John, "The Jesus Cult," Alan John Miller, Accessed March 15, 2016, http://www.aj-miller.com/

[317] Zarrella, J. & Oppmann, P., "Pastor with 666 Tattoo Claims to be Divine," *CNN,* February 19, 2007, http://www.cnn.com/2007/US/02/16/miami.preacher/index.html

[318] "Who is Jose Luis de Jesus Miranda? Is Jose Luis de Jesus Miranda the Antichrist?" Got Questions, http://www.gotquestions.org/Jose-Luis-Jesus-Miranda.html

[319] Malm, Sara, "Man Who Thinks He's Jesus... Along with Hundreds of Young Women Who Follow Him Across the World," *UK Daily Mail,* January 7, 2014, http://www.dailymail.co.uk/news/article-2535168/Man-thinks-hes-Jesus-hundreds-young-women-follow-world.html

[320] Obscura, Atlas, "Reincarnated Jesus' Secluded Siberian Sect," *Slate,* July 16, 2013, http://www.slate.com/blogs/atlas_obscura/2013/07/16/russian_cult_may_be_the_largest_religious_reservation_in_the_world.html

[321] Nemtsova, Anna, "The Vissarion Christ: Inside Russia's End-Times Cults, *Newsweek,* December 17, 1012, http://www.newsweek.com/vissarion-christ-inside-russias-end-times-cults-63607

[322] "Lord Our Righteousness Church," *Wikipedia,* Accessed March 15, 2016, https://en.wikipedia.org/wiki/Lord_Our_Righteousness_Church

[323] "NM Judge Wants to Cut Sex-Offense Sentence for Cult Leader Wayne Bent," *Albuquerque Journal,* January 5, 2016, http://www.abqjournal.com/701338/news/judge-wants-to-cut-sentence-for-cult-leader-wayne-bent.html

[324] Zaimov, Stoyan, "South African Man Claims He Is Jesus Christ; Believes He Is Immortal," *Christian Post,* June 6, 2013, http://www.christianpost.com/news/south-african-man-claims-he-is-jesus-christ-believes-he-is-immortal-97435/

[325] "South African Man Claims to Be Jesus," *NewsBite,* May 15, 2013, http://newsbite.it/index-id-weird+news-zk-15908.html

[326] Campbell, Andy, "Jett Simmons McBride Claimed to Be Jesus, Attacked Driver, Thwarted By Hitchhiker with Hatchet: Cops," *Huffington Post,* February 4, 2013, http://www.huffingtonpost.com/2013/02/04/jett-simmons-mcbride-jesus-hatchet-bear-hug_n_2616737.html

[327] Lesley, Alison, "Maitreya the World Teacher, the 'Second Coming,' Is on His Way, Evangelist Benjamin Creme Claims," *World Religion News,* June 17, 2015, http://www.worldreligionnews.com/?p=15001

[328] "Oral Sex, Orgies at Hedonism II, Guest Tells Travel Site," *Jamaica Observer,* March 8, 2010, http://www.jamaicaobserver.com/news/zein-issa_7469471

[329] Fox, Sandra Diamond, "Is Today's Society Too Self-Centered?" *News-Times,* Danbury, CT, January 9, 2012, http://www.newstimes.com/news/article/Is-today-s-society-too-self-centered-2450413.php

[330] "Bernard Madoff," *Wikipedia,* Accessed March 15, 2016, https://en.wikipedia.org/wiki/Bernard_Madoff

[331] Ford, Dana, "Florida Man Found Guilty of Wife's Murder After Posting Photo on Facebook," *CNN,* November 26, 2015, http://www.cnn.com/2015/11/25/us/florida-facebook-murder-guilty/

[332] Dougherty, Steve, "Facebook and Twitter Threat to Marriages: Social Media Now a Factor in One in Seven Divorces," *UK Daily Mail,* April 29, 2015, http://www.dailymail.co.uk/news/article-3061616/Facebook-Twitter-factor-one-seven-divorces.html/

[333] "Australian Singer Tina Arena Speaks Frankly About Youth and the Obsession with the Selfie Culture," August 29, 2015, News, Ltd, http://www.news.com.au/entertainment/music/australian-singer-tina-arena-speaks-frankly-about-youth-and-the-obsession-with-the-selfie-culture/story-e6frfn09-1227502883447

[334] "Preliminary Semiannual Uniform Crime Report, January to June, 2014-2015," FBI, https://www.fbi.gov/about-us/cjis/ucr/crime-in-the-u.s/2015/preliminary-semiannual-uniform-crime-report-januaryjune-2015/tables/table-1

[335] "Violent Crime Survey - Totals," Major Cities Chiefs Association, Q1 2016, https://assets.documentcloud.org/documents/2832727/MCCA-Violent-Crime-Data-1st-Quarter-2016-2015.pdf

[336] Reutter, Mark, "Baltimore Shootings Are Up 82.5%, or Nearly Double From Last Year," *Baltimore Brew,* June 31, 2015, https://baltimorebrew.com/2015/06/01/baltimore-shootings-are-up-82-5-or-nearly-double-from-last-year/

[337] Madhani, Aamer, "Murders, Shootings on the Rise in Chicago," *USA Today,* April 2, 2015, http://www.usatoday.com/story/news/2015/04/01/chicago-murders-shootings/70787110/

[338] Winton, R. & Poston, B., "LAPD Struggles with Spike in Violent Crime, Shootings," *Los Angeles Times,* March 24, 2015, http://www.latimes.com/local/lanow/la-me-ln-lapd-struggles-with-jump-in-violent-crime-20150324-story.html

[339] MacDonald, Heather, "The New Nationwide Crime Wave," *The Wall Street Journal,* May 29, 2015, http://www.wsj.com/articles/the-new-nationwide-crime-wave-1432938425

[340] *Ibid.*

[341] Pavlich, Katie, "Crime Wave: Murders Skyrocket Across the Country in St. Louis, Milwaukee, Chicago, Atlanta, New York City," *Townhall,* June 3, 2015, http://townhall.com/tipsheet/katiepavlich/2015/06/03/crime-wave-murders-skyrocket-across-the-country-in-st-louis-chicago-new-york-city-n2007487

[342] Siegel, Josh, "What Rising Murder Rates in US Cities Mean for 2016," *Daily Signal,* January 4, 2016, http://dailysignal.com/2016/01/04/what-rising-murder-rates-in-us-cities-means-for-2016/

[343] Kern, Soeren, "Germany: Migrant Crime Wave, Police Capitulate," Gatestone Institute, October 11, 2015, http://www.gatestoneinstitute.org/6668/germany-migrant-crime-wave

[344] *Ibid.*

[345] *Ibid.*

[346] *Ibid.*

[347] Zumwalt, James, "Sweden Opened Its Doors to Muslim Immigration, Today It's the Rape Capital of the West. Japan Didn't," *Daily Caller,* October 23, 2015, http://dailycaller.com/2015/10/23/sweden-opened-its-doors-to-muslim-immigration-today-its-the-rape-capital-of-the-west-japan-didnt/

[348] Hohmann, Leo, "We Will Cut the Heads Off Unbelieving Dogs Even in Europe." *WND,* October 26, 2015, http://www.wnd.com/2015/10/islamic-invasion-pulls-trigger-europeans-scramble-for-guns/

[349] *Ibid.*

[350] "Commission Proposals to Strengthen Control of Firearms: Questions & Answers," European Commission, November 18, 2015, http://europa.eu/rapid/press-release_MEMO-15-6111_en.htm

[351] "Saudi Arabian-led Intervention in Yemen," Wikipedia, Accessed March 19, 2016, https://en.wikipedia.org/wiki/Saudi_Arabian-led_intervention_in_Yemen

[352] Berstein, Lenny, "The Heroin Epidemic's Toll: One County, 70 Minutes, Eight Overdoses," *The Washington Post,* August 3, 2015, http://www.washingtonpost.com/national/health-science/the-heroin-epidemics-toll-one-county-70-minutes-eight-overdoses/2015/08/23/f616215e-48bc-11e5-846d-02792f854297_story.html

[353] Johnson, Kevin, "Heroin 'Apocalypse' Shadows New Hampshire Primary, *USA Today,* February 8, 2016, http://www.usatoday.com/story/news/politics/elections/2016/02/08/heroin-new-hampshire-primary/79720402/

[354] "Drug Facts: Nationwide Trends," National Institute on Drug Abuse, June 2015, Accessed March 20, 2016, https://www.drugabuse.gov/publications/drugfacts/nationwide-trends

[355] "World Drug Report," UNODC, 2015, https://www.unodc.org/documents/wdr2015/World_Drug_Report_2015.pdf, p. 42

[356] Vicens, AJ, "A Drug Warrior's Inside Look at the War on Afghanistan's Heroin Trade," *Mother Jones,* January 12, 2015, http://www.motherjones.com/politics/2015/01/ed-follis-dea-afghanistan-opium

[357] "Breaking Bad Blamed for Shocking Rise in Crystal Meth Usage," *UK Telegraph,* November 3, 2014, http://www.telegraph.co.uk/news/uknews/crime/11206140/Breaking-Bad-blamed-for-shocking-rise-in-crystal-meth-usage.html

[358] "Statistics: Worldwide," American Foundation for AIDS Research, Accessed February 29, 2016, http://www.amfar.org/worldwide-aids-stats/

[359] Parry, Lizzie, "New Aggressive Strain of HIV Can Progress to AIDS in Just Three Years, Scientists Warn, *UK Daily Mail,* February 15, 2015, http://www.dailymail.co.uk/health/article-2955486/New-aggressive-strain-HIV-progress-AIDS-just-three-years-scientists-warn.html

[360] Dalli, Kim, "We Work Hard to Dispel HIV Myths Such as the Virgin Cure," *Times of Malta,* August 18, 2012, http://www.timesofmalta.com/articles/view/20120818/local/-We-work-hard-to-dispel-HIV-myths-such-as-the-virgin-cure-.433297

[361] Flanagan, Jane, "South African Men Rape Babies as 'Cure' for AIDS," *UK Telegraph,* November 11, 2001, http://www.telegraph.co.uk/news/worldnews/africaandindianocean/southafrica/1362134/South-African-men-rape-babies-as-cure-for-Aids.html

[362] "Diagnoses of HIV Infection, by Transmission Category," CDC, November 2015, http://www.cdc.gov/hiv/statistics/overview/

[363] "Obama: We Are 5 Days From Fundamentally Transforming America," YouTube Video uploaded February 2, 1012, https://www.youtube.com/watch?v=oKxDdxzX0kI

[364] "Halper, Daniel, "Obama in 2004: 'I Don't Think Marriage Is a Civil Right'," *The Weekly Standard,* May 8, 2012, http://www.weeklystandard.com/blogs/obama-2004-i-dont-think-marriage-civil-right_644238.html

[365] Baim, Tracy, "Obama Seeks U.S. Senate Seat," *Windy City Times,* Chicago, February 4, 2004, http://www.windycitymediagroup.com/gay/lesbian/news/ARTICLE.php?AID=3931

[366] "Timeline of Obama's 'Evolving' on Same-Sex Marriage," *ABC News,* May 9, 2012, http://abcnews.go.com/blogs/politics/2012/05/timeline-of-obamas-evolving-on-same-sex-marriage/

[367] Sullivan, Andrew, "Andrew Sullivan on Barack Obama's Gay Marriage Evolution," *Newsweek,* May 13, 2012, http://www.newsweek.com/andrew-sullivan-barack-obamas-gay-marriage-evolution-65067

[368] *Ibid.*

[369] "Saddleback Presidential Candidates Forum," *CNN,* August 17, 2008, http://www.cnn.com/TRANSCRIPTS/0808/17/se.01.html

[370] "Mears, Bill, "Obama Views on Same-Sex Marriage Reflect Societal Shifts," *CNN,* March 3, 2013, http://www.cnn.com/2013/03/22/politics/court-same-sex-obama/

[371] Dwyer, Devin, "Timeline of Obama's 'Evolving' on Same-Sex Marriage," *ABC News,* May 9, 2012, http://abcnews.go.com/blogs/politics/2012/05/timeline-of-obamas-evolving-on-same-sex-marriage/

[372] Goldman, R. & Khan, H., "Obama Hails Victories of Lame Duck; Has 'Evolving Feelings' on Gay Marriage," *ABC News,* December 22, 2010, http://abcnews.go.com/Politics/hours-repealing-ban-gays-troops-obama-mulls-sex/story?id=12459702

[373] Dwyer, Devin, "Timeline of Obama's 'Evolving' on Same-Sex Marriage," *ABC News,* May 9, 2012, http://abcnews.go.com/blogs/politics/2012/05/timeline-of-obamas-evolving-on-same-sex-marriage/

[374] *Ibid.*

[375] Kurtz, Howard, "How President Obama, in Six Days, Decided to Come Out for Gay Marriage," *The Daily Beast,* May 10, 2012, http://www.thedailybeast.com/articles/2012/05/10/how-president-obama-in-six-days-decided-to-come-out-for-gay-marriage.html

[376] *Ibid.*

[377] Tashman, Brian, "Religious Right Slams Obama for Backing Marriage Equality," *Right Wing Watch,* May 9, 2012, http://www.rightwingwatch.org/content/religious-right-slams-obama-backing-marriage-equality

[378] *Ibid.*

[379] Boren, Zachary Davies, "Same-Sex Marriage: American Samoa May Be the Only Territory in the US Where the Historic Supreme Court Ruling Does Not Apply," *UK Independent,* July 10, 2015, http://www.independent.co.uk/news/world/americas/same-sex-marriage-american-samoa-may-be-the-only-territory-in-the-us-where-the-historic-supreme-10379804.html

[380] "Obergefell Et Al. v. Hodges, Director, Ohio Department of Health, Et All," October Term, 2014, Opinion June 26, 2015, p. 6, http://www.supremecourt.gov/opinions/14pdf/14-556_3204.pdf

[381] *Ibid.*, p. 5

[382] *Ibid.*, pp. 1-2

[383] *Ibid.*, p. 27

[384] *Ibid.*, p.101

[385] Somanader, Tanya, "Live Updates on #LoveWins: The Supreme Court Rules that Gay and Lesbian Couples Can Marry," The White House Blog, June 26, 2015, https://www.whitehouse.gov/blog/2015/06/26/live-updates-lovewins-supreme-court-rules-gay-and-lesbian-couples-can-marry-0

[386] Volokh, Eugene, "What Percentage of the U.S. Population Is Gay, Lesbian or Bisexual?" *The Washington Post,* July 15, 2014, http://www.washingtonpost.com/news/volokh-conspiracy/wp/2014/07/15/what-percentage-of-the-u-s-population-is-gay-lesbian-or-bisexual/

[387] Winter, Deena, "Nebraska School Suggests Teachers Avoid Calling Students Boys or Girls to Be 'Gender Inclusive'," Nebraska Watchdog, October 2, 2014, http://watchdog.org/174768/gender-inclusive/

[388] Payne, Ed, "Transgender First-Grader Wins the Right to Use Girls' Restroom," *CNN,* June 24, 2013, http://www.cnn.com/2013/06/24/us/colorado-transgender-girl-school/

[389] Tomlin, Gregory, "Open the Polygamous Gates: Montana Man Files for Marriage License to Second Wife, Cites #SCOTUS Same-Sex Ruling," *Christian Examiner,* July 2, 2015, http://www.christianexaminer.com/article/open.the.gates.montana.man.files.for.marriage.license.to.second.wife/49194.htm

[390] Charlton, Corey, "They Look Like a New Boy Band... But It's the World's First THREE-WAY Same-Sex Marriage: Gay Thai Men Tie the Knot in 'Fairytale Ceremony'," *UK Daily Mail,* February 27, 2015, http://www.dailymail.co.uk/news/article-2972542/They-look-like-new-boy-band-s-world-s-THREE-WAY-sex-marriage-Gay-Thai-men-tie-knot-fairytale-ceremony.html

[391] Newsome, Jude, "May Their Love Never Be Brought Down: A Woman Marries the Berlin Wall," *Ranker,* http://www.ranker.com/list/13-people-who-married-inanimate-objects/jude-newsome?format=SLIDESHOW&page=2

[392] Snow, K. & Brady, J., "Woman Proves Love for Eiffel Tower With Commitment Ceremony," *ABC News,* April 8, 2009, http://abcnews.go.com/GMA/story?id=7283494&page=1&singlePage=true

[393] Dugdale, Addy, "Technosexual: One Man's Tale of Robot Love," *Gizmodo,* March 25, 2008, http://gizmodo.com/367698/technosexual-one-mans-tale-of-robot-love

[394] *Ibid.*

[395] Beck, Julie, "Married to a Doll: Why One Man Advocates Synthetic Love," *The Atlantic,* September 6, 2013, http://www.theatlantic.com/health/archive/2013/09/married-to-a-doll-why-one-man-advocates-synthetic-love/279361/

[396] Beck, Julie, "Cure for Love: Fall for a Robot to Fend Off Heartache," *New Scientist,* February 14, 2014, https://www.newscientist.com/article/mg22129564.800-cure-for-love-fall-for-a-robot-to-fend-off-heartache/

[397] Phillips, Tom, "Man Marries Pillow," *UK Metro,* March 9, 2010, http://metro.co.uk/2010/03/09/man-marries-pillow-154906/

[398] Lim, John, "5 Bizarre Marriages Around Asia That Includes a Man Marrying a Pillow," *Says,* July 1, 2015, http://says.com/my/fun/bizzarre-marriages-in-asia

[399] "I, Robot, Now Pronounce You Man and Wife," *CBS News,* May 16, 2010, http://www.cbsnews.com/news/i-robot-now-pronounce-you-man-and-wife/

[400] Spindell, Mike, "Robot Love," *Jonathan Turley,* January 14, 2012, https://jonathanturley.org/2012/01/14/robot-love/

[401] Bogage, Jacob, "Companies Celebrate the Supreme Court's Same-Sex Marriage Ruling," *The Washington Post,* June 26, 2015, http://www.washingtonpost.com/blogs/wonkblog/wp/2015/06/26/companies-celebrate-the-supreme-courts-same-sex-marriage-ruling/

[402] Sanders, Catherine, "The Hidden Traps of Wicca," Focus on the Family, http://www.focusonthefamily.com/parenting/teens/hidden-traps-of-wicca

[403] Kosmin, B.A. & Keysar, A., "American Religious Identification Survey ARIS 2008," Trinity College, March 2009, http://commons.trincoll.edu/aris/files/2011/08/ARIS_Report_2008.pdf, p. 5

[404] Grossman, Cathy Lynn, "Pagans Wonder 'Witch' Way for the Next Generation as New Age Trend Ages," *Religion News Service,* August 1, 2014, http://www.religionnews.com/2014/08/01/pagan-wiccan-witch-religion/

[405] Brooks Alexander, "Witchcraft Goes Mainstream: Uncovering Its Alarming Impact on You and Your Family," Irvine: 2004, p. 50

406 "TV Shows Fuel Children's Interest in Witchcraft," *Annanova*, August 4, 2000, http://web.archive.org/web/20010406234209/http://ananova.com/entertainment/story/television_children-entertainment-religion-paganism_926320.html

407 The Pagan Federation, Accessed April 30, 3016, http://www.paganfed.org/

408 White, Hillary, "Under Influence of Harry Potter, Kids are Being Drawn into the "Language and Mechanics" of Occult," *Life Site News*, July 24, 2008, https://www.lifesitenews.com/news/under-influence-of-harry-potter-kids-are-being-drawn-into-the-language-and-

409 "Harry Potter Finale Sales Hit 11M," *BBC*, July 23, 2007, http://news.bbc.co.uk/2/hi/entertainment/6912529.stm

410 Brown, Celia, "Beyond Words: The Magic of the Harry Potter Brand," *Forbes*, October 31, 2014, http://www.forbes.com/sites/sap/2014/10/31/beyond-words-the-magic-of-the-harry-potter-brand/

411 "Author Contends Harry Potter Fuels Wiccan Growth Among Teens and that Witchcraft 'Spells Trouble' for Society," *Christian News Wire,* June 25, 2007, http://www.christiannewswire.com/news/208233477.html

412 "What Readers Think About 'Goblet'," *San Francisco Chronicle,* July 26, 2000, http://www.sfgate.com/books/article/What-Readers-Think-About-Goblet-2712173.php

413 *Ibid.*

414 Total Twilight Franchise Sales / Revenue, Statistic Brain, January 12, 2015, http://www.statisticbrain.com/total-twilight-franchise-sales-revenue/

415 "Profile - Stephenie Meyer: The Million-Dollar Vampire Mom," *The UK Telegraph,* November 27, 2008, http://www.telegraph.co.uk/news/worldnews/northamerica/usa/3531403/Profile-Stephanie-Meyer-the-million-dollar-vampire-mom.html

416 "Count von Count," Wikipedia, Accessed April 16, 2016, http://en.wikipedia.org/wiki/Count_von_Count

417 Witch/Pagan Web Sites: Main Index, http://www.witchvox.com/xlx.html

418 "Lackland Trainees Spellbound by Wiccan Faith Service at Base," KENS 5, San Antonio, November 24, 2013, http://www.kens5.com/story/news/local/2014/06/24/10303168/

419 *Ibid.*

420 *Ibid.*

421 *Ibid.*

422 *Ibid.*

423 Willis, Jennifer, "The Plight of Pagans in the Military," *Religion & Politics,* June 20, 2012, http://religionandpolitics.org/2012/06/20/the-plight-of-pagans-in-the-military/

424 *Ibid.*

425 Rosin, Hanna, "Wiccan Controversy Tests Military Religious Tolerance," *The Washington Post*, June 8, 1999, http://www.washingtonpost.com/wp-srv/national/daily/june99/wicca08.htm

426 Schulz, Cara, "Recovery & Healing for Military Pagans at Ft. Hood Open Circle," April 10, 2014, http://wildhunt.org/2014/04/recovery-healing-for-military-pagans-at-ft-hood-open-circle.html

427 Rosin, Hanna, "Wiccan Controversy Tests Military Religious Tolerance," *The Washington Post*, June 8, 1999, http://www.washingtonpost.com/wp-srv/national/daily/june99/wicca08.htm

428 Deam, Jenny, "Air Force Academy Adapts to Pagans, Druids, Witches and Wiccans," *Los Angeles Times,* November 26, 2011, http://articles.latimes.com/2011/nov/26/nation/la-na-air-force-pagans-20111127

429 Smith, Hayden, "Pagans and Witches Serving in the British Military," *UK Metro,* March 28, 2014, http://metro.co.uk/2014/03/28/pagans-and-witches-serving-in-the-british-military-4681211/

430 "Annual Halloween Expenditure in the United States from 2006 to 2014 (in Billion U.S. Dollars)," Accessed April 30, 2016, http://www.statista.com/statistics/275726/annual-halloween-expenditure-in-the-united-states/

431 Shaw, Hollie, "The $1-Billion Fright Economy: How Canadians Are Now Outspending Americans on Halloween," *Financial Post,* October 25, 2014, http://business.financialpost.com/news/retail-marketing/the-1-billion-fright-economy-how-canadians-are-now-outspending-americans-on-halloween

432 David, Curry, "Pray for Them: Christian Persecution at 'Biblical Proportions," *Fox News,* November 14, 2014, http://www.foxnews.com/opinion/2014/11/14/pray-for-them-christian-persecution-at-biblical-proportions/

433 Wooding, Dan, "Church History Timeline," *Christianity,* Accessed April 30, 2015, http://www.christianity.com/church/church-history/timeline/1901-2000/modern-persecution-11630665.html

434 Grimaldi, John, "Christian Persecution on the Rise Around the World, Says AMAC", Association of Mature American Citizens, April 30, 2015, http://amac.us/christian-persecution-on-the-rise-around-the-world-says-amac/

435 Blair, Leonardo, "Man Allegedly Urinates on, Crashes into Oklahoma's Controversial Ten Commandments Monument; Says Devil Made Him Do It," *Christian Post,* October 27, 2014, http://www.christianpost.com/news/man-allegedly-urinates-on-crashes-into-oklahomas-controversial-ten-commandments-monument-says-devil-made-him-do-it-128717/

436 "Naughty or Nice," American Family Association, December 13, 2011, Accessed April 30, 2015, http://web.archive.org/web/20120112113028/http://action.afa.net/item.aspx?id=2147486887

437 "Woman Claims "Merry Christmas" Got Her Fired," *NBC News,* December 23, 2008, http://www.nbcnews.com/id/28370145/ns/us_news-life/t/woman-claims-merry-christmas-got-her-fired/

[438] Huff, Richard, "NBC Apologizes for Cutting 'One Nation Under God' from Pledge of Allegiance During US Open Telecast," *NY Daily News,* June 20, 2011, http://www.foxnews.com/opinion/2015/01/08/nbc-omits-god-from-pledge-allegiance-again/

[439] Starnes, Todd, "NBC Left Out God From the Pledge of Allegiance... Again," *Fox News,* January 8, 2015, http://www.foxnews.com/opinion/2015/01/08/nbc-omits-god-from-pledge-allegiance-again/

[440] "Remove 'Under God'" from the U.S. Pledge of Allegiance," *Change,* https://www.change.org/p/remove-under-god-from-the-u-s-pledge-of-allegiance

[441] Ohlheiser, Abby, "Why President Obama Didn't Say 'Under God' While Reading the Gettysburg Address," *The Atlantic,* November 19, 2013, http://news.yahoo.com/why-president-obama-didnt-under-god-while-reading-191035734.html

[442] Klukowski, Ken, "Pentagon May Court Martial Soldiers Who Share Christian Faith," *Breitbart,* May 1, 2013, http://www.breitbart.com/national-security/2013/05/01/breaking-pentagon-confirms-will-court-martial-soldiers-who-share-christian-faith/

[443] Wilkins, Brett, "Oklahoma Teen Gage Pulliam Under Fire for Effort to Remove Ten Commandments from Muldrow High School," *Moral Low Ground,* May 13, 2013, http://morallowground.com/2013/05/13/oklahoma-teen-gage-pulliam-under-fire-for-effort-to-remove-ten-commandments-from-muldrow-high-school/

[444] *Ibid.*

[445] Wilkins, Brett, "Breathitt County Kentucky Removes Ten Commandments from Schools after FFRF Complaint," Moral Low Ground, April 13, 2013, http://morallowground.com/2013/04/13/breathitt-county-kentucky-removes-ten-commandments-from-schools-after-ffrf-complaint/

[446] Gryboski, Michael, "Atheist Group Demands Ten Commandments Display Be Removed From Pennsylvania School Grounds," *Christian Post,* June 11, 2014, http://www.christianpost.com/news/atheist-group-demands-ten-commandments-display-be-removed-from-pennsylvania-school-grounds-121344/

[447] Croft, Shelby, "10 Commandments Plaque Won't Return to Marion High School," WBNS-10TV, Columbus, OH; March 17, 2015, http://www.10tv.com/content/stories/2015/03/17/marion-high-school-10-commandments-plaque-decision.html

[448] Gibbs, Douglas V, "Shutting Down Christianity One Commandment at a Time," *Conservative Crusader,* May 5, 2012, http://www.conservativecrusader.com/articles/shutting-down-christianity-one-commandment-at-a-time

[449] "Tennessee: 5 Pillars of Islam Replace 10 Commandments in Public School, Tolerance Reigns Supreme," *Bradley County News,* August 9, 2013, https://bradleycountynews.wordpress.com/2013/08/09/tennessee-5-pillars-of-islam-replace-10-commandments-in-public-school-tolerance-reigns-supreme/

[450] Hallowell, Billy, "Atheists Demand NC Town Remove Ten Commandments From Town Hall, *The Blaze,* February 9, 2012, http://www.theblaze.com/stories/2012/02/09/atheists-demand-nc-town-remove-ten-commandments-from-town-hall/

[451] "Freedom From Religion Foundation," Wikipedia, Accessed July 13, 2015, http://en.wikipedia.org/wiki/Freedom_From_Religion_Foundation

[452] "Judge: Remove 10 Commandments from City Hall," *CBN,* August 12, 2014, http://www.cbn.com/cbnnews/us/2014/August/Judge-Remove-10-Commandments-from-City-Hall/

[453] "'Satan' Made Oklahoma Man Urinate on and Smash Ten Commandments Statue at State Capitol," *If You Only News,* October 28, 2014, http://www.ifyouonlynews.com/politics/satan-made-oklahoma-man-urinate-on-and-smash-ten-commandments-statue-at-state-capitol/

[454] Green, Rick, "Workers Remove Ten Commandments from Oklahoma Capitol Grounds," *The Oklahoman,* October 5, 2015, http://newsok.com/workers-remove-ten-commandments-from-oklahoma-capitol-grounds/article/5451584

[455] Hallowell, Billy, "'The Storm Is Coming': Famed Preacher Reveals the One Thing Obama Is Doing That He Believes Will Lead to Christian Persecution in America," *The Blaze,* March 3, 2015, http://www.theblaze.com/stories/2015/03/03/the-storm-is-coming-famed-preacher-reveals-the-one-thing-obama-is-doing-that-he-believes-will-lead-to-christian-persecution-in-america/

[456] Hitchens, Christopher, "Jefferson Versus the Muslim Pirates America's First Confrontation with the Islamic World Helped Forge a New Nation's Character," *City Journal,* Spring 2007, http://www.city-journal.org/html/17_2_urbanities-thomas_jefferson.html

[457] Thor, Brad, *"The Last Patriot,"* New York: Simon and Schuster, July 1, 2008, p. 82

[458] "Obama: We Are No Longer a Christian Nation," Video uploaded March 9, 2008, Accessed May 5, 2015, http://www.youtube.com/watch?v=tmC3IevZiik

[459] Remarks from President Obama, "Joint Press Availability With President Obama and President Gul of Turkey," The White House, April 6, 2009, https://www.whitehouse.gov/the_press_office/Joint-Press-Availability-With-President-Obama-And-President-Gul-Of-Turkey/

[460] "Remarks by the President in Closing of the Summit on Countering Violent Extremism," Office of the Press Secretary, February 18, 2015, https://www.whitehouse.gov/the-press-office/2015/02/18/remarks-president-closing-summit-countering-violent-extremism

[461] Shapiro, Ben, "Obama: Islam 'Woven into the Fabric of Our Country Since Founding'," *Breitbart,* February 20, 2015, http://www.breitbart.com/big-government/2015/02/20/obama-islamc-woven-into-the-fabric-of-our-country-since-founding/

[462] Chapman, Michael W., "Rev. Graham: 'This Country Was Built on Christian Principles' Not Islam," *CNS News,* January 20, 2015, http://cnsnews.com/blog/michael-w-chapman/rev-graham-country-was-built-christian-principles-not-islam

[463] Carter, Joe, "9 Things You Should Know About the 9/11 Attack Aftermath," *The Gospel Coalition,* September 10, 2013, http://www.thegospelcoalition.org/article/9-things-you-should-know-about-the-911-attack-aftermath

[464] Shukman, David, "Toxic Dust Legacy of 9/11 Plagues Thousands of People," *BBC,* September 1, 2011, http://www.bbc.com/news/world-us-canada-14738140

[465] Grohol, John M., "The Lingering Mental Health Effects of 9/11," *Psych Central,* September 9, 2012, http://psychcentral.com/blog/archives/2012/09/11/the-lingering-mental-health-effects-of-911/

[466] "Aftermath of the September 11 Attacks," Wikipedia, Accessed May 31, 2015, http://en.wikipedia.org/wiki/Aftermath_of_the_September_11_attacks

[467] Grabianowski, Ed, "What Was the Economic Impact of September 11" http://money.howstuffworks.com/september-11-economic-impact.htm

[468] "Aftermath of the September 11 Attacks," Wikipedia, Accessed May 31, 2015, http://en.wikipedia.org/wiki/Aftermath_of_the_September_11_attacks

[469] Grabianowski, Ed, "What Was the Economic Impact of September 11" http://money.howstuffworks.com/september-11-economic-impact.htm

[470] *Ibid.*

[471] *Ibid.*

[472] Londono, Ernesto, "Study: Iraq, Afghan War Costs to Top $4 Trillion," *The Washington Post,* March 28, 2013, http://www.washingtonpost.com/world/national-security/study-iraq-afghan-war-costs-to-top-4-trillion/2013/03/28/b82a5dce-97ed-11e2-814b-063623d80a60_story.html

[473] Kurman, Charles, "Terrorism Cases Involving Muslim-Amercans, 2014, Triangle Center on Terrorism and Homeland Security, Department of Sociology, University of North Carolina, http://sites.duke.edu/tcths/files/2013/06/Kurzman_Terrorism_Cases_Involving_Muslim-Americans_2014.pdf

[474] Prothero, Stephen, "How 9/11 Changed Religion in America," *USA Today,* September 10, 2011, http://usatoday30.usatoday.com/news/opinion/forum/story/2011-09-10/911-religion-islam-christianity/50354708/1

[475] Hoar, Jennifer, "Poll: Sinking Perceptions Of Islam," *CBS News,* April 12, 2006, http://www.cbsnews.com/news/poll-sinking-perceptions-of-islam

[476] Prothero, Stephen, "How 9/11 Changed Religion in America," *USA Today,* September 10, 2011, http://usatoday30.usatoday.com/news/opinion/forum/story/2011-09-10/911-religion-islam-christianity/50354708/1

[477] Kaleem, Jaweed, "More Than Half of Americans Have Unfavorable View of Islam, Poll Finds," *The Huffington Post,* April 10, 2015, http://www.huffingtonpost.com/2015/04/10/americans-islam-poll_n_7036574.html

[478] Chapman, Michael W., "Rev. Graham:'This Country Was Built on Christian Principles' Not Islam," *CNS News,* January 20, 2015, http://cnsnews.com/blog/michael-w-chapman/rev-graham-country-was-built-christian-principles-not-islam

[479] Bell, Stewart, "Outspoken Peshdary Was Swept Up During Project Samossa, But Not Charged," *Ottawa Citizen,* February 3, 2015, http://ottawacitizen.com/news/local-news/outspoken-peshdary-was-swept-up-during-project-samossa-but-not-charged

[480] Fatima, S. & Freeze, C., "Canada Trying to Deport Man Accused Plotting Terror Attack on Toronto," *The Globe and Mail,* March 11, 2015, http://www.theglobeandmail.com/news/national/man-plotted-terror-attack-on-toronto-financial-district-tribunal-told/article23403130/

[481] Bell, Stewart, "ISIS Takes Credit for Inspiring Terrorist Attacks That Killed Two Canadian Soldiers," *National Post,* November 21, 2014, http://news.nationalpost.com/news/canada/isis-takes-credit-for-inspiring-terrorist-attacks-that-killed-two-canadian-soldiers

[482] *Ibid.*

[483] "Canada Day Bomb Plot Suspects Were Kicked Out of Surrey Mosque," *Huffington Post,* July 3, 2013, http://www.huffingtonpost.ca/2013/07/03/john-nuttall-neighbour-amanda-korody_n_3538800.html

[484] Bell, Stewart, "Chiheb Esseghaier, Accused in Via Terror Plot, Considered Triggering Volcano in Northern U.S.," *National Post,* February 17, 2015, http://news.nationalpost.com/news/chiheb-esseghaier-accused-in-via-terror-plot-considered-triggering-volcano-in-northern-u-s

[485] Parry, Tom, "Al-Qaeda Affiliates Attracting Canadians, CSIS Head Says," *CBC News,* February 11, 2013, http://www.cbc.ca/news/politics/al-qaeda-affiliates-attracting-canadians-csis-head-says-1.1334343

[486] "New Charges Laid In Ottawa Terrorism Case," *Huffington Post,* September 17, 2014, http://www.huffingtonpost.ca/2012/05/16/project-samossa-ottawa-terrorism-case_n_1522925.html

[487] Press, Jordan, "Convicted Terrorist Khawaja Will Present Appeal to Supreme Court," *National Post,* June 30, 2011, http://news.nationalpost.com/news/canada/convicted-terrorist-khawaja-will-present-appeal-to-supreme-court

[488] "2006 Ontario Terrorism Plot," Wikipedia, Accessed June 3, 2015, http://en.wikipedia.org/wiki/2006_Ontario_terrorism_plot

[489] "Toronto 18: Key Events in the Case," *CBC News,* June 4, 2008, http://www.cbc.ca/news/canada/toronto-18-key-events-in-the-case-1.715266

[490] Bell, Stewart, "Man Admits to Plotting Attack," *The Windsor Star,* September 24, 2009, http://www2.canada.com/windsorstar/news/story.html?id=38d02f2f-5cee-49d6-9acb-5712c51224da

[491] "Timeline: Australia's Terror Threat," BBC, April 20, 2015, http://www.bbc.com/news/world-australia-30474414

[492] Cooper, Adam, "Terror Accused Wrote Death Plans Hours Before Raid, Court Told," *The Age,* May 26, 2015, http://www.theage.com.au/victoria/terror-accused-wrote-death-plans-hours-before-raid-court-told-20150526-gh9vdz.html

[493] "Sydney Terror Raid: Two Men Arrested, Hunting Knife And Flag Seized," *UK Daily Telegraph,* April 11, 2015, http://www.dailytelegraph.com.au/news/nsw/sydney-terror-raid-two-men-arrested-hunting-knife-and-flag-seized/story-fni0cx12-1227215449716

[494] "Timeline: Australia's Terror Threat," *BBC,* April 20, 2015, http://www.bbc.com/news/world-australia-30474414

[495] Johnston, C., Siddique, H., & Davidson, H., "Melbourne Teenager Shot Dead After Stabbing Two Police Officers," *BBC,* September 24, 2014, http://www.theguardian.com/world/2014/sep/24/melbourne-teenager-shot-dead-after-stabbing-two-police-officers

[496] "2014 Endeavour Hills Stabbings," Wikipedia, Accessed June 3, 2015, http://en.wikipedia.org/wiki/2014_Endeavour_Hills_stabbings

[497] "Australian ISIS Supporters Planned to Behead Randomly Selected Civilian to 'Shock, Horrify' Public: Officials," *New York Daily News,* September 17, 2014, http://www.nydailynews.com/news/world/australia-prime-minister-tony-abbott-knowledge-attack-led-counterterrorism-raids-article-1.1943735

[498] "Muslims Who Fled Civil War in Somalia and Lebanon and Got Asylum in Australia Sentenced for Plotting Jihad Murder at Army Base," *Jihad Watch,* December 16, 2011, http://www.jihadwatch.org/2011/12/muslims-who-fled-civil-war-in-somalia-and-lebanon-and-got-asylum-in-australia-sentenced-for-plotting

[499] Hansen, Jane, "Former Taliban Fighter Joseph 'Jihad Jack' Thomas Says Australian Muslims Should Take Back Islam from ISIS Extremists", *Daily Telegraph,* October 5, 2014, http://www.dailytelegraph.com.au/news/nsw/former-taliban-fighter-joseph-jihad-jack-thomas-says-australian-muslims-should-take-back-islam-from-isis-extremists/story-fni0cx12-1227079199555

[500] "Australia's Home-Grown Muslim Terrorists," *Australian News Commentary,* http://australian-news.net/articles/view.php?id=237

[501] "Who is Willie Brigitte?" *News Limited,* March 16, 2007, http://www.news.com.au/national/who-is-willie-brigitte/story-e6frfkw9-1111113165106

[502] "Terror Plotter Willie Brigitte Held After Raids in France," *The Australian,* April 1, 2012, http://www.theaustralian.com.au/news/world/terror-plotter-willie-brigitte-held-after-raids-in-france/story-e6frg6so-1226315576390

[503] "Terrorism in Australia," Wikipedia, Accessed June 10, 2015, http://en.wikipedia.org/wiki/Terrorism_in_Australia

[504] Schachtel, Jordan, "Revealed: Names of Seven American Muslim Leaders at White House 'Anti-Muslim Bigotry' Meeting," *Breitbart,* February 5, 2015, http://www.breitbart.com/national-security/2015/02/05/revealed-names-of-four-american-muslim-leaders-at-white-house-anti-muslim-bigotry-meeting/

[505] Twitter account of Hoda Hawa Elshishtawy, February 5, 2015, Accessed June 5, 2015, https://twitter.com/usislam/status/563435703317835777

[506] Elshishtawy, Hoda, "Meeting the President to Expand Muslim Civic Participation," Muslim Public Affairs Council, February 4, 2015, http://www.mpac.org/blog/meeting-the-president-to-expand-muslim-civic-participation.php

[507] Jackson, Kevin, "Devout Muslims in Key Positions in the White House," *The Black Sphere,* April 2013, http://theblacksphere.net/2013/04/devout-muslims-in-key-positions-in-the-white-house/

[508] Poole, Patrick, "Obama's Shariah Czar Mohamed Magid Hands Diversity Award to Jew-hater Dawud Walid," *PJ Media,* July 5, 2012, http://pjmedia.com/tatler/2012/07/05/obamas-shariah-czar-mohamed-magid-hands-diversity-award-to-jew-hater-dawud-walid/

[509] Warikoo, Niraj, "Muslim-American Leaders Meet with Obama at White House," *Detroit Free Press,* February 5, 2015, http://www.freep.com/story/news/local/michigan/2015/02/05/muslim-american-leaders-meet-obama-white-house/22919455/

[510] "America's Changing Religious Landscape," Pew Research, May 12, 2015, http://www.pewforum.org/2015/05/12/americas-changing-religious-landscape/

[511] Burke, Daniel, "The World's Fastest-Growing Religion Is...," *CNN,* April 3, 2015, http://www.cnn.com/2015/04/02/living/pew-study-religion/

[512] Romani, Rebecca, "Latino Family Reflects on Conversion to Islam," KPBS San Diego, CA, September 7, 2011, http://www.kpbs.org/news/2011/sep/07/latino-family-reflects-conversion-islam/

[513] "Christian Girl Given Zeroes for Her Beliefs," *WND,* May 4, 2015, http://www.wnd.com/2015/05/christian-girl-given-zero-grades-for-her-beliefs/

[514] Harrington, Elizabeth, "Feds Will Regulate Christmas Lights," *Washington Free Beacon,* May 5, 2015, http://freebeacon.com/issues/feds-will-regulate-christmas-lights/

[515] "Student Punished for Saying "God Bless America," *Christian Today,* February 12, 2015, http://www.christiantoday.com/article/student.punished.for.saying.god.bless.america/48018.htm

[516] Sims, Cliff, "N.J. Teacher Fired After Giving Student Bible Eager to Teach Again After Government Ruling," *New Jersey On-Line,* January 7, 2015, http://www.nj.com/warrenreporter/index.ssf/2015/01/bible_teacher_new_jersey_eeoc.html

[517] Cummins, Emily, "Perpetually Offended Atheist Group Targeted Alabama Town for Second Time – It Backfired," *Yellowhammer News,* December 7, 2014, http://yellowhammernews.com/faithandculture/perpetually-offended-atheist-group-targets-alabama-town-second-time-backfires/

[518] "Obama's 2014 White House Christmas Card Makes No Mention of Christmas," *The Right Pundit,* http://www.hapblog.com/2014/12/photos-obamas-2014-white-house.html

[519] Scarry, Eddie, "This Is the 2013 White House Holiday Card," *The Blaze,* December 9, 2013, http://www.theblaze.com/blog/2013/12/09/this-is-the-2013-white-house-holiday-card/

[520] Rao, Mallika, "2012 White House Christmas Card By Iowa Artist Features Bo and No Christmas Tree," *The Huffington Post,* December 7, 2012, http://www.huffingtonpost.com/2012/12/07/white-house-christmas-card-2012_n_2258812.html

[521] "White House Christmas Card 2011: As Usual, Not a Person in Sight," *The Washington Post,* http://www.washingtonpost.com/blogs/reliable-source/post/white-house-christmas-card-2011-as-usual-not-a-person-in-sight/2011/12/15/gIQAFBrlwO_blog.html

[522] "A Bo Type of Christmas," *History Is Elementary,* December 22, 2010, http://historyiselementary.blogspot.com/2010/12/bo-type-of-christmas.html

[523] O'Connor, Maureen, "Obama's Christmas Tree a Gay Communist Hotbed," *Gawker,* December 23, 2009, http://gawker.com/5432674/obamas-christmas-tree-a-gay-communist-hotbe

[524] Cummins, Emily, "Perpetually Offended Atheist Group Targeted Alabama Town for Second Time – It Backfired," *Yellowhammer News,* December 7, 2014, http://yellowhammernews.com/faithandculture/perpetually-offended-atheist-group-targets-alabama-town-second-time-backfires/

[525] West, Allen, "Openly Gay Houston Mayor Demands Pastors Turn Over Sermons," Allen B. West, October 15, 2014, http://allenbwest.com/2014/10/christian-persecution-us-openly-gay-houston-mayor-demands-pastors-turn-sermons/

[526] Smith, Peter Jesserer, "Christian Club Banned at Long Island Public School," *National Catholic Register,* October 9, 2014, http://www.ncregister.com/daily-news/christian-club-banned-at-long-island-public-school/

[527] Starnes, Todd, "College Orders Student to 'Dumb Down' Religious Show," *Fox News Radio,* October 4, 2014, http://www.foxnews.com/opinion/2014/10/04/college-orders-student-to-dumb-down-religious-show/

[528] Marsh, Kristine, "No 'Sectarian Materials' Allowed: California School Bans Christian Books from Library," *Newsbusters,* September 23, 2014, http://newsbusters.org/blogs/kristine-marsh/2014/09/23/school-bans-christian-books-library

[529] Wolken, Dan, "Arkansas State Removing Cross Decal From Football Helmets," *USA Today,* September 10, 2014, http://www.usatoday.com/story/sports/ncaaf/2014/09/10/arkansas-state-removes-memorial-crosses-from-helmets/15402697/

[530] West, Allen, "High School Student Barred from Mentioning Jesus in Graduation Speech," Allen B. West, June 17, 2014, http://allenbwest.com/2014/06/u-s-war-christians-high-school-student-barred-mentioning-jesus-graduation-speech/

[531] Seman, Sarah Jean, "Townhall, Other Conservative Sites Blocked at CT High School," *Townhall,* June 18, 2014, http://townhall.com/tipsheet/sarahjeanseman/2014/06/18/connecticut-high-school-allegedly-blocking-conservatives-sites-n1853037

[532] Starnes, Todd, "Atheists Strong Arm Wrestling Team over Bible Verse," *Fox News Radio,* April 22, 2014, http://radio.foxnews.com/toddstarnes/top-stories/atheists-strong-arm-wrestling-team-over-bible-verse.html

[533] Hopkins, K. & Oglesby, A., "N.J. School District Sued Over 'Under God' in Pledge," *USA Today,* April 21, 2014, http://www.usatoday.com/story/news/nation/2014/04/21/nj-school-district-sued-pledge-under-god/7982825/

[534] Christie, Joel, "Parents Outrage as 'Teacher Bans Little Girl, 5, from Praying Before She Eats Her Lunch at School'," *UK Daily Mail,* March 29, 2014, http://www.dailymail.co.uk/news/article-2592287/Parents-outrage-teacher-bans-little-girl-5-PRAYING-eats-lunch-school.html

[535] Starnes, Todd, "Georgia School Confiscates Christmas Cards," *Fox News Radio,* December 3, 2013, http://radio.foxnews.com/toddstarnes/top-stories/georgia-school-confiscates-christmas-cards.html

[536] Todd Starnes, "DOJ Defunds At-Risk Youth Programs over 'God' Reference," *Townhall*, June 25, 2013, http://townhall.com/columnists/toddstarnes/2013/06/25/doj-defunds-atrisk-youth-programs-over-god-reference-n1627526/page/full

[537] Ertelt, Steven, "Obama Admin's HHS Mandate Revision Likely Excludes Hobby Lobby," *Life News,* February 1, 2013, http://www.lifenews.com/2013/02/01/obama-admins-hhs-mandate-revision-excludes-hobby-lobby/

[538] Carmon, Irin, "Supreme Court rules for Hobby Lobby in Contraception Case," MSNBC, June 30, 2014, http://www.msnbc.com/msnbc/hobby-lobby-supreme-court-wins-narrow-ruling

[539] Stolberg, Sheryl Gay, "Minister Backs Out of Speech at Inaugural," *New York Times*, January 10, 2013, http://www.nytimes.com/2013/01/11/us/politics/minister-withdraws-from-inaugural-program-after-controversy-over-comments-on-gay-rights.html

[540] Hudson, Audrey, "Obama Administration Religious Service for Student Loan Forgiveness," *Human Events,* February 15, 2012, http://humanevents.com/2012/02/15/obama-administration-deletes-religious-service-for-student-loan-forgiveness/

[541] Clinton, Hillary Rodham, "Remarks in Recognition of International Human Rights Day," U.S. Dept. of State, December 6, 2011, http://m.state.gov/md178368.htm

[542] Starnes, Todd, "Obama Administration Opposes FDR Prayer at WWII Memorial," *Fox News,* November 4, 2011, http://www.foxnews.com/politics/2011/11/04/obama-administration-opposes-fdr-prayer-at-wwii-memorial/

[543] Siegel, Joel, "Obama Omits God From Thanksgiving Speech, Riles Critics," *ABC News,* November 25, 2011, http://abcnews.go.com/Politics/obama-omits-god-thanksgiving-address-riles-critics/story?id=15028644

[544] Donovan, Chuck, "HHS's New Health Guidelines Trample on Conscience," Heritage Foundation, August 2, 2011, http://www.heritage.org/research/reports/2011/08/hhss-new-health-guidelines-trample-on-conscience

[545] Richmond, Todd, "National Day of Prayer 2010: Federal Judge Rules Unconstitutional," *AP,* April 15, 2010, http://www.huffingtonpost.com/2010/04/15/national-day-of-prayer-un_n_539771.html

[546] Treleven, Ed, "Appeals Court Upholds National Day of Prayer, Overturns Judge Crabb's Ruling," *Wisconsin State Journal,* April 15, 2011, http://host.madison.com/news/local/crime_and_courts/appeals-court-upholds-national-day-of-prayer-overturns-judge-crabb/article_634facb2-66be-11e0-97d0-001cc4c002e0.html

[547] Johnson, Chris, "ENDA Passage Effort Renewed With Senate Introduction," *Washington Blade,* April 15, 2011, http://www.washingtonblade.com/2011/04/15/enda-passage-effort-renewed-with-senate-introduction/

[548] Medlin, Marrianne, "Amid Criticism, President Obama Moves to Fill Vacant Religious Ambassador Post," *Catholic News Agency,* February 9, 2011, http://www.catholicnewsagency.com/news/amid-criticism-president-obama-moves-to-fill-vacant-religious-ambassador-post/

[549] "Feds Sued by Veterans to Allow Stolen Mojave Desert Cross to Be Rebuilt," *Red State,* January 14, 2011, http://www.redstate.com/diary/ladyimpactohio/2011/01/14/feds-sued-by-veterans-to-allow-stolen-mojave-desert-cross-to-be-rebuilt/

[550] Klimas, Jacqueline, "U.S. Military 'Hostile' to Christians Under Obama; Morale, Retention Devastated," *The Washington Times,* April 15, 2015, http://www.washingtontimes.com/news/2015/apr/15/us-military-losing-christians-because-of-hostile-c/?page=all

[551] "Military Chaplains Told to Shy from Jesus," *The Washington Times,* December 21, 2005, http://www.washingtontimes.com/news/2005/dec/21/20051221-121224-6972r/?page=all

[552] *Ibid.*

[553] *Ibid.*

[554] "'Open Hostility' to Christians in U.S. Military," *WND,* May 3, 2013, http://www.wnd.com/2013/05/open-hostility-to-christians-in-u-s-military/

[555] *Ibid.*

[556] *Ibid.*

[557] Todd, Starnes, "Chaplain Ordered to Remove Religious Essay From Military Website," *Fox News Radio,* July 24, 2013 http://radio.foxnews.com/toddstarnes/top-stories/chaplain-ordered-to-remove-religious-essay-from-military-website.html

[558] *Ibid.*

[559] "Ron DiCianni Responds to Pentagon Censoring His Work," June 4, 2013, http://www.tapestryproductions.com/blog/rondicianni/rondiciannirespondstopen.php

[560] Haley, Garrett, "'Blessed Are the Peacemakers' Painting Removed from Idaho Air Force Base Following Complaint," *Christian News Network,* June 7, 2013, http://christiannews.net/2013/06/07/blessed-are-the-peacemakers-painting-removed-from-idaho-air-force-base-following-complaint/

[561] "U.S. Troops in Iraq Have Limited Body Armor," *Fox News,* October 24, 2003, http://www.foxnews.com/story/2003/10/24/us-troops-in-iraq-have-limited-body-armor/

[562] Leung, Rebecca, "GIs Lack Armor, Radios, Bullets," *CBS News,* October 31, 2004, http://www.cbsnews.com/news/gis-lack-armor-radios-bullets-31-10-2004/

[563] Tyson, Ann Scott, "Thousands of Army Humvees Lack Armor Upgrade," *The Washington Post,* February 12, 2007, http://www.washingtonpost.com/wp-dyn/content/article/2007/02/11/AR2007021101345.html

[564] Tilghman, Andrew, "Lawmakers Talk Big Cuts for Pentagon Budget," *Military Times,* February 11, 2015, http://www.militarytimes.com/story/military/capitol-hill/2015/02/11/budget-cuts-hearing/23231453/

[565] Simeone, Nick, "Hagel Outlines Budget Reducing Troop Strength, Force Structure," *American Forces Press Service,* February 24, 2014, http://archive.defense.gov/news/newsarticle.aspx?id=121703

[566] "Old Soldiers to Be Called to Action" *Fox News,* June 30, 2004, http://www.foxnews.com/story/2004/06/30/old-soldiers-to-be-called-to-action/

[567] "Repeated Deployments Weigh Heavily on U.S. Troops," *USA Today,* January 12, 2012, http://usatoday30.usatoday.com/news/military/2010-01-12-four-army-war-tours_N.htm

[568] Goodwin, Liz, "Multiple Combat Tours Linked to Mental Strain, Disease," *Yahoo News,* March 13, 2012, http://news.yahoo.com/blogs/lookout/multiple-combat-tours-linked-mental-strain-disease-174554188.html

[569] "One Every 18 Hours: Military Suicide Rate Still High Despite Hard Fight to Stem Deaths," *NBC News,* May 23, 2013, http://usnews.nbcnews.com/_news/2013/05/23/18447439-one-every-18-hours-military-suicide-rate-still-high-despite-hard-fight-to-stem-deaths

[570] Jaff, Alexandra, "Huckabee: Wait Until Obama Is Out of Office Before Joining the Military," *CNN,* April 20, 2015, http://www.cnn.com/2015/04/20/politics/huckabee-obama-administration-hostility-christians/

[571] Woodward, C. & Brown, J., "U.S. Navy Booting Bibles from Base Lodges," *One News Now,* April 12, 2014, http://www.onenewsnow.com/culture/2014/08/12/us-navy-booting-bibles-from-base-lodges

[572] "Report: Bible Controversy at Maxwell AFB," *Christian Fighter Pilot,* March 25, 2014, http://christianfighterpilot.com/blog/2014/03/25/report-bible-controversy-at-maxwell-afb/

[573] Schuster, Shawn, "Air Force Academy Promotes Atheist Event One Week After Forced Removal of Bible Verse," *Gospel Herald,* March 24, 2014, http://www.gospelherald.com/articles/50699/20140324/air-force-academy-promotes-atheist-event-one-week-after-forced-removal-of-bible-verse.htm

[574] "Outrage After US Marine Is Convicted By a Court Martial for Refusing to Remove a Bible Quote from Her Work Station", *UK Daily Mail,* May 27, 2015, http://www.dailymail.co.uk/news/article-3098272/Marine-prosecuted-refusing-remove-bible-verse-computer.html

[575] "Nativity Scenes Removed from Guantanamo Dining Halls After Complaints," *Fox News,* December 19, 2013, http://www.foxnews.com/us/2013/12/19/nativity-scenes-removed-from-guantanamo-dining-halls-after-complaints/

[576] Starnes, Todd, "Does Army Consider Christians, Tea Party, a Terror Threat," *Fox News,* October 23, 2013, http://www.foxnews.com/opinion/2013/10/23/does-army-consider-christians-tea-party-terror-threat/

[577] Starnes, Todd, "Catholic Priests in Military Face Arrest for Celebrating Mass," *Fox News,* October 5, 2013, http://www.foxnews.com/opinion/2013/10/04/catholic-priests-in-military-face-arrest-for-celebrating-mass/

[578] Elliott, Dan, "'So Help Me God' Optional in Air Force Honor Oath," *The Denver Post,* October 25, 2013, http://www.denverpost.com/news/ci_24388146/so-help-me-god-optional-air-force-test

[579] Salazar, Adan, "DoD Training Manual: 'Extremist' Founding Fathers 'Would Not Be Welcome in Today's Military'," *Infowars,* August 24, 2013, http://www.infowars.com/dod-training-manual-suggests-extremist-founding-fathers-would-not-be-welcome-in-todays-military/

[580] Klulowski, Ken, "Christian Airman Punished By Lesbian Commander Faces Possible Court Martial," *Breitbart,* September 6, 2013, http://www.breitbart.com/national-security/2013/09/06/christian-airman-punished-by-lesbian-commander-now-charged-with-crime-for-talking-to-media-court-martial-possible/

[581] "Military Gives Bonuses Only to Same-Sex Couples, *WND,* August 20, 2013, http://www.wnd.com/2013/08/military-gives-bonuses-only-to-same-sex-duos/

[582] Baklinski, Thaddeus, "Air Force Hosts Drag Queen Performance for 'Diversity Day'" *Life Site News,* August 23, 2013, https://www.lifesitenews.com/news/air-force-hosts-drag-queen-performance-for-diversity-day

[583] Groening, Chad, "Attorney Demands Answers for Air National Guard Sergeant Punished for Beliefs," *One News Now,* Monday, July 15, 2013, http://www.onenewsnow.com/culture/2013/07/15/attorney-demands-answers-for-air-national-guard-sergeant-punished-for-beliefs

[584] Starnes, Todd, "Obama 'Strongly Objects' to Religious Liberty Amendment," *Fox News Radio,* June 12, 2013, http://radio.foxnews.com/toddstarnes/top-stories/obama-strongly-objects-to-religious-liberty-amendment.html

[585] Brittingham, Rebecca, "Pentagon Orders the Removal of Air Force Video That Mentions God," *Liberty News,* June 10, 2013, http://libertynews.com/2013/06/pentagon-orders-the-removal-of-air-force-video-that-mentions-god/

[586] Chumley, Cheryl K., "Army Soldier Serves Chick-fil-A at Pro-DOMA Party, Is Punished," *The Washington Times,* June 6, 2013, http://www.washingtontimes.com/news/2013/jun/6/army-soldier-punished-chick-fil-a-pro-doma-party/

[587] Starnes, Todd, "Air Force Officer Told to Remove Bible from Desk," *Fox News Radio,* May 3, 2013, http://radio.foxnews.com/toddstarnes/top-stories/air-force-proselytizing-crosses-the-line.html

[588] Minor, Jack, "Military Warned 'Evangelicals' No. 1 Threat," *WND,* April 5, 2013, http://www.wnd.com/2013/04/military-warned-evangelicals-no-1-threat/

[589] Starnes, Todd, "Pentagon: Religious Proselytizing is Not Permitted," *Fox News Radio,* April 13, 2013, http://radio.foxnews.com/toddstarnes/top-stories/pentagon-religious-proselytizing-is-not-permitted.html

[590] Starnes, Todd, "Obama Calls Conscience Clause for Military Chaplains 'Ill-Advised'," *Fox News Radio,* January 4, 2013, http://radio.foxnews.com/toddstarnes/top-stories/obama-calls-conscience-clause-for-military-chaplains-ill-advised.html

[591] Jordan, Bryant, "DoD Yanks Consent for Military Seals on Bibles," *Military,* June 14, 2012, http://www.military.com/daily-news/2012/06/14/dod-yanks-consent-for-military-seals-on-bibles.html

[592] Blackwell, Ken, "Gen. Boykin Blocked at West Point," *CNS News,* February 1, 2012, http://cnsnews.com/node/508665

[593] Duell, Mark, "'It Sets a Dangerous Precedent': Fury as Air Force Removes God from Logo After Atheists Complain," *UK Daily Mail,* February 8, 2012, http://www.dailymail.co.uk/news/article-2098236/Rep-Randy-Forbes-shocked-U-S-Air-Force-removes-GOD-logo-atheists-complain.html

[594] Ertelt, Steven, "'Obama Admin Silenced Catholic Army Chaplain on New Mandate," *Life News,* February 7, 2012, http://www.lifenews.com/2012/02/07/obama-admin-silenced-catholic-army-chaplain-on-new-mandate/

[595] Roeder, Tom, "AFA Backs Away From Toy Drive That Sparked Flap," *The Gazette,* Colorado Springs, CO; November 3, 2011, http://gazette.com/update-afa-backs-away-from-toy-drive-that-sparked-flap/article/127840

[596] "Maintaining Government Neutrality Regarding Religion," Department of the Air Force, September 1, 2011, http://www.militaryreligiousfreedom.org/docs/gen_schwartz_letter_religion_neutralilty.pdf

[597] Callahan, C.W., "Wounded, Ill, and Injured Partners in Care Guidelines," Department of the Navy, September 14, 2011, http://forbes.house.gov/UploadedFiles/WalterReedMemo.pdf

[598] "US Navy Rescinds Ban on Bibles for Patients at Walter Reed Hospital," *Catholic World News,* December 6, 2011, http://www.catholicculture.org/news/headlines/index.cfm?storyid=12591

[599] Starnes, Todd, "Suspension of Air Force Class Over Bible Passages 'Misrepresents First Amendment,' Lawmaker Argues," *Fox News Radio,* September 5, 2011, http://radio.foxnews.com/toddstarnes/top-stories/pentagon-religious-proselytizing-is-not-permitted.html

[600] Wise, Lindsay, "Hit With Lawsuit, VA Denies Banning 'God' at Services," *Houston Chronicle,* June 30, 2011, http://www.chron.com/news/houston-texas/article/Hit-with-lawsuit-VA-denies-banning-God-at-2077968.php

[601] "Hidden Scriptures to be Removed from U.S. Weapons," *CBN News,* January 24, 2010, http://www.cbn.com/cbnnews/us/2010/January/Hidden-scriptures-to-be-Removed-from-US-Weapons/

[602] Todd, Starnes, "Chaplain Ordered to Remove Religious Essay From Military Website," *Fox News Radio,* July 24, 2013 http://radio.foxnews.com/toddstarnes/top-stories/chaplain-ordered-to-remove-religious-essay-from-military-website.html

[603] Gardiner, Lisa, "American Muslim Leader Urges Faithful to Spread Islam's Message," *San Ramon Valley Herald,* Pleasanton, CA, July 4, 1998, http://www.danielpipes.org/rr/394.pdf

[604] "Pervasive Religious Hostility In U.S. Irrefutable According to New, Extensive Survey," *PRNewswire-USNewswire,* August 15, 2012, http://www.prnewswire.com/news-releases-test/pervasive-religious-hostility-in-us-irrefutable-according-to-new-extensive-survey-166295186.html

[605] Greenfield, Daniel, "Islamic State Has 3,500 Sex Slaves," *Front Page Magazine,* January 19, 2016, http://www.frontpagemag.com/point/261527/islamic-state-has-3500-sex-slaves-daniel-greenfield

[606] "Goliath," Wikipedia, Accessed August 15, 2015, http://en.wikipedia.org/wiki/Goliath

[607] "Friedrich Lorenz," Wikipedia, Accessed August 15, 2015, http://en.wikipedia.org/wiki/Friedrich_Lorenz

[608] Walters, Guy, "How the Nazis Slaughtered 16,000 People By Guillotine: Found in a Munich Cellar, the Death Machine That Reveals a Forgotten Horror," *UK Daily Mail,* January 13, 2014, http://www.dailymail.co.uk/news/article-2538973/How-Nazis-slaughtered-16-000-people-guillotine-Found-Munich-cellar-death-machine-reveals-forgotten-horror.htm

[609] "Execution by Beheading (Decapitation)," http://www.capitalpunishmentuk.org/behead.html

[610] Daniel Pearl Foundation, http://www.danielpearl.org/home/about-us/about-danny/

[611] "Pentagon: South Korean Hostage Beheaded, Seoul Reaffirms Plans to Send More Troops to Iraq," *CNN,* June 23, 2004, http://edition.cnn.com/2004/WORLD/meast/06/22/iraq.hostage/index.html

[612] Martin, Arthur, "British Soldier's Alleged Killer 'Told Police He Went for Jugular as He Was Hacked to Death in London Street Because That Is How Animals Are Killed in Islam'," *UK Daily Mail*, December 5, 2013, http://www.dailymail.co.uk/news/article-2518738/Lee-Rigbys-killer-told-police-went-Fusiliers-jugular-animals-killed-Islam.html

[613] "Yusuf Ibrahim, of Jersey City, Indicted in 2013 Beheadings," April 28, 2014, *CBS Local,* New York; http://newyork.cbslocal.com/2014/04/28/yusuf-ibrahim-of-jersey-city-indicted-in-2013-beheadings/

[614] Whitehead, T., Malnick, E., Pollock, T. B. & Rayner, G., 'Woman Beheaded 'with Machete' in North London Garden', *The UK Telegraph,* September 4, 2014, http://www.telegraph.co.uk/news/uknews/crime/11075380/Woman-beheaded-in-north-London-garden.html

[615] Payne, Samantha, "UK Decapitation: Naveed Ahmed Jailed for Life After 'Barbaric' Murder of Wife Tahira," *International Business Times,* January 28, 2015, http://www.ibtimes.co.uk/uk-decapitation-naveed-ahmed-jailed-life-after-barbaric-murder-wife-tahira-1485612

[616] Lewis, Helen, "Are Beheadings Terrorism? Palmira Silva Was the Third Woman to be Decapitated in London This Year," *New Statesman,* September 5, 2014, http://www.newstatesman.com/politics/2014/09/are-beheadings-terrorism-palmira-silva-was-third-woman-be-decapitated-london-year

[617] "ISIS Burns Jordanian Pilot Moaz al-Kassasbeh Alive," *The Jawa Report,* February 3, 2015; http://mypetjawa.mu.nu/archives/219397.php

[618] Cohen, Ariel, "Obama Admin Called Out for Failing to Cite Christianity as Motive Behind ISIS Libya Beheading," *Jerusalem Post,* February 19, 2015, http://www.jpost.com/Christian-News/Obama-Admin-called-out-for-failing-to-cite-Christianity-as-motive-behind-IS-Libya-beheading-391518

[619] Zieve, Tamara, "Evangelist Franklin Graham Rejects Obama's Comparison Between ISIS, Crusaders," *Jerusalem Post,* February 8, 2015, http://www.jpost.com/Christian-News/Evangelist-Franklin-Graham-rejects-Obamas-comparison-between-ISIS-crusaders-390401

[620] Cohen, Ariel, "Obama Admin Called Out for Failing to Cite Christianity as Motive Behind ISIS Libya Beheading," *Jerusalem Post,* February 19, 2015, http://www.jpost.com/Christian-News/Obama-Admin-called-out-for-failing-to-cite-Christianity-as-motive-behind-IS-Libya-beheading-391518

[621] Ibid.

[622] Davis, Julie Hirschfeld, "Critics Seize on Obama's ISIS Remarks at Prayer Breakfast," *New York Times,* February 5, 2015, http://www.nytimes.com/2015/02/06/us/politics/obama-national-prayer-breakfast-terrorism-islam.html

[623] Jaffe, Alexandra, "Obama Takes Fire for Crusades Comparison," *CNN,* February 7, 2015, http://www.cnn.com/2015/02/06/politics/obama-isis-crusades-comparison/

[624] Davis, Julie Hirschfeld, "Critics Seize on Obama's ISIS Remarks at Prayer Breakfast," *New York Times,* February 5, 2015, http://www.nytimes.com/2015/02/06/us/politics/obama-national-prayer-breakfast-terrorism-islam.html

[625] Jaffe, Alexandra, "Obama Takes Fire for Crusades Comparison," *CNN,* February 7, 2015, http://www.cnn.com/2015/02/06/politics/obama-isis-crusades-comparison/

[626] Ibid.

[627] Zieve, Tamara, "Evangelist Franklin Graham Rejects Obama's Comparison Between ISIS, Crusaders," *Jerusalem Post,* February 8, 2015, http://www.jpost.com/Christian-News/Evangelist-Franklin-Graham-rejects-Obamas-comparison-between-ISIS-crusaders-390401

[628] Staff Reporter, "Coptic Church Recognizes Martyrdom of 21 Christians Killed By ISIS," *Catholic Herald,* February 23, 2015, http://www.catholicherald.co.uk/news/2015/02/23/coptic-church-recognises-martyrdom-of-21-egyptians-killed-by-isis/

[629] "ISIS kills 15 Christian hostages in Syria, Beheads Woman," *National Agency Associated Press,* February 26, 2015, http://www.ansamed.info/ansamed/en/news/sections/generalnews/2015/02/26/isis-kills-15-christian-hostages-in-syria-beheads-woman_1c61f6f6-5001-46e7-8fa8-5f1f0bed70ff.html

[630] Smith-Spark, Laura, "Activist: ISIS Now Holds 262 Christians Hostages in Syria," *CNN,* February 26, 2015, http://www.cnn.com/2015/02/26/middleeast/isis-syria-iraq/

[631] Perez, Chris, "ISIS Ransacks Museum, Destroys 2,000-Year-Old Artifacts," *New York Post,* February 26, 2015, http://nypost.com/2015/02/26/isis-destroys-ancient-iraqi-artifacts/

[632] Rasheed, Ahmed, "Iraq Says Islamic State Killed 500 Yazidis, Buried Some Victims Alive," *Reuters,* August 10, 2014, http://www.reuters.com/article/2014/08/10/us-iraq-security-yazidis-killings-idUSKBN0GA0FF20140810

[633] Stanton, Jenny, "ISIS Militants Slaughter More Than 300 Yazidi Captives in Northern Iraq After Thousands Were Taken Captive From Villages," *UK Daily Mail,* May 2, 2015, http://www.dailymail.co.uk/news/article-3065517/Isis-militants-slaughter-300-Yazidi-captives-northern-Iraq-thousands-taken-captive-villages.html

[634] McLaughlin, Eliott C., "ISIS Executes More Christians in Libya, Video Shows," *CNN,* April 19, 2015, http://www.cnn.com/2015/04/19/africa/libya-isis-executions-ethiopian-christians/

[635] Kirkpatrick, David D., "ISIS Video Appears to Show Executions of Ethiopian Christians in Libya," *New York Times,* April 19, 2015, http://www.nytimes.com/2015/04/20/world/middleeast/isis-video-purports-to-show-killing-of-ethiopian-christians.html

[636] Malm, Sara, "Muslim Migrants Threw 12 Christians Overboard to Their Deaths During Mediterranean Crossing From Libya, Say Italian Police," *UK Daily Mail,* April 16, 2015, http://www.dailymail.co.uk/news/article-3042001/Aid-agency-says-41-migrants-feared-dead-new-sea-tragedy.html

[637] "Terror Trainees: New ISIS Video Shows Indoctrination of Kids as Young as 5," *Fox News,* February 23, 2015, http://www.foxnews.com/world/2015/02/23/terror-trainees-new-isis-video-shows-indoctrination-kids-as-young-as-5

[638] "Guide to Understanding Islam, What Does the Religion of Peace Teach About Violence," *The Religion of Peace,* Accessed August 28, 2015, http://www.thereligionofpeace.com/quran/023-violence.htm

[639] "Civilian Death Toll in Iraq Doubles to 17,000 in 2014 'Due to Rise of ISIS'," *RT,* January 1, 2015, http://rt.com/news/219223-iraq-civilian-death-toll/

[640] Levy, Janet, "Turkey and the Restoration of the Caliphate," *American Thinker,* March 10, 2011, http://www.americanthinker.com/articles/2011/03/turkey_and_the_restoration_of.html

[641] Joe P. & Albayrak, A., "From His Refuge in the Poconos, Reclusive Imam Fethullah Gulen Roils Turkey," *The Wall Street Journal,* January 20, 2014, http://www.wsj.com/articles/SB10001424052702304027204579332670740491570

[642] Popp, Maximilian, "Altruistic Society or Sect? The Shadowy World of the Islamic Gulen Movement, Part 1," *Spiegel International,* August 8, 2012, http://www.spiegel.de/international/germany/guelen-movement-accused-of-being-a-sect-a-848763-2.html

[643] *Ibid.*

[644] *Ibid.*

[645] *Ibid.*

[646] Williams, Paul, "Islamic Armed Fortress Emerges from Pocono Mountains, Feds Turn Blind Eye," *Jihad Watch,* April 8, 2010, http://www.jihadwatch.org/2010/04/islamic-armed-fortress-emerges-from-pocono-mountains-feds-turn-blind-eye

[647] Baran, Zeyno, *Torn Country: Turkey Between Secularism and Islamism,* New York: Bloomsbury Publishing, July 1, 2010, p.145

[648] *Ibid.*

[649] Campbell, Andrew, "'Taqiyya': How Islamic Extremists Deceive the West," June 1, 2005, http://www.ci-ce-ct.com/index.php?option=com_content&view=article&id=3:taqiyya-how-islamic-extremists-deceive-the-west

[650] "Deception, Lying and Taqiyya," The Religion of Peace, Accessed May 1, 2016, http://www.thereligionofpeace.com/quran/011-taqiyya.htm

[651] Campbell, Andrew, "'Taqiyya': How Islamic Extremists Deceive the West," June 1, 2005, http://www.ci-ce-ct.com/index.php?option=com_content&view=article&id=3:taqiyya-how-islamic-extremists-deceive-the-west

[652] Palme, Louis, "Knowing Four Arabic Words May Save Our Civilization from Islamic Takeover," *Islam Watch,* July 31, 2012, http://www.islam-watch.org/home/139-louis-palme/1095-knowing-four-arabic-words-may-save-our-civilization-from-islamic-takeover.html

[653] *Ibid.*

[654] Ibrahim, Raymond, "Tawriya: New Islamic Doctrine Permits 'Creative Lying'," February 28, 2012, http://www.raymondibrahim.com/from-the-arab-world/tawriya-lying/

[655] Ibrahim, Raymond, "Top Muslim Cleric Qaradawi Urges Western Muslims to 'Liberalize' (Outwardly, Anyway)," July 23, 2010, http://www.raymondibrahim.com/islam/top-muslim-cleric-qaradawi-urges-western-muslims-to-liberalize/

[656] Jon M. C., "Some Islamic Doctrines," Faith Freedom, March 20, 2013, http://www.faithfreedom.org/some-islamic-doctrines-2/

[657] Shoebat, W. & Barrack, B., "Muruna: Violating Sharia to Fool the West: The Sunni Doctrine of Muruna Takes Taqiyya a Step Further," *Pajamas Media,* February 18, 2012, http://pjmedia.com/blog/muruna-violating-sharia-to-fool-the-west/?singlepage=true

[658] Palme, Louis, "Knowing Four Arabic Words May Save Our Civilization from Islamic Takeover," *Islam Watch,* July 31, 2012, http://www.islam-watch.org/home/139-louis-palme/1095-knowing-four-arabic-words-may-save-our-civilization-from-islamic-takeover.html

[659] Shoebat, W. & Barrack, B., "Muruna: Violating Sharia to Fool the West," *Pajamas Media,* February 18, 2012, http://pjmedia.com/blog/muruna-violating-sharia-to-fool-the-west/?singlepage=true

[660] Smith, Gregory, "America's Changing Religious Landscape, Summary Table: Religious Composition of U.S. Adults," Pew Research Center, p. 21, http://www.pewforum.org/2015/05/12/americas-changing-religious-landscape/

[661] "2015 Sees Sharp Rise in Post-Christian Population," Barna, August 12, 2015, https://barna.org/barna-update/culture/728-america-more-post-christian-than-two-years-ago

[662] Smith, Gregory, "U.S. Public Becoming Less Religious," Pew Research Center, November 3, 2015, http://www.pewforum.org/files/2015/11/201.11.03_RLS_II_full_report.pdf, p. 3

[663] *Ibid.,* p. 47

[664] *Ibid.*

[665] Hout, M., Fischer, C. S., & Chaves, M. A., "More Americans Have No Religious Preference" University of California; March 7, 2013, http://sociology.berkeley.edu/sites/default/files/faculty/fischer/Hout%20et%20al_No%20Relig%20Pref%202012_Release%20Mar%202013.pdf,

[666] Smith, Gregory, "America's Changing Religious Landscape, Summary Table: Religious Composition of U.S. Adults," Pew Research Center, http://www.pewforum.org/files/2015/05/RLS-08-26-full-report.pdf, p. 21

[667] Croucher, Shane, "How Rich Is the Vatican? So Wealthy It Can Stumble Across Millions of Euros Just 'Tucked Away'," *International Business Times,* December 5, 2014, http://www.ibtimes.co.uk/how-rich-vatican-so-wealthy-it-can-stumble-across-millions-euros-just-tucked-away-147821

[668] Thomas, Cal, "First Redistribute Vatican Wealth," *Townhall,* May 13, 2014, http://townhall.com/columnists/calthomas/2014/05/13/first-redistribute-vatican-wealth-n1837119/page/full

[669] "Scandals: No Apologies This Time," *Time,* October 28, 1991, http://content.time.com/time/magazine/article/0,9171,974120,00.html

[670] Gedeon, Kimberly, "Pick-Pocketin' Preachers! 10 Black Churches Caught Up In Embezzlement Scandals," *Madame Noire,* July 1, 2014, Accessed August 28, 2015, http://madamenoire.com/442410/holy-handcuffs-10-black-churches-caught-embezzlement-scandals/

[671] "Former Rockingham Co. Pastor Sentenced for Embezzling Money from Church," *Fox8 News,* November 5, 2014, http://myfox8.com/2014/11/05/former-rockingham-co-pastor-sentenced-for-embezzling-money-from-church/

[672] Gedeon, Kimberly, "Pick-Pocketin' Preachers! 10 Black Churches Caught Up in Embezzlement Scandals," *Madame Noire,* March 17, 2015, http://madamenoire.com/442410/holy-handcuffs-10-black-churches-caught-embezzlement-scandals/

[673] "Church Swindler Ephren Taylor Headed to Federal Prison for 19 Years," *Atlanta Journal,* July 1, 2014, http://www.ajc.com/news/news/church-swindler-ephren-taylor-headed-to-federal-pr/nkYhM/

[674] Ward, Clifford, "Pastor Gets 12 Years for Stealing $1.6M in Loans, Donations," *Chicago Tribune,* December 18, 2013, http://articles.chicagotribune.com/2013-12-18/news/chi-pastor-theft-sentencing-aurora-20131218_1_church-expansion-plan-howard-richmond-life-reach-ministries

[675] Futty, John, "Ex-pastor Ordered to Repay Church $54,000 He Stole," *Columbus Dispatch,* December 4, 2013, http://www.dispatch.com/content/stories/local/2013/12/04/ex-pastor-ordered-to-repay-near-east-side-church.html

[676] "Ex-pastor and His Wife Accused of Bilking $430,000 from Their Church, and Gambling It Away," *UK Daily Mail,* June 24, 2012, http://www.dailymail.co.uk/news/article-2163934/Ex-pastor-Charles-Gilford-wife-Adriane-Gilford-accused-bilking-430-000-church.html

[677] Geary, Jason, "Lakeland Pastor Sentenced In $100,000 Church Theft," *The Ledger,* October 16, 2013, http://www.theledger.com/article/20131016/NEWS/131019379

[678] "Ex-Chicago Pastor Gets 15 Years for Church Theft," *Journal Star,* May 5, 2014, http://www.pjstar.com/article/20140505/News/140509561

[679] Anderson, Glenda, "Former Pastor Sentenced in Lake County Church Embezzlement," *The Press Democrat,* February 19, 2014, http://www.pressdemocrat.com/csp/mediapool/sites/PressDemocrat/News/story.csp?cid=1856448

[680] Jackson, Barbara-Shae, "8 Church Scandals That May have Challenged Your Faith," *Atlanta Black Star,* April 28, 2014, http://atlantablackstar.com/2014/04/28/8-church-scandals-may-challenged-faith/6/

[681] *Ibid.*

[682] Paresh Dave, "Tony Alamo Victims Awarded $525 Million; L.A. Properties May Be Sold," *Los Angeles Times,* March 1, 2014, http://articles.latimes.com/2014/mar/01/nation/la-na-nn-tony-alamo-arkansas-victims-20140228

[683] Blair, Leonardo, "Founding Pastor of Va. Megachurch Caught in Sex Scandal Gets $115K Salary, Housing in Severance Deal," *Christian Post,* June 17, 2013, http://www.christianpost.com/news/founding-pastor-of-va-megachurch-caught-in-sex-scandal-gets-115k-salary-housing-in-severance-deal-98149/

[684] *Ibid.*

[685] Hipolit, Melissa, "Geronimo Aguilar, Former Mega-Church Pastor, Found Guilty of All Sex Crimes," WTVR-TV, Richmond, VA; June 25, 2015, http://wtvr.com/2015/06/24/geronimo-aguilar-former-mega-church-pastor-found-guilty-on-all-counts-of-sexual-assault/

[686] Jones, Sandra, "Former Richmond Pastor Geronimo Aguilar Sentenced to 40 Years in Prison for Sexually Abusing Children," WTVR-TV, Richmond, VA; October 13, 2015, http://wtvr.com/2015/10/13/former-richmond-pastor-geronimo-aguilar-sentenced-to-40-years-in-prison-for-sexually-abusing-children/

[687] Mueller, Mark, "Michael Fugee Expelled from Priesthood for Flouting Ban on Contact with Children," *New Jersey On-Line,* March 17, 2014, http://www.nj.com/news/index.ssf/2014/03/michael_fugee_expelled_from_priesthood_for_flouting_ban_on_contact_with_kids.html

[688] Townsend, Tim, "Ballwin Priest Sentenced to 3 Years for Child Pornography," *St. Louis Post-Dispatch,* April 30, 2013, http://www.stltoday.com/lifestyles/faith-and-values/ballwin-priest-sentenced-to-years-for-child-pornography/article_795e37f5-c883-5481-9507-960a0ac6d2c6.html

[689] Roberts, Hannah, "One in 50 Priests Is a Pedophile: Pope Francis Says Child Abuse Is 'Leprosy' Infecting the Catholic Church, *UK Daily Mail,* July 14, 2013, http://www.dailymail.co.uk/news/article-2690575/Pope-Francis-admits-two-cent-Roman-Catholic-priests-paedophiles-interview-Italian-newspaper.html

[690] "Catholic Church Sexual Abuse Cases," Wikipedia, Accessed August 28, 2015, http://en.wikipedia.org/wiki/Catholic_Church_sexual_abuse_cases

[691] Deveney, Catherine, "Catholic Priests Unmasked: 'God Doesn't Like Boys Who Cry'," *UK Guardian,* April 6, 2013, http://www.theguardian.com/world/2013/apr/07/catholic-priests-unmasked-god-boys

[692] Burns, John F, "Following Resignation, Top British Cardinal Acknowledges Sexual Misconduct," *New York Times,* March 3, 2013, http://www.nytimes.com/2013/03/04/world/europe/cardinal-keith-obrien-acknowledges-sexual-misconduct.html

[693] Deveney, Catherine, "O'Brien Priest Worries That Church Wants to 'Crush' Him," *The Observer,* March 2, 2013, http://www.theguardian.com/world/2013/mar/02/obrien-priest-catholic-church

[694] *Ibid.*

[695] Deveney, Catherine, "Catholic Priests Unmasked: 'God Doesn't Like Boys Who Cry'," *UK Guardian,* April 6, 2013, http://www.theguardian.com/world/2013/apr/07/catholic-priests-unmasked-god-boys

[696] *Ibid.*

[697] Leclaire, Jennifer, "Why Megachurch Pastors Keep Falling into Sexual Immorality," *Charisma Magazine,* May 8, 2013, http://www.charismamag.com/spirit/church-ministry/17654-why-megachurch-pastors-keep-falling-into-sexual-immorality

[698] Baker, P., Ahmed, A. & Yardley, J., "Pope Francis' Arrival in the U.S. Is a Low-Key Prelude to Pageantry," *New York Times,* September 23, 2015, http://www.nytimes.com/2015/09/23/world/americas/pope-francis-cuba-us.html

[699] Kaufman, Sarah, "By the Numbers: The Catholic Church's Sex Abuse Scandals," *Vocativ,* September 27, 2015, http://www.vocativ.com/news/235015/by-the-numbers-the-catholic-churchs-sex-abuse-scandals/

[700] *Ibid.*

[701] Allen Jr., J. L. & Schaeffer, P., "Reports of Abuse: AIDS Exacerbates Sexual Exploitation of Nuns, Reports Allege," *National Catholic Reporter,* 2001, http://natcath.org/NCR_Online/archives2/2001a/031601/031601a.htm

[702] *Ibid.*

[703] *Ibid.*

[704] "Senator Probes Megachurches' Finances," *NPR,* December 4, 2007, http://www.npr.org/templates/story/story.php?storyId=16860611

[705] Zoll, Rachel, "Televangelists Escape Penalty in Senate Inquiry," *NBC News / AP,* January 7, 2011, http://www.nbcnews.com/id/40960871/ns/politics-capitol_hill/t/televangelists-escape-penalty-senate-inquiry/

[706] Banks, Adelle M., "Evangelical Finance Probe Concluded By Senator," *Huffington Post,* January 8, 2011, http://www.huffingtonpost.com/2011/01/08/senator-concludes-probe-o_n_806202.html

[707] Dolan, Bill, "Ex-megachurch Pastor Blames Underage Victim, Wants Out of Prison," *The Times,* June 3, 2014, http://www.nwitimes.com/news/local/lake/hammond/ex-megachurch-pastor-blames-underage-victim-wants-out-of-prison/article_2ae9324b-eacf-546e-9f73-c12147f5726f.html

[708] Leclaire, Jennifer, "Why Megachurch Pastors Keep Falling Into Sexual Immorality," *Charisma Magazine,* May 8, 2013, http://www.charismamag.com/spirit/church-ministry/17654-why-megachurch-pastors-keep-falling-into-sexual-immorality

[709] Kunerth, Jeff, "Summit Megachurch Founder Isaac Hunter Found Dead in Apparent Suicide," *Orlando Sentinel,* December 13, 2013, http://articles.orlandosentinel.com/2013-12-10/news/os-isaac-hunter-suicide-20131210_1_rhonda-hunter-isaac-hunter-summit-church

[710] Kunerth, Jeff, "Discovery Church Pastor Resigns After Admitting to Affair," *Orlando Sentinel,* May 6, 2013, http://www.orlandosentinel.com/features/religion/os-discovery-church-pastor-admits-affair-20130506-story.html

[711] *Ibid.*

[712] Leclaire, Jennifer, "Why Megachurch Pastors Keep Falling into Sexual Immorality," *Charisma Magazine,* May 8, 2013, http://www.charismamag.com/spirit/church-ministry/17654-why-megachurch-pastors-keep-falling-into-sexual-immorality

[713] Tyler, Adrian, "Ex-wife Speaks Out on Bishop Terry Hornbuckle's Rape Conviction," *EEW Magazine,* September 30, 2014, http://buzz.eewmagazine.com/eew-magazine-buzz-blog/2014/9/30/ex-wife-speaks-out-on-bishop-terry-hornbuckles-rape-convicti.html

[714] "Wife of Convicted Rapist, Bishop Terry Hornbuckle, Speaks Out for the First Time Regarding that Horrible Situation and the Domestic Abuse that She Suffered," *Black Christian News Network,* September 27, 2014, http://blackchristiannews.com/2014/09/watch-wife-convicted-rapist-bishop-terry-hornbuckle-speaks-first-time/

[715] Jackson, Barbara-Shae, "8 Church Scandals That May have Challenged Your Faith," *Atlanta Black Star,* April 28, 2014, http://atlantablackstar.com/2014/04/28/8-church-scandals-may-challenged-faith/6/

[716] Brownie Marie, "Pastor Bob Coy scandal: Resigns from Calvary Chapel Fort Lauderdale Megachurch Amid Cheating, Affair Scandal, Leaving Congregants Heartbroken," *Christian Today,* April 8, 2014, http://www.christiantoday.com/article/pastor.bob.coy.resigns.affair.scandal.moral.failing.calvary.chapel.fort.lauderdale.congregants.heartbroken/36611.htm

[717] Marie, Brownie, "Pastor Bob Coy Scandal: Resigns from Calvary Chapel Fort Lauderdale Megachurch Amid Cheating, Affair Scandal, Leaving Congregants Heartbroken," *Christian Today,* April 8, 2014, http://www.christiantoday.com/article/pastor.-.-.resigns.affair.scandal.moral.failing.calvary.chapel.fort.lauderdale.congregants.heartbroken/36611.htm

[718] "Bob Coy," Wikipedia, Accessed August 28, 2015, http://en.wikipedia.org/wiki/Bob_Coy

[719] "Nate Morales Sentenced to 40 Years in Prison," *The Wartburg Watch,* August 15, 2014, http://thewartburgwatch.com/2014/08/15/nate-morales-sentenced-to-40-years-in-prison/

[720] Rodgers, Bob, "Setting the Record Straight on David Yonggi Cho," *Charisma Magazine,* February 25, 2014, http://www.charismamag.com/life/culture/19861-setting-the-record-straight-on-david-yonggi-cho

[721] Moon, Ruth, "Founder of World's Largest Megachurch Convicted of Embezzling $12 Million," *Christianity Today,* February 24, 2014, http://www.christianitytoday.com/gleanings/2014/february/founder-of-worlds-largest-megachurch-convicted-cho-yoido.html

[722] Hafiz, Yasmine, "Protesters Call for Pastor Mark Driscoll's Resignation After Multiple Scandals at Mars Hill Church," *The Huffington Post,* August 5, 2014, http://www.huffingtonpost.com/2014/08/05/pasotr-mark-driscoll-resign_n_5651088.html

[723] Krattenmaker, Tom, "'Rock Star' Pastors Lose Luster," *USA Today,* August 3, 2014, http://www.usatoday.com/story/opinion/2014/07/31/rock-star-pastors-church-celebrity-internet-column/13422869/

[724] Connelly, Joel, "Mark Driscoll Is Back and Wants Your Money," *Seattle Post Intelligence,* December 23, 2014, http://blog.seattlepi.com/seattlepolitics/2014/12/23/mark-driscoll-is-back-with-preaching-videos-and-a-mars-hill-like-website/

[725] "Jim Bakker," Wikipedia, Accessed August 30, 2015, http://en.wikipedia.org/wiki/Jim_Bakker

[726] "Jim Bakker Trial: 1989," Encyclopedia, Accessed August 30, 2015, http://www.encyclopedia.com/topic/Jim_Bakker.aspx

[727] "Jim Bakker," Wikipedia, Accessed August 30, 2015, http://en.wikipedia.org/wiki/Jim_Bakker

[728] Harris, Paul, "Ted Haggard, Mega-Church Founder Felled By Sex Scandal, Returns to Pulpit," *The UK Guardian,* June 5, 2010, http://www.theguardian.com/world/2010/jun/06/us-gay-scandal-pastor-church

[729] "Ted Haggard Talks" *The Oprah Winfrey Show,* June 30, 2009, http://www.oprah.com/oprahshow/Ted-Haggard-and-His-Wife-Talk-About-the-Gay-Sex-Scandal

[730] Beamon, Todd, "Glenn Beck: Legalizing Gay Marriage Will Cut Church Attendance in Half," *Newsmax,* May 2, 2015, http://www.newsmax.com/Newsfront/glenn-beck-gay-marriage-cut/2015/05/02/id/642228/

[731] Gumaer, David Emerson, "Apostasy – The National Council of Churches," Studies in Reformed Theology, 1999, http://www.reformed-theology.org/html/issue07/apostasy.htm

[732] Wildie, Duane L., Government, A Christian's Civic Responsibility. Bloomington: Westbow Press, 2014, pg.3

[733] Gumaer, David Emerson, "Apostasy – The National Council of Churches," Studies in Reformed Theology, 1999, http://www.reformed-theology.org/html/issue07/apostasy.htm

[734] *Ibid.*

[735] Midavaine, BreeAnn, "Federal Council of the Churches of Christ in America Records, 1905 – 1971," The Burke Library Archives, Columbia University Libraries, Union Theological Seminary; November 11, 2012, http://library.columbia.edu/content/dam/libraryweb/locations/burke/fa/wab/ldpd_4492697.pdf, p. 4

[736] Gumaer, David Emerson, "Apostasy – The National Council of Churches," Studies in Reformed Theology, 1999, http://www.reformed-theology.org/html/issue07/apostasy.htm

[737] Grossman, Cathy Lynn, "9/11 Traced New Spiritual Lines," *USA Today,* September 7, 2011, http://usatoday30.usatoday.com/news/religion/2011-08-19-spiritual-impact-sept-11_n.htm

[738] "The Impeachment of President Clinton," Eagleton Institute of Politics, Rutgers University, Accessed September 4, 2015, http://www.eagleton.rutgers.edu/research/americanhistory/ap_clintonimpeach.php

[739] Clinton, William, "Address Before a Joint Session of the Congress on the State of the Union," The American Presidency Project, January 23, 1996, http://www.presidency.ucsb.edu/ws/?pid=53091

[740] "'The Era of Big Government Is Over'," Transcript of President Clinton's radio address, CNN, January 27, 1996, http://www.cnn.com/US/9601/budget/01-27/clinton_radio/

[741] Bedard, Paul, "Happy 20th: Clinton's Top 10 First Year Scandals," *U.S. News & World Report,* September 30, 2011, http://www.usnews.com/news/blogs/washington-whispers/2011/09/30/happy-20th-clintons-top-10-first-year-scandals

[742] Bush, George Walker, State of the Union 2001, February, 27 2001, http://www.thisnation.com/library/sotu/2001gwb.html

[743] Hanson, Victor Davis, "Obama: Transforming America," *National Review,* October 1, 2013, http://www.nationalreview.com/article/359967/obama-transforming-america-victor-davis-hanson

[744] Luhby, Tami, "Can Bernie Sanders Deliver Free College For All? Not So Easily," CNN, February 3, 2016, http://www.cnn.com/2016/02/03/politics/bernie-sanders-free-college-costs/

[745] Velthoven, M., Kartch, J. & Ellis, R., "Obama Has Proposed 442 Tax Hikes Since Taking Office," Americans for Tax Reform, April 14, 2014, http://www.atr.org/obama-has-proposed-442-tax-hikes-taking-office

[746] Black, Simon, "Americans Renouncing US Citizenship Soars to Yet Another Record High…" Sovereign Man, October 27, 2015, https://www.sovereignman.com/trends/americans-renouncing-us-citizenship-soars-to-yet-another-record-high-18134/

[747] Smith, Allen W., "Ronald Reagan and the Great Social Security Heist," FedSmith, October 11, 2013, http://www.fedsmith.com/2013/10/11/ronald-reagan-and-the-great-social-security-heist/

[748] John, David C., "Three Social Security Fixes to Solve the Real Fiscal Crisis," Heritage Foundation, December 3, 2012, http://www.heritage.org/research/reports/2012/12/3-social-security-fixes-to-solve-the-real-fiscal-crisis

[749] "Size and Scope," US Post Office, Accessed September 15, 2015, https://about.usps.com/who-we-are/postal-facts/size-scope.htm

[750] Short, Doug, "September Median Household Income Slightly Off Last Month's Post-Recession High," Advisor Perspectives, October 23, 2015, http://www.advisorperspectives.com/dshort/updates/Median-Household-Income-Update.php

[751] Limitone, Julia, "Carson: Anyone Who Says You Can't Cut Spending is Full of Crap," *Fox Business,* October 8, 2015, http://www.foxbusiness.com/business-leaders/2015/10/08/carson-anyone-who-says-cant-cut-spending-is-full-crap/

[752] "2014 Annual Report: Additional Opportunities to Reduce Fragmentation, Overlap, and Duplication and Achieve Other Financial Benefits," GAO, April 8, 2014, http://www.gao.gov/assets/670/662327.pdf, p. 1

[753] *Ibid.,* p. 76

[754] *Ibid.,* p. 208

[755] *Ibid.,* pp. 207-208

[756] *Ibid.,* p. 6

[757] *Ibid.,* p. 83

[758] Korte, Gregory, "Government Often Has 10 Agencies Doing One Job," *USA Today,* April 8, 2014, http://www.usatoday.com/story/news/politics/2014/04/08/billions-spent-on-duplicate-federal-programs/7435221/

[759] Clark, Charles, "Senate Tries to Stop Agencies from Paying Dead People," *Government Executive,* July 30, 2015, http://www.govexec.com/oversight/2015/07/senate-tries-stop-agencies-paying-dead-people/118750/

[760] Clark, Charles, "How Many 112-Year-Olds Are Still Living, According to SSA?" *Government Executive,* March 9, 2015, http://www.govexec.com/management/2015/03/how-many-112-year-olds-still-collect-social-security/107019

[761] Paltrow, S. & Carr, K, "How the Pentagon's Payroll Quagmire Traps America's Soldiers," *Reuters,* July 2, 2013, http://www.reuters.com/investigates/pentagon/#article/part1

[762] Paltrow, Scot, "Behind the Pentagon's Doctored Ledgers, a Running Tally of Epic Waste," *Reuters,* November 18, 2013, http://www.reuters.com/investigates/pentagon/#article/part2

[763] *Ibid.*

[764] *Ibid.*

[765] Van Buren, Peter, "Dude, Where's My Humvee? Iraq Losing Equipment to Islamic State at Staggering Rate," *Reuters,* June 2, 2015, http://blogs.reuters.com/great-debate/2015/06/02/dude-wheres-my-humvee-iraqi-equipment-losses-to-islamic-state-are-out-of-control/

[766] Paltrow, Scott, "Behind the Pentagon's Doctored Ledgers, a Running Tally of Epic Waste," *Reuters,* November 18, 2013, http://www.reuters.com/investigates/pentagon/#article/part2

[767] Paltrow, Scot, "Why the Pentagon's Many Campaigns to Clean Up Its Accounts Are Failing," *Reuters,* December 23, 2013, http://www.reuters.com/investigates/pentagon/#article/part3

[768] Coburn, Tom, "Wastebook, What Washington Doesn't Want You to Read," 2014, http://showmethespending.com/wp-content/uploads/2014/10/wastebook2014.pdf, p. 2

[769] Smith, Jada F., "Eisenhower Memorial Moves Forward," *New York Times,* September 24, 2014, http://www.nytimes.com/2014/09/25/us/25eisenhower.html

[770] Boyle, Matthew, "Paul Ryan's Pelosi-Esque Obamatrade Moment: 'It's Declassified and Made Public Once It's Agreed to'," *Breitbart,* June 11, 2015, http://www.breitbart.com/big-government/2015/06/11/paul-ryans-pelosi-esque-obamatrade-moment-its-declassified-and-made-public-once-its-agreed-to/

[771] "Paper Nightmare! 20,000 Pages of Federal Regulations Create Obamacare Tower (Photo)" *Gateway Pundit,* March 12, 2013, http://www.thegatewaypundit.com/2013/03/horror-20000-pages-of-federal-regulations-create-obamacare-tower-photo/

[772] Richardson, Valerie, "Obamacare Website Won't Reveal Insurance Costs for 2015 Until After Election," *Washington Times,* October 14, 2014, http://www.washingtontimes.com/news/2014/oct/14/obamacare-website-wont-reveal-insurance-costs-for-/

[773] Pollock, Richard, "Obamacare Premiums to Soar 3 Times Faster Than Feds Claim," *Daily Caller,* November 1, 2014, http://dailycaller.com/2015/11/01/obamacare-premiums-to-soar-3-times-faster-than-feds-claim/

[774] Richardson, Valerie, "Obamacare Premiums Soar as Much as 78% to Help Cover 'Essential Health Benefits'," *Washington Times,* October 28, 2014, http://www.washingtontimes.com/news/2014/oct/28/obamacare-sends-health-premiums-skyrocketing-by-as/

[775] Phillips, Tim, "ObamaCare Cancellations, Again," *USA Today,* October 16, 2014, http://www.usatoday.com/story/opinion/2014/10/16/obama-health-care-insurance-cancellation-column/17353673/

[776] Turner, G-M & Hartsfield, T., "ObamaCare's Cascade of Taxes Pounds U.S. Taxpayers," Galen Institute, May 6, 2014, http://www.galen.org/topics/obamacares-cascade-of-taxes-pounds-u-s-taxpayers/

[777] Stiles, Andrew, "GAO Report: Obamacare Adds $6.2 Trillion to Long-Term Deficit," *National Review,* February 26, 2013, http://www.nationalreview.com/corner/341589/gao-report-obamacare-adds-62-trillion-long-term-deficit-andrew-stiles

[778] "Obama: 'If You Like Your Health Care Plan, You'll Be Able to Keep Your Health Care Plan'" *PolitiFact,* http://www.politifact.com/obama-like-health-care-keep/, NOTE: References for at least 37 instances of this exact phrase or a variation close to it.

[779] Phillips, Tim, "ObamaCare Cancellations, Again," *USA Today,* October 16, 2014, http://www.usatoday.com/story/opinion/2014/10/16/obama-health-care-insurance-cancellation-column/17353673/

[780] Carnevale, Mary Lu, "Obama: 'If You Like Your Doctor, You Can Keep Your Doctor'," *Wall Street Journal,* June 15, 2009, http://blogs.wsj.com/washwire/2009/06/15/obama-if-you-like-your-doctor-you-can-keep-your-doctor/

[781] Christensen, Jen, "Obamacare: Fewer Options for Many," October 29, 2013, *CNN,* http://www.cnn.com/2013/10/29/health/obamacare-doctors-limited/

[782] Beck, Melinda, "UnitedHealth Culls Doctors from Medicare Advantage Plans," *Wall Street Journal,* November 16, 2013, http://online.wsj.com/news/articles/SB10001424052702303559504579200190614501838

[783] Obama, Barack, "Remarks of Senator Barack Obama: Health Care Town Hall," Vote Smart, June 5, 2008, http://votesmart.org/public-statement/346763/remarks-of-senator-barack-obama-health-care-town-hall/

[784] Gonshorowski, Drew, "How Will You Fare in the Obamacare Exchanges?" Heritage Foundation Issue Brief No. 4068, October 16, 2013, http://www.heritage.org/research/reports/2013/10/enrollment-in-obamacare-exchanges-how-will-your-health-insurance-fare

[785] "News Conference by the President," The White House, Office of the Press Secretary, April 30, 2013, http://www.whitehouse.gov/the-press-office/2013/04/30/news-conference-president

[786] "Rules and Regulations," Federal Register, Vol. 75, No. 137, Government Publishing Office, July 19, 2010, http://www.gpo.gov/fdsys/pkg/FR-2010-07-19/pdf/2010-17242.pdf, pp. 41737

[787] Senger, Alyene, "When You Can't Actually Keep Your Health Care Plan," *The Daily Signal,* August 22, 2013, http://dailysignal.com/2013/08/22/when-you-cant-actually-keep-your-health-care-plan/

[788] Vespa, Matt, "Obamacare Shatters Obama's Promise on Fifth Anniversary of No-Tax-Hike Pledge," *CNS News,* September 12, 2013, http://dailysignal.com/2013/08/22/when-you-cant-actually-keep-your-health-care-plan/

[789] Turner, G-M & Hartsfield, T., "ObamaCare's Cascade of Taxes Pounds U.S. Taxpayers," Galen Institute, May 6, 2014, http://www.galen.org/topics/obamacares-cascade-of-taxes-pounds-u-s-taxpayers/

[790] "New Study Shows Obamacare Increases Deficit, Knocking Down President's Vow," *Fox News,* April 9, 2012, http://www.foxnews.com/politics/2012/04/09/study-claims-obamas-health-care-law-would-raise-deficit/

[791] Stiles, Andrew, "GAO Report: Obamacare Adds $6.2 Trillion to Long-Term Deficit," *National Review,* February 26, 2013, http://www.nationalreview.com/corner/341589/gao-report-obamacare-adds-62-trillion-long-term-deficit-andrew-stiles

[792] Obama, Barack, "Remarks by the President After Meeting with Senate Democrats," The White House, December 15, 2009, https://www.whitehouse.gov/the-press-office/remarks-president-after-meeting-with-senate-democrats

[793] Farley, Robert, "Obama Said Health Care Reform Will Reduce the Cost of Health Care," *PolitiFact,* April 9, 2012, http://www.politifact.com/truth-o-meter/statements/2009/dec/18/barack-obama/obama-said-health-care-reform-will-reduce-cost-hea/

[794] "Remarks By the President to a Joint Session of Congress on Health Care," The White House, September 9, 2009, https://www.whitehouse.gov/the_press_office/Remarks-by-the-President-to-a-Joint-Session-of-Congress-on-Health-Care/

[795] Kliff, Sara, "Romney's Right: Obamacare Cuts Medicare By $716 Billion. Here's How." *The Washington Post,* August 14, 2012, https://www.washingtonpost.com/news/wonk/wp/2012/08/14/romneys-right-obamacare-cuts-medicare-by-716-billion-heres-how/

[796] Contorno, S. & Holan, A. D., "5 Years Later, Medicaid Opt-Outs Create Holes in 'Universal' Bill," *PolitiFact,* March 25, 2015, http://www.politifact.com/truth-o-meter/promises/obameter/promise/433/sign-a-universal-health-care-bill/

[797] *Ibid.*

[798] "Remarks By the President on the Affordable Care Act and the Government Shutdown," The White House, October 1, 2013, http://www.whitehouse.gov/the-press-office/2013/10/01/remarks-president-affordable-care-act-and-government-shutdown

[799] Senger, Alyene, "Measuring Choice and Competition in the Exchanges: Still Worse than Before the ACA," The Heritage Foundation, December 22, 2014, http://www.heritage.org/research/reports/2014/12/measuring-choice-and-competition-in-the-exchanges-still-worse-than-before-the-aca

[800] Kocherga, Angela, "Border Patrol Agents Seeing Spike in Human Smuggling", KHOU, Houston, May 15, 2015, http://www.khou.com/story/news/local/texas/2015/05/15/border-patrol-agents-seeing-spike-in-human-smuggling/27393929/

[801] Cavenov, Damien, "In Middle of Mexico, a Middle Class Rises," *The New York Times,* November 18, 2013, http://www.nytimes.com/2013/11/19/world/americas/in-the-middle-of-mexico-a-middle-class-is-rising.html

[802] Booth, W. & Miroff, N., "As Mexico Claws Toward Prosperity, Some in Middle Class Slide Back," *The Washington Post,* December 19, 2012, http://www.washingtonpost.com/world/the_americas/as-mexico-claws-toward-prosperity-some-in-middle-class-slide-back/2012/12/19/93ecfe68-31c1-11e2-92f0-496af208bf23_story.html

[803] "Employed Foreign-Born and Native-Born Persons 16 Years and Over By Occupation and Sex, 2014 Annual Averages," U.S. Bureau of Labor Statistics, http://www.bls.gov/news.release/forbrn.t04.htm

[804] Camarota, S.A. & Zeigler, K., Who Got Jobs During the Obama Presidency?" Center for Immigration Studies, November 2012, http://cis.org/who-got-jobs-during-obama-presidency

[805] Horowitz, Ami, "Ami on the Street: America or Somalia - You Might Be Surprised," YouTube video, May 27, 2015, https://www.youtube.com/watch?v=PfmywzjdtRM

[806] Ryczkowski, Angela, "What Process Did Immigrants Go Through When They Arrived at Ellis Island in the Late 1800s," Synonym, http://classroom.synonym.com/process-did-immigrants-through-arrived-ellis-island-late-1800s-9519.html

[807] "Illegal Alien Minors Spreading TB, Dengue, Swine Flu," *Judicial Watch,* July 8, 2014, http://www.judicialwatch.org/blog/2014/07/illegal-alien-minors-spreading-tb-ebola-dengue-swine-flu/

[808] Forghani, Navideh, "Undocumented Immigrants Bringing Diseases Across Border," ABC 15 – Phoenix, June 6, 2014, http://www.abc15.com/news/national/immigrants-bringing-diseases-across-border

[809] Tate, Kristin, "Doctor: Risk of Diseases Brought by Migrants Not Being Taken Seriously," *Breitbart,* June 27, 2014, http://www.breitbart.com/texas/2014/06/27/doctor-risk-of-diseases-brought-by-migrants-not-being-taken-seriously/

[810] *Ibid.*

[811] *Ibid.*

[812] Mitchell, Paula Ann, "Historic Huguenot Street," *Scrollkit,* Accessed January 1, 2016, http://www.scrollkit.com/s/zoeNVOP

[813] "Judicial Watch Obtains New Border Patrol Apprehension Statistics for Illegal Alien Smugglers and 'Special Interest Aliens'," *Judicial Watch,* March 9, 2011, http://www.judicialwatch.org/press-room/press-releases/judicial-watch-obtains-new-border-patrol-apprehension-statistics-for-illegal-alien-smugglers-and-%E2%80%9Cspecial-interest-aliens%E2%80%9D/

[814] Yager, Jordy, "Napolitano at Immigration Hearing: US Borders Have 'Never Been Stronger'," *The Hill,* February 14, 2013, http://thehill.com/homenews/senate/282845-napolitano-says-us-borders-have-never-been-stronger

[815] Mora, Edwin, "Border Patrol Agent: 60 Percent of Illegal US-Mexican Border Crossers Succeed", *Breitbart,* March 17, 2015, http://www.breitbart.com/big-government/2015/03/17/border-patrol-agent-60-percent-of-illegal-us-mexican-border-crossers-succeed/

[816] Darby, Brandon, "Graphic Images Justify Border Patrol's Use of Deadly Force Against Rock Attacks," *Breitbart,* April 2, 2014, http://www.breitbart.com/Texas/2014/04/02/Graphic-Images-Justify-Border-Patrols-Use-Of-Deadly-Force/

[817] Groening, Chad, "What Is 'Insulting, Degrading, Ludicrous?' New Must-Retreat Rules for Border Patrol," *One News Now,* March 14, 2014, http://www.onenewsnow.com/national-security/2014/03/14/what-is-insulting-degrading-ludicrous-new-must-retreat-rules-for-border-patrol

[818] La Jeunesse, W. & Prabucki, L., "New Court Documents Reveal Final Moments of Border Agent Brian Terry's Life," *Fox News,* February 5, 2014, http://www.foxnews.com/politics/2014/02/05/new-court-documents-reveal-final-moments-border-agent-brian-terrys-life/

[819] Price, Bob, "Congressional Leaders Arrive in Laredo over Downed Chopper," *Breitbart,* June 7, 2015, http://www.breitbart.com/texas/2015/06/07/congressional-leaders-arrive-in-laredo-over-downed-chopper/

[820] Darby, Brandon, "Catch and Release 2.0 — Leaks Highlight Teardown of Immigration Enforcement," *Breitbart,* January 11, 2015, http://www.breitbart.com/big-government/2015/01/11/exclusive-catch-and-release-2-0-leaks-highlight-teardown-of-immigration-enforcement/

[821] "DHS Releases End of Fiscal Year 2015 Statistics," DHS Press Office, December 22, 2015, http://www.dhs.gov/news/2015/12/22/dhs-releases-end-fiscal-year-2015-statistics

[822] "Oversight of the Administration's Criminal Alien Removal Policies," Judiciary Hearing SD-226, Center for Immigration Studies, December 2, 2015, http://cis.org/Testimony/vaughan-Oversight-Administrations-Criminal-Alien-Removal-Policies

[823] "Interior Enforcement Disintegrates Further in 2015," December 2015, CIS, http://cis.org/Interior-Enforcement-2015-Deportations

[824] Picket, Kerry, "Source: DHS to Propose Moving ICE Border Funds to Other Agencies," *The Daily Caller*, August 6, 2015, http://dailycaller.com/2015/08/06/source-dhs-to-propose-moving-ice-border-funds-to-other-agencies

[825] *Ibid.*

[826] Pfeiffer, Alex, "Less Than 1 Percent of Immigrants Who Overstayed Visas Were Deported in 2015," *Daily Caller,* May 5, 2016, http://dailycaller.com/2016/05/06/less-than-1-percent-of-immigrants-who-overstayed-visas-were-deported-in-2015/

[827] Kouri, Jim, "Government Accused of Treating Imprisoned Border Patrol Agents Worse Than Terrorists," *Liberty Sentinel*, December 2007, http://www.libertysentinel.org/article.php?id=BorderPatrol

[828] "Illegal Alien Drug Smuggler in Border Agents' Case Arrested for... Smuggling Drugs," Center For Individual Freedom, November 30, 2007, http://www.cfif.org/htdocs/legislative_issues/federal_issues/hot_issues_in_congress/immigration/Aldrete-Davila-arrest.htm

[829] Carroll, Susan, "Judge Blasts Prosecutors in Ex-Border Agents' Case," *Houston Chronicle,* December 4, 2007, http://www.chron.com/news/article/Judge-blasts-prosecutors-in-ex-border-agents-case-1839725.php

[830] Corsi, Jerome R., "Ramos, Compean Freed From Prison – Congressman Calls for Probe of Prosecutor, Role of Mexico," *WND,* http://www.wnd.com/2009/02/89176/

[831] Hernandez, Kristian, "BP Council Says 'Catch and Release' Policy Continues Fueling Illegal Immigration," *The Monitor,* April 2016, http://www.themonitor.com/news/local/bp-council-says-catch-and-release-policy-continues-fueling-illegal/article_b48caa0c-f92c-11e5-914a-671ec164babb.html

[832] Dinan, Stephen, "Secret Report: Catch and Release for Low-Priority Illegals Proposed," *The Washington Times,* June 14, 2012, http://www.washingtontimes.com/news/2012/jun/14/catch-and-release-for-low-priority-illegals-propos/?page=all

[833] *Ibid.*

[834] Price, Bob, "Judicial Watch: 165,900 Criminal Aliens into US Population Through April 2014," *Breitbart,* March 25, 2015, http://www.breitbart.com/texas/2015/03/24/judicial-watch-165900-criminal-aliens-into-us-population-through-april-2014/

[835] *Ibid.*

[836] Dinan, Stephan, "DHS Released Another 30,000 Criminal Aliens onto Streets," *The Washington Times,* March 18, 2015, http://www.washingtontimes.com/news/2015/mar/18/dhs-released-another-30000-criminal-aliens-streets/

[837] Vaughan, Jessica, "Free to Kill: 124 Criminal Aliens Released By Obama Policies Charged with Homicide Since 2010," Center for Immigration Studies, March 14, 2016, http://cis.org/vaughan/Map-124-criminal-aliens-released-obama-policies-charged-homicide-2010

[838] Dinan, Stephen, "Nearly 20 Million Illegal Immigrants in U.S., Former Border Patrol Agents Say," *The Washington Times*, September 9, 2013, http://www.washingtontimes.com/news/2013/sep/9/nearly-20m-illegal-immigrants-us-ex-border-patrol/

[839] Tyler, Taylor, "30 Million Illegal Immigrants Live In U.S., Says Mexico's Former Ambassador, " HNGN, August 19, 2015, http://www.hngn.com/articles/121099/20150819/30-million-illegal-immigrants-live-u-s-mexicos-former-ambassador.htm

[840] "ICE Enforcement and Removal Operations Report," U.S. Immigration and Customs Enforcement, December 19, 2014, https://www.ice.gov/doclib/about/offices/ero/pdf/2014-ice-immigration-removals.pdf, p. 4

[841] Justich, R. & Ng, B., "The Underground Labor Force Is Rising to the Surface, Bear Stearns, January 3, 2005, http://www.steinreport.com/BearStearnsStudy.pdf, pp. 1-2

[842] Barlett, D. & Steele, J., "Illegal Aliens: Who Left the Door Open?" *Time Magazine,* March 30, 2006, http://content.time.com/time/magazine/article/0,9171,995145,00.html

[843] Dinan, Stephen, "Illegal immigrants release 'Bill of Rights'," *The Washington Times,* November 5, 2015, http://www.washingtontimes.com/news/2015/nov/5/illegal-immigrants-release-bill-rights/

[844] Malkin, Michelle, "How Mexico Treats Illegal Aliens, *National Review,* April 28, 2010, http://www.nationalreview.com/article/229641/how-mexico-treats-illegal-aliens-michelle-malkin

[845] Preston, Julia, "San Francisco Murder Case Exposes Lapses in Immigration Enforcement," *New York Times,* July 7, 2015, http://www.nytimes.com/2015/07/08/us/san-francisco-murder-case-exposes-lapses-in-immigration-enforcement.html

[846] Sernoffsky, E., Aleaziz, H. & Lyons, J., "Woman Mourned, Suspect Held in Random Killing on S.F. Pier," *San Francisco Chronicle,* July 5, 2015, http://www.sfgate.com/news/article/Woman-killed-on-San-Francisco-pier-identified-6363401.php

[847] Ross, Chuck, "Illegal Alien Arrested Four Times in Two Years Allegedly Beat California Woman with Hammer, Raped Her," *The Daily Caller,* August 4, 2015, http://dailycaller.com/2015/08/04/illegal-alien-arrested-four-times-in-two-years-allegedly-beat-california-woman-with-hammer-raped-her/

[848] Hicap, Jonah, "Illegal Alien Accused of Raping, Hammering California Woman, 64, Leading to her Death," *Christian Today,* August 7, 2015, http://www.christiantoday.com/article/illegal.alien.accused.of.raping.hammering.california.woman.64.leading.to.her.death/61311.htm

[849] Dinan, Stephen, "White House Defends Sanctuary Cities, Threatens to Veto Crackdown Bill," *The Washington Times,* July 23, 2015, http://www.washingtontimes.com/news/2015/jul/23/white-house-backs-sanctuary-cities-threatens-veto/

[850] "Sen. Cruz and Rep. Salmon Introduce 'Kate's Law,' the Establishing Mandatory Minimums for Illegal Reentry Act," Presser from Sen. Ted Cruz, July 21, 2015, http://www.cruz.senate.gov/?p=press_release&id=2395

[851] Nazarian, Adelle, "Sanctuary Cities Highlighted in GOP Debate," *Breitbart,* August 6, 2015, http://www.breitbart.com/california/2015/08/08/sanctuary-cities-highlighted-in-gop-debate/

[852] May, Caroline, "Harry Reid Blocks Kate's Law," *Breitbart,* November 4, 2015, http://www.breitbart.com/big-government/2015/11/04/harry-reid-blocks-kates-law/

[853] "Voters Favor 'Kate's Law' Sentences for Illegal Immigrant Felons," Rasmussen Reports, November 3, 2015, http://www.rasmussenreports.com/public_content/politics/current_events/immigration/october_2015/voters_favor_kate_s_law_sentences_for_illegal_immigrant_felons

[854] Gonzalez L. & Ixel, M., "80% of the Population, Poor or at Risk of Becoming: Coneval," *El Universal,* July 30, 2013, http://www.eluniversal.com.mx/primera-plana/2013/impreso/80-de-la-poblacion-pobre-o-en-riesgo-de-serlo-coneval-42648.html

[855] Nakamura, David, "Border Agents Decry 'Diaper Changing, Burrito Wrapping' with Influx of Children," *The Washington Post,* June 20, 2014, http://www.washingtonpost.com/politics/border-agents-decry-diaper-changing-burrito-wrapping-with-influx-of-children/2014/06/20/1a6b6714-f579-11e3-8aa9-dad2ec039789_story.html

[856] Darby, Brandon, "Leaked Border Crisis Intel Shreds Narrative from Media and Obama Admin," *Breitbart,* July 14, 2014, http://www.breitbart.com/Texas/2014/07/14/Leaked-Intel-Report-Violence-in-Central-America-Likely-Not-Primary-Factor-in-Border-Crisis/

[857] Coman, Julian, "Arab Terrorists 'Are Getting into the US Over Mexican Border'," *The Telegraph,* August 15, 2004, http://www.telegraph.co.uk/news/worldnews/northamerica/usa/1469466/Arab-terrorists-are-getting-into-the-US-over-Mexican-border.html

[858] Ibid.

[859] "Judicial Watch Obtains New Border Patrol Apprehension Statistics for Illegal Alien Smugglers and 'Special Interest Aliens'," *Judicial Watch,* March 9, 2011, https://www.judicialwatch.org/press-room/press-releases/judicial-watch-obtains-new-border-patrol-apprehension-statistics-for-illegal-alien-smugglers-and-%E2%80%9Cspecial-interest-aliens%E2%80%9D/

[860] Coman, Julian, "Arab Terrorists 'Are Getting into the US Over Mexican Border'," *UK Telegraph,* August 15, 2004, http://www.telegraph.co.uk/news/worldnews/northamerica/usa/1469466/Arab-terrorists-are-getting-into-the-US-over-Mexican-border.html

[861] Ibid.

[862] La Jeunesse, William, "Iranian Book Celebrating Suicide Bombers Found in Arizona Desert," Fox News, January 27, 2011, http://www.foxnews.com/us/2011/01/27/iranian-book-celebrating-suicide-bombers-arizona-desert/

[863] Ibid.

[864] Picket, Kerry, "Muslim Prayer Rug Found on Arizona Border by Independent American Security Contractors," *Breitbart,* July 9, 2014, http://www.breitbart.com/big-government/2014/07/09/muslim-prayer-rug-found-on-arizona-border-by-independendent-american-security-contractors/

[865] Carter, Sara, "The Odd Book One Texas Rancher Found Near the Border, *The Blaze,* July 14, 2014, http://www.theblaze.com/stories/2014/07/14/urdu-dictionary-found-on-texas-ranch-near-border-we-just-dont-know-whos-here-already/

[866] Baddour, Dylan, "David Dewhurst Says Prayer Rugs Found in Texas Brush Near Mexico Border," *Politifact,* October 19, 2014, http://www.politifact.com/texas/statements/2014/oct/19/david-dewhurst/david-dewhurst-says-prayer-rugs-found-texas-brush-/

[867] "Texas Sheriff: 'Muslim Clothing, Koran Books' Found on Border Trails, *Fox News,* September 15, 2014, http://insider.foxnews.com/2014/09/15/texas-sheriff-muslim-clothing-koran-books-found-along-mexican-border-trails

[868] "JW Confirms: 4 ISIS Terrorists Arrested in Texas in Last 36 Hours, *Judicial Watch,* October 8, 2014, http://www.judicialwatch.org/blog/2014/10/jw-confirms-4-isis-terrorists-arrested-texas-last-36-hours/

[869] Ibid.

[870] Baddour, Dylan, "David Dewhurst Says Prayer Rugs Found in Texas Brush Near Mexico Border," *Politifact,* October 19, 2014, http://www.politifact.com/texas/statements/2014/oct/19/david-dewhurst/david-dewhurst-says-prayer-rugs-found-texas-brush-/

[871] "Judicial Watch Obtains New Border Patrol Apprehension Statistics for Illegal Alien Smugglers and 'Special Interest Aliens'," *Judicial Watch,* March 9, 2011, https://www.judicialwatch.org/press-room/press-releases/judicial-watch-obtains-new-border-patrol-apprehension-statistics-for-illegal-alien-smugglers-and-%E2%80%9Cspecial-interest-aliens%E2%80%9D/

[872] Picket, Kerry, "Muslim Prayer Rug Found on Arizona Border by Independent American Security Contractors," *Breitbart,* July 9, 2014, http://www.breitbart.com/big-government/2014/07/09/muslim-prayer-rug-found-on-arizona-border-by-independendent-american-security-contractors/

[873] "U.S. Intel Center Wary of Terrorist Attack", *The Washington Times,* November 25, 2007, http://www.washingtontimes.com/news/2007/nov/25/us-intel-center-wary-of-terrorist-attack/?page=all

[874] Roberts, Chris, "More Iraqis Cross Southwest Border Seeking Asylum", *El Paso Times,* August 22, 2007, http://www.elpasotimes.com/news/ci_6684100

[875] "Terror-Linked Migrants Channeled Into U.S.", *AP,* July 3, 2005, http://www.foxnews.com/story/2005/07/03/terror-linked-migrants-channeled-into-us/

[876] "Flashback: Report said U.S. Seized 77 Mideastern Aliens in Southern Arizona", *The World Tribune,* August 2, 2004, http://www.worldtribune.com/2014/06/10/flashback-u-s-seized-77-mideastern-aliens-southern-arizona/

[877] "Chechen Terrorists Probed", *The Washington Times,* October 13, 2004, http://www.washingtontimes.com/news/2004/oct/13/20041013-121643-5028r/?page=all

[878] Moreno, S., & Mintz, J., "S. African Detained in Texas May Have Terrorist Ties", *The Washington Post,* August 1, 2004, http://www.washingtonpost.com/wp-dyn/articles/A30903-2004Jul31.html

[879] Spencer, Robert, "National Security At the Border," *Human Events,* February 19, 2008, http://humanevents.com/2008/02/19/national-security-at-the-border/

[880] "Hezbollah Terror Threat on U.S.-Mexico Border Is Real," *Arizona Capitol Times,* March 23, 2013, http://azcapitoltimes.com/news/2012/03/23/hezbollah-terror-threat-on-u-s-mexico-border-is-real/

[881] "Off the Record U.S. Responsibility for Enforced Disappearances in the 'War on Terror'," *Human Rights Watch,* http://www.hrw.org/legacy/backgrounder/usa/ct0607/ct0607web.pdf, p. 18

[882] "Rep. John Culberson", *Fox News,* November 21, 2005, http://www.foxnews.com/story/2005/11/21/exclusive-rep-john-culberson/

[883] Schilling, Chelsea, "Foreign 'terrorists' Breach U.S. Border, Illegals Coming from Afghanistan, Iran, Egypt, Pakistan, Sudan, Syria, Yemen, *WND,* May 20, 2010, http://www.wnd.com/2010/05/156441/

[884] *Ibid.*

[885] "U.S. Intel Center Wary of Terrorist Attack", *The Washington Times,* November 25, 2007, http://www.washingtontimes.com/news/2007/nov/25/us-intel-center-wary-of-terrorist-attack/?page=all

[886] *Ibid.*

[887] "Hezbollah Uses Mexican Drug Routes into U.S.", *The Washington Times,* March 27, 2009, http://www.washingtontimes.com/news/2009/mar/27/hezbollah-uses-mexican-drug-routes-into-us/?page=all/

[888] "Abdullah Al-Nafisi – A Biological Attack on USA," Al-Jazeera TV via YouTube video, February 2, 2009, https://www.youtube.com/watch?v=tsKEZ6QC2pQ

[889] Sundby, Alex, "Feds Worried About 300 Smuggled Somalis Gone Missing," *CBS News, April 13, 2010,* http://www.cbsnews.com/news/feds-worried-about-300-smuggled-somalis-gone-missing/

[890] Hohmann, Leo, "DHS Hides Crucial Fact on 'Terrorist Influx'", *WND,* February 23, 2015, http://www.wnd.com/2015/02/dhs-hides-crucial-fact-on-terrorist-influx/

[891] "Three Men Charged with Financing Hezbollah in Miami", *AP,* February 19, 2010, http://www.haaretz.com/news/three-men-charged-with-financing-hezbollah-in-miami-1.263655

[892] "Re: Ahmed Muhammed Dhakane", *The Global Intelligence Files,* February 2, 2013, https://wikileaks.org/gifiles/docs/52/5283004_re-ahmed-muhammed-dhakane-.html

[893] "Prosecutors: Somali Smuggled Jihadists into U.S.", *IPT News,* March 25, 2011, http://www.investigativeproject.org/2716/prosecutors-somali-smuggled-jihadists-into-us

[894] Mauro, Ryan, "Growing Hezbollah Presence in Southwest U.S.", *The Clarion Project,* October 13, 2013, http://m.clarionproject.org/analysis/hezbollah-tattoos-increasing-found-us-prison-inmates

[895] Wilkinson, Tracy, "Mexico Cartel Kills Four in Car Bombing" *Los Angeles Times,* July 17, 2010, http://articles.latimes.com/2010/jul/17/world/la-fg-mexico-car-bomb-20100717

[896] Bracamontes, Ramon, "Experts: Car Bomb in Juarez Mimics Middle East Terrorist Tactics," *El Paso Times,* July 17, 2010, http://www.elpasotimes.com/ci_15537113

[897] Stewart, Scott, "The Perceived Car Bomb Threat in Mexico", *Stratfor,* April 13, 2011, https://www.stratfor.com/weekly/20110413-perceived-car-bomb-threat-mexico

[898] Myrick, Rep. Sue, "MYRICK: Hezbollah Car Bombs on Our Border", *The Washington Times,* September 1, 2010, http://www.washingtontimes.com/news/2010/sep/1/hezbollah-car-bombs-on-our-border/

[899] La Jeunesse, William, "Iranian Book Celebrating Suicide Bombers Found in Arizona Desert," *Fox News,* January 27, 2011, http://www.foxnews.com/us/2011/01/27/iranian-book-celebrating-suicide-bombers-arizona-desert/

[900] Weiser, Benjamin, "Man Sentenced in Plot to Kill Saudi Ambassador," *New York Times,* May 30, 2013, http://www.nytimes.com/2013/05/31/nyregion/mansour-arbabsiar-sentenced-for-plot-to-kill-saudi-ambassador.html

[901] "Hezbollah Suspected Terrorist Arrested in Merida", *Yucatan Times,* September 10, 2012, http://www.theyucatantimes.com/2012/09/hezbollah-suspected-terrorist-arrested-in-merida/

[902] Kolb, Joseph, "Lawmaker Urges Feds to Monitor Hezbollah in Mexico", *Fox News,* October 29, 2012, http://www.foxnews.com/world/2012/10/29/lawmaker-urges-feds-to-monitor-hezbollah-in-mexico/

[903] Daly, Michael, "Terry Lee Loewen, the Mellow Kansas Man Who Dreamed of Jihad," *The Daily Beast,* December 16, 2013, http://www.thedailybeast.com/articles/2013/12/16/terry-lee-loewen-the-mellow-kansas-man-who-allegedly-dreamed-of-jihad.html

[904] "Austin Man Sentenced to Nearly 7 Years for Supporting Terrorism," *KXAN News,* June 5, 2015, http://kxan.com/2015/06/05/austin-man-sentenced-to-nearly-7-years-for-supporting-terrorism/

[905] "FBI: Ohio Man Planned to Bomb U.S. Capitol, Kill Officials," *Chicago Tribune,* January 15, 2015, http://www.chicagotribune.com/news/nationworld/chi-capitol-bomb-plot-20150115-story.html

[906] "Iraqi Caught Crossing US-Mexico Border was Military Trainer and Spoke Fluent Russian", *Breitbart,* April 7, 2015, http://www.breitbart.com/big-government/2015/04/07/exclusive-iraqi-caught-crossing-us-mexico-border-was-military-trainer-and-spoke-fluent-russian/

[907] "Syria-Trained Ohio Man Aimed to Kill Cops, Soldiers: Feds," *NBC News,* April 16, 2015, http://www.nbcnews.com/news/us-news/syria-trained-ohio-man-aimed-kill-cops-soldiers-feds-n342851

[908] Spencer, Robert, "Brooklyn: Three Muslims Charged With Plotting to Join Islamic State, Shoot Obama," *Jihad Watch,* February 25, 2015, http://www.jihadwatch.org/2015/02/brooklyn-three-muslims-charged-with-plotting-to-join-islamic-state-shoot-obama

[909] "ISIS-Inspired John Thomas Booker Jr. Charged in Kansas Military Bomb Plot," NBC News, April 10 2015, http://www.nbcnews.com/storyline/isis-terror/isis-inspired-john-thomas-booker-jr-kansas-charged-military-bomb-n339361

[910] "Illinois National Guardsman, Cousin Indicted in ISIS Plot," NBC News, April 3, 2015, http://www.nbcnews.com/storyline/isis-terror/illinois-national-guardsman-cousin-indicted-isis-plot-n335536

[911] Williams, P., & Connor, T., "Keonna Thomas, Philadelphia Mom, Charged With Plan to Join ISIS," NBC News, April 4, 2015, http://www.nbcnews.com/storyline/isis-terror/philadelphia-woman-keonna-thomas-charged-plan-join-isis-n335226

[912] Dienst, J., Valiquette, J., Nious, K., & Millman, J., "2 Queens Women Accused of Plotting to Plant Bombs in U.S. Talked Suicide Attacks, Had Propane Tanks: Complaint," NBC News, April 3, 2015, http://www.nbcnewyork.com/investigations/Terror-Arrest-New-York-FBI-NYPD-Police-297422441.html

[913] "Second Man Charged in Plot to Bomb Kansas Army Base for ISIS," NBC News, April 10 2015, http://www.nbcnews.com/storyline/isis-terror/second-man-charged-plot-bomb-kansas-army-base-n339701

[914] Boudin, Michelle, "Teen Charged with Plot to Support ISIS by Killing 1,000 Americans Has 'Shocked' Parents Standing by Him," People, June 22, 2105, http://www.people.com/article/north-carolina-teen-charged-plot-kill-americans-impress-isis

[915] Mueller, Benjamin, "College Student in Queens Is Charged With Conspiring to Support ISIS," New York Times, June 16, 2015, http://www.nytimes.com/2015/06/17/nyregion/college-student-in-queens-is-charged-with-conspiring-to-support-isis.html

[916] Pandey, Avaneesh, "From Pokemon to ISIS Terror Plots in 12 Months?" Vocativ, June 17, 2015, http://www.vocativ.com/world/isis-2/munther-omar-saleh-queens-college-isis-pokemon/

[917] "Feds: S.I. Man Tries To Stab FBI Agent With Knife During Terror Probe," CBS News, June 17, 2015, http://newyork.cbslocal.com/2015/06/17/queens-student-alleged-terror-plot/

[918] Ibid.

[919] Pugliese, Nicholas, "Alleged ISIS Hopeful from Fort Lee Has Unlikely Past," North Jersey, June 19, 2015, http://www.northjersey.com/news/alleged-isis-hopeful-has-unlikely-past-1.1359779

[920] Pandey, Avaneesh, "Who Is Samuel Rahamin Topaz? Alleged ISIS Sympathizer Arrested In New Jersey," International Business Times, June 19, 2015, http://www.ibtimes.com/who-samuel-rahamin-topaz-alleged-isis-sympathizer-arrested-new-jersey-1974451

[921] Marzulli, John, "New Jersey Man Arrested in ISIS Conspiracy: Federal Court Documents," New York Daily News, June 29, 2015, http://www.nydailynews.com/news/crime/nj-man-arrested-isis-conspiracy-federal-court-documents-article-1.2275181

[922] Mukhopadhyay, Sounak, "ISIS Suspect In New Jersey Had Plans For Beheading: Court Document," International Business Times, June 29, 2015, http://www.ibtimes.com/isis-suspect-new-jersey-had-plans-beheading-court-document-1988973

[923] "Total Number of Websites," Internet Live Stats, Accessed May 1, 2016, http://www.internetlivestats.com/total-number-of-websites/

[924] Hohmann, Leo, "We Are Charlie, Indeed! 22 Islamic Terror Camps in U.S," WND, January 13, 2015; http://www.wnd.com/2015/01/22-terror-camps-verified-inside-u-s/ '

[925] "35 Terror Training Camps Now Operating Inside U.S.," WND, January 2, 2012; http://www.wnd.com/2012/01/381953/

[926] Gertz, Bill, "DNI: 2014 Was Deadliest Year for Terror Attacks in 45 Years," Washington Free Beacon, February 27, 2014, http://freebeacon.com/national-security/dni-2014-was-deadliest-year-for-terror-attacks-in-45-years/

[927] "US Report: Sharp Rise in Global Terror Attacks in 2014," Aljazeera, June 20, 2015, http://www.aljazeera.com/news/2015/06/report-sharp-rise-global-terror-attacks-2014-150620013633463.html

[928] Ibid.

[929] Bennett, Brian, "White House Steps Up Warnings About Terrorism on U.S. Soil," Los Angeles Times, May 19, 2015, http://www.latimes.com/nation/la-na-terror-threat-20150518-story.html

[930] Davis, Melissa, "These 16 States Are Trying to Ban Sharia Law," US Herald, April 8, 2015, http://www.usherald.com/these-16-states-are-trying-to-ban-sharia-law/

[931] Burke, Caitlan, "Sharia Tribunal in Texas an Islamic Trojan Horse?" CBN News, March 8, 2015, http://www.cbn.com/cbnnews/us/2015/March/Sharia-Tribunal-in-Texas-an-Islamic-Trojan-Horse/

[932] "As Hamtramck's Polish Population Shrinks, a Muslim Sparks Controversy," Deadline Detroit, November 8, 2015, http://www.deadlinedetroit.com/articles/13611/as_hamtramck_s_polish_population_shrinks_a_muslim_s_remark_sparks_controversy

[933] Geller, Pamela, "New Muslim Majority City Council Member in Michigan Issues Warning," Breitbart, November 11, 2015, http://www.breitbart.com/big-government/2015/11/11/new-muslim-majority-city-council-member-in-michigan-issues-warning/

[934] "Hamtramck, Michigan Now Almost a Completely Muslim Community," Fox News Video, March 26, 2016, http://video.foxnews.com/v/4818427365001/hamtramck-michigan-now-almost-a-completely-muslim-community/

[935] Bailey, Sarah Pulliam, "In the First Majority-Muslim U.S. City, Residents Tense About Its Future," Washington Post, November 21, 2015, https://www.washingtonpost.com/national/for-the-first-majority-muslim-us-city-residents-tense-about-its-future/2015/11/21/45d0ea96-8a24-11e5-be39-0034bb576eee_story.html

[936] Burke, Caitlan, "Sharia Tribunal in Texas an Islamic Trojan Horse?" CBN News, March 8, 2015, http://www.cbn.com/cbnnews/us/2015/March/Sharia-Tribunal-in-Texas-an-Islamic-Trojan-Horse/

[937] "City in Michigan First to Fully Implement Sharia Law," National Report, July 27, 2015, http://nationalreport.net/city-michigan-first-fully-implement-sharia-law/

[938] "Sharia Law In America? - Hannity," YouTube Video, Uploaded June 2, 2015, https://www.youtube.com/watch?t=20&v=wDr8BCTqKK0

[939] Ibid.

[940] Qualls-Shehata, Nancy, "Okay, I Confess, We ARE Trying to Take Over the World!" Muslim Village, December 13, 2011, http://muslimvillage.com/2011/12/15/17236/okay-i-confess-we-are-trying-to-take-over-the-world/

[941] "New Jersey Judge Rules Islamic Sharia Law Trumps U.S. Law," *Creeping Sharia,* August 7, 2010, https://creepingsharia.wordpress.com/2010/08/07/new-jersey-judge-rules-islamic-sharia-law-trumps-u-s-law/

[942] Stimson, Cully "The Real Impact of Sharia Law in America," *The Daily Signal,* September 2, 2010, http://dailysignal.com/2010/09/02/the-real-impact-of-sharia-law-in-america/

[943] Madhani, Aamer, "Shariah Financing Growing Popular in the West, *USA Today,* October 13, 2014, http://www.usatoday.com/story/money/business/2014/10/11/shariah-compliant-islamic-financing-usa-europe/16828599/

[944] Wigglesworth, Robin, "Non-Muslims Tap Sukuk Market," *The Financial Times,* October 8, 2014, http://www.ft.com/intl/cms/s/0/8140af64-3feb-11e4-936b-00144feabdc0.html

[945] Turley, Jonathan, "Seattle Moves to Make Available "Sharia Mortgages" to Conform Mortgages to Islamic Law, July 23, 2015, http://jonathanturley.org/2015/07/23/seattle-moves-to-make-available-sharia-mortgages-to-conform-mortgages-to-islamic-law/

[946] Sacirbey, Omar, "Sharia Law in the USA 101: A Guide To What It Is and Why States Want to Ban It," *Huffington Post,* July 29, 2013, http://www.huffingtonpost.com/2013/07/29/sharia-law-usa-states-ban_n_3660813.html

[947] "How Is Sharia Law Dangerous for Western Society?" Video with Dr. John Ankerberg Interviewing Guests, Dr. Emir Caner, Kamal Saleem, and Lt. Gen. (Ret.) William G. "Jerry" Boykin, March 20, 2015, https://www.youtube.com/watch?v=JcpfZvt7iPY

[948] Fallaci, Oriana, from *The Force of Reason* via Wikiquote," 2004, https://en.wikiquote.org/wiki/Oriana_Fallaci

[949] Stakelbeck, Erick, "UK Islamist Leader: Islam Will Dominate America," *CBN News,* August 10, 2012, http://www.cbn.com/cbnnews/world/2012/august/uk-islamist-leader-islam-will-dominate-america/

[950] *Ibid.*

[951] Hizb ut-Tahrir America (About Us), Hizb ut-Tahrir, Accessed July 27, 2015,https://hizb-america.org/about-us/,

[952] Boniello, Kathianne, "'Ground Zero Mosque' Developer Sued Over Illegal Rental," *New York Post,* April 5, 2015, http://nypost.com/2015/04/05/ground-zero-mosque-developer-sued-over-illegal-rental/

[953] Redpath, Rhiannon, "Women Around the World Are Being Stoned to Death. Do You Know the Facts?" *Mic,* October 16, 2013, http://mic.com/articles/68431/women-around-the-world-are-being-stoned-to-death-do-you-know-the-facts

[954] "Mapping Stoning in Muslim Contexts," Women Living Under Muslim Laws, February 2012, http://www.wluml.org/sites/wluml.org/files/Mapping%20Stoning%20in%20Muslim%20Contexts_Final.pdf, p. 6

[955] "Iran: Death By Stoning, a Grotesque and Unacceptable Penalty," Amnesty International, January 15, 2008, https://www.amnesty.org/press-releases/2008/01/iran-death-stoning-grotesque-and-unacceptable-penalty-20080115/

[956] "Mapping Stoning in Muslim Contexts," Women Living Under Muslim Laws, February 2012, http://www.wluml.org/sites/wluml.org/files/Mapping%20Stoning%20in%20Muslim%20Contexts_Final.pdf, p. 10

[957] Clarke, Natalie, "The Girl Who Was Stoned to Death for Falling in Love," *UK Daily Mail,* May 17, 2007, http://www.dailymail.co.uk/femail/article-455400/The-girl-stoned-death-falling-love.html

[958] "Mapping Stoning in Muslim Contexts," Women Living Under Muslim Laws, February 2012, http://www.wluml.org/sites/wluml.org/files/Mapping%20Stoning%20in%20Muslim%20Contexts_Final.pdf, p. 10

[959] *Ibid.*, p. 3

[960] Batha, Emma, "Special Report: The Punishment Was Death By Stoning. The Crime? Having a Mobile Phone," *UK Independent,* September 29, 2013, http://www.independent.co.uk/news/world/politics/special-report-the-punishment-was-death-by-stoning-the-crime-having-a-mobile-phone-8846585.html

[961] "Pakistan: A Young Woman Stoned to Death for Having a Cell Phone After Ruling By a Panchayat," Asian Human Rights Commission, July 11, 2013, http://www.humanrights.asia/news/ahrc-news/AHRC-STM-128-2013

[962] Mroue, Bassem, "Women Stoned to Death in Syria for Adultery," *The Daily Star,* Lebanon, August 10, 2014, http://www.dailystar.com.lb/News/Middle-East/2014/Aug-10/266648-women-stoned-to-death-in-syria-for-adultery.ashx

[963] "Woman Stoned in Syria for Not Being a Virgin Was a Widow, ISIS Threaten 'Death By Sword,'" *The Inquisitr,* August 9, 2014, http://www.inquisitr.com/1402481/woman-stoned-in-syria-for-not-being-a-virgin-was-a-widow-isis-threaten-death-by-sword/

[964] Batha, Emma, "Stoning Victim 'Begged for Mercy'," *BBC News,* November 4, 2008, http://news.bbc.co.uk/2/hi/7708169.stm

[965] "Pakistani Woman Stoned to Death By Family for Marrying the Man She Loved," Reuters, May 27, 2014, http://www.reuters.com/article/2014/05/27/us-pakistan-honourkillings-idUSKBN0E711A20140527

[966] "State of Human Rights in 2013," HRCP, April 14, 2015, http://www.hrcp-web.org/hrcpweb/report14/AR2013.pdf, p. 6

[967] Bukhari, Mubasher, "Pakistani Woman Stoned to Death By Family for Marrying the Man She Loved," *Reuters,* May 27, 2014, http://www.reuters.com/article/2014/05/27/us-pakistan-honourkillings-idUSKBN0E711A20140527

[968] "Ending Violence Against Women and Girls," United Nations, http://www.un.org/en/globalissues/briefingpapers/endviol/index.shtml

[969] Chesler, Phyllis, "Worldwide Trends in Honor Killings," *Middle East Quarterly,* Spring 2010, pp. 3-11, http://www.meforum.org/2646/worldwide-trends-in-honor-killings

[970] *Ibid.*

[971] "What Is Honor Violence," AHA Foundation, Accessed October 13, 2015, http://www.theahafoundation.org/honor-violence/

[972] Treen, Joe, 'Die, My Daughter, Die!' *People Magazine,* January 20, 1992, http://www.people.com/people/archive/article/0,,20111801,00.html

[973] 'Terror and Death at Home Are Caught in F.B.I. Tape' *New York Times,* October 28, 1991, http://www.nytimes.com/1991/10/28/us/terror-and-death-at-home-are-caught-in-fbi-tape.html

[974] *Ibid.*

[975] Treen, Joe, 'Die, My Daughter, Die!' *People Magazine,* January 20, 1992, http://www.people.com/people/archive/article/0,,20111801,00.html

[976] Tarabay, James, "Man Accused of Killing Daughter for Family Honor," *NPR,* January 26, 2009, http://www.npr.org/templates/story/story.php?storyId=99616128

[977] "Court Upholds Man's Sentence In 'Honor Killing'," *CBS Atlanta,* January 22, 2013, http://atlanta.cbslocal.com/2013/01/22/court-upholds-mans-sentence-in-honor-killing/

[978] Tarabay, James, "Man Accused of Killing Daughter for Family Honor," *NPR,* January 26, 2009, http://www.npr.org/templates/story/story.php?storyId=99616128

[979] *Ibid.*

[980] Redlitz, Sean, "Dying Teen Names Dad as Killer," CNN, July 20, 2015, http://www.cnn.com/2015/07/08/us/yaser-said-the-hunt-john-walsh/

[981] *Ibid.*

[982] Mauro, Ryan, "Muslims of the Americas' Depositions Reveal New Enclaves," Clarion Project, May 4, 2014, http://www.clarionproject.org/analysis/muslims-americas-depositions-reveal-new-enclaves

[983] Kane, J. & Wall, A., "Identifying the Links Between White-Collar Crime and Terrorism," National Criminal Justice Reference Service, April 2005, https://www.ncjrs.gov/pdffiles1/nij/grants/209520.pdf, p. 93

[984] "Jamaat al-Fuqra; Gilani Followers Conducting Paramilitary Training in U.S.," Regional Organized Crime Information Center, 2006, http://info.publicintelligence.net/ROCICjamaatulfuqra.pdf, 93

[985] Mauro, Ryan, "Muslims of the Americas' Depositions Reveal New Enclaves," *Clarion Project,* May 4, 2014, http://www.clarionproject.org/analysis/muslims-americas-depositions-reveal-new-enclaves

[986] "Country Reports on Terrorism 2013," U.S. Department of State, Bureau of Counterterrorism, April 2014, http://www.state.gov/documents/organization/225886.pdf, p. 266

[987] "Terrorism-Related Inadmissibility Grounds (TRIG)," Immigration and Nationality Act, Section 212 (a)(3)(B), U.S. Citizenship and Immigration Services, October 1, 2014, http://www.uscis.gov/laws/terrorism-related-inadmissability-grounds/terrorism-related-inadmissibility-grounds-trig

[988] "Jamaat ul-Fuqra," South Asia Terrorism Portal, http://www.satp.org/satporgtp/countries/pakistan/terroristoutfits/jamaat-ul-fuqra.htm

[989] "Patterns of Global Terrorism 1999," U.S. Department of State, Bureau of Counterterrorism, April 2000, http://www.state.gov/www/global/terrorism/1999report/patterns.pdf, p. 120

[990] *Ibid.*

[991] Mauro, Ryan, "Exclusive: Islamist Terror Enclave Discovered in Texas," *The Clarion Project,* February 18, 2014, http://www.clarionproject.org/analysis/exclusive-clarion-project-discovers-texas-terror-enclave

[992] Lipton, Eric, "Homeland Report Says Threat From Terror-List Nations Is Declining," *New York Times,* March 31, 2005, http://www.nytimes.com/2005/03/31/politics/31threat.html

[993] Alfano, Sean, "Stopping Terror At The Border," *CBS News,* October 26, 2005, http://www.cbsnews.com/news/stopping-terror-at-the-border/

[994] "Illegal Immigrants Trash Border Lands With Tons of Waste," *Judicial Watch,* February 1, 2012, http://www.judicialwatch.org/blog/2012/02/illegal-immigrants-trash-border-lands-with-tons-of-waste/

[995] Alfano, Sean, "Stopping Terror At The Border," *CBS News,* October 26, 2005, http://www.cbsnews.com/news/stopping-terror-at-the-border/

[996] Williams, Linda, "Illegal immigrants smuggled across military range," *Fox 10 News,* Phoenix, November 17, 2015, http://www.fox10phoenix.com/news/arizona-news/50862876-story

[997] "ISIS Camp a Few Miles from Texas, Mexican Authorities Confirm," *Judicial Watch,* April 14, 2015, http://www.judicialwatch.org/blog/2015/04/isis-camp-a-few-miles-from-texas-mexican-authorities-confirm/

[998] Dinan, Stephen, "Border Patrol: Rules Hinder Effort to Oust Drug Spotters," *The Washington Times,* May 7, 2013, http://www.washingtontimes.com/news/2013/may/7/border-patrol-rules-hinder-effort-oust-drug-spotte/

[999] "ISIS Camp a Few Miles from Texas, Mexican Authorities Confirm," *Judicial Watch,* April 14, 2015, http://www.judicialwatch.org/blog/2015/04/isis-camp-a-few-miles-from-texas-mexican-authorities-confirm/

[1000] Murphy, Esme, "Former Minnesota Man Played Key Role In Inciting Texas Terror Attack," *CBS Minnesota,* May 4, 2015, http://minnesota.cbslocal.com/2015/05/04/former-minnesota-man-played-key-role-in-inciting-texas-terror-attack/

[1001] Onyanga-Omara, J. & Bacon, J., *USA Today,* May 5, 2015, http://www.usatoday.com/story/news/nation/2015/05/05/isil-texas-attack/26910117/

[1002] Price, Bob, "$10,000 Muhammad Art and Cartoon Contest to be Held at Site of 'Stand With the Prophet' Conference in Texas," *Breitbart,* February 11, 2015, http://www.breitbart.com/texas/2015/02/11/10000-muhammad-art-and-cartoon-contest-to-be-held-at-site-of-stand-with-the-prophet-conference-in-texas/

[1003] Yan, Holly, "Texas Attack: What We Know About Elton Simpson and Nadir Soofi," *CNN,* May 5, 2015, http://www.cnn.com/2015/05/05/us/texas-shooting-gunmen/

[1004] Engel, Pamela, "Texas Cartoon Contest Gunman Had Established Connections to ISIS on Twitter," *Business Insider,* May 12, 2015, http://www.businessinsider.com/texas-cartoon-contest-gunman-connected-to-isis-on-twitter-2015-5

[1005] "IS Says It Was Behind US Prophet Cartoon Attack," *BBC,* May 5, 2015, http://www.bbc.com/news/world-us-canada-32589546

[1006] Sweet, L., Cassidy, C. & McGovern, B., "Usaamah Rahim Called Dad to Say Goodbye Before Shooting," *Boston Herald,* June 4, 2015, http://www.bostonherald.com/news_opinion/local_coverage/2015/06/usaamah_rahim_called_dad_to_say_goodbye_before_shooting

[1007] Sanchez, R., Perez, E., & Prokupecz, S., "Boston Shooting: Suspect Plotted to Behead Pamela Geller, Sources Say," *CNN,* June 3, 2015, http://www.cnn.com/2015/06/03/us/boston-police-shooting/index.html

[1008] Sweet, L., Cassidy, C. & McGovern, B., "Usaamah Rahim Called Dad to Say Goodbye Before Shooting," *Boston Herald,* June 4, 2015, http://www.bostonherald.com/news_opinion/local_coverage/2015/06/usaamah_rahim_called_dad_to_say_goodbye_before_shooting

[1009] "FBI Has Nearly 1,000 Active ISIS Probes Inside U.S.," *Judicial Watch,* November 13, 2015, http://www.judicialwatch.org/blog/2015/11/fbi-has-nearly-1000-active-isis-probes-inside-u-s/

[1010] Chiaramonte, Perry, "ISIS Seizes Uranium From Lab; Experts Downplay 'Dirty Bomb' Threat," *Fox News,* July 10, 2014, http://www.foxnews.com/world/2014/07/10/isis-seized-uranium-compounds-from-lab-experts-downplay-threat/

[1011] Withnall, Adam, "ISIS's Dirty Bomb: Jihadists Have Seized 'Enough Radioactive Material to Build Their First WMD'," *The UK Independent,* June 10, 2015, http://www.independent.co.uk/news/world/middle-east/isiss-dirty-bomb-jihadists-have-seized-enough-radioactive-material-to-build-their-first-wmd-10309220.html

[1012] Chiaramonte, Perry, "ISIS Seizes Uranium From Lab; Experts Downplay 'Dirty Bomb' Threat," *Fox News,* July 10, 2014, http://www.foxnews.com/world/2014/07/10/isis-seized-uranium-compounds-from-lab-experts-downplay-threat/

[1013] *Ibid.*

[1014] Ward, Alexander, "ISIS Recruiting 'Highly Trained Foreigners' to Produce Chemical Weapons," *The UK Independent,* June 7, 2015, http://www.independent.co.uk/news/world/middle-east/isis-is-recruiting-highly-trained-professionals-in-a-bid-to-develop-chemical-weapons-10303031.html

[1015] Friedman, D. & Edelman, A., "ISIS Has Enough Radioactive Material to Make Dirty Bomb: Report," *New York Daily News,* June 11, 2015, http://www.nydailynews.com/news/politics/isis-nuclear-material-dirty-bomb-report-article-1.2253492

[1016] "The Perfect Storm," *Dabiq,* May 2015, https://azelin.files.wordpress.com/2015/05/the-islamic-state-e2809cdc481biq-magazine-9e280b3.pdf, p. 76-77

[1017] "US Confirms ISIS Made, Used Chemical Weapons," *Fox News,* February 9, 2016, http://www.foxnews.com/politics/2016/02/09/top-intel-official-confirms-isis-made-used-chemical-weapons.html

[1018] "Obama on ISIS Threat: 'Ideologies Are Not Defeated With Guns, They Are Defeated By Better Ideas'," *Real Clear Politics,* July 6, 2015, http://www.realclearpolitics.com/video/2015/07/06/obama_on_isis_threat_ideologies_are_not_defeated_with_guns_they_are_defeated_by_better_ideas.html

[1019] Remnick, David, "Going the Distance," *The New Yorker,* January 27, 2014, http://www.newyorker.com/magazine/2014/01/27/going-the-distance-david-remnick

[1020] "Obama: Paris Terror Rampage a 'Setback'," *Fox News,* November 16, 2015, http://www.foxnews.com/politics/2015/11/16/obama-facing-criticism-for-push-to-contain-isis/

[1021] "Gitmo Detainees Get Same Healthcare as Our Troops, Video Games and Movies," *Fox News,* February 24, 2016, http://insider.foxnews.com/2016/02/24/guantanamo-bay-detainees-get-same-healthcare-troops-movies-video-games-pete-hegseth

[1022] Feldman, Josh, "CNN's Amanpour: ISIS Not Contained, 'Pretty Incredible' for Obama to Say Strategy Working," *Mediaite,* November 16, 2015, http://www.mediaite.com/tv/cnns-amanpour-isis-not-contained-pretty-incredible-for-obama-to-say-strategy-working/

[1023] Hayward, John, "Al-Qaeda: Decimated, on the Run, and Closing in on Baghdad," *Human Events,* January 12, 2014, http://humanevents.com/2014/06/12/al-qaeda-decimated-on-the-run-and-closing-in-on-baghdad/

[1024] Crabtree, Susan, "Al Qaeda Is on 'a Path to Defeat'," *Washington Times,* May 23, 2013, http://www.washingtontimes.com/news/2013/may/23/obama-al-qaeda-is-on-a-path-to-defeat/?page=all

[1025] Harris, S. & Youssef, N., "Exclusive: 50 Spies Say ISIS Intelligence Was Cooked," *The Daily Beast,* September 9, 2015, http://www.thedailybeast.com/articles/2015/09/09/exclusive-50-spies-say-isis-intelligence-was-cooked.html

[1026] Ross, Chuck, "Shooter's Mother Active in US Branch of Pro-Caliphate Islamic Group, *Daily Caller,* December 5, 2015, http://dailycaller.com/2015/12/05/shooters-mother-active-in-us-branch-of-pro-caliphate-islamic-group/

[1027] Ashford, B., Styles, R., Rahman, K., Farberov, S. & De Graaf, M., "Radicalized US Muslim Was Teased By Colleagues About His Islamic Beard and Had Clashed With Jewish Co-Worker Over Religion Before He and Pakistani Wife Killed 14 at San Bernardino Holiday Party," *UK Daily Mail,* December 3, 2015, http://www.dailymail.co.uk/news/article-3344350/Devout-Muslim-citizen-Saudi-wife-living-American-Dream-identified-heavily-armed-duo-burst-office-holiday-party-slaughtered-14-leaving-baby-mother.html

[1028] "Official Reveals How Many Visas U.S. Revoked Over Terror Threats," *CBS News,* December 17, 2015, http://www.cbsnews.com/news/u-s-revokes-visas-based-on-threats-of-terrorism-official-says/

518

[1029] Leonard, Jack, "San Bernardino Gunman's Terrifying Plot to Bomb, Shoot Freeway Motorists Revealed in Court Records," *Los Angeles Times,* December 18, 2015, http://www.latimes.com/local/lanow/la-me-ln-san-bernardino-shooter-planned-deadly-bombing-shooting-on-91-freeway-records-show-20151217-story.html

[1030] Hamilton, M., Parvini, S. & Mejia, B., "San Bernardino Shooter's Friend Enrique Marquez Accused of Fraud in $200-Per-Month Marriage," *Los Angeles Times,* December 17, 2015, http://www.latimes.com/local/lanow/la-me-ln-enrique-marquez-immigration-fraud-marriage-20151217-story.html

[1031] CNN Wire, Kuzj, S., Hawkins, K. & Chambers, R., "Enrique Marquez Charged With Conspiring With San Bernardino Shooter in 2011, 2012," KTLA 5 News Los Angeles, December 17, 2015, http://ktla.com/2015/12/17/san-bernardino-mass-shooting-federal-prosecutors-expected-to-file-charges-against-gunmans-friend-enrique-marquez/

[1032] Ashford, B., Styles, R., Rahman, K. & Farberov, S., "Party Massacre Wife 'Pledged Allegiance to ISIS': Pakistani New Mother Swore Loyalty to Fanatical Leader Abu Bakr al-Baghdadi on Facebook Before Attack in Which She and Her Husband Killed 14," *UK Daily Mail,* December 4, 2015, http://www.dailymail.co.uk/news/article-3344350/Devout-Muslim-citizen-Saudi-wife-living-American-Dream-identified-heavily-armed-duo-burst-office-holiday-party-slaughtered-14-leaving-baby-mother.html

[1033] Serrano, R., Bennett, B. & Karlamangla, S, "San Bernardino Massacre Probed as Terrorism, FBI Says," *Los Angeles Times,* December 4, 2015, http://www.latimes.com/local/lanow/la-me-ln-san-bernardino-shooting-isis-20151204-story.html

[1034] McLaughlin, Kelly, "Did San Bernardino Gunman's Mother Know? FBI Say They Are 'Looking Very, Very Closely' at 'Momma's Boy' Parent Who Lived in Same House," *UK Daily Mail,* December 6, 2015, http://www.dailymail.co.uk/news/article-3348741/FBI-investigating-San-Bernardino-gunman-s-mother-lived-terror-couple-knew-attack-advance.html

[1035] Gorka, S. & Gorka, K., "ISIS: The Threat to the United States," *Threat Knowledge,* November 2015, http://threatknowledge.org/isis-threat-to-usa-report/

[1036] Ward, Alexander, "The Terrifying Rise of ISIS: Map That Shows How Terror Group's Tentacles Now Reach from Algeria to Afghanistan," *UK Daily Mail,* March 2, 2015, http://www.dailymail.co.uk/news/article-2960463/The-terrifying-rise-ISIS-Map-shows-terror-group-s-tentacles-reach-Algeria-Afghanistan.html

[1037] Young, Angelo, "ISIS Has $1B Worth of US Humvee Armored Vehicles; One Was Used in Monday's Suicide Bombing Near Baghdad," *International Business Times,* June 1, 2015, http://www.ibtimes.com/isis-has-1b-worth-us-humvee-armored-vehicles-one-was-used-mondays-suicide-bombing-1946521

[1038] Van Buren, Peter, "Dude, Where's My Humvee? Iraq Losing Equipment to Islamic State at Staggering Rate," *Reuters,* June 2, 2015, http://blogs.reuters.com/great-debate/2015/06/02/dude-wheres-my-humvee-iraqi-equipment-losses-to-islamic-state-are-out-of-control/

[1039] Mehta, Aaron, "Iraq Requests Abrams Tank, Humvee Sale," *Defense News,* December 2014, http://www.defensenews.com/story/defense/land/vehicles/2014/12/19/iraq-abrams-humvee-sale/20652483/

[1040] Menzies, Samantha, "How Are ISIS funded?" *Yahoo Finance,* November 17, 2015, https://au.finance.yahoo.com/news/how-are-isis-funded-041841110.html

[1041] Corcoran, Ann, "How Much of Your Tax Dollars Are the Federal Refugee Resettlement Contractors Receiving?" Refugee Resettlement Watch, January 16, 2015, https://refugeeresettlementwatch.wordpress.com/2015/01/16/how-much-of-your-tax-dollars-are-the-federal-refugee-resettlement-contractors-receiving/

[1042] Siemaszko, C., & Radford, M., "Earlier Arab Immigrants Also Wary of Syrian Refugees," *NBC News,* November 21, 2015, http://www.nbcnews.com/storyline/paris-terror-attacks/earlier-arab-immigrants-also-wary-syrian-refugees-n465641

[1043] Lott, Maxim, "Fact Check: Claims 'No Refugees' Since 9/11 Took Part in Terror Plots Ring False," *Fox News,* November 25, 2015, http://www.foxnews.com/us/2015/11/25/fact-check-claims-no-refugees-since-11-took-part-in-terror-plots-ring-false/

[1044] Diamant, Aaron, "2 Investigates: Local Refugees Deported for Violent Crimes," *WSB-TV2 Atlanta,* November 23, 2015, http://www.wsbtv.com/news/news/local/2-investigates-local-refugees-deported-violent-cri/npSxz/

[1045] Munro, Neil, "Sen. Sessions Reveals 12 Refugee-Jihadis Charged this Year, Hopes to Shrink Obama's 2016 Refugee Budget," *Breitbart,* November 24, 2015, http://www.breitbart.com/big-government/2015/11/24/sen-sessions-reveals-15-refugee-jihadis-hopes-shrink-obamas-2016-refugee-budget/

[1046] "Feds Can't Say Whereabouts of Those Whose Visas Were Revoked Over Terror Threat," *Fox News,* December 18, 2015, http://www.foxnews.com/politics/2015/12/18/feds-cant-say-whereabouts-those-whose-visas-were-revoked-over-terror-threat.html

[1047] Lott, Maxim, "Fact Check: Claims 'No Refugees' Since 9/11 Took Part in Terror Plots Ring False," *Fox News,* November 25, 2015, http://www.foxnews.com/us/2015/11/25/fact-check-claims-no-refugees-since-11-took-part-in-terror-plots-ring-false/

[1048] "Feds Can't Say Whereabouts of Those Whose Visas Were Revoked Over Terror Threat," *Fox News* Video Transcript, December 18, 2015, http://www.foxnews.com/politics/2015/12/18/feds-cant-say-whereabouts-those-whose-visas-were-revoked-over-terror-threat.html

[1049] Sabia, Carmine, "Clueless DHS Official Provides No Answers During Grilling on Immigration, Visa Waiver Program," *Bizpac Review,* December 11, 2015, http://www.bizpacreview.com/2015/12/11/clueless-dhs-official-has-no-answers-on-immigration-so-flustered-calls-k1-visa-program-ky-283178

[1050] Boss, O. & Dwinell, J., "Officials Investigate ISIS Faking Entry Documents," *Boston Herald,* December 12, 2015, http://www.bostonherald.com/news/local_coverage/2015/12/officials_investigate_isis_faking_entry_documents

[1051] Darby, Brandon, "30 Million Illegal Immigrants in US, Says Mexico's Former Ambassador," *Breitbart,* August 18, 2015, http://www.breitbart.com/big-government/2015/08/18/30-million-illegal-immigrants-in-us-says-mexicos-former-ambassador/

[1052] "Number Displaced Worldwide Hits Record High - UN Report," *BBC,* June 18, 2015, http://www.bbc.com/news/world-33178035

[1053] De Vries, Karl, "White House Issues Veto Threat Over Refugee Bill," *CNN,* November 18, 2015, http://www.cnn.com/2015/11/18/politics/white-house-issues-veto-threat-over-refugee-bill/index.html

[1054] "Obama Threatens to Veto House GOP Bill on Syrian Refugee Screening," *Fox News,* November 18, 2015, http://www.foxnews.com/politics/2015/11/18/obama-threatens-to-veto-bill-strengthening-syrian-refugee-screening/

[1055] *Ibid.*

[1056] *Ibid.*

[1057] Wooldridge, Frosty, "America's Population Predicament: Galloping People Growth, *Church and State,* January 26, 2013, http://churchandstate.org.uk/2013/01/americas-population-predicament-galloping-people-growth/

[1058] Clifton, Jim, "The Big Lie: 5.6% Unemployment," Gallup, February 3, 2015, http://www.gallup.com/opinion/chairman/181469/big-lie-unemployment.aspx

[1059] Kitroeff, Natalie, "Immigrants Pay Lower Fees to Send Money Home, Helping to Ease Poverty," *New York Times,* February 2011, http://www.nytimes.com/2013/04/28/us/politics/immigrants-find-it-cheaper-to-send-money-home.html

[1060] Martin, J. & Ruark, E., "The Fiscal Burden of Illegal Immigration on United States Taxpayers," FairUS, April 27, 2013, http://www.fairus.org/publications/the-fiscal-burden-of-illegal-immigration-on-united-states-taxpayers

[1061] Graham, Otis, Unguarded Gates: A History of America's Immigration Crisis. Lanham: Rowman & Littlefield, 2004, p. 201

[1062] "Number Displaced Worldwide Hits Record High - UN Report," *BBC,* June 18, 2015, http://www.bbc.com/news/world-33178035

[1063] "Census Bureau Reports at Least 350 Languages Spoken in U.S. Homes," Census Bureau Release Number: CB15-185, November 3, 2015, http://www.census.gov/newsroom/press-releases/2015/cb15-185.html

[1064] Teddy Roosevelt Speech to the Knights of Columbus at Carnegie Hall in New York City, Theodore Roosevelt, October 12, 1915, http://www.theodore-roosevelt.com/images/research/txtspeeches/781.pdf

[1065] Frosty Woolridge, Immigration and Population Expert in *Coast To Coast AM* interview, October, 27, 2015

[1066] Windrem, Robert, "ISIS Wannabes Focusing on U.S. Attacks, Study Says," *NBC News,* June 25, 2015, http://www.nbcnews.com/storyline/isis-terror/isis-wannabes-focusing-u-s-attacks-study-says-n381161

[1067] Windrem, Robert, "ISIS Wannabes: Inside the Minds of Jihadis Born in the USA," *NBC News,* April 17, 2015, http://www.nbcnews.com/storyline/isis-terror/born-u-s-inside-mind-isis-wannabes-n343181

[1068] Vidino, L. & Hughes, S., "ISIS in America, From Retweets to Raqqa," George Washington University, December 2015, https://cchs.gwu.edu/sites/cchs.gwu.edu/files/downloads/ISIS%20in%20America%20-%20Full%20Report.pdf, p. 7

[1069] Datoc, Christian, "FBI Director: It's Impossible to Vet Every Syrain Refugee," *The Daily Caller,* November 19, 2015, http://dailycaller.com/2015/11/19/fbi-director-its-impossible-to-vet-every-single-syrian-refugee-video/

[1070] Griffin, Andrew, "The Sun Could Spew Out Huge Superflares and Put Life on Earth in Danger," *UK Independent,* December 3, 2015, http://www.independent.co.uk/news/science/the-sun-could-spew-out-huge-superflares-and-put-life-on-earth-in-danger-a6758491.html

[1071] Zurbuchen, Thomas H., "How Likely Is a Space Weather–Induced U.S. Power Grid Catastrophe? JASON Weighs In," Space Weather, Wiley Online Library, August 30, 2012, http://onlinelibrary.wiley.com/doi/10.1029/2012SW000844/full

[1072] "Top 9 Things You Didn't Know About America's Power Grid," Dept. of Energy, November 20, 2014, http://energy.gov/articles/top-9-things-you-didnt-know-about-americas-power-grid

[1073] Ayre, James, "Power Outages to Become Much More Common & More Severe In Coming Years, Better to Start Adapting Now," Clean Technica, February 1, 2014, http://cleantechnica.com/2014/02/01/power-outages-become-much-common-severe-coming-years-better-start-adapting-now-research-finds/

[1074] Bullis, Kevin, "Could Electric Cars Threaten the Grid?" *MIT Technology Review,* August 16, 2013, http://www.technologyreview.com/news/518066/could-electric-cars-threaten-the-grid/

[1075] "Space Weather, Storms from the Sun," NOAA, http://www.srh.noaa.gov/srh/jetstream/downloads/space_weather_booklet.pdf, p. 1

[1076] "Near Miss: The Solar Superstorm of July 2012," *NASA Science,* July 23, 2014, http://science.nasa.gov/science-news/science-at-nasa/2014/23jul_superstorm/

[1077] "Severe Space Weather Events – Understanding Societal and Economic Impacts," National Academy of Sciences, *The National Academies Press,* 2008, http://lasp.colorado.edu/home/wp-content/uploads/2011/07/lowres-Severe-Space-Weather-FINAL.pdf, p.77

[1078] *Ibid.*, p.78

[1079] "Near Miss: The Solar Superstorm of July 2012," *NASA Science,* July 23, 2014, http://science.nasa.gov/science-news/science-at-nasa/2014/23jul_superstorm/

[1080] *Ibid.*

[1081] "Nuclear Environment Survivability," U.S. Army Report ADA278230, April 15 1994, http://www.dtic.mil/cgi-bin/GetTRDoc?AD=ADA278230&Location=U2&doc=GetTRDoc.pdf, p. D-7

[1082] "EMP Could Leave '9 Out of 10 Americans Dead'," *WND,* May 3, 2010, http://www.wnd.com/2010/05/149117/

[1083] "Severe Space Weather Events – Understanding Societal and Economic Impacts Workshop Report," National Academy of Sciences, *National Academies Press,* 2008, http://lasp.colorado.edu/home/wp-content/uploads/2011/07/lowres-Severe-Space-Weather-FINAL.pdf, p. 78

[1084] "Large Power Transformers and the U.S. Electric Grid, Dept. of Energy, April 2014, http://www.energy.gov/sites/prod/files/2014/04/f15/LPTStudyUpdate-040914.pdf, p. 9

[1085] Parfomak, Paul, W., "Physical Security of the U.S. Power Grid: High-Voltage Transformer Substations," Congressional Research Service, June 17, 2014, https://fas.org/sgp/crs/homesec/R43604.pdf, p. 12

[1086] Marsh, Rene, "Congressman: National Power Grid Frequently Attacked," *CNN,* October 21, 2015, http://www.cnn.com/2015/10/21/politics/national-power-grid-cyber-attacks/

[1087] "PowerEd Webinar: Physical Security (Part I) - How Secure Is Your Substation," *ABB,* October 16, 2015, http://www.abb.at/References/Default.aspx?db=db/db0048/db004888.nsf&c=61264a7fe60488f8c1257e76006594fe

[1088] Reilly, Steve, "Bracing for a Big Power Grid Attack: 'One Is Too Many'," *USA Today,* March 24, 2015, http://www.usatoday.com/story/news/2015/03/24/power-grid-physical-and-cyber-attacks-concern-security-experts/24892471/

[1089] *Ibid.*

[1090] Marsh, Rene, "U.S. Congressman: National Power Grid Frequently Attacked," OF Week, October 22, 2015, http://en.ofweek.com/news/U-S-Congressman-National-power-grid-frequently-attacked-35399

[1091] *Ibid.*

[1092] *Ibid.*

[1093] Bumiller, P. & Shanker, T., "Panetta Warns of Dire Threat of Cyberattack on U.S.," *New York Times,* October 11, 2012, http://www.nytimes.com/2012/10/12/world/panetta-warns-of-dire-threat-of-cyberattack.html

[1094] Farberov, S. & Evans, S.J., "Revealed: Security Expert Who 'Hacked a Commercial Flight and Made It Fly Sideways' Bragged That He Also Hacked the International Space Station," *UK Daily Mail,* May 20, 2015, http://www.dailymail.co.uk/news/article-3090288/Security-expert-admitted-FBI-took-control-commercial-flight-bragged-hacker-convention-2012-playing-International-Space-Station-getting-yelled-NASA.html

[1095] Bigelow, Pete, "Cars Aren't Target for Hackers; They're Gateway to Higher-Profile Attacks," Autoblog, February 19, 2015, http://www.autoblog.com/2015/02/19/cars-target-hackers-gateway-higher-profile-attacks/

[1096] Gorman, Siobhan, "Electricity Grid in U.S. Penetrated By Spies," *Wall Street Journal,* April 8, 2009, http://www.wsj.com/articles/SB123914805204099085

[1097] *Ibid.*

[1098] Pagliery, Jose, "U.S. Intel Officials Warn Hacking Is Getting Worse," *CNN,* September 29, 2015, http://money.cnn.com/2015/09/29/technology/nsa-china-spying/index.html

[1099] Dougherty, Joe, "Russian Hackers Have Burrowed into Critical U.S. Infrastructure Like the Electric Power Grid, Says Intelligence Director," *Glitch News,* September 22, 2015, http://www.wsj.com/articles/SB123914805204099085

[1100] Pagliery, Jose, "ISIS Is Attacking the U.S. Energy Grid (and Failing)," *CNN,* October 15, 2015, http://money.cnn.com/2015/10/15/technology/isis-energy-grid/

[1101] *Ibid.*

[1102] *Ibid.*

[1103] Crawford, Jamie, "The U.S. Government Thinks China Could Take Down the Power Grid," *CNN,* November 21, 2014, http://www.cnn.com/2014/11/20/politics/nsa-china-power-grid/

[1104] Levine, Mike, "Outgoing DHS Secretary Janet Napolitano Warns of 'Serious' Cyber Attack, Unprecedented Natural Disaster," *ABC News,* August 27, 2013, http://abcnews.go.com/blogs/politics/2013/08/outgoing-dhs-secretary-janet-napolitano-warns-of-serious-cyber-attackunprecedented-natural-disaster/

[1105] "In the Dark Over Power Grid Security," *CBS News,* November 1, 2015, http://www.cbsnews.com/news/in-the-dark-over-power-grid-security/2/

[1106] Rogers, Keith, "6 Congressmen Go Underground, Tour Yucca Mountain," *Las Vegas Review-Journal,* April 10, 2015, http://www.reviewjournal.com/news/yucca-mountain/6-congressmen-go-underground-tour-yucca-mountain

[1107] Goldsmith, Donald, "The $2 Trillion Economic Risk You Haven't Heard About," *PBS,* August 7, 2014, http://www.pbs.org/newshour/making-sense/the-2-trillion-economic-risk-you-havent-heard-about/

[1108] Gaffney, Frank, "Power Grid Vulnerable to Attacks," *Newsmax,* April 14, 2014, http://www.newsmax.com/FrankGaffney/Metcalf-Substation-EMP-Grid/2014/04/14/id/565456/

[1109] Congress: Job Ratings, Polling Report, Accessed January 10, 2016, http://www.pollingreport.com/CongJob1.htm

[1110] MacCormack, John, "Cibolo Creek Ranch Owner Recalls Scalia's Last Hours in Texas," *My San Antonio,* February 14, 2016, http://www.mysanantonio.com/news/local/article/Texas-ranch-owner-recalls-Scalia-s-last-hours-6830372.php

[1111] Urbanski, Dave, "Owner of Ranch Where Justice Scalia Was Found Dead Tries to Clear Up 'Pillow Over His Head' Questions," *The Blaze,* February 17, 2016, http://www.theblaze.com/stories/2016/02/17/owner-of-ranch-where-justice-scalia-was-found-dead-tries-to-clear-up-pillow-over-his-head-questions/

[1112] Moravec, E., Horwitz, S. & Markon, J., "The Death of Antonin Scalia: Chaos, Confusion and Conflicting Reports," *Washington Post,* February 14, 2016, https://www.washingtonpost.com/politics/texas-tv-station-scalia-died-of-a-heart-attack/2016/02/14/938e2170-d332-11e5-9823-02b905009f99_story.html

[1113] Duckett, Chris, "NSA Hunger Demands 29 Petabytes of Data a Day," *ZDNet,* August 12, 2013, http://www.zdnet.com/article/nsa-hunger-demands-29-petabytes-of-data-a-day/

[1114] Vasquez, Ian & Porcnik, Tanja, "Appendix L: 2012 Human Freedom Index Rankings and Democracy Index," The Human Freedom Index, 2015, pp. 102-105, http://www.fraserinstitute.org/uploadedFiles/fraser-ca/Content/research-news/research/publications/human-freedom-index-preliminary-report.pdf

[1115] "Report from the Field: The USA PATRIOT Act at Work," U.S. Department of Justice, July 2004, http://www.justice.gov/archive/olp/pdf/patriot_report_from_the_field0704.pdf, p. 1

[1116] Lott, Jr., John R., Report to the Parliament of Australia on "The Ability of Australian Law Enforcement Authorities to Eliminate Gun-Related Violence in the Community," Crime Prevention Research Center, August 15, 2014, http://crimepreventionresearchcenter.org/wp-content/uploads/2014/10/Report-on-gun-related-suicides-and-crime-for-the-Australian-Parliament-Rev.pdf, p. 2

[1117] Carter, Sara, "Blaze Sources: Obama Purging Military Commanders," *The Blaze,* October 13, 2013, http://www.theblaze.com/stories/2013/10/23/military-sources-obama-administration-purging-commanders/

[1118] Maloof, F. Michael, "Top Generals: Obama Is 'Purging the Military'," *WND,* October 31, 2013, http://www.wnd.com/2013/10/top-generals-obama-is-purging-the-military/

[1119] Maloof, F. Michael, "'Purge Surge': Obama Fires Another Commander," *WND,* November 4, 2013, http://www.wnd.com/2013/11/purge-surge-obama-fires-another-commander/

[1120] Carter, Sara, "Blaze Sources: Obama Purging Military Commanders," *The Blaze,* October 13, 2013, http://www.theblaze.com/stories/2013/10/23/military-sources-obama-administration-purging-commanders/

[1121] Coburn, Tom, "FRIENDLY FIRE: Death, Delay and Dismay at the VA," Accessed December 6, 2015, http://stripes.com/polopoly_fs/1.290429.1403627335!/menu/standard/file/Friendly%20Fire%20VA%20report.pdf, p. 4

[1122] *Ibid.*, p. 9

[1123] Roy, Avik, "No, The VA Isn't a Preview of Obamacare - It's Much Worse," *Forbes,* May 23, 2014, http://www.forbes.com/sites/merrillmatthews/2014/06/03/congress-will-not-drastically-change-the-va-because-too-many-benefit-from-the-status-quo/

[1124] Lapotin, Katie, "The Latest Veterans Affairs Scandal Is So Bad, The Department's Afraid of Leaving a Paper Trail," *Independent Journal,* August, 2014, http://www.ijreview.com/2015/08/396017-latest-veterans-affairs-scandal-bad-departments-afraid-leaving-paper-trail/

[1125] Coburn, Tom, "FRIENDLY FIRE: Death, Delay and Dismay at the VA," accessed December 6, 2015, http://stripes.com/polopoly_fs/1.290429.1403627335!/menu/standard/file/Friendly%20Fire%20VA%20report.pdf, p. 54

[1126] Assistant Inspector General for Audits and Evaluations, "Claims Folder Storage at the VA Regional Office, Winston-Salem, North Carolina," OIG's Management Advisory Memorandum, Dept. of Veterans Affairs, June 11, 2012, http://www.va.gov/oig/pubs/VAOIG-12-00244-241a.pdf, p. 2

[1127] Kennedy, Kelli, "Some Struggle to Live While Waiting More Than 2 Years for Social Security Disability Hearings," *U.S News & World Report,* November 28, 2015, http://www.usnews.com/news/us/articles/2015/11/28/long-wait-times-plague-social-security-disability-process

[1128] Nylan, Paul, "Child Care's Broken Promise: Parents Want Solutions," *Equal Voice News,* December 1, 2015, http://www.equalvoiceforfamilies.org/the-dignity-of-living-child-cares-broken-promise/

[1129] "Homeless People - Rebecca's Story," Rebeccas Community, http://www.homeless.org.au/people/rebecca.htm

[1130] Quinton, Andrew, "Panel Shares True Stories of Homelessness," *The Daily Gazette,* February 11, 2005, http://www.sccs.swarthmore.edu/users/05/maile/web0211.htm

[1131] Cosgrove-Mather, Bootie, "From Hero to Homeless," *CBS News,* March 25, 2005, http://www.cbsnews.com/news/from-hero-to-homeless/

[1132] Alarcon, Nefi, "22 Veterans Kill Themselves Every Day," *CNN,* April 17, 2014, http://www.cnn.com/2015/02/04/politics/22-veterans-kill-themselves-every-day/

[1133] "Homeless Veterans: Trying to Find Help and Hope," *CBS 60 Minutes,* July 10, 2012, http://www.cbsnews.com/news/homeless-veterans-trying-to-find-help-and-hope-10-07-2012/

[1134] "Chris – A Veteran's Success Story," Shelter for the Homeless, http://shelterforhomeless.org/about-us/success-stories

[1135] "Portraits of Homelessness in Las Vegas: Eight People Share Their Stories," *Las Vegas Sun,* December 8, 2015, http://lasvegassun.com/news/2015/nov/30/portraits-of-homelessness-in-las-vegas-eight-peopl/

[1136] Life Cycle of a Country, https://www.1215.org/lawnotes/work-in-progress/country-life-cycle.htm

[1137] Jenkins, Nash, "President Obama Says the U.S. Is Safe From an ISIS Attack," *Time,* December 3, 2015, http://time.com/4136061/barack-obama-isis-terrorism-attack-us/

[1138] "NICS Firearm Background Checks: Month/Year," NICS, November 30, 1998 - December 31, 2015, https://www.fbi.gov/about-us/cjis/nics/reports/nics_firearm_checks_-_month_year.pdf

[1139] Gutowski, Stephen, "2015: The Year of the Gun," *Washington Free Beacon,* January 4, 2016, http://freebeacon.com/issues/all-time-gun-sales-records-set-in-2015/

[1140] Shear, M. & Lichtblau, E., "Obama to Expand Gun Background Checks and Tighten Enforcement," *Alaska Dispatch News,* January 4, 2016, http://www.adn.com/article/20160104/obama-expand-gun-background-checks-and-tighten-enforcement

[1141] De Diego, J. & Machado, A., "In Wake of Terrorist Attacks, Sheriffs Call on Citizens to Take Up Arms," *CNN,* December 12, 2015, http://www.cnn.com/2015/12/12/us/sheriffs-urge-citizens-buy-guns/

[1142] "Gun Ownership By The Numbers," *Daily Caller,* November 4, 2014, http://dailycaller.com/2014/11/04/gun-ownership-by-the-numbers/

[1143] Cohn, D., Taylor, P., Lopez, M., Gallagher, C., Parker, K. & Maass, K., "Gun Homicide Rate Down 49% Since 1993 Peak; Pew Research," November 1, 2015, http://www.pewsocialtrends.org/2013/05/07/gun-homicide-rate-down-49-since-1993-peak-public-unaware/

[1144] Krouse, William, "Gun Control Legislation," Congressional Research Service, November 14, 2012, http://www.fas.org/sgp/crs/misc/RL32842.pdf, pp. 8-9

[1145] "Gun Homicide Rate Down 49% Since 1993 Peak; Public Unaware," May 7, 2013, http://www.pewsocialtrends.org/2013/05/07/gun-homicide-rate-down-49-since-1993-peak-public-unaware/

[1146] Hawkins, AWR, "Washington Post: Gun Violence Declining, Except in Gun-Free Zones," *Breitbart,* December 4, 2015, http://www.breitbart.com/big-journalism/2015/12/04/washington-post-gun-violence-declining-except-gun-free-zones/

[1147] Lott, John, "A Look at the Facts on Gun-Free Zones," *National Review,* October 20, 2015, http://www.nationalreview.com/article/425802/gun-free-zones-don't-save-lives-right-to-carry-laws-do

[1148] Gutowski, Stephen, "Gun Sales Set Record for Sixth Month in a Row," *Washington Free Beacon,* November 4, 2015, http://freebeacon.com/issues/gun-sales-set-record-for-sixth-month-in-a-row/

[1149] Hawkins, AWR, "Sheriff David Clarke: Obama Is on a 'Gun Confiscation Mission'," *Breitbart,* October 31, 2015, http://www.breitbart.com/big-government/2015/10/31/exclusive-sheriff-david-clarke-obama-gun-confiscation-mission/

[1150] "Wisconsin Sheriff Urges Residents to Arm Themselves," *Fox News,* January 27, 2013, http://www.foxnews.com/us/2013/01/26/wis-sheriff-urges-residents-to-get-gun-training/

[1151] Jones, Susan, "Milwaukee County Sheriff Challenges Obama: 'Forego Your Secret Service Protection'," *CNS News,* August 28, 2015, http://cnsnews.com/news/article/susan-jones/milwaukee-county-sheriff-challenges-obama-forego-your-secret-service

[1152] Roosevelt, Hunter, "Arizona Sheriff to Citizens: 'Get a Gun and Defend Yourselves'," *Controversial Times,* December 15, 2015, http://controversialtimes.com/issues/constitutional-rights/arizona-sheriff-to-citizens-get-a-gun-and-defend-yourselves/

[1153] Chesnut, Mark, "American Sheriffs Rally Concealed-Carry Permit Holders," America's 1st Freedom, December 11, 2015, http://www.americas1stfreedom.org/articles/2015/12/11/american-sheriffs-rally-concealed-carry-permit-holders/

[1154] Hawkins, AWR, "Florida Sheriff Asks Concealed-Carry Holders 'To Take on Terrorists'," *Breitbart,* December 7, 2015, http://www.breitbart.com/big-government/2015/12/07/florida-sheriff-asks-concealed-carry-holders-take-terrorists/

[1155] Chesnut, Mark, "American Sheriffs Rally Concealed-Carry Permit Holders," America's 1st Freedom, December 11, 2015, http://www.americas1stfreedom.org/articles/2015/12/11/american-sheriffs-rally-concealed-carry-permit-holders/

[1156] *Ibid.*

[1157] MacNeal, Caitlan, "Sheriff Lowers Concealed Carry Permit Cost, Citing Recent Terrorist Attacks," Talking Points Memo, December 10, 2015, http://talkingpointsmemo.com/livewire/wayne-merritt-missouri-concealed-carry

[1158] Stan Deyo on Alex Jones' InfoWars, April 10, 2014, https://www.youtube.com/watch?v=PpLPYA9MWcM

[1159] Greenfield, Daniel, "French City with 40% Muslim Population is the Most Dangerous City in Europe," *Front Page Magazine,* January 4, 2014, http://www.frontpagemag.com/point/214086/french-city-40-muslim-population-most-dangerous-daniel-greenfield

[1160] Hilburn, Matthew, "Americans Divided Over Calls to Remove Confederate Monuments," *Voice of America,* July 6, 2015, http://www.voanews.com/content/calls-to-remove-confederate-monuments-divides-americans/2851033.html

[1161] Sims, Cliff, "Army Officer from Alabama Nails It: 'I'm Offended That Everyone Is Offended By Something!'" *Yellowhammer News,* June 23, 2015, http://yellowhammernews.com/politics-2/army-officer-from-alabama-nails-it-im-offended-that-everyone-is-offended-by-something/

[1162] "Justice Dept. Stops Use of 'Disparaging' Terms Like 'Felons,' 'Convicts'," *Newsmax,* May 5, 2016, http://www.newsmax.com/Newsfront/justice-department-disparaging-terms/2016/05/05/id/727397/

[1163] Bennett, John, "The Knockout Game: Racial Violence and the Conspicuous Silence of the Media," *American Thinker,* July 14, 2011, http://www.americanthinker.com/articles/2011/07/the_knockout_game_racial_violence_and_the_conspicuous_silence_of_the_media.html

[1164] Cooper, A. & Smith, E., "Homicide Trends in the United States, 1980-2008," U.S. Department of Justice, Bureau of Justice Statistics, http://www.bjs.gov/content/pub/pdf/htus8008.pdf, p. 3

[1165] "Homicides Fall to Lowest Rate in Four Decades," *PRNewswire-USNewswire,* November 16, 2011, http://www.prnewswire.com/news-releases/homicides-fall-to-lowest-rate-in-four-decades-133967273.html

[1166] MacDonald, Heather, "The Shameful Liberal Exploitation of the Charleston Massacre," *National Review,* July 1, 2015, http://www.nationalreview.com/article/420565/charleston-shooting-obama-race-crime

[1167] Alvarez, L. & Williams, T., "Documents Tell Zimmerman's Side in Martin Case," *New York Times,* June 21, 2012, http://www.nytimes.com/2012/06/22/us/documents-tell-zimmermans-side-in-martin-shooting.html?pagewanted=all

[1168] Thompson, K. & Wilson, S., "Obama on Trayvon Martin: 'If I Had a Son, He'd Look Like Trayvon'," *Washington Post,* March 23, 2012, https://www.washingtonpost.com/politics/obama-if-i-had-a-son-hed-look-like-trayvon/2012/03/23/gIQApKPpVS_story.html

[1169] Oberman, Mira, "Church Shooting One of Deadliest US Hate Crimes," *AFP,* June 18, 2015, http://news.yahoo.com/church-shooting-one-deadliest-us-hate-crimes-214126157.html

[1170] Craven, Julia, "Black Lives Matter Co-Founder Reflects on the Origins of the Movement," *Huffington Post,* September 30, 2015, http://www.huffingtonpost.com/entry/black-lives-matter-opal-tometi_560c1c59e4b0768127003227

[1171] Monroe-Hamilton, Terresa, "We Ready, We Coming! #BlackBrunch Protesters Swarm Chicago, Shut Down 5 Locations," *Right Wing News,* January 2, 2016, http://rightwingnews.com/liberals/we-ready-we-coming-blackbrunch-protesters-swarm-chicago-shut-down-5-locations

[1172] "About the Black Lives Matter Network," Accessed January 4, 2016, http://blacklivesmatter.com/about/

[1173] "Study Shines Light on Wicker Park's More Integrated Past," Loyola University, Chicago; February 2, 2012, http://blogs.luc.edu/hubbub/writing-for-the-web/study-shines-light-on-wicker-parks-more-integrated-past/

[1174] "Michael Brown Anniversary Marked By Ferguson March, Minutes of Silence," *Penn Live,* August 9, 2015, http://www.pennlive.com/nation-world/2015/08/michael_brown_anniversary_mark.html

[1175] "Michael Brown's Robbery Accomplice Snags City Job in St. Louis," Mr. Conservative, December 2014, http://www.mrconservative.com/2014/12/53570-michael-browns-robbery-accomplice-snags-city-job-in-st-louis/

[1176] Basu, M. & Karimi, F., "Protesters Torch Police Car in Another Tense Night in Ferguson," *CNN,* November 26, 2014, http://www.cnn.com/2014/11/25/justice/ferguson-grand-jury-decision/

[1177] "Nicole Brown Simpson's Letter to O.J. Simpson," University of Missouri - Kansas, City, Accessed January 3, 2016, http://law2.umkc.edu/faculty/projects/ftrials/Simpson/brownletter.html

[1178] Mydans, Seth, "Los Angeles Policemen Acquitted in Taped Beating," *New York Times,* April 29, 1992, http://www.nytimes.com/learning/general/onthisday/big/0429.html

[1179] Shoichet, Catherine, "Is Racism on the Rise? More in U.S. Say It's a 'Big Problem,' CNN/KFF Poll Finds," *CNN,* November 25, 2015, http://www.cnn.com/2015/11/24/us/racism-problem-cnn-kff-poll/

[1180] "The Great Divider Is the 'Most Polarizing' President Ever," *Washington Examiner*, January 23, 2014, http://www.washingtonexaminer.com/examiner-editorial-the-great-divider-is-the-most-polarizing-president-ever/article/2542804

[1181] Jaoby, Jeff, "Obama Is the Great Divider," *Boston Globe*, September 26, 2012, https://www.bostonglobe.com/opinion/2012/09/26/jacoby/0t7V99K3QU2dlXvI8IEUnN/story.html

[1182] Cooper, A. & Smith, E., "Homicide Trends in the United States, 1980-2008," U.S. Department of Justice, November 2011, http://www.bjs.gov/content/pub/pdf/htus8008.pdf

[1183] "Murder Offenders by Age, Sex, Race, and Ethnicity 2013," FBI, 2013, https://www.fbi.gov/about-us/cjis/ucr/crime-in-the-u.s/2013/crime-in-the-u.s.-2013/offenses-known-to-law-enforcement/expanded-homicide/expanded_homicide_data_table_3_murder_offenders_by_age_sex_and_race_2013.xls

[1184] Murder Race, Ethnicity, and Sex of Victim by Race, Ethnicity, and Sex of Offender, 2014," FBI, 2014, https://www.fbi.gov/about-us/cjis/ucr/crime-in-the-u.s/2014/crime-in-the-u.s.-2014/tables/expanded-homicide-data/expanded_homicide_data_table_6_murder_race_and_sex_of_vicitm_by_race_and_sex_of_offender_2014.xls

[1185] "Race and Ethnicity in the United States," Wikipedia, Accessed January 13, 2016, https://en.wikipedia.org/wiki/Race_and_ethnicity_in_the_United_States

[1186] Watson, Paul Joseph, "Black Crime Facts That the White Liberal Media Daren't Talk About," *Infowars,* May 5, 2015, http://www.infowars.com/black-crime-facts-that-the-white-liberal-media-darent-talk-about/

[1187] Buchanan, Pat, "Black America's Real Problem Isn't White Racism," *Yahoo News,* July 19, 2013, http://news.yahoo.com/black-americas-real-problem-isnt-white-racism-070000529.html

[1188] "The Truth About Interracial Rape," *Conservative Headlines,* December 30, 2014, http://conservative-headlines.com/2014/12/the-truth-about-interracial-rape/

[1189] Espenshade, T. & Walton Radford, A., "No Longer Separate, Not Yet Equal: Race and Class in Elite College Admission and Campus Life," Princeton: Princeton University Press, 2009

[1190] "Lowering Test Standards for Police and Firefighters," *The Examiner,* March 15, 2011, http://www.examiner.com/article/lowering-test-standards-for-police-and-firefighters

[1191] Edelman, Susan, "Woman Who Failed FDNY Physical Test 6 Times Gets Another Chance," *New York Post,* December 27, 2015, http://nypost.com/2015/12/27/unfireable-female-firefighter-returns-to-the-fdny/

[1192] "Springs Officers Will No Longer Take Fitness Tests After Discrimination Lawsuit," *CBS Local* – Denver, November 10, 2015, http://denver.cbslocal.com/2015/11/10/female-springs-officers-win-lawsuit-no-longer-have-to-take-physical-fitness-tests/

[1193] Gates Jr., Henry Louis, "The Truth Behind '40 Acres and a Mule'," *The Root,* January 7, 2013, http://www.theroot.com/articles/history/2013/01/40_acres_and_a_mule_promise_to_slaves_the_real_story.html

[1194] Ibid.

[1195] Myers, Barton, "Sherman's Field Order No. 15," *New Georgia Encyclopedia,* September 17, 2014, http://www.georgiaencyclopedia.org/articles/history-archaeology/shermans-field-order-no-15

[1196] Main, Douglas, "Slavery Reparations Could Cost Up to $14 Trillion, According to New Calculation," *Newsweek*, August 19, 2015, http://www.newsweek.com/slavery-reparations-could-cost-14-trillion-according-new-calculation-364141

[1197] Cohen, Jennie, "Study Suggests Adolf Hitler Had Jewish and African Ancestors," *History Channel,* August 26, 2010, http://www.history.com/news/study-suggests-adolf-hitler-had-jewish-and-african-ancestors

[1198] "Selected Statistics on Slavery in the United States," Causes of the Civil War, http://www.civilwarcauses.org/stat.htm

[1199] Dewsbury, R. & Hall, A., "Did Hitler and Eva Braun Flee Berlin and Die (Divorced) of Old Age in Argentina?" *UK Daily Mail,* October 18, 2011, http://www.dailymail.co.uk/news/article-2050137/Did-Hitler-Eva-Braun-flee-Berlin-die-old-age-Argentina.html

[1200] Tozzi, John, "How Many Jobs Do Small Businesses Create? Depends What 'Small' Means," *Business Week,* October 17, 2011, http://www.businessweek.com/smallbiz/running_small_business/archives/2011/10/how_many_jobs_do_small_businesses_create_depends_what_small_means.html

[1201] Shah, Neil, "U.S. Household Net Worth Hits Record High," *Wall Street Journal,* March 6, 2014, http://www.wsj.com/articles/SB10001424052702303824204579423183397213204

[1202] "Global Wealth Report 2015," Credit Suisse, October 2015, https://publications.credit-suisse.com/tasks/render/file/?fileID=F2425415-DCA7-80B8-EAD989AF9341D47E, p. 46

[1203] Naim, Moises, "America's Coming Manufacturing Revolution," *The Atlantic,* April 21, 2014, http://www.theatlantic.com/business/archive/2014/04/americas-coming-manufacturing-revolution/360931/

[1204] Puzzanghera, Jim, "Economy Has Recovered 8.7 Million Jobs Lost in Great Recession," *Los Angeles Times,* June 6, 2014, http://www.latimes.com/business/la-fi-jobs-20140607-story.html

[1205] Rao, Rajiv, "H1B Fee Increase Sends Indo-US Relations South," *ZDNet,* January 8, 2016, http://www.zdnet.com/article/h1b-fee-increase-sends-indo-us-relations-south/

[1206] Munro, Neil, "Industry, Universities Hide Workforce of 100,000 Extra Foreign White-Collar H-1B Employees," *Breitbart,* January 5, 2016, http://www.breitbart.com/big-government/2016/01/05/industry-universities-hide-workforce-100000-extra-foreign-white-collar-h-1b-employees/

[1207] "H1B Visa & Status," Murthy Law Firm, http://www.murthy.com/worker/h1b-visa-status/

[1208] "Vision of Washington," April 10, 2014, http://www.ushistory.org/valleyforge/washington/vision.html

[1209] "Perry Stone Economic Crash Riots in America Then a Russian invasion," YouTube, July 15, 2012, https://www.youtube.com/watch?v=V6uiwfq2V9E

[1210] Wilkerson, David, March 7, 2009, http://davidwilkersontoday.blogspot.com/2009/03/urgent-message.html

[1211] "Perry Stone Economic Crash Riots in America Then a Russian invasion," YouTube, July 15, 2012,https://www.youtube.com/watch?v=V6uiwfq2V9E

[1212] "7 U.S. Cities on the Verge of Bankruptcy," *Wealth Daily,* October 14, 2011, http://www.wealthdaily.com/articles/7-us-cities-on-the-verge-of-bankruptcy/3263

"Eight New Cities on the Verge of Bankruptcy," Money Morning, July 7, 2013, http://moneymorning.com/2013/07/23/eight-new-cities-on-the-verge-of-bankruptcy/

Moore, Stephen, "20 Cities That May Face Bankruptcy After Detroit," *Newsmax,* August 6, 2013, http://www.newsmax.com/US/cities-bankruptcy-after-detroit/2013/08/06/id/519081/

Winegarden, Wayne, "Going Broke One City at a Time: Municipal Bankruptcies in America," Pacific Research, January 2014, https://www.pacificresearch.org/fileadmin/documents/Studies/PDFs/2013-2015/MunicipalBankruptcy2014_F.pdf, p. 3

Helms, M., "Detroit Files for Bankruptcy Protection," *USA Today,* July 18, 2013, http://www.usatoday.com/story/news/nation/2013/07/18/detroit-prepares-bankruptcy-filing-friday/2552819/

"Bankruptcy Option for Local Governments," Ballotpedia, Accessed December 7, 2015, https://ballotpedia.org/Bankruptcy_option_for_local_governments

[1213] "William M. Branham," Wikipedia, Accessed December 7, 2015, https://en.wikipedia.org/wiki/William_M._Branham

[1214] Gannes, Liz, "Google's New Self-Driving Car Ditches the Steering Wheel," *Recode,* May 27, 2014, http://recode.net/2014/05/27/googles-new-self-driving-car-ditches-the-steering-wheel/

[1215] "Baywatch Star's Lettuce Advice," *BBC,* April 9, 2003, http://news.bbc.co.uk/2/hi/uk_news/england/merseyside/2932505.stm

[1216] "Pantsuit," Wikipedia, Accessed January 5, 2016, https://en.wikipedia.org/wiki/Pantsuit

[1217] "1933 7 Visions of William Branham," http://www.williambranham.com/1933-7-visions-of-william-branham/

[1218] "A Warning to America by Dumitru Duduman," Video uploaded October 23, 2008, https://www.youtube.com/watch?v=6fGq279mE3Y

[1219] "Dreams and Visions of Dumitru Duduman and Michael Boldea," http://www.kennethmheckdownloads.com/dimitru%20duduman%20and%20michael%20boldea.pdf, p. 2

[1220] Duduman, Dimitru, "The Message for America," *Hand of Help Ministries,* 1984, http://www.handofhelp.com/vision_1.php

[1221] Duduman, Dimitru, "China and Russia Strike," *Hand of Help Ministries,* April 22, 1996, http://www.handofhelp.com/vision_36.php

[1222] Gruver, Henry, "The Prince Charles Vision & Russian Invasion, YouTube video published November 17, 2013, https://www.youtube.com/watch?v=h7rtg6iBlp0

[1223] Kinsella, Jack, "The Death of Alexander Lebed," *Omega Letter,* April 29, 2002, http://www.omegaletter.com/articles/articles.asp?ArticleID=156

[1224] Shrader, Katherine, "Suitcase Nukes Closer to Fiction Than Reality," *ABC News,* October 2015, http://abcnews.go.com/Technology/story?id=3848473&page=1

[1225] "Russian Roulette", PBS, February 23, 1999, http://www.pbs.org/wgbh/pages/frontline/shows/russia/

[1226] Shrader, Katherine, "Suitcase Nukes Closer to Fiction Than Reality," *ABC News,* October 2015, http://abcnews.go.com/Technology/story?id=3848473&page=1

[1227] "Backpack Nukes Small But Deadly," *UPI,* Dec. 20, 2001, http://www.upi.com/Science_News/2001/12/20/Backpack-nukes-small-but-deadly/38751008892483/

[1228] "Henry Gruver Russian Invasion of America," YouTube Video, accessed December 22, 2015, https://www.youtube.com/watch?v=4oB4feKSFUA

[1229] "Henry Gruver Vision 1: US Invaded By China," http://1080.plus/HhcOLtcmjmI.video

[1230] AA Allen, "My Vision of the Destruction of America," Stan Deyo, July 4, 1954, https://standeyo.com/NEWS/07_Prophecy/071111.AAAllen.destroy.USA.html

[1231] "Russia Says It Isn't Developing a Secret 'Superplague Powder'," *Desert News,* March 28 1994, http://www.deseretnews.com/article/344184/RUSSIA-SAYS-IT-ISNT-DEVELOPING-A-SECRET-SUPERPLAGUE-POWDER.html

[1232] "Use of Chemical Weapons in the Syrian Civil War," Wikipedia, Accessed December 27, 2015, https://en.wikipedia.org/wiki/Use_of_chemical_weapons_in_the_Syrian_Civil_War

[1233] Deutsch, Anthony, "U.S. Official Says Use of Chemical Weapons Is 'Routine' in Syria," *Reuters,* November 23, 2015, http://www.reuters.com/article/us-syria-crisis-chemicalweapons-idUSKBN0TC1E720151123

[1234] "Bill Gates Calls for One World Government," January 29, 2015, *TPNN,* http://www.tpnn.com/2015/01/29/bill-gates-calls-for-one-world-government/

[1235] State of the Union Address, January 29, 1991, http://www.thisnation.com/library/sotu/1991gb.html

[1236] "Bush's Letter to Students," MIT, January 16, 1991, http://tech.mit.edu/V110/N59/war6.59n.html

[1237] George Bush: "Address Before a Joint Session of the Congress on the Cessation of the Persian Gulf Conflict," March 6, 1991, The American Presidency Project, http://www.presidency.ucsb.edu/ws/?pid=19364

[1238] Transcript of Address Before a Joint Session of Congress, September 11, 1990, Miller Center, University of Virginia, http://millercenter.org/president/bush/speeches/speech-3425

[1239] Jimmy Carter: "Voyager Spacecraft Statement by the President," July 29, 1977, The American Presidency Project, http://www.presidency.ucsb.edu/ws/?pid=7890

[1240] "Remarks By the President at a DNC Event - Seattle, WA," The White House, Office of the Press Secretary, July 22, 2014, https://www.whitehouse.gov/the-press-office/2014/07/22/remarks-president-dnc-event-seattle-wa

[1241] Remarks By President Barack Obama in Prague as Delivered," The White House, Office of the Press Secretary, April 5, 2009, https://www.whitehouse.gov/the-press-office/remarks-president-barack-obama-prague-delivered

[1242] "Biden Calls for a New World Order'," *Infowars,* April 6, 2013, http://www.infowars.com/biden-calls-for-a-new-world-order/

[1243] Roeder, Tom, "Biden Challenges Graduating Air Force Academy Create 'a New World Order'," *The Gazette,* Colorado Springs, CO; May 28, 2014, http://gazette.com/biden-challenges-graduating-air-force-academy-cadets-to-create-a-new-world-order/article/1520651

[1244] "Joe Biden's New World Order Speech," Infowars, August 24, 2008, http://www.infowars.com/joe-bidens-new-world-order-speech/

[1245] Biden, Joe, "How I Learned to Love the New World Order," *Wall Street Journal,* April 23, 1992, http://www.pennsylvaniacrier.com/filemgmt_data/files/Biden-New%20World%20Order.pdf

[1246] Talbott, Strobe, "The Birth of the Global Nation," *Time*, July 20, 1992, http://www.worldbeyondborders.org/globalnation.htm

[1247] Pedraza, Rick, "Gore: Cap-and-Trade Will Bring Global Government," *Newsmax,* July 3, 2009, http://www.newsmax.com/InsideCover/gore-global-government/2009/07/13/id/331518

[1248] Garrison, Dean, "Biden: 'The Affirmative Task We Have Now, Is Uh, Is to Actually Um Uh Create Uh Uh a New World Order'," D.C. Clothesline, April 7, 2013, http://www.dcclothesline.com/2013/04/07/biden-the-affirmative-task-we-have-now-is-uh-is-to-actually-um-uh-create-uh-uh-a-new-world-order/

[1249] Nixon, Richard, "69 - Toasts of the President and Premier Chou En-lai of China at a Banquet Honoring the Premier in Peking," The American Presidency Project, http://www.presidency.ucsb.edu/ws/?pid=3751

[1250] "Revisiting Walter Cronkite and Hillary Clinton's Call for Global Government," *Renew America,* May 24, 2005, http://www.renewamerica.com/article/050524

[1251] Grice, Andrew, "PM Sets Out Vision for Life After Bush," *UK Independent,* October 22, 2011, http://www.independent.co.uk/news/world/politics/pm-sets-out-vision-for-life-after-bush-771708.html

[1252] "Brown: World Needs 'Global New Deal'," *CNN,* February 22, 2009, http://www.cnn.com/2009/WORLD/europe/02/22/germany.financial.summit/index.html

[1253] "Ahmadinejad: Iran and Syria Will Create a New World Order," *Haaretz,* July 1, 2010, http://www.haaretz.com/news/ahmadinejad-iran-and-syria-will-create-a-new-world-order-1.260993

[1254] Kissinger, Henry, "Henry Kissinger on the Assembly of a New World Order," *Wall Street Journal,* August 29, 2014, http://www.wsj.com/articles/henry-kissinger-on-the-assembly-of-a-new-world-order-1409328075

[1255] Francis, Diane, "Henry Kissinger's New World Order," *Financial Post,* November 1, 2014, http://business.financialpost.com/fp-comment/henry-kissingers-new-world-order

[1256] "Kissinger: Obama Primed to Create 'New World Order'" *WND,* January 6, 2009, http://www.wnd.com/2009/01/85442/

[1257] Kissinger, Henry A. "The Chance for a New World Order, *New York Times*, January 12, 2009, http://www.nytimes.com/2009/01/12/opinion/12iht-edkissinger.1.19281915.html

[1258] Rockefeller, David, <u>Memoirs</u>. New York: Random House, 2002, p. 405

[1259] "Larry McDonald – New World Order," YouTube video of McDonald interviewed by Tom Braden and Pat Buchanan on "In the Crossfire", May 1983, https://www.youtube.com/watch?v=puNCkwjuxJ0

[1260] Newman, Alex, "Putin: Key Player in the "New World Order"," *New American,* http://www.thenewamerican.com/world-news/europe/item/19164-putin-key-player-in-the-new-world-order

[1261] Jasper, William F., "Gorbachev: Pushing New World Order, World Government," *John Birch Society,* November 3, 2011, http://www.jbs.org/commentary/gorbachev-pushing-new-world-order-world-government

[1262] Newman, Alex, "Putin: Key Player in the "New World Order"," *New American,* http://www.nwotoday.com/the-new-world-orders-history/the-socialist-review-american-politicians

[1263] Chirac, Jacques, "Speech By Mr. Jacques Chirac French President to the 6th Conference of the Parties to the United Nations Framework Convention on Climate Change," *Climate Depot,* November 20, 2000, http://web.archive.org/web/20120418095206/http://sovereignty.net/center/chirac.html

[1264] Falk, Richard A., "Toward a New World Order: Modest Methods and Drastic Visions", from Saul H. Mendlovitz's book *On the Creation of a Just World Order, Preferred Worlds for the 1990's,* New York City: The Free Press, 1975

[1265] Griffiths, Martin, <u>Fifty Key Thinkers in International Relations</u>. Abingdon-on-Thames: Routledge, 1999, p. 120

[1266] McGovern, George, "I'm Ready to Run in '92," *New York Times,* February 14, 1991, http://www.nytimes.com/1991/02/14/opinion/i-m-ready-to-run-in-92.html

[1267] Kinman, Dwight L., *The World's Last Dictator,* New Kensington: Whitaker House, p. 81

[1268] Brace, Robin A, "Coming to a Church Near You... One World Religion!" UK Apologetics, November 21, 2008, http://www.ukapologetics.net/08/oneworldchurch.htm

[1269] Hooper, John, "Pope Calls for a New World Order," *UK Guardian,* January 1, 2004, http://www.guardian.co.uk/world/2004/jan/02/catholicism.religion

[1270] "Pope Calls on G-20 Nations to Serve Common Global Interests," *Business Ghana,* November 10, 2010, http://www.businessghana.com/portal/news/index.php?op=getNews&news_cat_id=&id=137401

[1271] "From Profits to Ethics: Pope Calls for a New Political and Financial World Order," *UK Guardian,* July 7, 2009, http://www.theguardian.com/world/2009/jul/07/pope-new-political-financial-order

[1272] Pope Benedict XVI, "Caritas in Veritate (Charity in Truth)," June 29, 2009, http://w2.vatican.va/content/benedict-xvi/en/encyclicals/documents/hf_ben-xvi_enc_20090629_caritas-in-veritate.html

[1273] Chua-Eoan, Howard, "Pope of the Americas," *Time,* March 13, 2013, http://world.time.com/2013/03/13/pope-of-the-americas/

[1274] "Pope Repeats Call for New World Order," *AP,* July 8, 2015, http://web.archive.org/web/20150711014830/http://www.onenewsnow.com/ap/religion/pope-repeats-call-for-new-world-order

[1275] Pullella, P. & Marsh, S., "Pope Calls for New Economic Order, Criticizes Capitalism," *Reuters,* July 9, 2015, http://www.reuters.com/article/us-pope-latam-bolivia-idUSKCN0PJ29B20150710

[1276] Flitter, Emily, "Pope Says Trump 'Not Christian' in a Sign of Global Concern," *Reuters,* February 18, 2016, https://ca.news.yahoo.com/pope-says-trump-not-christian-trump-calls-disgraceful-175531900.html

[1277] Lauter, D. & Bierman, N., "Trump and Pope Francis Clash Over Immigration, Another Extraordinary Campaign Twist," *Los Angeles Times,* February 18, 2016, http://www.latimes.com/world/la-fg-pope-on-trump-wall-20160218-story.html

[1278] Nolte, John, "Pope Francis: Tear Down the Vatican Wall!" *Breitbart,* September 24, 2015, http://www.breitbart.com/2016-presidential-race/2015/09/24/pope-francis-tear-down-the-vatican-wall/

[1279] Ibid.

[1280] Dinan, Stephen, "Obama Reinstates 'Catch-and-Release' Policy for Illegal Immigrants," *Washington Times,* February 4, 2106, http://www.washingtontimes.com/news/2016/feb/4/obama-reinstates-catch-and-release-policy-illegals/

[1281] O'Matz, Megan, "Number of Undocumented Cubans Entering US Up Sharply in 2015," *St. Augustine Record,* February 3, 2016, http://staugustine.com/news/florida-news/2016-02-03/number-undocumented-cubans-entering-us-sharply-2015

[1282] "Plans for Colorado Shelter for Immigrant Children Scrapped," AP, February 12, 2016, http://wtop.com/national/2016/02/plans-for-colorado-shelter-for-immigrant-children-scrapped/

[1283] Potter, M., & Chuck, E., "Surge in Children, Families at the U.S. Border May Be the 'New Normal'," NBC News, December 19, 2015, http://www.nbcnews.com/storyline/immigration-border-crisis/surge-children-families-u-s-border-may-be-new-normal-n482691

[1284] "Rush: What About Vatican's Border 'Walls'?" *WND,* February 18, 2016, http://www.wnd.com/2016/02/rush-what-about-vaticans-walls/

[1285] *Ibid.*

[1286] "23 Legal Medical Marijuana States and DC," ProCon, Accessed January 7, 2016, http://medicalmarijuana.procon.org/view.resource.php?resourceID=000881

[1287] Buchheit, Paul, "5 Facts About How America Is Rigged for a Massive Wealth Transfer to the Rich," *Alternet,* November 4, 2014, http://www.alternet.org/economy/5-facts-about-how-america-rigged-massive-wealth-transfer-rich

[1288] *Ibid.*

[1289] *Ibid.*

[1290] Buchheit, Paul, "The Stark Facts of Global Greed, a Disease as Challenging as Climate Change," *Alternet,* October 26, 2014, http://www.alternet.org/economy/stark-facts-global-greed-disease-challenging-climate-change

[1291] Coughlan, Sean, "Asia Tops Biggest Global School Rankings," *BBC,* Mary 13, 2015, http://www.bbc.com/news/business-32608772

[1292] "Agenda 21: How Will It Affect You?" April 30, 2013 Video from The John Birch Society, Accessed January 22, 2016, https://www.youtube.com/watch?v=rTE-3Fl7wgg

[1293] McManus, John F., "Local Governments Reject UN's Agenda 21," What Is Agenda 21, 2011, http://whatisagenda21.net/iclei.htm

[1294] "United Nations Conference on Environment & Development Rio de Janerio, Brazil, 3 to 14 June 1992," United Nations, https://sustainabledevelopment.un.org/content/documents/Agenda21.pdf, p.3

[1295] Goodenough, Patrick, "U.S. Pays $3B for UN--More Than 185 Other Countries Combined," *CNS News,* May 7, 2015, http://www.cnsnews.com/news/article/patrick-goodenough/us-pays-3b-un-more-185-other-countries-combined

[1296] Patrick, Goodenough, "U.S. Taxpayers Will Continue to Pay More Than One-Fifth of U.N. Budget," *CNS News,* December 28, 2012, http://cnsnews.com/news/article/us-taxpayers-will-continue-pay-more-one-fifth-un-budget

[1297] Goodenough, Patrick, "U.S. Pays $3B for UN--More Than 185 Other Countries Combined," *CNS News,* May 7, 2015, http://www.cnsnews.com/news/article/patrick-goodenough/us-pays-3b-un-more-185-other-countries-combined

[1298] "Headquarters of the United Nations," Wikipedia, accessed January 13, 2016, https://en.wikipedia.org/wiki/Headquarters_of_the_United_Nations

[1299] Chan, Sewell, "$2,100 a Square Foot for Vacant Land," *New York Times,* May 13, 2008, http://cityroom.blogs.nytimes.com/2008/05/13/2100-a-square-foot-for-vacant-land/

[1300] "Headquarters of the United Nations," Wikipedia, accessed January 14, 2016, https://en.wikipedia.org/wiki/Headquarters_of_the_United_Nations

[1301] "Transforming Our World: The 2030 Agenda for Sustainable Development," United Nations, 2015, https://sustainabledevelopment.un.org/content/documents/21252030%20Agenda%20for%20Sustainable%20Development%20web.pdf, p. 18

[1302] Wile, Anthony, "UN Plans to Expand the Phony Water Crisis ... 'Smart Water Meters' on the Way", *The Daily Bell,* June 16 2012, http://www.thedailybell.com/editorials/4001/Anthony-Wile-UN-Plans-to-Expand-the-Phony-Water-Crisis--Smart-Water-Meters-on-the-Way/

[1303] "USAID Global Climate Change Initiative Budget," Accessed January 14, 2016, https://www.usaid.gov/climate/strategy/budget

[1304] Deyo, Holly, Prudent Places USA. Pueblo West: Deyo Enterprises, 2014

[1305] Davenport, Coral, "Obama's Strategy on Climate Change, Part of Global Deal, Is Revealed," *New York Times,* March 31, 2015, http://www.nytimes.com/2015/04/01/us/obama-to-offer-major-blueprint-on-climate-change.html

[1306] *Ibid.*

[1307] "Napolitano: Supreme Sourt EPA Ruling a First in US History," *Fox News Video,* February 10, 2016, http://video.foxnews.com/v/4748755236001/napolitano-supreme-court-epa-ruling-a-first-in-us-history/

[1308] Bowerman, Mary, "GOP: Water Rule Is Murky," *Durango Herald,* May 29, 2014, http://www.durangoherald.com/article/20140529/NEWS01/140529480/article/20140529/NEWS01/140529480/GOP:-EPA-water-rule-muddies-the-water-

[1309] *Ibid.*

[1310] Davenport, Coral, "Nations Approve Landmark Climate Accord in Paris," *New York Times,* December 13, 2015, http://www.nytimes.com/2015/12/13/world/europe/climate-change-accord-paris.html

[1311] Davenport, Coral, "Obama's Strategy on Climate Change, Part of Global Deal, Is Revealed," *New York Times,* March 31, 2015, http://www.nytimes.com/2015/04/01/us/obama-to-offer-major-blueprint-on-climate-change.html

[1312] Bay Area Real Estate, "Tumbleweed: A Tiny House Company," *Nino's Realty News,* January 29, 2015, http://ninosrealtynews.org/2015/01/29/2846/

[1313] Spector, Julian, "A Big Turnout for a Tiny House 'Jamboree'," *Citylab,* August 17, 2015, http://www.citylab.com/housing/2015/08/a-big-turnout-for-a-tiny-house-jamboree/401498/

[1314] "One Planet Living," Bioregional, Accessed January 24, 2016, http://www.bioregional.com/

[1315] Bioregional, "BedZED," http://www.bioregional.com/bedzed/

[1316] "City Sustainability Initiative," City of Pueblo, Colorado, Accessed January 24, 2016, http://www.pueblo.us/371/City-Sustainability-Initiative

[1317] "New Strategies for Regional Economic Development," Lincoln Institute of Land Policy and Regional Plan Association, America 2050, March 29-31, 2009, http://www.america2050.org/pdf/2050_Report_Regional_Economic_Development_2009.pdf, P. 5

[1318] "States Explore Mileage-Based User Fees," Council of State Governments, April 2015, http://knowledgecenter.csg.org/kc/system/files/Mileage%20Based%20Fees.pdf

[1319] "Obama Admin Plans to 'Force' Americans to Move into Cities - 'Redistributing' the Wealth," *Fox News* video of Megyn Kelly interviewing Dr. Stanley Kurtz, published March 22, 2013, Accessed January 25, 2016, https://www.youtube.com/watch?v=jB2fexv5LDE

[1320] Kurtz, Stanley, "Obama's Plans for the Suburbs: And How to Stop Them," *National Review,* March 18, 2013, http://www.nationalreview.com/corner/343242/obamas-plans-suburbs-and-how-stop-them-stanley-kurtz

[1321] "Effects of the Built Environment on Transportation: Energy Use, Greenhouse Gas Emissions," and Other Factors," U.S. Department of Energy, March 2013, http://www.nrel.gov/docs/fy13osti/55634.pdf, p. 67

[1322] "How Many People Reside in Urban or Rural Areas for the 2010 Census," U.C. Census Bureau, Accessed January 26, 2016, https://ask.census.gov/faq.php?id=5000&faqId=5971

[1323] Heal, Loren, "The 57 States Gaffe Was No Joke," *Red State,* November 26, 2010, http://www.redstate.com/diary/Socrates/2010/11/26/the-57-states-gaffe-was-no-joke/

[1324] "Executive Order 13575 – Establishment of the White House Rural Council," Government Publishing Office, June 9, 2011, https://www.gpo.gov/fdsys/pkg/DCPD-201100431/pdf/DCPD-201100431.pdf, pp. 3-4

[1325] *Ibid.*, p. 2

[1326] "Quotes About Politics," http://quotes.cat-v.org/politics

[1327] The Cabinet, The White House, Accessed January 26, 2016, https://www.whitehouse.gov/administration/cabinet

[1328] Agenda 21, American Policy Center, https://americanpolicy.org/agenda21/

[1329] David Foreman, AZ Quotes, Accessed January 25, 2016, http://www.azquotes.com/quote/604920

[1330] Earth First! Target of Opportunity, Accessed January 25, 2016, http://www.targetofopportunity.com/earth_first.htm

[1331] "Wildlife Corridors Initiative Report," Western Governors' Association, June 29, 2008, https://www.nature.nps.gov/biology/migratoryspecies/documents/WGAWildlifeCorridorsInitiative.pdf

[1332] *Ibid.*

[1333] "Creating Landscapes for Life," Wildlands Network, Accessed January 25, 2016, http://www.wildlandsnetwork.org/wildways

[1334] Coffman, Michael S., "Explanation of the Biodiversity Treaty and the Wildlands Project," *Citizen Review Online,* September 13, 2003, http://www.citizenreviewonline.org/sept_2003/explanation.htm

[1335] "What is Rewilding Europe and What Are We Up To," Rewilding Europe, Accessed May 1, 2016, https://www.rewildingeurope.com/about/

[1336] Sylven, M. & Widstrand, S., "A Vision for a Wilder Europe", Rewilding Europe, January 2015, https://www.rewildingeurope.com/wp-content/uploads/2015/03/WILD10-Vison-for-a-Wilder-Europe-2015.pdf, p. 16

[1337] Hance, Jeremy, "Conservationists Turn Tiny New Zealand Island into Bold Wildlife Experiment," *The Guardian,* April 21, 2015, http://www.theguardian.com/environment/radical-conservation/2015/apr/21/rotoroa-new-zealand-birds-wildlife-rewilding

[1338] "Americans Think Islam Needs to Clean Up Its Act," Rasmussen Reports, January 13, 2015, http://www.rasmussenreports.com/public_content/politics/general_politics/january_2015/americans_think_islam_needs_to_clean_up_its_act

[1339] Marcus, Itamar, "PA TV Sermon: Jews Are "Apes and Pigs," *Palestinian Media Watch,* February 5, 2015, http://palwatch.org/main.aspx?fi=157&doc_id=13887

[1340] *Ibid.*

[1341] Kaufman, Joe, "Florida Muslim Leader Commemorates Hamas, Calls Jews Monkeys and Pigs," *Front Page Magazine,* December 28, 2015, http://www.frontpagemag.com/fpm/261255/florida-muslim-leader-commemorates-hamas-calls-joe-kaufman

[1342] *Ibid.*

[1343] Lane, Oliver LL, "Imam Calls Jews 'Pigs and Apes' in Mosque Rant," *Breitbart,* October 14, 2014, http://www.breitbart.com/london/2014/10/14/danish-imam-jews-apes-pigs/

[1344] Hooker, Richard, "Ancient Jewish History: The Diaspora," Jewish Virtual Library, http://www.compellingtruth.org/Jews-Arabs-Muslims.html

[1345] Schabb, Deborah Fineblu, "To Pray or Not to Pray: That is the Temple Mount Question," *Jewish and Israel News,* November 18, 2014, http://www.jns.org/latest-articles/2014/11/18/to-pray-or-not-to-pray-that-is-the-temple-mount-question

[1346] "Assassin Was a Serial Arsonist, Assaulted 3 Wardens in Prison," *Ynet News,* October 30, 3014, http://www.ynetnews.com/articles/0,7340,L-4586296,00.html

[1347] Hadid, Diaa, "Palestinian Women Join Effort to Keep Jews From Contested Holy Site," *New York Times,* April 16, 2015, http://www.nytimes.com/2015/04/17/world/middleeast/palestinian-women-join-effort-to-keep-jews-from-contested-holy-site.html

[1348] *Ibid.*

[1349] "Is Your Religion the True One," Jews for Judaism, https://jewsforjudaism.org/knowledge/articles/answers/ask-the-rabbi/is-your-religion-the-true-one/

[1350] Slick, Matt, "Jihad: Holy Struggle or Holy War?" Christian Apologetics & Research Ministry, https://carm.org/jihad-holy-struggle-or-holy-war

[1351] "What Has Been Related About What Bounties There Are for the Lowest Inhabitants of Paradise," Book of Sunah, Hadith Al-Tirmidh, Chapter 23, https://futureislam.files.wordpress.com/2013/06/jami-at-tirmidhi-vol-4-ahadith-1897-2605.pdf, p. 549

[1352] "The House of One", http://house-of-one.org/en/idea

[1353] "About URI," URI, Accessed January 12, 2016, http://www.uri.org/about_uri

[1354] "Explore Regions," URI, Accessed January 12, 2016, http://www.uri.org/cooperation_circles/explore_regions

[1355] "Get Started," URI, Accessed February 1, 2016, http://www.uri.org/cooperation_circles/create_a_cooperation_circle/get_started

[1356] "Preamble, Purpose and Principles," URI, Accessed January 30, 2016, http://www.uri.org/about_uri/charter/preamble_purpose_and_principles

[1357] *Ibid.*

[1358] "Environment," URI, Accessed January 12, 2016, http://www.uri.org/action_areas/environment

[1359] Blake, John, "How the Ultimate Scandal Saved One Pastor," CNN, March 2015, http://www.cnn.com/interactive/2015/03/living/ultimate-scandal-paulk/

[1360] Paulk, D.E., "Faith and Free Will," *Weekly Eureka,* http://archive.constantcontact.com/fs070/1102200732777/archive/1109522110852.html

[1361] Pullella, Philip, "Shimon Peres Floats Idea of U.N.-style "United Religions" with Pope Francis," *Reuters,* September 5, 2014, http://blogs.reuters.com/faithworld/2014/09/05/shimon-peres-floats-idea-of-u-n-style-united-religions-with-pope-francis/

[1362] Heneghan, Tom, "Pope Sends Olive Branch to Worried French Protestants," *Times of Malta,* May 9, 2005, http://www.timesofmalta.com/articles/view/20050509/local/pope-sends-olive-branch-to-worried-french-protestants.90910

[1363] Stewart, Phil, "Vatican Says Other Christian Churches 'Wounded'," *Reuters,* July 10, 2007, http://www.reuters.com/article/us-pope-christians-idUSL1048495520070710

[1364] Jenkins, Mark, "Vatican: Catholic Church Still the Only Real Church," *The Trumpet,* July 12, 2007, https://www.thetrumpet.com/article/3945.2.0.0/religion/vatican-catholic-church-still-the-only-real-church

[1365] *"Ut Unum Sint,"* John Paul II Encyclical, May 25, 1995, http://w2.vatican.va/content/john-paul-ii/en/encyclicals/documents/hf_jp-ii_enc_25051995_ut-unum-sint.html

[1366] "Orthodox and Catholic Unity a 'Duty'," *The Trumpet,* December 4, 2008, https://www.thetrumpet.com/article/5730.1.0.0/world/war/orthodox-and-catholic-unity-a-duty

[1367] Blake, John, "The 'Obamification' of Pope Francis," *CNN,* July 8, 2015, http://www.cnn.com/2015/09/13/us/pope-obama-critics/

[1368] "Pope Wraps Ecuador Leg of South America Trip After Calling for New Ecological, Economic Order," *Fox News,* September 13, 2015, http://www.foxnews.com/world/2015/07/08/pope-wraps-ecuador-leg-south-america-trip-after-calling-for-new-ecological.html

[1369] On Care for Our Common Home," Francis Encyclical, May 24, 2015, http://w2.vatican.va/content/francesco/en/encyclicals/documents/papa-francesco_20150524_enciclica-laudato-si.html

[1370] "Pope Francis' Prayer Intentions for January 2016," YouTube video Accessed February 4, 2016, uploaded January 6, 2016, https://www.youtube.com/watch?v=-6FfTxwTX34

[1371] "Anglican Leader Urges Acceptance of Pope, *Deseret News,* October 1, 1989, http://www.deseretnews.com/article/66321/ANGLICAN-LEADER-URGES-ACCEPTANCE-OF-POPE.html?pg=all

[1372] Ross, Hugh, "Fulfilled Prophecy: Evidence for the Reliability of the Bible," Reasons to Believe, August 22, 2003, http://www.reasons.org/articles/articles/fulfilled-prophecy-evidence-for-the-reliability-of-the-bible

[1373] Maoz, Jason, "Lyndon Johnson, Friend of the Jews," *Commentary Magazine,* August 22, 2008, http://www.commentarymagazine.com/2008/08/22/lyndon-johnson-friend-of-the-jews

[1374] McCullough, David, Truman. New York: Simon & Schuster, 1992, p. 336

[1375] "United States Policy Toward Jewish Refugees, 1941-1952," Holocaust Encyclopedia, http://www.ushmm.org/wlc/en/article.php?ModuleId=10007094

[1376] Bard, Mitchell G., "The Sinai-Suez Campaign: President Eisenhower & PM Ben-Gurion on Israeli Withdrawal from Sinai," Jewish Virtual Library, http://www.jewishvirtuallibrary.org/jsource/US-Israel/phantom.html

[1377] "Foreign policy of the John F. Kennedy Administration," Wikipedia, Accessed February 6, 2016, https://en.wikipedia.org/wiki/Foreign_policy_of_the_John_F._Kennedy_administration

[1378] Kinzer, Stephen, "Shot Heard Round the World," *UK Guardian,* June 13, 2008, http://www.theguardian.com/commentisfree/2008/jun/13/israelandthepalestinians.usa

[1379] Smith, Morris, "Our First Jewish President Lyndon Johnson? - An Update," *5 Towns Jewish Times,* http://5tjt.com/our-first-jewish-president-lyndon-johnson-an-update/

[1380] Byron, Jim, "How Richard Nixon Saved Israel," http://web.archive.org/web/20150622022340/http://blog.nixonfoundation.org/2010/10/how-richard-nixon-saved-israel/

[1381] Stone, Roger, "How Nixon Saved the State of Israel," *Lew Rockwell,* August 19, 2014, http://www.lewrockwell.com/2014/08/roger-stone/nixon-on-jews-and-israel/

[1382] "Gerald Ford, the U.S. President Who Reassessed Policy Toward Israel, Dies at 93," *Haaretz,* December 28, 2006, http://www.haaretz.com/gerald-ford-the-u-s-president-who-reassessed-policy-toward-israel-dies-at-93-1.208477

[1383] Gwertzman, Bernard, "Egypt and Israel Sign Formal Treaty, Ending a State of War After 30 Years; Sadat and Begin Praise Carter's Role" *New York Times,* March 26, 1979, http://www.nytimes.com/learning/general/onthisday/big/0326.html

[1384] Pompi, Jennifer, "Jimmy Carter Slams Israel in Pro-Palestine Op-Ed," *The Washington Times,* August 5, 2014, http://www.washingtontimes.com/news/2014/aug/5/jimmy-carter-slams-israel-in-pro-palestine-op-ed/

[1385] Boteach, Shmuley, "The Moral Disintegration of Jimmy Carter," *The Observer,* August 11, 2014, http://observer.com/2014/08/the-moral-disintegration-of-jimmy-carter/

[1386] Benoit, Sammy, "Jimmy Carter, the Jew-Hater Who Cried Racist," *American Thinker,* September 17, 2009, http://www.americanthinker.com/blog/2009/09/jimmy_carter_the_jewhater_who.html

[1387] Schachtel, Jordan, "Bibi Declines Jimmy Carter Meeting Over His 'Anti-Israel,' Pro-Hamas Views," *Breitbart,* April 21, 2015, http://www.breitbart.com/national-security/2015/04/21/bibi-declines-jimmy-carter-meeting-over-his-anti-israel-pro-hamas-views/

[1388] Shalev, Chemi, "If Obama Treated Israel Like Reagan Did, He'd Be Impeached," *Haaretz,* December 9, 2011, http://www.haaretz.com/blogs/west-of-eden/if-obama-treated-israel-like-reagandid-he-d-be-impeached-1.400542

[1389] Bard, Mitchell, "Reagan's Legacy on Israel," 2013, http://www.mitchellbard.com/articles/reagan.html

[1390] Singer, Jay Saul, "George Bush, James Baker, and the Jews," *Haaretz,* March 12, 2015, http://www.haaretz.com/gerald-ford-the-u-s-president-who-reassessed-policy-toward-israel-dies-at-93-1.208477

[1391] "The Madrid Conference, 1991," U.S. Department of State, Office of the Historian, Accessed February 10, 2016, https://history.state.gov/milestones/1989-1992/madrid-conference

[1392] "William 'Bill' Clinton," Jewish Virtual Library, http://www.jewishvirtuallibrary.org/jsource/biography/billclinton.html

[1393] Au, Ceri, "Sixteen Years of Israeli-Palestinian Summits: Wye River Summit," *Time,* 2007, http://content.time.com/time/specials/2007/article/0,28804,1644149_1644147_1644132,00.html

[1394] "President Bush's Freedom Agenda Helped Protect the American People," The White House, January 12, 2009, http://georgewbush-whitehouse.archives.gov/infocus/bushrecord/factsheets/freedomagenda.html

[1395] Obama, Barack, "Remarks by the President at Cairo University" The White House, Office of the Press Secretary, June 4, 2009, http://www.whitehouse.gov/the_press_office/remarks-by-the-President-at-Cairo-University-6-04-09

[1396] Wilson, Scott, "Obama Searches for Middle East Peace, *Washington Post,* July 14, 2012, https://www.washingtonpost.com/politics/obama-searches-for-middle-east-peace/2012/07/14/gJQAQQiKlW_story.html

[1397] Cohen, Tom, "Obama Calls for Israel's Return to Pre-1967 Borders," *CNN,* May 19, 2011, http://www.cnn.com/2011/POLITICS/05/19/obama.israel.palestinians

[1398] Gabbay, Tiffany, "Obama Caught on Live Mic Blasting Netanyahu to French PM: 'You're Fed Up With Him But I Have to Deal With Him Every Day!'" *The Blaze,* November 7, 2011, http://www.theblaze.com/stories/obama-caught-on-live-mic-blasting-netanyahu-to-french-pm-you%E2%80%99re-fed-up-with-him-but-i-have-to-deal-with-him-every-day/

[1399] Obama, Barack, "Remarks by the President to the UN General Assembly," The White House, Office of the Press Secretary, September 25, 2012, http://www.whitehouse.gov/the-press-office/2012/09/25/remarks-president-un-general-assembly

[1400] Rubin, Jennifer, "Reversing Obama's Latest Anti-Israel Move," *CNN,* https://www.washingtonpost.com/blogs/right-turn/wp/2016/02/01/reversing-obamas-latest-anti-israel-move/

[1401] "Obama and Israel," Discover the Networks, http://www.discoverthenetworks.org/viewSubCategory.asp?id=1521

[1402] Obama Blocked Arms Deliveries to Israel, Ordered No Shipments Be Made Without His Approval," *World Tribune,* August 15, 2014, http://web.archive.org/web/20150319021805/http://www.worldtribune.com/2014/08/15/furious-obama-blocked-arms-deliveries-israel-state-dept-approved-july-request/

[1403] Yashar, A. & Wanderman, M., "US Declassifies Document Revealing Israel's Nuclear Program," *Arutz Sheva,* March 25, 2015, http://www.israelnationalnews.com/News/News.aspx/193175

[1404] Zuckerman, Mortimer, B., "Obama's Unforgivable Betrayal," *U.S. News & World Report,* April 17, 2015, http://www.usnews.com/opinion/articles/2015/04/17/obamas-iran-nuclear-deal-is-an-unforgivable-betrayal-of-israel

[1405] "Assassination of Yitzhak Rabin," Wikipedia, Accessed February 6, 2016, https://en.wikipedia.org/wiki/Assassination_of_Yitzhak_Rabin

[1406] "1991: Bush Opens Historic Mid East Peace Conference," *BBC,* http://news.bbc.co.uk/onthisday/hi/dates/stories/october/30/newsid_2465000/2465725.stm

[1407] "Billion-Dollar Weather and Climate Disasters: Table of Events," NOAA, Accessed February 6, 2016, https://www.ncdc.noaa.gov/billions/events

[1408] "Warren M. Christopher," U.S. State Department Archive, Accessed February 6, 2016, http://2001-2009.state.gov/r/pa/ho/trvl/ls/13043.htm

[1409] "1993 World Trade Center Bombing Fast Facts," *CNN,* February 13, 2015, http://www.cnn.com/2013/11/05/us/1993-world-trade-center-bombing-fast-facts/

[1410] "Oslo I Accord," Wikipedia, Accessed February 6, 2016, https://en.wikipedia.org/wiki/Oslo_I_Accord

[1411] "Billion-Dollar Weather and Climate Disasters: Table of Events," NOAA, Accessed February 6, 2016, https://www.ncdc.noaa.gov/billions/event

[1412] "Arafat, Netanyahu to Restart Stalled Mideast Peace Process," *CNN,* September 28, 1998, http://www.cnn.com/WORLD/meast/9809/28/mideast.05/index.html

[1413] "Billion-Dollar Weather and Climate Disasters: Table of Events," NOAA, Accessed February 6, 2016, https://www.ncdc.noaa.gov/billions/events

[1414] "Clinton: Gap Narrowed Over Mideast Peace," *CNN,* September 28, 1998, http://web.archive.org/web/20060823082644/http://www.cnn.com/WORLD/meast/9809/28/mideast.04/index.html

[1415] "Billion-Dollar Weather and Climate Disasters: Table of Events," NOAA, Accessed February 6, 2016, https://www.ncdc.noaa.gov/billions/events

[1416] "American Minute with Bill Federer, Jerusalem Temple Destroyed - Tisha B'Av," http://archive.constantcontact.com/fs155/1108762609255/archive/1118467773266.html

[1417] "Billion-Dollar Weather and Climate Disasters: Table of Events," NOAA, Accessed February 6, 2016, https://www.ncdc.noaa.gov/billions/events

[1418] Koenig, William, Eye to Eye - Facing the Consequences of Dividing Israel. McLean: About Him Publishing, 2008, p. 138

[1419] "President George W. Bush Addresses the 106th Convention of the Veterans of Foreign Wars," *CNN Transcripts,* Aired August 22, 2005, http://edition.cnn.com/TRANSCRIPTS/0508/22/se.01.html

[1420] "President Discusses Iraqi Constitution With Press Pool," U.S. State Department Archive, August 23, 2005, http://2001-2009.state.gov/p/nea/rls/rm/51372.htm

[1421] "Billion-Dollar Weather and Climate Disasters: Table of Events," NOAA, Accessed February 6, 2016, https://www.ncdc.noaa.gov/billions/events

[1422] Julian, Hana Levi, "Obama Tells Abbas: I Support Dividing Jerusalem," *Israeli National News,* November 4, 2008, http://www.israelnationalnews.com/News/News.aspx/128225

[1423] "Billion-Dollar Weather and Climate Disasters: Table of Events," NOAA, Accessed February 6, 2016, https://www.ncdc.noaa.gov/billions/events

[1424] *Ibid.*

[1425] Wilner, Michael, "No Two-State Solution During Obama Presidency, White House Assesses," *Jerusalem Post,* November 6, 2015, http://www.jpost.com/Israel-News/Politics-And-Diplomacy/No-two-state-solution-during-Obama-presidency-White-House-assesses-432227

[1426] "Anti-Semitism: A Hoax of Hate," Jewish Virtual Library, https://www.jewishvirtuallibrary.org/jsource/anti-semitism/hoax.html

[1427] Adachi, Ken, "The Protocols of the Learned Elders of Zion," Educate Yourself, September 17, 2014, http://educate-yourself.org/cn/protocolsofsion.shtml

[1428] Sherr, Dean, "Why Does the Left Downplay Antisemitism? All Forms of racism Should Be Abhorred," *The Guardian,* March 19, 2015, http://www.theguardian.com/commentisfree/2015/mar/20/why-does-the-left-ignore-antisemitism-all-forms-of-racism-should-be-abhorred

[1429] Edmunds, Donna Rachel, "Anti-Semitism on the Rise: European Terror Attacks Fuel Hate Crimes Against Jews," *Breitbart,* July 30, 2015, http://www.breitbart.com/london/2015/07/30/anti-semitism-on-the-rise-european-terror-attacks-fuel-hate-crimes-against-jews/

[1430] "Coordination Forum for Countering Antisemitism, Annual Evaluation 2015 – Present Situation and Tendencies," Coordination Forum for Countering Antisemitism, 2015, http://antisemitism.org.il/webfm_send/151, p. 25

[1431] Hackett, Conrad, "5 Facts About the Muslim Population in Europe," Pew Research Center, November 17, 2015, http://www.pewresearch.org/fact-tank/2015/11/17/5-facts-about-the-muslim-population-in-europe/

[1432] Drury, Ian, "The Number of Muslims in Europe Reaches 44M: Serious Concerns Raised About the Challenges of Integration Following Attacks on Paris," *UK Daily Mail,* November 15, 2015, http://www.dailymail.co.uk/news/article-3319890/The-Paris-attacks-drawn-renewed-attention-Europe-s-growing-Muslim-population.html

[1433] Edmunds, Donna Rachel, "Anti-Semitism on the Rise: European Terror Attacks Fuel Hate Crimes Against Jews," *Breitbart,* July 30, 2015, http://www.breitbart.com/london/2015/07/30/anti-semitism-on-the-rise-european-terror-attacks-fuel-hate-crimes-against-jews/

[1434] *Ibid.*

[1435] Prince, Cathryn, "Anti-Semitism Now 'Fashionable' in the US, Warn Experts," *Times of Israel,* February 18, 2015, http://www.timesofisrael.com/anti-semitism-now-fashionable-in-the-us-warn-experts/

[1436] "Antisemitism Tracker Organized by State," Accessed February 9, 2016, http://www.amchainitiative.org/antisemitism-tracker

[1437] "Muslims in America – A Statistical Portrait," Embassy of the United States – Baghdad, Iraq, Accessed February 9, 2016, http://iraq.usembassy.gov/resources/information/current/american/statistical.html

[1438] Kredo, Adam, "Anti-Semitic Incidents on U.S. College Campuses Spike," *Washington Free Beacon,* January 22, 2016, http://freebeacon.com/issues/anti-semitic-incidents-us-college-campuses-spike/

[1439] Zarmi, Avner, "30 Wisconsin Homes Vandalized with Swastikas and Anti-Semitic Slogans," *PJ Media,* February 15, 2015, https://pjmedia.com/blog/30-wisconsin-homes-vandalized-with-swastikas-and-anti-semitic-slogans/

[1440] Durkin, Erin, "Pro-Palestinian Activists Disrupt City Council Meeting," *New York Daily News,* January 22, 2015, http://www.nydailynews.com/blogs/dailypolitics/pro-palestinian-activists-disrupt-city-council-meeting-blog-entry-1.2088801

[1441] Prince, Cathryn, "Anti-Semitism Now 'Fashionable' in the US, Warn Experts," *Times of Israel,* February 18, 2015, http://www.timesofisrael.com/anti-semitism-now-fashionable-in-the-us-warn-experts/

[1442] *Ibid.*

[1443] Kredo, Adam, "Study: Anti-Semitism Skyrockets in Canada," *Washington Free Beacon,* June 16, 2015, http://freebeacon.com/issues/study-anti-semitism-skyrockets-in-canada/

[1444] Marcus, Lori Lowenthal, "Why is Antisemitism in Canada Soaring?" *Jewish Press,* June 17, 2015, http://www.jewishpress.com/news/breaking-news/why-is-antisemitism-in-canada-soaring/2015/06/17/0/

[1445] Gordon, Erin, "I'm Tired of Being Scared to Tell Friends I'm Jewish," *Mama Mia,* March 13, 2015, http://www.mamamia.com.au/anti-semitism-australia/

[1446] Kemp, Richard, "Letter from Colonel Richard Kemp to Vice Chancellor USYD, March 12, 2015, *Jews Down Under,* http://jewsdownunder.com/2015/03/14/letter-from-colonel-richard-kemp-to-vice-chancellor-usyd/

[1447] Goldberg, Dan, "Rising anti-Semitism in Australia Leaves Jews Feeling Vulnerable," *Haaretz,* August 26, 2014, http://www.haaretz.com/jewish/news/.premium-1.612430

[1448] "Anti-Semitic attack in Melbourne," *Jewish News,* November 12, 2015, http://www.jewishnews.net.au/anti-semitic-attack-in-melbourne/50547

[1449] "Australian Jews' Safety at 'High Warning Level'," *Times of Israel,* July 22, 2014, http://www.timesofisrael.com/australian-jews-safety-at-high-warning-level/

[1450] Massey, Alex, "Jews Abused at Perth Shopping Centre," *West Australian,* August 4, 2014, https://au.news.yahoo.com/thewest/a/24629519/anti-semitic-abuse-at-perth-shopping-centre/

[1451] "Israeli Rabbi Attacked Visiting Mall in Australia," *Haaretz,* August 5, 2014, http://www.haaretz.com/jewish/news/1.609019

[1452] *Ibid.*

[1453] Goldberg, Dan, "Rising anti-Semitism in Australia Leaves Jews Feeling Vulnerable," *Haaretz,* August 26, 2014, http://www.haaretz.com/jewish/news/.premium-1.612430

[1454] Manning, Brendan, "'Vile' Desecration of Jewish Headstones," *New Zealand Herald,* October 19, 2012, http://www.nzherald.co.nz/nz/news/article.cfm?c_id=1&objectid=10841595

[1455] "Anti-Semite Assaults 4-year-old Boy in New Zealand," *Jewish Journal,* August 15, 2014, http://www.haaretz.com/jewish/news/1.628096

[1456] "New Zealand Election Posters Defaced with Anti-Semitic Messages," *Haaretz,* November 23, 2014, http://www.haaretz.com/jewish/news/1.628096

[1457] Krauthammer, Charles, "At Last, Zion: Israel and the Fate of the Jews," *The Weekly Standard,* May 11, 1998, http://www.freeman.org/m_online/aug98/krauthmr.htm

[1458] "*Fiddler on the Roof* Quotes," IMDB, http://www.imdb.com/title/tt0067093/quotes

[1459] Booth, William, "Here's What Really Happened in the Gaza War (According to the Israelis)," *Washington Post,* September 3, 2014, https://www.washingtonpost.com/news/worldviews/wp/2014/09/03/heres-what-really-happened-in-the-gaza-war-according-to-the-israelis/

[1460] Goldberg, Jeffrey, "The Iranian Regime on Israel's Right to Exist," *The Atlantic,* March 9, 2015, http://www.theatlantic.com/international/archive/2015/03/Iranian-View-of-Israel/387085/

[1461] McElroy, D & Vahdat, A., "Mahmoud Ahmadinejad Revealed to Have Jewish Past," *UK Telegraph*, October 3, 2009, http://www.telegraph.co.uk/news/worldnews/middleeast/iran/6256173/Mahmoud-Ahmadinejad-revealed-to-have-Jewish-past.html

[1462] "DNA Tests Reveal Hitler's Jewish and African Roots," *Haaretz,* August 24, 2010, http://www.haaretz.com/jewish/dna-tests-reveal-hitler-s-jewish-and-african-roots-1.309938

[1463] "Sanhedrin Court Notes," Jewish Roots, http://www.jewishroots.net/library/end-times/sanhedrin.html

[1464] Weiss, Hillel, "The Sanhedrin's Decision Regarding the Holy Temple, the Temple Mount, and Jerusalem," The Temple Institute, June 2005, https://www.templeinstitute.org/sanhedrin-declaration.htm

[1465] Mitchell, Chris, "'Temple in Waiting' Prepared in Jerusalem," *CBN,* September 8, 2014, http://www1.cbn.com/cbnnews/shows/cwn/2009/September/Temple-in-Waiting-Prepared-in-Jerusalem

[1466] Sales, Ben, "Laying the groundwork for a Third Temple in Jerusalem," *Times of Israel,* July 16, 2013, http://www.timesofisrael.com/laying-the-groundwork-for-a-third-temple-in-jerusalem/

[1467] Gano, Ray, "Ready to Rebuild?" Lambert Dolphin Library, Accessed February 25, 2016, http://www.ldolphin.org/gano.html

[1468] Ben David, Amir, "Israel's Natural Gas Potential Triple What Was Thought," *Ynet News,* February 24, 2016, http://www.ynetnews.com/articles/0,7340,L-4770058,00.html

[1469] "Russia," U.S. Energy Information Administration, July 28, 2015, https://www.eia.gov/beta/international/analysis.cfm?iso=RUS

[1470] Withnall, Adam, "Vladimir Putin 'Corruption': Five Things We Learned About the Russian President's Secret Wealth," *UK Independent,* January 26, 2016, http://www.independent.co.uk/news/people/vladimir-putin-corruption-five-things-we-learned-about-the-russian-presidents-secret-wealth-a6834171.html

[1471] Kelley, Michael B., "Russia's Former Largest Foreign Investor: Putin Is Worth $200 Billion," *Business Insider,* February 15, 2015, http://www.businessinsider.com/russias-former-largest-foreign-investor-putin-is-worth-200-billion-2015-2

[1472] MacFarquhar, Neil, "Russians' Anxiety Swells as Oil Prices Collapse," *New York Times,* January 22, 2016, http://www.nytimes.com/2016/01/23/world/europe/russians-anxiety-swells-as-oil-prices-collapse.html

[1473] By Evans-Pritchard, Ambrose, "The Week the Dam Broke in Russia and Ended Putin's Dreams," *UK Telegraph,* December 23, 2014, http://www.telegraph.co.uk/finance/economics/11305146/The-week-the-dam-broke-in-Russia-and-ended-Putins-dreams.html

[1474] Bennett, Kate, "Four Seasons Rolls Out the Red Carpet for King Salman," *Politico,* September 3, 2015, http://www.politico.com/story/2015/09/four-seasons-king-salman-visit-red-carpet-213324

[1475] "Oil downturn," *Hurriyet Daily News,* February 20, 2016, http://www.hurriyetdailynews.com/oil-downturn.aspx?PageID=238&NID=95448

[1476] "Tel Megiddo," Shalom Israel, Accessed February 22, 2016, http://www.shalomil.com/places/tel-megiddo

[1477] Barber, Matt, "Today's Baal Worshipers," *WND,* December 19, 2008, http://www.wnd.com/2008/12/83960/

[1478] Kristensen, H. & Norris, R, "Israeli Nuclear Weapons, 2014," *Bulletin of the Atomic Scientists,* October 28, 2014, http://bos.sagepub.com/content/early/2014/10/28/0096340214555409.full.pdf+html, p. 15

[1479] Gilbert, Joseph, "'High Probability' Chemical Weapons Used in Syria, *Watertown International News Examiner,* March 19, 2013, http://www.examiner.com/article/high-probability-chemical-weapons-used-syria

[1480] "Syria Facilities," Nuclear Threat Initiative, Accessed March 5, 2016, http://www.nti.org/gmap/nuclear_syria.html

[1481] Gordon, Jerry, "Syria's Bio-Warfare Threat: an Interview with Dr. Jill Dekker," *New English Review,* July 16, 2012, http://www.newenglishreview.org/custpage.cfm/frm/13108/sec_id/13108

[1482] Al-Sughair, Sultan, "'North Thunder' Sends a Message of Unity, Power," *Arab News,* February 17, 2016, http://www.arabnews.com/featured/news/881886

[1483] "Sanaa Is the Fourth Arab Capital to Join the Iranian Revolution," *Middle East Monitor,* September 27, 2014, https://www.middleeastmonitor.com/news/middle-east/14389-sanaa-is-the-fourth-arab-capital-to-join-the-iranian-revolution

[1484] Lieberman, Julia Rebollo. Sephardi Family Life in the Early Modern Diaspora. Waltham: Brandeis University Press, 2010

[1485] Prager, D. & Telushkin, J. The Nine Questions People Ask About Judaism. New York: Simon & Shuster, 1981

[1486] "Semitic Neopaganism," Wikipedia, Accessed February 28, 2016, https://en.wikipedia.org/wiki/Semitic_neopaganism

[1487] "Commission Rejects Russia Syria Arms Deal," Foundation for Defense of Democracies, March 5, 2016, http://www.defenddemocracy.org/media-hit/commission-rejects-russia-syria-arms-deal/

[1488] Sanamyan, Emil, "Russia Details USD200 Million Arms Sale to Armenia," *Jane's Defence Weekly,* February 25, 2016, https://therearenosunglasses.wordpress.com/2016/02/25/russia-pours-200-million-heavy-weapons-into-armenia-eat-that-turkey/

[1489] Chastain, Mary, "Russia Announces Closer Military Cooperation with Iran in Syria," *Breitbart,* February 19, 2016, http://www.breitbart.com/national-security/2016/02/19/russia-iran-to-increase-military-cooperation/

[1490] Sobecki, Nichole, "Turkey Moves Away from the West, *Huffington Post,* May 25, 2011, http://www.huffingtonpost.com/2009/05/29/turkey-moves-away-from-th_n_209131.html

[1491] "Saudi Arabia to Invest in Turkey 613 Billion Dollar," Report.Az, December 30, 2015, http://report.az/en/other-countries/saudi-arabia-to-cooperate-with-turkish-companies-on-613-billion-dollar-investment/

[1492] Rubin, Michael, " Turkey, From Ally to Enemy," *Commentary,* July 1, 2010, https://www.commentarymagazine.com/articles/turkey-from-ally-to-enemy/

[1493] "Oil Embargo, 1973–1974," U.S. Department of State, Office of the Historian, https://history.state.gov/milestones/1969-1976/oil-embargo

[1494] "Frontline," *PBS,* Accessed March 7, 2016, http://www.pbs.org/wgbh/pages/frontline/shows/saudi/etc/cron.html

[1495] Blanchard, Christopher M., "Saudi Arabia: Background and U.S. Relations," Congressional Research Service, February 5, 2016, https://www.fas.org/sgp/crs/mideast/RL33533.pdf, p. 29

[1496] *Ibid.*, p. 32

[1497] "U.S. Imports by Country of Origin," U.S. Energy Information Administration, Accessed March 8, 2016, https://www.eia.gov/dnav/pet/pet_move_impcus_a2_nus_epc0_im0_mbblpd_a.htm

[1498] Krauthammer, Charles, "The Worst Agreement in U.S. Diplomatic History," *Washington Post*, July 2, 2015, https://www.washingtonpost.com/opinions/the-worst-agreement-in-us-diplomatic-history/2015/07/02/960e8cf2-20e8-11e5-aeb9-a411a84c9d55_story.html

[1499] Tyler, Taylor, "Iran: $100 Billion In Previously Frozen Assets 'Fully Released' Per Nuclear Deal," HNGN, February 1, 2016, http://www.hngn.com/articles/175070/20160201/iran-100-billion-previously-frozen-assets-fully-released-per-nuclear.htm

[1500] McCarthy, Kevin, "21 Reasons the Iran Deal is a Bad Deal," July 22, 2015, Kevin McCarthy Majority Leader, http://www.majorityleader.gov/2015/07/22/21-reasons-iran-deal-bad-deal/

[1501] Onyanga-Omara, Jane, "Reports: Iran Fires Missile Marked with 'Israel Should Be Wiped'," *USA Today,* March 9, 2016, http://www.usatoday.com/story/news/world/2016/03/09/reports-iran-fires-missiles-marked-israel-must-wiped-out/81517488/

[1502] Gladwell, Malcolm, "David and Goliath Quotes," Accessed March 8, 2016, https://www.goodreads.com/work/quotes/21445709-david-and-goliath

[1503] "Netanyahu on Iran: I'm Trying to Kill a Bad Deal," *NBC News,* April 5, 2015, http://www.nbcnews.com/storyline/iran-nuclear-talks/netanyahu-iran-im-trying-kill-bad-deal-n335961

[1504] "Iran's Nuclear Timetable," *Iran Watch,* November 18, 2015, http://www.iranwatch.org/our-publications/articles-reports/irans-nuclear-timetable

[1505] Read, Russ, "Iran Wrote 'Israel Should Be Wiped off the Earth' on the Side of Tested Missile," *Daily Caller,* March 9, 2016, http://dailycaller.com/2016/03/09/white-house-quiet-as-iran-brazenly-touts-that-israel-should-be-wiped-off-the-earth-was-written-on-recently-tested-missiles/

[1506] Vick, Karl, "The Middle East Nuclear Race Is Already Under Way," *Time,* March 23, 2015, http://time.com/3751676/iran-talks-nuclear-race-middle-east/

[1507] Piggott, Mark, "Middle East 'Nuclear Arms Race' in Progress Says Israeli Defence Minister Moshe Ya'alon," *International Business Times,* February 16, 2106, http://www.ibtimes.co.uk/middle-east-nuclear-arms-race-progress-says-israeli-defence-minister-moshe-yaalon-1544022

[1508] Khatri, Shabina S., "US to Expedite Arms Shipments to Qatar, Other GCC Nations, Kerry Says," *Doha News,* August 4, 2015, http://dohanews.co/us-to-expedite-arms-shipments-to-qatar-other-gcc-nations-kerry-says/

[1509] Majumdar, Dave, "Russia Bolsters Iran's Air Defense with Lethal S-300," *The National Interest,* December 7, 2015, http://nationalinterest.org/blog/the-buzz/russia-bolsters-irans-air-defense-lethal-s-300-14536

[1510] *Ibid.*

[1511] "S-300VM," Wikipedia, Accessed March 11, 2016, https://en.wikipedia.org/wiki/S-300VM

[1512] "Future Outlook of Military Cooperation Between Iran and Russia – Analysis," *Eurasia Review,* March 7, 2016, http://www.eurasiareview.com/07032016-future-outlook-of-military-cooperation-between-iran-and-russia-analysis/

[1513] Wagner, Stephen, "The "Old Hag" Syndrome," About Paranormal, http://paranormal.about.com/od/humanenigmas/a/Old-Hag-Syndrome.htm

[1514] Wagner, Stephen, "Scariest Old Hag Experiences," About Paranormal, http://paranormal.about.com/od/humanmysteries/a/Scariest-Old-Hag-Experiences.htm

[1515] Wagner, Stephen, "Scariest Old Hag Experiences," About Paranormal, http://paranormal.about.com/od/humanmysteries/a/Scariest-Old-Hag-Experiences_2.htm

[1516] *Ibid.*

[1517] *Ibid.*

[1518] "Town Gets Snippy About Skeleton of Mutilated Horse," *Denver Post*, December 9, 2009, http://www.denverpost.com/news/ci_4809131

[1519] Duran, Frank, "Snippy the Horse - the Most Famous Horse in the World!" Accessed March 13, 2016, http://www.snippy.com/

[1520] Murphy, Jan. Mysteries and Legends of Colorado: True Stories of the Unsolved and Unexplained. Guilford: Globe Pequot, 2007 p. 94

[1521] Speigel, Lee, "Colorado's San Luis Valley Is A UFO Hotspot With A Specially Built UFO Watchtower," *Huffington Post,* November 16, 2011, http://www.huffingtonpost.com/2011/05/25/colorado-san-luis-valley-ufos-watchtower-judy-messoline_n_865682.html

[1522] *Ibid.*, p. 96

[1523] Sanders, Ed, "The Mutilation Mystery," *Oui Magazine,* September 1976 issue, https://vault.fbi.gov/Animal%20Mutilation/Animal%20Mutilation%20Part%202%20of%205/view

[1524] Howe, Linda Moulton, "Strange Harvest," 1999 made-for-TV documentary

[1525] Rose, Joseph, "UFOs, Mutilated Cows and Oregon: What's the Link?" *Oregon Live,* February 17, 2016, http://www.oregonlive.com/entertainment/index.ssf/2016/02/ufo_cow_mutilations_oregon_no.html

534

[1526] Blevins, Jason, "Colorado Cow Mutilations Baffle Ranchers, Cops, UFO Believer," *Denver Post*, December 9, 2009, http://www.denverpost.com/ci_13956752

[1527] "Cattle Mutilation," Wikipedia, Accessed March 13, 2016, https://en.wikipedia.org/wiki/Cattle_mutilation

[1528] Dahlgreen, Will, "You Are Not Alone: Most People Believe That Aliens Exist," *YouGov*, September 28, 2015, https://today.yougov.com/news/2015/09/28/you-are-not-alone-most-people-believe-aliens-exist/

[1529] Main, Douglas, "Most People Believe Intelligent Aliens Exist, Poll Says," *Newsweek*, September 29, 2015, http://www.newsweek.com/most-people-believe-intelligent-aliens-exist-377965

[1530] DiBlasio, Natalie, "A Third of Earthlings Believe in UFOs, Would Befriend Aliens," *USA Today*, June 26, 2012, http://usatoday30.usatoday.com/news/nation/story/2012-06-26/ufo-survey/55843742/1

[1531] Gannon, Megan, "60 Billion Alien Planets Could Support Life, Study Suggests," *Space*, July 1, 2013, http://www.space.com/21800-alien-planets-60-billion-habitable-exoplanets.html

[1532] Choi, Charles, "Milky Way Could Have 100 Million Planets Hospitable for Complex Life," *Popular Mechanics*, June 5, 2014, http://www.popularmechanics.com/space/deep-space/a12955/milky-way-could-have-100-million-planets-hospitable-for-complex-life-16863392/

[1533] Withnall, Adam, "Pope Francis Says He Would Baptise Aliens: 'Who Are We to Close Doors?'" *UK Independent*, May 13, 2014, http://www.independent.co.uk/news/world/europe/pope-francis-says-he-would-baptise-aliens-9360632.html

[1534] Lusher, Adam, "Meeting Extraterrestrials: Should We Contact Aliens?" *UK Independent*, July 27, 2015, http://www.independent.co.uk/news/science/meeting-extraterrestrials-should-we-contact-aliens-10420032.html

[1535] "Alien Life and UFOs: 10 Top 'Believers,'" *UK Telegraph*, February 21, 2011, http://www.telegraph.co.uk/news/newstopics/howaboutthat/ufo/8337299/Alien-life-and-UFOs-10-top-believers.html

[1536] *Ibid.*

[1537] Carter, Jimmy, "Voyager Spacecraft Statement by the President," July 29, 1977, The American Presidency Project, http://www.presidency.ucsb.edu/ws/?pid=7890

[1538] "Alien Life and UFOs: 10 Top 'Believers,'" *UK Telegraph*, February 21, 2011, http://www.telegraph.co.uk/news/newstopics/howaboutthat/ufo/8337299/Alien-life-and-UFOs-10-top-believers.html

[1539] *Ibid.*

[1540] *Ibid.*

[1541] "UK Has Anti-Alien War Weapons, Former Defense Adviser," *GMA News*, October 16, 2012, http://www.gmanetwork.com/news/story/278438/scitech/technology/uk-has-anti-alien-war-weapons-former-defense-adviser-claims

[1542] Cannon, Lou. President Reagan: The Role of a Lifetime. New York: Simon & Schuster, 1991, p. 42

[1543] Carter, Claire, "All the President's (Little Green) Men: How Ronald Reagan Asked Soviet Rival Mikhail Gorbachev for Help Fighting Alien Invasion," *UK Daily Mail*, April 19, 2015, http://www.dailymail.co.uk/news/article-3045894/How-Ronald-Reagan-asked-Soviet-rival-Mikhail-Gorbachev-help-fighting-alien-invasion.html

[1544] "Alien Life and UFOs: 10 Top 'Believers,'" *UK Telegraph*, February 21, 2011, http://www.telegraph.co.uk/news/newstopics/howaboutthat/ufo/8337299/Alien-life-and-UFOs-10-top-believers.html

[1545] "UK Has Anti-Alien War Weapons, Former Defense Adviser," *GMA News*, October 16, 2012, http://www.gmanetwork.com/news/story/278438/scitech/technology/uk-has-anti-alien-war-weapons-former-defense-adviser-claims

[1546] "Former Canadian Minister of Defence Asks Canadian Parliament Asked to Hold Hearings on Relations with Alien "ET" Civilizations," *UFO Digest*, November 24, 2005, http://www.ufodigest.com/parliament.html

[1547] Salucop, Sigrid, "UFOs, Aliens: 20 of Most Famous People Who Believe in Extraterrestrials," *International Business Times*, October 14, 2013, http://www.ibtimes.com.au/ufos-aliens-20-most-famous-people-who-believe-extraterrestrials-photos-1268495

[1548] *Ibid.*

[1549] *Ibid.*

[1550] *Ibid.*

[1551] Cooke, John, "Astronaut Gordon Cooper Witnesses UFO Landing at Edwards AFB," *UFO Evidence*, Undated, http://www.ufoevidence.org/cases/case357.htm

[1552] Salucop, Sigrid, "UFOs, Aliens: 20 of Most Famous People Who Believe in Extraterrestrials," *International Business Times*, October 14, 2013, http://www.ibtimes.com.au/ufos-aliens-20-most-famous-people-who-believe-extraterrestrials-photos-1268495

[1553] *Ibid.*

[1554] Hickman, Jim, "Walter Cronkite's UFO Encounter," Rense, July 6, 2000, http://www.rense.com/general2/celeb.htm

[1555] "Clips and Quotes," The SETI League, October 14 2002, http://www.setileague.org/press/pressquo.htm

[1556] Darrach, H.B. & Ginna, R., "Have We Visitors From Outer Space?" *LIFE Magazine*, April 7, 1952, p. 92

[1557] "Former Canadian Minister of Defense Asks Canadian Parliament to Hold Hearings on Relations with Alien "ET" Civilizations," Rense, November 24, 2005, http://www.rense.com/general68/eurdo.htm

[1558] "'I Believe in UFOs... and I've Seen Them': Former Canadian Defense Minister Accuses American Government of Cover-Up," *UK Daily Mail*, February 25, 2011, http://www.dailymail.co.uk/news/article-1360737/I-believe-UFOs--Ive-seen-says-ex-defence-minister-Paul-Hellyer.html

[1559] Corso, P. & Burns, W. The Day After Roswell. New York: Pocket Books, 1997, p. 293

[1560] "1962 - 2015 – RTG's; Multiple Plutonium Containing Satellites Melt Down And Burn Up on Reentry, 34 Total In Orbit Just from US Military," A Green Road, April 29, 2014, http://agreenroad.blogspot.com/2014/04/1962-1964-indian-ocean-multiple.html

[1561] "Dr. Helen Caldicott Fukushima Nuclear Disaster You Won't Hear This on the Main Stream News," YouTube Video of Press Conference on "The Dangers of Nuclear War," Accessed April 1, 2016, https://www.youtube.com/watch?v=tZ_mzaAZqsw

[1562] "The Nuclear Disaster of Kosmos 954," *Historic Wings,* January 24, 2013, http://fly.historicwings.com/2013/01/the-nuclear-disaster-of-kosmos-954/

[1563] Benko, Marietta. Space Law in the United Nations. Dordrecht: Martinus Nijhoff Publishers, 1985

[1564] "NASA Needs Strategic Plan to Manage Orbital Debris Efforts; Risks Increasing for Satellites, Space Station," National Research Council, September 1, 2011, http://www8.nationalacademies.org/onpinews/newsitem.aspx?RecordID=13244

[1565] "Ronald Reagan Quotes," Think Exist, http://thinkexist.com/quotation/i_couldn-t_help_but_say_to_mr_gorbachev-just/337349.html

[1566] "Ronald Reagan's Address to the 42nd Session of the United Nations General Assembly in New York, New York," September 21, 1987, Video Accessed March 31, 2016, https://www.youtube.com/watch?v=dL6PIM24JBQ

[1567] "Reagan Comments on ET Alien Threat," Video Accessed March 31, 2016, https://www.youtube.com/watch?v=CfejBpD_wm4

[1568] Blumenthal, Ralph, "Alien Nation: Have Humans Been Abducted by Extraterrestrials?" *Vanity Fair,* May 10, 2013, http://www.vanityfair.com/culture/2013/05/americans-alien-abduction-science

[1569] Cho, Adrian, "Gravitational Waves, Einstein's Ripples in Spacetime, Spotted for First Time," *Science Magazine,* February 11, 2016, http://www.sciencemag.org/news/2016/02/gravitational-waves-einsteins-ripples-spacetime-spotted-first-time

[1570] Ghose, Tia, "Wormhole Created in Lab Makes Invisible Magnetic Field," *Live Science,* August 20, 2015, http://www.livescience.com/51925-magnetic-wormhole-created.html

[1571] "CERN's LHC: "Parallel Universes Could be Hidden Within the Four Dimensions," *Digital Galaxy,* May 6, 2011, http://www.dailygalaxy.com/my_weblog/2011/05/cerns-lhc-parallel-universes-could-be-hidden-within-the-four-dimensions.html

[1572] Hawking, Stephen, "Life in the Universe," Accessed March 25, 2016, http://www.hawking.org.uk/life-in-the-universe.html

[1573] Jha, Alok, "Is Stephen Hawking Right About Aliens?" *UK Guardian,* April 30, 2010, https://www.theguardian.com/science/2010/apr/30/stephen-hawking-right-aliens

[1574] Lusher, Adam, "Meeting Extraterrestrials: Should We Contact Aliens?" *UK Independent,* July 27, 2015, http://www.independent.co.uk/news/science/meeting-extraterrestrials-should-we-contact-aliens-10420032.html

[1575] DiBlasio, Natalie, "A Third of Earthlings Believe in UFOs, Would Befriend Aliens," *USA Today,* June 26, 2012, http://usatoday30.usatoday.com/news/nation/story/2012-06-26/ufo-survey/55843742/1

[1576] "An Urgent Message to Humanity," The Ground Crew Project, August 1997, http://wwwuser.gwdg.de/~agruens/UFO/ufo_apdx/messhum2.htm

[1577] "Sheldan Nidle," Wikipedia, Accessed March 25, 2016, https://en.wikipedia.org/wiki/Sheldan_Nidle

[1578] Bloxham, Andy, "Aliens Have Deactivated British and US Nuclear Missiles, Say US Military Pilots," *UK Telegraph,* September 10, 2010, http://www.telegraph.co.uk/news/newstopics/howaboutthat/ufo/8026971/Aliens-have-deactivated-British-and-US-nuclear-missiles-say-US-military-pilots.html

[1579] "Ex-Air Force Personnel: UFOs Deactivated Nukes," *CBS News,* September 28, 2010, http://www.cbsnews.com/news/ex-air-force-personnel-ufos-deactivated-nukes/

[1580] *Ibid.*

[1581] Ribas, Jorge, "UFOs Spying on Our Nukes, Airmen Claim," *Discovery,* September 28, 2010, http://news.discovery.com/space/ufos-spying-on-our-nukes-airmen-claim.htm

[1582] Johnson, Donald A, "Do Nuclear Facilities Attract UFOs?" Computer UFO Network, July 14, 2002, http://www.cufon.org/contributors/DJ/Do Nuclear Facilities Attract UFOs.htm

[1583] Stanglin, D. & Rice, D, "Wildfire Guts Large Swath of Canadian City; 88,000 Flee," *USA Today,* May 4, 2016, http://www.usatoday.com/story/news/world/2016/05/04/over-80000-evacuated-fires-threaten-canada-town/83912738/

[1584] "Arnie Gundersen on CCTV- Nuclear Free Future: Fukushima at 5 and the Vermont Yankee Shutdown: What Do They Mean," April 5, 2016, Fairwinds, http://www.fairewinds.org/nuclear-energy-education//arnie-gundersen-on-cctv-nuclear-free-future-fukushima-at-5-and-the-vermont-yankee-shutdown-what-do-they-mean

[1585] Melvin, D., Sciutto, J. & Ripley, W, "North Korea Launches Missile From Submarine," *CNN,* April 25, 2016, http://edition.cnn.com/2016/04/23/asia/north-korea-launches-missile-from-submarine/index.html

[1586] "About Us," Vital Ground, Accessed May 2, 2016, http://www.vitalground.org/about/about-us/

[1587] "Policy Concerning Access of Immigrants to City Services," Accessed August 6, 2015, http://www.phila.gov/ExecutiveOrders/Executive%20Orders/2009_EO08-09.pdf

[1588] Romboy, Dennis, "Utah Legislature Passes Package of Immigration Bills," *Deseret News,* March 4, 2011, http://www.deseretnews.com/article/705368042/Utah-Legislature-passes-package-of-immigration-bills.html?pg=all